More Career Resources
for a Life in the Law

Order Now from DecisionBooks.com*

■ ■ ■

What Can You Do With a Law Degree?
A Lawyer Guide to Career Alternatives Inside, Outside & Around the Law
By Deborah Arron, JD
$29.95, 360 pages/5th edition Companion workbook due Spring 2004; $21.95

Should You Marry a Lawyer?
A Couple's Guide to Balancing Work, Love & Ambition
By Fiona Travis, Ph.D.
$18.95, 160 pages

Should You Really Become a Lawyer?
A Guide to the Biggest (and Most Expensive) Career Decision You'll Ever Make
By Deborah Schneider, JD & Gary Belsky
$21.95, 224 pages (due Spring 2004)

Should You Become a Freelance Lawyer?
What Every Lawyer & Law Firm Needs to Know About Temporary Legal Services.
By Deborah Arron, JD & Deborah Guyol, JD
$29.95, 288 pages/3rd edition

Running From the Law
Why Good Lawyers Are Getting Out of the Legal Profession
By Deborah Arron, JD
$16.95, 192 pages/3rd edition

■ ■ ■

To order, call **1-800-359-9629**. Or order online from **www.DecisionBooks.com**.

Dedication

To Deborah, whose influence continues to be felt

WHAT CAN YOU DO WITH A

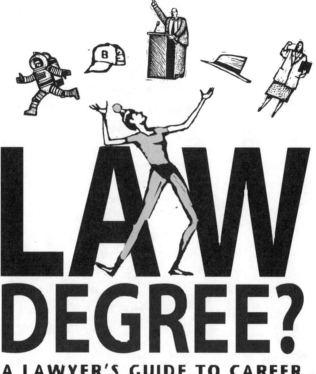

LAW
DEGREE?

A LAWYER'S GUIDE TO CAREER ALTERNATIVES INSIDE, OUTSIDE & AROUND THE LAW

• • •

DEBORAH ARRON

DecisionBooks™
SEATTLE WASHINGTON

DecisionBooks
Published by Niche Press LLC
PO Box 99477 Seattle WA 98139 U.S.A.

DecisionBooks is a registered trademarked imprint of
    Niche Press LLC

Library of Congress Cataloging-in-Publication Data

Arron, Deborah L.
    What can you do with a law degree?: A lawyer's
guide to career alternatives inside, outside & around the
law / by Deborah Arron.
        p.   cm.
    Includes index.
    ISBN 0-940675-51-X
    1. Law—Vocational guidance—United States.
    2. Lawyers—United States.   I. Title.
KF297.A875   1997
340'.02373—dc21   96-49539
                                                            CIP

ISBN 0-940675-51-X

New Career
wanted

Cover and interior design by Elizabeth Watson
Book layout by Hargrave Design

DecisionBooks are available at special discounts for bulk
purchases. For more information, write to Special Markets,
DecisionBooks, PO Box 99477, Seattle WA 98139,
or e-mail DecisionBooks@aol.com

Publisher's Introduction

Of the million-plus lawyers in the US today, at least half are said to be unhappy in their chosen profession and considering leaving the law. That's no secret anymore. Back in the 1990s, though, it was big news. And the first to break the profession's code of silence was Seattle lawyer Deborah Arron in her book, *Running From the Law*.

Soon after its publication, the book was given the imprimatur of success by *Time Magazine*, the *ABA Journal,* and many other major publications. Two years later, Arron, by now a successful author and national public speaker, followed with another hit — *What Can You Do With a Law Degree*? It sold more than 100,000 copies, and created a new niche among professional career books. Unfortunately, tragedy struck as Arron was preparing this new 5th edition of her book. The author developed a serious illness and passed away. Deborah Arron loved the law but loved lawyers more, and for that reason we felt there was no more fitting tribute than to make sure her work remained available. We wish to thank all the lawyers, law students, and law school career services professionals who contributed to the evolution of Arron's work. And a very special thanks for editorial generosity to Rita Carey, JD; Jill Eckert, JD; Angelique Electra, JD; Ed Honnold, JD; Carol Kanarek, JD; Janina Latack, Ph.D.; Irene Leonard, JD; Kathy Morris, JD; Celia Paul, Camille Walker, JD; and J. Kim Wright, JD.

Years ago, *Wisconsin Lawyer* magazine suggested in a review of one of Ms. Arron's books that its contents were so provocative that — after reading it — one might be doing "a public service" by passing it along to some bright kid headed for law school. That's still good advice.

Contents

Foreword

Most of you recognize this classified ad for what it is: a piece of fiction.

Even so, at some level, you may want to believe the ad could be real. "After all," you say. "I'm a lawyer. I've paid my dues. *Someone* out there must recognize my value." I remember having the same thoughts before I finally closed my law practice. In fact, in my fantasy, I actually imagined running into a colleague who would offer me a terrific, well-paying job that not only relieved me of everything I disliked about my law practice, but provide unlimited opportunities for self-expression. Like most fantasies, the offer never materialized. I learned that I had to build a new career on my own one brick at a time and so will you.

Many of you will open this book in the middle of a career crisis. Maybe you're facing involuntary unemployment or retirement ... maybe you're graduating from law school with no clear career path or job offers ... maybe you're wondering how to return from parental leave or whether you should pursue a part-time track. Others may be terminally bored with your practice, and still others may be feeling so burned out and frustrated it's all you can do to drag yourself into the office each morning. With so much confusion and pain in the legal profession these days, it would be nice to find concrete answers. You'll find answers here, but they *won't* be easy answers or quick fixes.

This book was written by a lawyer for lawyers. So, expect a pragmatic, down-to-earth approach to career development whose job-finding techniques have been successfully tested by thousands of lawyers and law students over a 10-year period. And whether you read this book in sequence — or not, as time permits — you'll find many helpful resources, including the latest Internet resources for lawyers. Our profession faces a new business reality — layoffs, consolidations, firm dissolutions. These are the times in which we live, and that's why — as never before — your career is in your hands. I hope you will make good use of the resources here ... not just now, but at your next career crossroads as well.

Deborah Arron
Seattle, Washington

CHAPTER 1

SUCCESSFUL CAREER DEVELOPMENT

In a Buddhist fable, a man falls from a steep ledge. On his way down, he grabs a branch on the side of the cliff. Clinging to the branch, he sees a small, grassy plateau nearby. If he could only get to it, his life would be saved. Suddenly, from nowhere, the man hears a voice, *Let go of the branch and jump. You can make it!* The man is paralyzed. Should he trust the voice? One wrong move might cost him his life. On the other hand, dangling from a branch is no way to live either. What to do, what to do? Hanging off the side of the cliff, the man weighs his options. What would it take to trust the voice?

A leap of faith.

What It's All About?

"To my clients, I'm nothing more than a utility like the lights or water. They flip my switch and I'm just supposed to turn on. Well, I don't want to be a utility anymore. I want to watch my daughter grow up."

— *Steve, a former California practitioner*

· · ·

What can you do with your law degree?

Honestly?

After 11 years of working and consulting with lawyers and law students, I really believe you can do just about anything you want with your law degree. The choices are limited only by imagination and perseverance.

Maybe you were meant to be a painter, a screenwriter, a horse-breeder or small-town minister; maybe you want to find a practice area where your weekends are your own; maybe you want a job in Big Law to pay off your student loans, maybe you want to find a small practice where you won't get lost in the crowd; maybe you were caught up in a layoff and need something — anything — right now. Whatever you want to do, it is possible if you're willing to stretch a little, dream a little, and risk a little.

> Anything is possible if you can stretch, dream, and risk.

That's what this book is all about — stretching, dreaming, risking.

Take **Mike**, for example. A small-firm personal injury lawyer. He was unhappy, unchallenged, and bored out of his mind. Finally, he jumped ship. But instead of limiting himself to what he'd always done, he decided to expand his field of view. He set his sights on becoming in-house counsel for a technology company. Along the way, he became knowledgeable about emerging corporate law issues, repackaged his skills, joined some new organizations, and networked faithfully until he landed a new job.

Or consider **Elizabeth**: A Harvard law grad who was handling routine land-use

3

cases for a small municipality in the Pacific Northwest. On a whim, she took a scuba class. Over time, she became an experienced diving enthusiast, and took advanced courses in marine law and marine biology. While vacationing in the Cayman Islands, she had a chance conversation with a Caymanian local who told her (and I'm not making this up) that the island municipality needed a lawyer who was an experienced diver to help draft and enforce new environmental legislation. As far as I know, Elizabeth is still there, happily working as a diver-environmental planner.

And finally, there's **Garry**. An unhappy man with 20 years in practice, Garry approached the idea of getting out of the law soon after the death of his sister. One day he told me that he read an article about mid-life career changers and decided life was too short to be unhappy. So, he decided to enroll in some graduate classes and went on to earn a Masters in psychology. He has since developed a successful counseling practice.

"*Okay,*" you say, "*I get it. If I want work that's right for me, I shouldn't limit myself to the obvious choices. But I just want something better than I have now. Where are those jobs?*"

I understand your impatience. But it's too soon to ask. Besides, once you've worked through all the exercises between Chapters 3 and 5, your question will have answered itself. All that's important now is that you trust that a process does exist to identify and find more satisfying employment, and that — for now — you're willing to stretch a little, dream a little, and risk a little.

Despite the current economy and whatever you've heard, your law degree — and any professional experience you've subsequently gained — are valuable credentials in even the softest, most competitive job market. And, contrary to what you may believe about yourself, merely having succeeded through law school — last month, last year or 20 years ago — tells the world that you are a competent, intelligent and responsible person who attains the goals you set, and that you're someone who commands respect. And just because your law school classmates got better grades, or they win more cases, or they drive a Jag or a Lexus and earn more money, doesn't mean that you've failed. Their *apparent* success only signifies that they're in the right place and you're not ... not yet. Let me assure you, whatever pain or frustration you're experiencing now, will vanish when you find a work environment more suited to your strengths, interests and values. It's as simple as that.

Shall we begin?

Four Steps to Career Transition

"The legal profession is very narrowing to the soul. That's why lawyers need to get away and do something else ... to discover there's a whole world out there that doesn't know there are two court systems."

—*A Fordham Law School grad*

■ ■ ■

A law degree is a valuable credential, and earning one tells the world you're worth paying attention to. But it's not a passport; it's not an automatic entree to any job or career.

Leveraging your legal background requires serious effort — and a well-thought plan. In fact, in a soft job market, a job- or career-transition may be the toughest work you ever do (just ask anyone laid off in a recession). In fact, the first phase of your transition — self-assessment — is a lot like taking on a new case: you've got to develop the essential facts, research the field, learn as much as you can about the client (in this case, you), and commit whatever time, energy, and money it takes to prevail.

> Changing careers may be the toughest work you ever do.

Did you ever see the Al Brooks film comedy, *Lost in America*? It's a brilliant satire on the American attitude toward work. Brooks plays a displaced advertising executive trapped in a seedy desert town, desperate for a job. At the employment office, he sits across from a clerk who is sifting through a cardboard box that contains job notices for dishwashers and crossing guards. Brooks says he wants a job, any job, but he's accustomed to making a $100,000 a year. "Are there any jobs like that around town?" he asks.

"Oh, sure," says the clerk with a demonic smile. "One moment, please. I'll check my $100,000 box."

Brooks (and the rest of us) all want work commensurate with our education and status, and — when times get tough — we will often sacrifice job satisfaction to get our foot in the door. But the truth about finding satisfying employment (and career consultants are in agreement on this), is that job seekers who *narrow* the scope of their search to areas that excite and interest them, are far more successful in securing employment than those who are willing to take anything that comes their way. "People who offer themselves as a kind of jack-of-all-trades are generally unsuccessful in their job hunt," says lawyer/psychologist Larry Richard. "Employers are interested in somebody who has enthusiasm and motivation, and who has formulated a game plan. Because they believe that a goal-directed person will apply that same single-mindedness to their businesses."

That brings me to the four steps to a successful career transition.

Step One — Self-assessment. You can do it on your own (see Chapters 3 to 5), or you can work with a career counselor, a career coach, or — as a law school alumnus — you can seek out the assistance of a law school career services professional. Whichever you choose, self-assessment is absolutely, positively critical to a successful job-finding process. For additional assessment options, turn to Appendices 3, 4 and 5. And for names of career counselors and coaches experienced at working with lawyers, go to **www.DecisionBooks.com**.

Step Two — Once you've assessed your personal work preferences, you need to research where you fit in the employment scene. I can't emphasize this point too strongly: you must define the specifics of the environment and type of work that will suit you before you explore the marketplace, rather than expecting the marketplace to define the options for you. I don't know why, but this seems to be a difficult notion for many lawyers and law students to accept. Although there are hundreds of fields for which your legal background would be helpful, your background alone will not get you employed. Not anymore; not in this economy. Nowadays, you have to demonstrate a deep, personal connection to the work you seek. Anything less and you're just contributing to the résumé spam. So, knowing what jobs that others are pursuing is completely irrelevant. You only need to know what jobs or careers interest you enough to pursue them with full commitment. And you won't learn this in the classifieds or online job boards; it's the sort of knowledge that only comes from self-assessment and from talking to people with experience in your areas of interest.

Step Three — After identifying a suitable job target, you begin networking, mining job leads, and fine-tuning your résumé and cover letter(s). See Chapter 6.

Step Four — This is when you involve family, friends, or associates ... or all three.

It won't be easy. Your job- or career-dissatisfaction may be unsettling to the people closest to you, and be prepared for a less-than-sympathetic response. West Coast

PLANNING YOUR TRIP

Career development resembles a road trip.

► First, you get your bearings; you evaluate where you are now and where you want to go. "Where you are now" is your background, your unique combination of strengths and preferences, and your credentials. "Where you want to go" is your vision of the future, the qualities you hope to find in your work, and the contribution you want to make.

► When you've identified starting and ending points, decide what the trip itself should be like. Do you find a flight on the Concorde tempting, trading speed for expense? Or are you more interested in country roads that allow you time to meander, explore and learn unexpected lessons? Perhaps you'd like to take a detour before heading for your ultimate destination by building a family, achieving financial security where you are, or taking a sabbatical or vacation.

► In other words, you must decide which road to take.

► Poet Robert Frost recommended "the road less traveled." Cartoonist Gary Larsen suggests the "scary or weird" road. There are the roads everyone else can see, and the ones that are apparent only to you. In every case, though, the most exciting and rewarding trip is on your own road, one you've chosen and built for yourself.

► Sometimes, the only way to locate the path that's right for you is to start on a road with everyone else and then branch off. Don't be discouraged if it takes a while to find the right alternative route. Depending upon how boxed in you are, you may have to turn around, travel around a corner, or wade through the underbrush to find a meaningful road. You might also have to stay in one place while you construct a new thoroughfare.

► The last step, of course, is to start the trip. Do something that gets you on that road, and then persist in your journey. "Don't stare up the steps," says motivational speaker Zig Ziglar. "Step up the stairs."

career consultant Ava Butler says she's worked with many lawyers who shared their unhappiness with their families, and the situation usually ended with someone — a spouse or a parent — in tears, wondering "what-the-hell-is-wrong-with-you?"

But if you don't risk revealing what's going on with you, then the family and colleagues closest to you won't be able to provide emotional support, job leads or contacts. They'll just assume you're happy doing what you're doing. Says one ex-solo practitioner, "I kept waiting for my clients to notice what a great job I was doing so they would invite me in-house. But I was so clever at concealing my feelings, they had no idea I was dissatisfied, and I was caught in this vicious cycle: I couldn't tell them, because if I did I worried they would want to find another lawyer."

So, what do I mean when I say "support"? This simply involves asking for what you want — empathy, inspiration, financial resources, referrals — from family, friends, acquaintances or business associates. You also need to identify others who have made successful transitions and use their examples to find solutions to your own

Self-Defeating and Dangerous Career Strategies

- ▶ Trying to do something about your career only when you're unhappy with it.
- ▶ Waiting for opportunities to fall in your lap.
- ▶ Intellectualizing where to go next and how to get there.
- ▶ Hoping to fall into something interesting by being a generalist.
- ▶ Deciding at the outset that your next job must provide the same amount of money, or maintain the same level of responsibility or prestige.
- ▶ Believing that you'll only be hired to do something for which you have been formally trained or educated.
- ▶ Getting yet another educational degree simply to postpone your job hunt, or when it isn't a requirement for the work you'd like to do.
- ▶ Putting off decisions until you lose your job or you burn out.
- ▶ Keeping your feelings of dissatisfaction to yourself, or dumping them only on your family.
- ▶ Expecting your work to bring you complete personal fulfillment or believing it's unrealistic to expect work-related gratification.
- ▶ Staying where you are because you're afraid of failing in the next endeavor.
- ▶ Believing you owe a lifetime commitment to your current employer or partners, your next job, or even your legal career.

problems, or find support from those who are currently undergoing a similar experience. Of course, if you want to leave the law and your family thinks you're crazy, and
you don't want to be too candid with friends or associates, you must seek outside
support — from a career counselor, a career coach, a law school career services
office, or your bar association's lawyer assistance program (for a state-by-state directory, visit the ABA's lawyer assistance program Web site at **www.abanet.org/
legalservices/colap/home.html**. You might also consider forming your own lawyer
support group, or take career development workshops at a community college, or
reach out to a local non-profit that provides support to job-seekers.

Does all this seem too unnecessary ... too time-consuming ... too "touchy-feely"?
Sorry. But if you go in search of work without pausing to examine where you are
now, where you want to go and how to get there, you run the risk of ending up in a
worse environment. Indeed, you may ...

- ▶ Discover you've become one of those aimless associates who, in the
  words of one lawyer, secured "the same terrible job in two different
  buildings";
- ▶ Find yourself trapped by "golden handcuffs";
- ▶ Pigeonhole yourself in a specialty you didn't really choose;
- ▶ Wind up as one of the long-term un- or under-employed;
- ▶ Reach a dead-end, with no place to go for challenge and or increased
  responsibility;
- ▶ Or, bounce from job to job until your résumé establishes only your ability
  to find work.

CHAPTER 2

THE ROOTS OF DISSATISFACTION

The Seasons of Your Career

"When I was in private practice, I sometimes arrived at the office looking at my watch and wondered, 'Oh, my God, how am I going to get through the rest of the day?'"

— *Sarah, a former New York practitioner*

■ ■ ■

A career in trouble is like a badly made stew. You add too little of this or too much of that, and your meal is less than satisfying. In the same way, your career — your stew — also depends on the right balance of ingredients and proportions. For example, you may be engaged in the wrong kind of activity or you work with the wrong group of people. On the other hand, your job and the environment may be terrific, but you've neglected to balance the time spent on work, family and your own needs. Whatever your situation, I've identified six important factors that are work *dissatisfiers* among lawyers, and I'll explore them in detail as we go along:

> The only way to better your situation is to carefully analyze your life and pinpoint the trouble spots.

- ▶ Experiencing unreasonable expectations about the law;
- ▶ An uncomfortable phase in your career;
- ▶ Living life out of balance;
- ▶ Failing to set appropriate limits with clients and colleagues;
- ▶ Working in an unpleasant work environment;
- ▶ Lacking work that calls upon your talents and preferences.

Unreasonable Expectations

Dissatisfaction results when expectations collide with reality. Vague or ill-conceived reasons for deciding to go to law school, or going into private practice, can lead to sharp disappointment in later years. You might have headed to law school with the expectation that your education would be a magic ticket to a dream destination. Said one practitioner, "I went to law school and thought it was interesting, but did I know anything about what lawyers did ... did I ever know a lawyer ... had I ever been inside a law firm? No, but that didn't daunt me. I figured that after all those years in school, I'd be a professional, have some flexibility, and work a nice schedule." Or consider this woman, who accepted her first job with no real appreciation of the nature of the work or the work environment:

> ► "I was a first-year law student when I heard you speak at my law school.
> At that time, I could not imagine anyone wanting to give up a career in
> the law to work in another field. In fact, I thought your presentation was
> close to blasphemy. I have now been practicing law for almost two years,
> not including the summers and semesters of internships. I am a city
> prosecutor and am in court every day — just the way I always dreamed.
> I hate it."

Once in practice, you might have thought that the profession would afford you continuing opportunities for advancement and challenge, or that your practice would be steady and predictable. This is not the reality of law practice. One Chicago practitioner describes it like this:

> ► "To do it (practice law) right is a hard job. You cannot try cases without
> very long hours. Your life is not your own. Judges and others control your
> schedule. You have only yourself and your wits and experience. You have
> no 'investment' or equity in a company. You are only as good as what you
> did today."

If you entered the practice of law thinking otherwise, you're probably dissatisfied now. So what were you expecting when you enrolled in law school, or when you first entered the practice of law? Look at the three charts I've included in this section. Do any of these frequently expressed expectations about law practice sound familiar? Are you now experiencing the disappointing reality? If your legal career has not met your

The Good Things about Practicing Law	The Downsides of Practicing Law
Money	Not enough money
Intellectual challenge	The billable hour
Status	Working with, against or around difficult people
Prestige	Limits to your ability to help
Autonomy	Guilt about not being able to fix everything
Variety	Being on a financial treadmill
Camaraderie	Repetition
Winning	The poor public image of lawyers
Flexibility	The lessening need for lawyers
Professional longevity	Being vulnerable to public opinion
Relationships with clients	Having no control over time
Access to organizations and events	Performance anxiety
Being in a project-driven business	Too little time for contemplation
Intellectual engagement and stimulation	Client demands and expectations
Ability to facilitate change	Being responsible for serious consequences
Ability to help others in need	Guilt from knowing the client will pay for your mistakes
Accumulated knowledge	Increasing overhead
Focus on problem solving	Exposure to malpractice claims and the high cost of premiums
Networking opportunities	Long hours
Power to influence others and society	Constant deadlines and time pressures
Professional identity	The way it takes over your life
The thrill of trying cases	The interminable nature of the problems and process
Having a socially acceptable outlet for aggressive behavior	Having to keep emotional distance from your clients
	Unpredictability
	Office and legal system politics
	Law office administration
	Competition
	Current turmoil in the profession
	High expectations of clients, colleagues, court system, society
	Isolation
	The adversarial system
	Having to keep too many balls in the air
	Having to live with wrong or unfair outcomes
	Knowing that legal services are expensive

expectations, and you fail to accept that reality, you will be dissatisfied. Says author Stephen Levine, "Suffering ... is wishing things were different from the way they are." There are only two cures for career dissatisfaction caused by unrealized or unrealistic expectations: If you don't like it, change it. If you can't change it, don't worry about it. Either take steps to remedy the situation, or accept it as it is.

An Uncomfortable Phase in Your Career

Every career moves along a predictable arc, progressing through at least five distinct phases of development.

Stage One (Orientation) — You figure out the rules of the game.

Stage Two (Challenge) — You prove your competence.

Stage Three (Establishment) — You climb the ladder.

Stage Four (Cruising) — You operate on a comfortable plateau.

Stage Five: (Disengagement) — You begin to let go.

Some people cycle through all five phases as they move from job to job, or as they handle a variety of projects for the same employer. At any stage, difficulties can create the urge to change just to escape the discomfort. Take a few moments to consider where you are in the arc of your law career.

Orientation

At this stage, you learn the rules of the game while engaging in a variety of tasks for the very first time. The experience varies with the environment you've chosen. If you choose to practice law, you have to familiarize yourself with its procedures and peculiarities. **Marla McGeorge**, a lawyer-turned-veterinarian, remembers the difference between "actually learning the craft" and floundering every time she walked into court, "trying to figure out which seat to sit in and what side of the courtroom table to choose." (Author's note: In my own case, I'll never forget the anxiety of trying to figure out when to say, "May it please the court" and when not to. After a while, I realized it didn't make any difference.)

> Every career moves along a predictable arc with at least five distinct phases.

Your task — To act without always knowing what you're doing — an uncomfortable feeling when you're accustomed to being competent and in control. Simply living through the discomfort of feeling foolishly incompetent — getting to the point of doing something the second or the third time — will sometimes cure your career ills. To allay your discomfort, identify lawyers, paralegals or even legal secretaries to whom you can turn for help. If you're working alone or have difficulty getting support from others in your office, join a relevant bar association section. This contact will provide a network of friendly experts. You can repay their kindness by assisting them with research or by making simple court appearances for them at no charge.

Challenge

This is the competence-building stage. During these years, you operate along a stimulating learning curve, becoming more and more skilled as a fourth motion is followed by a fifth and a first trial is followed by a second. The risk during this phase is that you handle cases or matters before you've developed the necessary expertise, or that you take on more work than you can competently handle. To avoid these pitfalls, develop working associations with more experienced practitioners. The challenge phase is particularly stimulating and engaging.

Your task — Few lawyers choose to make career changes during this period. Some of you, though, may be forced to look for other work due to financial pressures, employer instability, downsizing, or layoff. Being forced to make a change can be demoralizing, and may cause you to reconsider, or even abandon, your commitment to the legal profession. Don't act rashly; it would be unwise to make a career-changing decision based on hurt and disappointment.

Establishment

Here, the goal is to climb the ladder of success. Everyone defines the word "success" differently. For some, the end is purely financial — a bigger salary. Others seek increased responsibility, flexibility, respect, security, influence or recognition. Sometimes a long-range target — becoming a judge, or securing a high-level management position with a former client — is the definition of success.

Beware of the risks:

▶ You allow your desire for a good income and a good reputation to control your actions to the point where you neglect personal relationships, especially your marriage and your role as parent.
▶ You drive so hard without thinking about where you're going that you become trapped by "golden handcuffs" or, as author Joseph Campbell

puts it, you climb the ladder of success only to discover you put the ladder against the wrong wall.

▶ As you compete with more people for fewer opportunities, you might find your ladder more crowded than expected. For example, after eight years of apprenticeship in a large law firm, you might discover you're no longer on partnership track. Or, as an associate counsel in a corporate legal department, you might have to accept that the current general counsel is young, healthy, and committed, and blocking your upward mobility.

Your task — Accept the situation, find new work, or redefine success.

Cruising

The cruising stage begins when you've mastered the practice of law, and reached a comfortable plateau: a place where you know your job, you can easily meet its challenges, and you feel both personally and financially secure. Some lawyers cruise happily until retirement. Others feel restless or bored, especially those who thrive on the excitement and tension fueled by having to learn. The danger here is that boredom sets in when you stop taking calculated risks, the very quality that created success for you in the first place. Risk-avoidance can also result in job insecurity. Studies have shown that as professionals gain seniority, they lose the very quality that created their success in the first place — their willingness to risk. This immediately lowers their self-esteem, and leads to lower productivity and work quality. When law firm policies or financial reversals call for layoffs, these individuals are targeted for termination.

Your task — You can improve your longevity while also reinvigorating your career by adding an element of risk to your workday. As a subject matter specialist, you might experiment with new projects, branch into another area of practice, or strike out on your own. Long-time litigators might take a case or two to trial rather than pushing for settlement or letting a younger associate get the experience. Experiment with esoteric ventures to stretch your mental muscles. For example, several lawyers at a San Francisco firm designed a CD-ROM full of advice on preparing clients for depositions. A group in Seattle put together a video for their clients to help them get ready for their initial estate-planning meeting; it's now being sold nationally.

If you've saved a lot of money or have no immediate concerns about being let go, you might accept the level of accomplishment you've already attained, relax into a less grueling pace, and look outside work for new personal challenges. Or you might regard yourself as a part-time practitioner while marketing such personal services as teaching, designing seminars or law office software, or writing how-to manuals.

Senior associates and partners in larger firms may be able to get others to recognize the value of the roles you do find rewarding — teaching, training, mentoring, research, efficiency — without having to continue to grind away at more tedious duties. One lawyer turned down two offers to join other law firms after his firm finally recognized his leadership ability and asked him to chair the litigation department. Other lawyers have accomplished this goal by creating new roles within their firms — for example, client services manager, recruiting administrator and director of professional development.

Disengagement

If you believe you are at the cruising stage of your career, you may in fact have already begun to disengage. Disengagement can lead to retirement or a new career, or it can lead to procrastination, loss of interest, or depression. In the words of one HR manager, you can become a person who has "retired but forgotten to announce it." Our nation has operated for decades with the expectation that everyone first gets educated, then works and raises a family, and retires at 65, at which time the "leisure" years begin. But author/sociologist Ken Dychtwald points out in his book, *Age Wave*, that with life expectancies moving into the 80s and 90s, it's unrealistic to expect to have only one career in a lifetime. Any activity will become less stimulating and enjoyable after 20 or 30 years. It's also unrealistic, especially in these times of rapidly developing technology, to believe that you can stop educating yourself in your 20s. And how can anyone delay having fun until age 65 and actually live that long!

> Do something that makes you feel exhilarated, and a little afraid.

Your task — Negotiate a retirement package; train others to handle those aspects of practice for which you have lost interest; switch to a mentoring role; get involved in community activities. Do something that makes you feel exhilarated and a little afraid. That new "something" may just lead you to a new career, where the five-stage cycle will begin anew.

Living Life Out of Balance

By itself, fulfilling work does not create a fulfilling life. For that, you need to achieve a balance between work, family, leisure and personal challenge (and many would add a fifth dimension — spiritual development). Without that, no job — no matter how engaging or well-paid — can ever fill the gap. Indeed, many lawyers err by blaming their work environment for inadequacies in the other dimensions of their lives. But even if you feel completely engaged at work, it's only natural that in time it will lose its luster. And, as has been said for a long time, all work and no play makes Jack a dull fellow.

If you're living life out of balance, you need to tend to the primary connections in your life: developing emotional closeness with your children, taking steps to revive a failing marriage, or taking steps to develop a long-term romantic relationship. More than anything else, the quality of life depends on two factors: how we experience work, and our relations with other people. In his book, *The Pursuit of Happiness*, author David Myers even says that studies show that "supportive, intimate connections with other people are tremendously important" to feelings of happiness or well-being. For additional thoughts on this issue, read, *Should You Marry a Lawyer? A Couple's Guide to Balancing Work, Love & Ambition*, by Fiona Travis, Ph.D. (DecisionBooks, 2004).

Another way to live life in balance is by introducing some new challenge to your routine. Here is what two practitioners did to balance their lives:

▶ As counsel for the Seattle City Council, **Elizabeth** — introduced in Chapter 1 — felt stuck in her job and personal life. To compensate, she accepted a friend's challenge to try scuba diving. She loved it, and soon began diving in her spare time. Her passion for the sport led her to the Caribbean for a vacation. There, she learned from an island local that the local government needed someone with unusual qualifications: a law degree and good diving skills who could examine the coastal waters first-hand, and write and enforce regulations to protect their environment. Elizabeth grabbed the job.

▶ Or, take **Jim**: A veteran tax lawyer, his high school fantasy had been to fly for one of the airlines. That dream went into a tailspin when he lost out on a competition for Air Force ROTC. Jim's Plan B was to attend and graduate from law school. Ten years later, and feeling bored with his practice, Jim wondered whether it was too late to become a commercial pilot. In the course of his investigation, a friend and lawyer-turned-pilot told him he could still get into commercial aviation ... but he'd have to log the necessary flight time. Just one small problem: in all these years, Jim had never flown a plane. At that point, though, Jim signed up for lessons.

A year later, Jim had soloed and was having fun balancing time with his
family, his tax practice, and flying his own small plane. Simply scratching
an old itch, Jim didn't have to leave the profession to find happiness.

Are you living life in — or out — of balance?

In my work as a career consultant, I'm always struck at how many lawyers point
to their career choice as the sole cause of their unhappiness when the problem is
actually a life out of balance. With profits decreasing, and competition and overhead
increasing, it's no wonder so many of you find your lives increasingly out of balance;
you simply have no time for other interests, family and friends, not to mention your
own needs. This lack of balance is one of the six Roots of Dissatisfaction. But without
addressing this first, leaving the legal profession would be a big mistake.

Failing to Set Limits with Clients & Colleagues

Directors of the nation's lawyer assistance programs have observed a pattern
common to lawyers: they define "responsibility" in terms of their obligations to others without giving equal consideration to their own needs or the needs of their families. This unwillingness to disappoint others could very well be the sole cause of living
life out of balance. If this is your issue, the solution is to learn how to say "no" without jeopardizing your relationship with your clients, your partners or your boss. I'm
not unaware that heightened competition — not only between firms but among
lawyers within the same firm — has raised the threat level for those who would turn
down billable hours. So, if saying "no" is an issue in your life, the first step is to identify what's stopping you. After all, failing to set appropriate limits is one of the six
Roots of Dissatisfaction. But what's causing it?

▶ Not meeting the expectations of your boss?
▶ Angering or disappointing your clients?
▶ Angering or disappointing the person who referred the matter to you?
▶ Never getting another case if you turn this one down?
▶ Not making a good impression?
▶ Compromising your income or future opportunity for advancement?

Now, evaluate how realistic your fear really is, considering the experience of others you know. For example, are there any other associates or partners in your firm who
seem to be able to turn work away without losing respect or income? How can you

model yourself after them? The fear of repercussions are usually much worse than the repercussions themselves. In fact, saying "no" to a client may keep the client from spending money needlessly, and might actually lead to gratitude instead of resentment. Saying "no" to your boss may demonstrate your sense of responsibility to other commitments or your common sense in handling your legal work. And saying "no" to new clients may lead to the perception that you are so good and so busy that only the special few clients get to come in your door. There is an upside to saying "no".

Working in an Unpleasant Work Environment

According to a Newsweek study, 87 percent of those polled considered their workplace "a pleasant environment." Do you feel the same way? If it's the environment that's not working for you — that is, the people with whom you work, or the office atmosphere itself — you need to recognize it as one of the Roots of Dissatisfaction. But how can you know if environmental factors are the cause of your discomfort? One young lawyer tells of her mistaken diagnosis:

> ► The only woman in a firm of 10 lawyers, Cheryl decided that life would
> be better in a firm with more women. About that time, she got a call
> from a headhunter who was looking for a real estate associate for a large
> firm. "It was destiny," recalls Cheryl. "I was thinking about going to a
> large firm and, out of the blue, I get call from a headhunter. It seemed like
> a match made in heaven." It wasn't. "I thought I just needed to work
> with more women," said Cheryl. "The problem was deeper than that, and
> it took me a long time to wake up and say, 'Hey, Cheryl, practicing law is
> not going to get any better.'" She left after two years.

There's nothing wrong with changing jobs if, along the way, you achieve some insight to your dissatisfaction. But Danny Hoffman, a Stanford Law School grad who became a legal headhunter, sees many lawyers changing jobs needlessly just to escape their environmental concerns. The first move occurs, Hoffman says, when the thrill of getting a job out of law school wears off, and you wake up to the discomfort of living in a particular city or undertaking a lengthy commute. In the second stage, the firm itself is the defined problem. Whether working for an unpleasant partner, a boss-from-hell, or hating the workaholic atmosphere, the unhappy associate searches for a more congenial environment. After the next move, the young lawyer unhappily concludes, as one disillusioned associate put it, that "I've had the same terrible job in

two different buildings." At that point, it becomes apparent that it may be the practice of law itself that is the problem.

Though the prospect of working one more day in an uncomfortable environment is painful, resist the temptation to flee until after some reflection. Your boss may
be difficult, your office may be too stuffy, or you may want more flexible work hours.
But if you move to another job that satisfies only your environmental concerns, you
may soon discover that you dislike the work there as well. By then, you may not have
the emotional or physical energy, or the money, for another disruptive career move.
The bottom line is that you must examine whether the practice of law suits you
before you can determine whether your environment is the root cause of your dissatisfaction. For real-life examples, see another of my books, *Running From the Law: Why
Good Lawyers Are Getting Out of the Legal Profession* (DecisionBooks, 2004).

Not Using Your Talents and Preferences

Every person is born with, and continues to develop, a unique personality profile.
It's an ever-evolving combination of interests, skills, values, and preferences. But harnessing those talents and preferences inappropriately makes for one of the most
common roots of lawyer dissatisfaction.

Going to work every day is like trying to sign your name with your non-domi-
nant hand. Sure, you can do it. But it just never feels right.

The work of a lawyer involves an extraordinarily wide range of skills. You might
procrastinate when facing some tasks, but feel great energy to accomplish others. For
example, you might love meeting and communicating with clients, but hate having
to research a brief. So you'll gladly take interruptive phone calls and schedule emergency conferences with clients, but never seem to find the time to draft a summary
judgment motion or probate inventory. Many lawyers find their skills misapplied in
this way. For example, young lawyers with good people-skills apprentice by spending
solitary years in the library, while lawyers who loved the legal analysis, research and
writing they did in their early years, are expected to become rainmakers or engage in
client development as they mature.

To help you determine whether your work is compatible with your skills and
values, pay attention to your emotional responses. When you're in the right line
of work:

▶ You approach your work with enthusiasm and high energy, not anger,
   boredom or lethargy.

▶ You tend to initiate work rather than avoid it.

▶ You want to lead or join in activities rather than complain about them or withdraw from them.

▶ When faced with a new project, you feel stimulated to learn rather than tempted to procrastinate.

▶ When you've finished a task, you feel proud of the accomplishment rather than relieved that you're done.

Review the list of character traits shared by contented lawyers and the Personality Preference Quiz that follows. If you find yourself out of sync, invest time in completing the exercises in Chapter 3 (*Self-Assessment*) before making any other changes.

A Dozen Traits Shared by Contented Lawyers

1. Display a love of learning
2. Pay attention to details
3. Respect the rules
4. Possess strong analytical abilities
5. Achievement-oriented
6. Competitive
7. Steady and stable
8. Patient and persistent
9. More realistic than idealistic
10. More conventional than innovative
11. More dispassionate than emotional
12. Thick-skinned

Personality Preference Quiz*   *yes/no*

1. Do you like to get emotionally involved with your work?
2. Do you dislike or attempt to avoid conflict?
3. In resolving conflict, do you prefer deciding what's fair based on the circumstances of each situation?
4. Do you like to create or start projects and let others finish or maintain them?
5. Do you dislike paying attention to details?
6. Do you prefer short-term projects?
7. Do you value efficiency?
8. Do you like to do things your own way, on your own schedule, and in order of your own priorities?
9. Do you get more satisfaction being part of a team than being a solo act?
10. Do you want to change the world?

A "yes" answer to any of these questions ought to raise serious reservations about the wisdom of using your law degree to practice law. There may be some appropriate options for you in the legal profession, but you should take time for self-assessment and more thorough research of alternative career directions.

*Excerpted from *Running from the Law.*

Is It Burnout or Dissatisfaction?

"The two most thrilling days of my life were graduating from law school and being sworn into the bar. But when it came to actually practicing law, I was almost instantly miserable."

—*Valerie, a lawyer-turned-foundation director*

▪ ▪ ▪

In the last six months, have you noticed that:

▶ You used to love your work but now it exhausts you emotionally or physically?

▶ You feel you're accomplishing much less compared with your past performance?

▶ You're dedicated to your clients and colleagues but no one seems to appreciate it?

▶ You feel cynical about your work, your employer, and/or your clients?

▶ You believe only you can do the work you do as well as you do it, and that your clients and colleagues would be harmed if you quit?

▶ You're no longer interested in the hobbies or pastimes you used to enjoy?

▶ You feel tired rather than energetic?

▶ People wonder why you look tired or "not so good"?

▶ You're increasingly forgetful about appointments, or overlooking deadlines?

▶ You need more time alone than you used to?

> Burnout is an unacknowledged state of exhaustion that occurs when you consistently make choices for the benefit of others at the expense of your own needs.

▶ You're more irritable now when driving in traffic or waiting in lines?

▶ You're getting unexplained headaches or stomachaches or backaches?

▶ You find yourself frequently feeling angry and striking out at others?

If you answer "yes" to any of these questions, you're probably exhibiting one or more symptoms of burnout. Although you can burn out from devoting yourself to work you don't enjoy, burnout is not the same as dissatisfaction with your job or career. This section will help you determine whether it's your work or your attitude toward your work that is the problem.

What Is Burnout?

To begin with, burnout is more than simply fatigue.

Much more.

By definition, burnout is an unacknowledged state of exhaustion that occurs when you consistently make choices for the benefit of others at the expense of your own needs. For example, if you just completed a long trial or brief, or you concluded a complicated business deal after working night and day for weeks, you might be tempted to describe your exhaustion as *burnout*. But it could just as easily be overwork. How to distinguish between the two? Here's a quick test: If tomorrow you were given an opportunity to take some time off, and you accepted, then you're not burned out. But you probably *do* have a problem with burnout if you respond this way:

> I can't take time off. What would my clients (or boss) say?
> There's too much on my plate right now; I can't leave. Maybe in a few months.
> They need me here. I'm the only one who can do this work

According to Dr. Herbert J. Freudenberger, author of *Burn Out*, the victims of this syndrome are usually "dynamic, charismatic, goal-oriented people" or "determined idealists." Burnout, says Freudenberger, "usually has its roots in the area of your life that seems to hold the most promise." And for lawyers, that area is work. Lawyers tend to exhibit two signs of chronic burnout: an I-just-don't-care-anymore attitude which is often accompanied by heavy drinking, or overeating, or increasingly compulsive activity. "The manic defense against depression," says author James Hillman, "is to keep extremely busy — and to be very irritated when interrupted. Your schedule is one of your biggest defenses."

The Roots of Burnout

Burnout among lawyers can occur from consistently working too much to meet daily demands ... from having to perform in ways that violate your sense of right and wrong ... from being caught between bosses demanding your time and attention ... or from never getting any praise from your superiors no matter how impressive your work. More commonly, though, the problem is a result of the lawyer work style. The following 10 symptoms are among the Roots of Burnout. Can you identify with any of them?

▶ *A pressure to succeed* — You don't just imagine this pressure; it's inherent in your role as an attorney. Your clients bring you problems. It's your job to take on their burdens so they feel better and you feel responsible.

▶ *A need for continual stimulation* — Trial lawyers and mergers and acquisitions specialists are especially prone to this affliction. As one former practitioner put it, "I think I was a law addict." There may also be an institutional fear of, or scorn for, relaxation. This alone leads to burnout.

▶ *A lack of balance* — Clients demand that you meet their needs before you think about anything else. Firms expect you to put your work first. Lawyers are often competitive about how hard they work. Think about it: do you know of a law firm that rewards the lawyer who regularly gets home in time to eat dinner with the kids as generously as the one who bills 2,500 hours a year? In an office standard of overwork, a macho attitude prevails that suggests "you're not committed to the firm unless you share our work habits."

▶ *Inflexibility* — Being inflexible once you've taken a stand on something. In agreeing to represent a client, you've agreed to promote that client's best interests. You can't suddenly decide the other side's position is the better one; you must stick to your guns.

▶ *Lack of intimacy* — Feeling a lack of intimacy with the people around you. You're a lawyer; you're expected to separate yourself from the problem and remain rational at all times. You often submerge your own beliefs and values when you advocate a client's position. You can generate inner confusion when you advocate a position for one client one moment and the opposite for another client the next.

More on Lawyer Stress & Burnout

Stephen Feldman practiced law for five years in the 1960's, and then taught law for another 11 while he earned a Ph.D. in psychology. Since 1982, he's practiced as a clinical psychologist, working with many lawyers and their families. Here he shares his unique perspective on the stresses peculiar to practicing lawyers.

Feldman's Statement: Law was a tough thing to get up in the morning to do. I used to wake up and think, "Maybe it's World War III and I won't have to go to the office. Maybe everything will be called off today."

For me, the anxiety started as far back as law school. I remember once sitting in a class, saying to myself, "I am paying attention, I have read the material, and I don't know what they are talking about. This is frightening." The only thing I could hold onto, I thought, was that I was fourth in the class and there were only three other guys who might be understanding it. If I was at the bottom of the class, I think I would have walked out.

I continued through law school like a little pigeon. I kept pecking, they kept rewarding me, and I continued to be a good student. I remember how tense law school was and how massive the workload seemed to be. The horrible news is that things are probably still that way for most lawyers, but they have just gotten used to it.

Stress is not just a matter of staying late at the office or becoming irritable at home. It is a serious business that can affect the quality and indeed the length of life. And there are stresses peculiar to a lawyer's work.

First, practicing law is the only profession in which there is an equal and opposite professional whose job it is to prove that you are wrong. A doctor does not ordinarily face a second doctor objecting to what he or she does. No opposing preacher is there to argue for the devil. The adversary system means there is little margin for error, as opposing counsel forever lurks, waiting to pounce on any mistake. Additionally, any error is forever part of the record, able to come back to haunt you long after you have retired to Hawaii and quit paying for malpractice insurance.

Besides opposing counsel, the work is often subject to criticism or praise by a third person, namely a judge or a jury. In law, someone wins and somebody loses. Judgments of your work are made virtually every day.

And lawyers continually deal with the heavy responsibility of someone else's money, property, quality of life, family or even life and death. A lawyers faces these issues, and usually several client's problems, all in one day.

One lawyer described the essence of his practice as absorbing the client's energy. The client relieves himself of his stress by passing it on to you. You accept it from the client so the client can leave your office saying, "I feel better." That way, the client will be back.

The pressure never ends. One night, I was lying in bed reading a detective novel. I got to this steamy part that read, "Slowly, he ran his hand along Babs' thigh," and I suddenly found myself wondering whether I'd remembered to file for an extension in the Babs Smith case? Then it hit me. I couldn't even read a dirty book without the law intruding.

Lawyers also continually deal with deadlines. Law is the business of deadlines, and woe to you if you miss that 10 days to file a notice of appeal (or is it 30?), the 20 days to answer a complaint, the statutes of limitations, the interrogatories, and so on and so on. There isn't an event that happens in a lawyer's professional life that doesn't have a time frame and a penalty attached to it.

Along with winning and losing comes conflict. The lawyer's professional life is filled with dispute, confrontation, and occasionally actual hatred. It is rare that a case will be pleasant; even adoptions can have snags. That unhappiness and conflict is reflected in the public's generally low opinion of lawyers as compared to other professionals. This also adds to the stress.

And you are the person expected to have the knowledge and expertise to give answers. Clients don't understand that you usually can't say either "yes" or "no," "black" or "white."

Being both a psychologist and a lawyer, I can speak to the difference in client attitudes. As a psychologist, when I call a client to make an appointment to come in, the response is usually pleasure in some form. It might be relief or gratitude. Almost always there is compliance. As an attorney doing the same task, there is usually hostility or suspicion. At the very least, there is apprehension, fear, tension, distance or coolness.

Similarly, when the phone rings for lawyers, it's like a time bomb going off. You can never tell what kind of crisis or attitude is going to come at you through the receiver.

None of the phone calls may be actual Big Events. But just one may be, and it may be the next call.

I believe it's quite true that as people go forward in the practice of law they learn more and more about less and less. The legal profession is very narrowing to the soul. That's why lawyers need to get away and do something else; to discover there's a whole world out there that doesn't know there are two court systems. They need to remind themselves that the universe that has become so important to them is just a footnote in most other people's lives.

I once said to a nurse I was working with that I had found the secret to happiness in life.

She said, "Great, what's that?"

"What you have to do," I said, "is first figure out what you like to do and then figure out how to make money at it."

She thought for a minute, and then said, "I think that's prostitution!"

It was a great answer, but I still think I had the right idea. It's the whole reason I went into psychology. I like to talk to people; I like to listen to people. Hell, if I like to do that, why not do it and make money too?

Most lawyers don't see their work that way.

How can other people get close to you if they can't see through your camouflage?

▶ *An inability to relax* — Who can relax when six deadlines are converging, or when everyone around you is questioning your decisions? Technology has only accelerated the process to the point where a crisis mentality is the norm. How many times have you received something by e-mail, fax, or overnight delivery and, without regard for its contents, assumed that it was more important and required a quicker response than if you had received it through the postal system? The court system aggravates the problem by creating programs to speed trials and discovery, and to schedule motions and trials with shorter notice periods. And the lack of civility among lawyers results in more surprise motions with little notice. Then, of course, clients often delay seeking out your help for their problems until the very last minute.

▶ *Can't focus on priorities* — This symptom is characterized by shifting back and forth between long-range and immediate goals. You don't control your schedule; it's in the hands of other lawyers, the whims of clients and the court system. Who can focus on long range goals when urgent short-term matters continually interrupt?

▶ *Hyper self-conscious* — Always being worried about preserving your image. You aren't imagining the pressure to look and act a certain way. The rules of ethics require that you uphold a high standard and noble image as an agent of justice and the court system.

▶ *Taking yourself too seriously* — If you don't take yourself seriously, who else will? Your entire mission is to be taken seriously by your clients, opposing counsel and their clients, and the court system.

▶ *Identity issues* — Identifying so closely with your activities that if they fail, you fall apart. Your clients hire you to win for them. When you lose a trial, you've failed them and that means you've failed as a lawyer. It's even worse if you get caught in an act of legal malpractice; you have a fiduciary obligation to act in your client's best interests. It's a rare lawyer who can get through either of those events without feeling personally destroyed.

A seminar participant once asked me, "How do you address the fundamental psychological barrier of turning to a non-professional career without feeling that you're stepping into a job that anyone with less smarts and skills could do?" Now there's a lawyer who has over-identified with the title and role of lawyer, and is a clear candidate for burnout.

Distinguishing Burnout from Dissatisfaction

Whether you're burned out or dissatisfied with your work, the solutions are the same: a need for serious reflection, and the development of supportive relationships. But don't expect instant results. As you begin to explore your relationship with your work, you may feel even more confused. Insight develops gradually; but it will happen. The importance of outside support, especially by peers, cannot be overemphasized. Isolation is one symptom of burnout. The more dissatisfied you become, the less willing you are to admit it and to discuss your malaise with others.

In the case of one successful practitioner, he developed — and finally acknowledged — a drinking problem. With the support of Alcoholics Anonymous, he admitted his vulnerability, and then confided his turmoil about his professional direction to some of his more successful colleagues. He was surprised to find they, too, were unhappy despite their self-satisfied public image. Suddenly, he realized that for years he had assumed that he alone was struggling. That fateful connection with other lawyers caused him to rethink, and successfully redirect, his career. Increasing your contact with others can provide you the insight and courage that leads to change. This next chapter will put the notion of change is sharper relief. For additional resources, turn to Appendices 2-6.

CHAPTER 3

COMING TO TERMS WITH CHANGE

Managing the Natural Resistance to Change

"If someone said I could make as much money writing as practicing law, I'd quit the law in a minute. But I need to stick it out. I make four times as much money lawyering as writing, and I have a wife and two kids to consider."

—*Walter Walker, a lawyer/novelist*

■ ■ ■

I spent 10 years in the practice of law.

One night at dinner, I found myself confiding to a lawyer friend that I doubted I could practice law for the rest of my life. "I guess I ... just ... don't ... want to be a lawyer anymore," I said. Even as the words tumbled out, I felt I was confessing to treason.

I remember my friend's expression. "That's crazy," he said. "The profession suits you. You'd be making a huge, huge, mistake to think about doing anything else."

> Resistance to change is real and justified.

So, I didn't. I put the handcuffs back on for another six years. During that time, I adapted (we're great at adapting, aren't we?) And bit by bit, I began adjusting my practice — or "reinventing" as we said back then — to emphasize what I enjoyed doing, and to minimize what I didn't. I turned down clients I knew would be trouble — either personality-wise or financially — and I declined cases that didn't interest me enough to want to learn the law.

Eventually, I narrowed my practice to matters involving families or residential real estate, the two subject matters that engaged me, and which allowed a high level of client contact, and in which the law itself was not too complex. I invested in a good computer system so I could draft my own work, I cut down on overhead and reduced the hours I had to bill. At that point, having withdrawn from a small partnership to practice on my own, I even added fiction writing into the mix. All the while, I was diligent about putting money into savings for an unknown future.

Finally, though, I was just so frustrated with my life and law career I wanted out. For awhile, Tahiti was sounding real good. But, like the guy in the Buddhist fable (see Page 2), I couldn't let go of the branch of the tree. I was so tied to my professional identity, and to the belief that my clients would never forgive me for quitting, I put it off. A month went by, two months. Then, at the gym, another friend suggested a long sabbatical. A sabbatical? Was she insane? I couldn't do that. My clients depended upon me. I would be throwing away a stable, lucrative practice. Everyone would think I was irresponsible, unreliable. And, yet ... and yet, an hour later, still a little high from exercise, I decided a sabbatical was possible. I hurried back to the office and projected cash flow and expenses, determined which files I could transfer to other lawyers and which ones I felt morally committed to completing, and I scheduled my sabbatical six months from that very day!

Of course, when I finally did close the doors to my office, I suffered a deep reactive depression. After all, if I wasn't a lawyer, what was I? If I wasn't billing for time, what value did I have as a person? It was only while researching and writing my first book — *Running from the Law: Why Good Lawyers Are Getting Out of the Legal Profession* — and I established a support group for lawyers in transition, that I was able to see through the fog and move on. Soon after my book was published, I saw a review in *California Lawyer*. I laughed. The reviewer criticized the lawyers I profiled in the book, and wrote that any lawyer who wants to switch careers should, in the words of the Nike slogan, "just do it." Oh, right. If it was only that easy. We all put so much of our lives into becoming lawyers that resistance to change is real and justified. And you know what I'm talking about. Indeed, there many logical reasons to simply put this book back on the shelf and stay where you are.

How many of these reasons sound familiar?   **Just do it!**

- ▶ I can't let my partners down (how will they function without me?).
- ▶ I can't let my clients down (how will they get along without me?).
- ▶ I have my family to think about. Changing careers now would create big problems for them.
- ▶ My work offers intellectual challenge and financial security (where else can I get that?)

▶ I like the predictability of being a lawyer.

▶ Some days are better than others, but even on the bad days I survive.

▶ I like my corner office.

▶ The job market is awful right now. I have friends who jumped ship and were out of work for months ... and some are still looking.

▶ I really don't have time to think about this now.

These are just a few; feel free to add a few of your own excuses.

It's only natural to experience resistance when we think about leaving the law. But the problems really begin when we procrastinate. The trick is to recognize when we've crossed the line. "In the Air Force, one of the big lessons they tried to get across to us was when to bail out," said former practicing lawyer Rick Rogovy, now a successful entrepreneur. "Too often, pilots would ride their planes into the ground because it was more familiar inside the cockpit — even in a crippled plane — than depending on an ejection system and parachute." In an interesting biological parallel, studies have shown that if frogs are dropped into boiling water, they will instantly hop out for safety. But put them into cold water that is slowly brought to the boiling point, they stay until it's too late.

Why do we remain where we are?

Because we're afraid of jeopardizing our sense of security, our primary relationships, our self-esteem, even our identities. Lawyers, who are trained to find precedents for every choice, just naturally avoid risk. "Lawyers want to know for sure that career planning is going to work," says Washington State career consultant Ava Butler. "They want facts and evidence. But there are so many unknowns involved that it keeps many lawyers unhappy and stuck."

But without taking the risk of letting something end, there can be no beginning of something better.

You must let go of your commitment or attachment to the old before you can develop something new. That ending and those feelings of loss are the starting point for the change. In fact, you know you've initiated an ending when you find yourself feeling unhappy or anxious for no apparent reason. Unfortunately, between the ending of the old and the beginning of the new is a middle, an uncomfortable place full of confusion, doubt, tension and frustration. This time of inertia, according to career consultant Lesah Beckhusen, may even serve to buffer you "from making another wrong decision or from realizing your worst fears, that there might not be anything better out there."

Coming to Terms
with Change

Some lawyers try to ignore the messy process of change and all its discomfort and uncertainty. Instead, they remain stuck in their dissatisfaction until some external event galvanizes them into action — getting fired or laid off, or developing a precarious medical condition. Other lawyers keep working until they burn out, and then quit in a huff with nowhere else to turn.

At a time when you most need energy and confidence, avoiding change can leave you exhausted and with badly damaged self-esteem. Let's face it. When you initiate change, you enter an awkward, uncomfortable, even depressing period of time,

Some Little-Known Facts about Change

▶ The average American changes jobs every three years and careers every ten.

▶ Contrary to general perception, positive feelings motivate most change.

▶ A sudden insight or unpredictable event, rather than a carefully-developed plan, usually triggers action.

▶ You are more likely to change on your own volition than at the urging of colleagues, relatives or self-help groups, or doctors, therapists or other professional advisors.

▶ In order to change, you have to step out of your "comfort zone" and face your fears of humiliation, failure, discomfort or pain.

▶ In order to change, you have to think about old situations in new ways.

▶ Outward change happens to us. Inner change occurs only with intention.

▶ Change does not occur in a straight line.

▶ There is no timeline for change. Everyone changes at his or her own pace.

▶ Change is always stressful.

▶ Confusion and dissatisfaction are the two most obvious signals that something needs to change. They are symptoms that something is wrong in your life and that you're going to end up exactly where you don't want to be if you don't change directions.

▶ Stress and frustration may be the first signs that you are changing.

▶ You have less to give to others when you are changing.

▶ Change always triggers loss and the emotional reactions that accompany it: shock, denial or resistance, bargaining, grief and acceptance.

▶ Planning for change provides a measure of security, but it is impossible to plan for the range of emotions that accompany it.

a time when you no longer want to wear your current identity but you haven't found a new one to put on. Those uncomfortable feelings persist even after you've chosen a new career if you haven't progressed far enough to create the same kind of firm-footed sense of belonging you had before. The discomfort eventually recedes as you become more a part of your new career and less identified with what you've left behind. But it's important to recognize that you cannot — let me repeat, cannot — move from the old to the new without passing through that uncomfortable place in between.

The good news is that every lawyer who truly wants to make a change will do so. This chapter will begin to help you do that.

Reasons to Maintain
the Status Quo

"I don't want to leave hell. I know the names of all the streets."

—a lawyer

■ ■ ■

The first step to moving past your resistance to change is to define what's good about where you are now. You may dislike your job, your practice area, even your lack of a secure future, but there are probably several good reasons you maintain the status quo. Those reasons are sufficient to create a level of resistance that mere dissatisfaction cannot budge. That's why you've been "bitching and moaning" to your friends, or why you always resolve your criticism of your current situation by telling yourself, "Oh well, at least I'm working." You can also look at your resistance to change in the opposite way: What's so bad about where you're going?

> "Often what holds us back is an undefined fear."

Peter C. Jenkins, a lawyer and consultant from Gaithersburg, Maryland, suggests making a detailed list of what it is you fear most. "Often what holds us back," he says, "is an undefined fear." To identify your fears, grab a legal pad and jot down your thoughts about the following questions:

▶ What am I afraid I'll lose?
▶ What is the worst ending I can imagine?
▶ What do I hope to gain?
▶ What would an ideal ending look like?
▶ Who will have to let go of what when the change occurs?

In the chart that follows, I've identified nearly four dozen barriers to change that are commonly mentioned by lawyers in distress. After reading them, return to your answers to the questions above, and jot down a few barriers of your own. Don't be timid; be specific. When you make a list of the fears that are holding you back, your reasons to maintain the status quo can appear insurmountable. And they will be, until you begin the process explained later in this chapter.

The Unknown	Lack of Time or Timing
▶ Not knowing what else to do	▶ Having no time to look for something else
▶ Not knowing about other options	
▶ Not knowing where to start	▶ Having no time to think about doing something else
▶ Not being able to imagine having work you love	▶ Thinking you'll have more time after a certain case ends
▶ Not believing you could ever earn enough money doing what you really love	▶ Having a hard time concentrating on transition when the demands of your caseload keep interfering
▶ Not having the right background to do what you really want to do	▶ Needing to give the profession more of a chance
▶ Having to make a decision about which direction to take	▶ Worrying that you're giving up too soon
▶ Only knowing how to practice law	▶ Hoping it will be better when you're a partner
▶ Fear of not finding anything else	
▶ Fear of being under-employed	▶ Hoping the situation will improve (e.g., the partner you hate might die, leave or miraculously change)
▶ Fear of getting into a profession with even fewer women or minorities	
▶ Fear of getting into something that's no better—and could be even worse	▶ Waiting for things to get bad enough
▶ Fear of having regrets	▶ Believing it will look bad on your résumé to change employment after only a year
▶ Fear of losing or wasting your investment in time or education	▶ Feeling that your investment hasn't paid off enough to justify leaving
▶ Losing the comfort of knowing what's expected of you	▶ Thinking you're too old to change
▶ Knowing you will have to make a big investment in any new venture	
▶ Wondering if you could just make an adjustment where you are	

41

Money Concerns	**The Reaction of Others**
▶ Thinking it's smarter to wait until you get fired or laid off so you can collect unemployment	▶ Not wanting to let your [partners, clients, parents, spouse, kids, relatives] down
▶ Knowing your children will be going to college soon, and that you have to pay for their schooling	▶ Knowing your [clients, partners, boss] need you
▶ Realizing that you're deeply in debt	▶ Feeling that your family expects you to continue to support them in the style to which you have all become accustomed
▶ Refusing to accept the prospect of earning less money	▶ Reneging on your commitment to put your kids through private school or college
▶ Not knowing how you'll pay your student loans	▶ Knowing your family expects you to be a "professional"
▶ Being attached to the lifestyle your high income provides	▶ Fear of losing the respect of your colleagues
▶ Hating your work, but loving the security	▶ Fear of invoking the wrath of your parents or spouse
▶ Having a spouse and children to support	▶ Fear of setting a bad example for other women or minorities
▶ Having to pay the kids' private school tuition	▶ Feeling that a certain project or client needs you to handle it right
▶ Needing $100,000 per year just to survive	▶ Fearing failure to live up to your potential
▶ Worrying that you'll end up a bag lady or homeless	▶ Fearing being seen as a failure
▶ Worrying that the bank will take back your house	▶ Not wanting to lose the relationships you've built
▶ Worrying that you'll never have financial security or a respectable income again	▶ Fearing you'll be rejected by your social network
▶ Missing the good life from law firm parties	▶ Fearing your friends will turn on you
▶ Being reluctant to give up staying in nice hotels on someone else's dime	▶ Fearing your colleagues will shun you
▶ Giving up benefits like health insurance, paid vacation, pension plan	
▶ Missing perks like a secretarial staff, copy room, library, free lunches	

Self-Esteem and Identity Issues

▶ Not believing in yourself

▶ Feeling lucky that you have so much and guilty that you would give it all up

▶ Hating to give up the prestige, automatic respect and ego boost that come from being identified as a lawyer

▶ Liking the professionalism of the business

▶ Wanting to keep the credibility and recognition you've earned

▶ Not wanting to feel like a quitter or a failure

▶ Appreciating the power, control or autonomy you now have

▶ Liking your freedom and flexibility

▶ Not wanting to give up the intellectual validation and challenge of your work

▶ Hating to start again at the bottom

▶ Worrying that you won't be taken seriously in the next endeavor

Realistic Guidelines for Change

By Ed Honnold*

"We prefer the security of a known misery, to the misery of an unfamiliar insecurity."

—*Stan McCleary, lawyer-turned-psychologist*

■ ■ ■

Though a lateral move within law can sometimes occur quickly, a more radical career change may take considerable time to accomplish. Years, in fact.

In my experience as a legal career counselor, radical change typically occurs in four phases: 1) assessing the nature and causes of your discontent; 2) overcoming the influences that lead you to continue your current work, even if it makes you unhappy; 3) envisioning an alternative to your current work that suits your interests, skills and values, and that deeply excites you; and, 4) seeking (or creating) a new job or profession. Let's look at each phase in detail:

Assessing the Nature and Causes of Your Discontent

The Misery Index — The first step is to take a rigorous account of your current professional experience. Ask yourself what elements in your work you enjoy or don't enjoy. Take a reading of what I call your "misery index". On a scale of 1 to 10 (with 10 being the most miserable), what tasks generally prompt the highest and lowest stages of discomfort. Now, ask yourself whether there is a way to salvage your legal career, or even your current job, by seeking more of the types of work you enjoy and less of the other. Seeking a different practice area, avoid-

> The Misery Index – the first step to salvaging your career.

ing or pursuing further litigation work, or moving from the private to public sector, may be worth considering. At least it would buy you more time while you consider more radical alternatives.

Take note of your pain — Physical and emotional pain are powerful motivators for change. The lawyers who are most successful in achieving a bold alternative to their current work are often those who start out being the most miserable in their current law practice. So, pay close attention to several things:

▶ Notice how often you get headaches, backaches, stomach pain;
▶ Notice symptoms such as insomnia, fearfulness, anxiety, loss of energy and enthusiasm;
▶ Notice the experience reported by many lawyers that "it just doesn't feel right" to be at work, or feelings of detachment, lack of motivation, or resentment toward the demands of work;
▶ Notice the language you use to describe your professional life to friends and family, especially when you are being ruthlessly honest.

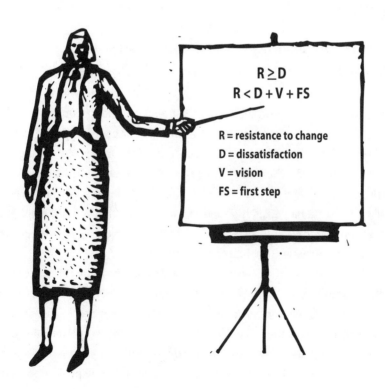

$$R \geq D$$
$$R < D + V + FS$$

R = resistance to change
D = dissatisfaction
V = vision
FS = first step

Instead of distracting yourself by doing more legal work, or planning exotic vacations, or shopping, drinking or surfing the Internet, practice sitting with your feelings and writing about them to yourself. This attention to your experience will increase your awareness of how unhappy you are and strengthen your resolve to making change. Try to see your discomfort as an ally to your change process rather than its enemy.

Rule out alternative sources of discontent — In assessing and interpreting your state of mind, consider whether other factors may be governing your experiences at work. For example, how well is your primary relationship working? If you are single (or even in a relationship), are you lonely? Are you neglecting to pay attention to important friendships? Are you neglecting to exercise, get enough sleep, eat a healthy diet, or plan for fun? Are you victimized by high standards of performance which may have helped you to achieve success in law, but may also prevent you from enjoying your success? If your primary issue is that you have not yet learned how to find happiness in any sector of life, and you have poor coping skills, a career change alone may bring little relief. As the Buddhists say, "wherever you go, there you are." Instead of changing your practice, you may wish to consider counseling, meditation, yoga, or other healing practice.

The Influences That Keep You "Stuck"

Count the money — Many lawyers feel "stuck" in unhappy careers because of law school debt, large mortgages, expensive tastes, financially dependent family members, and aspirations to an early or comfortable retirement. Though financial considerations can be significant, ask yourself whether money concerns may be "standing in" for other, more intangible and inaccessible issues. For example, how much is it worth to you to be happy? When your life ends, will it seem worthwhile to have earned an impressive income over the course of your life by doing meaningless work? And realistically, how sustainable is a high income in law practice if you are unhappy, resentful and unmotivated? Keep in mind that many unhappy lawyers eventually move on to highly successful and profitable alternative careers.

Unproductivity happens — If you come to believe that your current career must end (especially if, despite your best efforts, it is ending), accept the fact that your work output and quality of work product will suffer in the final months. Most lawyers find it impossible to maintain their accustomed high standards of performance during their career's terminal stage, when their personal misery index is high and their thoughts are turning to what they will do next. Ending an unhappy professional life is often the most painful stage in career transition. Many lawyers exert massive and costly efforts to conceal their unproductivity, hoping that no one will notice ... at least not before they depart. Many lawyers fail to acknowledge this loss of productivity to others and themselves because it engenders such profound shame and mortification. If you are experiencing some degree of "end stage" unproductivity, keep this in mind — it's normal. In fact, it may be essential to build the momentum needed to make a change.

Honor your resistance — Even up to the last possible moment (and long past any logical point-of-no-return) many lawyers will "bargain" with the death of their careers. They will find logical and persuasive reasons to continue doing what they have been doing. A career change process inevitably encounters various manifestations of psychological resistance — fears that family, friends and colleagues will disapprove of the change; that the alternatives are not sufficiently clear in mind; or fears that financial obligations demand that you put off your departure. If you have a high tolerance for pain, fear and self-doubt, such resistance can keep you blocked indefinitely. There should be no dishonor in experiencing such resistance. Without psychological defenses of this and other kinds, we would all be emotionally unbalanced. Try to develop a compassionate and nonjudgmental stance toward your doubts.

> The right career begins with a rigorous personal inventory.

Envisioning a Career Alternative

Mobilize your vision for an alternative — A transition toward a new career may be motivated initially by pain. But it will be consummated only by a rigorous assessment of your skills, values and passionate interests. A common flaw in career change is the belief that the "right" choice of career can be "found" somewhere and "pursued" like a hound chasing a fox. It is more realistic to expect that a sustainable career choice arises from a rigorous inventory of the process of your own life as you currently live it. Most important is to take account of your interests, which will usually reflect your aptitudes and values.

Envisioning a new career resembles solving a mystery. The clues are all available within yourself and in your current behavior. So, begin to look for clues in the nature of the books and magazines you read, in the content of your social conversations, in your fantasies and dreams, and in your weekend and other "spare time" activities. What activities do you most enjoy when you aren't obligated to do anything for someone else? Many lawyers discover that the best career move has already been taking shape naturally "around the edges" of everyday life. A professional job should deeply engage and excite you, involving interests that are deeply grounded in an experience of your true self.

Career assessment — At this time, it may be useful to take one of the widely available career assessment tests administered by career counselors and by law school placement and alumni offices (see **www.DecisionBooks.com** for names of career counselors), and read Appendix 3 for a list of online self-assessment tools. These tests may be particularly useful if you are considering a wide range of career options, or if you feel clueless or overwhelmed by available options. The tests, though, will not provide a definitive answer to your inquiry because they cannot substitute for the hard work of identifying who you are and the nature of your mission in life.

Envision an ideal job — It is often helpful to imagine an ideal job for yourself, assuming that you have all the needed skills and that your financial needs will be met. Many lawyers discover that their ideal job is not as unrealistic or unattainable as they initially expect, and that their best career moves point toward implementation of some variation of their "ideal job".

Identify a range of possibilities — Open a file for each "possibility", and investigate each option systematically. Talk with people already doing this kind of work; attend professional meetings and training programs for people in each field; gather articles and other source materials for each field; and assess the entry requirements, pay scales and economic prospects for each option. Most important, notice your level of interest and excitement about each one. Do you feel "called" to learn more and more about certain ones? Keep these files open as you investigate further, and close the files that register little activity.

Seeking or Creating, a New Job or Career

Develop a working hypothesis — From your investigation of job possibilities, you will eventually choose one which you will explore more intensively. Proceed with a "working hypothesis" that this will be your next career, until you either prove or disprove the hypothesis. Continue to assess your level of excitement and interest. You will know you have made the right choice if you experience a sustaining desire to pursue it further. If you find your interest waning, replace this option with one of the others from your possibility set, and test the next hypothesis the same way. Eventually, your "right livelihood" will arise and supplant all the other possibilities.

Bring your new career into being — Put your working hypothesis to its final test by taking a course, reading books, actively networking, and applying for jobs — or preparing to create a job — in the new field. If you are on the right track, options will open in front of you as you take initiative.

Relax — Career transition need not be continuously painful; it can often prove enjoyable, especially as momentum builds toward a satisfying outcome. If you approach this process with a relaxed, non-judgmental, self-compassionate attitude, the results are more likely to satisfy your deeper desires. Congratulations ... and good luck.

Ed Honnold, JD/LICSW — Honnold is a former law clerk for the US Court of Appeals, a private law firm associate, and a legislative director to a member of Congress. He is currently a Washington DC-based clinical social worker specializing in transition counseling to help attorneys explore career options, match skills with vocations, and overcome obstacles to change. Contact — (202) 244-2886.

The Lawyer's Dilemma

"Between the ages of 21 and 65, we spend about 11,000 days at work. That's a staggering amount of time to commit to any one activity."

—*Richard Koonce, career counselor*

■ ■ ■

Why did you choose to study law?

This is not a trick question. Because you might be surprised at how often the decision to enter law school is made with the most meager self-reflection. Indeed, a sample of first-year students offered the following reasons:

> The dilemma of career planning — passion or logic?

- ▶ I wanted to help others.
- ▶ I would have gone to medical school but didn't like the sight of blood.
- ▶ I thought accounting would be boring.
- ▶ I thought a JD would be more versatile than an MBA.
- ▶ I thought the education would assure me a good job.
- ▶ I wanted a profession with status and prestige.
- ▶ I wanted intellectual challenge in my work.
- ▶ I wanted to do something that mattered.
- ▶ I didn't know what else to do with my life.
- ▶ I wanted to earn a ton of money.

A few years later, these same students graduate. And, if they're like you and I, they will head into practice or a judicial clerkship for reasons just as flimsy as the ones cited above:

- ► I got good grades.
- ► I didn't want to waste my education.
- ► I didn't want to disappoint my father.
- ► I figured that maybe I'd like the law once I tried it.
- ► I had student loans to pay off.
- ► I was offered a job.
- ► That's where everyone else in law school was going.
- ► The money was good.

I'm not sure why, but — in my capacity as a legal career consultant — I find that lawyers and law students bristle at the prospect of career self-assessment. I don't know why. But it's often accompanied by what I call "magical thinking" — a belief that the perfect job will just materialize if they're patient. Or perhaps they believe the usual rules of job-finding don't apply; that one's legal credentials are so superior that employers and headhunters should be clamoring for your services.

"Maybe the fault is our legal education", a former practitioner once told me. "After all," he said, "we're trained to accept tradition and precedent as the primary rule of law, but we're not encouraged to seek the unconventional. It is extremely difficult to break away from our professional training and not practice law — especially to do something that is completely creative and has no rules or boundaries.

"It's just not in us," he said.

Well, let me explain the dilemma:

Successful careers are built on passion not logic, and to make a serious job or career transition requires risk and an embrace of the unconventional. I can't tell you how many letters I've received from lawyers who finally mustered the courage to leave the law — and succeeded — even though their actions seemed reckless at the time. What I hope you will discover — like so many lawyers and law students before you — is that the transition process is frequently illogical and without precedent. That the process often only makes sense in hindsight. That's why whatever self-reflection and self-assessment you engage in the sections ahead will almost certainly be worth the investment later.

Here's why:

The importance of credibility

You probably believe that your achievements matter most; that you'll be hired because of your credentials.

3 Coming to Terms with Change

Well, it's true that credentials — the achievements that prove your competence — are critical to job-finding success, but most employers are looking for something more. Authors James Kouzes and Barry Posner, experts on the subject of leadership, wrote a respected book on the subject of credibility. They discovered that instead of the right credentials, it's far more important a) to be honest with others about yourself and your motivations, b) to have a vision for the future, and c) to be able to articulate your honesty and vision in a way that inspires others. In other words, your credibility as a job-seeker is based more on the subjective qualities of honesty, vision and enthusiasm than on competence!

As David Maister, a Boston management consultant and former Harvard professor, puts it: "*People don't care how much you know until they know how much you care. Enthusiasm and the hard work it inspires count for more than an extra piece of ability.*"

Take a moment to re-read that quotation. It's important.

All of you have competencies and credentials. You couldn't have entered law school, passed the bar exam or practiced law without them. In short, you already can claim one of the foundations of credibility. But you undermine your chances of getting hired when you place too much emphasis on your credentials while ignoring your occupational passions.

The importance of self-awareness

Steve Gustaveson didn't feel fulfilled as a litigator in the Attorney General's office. So he enrolled in a career evaluation workshop, and discovered that he preferred a more advisory role and an opportunity to teach. The self-awareness that Steve gained by exploring his preferences and strengths paid off. Six months later, the A.G.'s office created a new position with a job description that seemed to have been written just for Steve: program advisor to the Division of Children and Family Services. It involved consultations with managers on legal and policy issues, legislative work and training.

After getting hired, Steve's new boss told him that he was chosen over more experienced candidates because he was able clearly to articulate what it was about the job that appealed to him, and precisely why he was qualified to handle it.

As a lawyer, you tend to be goal-oriented, and intent on achieving results and closure. With that single-mindedness, it's possible you may suppress or ignore your own preferences, and end up competing with those whose own preferences naturally lead them to that type of work. The result is often failure, either because you can't muster the enthusiasm that impresses employers, or you lack the commitment that motivates you to hammer away at potential leads. With greater self-awareness, you'll be able to create a vision based on your strengths and preferences, and be motivated enough to bring that vision to life. The alternative is too awful to think about. To paraphrase career consultant David Maister, there's nothing more depressing than to be rejected for a job you didn't want in the first place.

The importance of self-assessment

Self-assessment, says one psychologist and former practicing lawyer, helps you avoid a career move that "merely changes staterooms on the Titanic." Through careful, deliberate introspection, you can figure out what you would like to be doing with your time, not what you think you could get paid to do.

The Case for
Self-Assessment

"Get a job you love and you'll never have to work a day in your life."

—anon

Career self-assessment boils down to answering three questions:

Who am I?
What do I want?
What am I willing to give up to get what I want?

I. Who Am I?

This is not the beginning of some frivolous exercise on The Meaning of Life. On the contrary, this deceptively simple question goes to the heart of your career search, and it demands the most rigorous investigation of your personal strengths and preferences in five areas:

▶ interests;
▶ skills;
▶ values;
▶ people contact; and
▶ work environment.

> Who am I?
> The question
> goes to the
> heart of
> self-assessment.

Interests — Interests are subjects to which you are drawn, topics about which you read and inquire, and activities and areas of knowledge that are intriguing (see the Ideal Job Grid section at the end of this chapter for interests common to lawyers). Some people are generalists with broad interests that frequently change; others are specialists who like to focus on one subject or field. Subject matters that many lawyers find appealing include international affairs, human behavior, social policy, constitutional law and high technology.

Skills — Skills are your natural abilities and those you have developed through experience. (Go to the end of the chapter for skills common to lawyers.) Analyzing these skills, as well as the skills you most enjoying using, is the foundation of a Transferable Skills Analysis, and the key to successfully making a shift in your employment status. Behavioral research confirms that we enjoy jobs that call upon our natural aptitudes (those skills that come most readily to us), and that we dislike work that asks us to rely on skills we don't have. Likewise, many studies prove what we know instinctively; that the tasks that come easily are the ones we do best. So, it follows that the closer we can get to work that draws upon our natural aptitudes, the more we reduce our risk of layoff, and increase both our career satisfaction and the chance of reaching your greatest potential.

John, a small-firm practitioner for 15 years, is a perfect example.

John spent most of his time at work meeting and talking with others. He loved to meet with clients and brainstorm solutions to their problems. In the meantime, files stacked up on his desk, begging for completion, especially when the matter involved a lot of details, rules or complex documentation. On reflection, John realized that his procrastination was not a personal failing, but an indication of his preference to work with others in a fast-paced environment. Soon after, he closed his law practice. He went to work for law firm software company large enough to provide substantial support and follow-up. Most people possess a narrow but compatible range of natural aptitudes, which are easily found in one type of employment. Some claim a broad range of talents; for these individuals, it's harder to find a single occupation that is sufficiently challenging and engaging. If you are one of these people, I suggest you devote yourself to a social cause, or involve yourself in leisure activities that make use of the unused aptitudes, or split your time between two careers to keep dissatisfaction from taking root.

Values — Values are the intangible guiding principles and goals that bring meaning to your work and motivate your involvement and commitment. Some values shift as you mature and grow, but most guide your choices throughout a lifetime. Common values preferences among law school graduates include recognition, autonomy, variety, intellectual challenge and helping others. (Go to the end of the chapter for values preferred by lawyers.) If your work clashes with your values, you may pro-

duce easily enough, but you won't feel good about it. You'll experience a gut conflict, an unsettling doubt about whether you're doing the right thing. If your work is
consistent with your values, however, you'll feel motivated to do more, even if the
work itself is difficult. You'll want to accomplish your goals in order to express that
value.

People contact — Your preferences in this category are all the ways you like to
interact with coworkers and clients. Here you need to define the personality traits and
cultural backgrounds of the people you prefer as colleagues and clients. Consider also
whether you prefer to work alone, with a handful of others, or with larger groups. At
least one lawyer in any group of 10 prefers an isolated environment for introspective,
analytical work. Others prefer a team approach, working together with a compatible
group toward a common goal. There are also those who prefer to have many and
varied personal interactions in their workday. (Go to the end of the chapter for the
people preferences expressed by lawyers.)

Work environment — Environmental preferences involve the physical and intangible aspects of the workplace itself: the office atmosphere, the work schedule, the aesthetics of the physical setting, the degree of flexibility in office management, even
the dress code. Some of you feel uncomfortable the moment you dress up for the
office and would much rather throw on a pair of denims and a sweatshirt. Others
hate "dress down" Fridays. Some of you might feel claustrophobic in an office without windows that open, while your colleague down the hall loves his corner office in
a gleaming glass-and-steel tower. It's important to explore and define all five areas,
and prepare a complete view of your preferences, if you want to make a meaningful
change. Lawyer/psychologist Larry Richard of Philadelphia explains why:

> ▶ "When a psychological need is met, it recedes, and you don't think about
> it. You may decide to leave one job because you can't stand the high
> pressure and demanding work hours. But the new job, with its set hours,
> doesn't offer the variety and intellectual challenge you did like — *but
> didn't realize you liked* — in the last job. And there's no way to know what
> your psychological needs are without self-assessment."

The most reliable way to identify your preferences is to analyze your past experiences — good and bad — and define the qualities that tie them together. This type of
analysis is often more accurate and revealing than what you've learned about yourself

from family and friends, or from experiences in past employment. When you complete your Ideal Job Grid (see the Ideal Job Grid section at the end of the chapter), you will have developed at least a preliminary answer to the question of who you are.

II. What Do I Want?

Every career self-assessment asks you to consider the practical and measurable, and the fantastic and illogical.

The career transition process in this book is no exception, and this second of three vital questions begins to examine your dreams for the future, and the motivations that will help you establish links to a task, a job, a goal, and an employer. But first, you'll have to give yourself permission to consider the fantastic and illogical.

"If I had to come up with the major issue that makes working with attorneys such a challenge," says San Francisco career counselor Lesah Beckhusen, "it is their almost exclusively left-brained thinking about how the world works." Lawyers, she says, are trained to rely upon rational, linear, organized thought. But down deep, all of us are motivated by what we want, not by what is logical or practical. Beckhusen advises lawyers to trust their right-brained intuition and feelings for a vision of what they want ... and then let their left-brain skills get them there.

> What do I want? Let yourself be practical and illogical.

Acknowledging your occupational dreams can be unnerving if you have spent your life concentrating on the expectations and needs of others. But meeting your own needs by pursuing what you want creates an important paradox: It motivates you to achieve career success, thereby also allowing you to meet the needs of those who depend upon you.

Some career consultants suggest exploring the question of what you want in terms of the impact you'd like to have on the world. Richard Bolles, author of the classic *What Color Is Your Parachute?*, calls this motivation the "integrating factor," and he defines it as that which you think most needs fixing in the world. The question of what do you want can also be posed in terms ... such as motivation. Dr. Dennis Jaffe, co-author of *Take This Job and Love It*, find three basic motivations:

► External reward (e.g., salary, advancement, bonus, job titles or special perks, and even termination or reproval);

- ▶ Peer respect or a feeling of importance or connection to a group; and
- ▶ Internal validation or meaning, usually as a result of using your creative capacity and growing in your work, learning, meeting challenges or participating in decision-making.

Similarly, author and MIT Sloan Fellows Professor Edgar H. Schein, defines job contentment in terms of eight "career anchors":

- ▶ Technical/functional competence;
- ▶ General managerial competence;
- ▶ Autonomy/independence;
- ▶ Security/stability;
- ▶ Entrepreneurial creativity;
- ▶ Service/dedication to a cause;
- ▶ Pure challenge; and
- ▶ Lifestyle.

Finally, you might look at what you want by monitoring how you currently spend your time. Lawyer **Nancy Ashley**, a veteran practitioner who moved from private practice to human services consulting, described her own transition: "For years, I had done volunteer work in human services — child advocacy issues, food banks, starting a domestic violence shelter. If only I had looked at how I used my time when it was my own choice, I could have saved years of trying to figure out a new direction for myself. But it just took me a while to recognize the signals that everyone else could see."

Ultimately, your answer to the question, "What do I want?" is your own personal definition of success. And it may not be motivated by noble urges. In the words of former Harvard professor David Maister: "The keys to what you really want are the things you don't like to admit. For example, maybe you don't like to admit it, but you need to be the center of attention. Okay, then find a job that will let you show off. Or, maybe you're someone who doesn't want to admit it, but you really want to be rich. Fine, go out and make lots of money. I'm saying, play to your evil secrets; don't suppress them."

Lawyer **Barbara Boivin**, who succeeded at general practice, and at both criminal prosecution and defense, was in a workshop audience when I introduced the concept of "evil secrets". Afterward, Barbara told me that she didn't want to acknowledge her own "evil secret" — that even as a successful lawyer, she wasn't interested in a career at all! She preferred to work on well-defined, short-term projects in a variety of fields. Eventually, she was put a positive spin on her "evil secret" — that she had an ability to orient herself quickly to new areas and environments, especially when the tasks involved research and mediation. Once she accepted this truth about herself, she was able to find a series of temporary, diverse and well-paid assignments: completing a research project for a mediation practitioner, designing a plan for coordinating solid waste and recycling contracts, reviewing municipal codes for statutory and constitutional inconsistencies, and filling in for a hearing examiner on maternity leave.

Like Barbara, you'll progress in developing a satisfying career when you get to the point where your secret is no longer "evil" but a quality you can not only live with but verbalize proudly to others.

III. What Am I Willing to Give Up to Get What I Want?

Imagine a child with an armful of toys who wants one more. As she reaches for the new toy, she accidental drops one of the others. As she tries to retrieve it, she loses the new one. In this way, the child learns she must be willing to give up something to get what she wants. I believe the child's experience and the process of career transition have parallels. Because the transition process almost always involves sacrifice; every change — no matter how desired and fortunate — involves a loss of some kind. And it is difficult to choose what to let go of, what to set aside, what to accept less of; when everything seems essential.

But if you resolve the first two questions — *Who am I?* and *What do I want?* — the third question is likely to take care of itself.

Below are the three main issues that concern lawyers:

Letting go of your lawyer identity — Those of you who consider yourselves "successful lawyers" may have to give up the external rewards associated with your position — the status, the prestige, the financial resources. When you discard your title, you may also have to sacrifice the self-esteem it generated. Leaving the profession is especially traumatic for lawyers who never found success in the law. They may have felt like failures from the time they entered law school until they handled their last court case. And even though they know they would be more suited in another profession, their self-esteem has been so battered that change is equated with failure and frustration. Their professional identity — the ability to introduce themselves as a lawyer or a law school graduate — may be their greatest sense of pride. If they renounce even this accomplishment, what have they left to offer? In a study done by two Minnesota career services offices, many lawyers considering leaving the profession were concerned that their colleagues would look down on their new careers as having less prestige. The anxiety didn't last long, though, Once they'd made the move, they didn't look back. And they appreciated the improvement in their quality of life, the greater independence, flexibility and family time, and the reduction in stress.

The conflict between money and meaning — Despite all the evidence that money does not buy happiness, the conflict between money and meaning is doubtless the most difficult for lawyers to resolve. Those of you who are experienced practitioners might now be earning good money, but perhaps you're no longer satisfied with your work. To find fulfillment, you must trade the assurance of a comfortable, or even regular, income for the risk and invigoration of a meaningful change. Others of you — especially solo practitioners, small town lawyers, or public interest lawyers — might be earning too little money. It could be that you place a higher priority on the meaning you derive from your work — whether contribution to society or to your individual clients — or on your lack of pretentiousness, than on the money you earn. You're afraid that if you move into better paying work, you'll sacrifice your integrity. You might also envy those in lucrative practices or those receiving regular salaries in private industry or government, but you can't overcome what you believe is your inadequacy to find that type of work. You may be placing a higher priority on autonomy, self-direction, and control than on the income you generate.

The conflict between work and family — Some of you may love your work but wish you could spend more time with family and friends. Those of you who are parents might like to quit working, or reduce your workload to a part-time schedule. But you fear you will never regain career momentum. Still others never find the time to explore personal interests or simply relax. You may all believe that your families are your highest priorities. But think a moment about these situations. If you work long, hard hours for a good income but seldom see your families, you might be placing a higher priority on the needs of your clients or coworkers, or on supporting your family's lifestyle, than on actually spending time with your family. Likewise, those of you who don't want to "get off the partnership track" are placing a higher priority on that goal. If you don't have time for yourself, you may be acting quite consistently with your priority of spending time with your family, or you might be placing an even higher priority on your work, with time for self coming last. None of these choices are wrong per se, but refusing to acknowledge that all your priorities cannot be weighted equally can cause frustration and guilt.

Gordon, with nearly 20 years of law practice behind him, hated his work but at a group workshop confided that something was preventing him from leaving the law. He had promised to put his sons through college, and the only way he could meet that commitment was to keep practicing law. When someone in the workshop asked whether he'd shared his dilemma with his sons, Gordon looked shocked. "I can't do that," he said. After all, he'd given his word, and that was that. He arrived at the next meeting looking 10 years younger and 100 times happier. He had told his eldest son about his career conflict and was astonished by his son's response. The young man urged him to quit. He said he admired his father for putting him through college and wanted his father to enjoy the same opportunity to prove himself. More importantly, he missed the supportive, fun-loving father he had before Gordon's depression set in. Two years later, I ran into Gordon at a CLE seminar. He was wearing a bus driver's uniform and had a big smile. He'd left his partnership six months after the workshop ended. Now, he supports his family — and his interest in fiction writing — by driving a city bus, teaching in a paralegal program and handling a little bit of legal work out of his house. You might not make the same choice, but it worked for him.

None of these conflicts require all-or-nothing solutions. You don't have to give up money to find meaning in your work. You don't have to drive a bus just to spend quality time with your family. You don't have to go bankrupt to achieve career satisfaction. You simply need to clarify your values, and make the compromises that bring your priorities and the realities of your life into alignment. Until you identify a next step and engage in some personal research, though, you can't know how much you're going to have to give up or whether the sacrifice will be worthwhile. The point is to begin your introspection and analysis and deal with this last issue when required. You won't have to make decisions about household expenses and outside obligations until you choose a direction and confirm the sacrifices it will require. By then, you'll know whether the loss will be worth the reward.

Today's Assignment

"Listen to your stomach not to your head. Your head will only rationalize you into a job you shouldn't have."

—*Ray Bradbury, novelist*

■ ■ ■

This section contains a series of self-assessment exercises that will help reveal your employment preferences. If you need results fast, I suggest you focus on three exercises — *Your History of Achievement, The Self-Assessment 10* , and *Passions*. But for greater, more accurate detail, it's best if you complete most if not all the exercises. This and the next two sections are at the heart of this book. And, as busy as you are, I urge you to complete as much self-assessment as you can. You'll get more done if you ...

▶ Work with a process in mind (this book will provide that)
▶ Commit yourself to a time-frame (a weekend, or an hour a day for a period of weeks).
▶ Find a friend with whom you can work you (input from others — especially those who have nothing to gain or lose from your choices — will add to your self-knowledge).
▶ Record your responses in a journal or binder.

> You'll find you discover new aspects of yourself, and clarify your overall preferences.

Self-assessment is like peeling an onion; just when you think you've revealed all the important layers, a few more are revealed. For that reason, I suggest you consider enrolling in a career workshop, or take advantage of the many online assessment resources (see Appendix 3), or hire a career consultant or career coach who has experience working with lawyers (**see www.DecisionBooks.com** for a list of counselors). If you apply only a fraction of the time to the self-assessment process that you devoted to obtaining your law license, you'll greatly improve your chances of finding new, more satisfying work.

Assignment #1: Your History of Achievement

List the achievements and accomplishments of your life; the things for which you have bragging rights. Begin with childhood and work your way to the present. For each citation, describe the highlights about your involvement, the nature of the project and the results achieved. Note: These achievements or accomplishments need not have been acknowledged by others. List any activity in which you took a leadership role, or in which you helped to create a product, or in which you wrote, spoke, taught, researched, coordinated or constructed, no matter how insignificant that contribution might seem now. When you finish gathering the information, organize your list chronologically to serve as a data bank for future résumé writing.

Assignment #2: The Self-Assessment Ten

▶ Describe what you learned about money and work from your parents.
▶ Describe what you'd like to do if your life expectancy was just a matter of months.
▶ Finish these sentences in some detail:
  I don't like to admit it, but I really need …
  I feel happiest when I'm …
  If money and education were not considerations, the kind of work I prefer would be …
  When I was a child, I always want to be a …
  Time passes most quickly for me when I'm …
  One thing I've always done well is …
▶ Imagine you've won a $200,000 lottery annuity. Describe how it would change your daily existence.
▶ For one week, take a few minutes every day to jot a few key thoughts about your ideal work place. Describe your ideal work place in detail. If others are there, who are they and what are they doing?
▶ For a full month, note on your desk calendar (or computer or PDA) which daily activities you enjoyed the most and the least. At the end of the month, summarize and categorize your preferences.

- ► For a full month, take a few minutes every day to visualize your ideal day. Describe it even it has nothing to do with work.
- ► In 10 minutes of continuous writing (without removing your pen from the paper or your fingers from the keyboard), describe what you enjoy doing when you're not working.
- ► Write a description of yourself. Describe your interests and define your personal style, including the way you like to dress, live, and interact with others. Be certain to list those skills at which you excel, and those you enjoy using, whether or not they have anything to do with work.
- ► Describe what you know of your long-range career goals, and identify what contributions you would like to make to yourself, to your family, to your community, and to the world.

At the end of this exercise, read over your answers and look for themes and contradictions. Summarize the results in writing.

Assignment #3: Passions

Describe up to 50 of the most enjoyable events of your life. Focus on experiences you remember as fun or fulfilling, and when time seem to pass without notice. Choose events you enjoyed as they were unfolding, not because of any outcome or positive feedback. Be sure to include at least a dozen experiences from childhood — anything from finger-painting to camping to shooting hoops. One of your 50 events might be something as simple enjoying a memorable Tuscan sunset, or hiking the Sierra range, or delivering meals to seniors. The point is to get in touch with experiences that lifted your spirits and that you would gladly repeat. Afterward, compile a list of 10 awful experiences — when time dragged or was filled with frustration, dread or fear. Again, consider only the process and not the result. When both lists are complete, spend some time answering the following questions:

- ► How often were you alone and how often with others? What were you doing when you were alone? How did those activities differ from your activities with others?
- ► How many others were with you? What was the nature of your interaction with them? Were you conversing or participating with them, or quietly working alongside them? Were you engaged in group activity? What kind?

▶ What were the characteristics of the people around you? Up-beat? Analytical? Daring? Supportive? Competitive? Challenging? Smart? Artistic? Athletic?

▶ What were you doing? Was it physical, mental or both? Were you passive or active, moving around or staying in one place; conveying or receiving information?

▶ What was the purpose of your participation in each event? Personal growth, building something, enjoyment, making change, helping others, competition?

▶ In what environments did you find yourself? Indoors or outside, sunny, rainy, dark, bright, crowded, spacious, formal, informal?

▶ Were you relating emotionally, intellectually, physically or spiritually to your surroundings?

▶ Were your activities internalized-that is, thoughtful or meditative — or external to yourself — for example, teaching, advising, coaching, viewing entertainment?

▶ What was the tempo of each event? Fast-paced, relaxed?

Note that the answers to these questions may be contradictory. You may enjoy being alone and being with others, or engaging in high-energy activities and sitting peacefully outside in the sunshine. Include these observations in your answers to the questions.

Assignment #4: Show and Tell

Go through your files and mementos to create a "brag" or "show and tell" file. Look through records of your accomplishments and involvement in any kind of activity. This, too, will help update and target your résumé, and can sometimes be used for illustrative purposes during an interview. You might also look for additional underlying themes.

Assignment #5: Newsmagazine Review

This is an exercise for a small group of three to five individuals. Invite each person to bring with them a half-dozen news magazine articles of personal interest. Give each person 10 to 15 minutes to spread the articles out on a table, and explain the reasons behind their choice and what themes the articles represent. Ask the group for its impressions of each presentation.

Assignment #6: Classified Ads Review

Read through the Sunday classifieds in a large metropolitan newspaper, or scan a variety of online job boards (see Appendix 2). Search for ads or online job posts that appeal to you for any reason regardless of salary or lack of qualifications. Clip or copy your samples and put them in a notebook; select about a dozen. Describe the appealing and not-so-appealing characteristics of each position. Also, summarize what if any themes link these ads or posts. By the way, this makes a powerful group exercise.

Assignment #7: What Makes Work Meaningful to You?

Read the six qualities listed below and rank them in order of their importance to you (with 1 being most important). Be certain to answer the way you really feel, and not the way you think you should!

THE BEST WORK FOR ME WOULD:	Rank	
1. Make use of my special talents	2	4
2. Pay me well.	1	3
3. Let me be creative and original.	6	5
4. Make me well-known and respected.	4	6
5. Let me work with people, rather than things.	3	1
6. Give me an opportunity to help others.	5	2

Add the points for the statements paired below and write the totals in the space provided.

_7_ Statements 1 and 3 (SE)   9
_10_ Statements 5 and 6 (PO)   3
_5_ Statements 2 and 4 (ER)   9

Now, rank the three pairs, with the lowest total ranked number one (your highest value) and the highest, number three (your lowest value).

*Adapted from *The Book of Tests,* Michael Nathanson.

Explanation of Results

ER (external-reward) — If this is your highest value, then what brings you personal fulfillment is that which offers wealth, prestige, power, security, status, respect or similar rewards. If external reward is your highest value, you are well-suited to the law. If you value external reward and are just starting your legal career, your best bets are employment in conventional areas of practice with private, corporate, public interest or government legal employers. As you proceed through your career, you might want to run for political office, lobby for a judicial appointment, or network your way into a management position with a former corporate client.

PO (people-orientation) — If this is your highest value, you need to work with or help other people, rather than concentrating on data, ideas or things. In law, those with a people orientation ought to represent individual clients — not business entities or faceless classes — or they should have frequent interaction with others. You also will prefer to work with client needs and problems that the legal system can directly remedy such as plaintiffs' personal injury or employment law work, legal services to the poor or disadvantaged, guardianship and probate, family or elder law, and consumer problems. Outside the profession, you might enjoy a retail environment, being a therapist or counselor, or working in education, placement, or employment counseling.

SE (self-expression) — If this is your highest value, the need to be creative and to express yourself in your work is very important to you. Those who value self-expression need to deal in more creative areas of practice, such as fast-paced trial work, deal-making, or emerging or rapidly changing areas of law. Also, the more autonomy you can create for yourself, the more chance for creativity you will find. For that reason, self-employment is often attractive to those with this preference. Legal writing, especially for a newspaper or magazine, could provide an opportunity for self-expression. Outside the legal profession, journalism, entrepreneurial ventures and the arts can be satisfying options. Those with a strong preference for self-expression are likely to become dissatisfied with law over time. Early in your career, you'll have much to learn and many opportunities to talk, write and create solutions. Later, you'll probably discover that the rules and repetition of the legal environment, as well as your role representing someone else's interests, stifles your ability to express yourself. To avoid dissatisfaction, you'll have to find outlets for your creativity, whether in your work or free time.

The emphasis you place on certain values can change during the course of a career. Many lawyers start out seeking external reward in the form of the certainty of employment after graduation. Once they become established in the profession and enjoy the financial security and status they sought, a need for self-expression or helping others might take precedence.

Assignment #8: Things I Really Love to Do

Draw a line down the center of a legal pad. In the left column, record all the activities you enjoy in any aspect of your life. For each entry, describe in the opposite column what skills you use to accomplish that activity. For a sample list of skills, refer to the Ideal Job Grid section at the end of the chapter.

Assignment #9: What Do You Value?

Read the 29 values listed below. Draw a line through those of less importance to you, and circle those values that have the greatest importance. Now, if you had $1,000 to "buy" the values you've just circled, how would you allocate the money? For the purposes of this exercise, assume you have none of these qualities now:

___Achievement (accomplishment, results brought about by persistence)

___Adventure/Excitement (action, risk and a fast pace)

___Beauty/Aesthetic Value (appreciation and enjoyment of beauty)

___Autonomy (independence, personal freedom, making your own choices)

___Creativity/Self-Expression (innovating new ideas, designs or solutions)

___Emotional Well-Being (peace of mind, quickly resolving inner conflicts)

___Physical Health (physically well, sound and strong in body)

___Honesty/Authenticity (being frank and genuinely yourself with others)

___Humor/Wit (a sense of humor, holding things in perspective)

___Intellectual Challenge (learning new things, stimulating the mind)

___Justice/Fairness (treating others impartially, wanting equity for others)

___Knowledge (seeking truth, information or principles out of curiosity)

___Love/Family (affection, intimacy, caring, attachment to a family)

___Loyalty (maintaining allegiance to a person, group or cause)

___Morality/Personal Integrity (maintaining ethical standards or honor)

___Nature (contact with or appreciation of the natural world)

___Physical Appearance (concern for one's physical attractiveness)

___Pleasure/Fun (enjoyment, gratification, playfulness)

___Power/Influence (having authority; power to get things done)

___Recognition (acknowledged as important or significant, respected)

___Religious Conviction (communion with or activity on behalf of God)

___Safety/Security (protection from threat or danger)

___Service/Helping Others (devotion to others' interests, serving a cause)

___Skill/Competence (being good at something)

___Tangible Results (see, touch, hear, smell or taste the results of your effort)

___Variety (regular contact with a broad number and type of experiences)

___Wealth/Possessions (owning things, ample money for things you want)

___Wisdom (mature understanding, insight, good sense, and judgment)

___Work Productivity (being actively productive)

When you have allocated the entire sum, list the six items for which you spent the most money. These are the qualities you value most highly and that you should emphasize in your work. Make certain these values are included on the "Must Have" side of your Ideal Job Grid at the end of the chapter.

Assignment #10: Your Lasting Contribution

Imagine learning you have three years to live. How would you spend the time? Probably devote a year or so to traveling and visiting family and friends. But after that, what? If money and energy were not a factor, you might look at opportunities to create a legacy. In this exercise, answer three questions: What would you devote yourself to in the last years of life ... how might others be impacted by your legacy ... and what might others say about you and your legacy after your passing?

Assignment #11: Your Fantasy Employment

Imagine yourself working at a fantasy job, and describe a day-in-the-life in this role. Be as specific and detailed as you like, and imagine yourself in this role from your first cup of coffee to the end of the day.

▶ Where are you?

▶ What are your surroundings?

▶ What activities are underway around you?

▶ Who, if anyone, are you working with?

▶ What are the others doing, and what are you doing in relation to them? If no one else is around, what are you doing?

Assignment #12: The Real Costs of Change

This assignment asks that you project yourself through time — 1, 5, 10, even 20 years — and describe what your life might look like if you remained on your present course. Describe your life in terms of opportunities, relationships, and your emotional and physical well-being.

Assignment #13: Setting Your Priorities

Tear off four sheets from a legal pad and draw a line down the middle of each.

On each sheet, identify one of four jobs, career paths or work-time arrangements that you currently have under consideration. In the left column, describe what attracts to that option, and on the opposite side all the reasons you don't want to, or feel you can't, make that choice. When you finish, draw a line through any reasons that duplicate or contradict one another.

Now, rewrite each reason — pro and con — in a way that reflects a core personal value (you can refer to the values listed at the end of the chapter). For example, if you're avoiding private practice because it's "too cutthroat," explore what it is that's actually behind your reason, i.e., you prefer a non-competitive environment, or you want a relaxed work pace, or you prefer more collegiality and cooperation. When you finish exploring each pro and con, you have all the reasons you're in a state of conflict.

Review your list and allocate $1,000 to "buy" the five values most important to you, and list them in descending order.   If you want to take this exercise one more level, fill out a time log. At the end of seven days, add up the number of hours spent on all your activities, and compare your log with the values you have just prioritized.

Congratulations, you've just completed your self-assessment. I'm certain you know more about your work and life preferences than you did before you began. But if you need some structured assistance, go online to **www.DecisionBooks.com** for names of career counselors and coaches who specialize in working with lawyers. Or go to Appendix 3 for a list of online self-assessment tools.   Now, let's take what you've learned into the next two sections — *A Transferable Skills Analysis* and *Creating your Ideal Job Grid*. As I said earlier, you won't regret the time you spent here.

A Transferable
Skills Analysis

"If you think of your job as a series of separate skills, then the parts can be reassembled anywhere."

— *Carole Hyatt and Linda Gottlieb, authors*

■ ■ ■

"Legal training is broad training," says Celia Paul, a New York City career and outplacement counselor. "My clients know they'll be hired on the basis of their skills, but it's up to them to translate those skills into something marketable."

How successful you are at translating those skills depends on what career consultants call a Transferable Skills Analysis. It requires that you identify your core skills in three areas — the skills you develop as a practicing lawyer or law student, the skills you enjoy using on a daily basis, and the skills you want to market to employers. As lawyers and law students, we really are quite skillful individuals. And if you ever had the least doubt, just examine the charts on the next three pages, where I describe skills we developed in law

> The application of skills from field to field is the essence of transferable skills analysis.

school, and — if you're currently in practice — the skills you use every day. While you're working in this section, take a moment to visit Appendix 1 (*The 7 Lawyer Profiles: Types, Motivations, Challenges & Career Options*). It describes seven distinct lawyer motivational types, and explains what professional options exist that would help practicing or aspiring lawyers optimize their natural gifts and have more professional fulfillment.

Now, to begin this analysis, you'll need to break down the tasks, cases and projects you've handled into the skill sets you use to complete the work. I'll illustrate by

Skills Developed in Law School

Reading Casebooks	digest large quantities of material learn technical jargon read a lot	**Memo Writing**	clarify information communicate technical concepts compare for accuracy and content edit generate solutions proofread research solve problems write persuasively
Classroom Attendance	concentrate listen intently and thoughtfully deal with difficult people withstand or flourish in a highly competitive environment withstand pressure respond to challenges		
		Moot Court	listen critically and intently speak cogently and persuasively speak in public think quickly on one's feet articulate or advocate a position
Studying	discipline exchange information and ideas with others organize time and materials prioritize work with others		
Briefing	analyze logically and in linear progression generalize ideas from extensive reading material identify issues interpret technical jargon synthesize information think critically	**Clinical Education**	negotiate active listening interpret for others convey complex notions in simple terms meet deadlines counsel or advise work in a team assist others with less education and knowledge

Data-Related Skills Developed by Lawyers

CASE MANAGEMENT

accurate memory for details

analyze

anticipate problems or needs

classify expertly

conceptualize

coordinate operations or data

discover similarities or dissimilarities

establish priorities among competing
   requirements

experiment with new approaches

file so as to facilitate retrieval

gather information

handle many tasks and responsibilities
   efficiently

innovate

interview individuals to obtain
   information

keep track of details

manage

memorize rules and procedures

organize

plan

plan on the basis of lessons
   from the past

recognize the need for, and locate,
   outside experts

recognize when more information is
   needed

research

see the big picture

strategize

summarize

synthesize

troubleshoot

OFFICE MANAGEMENT

allocate scarce financial resources

budget

maintain fiscal controls

project costs

OPEN NEW FILES

assimilate new data quickly

learn new things

read quickly and comprehensively

WORK PRODUCT

apply what others have developed to
   new situations

communicate technical information

compose

conceive new interpretations
   and approaches

consolidate

edit

interpret documents

keep others informed

make practical applications of
   theoretical ideas

persuade

persuasive writing

summarize

technical writing

update

People-Related Skills Developed by Lawyers

CASE/OFFICE MANAGEMENT
- brainstorm
- bring projects in on time and
  within budget
- critique
- delegate authority
- develop projects
- lead
- make hard decisions
- manage
- prioritize
- supervise

COURT APPEARANCES
- act immediately on new information
- deal well with the unexpected or
  critical event
- decisive in emergencies
- easily remember faces
- improvise
- make presentations
- quickly size up situations
- speak clearly, articulately and
  engagingly

PRACTICE DEVELOPMENT
- collaborate
- identify needs and solutions
- network
- reciprocate
- sell

PRACTICE MANAGEMENT
- continually seek more responsibility
- follow through
- organize time expertly
- responsibility

- self-direction
- systematically accomplish tasks in
  order to obtain objectives
- work well without supervision

SETTLE CASES
- negotiate
- persuade
- sell a program or course of action
  to decision-makers

WORK WITH CLIENTS
- allay fears
- clarify values and goals of others
- confront others with difficult
  personal matters
- counsel
- develop rapport and trust
- disseminate information accurately
- empathize
- employ "active listening"
- explain complicated theories or
  procedures in simple terms
- gain cooperation among
  diverse interests
- give professional advice
- handle emotional outbursts
- hone and use powers of observation
- identify problems, needs and solutions
- inspire others
- intuit
- keep confidences and secrets
- perceive and assess the potential
  of others
- resolve conflicts
- train, teach, educate

analyzing the deposition of a medical expert. The main components of accomplishing that task are as follows:

- ▶ review file;
- ▶ consult partner about opposing counsel and the case;
- ▶ review the medical records;
- ▶ read articles about the medical problem;
- ▶ plan deposition questions;
- ▶ analyze questions asked by opposing counsel;
- ▶ make objections.

The core skills used to accomplish each part of the process were as follows:

- ▶ you review file: assimilate new data quickly, read quickly and comprehensively.
- ▶ you consult partner about opposing counsel and the case: collaborate; anticipate problems; identify problems, needs and solutions; recognize when more information is needed before making decisions; plan; come up with a strategy.
- ▶ you review the medical records: learn medical terminology; read and understand medical records; extract and evaluate information; interpret medical terms.
- ▶ you read articles about the medical problem: recognize the need for and locate outside experts.
- ▶ you plan deposition questions: investigate, gather information.
- ▶ you analyze questions asked by opposing counsel: apply standards to another's performance; make practical applications of theoretical ideas.
- ▶ you ask questions: interview; pose technical questions; respond to unexpected answers.
- ▶ you make objections: think quickly; apply standards to facts; explain.

Now it's your turn.

Analyze the following tasks common to law practice in the same way, first breaking them down into their component parts and then locating the "generic" name for the skills used to complete each part of the process. (Refer to the preceding skills listings, and those in the next section). Limit yourself to tasks you've actually performed. And if you haven't worked as a lawyer or law clerk, then analyze tasks from other jobs you've held, or from school or volunteer projects.

▶ Advising a corporate department manager
▶ Answering interrogatories
▶ Arguing an appeal or motion
▶ Attending the deposition of a client
▶ Litigating a jury trial
▶ Mediating a dispute
▶ Meeting with a client for the first time
▶ Negotiating an agreement
▶ Preparing a complaint
▶ Preparing a trial brief
▶ Preparing for trial
▶ Presenting a trial to the court
▶ Writing a contract
▶ Writing a legal research memorandum

Once you have the process down, you'll want to compile a list of the core skills you've developed so far. Review the exercises you completed in the Ideal Job Grid

Sample Skills Evaluation

PROFICIENT	COMPETENT	INEPT
reading	calculating	abstract analysis
public speaking	editing	keeping track of details
developing rapport	organizing	administering
coming up with ideas	technical writing	small tool work
explanatory writing	designing	coordinating
motivating	researching	detail work
synthesizing	supervising	planning
leading	implementing	
listening		

section, especially *My History of Achievement* and *Things I Really Love to Do.* Compare those experiences to the lists of skills in this and the next section, and make a running list of the skills you identify.

Now, sort the skills into a hierarchy of competency. For example, put an asterisk next to those you perform particularly well, and a downward arrow next to those you only stumble through. The rest will be considered average. Or create a chart like the one in my Sample Skills Evaluation. Remember, the fact that you have a skill does not mean you ought to seek work that uses it. You'll do a better job, and enjoy your work more, if you focus on those skills you both enjoy using and can do well. The last part of this Transferable Skills Analysis is to identify which of the skills you've developed you'd really like to use. So, go back over your list of skills and circle those you most enjoy. You'll need this when you create your Ideal Job Grid in the next section.

Creating Your
Ideal Job Grid

"I was a lawyer for seven years. I thought about leaving after the first two years, and stayed five more because I couldn't figure a way out. What I want to do now is something that has an effect on the way people live."

— a University of Colorado Law School graduate

■ ■ ■

This section approaches the midpoint of the book, and its placement is no accident. Of all the resources here, I consider the *Ideal Job Grid* as among the most important. Why? Because with all the analysis you've done in the previous two sections, you're now ready to plot out the best work and work environment you can imagine. Not just for now, but whenever your work or career hits a snag. Of course, you may be thinking, "Great, just what I need — more analysis. In this economy, I'll be lucky if I find a job."

> Career-change requires even more analysis & preparation in a weak economy.

But it's *because* of the economy that your preparation here is so critical.

In this section, you will broaden your field of view and multiply your options, you'll create a more complete picture of the work and environment in which you thrive, and — most important — you'll emerge better able to articulate why you have more of what your potential employer needs than your competitor. What's ahead is no quicky exercise. Creating an *Idea Job Grid* is a five-step process that requires several hours. So, turn off your cell phone or pager, and find a place at home or away where you can work without distraction.

Step #1 — Review the sample Ideal Job Grids in this section to get a sense of the end-product. Remember, this grid represents extremes — the very best qualities of the best work you could possibly have. (Some people prefer to also look at the grid as a synthesis of the qualities they want in life.)

Step #2 — Review the results of the exercises in the last two sections, as well as any career-testing or prior self-assessment work you've completed. Highlight the words and phrases that appear repeatedly in the exercises, as well as those qualities that attract you. Place those words and phrases in the most appropriate category. Please include interests, skills and other preferences even if you cannot imagine how you'd get paid to use them, or you are afraid using them would require you to change careers, go back to school, or take a pay cut.

To review from the last section:

▶ *Interests* are subject matters to which you are drawn, topics about which you read and inquire.
▶ *Skills* are the abilities you've developed.
▶ Values are the intangible guiding principles and goals that bring meaning to your work and motivate your involvement and commitment.
▶ *People preferences* refer to the kind of contact you'd like to have with others, both co-workers and clients, including the nature of the interaction you favor and how many others you prefer to work with at any one time.
▶ *Environment* involves both the physical and intangible aspects of the workplace itself: the office atmosphere, your work schedule, the aesthetics of the physical setting, the degree of freedom and flexibility in office management.

Step #3 — Your first draft will include dozens of entries under some categories and none in others. Eliminate the repetition by including any particular term only in one category. For example, creativity could be a talent of yours that you list under Skills, or a fascination with other people's creativity that you place in the Interests box, or a preference to work with creative people that you'd place in the People box, or the kind of love of new ideas and things that makes your entire work meaningful and is therefore included as a "Must Have" value. If you have a hard time deciding — and you will — it probably belongs under Values.

Avoid putting opposites of the same quality on both sides of the grid. For example, under "Environment," either indicate that you want a light and spacious atmosphere on the "Must Have" side or write on the "Must Avoid" side that you don't want a crowded, dark workplace, but do not include both. After you delete repetitive entries, think about the remaining words and phrases. Delete any to which you respond neutrally, with two exceptions:

► Include any words that emerged in a majority of the exercises even if you don't think they're that important to you.
► With respect to interests, include subject matters that are appealing but may not rise to the level of a "must." List up to a dozen interests you find appealing or would be happy to learn about.

Step #4 — Make certain that anything you include is a "must have" — an element that if absent would make your work feel unsatisfying or, if it's on the "Must Avoid" side, makes work intolerable. The only exception is that your interests do not have to rise to the level of a "must." Refrain from including by-products such as *enjoying my work, feeling like I'm contributing to society, fulfillment,* and *work that is meaningful to me.* The assumption is that if you found your ideal position, those responses would naturally occur. One more thing: avoid terms that can have ambiguous meaning. For example, "professionalism" could as easily mean that you wish to wear a suit and tie and carry a briefcase. Instead, choose the word or phrase that precisely conveys your requirements.

Step #5 — Finally, narrow your entries to no more than a dozen per category on the "Must Have" side, while making sure you list at least eight preferred interests, skills and values. Limit yourself to 10 entries under each category on the "Must Avoid" side, but there are no minimum requirements on this side of the grid. If no strong preference stands out for a "Must Avoid," leave it blank. Notice that the grid does not include the level of compensation you require for your next position. Assume you would earn as much money as you need to support yourself and your family.

interests, skills, values, people, environment

Ideal Job Grid

	MUST HAVE	MUST AVOID
Interests		
Skills		
Values		
People		
Environment		

Sample Ideal Job Grid #1		
	MUST HAVE	**MUST AVOID**
Interests	medicine/health human behavior children movies/TV fiction & self-help books fads/trends	physics advanced math military strategy
Skills	idea generation sharing insights advising listening public speaking reading, writing & editing designing or creating identifying root issues	sole responsibility for clerical tasks purely abstract pursuits keeping track of details
Values	autonomy variety innovation tangible goals or products focus on a "cause" influence	"win at all costs" attitude doing it only for the money
People	communicative growing cooperative working independently but with others around	closed-minded adults isolation
Environment	flexibility natural light complex but harmonious mobility	smoky air rigidly competing deadlines

Sample Ideal Job Grid #2

	MUST HAVE	MUST AVOID
Interests	recreation/the outdoors real estate business new things publishing	religion mental health
Skills	problem solving building or repairing creativity business start-up analyzing planning	purely theoretical work repetitive or procedural work people management
Values	variety the unusual challenge competition curiosity	
People	smart humorous upbeat supportive appreciative	emotionally trying situations women superiors incompetence autocratic leaders
Environment	informal flexible hours seasonally Western Washington in the summer	fast-paced totally outdoors

A Note on Interest in "Travel"

Many lawyers list "travel" as one of their "interests." Before you place the word in your own Interest column, explore what it is about travel that appeals to you. Is it the opportunity to learn about other cultures (interest: cultural diversity, foreign cultures) or simply to learn new things or to adapt? Do you crave the mobility (Environment), the variety (Value or Environment), or the time away from work (Environment)? Or are you interested in the travel industry itself? If it's the latter, then list travel in the Interest column. If it's any of the others, or some other reason, place that characteristic in the appropriate category.

A Dozen Skills Preferred by Lawyers in Transition

I reviewed the Ideal Job Grids of over 200 graduates of my career evaluation workshops to come up with a list of a dozen common "building-block" skills preferred by lawyers. I use the term *building block* deliberately. Problem-solving was the most frequently mentioned skill preference, but that skill is actually a compilation of other basic skills: analyzing, researching, organizing and planning, and often speaking, writing, advising, persuading and developing rapport. In order of preference, the 12 basic skills preferred by lawyers are:

TRAVEL
cultural diversity?
learn new things?
mobility? variety?
time away from work?

Analyze (including evaluate, clarify and interpret) — Every job listed in this book demands the skill of analysis. Be specific. This preference really reflects more what you like to analyze — abstract, theoretical issues or more concrete and structural problems — and how — using common sense, logic or intuition, or having time to study the problem in depth versus having to size up a situation quickly for an on-the-spot solution.

Organize (including synthesize, conceptualize and simplify) — This skill usually refers to the ability to take something that has been randomly arranged and put it into better order. The "something" being organized might be people, data, objects or time. You may enjoy creating a new system, or maintaining an old one. Some prefer to tackle highly complex projects; others like to keep the routine moving along smoothly and predictably.

Write (including read and edit) — The writing can be creative, technical, investigative, reportage, or persuasive. The pieces can be of any length, from essays to legal thrillers. You might enjoy going into depth or remaining superficial. Writing style should also be considered: Do you prefer writing with a deadline, having all the time in the world to express yourself completely and accurately, or taking moments here and there to dash off a quick thought?

Create (including innovate, design, generate ideas and brainstorm) — Many lawyers associate creativity only with the arts. But problem-solving of all types also calls upon one's creativity. For example, do you prefer coming up with your own ideas or to implement the ideas of others? Do you like to start projects and creating something from nothing, or do you prefer dealing with issues in projects that someone else initiated? Do you have more fun figuring out how to get something going, or prefer to keep something going?

Research (including investigate, interview and gather facts or information) — This skill stems from your curiosity and love of learning, but the preference often falls into one of two categories: oral versus written and personal versus statistical or factual. You may like to spend hours in the library or on-line gathering data; you may prefer to hear the stories of many people. It's all research.

Interests

accounting	current events	human relations	movies	self-help
acting	design	human rights	music	skiing
animal rights	ecology	indigenous	music therapy	social issues
animals	economics	cultures	musicians	social justice
anthropology	education	information	mysteries	social science
antiques	electronics	inner city	mythology	sociopathic
architecture	entertaining	problems	nature	behavior
art	environment	insurance	nutrition	software
astrophysics	fads & trends	intellectual	organizational	applications
athletics	fantasy	property	psychology	spirituality
bankruptcy	fashion	interior design/	other cultures	sports
bicycling	fiction	decorating	outdoors	swimming
books	finance	international law	parenting	technology
business	fine arts and	inventions	people	television
career choices	artists	investments	philosophy	the decision-
children	fitness	irony	photography	making process
civil rights	food	issues of the	physics	the past
classical ballet	foreign cultures	elderly	physiology	the unusual
community	foreign relations	journalism	poetry	toys
activism	foreign trade	jurisprudence	political satire	travel industry
computers	furniture	labor law	politics	wilderness
constitutional	gardening	language	poverty law	women's issues
law	group dynamics	law	psychology	words
consumer	health	legal theory	public issues	work safety
protection	history	lifestyles	public policy	youth
cooking	history of law	literature	publishing	
crafts	horses	magazines	religion	
criminal law	housing	math	residential real	
criminal	how things work	mechanical	estate	
psychology	human behavior	things	rhetoric	
criminality	human	medicine	science	
culinary arts	motivation	modern jazz	science fiction	
cultures	human potential	morality	securities	

Skills

achieve goals	create solutions	focused	manage people	public speaking
act on gut	creative writing	concentration	manage projects	quick thinking
reactions	creativity	follow rules	mechanical	read
active listening	critical thinking	forecast	tinkering	remember details
adapt to new	critical/precise	fundraising	mediate	repair
situations	writing	gather	memory work	research
adjudicate	curiosity	information	mentor	resolve conflict
administer	decision-making	generate	monitor	resourcefulness
advise	decisiveness	enthusiasm	monitor details	review
agility	dependability	guide	motivate	information
analyze	design	identify issues	musicality	see potential
analyze	detail work	identify problems	negotiate	possibilities
information	develop expertise	imagination	notice details	sell
answer questions	develop intimacy	implement	nurture	share
assist leaders	develop	implement	object	share insights
athletic ability	programs	projects	observation	simplify
attention to	develop rapport	influence others	objectivity	complexity
details	diplomacy	initiate	obtain	size-up accurately
brainstorm	directness	innovate	cooperation	speak
budget	discipline	inspire others	oral advocacy	stage a
build	dispassionate	instruct	oral	production
calculate	analysis	integrate	communication	strategize
calm others	edit	components	organize	summarize
close observation	educate	intellectual	organize groups	supervise
coach	efficiency	tinkering	paint	support
communicate	empathy	interview	perceive	synthesize
compose	empirical	intuit	perform	take inventory
computer work	observation	investigate	persevere	take the initiative
conceptualize	empirical research	lead	persist	teach
conflict resolution	empower others	learn new things	persuade	team build
connect people	entertain	learn quickly	physical strength	theorize
to resources	establish rapport	listen	plan	versatility
consensus	evaluate	logical thinking	plan concrete	visual awareness
building	exercise common	long-range	action	win confidence
contemplation	sense	planning	practicality	work under
coordinate	experiment	make people	pragmatism	pressure
cost-	explain	laugh	prioritize	work with
consciousness	expressiveness	make quick	problem solve	animals
counsel	eye/hand	decisions	process	work with hands
count	coordination	manage	information	write
create	facilitate	manage details	provide expertise	
create documents	film	manage money	provide feedback	

Plan (including develop a strategy) — Anyone who likes to plan also enjoys analysis, but analyzers don't always like to plan. Planning requires foresight, the ability to anticipate and prepare for future contingencies. It demands a thoughtful approach to problem solving, weighing the possibilities and balancing resources. Planners have a deliberative rather than a spontaneous approach to life.

Speak (including performance and public speaking) — The size of the crowd may vary, but by and large, those who enjoy speaking thrive when they're in the public eye. The topic may be humorous, entertaining, educational, political or religious; the

Values

achievement	control over	helping others	moderation	safety
action	decisions	high drama	morality	security
adventure	cooperation	high profile	novelty	self-expression
aesthetics	courage	high risk	order	sensuality
alleviate	creativity	holistic view	originality	shared
suffering	diversity	honesty	personal growth	enjoyment
authenticity	effectiveness	hope	playfulness	sharing
autonomy	ethics	improvement	pleasure	simplicity
balanced lifestyle	excellence	independence	power	social relevance
beauty	excitement	individuality	practicality	social utility
cause-orientation	expertise	influence	predictability	solitude
challenge	fairness	innovation	prestige	spontaneity
change	family	integrity	productivity	stability
client-centered	flexibility	intellectual	push personal	structure
closure	focus	challenge	limits	tangible results
comfort	forthrightness	intellectual	relationships	the unusual
competence	freedom	stimulation	religious	usefulness
complexity	gaiety	justice	conviction	variety
concrete goals	hands-on	knowledge	respect	wholesomeness
conformity	harmony	loyalty	responsibility	
connection	health	measurable	risk	
control	helping a cause	results	routine	

style may be extemporaneous or carefully planned. But the goal is almost always to influence, teach or inspire.

Persuade (including advocate, sell, negotiate, inspire, and motivate) — This is the main skill you learn in law school; it's odd that it isn't higher on the list of preferences. You can persuade orally or in writing. Some view the skill as something close to coercion; others see it rather as motivating others to follow the most reasonable path.

Manage (including coordinate details or people, supervise, monitor, administer and pay attention to details) — Planners often like to manage, because the two skills require the same foresight. The big difference between the two is the degree to which attention to detail is required. Planners notice the detail in order to come up with the plan; managers must keep track of the detail in order to keep progressing. Some only like to manage people, others only data. Project managers often oversee both.

Develop rapport (including empathize and active listening) — This is the preference that shows you're a "people person". You prefer to relate to others on a feeling basis, making connections on a gut rather than an intellectual level. You may want to use the skill in a counseling session, to market a product or service, or to generate enthusiasm. The goal is always to build trust.

> Your ideal job grid will multiply your options and clarify the best work and work environment for you.

Observe (including listen, perceive and visual awareness) — You must observe to develop rapport, but you can also observe without developing rapport. This talent involves either noticing details in your surroundings or reading body language and other non-verbal communications. Trial lawyers use this skill to read juries and to determine whether their message is getting across. Negotiators and mediators must be good observers to uncover the unspoken positions that are impeding agreement.

Do You Prefer Independence, Autonomy or Teamwork?

Independence is the quality or state of not being dependent, or not subject to control by others, or not affiliated with a larger controlling unit, or not requiring or relying on something else and not looking to others for guidance in conduct.

Autonomy means the quality or state of being self-governing, i.e., having control or rule over oneself. Many lawyers initially define their desire for self-governance as independence, but upon further reflection realize they really value autonomy. They want to be able to control their own environment, make decisions in their work based on their own notions of right and wrong, but want to work collaboratively or at least with others around to share ideas and the workload.

Teamwork is work done by several associates, each performing a part, but all subordinating their personal prominence to the efficiency of the whole. This type of work arrangement is unusual among lawyers. Lawyers tend to organize themselves in projects where one, usually senior, lawyer is responsible for guiding and controlling the effort and everyone else works in a lesser role. The senior lawyer takes all the credit for a job well done and usually takes the heat for failure. This is not teamwork. Some lawyers confuse the notion of teamwork with a preference to have competent help in completing tasks, to work with other people around, or to be able to brainstorm and discuss cases. Determine whether you in fact are willing to subordinate your need for recognition or prestige to the success of the group before deciding that teamwork is one of your preferences.

When you're deciding which value best reflects your preference, remember that independence is a more broad-based desire to be free from the constraints of working with others, either above or below you. Autonomy is more limited: the desire to control your own work environment and decision-making on your own projects, but not necessarily to work alone or to have sole responsibility and power to affect the course of a project or case.

The Work-Hours Question

With demands escalating in the practice of law, many lawyers yearn for work that gives you more control over your time. You might define it in terms of a part-time schedule or working a steady 40-50-hour week. Regular hours, regular vacations or taking comp time might be your goals. Again, consider carefully what you want. Would you mind occasional long hours and intense pressure if you loved the work and believed in the goal? Or do you want a set schedule with no variation in work-load, pace, pressure or time commitment? Is it okay to work long hours as long as you get to pick the hours and where you perform the work? Do you like the idea of working on projects that demand a lot of time and attention for three or four months and are followed by a similar period off? Concentrate on the rhythms you prefer rather than merely reacting to the demands of the typical workplace.

People				
adversial roles	dependable	insightful	practical	tactful
appreciative	eccentric	intelligent	reasonable	team work
be in authority	enthusiastic	interactive	relaxed	trustworthy
bohemian	fair	large institution	reserved	undemanding
business-like	flexible	leader	respect	urbane
camaraderie	forthright	liberal	differences	value driven
collaborative	frequent	lively	respectful	well-informed
committed	interaction	loyal	responsible	wholesome
compassionate	friendly	mature	self-aware	women in
competence	gentle	meet new	sense of humor	authority
congenial	genuine	people often	sensitive	work alone
considerate	goal-oriented	mutual respect	shared values	work
cooperative	great minds	one-on-one	small group	collaboratively
creative	honest	open	smart	work
dedicated	humor	people-oriented	sophisticated	independently
democratic	independent	positive	supportive	

3 Coming to Terms with Change

Now that you have worked through the self-assessment process, and you've generated a list of job options inspired by your Ideal Job Grid, it's time to narrow your focus to the one or two fields. The ones that most intrigue you. At this point, though, you might not know enough about the options you've gathered to decide what interests you most — or whether you ought to be interested at all! The next chapter (and Appendices 2, 5 and 6) will help you research your options inside, outside and around the law.

Environment

a lot going on	frequent travel	predictable	steady work pace
access to the outdoors	friendly competition	private office	stylish
active	full days	private spaces	support staff
aesthetically pleasing	group setting	regular hours	telecommuting
automated	growth encouraged	relaxed	time for exercise
calm	informal	respect for diversity	time for reflection
casual	intense	rural	uncomplicated
changing	light	schedule control	uncrowded
close to nature	long vacations	security	unstructured
competitive	long-term projects	semi-arid	upscale
consistent work flow	mobility	sense of community	urban
constant work flow	natural light	short-term projects	visually stimulating
control over time	okay to be average	smoke free	well-defined duties
commitment	ordered	social	well-equipped office
discrete projects	organized	sophisticated	wide open space
fast-paced	outdoors	spacious	work at home
flexible	peaceful	stable	work at own pace
formal	physical activity	state-of-the-art	

CHAPTER 4

RESEARCH

Researching
Your Options

"People say I was courageous to do what I did. But leaving the law was actually a necessity. It was like having an illness. I either had to cure myself or watch a big part of me die."

—*Barry, a lawyer-turned-sculptor*

▪ ▪ ▪

Speculation has it that more than half of all existing jobs will change fundamentally over the next 10 years.

Furthermore, that a third of all current jobs will no longer exist.

More important, many of the jobs of the future do not even exist today; they will reflect changes in technology, or deal with concepts and products that are now being developed or that may only be a gleam in someone's imagination. Take law libraries, for example. "The law firm library may one day become a casualty of the Information Age," writes The National Law Journal. "Indeed, the ease of access to information brought about by networked CD-ROM technology and online services may render the traditional conception of the library obsolete."

> A good search engine is invaluable, but it's not the only research option.

Written Research

Of course, the obvious first option is to go online with the help of good search engines. Two of the most popular are **www.Google.com** and **www.Dogpile.com**. You'll find even more online job-finding references online in Chapter 6 (*Taking Advantage of the Internet*), and in Appendices 3 and 4. For all the speed and convenience of the web, though, don't ignore your local public library, or even the free business library at any one of the Fed's many regional Small Business Administration offices. Taken together, there is nothing you can't find on any field of interest.

Pay particular attention to the Web sites of professional associations in your areas of interest (see Appendices 4 and 6). These groups serve as both clearinghouses of information (newsletters, magazines, journals, employment guides and seminars) and job-search vehicles (announcements of job vacancies, job banks, and networking opportunities). Reading the association newsletters and reviewing their program announcements may give you a preliminary sense of whether the subject matter and issues facing those working in this field genuinely interest you. And the well-regarded Encyclopedia of Associations is on the shelf of most public libraries.

To brush up on effective research techniques, I also recommend Karmen Crowther's book, *"Researching Your Way to a Good Job: How to Find and Use Information on Industries, Companies, Jobs and Careers."*

Of course, anything published—in books or articles—is no substitute for substantive discussions with individuals currently working in your targeted field. Attending programs sponsored by local chapters of national organizations will also help you determine whether the industry is all you expected it to be, or whether you have some misconceptions about its scope and function. But, again, it's important to talk directly to those who work in the industry. There's even a name for it; it's called "informational interviewing."

Informational Interviewing

An informational interview is an opportunity to learn about a field of interest, or one specific person's job duties, or a business environment. It is not (nor should be) a veiled plea for employment. It is also not intended to result in a job with that person or firm (although sometimes it does). Your invitation to talk should be based on your genuine need to know more about a career field before determining what you want to do and where you want to work. Informational interviewing not only helps you determine what direction to head, it also has proved to be one foundation of successful job hunting.

When Richard *What-Color-is-Your-Parachute* Bolles, and his co-author John Crystal, first studied job hunters, they discovered that the most successful had interviewed lots of people simply for information before they ever went out on an actual job interview. The two authors screened potential fields, then individual industries, and finally organizations to confirm their interest in a particular career direction. Bolles, and other authors and consultants like him, advised others to mimic these successful job hunters by engaging in the person-to-person research process they named "informational interviewing."

As you may have guessed, job-seekers besieged corporate HR departments with requests for informational interviews when the individuals were actually fishing for a job. The subterfuge led some employers to look upon the strategy with suspicion; in fact, many with hiring authority still refuse to respond to such requests. But even HR employees under orders to avoid informational interviews will talk to a friend of a friend about their job and company. Be certain, then, that your request for an informational interview is just that, and not a ploy to get hired.

Getting Started with Informational Interviewing

Once you start the process of talking to other people, it seems easy. But it's often hard to make that first call or write that first letter. Fear keeps getting in the way: fear that the people you contact will reject you or won't have time for your questions; fear that your mind will go blank, or you'll say something stupid. You may procrastinate and worry rather than take the first step. You may even develop what lawyer/psychologist Stephen Feldman calls "phone phobia." As he puts it, "When the phone rings for lawyers, it's like a time bomb going off. You can never tell what kind of crisis or attitude is going to come at you through the receiver."

After 10 years of intermittent telephone unpleasantness with clients, witnesses and opposing counsel, I know that I developed resistance to telephone networking. To overcome the fear, I suggest you start modestly. Talk to your best friends on the phone about the career direction you're considering. For additional practice, also interview people about subjects that interest you, but not for reasons of employment. One Texas lawyer in transition started by talking to artisans she admired—quilters, watercolor painters, folk art collectors — even though she was planning to find a job in nonprofit fund-raising. Her experiment taught her that most people like to be asked questions about themselves and their interests, and are usually generous with their time and information.

There are some helpful books on "cold calling" technique. In the meantime, if you're reluctant to reach out by phone, here are three suggestions:

▶ Send an e-mail or write a note introducing yourself first, and indicate when you will be following up with a telephone call.

▶ Attend a lecture or class on a relevant subject matter. Ask questions of the speaker and talk to at least one other attendee.

▶ If you cannot find anyone who works in a field of interest, turn to the experts you've discovered in your library research. Call or write the author of an article you found interesting, or someone who was profiled in a newspaper or magazine. Go ahead and reach to the top. Don't assume that those people would not be interested in speaking with you. Usually they're flattered that you are seeking advice from them. Some will even remember what it was like to be looking for work!

Do be cautious, though, about deciding your career direction after talking to a single source. "Find at least three people for each career field," says Cindy Chernow, former Director of Alumni Career Services at UCLA. "If you find only one person in a field and they have a poor attitude, it could skew your impression about the work and dampen your interest." Of course, the opposite can also occur; one person's great experience may be equally atypical.

Informational Interviewing Etiquette

The best way to arrange an informational interview is to make your request as non-invasive as possible and to communicate your enthusiasm. You might start by introducing yourself and explaining how you got that person's name. For example, "I saw the announcement of your career change in the Business Journal," or "My friend, Jane Doe, who I understand you also know, told me about your new teaching job, and suggested that I give you a call." Then state the purpose of your call: "I've been thinking about going into elementary education myself, and I thought I ought to talk to another lawyer who has made the change before I enroll in the local certification course. I'd love to know how the change has worked for you."

Don't assume your contact will be delighted to spend time with you. Inquire directly: "May I buy you a cup of coffee, or meet you, to ask you some questions about your work?"

If you sense resistance, assure your contact that you are not seeking employment at this time, and that you don't expect to be told about any current openings, that you don't care if there are any such openings at his or her company. Instead, explain — but only if it's true — that you are researching your ideal job and want to learn more about a particular job function, or industry, or the

Suggested Interpersonal Research Questions

▶ Could you describe some of your daily activities in the position you now hold?

▶ What tasks do you typically perform in your work?

▶ What skills do you need for this work?

▶ What is the overall objective of this job (i.e., why do you do what you do)?

▶ What do you like and dislike about your work?

▶ What are the major benefits and drawbacks of this work?

▶ What is the work environment like? If there are different environments in which this work is performed, what are they like?

▶ How did you get into this work? How did you get into your current position?

▶ What qualifications are necessary or desirable to become employed in this area or to succeed in this field?

▶ How can my legal training or skills be of benefit in this field?

▶ What is the best way to obtain a position that will start me on a career in this field?

▶ At what level could I enter this field with my current qualifications?

▶ What is the top job you can have in this career?

▶ Are there other areas of this field to which people may be transferred, and what are they?

▶ What current demand is there for people in this field? Do you expect that level of demand to continue?

▶ What future opportunities or developments do you see in this field?

▶ What is the compensation range for this field/work?

▶ What are the employment prospects in this field?

▶ If I want to change to this type of work, what are the best ways to find out what is available?

▶ Who else should I talk to, and where else should I go for more information? May I use you name as a referral?

background you ought to have for the kind of work you envision. Sometimes the referral name will provide an instant entree; other times you'll be turned down. In any event, don't take it personally. The contact may:

▶ have a strained relationship with your friend;

▶ be extremely busy or in a lousy mood;

▶ honestly believe she has nothing to offer you; or

▶ not be a particularly helpful person.

If you're unlucky enough to be turned down by your first contact, be sure to call another contact right away. You're not likely to receive the same treatment twice in a row. Most people really want to help and will be surprisingly generous with their time and knowledge. Talk to as many people as possible. Nearly every informational interview produces at least one bit of useful information, and you can't know in advance which ones will be most helpful. Be gracious in receiving the information as well. Never say, "I've already tried that and it didn't work," or, "That doesn't interest me." The people you contact are trying to help. If you respond negatively or ungratefully, they probably won't think of you in the future when opportunities do arise.

Nor should you go into the meeting without preparation, expecting the interviewee to know what you need to be told. Do as much research as possible online or at the library beforehand so you'll know what to ask. Write your questions down and bring them with you. Have enough focus (in terms of questions or requests for information) so that you don't make your contact feel you're both wasting time.

You might wonder whether you should "waste" an informational interview on a networking contact who might actually have a job opening. If your intention in meeting with the contact is to get a jump on the position, don't ask for an informational interview. Be honest and ask for what you really want — a job interview. Assuming you're still in the clarification process, however, go ahead and schedule a research meeting. You may discover that you don't want to work in that field or in that firm. You may also develop a solid rapport with the person that could lead to future employment. Whatever happens, be sincere. If an opening arises later, realistically appraise the degree of rapport you developed with that contact. If it was cold, you're not likely to get far on a second call. If it was good, remind the contact of your prior meeting, and let him or her know of your interest in the position. If you really hit it off, your contact will remember you and be happy to help. He or she might even be embarrassed about the oversight in not contacting you first, and be even more eager to provide assistance.

Keeping at It

At first, talk to as many of the people who are suggested as possible and ask each contact for the names of others who might be helpful. As you get further into your research process and refine your focus, you'll want to be more discriminating in following up. But beware of being too selective. Nearly every interview produces some information, and you can't know what you will learn, which interviews will be most helpful, or which bit of information could change your life, until after the fact. If you follow this process of researching the fields that interest you, especially through personal contacts, your job-search may take you in unexpected directions. It's the same as a new lawsuit; as you progress through the discovery process you sometimes realize that you're working with an entirely different cause of action. Similarly, when you begin to research one potential career direction, you may realize that you were mistaken about what the work entailed, but you discover another path more closely matches your requirements. The point is to let the research process evolve. Sticking to the process, and keeping an open mind when making contacts, will ultimately help you find a new direction.

Failed the Bar! Now What?

By Michael Moiso, JD

Only about one out of every four law school graduates passes the bar the first time out.

This is a national average. Your own state will have its own higher — or lower — pass rate. As an attorney and bar exam coach, though, I can't fully explain why some grads pass the bar and others don't. The reasons are both personal and mysterious. Some grads are not as organized or as disciplined going into the exam as they could be, others can't afford a bar prep course or can't dedicate a full six-to-eight weeks in preparation because of work or family obligations, and still others are better in class and mock court than they are in a testing environment. And let's be fair: the idiosyncrasies in some jurisdictions (e.g., New York, California) make the exam a grueling rite of passage with first-time pass rates in the 50-to-60 range!

I've been practicing in Oregon for 10 years now, but I still remember what it was it like to fail the bar exam the first time. It's a source of great sadness, disappointment, and embarrassment. And why not? For three years, you dedicate yourself to one single goal, sacrificing time, effort, and financial resources (and sometimes even relationships) only to be denied access to The Club. Well, I've got good news: If you fail, the following months will certainly be a test of fortitude, but not a death sentence. You can take the bar exam as many times as necessary to pass (note: Charles Evans Hughes, a former Chief Justice of the Supreme Court, failed the New

York bar seven times before he was finally allowed to practice law). The important thing is not to let it keep you down. You must accept the reality for what it is — a minor setback in your goal to become a practicing attorney.

So, what can you do now? Plenty. In this short article, I'd like to offer a few quick tips so that you can finally pass the bar exam and move on to your life's true purpose:

1. *Are you sure you want to practice law?* — As a bar exam coach, this is the very first issue I raise with my clients. Passing the bar is not the only path to a successful career in law. Your JD can be invaluable throughout the corporate, government, or nonprofit sectors. If you decide not to practice law, this book will help you explore career alternatives. If you're sure you want to practice, read on.

2. *Get back on the horse* — Take a little time to lick your wounds ... but not too long. Make plans now to take the very next exam. Many of you will be preoccupied with work, financial, or child-care issues, but I strongly urge you not to let a year elapse before retaking the test. Otherwise you risk forgetting what you learned in bar review. And if you do take the next test, you may be able to skip the expense of another bar review course.

3. *Get professional assistance* — Don't let pride and ego get in the way. This is one of those times when you have to pull over to the gas station and ask for directions. Request the return of your exam materials and review them with the help of a mentor or tutor. Ex-bar examiners are the best (contact your state bar for names), but I also recommend calling on one or more law professors or practicing attorneys.

4. *Think strategically* — Don't wait for your exam results before looking for work. Jump in now, and stay in the legal field. Large firms have legal assistant and paralegal positions, but your status will be tenuous if you fail the bar a second time. On the other hand, there are research and/or investigative positions in the DA or Public Defender's offices, or you can intern at legal services, all of which are a lot more forgiving if you need to take the bar exam on more than one or two occasions. Better still, seek out small law firms (under 15 lawyers), where a JD can do all sorts of hands-on lawyer stuff that wouldn't be permitted in large firms. And finally, if you're willing to look outside the immediate legal environment, consider working at state or federal think tanks, legislative councils or lobbying organizations.

5. *Don't be picky* — The job market now is the roughest in decades. So don't hold out for your dream job. Find a stepping-stone job ... a bridge job ... that earns you a

living, keeps your brain cells working, and allows some flexibility as you prepare to retake the bar. The next bar.

Whatever you choose to do, don't let the bar exam break your legal spirit. Know that how you perform on the bar exam relates only to the bar exam. Whatever happens, you are a Doctor of Jurisprudence, and no one can take that away.

Michael J. Moiso, Esq. — *Moiso, a bar exam coach and author of Don't Stress The Bar Exam, has a law practice in Beaverton, Oregon, that focuses on small business and real estate law.*

An Overview of Alternative Careers

"I still consider getting out of law once in a while. The last time was about a year ago, when we were in the middle of a big trade secrets lawsuit. The case was very combative, and it drove me crazy. Pretty soon, I contracted "Sunday Syndrome", dreading Monday on Sunday morning. Eventually, the only good time of the week was Friday night because then I still had all day Saturday before I felt the dread of going into the office."

— *a George Washington University graduate*

■ ■ ■

What can you do with your law degree and practice experience besides practicing law? The options are staggering. Nearly a thousand options alone are listed in Appendices 1 and 4, and all of them available to someone with a law degree or legal background. Of course, the temptation is to aim toward a "hot" specialty. Ten years ago, bankruptcy and environmental law were supposed to carry the legal profession for the foreseeable future. Just a few years later, they were the only ones *declining* in a booming legal market, and were replaced by intellectual property and employment law. One National Law Journal study showed that litigation was the only practice area that remained stable and large, at almost one-third of all practitioners. As you read through this section, remember that the best career direction for you has to do less with what's "hot" than what you are capable of doing and are impassioned enough to pursue at all cost.

> The options for what you can do with your law degree besides practicing law are almost unlimited.

Nontraditional Law Practice Alternatives

The real opportunities are in emerging practices ... such as contract (or temporary) lawyering, independent general counsel arrangements, and legal research services.

Contract lawyers perform legal services for other lawyers on an intermittent or impermanent basis. Their prominence in the legal profession coincides with tremendous growth in the entire temporary services industry. Many large and specialty law firms hire contract lawyers, often through placement agencies, as temporary associates, paying them on an hourly basis to work full-time (that is, overtime!) in the law firm for a minimum of three months or until they are no longer needed. Other contract lawyers work on a project, or a rush, or an as-needed basis with a number of different solo and small firm practitioners, government agencies or in-house legal departments. Neither the contract lawyer nor the hiring lawyer has any guarantee that the relationship will continue beyond the agreed-upon period or project.

Independent general counsel (also known as part-time in-house counsel) are private practitioners who contract with a number of corporations to provide in-house legal services on a less than full-time basis. They usually charge hourly rates significantly lower than those of comparable outside counsel, or a guaranteed monthly retainer, and work on-site at the corporations. Legal research services contract with law firms to produce memoranda on requested points of law. The research may or may not be generated by lawyers; sometimes a computer-research specialist or law student performs the services.

Working Within the Legal Profession as a Non-Practitioner

The rapid growth of the profession, as well as technological advances, and changes in client expectations, have provided tremendous opportunity to law school graduates who want to work within the profession without practicing law.

In some law firms, former practitioners with business skills have created niches for themselves as managers and office administrators. Those with marketing instincts have taken positions as directors of practice development, client services or marketing. To pursue interests in education, training and human resources, still others now manage in-house professional development programs or associate recruiting. In fact, an entire industry has emerged of service providers to the profession, many founded, operated or staffed by former lawyers. Any edition of The National Law Journal or the ABA Journal offers dozens of examples: computer software vendors, contract lawyer placement agencies, and jury, marketing or management consultants, among others.

The New York Times called legal publishing a "new growth industry," and some former practitioners have taken advantage by publishing, writing for, or distributing newsletters and journals catering to legal specialties. Legal publishers (see Appendix 6) and legal research services also hire former practitioners in departments as diverse as sales, management, marketing, training and acquisitions. I've also witnessed dramatic growth in the mediation field. Former (and current) practicing lawyers act as mediators, and participate in the training, marketing and administration of alternative dispute resolution services. At the current time, though, there are more lawyers who want to be mediators than the market will support. For access to online mediation resources, see Appendix 4.

Providing Legal Information to the General Public

Lawyers have also designed products and services that explain legal issues and procedures to the lay public. Examples include do-it-yourself divorce and estate planning books and software programs, seminars that explain the defamation laws to journalists, and systems designed for intellectual property protection. Those who wish to teach, or speak more and write less, might move into the burgeoning "preventive law" seminar business. Former practicing lawyers are frequently hired to teach corporate employees to deal with a diverse workforce, avoid sexual harassment and learn to resolve conflicts without involving the legal staff.

Educational Administration

Law schools are feeling the pinch of competition. Students now demand more services for their tuition dollars, hence the growth in law school career services and counseling offices. The schools also must develop better relationships with alumni to encourage their financial contributions. You might consider a position in career services, alumni relations, fund-raising, and CLE programming. General university administration also offers opportunities. Universities want to limit the number of EEO and ADA complaints that end up in court by hiring investigators to look into the complaints and work out "reasonable accommodations" with the professor and the student. Other aspects of risk management, HR, technology transfer and contract negotiation and administration also provide spots for those with legal backgrounds.

Regulation or Enforcement Specialist
Within Business or Government

Similar positions can be found in the corporate and public sectors. As the law has become more complex, the demand has grown for lawyers to act as interpreters for non-lawyers. Some lawyers find positions inside corporations or the government in which their familiarity with the law is used on a daily basis.

For example, **Tom**, a sixth-year associate in a large law firm, found work as a training administrator with an aircraft manufacturer in which he ensures that federal and state health, safety and environmental regulations are being met by the company's training departments. In this job, he uses the skills he developed in trial practice: the ability to understand the intent of the regulations, to organize materials for training consortiums, and to mediate discussions among groups of people with vastly different opinions and agendas.

In general, corporations are interested in lawyers with knowledge relevant to compliance and enforcement functions (e.g., EEOC, ADA, affirmative action, environmental or other regulatory matters, employee benefits, internal ethics consultant, labor relations manager). Purchasing agent and contract administration positions are also prevalent in government offices, especially civilian positions with the military. Corporations and federal, state and local governments all want to limit the number of suits filed against them, thereby reducing legal fees and the disruption caused by employee involvement in the matter. Many employ former practicing lawyers in-house to intervene in conflicts before they reach the point of a lawsuit. These entities also hire lawyers for litigation oversight.

Nonprofit Management

The growing number of practicing lawyers, combined with new specialization and mandatory continuing education requirements, have led to increases in bar association size and numbers. Every new bar group or function provides opportunities for practitioners to manage or supervise the operations. Discipline, CLE, attorney assistance, mentoring, public affairs and lobbying functions are frequently handled by lawyers.

Nonprofit organizations outside of the legal profession often hire lawyers as directors or project managers, or as specialists in development or planned giving.

Mark spent six years working in a Manhattan insurance defense firm, and one year as a lawyer in city government, then accepted a planned-giving position in the development office of New York University. He designs testamentary plans that maximize benefits to both the donor and the beneficiary. Although Mark had no experience in estate planning before this job, he impressed his new employers with his ability to learn what was needed, a skill he developed in handling a wide variety of court cases.

Leaving the Law Behind

It's hard to imagine a career that wouldn't use any of the background we develop as lawyers. Those who return to school to become secondary school teachers make use of the insight, self-discipline, and knowledge they developed as lawyers. One pair of entrepreneurs even called upon their legal experience to navigate the licensing process to start an alpine travel company using llamas as pack animals. Those lawyers who move the farthest from the profession, though, seem to gravitate toward the following fields and positions:

► Entrepreneurial ventures — It can range from restaurants like the California Pizza Kitchen chain developed by two lawyers, to retail operations like the Sharper Image, founded by former practicing lawyer Richard Thalheimer; and publishing successes like Nolo Press and The Zagat (restaurant rating) guides.

► Communications — It includes publishing, editing, writing, and reporting for newspapers, magazines, television, radio and public relations companies. Three such celebrity ex-lawyers are author John Grisham, TV producer David Kelley (The Practice), and journalist Tim Russert, host of NBC's Meet the Press.

► Real estate — It includes real estate development, property management, construction, remodeling and interior decoration.

► Teaching — Many ex-lawyers have sought out teaching positions in both public and private schools at all levels, from grade school to graduate level work.

► Counseling — Another area popular with ex-lawyers are positions as psychotherapists, marriage-and-family counselors, and as career coaches.

The Big Decision: For Women Only

By Camille Walker

I've spoken to many women attorneys about their decision to become lawyers, and whether they felt it was the right choice. What surprises me is the number of women who appear to be just going through the motions without regard to whether the practice of law is fulfilling some purpose in their life. In this sidebar, you'll read about five women — myself included — and what we learned about finding work that fit our lifestyle, interests and values:

Camille's story — "I got started as an assistant city attorney. I was good at municipal law, but was bored the more comfortable I became. It didn't help that my colleagues were saying things like, 'Only 15 more years until retirement.' I left and tried a variety of jobs. But it was the same wherever I went; the moment I settled into a routine, I was bored and restless. This time, though, instead of ignoring my feelings, I decided to explore my dissatisfaction. I spent several months soul-searching. I finally had to admit that my dream of being a lawyer since the age of 12 wasn't fulfilling my life as an adult. About that time, I read a copy of Barbara Sher's book, *I Could Do Anything if I Only Knew What it Was*. What surfaced was my love for training, communications, and helping others. Before long, I was reading everything about career transition. In 2002, I launched a career consulting business just for women. My own transition took more than 10 years but it was worth the wait. I love this work.

What did I learn? — "Sometimes finding your niche takes longer than you expect."

Lisa's story — After five years, I became partner in a medium-sized firm. I handled intellectual property, and had a growing client base. I was also a mom with two toddlers, and it was increasingly difficult to balance work with the needs of my children. Fortunately, I was able to negotiate leaving in the afternoon. My mistake was not telling my clients, and I usually ended up working the phone with my children screaming in the background. I had to leave. My schedule was draining me. I was just plain cranky all the time. One day, I met a friend for lunch. She said a nonprofit was looking for a contract manager. The work was narrow in scope, and it didn't pay much. I told them I can't work full-time for that amount, so they countered with a three-quarter-time position. I'm happy I took the job. It expanded into areas I never anticipated, and I'm practicing an area of law that really enhances peoples lives.

What did I learn? — "That I just wanted to be a good parent and good at work, and that I had to persist to find the right combination."

Chris' story — When I was younger, I didn't have any grand dreams about practicing law. It was my college roommate who suggested the law because I liked working with people. So I thought, 'Well, OK, it sounds like a way to make a living and help people at the same time.' Big mistake. I thrive on harmony, and here I was in the middle of an adversarial system. After nine years in family and juvenile law, and a few more at the AG's office, I turned 40, and was chronically depressed. My problem was, I didn't have goals of my own. That was the turning point. So, I returned to graduate school. Spent the next five years working my day job, and studying toward a degree in mental health. A day before the deadline, I applied for — and got — a job working with the state bar's lawyer assistance program. Now I work with lawyers on substance abuse issues. It suits me perfectly.

What did I learn? — "Don't settle for any job that means a spiritual death for you."

Darlene's story — "I grew up in a small Southern town. My family knew all the lawyers in town, and when I was old enough they told me about the law. Too stressful, too demanding, too many long hours, they said. But my father argued the other side, and that was enough for me. Best decision I ever made. I started as a legal secretary, and loved the client work. Became a bankruptcy paralegal, and loved the courtroom work. By then, it just seemed natural to go to law school. So I did ... but my dream was to one day become a judge. After practicing general civil litigation for 10 years, I got a chance to be a district court judge. Later, I was elected to the state district court. I love the law, and I like analyzing the issues. I would say my personality seems better suited to the judiciary instead of the constant advocacy for one party. Besides, the hours are more predictable than litigation, and I can have a life outside the law.

What did I learn? — "Your career should reflect who you are and what you value."

Victoria's story — "My first job out of law school was with a small civil litigation firm. I really hated the practice, especially the ligation because it was always so full of conflict and stress. It was a rude awakening to learn that clients don't always tell the truth, and you're at the mercy of some judge who could make his or her own decision despite the evidence. I would go to court knowing I was right, but might still lose ... and I hated losing. That's when I began to seriously give some thought to a teaching career. I returned to get an LLM in real property and was recruited to teach law students. I always knew I wanted to teach. I just didn't know I'd have to become a lawyer to do it.

What did I learn? — "That sometimes I take for granted the things that I love, the things that come easily to me."

Camille Walker, Esq. — *Ms. Walker is the principal of Career Strategy, a national provider of career development seminars and workshops for law students and attorneys. Ms. Walker has a business degree from Texas Tech University and a law degree from the University of Houston. She also serves as an advisor and volunteer mentor for the State Bar of Texas, Lawyer Assistance Program. Contact — www.mylawcareer.com.*

CHAPTER 5

BEING REALISTIC ABOUT TRANSITION

Three Major Barriers

"Most lawyers are interested in hearing about others who left the law because 95 percent of us secretly want to leave ourselves. I left, and my only advice is that when you begin to be unhappy with what you do, take the time to analyze why. If you find that you can't change things, it's time to leave."

—*Former assistant U.S. attorney*

■ ■ ■

Now that you've chosen a direction and researched what you might find there, it's time to think about the barriers that lay ahead. Not just any barriers — your barriers. The biggest barrier to change is usually *timing*: is it the right time for you to contemplate major change?

Of course, you may have no choice; you may have been pushed into action by an external circumstance — a lay-off, a forced retirement, loss of a big client, illness, or the merger or dissolution of your firm. For others, the barrier to change may be *lack of clarity*. That is, you're still unclear about whether to head off in a new direction or to find different work within your field or practice area. In my opinion, you should postpone any major career change if, after all the self-assessment you've done here (and elsewhere), you're still feeling unsure. This is especially true if your disenchantment is less than three years in duration ... or you aren't strongly drawn yet to any alternative ...or you aren't sure what field attracts you ... or you have a job that gives you the flexibility or financial security to let you continue assessing and researching.

> The 3 biggest barriers to change: timing, clarity, money.

That's why you're ready for career change if ... and only if ... you can honestly say:

▶ You're dissatisfied with the practice of law and you're strongly drawn to an identified new career; or
▶ You feel you've reached the end of your career path in law and are unlikely to grow further in the profession; or
▶ You never had the opportunity to pursue another more appealing career, and you now wish to act upon that long-suppressed desire; or
▶ You've experienced a seismic shift in your life interests, goals or values that has capped your interest or belief in the law, and you wish to move toward your new objectives in another line of work.

While timing and clarity are two major barriers, another is financial — you don't yet have the resources to support yourself or your family for the three to 12 months needed to locate a better job, or from six months-to-two years to switch to another field. Or, you can't afford the pay cut that would accompany a new line of work. Or, you want to buy a house and need your current income to qualify for a mortgage.

For others, the issue may be that you have too many demands on your time and energy right now. For example, this is not the right time for change if you're undergoing a marital separation or divorce ... grieving over a recent death ... caring for someone in your family who is grievously ill ... you're experiencing a serious health problem ... or you're preparing for a major trial or transaction closing. Certainly you must resolve the current crisis before you initiate another.

On the other hand, if there are always unusual demands on your time, you need to look at those demands more critically. Let's face it: what difference does it make if you bill the most hours in your department if you're planning to leave in six months? Who cares if you can't meet all the requests of your most unreasonable clients if they're going to be someone else's clients soon? Those demands may be getting in the way simply because you haven't made peace with the status quo. Maybe you need to tell your current employer or partners about your dissatisfaction and ask for some accommodations. If your only motivation for making a change is financial, consider whether your employer rewards longevity with increased pay or offers training that could make you more valuable when you do move on. It might be prudent to hold off on your transition until you feel comfortable that you've given your current situation a chance to prove itself.

But if you experience a queasy feeling every time you think about heading off in a direction in your career, or it terrifies you to think about not being a lawyer, re-read chapters 2 (*Realistic Guidelines to Change*) and 5 (*Finding Stepping-Stones, Filling in the Gaps,* and *Should I Leave the Law?*).

Improving Your Financial Situation

"Money is better than poverty, if only for financial reasons."

—Woody Allen, film-maker

■ ■ ■

Financial barriers can appear insurmountable at the beginning of a transition. Consider the story of one practitioner, contract lawyer **Deborah G**:

> I come from a family of modest means. We lived in a kind of impoverished intelligentsia where it was almost a disgrace if you made too much money using your mind. I carried on that tradition into my 20's, and worked part-time as a secretary so I could be involved in politics, art and literature. But when I turned 30, I still wasn't making any money, I wasn't married, and I hadn't written a best-selling novel.
>
> I decided to go to law school. I was desperately poor the whole time I was there. By the time I graduated, I really wanted some creature comforts. I wanted all the stuff that hard work can get you, so I bought it all. I bet on my future high income. The trouble was I was already having fantasies about leaving the law in my second year of practice. I had a $20,000 fantasy, where I could pay off short-term debt and start fresh without having to go through bankruptcy. Then there was my $50,000 fantasy where I paid off my debts and lived for a year without working. And then there was my $100,000 fantasy, where I could pay off debts, and live for two years without working ... *and* remodel my kitchen.

> Money is always a problem in transition, but it seldom stops those who are committed to their change.

Ten years later I was still having those fantasies ... and still practicing.

I was also whining and moaning about how I didn't have time to be creative, and how the practice of law was so soul-deadening. One day, a friend of mine who was tired of hearing my complaints, said, 'Well, you ought to just sell your house and car and go be a starving artist.' That was my wake-up call. At that moment, I realized that money issues were a cop-out. They were just an excuse for all the unhappiness I felt practicing law.

Money is always a problem in transition. No matter how much you've saved or how much you owe, just the prospect of doing without income for a while, or facing a big pay cut, can be daunting. But if you're committed to your transition, money should not be a reason to stop you. Indeed, when Deborah G quit her job, her financial anxiety vanished. It didn't mean her money worries were all in her head ... just that they took a back seat to the larger issue: career satisfaction. Face it, though: Changing jobs or making a career-transition will cost you something ... in time, money or worry, or all three. But there are ways to minimize the negative impact of that investment. Consider these suggestions:

Look at the Details

In my individual consultations with lawyers, I always ask, *How little money can you get by on*? Most of them don't know; they've never thought about it. Then, my follow-up question — *how much are you spending now*? — usually gets the same response: they don't have a clue. To make sure that finances don't become your barrier to change, you must begin attending to these "details." Most lawyers don't want to go there. Doing so — and this is the real psychological barrier — might confirm that they (you) don't have the resources to make the change. Even more threatening is the prospect that you do have enough money, thus eliminating a convenient excuse for staying stuck.

Let's look at the "details":

▶ *Create a balance sheet* — List all of your assets (e.g., savings and checking account balances, stocks, bonds, other investments, retirement fund, pension and profit-sharing plans, expected inheritance, accounts receivable, real estate, personal property) and their estimated values. Then deduct all liabilities (e.g., mortgage, car loan, credit card debt, student and other personal loans). A loan application form from your local banker can help you organize this information. You can probably get one online. The process may be painful, but the balance sheet will tell you whether you have assets that could be available for spending or borrowing against while in transition. One lawyer decided she would tap her IRA account if necessary (it wasn't). Another lawyer's transition was so important to him that he reallocated the $25,000 he'd saved for a down-payment on a house. Your own analysis will help you clarify what liabilities to reduce before starting the change process.

▶ *Evaluate your spending patterns* — Review your checking account records for the last full year. Calculate expenditures for housing, utilities, insurance, food, clothing, transportation, entertainment, travel, un-reimbursed work expense, uninsured medical and dental expenses, and any other relevant categories. This is no time for guesstimates (most people substantially underestimate their outlay for entertainment and dining out.) If any of your expenses turn out higher than you think you're actually spending, or if you spend more than $100 per month in cash, keep track of every dollar you pay out for another month to confirm or adjust the figures. Save receipts for all cash purchases. If you're not offered a receipt, ask for one or make an immediate notation on a slip of paper. Then add those expenditures to the total.

▶ *Calculate your total expenditures* — Do this on an annual and monthly basis to determine the reserves or resources you'd need to maintain your current spending patterns. This analysis will help you pinpoint what may be self-defeating spending patterns. Deborah G spent a frustrating year trying to reduce her credit card debt before taking a closer look at her habits. "What I discovered was that clothing was my luxury item," she said. "I had to buy a lot of really nice clothes to keep from going crazy in my job. Once I decided I was going to leave, it was easy for me to say, 'Okay, no more new clothes.'"

▶ *Big-ticket items* — Postpone major expenditures. I've noticed that many lawyers who contemplate a career change burden themselves with a new financial commitment right about the same time — a new car, a home, a remodel, a vacation. The issue isn't the items themselves; it's the timing. If you're thinking about a career change, a big-ticket purchase could be interpreted as a substitute for the change you really want. So, it's wise to postpone major expenditures if you really want to leave your job ... or the law itself.

▶ *Advanced penny-pinching* — Cutting back on a muffin and morning latte will save you about $1,800 a year that would make more sense sitting in your 401(k). But while you're at it, there is another level of penny-pinching to consider. Have you calculated lately how much of your household budget goes to link up with the outside world? Some families are paying between $200 and $600 a month in subscription services for cable TV, local, long-distance, cell-phone, and wireless e-mail services, as well as for high-speed Internet connections. So, if you really want to squeeze out the fat, reevaluate your communications needs. While you're at it, take a second look at your utility bills and what you pay for auto and homeowners insurance. Insurance premiums were up 9 percent in 2003; maybe it's time you raised your deductible and took advantage of some savings.

▶ *Impulse buying* — Put away your credit cards and pay off any debt. Do you really need to dine out as often as you do?

▶ *Involve the family* — Create an agreement among your family members to discuss and agree on every purchase above a specified price before making it. Change your attitude toward the money you earn from one of expectation to one of gratitude and scarcity.

▶ *Retirement planning* — If you're considering going out on your own, consider setting up a Solo(k), a fantastic new retirement-savings vehicle created for the self-employed. You can bank up to $40,000 a year and, as with a traditional 401(k), even borrow money from your account. Plan fees vary widely, so shop around on sites like **www.401khelpcenter.com**.

Cutting back on your spending needn't be a form of punishment. Acknowledge your need for play and pampering while you accept the fact that the way you meet those needs might have to change. Even though Deborah G stopped being a fash-ionista , she decided it was important to keep the small treats in her life. "It's like a diet," she says. "If you try to cut out everything that's fun, you won't be able to stick to your plan." So, Deborah kept her "little luxury" of a daily cappuccino and brown-ie. Recognize your modest lifestyle for the tradeoff it is: Spending less money is an investment in your future well-being and success. "Simple living is not about being deprived," says Janet Luhrs, a former practicing lawyer who now publishes a national newsletter. "Simple living is about freedom. The freedom to choose the kind of life you want. Freedom to enjoy what is important to you." Luhr's newsletter is at **www.simpleliving.org**.

Budget for Transition

When you get close to making the move, calculate a projected budget for your job or career change. Identify expenses directly caused by your current employment (e.g., commuting, parking, clothing, dry-cleaning, lunches, client entertainment). You might find when you quit your current job, that some burdensome expenses will disappear — for example, you can do more of the household chores that you might otherwise hire out, or it might be more economical to do your work-out at home or in the neighborhood rather than to maintain a gym membership. Be sure to include your estimated costs of self-assessment and job hunting (e.g., career or psychological counseling, assessment-testing costs, workshops, résumé production, research materials, travel, networking meals). Don't be afraid to allocate liberal sums here. Your investments will be returned in the results they produce.

Once you've gathered all the necessary data, write a detailed description of your goal without concern for its economic viability. Define the specific work you are seeking (by now you should know), and how long it will take to find it. By an industry rule of thumb, a change in employ-ment takes from three to six months, or one month for every $10,000 in salary. If you plan a career change —

> Before you make a move, prepare a budget.

especially if you expect an elevated compensation — assume it will take one to two years! Be sure to include time for a sabbatical, travel, additional education, or child-rearing, if that is part of an ideal scenario for you. Remember, at this point you are not concerned about the feasibility of your plan. You are simply exploring a "worst case" scenario.

Then calculate the reserves you'll need to fund the change you contemplate. Multiply the number of months you believe your transition will take by the expenses you believe you will incur. If you are concerned that you're going to be laid off (see Chapter 5), or if you would like to quit your job while you're job hunting, this nest egg should provide adequate funds for your period of unemployment. Or, decide how much money you are willing to invest in your career reformation. The amount you need is your financial "nut".

Tackle Your Debt

Those of you who have accumulated more debt than you can carry must simply take steps to reduce your load. As I've said before, what are you willing to give up to get what you want? The most obvious approach is to stop incurring new charges and start making more than the minimum payments each month. That's a tall order if you're habituated to the credit card life. Here are some other suggestions for shrinking the size of your debt.

- ▶ Use cash (or a debit) card whenever possible.
- ▶ List your credit card accounts and minimum payments in descending order of current balance. Determine how much beyond the minimum payment you can afford to pay each month. You need to stretch here; this number assumes you're cutting back each expense as recommended earlier. Every month, make the minimum payment on all accounts and add the extra amount to the first card listed. When that card has been paid off, apply the extra payment to the next one down.
- ▶ If you're facing student loans, negotiate an extended payment schedule with each lender or try to consolidate all of the debt into a new loan with a longer term. That should reduce your monthly obligation. And with interest rates as low as they are, you might also want to pay off the debt by refinancing your home.

Build a War Chest

Your calculations will tell you what to do next. You may already have saved the money to take the steps you envision. At this point, you just need to decide that your future well-being is worth the investment. (One former practitioner renamed her security savings her *freedom fund* in order to reflect this decision.) You may also be able to tap some assets you hadn't previously considered.

- ▶ Borrow from a relative, or from your retirement plan or life insurance policy. Draw upon credit card or home equity lines of credit only as a last resort.
- ▶ Loot the kids' college accounts. If college is years away, you'll have plenty of time to repay what you withdrew. If college is right around the corner, the drop in your income and assets could help your child qualify for financial aid and government loans.

Sometimes just being willing to use the money is enough. Deborah G's decision to tap her IRA account if she needed it gave her the courage to quit her job. Almost immediately, she started to receive contract legal assignments. She never had to touch those funds. If you don't currently have the funds, work toward accumulating the money. Find creative ways to supplement your income. Here's what some lawyers do:

- ▶ Take a second job (some lawyers teach evening classes at community colleges, or serve as a live-in manager of an apartment building).
- ▶ Figure out what freelance legal services you can sell.
- ▶ Sell items you aren't using or that you are willing to trade for a more fulfilling work life. Don't sell your house if you can avoid it. Depending on the market, the cost of replacement housing could exceed what you're paying now. And you'll only aggravate the stress of a career transition by imposing another major change upon yourself.
- ▶ Use (or be certain to be compensated for) all of your accrued vacation and sick leave, and take advantage of a law firm sabbatical policy.

If the "nut" (the monthly amount you need) is too large, redefine your goals until you reach an amount you think you can manage. Then, save this amount of money as a cushion. Or, think about ways to maintain your cash flow while still having time to search for work. Inquire about opportunities for contract legal work, or suggest a part-time or freelance arrangement with your current employer or partners. Look for an interim, less pressured position that will bring in money while you're networking. You may even want to take a low-paying "McJob" just to keep the cash flowing ... though there can be unexpected downsides. For example, lawyer **Bob McSweeney** recalls making pizza deliveries before finding work as the director of a local nonprofit. Says Bob, "I'll never forget the day I drove up with a pizza order to the home of one of our county DA's. He knew who I was. As he was pulling out his wallet to pay for the pizzas, he looks at me and says, 'What the hell are you doing?' I told him pizza delivery was my 'bridge job', and I was having a wonderful time!"

Keep at It

Persist toward your financial goals. Evaluate your progress periodically and adjust your spending habits as you go. If after a few months you see little or no progress toward accumulating your "nut," reevaluate your goal, or ask friends to help you brainstorm new ways to generate money or reduce expenses. You might also consider postponing your career change, perhaps until you conclude a matter that could generate additional cash, or until your children are in school full time and your day-care expenses are lower. In the interim, lay the groundwork for your transition by getting active in appropriate industry or professional organizations, enrolling in educational programs, or polishing the skills you plan to use in your next venture. All the while, remain conscious of your spending and saving.

Finding Stepping-Stones

"The transitions of life's *afternoon* are more mysterious than those of its *morning*, and so we tend to pass them off as the effects of physical aging. But something deeper is going on. It involves letting go of a particular kind of self-image and a style of coping with the world."

—*William Bridges, Transitions*

• • •

If the time is right, but you still don't feel ready for transition, it may be necessary to work on the process in phases. This was true for Nancy Ashley, a partner in a commercial law firm who later moved into HR consulting. She shared with me this summary of the steps (and time) she took to finally accomplish her career transition:

▶ Understanding the difference between career dissatisfaction and fatigue (two years);

▶ Worked with my first career counselor (six months);

▶ Put off my career change to get married and buy a house (18 months);

▶ Attended career workshop for lawyers and continued with support meetings (six months);

▶ Began working with a new career counselor (nine months);

▶ Quit my job to conduct about 60 informational interviews, found contract lawyer work to keep me afloat financially, and volunteered in human services field (six months);

▶ Worked in two part-time human services planning jobs (three months);

▶ Received full-time job offers from both employers.

> Even if the time is right, you may need to break down the process into small steps.

Often, it's not possible to jump from where we are without serious consequences. The result? We experience inertia. The prospect of change is simply too great, so we fall back and do nothing and then blame ourselves. What exacerbates the situation is that our current job robs us of the time and energy we would otherwise spend on a transition. The solution is to divide the transition process into phases ... or, a series of stepping-stones. A few of them, listed in order of effectiveness, are:

▶ You make some internal changes where you're working now;
▶ You take some time off for reflection;
▶ You switch to an alternative work schedule arrangement;
▶ You work as a contract lawyer; or
▶ You take one or more steps in the wrong direction and accept that detours are just par for the course.

Changing Things Where You Are

According to San Francisco career consultant Lesah Beckhusen, if you feel you have no control over your current work environment, it helps to look at making changes where you are now. This alone may be sufficient. After all, minor adaptations to your work environment often result in major shifts in satisfaction. If your situation does not improve, at least you'll know you gave your current job (or the law itself) a fair chance, and be more willing to pursue other options. To start the change-where-you-are process, write down what you do each day in your job for a couple of months (review your past time slips.) Where appropriate, break down the experiences into their component skills, values and other preferences. For each task (or skill, value, preference) indicate your feeling for it — liked, disliked, neutral. Compare the results to your Ideal Job Grid.

▶ What tasks do you perform frequently that require the skills you listed in the "must avoid" column?
▶ How often and in what fashion do you work with other people, and how does this compare to what's in the "must have" side of your Grid?
▶ What if any gap exists between the values you want to express and those you are expressing in your work?

Once you've pinpointed the most troubling conflicts, consider what you have the power to change. Don't rely only on your appraisal. Get advice from others who also know the players involved. Of course, some changes are within your power to make — saying "no" to clients more often, firing your worst clients, hiring someone else to collect money or handle the type of work you dislike, changing your retainer policies, requesting better compensation or more feedback, and taking workshops to help you learn to deal with difficult people.

Now for the hard part:

If the change you seek is not under your control, ask for what you want from your employer. If an obnoxious partner is making your life miserable, ask to be relieved from working with him or her. If you think you'd be happier working on deals than going to court, request a change in departments, or accepting a reduction in pay or seniority if necessary. And discuss the possibility of reduced pay in return for a four-day week, two months off a year, or some other adjustment to your billable requirements.

Recently, I consulted with a lawyer — the parent of a young child — who was commuting about three hours a day and becoming increasing dissatisfied with her work environment. When she studied the situation, she realized that she enjoyed the work but hated the way it consumed her life, and she felt uncomfortable with the work style and personalities of some of her colleagues. She was expecting a $4,000 raise, but in lieu of that she proposed that her firm pay for a small office near her home. She would work there three days per week, and use the time she saved on commuting to develop business contacts and potential new clients in that city. Happily, the firm agreed to the proposal.

What conversations could you be having with your boss?

▶ If you want a review, request one.
▶ If the issue is purely financial, confront it head on.
▶ If you're not compensated fairly, figure out exactly how much you want and ask for it.
▶ If you think you should receive a bonus for the business you bring into the firm, ask for that kind of compensation arrangement.
▶ If you are interested in becoming a partner in the firm, start bringing up the subject.

Your employers are busy people who, unless you make yourself a priority, will always respond first to the demands of their cases and their families. If you want their attention, ask for it firmly but politely. But don't let the situation get to the point where your resentment might erode what would otherwise be a good working relationship. Now, if the change is under your control, you might want to model your efforts after those of other lawyers:

- ▶ Figure out what kinds of clients you like to work with and solicit only those clients. Turn down clients who you know will end up being a thorn in your side.
- ▶ Cut yourself loose from clients who drive you crazy. I know one small firm that celebrates with an "ex-client-of-the-month" party.
- ▶ Practice the kind of law that invigorates you, or about which you are passionate. If this is a new area for you, take on only one case at a time, perhaps working pro bono, to build your expertise.
- ▶ Turn down all clients who can't pay, no matter how sorry you feel for them, unless you make a deliberate decision to take the case pro bono. Demand substantial up-front retainers from all paying clients. If a client can't come up with the money, you won't spend the time on the case.
- ▶ Add to the variety of services you offer, mixing bread-and-butter work with more esoteric ventures. Work at a wider range of competency levels.
- ▶ Delegate those aspects of your practice that you feel responsible for but that others could do more efficiently and effectively. The cost should be recovered by your increased productivity in the areas you do enjoy.

Taking Some Time Off

Sometimes you just have to create an end to one commitment before you discover energy for something new. Philosopher Andre Gide put this so well when he said, *"You cannot discover new lands unless you leave shore for a very long time."*

Sabbaticals, vacations, and leaves of absence may provide just the break you need.

One new grad, **Bill**, started his career by working in a small corporate law firm, first on a contract basis and then as an associate. After nine months, though, Bill realized he was in the wrong environment. So, he quit to attend an international law conference in Australia. On his return a month later, he was sure he didn't want to go into corporate law again ... but he didn't know what else to do. Rather than accepting an offer for his old job, Bill devoted himself to self-assessment. A few months later, he had a much better sense of direction: he wanted to a job in international affairs or human rights, and he told everyone. Soon after, he got a job as the director for policy and legislative affairs for a nonprofit that sponsors conferences on economic and political issues. Bill's duties included gathering and disseminating information, writing letters and promotional materials, creating educational packages and helping to coordinate the international conferences sponsored by the foundation.

In another example, Denver lawyer **Connie Talmadge** walked away from a lucrative "big time" litigation practice to spend the next two years on hiatus. She was shocked to discover how much of her identity and self-esteem was tied to being a lawyer. As a result, it took a considerable amount of time and energy to sort through the "who-am-I?" question. In the end, she says, "I was able to empty my closet of all the clothes — the lawyer clothes — that belonged to the person who used to live in this house, and now I feel more at home than ever." Connie became director of the statewide ADR office for the Colorado Judicial Branch, a job that better suited her skills and values.

If you believe you can't afford to take time off, I recommend reading, *Six Months Off: The Sabbatical Book*, by James Scott and David Sharp. It suggests a variety of ways to make a sabbatical feasible.

On the other hand, sabbaticals are not for everyone

Jon, for example, is a top-rate litigation partner who handles the most complex and crucial of his firm's court cases. While the glamour and challenge of being in the courtroom excite him, trial work these days mostly occurs in his or some other lawyer's office. While still an associate at the firm, Jon took a three-month unpaid sabbatical. Later, when he qualified for a paid sabbatical, he again left the country. Would he do it again? I'll let him tell you:

Jon's Story

BA, Williams College
JD, Columbia Law School
Assistant U.S. attorney
Became a litigation partner, corporate law firm

Jon's Statement: "Both of my sabbaticals lasted three months. On the first, I traveled through Asia, and it really gave me a different perspective on life. When you go somewhere like Bombay and see people in loincloths sleeping in the streets, or living in little cardboard shacks, you come back thinking your problems aren't quite so big. On my next sabbatical, I traveled through the South Pacific

"Both times, I took my watch off the day that I left, and didn't put it on again until the day I came back. There was no worrying about billable hours, or accounts receivable, or getting clients. The big issues in life became 'What am I going to eat today' and 'What am I going to do?' I ate when I was hungry; slept when I was tired. For me, high stress was missing a flight I planned to take on my open-ended ticket.

"On a sabbatical, you aren't judged. No one figures out who you are by what you do. You're just another traveler. You don't have 25 phone messages to return that day. You don't have all these hassles of deadlines and clients and judges and other lawyers on your ass. You're not constantly competing. You're not always trying to achieve something; to maintain some prescribed level of success.

"In my experience, though, the effects of each sabbatical lasted little more than two months. After a short while-this happened to me each time-I'd be back on a fast track for trial, getting tense and biting my fingernails; in the middle of the same old scene. Last year, after the second sabbatical, I had four trials from April to December and ended up working our law firm billable hour average, even though I was only there about eight months of the year. I was the first person in the firm to get a bonus in the year of my sabbatical because I put in so many hours.

> ... time to think about what I really want to do; whether I should be practicing law at all ...

"In the long run, I'm not sure sabbaticals do anything for you, other than create great anticipation for the next one. Three months off might seem like a lot of time to some people. But let me tell you. It's not long enough to make you seriously think about getting out. Halfway through both sabbaticals, I remember thinking, 'Gee, it's half gone and pretty soon I have to go back.' Then, before I knew it, the end was only two or three weeks away and I was disappointed and sad that it was all coming to a close. In terms of long-range career implications, I don't think my sabbaticals were of any benefit to me.

"Taking a longer sabbatical might be more helpful, or even spending three months by myself in a cabin in the woods. It might give me more time to think about what I really want to do; whether I should be practicing law at all, or practicing a different kind of law, or in a different environment.

"We used to have a deal where you could skip sabbaticals and double up.

Instead of taking one every three years, you could take six months every six years. About two years ago, for economic reasons alone, the partners not only barred doubling up, but extended the time between sabbaticals from three years to four. I won't qualify again until 1992 and that's a long way off. Even though I'm skeptical about the lasting benefits of sabbaticals, I still would rather make a lot less money and have a lot more time off."

Switching to an Alternative Work-Schedule Arrangement

A less drastic way to create more time for career transition is to negotiate with your boss or partners a part-time or other alternative work schedule arrangement. One lawyer worked part-time in her law firm for two years so she had time to volunteer for a nonprofit organization. The group eventually created a position for her as its first public policy advocate.

Solo practitioners can also create part-time practices.

The first step is to lower your overhead, to move your office into your home, pay for a good answering service, and meet clients in a conference room rented by the hour from another law firm. But the real secret is to pick a narrow practice area that involves almost no unexpected court appearances, such as estate planning, tax, adoption, bankruptcy and guardianship. More problematic would be contested divorces and custody battles, personal injury and criminal work.

Telecommuting is another stepping-stone to change.

Some lawyers telecommute daily; others spend two or three days each week at home; still others leave town for months at a time while taking their office with them. By working from home, the time and cost of commuting and dressing for success drop sharply. And the luxury of e-mail and the growing popularity in wireless computing, now allow you to work from anywhere, and maintain a relationship with the firm or your clients as if they were just down the hall.

There's one more way to buy more time away from the office. Negotiate with your boss (even if that boss is you) for two more weeks of vacation or a couple three-day weekends each month, rather than an annual raise. Or for every week, work at least one full day out of your home. Discover how much more efficient you can be in a day's time when you don't have the constant interruptions that occur in an office environment. During the natural breaks you take during a day, you can head to the library to research careers that interest you, take contacts to lunch, enroll in educational programs that will enhance your credibility or volunteer for the right organizations.

For additional online resources, turn to Appendices 2 and 3.

How to Negotiate a Part-Time Schedule with Your Current Employer

According to New York's Families and Work Institute, more than half the work force wants some kind of change in their hours on the job. But unless your employer is among a minority that has adopted and truly embraces clear, fair, alternative-work policies, surmounting obstacles to changing your work setup can be daunting. In the first place, you'll need plenty of goodwill with your bosses — earned through hard work — and a good track record on the job to lend your proposal credibility. You'll also need a fundamental understanding of the objectives of your business, to show how your proposed new setup will serve its needs.

Take a look at yourself — Are your skills and experiences in demand? You're in a better position to proceed if you know what you have to offer.

Take a look at the employer you want to approach — Is the organization considered innovative or conservative? Some employers discourage the practice, and others encourage it only for certain groups like new parents, pre-retirees and students.

Take a look at the job itself — Does it have some of these special characteristics that might make it easier to do on a part-time basis:

▶ Self-contained (in terms of time);

▶ Independent projects or cases;

▶ Peak workloads;

▶ Potential for overlapping coverage;

▶ Multiple skills needed; and

▶ High stress.

Put yourself in your employer's shoes — What arguments would you need to hear to be convinced that a part-time arrangement could be as beneficial to the organization as to you? Prepare yourself to be an advocate of part-time employment.

Draft a proposal — Include the tasks and responsibilities you would handle working part-time, a suggested schedule, techniques for communication, your ideas on fair handling of salary and benefits, the advantages to the employer and answers to other anticipated employer concerns.

Be positive — Don't apologize for wanting to work less than full-time. Many lawyers work part-time and are high-quality, committed professionals.

And don't forget the Internet to provide you with some of the best strategies that have come out of more than a decade of job flexibility research and practice. Online you can find templates for a detailed written proposal, background on the business reasons for offering flex-jobs, expert Q&A's, and even an online assessment to help you figure out whether you're suited to work independently. Here are some helpful Web sites:

▶ **www.workoptions.com** — Offers checklists of things to do before approaching your boss.

▶ **www.gilgordon.com** — Flex-job consultant offers expert Q&A's about telecommuting issues.

▶ **www.joannepratt.com** — Click on "wannabes" for a self-quiz to see if you're temperamentally suited to working at home.

▶ **www.att.com** — Click on "Telework Guide" in the A-to-Z Index, then click again on Getting Started.

Work as a Contract Lawyer

As many as 33 million American workers — up 25 per cent from 1998 — are estimated to be free agents untethered to a large organization. Among lawyers, the most common free agent arrangement is known as "contract lawyering".

Contract lawyers, many of them former partners or associates of the law firm, offer their services on a freelance or hourly basis. They are often paid for every hour billed to a client. Most lawyers negotiate directly with one or more law firms to work a fixed number of hours per week, or on an irregular, project-by-project basis. Others receive assignments through temporary agencies. For a complete discussion of the pros and cons of contract work, see *Should You Become a Freelance Lawyer?*, 3rd edition (DecisionBooks, 2004). Most large legal communities nationwide now support several agencies that place lawyers with the appropriate skills in law firms that need short-term, specialized assistance. Some concentrate on corporate placements; others place lawyers in a wide geographic area, even internationally. Placement agencies usually tack a surcharge onto the hourly fee you are paid and are responsible for collecting from the law firm. At times, the lawyer is brought in to complete one project, e.g., researching and writing an appellate brief or attending a deposition; other assignments are longer term and cover a number of different projects.

Contract employment provides benefits to both law firm and lawyer. Law firms gain the tangible benefits of handling fluctuations in workload cost-effectively and passing on the contract employee's fee, usually with a surcharge, to the client. They also confirm the value and compatibility of a potential permanent employee before making a long-term commitment. The advantages include:

► Higher compensation for every hour worked than would be received on a part-time employee basis;

► More control over scheduling and the ability to take off time for research and networking;

► The ability to maintain cash flow while searching for work or changing careers, without making a long-term commitment.

The flexible work schedule of contract legal work may give you time to study, write, network or start a small business. New York City lawyer **Peter Zerilli** uses contract work to pay the bills while he tries to establish himself as a writer. "It's not a permanent job, which is a very important psychological factor for me," he says. "I can still feel I'm doing something leading toward the goal of supporting myself by writing full time."

Sometimes contract work is a way to test one's misgivings about the law. Lawyers Michael Goldenkranz and Robert Hoon both had families to support when they decided to try it. Ironically, their freelance relationships were such unpleasant reminders of why they wanted to leave the law in the first place, that they both became even more motivated. Both worked about six months as contract lawyers before securing new permanent positions outside the profession.

Taking One or More Steps in the Wrong Direction

Sometimes it doesn't even matter what you choose to do; taking any step at all redirects your career.

One day, **Nancy Walseth** quit her job as an associate in a medical malpractice firm. After two months of readjustment, she enrolled in a college certification program to become a grade-school teacher. Her first course was called Art for Elementary Teachers.

"As part of that course," she says, "we were required to have colored pens and to doodle if we had time. I finished early one day and drew a cartoon that was a parody of myself. I threw it in my portfolio and forgot about it." Sometime later, Nancy dropped out of the program. But her art teacher tracked her down and said she had a gift for cartooning. Soon after, Nancy was penning Doonesbury-like cartoons featuring a sardonic woman lawyer as the central character. Those cartoons were later published in a book. But Nancy didn't stop there.

About three months after she quit her full-time job, she started to get telephone calls from lawyers asking if she could help with their legal work. For three years, she had enough contract assignments to earn as much working five hours a day, five days a week as she had made as a full-time lawyer! At that point, she met someone who owned a sailboat brokerage. The company was in a growth phase and needed help with computerization. "I ended up working half-time downtown as a lawyer and half-time out at the boat place helping set up systems," she recalls. A year after that, she finally dropped her malpractice insurance coverage and stopped practicing law altogether. She now co-manages the business.

"The uniform of the day is jeans, tennis shoes, sweatshirts," she says. "I sweep the place and kill the spiders. It's like what I wanted to do when I was five years old and used to fantasize about being a grocery store owner, except we're selling boats instead of candy bars."

As you see from Nancy's story, when you're in transition your compass needle may point in many unexpected directions, and yet still lead you to a place you want to be. Although making the first move may feel like jumping off a cliff, take heart. You're actually just stepping off a curb ... and onto a path that leads to change.

Filling the Gaps

"In a dark time, the eye begins to see."

— Theodore Roethke, poet

■ ■ ■

If the work you seek differs from what you do now, you need to add to your résumé the kind of credentials that will get you where you're going.

As an educated person, you're conditioned to look at formal education as the best way to expand your knowledge base, and to establish your qualification for the next field. The problem is that education will only provide a knowledge base; even after you've earned the degree, you still have to get experience. Getting more education isn't automatically a bad idea. But it is expensive and time-consuming, and may not advance your career any faster than the other techniques outlined in this section.

I've seen many lawyers head back to school, but only two kinds of lawyers actually required their new degrees to do what they wanted to do: those who wanted to teach in public school, and those who wanted to be licensed therapists. In most other situations, advanced degrees were superfluous and a waste of money. In my experience, LLMs, except perhaps in tax, are rarely useful.

> A law degree provides enough education to qualify you for employment in almost any field.

The good news is that a law degree provides enough education to qualify you for employment in almost any field, even teaching and counseling. It's true that the conventional jobs in those fields — teachers and clinical psychologists — have rigid educational licensing requirements of their own. But you can teach or counsel with no more background than your law degree, your legal experience and your other "life credits."

For example, the Oregon State Bar's Attorney Assistance Program is staffed solely by former practicing lawyers, not licensed therapists, and they manage and facilitate its peer counseling programs. In the teaching field, lawyers work as paralegal, CLE and law firm training instructors, and teach law-related courses such as political science, criminal justice, sports management, and business law in colleges across the country. In fact, over 1,000 such teachers have formed the Academy of Legal Studies in Business (**www.alsb.org**).

So before you enroll in the local university, consider whether one of the following outlets will be equally effective in making you an attractive candidate for your chosen field:

- ▶ Volunteer work;
- ▶ Internships;
- ▶ Freelancing;
- ▶ Consulting;
- ▶ Experience-building interim jobs;
- ▶ Building a business; or
- ▶ Non-degree course work.

Volunteering

Many of you already volunteer for nonprofit organizations. You might be sitting on the board of directors; chairing a committee, a fund-raising drive or program; or leading lobbying efforts. In the course of your involvement, you're developing friendly relationships based on mutual respect. Those relationships can lead to wonderful work opportunities.

Mary was employed as a public defender for several years and grew tired of the one-on-one helper role. After engaging in self-assessment and some research, she targeted waste management as an area with great social utility and less of the futility she felt as a public defender. She volunteered for a citizen recycling group for another year while continuing to practice criminal defense. That experience gave her the background she needed to land a one-year contract as a recycling coordinator in another state. In her position, she managed about 10 different waste reduction and recycling projects back in her hometown.

Working in professional associations is an especially effective way of escaping your current legal specialty. If, for example, you're a civil litigator who would like to move into transactional work or environmental litigation, join the appropriate interest section of the ABA, or your state or local bar association. You'll receive publications that will identify the heavy hitters in that field. You'll educate yourself about emerging issues in that area of law. And if you also attend general membership meetings, special events and educational seminars, you'll meet people who may be able to assist you in your transition.

Freelancing

In certain fields, getting practical experience on your own is essential. As executive editor of the New Jersey Law Journal, Pamela Brownstein was in a position to see a number of résumés from lawyers seeking editing and reporting jobs. "The most impressive résumés were accompanied by a [non-brief] writing sample because I got the feel for the candidate's skill, potential and initiative." If you are interested in making the transition into journalism, you need published clips. One way to get them is to send one-page "query letters" to local, regional or national publications about a topic of interest, and also let them know you are available for assignments. "There's a truism," says lawyer/journalist Monica Bay. "It's that writers ... write. So, start writing, even if it's just letters to the editor. Most papers welcome commentaries and opinions, and if you become a regular contributor you will get to know the staff." Note: Offering Bar association magazines and regional business journals a 500-750-word essay or column about a current issue is a proven way to get your foot in the door.

Consulting

Bob McSweeney served as counsel for several nonprofit organizations, and he noticed how the people at the top, like so many small business owners, didn't know much about running their organization. So, after taking some classes on nonprofit management, Bob started a consulting practice and in two years had helped 12 groups improve their management practices. Said Bob, "But I was so busy doing this for other people, it was like passing out the dinners but not getting to eat yourself." He finally got to the table when one of his clients hired him as its new executive director. It can be difficult to convert volunteer work into paid consulting, but this is one of the most common ways to build a new career. Jane Lynch decided that nonprofit work was more appealing than family law practice. Her first step was to get involved with half a dozen organizations in her community, all of them concerned with family violence education. One group needed an executive director. She negotiated a stipend to handle the work until a search could be completed. That experience opened her eyes to the opportunity for project work with others. Jane developed a consulting business that she hoped would eventually replace her law practice income.

Bridge Jobs

It's often difficult to tell when a replacement, or "bridge", job is a path to more satisfying employment or an end in itself.

For example, one woman wanted to move away from practicing law and into nonprofit management. In order to get some experience, she accepted what she thought would be a short-term position as head of a bar association pro bono program. Eight years later, she was still happily running the program — and still practicing law, but only in a supervisory capacity. In another example, Gail Hunter realized that civil litigation was not for her. She enrolled in a self-assessment program and discovered that her interests, skills, values and workplace preferences translated into a job in sports management. Gail was a good athlete and had worked with amateur sports organizations as both player and manager. Even so, it took a year of research and national networking to land a relatively low-level management position 2,000 miles from her home supervising the awards program for the NCAA Championships Department. That job, however, led to a more challenging position with Major League Baseball Properties in New York City.

Building a Business

Earl and Kate, partners in marriage and law, spent more than a year developing a home-based business in ceramic holiday ornaments. First, they researched the market, and then they experimented with manufacturing different products to see what retailers preferred. Earl and Kate did all this while maintaining a full-time bankruptcy practice. "I was only able to do both because we found ways to cut out every ounce of dead weight out of our practice," says Earl. "Every minute at the office was productive so I could have lots of time to devote to the ornaments. It got to the point where I was working at the law office only as long as the parking meter would last — 120 minutes at a time. I'd go in and move through my work as fast I could." As soon as it appeared Earl and Kate could make enough money selling holiday ornaments, they closed their office.

Non-Degree Course Work

If there's anything you really do need to learn, don't hesitate to enroll in a university extension or other continuing education course. Through a self-assessment workshop, Eduardo Munoz discovered he loved technical analysis and working with computers in a team environment. When he researched his options, he realized that he needed more technical knowledge before he would be employable as a software designer or engineer. He enrolled in a nine-month university certification program in software engineering; soon after completing it, he joined a small design team for a fast-growing computer company.

At this point, let's return to the question of additional formal educational credentials. Sometimes, another degree is essential to your career plan. But before you enroll, make sure you are not falling into the trap of postponing your career decision, rather than pursuing it. First, you need to know what field you want to enter, not what degree will make it easier for you to get work. You probably earned your law degree to make yourself more marketable and look where that got you! "The legal job market," says District of Columbia career counselor Linda Sutherland, "is littered with disappointed attorneys who paid tens of thousands of dollars for advanced degrees without first performing a 'due diligence' about whether the effort would pay off in enhanced career opportunities."

So, the next issue to explore is what practical advantages you think your educational investment will yield. To find out, answer these questions:

- ► How much will it cost?
- ► How long will it take?
- ► How much more money or opportunity will it yield?
- ► What positions could you obtain *without* earning another degree or certificate?
- ► How long will it take you to go from an entry-level position in the new area to the type of position you hope the extra credential will qualify you for?
- ► Where have recent law graduates landed, and can you contact them?

I suggest you put these questions to your law school career services representatives, as well as to prospective employers and related professional or trade associations. Ask the schools about the track record of their graduates. Whatever you learn about the marketability of this or that degree, you may still want to return to school even if a cost-benefit analysis doesn't warrant the financial investment. It may be that conventional employment suits you better. Or your motivation — perhaps a love of learning or a well-earned break from salaried employment — outweigh any financial considerations. It's also possible that the education you receive will make you appreciate your legal work all the more. One personal injury lawyer wanted to help others more than she could as a lawyer. She earned a Masters Degree in psychology with the intent of becoming a therapist. Rather than leave the profession, however, she changed her practice focus. She now specializes in lawsuits brought by abused women against their abusers, and uses her new education to help clients cope with both their original trauma and the stress of the lawsuit itself.

Making Part-Time Practice Work

Robin entered the legal profession determined to succeed on her own terms. After a few years with a small law firm, she hung out her own shingle to practice with a style and focus that was totally her own. After the birth of her first child, she reduced her practice by half. Now, divorced and sharing custody of her two children, Robin has learned what works, and what doesn't, in running a part-time practice.

Robin's Statement: With many years of experience practicing law part time, I know exactly what's necessary to do it.

▶ "First, you have to cut your overhead.
▶ "Second, you have to narrow your scope.
▶ "Third, you have to swallow your pride.

"I was prepared for my income to drop 30 percent when I switched to half time, but actually I make as much money now as I did when I was working full time. The key is keeping my overhead down. I work primarily out of my house. In order to sit down with clients occasionally, I rent a tiny office from a law firm with leftover space. For typing, I use a local entrepreneur who does freelance word processing at a very reasonable price. I keep my eye on the cost of supplies, malpractice insurance and accounting fees.

"The next requirement is to narrow your scope. I accomplished that goal at the outset by firing the clients who either didn't pay me, or who forced me to beg for a percentage on the dollar. By the time I moved my business home, I could tell on the telephone which clients were not likely to pay. They usually tipped their hand by making the same sort of remarks as the last ten people who wound up not paying. I got rid of all those cases, and now I regularly turn away new business that looks like trouble. I only take cases that are interesting, with people I like and who are likely to pay me. I've lowered my stress and increased my income. The time I work is time well spent.

"I have a lot more control over my income by running a much tighter ship. When I worked full time, I'd have 60, 70, even 80 cases going at a time. I was occasionally out of control and always working too hard. Now I'm down to 20 to 25 cases of different sizes, but mostly fairly small. The smaller my operation gets, the more control I have. I'm not under stress, because I weed out most of the bad cases and I know what I'm doing.

"Which leads to another element of narrowing your scope: carving out a specialty. When I started my practice, I would take the case of anyone who walked in my door. No

more. General practice is too hard now, period. And if you are going to work part-time, it's ridiculous. Now my practice is limited to guardianship and probate, a specialty that's affected by only one section of the legislative code. I don't have to worry as much about keeping up with changes in the law.

"It's important to pick a specialty that avoids complex matters and high-stress litigation. The only exception I would make is a wrongful death case with no liability issues, like a father of three getting run over in a crosswalk by a well-insured driver. But how many cases like that are you likely to get? In 20 years of practice, I haven't gotten one. If you don't have the support you need, you cannot handle a complicated lawsuit against a big corporation. You have to leave that for the full-time lawyers. The case may look attractive, but if it's stressful and will require costs to be advanced, you're getting yourself right back into what you just finished leaving.

"Swallowing your pride — the last requirement — means using voice mail instead of employing a full-time receptionist or paying for an answering service. It means doing without the fancy office and the personal secretary. It means that when someone asks if they can schedule a motion on Thursday afternoon, you have to admit that your preschooler's play takes priority. Fortunately, I find other lawyers to be much more responsive to that kind of scheduling problem than they would be if my conflict involved a very important deposition in 'my Union Oil case.'

"I found full-time law practice relentless. There was never any time to breathe. Even if I was vacationing, I was always worrying about my cases. On a part-time basis, things are not as relentless. I work about 25 hours per week. My kids are finally in school, and I have some free time. There's only one problem with this whole arrangement. If you develop a good part-time schedule, it's difficult to imagine going back to work full time."

Should I Leave the Law?

"It was tough going in every morning to practice law. I used to wake up and think, 'Maybe they'll declare World War III, and I won't have to go into the office.'"

—*Stephen, a lawyer-turned-psychologist*

■ ■ ■

"I wore a tie for eight years, every week day and sometimes seven days a week while I was practicing law. One of the adjustments I had to make — a friend dubbed it "tie therapy" — was to learn that I didn't have to have a tie on to have my brain work. It may sound funny now, but it was a major adjustment. I truly thought you had to choke the blood supply off to get your brain working. It took me about six months to get to the point where I could go to work and feel good about myself without the tie. It sounds silly now, but those are the type of hurdles that I think you have to overcome when you leave the law."

> No question about it. Leaving the law is a difficult choice.

In moments of reflection, many practitioners will admit that one of their main reasons for attending law school was for the external rewards — money, prestige, respect, security. Later, if they decide to leave the profession, they talk about the difficulty of giving up their lawyer identity. For some, this change is especially disorienting. And what can make it especially difficult are the reactions of others.

"There's a stigma to changing careers after practicing law," says ex-lawyer Wendy Leibowitz, now of American Lawyer Media. "Believe it or not, it is more acceptable to change firms many times, or to hang out your own shingle, than to leave the practice of law."

Says another former practicing lawyer, "When I practiced, one of the most self-defeating things I did was in believing something wrong with me for not liking my work. I had this perception that everybody else in my firm was doing quite well, and that they all loved their work. I'd look at them and wonder, 'How is it that you like it?', and try to figure out what was wrong with me. I thought that if I just fixed me, I could be like them and enjoy the law."

Maybe you're worried that if you admit to being tempted to leave the law that you'll invite an onslaught of negative comments ... or that your family and colleagues will see you as a failure. According to a survey of Minnesota law school graduates working in nontraditional environments, the most common personal obstacle in the transition process was opposition from friends, family and colleagues. This barrier was bigger than the grads' own anxiety, the loss of prestige, the feelings of shame or failure, and even their worries about financial sacrifice.

Michael Whithers tells the story of leaving the law to become executive director of one of the largest nonprofit organizations in Portland, Oregon. Walking downtown one day, Michael bumped into some of his old law buddies. "Before I could even say what I was doing," says Michael, "my friends all lowered their eyes out of embarrassment for me. After all, I used to be a partner in an A-rated law firm. What happened to me?"

Doug Stam, who also left the law — to manage sports marketing at Nike — also remembers the confusion his decision created among some of his colleagues:

"The first month after I announced I was leaving, other lawyers would meet me on the street and say, 'You can't leave.' I'd say, 'Why can't I?' And they'd say, 'Well, you've got a great practice.' And my response was always, 'Yeah, but I don't like it.' So, they would look down at their shoes and just walk away. But after I started working at Nike, I began getting calls from these same guys. They'd say things like, 'I'm really kind of dissatisfied with private practice, but I can't seem to pull the plug. Could I come out and talk to you?'"

No matter what your professional status, your choice to trade your lawyer identity for a different one will trigger a period of emotional ups and downs. Consider this lawyer's experience:

> I practiced general civil law for nearly 15 years, the last ten of which I operated as a solo practitioner. I maintained a diverse clientele and rendered services in nearly every discipline of law. Despite the variety of my career experiences, I had no passion for my work. About a year ago, I simply burned out and quit my practice without any career plans. My business telephone line and stationery are my only remaining ties to the legal profession.

145

The past year has been filled with near-equal doses of doubt, anxiety, frustration and self-discovery. Reading about others who have dropped out of law has been a newfound source of reassurance and inspiration and, in that regard, has provided much needed relief to my understanding wife. Only recently have I begun my search in earnest for a new career.

Breaking ties to the profession leaves you without a sense of belonging. And that's one very uncomfortable state of being. The good news is that once you start the process of moving closer to finding satisfaction, you will eventually feel better. On the other hand, if your fear of the future keeps you stuck, you'll be doomed to be in the doldrums for a lot longer. "Before you make a break," says one former practicing lawyer, "you have to overcome your own ego. My ego was right there in front of me all the time. It said, 'I'm a lawyer', and I kept running into it."

How can you break through this daunting barrier?

The most important ingredient is support; reaching out to others who have already made the change or who themselves are struggling through the same process.

I'll illustrate with my own experience:

Most of my self-esteem was tied up with my success in law — as a student, in practice and as a bar association leader. And when I realized that my one-year sabbatical was really my first step out of the profession, my confidence sank. I felt insecure and afraid. I didn't even want to set foot in any law offices because I felt like such a failure. A year later, I knew I would never return to the practice of law. But other than a vague notion of being a writer, I still hadn't pursued any concrete options. I gradually fell into a low-grade but persistent depression and avoided locations and social events that might attract other lawyers.

Strangely, my unhappiness didn't lift until I started to research my first book, *Running from the Law: Why Good Lawyers Are Getting Out of the Legal Profession*. By reaching out to lawyers who had experienced the same hell, I didn't feel so alone. Moreover, I could look at them, see what remarkable people they were and how much they enjoyed their lives. It began to dawn on me that I had the same potential for change. The more involved I became with the issue of career change for lawyers, the better I felt about my decision, although I wasn't free of insecurity. Because as much fun as I was having, it was hard to admit that my early income as the founder of a support group for transitioning lawyers was so much less than what I earned before.

Eventually, I replaced my lawyer persona with others: human being, author and public speaker, wife, friend and former practicing lawyer. Now, nearly 15 years from the day I closed my office doors, I'm proud of my flexible and creative lifestyle and can say, quite honestly, that I have absolutely no regrets about my choice to leave the practice of law. But I would never have completed my transition if I hadn't reached out to others.

Should I Stay? A Case for Renaissance Lawyering

By J. Kim Wright, JD & Kevin Ginsberg, JD

Do you like to solve problems?
Do you like to use your creativity to help people?

You probably answered "yes" to both questions because lawyers are basically creative problem-solvers who like to help people. Here are some other generalizations that come to mind about practicing or aspiring lawyers:

▶ You went to law school with a deep desire to help people and make the world a better place.
▶ You find it difficult to have your law practice match your highest ideals because of the stress in your work.
▶ You'll leave the law one day, or end up practicing as a way to make a living rather than as a vocation.

Should you stay in the law?

If you do, there is a better way.

In the last few years, a movement among thousands of lawyers has gained attention and momentum. You may have read about it in your state or local bar journal, or even the Wall Street Journal. This movement is known by many names: visionary law, transformational law, comprehensive law. Others, including myself, call it renaissance law. And while we hear about all the lawyers who leave the law because of stress and other factors, I believe the "renaissance" models offer some exciting new approaches to our work.

There is an increasingly popular process called *collaborative law* that is less emotionally taxing on everyone involved. Collaborative law is part of a continuing effort to accomplish the impossible — smooth, pain-free divorces. The main distinction is that the couple and their lawyers try to resolve all issues themselves, then present their agreement to a judge for approval. It makes for a relatively brief process (about three months compared with an average of 20 months for a courtroom divorce).

Of course, as with anything new, collaborative law is scorned by some lawyers for its New Age approach. One New England lawyer with a general practice says his "holistic" approach has taken some heat for being "wimpy law." But what's wimpy about a model that's been adopted some 3,000 practitioners in more than two dozen states? The numbers alone suggest that collaborative (renaissance) law is going mainstream. It's become especially popular in San Francisco, Atlanta, Dallas, Boston, and Miami. The San Francisco-based International Academy of Collaborative Professionals (**www.collabgroup.com**) says nearly 100 firms are in its directory, up from 16 in 1999. And in Cincinnati, more than two-thirds of the city's 110 divorce lawyers practice the collaborative model first developed by Minnesota family lawyer Stu Webb (**www.collaborativelaw.org**).

What collaborative, or renaissance, lawyers are doing is nothing less than reclaiming their practice; finding creative ways to resolve conflicts and to utilize the legal system in a way that has clients, lawyers, judges and society all winning. There's nothing "wimpy" about a lawyer whose vision of the legal system takes in the human element. At the end of the day, when we make choices that are out of integrity for us, our lives lose balance and are unfulfilled. When we make choices that are in integrity, we improve the quality of our lives and the satisfaction with our jobs. So, stay in the law and build your own renaissance practice.

What follows are a few online resources, and you'll find additional resources in Appendix 5.

Collaborative Law — A family law model in which the parties and their attorneys contractually agree at the outset that they will not litigate. For more information, visit the International Academy of Collaborative Professionals Web site (**www.collabgroup.com**).

Community Lawyering, or *Community-Oriented Lawyering* — A movement where the lawyers, especially those in government, public interest, etc., work together to address the underlying problems that result in clients being in court, as well as to promote the welfare of the community and their clients in relationship to one another. For examples, see attorney Roger Conner's Web site at **www.community lawyering.org**. Conner describes community lawyering as a way for attorneys to take a direct working interest in the peace and safety of particular places, and to work to not only win cases but generate outcomes that the community values.

Holistic Justice, or *Holistic Law* — An approach to law that attempts to see the whole picture—the lawyer's role, the client's responsibility, the impact on the community—seeking answers that benefit the greatest good while promoting healing and completion. Visit the International Alliance of Holistic Lawyers online at **www.iahl.org**. The organization hosts annual conferences.

Preventive Law — Based on the premise that "the legal profession can better serve clients by investing resources in consultation and planning rather than relying on litigation as the primary means of addressing legal problems." For more information, read The Preventive Law Reporter at **www.preventive-law.org**.

Restorative Justice — In a typical RJ conference, victim, offender, community members, and members of the court system all sit down in a facilitated conference, discussing the impact of the event and creating a resolution that works for everyone. For more information, visit the International Centre for Justice and Reconciliation at **www.restorativejustice.org**.

The Project on Integrating Law, Politics and Spirituality — A group of lawyers and legal educators committed to the integration of spirituality and politics, and the incorporation of a spiritual-political understanding into American legal culture. The Project was founded at New College of California, where its leader, Peter Gabel, teaches in its public interest law school. Gabel is a founder of the Critical Legal Studies movement. For more information, call Coordinator Wendy Ervin at 415-437-3496 or email wervin@newcollege.edu. If you want to transform your law practice, there are dozens of visionary models, trends and approaches to choose from. If you'd like additional references, see Appendix 5 .

J. Kim Wright, Esq. & Kevin Ginsberg, Esq. — Both Wright and Ginsberg are principals at Renaissance Lawyer Society, a non-profit organization that serves as a clearinghouse and resource center for innovative approaches to law practice that are based on connecting people, solving problems and resolving conflict. Contact — www.RenaissanceLawyer.com.

Is There a Layoff in Your Future?

By Janina Latack, Ph.D.

"Loyalty is something to be considered carefully. While an extended period of employment can look good on a résumé, the goal is to balance loyalty with prudent self-interest in case the picture changes quickly."

—*Kris Maher, Wall Street Journal*

■ ■ ■

Do any of these scenarios sound familiar?

- ▶ You're hearing rumors that your firm is having financial difficulties, or ...
- ▶ Your firm's revenues are down, and you're seeing more memos to cut expenses, or ...
- ▶ Your firm's partners are meeting behind closed doors more often, and your questions are being met with unusual evasiveness, or ...
- ▶ Your co-workers aren't being replaced, and you suspect there's more to it than "natural attrition".

These days, the possibility of forced job change is an unpleasant new reality in the law, and — as never before — associates and partners must take steps to deal with the likelihood of getting pink-slipped. So, how vulnerable are you?

> Polish your résumé, talk to some recruiters. No one is immune to layoff.

7 Categories of Vulnerability

After many years, Jeanne Svikhart, a Washington, D.C. law firm consultant, says there are at least seven leading indicators suggesting you're at greater risk of getting laid off. In fact, she says, if you fall into one of these categories, it would be prudent to polish your résumé and have some friendly recruiters in your back pocket.

The 7 categories are:

▶ You're a service partner who doesn't control significant client portfolios.
▶ You're partner who practices in an area hit hard by the recession.
▶ You're a senior associate or partner whose work was tied to a rainmaker who has since left the firm.
▶ You're a laterally transferred senior associate (or of counsel, or contract partner) who hasn't delivered on new business you promised.
▶ You're a newly merged partner who doesn't control firm business.
▶ You're a senior lateral hire who isn't performing as expected.
▶ You're an associate who was hired through a merger but who doesn't mesh with the culture.
▶ You're a partner with substantial management responsibilities, but whose non-billable work is no longer valued.

Svikhart's list is pretty definitive, and easily sorted out — you either fit one of her categories or not. If not, don't break out the champagne yet; the axe could still fall. Because there are other, more complex clues that point to your vulnerability. For example, have any of these situations happened to you?

▶ You've expressed a clear interest, and requested work from associates you admire, but it's not happening You aren't getting case assignments that might have developed your career potential.
▶ You're put off, or get a waffling response, when you ask for performance feedback or for suggestions for improvement (this could be especially worrisome if it comes after establishing a track record of only moderately positive reviews).
▶ You're advised to develop new skills or clients, but you haven't done anything about it yet.
▶ Your most recent performance reviews are lukewarm-to-negative (note: such reviews may not be a sign of impending doom, according to Harrison Barnes, CEO of BCG Attorney Search, "When young attorneys join larger or mid-sized firms," he says, "there is a sorting process, almost

like a 'hazing'". He says that if the firm likes you and sees potential, you may actually receive a harsher review precisely because you're seen as talented and as someone who can improve. But, if your performance contains no positive feedback, the handwriting is on the wall.) For additional articles, go to www.bcgsearch.com.

If the Handwriting is On the Wall.

It's surprising how many lawyers recognize the warning signs, and yet prefer to keep their heads down in hopes the "tornado" doesn't hit their house. Don't be one of them; take action now, and watch for signals. Here are 10 suggestions if the handwriting is on the wall at your firm:

Do a career-progress analysis — Review your contributions and accomplishments, evaluate your CLE and other professional development activities. Let key partners know about the good results you are delivering, and what you're doing to further develop your potential.

Get feedback — Arrange for short, individual meetings with the partners for whom you do the most work. Get their evaluation(s). Find out what you do well, where you need to improve, and what skills you need to add to position yourself for the next few years. In short, learn how to support the firm's long-term strategy.

Re-invent yourself — If work is flagging in your practice area, consider developing

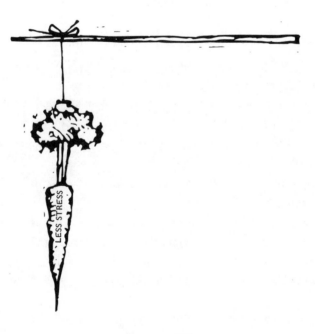

another specialty, or offer to support a busier area of the firm. Ask what the partners in another practice area can hand off to you that would make their lives easier.

Start rainmaking — Promote your firm more, raise your visibility, start bringing in some business. Rainmaking isn't rocket science, it's the art of building relationships. And, in a soft economy, it's everyone's responsibility.

Volunteerism — Propose a high-profile pro bono assignment that will enhance the firm's reputation. Or, if you can afford it, volunteer to take unpaid leave and use the time to increase your community ties and help build your practice at the same time. (Note: the number of lawyers doing pro bono work across the country is at record levels after a decade-long decline.)

Evaluate your practice mix — Look at the firm's practice mix as you would an investment portfolio. Is it diversified or concentrated in a few economic sectors? Has the firm extended itself with rapid expansion at the expense of profitability? Did it expand and offer big salaries during a market upswing only to become vulnerable now?

Improve your finances — If the handwriting is on the wall where you work, start paying down personal debt and begin building up an emergency fund of six to nine months of salary. And, with current low rates of bank interest, you also might consider a home line of credit. If you're considering going out on your own, consider setting up a Solo(k), a fantastic retirement-savings vehicle created in 2002 for the self-employed. You can bank up to $40,000 a year and, as with a traditional 401(k), even borrow money from your account. Plan fees vary widely, so shop around on sites like **www.401khelpcenter.com**. For more suggestions, see Chapter 5.

Do more networking — Attend more professional gatherings. Keep in touch with small legal search firms. Find out what searches they're working on and refer colleagues if you can. If a search firm calls and you're not interested, be courteous. Cultivate the relationship, and save their business card. You never know.

Propose relocating — If your firm has multiple offices, consider moving where its business is growing. Relocation is less common among law firms than it is in the corporate sector. Also, relocation could disrupt your career for a short term fix that doesn't serve you well. If it still interests you, be prepared to make a business case (what's in it for the firm). Ask for moving expenses, but be ready to pay them yourself.

Leave before you're asked — You'll make a stronger re-employment candidate if your job-search doesn't have the stigma of "termination" hanging over it, even if the firm makes it clear that you were not let go for performance reasons. At the very least, leaving on your own will do more for your self-esteem.

If all else fails ...

Consider these steps if you are going to be laid off:

Educate yourself about termination benefits — All companies with more than 20 employees must comply with the government's Consolidated Omnibus Budget Reconciliation Act (COBRA). Under this Act, continuing group health insurance coverage must be offered to all employees who either leave the company or are terminated, or who voluntarily or involuntarily cut back to part-time work or retire before becoming eligible for Medicare, or who become disabled. Your spouse and children will also qualify for coverage. COBRA rules are very specific, and many employers will cut you off if you don't comply to the letter, which means you must make your premium payments on time.

Negotiate your severance — Don't worry about how your departure is characterized — layoff, termination, or resignation. Keep your eyes on the prize: negotiate a good severance package, and if you think you're entitled to more, hire a good lawyer (no kidding!) Getting between a month and a year's salary (depending on your tenure with the firm), along with health and insurance coverage, are not unreasonable severance terms. And don't forget to take the tax ramifications into account. Severance pay is taxable. Outplacement assistance is also taxable when offered in lieu of severance, but is exempt when the employer receives a business benefit. As far as outplacement help, seek out a firm specializing in attorneys. On the other hand, if you're interested in going in-house, you may benefit from a corporate outplacement firm that has a broader business perspective and a wider range of clientele.

Leave on good terms — Meet with the partners and confirm your understanding and acceptance of the reasons for the layoff. If performance deficiencies played a role, this is not the time to discuss them. Express your appreciation for the experience you gained and for any severance or outplacement benefits. Determine who will be serving as a reference for you, and what they are able to say on your behalf. Ask for the partners' assistance in networking contacts and in keeping you in mind if they hear of firms that are hiring. You may or may not want to send a short e-mail to your colleagues, depending on the firm's culture and politics. If appropriate, pay your respects and emphasize that you look forward to staying in touch with your associates; if it isn't, confine your good-byes to those with whom you worked most closely.

Don't slam the door behind you — It's difficult to feel warm and fuzzy toward those who let you go. Nevertheless, take the high road, and keep your professionalism intact. In the months ahead, you'll need references for your next job, and you'll want your colleagues looking out for opportunities that might be a fit for you.

Unemployment is not a synonym for vacation

Some years ago, psychologists asked a group of unemployed, middle-aged professionals to write for 20 minutes day for five consecutive days about the trauma of their job loss (or any topic of their choice). Curiously, more than half of those who had written about job loss were re-employed within a few months, while only 25 percent of those who wrote on other topics, and only 14 percent who didn't write at all, had found work. Researchers theorized that those who wrote about the loss were able to rid themselves of some of the bitterness that could have sabotaged their job interviews. Try the exercise yourself, or even better — start a daily journal. It's clear that the act of writing helped the job-seekers move into a more hopeful frame of mind. Here are some other suggestions:

Maintain a daily routine — Have a plan for each day; calls to make, people to meet, job postings to respond to, and self-marketing letters to send or post.

Stay involved — More lawyers are doing pro bono work than they have in decades. For some, it's the opportunity to network or make themselves more marketable to firms; for others, it has something to do with post-September 11 altruism. Whatever your motivation, get involved. Volunteer work offers tremendous psychological benefits.

Stay well — Take care of yourself physically, spiritually and emotionally. This is not the time to slack off on health-maintaining regimens; jogging, walking, rowing, skipping rope, dancing; whatever. If you don't have a regular exercise program, now is the time to start one. It's also an ideal time to turn to whatever spiritual practices help you stay grounded — and to tap the counseling and support available in your community.

Don't jump at the first job offer — Consider project or contract work. It's much more common now, and many law firms are adopting a "let's-dance-before-we-get married" strategy, especially with mid-level associates who have been in practice a while (re-read Chapter 5, *Finding Stepping Stones*). If you do accept a permanent position, negotiate a severance package beforehand, or at least enter into an employment contract before you start.

Janina C. Latack, Ph.D. — *Dr. Latack is a career consultant, executive coach, and ABA and Arizona State Bar presenter. She contributed to two ABA books, and is the author of the* What Can You Do With a Law Degree Workbook. *Dr. Latack is a former faculty member in the College of Business at Ohio State University, and has been on the adjunct faculty at the University of Arizona College of Business. Contact —* www.JaninaLatack.com.

CHAPTER 6

THE JOB HUNT

Making Opportunities

"The people who get on in this world are the ones who get up and look for the circumstances they want, and if they can't find them — they make them."

— George Bernard Shaw, author

■ ■ ■

How would you describe today's employment market? Competitive, depressing, frustrating ... or, is it interesting, challenging and provocative? The truth is that in spite of the competition and the soft economy, today's market is as rich as ever with opportunities for those who employ a highly personalized and focused search.

And that's the theme of this chapter — opportunity.

I hope by now you understand the limits of the scattered, I'll-take-anything approach. That sending out a blizzard of résumés (paper or electronic), and that responding to every remotely relevant classified ad, just builds frustration and despair. There's no ignoring the fact that finding work or changing careers takes considerable time and effort, and that the most meaningful opportunities come from deep reflection and self-assessment. If you haven't already generated some opportunities, these last few sections are for you. In them are what I believe are the three keys to a successful job hunt:

> Successful job hunts are based on initiative, and take time and effort.

▶ Focus on the employer's needs — To paraphrase President Kennedy, "*Ask not what the employer can do for you, ask what you can do for the employer.*" See *Focusing on the Employer's Needs* in this chapter.

▶ Stay visible — Concentrate your marketing efforts on active, personal contact with others. Only if you have impeccable, directly relevant credentials should you gamble on passive methods like classified ads, résumés or cover letters. In this chapter, see the sections on *Pursuing Your*

159

Goal and *Reaching Your Goal* for many interactive strategies.

▶ Be flexible — The opportunities you seek may be elusive; the ones you do encounter may not, at first glance, appear to meet your needs. Keep an open mind and follow through anyway. The suggestions in the *Marketing Techniques* section will help you strike a balance between persistence and flexibility.

Career Resilience: Your Personal Safety Net

By Rita Carey

In my work as a career consultant, I deal with the anger, anxiety, hurt, and sadness — the emotional upheaval — caused by job loss. In time, these feelings all channel into one ... fear. Which explains why when I hear lawyers talk about job loss the image they most often use is one of being suspended between one trapeze and another, and with both out of reach. The reason it's so scary is that they don't see a safety net. And that's where our career consultation begins. Because in a soft economy, it's important to understand that the only true safety net is a concept called *career resilience*. There are at least four elements to it:

▶ *Adaptability* — Being adaptable requires an acceptance that change is a way of life. It means that you shouldn't expend energy trying to prevent change; instead, you need to put your efforts into taking responsibility for your own employment. The goal must be to remain "employable" rather than getting "employed." To be adaptable, you need to look at yourself as self-employed, not technically, perhaps, but professionally. You need to recognize that your knowledge, skills and abilities are your products. As long as there is a demand for them, you are employable.

▶ *Lifelong learning* — Your "product" must be consistently improved, updated, or refined to meet the changing needs of the marketplace. Avail yourself of every opportunity to upgrade you skills and increase your value in your area of competency. It concerns me when I hear people say that their company won't pay for them to get additional training, therefore they can't get it. If your company does not pay for training, invest in it yourself. It is short-sighted to do otherwise. Lifelong earning demands lifelong learning.

▶ *Visibility* — Become known beyond your workplace. Participate in professional associations related to your field and join organizations that give you access to employers such as the Chamber of Commerce or Rotary. One caveat: joining is not synonymous with participating. It is through participation that relationships are formed and talents are noticed. Be a contributor!

► *Financial Viability* — The clients of mine that are most successful in their career transitions are those who find ways to manage the financial demands while making a transition. They aren't wealthy. Rather, they become credit card-debt free, and make sure they have some savings and/or find ways to earn through part-time work while making the transition.

Now, the challenge: you must add to what is an already-demanding schedule, some activities that will ensure your career resilience. It won't be easy, here are a few suggestions :

► Look for ways to learn while networking. For example, professional associations offer evening and breakfast meetings that both inform and provide opportunities for meeting others in your field.

► Identify someone who appears to be on the cutting edge of her/his field and get together for lunch. Talk about the trends, what employers find most valuable, etc. Ask about other people who might meet with you. And, give something back! Share your knowledge and experience. Each of us has much to offer.

► Check out the online learning opportunities that abound today. Once you know what additional knowledge or skills would be most valued in your field, find a program that provides that training in an online format. That will allow you to complete the work at the most convenient time for you.

► When it comes to financial security, there is only one way to go. Cut back on all unnecessary purchases and keep your eye on your goal. Write your goal or vision on a Post-It and put it up on the refrigerator or your bathroom mirror to remind you what you are working toward.

There is a safety net, and it's woven together with your skill and abilities, your financial resources, your sensitivity to the labor market, your willingness to expand your professional relationships ... and your openness to change. There's a catch, though — your safety net must already be in place *before* you let go of the trapeze.

Rita Carey, Ed.D. — *Dr. Carey is a former law school career planning director and career center manager for General Electric. Currently a certified professional career and executive coach, Dr. Carey is reccognized as a national leader in workforce development and corporate transitions, and has been consulted by the* Wall Street Journal *and National Public Radio. Contact — rita@rcmassociates.com.*

Taking Advantage of the Internet

By Jill Eckert, JD

"Paper résumés are last century."
— Marilyn Kennedy, syndicated career columnist

■ ■ ■

Research shows that many of us will change jobs nearly a dozen times in our lifetime, and that we can expect to have three career changes. This phenomenon is why harnessing the power of computing is now becoming such a vital skill in the job-search process, and why the need for that skill is only escalating. Indeed, the distinguishing factor between you and another lawyer with similar knowledge, skills and abilities, may one day come down to the first person who goes to their computer and hits "send". This section offers a wide variety of resources on how lawyers and law students can get the edge in their search for work online, and the section will include the following topics:

> Harnessing the Internet is a vital job-search skill.

- ▶ Search engines
- ▶ Law firm research
- ▶ Job boards
- ▶ For law students only
- ▶ Salaries

- ▶ Corporate Search
- ▶ Posting your résumé
- ▶ Electronic résumé techniques
- ▶ Basic search techniques

Search Engines

Rule #1, no one search engine exists for all your job online needs. Use several engines, depending on the nature of your search. For example, you might start with **www.Google.com**, the Web's leading search engine (200 million queries a day from more than 100 countries). Better yet, use a "meta-search engine," which scours several search engines simultaneously without repetition. One of many such engines is **www.Dogpile.com**. When you click on a keyword or phrase, Dogpile will produce results from the following search engines — Ah-ha, Ask Jeeves, Excite Precision Search, Fast, FindWhat, Google, Inktomi, Looksmart, OpenDirector, Overture, SearchHippo, and Sprinks!

Whether your job-search takes you in or out of the legal arena, start with the online job board at the Web site of a legal association in your area(s) of interest. You'll find a detailed list of such sites in appendices 2, 4 and 6. If you wish to throw a wider net, visit the Web site of the American Society of Association Executives (**www.info.asanet.org**), or go to Weddle's Association Directory (**www.weddles. com**). And don't overlook the ABA's own Legal Technology Resource Center (**www.lawtechnology.org**) for additional hints and Web info for lawyers.

In each case, start at the homepage and click on links variously called, "About Us", Opportunities," "Jobs," "Employment Information," "Career", or simply "Company Information".

Law Firm Research

If you want to research law firms around the country, you can't do better than the Web sites of legal publisher Martindale-Hubbell (**www.martindale.com**) and the National Association of Law Placement's Directory of Legal Employers (**www.nalpdirectory.com**). Also visit the career page at Findlaw (**www.careers.findlaw.com**) and InFIRMation (**www.infirmation.com**), both of which include detailed salary information, a job bank, and Web discussion boards. For information on general legal trends, try **www.law.com** and the ABA's own site at**www.abanet.org**. If working at a law firm in England interests you, visit **www.lexonthenet.co.uk**.

Job Boards

There are some 10,000 job boards, and the number keeps rising despite the soft economy. It's worth paying a visit to the general job banks. A comprehensive list of such sites can be found at **www.rileyguide.com/jobs.html**. Some of the most popu-lar boards include:

- ▶ **www.recruitersnetwork.com** — Rates and indexes job boards.
- ▶ **www.careerbuilder.com** — A network of sites offering a personal search agent.
- ▶ **www.CareerMosaic.com** — One of the biggest; can do a "radius search" in specific areas.
- ▶ **www.CareerSite.com** — Cross-posts to other sites.
- ▶ **www.hotjobs.yahoo.com** — A large general site; millions of hits a month.
- ▶ **www.JobOptions.com** — Specializes in managerial, technical and professional positions.
- ▶ **www.monster.com** — The nation's largest online job service.
- ▶ **www.netshare.com** — Specializes in confidential senior executive recruitment; base salary must equal or exceed $80k. Named in Fortune's list of "Best Search Sites."

Some of the lesser-known but effective job sites include America's Job Bank (**www.ajb.dni.us**) created by the U.S. Department of Labor, **www.directemploy-ers.com** , and **www.truecareers.com**. Altogether, these sites publish hundreds of thousands of searchable job postings (including some legal postings), and some will notify you by e-mail when new postings appear that meet your criteria.

For lawyers, my Top Six job board recommendations include:

- ▶ eAttorney (**www.eattorney.com**)
- ▶ EmplawyerNet (**www.emplawyernet.com**)
- ▶ LawJobs (**www.law.com**)
- ▶ LawMatch (**www.lawmatch.com**)
- ▶ Legalstaff (**www.legalstaff.com**)
- ▶ Hieros Gamos (**www.hg.org**)

If you want to move in-house, visit the American Corporate Counsel Association's job line **www.jobline.acca.com**or the site co-hosted by the Minority Corporate Counsel Association and Dupont at **www.dbkoncepts. net/MCCA.**

For government work, I suggest beginning with the federal Office of Personnel Management's USAJOBS site (**www.usajobs.opm.gov**), and one other site that organizes jobs by state, grade, series and beyond (**www.fedworld.gov/jobs/jobsearch. html**). Note: some federal agencies (e.g., the Federal Communications Commission, **www.fcc.gov/jobs** have job boards of their own.

For non-profit positions, visit the Institute for Global Communications (**www. ig.org/jobs.html**). It offers a list of non-profit job banks and helpful links to such sites as **www.idealist.org** and **www.NonprofitOyster.com.**

For academic positions, The Chronicle of Higher Education (**www.chronicle. com/jobs**) offers news, advice, and an updated posting board with state-by-state positions. In journalism: **www.newslink.org** hosts a strong job bank for journalists. And in the technical and managerial areas, visit **www.nationaladsearch. com**. It hosts relevant classified ads from 60 metropolitan US cities.

What the Career Coaches Say

Career coaches advise job seekers to post several résumés tailored to different sorts of opportunities to at least two of the major boards. They also suggest regularly editing or reposting your résumés because many job boards (and many corporate systems) rank newer résumés closer to the top. In fact, some sites (Monster.com is one) automatically resend résumés to employers whenever a résumé has been edited.

For Law Students Only

Most law-related job boards are geared toward practicing lawyers. But some — like **www.eattorney.com** — do have special sections for law students. And there are also specialty Web sites such as **www.internships-usa.com**. To get access to this one site, you'll need an ID and password from your law career services. But once you're signed on, you can surf their Non-Traditional Jobs of the Week, their listings of prosecutors' offices, and their job opportunities

> Career coaches suggest you post résumés to at least two major job boards.

in international affairs, women's rights, local and federal government, sports, education, the environment, human rights, and mid-size firms. Over at L Magazine's job board (**www. SummerClerk.com**), you can post a personal profile at no cost. One more suggestion: some employers, including the Department of Justice (**www. usdoj.gov/oarm/oarmlaw.html**), and the Chicago megafirm of Kirkland & Ellis (**www.kirkland.com**), also host law student information.

Salaries/Benefits

Yahoo's salary calculator (**www.careers.yahoo.com**) can be adjusted by zip code and profession, while JobStar (**www.jobstar.org**) offers a long list of position-specific salary data links. Although still reflecting Year 2000 data, the salary calculator at America's Career InfoNet (**www.acinet.org**) predicts trends and wages and sorts legal positions into eight categories. And here's a calculator with a twist: at Wall Street Journal online (**www.careers.wsj.com/salaries/calculator/index.html**), you can see what a $100k salary would be worth in hundreds of cities. If you're interested in alternative careers, try the salary links at **www.wageweb.com**. Or if you prefer a government job, learn about pay scales at **www.opm.gov/oca/payrates/index.asp**, and cross-check them with job titles at **www.fedworld.gov/jobs-occ.tx**.

Finally, if you're making plans to move, visit www.homefair.com or CNN/ Money Magazine's Best Places to Live survey (**www.money.cnn.com/best/bplive**) for information on a variety of home front issues.

Corporate Search

While the big job boards provide lots of leads, many more are to be found at the Web sites of employers. At **www.flipdog.com**, the site regularly scans the Web for job postings at employer web sites, gathers its findings and publishes them in its own searchable database. Another handy resource is **www.job-hunt.org/employers. shtml**.

If you begin your own corporate search, try **www.corporateinformation.com**, which links to a free database that helps you compare US companies with background on ownership and earnings. Hoover's (**www.hoovers.com**) is another site that offers general information at no cost, and has a short list of competitors and key officers. Most government filings, including SEC Filings & Forms, are available online at **www.sec.gov/edgar.shtml**. For work overseas, visit www.europages.com and **www.careercenter.umd.edu/crws/longdist.htm**. A survey found that most Global 500 companies use corporate Web sites in their recruiting efforts. For corporate legal department trends, visit the American Corporate Counsel Association (**www.acca.**

com), and for general business trends, visit the Wall Street Journal Online (**www.wsj.com**). If you have Lexis access, visit **www.support.lexis-nexis.com** for instructions on how to take advantage of their law firm, corporate, judicial, government/public interest, tax, and international directories.

Finally, check out what the media have to say about a prospective employer at **www.newslink.org**, **www.onlinenewspapers.com**, and **www.NewsDirectory.com**.

Specialty Job Sites

Specialty job sites can also be good sources of leads. These niche sites publish postings for specific professions, industries or salary levels, and are increasingly used by employers. Some notable examples include **www.6figurejobs.com**, **www.sciencejobs.com**, **www.higheredjobs.com** (higher education), **www.jobsinthe-money.com** (finance and accounting), and **www.mediabistro.com** (For media jobs). A list of specialty sites can be found at **www.job-hunt.org**.

Posting your résumé

Posting your résumé couldn't be simpler; you merely type your résumé into blank fields at a host site. As the name implies, "posting" allows potential employers to seek you out. Most job Web sites, including Legalstaff (**www.legalstaff.com**), and some employer Web sites (**www.company.blackboard.com**) offer résumé posting. Most don't recognize fancy graphics or fonts, but those that do — such as **www.Monster.com** — charge a few dollars a month for the privilege.

Should you "post" or not?

Yes — Posting increases your exposure to a wider population of potential employers. Most companies don't advertise open positions. Besides that, posting is easier and less expensive considering the time and expense of redrafting your résumé the conventional way.

No — You have less control who sees your personal data, where it ends up, and how it is used. One disturbing new trend is the sale of résumés and e-mails from one Web site to another (for as little as 33 cents each, according to the Wall Street Journal) without the job seeker's knowledge. There are also growing reports of Web hosts looting thousands of résumés from competing sites. "Posting a résumé on the Internet," says one consultant, "is like putting some of your most private information on a highway billboard." Further complicating the issue, is the occasional appearance of fake job listings for the purposes of identity theft and annoying e-mail spam. In 2003 Monster, the largest Internet job board, notified millions of job seekers that "from time to time, false job postings are being listed online to illegally collect personal information from unsuspecting job-seekers."

Electronic résumés

Most Web sites accept electronic résumés via email. By all means, take advantage of this efficiency, but understand that any job posted to job boards will invite a flood of résumés (so don't take it personally if you don't get a "call-back"). Here are some suggestions:

Anonymity — You're safer divulging personal details when you apply through corporate Web sites. Even then, you should note in your posting that your résumé is being "submitted in confidence." But if you post a résumé to a job board, do your best to make it "cybersafe" by either suppressing contact information or sending the résumé through a legitimate and anonymous e-mail address like those available at Hotmail or Yahoo. Such steps can also help guard against identity theft or unscrupulous headhunters who might bring your résumé to an employer to earn a contingency fee (thus reducing your chances than if you had approached the employer on your own).

Home base — Conduct your job-search from home. You'll need a separate e-mail account, fax machine, and even an additional phone line with, ideally, a professional answering service (potential employers aren't impressed when your four-year-old answers the phone and shouts over the sound of barking dogs that you're in the shower).

Your email address — Before composing your virtual correspondence, select your e-mail name with care. An odd nickname or catch phrase (i.e., princess@aol.com), or using your current work email account, will seem unprofessional. It's best if you set up a commercial account using a version of your own name (i.e., YourName@hotmail.com).

References — With jobs tight, references matter again. Assemble a solid cadre of references and coach them well. Use someone who can speak enthusiastically about you and will elaborate on your strengths and accomplishments; use someone with excellent oral and written communication skills; and if you're laid off, request as part of your separation agreement a "to whom it may concern" letter from a current or past supervisor. Best of all, if you've selected a prospective employer, try to get someone inside that firm to recommend you.

Interviews — Arrange job interviews for non-work hours, or use vacation time.

A personal Web site — Consider creating a personal Web site to manage and define your portfolio. Personal Web sites can help employers learn more about you from your résumé, references, writing samples, and picture. Some sources (**www.careermag.com**) offer free web hosting. You'll need a Web hosting company (at $10-$30 a month), and you can find lists of them at **www.webhostingtalk.com** or **www.hostsearch.com**.

Online language — If the job you're applying for is described online, make sure your email and/or your Web site contain the relevant keywords. If the job description is not available online, search the Internet for comparable positions and use similar language where possible.

Sending attachments — If you can submit your résumé as an attachment, send it in a Portable Document Format (PDF) file. Employers that cannot open the document can always download free reading software such as Adobe Acrobat at **www.Adobe.com**. Another option is to save your résumé in Rich Text Format (RTF). Although your formatting may not be retained this way, your data can be read via any word processing program. For information on sending "scannable" résumés, see *Résumés and Cover Letters* in this chapter.

Research and Interviewing

Blind ads — Some so-called "blind ads" only list an email address. But that shouldn't stop you from doing a little reconnaissance. To begin, go to **www.Dogpile.com** and type in the email address. You may be able to find the name of the employer, perhaps even the names of one or more contacts with whom to follow up after submitting your résumé. Next, seek out the company's web page and study its links. You'll learn all sorts of interesting things about the company's history, mission and goals. And don't forget to alert friends, colleagues, relatives — and your alumni office — and ask if they've had contact with the company or whether they know anyone with whom you could talk.

Online chat — Chat rooms discussion boards, and discussion groups are a great way to hear what's hot and what's not. For example, visit **www.infirmation.com/bboard/clubs-top.tcl** or **www.greedyassociates.com**. If you haven't visited Greedy Associates yet, get ready for the wild, wild West of online conversation. The Web site was created to "provide an outlet for lawyers to communicate anonymously to each other about topics like salaries, benefits, perks, rumors about mergers, personality issues, statistics, law firm reputations, etc." Even law librarians find Greedy and other chat groups an important source of law firm news and gossip. Another goldmine of information are Weblogs (commonly called "blogs") — a form of hyperlinked online journal — that lawyers and hundreds of thousands of other computer-users give voice to subjects ranging from the very personal to the highly polemical. For an example, go to **www.Insta Pundit.com** authored by University of Tennessee law professor Glenn Reynolds. Or, for a list of attorney blogs, visit Ernie the Attorney at **http://radio.weblogs.com/0104634**). Once you're there, click on Law Stuff and then on LawBlogs.

When you are online, be sure to visit some of the general networking sites. Among them are the Excite Community (**www.communicate.excite.com/index. html**), Google Groups (**www.groups.google.com**), and Yahoo Groups (**www.groups. yahoo.com**).

List Serves — To stay current with trends in your area(s) of interest, I recommend signing up for their online bulletin boards. List serves (otherwise known as news groups or email communities) are valuable sources of information on a particular area of interest or a particular company. Visit the catalog of listservs at **www.lsoft.com/lists/listref.html**, or go to the Publicly Accessible Mailing Lists at **www.paml.alastra.com/sources.html**. Associations in most areas of interest have their own list serves (e.g., **www.abanet.org/discussions/home.html**); and most require some basic information before adding you to the roster.

Buyer beware — According to consumer advocates, more unethical career-advisory firms are coming out of the woodwork as the job market continues to languish. There are at least two Web sites — **www.execcareer.com** and **www.ripoffreport. com** — that offer background articles on deceptive sales practices and post comments from past clients.

A Word About Online Security

Don't let your security fears prevent you from using technology. Just use common sense when considering the security of your submissions. For example:

► Don't give out more information than required, especially if you do not yet trust the source.
► Don't include your social security number when posting a résumé or online application even if a potential employer insist it is for a background check.
► Don't include credit card or bank information during the application process.
► Be wary of where you are being listed and the personal information you post there. And remember to click on the "opt out" option for promotion materials when signing up for job-search list serves and web boards.
► Don't include a home mailing address; most employers will make contact by e–mail, telephone or fax.

Jill Eckert, Esq. — Ms. Eckert is an attorney and legal career specialist at the ABA's Career Resource Center in Chicago. Ms. Eckert contributed to the Commission on Billable Hours report for the ABA, and co-authored Direct Examination: A Workbook for Lawyer Career Satisfaction. *Contact — www.abanet.org/careercounsel.*

Focusing on the Employer's Needs

"Help thy brother's boat across, and lo! thine own has reached the shore."
—*Hindu proverb*

■ ■ ■

Lawyer Melanie Rowland wanted to leave government for environmental activism, but was finding it difficult to get work. Then she had a brainstorm: she would research an environmental group she had great respect for — The Wilderness Society — to see if she might create her own position. Indeed, in the course of her research, she discovered the Society lacked someone to handle the legal challenges presented by the spotted owl controversy. So, she studied the organization's budget. She specifically looked into the available grants so she could persuade the agency's director that he could afford to hire someone to oversee that activity. Melanie also wrote a job description for the position (including lobbying, public relations, fund-raising, grant writing, training and evaluating emerging litigation), and, of course, her job description just happened to reflect the sum of her own work and volunteer experience. Did she get the job? You bet she did.

> Employers hire new people for three reasons: they have a need, they accept the cost, and they recognize the fit.

Organizations hire new people for three main reasons, and Melanie's story illustrates them well:

> ▶ An employer has an emerging need that can't be accomplished with existing staff.
> ▶ An employer is willing to take on a new employee because he believes

the new-hire can save the organization money or add value that isn't available now.

▶ An employer is convinced that one particular person (you) will do a better job of performing the work than anyone else under consideration.

Your task as a job-hunter is to satisfy as many of the criteria as you can ... and all of them, hopefully. Let's examine each criteria in detail:

An Emerging Need

Work opportunities develop for two reasons — maintenance and growth. To minimize competition and maximize your chances of finding work, don't wait until an employer has posted a job or is already into the hiring process. Assess what a company needs before they recognize it or while they're still making their own assessments. How do you find out what companies need? Traditional business reconnaissance: Subscribe to the local business press and bar journals, and read between the lines. As you get practice, emerging company needs will begin to leap out at you. Also, watch the court dockets: if a company is appearing often as a defendant, it may need preventive law help or litigation oversight. Talk to employees about what they see as the company's challenges. Talk to competitors to get the same information.

With 15 years of legal experience, more than half as senior law department manager and assistant general counsel for a health insurance company, **Michael**

Special Advice for the Small Business Market

Did you know that:

▶ Small businesses add virtually all of the net new jobs to the economy?

▶ Small businesses employ over half of the country's private labor force?

▶ Small firms hire more employees who are younger workers, older workers, women and part-timers?

▶ The small business sector comprises nearly 95 percent of privately-held firms?

▶ Small businesses account for 39 percent of America's gross national product?

▶ Small companies produce two and a half times as many innovations per employee as large firms?

For all these reasons and more, if you're moving from the practice of law to a nontraditional alternative, look for opportunities in the small business sector. When approaching a small business, keep these points in mind:

▶ Small businesses tend to want applicants with a demonstrated willingness to assume responsibility; commitment to hard work and doing the job; a high energy level; a team spirit; and good oral communication and interpersonal skills.

▶ Most jobs with small businesses are filled only as the need arises and begin immediately, unlike larger companies with long-term personnel forecasting and predetermined job categories.

▶ A small business probably will not have a personnel department, standard hiring procedures or fixed job duties, salaries and benefits.

▶ The top two hiring methods used by small businesses are non-employee referrals and employee referrals.

▶ In most cases, you will interview with the company founder, who probably is not a trained recruiter and who is taking valuable time from other concerns to talk with you. Interviewing with a company founder is a lot like talking to a parent about his or her child. The company represents a substantial personal and financial investment for the owner. The owner is looking for employees who will share that passion for the company and its future.

▶ Since everyone in the organization may want to get in on the hiring decision, you may have to talk to many people before you are hired.

▶ Small companies do not have the time or budget for extensive training. You must convince the interviewer that you know (or can quickly learn) about the business and can work without direct supervision.

▶ In a small company, you will probably be called upon to perform many roles. Emphasize your flexibility and willingness to perform whatever is necessary. You will likely be involved in decision-making and planning, so also emphasize your leadership and teamwork skills.

▶ Do not express fear of risk or uncertainty. (But research the stability of the company before you sign on.)

▶ You probably will have to negotiate your salary. Consider salary components that tie your compensation to your or the company's performance. (See discussion in *Reaching Your Goal*, Chapter 6).

Goldenkranz wanted to be more in the "happiness business." Through a careful self-assessment, he mapped out four major professional interests: hospital service providers, in-house legal, community service and education. Then he began to make contacts.

In the course of his networking, he heard that a local hospital was in danger of losing its not-for-profit status because of a failure to contribute to the community. First, he studied the hospital's operations. Then he began a dialogue with the senior staff about what they saw to be the hospital's needs. Within a few months, he'd successfully proposed a new position for himself as assistant to the president. His job description, which he wrote himself, included counseling the hospital staff on risk management; advising on governmental, legislative and regulatory issues; serving as employee ombudsman and advocate; and maintaining the hospital's not-for-profit status by assessing community needs and recommending community service projects.

"The most efficient way to [find out about a company] today is by studying a company's Web site," says Microsoft founder Bill Gates. "On a Web site you can learn not only about employment opportunities but also about the needs and challenges the company faces. In fact you can often learn more about a company on the Web than you would by actually spending a day at the company."

> A potential employer wants to know two things: can you add value or save him money?

Saving Money or Adding Value

Figure out how you can save or make the employer money, or how your presence will make life easier for the employer without being too costly. One of the best places to begin is your own client list. One former practicing lawyer believes there's real opportunity for people to convince business clients that they need you. "If it's a client you've known for years, you probably know a lot about their business," says lawyer Doug Stam. "Tell them what it will cost them a year for you to come on their payroll and what you can provide: contract writing and review, outside counsel supervision, discovery work, personnel problem intervention or workers' comp claim review and resolution."

One lawyer with private practice litigation experience read that a local corporation without in-house counsel was involved in extensive litigation. With some accuracy, he calculated the company's legal costs, arranged to meet the company president and showed how much money would be saved by hiring him to oversee the litigation and handle routine discovery work in-house. By focusing on the realities of today's cost-conscious professional environment, he overcame the president's reluctance to add another full-time salary to operating expense by demonstrating a clear financial benefit. In your own case, this same tactic may lead to temporary or project assignments that eventually turn into long-term employment.

If you want to sell yourself into something temporary that's likely to become something permanent, here are some tips:

Target the right employers — Start your search with small to mid-sized companies. Lawyers with experience in civil litigation or transactional work may discover good contract opportunities with corporate legal departments. Small but growing companies with only one in-house lawyer may need temporary assistance with product chronologies, due diligence, routine filings or discovery work that may evolve into a permanent position as the company grows.

Be flexible — Whenever you talk with potential employers, make clear that you are willing to prove your suitability for a permanent position by starting out with a temporary assignment. But don't offer to take on a project without compensation when you already have experience in the area. That signals more desperation than talent.

Do your best work — When an employer is dissatisfied with the work of a temp, there are no second chances. For that reason, accept only assignments within your competency and experience. Get clear instructions up front and repeat what you've been told to confirm you heard it correctly. If you'll be creating a written product, ask for samples so you can meet the employer's expectations of style and format. Then check in regularly as you progress to make sure you're still on track, and offer the very best product you can on a timely basis.

Make yourself indispensable — The employer wants you there to meet an urgent need at the right cost. Produce cost-effective results on that project while remaining alert to — and suggesting — other ways you can help out. Your temporary role will become permanent if you find a way to assimilate yourself into the company's operations and your presence is taken for granted.

The Best Person for the Job

Your task is to demonstrate to a prospective employer that you'll be a better worker than anyone else under consideration. "My general advice to job applicants," says Microsoft's Bill Gates, "is to find out as much as possible about a company in advance. A demonstration of deep corporate knowledge on the part of a job applicant impresses me — and almost any other prospective employer."

Once you understand an employer's needs, your next challenge is to communicate your value in terms the employer can understand. This is true whether you're looking for work outside the law or you just want to practice a different practice area. For example, the meaning of technical terms may differ from jurisdiction to jurisdiction or practice to practice. "Taking a deposition" means the same thing as "writing an affidavit" in some areas; in others, it refers only to a recorded question-and-answer session with both sides present. An instruction to "write a memorandum" in a transactional practice usually refers to a request for legal research on an issue of law. In a trial practice, it could refer to the same thing, or to a "memorandum of points and authorities" filed with a motion.

The bottom line: if you prepare a résumé or speak using legal jargon, whether you're taking a nontraditional step in law or looking for work outside the profession, you'll probably be misunderstood. Describing yourself as a civil litigator, or listing a job function of "motion practice" will be meaningless to many hiring personnel; they may have absolutely no idea what tasks you accomplished and what skills were demanded by your work.

I remember one lawyer telling me the difficulty he had getting a management position with a prominent sports manufacturer. At first, the lawyer sent out dozens of cover letters, enclosing a standard chronological résumé. He had an impressive legal background, and he thought he would be overwhelmed with offers. Instead, he didn't get a single call-back. The lawyer said he thought his legal background might have been off-putting, so he took another swing. He rewrote his résumé, this time emphasizing his experience in financial management and in the sports industry, and his new cover letters told of his interest in acquiring both a management and a financial interest in a start-up sports manufacturer. By speaking directly to the recipient's needs (without legal jargon), he was able to uncover some intriguing opportunities.

It's your responsibility to translate what you've actually learned into plain English.

The good news is that once you finish the self-assessment in Chapter 3, it will be easier to articulate your strengths and qualifications in terms both legal and non-legal employers will understand. And when you add the research you've done on each prospective employer, you're prepared to handle an effective search. Remember, your pitch should be tailored to each potential employer, highlighting those aspects of your background and experience that align with their needs.

Overcoming Objections to Background & Experience

"Your objective isn't to turn someone who's against you, or who believes in negative stereotypes, into an avid supporter. Your goal is to simply reduce that person's negativity sufficiently enough so that it doesn't hinder your career."

— *Michael Kastre, author*

■ ■ ■

A few years ago, a Minnesota study of law school alums found that nearly half of those who chose nontraditional careers faced resistance and stereotypes from potential employers. For some, the objection stemmed from a prejudice against lawyers; for others it was simply the employer's inability to recognize the transferability of a lawyer's skills and background.

Stereotypes about lawyers are an "easy roadblock for an interviewer to throw in the way of an applicant," says Ken, a lawyer-stockbroker. When Ken wanted to change from law to institutional equity sales, he formulated answers to many legal stereotypes. "It really doesn't matter what you say as long as it is plausible," he discovered. "All you have to do is be prepared to answer the stereotype questions."

> All you have to do is be prepared to answer the stereotypical questions.

Before we get into the 13 most-often encountered objections, consider these five job interview suggestions:

▶ *Tip #1* (prepare) — Most interviewers begin by asking about your vision of the ideal job and boss, and the reason for your current job search. After that, expect to be asked about any unique qualifications or experiences that distinguish you from other candidates. Then it's show time, and the four most-often asked questions are these — *What are your short-term/long-term goals ...What are the best and worst aspects of your previous job ... What do you know about our company ...* and, *What would your former boss/colleagues say about you?* Of course, expect some questioning about your legal background. And be sure to have some better reason for your job search than you aren't making enough money where you are now.

▶ *Tip #2* (research) — If you have contacts in this new field, ask them what stereotypes or objections someone with your background might encounter. Honestly evaluate whether those objections apply to you. If they do, find a way to turn them into advantages for your prospective employer. Of course, if the objections don't apply to you, be prepared to offer examples from your past. Overall, my advice is to prepare at least one story for every objection you anticipate. Then you can weave into your conversation examples of things you have done that show you do not fit their stereotype. For instance, if your interviewer wonders about your ability to be a team player, you might — in the course of the conversation — say something like, "The best part of practicing law for me has been working as part of a team to close a large commercial transaction."

▶ *Tip #3* (reveal) — Don't conceal a truth, hoping the employer won't care. You may have learned how to hide your feelings in court, but it's harder to remain impassive in a job interview. Your anxiety triggered by a half-truth may reveal itself in your body language or voice quality, and be perceived as deception or dishonesty. Don't wait for the employer to bring up a subject. Instead, raise an objection yourself as soon as you feel you've developed some rapport. You needn't linger on it, though. Simply point out the situation, acknowledge that the employer may be concerned about it, and explain why it will not interfere with your ability to meet the demands of this job.

▶ *Tip #4* (reverse) — Turn an apparent vulnerability into a virtue. If you were fired from your last job, explain how you grew from the experience (it indicates your competence in dealing with adverse situations). Or a new graduate can point out that he or she is ready to be groomed into the type of lawyer the employer needs — and that you're willing to accept a lower salary to get the experience. The experienced lawyer can tout his or her ability to be profitable from the very first hour, pointing to the wisdom and maturity that come with age.

Now let's take a look at some objections you can expect, and how you might want to handle them:

Objection #1: You have no directly relevant experience

This is where transferable skills analysis will play a very big role in whether you get the job. Because if there's nothing on your résumé that leads an employer to believe you can do the job, you need to make a compelling oral argument about how your background has prepared you for the work. "When I was looking to change from law to institutional equity sales," says one former lawyer, "I formulated answers to many legal stereotypes. For example, when someone mentioned that law school trained lawyers for litigation, not sales, I made the point that presenting a case in court really was a matter of presenting your facts or arguments in the most attractive, concise and forceful manner ... exactly what a good salesperson should do."

Sharon Gerber used a similar argument when she applied for a managerial position with a Los Angeles temporary placement agency after several years as a family law lawyer followed by a stint as a professional liability claims specialist. She pointed out to her interviewer that to be effective in her work, she had to develop strong people skills, manage outside counsel and deal effectively with many very stressed lawyer insureds. "There is not a tougher group to manage than lawyers," she said. "I think I'll do just fine with staffing specialists."

The strongest point most lawyers can make is their ability to learn quickly. For example, you might say: "In the practice of law, I've worked under pressure to solve a wide variety of problems in many different industries and fields, and for diverse clientele. One of the reasons I've been able to perform this work is my ability to get up to speed rapidly in new areas. I'm certain that ability compensates for whatever I lack in actual experience."

Sometimes, though, just dealing candidly with an employer's objection can get you the job. Soon after graduating from law school, Deborah Moore began helping her parents resolve employment law matters in the family business. After about a year, Deborah applied to be a human rights advocate in city government. When the interviewing panel wondered about her lack of experience, she was frank: "You're right, I don't have a background in human rights," she said. "But the work I've done representing individual rights in the workforce, and doing employment law work, has taught me how to advocate for people without power." One of the interviewers later told Deborah that the hiring committee admired her honesty. When she was hired, she was simply told to "brush up" on the city's human rights statute before her first day of work.

Objection #2: We don't want a lawyer in this job

According to a story in the New York Times, "… Lawyers trying to switch careers say they are often typecast as narrow-minded, confrontational and unimaginative."

Against such opposition, career consultants agree that one's best strategy is to deal head-on with these stereotypes. One tactic is to take the high ground, explaining that you left the law because you just didn't have "the killer instinct." Or perhaps introduce a little self-deprecating humor before an interviewer has a chance to say, "We don't want to hire a lawyer because they're too argumentative and competitive."Another objection is that all lawyers are "glory-seekers" … they're not team players. This one will be a little tougher to overcome because lawyers are rewarded for achieving a high profile. Think about it: How do lawyers get new clients or partnership slots? By being recognized for being exceptional in some way — winning the most cases, bringing in the most business, billing the most hours. In contrast, corporate accomplishments are owned by the division, the department, the team; not any one individual.

> Lawyers need to emphasize their capacity as team players.

So, you will need to extinguish any doubts about your capacity to be a team player by describing your accomplishments with phrases like "contributed to," or "participated in" or "worked as part of a group."

In short, play up your team spirit.

You can also be more assertive. If you think the interviewer holds — but isn't voicing — some prejudices against lawyers, bring them up yourself and explain why they don't apply to you. One non-threatening way to bring up the subject is to acknowledge your awareness of lawyer stereotypes, and tell the interviewer that you've done a lot of thinking about how you would present yourself to fellow employees or potential clients to overcome their prejudices.

For example:

▶ Some might believe that with my law background I'm not a team player. My experience shows that not to be true. In my position as volunteer coordinator of the hospital fund-raising project, I managed a team of 20 volunteers. All but one of them worked with me on the project from start to finish, and we raised 20 percent more money than in any previous year.

▶ One of my frustrations practicing law was the tendency of my peers to find fault with ideas and then reject them before researching and developing them further. That's one of the main reasons I'd prefer to get into an idea-business like public relations. I consider myself a good brainstormer and creative problem-solver. I want to generate and implement new possibilities, not strike them down before we've had a chance to explore them.

▶ I know that some employers regard lawyers in sales environments as deal-breakers rather than deal-makers. One thing I prided myself in when I was practicing law was my ability to get people who seemed pretty far apart to agree on something reasonable for all of them. As an example, I was able to settle a real estate lawsuit that had been pending for seven years and involved 15 parties.

In the process of separating yourself from negative associations with lawyers, you don't want to go so far as to dismiss your legal background. You simply want to demonstrate how your legal background makes you a bonus employee (or as one career consultant puts it, a "two-in-one" employee). You'll be able to understand lawyers and the legal system, interpret legalities for the rest of the organization, and use your non-legal people and team skills to get the job done. In other words, you're a value-added employee; your legal knowledge will add another valuable dimension to the organization.

On the other hand, if any of these stereotypes do apply to you, don't argue that they don't (after all, if you're accused of being contentious and confrontational, you'll only prove the point!) Instead, show how that characteristic only strengthens your credentials. For example, "Sometimes being confrontational is an advantage in a management position. You need to have the courage to deal with difficult people, to confront them and get the issues resolved. My legal training has taught me not to fear conflict and to hit problems head on."

Objections #3: Why would a lawyer want a job outside the profession?

"You must be a loser lawyer."

As many years as I've been out of the law, that phrase still offends me. And while a prospective employer wouldn't be so insensitive to utter it, it doesn't mean it wouldn't occur to them. No matter how well you write cover letters and résumés; no matter how sincere your enthusiasm and commitment to a new endeavor, you must be fully prepared for the question: "Why do you want to leave the profession?" First, be flattered. The question suggests the interviewer holds you in high regard. After all, it is possible the interviewer wanted to be a lawyer and can't understand why anyone in your position would be dissatisfied. Many members of the general public regard law as a glamorous field they might have pursued if only they had the talent and persistence. To some, anyone who would leave the profession is suspect.

If you can't find a job practicing law, or if you haven't yet come to terms with leaving the legal profession, the question — Why do you want to leave? — will sting. In fact, you might be asking yourself the same question and wondering, "Am I a failure?" In which case, it may cause you to behave as though you have failed. One former lawyer was complimented by an interviewer for having a "very, very great" background. The lawyer's response was, "I do?" The interviewer replied, "Yes, but you still think there's something wrong with not wanting to practice law anymore." The lawyer hadn't mentioned her feelings, but her body language apparently signaled "failure".

Remember, people want to hire successes. So, present yourself as somebody who has made a conscious, well-considered decision to do what you're doing. It's easier to explain your new direction when you've taken the time for self-assessment. It's nearly impossible when you haven't. The point is to come up with your own heartfelt explanation for wanting to move toward the position under discussion ... rather than fleeing from your current one. For example, one successful candidate for a position as assistant director of a law school career services office explained her motivation this way:

"I've been working with families in crisis as a matrimonial lawyer for three years; client contact has been the most enjoyable part of my work. Career services work appeals to me because I want to remain involved in a field where I'm in close contact with people in the midst of change. But I'd prefer to work in a cooperative, rather than adversarial, environment. I see myself as a lifelong learner, and would very much enjoy being with the law school."

Objection #4: You can't afford to take this job

The subtext is similar to Objection #3: "Why would someone as well-educated as you consider taking a job that pays so little money? Something must be wrong." It could also be that the employer is worried you'll quit as soon as you find a job in law that pays better (a separate topic handled at the end of this section). Usually though, Objection #4 surfaces when the employer assumes your salary demands will be excessive. Consider the case of **Alison Cooper**: She was a well-paid — but unhappy — third-year associate at a Dallas law firm. She decided to seek work in university management, and — in anticipation of a huge pay-cut — moved into an inexpensive apartment and paid off her credit cards. When a job opened up at a Texas law school, Alison promptly sent in her résumé. But the review committee assumed she wasn't aware of the huge pay-cut, and discarded her résumé. Undaunted, Alison obtained an interview by contacting several employees of the law school, described to them the steps she'd taken, and assured them of her willingness to accept a substantial pay cut. She was hired. Within two years, she was promoted to assistant dean for alumni relations at double her associate's salary.

Objection #5: You're too young

If you're under 30, you've got other stereotypes to confront, and you must be prepared to counter them with concrete examples of competence. Many employers complain about being burned by younger workers who failed to demonstrate sufficient commitment to the firm, or to follow rules of etiquette in dress or communication, or to give adequate notice of quitting. Your personal demeanor in a job inter-view will speak volumes. At the same time, you must be prepared with stories of pro-jects you saw through to the end, of commendations you received for good attendance, and other examples of how you've met the expectations of prior employers. You can also point out the advantages of your youth:

- ▶ Being as young as I am, I have the energy to devote to my work. I have no ties keeping me in the city and I'm willing to relocate and travel regularly.
- ▶ I'm aware that I don't have a lot of experience, I'm willing to take on extra projects and do what needs to be done. With me, you'll be getting more than your money's worth.
- ▶ I'm not likely to make the mistake of thinking that I know something I don't.

Objection #6: You're overqualified

Second-career lawyers, especially those who reached a high level of professional responsibility before enrolling in law school, must defer to those who will be your teachers, even if they have fewer "life credits" than you. Susan Gainen, career ser-vices director at the University of Minnesota School of Law, says that second-career lawyers need to express their interest in, and willingness to be, a junior member of a team. Younger employers may expect someone with your experience to disrupt the balance of power. It's your job to make them comfortable that you won't.

Objection #7: You're too old

This unspoken (and illegal) objection actually suggests a number of questions: Will you work well with younger managers? Will your salary expectations be too high? How long will you stay with the organization before you retire? Do you have any illness or disability that would interfere with your performance? The American Association of Retired Persons suggests that you emphasize the positive attributes of your age, including your accumulated experience, maturity, judgment, perspective, increasing responsibility, and consistent achievement. You can also point to your sta-bility. The Bureau of Labor Statistics estimates that only three percent of workers in their 50s change occupations in any given year, while 12 percent of those age 25 to 34 take the plunge, and the annual career change rate for all ages is around 10 per-cent. As a result, according to the national outplacement firm Challenger, Gray &

Christmas, corporations believe that younger workers will stay an average of three to five years, while those in their early 50s are likely to remain until at least age 65. Since low turnover generally translates into increased efficiency, the older worker recoups for the employer any losses resulting from a higher salary or a shorter period of employment before drawing retirement benefits.

You might also try some of these arguments:

▶ Because of my age and status, I don't have the "family v. work" conflicts of so many other applicants. I can stay at work as long as it takes to get the job done.
▶ I pride myself on my flexibility, and am a very quick study when new approaches are needed.
▶ I have enough life experience to know that no job is perfect 100 percent of the time; I've learned to appreciate the positive factors of each assignment.
▶ I'm a seasoned veteran. I won't require training or orientation; I can dive right in without supervision and make a contribution immediately (as opposed to a younger job seeker's untested potential). Therefore, I'm worth a somewhat higher salary.

Objection #8: You were fired from your last job

Syndicated career columnist Joyce Lain Kennedy suggests you tell the truth about losing your job, but take the opportunity to demonstrate how you've grown from the experience. In an interview, honestly but briefly recount the reasons for your termination, taking responsibility for everything including a difficult boss. Explain why you will not repeat the same pattern in this job. For example, you now believe in deferring to your boss's expertise, or your personal problems have ended, or you've learned to ask for help when you don't have the experience or knowledge to handle something. Don't try to hide the truth, hoping that you won't be found out. Many employers want to know about your last employment, even if you don't list a reference. It's best to provide the name of a contact who will speak fairly of your work. Be aware, though, that sometimes the hiring personnel will sidestep your recommendation and contact an acquaintance of theirs to confirm your explanation. Anticipate the worst of

> Don't try to hide the truth, hoping that you won't be found out

what your former employer might say, accept responsibility for that evaluation, and explain what you learned from the experience.

Objection #9: Your résumé has a noticeable time gap

If you've been unemployed for a long time, determine why and how it relates to this job application. Have you now broadened your job-search after evaluating the transferability of your skills? Were you trying to move into a different field but realize now you're more suited to this area? Career columnist Kennedy suggests that if you've had an illness and are now completely recovered, "stress that your illness is not likely to recur and briefly speak of your doctor's encouragement to get back to work. If your health outlook isn't that rosy, bone up on the provisions of the Americans with Disabilities Act."

If, instead, you took a long, unpaid "sabbatical" to travel, raise children, or just recover from burnout, seek employers who understand and appreciate adventure, balance, or personal growth. Before applying, review the lessons you learned during your break. Then present that detour in its most positive light, turning it into a strong selling point. As an example, one young lawyer spent a small inheritance skiing in Europe and general fooling around during a two-year sabbatical from private practice. He later obtained a position in-house with a sports manufacturer by explaining how pleased he was that he'd taken time out when he was young enough to enjoy it, and how eager he now was to get back to work.

Objection #10: You're a woman

You'd think by now gender would be less of a hiring issue than it is.

But statistics prove that women are still being penalized for not being men. ABA studies indicate that, even after 10 years in private practice, only a fraction of women lawyers make partner. And while the Bureau of Labor Statistics assures us that the gap between the men and women's wages continues to narrow, full-time female workers still only make 77.5 percent of what their male counterparts earn.

Female applicants face one main prejudice: that they may be more committed to their personal lives than to their job (as evidenced by the probability that they may want time to have children and raise them). One female partner of an overwhelmingly male megafirm attributes her success to her fierce loyalty to the firm. She believes that this characteristic is the one which male partners and clients expect without qualification from their colleagues. But at what a price — at last report, she was still unmarried and childless throughout her 20-year career.

To overcome this subtle and always unexpressed prejudice against women, let the interviewer know that have experience juggling multiple responsibilities. For example, you might have been a parent while going to law school or when you studied for the bar exam. You might have taken on a demanding volunteer project while handling a heavy caseload? Maybe you nursed someone close to you back to health while also holding down a full-time job? The more examples you have of when you successfully balanced conflicting demands, the stronger your case will be.

Objection #11: You're a member of a minority group

"Your objective isn't to turn someone who's against you, or who believes in negative stereotypes, into an avid supporter," say author Michael Kastre in *The Minority Career Guide*. "Your goal is to simply reduce that person's negativity sufficiently enough so that it doesn't hinder your career." Most of the prejudice you'll encounter will relate directly to the question of whether you'll be compatible with the organization. Demonstrate your conformity through your actions and past history. If you cannot show a fit, ask yourself how much you want to join a club that doesn't want you as a member. In other words, expect prejudice, and choose potential employers based on your tolerance for bigotry. Either seek employers with reputations for open-mindedness, or set out to be a paradigm-shifter or trailblazer. No matter what choice you make, you must show the employer not only that you can do the job, but that you will fit in.

One law student with stellar credentials sought a position with one of the major large firms in town. Her goal would have been completely reasonable, except that she was a transsexual who liked to wear provocative attire and heavy make-up. Her look and style excluded her from consideration by any conservative law firm; she also let every interviewer know she was in the midst of a change in sexual identity. She deserves credit for being courageous, but she only reinforced the stereotypes and prejudices she tried to overcome.

Objection #12: You have a disability

Don't hide your disability. The fact that you've gotten as far as you have speaks well for you. As opportunistic as this may sound, your disability may give you an edge when applying to large private and public employers who wish to demonstrate their commitment to a diverse workforce.

Your attempts to cover up your disability may also backfire. One hearing-impaired lawyer with excellent law school credentials wanted to keep her difficulties secret, fearing employers would see her impairment as interfering with her ability to do a good job. In several interviews, she did not hear the questions posed and responded inappropriately. By failing to reveal her hearing loss, she conveyed exactly what she feared she would: The employers thought she was inattentive or unintelligent. The best approach is to be straightforward about your disability without asking for sympathy. Show through your accomplishments (and a couple of glowing recommendations) how capably you've met the challenges of your disability in other environments.

Objection #13: You'll quit as soon as you find a job in the law

If it's true, play fair. Admit that you'll continue your search for legal employment and point out what you'll be able to contribute to their operation in the meantime. Also assure them that you'll provide whatever length of notice they require. But don't expect this argument to sell very well, except for temporary or project assignments.

These 13 examples are only the most obvious objections; I'm sure you will hear or experience others. One of the most egregious (reported in the New York Times) was a demonstrated prejudice of some employers to résumés with nonwhite-sounding names. As effective as you are at countering all these objections, it does not mean you will overcome them or even that you'll get hired. After all, one's prejudice may be intractable and, of course, you may be simply be competing with others who are more qualified. But you'll never get anywhere if you can't at least address the employer's concerns. And if you seem to be running into the same objections repeatedly, it may mean one thing — you need to get some educational, volunteer, or internship credits behind you. Or, maybe you should target different employers. Author's note: if you want additional perspectives on how to handle specific employer objections, be sure to visit **www.GreedyAssociates.com,** a popular online lawyer/law student chat group.

Marketing Techniques

"There's a rule of thumb that 80 percent of the important contacts you need to find your next job are through informal networks. If you ask me, I think 80 per cent is an underestimate."

—a career consultant

．．．

One debate among career counselors concerns the success rate of various employment marketing techniques. For example, they wonder, what percentage of job-hunters get jobs through networking ... 85 percent? 75 percent? Fewer? How many employers rely upon classified ads, mail campaigns, headhunters? And how many people are hired through the Internet? You won't find anything close to a consensus. The percentages are irrelevant, though, because the experts generally do agree on one thing — a job-search that emphasizes active, personal contact is more effective than not.

> A job search emphasizing active, personal contact with others is much more effective.

Yes, it's okay to mail out résumés and respond to classified ads. But if you really want a campaign to be a success, you need to spend most of your time on job-finding techniques that are warm not cold, interactive not solo, active not passive.

> ▶ By a *warm* technique, I mean that you have some direct or indirect connection to your contact. Either you've been referred by someone who's given you permission to use their name, or you and your contact were graduated from the same school, or you attend the same Sunday services, or you belong to the same special-interest group; or you're contacting someone whose article you read or presentation you heard. Warm is the opposite of cold-calling, which is contacting someone you know nothing about and who knows nothing about you. One cold (i.e.,

ineffective) technique is mailing résumés to everyone listed in Martindale-Hubbell in your area of interest.

▶ By an *interactive* technique, I mean you have an active, personal contact with someone already working for the hiring company.

▶ By an *active* technique, I mean it's a contact you initiate yourself.

In a soft economy, you simply cannot afford to wait for someone to read your résumé and pick up the telephone to call you. You must follow up your letter with a telephone call so that your contact becomes not only "warm" but "interactive." In my experience, lawyers and new grads tend to resist the more personalized techniques. "Lawyers like to feel special, that their career issues are different from the average Joe," explains consultant Ava Butler. "They feel that because they have paid their dues in law, that they're paid up forever."

The SGOL Method

Lawyers are special but not different. And, as far as the job-search goes, you will need to jump through the same hoops as everyone else. In this section, I've organized a variety of job-finding techniques that will give you an edge as you jump through those hoops. The techniques are bundled into what I call the *SGOL Method* — S is solo techniques, G is for group techniques, O is for one-on-one techniques, and L is for leadership techniques. By the way, for over a year, I surveyed lawyers and law students about which techniques they used to get their last job. At least three-quarters said their most successful techniques were in Category O — one-on-one.

Category S (solo techniques)

Responding to Classified Advertisements — Ever scan the classified section of your local newspaper or bar association publication and wonder where all the good jobs are? And then a few weeks later, you hear about a friend who gets a fantastic job that you know was never posted. Many job-hunters delude themselves that all jobs are published or posted somewhere. Some even believe it's a legal requirement for employers to do so. Or they're under the common misconception that jobs are advertised solely to communicate news of an opening. In fact, advertisements are placed for many other reasons as well:

▶ To satisfy EEO requirements;

▶ When there's no one in-house who wants the position;

► To comply with regulations requiring the posting of open government
positions;

► To justify the hiring of a non-resident alien;

► When the position pays a below-market salary;

The Marketing Grid

Category S/solo techniques

Respond to a classified advertisement

Mass mail letters/résumés

Mail résumés to targeted employers
   without follow up

Post announcements in law libraries

Place a "position wanted" ad

Respond to a government job posting

Work with a legal search consultant

Post a home page on the Internet

Mail letters/résumés to colleagues

Write author of relevant article or book

Category O/one-on-one techniques

Ask friends and family for leads

Talk to colleagues about openings

Ask neighbors & acquaintances for leads

Call on individual employers

Converse with other lawyers
   on the Internet

Do cold-calling

Follow up letters/résumés by telephone

Contact those to whom you've
   been referred

Go door-to-door

Initiate conversations at any function

Initiate conversations in the law library

Take a contact to lunch

Category G/group techniques

Attend a job fair

Attend a law school recruiting interview

Attend alumni association meetings

Attend religious gatherings

Attend seminars/lectures

Attend social functions

Attend sports events

Perform nonprofit volunteer work

Seek out a campaign volunteer position

Take on committee work

Category L/leadership techniques

Write a column for a newsletter/journal

Accept or solicit speaking engagements

Write and publish articles

Chair a fundraising campaign

Chair a volunteer project

Chair a bar association committee

Direct a political campaign

Edit a bar association publication

Found an information-and-support group

Involve yourself as a community activist

Lead reform or investigation efforts

Run for a professional association office

▶ When the employer seeks applicants unfamiliar with its poor reputation;

▶ When the employer needs to combat high turnover;

▶ When the employer plans to hire from within or has already identified another outside candidate, but wants to confirm there's no better applicant available.

Even when a job is advertised, the person who gets it is often someone who learned about it using a networking, or one-on-one technique. That is, one of their friends has a contact at the company, and passes the information on. Then, with a single call, the job-seeker jumps to the head of the line for an interview.

Here's an example of what I mean: **David**, a lawyer and CPA, saw a classified ad for a company controller and mailed his résumé. He casually mentioned the job

Networking Success Story #1

Rob H., an unhappy fifth-year associate at a mid-sized insurance defense firm, was given an ultimatum — commit to the firm or leave. His gut told him to leave, but he worried that leaving the firm might mean leaving the law. So, Rob reached out to a career counselor. The counselor suggested that since Rob had only practiced in one type of legal environment, he ought first to spend time evaluating his preferences, and then research the legal profession to see where else he might apply his talents.

Rob enrolled in a self-assessment workshop for lawyers.

Through that process, he got in touch with his love of troubleshooting, i.e., anticipating potential problems in complex organizations and brainstorming solutions to those minor problems before they could blow up into crises. Remembering peak experiences from his college days, Rob targeted higher education as the right environment for him. Once again, he reached out. By talking to other practitioners, he discovered that the work of lawyers in the Higher Education Division of the Attorney General's office closely matched his profile of an ideal job.

Like many other lawyers in transition, Rob accepted a temporary contract position with a litigation firm to cover family expenses while he was working toward his goal. This experience only confirmed what he had learned through the workshop process: He did not want to practice civil litigation. Despite his persistence, it took Rob much longer than he'd anticipated to secure the position he really wanted. He became discouraged and was tempted to accept a less appealing alternative. But once again, he reached out ... this time to a lawyer already employed in the Attorney General's office.

"Don't give up on the slow hiring process," the lawyer said. "Just stay flexible enough to jump when the right offer comes along."

A short time later, Rob did get the right offer — to work in the Attorney General's office at Washington State University in Pullman, Washington. By coincidence, the offer occurred almost simultaneously with the decision he and his wife made to move to a small town so they could afford to live on one paycheck. (They were expecting the arrival of their second child at the time.) Rob's new position turned out to be 90 percent advisory and problem-solving, involving conversations and group meetings rather than memos and the library. Through introspection, patience, persistence, and reaching out, Rob, in his own words, "put [him]self in the position to get a little lucky." He thrived so well in the university environment that he was soon promoted out of the AG's office and into a position in general administration as executive assistant for business affairs.

Rob didn't get where he wanted on his own — he reached out to others. His is a classic networking success story.

opening to a neighbor who, by coincidence, knew the company president. The neighbor suggested that David call the man and use his name as a reference. David followed up, was interviewed and ... got the job. His first day at work, he found a stack of never-reviewed résumés and cover letters waiting for his reply. His own résumé was in the middle of the pile.

Here are some other solo job-finding techniques:

Search Firms ("Headhunters") — Executive or legal search consultants, otherwise known as "headhunters," are hired by law firms, government agencies, universities and corporations to find the ideal person to fill a high-level position. Some head-hunters work on retainer from the employer, usually to fill a key position in a large corporation or public agency. Others are compensated only if they successfully place an applicant. In either event, they are paid a substantial fee (as much as 40 percent of an annual salary) to locate candidates whose experience closely matches the job profile provided to them. For a thorough understanding of legal search firms, outplacement consultants, and career coaches, read Chapter 7.

Mail Campaigns — It shouldn't surprise you, but employers today receive more unsolicited résumés than they can handle. The problem is so acute that corporate HR departments even have a name for the tidal wave of paper and e-mail — *résumé spam*. For that reason, the "broadcast" or mass-mailing approach usually yields disappointing results. Done right, however, selective mailings can be an effective. To distinguish your résumé from the rest, personalize your correspondence. Before you send it, learn more about each recipient. Better yet, locate someone who actually knows the employer and will let you use his or her name in introduc-  tion. Then, begin your letter referencing that person, or by mentioning the recipient's practice area, affiliation or latest high-profile case. Follow up every letter with a telephone call a few days later. Don't expect your contacts to telephone you; this happens rarely. And don't mail so many letters at once that it would take weeks to reach everyone. Networking expert Cynthia Chin-Lee, author of *It's Who You Know*, says that you don't want to wait so long that the person could have read your letter and forgotten about it, or so long that you yourself have lost interest.

Category G (group techniques)

Volunteering and Affiliating — Volunteer work is a great way to develop the contacts you need in a job-search, especially if you are reluctant to calling strangers on the phone. And a volunteer leadership role will get you further faster; even support roles like registering attendees at seminars or editing the newsletter will introduce you to the players in the field. A new University of Connecticut Law School graduate got her first "job" by volunteering for a community organization. One member of the board alerted her to a city government opening as a discrimination investigator; other board members lobbied hard for her to get selected out of 75 applicants. The more involved you get in the organization the more connected you become.

Example 1 — **Doris** successfully led the local Humane Society's effort to legislate anti-vivisection laws. With this high profile involvement, she became well-known and respected by the Society. A year later, the organization's director resigned and a search began for a replacement. Even though Doris's employment background was strictly limited to public service law practice in a non-supervisory role, she sold her leadership abilities to the organization's board of directors by pointing to her efforts on the anti-vivisection campaign. She was hired because they knew her, liked her and respected her. Joining — and participating in — professional associations related to the area you'd like to enter is another great way to develop contacts, build credibility and get the inside track on job openings. Some associations even operate job hot-

Who Are Your Contacts?

- Family
- Prior coworkers
- Current coworkers
- Judges
- Law school professors
- Law school students
- Law school staff
- College acquaintances
- Sorority or fraternity members
- Alumni association
- Professional associations
- Volunteer affiliations

- Children
- Neighbors
- Customers or clients
- Armed Forces
- Doctors
- Dentists
- Accountants
- Bankers
- Insurance agents
- Sports team members
- Athletic club members
- Counselors

lines for their active members (see the Index to Legal Organizations in Appendix 6; the organizations listed there all have Web sites, many of them with job boards).

Example 2 — **Peter** was drawn to alternative dispute resolution while practicing in a small litigation firm, and decided to learn everything he could about ADR. He joined and then chaired the ABA's ADR committee, spending his own money to attend functions across the country. When his job situation soured, he spread the word among his ADR contacts that he was looking for new employment. At the same time, he continued his commitment to ADR by volunteering to assist with a lawyer-sponsored nonprofit mediation program in his area. Another volunteer for the program was so impressed by Peter's experience, enthusiasm and commitment, that he immediately hired him when a position opened up in his corporate law department.

When you get a chance to work with someone you respect, whether you're volunteering, or being paid for your services, do your best. As in Peter's situation, your enthusiasm and the quality of your work will be the keys to your future networking success.

To make your affiliations and volunteer work really count, join an organization with a goal or mission you endorse, or that has a subject focus you find truly fascinating. Don't be so calculated as to choose a group based on the number of potential employers as members. The point is to connect with people with whom you have an innate bond.

Category O (one-on-one techniques)

Career counselor Lesah Beckhusen once worked with a group of unemployed law school graduates to help them in proactive marketing. The group had "incredible resistance" to networking as a way to uncover positions, says Beckhusen. It took several discussions to break through their cynicism and resistance. But those who actually tried the ideas while still in class came back feeling empowered. "The real job market is conducted by word-of-mouth," says Jeffrey J. Mayer, author of *Find the Job You've Always Wanted in Half the Time with Half the Effort.* In fact, he says, the conventional wisdom in the career counseling and job-search industries is that four out of five job hunters find new employment in this "hidden" job market. Lee Hecht Harrison, a national outplacement firm, defines this market as those unadvertised, often even unidentified, positions that someone gets because they talked to the right person at the right time.

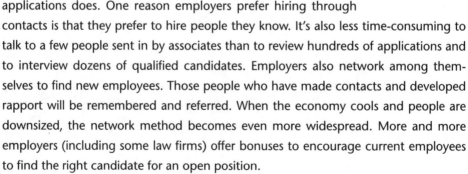

According to one employment industry newsletter, only one percent of employers they studied had ever hired an applicant on the basis of a mailed-in résumé. On the other hand, 99 percent of the same companies hired individuals who contacted them directly! The U. S. Department of Labor and the Harvard Business Review confirm this result. According to studies conducted by both, approximately 75 percent of all jobs are found through personal and professional contacts. We know this process as "networking".

How Employers Use Networking — Employers want to find the best person for the job, but at the same time they want expend the least possible effort and expense. Placing an advertisement in a local newspaper doesn't cost much, but following up on all the applications does. One reason employers prefer hiring through contacts is that they prefer to hire people they know. It's also less time-consuming to talk to a few people sent in by associates than to review hundreds of applications and to interview dozens of qualified candidates. Employers also network among themselves to find new employees. Those people who have made contacts and developed rapport will be remembered and referred. When the economy cools and people are downsized, the network method becomes even more widespread. More and more employers (including some law firms) offer bonuses to encourage current employees to find the right candidate for an open position.

Jim Rupp was a sixth-year associate when he started his hunt for an in-house corporate position. About nine months into his search, he noticed a position advertised for a lawyer with two to three years corporate experience. He mailed a cover letter and résumé. A week later, he was notified that he was overqualified for the position, but that his résumé would be "kept on file." Some months later, the company realized its error; it needed a more experienced lawyer. But rather than advertising again or looking through résumés, the company's general counsel called around for the name of a qualified candidate. Jim's name was passed along, and he was hired. At a seminar on job finding, Jim said he thought his employment was a stroke of luck. Upon reconsideration, he realized it was more a matter of hard work. If he hadn't made personal contacts with dozens of potential employers, his name wouldn't have gotten to the right people. At the end of his presentation, he quoted the entrepreneur Armand Hammer — "Luck seems to come to you when you work 17 hours a day!"

How Networking Really Works — Networking is simply a process of community-building. It is "the ability to create and maintain an effective, widely-based system of resources that works to the mutual benefit of yourself and others." Most of us network in some form every day:

▶ You network when you ask a fellow lawyer for input on case strategy.
▶ You network when you investigate a client's case by telephoning potential witnesses.
▶ You network when you contact experts and acquaintances for leads and information about purchasing a new house or car.

To start networking, flip through your address book and your memory to make a working list of everyone you know — from your best friend to your pharmacist. Read *Who Are Your Contacts?* in this section. It may jump-start your memory with networking possibilities. At this point, don't even think about whether they might have any information about your area of interest, or whether they might know anyone who does.

Once you have your list, identify which of your acquaintances are most likely to have contacts — or to know others who do — in your fields of interest. Ask friends, relatives, acquaintances, and business associates for names of individuals who might be able to provide job leads or information. You can also use your list to locate someone who is acquainted with the person responsible for hiring a specific position, and use that person's name to obtain an in-person interview. Some of your best sources will be friends, colleagues and acquaintances. Because in a job-search, no connection is too remote.

Let me repeat, no connection is too remote.

According to Jack Erdlen, CEO of an outplacement and human resources consulting firm, people tend to give preferential treatment to those people they or their friends know. And don't underestimate the contacts family members can provide, says former practicing lawyer and now Minneapolis career consultant Joan Bibelhausen. One of Joan's clients discussed his career goals with his future mother-in-law at a holiday dinner party. As it turned out, his future in-law had a friend who was well-placed in an organization he had been pursuing. The friend in the company clued him into a temporary position, and he was hired within a week. That experience gave him the credibility he needed to secure another permanent position later.

Be sensitive to how you approach people.

"If you call someone up and ask them to help you to do something that they cannot do effectively, you create guilt," says Chicago career counselor and former practicing lawyer Sheila Nielsen. "Your friends feel uncomfortable because they don't know of a job for you. That is why they cut short their conversation." Sheila suggests that you ask your contacts to assume a role they can handle effectively, such as advising you on the marketplace or counseling you on job-search techniques.

It's natural not to feel entirely comfortable calling people you don't know, no matter what the subject. If that's true for you, call people you do know, write letters, send an e-mail or seek out information through one of the many online communities for lawyers (see Ch. 6, *Taking Advantage of the Internet*). The community-building process has all sorts of channels. For tips about the etiquette of networking, reread the discussion about informational interviewing in Chapter 4 (*Researching Your Options*). In brief, it works like this: Whenever you meet or talk to someone new, ask that person for names of at least three others who might be able to help you, and request permission to use your contact's name in making your introductions. Never use a contact's name without prior approval.

When you contact a lead, be specific:

▶ Who should I contact at your company to find out about job openings in my field?
▶ Do you know anyone who might be aware of current openings?
▶ I'd really appreciate some advice about my job hunting tactics.

Networking Success Story #2

Jim Latting was an associate at a prestigious but very demanding law firm when he decided to look for a firm that encouraged a balance between one's personal and professional life. Based on his impression of the legal job market, Jim targeted in-house corporate counsel as a position that would permit the lifestyle he sought. He arranged to meet with a former associate of his firm, now employed by a corporation, to explore this possibility. This lawyer disabused him of the notion that an in-house legal department would encourage a balanced life. But he suggested that a small-firm environment might be more to Jim's taste, so he referred Jim to another former associate. Even though he had ruled out small firm practice, Jim continued to keep an open mind, and followed up the lead. The second associate referred him to a third person, a partner in a small business-oriented law partnership. That firm, which emphasized life outside the office and required lower billable hours as a result, just happened to be looking for another compatible associate.

Jim was hired and soon after became a contented partner.

Another networking success.

▶ Could you review my résumé to see if it adequately addresses the needs of my market?

▶ Would you be willing to drop off a copy of my résumé with the head of a particular department?

▶ Could you arrange an interview for me with the hiring authority?

▶ Could you put in a good word for me with the hiring director?

If you know someone who is hiring for a job, call that person, explain that you are looking for work and, if you feel comfortable, indicate that you are aware of the opening. If your contact does not associate you with the position or encourage you to apply, either she's looking for different qualities than you possess or she has already picked someone for the position.

Meeting with Your Contact — Ask your contacts and their referrals for short, face-to-face meetings rather than conducting your questioning over the telephone. This way your contact will be able to attach a face and personality to your name. You might also develop a rapport that will assist you in the future. Sometimes it helps to request a very short period of time — 15 minutes to half an hour. If you are granted an interview based on that representation, be prepared to leave when the agreed-upon period has elapsed. The contact may wish to extend your meeting, but leave the choice to him or her. Offer to pick up the tab for both of you if you meet over coffee or a meal. Walk in with an agenda: to gather information about the job or employer, to identify the background they expect when filling positions, or to obtain direct leads and specific help in getting an interview.

Following Up — Send a personalized note of thanks to every person who helps you. Tailor each note to the recipient, letting the person know how you plan to use the information you received. Have you contacted one of their referrals? Did you read the magazine article they cited? At their suggestion, are you now exploring a different market than before? You might also enclose some information you believe your contact would find useful. Stay in touch with your contacts over the course of your job-search by telephoning or sending a short note every couple months. While your job-search is primary in your mind, it's not their major concern. If they fail to hear from you, they may forget about you, assume you've found a new position, or conclude you are no longer interested in working with them. Have others network for you? Call past employers and coworkers who respect you and your work to ask for their help. See if they'll make the appointment for you.

Category L (leadership techniques)

You might be able to get away with cold calls if you make yourself visible in a leadership role. This type of activity tends to attract consulting contracts, political appointments, calls from headhunters and inquiries from other employers in your specialty area. Although many of the examples listed in Category L are solo and cold techniques, none of them are passive. Becoming a leader demands that you expend substantial unpaid hours in the public eye.

One lawyer with 10 years of civil litigation experience put years into a variety of nonprofit groups. She finally consolidated her efforts into one very high profile campaign for the largest nonprofit organization in her area. Her contribution included researching and drafting public policy statements on such controversial issues as fetal tissue research and late-term abortion, and speaking before legislative hearings and community information meetings. The organization's management was so impressed with her ability to articulate the group's mission in a way that professional and lay listeners alike could understand that it created a new policy advocate position for her.

Expose Your Limiting Beliefs

By Irene Leonard

Limiting beliefs.

Everyone, and I mean everyone, has them. Conscious or not, they are beliefs that stop ... or limit us ... from doing something we say we want to do.

How do limiting beliefs affect our job-search? Consider this: Some lawyers will put a lot of energy into self-assessment, they will work intensively with a career coach or counselor, and they'll even generate a great personal marketing plan. But as motivated as they appear to be, they won't go the distance; they will stop short of actually calling on strangers for help in their job-search. They'll have many explanations for this, but they won't really understand why.

That's the way it is with *limiting beliefs.*

For example, take Joe, a lawyer-client who promised he would make five calls to get new job leads. Joe knew he should make the calls; he even set a reasonable time period to do them. But by our next session, he hadn't made a single call. He said he was embarrassed because he didn't want anyone to know he was dissatisfied with his current job. Joe's *limiting belief* was this: He felt there was something wrong with him for giving up a job so many other people thought was great. Through coaching, Joe devised a plan — and a script — that helped him deal with the obstacles he threw in his own path.

What are your *limiting beliefs*?

One way to learn what they are, and to deal with them, is to work with a professional coach or a career counselor. Or, engage a friend in conversation, asking them to help you examine why you aren't doing those things you need to do. It requires that your partner — your coach or your friend — to ask you "what" and "how" questions about what is keeping you from taking action, and then to listen without offering advice. This simple technique really works, and will help expand your self-awareness. I suggest you also begin a journal, writing at least two pages that take you through the questions that develop in your self-talk. For example:

Q: How come you haven't made any calls this week?

A: *I don't know.*

Q: If you did know, what do you think would be the reason?

A: *Well, maybe fear.*

Q: Fear of what?

A: *Fear ... that ... they won't help me.*

Q: What are the reasons they won't help you?

A: *They're too busy.*

Q: How do you know they are too busy?

And so on. Continue with the self-talk (or the conversation with a partner) through each objection.

When fear or limiting beliefs hinder our course of action, it is important to realize that fear is generally the reason we're not making taking action. To help you get started with the Q&A technique, here are some other common limiting beliefs related to job-change:

- ▶ They wouldn't know anyone that can help me
- ▶ I don't have the experience
- ▶ They'll hang up on me
- ▶ They'll never talk to me again
- ▶ It is not professional to ask for help
- ▶ I'll only embarrass myself
- ▶ The economy is terrible, no one is hiring at this time

Don't stop your analysis too soon. Continue talking (and/or writing) until you realize that fear isn't based on anything you can't handle. Again, it is important to identify the limiting belief so you can develop more useful interpretations. In my experience, the "ah-ha" will come. Indeed, where once you might have said, '*They won't take my call*', it will become, '*Some people would be happy to help me.*'"

Once the nature of limiting beliefs is understood, it's a short distance to working on a strategy to cope with them. Start small, but be tenacious. Make just one call based on an outline or script, and see what happens. You could even start tomorrow morning.

Irene Leonard, Esq. — *Ms. Leonard is an international business and professional development coach specializing in lawyer career issues, and is the author of* Create the Practice You Want. *She is a member of the Washington State Bar and the Law Society of British Columbia. Contact — www.CoachingforChange.com.*

The point is to be visible. Your reputation will eventually attract new opportunities if you let others know that you're interested in considering them.

Picking the Right Methods for You

From the methods listed in the Marketing Grid, select three interactive, warm and active techniques you haven't yet used but are willing to try. Then commit to using them in your job-search in the next week. You earn a gold star if you try just one, a solid job lead if you try two of these techniques, and you may end up with a great new job if you make regular use of all three.

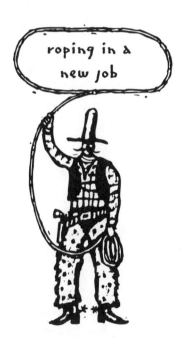

Résumés and Cover Letters

"People no longer look at job hunting as a skill that takes time and effort to develop, but simply a task that requires repetition. They e-mail several hundred résumés and wait for the phone to ring."

—Jay Guard, CFO for Isomedia, Inc.

■ ■ ■

Until recently, most job candidates prepared résumés and cover letters on crisp white bond paper, and sent them off with a postage stamp.

That's still true throughout most of the legal profession.

But there's no denying the growth and acceptance of electronic résumés. Among applicants and HR personnel, e-résumés are increasingly popular given the ease of e-mail and the efficiency of scanning and tracking those résumés in a company database. In fact, Marilyn Moats Kennedy, managing partner of Career Strategies, a Midwest consulting firm, goes so far as to say, "Paper résumés are last-century ... it's just a matter of time before electronic résumés become the rule in the hiring process."

> Form is less important than substance in delivering a positive message.

Still, for all their popularity, e-résumés can't match paper-based marketing materials for creativity and personalization. In fact, the HR director at one West Coast accounting firm, says most résumés come to him electronically these days, but "I still like getting them the old-fashioned way." Indeed, any lawyer looking for work inside, outside or around the legal profession, would be committing a serious error by not making marketing materials an essential part of their job-search campaign.

This section focuses on the best way to present that information.

Writing Résumés & Professional Profiles

An effective résumé is nothing less than your Personal Marketing Tool. It presents a dynamic view of what you can do and why you are qualified to do it. It answers the question posed by every employer — *What can you do for my business*, and *why should I interview you or even hire you*? The way to respond to the question is to focus more on the employer's needs and less on your credentials or goals. And if you feel awkward as you prepare your résumé, it suggests you're not yet clear about the connection between you and the job. In that case, return to Chapter 3 for greater clarity about what you want to do.

To prepare to write a résumé, ask yourself these questions:

1. What skills are required to perform this job?
2. What other skills and personal qualities will the employer find attractive?
3. Which of my work, volunteer or educational experiences prove that I match those skills and qualities?
4. What results did I achieve in those experiences?
5. Who among my references will confirm those achievements?

To answer Questions 1 and 2, find out as much as you can about the position. If you're drafting a résumé for a position rather than a particular opening, make certain that you've talked to people in the field to confirm your understanding of the skills and characteristics demanded by the work. Failure to do so can result in many wasted hours. One woman initiated a job-hunt for project management work, believing that her general legal background in handling cases and clients would suit that employment splendidly. Later, she learned that project managers must possess technical expertise in the area being managed; that her management skills were secondary. It's a little easier to get the information when you are applying for an actual job opening. Some employers, especially government, universities and other large institutions, will provide a lengthy job description upon request. With smaller organizations or positions under development, you must be more resourceful. Talk to the hiring person or others in the department. Ask what problems led to the creation of this vacancy or new position. Find out as much as you can about the business atmosphere.

For Questions 3 and 4, refer to the exercises you completed in the self-assessment section, especially *Your History of Achievements* and *Passions*, and the Chapter 3 section on Transferable Skills Analysis. Identify which achievements demonstrate that you can meet the needs of your targeted employers. Don't limit your selections to work experiences. Consider also volunteer, community, personal, religious, and school projects. Focus on the skills you used and the specific results you achieved (for example, the money you generated or saved, or the numbers of people you led). Then, extract information from that list that will reinforce your qualifications.

As to references (Question 5), they needn't be included on your résumé. Most experts claim that references are superfluous. They say that because employers assume you have them and will request the information if they're interested in you.

It must now be obvious that you need to write your own résumé. Although it's tempting to hire the services of a pro, it may not be the smartest play:

▶ The professional résumé services tend to use similar résumé formats in their work. As a result, employers might recognize a canned résumé and

Résumé Writing Guidelines

▶ Write your own résumé.

▶ Rewrite your résumé for each job opening.

▶ Write your résumé as you would a short, persuasive brief.

▶ Organize your résumé to give immediate visibility to your strongest selling points.

▶ Show results, not just titles.

▶ Be descriptive.

▶ Be selective about what you include in your résumé.

▶ Sell your relevant volunteer experience.

▶ Highlight only impressive educational credentials, or those that directly contribute to your qualification for the position.

▶ Include irrelevant honors and awards only if they are prestigious and well-known.

▶ Exclude irrelevant and potentially prejudicial information.

▶ Ask someone else to proofread your résumé for typos and misspellings.

▶ Make certain you can be reached at the telephone number you provide.

wonder whether they want to hire an applicant who hasn't the confidence or ability to communicate for themselves.

▶ The pros may also emphasize skills and experience they believe will create a strong impression. But they may emphasize the wrong skills and accomplishments because they can't begin to know all the ways you will use the résumé.

▶ If you invest in a professional résumé, it's only natural to want to make the most of your investment by using the résumé over and over without tailoring it. This will only diminish the effectiveness of your job-search efforts. For example, government agencies and some large corporations use software, or assign staff, to search for key words that apply to specific job descriptions. Only résumés that use the specific language included in the job description will be passed to the decision makers. If you use a "one-size-fits-all" résumé, you probably won't even make the first cut.

▶ Most significant, having someone else prepare your résumé deprives you of a vital opportunity. The process of thinking through and putting your own skills and accomplishments down on paper is crucial to building your confidence and to making a case to a prospective employer. If you can't convey your suitability in person as persuasively as your résumé does, then you won't get hired ... no matter the quality of your résumé. Caveat emptor: According to consumer advocates, more unethical career-advisory firms are coming out of the woodwork as the job market continues to languish. There are at least two Web sites — **www.execcareer.com** and **www.ripoffreport.com** — that offer background articles on deceptive sales practices and offer comments from past clients.

Once you've gathered the necessary information, you need to put together a document that will catch the reader's attention. Employers are no longer looking for someone with the right title; in the current buyer's market, employers have the luxury of looking for someone with the right skills, and the right knowledge base, motivation and results. That means you cannot afford to write an effective résumé in "shorthand," listing titles, dates of employment, salaries, and employers, without any narrative. As noted in Business Week, forget the titles, and illustrate your résumé with specific examples of the skills, experience and credentials that raise your "employability quotient."

Compare these two descriptions:

Partner, Smith & Jones, Attorneys at Law
January 1991 through June 1998
Civil litigation practice

Partner, Smith & Jones, Attorneys at Law
From 1991 to 1998, handled civil litigation matters primarily relating to personal and real property. 90 percent of jury and bench trials resulted in verdicts better than offers of settlement, taking into consideration expenses of trial. Averaged 2,000 billable hours annually.

The most powerful résumé reads like a persuasive brief. Underlying its content is the premise that you are well qualified to perform a specific job. The content itself has only one purpose: to prove that premise. The first step in drafting your résumé, then, is to define what it is you want to prove. Some résumés contain a job objective at the very beginning; it is, in essence, the résumé's thesis. It's not necessary — some would say it's not even desirable — to include that statement on your résumé. But I recommend that you place it at the top of the page while drafting to keep reminding yourself what you want to prove.

Once you define your thesis, organize your qualifications around the requirements of the work. Imagine you are creating a magazine advertisement. How can you get the reader to absorb the essence of your résumé in a single glance? One strategy is to summarize your background in impressive terms right at the beginning. For example, you could present your strongest qualifications in capsule form:

- ► Proven Leader
- ► Experienced Trial Lawyer
- ► Attorney Licensed in New York and California

You might also use such headlines as "Management Experience" or "Legal Background" to emphasize your areas of expertise (see sample résumés in this section), or highlight your accomplishments with an opening category of "Representative Achievements". Choosing the correct format — a one-page profile, or a chronological, functional, targeted format — will also strengthen your presentation.

Sample Professional Profile (see Page 213) — In recent years, some lawyers have begun adapting the one-page profile, a format written in the third person and more commonly used by partners for business development. Some consultants say this format is more effective than résumés, especially if one's career is heading in a new direction.

Selected Transactions (see Page 214) — A Transaction List usually accompanies a corporate lawyer's résumé to give greater detail

Sample Chronological Résumé (see Page 215) — This format displays your employment background, education and other relevant experience in order of date, with the most recent occurrences listed first. This is the type of résumé most commonly seen in the legal profession. Its purpose is to demonstrate your qualification for a position similar to what you have now, preferably a next step up the ladder of responsibility. It is also the expected form of résumé for traditional employers like law firms, universities, government agencies and large corporations, where the fact that you worked for a specific employer or earned a particular title may be of paramount

Special Rules for the "Scannable" Résumé

With today's technological advances, most big businesses, company recruiters, and headhunters, use electronic scanners to sort through the flood of résumés. Scanned information allows computers to zero in on key words and phrases that match a job's qualifications. For this reason, your résumé should make maximum use of words and phrases that relate to the position for which you are applying. For example, an employer looking for a lawyer to head its HR department might program its computers with key words such as lawyer, employment law, manager to begin sorting through the résumés. Be sure to describe your skills, experience, education, achievements, affiliations, and languages spoken, with appropriate industry jargon, abbreviations, keywords and nouns. And begin the "employment" portion of your résumé with key action words and phrases (i.e., developed, delivered, consulted, negotiated, implemented, analyzed, managed, etc). And if, as is likely now, your résumé is to be scanned, make it computer-friendly — use simple fonts (Arial, Times Roman, Courier, or Helvetica), and avoid italics, bullets, columns, underlining, graphics, shaded lines, or staples. Print your résumé on one side only.

For additional help on how to take advantage of the Internet in your job-search, read Appendix 2.

importance. A chronological résumé is effective only if you have made steady progress in one field and are seeking a position that is a step up the same ladder. In my opinion, you should not use this format if a) you are leaving the law, b) if you changed employers frequently, c) have been absent from the job market for a while, or d) have a short work history in two or more fields.

Sample Functional Résumé (see Page 216) — This format works well if you have a strong background in two areas — for example, law and management, or trial work and sales — applicable to the position you seek. It is also useful if you want to emphasize capabilities not used in your most recent work or if you have had a variety of different, seemingly unconnected work experiences, such as in temporary, freelance or consulting jobs. A functional résumé organizes your background by category, rather than in chronological order, to support your thesis. For example, a lawyer who wishes to combine his law and volunteer fund-raising experience in a new career as a planned-giving specialist with a nonprofit organization might mix educational, volunteer, and work experience under the two categories of "legal" and "fund-raising."

Sample Targeted Résumé (see Page 217) — This format focuses on skills and achievements that establish your qualification for a specific position. It is similar to a functional résumé in that it downplays the chronology of your background and emphasizes its substance. Use a targeted résumé when you are very clear about your job goals; when you have several directions to go, and want a different résumé for each; or when you want to emphasize capabilities for which you have never been paid. For example, a lawyer without management experience who wants a job as the executive director of a nonprofit organization might begin with a list of results that establish his credibility as a leader, and then follow with specific job and volunteer experience and educational credentials. Once you have defined your thesis and chosen the best format, you need to prove that you're worth interviewing. You do this by showing, not telling, your qualifications. That means describing actual accomplishments rather than listing job titles and dates.

Go back to the list of accomplishments that demonstrate your suitability for the work you've targeted. Select the strongest examples and describe the incidents in an anecdotal manner. Use dynamic nouns and verbs and make every word count. Don't use self-serving adjectives like "excellent" communicator or "outstanding" negotiator. Let the results of your efforts speak for themselves (e.g., resolved without trial a real estate lawsuit pending 14 years involving over 700 claimants).

Tell what you accomplished in terms of dollars or other metrics (i.e., the money

Sample Professional Profile*

Note: In recent years, some lawyers have begun adapting the one-page profile, a format written in the third person and more commonly used by partners for business development. Some consultants say this format is more effective than résumés, especially if one's career is heading in a new direction.

Jane Doe, Esq.

123 Main Street
Chicago, IL 60601
(312) 555-1212

Jane Doe is an associate at the New York City law firm of Skadden, Arps, Slate, Meagher & Flom, where she primarily focuses on corporate intellectual property matters. Her assignments include drafting and negotiating license agreements for clients whose businesses range from software products to international pharmaceutical companies to international manufacturing companies. She also gained experience in the field of international corporate finance and mergers and acquisitions for companies whose major assets are intellectual property.

She has been the principal negotiator for Dow Chemical Corporation for its acquisition of a technological research and development company previously owned by Union Carbide. She also has negotiated acquired transactions for RJR/Nabisco's sale of trademark and business of one of its affiliates. She has represented financial institutions such as Salomon Brothers Inc., and Seligman & Co., in software licensing and other intellectual property matters.

Ms. Doe was graduated from New York University School of Law in May 1990 with honors, including a Vanderbilt Medal and the Lilly Foundation Fellowship for International Studies, and she has published two law review articles while in law school. Her undergraduate and graduate years were spent at the University of Geneva and the Graduate School of International Studies in Geneva, Switzerland, where in 1983 she received a *Licence es Sciences Politiques*, specializing in political science and international relations.

Ms. Doe is also a board member of a not-for-profit organization, Justice Today, that focuses on the human rights of girls and women around the world. Skadden Arps, as Justice Today's pro bono counsel, has performed a considerable amount of legal work for the organization, including the prosecution of their trademark and logo with the United States Patent and Trade Office.

Ms. Doe was born in New York City, where she currently resides. From the age of ten to adulthood, she was reared in Geneva, Switzerland. She is bilingual in French and English and has knowledge of Spanish and German.

---

* Where indicated, the sample letters were provided by **Celia Paul** — Ms. Paul's New York City-based career consulting and outplacement firm has helped thousands of lawyers through the career change process since 1980. Ms. Paul speaks regularly at Harvard Law School and the New York Bar Association. Contact — www.CareerChangeability.com.

Selected Transactions*

Note: A transaction list usually accompanies a corporate lawyer's résumé to give greater detail.

Conrad Wilberforce

Senior Associate — Corporate Department — M&A Group
Paul, Weiss, Rifkind, Wharton & Garrison
October 1990 — Present

Selected Transactions

Mergers & Acquisitions

Currently advising Morgan Stanley Dean Witter, as financial advisor to Time Warner, in connection with the proposed merger between Time Warner and AOL.

Advised a major Japanese technology company in a proposed joint acquisition, with a major US technology firm, in a $1.0 billion transaction; acquisition aborted after substantial negotiations in Fall 1998.

Advised Goldman, Sachs & Co., as financial advisor to Ameritech, in the recent merger between SBC and Ameritech, and advised Goldman Sachs, as financial advisor, in a variety of other M&A transactions in 1998, 1999, and 2000.

Securities

Private placements of over $1.0 billion of debt securities under Rule 144A for Time Warner, Inc., and its subsidiary, Time Warner Entertainment Company, LP — each closed Spring 1993.

$310 million Rule 144A offering of senior debt to finance a tender offer for Plygem Inc., by the issuer, Nortek Inc., a public building materials company, for Wasserstein Perella Securities, Inc., and Bear, Stearns & Co., Inc., the initial purchasers closed August, 1997.

Joint Ventures

Dissolution of a joint venture between Thorn-EMI and M.C. Hammer, for Thorn-EMI — closed Summer 1992.

Finance

Represented FLAG Limited, a special purpose entity formed by NYNEX and other investors to build a fiber-optic cable between Asia and Europe, in connection with $1.6 billion bank and preferred stock project financing — closed October 1995.

Venture Capital/Investment Funds/Limited Partnerships

Represented the principals of a new $1.0 billion telecommunications and media private equity fund and M&A advisory boutique in the formation of the companies — closed 1999.

Sample Chronological Résumé

Note: The objective of this résumé is to demonstrate the applicant's suitability as managing partner of the commercial law department of a national law firm.

Jane Doe, Esq.

123 Main Street
Chicago, IL 60601
(312) 555-1212

Chronological Employment History

Partner, Doe & Smith, Chicago, IL   *1992- present*

In nine years, built a start-up, two-partner commercial law firm into an enterprise with average annual receipts exceeding $1,000,000. Limited overhead to 40 percent of gross revenues through efficiency study and implementation. Hired and trained both clerical and professional staff, accomplished all financial forecasting and planning, and introduced computer technology into the office.

Personal law practice emphasized commercial law (transactions and litigation), real estate (leases, financing and sales) and franchise law. Representative practice accomplishments include forming or terminating over 100 closely-held corporations and partnerships, and resolving a real estate lawsuit that involved over 700 claimants and had lasted 14 years before I took over.

Instructor, University of Illinois Extension, Chicago, IL   *1993 - present*

Teach general corporate and commercial law to those currently working in business management.

Partner & Associate Attorney, Rich, Richer & Doe, Lansing, MI   *1985 - 1992*

Engaged in general practice of law including domestic relations, landlord/tenant, business and estate planning and municipal law. Arranged a comprehensive right-of-way agreement between a telecommunications utility and municipality. Served as administrative partner for the firm with responsibility for budget, management reports, and personnel.

Financial Specialist, Federal Highway Administration, Lansing, Michigan   *1979-1983*

Conducted compliance reviews. Assisted in management, fiscal and personnel activities.

Community Contribution

Vice President, North Chicago Youth Services   *1996 to present*

Coordinated the start-up of a project to strengthen child care and health services for homeless children. Developed a system for linking programs, and negotiated and drafted interagency agreements.

Chairperson, Livingston Area Council Against Spouse Abuse   *1989 to 1990*

Initiated a spouse abuse treatment and prevention program. Took the lead role in budget preparation, staffing, fundraising and community involvement.

Professional Credentials

Juris Doctor (Ranked 1st out of 113), 1985
Thomas M. Cooley Law School, Lansing, Michigan
Courses toward MBA, 1980-1981, Michigan State University
Bachelor of Arts, 1979, summa cum laude, Central Michigan University
Admitted to practice law in Michigan and Illinois

Sample Functional Résumé

Note: The objective of this résumé is to combine law practice and human services volunteer experience into a position as a human services program analyst, coordinator or planner.

Jane Doe, Esq.

123 Main Street
Chicago, IL
(312) 555-1212

Human Services Experience

Vice President, North Chicago Youth Services   *1996 to present*
Coordinated the start-up of a project to strengthen child care and health services for homeless children. Developed a system for linking programs, and negotiated and drafted interagency agreements.

Chairperson, Livingston Area Council Against Spouse Abuse, Inc.   *1989-90*
Initiated a spouse abuse treatment and prevention program. Took the lead role in budget preparation, staffing, fundraising and community involvement.

Child Advocate, Kings and Livingston County Juvenile Courts   *1988 to 1997*
Served as an advocate for abused and neglected children for over eight years.

Legal Experience

Partner, Doe & Smith, Chicago, IL   *1992 - present*
Successfully represented a disabled father against two sons who had stolen and mismanaged his assets. Resolved a real estate lawsuit pending 14 years involving over 700 claimants. Structured the formation or termination of over 100 closely-held corporations and partnerships, accommodating the needs of all parties.

Partner & Associate Attorney, Rich, Richer & Doe, Lansing, MI   *1985 - 1992*
Engaged in the general practice of law including domestic relations, landlord/ tenant, business and estate planning, and municipal law. Analyzed issues and prepared a persuasive paper on representing the best interests of mentally disabled parents in child abuse and neglect cases. Served as administrative partner for the firm with responsibility for budget, management reports, and personnel.

Professional Credentials

Juris Doctor (Ranked 1st of 113), 1985
Thomas M. Cooley Law School, Lansing, Michigan
Bachelor of Arts, summa cum laude, Central Michigan University, 1979
Admitted to practice law in Michigan and Illinois

Sample Targeted Résumé

Note: The objective of this résumé is to obtain a planning, policy or analyst position in the human, health or public service fields.

Jane Doe, Esq.

123 Main Street
Chicago, IL
(312) 555-1212

Qualifications

Ten years of human services volunteer and progressive legal experience, with special expertise to:

- Research original issues
- Synthesize data
- Clarify and communicate fundamental points
- Coordinate case management
- Negotiate among various constituencies
- Comprehend and apply laws and regulations

Representative Achievements

Initiated a spouse abuse treatment and prevention program. Took the lead role in needs assessment, budget preparation, staffing, fundraising and community involvement.

Coordinated the start-up of a project to strengthen child care and health services for homeless children. Developed a system for linking programs, and negotiated and drafted interagency agreements.

Resolved a real estate lawsuit pending 14 years involving over 700 claimants.

Arranged a comprehensive right-of-way agreement between a telecommunications utility and a municipality.

Advocated successfully on behalf of a disabled father against two sons who had stolen and mismanaged his assets.

Analyzed issues and researched and wrote a persuasive paper on representing the best interests of mentally disabled parents in child abuse and neglect cases.

Structured the formation or termination of over 100 closely-held corporations and partnerships, accommodating the needs of all parties.

Served as an advocate for abused and neglected children for over eight years.

Chronological Employment History

Partner, Doe & Smith, Chicago, IL	1992 - present
Instructor, University of Illinois Extension, Chicago, IL	1993 - present
Partner & Associate Attorney, Rich, Richer & Doe, Lansing, MI	1985 - 1992
Law Clerk, J. David Rich, Lansing, MI	1983 - 1985
Financial Specialist, Federal Highway Administration, Lansing, MI	1979 - 1983

Professional Credentials

Juris Doctor (Ranked 1st of 113), 1985
Thomas M. Cooley Law School, Lansing, Michigan
Bachelor of Arts, summa cum laude, 1979
Central Michigan University, Mt. Pleasant, Michigan
Admitted to practice law in Michigan and Illinois

you saved or generated in terms of dollars or percentages, or the number of people, papers or projects you handled). If your results are hard to measure, describe the scope of your responsibility and the impact of the project on its intended marketplace.

Describe your volunteer activities in the legal profession, or religious or other community organizations, if they demonstrate your ability to meet the needs of prospective employers. Have you served on the board of a nonprofit, taught Sunday school, organized fund-raising drives or programs, or provided hands-on assistance to those in need? Those experiences may reinforce your value to the right employers. Look at the Sample Targeted Résumé (previous page). That lawyer successfully marketed her extensive volunteer experience, combined with the skills she developed as a lawyer, and was hired for a human services consulting position. If your volunteer experience does not seem relevant to the jobs you are targeting, rethink your career direction. Should you be looking in another field?

Most of your résumé should focus on accomplishments that prove your suitability for a specific type of work. But throwing in a few unrelated but impressive credentials won't hurt; it always helps to show depth of character and a history of high achievement. Mention honors such as Rhodes Scholarships, a Phi Beta Kappa, or high class standing, but omit obscure awards, especially if they occurred prior to law school or were earned more than five years ago. Knowledge of foreign languages is appropriately included if it relates to your job objective.

It may not feel like it right now, but your law degree falls into the category of an "impressive credential." That means you ought to include it on your résumé, but its location on the résumé will depend upon the thesis you're trying to prove.

Most experts in the legal profession recommend that you place information about your legal education at the top of your résumé if you've just earned it and are applying for a position that will use it. You also want to place your legal education at the beginning of the page if you earned your degree within the last five years from a prestigious law school or graduated at the top of your class and are applying for legal positions. On the other hand, if you earned your degree more than five years ago, no matter how impressive your school or honors, put it at the bottom of the résumé. Solid post-graduate accomplishments are necessary to impress potential employers now.

If you're applying for a position that makes no obvious use of your legal background, downplay your legal background and explain your commitment to and interest in your new field. Reference special courses, seminars or workshops that do relate to your job objective in a prominent location, and place your law degree in an

Special Rules for Government Applications

The hiring process for most merit-protected positions in government involves specific, often burdensome application requirements. You cannot just mail in a résumé and cover letter and expect to get anywhere. "The first place to start," says Brian C. Conelley in his pamphlet, *Federal Attorney Employment Guide,* "is to recognize that finding a job as an attorney in government is a job itself. To find that job you will need *more* than your professional qualifications."

Because of the complex and strict requirements for each agency, it's better to narrow your search to specific agencies that interest you. If possible, request a copy of each agency's application procedure, and prepare the necessary documentation before you hear of any particular opening.

If you do come across an interesting opening, but the job title does not clearly indicate whether the position is law-related, request a copy of the complete job announcement and description. This form will list all qualification requirements, application procedures and deadlines.

Often, you're asked to complete a statement of experience and training (E & T). This is where the government hiring process diverges from the norm. In this statement, you must outline your job experience and educational background by *using the exact words* contained in the job description, the more frequently the better. The reason for using the exact words is simple: Your application will likely be screened initially by a clerk with little or no knowledge of the demands of the position. These clerks are trained to assign points to applications based on specific, literal satisfaction of posted job requirements. They score your E & T mechanically, without extrapolation or interpretation. For example, if the application asks you to list your supervisory experience, and you indicate that you were a partner in a small law firm, the clerk will not presume that you supervised a secretary, a legal assistant and several associates in that position. You must spell it out specifically, using the word "supervise" over and over again.

Another hint: If the E & T asks you to provide detailed information about a particular kind of work experience, mention that background more than once on your completed submission. "Disconnect your natural intelligence and creativity and break up your education and employment history into a large number of tedious, redundant paragraphs," suggests one successful lawyer applicant. "Restrain the impulse to shout, 'To heck with this! I'm just going to send them my résumé; all the information they want is there.'"

unobtrusive location. You want the employer to see you first as someone qualified for the position under consideration and then be surprised to learn that you've also been educated as a lawyer.

Your résumé should be organized to show that you can focus on the big picture. That means leaving out detail. To pare down your résumé, ask the following about every bit of information:

► Does the information clearly support your qualification for the position sought? What specifically does it add to the total picture?

► Do the facts translate into benefits for the employer, or do they merely recite history?

► Does the information raise more questions about your suitability for the position than it answers? If so, is it worth the risk, or important enough to you that you must include it?

Disclosing political or religious affiliations may trigger negative responses. Decide whether that affiliation, or your involvement, is relevant to your qualification for the position under consideration. If not, exclude any reference to it. For example, if you were applying for a position with the Democratic or Republican national headquarters, you would list your affiliation with party organizations in your area. If you're applying for a position as a litigation associate with a conservative law firm, you'd be better off omitting your party affiliation unless you can show that it would be a potential source of business. Of course, if the firm's acceptance of your affiliation is a condition to your interest in a position, keep that information in your résumé.

References to height, weight, sex, marital status, health and hobbies are not relevant and should be excluded. Employers don't even want to look at most of that information because of its potential for exposing them to liability for employment discrimination. One thing you want to avoid is making potential employers uncomfortable with you and your application before they even meet you. Your goal is to create a condensed but persuasive document. It's been said that employers spend less than a minute perusing each résumé. A short résumé forces you to be clear and concise while leaving enough mystery to pique the reader's curiosity. As a general rule, limit your résumé to one page for every 10 years' combined educational and employment background, up to a maximum of two pages. Those with more than 20 years experience may shorten their résumé by focusing on accomplishments during the last 10 years.

A final note: Be sure to mention how you can be reached. Some lawyers are afraid of being found out so they list their home telephone number. Employers facing a flood of applicants may not try again if they can't reach you the first time. So, make sure your home line has voicemail or a reliable answering machine with a professional-sounding greeting. Or, provide a telephone number where someone else is available to answer in an appropriate manner, and can take messages and promptly convey them to you.

For additional information, see Special Rules for "Scannable" résumés and for Government Applications elsewhere in this section.) For information on electronic résumés, read *Electronic Résumés: A Complete Guide to Putting Your Résumé On-Line*, or Mark Mehler's *CareerXRoad*, an annual directory to jobs, résumés and career management on the Web.

Also, for instructions on how to send résumés by e-mail, go to Chapter 6 (*Taking Advantage of the Internet*).

Writing Effective Cover Letters

A résumé and cover letter sent blindly to a company address is no better than junk mail.

Before you send anything to a prospective employer, make sure you're sending to a specific individual, and that you have a "warm" connection to that person. And if you have no specific information about the person to whom you're writing, wait until you do! If you want good results, you must personalize your correspondence with an introduction that relates you specifically to the recipient. Refer to the name of any mutual acquaintance since it immediately links you with the recipient. If you can find a point of mutual interest (for example, an article written by the recipient), reference it in the opening. And if you have achievements the recipient would find compelling, cite them. The rest of your letter should motivate the recipient to interview you or help you with other referrals. To accomplish that purpose, answer these two questions engagingly:

► Why have you contacted me?
► Why should I be interested in meeting or helping you?

You can answer those questions best by concentrating on the first rule of effective job hunting: Focus on the employer's needs. Emphasize your value to the recipient, not the features of your background or education. A marketing expert with the

Seattle law firm of Davis Wright Tremaine suggests that in the first few lines you should respond to the firm's unspoken question, "What's in it for us?" Don't waste the reader's time with too much detail. Present one or two pieces of information from your résumé that best answer this question.

Although the sample cover letters that follow use different techniques, they all highlight representative accomplishments, relate them to the needs of the employer or industry, and refer to future action. They also avoid the writing flaws common to lawyers: writing in a cold and impersonal tone, using the passive voice and using overly complex words and sentences. Letters that invite the reader to respond are not written like a business transmittal letter. Starting a letter with stilted language like "Enclosed please find my résumé" is impersonal and remote. An opening sentence like, "I'm writing to introduce myself to you," is equally professional but more friendly. The passive voice also creates an awkward impression.

Compare this sentence written in the passive voice — "It was suggested by John Doe that I contact you" — with this: John Doe suggested that I contact you." The active voice moves the eyes along while the passive voice slows them down. The passive voice is also the language of irresponsibility; its purpose is to mislead, distort or disguise (some would argue that lawyers write in the passive voice for exactly that purpose!) Make sure your letter is written in the active voice so it conveys the impression that you are trustworthy and straightforward.

"Generally speaking," says Richard Andersen, author of *Powerful Writing Skills*, "the more natural the tone of your writing, the more appealing your message will be."

You not only want to be considered approachable and honest, you also want your letter to be easily understood. Convoluted sentences kill good ideas. Notice how the complexity of this sentence — taken from an actual cover letter — weakens the writer's presentation:

> ▶ I believe that the breadth of my legal experience at the bank, as detailed in my résumé, would qualify me for an in-house position with a company/ corporation which may need a generalist who is comfortable with and proficient in various legal subject areas which may affect its business operations.

Simplicity is the key. Say what you want to say in unadorned, straightforward language. Don't write complex sentences or pick fancy words. They'll only make you sound "obscure and affected", says Andersen. See how much stronger the sample sentence above becomes when it's rewritten to follow all these rules:

► As you can see from my résumé, I've been working as a generalist in banking. With this breadth of experience, I will be able to tackle most of the legal issues you encounter in your business.

Respond to anticipated questions about why you left, or want to leave, your current position or the law in a simple paragraph, without using chatty language such as "You might be wondering why." Here are two examples of straightforward but unapologetic explanations:

► In the last year, I have been devoting less time to the practice of law and more to volunteer activities in my three main areas of interest: children, human behavior and adult education. I was attracted to your advertisement [for a new director of a small children's nonprofit organization] because it is hard to imagine an effective program to benefit children that would not also strive to educate adults and foster an understanding of human behavior. I have decided to move from the practice of law to a position as a pre-law counselor for two reasons. First, I want to continue to assist adults who are in the midst of personal change — the most gratifying aspect of my work as a family law practitioner. At the same time, I would prefer to operate in an environment that relies on education and collaboration, rather than adversarial action.

My last suggestion is that you use an active closing. Request a meeting and tell the recipient when you'll call to follow up. If you're writing a thank-you letter, let the recipient know what you intend to do as a next step.

You'll find a an example of a Thank-You letter and several other sample cover letters on the pages that follow.

Letter 1: Self-Marketing Letter Without Résumé*

Mr. John Smith
Literary Representation, Inc.
15 Park Avenue
New York, NY 10012

Dear Mr. Smith:

Our mutual client, John Doe, suggested that I contact you.

I am an experienced intellectual property lawyer and negotiator, but I would like to increase my contact with authors and publishers by becoming a literary agent. My relevant accomplishments include:

▶ Negotiating a publishing contract for a celebrated author that was one-third more generous than his last contract;

▶ Obtaining a $25,000 advance for an unknown author;

▶ Publishing articles on intellectual property law and negotiations in *The Writer's Market* and attracting three new clients as a result;

▶ Helping six students sell their manuscripts by teaching a seminar at New York University on how to negotiate with publishers.

As you can see from these accomplishments, I have polished my negotiation, persuasion, analysis and editing skills in my legal career. I am eager to perfect my innate marketing ability, and combine it with my existing skills, in a new career as a literary agent.

I look forward to discussing in greater detail how my background can match your firm's needs. I will call you next week to set up a meeting at your convenience.

Sincerely,

---

* Provided by Celia Paul, www.celiapaulassociates.com

Letter 2: Cover Letter With Résumé*

Mr. Harold D. Martin, Esq.
General Counsel
American Bar Association
750 North Lake Shore Drive

Dear Mr. Martin:

As can be seen from my enclosed résumé, which I am submitting in response to the ABA's search for an Administrative Officer, I am an experienced attorney and manager with an extensive legal and financial background. I am greatly interested in the opportunity to manage the ABA in an effective manner, and feel that I am particularly well-suited for the opportunity by background and experience.

Among my most relevant accomplishments are the following:

▶ Worked for seven years as a corporate attorney at one of the country's premier law firms, six years as vice president and assistant general counsel of two major financial institutions, and three years as vice president and general counsel of a significant corporation.

▶ Negotiated multi-million-dollar deals in various parts of the country and the world. Wrote a wide variety of different documents; administered and supervised the work of many different types of people in different locations.

▶ Successfully completed diverse legal matters for numerous clients under severe time pressure and budgetary constraints.

In addition, I have always been active in various bar-related organizations. For the past 16 years, I have taken an active role in the American Bar Association, the New York State Bar Association, the Association of the Bar of the City of New York, and the Westchester-Fairfield Corporate Counsel Association. I welcome the opportunity to make these kinds of activities an even larger part of my life.

I look forward to discussing with you in greater detail how my background can match the ABA's needs. I will call you next week to set up a personal meeting at your convenience.

Very truly yours,

---

* Provided by Celia Paul, www.celiapaulassociates.com

Letter 3: Cover Letter in Response to Advertised Position*

Mr. John Doe, Chairman
New York City Bank
1000 42nd Street
New York City, N.Y. 10012

Dear Mr. Smith:

In response to your advertisement in the *Wall Street Journal,* I have highlighted my qualifications that parallel your stated requirements:

You Require a Background in:	I Offer these Accomplishments:
Calling on major accounts	Attracted new clients to my law firm, which resulted in a 30 percent increase in banking business for the firm.
	Developed additional legal work from existing clients, resulting in a $200,000 increase in legal fees.
Securing loans	Secured loans of up to $250 million for numerous legal clients.
General business development	Negotiated business deals, analyzed agreements and organized transactions as both in-house counsel and law firm partner specializing in banking.
5 years commercial lending	5 years as in-house attorney for major New York City commercial bank.
In-depth knowledge of credit	Completed bank credit training program.

I will be happy to discuss how I can meet your needs in a personal meeting. I look forward to your response.

Sincerely,

---

* Provided by Celia Paul, www.celiapaulassociates.com

Letter 4: Interview Thank-You Letter*

Mr. Sam Partridge
SIA Director of Development
3989 Fifth Avenue
New York, NY 10016

Dear Sam:

I want to thank you for meeting with me yesterday. I enjoyed speaking with you and your colleagues and having the opportunity to see the SIA offices.

I am genuinely enthusiastic about the SIA position. It would give me an opportunity to use my legal skills and expertise in a way that I think would be both personally challenging and constructive for the industry.

I have the background that you are looking for in terms of banking law. As someone who has served as inside counsel at a major bank with a broker-dealer affiliate, I have had an opportunity to see the issues that are important to the banking side of the industry.

As we discussed, I have demonstrated my analytical skills by successfully handling a number of very unusual regulatory questions in connection with the Texas Commerce and Horizon BancShares acquistions, the ManHan and Chase mergers, and the transfer of the emerging markets area of Chase from the bank to the broker-dealer. I have given legal advice concerning a number of complex emerging markets instruments and derivatives, that were made more challenging due to the cross-border nature of both the product and the transaction. I have also handled some very delicate responses to the regulatory inquiries, and the preparation of some unique applications and several esoteric comments letters.

Most importantly, I think I have consistently demonstrated good people skills, and I have the ability to be both a consensus builder and an advocate.

I look forward to getting the chance to talk further. In the meantime, attached is a copy of the writing sample you requested.

Sincerely,

_____

Pursuing Your Goal

"Studies show that in the job market optimists and pessimists have the same rate of failure. The difference is that pessimists attribute failure to personal inadequacy and give up, while optimists attribute failure to external factors and keep trying."

—*Daneen Skube, career columnist*

■ ■ ■

The process of job- or career-transition is not linear in nature. "Most people feel like they're going in circles looking for work," said one career counselor. "They bounce from excitement to depression and back again. What's really happening is that they're moving along a spiral. If they could just hang in there and accept a certain amount of confusion, they would find what they're looking for." If we accept this advice, then the key to a successful transition is flexibility and persistence. Let's explore both in greater detail:

> Perseverance and flexibility will usually lead you to your goal.

Persistence

In the first place, no one has to teach a JD about perseverance or commitment.

You survived law school and the bar exam (and probably an endless lawsuit or two). Sometimes, though, the effort involved in job- or career-transition seems futile and harder because it's more personal. It's about you, not a case. So, you make a few inquiries or send out a new batch of résumés when your job seems intolerable or especially insecure. But when those efforts fail to produce a satisfying outcome, or pressure at work slacks off, you put your career plans back on the shelf. Later, when the work becomes unbearable, the oppressive cycle begins all over again.

Persistence is continuing your search through the bad times ... and the good.

Persistence also means disciplined follow-up — checking within a few days of mailing to assure that your application or résumé was received. For a status report about your job application with a government agency or large corporation, you can wait up to a month after the closing period to inquire. But if it's a small organization, a follow-up call within a week is appropriate. And if you get an interview, persistence requires that you follow-up every interview with a personal letter. It reminds your interviewer how interested you are in the position (if indeed you are), and provides any additional information about yourself you think might be helpful.

Having a system — your day-timer, your PDA, whatever — will assure that you actually make the calls and write the letters. Here are some other suggestions:

▶ Maintain a card file, a 3-ring binder, or an electronic record of all your contacts, noting a date and description for every move. This is a perfect opportunity to use your Palm Pilot.

▶ Keep copies of every version of your résumé, noting on the reverse which employers received each one. When you get a response, or make a follow-up phone call, note the date and result on your copy of the cover letter.

▶ Use a "tickler" system to remind you of the follow-up calls and letters you need to send. Tuck notes into your calendar or scheduling software, or create a card file of reminders organized by day and month.

Assume your search will take longer and require more effort than you think. And, despite your best efforts, there will be times when every inquiry is met with a "Sorry, we're not hiring," and each lead you follow seems to be a dead-end. During those times, you'll feel as if you're heading backwards; you will be tempted to suspend any further efforts. But "try, try, try to be positive," says one former litigator who marketed herself into an in-house transactional position with a bank. You must fight the tendency to be negative, or to draw negative inferences from rejections or what you assume to be your failure to get the right job."

Flexibility

Be persistent in working toward your goal, but stay flexible.

Remember the Energizer Bunny? Just imagine him making his way across the floor and smacking into a wall. Without an ability to change direction, even the Energizer Bunny will run out of juice. Same thing can happen to us. We send out 500 more résumés, make 100 more calls, wait another six months, and hope that something — anything — will happen. It does — we run out of juice.

Cindy fell into this trap.

By her third year of law school, Cindy had answered scores of legal Help Wanted ads, sent out hundreds of résumés, and sought out friends and relatives for leads. Like every other grad she simply wanted to practice law full time. But 18 months after graduation, Cindy was still unemployed ... and losing hope. Then, she tried a new approach. She called a family friend with a real estate practice. She asked if she could do some project work ... just something to get her through the Christmas holidays. The family friend had been reluctant to take on an associate the first time she called. But this time, he really did need some project help ... and so did another solo he knew. By spring, Cindy was working almost full time on projects for both lawyers. She got her wish — she just didn't realize how flexible she needed to be to get it. Six years later, Cindy still has a full-time practice, and she earns a very comfortable living.

My point is this: the rate of success will be so much greater if you stay flexible about the form your search takes, and the kind of work you accept.

It means, you say "yes" to every lead instead of finding reasons why it wouldn't get you where you think you want to go.

It means, when one job-search method doesn't work, you get creative and try another.

It means, if efforts to get into one market or practice area seem futile, then brainstorm other options. And question your assumptions. Don't assume that a particular company is not hiring, or that you won't qualify, or that the organization probably doesn't pay enough, or that you wouldn't enjoy that kind of job. Don't sabotage your efforts until you've made enough inquiries to confirm your suspicions.

For example, **Robin** targeted human resources as a field in which she could work with other people to set and achieve team goals. During her networking, she heard that an employee benefits consulting firm was looking for someone with her qualifications to work in the "gain-sharing" area. Initially, Robin rejected the suggestion because it involved employee benefits work, something she associated only with numbers. The next day, her intuition urged her to make the appointment anyway. She discovered that "gain-sharing" groups assist employee teams in setting and achieving continuous improvement goals. If she had turned down the opportunity to find out more about the position, she would never have discovered this exciting new area.

For every person who has traveled a straight path from law school to senior partner, you'll find many others who have turned a conventional legal background into a novel career by remaining open to new possibilities. Here are a few more examples:

▶ **Rees** was a bankruptcy associate who commuted by train each day, using the time to work on his laptop. One day he struck up a conversation with another passenger using a wireless laptop, and someone who just happened to own a law office software company. Soon after, Rees accepted an equity position with the company, and later became a law firm management consultant with Price Waterhouse Coopers.

▶ **Joseph** had only a few years of legal experience when he seized upon an idea to develop high-end shopping malls in Europe. He tried to persuade Sharper Image owner Richard Thalheimer to go in with him. Thalheimer turned Joe down, but offered him a job instead — in a division that selects new sites for Sharper Image outlets. Believing that Thalheimer's rejection might be a blessing in disguise, Joe accepted the offer. In time, Joe leveraged his experience there to start his own company, counseling specialty stores on how to select and negotiate the best malls for their businesses.

▶ **Michael** was a transactional lawyer who wanted to move in-house but was repeatedly told by companies that they could not afford to hire him. Rather than letting their responses stop his search, he proposed that he work for several companies on a part-time basis. He turned his rejections into a full-time living, and later secured a full-time in-house position with another corporation.

As a "pick-me-up" during those times when you seem to be spiraling away from your goal, try one of more of these course corrections:

▶ Get a sense of accomplishment from tasks you can do in a day instead of believing that the only measure of success is getting a job. Consider your day successful if you nail down an appointment, research an employer or industry, make three telephone calls, write a thank-you letter the same day as an appointment, or put in a full job-search day.

▶ Review your self-assessment materials and reconfirm your commitment to your goals. Are you looking only for work you think you can get instead of aiming for what you would really like to do?

▶ Reevaluate the way you're pursuing your ultimate goal. Are you trying to make too big a leap to your chosen career? Should you be looking at a "stepping stone" instead?

▶ Examine your assumptions — e.g., targeting companies within a one-hour radius of your home, looking at only one industry, or staying within a tight salary range — and remain open to new approaches.

▶ Search for project or consulting work instead of a job. Those temp legal assignments often turn into permanent arrangements. Even if they don't, you gain experience and make what could turn out to be valuable contacts.

▶ Ask yourself if you are defeating your job-search efforts by pursuing too many different geographical areas or fields at the same time.

▶ Be courageous. Ask friends and professional acquaintances if they know why you haven't been successful in your job-search. You could be doing something ineffective that is apparent to others, but not to you.

▶ Be certain that you are tailoring your cover letters to the specific requirements of the position for which you are applying, and that your résumé is directed to the actual person or persons who will hire you.

▶ Consider whether you are being negative, vague, evasive, indirect or dishonest about your credentials or past employment.

▶ Determine whether your stated salary requirements are out of line with the marketplace — either too high or too low.

▶ Spend more time developing contacts who can give you direct introductions to the decision-makers within a company.

▶ Bring your résumé to a career counselor, placement director, or legal search consultant for a critique. You may not be aware of the impression it conveys. Maybe it needs a make-over.

▶ Seek out professional assistance, whether with a career counselor, a reputable employment service, an image consultant, therapist, personal

The Long-Distance Job Hunt

Many who decide to change jobs or careers, also choose to change geographic locations. Job hunting from a distance creates some additional complications.

If you're lucky enough to have a profile that is unique and in high demand, you can pretty much write your ticket to any city in the country. Headhunters will be happy to assist you, and employers will gladly pay the expenses of interviewing, house-hunting and transporting your goods to the new location.

If you're seeking a move into the same or a similar line of work in a location that's not very popular—places like New York City or Los Angeles, or smaller towns throughout most of the country—you may be able to find work before you leave home. You also may be flown out for interviews and receive a subsidy for your moving expenses.

Those who want to move to a popular area like Boston, Denver, San Francisco or Seattle, or who offer skills that can easily be found locally, will first have to prove their commitment to the new location by moving there, sitting for (and, of course, passing) the bar exam in the new state, or at a minimum, investing in several networking trips.

No matter where you're planning to move, be sure to subscribe to the local newspapers and commercial publications to obtain information about trends, potential employers and job openings in that area. Some of these periodicals publish special directories of law firms and businesses, or profile local law firms, lawyers and business owners. Contact any relevant bar associations, other professional societies, law schools or universities with courses of study in your area of interest to get their publications. Monthly journals and newsletters often contain announcements of job openings. Your knowledge of local issues, lingo and neighborhoods will make you seem less of an outsider.

Act now. As one executive search consultant has observed, good things may indeed come to those who wait ... but they'll be the opportunities passed over by people who didn't wait.

effectiveness training course, or other career-related seminar or workshop.

▶ Contact more small- to medium-sized businesses and organizations, where most of today's employment growth occurs.

▶ Devote more time to your marketing efforts. If you're making five contacts per day, bump it up to 10.

▶ Ask for feedback from those who have interviewed you for job openings.

▶ Polish your interviewing skills by role-playing with a friend. Better yet, record the mock interview on a camcorder and review your performance with your friend.

▶ Join a job-hunters' support group, or contact your local college or university career center for leads. If you can't find an appropriate group, create your own. Reserve space in a central location like a public library or the bar association and announce a meeting in your local bar association publication.

▶ Take a break. Do something relaxing; better yet, go help out someone who needs it. One executive who spent six months looking for a job said his interim nonprofit work as an executive director was an important morale-booster. "The work I did, and the appreciation I got, gave me back my self-esteem," he said, "and it kept me in contact with all sorts of people and organizations."

Reaching Your Goal

"The first thing we have to do is figure out what we like to do, and then figure out how to make money at it. If we do any less, we're just rearranging deck chairs on the Titanic."

—a former practicing lawyer

■ ■ ■

So, now you've got a résumé and a cover letter, and you're contacting individuals in your target field. Now what? This section looks at the ins and outs of interviewing and negotiating compensation.

> Your genuine interest in the work and field makes the crucial difference in getting hired.

Interviewing

Before the end of a job interviewer, every employer will want to have resolved two questions about you:

- ▶ Will you do a good job?
- ▶ Will you fit in?

To make sure those questions are answered in your favor, you must accomplish two objectives — develop a rapport with your interviewer, and articulate how your strengths and abilities mesh with the company's mission and environment. Your genuine interest in the work and the field makes the crucial difference. Anything short of that; anything suggesting you don't care enough about the company or the work, will sharply reduce your chances of success. Your legal training should help. If you know how to do anything, it's how to persuade others to take your side when there's an arguable reason not to. You do it by knowing the opposition's position as well as your own, and by showing logically and passionately why your position is the better one.

The most important preparation for any particular interview, then, is to research the company's needs, growth patterns, and conflicts. As one executive search consultant has observed, good things may come to those who wait ... but they will be the opportunities passed over by the people who didn't wait. For that reason, you must be diligent about researching the company; on and off the Web, and in conversations with others. Seek out information such as:

▶ potential new markets, products or services;

▶ potential for growth in the industry;

▶ the relative size of the firm in the industry (profession);

▶ percent of annual sales growth over the last five years;

▶ their services, product lines, practice areas;

▶ price points in the product or service line;

▶ the competition;

▶ organizational structure including number of branch offices, stores, plants or outlets;

▶ training programs and policies for employees;

▶ average time commitments for those in this position;

▶ typical career path in your field;

▶ the corporate culture.

Once you've finished your research, review *Today's Assignment* in Chapter 3 to find examples in your experience that prove you have the requisite skills, motivation and enthusiasm to perform the work. Then, draft a one-paragraph summary of yourself that establishes your credibility — one that conveys your honesty, vision, enthusiasm and competence. What do you have to offer this employer? What kind of employee will you make? Where are you heading in your career and how does this opportunity fit into your plans?

Once you get your thesis down, identify stories you can tell about your accomplishments that convey the same message. More than anything, story-telling will illustrate your ability and personal style much more vividly and convincingly than any conclusions you draw about yourself. After all, if you were the employer, which candidate — A or B — would you remember more favorably?

Candidate A — "I think fast under pressure and get along well with others. People often turn to me as a leader."

Candidate B — "I've been volunteering at the Red Cross for three years. About a year ago, there was an explosion at an apartment building in my neighborhood. I got a call from the office asking if I could help. I got permission from my boss to take the rest of the day off and drove out to the site. Six volunteers were standing around waiting for the official site supervisor to arrive. It seemed odd to me that he wasn't there. I telephoned his office; they said he'd left 30 minutes ago. I asked the police if they could check the radio to see if there was any obvious reason for his delay. Sure enough, a freeway accident had tied up access. I suggested that in his absence we get going by identifying who needed what kind of relocation assistance. From then on, the other volunteers came to me for instruction and the police and medical personnel kept checking in with me. I was promoted to volunteer emergency supervisor after that event."

Besides being a leader who thinks fast and gets along well with others, we see in Candidate B a person who genuinely cares about the community, is responsible enough to ask permission before dashing out to help, doesn't jump to conclusions, understands protocol, and respects the system. This is an example of how a story can convey more than is intended, and sends a stronger, more dramatic message than merely drawing a conclusion ("I think fast under pressure," etc.) The next step is to practice articulating your presentation. Describe yourself to your closest friends and most trusted colleagues and ask for their honest feedback about the impact, accuracy

Ten Selling Points in an Interview

- ▶ You know what the company does.
- ▶ You're aware of the most recent developments in the industry.
- ▶ You know what the challenges are for this industry and company and you relish the opportunity to tackle them.
- ▶ You clearly want to work for this company.
- ▶ You display no ambivalence about your desires.
- ▶ You don't appear to be desperate.
- ▶ You can point out tangible ways you have benefited previous employers.
- ▶ You're clear about what you do and don't know.
- ▶ You are computer literate in ways relevant to the industry.
- ▶ You accept and embrace change.

and effectiveness of your presentation. You'll also want to role play an interview with a career counselor or savvy colleague, using these common interview questions:

previous
boss

- ▶ What can you tell me about yourself?
- ▶ What are your weaknesses?
- ▶ What are your strengths?
- ▶ Why should I hire you?
- ▶ Where do you see yourself in five years?
- ▶ Why did you decide to leave your last job (or the legal profession)?
- ▶ What kind of salary are you looking for?
- ▶ What is your work style?
- ▶ What were your responsibilities in your last job?
- ▶ What do you think of your last boss?
- ▶ How would your previous supervisor describe you as a worker?
- ▶ What do you know about our company?
- ▶ Why are you interested in our company?
- ▶ Are you willing to work overtime?
- ▶ Aren't you over- or under-qualified for this position?
- ▶ When are you available to begin work?
- ▶ Have you applied with other companies?
- ▶ How do you define success, and how do you measure up to your own definition?
- ▶ What would you do if you won a $10 million lottery?
- ▶ Why should I hire you when I could promote someone from within?
- ▶ Tell me something negative you've heard about our company.

Your goal is to plant the message that you can meet the employer's needs in a way that is compatible with the company style. Be certain to support any general statements (e.g., "I have substantial experience in negotiation") with a specific achievement (e.g., "Last year I settled 15 out of 16 cases scheduled for trial") or illustrative story. Again, the proof is in the details; the right stories will convey your message much more convincingly than any assurances of your ability and commitment.

Whenever you're confronted with a question that raises a negative, offer the most neutral response you can, even if it's not the whole truth. For example, if you left your last job because you weren't willing to commute an hour each way to work for the Boss from Hell, say that you wanted work closer to home — if this job is indeed an easier commute.

Avoid badmouthing your prior employer, no matter how unfairly you were treated.

Be prepared with astute questions of your own. Avoid asking about anything that can be learned by reviewing the company's Web site, annual report, or brochure. Feel free, though, to ask for clarification of information contained in any of those sources, or in a magazine or newspaper article about the company. But don't bring up embarrassing information like lawsuits or labor problems unless they are directly relevant to the position for which you have applied. Employers learn a lot about by the questions you ask — how seriously you've been thinking about the job ... how well you understand the demands of the work ... and what your expectations are of are the job. This is why it's so important to avoid asking questions about overtime and vacations until an offer is actually extended. Such an inquiry suggests you may be more committed to your free time than to your work!

Here are some questions you might ask:

- ▶ How are employees evaluated? Is it company policy to promote from within?
- ▶ If I was hired, what would I need to do over the next months to prove that I was the right person for the job?
- ▶ How would you describe your company's personality and management style? How is work assigned to employees?
- ▶ What are the company's growth plans?
- ▶ How are you responding to a particular industry trend?

"During the interview, you must let the prospective employer know that you have decided — without regret or hesitation — to focus on this job, with this company, in this industry," says Brandon Toropox, author of *Last Minute Interview Tips*. "You must show you have a clear idea of exactly what you want to accomplish, and that you are itching to start. Most employers can sense this passion. It is an extremely attractive trait, one that interviewers respond to in a positive way."

But don't be too hasty about getting started. Any prospective employer will notice how you plan to treat your current employer. A seemingly innocent question like, "When can you start?" may be posed as much to expose your sense of responsibility and loyalty as to find out how available you are. Two weeks is the absolute minimum

Dressing for an Interview

The day before the interview, try on the clothes you plan to wear, checking for spots, tears and fit. (One man, who met with me immediately after a job interview, arrived with a long split in the seam of his trousers; another had a series of pen leaks across his belly.) Male or female, you can't go wrong by purchasing and keeping clean one conservative navy blue, gray or taupe gabardine suit, a neutral-colored shirt or blouse, and polished leather shoes, and wearing the same outfit to every initial meeting. That way, you'll only have to worry about your selection when you get called back for a second round—but by then you'll have a better sense of the employer's dress code.

If you're going to be interviewed by video conference, avoid white, plaids and any busy print that may seem psychedelic on the television screen. Look straight into the camera; that's the equivalent of good eye contact. Avoid broad gestures or abrupt motions.

Don't worry *too* much about your attire though. A survey reported in the *Los Angeles Times* found that inappropriate attire was at the bottom of the list of ways to undermine an interview. (Arrogance was first.)

unless your current employer wants you gone sooner and the new employer is aware of it. A month is not unreasonable if you have cases to reassign or a practice to close.

Requesting time off before you start is another matter. There's nothing wrong with asking for a break if you know of no reason why your presence is needed more urgently. But if you're being hired to handle a huge backlog or you get the impression they want you there as soon as possible, don't even ask. Just make sure that they understand you haven't had a break for a while and would like to qualify for vacation before a full year has elapsed.

In summary, your goal in any interview is not only to impress the interviewer with your ability to do what the job requires, but to convince him or her that you'll be easy to work with, that you have integrity, and that your enthusiasm for the job will place you in the "bonus employee" category.

Compensation Negotiations

The rule of thumb about salary talks is to defer the issue until you've had a chance to learn more about the company, and to convince those with the authority that you'll be a great resource. In interviews before a formal offer is extended, keep the salary issue in abeyance with a comment like, "I think we can work that issue out." If it looks like an offer will be extended, prepare for the negotiation by following these steps.

First, research your value in the marketplace.

Look for compensation surveys, and salary updates by the Bureau of Labor Statistics, at your local library.

Check regional business newspapers and legal periodicals for salary surveys. For example, The National Law Journal offers a spring survey called, "What Lawyers Earn." It covers salaries for lawyers in corporate, law firm, private practice, public interest, law school and judicial environments.

Study bar journal classifieds, and talk to executive recruiters and career counselors.

Ask colleagues and networking contacts about salary ranges in their firms or companies. Check with relevant professional associations to see if they've conducted any recent surveys. WorldatWork, a professional association for compensation and benefits personnel (formerly the American Compensation Association) is a good source for online salary information. You can find them at **www.WorldatWork.org**. Or go to the Bureau of Labor Statistics Web site at **http://stats.bls.gov**. A third resource is **www.jobstar.org**. Jobstar has hundreds of salary survey links, at least a dozen of which apply to the legal profession.

Of course, be sure you're comparing apples with apples. Don't study large or mid-sized law firm salaries when you're going to be hired by a solo practitioner.

Another thing: you must make certain you know the requirements of the job. Obtain a complete description of your duties and responsibilities. If there's nothing in writing, ask specific questions and confirm the answers in a letter of agreement. If you're going to be hired for a position that requires something more or less than the standard, adjust your salary expectations accordingly. Then study the benefits package and take into consideration the added value of perquisites like these:

► Medical/dental plans;
► Life/disability insurance;
► CLE/licensing reimbursement;
► Vacation;
► Parking;
► Health or country club dues;
► Profit-sharing;

- Company car, or gas or bus allowance;
- Child-care/family leave policy;
- Van pools or public transportation subsidy;
- Pension plans;
- Legal assistance/counseling;
- Reimbursement for moving expenses;
- Training and educational expenses;
- Seminars;
- Bonuses.

Be prepared to trade perks for salary, especially if your compensation will exceed that of your peers. Consider incentive compensation (remember when it used to be stock options?), or a percentage of the work you bring in, or fees collected above a base monthly or annual amount. Your willingness to share the risk with the employer may make you a more attractive candidate.

Know your salary history. Make a list of the highest salary you earned at each preceding job. Explain salaries that are artificially low because of unusual perks. If you've been freelancing or consulting for a while, disclose the project or hourly rate you received from sample employers. It's not necessary to provide tax returns to prove your claims. Allow enough time for both sides to consider offers. You may be eager to begin or desperate about your cash flow, but don't let that control you. This is a big decision for both you and the employer; so demonstrate your maturity by taking the time to study their proposal and giving them the time to study yours.

Whether you're being hired as a permanent or temporary employee, providing consulting services or joining as a partner or owner, get everything in writing. If you haven't been given a contract or letter to sign, send your own letter confirming what you understand to be the terms of your engagement. You'll quickly receive a response in writing if you're incorrect!

As lawyers, you've learned to advocate for others, not for yourself. As an American, we learn that, conversationally, the subject of money is almost taboo. To land the job you want on terms that will make you feel valued, you must set aside your attitudes about money. If you apply the same skill and forthrightness to your own interests that you use in representing your clients, you'll successfully conclude this career move, and prepare yourself for the next.

Law Firm Partnership Negotiations

Two consultants in Brookline, Massachusetts, Deborah Heller and Linda Cunningham, studied professional organizations and discovered these three key elements to partnership success:

▶ The partners must respect each other's professional competence.

▶ The partners must clearly set forth the parameters of their business relationship.

▶ The partners must respect each other's personality differences, although they don't have to be compatible as individuals.

In Maryland, David Coleman, Ph.D., of Transition Management Services, believes that the first two requirements are more important than the third. Personality differences, he claims, can be managed effectively by timely professional intervention.

It is always wise to investigate the reputations of your future partners. Ask lawyers in your community, and judges if they have trial practices, about the quality of their work.

Next, discuss specific partnership terms. Don't be afraid to bring up uncomfortable topics like how much money they're now generating, what they're spending on overhead, their debt load, and what happens if one of them dies. (Of course, you should be prepared to divulge similar details about your own practice.) Their discomfort with the topics, or reluctance to disclose what's really going on in their firm, could be warning signals.

Hammer out the terms of your agreement. Include descriptions of your business goals, degree of autonomy, compensation, decision-making methods, overhead, entrance and dissolution procedures, equity ownership, and management methods and responsibilities. An ABA publication, *Compensation Plans for Law Firms,* describes ways of distributing profits to partners. *Getting Started: Basics for a Successful Law Firm,* covers successful practice arrangements, ownership options, and partnership agreements, and includes a model partnership agreement on an accompanying diskette.

You might also consider a one-year "of counsel" or space-sharing arrangement to get to know your prospective partners and their operation better. Use this time to discuss fully the terms of any future agreement. The ABA publishes another book that might be helpful here, *The Of Counsel Agreement: A Guide for Law Firm & Practitioner.*

Steps to Take If You Leave the Profession

"If you do decide to leave, don't slam the door behind you ... and keep up your malpractice insurance."

—anon

■ ■ ■

Withdrawing from the legal profession often seems as complicated and time-intensive as entering it. Here are some steps that will allow you to make the transition in a way that won't come back to haunt you:

Associates/Partners Leaving Their Firm

Educate yourself about termination benefits — All companies with more than 20 employees must comply with the government's Consolidated Omnibus Budget Reconciliation Act (COBRA). Under this Act, continuing group health insurance coverage must be offered for 18 months to all employees who either leave the company or are terminated, or who voluntarily or involuntarily cut back to part-time work or retire before becoming eligible for Medicare, or who become disabled. Your spouse and children will also qualify for coverage. You have to pay everything that your employer was paying each month, along with your own contribution — and a two percent management fee. COBRA rules are very specific, and many employers will cut you off if you don't comply to the letter, which means you must make your premium payments on time.

> If you do leave, stay in touch. And don't slam the door behind you.

Your 401(k) — The money you've saved in your 401(k) account raises myriad questions. First, do you want to park it with your former employer, or move it to an

IRA? You can leave the money with your employer until you reach the age of 65 (this applies only if you have more than $5,000 in your account. If the account dips below $5,000, the employer will deduct 20 percent for taxes and send you the balance). Another route is to move the money into an IRA account. This will provide flexibility with your investments and maintain the tax advantages. When you find your next job, you can always rolls it into your new 401(k) account.

Negotiate your severance — Don't worry about how your departure is characterized — layoff, termination, or resignation. Keep your eyes on the prize: negotiate a good severance package, and if you think you're entitled to more, hire a good lawyer (no kidding!) Getting between a month and a year's salary (depending on your tenure with the firm), along with health and insurance coverage, are not unreasonable severance terms. And don't forget to take the tax ramifications into account. Severance pay is taxable. Outplacement assistance is also taxable when offered in lieu of severance, but is exempt when the employer receives a business benefit. As far as outplacement help, seek out a firm specializing in attorneys. On the other hand, if you're interested in going in-house, you may benefit from a corporate outplacement firm that has a broader business perspective and a wider range of clientele.

Leave on good terms — Meet with the partners and confirm your understanding and acceptance of the reasons for the layoff. If performance deficiencies played a role, this is not the time to discuss them. Express your appreciation for the experience you gained and for any severance or outplacement benefits. Determine who will be serving as a reference for you, and what they are able to say on your behalf. Ask for the partners' assistance in networking contacts and in keeping you in mind if they hear of firms that are hiring. You may or may not want to send a short e-mail to your colleagues, depending on the firm's culture and politics. If appropriate, pay your respects and emphasize that you look forward to staying in touch with your associates; if it isn't, confine your good-byes to those with whom you worked most closely.

Don't slam the door behind you — It's difficult to feel warm and fuzzy toward those who decided to let you go. Nevertheless, take the high road, and keep your professionalism intact. In the months ahead, you'll need references for your next job, and you'll want your colleagues looking out for opportunities that might be a fit for you

For additional suggestions, refer to Chapter 5 (*Is There a Lay-off in Your Future?*)

Closing an Active Practice

Ethically, you must be certain that every client in your office with an active case knows that you are leaving the practice, and that they have an opportunity to find replacement counsel. You can let them know your recommendation for substitute counsel, but you must obtain their express permission before transferring their case to another lawyer. When you do transfer a file, send it to the new attorney with a cover letter copied to the client. For pending court cases, file a "Notice of Withdrawal and Substitution of Attorneys" and make certain opposing counsel receives a copy.

Those clients who wish to postpone hiring another lawyer, or who cannot decide on a replacement, can take their files. But before they leave, have them sign a receipt for the file which acknowledges your withdrawal from the case and advice that they promptly find other representation. Then file the "Notice of Withdrawal" with the court and opposing counsel.

Clients with wills or other ongoing but inactive matters should also be notified of your status. Send them a letter which recommends substitute counsel should they need legal services in the future and lets them know where their file is maintained. Also, try to return — by certified mail or personal delivery — any original documents you've been holding for safekeeping.

Cases that Won't Go Away

There may be matters from which the court will not permit you to withdraw. They're usually the ones with a trial or other significant hearing scheduled for the near future, or a client who doesn't want to pay a new attorney to become familiar with the case. If this occurs, you have only three good options:

▶ Postpone your departure until every case is concluded.
▶ Close your office, but make arrangements with another firm to accept pleadings and provide occasional conference room space, or set up a temporary home office until you complete the matter.
▶ Associate with another lawyer (with your client's permission), and assume the cost of getting that lawyer familiar with the case.

There is another option, but I certainly wouldn't recommend it: You can withdraw anyway, and face the consequences. One lawyer who actually did that explained away his abrupt actions this way: "What are they going to do? Disbar me? I quit!"

Selling Your Practice

Historically, most state ethics codes prohibited the sale of a law practice as a going business.

Lawyers attempted to circumvent these proscriptions by:

▶ Inflating the value of the law practice's physical assets and agreeing to refer clients to the purchaser, or
▶ Creating a "quickie" partnership from which one partner would soon retire and receive compensation, leaving the remaining partner with the client base.

Such sales contracts, however, were invariably ruled unenforceable as violations of public policy. The ABA's Model Rule of Professional Conduct 1.17 outlines the following terms under which a lawyer may sell a practice, including goodwill:

▶ The seller must cease to engage in the private practice of law in the jurisdiction or geographic area in which the practice was conducted.
▶ The practice must be sold in its entirety.
▶ Actual written notice must be given to each client regarding, among other information, the client's right to retain other counsel or to take possession of the file.

At this time, Rule 1.17 is being adopted by selected states. Even if not endorsed in your state, the existence of this Model Rule could argue against the voiding of a sales contract. In any event, you would be wise to review the provisions of Model Rule 1.17.

Transferring Files with Potential Malpractice Claims

One day, seven years after I closed my practice, I found an official notice in my mailbox: an Attempt to Deliver a Certified Letter. I couldn't sleep that night, agonizing about which "time bomb" had just gone off among my long-closed files! To my relief, the undelivered mail turned out to be only airline tickets ... not a threatening letter. But that experience reminded me of the haunting stress of practicing law. It's a rare (and probably deluded) lawyer who hasn't made a mistake along the way. As a result, almost every lawyer has a case or two that raises fears of malpractice claims. This common experience will probably result in some pretty sympathetic ears when it comes time for you to transfer those troublesome files to other lawyers.

In order to assure a supportive ear, scan your memory for the lawyers you most trust and respect, and who practice in the appropriate areas of law. Look especially for those with accepting, non-adversarial natures, and approach them one at a time. Be straightforward about your anxiety, and come prepared with specific examples of cases you think you've handled badly. The lawyers you consult will probably know how to get the cases back on track.

If you have made errors or oversights that will require your clients to invest in additional legal work, offer right up front to pay the cost. That investment will likely avert any subsequent malpractice claims.

In some cases, your actions will have caused irreparable injury to your client. If you're covered by a "claims-made" policy, notify your carrier of any potential claims before you terminate the policy. Better yet, purchase "tail" coverage (see below) to insure you against claims that are raised after you quit practicing law. One consolation: You won't have to worry that your mistakes will increase your malpractice premiums ... because you won't be practicing law any more!

Malpractice Insurance Coverage

Most current policies are "claims made." In other words, you are covered in every annual policy period only for those claims that are actually filed (or sometimes, for those you notified the insurance company might arise in the future). If you have been self-employed or part of a partnership, purchase a "tail" policy (known as an "extended reporting form endorsement"). This policy will protect you against all errors and omissions that occurred before you quit practicing but weren't filed until after you closed your doors. Depending upon what you buy, the coverage may last until your death, or for only a limited period. "Tail" policies can cost up to three times the last annual premium, but the investment is essential for peace of mind. On the other hand, if you were a law firm or agency employee, your actions will probably be covered by the continuing policy of your employer — unless they have also dissolved. In that case, make certain that they have purchased the appropriate "tail" coverage. Remember, that if you continue to do a "little bit" of law practicing on the side, you will be personally liable for any claims which arise after policy termination.

Health Insurance

If you will be unemployed or self-employed after you quit, or if the health plan at your new company legally excludes coverage for pre-existing conditions, be certain to investigate the requirements for continuation coverage under any prior group plan. Before you leave your current job, make certain that your employer sends you

the legally required notice of the right to continue coverage. (See discussion of COBRA benefits in Chapter 5, *Is There a Layoff in Your Future?*) Then, request continuation coverage in writing, following the company's procedures exactly.

Bar Association Membership

It took me eight years before I converted my Washington State bar membership to inactive status. I only took the step when I learned I could go inactive for three years without retaking the bar examination. By the end of that period, though, I was certain I would never practice law again, and I chose to remain inactive. My reluctance to give up an active license is not at all unusual among former practicing attorneys. Most continue to maintain an active license in at least one jurisdiction. Some remain active in one state and convert to inactive membership elsewhere. Others choose to switch to an inactive membership (especially in states like California, where annual dues are so high and you can reactivate without retaking the bar examination). If you do choose inactive status, make certain that you know what is required to become active again should you ever want or need to use your license.

Keeping in Touch

Don't slam the door behind you if you do leave the law.

You may be thinking "good riddance" now. But after you get some emotional distance, you may come to appreciate the people you knew and the support you received. Your legal education and experience served you well enough to get you where you are now. It will continue to serve you in the future if you respect the commitment of all your former colleagues, and you keep in touch with those you knew best. Who knows? There may come a day when you need their advice — or they need yours!

CHAPTER 7

PROFESSIONAL CAREER ASSISTANCE

Where to Turn If You Need More Help

By Carol Kanarek

"Changing careers may be the toughest work you ever do."

—anon

■ ■ ■

For many readers, the information and guidance provided in this book will be sufficient to serve as a template for a self-guided career change. Others, however, may feel the need to consult with a professional career change agent for more hands-on assistance with the transition process.

Many lawyers have serious misconceptions about the roles that various third parties — including legal search firms, career counselors, outplacement consultants, and career coaches — can play in the career planning and job-search process. Before you hand over your résumé or write a check to someone, read on for some guidance in determining whether or not one of more of these third parties can provide the assistance you need.

> Each of us must take on the quest of finding work we care about.

Legal Search Firms

Most lawyers know that legal search firms (or "headhunters") exist, yet few understand that they are not the primary means by which lawyers find new jobs. Although there are hundreds of legal headhunters in the United States, the reality is that these firms provide access to only a tiny percentage of jobs for lawyers, and — of particular significance to many readers of this book — they are almost always used to find "square pegs for square holes". Search firms represent the employer, and not the candidate; the employer pays a hefty fee if the search firm finds a lawyer to fit the employer's specific needs. Consequently, if you are seeking a non-legal position or wish to change to a new area of practice, a legal search firm will rarely be of help.

Non-legal search firms in other business sectors that interest you may provide information about the overall availability of jobs in those sectors, as well as insight regarding the skills and experience employers in that sector are seeking. As a general rule, however, they will not be able to assist you in finding your first position in a non-legal field.

Legal search firms are used only by those law firms and companies that are seeking lawyers with very specific expertise whom they cannot easily recruit through advertising, word of mouth, law school career services offices, and unsolicited résumés. Because there is no shortage of lawyers to fill most jobs, the vast majority of employers of lawyers — including most small law firms, many corporations, and virtually all governmental agencies, academic institutions, and nonprofit organizations — do not use search firms. The reason for this is simple: it is very expensive to hire lawyers this way. Most search firms work on a contingency basis, and charge employers a fee ranging from 20 to 30 percent of the initial annual compensation of any lawyer placed with that employer. The employers most likely to use legal search firms are law firms and corporations who require lawyers with sophisticated commercial expertise and/or experience representing corporations or financial institutions in such matters as mergers and acquisitions, corporate or project finance, commercial real estate, securities and other corporate or banking regulatory matters, complex commercial litigation, tax, ERISA and bankruptcy. Most legal employers which represent individuals or small businesses do not use legal search firms, yet those constitute the vast majority of employers of lawyers in the United States.

There are also geographic limitations. Most legal employers in suburban and rural areas do not use search firms. States with significant numbers of legal employers that use search firms include California, Connecticut, the District of Columbia, Florida, Georgia, Illinois, Maryland, Massachusetts, Michigan, New Jersey, New York, North Carolina, Ohio, Pennsylvania, Tennessee and Texas. If you are seeking to relocate to another geographic area, you will generally get the best results by working with a search firm in the state or region in which you wish to practice.

The ideal candidate for most legal search firms is a lawyer with experience representing large corporations or financial institutions, who is looking for a position practicing law with a firm which represents similar clients, or with a corporation or financial institution. Many legal search firms only have positions with large law firms (or branch offices or small firm "spin-offs" of large law firms), as large law firms constitute the vast majority of employers who use search firms. Law firm experience is generally preferred, although many large corporations that use search firms request candidates who have experience in both a large law firm and a corporation, and some law firms will accept candidates through search firms who have specialized governmental experience (e.g. the SEC or a U.S. Attorneys office).

The vast majority of jobs listed by corporations with search firms require general corporate, transactional or regulatory — as opposed to litigation — experience, with the exception of litigation-intensive companies, which may list positions with search firms for litigators with insurance, securities, employment or products liability experience. Many employers who list jobs with search firms specify that candidates must have graduated from "national" law schools, and/or must have high law school grade point averages. Legal search firms do not establish these parameters; employers do.

So what does this mean to you?

- ▶ If you have tried unsuccessfully to find a position through a legal search firm, you are not alone. At least 90 percent of all lawyers are similarly situated.
- ▶ You should have a fairly clear idea of what you are looking for before you make an appointment to meet with a legal search firm. Search firms are not career counselors, and you should not forget that the only way in which they make money is by finding suitable lawyers to meet the specific needs of their employer clients.

Many national and local legal periodicals publish annual lists of search firms. The American Lawyer Directory of Legal Search Firms is the largest national directory of legal headhunters. It is published each January as a supplemental pull-out to the American Lawyer Magazine.

Career Counselors

Career counselors have very little in common with legal search firms, yet many lawyers mistakenly believe they do the same things. The most fundamental difference between them is that a career counselor's objective is to help you make sound career decisions and present yourself to the job market, while legal search firms are exclusively focused on finding lawyers to fill their employer clients' job orders. The primary role of a career counselor is to guide you through the process of career planning — including self-assessment and market assessment — with the goal of helping you to identify career options that will be both satisfying and realistic. A career counselor also can assist in the job-search process by providing guidance in résumé and cover letter writing, networking strategies, and interviewing techniques.

> You can do what is safe, or take a risk by moving toward what thrills you.

When you work with a career counselor, you are the client and you pay the fee. Consequently, you should perform the "due diligence" necessary to satisfy yourself that the counselor's approach is compatible with your particular needs and objectives. Career counselors are not employment agencies, so be wary of any counseling service that lures you in with vague promises of "high-level contacts", and then charges a large fee for what is essentially a mass-mailing service. Some lawyers only want or need assistance with the nuts and bolts of the job change process: résumé preparation, cover letter writing and/or interview skills. If this is the case for you, look for a career counselor who will bill you by the hour or by the task.

Many career counselors place a strong emphasis on interests, skills, and values clarification. These counselors may use one or more of a variety of tools, including the Myers-Briggs Type Indicator, the Strong Interest Inventory, and various other self-assessment exercises. The interpretation of these exercises may help you to determine what careers and work settings are most likely to give you satisfaction. Counselors who are strongly oriented towards this aspect of the career-planning process may be particularly appropriate for lawyers who are unhappy in the practice of law, but unsure about where to turn next. Here's how they can help you:

▶ A career counselor can guide you through the process of market analysis, the goal of which is to gather as much specific information as possible about the jobs or careers that you have identified as being potentially of interest to you so that you can decide whether and how to pursue them.

▶ A career counselor can show you strategies for networking and obtaining informational interviews to help you to answer critical questions about market demand, salary, opportunity for advancement, and skills or educational requirements for particular jobs or careers. This is the "real-world" half of the career-planning equation, and is it very important. Without it, you might formulate a career objective that is theoretically satisfying, but also totally unrealistic, since most standardized tests do not take into account such factors as age, minimum income requirements, or job availability. Once you have completed the career planning process (self-analysis plus market analysis), you might proceed directly to the job-search process.

► A career counselor can provide advice on the most effective ways to present yourself to potential employers. For this phase, it can be particularly useful to work with a career counselor who has extensive experience with lawyers (for recommendations, go to **www.DecisionBooks.com**). A counselor who has a strong understanding of the legal profession can help you to "functionalize your credentials" in order to emphasize those aspects of your training and experience that are relevant to the new job you are seeking. He or she also can provide assistance with respect to many other matters, including difficult questions in interviews, salary negotiations, and reference checks.

Your local bar association or law school career services office can help you to identify career counselors in your geographic area who may be most helpful to you. In addition, many universities with counselor training programs offer career testing and post-testing follow-up to members of the public at prices substantially below those charged by most counselors in private practice.

Outplacement Consultants

Outplacement assistance is now routinely provided by many law firms and corporate legal departments, particularly when lawyers are laid off for economic reasons. An outplacement consultant performs essentially the same functions as a career counselor, although time constraints often dictate that the focus be on rapidly securing new employment that will not be inconsistent with the lawyer's long-term goals. The fee for the outplacement counseling is paid by the employer who is asking the lawyer to find new employment. Many legal employers only provide such assistance upon request. If you are fired and believe that outplacement might be helpful to you, be sure to ask your employer if it is available. Some employers may not be willing to pay the large fees typically charged for office space and secretarial services by the large outplacement firms, but might agree to pay for a specified number of hours of career counseling.

The outplacement consultant is not involved in establishing the terms of the lawyer's severance, and conversations between the lawyer and the consultant should be strictly confidential. In some instances the lawyer may wish to have the outplacement consultant discuss a particular issue with his or her employer, but such conversations should take place only at the lawyer's request. Assistance provided by an outplacement consultant typically covers a range of areas:

- ► Market analysis.
- ► A network of contacts.
- ► A data bases of employers and job openings.
- ► Assistance in drafting résumés and cover letters.
- ► Interviewing strategies.
- ► Help in negotiating terms of employment.

Some of the larger outplacement firms also offer group sessions in which current clients can exchange ideas with one another regarding professional networking and job-search strategies. Be wary, however, of following approaches or using form letters provided by a "one-size-fits-all" outplacement firm. If you are looking for a new legal position, make sure that the outplacement consultant has specific experience working with lawyers. This is important for both substantive and stylistic reasons. You will need someone who can assist you in describing your experience — both on your résumé and interviews — in ways that will be meaningful and attractive to other lawyers, and who can help you to draft a résumé that will be free of the jargon that most legal employers find annoying.

The best outplacement consultant is one who has direct knowledge of the specifics of the job market that is relevant to you. For example, a consultant who understands the mind-set of legal employers can help lawyers draft customized cover letters that demonstrate an awareness of the substantive needs and bottom-line concerns of the law firms or companies with which the lawyer is seeking employment. Such a consultant also can provide guidelines to senior associates and partners for the preparation of detailed experience summaries and practice development plans — both of which are increasingly essential elements of a successful search for legal employment.

A lawyer who is under time pressure to leave his or her current job is particularly vulnerable to pressure to accept a position that may not be appropriate. Unlike a legal search firm, the outplacement consultant (who is generally paid a fixed fee by the current employer) does not have a financial stake in the lawyer's decision to accept or reject a particular job offer. Consequently, he or she can help you to evaluate your options, and provide guidelines for negotiating the terms of your new employment.

Directors of legal personnel of large law firms and human resource directors of corporate legal departments can provide you with the names of local outplacement consultants who work with lawyers. In addition, many career counselors will provide outplacement services on an hourly or monthly basis.

Career Coaches

Career coaching is a relatively new phenomenon — related to career counseling, but with more of a focus on specific problem-solving as a catalyst for career growth or change. The ideal career coach is the functional equivalent of a mentor; he or she may serve as a guide, teacher, sounding board, or troubleshooter. A coach provides feedback, monitors performance and experience, provides advice about career decisions and workplace dilemmas, and generally encourages professional development. You may wish to consult a career coach if you feel "stuck" in a job that has been generally satisfying, if you are encountering political barriers in your workplace, or if you have received negative feedback regarding your relationships with co-workers or clients. Working with a coach for a few months may help you to decide whether dissatisfaction you are feeling can be cured by taking a new approach to your current work environment, or whether a more fundamental job or career change is needed.

Many career coaches are also career counselors or licensed clinical social workers or psychologists. However, the coaching profession is not licensed, so anyone may call him or herself a coach. Here are some suggestions about how to choose a career coach:

► Inquire about a coach's specific credentials and experience in order to determine whether or not he or she will be attuned to your specific situation and needs. (Note: for lawyers, the appropriate coaches will most likely have graduate degrees — an MA or Ph.D., though not necessarily a JD).

▶ Because you will be seeking advice on important issues that arise on the job, it is critical that your advisor be well-versed on the written and unwritten rules of your particular workplace culture, and that he or she has a strong knowledge of the demands and requirements of a professional service career.

▶ If you are depressed, worried about substance abuse, or facing personal issues that are exacerbating your professional problems, you may wish to choose a coach who is also a licensed psychotherapist. In most parts of the country there are coaches who work exclusively with lawyers, and many coaches will provide services by telephone or email to clients who are geographically remote from them.

Career coaches usually charge by the hour, and many are willing to be flexible in terms of availability to deal with critical situations as they arise. As is the case with psychotherapists, some coaches have a long-term orientation, while others are more comfortable with a short- term, goal-oriented approach. Be sure to discuss your needs and desires with the coach at the outset of the relationship, so that you can determine what time frame and approach will work best for you.

Coaching sessions are generally highly interactive, with the client generally summarizing events that have occurred since the previous session, and then requesting advice or assistance in resolving current dissatisfactions or conflicts. Unlike a mentor from within your own workplace, a coach has no connection with — or obligation to — your employer. Consequently, he or she is someone with whom you can speak freely, without fear of personal or professional repercussions. If you have career goals that are inconsistent with your employer's desires for you, a coach is usually a better and safer confidante than someone from your current place of employment.

Many career counselors and psychotherapists provide coaching services directly, or can recommend colleagues who have career coaching skills. In addition, many bar associations and law school counseling or career services offices can provide you with information on how to find a career coach.

Carol Kanarek, JD/MA/MSW — Ms. Kanarek is a former corporate lawyer, and is currently a clinical social worker who for the past 20 years has provided outplacement, career counseling and career coaching services to lawyers in New York City. Contact — ckanarek@aol.com.

Epilogue
A Glass Half-Full

By Kathy Morris, JD

" ... The very first condition of lasting happiness is that a life should be full of purpose, aiming at something outside itself."

—*Hugo L. Black, Justice of the Supreme Court*

■ ■ ■

The pursuit of happiness is an inalienable right.

And for us lawyers, it is also a career goal of the highest order. But don't take my word for it.

In his book, *Authentic Happiness*, Psychologist Martin E.P. Seligman says the law is one of America's most highly paid professions, but not composed of very happy human beings. Why? He says the problem is that lawyers must find ways to have more personal control over their work ... a better sense of the big picture ... and to regularly engage their enthusiasm and originality. Sociologist Frederick Hertzberg goes further. He says occupational satisfaction includes achievement, recognition, enjoyment of the work itself, responsibility, advancement, and opportunity for growth. What does this tell us? That each of us must take on the quest of finding work that we care about, and caring about the way we work.

> Each of us must take on the quest of finding work we care about.

Over the years, I've worked with and counseled many lawyers. I believe that in order to see our glass as half-full we need to assess who we are, and identify our native talents and personality preferences. Only from there can we begin assessing how suited we are to our current position. The challenge is to seek an environment

261

that plays to our strengths and preferences, and to be adaptive as we progress in our career.

I know some young lawyers with very good people skills but who are chafing at all the solitary time they spend in the library. And I know other lawyers who love all the legal analysis, the research and writing, but hate to become supervisors and rain-makers. There are litigators who hate the contentiousness and competition of the courtroom; there are others frustrated at the document-intensive, time-sensitive pre-trial process. No practice area comes in one-size fits all, and all aspects of any one role do not satisfy individual attorneys equally.

So, how do we know when you're happy? You'll know you're in the right line of work, and at the right place for you when ...

- ▶ You approach your work with enthusiasm and high energy, not anger, boredom or lethargy.
- ▶ You tend to initiate work rather than avoid it.
- ▶ You want to lead or join in activities rather than complain about them or withdraw from them.
- ▶ You feel motivated, when faced with a new project, to learn rather than to procrastinate.
- ▶ You feel proud of your accomplishment, rather than simply relieved that you're done, when you've finished a task.

In my experience, people truly engaged in careers they care about are highly involved with their work and their clients, and have integrated personal and professional concerns. They have been innovative in staking their claim to contentment. And they make career moves not by some linear approach, but by a commitment to embrace change and growth, whether that means changing jobs or the way they adapt as their job changes.

I know the difficulty of examining your job, your profession, at the same time you've got your day-to-day assignments, your monthly billing requirements, and your annual performance challenges. Author Deborah Arron's own evolution from a practicing lawyer to an author and career counselor began with a sabbatical. Have you considered that possibility? If you're junior or new to your job, it may not be a possibility right away, but it is something everyone should consider as you move along your career path. In the book, *Rest Assured, The Sabbatical Solution for Lawyers*, author Lori Simon Gordon writes about her own life-changing decision to take a sabbatical from a big firm. Says Ms. Gordon, "The time I took had a profound effect on my career, my non-professional endeavors, my friendships, and my sense of myself in the world."

Don't make the mistake of keeping up with the Jones'. No matter what you have or what you do, there will always be someone with more. Just focus on living and doing what you enjoy ... doing it well ... and feeling your sense of success and satisfaction. One of the simplest pieces of career advice I ever heard was this: "Find out what you like doing best, and get someone to pay you for doing it."

That's how you keep the glass half-full.

Isn't that worth the quest?

Kathy Morris, Esq. — *Ms. Morris, a former trial lawyer and director of law school placement and counseling, has authored three ABA books, and is the founder of the ABA's Career Resource Center. She has her own Chicago-based career counseling firm for lawyers, and has provided outplacement assistance for lawyers since 1988. Contact — www.UnderAdvisement.com.*

THE 7

LAWYER PROFILES:

TYPES, MOTIVATIONS,

CHALLENGES & CAREER OPTIONS

By Angelique Electra, JD/MBA

In recent years, numerous publications, from the *ABA Journal* to the *Wall Street Journal,* have written about lawyer dissatisfaction. These were never just stories to me because — as both a lawyer and career consultant — I knew first-hand how many practitioners were angry, frustrated, confused, discontent ... and trapped.

There are many well-established diagnostic tools for career assessment, and most of them focus on personality and behavioral typing. In my own consulting work, however, I didn't feel the existing tools could assist my lawyer clients in understanding their inner "ache" or their desire for more meaning or career-fulfillment. For that reason, I developed a self-assessment process and instrument called, The *JurisDoctor Profiles™.* It describes what I believe are seven distinct lawyer motivational types, and it explains what professional options exist for practicing or aspiring lawyers to optimize their natural gifts and to achieve more fulfillment. Look closely at the pages that follow. I'm sure you'll find yourself in one or more of the seven categories:

- ▶ *The Warrior/Libertarian* — Strong and enduring. An ability to demonstrate fortitude, and to apply power and leadership purposefully and dynamically to reach goals.
- ▶ *The Counselor/Teacher* — Attracting, empowering, and wise. An ability to teach, empower, mentor, and understand others with great perception; an intuitive and synthesizing mind.
- ▶ *The Rainmaker/Innovator* — Promoting, versatile, creative, mentally astute. An ability to act, enroll others with a high degree of creative, strategic ideas.
- ▶ *The Negotiator/Diplomat* — Imaginative and adept at promoting rapport and agreement. An ability to move people toward agreement and create alliances.
- ▶ *The Problem Solver/Expert* — Precise with a passion for progressive knowledge; an

ability to arrive at solutions through focused thinking and analytical experimentation.
- ▶ *The Activist/Moralist* — Steadfastly and ardently focused. An ability to devote self to a great purpose or cause, and live and work according to your highest ideals, beliefs, and vision.
- ▶ *The Manager/Reformer* — Organized and skillful. An ability to demonstrate a high degree of organizational and managerial prowess by means of skillful coordination, practical efficiency and diplomacy.

THE WARRIOR/LIBERTARIAN

They enjoy being a leader or "boss" — in the firm, in an organization, or within the family. They exude a sense of power, and the ability to empower others. They are goal-oriented, purposeful and single-minded with respect to attaining their objectives. They are task-oriented, and do not focus on the quality of interaction with others toward an end. Others may find their communication style to be forceful, direct, and sometimes very blunt. Professional theme — "*I control.*"

Characteristics — Independent, powerful, aggressive, willful, dominating, self-confident, decisive, controlling, confrontational, competitive, relentless, courageous, stoic, able to detach emotionally.

Challenges — Egotism, excessive pride, arrogance, insensitivity, impatience, stubbornness, obsession to "look good", and to avoid being controlled or dominated.

Core motivation — To be self-reliant, controlling, and to avoid weakness and submission to others.

Vocational qualities — They have the disciplined ability to control, assert, direct, lead, inspire a following, and to achieve any desired goals regardless of obstacles. They have the strength and power to unravel oppressive systems and initiate democratic solutions.

Career Options

General practice lawyer
Criminal lawyer
Personal injury lawyer
Plaintiff's class action lawyer
Trial lawyer
Prosecutor
Anti-trust litigator
IP litigator
Takeover/mergers and acquisitions litigator
Environmental litigator
Judge
Politician
First Amendment lawyer
Defamation lawyer
IP infringement lawyer
Appellate specialist
Trial strategist
Tax litigator (against IRS)
General counsel
Independent general counsel
Chief or supervising public defender
Chief legal counsel for state ethics board
Collector
Contract (freelance) lawyer
Deputy public defender
Deputy district/prosecuting attorney
Deputy US attorney
Deputy attorney general
Disciplinary proceedings prosecutor for bar association
District/prosecuting attorney
Ethics defense counsel
Federal public defender
Judge Advocate General (any military branch, active or reserve)
Labor union counsel
Litigation counsel
Partner in start-up firm
Pro bono director for law firm

Solo practitioner
Sports lawyer in private practice
State attorney general
Supervising attorney
US Attorney
US counsel for foreign companies/investors

THE COUNSELOR/TEACHER

Their orientation in life is to help and support others. They especially like to teach, inform, enlighten, heal and develop others. They are expressing their highest values when they are helping others in difficulty or contributing to human welfare. They have a strong drive to learn and understand the underlying nature of people and of life itself. Obtaining knowledge supports their need to give and receive wisdom. Professional theme — "*I understand.*"

Characteristics — Friendly, helpful, patient, perceptive, intuitive, empathetic, caring, trustworthy, tolerant, honest, reassuring, connecting, facilitating, tactful, collaborative, enthusiastic, sociable, generous.

Challenges — Too accommodating, self-devaluing, overly sensitive, inability to say "no", lacks objectivity, too emotional, negatively reactive to being underappreciated.

Core motivation — To be loved and appreciated, to express positive feelings toward others.

Vocational qualities — They exercise their personal magnetism and calm wisdom by being warm, friendly, kind and likeable. They're able to use well-developed intuitive understanding to show concern for others.

Career Options

Appellate specialist
CLE instructor
Consulting lawyer:
    associate training
    client relations

communications regarding juries, clients &
employee selection
jury selection
law firm management
Counsel to company president
Domestic affairs lawyer
EEOC specialist
Employment lawyer within company
Estate planning lawyer
Family law lawyer
Financial & tax planner
Geriatric/elder law lawyer
Guardianship lawyer
Involuntary commitment lawyer
Law or university professor
Lawyer for family business
Lawyer for start-up business
Lawyer representing aggrieved employees
Lawyer-agent for sports/entertainment figure
Nonprofit executive director
Plaintiff's class action lawyer
Probate lawyer
Public defender
Solo practitioner
Solo practice with direct client contact
Trust and estates lawyer

THE RAINMAKER/INNOVATOR

They have a quick, agile mind and a keen, powerful intellect. They are self-reliant and attract others with their ingenuity. Their ideas, while formulated from abstract concepts in many cases, are designed to lead to practical and constructive "real world" applicability. They are the consummate "orchestra leader", combining and directing the elements of new projects until their vision is realized. Unlike the Warrior/Libertarian, the Rainmaker/Innovator is not motivated by control or power. Professional theme — "*I create.*"

Characteristics — Skillful communicator, mentally agile, highly adaptable, open-minded, ability to conceptualize and concretize, executive aptitudes, capacity to be rigorously analytical, good sense of financial issues/matters, strategic thinker.

Challenges — Intellectual pride, overly critical, absent-minded, manipulating, calculating, opportunistic, hyperactive, restless, scattered.

Core motivation — To be affirmed, admired and validated by others; to create an attractive. image of themselves and to avoid failure.

Vocational qualities — They are able to successfully adapt themselves to intellectual or circumstantial challenges, and use their creative abilities to male all the necessary plans and arrangements for successful outcomes.

Career Options

Client development partner
Consulting lawyer:
    increasing law firm profitability
    interpersonal communication
    jury selection
    law firm management
    marketing and promotion
    marketing consulting
    mergers and acquisition
    negotiation skills
    strategic planning
Corporate partner in law firm
Counsel to venture capital firm
Entertainment lawyer
In-house counsel, arts organization
In-house counsel for multinational company
Inside/outside counsel for institutional investor
International transactions lawyer
IP lawyer
Law firm practice:
antitrust, appellate, business organizations,
    commercial finance, communications,
    computing, corporate transactions,
    entertainment, environmental, IP,
    international finance, international, lobbying,
    mergers/acquisitions, patent, real estate,
    small business formation, sports, technology
    licensing, venture capital.

Licensing rights lawyer
Politician
Solo practitioner
Speaker/presenter
Staff counsel, investment bank
US counsel for foreign companies/investors
Venture capitalist

THE NEGOTIATOR/DIPLOMAT

They have a creative, expressive and energetic spirit, and are perceived as gifted, charming and captivating. They're optimistic, imaginative, verbal, stimulating and open-minded, and seek self-actualization and self-fulfillment. While they have a need to bring others together to achieve some end, they are loners by nature. Professional theme — "I harmonize."

Characteristics — Peacemaker, tenacious facility to reconcile opposite forces and bring harmony out of conflict, creative, highly intuitive, spontaneous, flexible.

Challenges — Worry, moody, lack of composure, temperamental, unpredictable, overeager, indecisive, impatient, not careful with details.

Core motivation — To live in unit and harmony with others; to maintain peace, avoid conflict.

Vocational qualities — An innate ability to see and experience both sides of any issue or conflict. An eye for harmony, color, beauty. A gentility, spontaneity and eloquent self-expression that serves them well in interpersonal activities.

Career Options
Bankruptcy/creditors' representative
Commercial real estate lawyer
Consulting lawyer:
  building client relationships
  communication with clients, juries
  interpersonal communications
  negotiation skills

jury selection
professional development
marketing and promotion
marketing coaching
wardrobe/personal appearance for jury
  presentations
writing
Corporate transaction lawyer
Foreign affairs officer
In-house counsel for arts organization
Investment banking lawyer
Labor negotiator
Law firm practice:
ADR, business organizations, communications,
  entertainment, environmental, franchising,
  governmental relations/lobbying, intellectual
  property transactions, matrimonial, mergers
  & acquisitions, real estate, small business
  formation, sports, venture capital.
Lawyer for multi-media or the Internet
Lawyer for software/technology licensing
Lawyer for entrepreneurs, start-ups, new IPOs
Mediator/ADR professional
Sports lawyer/agent for media/entertainment
  figure
Staff lawyer, parent company

THE PROBLEM SOLVER/EXPERT

They like to observe, learn, experiment, investigate, analyze, evaluate, and solve problems. They like to explore patterns, categories and relationships from a scientific or philosophical perspective. Facts are the primary language of their lives; accuracy and comprehensiveness their hallmarks. In business, their goal is to investigate their clients' needs, gather and analyze as much as possible, research the facts, and bring back a perfect, customized solution. Professional theme — "I know."

Characteristics — They have the capacity to absorb, analyze, and manipulate large amounts of information and data. They have highly developed powers of logic, analysis

270

and precision in thought and action.

Challenges — Excessively objective, overly technical, skeptical, hardheaded, harshly critical, socially awkward.

Core motivation — To know and understand everything with certainty; to avoid ignorance and not having the answer or looking foolish.

Vocational qualities — A tenacious ability to attack problems until solved, and apply precision and accuracy to all they do. They tend to have a recognized command of the facts in some area of specialized study or application. They prefer handling data over people.

Career Options

Accounting firm lawyer
Consulting lawyer
    automation
    business valuation expert
    case management systems
    computing (training, systems purchase)
    expert witness on business and real estate
    failure, partnership disputes, insurance
    coverage, bad faith and underwriting issues
    law firm systems
    marketing research
    network design
    pension and profit-sharing programs
    pricing legal services
Immigration lawyer
Insurance defense
Insurance/risk management lawyer
Law firm or in-house lawyer
    Antitrust, banking, bankruptcy, biomedical
    issues, corporate tax, IP, trusts and estates,
    environmental, regulatory, ERISA, employment,
    administrative, mergers and acquisitions
    multimedia/telecommunications, technology,
    finance, probate, tax, workers comp.
Legal research and writing specialist
Medical malpractice lawyer
Tax litigator (against the IRS)
Tax lawyer for individuals

THE ACTIVIST/MORALIST

Of all the types, the Activist/Moralist is most defined by idealism, passion and enthusiasm.

They have a sincerity, enthusiasm and optimism which inspires and captivates others. They rely on inner guidance to settle their dilemmas in life. Their faith is critical to their sense of well-being. Professional theme — "*I believe.*"

Characteristics — Idealistic, devoted, single-minded, earnest, sincere, humble, persistent, able to arouse/inspire/persuade, optimistic, relentless, selfless, altruistic, die-hard, forceful, hardworking, tireless.

Challenges — Overbearing, intolerant of others' ideas, rigid, given to unreasoned devotion, blind faith, fanaticism, emotionalism, over-excitable, gullible, self-abasing, impractical.

Core motivation — To make a difference and validate oneself (and avoid one's life as insignificant or lacking in purpose).

Vocational Qualities — When they have a goal or vision, they exude the enthusiasm, idealistic commitment and singlemindedness to make it a reality. Tireless and unrelenting, they tend to honor and pursue their object with fervor and passion.

Career options

Anti-discrimination lawyer
Bar association professionalism counsel
Bar association disciplinary counsel
Child advocacy lawyer
Civil rights lawyer
Constitutional lawyer
Defamation lawyer
Expert witness on legal ethics or lawyer standard
    of care
Foreign adoption lawyer
Foundation or nonprofit lawyer
Geriatric/elder law lawyer
Immigration lawyer
Judge
Law or university professor

Legal columnist/commentator
Legislator
Lobbyist
Nonprofit executive director or counsel
Politician
Public defender prosecutor
Public interest lawyer

MANAGER/REFORMER

They enjoy bringing order out of chaos, and are best at organizing information, data and task. They are precise, disciplined, dependable and accurate in their approach to tasks. They have a follow-through capacity essential in organizational life, and are comfortable with the operation and necessity of hierarchy, structure and rules. They value productivity, economic success and financial security for themselves and those they serve. Professional theme — "*I orchestrate.*"

Characteristics — Organizer, self-reliant, accurate, moral, ethical, risk-averse, formal, structured, productive, loyal, follower, appreciates structure, routine, rules and predictability.
Challenges — Over-reliance on authority, routines and habits; overly conforming, perfectionism, intolerance, prideful, analysis paralysis, skeptical, slow to trust.
Core motivation — To be safe and secure.
Vocational qualities — A natural ability to organize people and processes in right relationship to one another, and manage it all toward the accomplishment of defined goals. A precision and commitment to quality resulting in a strong work ethic.

Career options
Advertising-compliance lawyer
Appellate lawyer
Banking lawyer
Contract (freelance) lawyer
Consulting lawyer

computing (training, systems purchase)
document assembly systems
expert witness on legal ethics
improving quality/cost-effectiveness of inside counsel
increasing law firm profitability
law firm management
law firm systems
outsourcing legal services
network design
pension and profit-sharing programs
time management
trial management
Corporate staff lawyer
Corporate compliance officer
General counsel of public company
General counsel for bar association
Government agency lawyer
In-house counsel for accounting firm
Insurance defense
Insurance company lawyer
Law firm practice:
    administrative
    banking
    bankruptcy
    general corporate
    complex civil litigation
    disciplinary action by licensing boards
    employee benefits
    employment
    employment relations
    public contracts
    due diligence specialist
Legal assistant or paralegal
Legal research and writing specialist
Legislator
Litigation management
Managing partner
Pro bono director for law firm
Regulatory lawyer
Researcher
Risk management specialist
Securities lawyer
Staff lawyer for foundations/nonprofits

THE LAWYER TYPES

Here's a simple sort mechanism to help students identify an initial career direction, and lawyers evaluate how well suited they are to the practice of law. Begin by answering these three simple questions:

1. *Are you more drawn to issues involving people and human behavior, or to financial, technical, scientific or business matters?*

2. *Are you more excited by solving problems or analyzing issues?* "Problem solvers" prefer the practical; "analyzers" the theoretical. "Problem solvers" like to focus on concrete issues with a good chance of closure. "Analyzers" prefer to explore complex issues; they often don't care if they find an absolute answer or conclusion as long as they've evaluated the situation thoroughly and correctly.

3. *Do you prefer to communicate and investigate orally or through the written word?* This is usually the hardest to answer, since most who choose law school enjoy communicating and are proficient both orally and in writing. Ask yourself which comes more easily to you. As a law student, thriving in the library or when you prepare class notes is a good clue that you tend to prefer writing. Enjoying your study group experiences or loving moot court and clinical education classes means you're happier when you're talking. In practice, if you most enjoy tasks like meeting with clients, talking on the telephone, attending depositions and appearing in court, you probably prefer oral communication and investigation. If instead, you'd rather be researching and writing briefs, composing letters and settlement proposals, and communicating by e-mail, you'd prefer written communication. You might also ask yourself whether your best ideas and insights emerge when you're speaking or when you're writing, or whether you like to investigate by talking to people or by using the library and the Internet. Looking at it from the negative, which tasks are you facing when you procrastinate? Are they those done orally or in writing? You may not have a strong preference either way, but most of us lean to one side or the other.

Now that you've declared yourself, let's explore what each choice means.

People and human behavior v. financial, technical, scientific or business: Law is by its nature mostly a process of evaluating data and numbers, and exploring systems and ideas. In certain areas of law, the data and ideas spring directly from human behavior and the problems that are solved directly impact people rather than businesses, systems or processes. People-oriented areas of practice include criminal and juvenile law, domestic relations, guardianship, elder law, adoption, employment law, professional liability or license revocation, immigration, and personal injury. Other areas of law typically involve some people contact, but the issues themselves are more removed from human foibles. Those areas include corporate and international transactions, commercial litigation, insurance coverage, real estate, construction, employee benefits work and creditor representation in bankruptcy. A few areas, like consumer bankruptcy and estate planning, are hybrids, but legal work still involves more financial and technical analysis than people understanding.

Solving v. analyzing: The goal in law is eventually to achieve closure, usually by proving a point or winning. Working to create agreement and therefore solve the problem typically comes after a protracted process of analysis and posturing. This is especially true with complex litigation—class actions, antitrust, products liability, medical malpractice, employment claims, commercial transactions, construction disputes—and transactions involving significant sums of money. Lawyers who like to solve problems more than analyze them should focus on matters requiring faster turnaround and involving smaller amounts of money—consumer disputes, simple estate planning, adoption, employment law advising, residential real estate, and consumer bankruptcy as examples.

Speaking and investigating v. writing and researching: At the beginning of your legal career, you won't have much opportunity to communicate orally unless you choose a general practice, criminal or quasi-criminal advocacy, or litigation in a law firm that handles small matters. For the most part, you'll be learning the ropes by spending considerable time researching and writing briefs and memoranda and drafting pleadings and contracts. Later in your career, especially if it's up to you to maintain client relationships, you'll find it hard to concentrate on research and writing unless you develop a career in appellate work, insurance coverage, intellectual property, employee benefits or complex business transactions.

Overall, you'll find much to commend itself in the practice of law if you prefer to analyze problems rather than solve them, written communication, and if you build your practice in a subject matter that reflects your preference as to focus (i.e. people issues v. technical matters). Those who like to solve problems, to communicate orally and to deal with people issues will have be very selective in developing their legal careers. First and foremost, target one of the practice areas where you'll be working with a variety of individuals on short-term projects: general practice, domestic relations, criminal prosecution and defense, adoption, immigration, elder law including simple estate planning, and employment law advising as examples. If those areas of practice hold no appeal to you, look outside the conventional practice of law to positions in bar association or law school administration, training, customer service (perhaps for a legal publisher), public relations, human resources, information and referral, or investigative functions.

Angelique Electra, JD/MBA — *Angelique Electra is the principal of The JurisDoctor™, a national career development and coaching firm serving law students, JDs and other members of the legal profession. She coaches and facilitates individuals and groups to realize their career and professional goals by activating a dynamically empowered life purpose and vision. A seasoned business professional and attorney, she also continues to enjoy a long-term corporate practice supporting business development initiatives of Fortune 500 companies. Ms. Electra earned her law degree from Yale Law School and her Masters in Business Administration from the Yale School of Organization & Management. For more information about The JurisDoctor™ and The JurisDoctor Profiles™, please visit www.TheJurisDoctor.com or www.TheJurisDr.com.*

ONLINE JOB-SEARCH

RESOURCES

By Jill Eckert, JD

LAWYER-SPECIFIC WEB SITES

eAttorney (www.eAttorney.com) — Online recruiting site focusing on lawyer and law student positions.

EmplawyerNet (www.emplawyernet.com) — Monthly fee for job seekers.

FindLaw Career Center (www.careers.findlaw.com) — Post your résumé, peruse employer listings, visit the job bank, and discuss the market with others.

Hieros Gamos Legal Employment Classifieds (www.hg.org/employment.html) — A job bank with career links.

LawJobs (www.lawjobs.com) — See their career area.

LawMatch (www.lawmatch.com) — Searchable résumé bank for lawyers and others in the legal field.

Law school career services/placement offices (www.hg.org/schools.html) - The law school Web sites usually offer job hunt suggestions and sometimes post job announcements. Many also distribute employment announcements and information on networking opportunities by email or mail.

Legal Employment Search Site (www.legalemploy.com) — Links to legal, law school, and general career sites.

Legalstaff.com (www.legalstaff.com) — Offers a job bank and job seeker resources and articles.

National & Federal Legal Employment Report (www.attorneyjobs.com) — A monthly listing of available attorney, court, and law-related professional positions organized by openings within the federal government in Washington, DC, and the rest of the country and other positions in and outside of Washington, DC. Available through Federal Reports, Inc.

State and Local Bar Association Online Career Resources (www.abanet.org/careercounsel/statebar.html) — The directory offers a state-by-state listing of local bar associations hosting online career information.

WashLaw WEB (www.washlaw.edu/postlaw/postlaw.htm) — Career services overview, bar preparation, employment opportunities and links to other career planning centers for lawyers and law students.

GENERAL LEGAL CAREER RESOURCES

ABA Career Counsel (www.abanet.org/careercounsel) — The ABA's Career Resource Center maintains this Web site, which offers ABA-wide job-search and career enhancement resources for lawyers, students, and employers.

ABA Journal (www.abanet.org/journal) — The ABA's monthly magazine, in conjunction with its weekly eReport, contains articles of interest to a broad range of lawyers and law firm managers as well as some classified advertisements for law firm, corporate and law school positions.

BCG Attorney Search (www.bcgsearch.com) — National search consultants whose Web site offers lawyers helpful articles on the job-search process, including a detailed analysis, "How Attorneys Choose Law Firms."

The National Association for Law Placement Directory of Legal Employers (www.nalpdirectory.com) — This directory can now be searched or browsed online.

Law and Legal Information Directory (Gale Research; 13th edition, 2002) — Descriptions and contact information for law-related institutions, services and facilities including bar associations, court systems, law schools, legal periodicals, lawyer referral services, legal aid offices, public defender offices and more. Hardcover.

Law Info's Legal Career Center (www.jobs.lawinfo.com) — Not only can you read job postings or post your résumé, you can also search through the employer profiles and other career resources.

Legal Researcher's Desk Reference (www.infosourcespub.com) — This helpful book lists federal and state elected and appointed officials, attorney general offices, law library suppliers, law-related associations, law schools, legal periodicals and more. Paperback; 2002/3.

Martindale-Hubbell (www.martindale.com) — You can look up interviewing attorneys and information about potential employers with their Lawyer Locator.

National Association for Law Placement (www.nalp.org) — An organization of the career services offices of accredited law schools, as well as over 1,000 legal employers actively engaged in the recruitment and placement of lawyers.

National Law Journal (www.nlj.com) — A weekly newspaper that regularly covers trends in the legal profession, law firm mergers, dissolutions and other changes. Classified advertising section, mostly for positions being filled by headhunters and corporations.

Jill Eckert, JD/MBA — *Ms. Eckert is an attorney and legal career specialist at the ABA's Career Resource Center in Chicago. Ms. Eckert contributed to the Commission on Billable Hours report for the ABA, and co-authored* Direct Examination: A Workbook for Lawyer Career Satisfaction. *Contact — www.abanet.org/careercounsel.*

CAREER COUNSELING, TESTING & ONLINE SELF-ASSESSMENT

If you feel the need for additional resources to begin your career-change process, we recommend the following in the areas of career counseling, assessment testing, and the fast-growing number of ABA-sponsored Lawyer Assistance Programs that offer career assistance:

CAREER COUNSELING

The National Board for Certified Counselors (www.nbcc.org) — Offers a free state-by-state listing of certified career counselors. To receive NBCC certification, a career counselor must hold a Master's or Doctorate in counseling or a closely-related field. Their university course work must have included lifestyle and career development, tests and measurements, and a career counseling practicum or internship. They must also have at least three years professional career counseling experience, and must pass the NBCC's examination.

Law School — Check with the law school career services directors in your area for referrals to well-regarded career counselors or other programs for lawyers in transition. From time to time, the law schools also sponsor seminars and workshops for students, recent graduates and alumni.

DecisionBooks (www.DecisionBooks.com) — The publisher of this volume maintains a database of career counselors and coaches — all of whom specialize in the career issues of lawyers, and some of whom have JD's themselves. This region-by-region roster is available free by email or by calling 1 (800) 359-9629.

TESTING RESOURCES

We recommend two well-regarded, career-related testing instruments — the Myers-Briggs Type Indicator (MBTI), and the Johnson O'Connor Inventory of Aptitudes and Knowledge. The MBTI evaluates personality preferences and helps those who sense they don't fit into a particular work environment but don't know why. The Johnson O'Connor test identifies your natural aptitudes or skills.

Myers-Briggs Type Indicator — The MBTI is a well-validated personality evaluator that studies four sets of character traits, and draws conclusions about your preferences as one of 16 types. The test has nearly 50 years of research, development and application behind it, including extensive use in the Fortune 500. According to studies, certain proclivities are shared by satisfied attorneys in different areas of the law, and this test can tell you whether you fit into the right pattern. For information about licensed MBTI administrators in your area, contact Consulting Psychologists Press (www.cpp-db.com).

Johnson O'Connor Research Foundation (www.jocrf.org) — The nation's oldest center for the study of human aptitudes. The organization believes that true job satisfaction depends upon using those aptitudes (or natural talents and skills) with which you were born. Testing at one of 11 US locations takes a day and a half and yields a useful and individualized job profile and post-test consulting. Fee $600; free follow-up the first year.

ONLINE ASSESSMENTS

CareerLeader (www.CareerDiscovery.com) — A self-assessment developed by two former Harvard business and career psychologists. Their Business Career Interest Inventory, adopted by more than 160 MBA programs and corporations, defines a "universe of possible business careers" in which you could express your interests. Available online, $95.

CareerKey (www.CareerKey.org) — A self-assessment that assigns users to one or more of six personality types and helps identify occupations most likely to fit their profile. Developed at North Carolina State University's College of Education. Available online, free.

DISC Personal Profiles (www.DiscProfile.com) — A self-scoring, self-interpreting assessment that identifies work style patterns, and measures them in four personality categories (Dominance, Influence, Steadiness, and Compliance). A popular assessment tool in use for more than 25 years. Available online with a personalized written report; $25.95.

The Enneagram (www.EnneagramInstitute.com) — In 144 forced-pair questions, this instrument looks at nine personality types and determines your basic type, and what that means for you in the workplace and in relationship. Test takes about 30 minutes; available online and in booklet form; $10

Focus (www.FocusCareer.com) — A career development system developed by the same design team that pioneered IBM's computer-based, career-planning program. Focus is reputed to be one of the three most widely used career-planning systems in the US. Available online with a personalized written report; $18.95.

Highlands Program (www.HighlandsProgram. com) — A comprehensive and thorough personal strategic planning program. The Highland Ability Battery is a CD-based assessment that identifies your natural abilities (communications, learning, problem-solving, decision-making) and how they work together. The package includes testing, a written report, a two-hour consultant (phone or on-site) and an audiotape of the consultation. $400.

HumanMetrics (www.HumanMetrics.com) — This Israeli company provides online testing in the field of human typology and personal relations. Their 72-question Typology Test assigns users to one of 16 "types" and offers links for a full explanation. Free.

Jackson Vocational Interest Survey (www.jvis.com) — An educational and career-planning tool that offers a detailed snapshot of your interests and how they relate to the world of work. JVIS was written by a former President of the American Psychological Association Divison of Measurement, Evaluation and Statistics, and who developed an intelligence test for NASA astronauts. Available online, $14.95.

Keirsey Temperament Sorter (www.keirsey.com) — David Keirsey's book on human typology has sold millions of copies in 20 years. His typology sorter isn't as famous as the Myers-Briggs Temperament Instrument, but both are valid assessments based on Carl Jung's original work. The Keirsey Sorter is a free, 15-minute, online assessment; a personalized, 10-page report is available for $14.95.

Kuder Career Assessment Services (www.kuder.com) — Many of today's adult vocational concepts are based on the work of Dr. Frederic Kuder in the 1930s. Kuder's updated Career Planning System is designed to help individuals discover their career interests, skills, and work values. The online package offers a suite of tools, including an Electronic Career Portfolio, Interest Inventory, Skills Assessment and Work Values Inventory. $14.95.

MAPP (www.assessment.com) — First developed in the 1960s, MAPP — Motivational Appraisal of Personal Potential — is now an online assessment that measures your motivation toward specific work areas. The CareerSeeker package offers a vocational analysis, a narrative interpretation of your ratings in nine trait groups, a personalized 20-page report, and a summary of your top six motivators. $39.95.

Self-Directed Search (www.self-directed-search. com) — Discover the careers that best match your interests. This online assessment is based on the occupation codes popularized by Dr. John Holland. The assessment takes 20 minutes. A personalized report is e-mailed to

MORE ENCOURAGEMENT ABOUT SELF-ASSESSMENT

Some attorneys respond to their inner signals with the same conscientiousness and attention to detail they applied to their lawyering. They carefully investigate other career possibilities, sometimes on their own but more often with the assistance of a professional career counselor.

Other practitioners work together to plot a reasoned path out of the profession. As an example, two San Francisco lawyers noticed how much time they spent grousing with coworkers about their work. Once they realized that their negative attitude was not going to create a better work environment, they made a pact with each other to take a moment each day to write down the one thing they most enjoyed doing. Even this short mental break helped each of them to focus on what elements in a job would be most satisfying. Within a year, both of them had moved into equally respectable but more enjoyable non-legal positions.

Those who are methodical about their leave-taking are in the minority. Still, their numbers are growing and, to help them, there are an increasing number of career counselors specializing in law—many of them former practicing lawyers. Many other career planning books designed especially for lawyers have been published in the last few years. And seminars about how lawyers can make the best use of their degrees and backgrounds are attracting lawyers in every major city.

For Robert, law school represented a continuance of his long-time drive toward achievement. After only a few years in the profession, on a day he will long remember, Robert realized that while what he'd attained impressed others, it would never be personally satisfying. Once he was able to

acknowledge that, he turned to a career counselor. With guidance and encouragement, Robert carefully plotted his departure from law practice.

Robert's Statement: After three years of practice, I was working on a month-long project in Washington, DC, when the associate review committee called me from New York to give me my annual critique. They said, "You're doing fine, blah, blah, blah, but you don't have enough initiative."

"There's a good reason for that," I wanted to say. "I hate doing this."

I realized then that I could only continue pretending for so long. I didn't like what I was doing, and it was bound to show one way or another. When I realized that, I began asking myself why a perfectly competent person like me was subjecting myself to criticism.

That very same day, I saw a copy of the *National Law Journal* with a front page article about lawyer dissatisfaction. It was a moment I'll always remember; an epiphany. The article appeared at the right time with the message I needed to hear: that I wasn't unusual, or alone, feeling as I did. That what I was feeling wasn't a flaw in my character. That the law is right for some people and not right for others. And that there were people I could turn to for help.

Right then, I decided I was going to get out of law. I circled in red the names of the two career counselors mentioned in the article and investigated them the minute I returned to New York. My counseling sessions started a few weeks later.

We started out by talking about what I would do if I could do anything I wanted. Although I was suspicious at first, that exercise helped me understand that I like to solve problems, to nurture things and make them bloom into something. I don't like to fight, nor do I share those values held in high esteem by most lawyers—competition, aggressiveness, a fast pace, being considered an expert, or getting a case exactly right down to the last detail. I also came to realize that my creativity is severely restricted in law. My writing style is restricted by its conventions, and I can't be as emotional as I would like.

I enjoy writing, researching and advising—things I do in law—but charging a lot of money to shift dollars around from one person to the next isn't enough to sustain me. What I need to do is work toward a purpose which transcends a corporation's goal of making money. From all that analysis, I've concluded that I want to work for a nonprofit organization, doing what I'm doing now but without the fighting.

With my counselor's help, I've picked out a career that is more in tune with my interests and personality and overall values.

And I've decided to quit my law job to look for other work. I've never taken a risk like that before. Now that I think about it, going to law school was a choice I made to avoid risk. By applying, I didn't have to think about finding a job, didn't have to worry about my student loan payments starting. I pushed off thinking about my life, my future and my interests.

I feel proud of myself because, at last, I've taken the time to figure out what I want to do with my life. I no longer want to be a lawyer by default. I'm prepared for the downsides, especially the financial loss. I make $75,000 a year now, but I'm willing to drop to $35,000.

I can't help but think about something my mother told me when I was in law school. I had said something like "I can't wait until the semester is over," and she asked me, "What are you going to do, wish your life away?" That's exactly what I've been doing here. I can't wait until this brief is done; can't wait until this case settles, or until this trial is over. I'm done wishing my life away.

users along with a list of the occupations and fields of study that most closely match their interests. $8.95.

Storm Navigator (www.careerstorm.com/ stormnavigator) — One of a series of free career assessment tools developed by a European company specializing in web-based career products. Assesses your values, skills, work style and subjects of interest in a series of short, 10-to-20-minute modules.

StrengthsFinders (www.strengthsfinder.com) — One of the most unusual online assessments here begins with the purchase of a self-help book — *Now Discover Your Strengths* — co-published by the Gallup research

organization. Gallup interviewed nearly two million employees and identified 34 themes that translate into personal and career success. Each copy of the book has a PIN number that allows readers to access an online assessment.

Strong Interest Inventory (www.careers-by-design/strong_interest_inventory.htm) — The Strong Inventory is based on the idea that individuals are more satisfied and productive when they work in jobs or at tasks that they find interesting, and when they work with people whose interests are similar to their own. Available online; $75 (includes six-page profile). Separate packages include a Myers-

Briggs test, and career and entrepreneur assessments; $90-$125. All packages include a half-hour phone counseling session to review your results.

LAWYER ASSISTANCE PROGRAMS

In recent years, a growing number of state bar Lawyer Assistance Programs (LAP) have begun sponsoring career transition workshops, seminars, presentations, CLE's, and individual career counseling, as well as making referrals to local attorneys who will lend a hand as "job coaches." Some LAP's even offer periodic programs on non-traditional practice options. The following state LAP programs are known to offer some, but not all, of the aforementioned career programs:

Arizona — Contact Diane Ellis, LAP director; diane.ellis@staff.azbar.org,

British Columbia — Contact Derek LaCroix, director; (604) 685-2171, 1 (888) 685-2171.

California — Contact Richard Carlton, LAP director; Richard.Carlton@calbar.ca.gov.

Colorado — Inquiries to www.clhp.org

District of Columbia — Contact Lynn Phillips, director, (202) 347-313, Lphillips@dcbar.org.

Minnesota — Contact Emil Jalonen, director, ejalonen@mnlc.org.

Mississippi — Contact Betty Daugherty, director of the Lawyers and Judges Assistance Program, bdaugherty@msbar.org.

New Jersey — Contact William John Kane, director, 1 (800) 246-5527, (732) 937-7549, njlap@aol.com.

North Carolina — Contact Dr. Charles Cooper of the Human Resource Consultants, (919) 929-1227; www.hrcchapelhill.citysearch.com.

Oregon — Contact Mike Long, program attorney at the Oregon Attorney Assistance Program, (503) 226-1057; MikeL@oaap.org.

Tennessee — Contact Robert Albury Jr., executive director, at (615) 591-5801; www.tlap.org.

Washington State — Contact Barbara Harper, director, barbarah@wsba.org.

For a state-by-state list of LAP's , go to the Web site for the ABA's Commission on Lawyer Assistance Programs at www.abalegalservices.org/colap/home.html.

JOB OPTIONS

INSIDE, OUTSIDE

& AROUND

THE LAW

What can you do with a law degree?

On the following pages, you will find hundreds of job options in dozens of categories.. The bold-faced subheadings (e.g., **Alternative Dispute Resolution, Arts and Entertainment, Bar Associations**, etc.) identify resources and job options in three separate categories — *Practicing Law, Nonlegal* or *Law-Related*. The occupations described in the *Practicing Law* category require an active license to practice, but this does not apply to the other two categories. The Web and phone listings in this 5th edition have all been updated, and are current through August 1, 2003.

Note: It is important to keep in mind that every occupational title listed here is now, or has once been held, by a lawyer or law school graduate ... and the opportunities described here are just a small fraction what you will find Out There:

Alternative Dispute Resolution
Arts and Entertainment
Bar Associations
Communications
Consulting
Corporate, Business, Banking
Counseling
Education
Entrepreneurial Ventures
Environmental
Ethics
Foundations and Nonprofit Organizations
Government
Healthcare
International
Judiciary
Labor Unions
Law Enforcement
Law Firms
Legal Information Science
Lobbying & Public Affairs
Military
Publishing
Real Estate
Sports
Technology

ALTERNATIVE DISPUTE RESOLUTION

Possible Employers:

colleges and universities
community dispute resolution boards or panels
corporations
court-sponsored programs
federal, state and local government
for-profit mediation services
labor unions
law firms
newspapers
nonprofit organizations
American Arbitration Association panels
private solo practice

Common Subject Matters:

boundary disputes
child custody/visitation
commercial litigation
construction disputes
dissolution of marriage
environmental compliance
insurance coverage
landlord-tenant disputes
partnership/business dissolution
personal injury claims

Service Positions:

ADR specialist
arbitrator
contract mediator
director of legal services
dispute resolution trainer
employee grievance mediator
mediator
ombuds
settlement conference referee
staff mediator
volunteer mediator

Administrative Positions:

director/manager
director of training
marketing director

A NOTE ABOUT MEDIATION

Many lawyers today face significant barriers when they attempt to enter the mediation field. First, they often compete for business with free community- and court-sponsored programs founded to lessen the backlog of lawsuits and to remove from the legal system altogether matters involving small amounts of money or emotional issues like child custody and visitation. Competition is exacerbated by companies that retain retired judges to serve as mediators (although most actually conduct their sessions more like settlement conferences). Most important of all, interest in serving as a mediator continues to outpace consumer demand.

The combination of all three factors makes paying customers hard to come by. As a result, most lawyers who are drawn to mediation find they must mix a regular law practice with their mediation cases, or be paid to train others in the art of dispute resolution.

Lawyers who attract most of the mediation referrals usually have followed one of these paths:

- They've established a reputation for fairness and competence as practitioners in such specialties as environmental, construction, personal injury or family law.
- They retired from the trial court bench with reputations as effective settlement judges.
- They combined their legal backgrounds with degrees in psychology, social work or counseling. Then, they networked with former colleagues to generate referrals and now focus primarily on mediating family or interpersonal disputes.
- They operate an alternative dispute resolution service which handles all marketing and logistics, but they generally do not mediate the disputes themselves. Instead, they rely upon a panel of mediators (primarily those from the first three categories) to whom they pay a portion of the fees collected.
- They volunteered for a well-regarded community mediation program long enough to develop a reputation for effectiveness, then let the agency know of their interest in receiving referrals of matters outside the agency's jurisdiction.

Considering these restrictions, it's difficult for all but the elite few in any area or field to obtain enough private mediation work to make a decent living. Fortunately, lawyers can obtain other positions which make use of their conflict resolution skills. The broadest range of opportunities fall under the categories of ombuds and grievance investigator.

An ombuds is a neutral party who investigates complaints, issues reports, and provides assistance in resolving disputes. A classical ombuds conducts formal investigations, often in a public setting, and has powers of subpoena; an organizational ombuds conducts informal interviews, preserving the confidentiality of those involved. An organizational ombuds may work internally, that is, as an employee of the company, or as an external consultant on an outsourced basis.

Most ombuds positions are found in large institutions (e.g., government, universities, hospitals, newspaper publishing, corporations) and deal with grievances filed by students, customers, citizens, suppliers or employees. This field has grown—and is likely to continue to grow—because businesses recognize the cost-savings and improved morale of avoiding litigation.

A similar role is that of a grievance investigator in a corporate, university or government environment. The ADA has triggered an enormous number of employee and student complaints of failure to accommodate their physical, mental or learning disabilities. In many environments, the human rights or equal opportunity department handles these complaints, but some organizations have moved the investigations to the risk management department. Investigators are hired, therefore, not only to get to the truth of the complaint, but to work with the complainant and respondent to resolve their differences amicably.

owner/founder
program administrator/coordinator
volunteer coordinator

Law-Related Resources

ABA Section of Dispute Resolution (www.abanet. org/dispute) — Maintains a National Dispute Resolution Resource Center in Washington, DC 20005; (202) 662-1680. Publishes Dispute Resolution Magazine, containing updates on events and resources in ADR.

Association for Conflict Resolution (formerly Academy of Family Mediators) www.mediators.org — A national membership organization for lawyers and mental health professionals involved in the resolution of domestic relations issues. Publishes annual membership directory, and quarterly newsletter and journal. Provides public referral service. (202) 667-9700.

American Arbitration Association (www.adr.org) — Publishes the quarterly Dispute Resolution Journal, Dispute Resolution Times, and ADR Currents. Branch offices maintain panels of arbitration and mediation attorneys available for referral mostly in construction, securities, computers or commercial law disputes. You'll find branch office listings in your local telephone directory or go online for a directory of regional offices. (212) 716-5800.

Association of Family and Conciliation Courts (www.afccnet.org) — An organization of judges, counselors, lawyers, mediators and others interested in the resolution of family disputes as they affect children. (608) 664-3750.

Council of Better Business Bureaus (www.bbb.org) — The Web site has an office directory organized by state and zip code. Includes the Auto Line Program, a mediation and arbitration service for disputes between consumers and participating manufacturers. (703) 276-0100.

CPR Institute for Dispute Resolution, www.cpradr.org; (212) 949-6490. Nonprofit organization of general counsel from major corporations, senior partners in leading law firms and legal scholars interested in installing ADR into the mainstream of corporate law departments and law firm practices.

Directory of Law School ADR Courses & Programs. Lists professors, course descriptions and teaching methods for ADR courses around the country. Available from the ABA, www.abanet.org.

Federal Mediation & Conciliation Service (www.fmcs.gov) — A federal agency that mediates labor disputes. Regional offices located nationwide.

Journal of Dispute Resolution (www.law.missouri. edu/csdr) — A semiannual magazine published by the University of Missouri-

Columbia School of Law in cooperation with its Center for Dispute Resolution.

Martindale-Hubbell Dispute Resolution Directory (www.martindale.com) — State-by-state listing of over 45,000 professionals participating in alternative dispute resolution.

National Institute for Dispute Resolution (www.crenet.org) — Posts employment and volunteer opportunities on its Web site. Circulates a catalogue of conflict resolution resources. (202) 466-4764.

Society of Professionals in Dispute Resolution (www.spidr.org) — Organization of professionals and volunteers interested in alternative dispute resolution. Annual conference, newsletter, clearinghouse of information about dispute resolution in many arenas, annual membership directory. (202) 265-1927.

US Arbitration & Mediation (www.usam.com) Franchise operation with offices in the US, Canada and abroad. Contact local arbitration and mediation service providers. Listed in local telephone directories under "Arbitration Services" and "Mediation Services." (800) 318-2700.

Negotiation Resources

The Negotiation Journal. A quarterly magazine containing articles on the subject of dispute settlement. Published in collaboration with the Harvard Law School Program on Negotiation, www.law.harvard.edu. Available from Kluwer academic publishers (www.wkap.nl/).

Ombuds Resources

The Ombudsman Association (www.ombuds-toa.org) — Membership organization consisting of those currently involved as internal and external organizational ombuds, as well as those interested in the field. Publishes the Ombudsman's Handbook, and a code of ethics and standards of practice. Offers training programs.

ARTS AND ENTERTAINMENT

Practicing Law:
entertainment lawyer
First Amendment lawyer
in-house counsel for an arts organization
intellectual property lawyer

Law-Related Positions:
art sales to law firms
computer-aided trial exhibits designer
consultant on visual aids for trial
producer, associate producer, or assistant
    producer of a courtroom TV program
supervising producer of TV programs about
    lawyers

The Talent:
actor
classical musician
comedian
commercial voice-over work
composer
fashion model
film maker
furniture art designer
graphic artist
jazz band member
jewelry designer
lyricist
folk musician
painter
rock musician
sculptor
singer
songwriter
storyteller
woodworker

The Business Angle:
art gallery owner
artist's agent or representative
assistant artistic director
associate producer
co-creator of television show

RELEASING THE ARTIST WITHIN

Barry held an enviable position as senior partner of a prestigious New York City law firm. After many years of working almost around-the-clock, his life had eased into a pleasant routine of practicing law by day and, in the evenings, painting and sculpting. When a voice inside him announced the time to follow his passion in art, Barry was attentive enough to finally leave the law.

Barry's Statement: I wish I'd left law sooner. But like everything else it happened at one of those times when I least expected it.

I was actually happier practicing law than I had been in years. My workload was much easier because I had more help. I was doing much more supervisory work rather than all the detailed stuff that used to consume me. Life was a lot better than it had been, but by then I had already crossed over the line.

I was on my way home from Norway where I had obtained lengthy affidavits for an international bankruptcy matter. It had been a wonderful week, full of intellectual stimulation. When I was on the plane home, all of a sudden, I had this overwhelming feeling that I had to stop practicing law. Before that moment one of my biggest barriers to leaving was that I could not walk away from my partners; that I owed it to everybody to stay put for the rest of my life. At that moment, though, it all became crystal clear; I knew exactly what I had to do, and how I would tell them. The relief was so great that I started to cry. That clinched it. There was no turning back.

When I practiced commercial law, I never had the sense I was doing anything of great social value. It was more a matter of getting satisfaction out of presenting the best legal case I could with the facts and legal precedent I had. Although the work was very challenging, it was also totally consuming. We were a very small firm and worked harder than everybody else because we had to make up for the lack of numbers. The workload was incredible: seven days and seven nights at the beginning. It was a grind.

After the first seven years, I started to question what I was doing. As a way of expanding my life, I invested in an art gallery with three others. I participated in the planning, visited artists' studios and helped to select artists to represent. On weekends, I would go down to see what was going on. Before long, I began to read and study obsessively about art.

About a year after we opened the gallery, I started drawing after I came home from work, sometimes feeling so driven that I was at it until almost dawn. A few hours later, I'd go back to the office. The more I indulged my interest in art, though, the more frustrated I got with the life I was leading as a successful commercial lawyer. Other lawyers in the firm seemed totally obsessed with practicing law, that being the major impulse in their lives. With only a few exceptions, it seemed they didn't resent the demands because they weren't actively involved in anything else. On the other hand, my life was becoming schizophrenic. I tried to put my energies into the law as fully as I could, but art engaged me more and more.

Initially, I was just discontent. Then I started to realize how I was not living the kind of life that I really wanted to live.

Deciding whether or not to leave presented a multi-faceted conflict. On the one hand, there were the non-material rewards—the excitement of cases; the intellectual challenge; the prestige of being with a successful firm; the good feeling of being accepted as a successful lawyer. There were also the material rewards. As unhappy as I was, those things were hard to give up.

One the other hand, I was really in love with, and excited by, painting and art, and I hadn't felt that way about law for a long time. I had this feeling that I could do something significant with my life by devoting myself to art. Sure, I had doubts about starting a new career. Was I fooling myself? Did I only want to escape from law, or did I truly believe that I could do something meaningful? Did I have enough money to make the change and still maintain

a reasonable lifestyle until I established myself again? What would it mean to my family?

Most lawyers I know are extremely interested in hearing about others who have left the law because 95 percent of them have secret yearnings to leave themselves. The only advice I can give is that when you begin to be unhappy with what you are doing, take the time to isolate the reasons why. If you find that you can't change them, then leave.

People say I was courageous to do what I did. But leaving law was a necessity for me. It was like having an illness. The way I see it, I either had to cure myself, or watch a big part of me die.

dance instructor
executive film producer
executive TV producer
founder of recording company
literary agent
manager for actors, musicians, or musical groups
managing director of theatrical production
    company
movie producer
museum curator
theatrical agent
theatrical producer

Law-Related Resources

Volunteer Lawyers for the Arts (www.vlany.org) — Maintains an annually updated listing of affiliated groups across the country, called the Volunteer Lawyers for the Arts National Directory. (212) 319-2787.

Art Resources

American Association of Museums (www.aam-us.org) — Web site contains articles on issues of interest to the museum community (fair use, ADA, intellectual property). (202) 289-1818.

National Guild of Community Schools of the Arts (www.nationalguild.org) — Monthly announcements of administrative openings in the field of community arts education available to members of the www.natguild.org; (212) 268-3337. The Guild focuses on nonprofit, non-degree granting community schools offering instruction in the performance and visual arts.

Theatre of Communication's ArtSearch (www.tcg.org) — A national employment service bulletin for the performing arts issued twice monthly. Covers positions in the areas of artistic, administrative, career development, production and education.

BAR ASSOCIATIONS

Practicing Law:
disciplinary counsel
general counsel
lawyer referral service supervising attorney
lawyer referral service telephone intake attorney
legal education staff attorney
professionalism counsel

volunteer legal service project intake or staff
attorney
volunteer legal service project supervising
attorney

Administrative and Program Positions:
admissions/licensing director
assistant director
continuing legal education director
convention planner
coordinator of Lawyer Helpline service
director, assistant director or program
coordinator for CLE
director of Lawyers Concerned with Lawyers
program
director of professional competence, planning &
development
director, special funds
executive director
fee arbitration program director
law-related education director
lawyers' assistance program director
legal information answer line coordinator
legislative representative
membership services director
program planning advisor
programming director
public affairs director
publications manager
special project coordinator
volunteer legal services project director
Web site developer

Law-Related Resources
American Bar Association (www.abanet.org) —
Functions at the Chicago headquarters
include membership, communications,
meetings, CLE, publishing and young lawyers
as well as most sections and committees. The
Washington, DC, offices include
governmental affairs, ADR and public service
departments. (312) 988-5000. Directory of
Lawyer Referral Services. Programs in the US
and Canada. Available from the American Bar
Association, www.abanet.org. Job

Descriptions & Association Personnel Policies.
A collection of over 100 sample descriptions
of bar association positions from executive
director to secretary. Published by the ABA.
National Association of Bar Executives
(www.abanet.org/nabe) — An organization
of managing directors, public information
officers, CLE directors, counsel and other
professional staff of state, county and city bar
associations. Online job listings.
National Organization of Bar Counsel
(www.nobc.org) — A nonprofit group of
disciplinary counsel to state and federal
courts, and bar associations. Membership
directory online. Holds semiannual
conventions in February and August, in
conjunction with ABA meetings.
(202) 638-1501.

COMMUNICATIONS

Practicing Law:
defamation lawyer
First Amendment lawyer
intellectual property lawyer
in-house lawyer for media organization

Law-Related Positions:
crisis PR for law firms
freelance writer for any legal magazine,
newspaper, or newsletter
legal correspondent for television
PR account rep working with law firms
radio network news
reporter for legal newspaper
reporter on legal issues for general circulation
magazine or newspaper
scriptwriter for TV program about lawyers
speaker on career issues for law students
staff writer or editor for a law book publisher
staff writer for legal magazine or journal
Web site developer or editor
writer for a law-related TV program
writer of legal career books
writer of substantive law books

The Business Angle:

agent

business affairs manager at media company

corporate communications

company president

literary agent

ombuds person

PR account executive

radio adman

television broadcast sales

Other Editorial Positions:

assistant editor for collegiate dictionary

associate food editor for women's magazine

copy editor

editor (book, magazine, newspaper, newsletter)

editorial page editor

industry newsletter editor

proofreader

publications director

Talent:

advice columnist

author of nonfiction book

dance critic

disc jockey

editorial columnist

essayist

fiction writer

food critic

freelance corporate communications

freelance magazine writer

freelance news reporter

historical romance novelist

humor columnist

corporate communications specialist

journalist

motivational speaker

newspaper columnist

newspaper or magazine reporter

news writer and producer for network

television affiliate

playwright

public affairs producer

professional speaker

published novelist

radio talk-show host

restaurant reviewer

screenwriter

sportscaster

stand-up comedian

syndicated columnist

talk show host

technical writer

television news reporter

television scriptwriter

Law-Related Resources

Careers in Entertainment Law — by William D. Henslee. What to expect as an entertainment lawyer, including recommended academic background and work experience. An ABA paperback.

Communications Lawyer — A quarterly newsletter produced by the ABA's Communication Law Section. Reviews significant activities and developments in communications law.

Creative Writing for Lawyers, Michael H. Cohen; paperback.

Forum on Communications Law (www.abanet. org/forums/communication/colead.html) — Encourages discussion and information exchange relating to legal counseling of print media, the telecommunications industry and electronic media.

Advertising Resources

American Association of Advertising Agencies (www.aaaa.org) — A national trade association representing the advertising business. A roster of members is available online, as well as references to about 150 other publications on the advertising field. (212) 682-2500.

Broadcasting

National Association of Broadcasters (www.nab. org) — Representatives of radio and TV stations and networks; associate members include freelance producers. An extensive career center online lists both employee and employer job announcements and permits résumé posting. (202) 429-5300.

Radio-Television News Directors Association (www.rtnda.org/rtnda) — The trade association for the electronic journalism profession. Offers a 25-page booklet entitled Careers in Radio & Television, as well as an annual salary survey. (202) 659-6510.

Public Relations & Business Communication Resources

International Association of Business Communicators (www.iabc.com) — A professional association and information network for communication managers, public relations directors, writers, editors, audiovisual specialists and consultants. Publishes Communication World magazine, other books, a bibliography of communication-related books, and an annual directory of members. Offers an accreditation program. Many chapters operate job listings which nonmembers may access for a nominal fee. (415) 544-4700.

Public Relations Society of America (www.prsa.org) — Publish a subscription database of current public relations opportunities. Publish Careers in Public Relations, an eight-page booklet, the PRSA Salary Survey, a Green Book identifying PR service companies nationwide and a Red Book identifying PR firms and consultants nationwide. (212) 995-2230.

Speaking Career Resources

National Speakers Association (www.nsaspeaker. org) — Publishes Who's Who in Professional Speaking and Professional Speaker magazine. Excellent mid-year and annual educational conferences as well as local chapter programming.

Toastmasters International (www.toastmasters.org) — Thousands of

chapters meet all over the world on a weekly basis to help professionals improve their presentation skills. (949) 858-8255.

Writing Resources

Society of Professional Journalists (www.spj.org) — Promotes journalism as a career. Maintains a placement service and publishes the SPJ Internship Directory and the Writer's Guide to Magazine Editors and Publishers. Membership includes lawyers interested in their Freedom of Information committee. (317) 927-8000.

Society for Technical Communication (www.stc.org) — An association of technical writers, editors, publishers, graphic designers and others whose work involves making technical information understandable to the general public. Members have access to their web-based job-search database. (703) 522-4114.

CONSULTING

Practicing Law:

appellate specialist
consulting lawyer
legal research & writing specialist

With Law Firms, Lawyers and In-House Legal Departments:

associate training
automation
building good client relationships
business acquisition
business valuations expert
case management systems
communication with clients and juries
computer systems purchase or training
document assembly or management systems
employee selection, both professional and staff
expert witness on business and real estate
   failures
expert witness on general/limited
partnership disputes

expert witness on insurance coverage, bad faith and underwriting issues

expert witness on lawyer standard of care or legal ethics

improving the quality and effectiveness of inside counsel

increasing law firm profitability

interpersonal communication

jury selection

law firm management

law firm systems

lawyer training (i.e., professional development)

marketing and promotion

marketing coaching

market research

mergers and acquisitions

office space design

outsourcing legal services

network design

pension and profit-sharing plans

strategic planning

structuring alternative fee arrangements

telephone systems selection

time management

trial preparation

trial strategy

visual aids for trial

wardrobe and personal appearance, especially for jury presentations

writing

Law-Related Consulting with Other Types of Businesses:

acquisition consulting

advising veterinarians about legal/business aspects of their practices

consulting in cost, quality and effective use of legal services

designing corporate compliance programs

dispute resolution training

employment law/human resources

freelance negotiator

intellectual property protection systems design

internal dispute resolution

international business

IRS compliance analyst

labor-management relations

litigation avoidance or management

pension benefits programs

real estate syndication

seminars that teach law to non-lawyers

sexual harassment avoidance training

training managers to avoid employee lawsuits

Non-Legal Consulting:

business & entrepreneurial coaching

business management

executive search

financing

human resources

human services

international relations

Law-Related Resources

Altman Weil Pensa (www.altmanweil.com) — East coast (610) 886-2000, West Coast (925) 287-8211, Midwest (414) 427-5400. Management consulting exclusively to the legal profession. Web site includes many articles on law firm management consulting topics.

Hildebrandt Law Firm Consulting Services (www.hildebrandt.com) — Management consulting services exclusively for law firms, corporate law departments and others in the legal profession. Offer executive search services for their clients as well. (732) 560-8888.

Law Practice Management, www.abanet.org (click on Publications and then on Browse index) — Published eight times annually by the ABA's Law Practice Management Section. Often features articles contributed by consultants to the legal profession.

Technical Advisory Services for Attorneys (www.tasanet.com) — An expert referral service for lawyers which claims access to 24,000 experts, some of whom are non-practicing lawyers. (800) 523-2319.

CORPORATE, BUSINESS AND BANKING

Practicing Law:
associate general counsel
department (tax, real estate, labor relations,
    contracts, public information, finance,
    acquisitions) legal advisor
director, intellectual property
general counsel
independent general counsel
in-house insurance defense
in-house intellectual property auditor
litigation management
medical division counsel
part-time in-house counsel
patent attorney
tax department of public accounting firm
VP, legal administration

Law-Related Employers:
accounting firms
banks
collection companies
law firm consulting companies
insurance companies
legal publishers
management consulting companies
mortgage companies
public accounting firms
retailers of products or services for lawyers and
    law firms
Section 1031 exchange intermediaries
software developers for law firms
wealth management companies

Examples of Law-Related Products:
advertisements in legal newspapers and
    magazines
communications systems
computer animation/graphics
computer hardware/software
computerized legal forms
computer systems and components
corporate kits
educational videos

executive gifts (i.e., premium sales)
law books and directories
legal applications computer software
legal forms
mail order products with a lawyer theme
office furniture, supplies, equipment
printing
training films on legal ethics & overcoming
    discrimination
visual aids for trial

Examples of Law-Related Services:
accounting/bookkeeping
advertising
appraisals (personal property; residential and
    commercial real estate)
career and life planning for lawyers
CLE-accredited seminars
completion of legal forms
computer-assisted research and retrieval
computer-generated accident reconstruction
contract lawyer placement
corporate communications
courier/messenger service
courtroom exhibit preparation and design
deposition and trial transcript summaries
expert witness clearinghouse and referral
    service
facilities management
graphic design
in-firm training programs
in-house continuing legal education
independent paralegal
insurance coverage, such as malpractice, office
    liability, disability, life, and health insurance
interactive CLE videos
investigator, criminal or civil
judgment purchase
language/interpretation services
legal research services
legal search consultant ("headhunter")
linguistic analysis
litigation management, oversight, research,
    support
management consulting

market analysis

"mastery of practice" training seminars

medical illustration

medical research

office machine maintenance and repair

outplacement services

paralegal and clerical staff placement

paralegal services (e.g., document organization, indexing, and retrieval)

polygraphs

probate administration

professional development courses

public relations

strategic automation

strategic planning retreats

systems integration

videotaping depositions, will-signings, accident scenes, etc.

Positions with Law-Related Employers:

acquisitions counselor or evaluator

adjuster in claims department of insurance company or self-insured corporation

attorney-pension operations for insurance company

attorney-underwriter

bank investment compliance officer, probate administrator, analyst, trust department consultant, trust officer

claims adjuster

claims examiner

client service representative for trust company

commercial loan administrator

contract lawyer placement specialist

estate administrator

insurance claims representative, bonding specialist

INDEPENDENT GENERAL COUNSEL OR PART-TIME IN-HOUSE COUNSEL

Some years ago, Michael came up with an idea for a new service:

He would act as in-house counsel for several corporations on a part-time basis, charging a reduced hourly rate in exchange for an as-needed office and occasional secretarial assistance. He contacted companies in his area that were too small to justify an in-house legal department, but had enough legal expense to be interested in the cost-savings he was suggesting. Several bought the idea. One of them eventually offered him a full-time position as general counsel as they expanded.

Jerry's 10-year stint as house counsel for a real estate development company ended when the company went bankrupt. After some serious soul-searching, researching the market and discovering how slim were his prospects for another in-house position — and hearing Michael speak at a gathering of disgruntled lawyers — Jerry copied Michael's idea. He marketed his services exclusively to privately-held property management and real estate development companies. His efforts resulted in relationships with four companies and an income which doubled the salary he lost.

Now, innovative law firms across the country market themselves as "independent general counsel." They take on routine corporate assignments for mostly new and emerging high-technology companies with little or no in-house staff. Firms that have done well enough to get in the news include the General Counsel Group in Pennsylvania; General Counsel Associates in Mountain View; The General Counsel, Ltd., in Minneapolis; the Association of Independent General Counsel in the Boston area; and Venture Counsel in Portland, OR.

loan administrator
life insurance agent
manager
prepaid legal plan administrator
sales manager, national collection company
trust examiner, officer
vice-president, loan review

**Law-Related Positions for
Non-Legal Employers:**
account executive for private wealth
    management group
ADA compliance specialist
ADA coordinator
affirmative action director
associate director of business affairs
chief operating officer (COO)
contract compliance administrator
contract negotiator
contracting director or staff
corporate quality and technical affairs director or
    staff
dispute resolution specialist
EEOC compliance officer
employee benefit plan administrator, designer,
    products and development director, analyst,
    benefits consultant
employee relations officer
employe/labor relations director or staff
errors and omissions examiner
estate planning specialist
ethics officer
human resources consultant
IRS compliance analyst
labor administration
leasing contract administrator
legal compliance manager
legal editor
legal translation specialist
litigation oversight
loan administrator
ombuds person
procurement analyst
product licensing director or staff
property protection specialist

purchasing director
regulation analyst
retirement plan consultant
risk management advisor
SEC compliance monitor
tax consulting
tax law analyst
training administrator
workers' compensation claims examiner

Other Management Positions:
board chairman
CEO
director of field human resources
manager of management practices
president of film distribution company
senior vice-president for business management
VP, job-placement firm
VP/manager, administration
VP/manager, community relations
VP/manager, development
VP/manager, financial planning
VP/manager, research

Other Sales Positions:
automotive sales
corporate marketing
financial plans sales director
financial products sales
institutional sales
insurance broker
manufacturer's representative
stockbroker
VP, equity sales

Other Staff Positions:
actuary
airline pilot
computer systems analyst
conference planner
convention planner
director of field human resources
director of special projects
documentary producer
employee relations officer

employee training
executive search consultant
field education director
human resources manager
human services consulting
independent insurance adjuster
international business development advisor
investment banking, analyst, strategist
linguist
merchandising
mergers and acquisitions specialist
pension & profit sharing analyst
program development director at a health resort
public insurance adjuster
public relations director
purchasing agent
risk arbitrage analyst
senior account manager
senior internal auditor
software design
supervising environmental scientist
trainer

Law-Related Resources

American Corporate Counsel Association (www.acca.com) — An organization of attorneys employed in corporate law departments, with nationwide chapters. Publishes a membership directory and online job listings. (202) 293-4103.

National Contract Managers Association (www.ncmahq.org) — An organization of contract administrators, negotiators and others involved in contract management and procurement for private business and government. Web site offers job announcements, information about the profession and links to regional and local chapters. (703) 448-0939.

Financial Services (Banking, Insurance, Finance) Resources:

American Bankers Association (www.aba.com) —

Career services online. (800)-BANKERS.

American Banker Online (www.american banker. com) — The Web site of this financial services daily includes a Career Zone with articles on employment issues and job announcements.

Human Resources

World at Work (formerly American Compensation Association) www.worldatwork.org — A nonprofit organization of human resources practitioners who design and manage employee compensation and benefit programs. Confers certified compensation and certified benefits professional designations. (877) 951-9191.

American Staffing Association (www.natss.com) — An nationwide organization of companies that supply workers on a temporary basis. (703) 253-2020.

Society for Human Resource Management (www. shrm.org) — An international organization; online job listings for careers in personnel and industrial relations. (800) 283-SHRM.

Marketing and Sales Resources

American Marketing Association (www.ama.org) — Publishes many resources on marketing as well as an International Membership Directory. Their extensive Web site includes announcements of job vacancies around the country. (312) 648-0536.

Organizational Development

Organizational Development Network (www.ODNetwork.org) — Practitioners, academics, managers and students employed or interested in organizational development, a process of analyzing group psychology and assisting with change. (973) 763-7337.

Trade Shows and Conventions

Meeting Professionals International (www. mpiweb.org) — An association of corporate, association and independent conference, retreat and convention planners. Publishes an annual directory. Chapters nationwide maintain job banks; membership also provides access to the organization's online Career Resource Service. (972) 702-3000.

Training

American Management Association International (www.amanet.org) — Focuses on development and training within the corporate environment. (212) 586-8100.

American Society for Training and Development (www.astd.org) — A national organization for professionals in business, industry, education, and government who concentrate on workplace learning and performance. (703) 683-8100.

Multidisciplinary Associations

Association for Quality and Participation (www.aqp.org) — A national organization of managers, manufacturing executives, HR professionals, and trainers, facilitators and coordinators, who promote quality and participation in the workplace. Operates nine regional groups. (800) 733-3310.

Chamber of Commerce (www.uschamber.org) — Online links to their local chapters, which provide excellent networking, educational and information gathering opportunities. Also publishes Nation's Business, a monthly magazine with an emphasis on small business. (202) 659-6000.

COUNSELING

Practicing Law:

elder law lawyer
estate planning lawyer
guardianship lawyer
involuntary commitment lawyer
matrimonial (family law) lawyer
probate lawyer

Law-Related Positions:

career counselor at a law school
career counselor for lawyers
family therapist specializing in child custody/divorce actions
forensic psychologist
individual therapist specializing in lawyers and their families
lawyers assistance program counselor

Other Counseling Positions:

after-care coordinator at residential treatment facility
career counselor
corporate counseling via a masters in applied behavioral science
employee assistance program (EAP) counselor
experimental psychology and cognitive science via a doctoral degree
hypnotherapist
minister, rabbi
social worker, personal coach
psychological counseling via a masters or Ph.D. in psychology

Law-Related Resources

Directory of Lawyer Assistance Programs — Offers online contact information for bar association committee chairs and program managers for approximately 100 lawyer assistance programs in the US and Canada. (800) 285-2221.

American Academy of Matrimonial Lawyers (www.aaml.org) — Publishes annual membership roster, journal and newsletter. Articles and a divorce manual accessible on their Web site.

Commission on Lawyers Assistance Programs (312) 988-5359 — The governing body for programs that assist lawyers with drug and alcohol problems; some programs also provide outreach to lawyers suffering from depression or other mental illness, and career dissatisfaction. You'll find announcements about open positions with lawyers assistance programs nationwide on their Web site.

Family Advocate — A quarterly journal produced by the ABA Family Law Section. Contains information on current trends in divorce, mental health, custody, support and problems of aging.

National Association for Law Placement Bulletin (www.nalp.org) — Publishes a monthly newsletter that goes to the career services offices of all the accredited law schools. The Web site posts job notices, many of them counseling-related. (202) 835-1001.

General Resources

American Counseling Association (www.counseling.org) — Counseling and human development professionals in government, education, nonprofit, business, and private practice dealing with career, mental health, school and rehabilitation matters. Also publishes Career Development Quarterly and Counseling Today.

Career Planning and Adult Development Network (www.careernetwork.org) — A nonprofit organization of professionals who work with adults in job and career transition. Publishes a monthly newsletter and a quarterly journal.

Employee Assistance Professionals Association (www.eapassn.org) — International organization that assist in identifying and resolving productivity problems caused by employee impairment from alcoholism, divorce, depression and other personal issues. Publishes an Employee Assistance Law Book and a member resource directory.

National Association of Social Workers (www.social workers.org) — The nation's largest organization of professional social workers. Includes links to other online job boards, and information on developing a career in social work.

National Board for Certified Counselors (www.nbcc.org) — Confers counseling

certification. Maintains a state-by-state list of certified counselors in your area.

EDUCATION

Possible Employers:
adult education companies
bar review courses
CLE providers
colleges and universities
community colleges
corporate training companies
corporations
court reporting schools
law schools
private schools
school districts

Practicing Law Positions:
general counsel
outside counsel
plaintiff's lawyer for ADA and other claims
in-house staff attorney

Teaching Law School:
adjunct professor
director of law center
director/supervising attorney of clinical
    education program
instructor
lecturer
legal writing instructor
tenured professor
tenure-track professor
tutor

Law School Administrative Positions:
academic compliance manager
dean, assistant dean, dean of students
cooperative legal education director
director or assistant director of admissions
director of alumni affairs
director of legal externship program
director or assistant director of career services,
    career development or placement

BREAKING INTO LAW SCHOOL ADMINISTRATION

In the eight years after she graduated from law school, Sharon held four different jobs as a lawyer. She tried academia, public interest law, legal publishing and private practice. Her focus ranged from counseling to administration; from litigation to legal research and writing; from day care regulation to school bond issues. None of it, though, complemented her roles as wife and mother until she moved into law school administration. Here's her story of how she made the switch and what her job now entails.

Sharon's Statement: I'm one of those people who was headed for an academic career and then shifted when it seemed that teaching English at the college level full time had become an impossibility. I always knew that I was going to do something serious—whatever that means—so when the time came to take the next step, I went into law.

My first job as a practicing attorney—director of a public interest project devoted to children's issues—was originally set up as a 30-hour per week commitment. I noticed a huge difference between being a law student with three young children and being an attorney with three young children. As a student, I could do what I needed to do fairly easily. As a lawyer, it was very hard. I was always frantic and conflicted, thinking, "I should be home with the children; I should be here at work." Everything had to be so carefully calculated in terms of time and who was responsible when. It seemed that there was a constant crisis or near-crisis all of the time. I was always juggling too many things.

I was dedicated to a part-time arrangement. But the conventional wisdom was that practicing law part-time could not be done if you wanted to have a serious practice. So, after the first year, the board voted to switch my position to full time with a proportionate increase in income. I fought the decision long and hard but eventually lost.

It was not a good trade-off for me. Full-time practice meant spending all day in the city, bringing a lot of work home, attending many night meetings and sometimes working through the weekend. I had to do all of the fundraising, manage the office, and take care of the clients. It was much more than I could handle given that it didn't pay enough for me to have the amount of child care I really needed. When I look back at what made me leave the children's rights project, it was, ironically, the demands of my own family.

When I am under a lot of stress, I wake up at two in the morning and can't go back to sleep. Back then, I was doing it constantly. At one point, I had a serious bout of pneumonia, which I am sure was 90 percent stress-related. I got to thinking that there had to be a better way to live.

Fortunately, my husband got a job offer in Denver. It was a difficult decision, but we were both ready for a change. We thought a less high-powered environment would make our marriage work better.

I worked for a midsize Denver firm for a year, slowly working into advising school districts on their elections. We did some corporate work for hospitals. The firm was generous in paying for the bar, and giving me a month off with salary to study for it.

I thought I had actually achieved a balance among my obligations. But the moment I was to take the bar, my husband told me that he was moving back to Illinois—whether or not I wanted to come—and that he was inviting our teenage kids to return to the Chicago area with him. We moved back together, but that episode finished our marriage.

After my husband moved out, I took a job with a legal publisher. I wondered if I would be happier in a job with less stress and excitement, and with regular hours. All I discovered was that working at something too easy and boring has its own stresses.

At some point, I began to make lists of what I liked and didn't like. By conducting some research, I figured out that my lists pointed to university administration of one sort or another. I applied for a position as a placement director at a local law school and called the director of career services at my alma mater to tell her what I was doing and ask if she would write a letter of reference. She told me in confidence that she was about to leave her job and would love to recommend me as a replacement.

In my present job at the law school, I do a lot of individual student counseling and some teaching about careers and job hunting. I've written handouts and guides on different types of legal careers and how to go about preparing for and finding those jobs. I'm working in a legal environment, but my schedule is manageable and predictable. The summer, when my children are on vacation, is quiet; a time for me to catch up and reassess what I am doing. The upside of the job is that I have a lot of autonomy. The downside is the isolation; I'm not faculty and there is no one at the law school at my level who is working with the same issues and concerns.

People often ask if I'm ever going to go back into practice. The answer is yes, probably. But not until I feel less of an obligation to be available to my last child at home and very likely, even then, on a volunteer basis only. You see, to be truthful, I do not miss the practice of law at all.

director or assistant director of continuing legal education
director or assistant director of development or fund-raising
director or assistant director of community relations
director or assistant director of marketing
director or assistant director of student affairs
faculty computer consultant
law librarian
publication support specialist

Other Law-Related Administrative Positions:
affirmative action/EEO officer
bar review course administrator
director or assistant director of the office of technology transfer
campus ombuds

campus security/compliance officer
coordinator for a CLE provider
course designer for a CLE provider
contract staff analyst
corporate liaison officer
director of federal/state relations
director of a legal assistant/paralegal program
director or assistant director of legislative and regulatory affairs
director of cooperative legal education
director of planned giving
diversity management director
equal opportunity officer
executive director or manager of CLE provider
executive director, center for law-related education
faculty director of master's degree in dispute resolution
investigation and resolution specialist

planned or deferred giving officer or director
pre-law advisor
risk management director
special assistant to the president
technology licensing associate

Law-Related Subject Matters
business ethics, business law
constitutional law
criminal justice
juvenile justice
dispute resolution
environmental law or policy
estate planning
labor relations
law and society
legal studies
marketing for lawyers
negotiation
paralegal education
political science
real estate law
securities law
sexual harassment avoidance
tax

Law-Related Teaching Positions:
bar review course instructor
bar review tutor
community college instructor
corporate trainer
full or associate professor
instructor
lecturer

Other Administrative Positions:
administrative vice chancellor and CFO
assistant dean or dean of students
assistant to the President or Dean
assistant director of office of technology transfer
director of alumni affairs
director, professional development centers and
    institutes
program coordinator of academic support
provost for faculty recruitment and retention

researcher, educational "think tank"
university administrator
vice-president., community college

Other Teaching Positions:
elementary school teacher
facilitator of personal growth seminar
junior or senior high school teacher
instructor, college prep course offered on-site in
    a corporation
instructor, professional writing skills for trainers
outdoor leadership instructor
professor at an art academy
secondary-education teacher
team-building & leadership instructor

Law-Related Resources
Academy of Legal Studies in Business
    (www.alsb.org) — An organization of
    teachers and scholars who work in the field
    of business law, legal environment and law-
    related courses outside of professional law
    schools. Their quarterly contains job listings.
    Networks with 11 regional associations.
    Welcomes inquiries about the educational job
    market, job-search and the drafting of
    effective résumés.
ALI-ABA Committee on Continuing Professional
    Education (www.ali-aba.org) — Assists in the
    development, organization and
    implementation of educational tools for
    lawyers, including a satellite broadcast
    network, publications and live programs.
American Association of Law Schools
    (www.aals.org) — Web site lists faculty,
    administrative and law library job openings at
    US law schools. You can also receive these
    postings through their Placement Bulletin,
    published three times a semester.
American Association for Paralegal Education
    (www.aafpe.org) — An association of
    paralegal educators and institutions of higher
    learning offering paralegal programs.
American Institute for Law Training Within the
    Office (www.aliaba.org/aliaba/ailto.htm) —

A project of ALI-ABA in cooperation with the ABA Standing Committee on Continuing Education of the Bar. Assists law firms in establishing in-firm training programs for lawyers.

Association of Continuing Legal Education (www.aclea.org) — Coordinating group for CLE providers (nonprofit and profit-making) across the country. Membership open to bar associations, law schools, legal publishers, for-profit companies, adult ed specialists, editors, publishers, marketing and media specialists and in-house educators that present a minimum number of CLE-accredited programs annually. Publishes a quarterly newsletter and holds annual and mid-year conferences, often in conjunction with ABA meetings.

National Federation of Paralegal Associations (www.paralegals.org) — Publishes a directory of paralegal training programs.

National Association for Law Placement (www.nalp.org) — An organization of law school career services offices and law firm recruiters. Monthly NALP Bulletin posts job notices for law school career services positions in every edition. Available in your law school career services office.

National Association of College and University Attorneys (www.nacua.org) — Attorneys representing US and Canadian college and university campuses in legal matters. You'll find a good summary of the legal issues involved in university representation on their Web site.

NSBA Council of School Attorneys (www.nsba.org/cosa) — Primarily private practitioners representing school districts nationwide. Employment opportunities posted online. Web site offers insight into the legal issues facing those who represent school districts.

General Resources:

Academic Employment Network

(www.academploy.com) — Lists available positions across the country in colleges and primary and secondary institutions for faculty, staff and administrative professionals.

American Association for Adult and Continuing Education (www.aaace.org) — An association of administrators and professors involved in adult education programs. Publishes three respected periodicals on education and training: Adult Learning magazine, Adult Education Quarterly, and Adult Basic Education.

American Association for Employment in Education (www.aaee.org) — Publishes the National Directory for Employment in Education (a directory of member schools) and the National Directory of Job & Career Fairs for Educators.

American Association for Higher Education (www.aahe.org) — Addresses the needs of individuals and institutions in higher education.

American Association of Community Colleges (www.aacc.nche.edu) — Online job listings and a membership directory.

Chronicle of Higher Education (www.chronicle.com) — A weekly publication with an extensive listing of education-related positions. Copies available in many public libraries.

Education World (www.education-world.com) — Posts K-12 job openings.

National Association of Student Personnel Administrators (www.naspa.org) — The leading national association for college and university student affairs administrators. Online job announcements.

National Educators Employment Review (www.thereview.com) — Job announcements nationwide for K-12 teachers, specialists, administrators and superintendents.

Teacher Job Links (www.geocities.com/Athens/Forum/2080) — Links to national and international teaching jobs; updated weekly. Also provides information about and references for alternative certification methods.

ENTREPRENEURIAL VENTURES

Practicing Law:
consulting lawyer
contract or temporary lawyer
partner in a start-up firm
solo practitioner
solo practice with direct client contact

solo practice as consulting expert (e.g., appellate work, subject matter specialist)

Law-Related Service Businesses:
consumer advocate
contract lawyer placement
dispute resolution training
diversity training
ghost-writing and researching legal issues for books and media.
heirfinder

THE LAWYER-ENTREPRENEUR

Earl expressed a strong entrepreneurial spirit from the moment he left the Air Force in 1973. He put himself through law school by making wind chimes, then founded a general law practice when he graduated and later narrowed it into the first bankruptcy law clinic in his area. In the early 1980's, he decided to get out of law by getting back into crafts. His ceramic Christmas tree ornament business netted close to $100,000 a year. When the market dropped for that product, he designed well-received bankruptcy software for the Macintosh platform, and later, for Windows. Here is his story about becoming an entrepreneur, and his suggestions for how other lawyers can follow in his footsteps:

Earl's Statement: In 1982 I happened to see some ceramic Christmas tree ornaments that appealed to me. I knew nothing about the technique of making them, but I bought one anyway and went around to ceramics stores and crafts outlets, trying to figure out what glaze was used and how the colors were applied.

After hundreds of false starts, I made a small run of my own ornaments. They sold

pretty well. The following spring, my wife and I entered ourselves in a gift show and got a sales rep. A few months later, I was already spending far more of my time making Christmas ornaments than practicing law. Ceramics became my first priority. I told the secretaries that if I was on the phone talking about selling the ornaments, I didn't care if a Supreme Court Justice called, everything else went on hold. It got to the point where I was working at the law office only as long as the parking meter would last—120 minutes at a time. I went in and moved through all of my work as fast as I could. I booked clients every quarter hour. The minute it looked like bankruptcy wasn't an appropriate option, I sent them out the door. I wasn't there serving coffee to people.

I cut out every ounce of dead weight. Every minute at the office was productive so I had big blocks of time to devote to the ornaments. By the Fall, it looked like the business would fly and we packed up our office and left.

Those ornaments gave us a good ride for six years. We were able to make a killing in the crafts business for the simple reason that we regarded it as a business, not a hobby or an artistic endeavor. As in any business, though, you have to keep creating new products in order to survive. I did at first, but then I lost interest. Computer programming hooked me instead.

That's where I was able to combine my legal background with a nonlegal venture. I designed a software program that took all the effort out of bankruptcy filings. It took a while to get the bugs out, but now it's selling well and paying off.

After 25 years of personal experience, I've learned a lot about how lawyers become successful entrepreneurs.

1. Be on the lookout for opportunities. You need to be in the right frame of mind for a fairly long period so that you view opportunities that come your way with a different mind than you would if you were committed to your current position. One of the common fallacies is that if it's such a good idea, why hasn't someone else done it? Look at the converse of that right in the legal profession. How can so many people who are so smart do something that makes them so unhappy? The reason is inertia, or they don't understand how to implement a change, not that it's a bad idea.

2. Set aside some serious non-law time to coming up with something that will work. Get out of the office and look at ideas. See what's out there. Go to suppliers and see what can be made. Go to stores to see what people are buying. Ask questions.

3. Pick a product or service with a big margin. That way you can make lots of mistakes. It lets you be very generous with everybody. You can treat them to generous terms, give discounts, pay for shipping.

4. Research, research and research some more. If somebody came to you with a

contract problem, you would do what you could to understand their business in order to write the contract. With lawsuits, you do the same thing. Why can't you use the same skills for your own benefit?

5. Build your new business little by little. You don't have to shut down your practice and devote all your time to the new. You can see what happens with a smaller effort, then make some hard decisions.

6. Write up a business plan. What do potential customers need? Where do you want to be in three to five years? How can you win the market? Project revenues and expenses.

7. Stop thinking like a lawyer. Lawyers are extremely pessimistic people, always looking for what can go wrong. Business people don't care. Their thinking is, "Try to do it; what have you got to lose?" Consider what you've got to lose, do it and try to minimize the losses.

8. Lawyers are used to delaying gratification. You do it all the time by waiting for the big one to come in the door, or for the next case to settle. You can't do that. Take a lesson from your clients. Get a little flaky. Do it now.

9. Lawyers are aggressive; aggression doesn't work in the business world. It scares people. They think you're pushy. You have to be a nice, honest, hand-shaking sort of person. A good example is contracts. Business people think that contracts are either for sissies or crooks. You don't need contracts unless you're going to pull a fast one on somebody.

10. Lawyers are always obsessed with details. There's no time for that when you're in business. You can't worry about the small stuff. You have to accept and trust people and go with the flow.

legal headhunting

mediation

nonprofit lawyer selection service

private investigator

sexual harassment avoidance training

training in the law for therapists working with
divorcing clients

Law-Related Manufacturing Businesses:

computer-based legal compliance training
program

court coach

do-it-yourself divorce books/software

do-it-yourself probate books/software

do-it-yourself will writing books/software

legal information to non-lawyers

self-help law book publisher

Law-Related Design Business:

bankruptcy software

office space planning

trial exhibits

Law-Related Retail Businesses:

catalogue sales

law office software

Other Service Businesses:

accounts payable auditing

ballet school

business coach

catering

consumer advocacy

desktop publishing

film financing

fitness trainer

hair salon

horse wrangler

licensing agency

landscape gardener

massage therapist

personal fitness trainer

personal growth seminars

self-defense training

seminars

social matchmaker

telemarketing

tour company operator

training and placing hearing and
service dogs

venture capital firm

yacht parties

Retail Businesses:

aircraft leasing

automobile dealership

bakery franchise

beach resort

bed-and-breakfast

careers & job-finding resources
catalogue

commercial airline

computerized information services

custom pottery painting store

fast food franchisee

fishing tackle and other equipment

furniture sales

high-end gadgets

indoor playground for children

jazz club

laundry owner

multi-level marketing

night club owner

restaurant franchise owner

restaurant owner/operator

sailboat broker

semi-professional and professional baseball
teams

ski resort

small hotel

travel store

Wholesale Businesses:

cattle ranch

tree farm

horse farm

imported specialty items

wine importing

alternative baseball magazine

audio and videotape course instruction

ARE YOU CUT OUT TO BE AN ENTREPRENEUR?

Successful entrepreneurs:

☞ Are very realistic;

☞ Possess superior conceptual abilities and the broad thinking of a generalist;

☞ Bristle against standard operating procedures;

☞ Don't make good team players;

☞ Are willing to gamble their own money on a great idea;

☞ Like to get something going much more than maintaining it once it's established;

☞ Possess above-average energy and persistence;

☞ Often neglect their personal lives;

☞ Will readily "steal" the ideas of others and improve upon them;

☞ Invest in substantial market research before launching their business;

☞ Are highly ethical and trustworthy;

☞ Are confident enough to make mistakes . . . and often do!

ceramic Christmas tree ornaments
direct mail marketing
educational and entertainment software
jewelry
records and tapes
restaurant and hotel guides
tomato sauce for pizza restaurants
toy that teaches phonics
video lectures
wine

Law-Related Resources

Flying Solo: A Survival Guide for Solo Lawyers —
A 320-page publication in which successful solo practitioners share their methods and systems. An ABA paperback (3rd ed., 2001).

The Compleat Lawyer — Published quarterly by the General Practice Section of the ABA. Includes a practice management section addressed to solo practitioners.

Running a Law Practice on a Shoestring —
Cost-cutting techniques for the frugal or new practitioner. An ABA paperback.

ENVIRONMENTAL

Practicing Law:
environmental lawyer in private practice
environmental specialist for government
environmental specialist for in-house corporate legal department
litigator for environmental public interest group
real estate lawyer for preservationist organization

Law-Related Positions:
environmental and energy policy manager for corporation
environmental consulting
environmental policy analyst
environmental protection specialist
environmental regulation/compliance analyst
landman
negotiator for preservationist organization

Non-Legal Positions:
managing director of multinational alternative energy company
recycling coordinator for local government

secretary, Environmental Regulation Department

waste reduction and recycling supervisor for local government

waste management planning

Law-Related Resources

American Association of Professional Landmen (www.landman.org) — A group of law school graduates and others who negotiate mineral rights and exploration agreements for energy companies. Maintains a members-only online job bank.

General Resources

Econet (www.econet.apc.org) — Links to environmental activity on the net. Online environmental job postings.

Envirolink (www.envirolink.org) — An online environmental community. Web site includes "green internships" and "green dream jobs" in consulting, universities and at the executive, mid-career and entry levels.

Environmental Career Opportunities Newsletter (www.ecojobs.com).

ETHICS

Practicing Law:

complaint audit and review for bar association

defense counsel

disciplinary proceedings prosecutor for bar association

state bar court staff

Law-Related Positions:

associate director, AMA division on medical ethics

bioethicist

business ethics instructor

corporate or governmental ethics officer

ethics officer

ethics professor at law school

undergraduate ethics instructor or professor

Law-Related Resources

Academy of Legal Studies in Business (www.aslb. org) — JD's who teach ethics (among other subjects) in the university setting.

Association of Professional Responsibility Lawyers (www.aprl.net) — An organization of consultants, teachers and practitioners in attorney discipline, ethics and risk management.

Directory of Lawyer Disciplinary Agencies and Client Protection Funds (www.abanet.org/cpr/disciplinary.html) — A state-by-state listing assembled by the ABA Center for Professional Responsibility.

The Professional Lawyer — A quarterly magazine produced by the ABA Center for Professional Responsibility that examines professionalism, regulation and ethical issues impacting the legal profession.

General Resources

Applied Ethics Resources (www.ethics.ubc.ca/resources) — Links to ethics Web sites in the fields of healthcare, business, high technology, environmental, media, animal welfare, professionals and more.

Association for Practical and Professional Ethics (http://php.indiana.edu/~appe/home.html) — An organization of scholars and professionals interested in practical and professional ethics. Profiles in Ethics online offers a comprehensive list of member ethics centers.

Council on Governmental Ethics Laws (www.cogel.org) — An organization for government agencies, organizations and individuals with responsibilities or interests in governmental ethics, elections, campaign finance, lobby law and open public meetings and records regulation. Individual associate membership available. Publishes guidebooks to such governmental ethics issues as campaign finance, lobbying and freedom of information.

FOUNDATIONS AND NONPROFIT ORGANIZATIONS

Practicing Law:
directing attorney
director of law firm pro bono work
director of legal affairs
director of legal project
fund-raising counsel
litigation coordinator
special counsel to the president
staff attorney
staff researcher
supervising attorney
Law-Related Organizations:
legal foundations
legal services offices
public defender offices
public interest law centers

Law-Related Positions:
development officer
director of education, effective incarceration
    project
director of governmental relations
director of national training project
director of planned giving
executive director
freelance development/fund-raising assistant
government relations assistant
intake worker
legal information answer line coordinator
legal outreach program developer
organizer for law-related organization
pro bono foundation (IOLTA) administrator
pro bono foundation (IOLTA) director
program developer

Non-Legal Positions:
administrator of small agency
campaign director
CEO of public policy think tank
consumer advocate
director of awards programs
director of planning

director of private family charitable foundation
eligibility investigator for the NCAA
executive director
founder & executive director of nonprofit
    focusing on dating violence prevention
fundraiser
grant writer
organizer
Outward Bound facilitator
president, amateur athletic foundation
president, regional trade association
project director
publications director for theater
public information officer
vice-president, community relations
vice-president, donor and board relations

Law-Related Resources
American Civil Liberties Union (www.aclu.org).
Equal Justice Works (formerly National
    Association for Public Interest Law
    (www.napil.org) - A national coalition of
    student groups mostly from ABA-approved
    law schools. Publishes a public interest career
    resources guide and the Yale Law School
    Public Interest Fellowships Guide.
National Conference of Bar Foundations
    (www.abanet.org/barserv/ncbf/home.html)
    — You'll find a list of member foundations
    online.
National Legal Aid & Defender Association
    (www.nlada.org) — Publishes the Directory
    of Legal Aid and Defender Offices in the US
    biennially. Employment opportunities are
    listed in NLADA's quarterly newsletter.
Public Service JobNet
    (www.law.umich.edu/_Jobnet/main.asp) —
    An online database of public interest jobs by
    location, practice area, eligibility and type of
    position.

General Resources
ACCESS: Networking in the Public Interest
    (www.communityjobs.org) — Offers career
    consulting and job leads to those interested

GETTING INTO NONPROFIT WORK

The road from law school or law practice to nonprofit employment is a relatively easy one: Just be a committed volunteer. Catherine worked as both a legal services lawyer and solo practitioner in Michigan before moving into nonprofit management. Here is her story, and her advice about making your own transition.

Catherine's Statement: All the time I practiced law I was angry. I was angry when my clients were evicted. I was angry when my clients were arrested (even though they were usually guilty). I was even angry when I managed to protect a client, or get a good result for one, because I knew that my clients needed money or a social worker a lot more than they needed me. Before long, I realized that practicing law was encouraging certain, maybe primal, anger in me. It encouraged me to be fairly pugnacious about almost everything. I wasn't sleeping well. I worried about my clients; but I worried more about losing.

At the same time that I was practicing law, I was volunteering at the local animal shelter. I started out cleaning kennels, working in the front office, doing anything and everything the staff asked me to do. I put in a lot of time and made it clear that I was willing to learn. Eventually, I was asked both to sit on the Board of Directors and to do some legal research on antivivisection statutes for a number of national organizations. I came away from all of those experiences feeling up, excited and almost never being angry or losing any sleep.

Opportunity knocked when the current executive director resigned and there was an opening. I was on the search committee and as I reviewed candidates, I realized that none

of them were as well-qualified as I thought I was. So I resigned from the Board and applied for the job. They had known me for several years and liked me, as well as my credentials. It was a small organization without a lot of credibility in the community and they thought my legal background would boost their image.

They hired me. It was an easy transition in some ways, but a difficult one in that I had to give up a dream. I was the youngest of seven children of an immigrant family. My family was very proud of my accomplishments and that felt really good. I also liked the idea of being empowered as a professional, of having the opportunity not only to earn a good living but to do something important. I had to leave that dream behind when I made the transition. Even now, I have some misgivings when I look at my paycheck, but never when I look at my life.

Only in retrospect, though, do I feel bad. My work in animal welfare has always been very absorbing. I started out with strong feelings for animals and their welfare. But I didn't know much about running a business, or about animals, and I had to learn very fast. I spent two years at the humane society in Michigan. That gave me the background to get a position as executive director of a much larger, very prestigious and influential humane society in California.

Some of the things I do in my current job I could not do as well if I had not been to law school or practiced law for five years. I negotiate contracts with dealers for fleet automobiles, with counties and cities to provide animal services, and with private citizens for the purchase and sale of property. I deal with lawyers on trust and estate issues. I talk to legal groups about encouraging clients to provide for animal welfare organizations in their estate planning. I work on planned giving programs. One of the skills I use most often from practicing law is problem solving, looking at issues and developing a strategy. At the same time I find the experience significantly different from practicing law because I am working with a team within a community effort.

Being connected to an organization or a cause is essential to getting a job in a nonprofit. I would be very suspicious if I got a résumé from a lawyer I didn't know. I would suspect the applicant was a self-centered, egotistical,

difficult person who was trying to escape to something less stressful. It would be different if the person had volunteered for our organization and I could see that he was a genuinely committed person with good people skills on top of being well-educated. You need to volunteer, get on the board, offer to help free of charge so that you have a relationship with a particular organization or the substantive community. At least three-quarters of the executive directors of nonprofits in my area volunteered for those organizations before their appointment. It's the single most important key to getting a paid position.

in working for nonprofits. Publishes The National Employment Newspaper for the Non-Profit Sector, a job register updated monthly with hundreds of job-listings from nonprofit organizations around the country. Also features resource lists, book reviews and profiles of nonprofit organizations. Available online, in college career centers, public libraries and other referral centers.

American Society of Association Executives (www.asaenet.org) — A professional society of paid executives of national, state and local trade, professional and philanthropic organizations. Publishes Who's Who in Association Management, and offers a certified association executive program, and other education on effective association management. Maintains an online job board.

Association of Fund-raising Professionals (formerly National Society of Fund-raising Executives), www.nsfre.org — Publishes the Employment Opportunities Newsletter, available only to members, the NSFRE Fund-Raising Dictionary (definitions for 1,400 terms used in the fund-raising field) and other books about the industry. Offers courses like "First Course on Fund-Raising" as

well as certification in fund-raising.

Council on Foundations (www.cof.org) — An association of grant-making foundations and corporations. Publishes a membership list, newsletter and journal. Their Web site offers information on foundation basics.

Essential Information (www.essential.org) — Links to nonprofit organizations.

National Committee on Planned Giving (www.ncpg.org) — A group involved in fund-raising, accounting, estate planning and insurance who specialize in developing charitable gifts through bequests, trusts, annuities, life insurance and real estate. Publishes the Directory of Counsel Members.

Society for Nonprofit Organizations (http://danenet.wicip.org/snpo) — Publishes bimonthly Nonprofit World, a leadership and management magazine for the nonprofit sector. Articles on the legal, legislative, marketing, fund-raising and planning aspects of nonprofit management online.

The Foundation Center (www.fdncenter.org) — A national nonprofit clearinghouse of information on foundations, grants and corporate giving. Maintains an extensive resource library in New York, fully-staffed branch libraries in San Francisco, Washington, Atlanta and Cleveland, and cooperating collections nationwide. Their online library includes a short course on proposal writing as well as regional and international directories. Foundation Center's Guide to Proposal Writing. Includes sample proposals and advice for pre-proposal planning.

GOVERNMENT

Practicing Law in the Federal Jurisdiction:
administrative law judge in agency or
    department
attorney advisor
circuit mediator for US Court of Appeals
deputy general counsel, US Sentencing
    Commission
deputy US attorney
federal public defender
Judge Advocate General (JAG) in any military
    branch, active or reserve
staff attorney in agency or department
technology licensing
US Attorney
US trustee in bankruptcy

Practicing Law in State Jurisdiction:
administrative law judge
attorney general
chief legal counsel for State Ethics Board
condemnation specialist
deputy attorney general
deputy chief counsel for coastal commission
hearing officer for agency or department
legislative analyst
probate referee
program advisor
staff attorney for agency or department
Practicing Law in Local Jurisdictions:
chief or supervising public defender
city attorney
city or county council legal advisor
deputy city attorney

deputy district/prosecuting attorney
deputy public defender
district/prosecuting attorney
hearing officer or administrative law judge

Law-Related Positions:
ADA investigator
bank fraud investigator
child support enforcement case analyst
claims officer
code research analyst (i.e., code reviser)
commissioner, anti-discrimination commission
community relations coordinator
complaint investigator
condemnation specialist
congressional aide
contract compliance administrator
crime prevention coordinator
criminal investigator
deputy planning commissioner
director of ethics commission
director of human relations commission
elected official
ethics officer
executive assistant to Director of Natural
    Resources
forensic investigator
human relations coordinator for Office of
    Women's Rights
immigration inspector
insurance regulation analyst
international or interstate trade relations
    specialist
investigation & resolution specialist
land use examiner
legal documents officer
legal investigator
legislative director
lobbyist
Medicaid/Medicare fraud investigator
member of Labor Relations Board
ombuds person
postal inspector
program advisor
public disclosure commission director

purchasing agent
regulation analyst
research staff for congressional committee
retail application analyst for state lottery
supervisor of public trust accounts
victim's compensation investigator or advocate
waste fraud abuse

Non-Legal Positions:
bus driver
campaign manager
city/county clerk
city manager
city parks landscape laborer
director of commission or agency
director of human relations commission
elected official
executive director of the governor's council on
   disabilities
fund-raiser
human services project manager
mail carrier
mayor
special project administrator

Law-Related Resources
Air Force Attorney Recruiting Office,
   www.jagusaf.hq.af.mil, 1 (800) JAG-USAF.
American Association of Public Welfare Attorneys
   (www.aphsa.org) — An affiliate of the
   American Public Human Services Association.
   Provides an online forum at the national,
   state and regional levels for discussion of
   legal matters pertaining to public welfare.
Army Civilian Attorney Program
   (www.jagnet.army.mil/ppto).
Army JAG Corps Recruiting & Placement Office
   (www.jagcnet.army.mil/recruit.nsf).
Department of Justice (www.usdoj.gov/oam) —
   Posts current job openings in US Attorney
   offices nationwide and in DC.
Federal Bar Association, www.fedbar.org; (202)
   785-1614. Monthly job listings in federal
   government nationwide, plus occasional
   other job tips.

The Federal Law-Related Careers Book — Job
   descriptions and contact information for
   nearly 200 federal positions that are not
   designated "attorney" but which require a
   strong legal background. Paperback; Federal
   Reports, Inc.
Military Lawyers Conference
   (www.jaa.org/MALC-2002.htm) — An
   organization of active, reserve and retired
   military lawyers. Annual conference held in
   conjunction with the ABA's annual meeting.
   Publishes a newsletter.
Navy JAG Recruiting Office (www.jag.navy.mil)
   — Information about both law student
   recruitment and direct commissions for
   experienced lawyers.
Now Hiring: Government Jobs for Lawyers —
   A directory of agencies that hires lawyers.
   Geared to law students, or entry-level
   positions in the executive, legislative and
   judicial branches, and in independent
   agencies of federal government. An ABA
   paperback.
State and Local Law News — A quarterly
   newsletter published by the ABA State and
   Local Government Law section.
US Coast Guard Direct Commission Lawyer
   Program (www.uscg.mil/legal/recruit/
   dclinterinfo.htm) — Information about
   requirements and application procedures, as
   well as duties, salary and assignments.
Contact city attorney offices — Located in all
   incorporated communities. Call the
   personnel or human resources office for
   current job openings and application
   procedures.

General Resources
Army Civilian Personnel Online
   (www.cpol.army.mil/index.html).
Career America Connection — A telephone
   system of worldwide federal job opportunities.
   Online information and application packages
   mailed to you. Salaries and employee benefits
   information. Special recruitment messages.

Available worldwide 24 hours a day, 7 days a week. Phone (912) 757-3100.

FedWorld Information Network (www.fedworld.gov) — Job postings from the federal government.

FirstGov (www.firstgov.gov) — A retrieval site that provides access to nearly 850,000 US government and military Web sites.

HEALTHCARE

Practicing Law:
in-house hospital lawyer
managed care attorney
medical malpractice lawyer
outside counsel for healthcare organization

Law-Related Positions:
bioethicist
compliance officer
director of corporate integrity & compliance
editor for health law digest
healthcare licensing manager
managed care specialist
risk management advisor

Management Positions:
assistant to the president of a community hospital
hospital administrator
marketing director for private health-care provider
vice-president, corporate finance

Law-Related Resources
The Health Lawyer — A periodic newsletter published by the ABA Health Law Section on current trends in health law.

American Health Lawyers Association (www.healthlawyers.org) — An organization of health lawyers and clients formed in a merger of the National Health Lawyers Association and the American Academy of Healthcare Attorneys. Web site includes a national job bank. (202) 833-1100.

General Resources:
American Academy of Medical Administrators (www.aameda.org) — An umbrella organization for administrators in managed care, healthcare information, home health, oncology and cardiovascular clinics. Publishes a bimonthly newsletter with administrative positions. (847) 759-8601.

American Association of Health Plans (www.aahp.org) — National trade association for HMO's, PPO's and other network-based plans. Publishes Healthplan Magazine containing articles about healthcare trends and Managed Care Careers newsletter which contains ads for directors, executives and administrators in sales, marketing, research, projects and personnel.

American College of Healthcare Executives (www.ache.org) — Publishes a members-only executive employment newsletter. (312) 424-2800.

American Medical Group Association (www.amga.org) — A group of about 200 medical groups nationwide that focus on the business aspects of medical group practice. (703) 838-0033.

Healthcare Financial Management Association (www.hfma.org) — An organization of CEOs, CFOs, controllers, patient accounts managers, information management specialists, consultants and others involved in the financial management of integrated health systems and other healthcare organizations. Publishes Modern Healthcare (www. modernhealthcare. com), a weekly newsmagazine covering federal and state legislation and regulations, political activity and financial news of interest to healthcare organizations. (708) 531-9600.

INTERNATIONAL

Practicing Law:
immigration lawyer
international transactions lawyer

TIPS FOR GETTING INTO HOSPITAL LAW

Suzanne Mitchell, former assistant dean for Career Services at the University of Chicago Law School, spent many years as a hospital lawyer before entering career service, and returned to that milieu in 1998. She cautions those aspiring to this work to expect an extremely tight and demanding market. Most hospitals will not hire inexperienced law school graduates because they are:

- too small to devote any resources to training a new lawyer;
- too busy to hire anyone who needs supervision or orientation; and
- too under-funded to maintain an adequate library for the lawyer who needs to research before issuing an answer.

Consider the following positions as a career path into a hospital position, says Mitchell:

- a law firm with a healthcare, general corporate, medical malpractice, labor and employment, tax or real estate practice;
- federal or state health, human services, or social services agencies;
- managed care companies;
- insurance companies;
- nonprofit organizations with a health and human services focus.

In addition, consider:

- volunteering in a hospital legal office, or health-related agency (e.g. providing legal advice at a clinic for AIDS patients, working at Planned Parenthood);
- joining the American Health Lawyers Association (see reference under law-related resources);
- joining local, state and national associations with sections that pertain to health law;
- applying for law-related positions like human resources manager, regulatory compliance, or grants, contract or risk management.

"One last bit of advice," says Mitchell. "The healthcare field is not the place for people who like to master a body of law in a relatively short period of time. This is an area where the issues—political, legal, economic and ethical—change rapidly."

in-house counsel for multi-national company
US counsel for foreign companies or investors

Law-Related Positions:
business agent for import/export company
executive director, International Development
    Law Institute
international trade development
international trade services (country-of-origin
    verification & ISO 9000 consultation)
legal translator for foreign law firm

Non-Legal Positions:
adventure travel leader

bicycle tour organizer and leader
foreign service officer
international or interstate trade relations
    specialist
leader of scuba diving trips to Southeast Asia
managing director of an alternative energy
    company
program developer for trade education
    foundation

Law-Related Resources:
ABA Guide to Foreign Law Firms — Contains
    listings of law firms in foreign jurisdictions.
American Immigration Lawyers Association

(www.aila.org) — A group of lawyers who specialize in assisting families and businesses with immigration issues. Web site includes information about immigration law and a chapter index. (202) 216-2400.

American Society of International Law (www.asil.org) — Publishes the International Law Career Guide with information on international careers in human rights, international trade, environment, telecommunications, finance & banking, international development and dispute resolution.

International Lawyer's Newsletter — A 24-36 page bimonthly issue-oriented publication for lawyers interested in international law. Each issue contains job announcements, and references to international employment placement agencies. For more information,

contact Kluwer Law & Taxation Publishers, www.kluwerlaw.com, (212) 620-8080.

International Lawyer — A quarterly journal produced by the ABA International Law and Practice Section. Contains articles for lawyers with an interest in international business transactions, public international law, and comparative law.

General Resources:

Foreign Service Exam — Contact The State Department, Recruitment Division — FSWE, PO Box 12226, Arlington, VA 22219, for information about testing dates and requirements.

International Career Employment Center, www.internationaljobs.org. A biweekly publication listing over 600 open positions with international health and welfare

WORKING ABROAD

Ahhh, the romance of a job overseas. Wouldn't it be nice to study French for six years, catch the travel bug on a post-college tour of Europe, and snag a job in a French law firm upon graduation from law school? It's a wonderful fantasy, but far from the reality of obtaining international positions.

The most common way for a law school graduate to work abroad as a lawyer is to get hired by the international law department of a large, big city law firm and be assigned to a foreign locale for a year or so. European placements out of New York City and Asian placements out of Los Angeles, San Francisco and Seattle, are customary under those circumstances. If you practice any place else, finding well-paid work in a foreign country will be a tremendous challenge.

Notice that I said "well-paid" work. Most law school graduates without a law firm or business affiliation who end up working

abroad start out with volunteer work, internships or acting as interpreters for foreign law firms. One graduate of the University of South Carolina School of Law who was fluent in French and Spanish got a job in Italy by offering to work unpaid to get the experience, telling them she was going to be living there anyway. A University of Texas graduate obtained a position in a German law firm translating English contracts into German and vice versa. She could not practice law, and as a result, her position was low paid with no prestige, but she did gain valuable experience in the international arena.

If you really want to practice law abroad and aren't qualified for employment with the international law department of a major US firm or the in-house legal department of a multinational company, move to the country of your choice and start making contacts!

organizations, state governments, universities, federal agencies, government contractors, corporations involved in international trade and finance, export management firms, engineering companies, associations, foundations, student exchange organizations and international government agencies including the UN.

United Nations (www.un.org) — Current employment openings online.

JUDICIARY

Possible Jurisdictions:
county trial court system
federal court of appeals
federal district court
government agency or department
municipal or small claims court
state appellate court system
US Supreme Court

Positions Practicing Law:
central research staff
staff attorney
hearing officer or administrative law
    judge
judge or justice
justice of the peace
law clerk
court commissioner/magistrate
pro-tem judge
supervising staff attorney

Law-Related Positions
bankruptcy administrator
bankruptcy case administration manager
bankruptcy examiner
circuit mediator
court administrator
court clerk
court interpreter
director of training for judicial district
guardianship clerk
probate clerk

Law-Related Resources
Council of Appellate Staff Attorneys — A subdivision of the Judicial Division of the American Bar Association, consisting of about 300 lawyers who work as permanent staff lawyers for appellate courts nationwide. Publishes the CASA Quarterly, a newsletter, and a Directory of Appellate Central Staff Counsel.

Federal and State Judicial Clerkship Directory — Application procedures, hiring criteria and employment opportunities for hundreds of federal and state court judges. Paperback; National Association for Law Placement, annually updated.

Federal Judiciary Home Page (www.uscourts. gov) — Posts employment opportunities online for many, but not all, federal courts. Also publishes a monthly newsletter that announces vacancies in magistrate and judicial positions.

National Association of Administrative Law Judges (www.aalj.org) — Nonprofit group dedicated to promoting the legal education, training and professional standing of social security administrative law judges. Members include anyone appointed to the position of administrative law judge. Web site offers links to social security offices, federal courts, and other related sites.

National Association of Hearing Officials, www.naho.org. Members include attorney and non-attorney hearing officials, ALJ's and managers in the resolution of human services-related administrative matters.

National Conference of Appellate Court Clerks (http://ncacc.ncsconline.org) — An organization of court administrators. Publishes a bimonthly newsletter.

Supreme Court Judicial Fellows Program — One-year appointment working on projects concerning the federal court system and the administration of justice. Requires 2+ years professional experience with a record of high performance. Paid as federal employee.

A JUDGE'S PERSPECTIVE

A seat on the bench is an attractive way to avoid many of the stresses that plague the general practitioner. Although some attorneys forsake high incomes for an appointment to the judiciary, judges still earn comfortable salaries and in most jurisdictions receive generous retirement benefits. They never have to worry about billing clients or collecting fees, nor about rising overhead. The cases judges decide have beginnings, middles and ends that generally occur over the span of a few days. Most importantly, they exercise the power to bring closure to those conflicts.

The choice to move to the bench is not, of course, available to every practicing lawyer. The lawyer must either be well-respected among those with the power to make appointments, or capable of waging a campaign and winning an election for the seat. More significantly, judges must find enough value in the adversarial system to tolerate sitting in the middle of argument and hostility. And, they must learn to endure constant public scrutiny, second-guessing and criticism.

Judge Smith entered the profession at a time when there were few women lawyers, and female litigators were even rarer. In defense against anonymity, she resorted to wearing loud hats and eccentric clothing in court, and brandishing her advocacy like a weapon. But as her legal reputation grew, she gradually relaxed and started each lawsuit in a novel fashion: by agreeing with opposing counsel to avoid mutual hostility. Eventually, she wearied of private practice. After four years of active lobbying, she was appointed to the state trial court bench.

Judge Smith's Statement: Back in 1970, the senior partner of the firm I joined said to me, "Someday you're going to be on the bench." I laughed it off because that was not what I saw for myself. I saw myself as a fire-breathing litigator.

In my first four years of practice, it was my goal to do every kind of proceeding and action at least once. What I ended up enjoying most was the trial work. As a woman lawyer in the early 1970's, I didn't have many examples to follow. At one extreme, there were women lawyers in title companies, and at the other, there was "Bernice the Bitch." By the time I was ready to go out on my own, I decided that if I had to choose one image, I'd be like Bernice, which in those days meant being pretty abrasive and strident. But remember. Back then, a woman got run over if she didn't throw down the gauntlet right away.

I worked horrendous hours, because when men opposed me (which was almost all the time) they tended to prepare harder. They took it very personally if they lost a case to a woman, as if it was somehow a challenge to their manhood. Fortunately, as my reputation preceded me, men expected a female barracuda, and I could afford to be nicer.

As I became more experienced, the first thing I would do in almost every major case was to take the opposing counsel to lunch. I spent half the time talking about the case and the other half speaking personally, finding out whether the lawyer was married and had kids, what his hobbies were, what other pressures he might be experiencing in addition to the case we had in common, and how all these factors might affect the progress of our case. If possible, I'd make a little pact to avoid hostility between us even as we advocated the clients' hostilities.

As the years went by though, I noticed that attorneys were becoming less and less cooperative. There was no such thing as settling a case over a cup of coffee. It was all so stress-producing that I used to come home like a helicopter setting down. I was all wired up, outraged and upset. In time, all that combat steered me into the judiciary.

I still feel the wear and tear of the adversarial system. In fact, the hardest adjustment in moving to the bench was shedding the adversarial role. As a judge, you have to sit back and wait for the other side to wage their attack. With my background as a litigator, that was difficult. I would listen to one side's arguments and force myself not to cut in and say, "Well what about this?" and "What about that?" and Gee, haven't you considered this, this and this?" I had to

consciously jump back from an adversarial orientation to become the decider. That's turned out to be the best thing about being a judge—the opportunity to do what I think is right. And, in some ways, it's the worst too, because it is an awesome challenge.

There are downsides to being a judge. First of all, the loneliness of the judiciary is not overrated. I'm definitely more restricted in my public interaction, having to watch what I say about everything. I'm never sure if some inadvertent statement I make is going to end up being lambasted on the front page of the newspaper.

All in all, though, I find this very satisfying. My years on the bench have been the best of my life.

Application deadline mid-November every year. Contact the Administrative Director, Judicial Fellows Program, Room (202) 479-3415.

Contact state and local bar associations. Often publish membership directories that include current listings of court personnel.

LABOR UNIONS

Practicing Law:
grievance counsel for union member
in-house labor counsel for employer
in-house lawyer for labor union
outside counsel for labor union
outside counsel for employer

Law-Related Positions
administrator/manager
labor mediator
labor negotiator
union representative

Law-Related Resources
National Lawyers Guild (www.nlg.org/committees/labor/newsletter_index.htm) — The AFL-CIO Lawyers Coordinating Committee puts online a state-by-state listing of AFL-CIO counsel, both private and in-house. Available only to member attorneys (those who verify by letter that 50 percent or more of their practice consists of union-side representation).

General Resources
Directory of US Labor Organizations, edited by Courtney Clifford. 200 national unions, professional and state employee associations engaged in labor representation. Paperback; Bureau of National Affairs.

Encyclopedia of Associations, "Section 15: Labor Unions, Associations and Federations." Over 200 national collective bargaining groups listed. Published by Gale Research, annual.

LAW ENFORCEMENT

Practicing Law:
criminal defense lawyer in private practice
criminal prosecutor
department legal advisor
law enforcement legal advisor
legal counsel to sheriff's office
public defense lawyer

Law-Related Positions:
agent for CIA, DEA or FBI
court bailiff
customs inspector
fines, penalties and forfeiture specialist
immigration inspector
juvenile justice
ombuds person
parole officer
police administration
police officer
postal inspector
special agent (customs, narcotics, US Marshall
    service, border patrol, secret service)
state patrol chief

Law-Related Resources
Association of Trial Lawyers of America
    (www.atlanet.org) — An organization of
    lawyers, law professors and law students
    interested in criminal defense advocacy.
    Publishes an annual directory of members
    and various journals. Affiliated regional
    associations operate nationwide.
    (800) 424-2725.
Criminal Justice — A quarterly ABA magazine
    providing practical treatment of aspects of
    criminal law.
National Association of Criminal Defense Lawyers
    (www.criminaljustice.org).
National Directory of Prosecuting Attorneys
    (www.ndaa-apri.org) — Members include
    prosecuting attorneys and assistant

prosecuting attorneys nationwide. Provides a
guide to each state's prosecution system.
Published annually. For a copy, call (703)
549-9222.
National Legal Aid & Defender Association
    (www.nlada.org).

LAW FIRMS

Positions Practicing Law:
contract (temporary or freelance) lawyer
department manager
managing attorney
managing partner
non-equity partner
participating attorney
partner
partnership-track associate
of counsel
public, pro bono or public service counsel
referral attorney
regional partner
senior attorney
staff attorney
special counsel

Areas of Practice:
administrative
adoption
agricultural
alternative-dispute resolution
antitrust
appellate
banking
bankruptcy
biomedical issues
bond
business organization
commercial finance
commercial litigation
commercial banking
communications
computer

constitutional
construction
copyright
corporate
corporate reorganization
disciplinary action by licensing boards
discrimination
domestic relations
elder
employee benefits
employment
employment relations
energy
entertainment
environmental
estate planning
family
franchising
general practice
governmental relations/ lobbying
guardianship
healthcare
immigration
insurance
insurance defense
intellectual property
international finance
international
labor
litigation
lobbying
matrimonial
mergers & acquisitions
natural resources
patent
pensions
probate
public contracts
public utility
real estate
social security
sports
taxation
trademark
transportation

trust
workers' compensation

Law-Related Positions:
client services manager
director of business development
director of client relations
director of legal information services
director of management and
legal information services
director of practice development
director of professional development
director of training (clerical/paralegal)
firm manager
in-house corporate communications
in-house editor
law firm administrator
law librarian
legal assistant manager
marketing manager
paralegal/legal assistant
personnel director
professional development training officer
public relations director
recruiting administrator/director
strategic planner

Law-Office Management Resources
Altman Weil Pensa (www.altmanweil.com) —
    Articles available online on law firm
    management topics like strategic planning
    and human resources. Publishes an annually
    updated overview of median salaries
    nationwide for law firm support staff.
Association of Legal Administrators
    (www.alanet.org) — Chapter contacts listed
    online. ALA Management Connections offers
    a nationwide job bank. Also offers Career
    Talk, a series of career development articles.
    (847) 816-1212.
Law Partnership: Its Rights and Responsibilities, by
    George H. Cain. Offers advice on drafting an
    effective agreement, legal requirements in
    the relationship of partners to associates,
    potential difficulties brought by dissolution

INTELLECTUAL PROPERTY LITIGATION: A "GENTLY ADVERSARIAL" PRACTICE

Many lawyers who tire of conflict and hostility neither want to nor feel able to walk away from the profession. Concerned that they give their career every consideration, they trade one job for another within the profession until they find the right niche. Some move from private practice to public practice or corporate counsel; others from one area of law to another. With enough exploration and persistence, many settle into a less adversarial alternative.

Tom made two mistakes in getting his legal career off the ground. First, he went to law school before he was ready to make a commitment to the profession. Then, when he finally decided to take his degree seriously, he accepted the first job he was offered without exploring whether the subject matter, or style of his employer, suited his talents and personality. As a result, he was pigeonholed for five years in an intolerable environment. Only through a series of lucky breaks did he finally discover a specialty he now finds thoroughly enjoyable.

Tom's Statement: I went to law school without any expectation of ever practicing. I just wanted to stay out of the Army. Once I accomplished that, I didn't take my career seriously until almost 10 years later.

When I got married, I approached a solo practitioner for a job as an associate. I walked in, said "Here I am," and he said, "Okay. You're hired." The next four years consisted of a series of emergencies. It was Band Aid law; I was always patching up this guy's mistakes. I learned a little bit about all of his work, mostly personal injury lawsuits with some real estate, probate and misdemeanors thrown in. But I never felt comfortable with any of it.

Once, I quit to write science fiction for a few months. For the first time in years, I felt I was doing the right thing. But then we needed money and I didn't know how else to earn it. So I went back to work for him again. By the time I left for good, I had two children and didn't see fiction writing as a viable option to support them. Instead, I advertised in the legal newspapers for work assignments from other attorneys, set up an office in my home and waited for the calls to come in.

Rather than generating freelance work, the advertisement led to my next job. A three-person firm handling a huge patent case was facing three firms on the other side and was dying for help. I joined them on a provisional basis to write responses to summary judgment motions. They liked my work so well that I was asked to join the firm.

That was where law opened up for me. There was a whole new area to explore—patents, copyrights, trademarks—and I was pleasantly surprised to discover how well it suited my style. The litigation moves more slowly. Writing is very important. Cases are often won on the briefs I produce.

I worked for six years as part of that firm. Now, I do the same kind of work as an independent contractor for one of the partners, but the bulk of my practice is with my own clients. I emphasize "own," because this is where the satisfaction comes: from making the decisions, being the one in charge, taking the risks and reaping the rewards myself.

I still consider getting out of law every once in a while. The last time was about a year ago when we were in the middle of a big trade secrets lawsuit. The case took on a terribly combative tone, and it drove me crazy. At first, it was horrible waking up Monday morning. Pretty soon I contracted "Sunday Syndrome," dreading Monday when I awoke on Sunday. Eventually, the only good time of the week was Friday night because I still had all of Saturday before I felt that dread of heading back to the office again.

Other lawyers might crave winning; speaking the loudest and the most quickly to get the judge to believe them. But that's not for me. I've set limits now on my practice. When I accept a big litigation case, I associate a trial counsel to handle the things I don't like, leaving me to do what I enjoy most: the client contact, research, motion and appeals practice, being the lead counsel. My practice is gently adversarial and scholarly, and I no longer feel any pressing urge to flee.

and retirement. An ABA paperback.

Law Practice Management section of the American Bar Association (www.abanet.org/lpm/home.html) — One of the better-organized and most active sections of the ABA. Publishes Law Practice Management magazine.

Legal Marketing Association, formerly National Law Firm Marketing Association (www.legalmarketing.org) — Maintains a job bank of marketing positions. Publishes Strategies: The Journal of Legal Marketing, The View from Within: A National Survey of Legal Marketing Directors and a compensation & benefits survey.

Survey of Legal Recruitment & Attorney Management Personnel. Job responsibilities and salaries of legal recruitment administrators and legal personnel directors. Available from the National Association for Law Placement. (847) 657-6717.

Subject Matter Specialty Resources

American Bar Association (www.abanet.org) — Special interest sections and committees include administrative law & regulatory practice; affordable housing and community development law; air and space law; antitrust; business law; children and the law; communications law; construction industry; criminal justice; disability law; dispute resolution; domestic violence; entertainment and sports industries; family law; franchising; general practice; health law; individual rights and responsibilities; intellectual property law; international law and practice; labor and employment; law practice management; legal problems of the elderly; litigation; natural resources, energy and environmental law; public contract law; public utility, communication and transportation law; real property, probate and trust law; science and technology; state and local government law; tax; and tort and insurance practice. Many sections and committees publish periodic newsletters and journals. (312) 988-5522.

National Law Journal — Publishes periodic special pullout sections on various specialty areas (e.g., sports law, intellectual property, corporate law, employment law, technology).

Careers in Admiralty & Maritime Law — By Robert M. Jarvis. Basic information about this practice field. An ABA pamphlet.

Air and Space Lawyer — A quarterly newsletter on significant developments in the field produced by the ABA's Air and Space Law Section.

Lawyer-Pilots Bar Association (www.lpba.org) — For lawyers who are licensed pilots or engaged or interested in aviation law.

Antitrust — A magazine on developments in antitrust law produced three times a year by the ABA's Antitrust Law Section.

National Association of Bond Lawyers

(www.nabl.org) — Lawyers involved with state and municipal bond work. Web site includes a job service and interactive news groups. (312) 648-9590.

American Association of Attorney-CPAs (www.attorney-cpa.com) — Publishes an annual membership directory and a quarterly newsletter To join, must be licensed both as a lawyer and a CPA, or be licensed in one and in the process of obtaining a license for the other. Call 1-888-ATTYCPA.

Business Law Today — A bimonthly magazine produced by the ABA Business Law Section. Features substantive articles, lifestyle pieces on being a business lawyer and practice forms.

National Academy of Elder Law Attorneys (www.naela.org) — Lawyers nationwide with practices involving estate planning, probate and guardianship, nursing home placement, public benefits planning, trusts, healthcare and other issues involving legal services to the elderly and disabled. Publishes a registry of members, including areas of expertise, and a series of pamphlets on aging. (520) 881-4005.

Entertainment and Sports Lawyer — A quarterly newsletter of the ABA Entertainment and Sports Industries Forum.

American Association of Nurse Attorneys (www.taana.org) — Acts as an employment network and assists new nurse attorneys. Publishes quarterly Inside TAANA and annual membership directory. (877) 538-2262.

Probate and Property — A bimonthly magazine aimed at lawyers who devote a large part of their practice to real estate law or wills, trusts and estates. Published by the American Bar Association.

Section of Taxation Newsletter — A quarterly publication of the ABA Taxation Section. Updates current tax developments and reports on work of the section.

Transportation Lawyers Association (www.translaw.org) — Publishes Transportation Lawyer five times a year, and a biennial roster of members.

American College of Trust & Estate Counsel (www.actec.org) — A national group of nearly 3000 lawyers invited to be members due to their high standards of practice. (310) 398-1888.

Should You Become a Freelance Lawyer? What Every Lawyer & Law Firm Needs to Know About Temporary Legal Services. (3rd edition, 2004) — By Deborah Arron & Deborah Guyol. How to hire and work with, and how to practice as, a lawyer on a temporary or freelance basis. See order information on the inside front and back cover.

Litigation Practice Resources

Defense Research Institute (www.dri.org) — An organization for insurance defense lawyers. Member directory online as well as expanded attorney profiles and links to state and local defense organizations. (312) 795-1101.

Association of Trial Lawyers of America (www.atlanet.org) — An organization of lawyers, judges, law professors and law students interested in civil plaintiff and criminal defense advocacy. Online job bank. Affiliated regional associations operate nationwide.

The Brief — News and feature magazine on current events in the fields of tort and insurance law. Produced quarterly by the ABA Tort and Insurance Practice Section.

Litigation — A quarterly journal in the style of a magazine that focuses on a specific trial practice topic in each issue. Produced by the ABA Litigation Section.

General Resources

Associate Salary Survey — Based on a survey of law firms nationwide, this report details salary ranges for associates through the 8th year, bonus structures and timing of salary increases by firm size. Available from the National Association for Law Placement (www.nalp.org).

American Lawyer — A weekly newsmagazine focusing on the legal profession, especially from a large law firm perspective. Publishes lists of law firms by specialty, size or other category and special features on different areas of law.

Christian Legal Society (www.clsnet.org) — A national organization established in 1961 for lawyers, judges, law professors, students and non-lawyers. (703) 642-1070.

Getting Started: Basics for a Successful Law Firm — Edited by Arthur C. Greene. Covers the life cycle of the law firm, characteristics of successful practice arrangements, ownership options, content of partnership agreements and financing the new law firm. An ABA paperback.

Guide to Small Firm Employment — A booklet addressing the advantages and disadvantages of small firm employment, including methods and resources for the job-search. Brochure available from the National Association for Law Placement (www.nalp.org).

International Alliance of Holistic Lawyers (www.iahl.org) — A nonprofit association of lawyers interested in supporting each other in practicing law from a whole systems approach, increasing their career satisfaction, and transforming the nature of conflict resolution in the US. Emphasizes personal and professional change through educational outreach. (802) 388-7478. For additional information, see Chapter 5 and Appendix 5.

Law Firm Partnership Agreements — By Leslie D. Corwin and Arthur J. Ciampi. A detailed study of law firm partnership, including sample agreements. Looseleaf; Law Journal Seminars Press.

Lawyer's Weekly USA (www.masslaw.com) — A 40-page tabloid for small firm lawyers.

Martindale-Hubbell Law Directory — Published in 26 volumes and annually updated. Identifies over 700,000 lawyers, law firms and corporate legal departments in the US, Canada, and the international community. Extensive biographical and practice information for law firms which pay for a listing; others referenced in brief. Published in CD-ROM. Accessible on Lexis-Nexis.

The Of Counsel Agreement: A Guide for Law Firm & Practitioner — Harold G. Wren & Beverly J. Glascock. A 97-page examination of various of-counsel arrangements, including sample agreements. An ABA paperback.

Contact state and/or local bar associations. Most maintain special interest sections and produce newsletters and other publications.

LEGAL INFORMATION SCIENCE

corporate libraries
court libraries
data management companies
government agencies
law firms
law schools
public libraries
publishers

Possible Positions:

director of legal information services
independent law librarian
law librarian
manager of information systems
staff attorney for municipal research service
vice-president for information services

Law-Related Resources

American Association of Law Libraries (www.aallnet.org) — Librarians for courts, bar associations, law schools, private law firms, corporations and government. Publishes a monthly newsletter that contains job announcements. Career Hotline updated on Fridays. Online database of members and biennial salary survey. (312) 939-4764.

LOBBYING & PUBLIC AFFAIRS

Practicing Law:
administrative law attorney
governmental relations lawyer
regulatory lawyer

Law-Related Positions
corporate director, federal affairs
director of corporate affairs
fundraiser
governmental relations assistant
lobbyist
policy and legislative affairs director or staff
public relations or public affairs for a
bar association
regional marketing director

Other Positions:
campaign manager
political campaign planning
political consultant
public affairs officer
public affairs producer
public affairs director or staff
public information officer
VP/manager, public affairs

Law-Related Resources
ABA Legislative & Government Advocacy,
www.abanet.org/legadv/home.html. The
lobbying arm for the ABA.
*Lobbying Manual: A Compliance Guide for Lawyers
and Lobbyists.* Real-world examples demystify
complex world of federal lobbying laws. An
ABA paperback.

PUBLISHING

Practicing Law:
author representation
defamation lawyer
First Amendment lawyer
in-house counsel for publishing company
outside counsel for publishing company

Management Positions with Legal Publishers:
acquisitions director
editor of legal magazine, newspaper or
journal
manager, educational services
publisher of career books for lawyers
publisher of marketing books for lawyers
vice-president for governmental relations

Staff Positions with Legal Publishers:
access specialist
account representative
applications consultant
client support specialist
computer-aided legal research
trainer
copy editor
database development
developing Internet tools for lawyers
documentation specialist
legal reporting
legal research & writing
marketing specialist
purchasing
quality assurance
reference attorney
research associate
sales representative
search representative
software development
Non-Legal Positions:
author's agent
independent publisher
publisher or editor of an industry
newsletter
publisher or editor of an investment advisory
newsletter
publisher of a city magazine
owner and publisher of a neighborhood weekly
newspaper

Law-Related Publishers (all have online job listings)
Aspen Publishers (www.aspenpub.com).

MAKING MONEY ON SELF-HELP LAW

Ralph Warner was a self-described "quintessential hippie lawyer" who went to law school to change the world. When he became disillusioned with the law's ability to change anything, he dropped out of lawyering without sacrificing his notion of making a significant contribution to society. What began as a service to the poor evolved into a thriving legal self-help publishing company, Nolo Press, which offers affordable legal information and advice to the average citizen. This is his story:

Warner's Statement: I went into law because I somehow saw it as a way to make money while, at the same time, doing good. Since then, I've learned that life doesn't compensate poets well.

After graduation, I ran out and did what a whole lot of other people did: I joined Legal Aid and immediately filed a bunch of court actions against all of these huge and gross unfairnesses. We were able to shift some money from here to there; to win some individual cases. But I saw so many of these cases as merely winning $30 million here and moving it there without any more money being spent on the poor. The federal courts didn't make the poor less poor. They just took money away from somebody else who needed it just as badly so the game could go on forever. It got to the point that I couldn't write another grant, or go before another unresponsive legislative committee, or file another court action that was going to be buried.

After five years, most of the people who went into law for altruistic reasons—myself included—were burned out and unhappy. I looked very hard for another way to live because it seemed that law didn't work. It produced a certain amount of money, but it didn't produce any poetry. And I really wanted to do something to change things for the better. Why? Because I was one of the people for whom the whole American dream worked: I grew up in the suburbs, passed all the SATs with flying colors, went to exactly the right schools, and got all the right degrees. But by the time I was 25 years old, I felt like I had done it all. At age 28, I quit everything.

Ed Sherman, my former partner here at Nolo Press, worked with me at Contra Costa Legal Services and quit about nine months before I did. Between the two of us we had five kids, and neither he nor I knew what to do next. So we ran a legal clinic out of the backyard. While running this clinic, Ed and I realized that half of the employees at Legal Aid only existed to tell people they weren't poor and miserable enough to qualify for free legal services. And yet those people had no other place to go. At some point, Ed wrote instructions to do your own divorce, put some staples in the side of it and ran it off as a quasi-book. It sold 500 copies.

Fortunately, the bar association attacked it as dangerous without ever having read it. What luck! Suddenly we were selling a couple thousand copies a month. Since then, we've sold more than 500,000 copies of the divorce book in California, and 35 percent of the population handles their own divorces. Now, twenty-seven years after we started writing plain-English law books for non-lawyers, Nolo Press publishes more than 120 titles—books, software, legal forms, audio and video tapes—and has over five million copies in print. Our products have helped more people take care of their legal work than any lawyer or law firm in history.

I don't have a grand plan in running this business, but I do have my own personal plan. I don't want to commute. I don't want to work 90 hours a week. I don't want to be too greedy. I want to continue to have fun. What appeals to me is the notion of empowering people with the tools to represent themselves. It satisfies a part of me that needs to be on the right side of the world.

I don't know that anybody is ever going to change the world's view about sharing everything. We are basically pretty greedy monkeys and the world's always been a pretty unfair place. But to the extent that anybody changes anything, they get there by walking step by step from where they are to where they want to be.

Talking about it, arguing in court, filing papers doesn't change it. Doing it changes it. In that sense, I hope my experience with Nolo serves as a model for others.

Bureau of National Affairs, Inc. (www.bna.com).
Commerce Clearinghouse (www.cch.com)
James Publishing (www.jamespublishing.com)
Lexis/Nexis (www.lexis-nexis.com).
Lexis Law Publishing
    (www.lexislawpublishing.com).
Martindale-Hubbell (www.martindale.com).
Matthew Bender & Co.
    (www.bender.com).
Nolo Press (www.nolo.com).
Reed Elsevier (www.reed-elsevier.com).
Research Institute of America
    (www.riahome.com).
Shepard's/McGraw-Hill, Inc.
    (www.shepards.com).
Thomson Corporation (www.thomcorp.com).
VersusLaw (www.versuslaw.com).
West Information Publishing Group
    (www.westgroup.com).

REAL ESTATE

Practicing Law:
associate counsel for real estate
    association
construction lawyer
in-house lawyer for real estate company
in-house lawyer for closing company
in-house lawyer for mortgage company
real estate lawyer

Law-Related Positions
land use examiner
real estate law newsletter editor
title examiner
zoning and short-platting specialist

Non-Legal Positions
carpenter
commercial property manager
commercial real estate broker
co-founder and CEO of national resort
    communities development company
developer of affordable housing for the elderly
director of development company building
    housing for the homeless
director of human relations commission
director of planning, community redevelopment
    project
head of real estate subsidiary of major corporation
house painter
independent commercial real estate developer
independent residential real estate developer
on-site condominium sales
project manager for residential real estate
    development
real estate developer
real estate licensing course instructor
residential property manager
residential real estate agent or broker
residential rehabilitation

residential remodel contractor
restoration specialist
unimproved property management

Law-Related Resources:
American College of Real Estate Lawyers
(www.acrel.org) — An organization of real
estate lawyers. Invited to be members for

their reputation for quality legal work.
(301) 816-9811.
The Construction Lawyer — A quarterly
newsletter produced by the ABA Forum on
the Construction Industry containing articles
on recent developments in the construction
industry as well as announcements of
organizations in the field.

THE ROAD TO REAL ESTATE DEVELOPMENT

Law is a profession of abstractions and
vicarious involvement. Real estate
development couldn't be more different; it's
hands-on, risky and at the end of the project,
you can see the results of your labor.

Alan practiced law for 12 years before
founding his own real estate development
company. He loves what he is doing; it is his
passion. Not only does he have time to enjoy
his family, but he gets a kick out of the
characters who inhabit the industry. More
rewarding to him, though, is the challenge
that comes from investing his creativity, time
and ingenuity where the potential for a large
financial return is so great. This is his story:

Alan's Statement: I don't regret having
gone into the practice of law, or even having
stayed long enough to get some sense of
what it was about. And I have no regrets
about leaving. None. Not for a minute.

What I do regret is having practiced for as
long as I did. It irritates me that, in 10 or 11
years of practice, I probably put in four or
five years too many.

What tied me to the law for so long? My
perception is that people either have stable
relationships or they don't. I've been married
for almost 20 years. I worked with lawyers I
liked. No one was driving me away from law.
I was under no compulsion to get out of the

practice. Unlike some of my friends, I was not
unhappy. But I didn't feel great about practicing
law. It wasn't fulfilling. And it got boring.

Before I entered law school, I had no idea
what lawyers did. I had no lawyer-mentors or
other examples to follow. My mentor was my
father. He was a good businessman in a small
town sort of way; he ran a garage and fixed
cars. I remember when I was a kid, my father
asked if I wanted to go into his auto repair
business with him. Even though I loved fixing
cars, I said no. I was too young to be asked
the question, and too stupid to realize I'd
answered too quickly.

Thereafter, it was generally accepted that
I was going to do something of a professional
nature; something that would help me avoid
what my parents saw as the hardship in their
own lives. I didn't want to be a doctor. What
I looked forward to was law school and then
going into business.

As time went by, I lost sight of the fact
that I never intended to be a lawyer in the
first place; that I'd gone to law school only as
a means of learning how business is done.
And while practicing, I fooled myself into
believing that I was participating in my
clients' businesses, and was therefore a
businessman myself.

What I've learned since is that when a
client called me to do what I thought of as

General Resources

National Association of Women in Construction (www.nawic.org) — More than 200 local chapters nationwide provide networking and information-gathering opportunities. (817) 877-5551.

Society for Marketing Professional Services (www.smps.org) — Business development for design- and construction-related firms. Publishes Marketing Salary & Expense Survey. Online job listing. (800) 292-7677.

SPORTS

Practicing Law:

in-house counsel for league

---

initiating a transaction, he was really calling me to finish it. You see, to me that phone call was the beginning of the excitement. To the client, it was the end of it. He'd been pursuing the deal for a long time, and finally he had it put together. All he wanted me to do was to get it in writing and not screw it up in the process. The client didn't want to hear from me six reasons why he couldn't, or shouldn't, complete a deal. He just wanted to be told where to sign. As a lawyer, I wasn't really involved in their businesses. I only handled their legal matters. One day, I woke up and realized that I was just kidding myself if I thought that somehow I would get more involved in a business way with some of my clients.

I spent nearly a year wrestling with how I could both develop real estate and practice law. I wanted to structure an arrangement that my partners would find acceptable and, at the same time, give me enough latitude to pursue my real passion. What finally helped me make my break was the realization that I could not wear two hats effectively.

Practicing law was in some ways easier than what I am doing now. Friends of mine who are happy as lawyers wouldn't be able to stand the risky, episodic and uncertain nature of what I do. Law may have been more intellectually challenging in an abstract way, but I actually find real estate problems to be much more stimulating. The builder calls and says there is a problem with the plan—a wall is supposed to be somewhere that conflicts with something else—and we figure out a solution. You don't have to be a genius to do that, but I like that kind of practical, structural problem solving.

I also meet a lot of characters in this business; you don't find your average securities lawyer in real estate development. Many of these men couldn't write a single sentence in correct English, but they are very good at what they do. I also like the fact that there's more independence than being a lawyer. You are driven by vicissitudes within the business, but you make your own choices along the way.

I'm much more satisfied with the buildings I construct than I ever was drafting a contract, no matter how brilliantly I might have conceived it. To build this last building took gasping at the price of paying for the land, then going through the approval process for a year with delay after delay, and then more problems of this and that, but ultimately the building is up. I take pride in knowing that what I have accomplished over the years, I've done by sticking it out, working hard, taking the bad news and rolling with it, and staying in.

in-house counsel for player's association
sports lawyer in private practice (i.e. outside
  counsel for leagues, unions or players)
team lawyer
vice-president & general counsel for professional
  football team

Law-Related Positions:
instructor in sports management
manager, Major League Baseball properties
player's agent

Other Positions
business manager for sports network
manager of a professional or semi-professional
  athletic team
"scout" for professional athletic team
sportscaster
sports stadium development consultant

Law-Related Resources
Sports Lawyers Association
  (www.sportslaw.org/sla) — An international
  educational nonprofit devoted to the
  understanding, advancement and ethical
  practice of sports law. Publishes The Sports
  Lawyer, a bimonthly newsletter, and the
  annual Sports Lawyers Journal.
  (703) 437-4377.

General Resources
Institute for Sports Advancement
  (www.isacentral.org) — An annual
  conference held in New York City in January
  to assist individuals interested in gaining
  employment in the sports industry.
  (301) 986-7800.
Sports Careers and CBS Sportsline
  (www.sportscareers.com) — A career
  development organization that focuses
  exclusively on jobs within the sports industry
  including special events, TV and cable,
  sporting goods, colleges/universities, facilities
  management, corporate sponsorship, athletic

representation, front office, print and radio,
and health and fitness. Publishes (through
Franklin Covey) the Sports Market Place
Directory, a detailed list of over 27,000
national and international sports contacts
and Career Connections, a semi-monthly
newsletter with listings of job opportunities
and market research on major career paths.
Online job listings.

TECHNOLOGY

Practicing Law:
computer law specialist
intellectual property auditor
intellectual property lawyer
patent lawyer

Law-Related Positions:
co-designer of Web-based communication
  systems for lawyers
consulting webmaster to law firms
designer & seller of a bankruptcy program
in-house law firm technology adviser
intellectual property protection systems design
manager of intranet development for law firms
selling customized web-links to law firms
software development intern
telecommunications fraud consultant
VP of sales, legal accounting software company

Non-Law Positions
director of marketing & sales for ISP
freelance computer training manual writer
program manager
regional sales coordinator
systems analyst
software designer
software development
technical writer
Web project manager

Law-Related Resources
American Intellectual Property Association

(www.aipla.org) — More than 10,000 lawyers nationwide specializing in the practice of intellectual property law. (703) 415-0780.

Attorneys and Agents Registered to Practice Before the US Patent & Trademark Office. An annual publication of the US Patent & Trademark Office; (703) 308-4357.

Computer Law Association (www.cla.org) — An international organization of technology lawyers. Online job openings. (703) 560-7747.

International Trademark Association (www.inta.org) — Members include trademark holding companies and intellectual property lawyers, among others. Extensive publication list on international and US trademark issues. (212) 768-9887.

General Resources

Association for Multimedia Communications (www.amcomm.org) — An organization of individuals, small businesses, corporations and educational institutions interested in interactive multimedia and the Internet as communications tools. Online job opportunities. (773) 276-9320.

International Interactive Communications Society (www.iics.org) — An organization of those who work in a full spectrum of new media discipline. (510) 608-5930.

Software Publishers Association (www.spa.org) — A full service association for software publishers and developers; associate members include law firms that represent software companies. Publishes SPA Guide to Contracts and the Legal Protection of Software. (202) 289-7442.

OPPORTUNITIES

FOR TRANSFORMING

YOUR PRACTICE

By J. Kim Wright, JD, and Dolly Garlo, JD

RENAISSANCE LAWYERING: RESOURCES

Collaborative Law

A family law model in which the parties and their attorneys contractually agree at the outset that they will not litigate. Unlike other forms of alternative dispute resolution, mutually satisfactory cooperative resolution is the focus of all parties from the outset. For more information, visit the International Academy of Collaborative Professionals Web site (**www.collabgroup.com**).

Community Lawyering, or Community-Oriented Lawyering

A movement where the lawyers, especially those in government, public interest, etc., work together to address the underlying problems that result in clients being in court, as well as to promote the welfare of the community and their clients in relationship to one another. Community Lawyers take on projects that get to the source of cases that recur in the court system. For example, in housing issues, instead of litigating one tenant issue after another, a Community Lawyer might work to create standards for rental units. For other examples, see attorney Roger Conner's Web site at **www.communitylawyering.org**. Conner describes community lawyering as a way for attorneys to take a direct working interest in the peace and safety of particular places, and to work to not only win cases but generate outcomes that the community values.

Contemplative Practice

The Center for Contemplative Mind in Society (**www.contemplativemind.org**) has a program that focuses on the law. The program offers retreats that address the contemplative and legal perspectives of winning and losing, the role of compassion in adversarial situations, truth and "right speech," Socratic and contemplative methods of inquiry, action and non-action, separation and connection, and listening. Many lawyers are beginning to integrate spiritual and religious practices into their legal life. For a discussion of spiritu-al values in the law, read Steven Keeva's Transforming Practices, Finding Joy and Satisfaction in the Legal Life. Also visit the author's Web site at **www.transformingpractices.com**.

Creative Problem-Solving

One of the newest accredited law schools — California Western School of Law, San Diego, CA — teaches creative thinking processes usually found in the most progressive MBA programs. This approach encourages new grads lawyers to use the broadest array of creative problem-solving techniques to achieve better results for their clients. It is a caring approach that seeks transformative solutions to redefine problems, expand resources and facilitate enhanced relationships between the parties. For more information, go to Cal Western's Web site — **www.cps.cwsl.edu**.

Holistic Justice, or Holistic Law

An approach to law that attempts to see the whole picture — the lawyer's role, the client's responsibility, the impact on the community — seeking answers that benefit the greatest good while promoting healing and completion. Holistic lawyers are often trained in other disciplines, from counseling to energetic healing and may use those skills in their legal work as well. Visit the International Alliance of Holistic Lawyers online at **www.iahl.org**. The organization hosts annual conferences.

Peacemaking

Many lawyers consider themselves to be peacemakers; they express it in many ways. Some actually create organizations dealing with international conflict, like attorney and former Ambassador John McDonald, whose work with the Institute for Multi-Track Diplomacy can be reviewed at www.imtd.org.

Sharif M. Abdullah, a former North Carolina lawyer now in Oregon, has written and spoken on campaigns for expanding the consciousness for peace, as the founder and director of **www.commonway.org**.

Others seek to heal and bring peace at a more personal, energetic level like Jill Dahlquist at **www.grouppeace.com**.

Preventive Law

Based on the premise that "the legal profession can better serve clients by investing resources in consultation and planning rather than relying on litigation as the primary means of addressing legal problems." This theory of the late Louis Brown recognizes that while litigation is sometimes necessary to address past wrongs, the fact that one ends up in an adversarial proceeding may be evidence of a lack of planning or communication. By applying foresight, lawyers may limit the frequency and scope of future legal problems. Preventive Law is the now-recognized term to describe "minimiz[ing] the risk of legal disputes and maximiz[ing] professional opportunities [and providing] suggestions for practicing law or business in compliance with the law so that individuals and corporations can best use their resources and capitalize on their profits. For more information, see The Preventive Law Reporter, a University of Denver College of Law quarterly www.preventive-law.org. The National Center for Preventive Law, is now housed at California Western School of Law **www.cwsl.edu/mcgill/mc_brown.html**.

Problem Solving and Drug Treatment Court

Problem-solving courts provide another opportunity to implement a visionary legal approach. For example, Drug Treatment Courts are designed to interrupt the cycle of substance abuse. Using this holistic process, defendants identified as addicted enter a structured recovery program with built-in incentives for their success. The judges and attorneys involved report much higher satisfaction with the court system and fulfillment. For more information, see the Justice Programs Office of the School of Public Affairs (SPA) at The American University in Washington, D.C., at **www.ameri-can.edu/justice/drugcourts.html** or **www.prob-lemsolvingcourts.com**.

Restorative Justice

In a typical RJ conference, victim, offender, community members, and members of the court system all sit down in a facilitated conference, discussing the impact of the event and creating a resolution that works for everyone. This approach seeks to advance restorative purposes that will identify and involve all stakeholders, take steps to repair harm done, and to transform the traditional relationship between communities and their governments. In some RJ approaches the focus is on the impact of the legal process on communities and the victims of crime. For more information, go online to the International Centre for Justice and Reconciliation, **www.restorativejustice.org** and **www.restorativejustice.com**.

Project on Integrating Law, Politics and Spirituality

A group of lawyers and legal educators committed to the integration of spirituality and politics, and the incorporation of a spiritual-political understanding into American legal culture. Members of the task force have written and spoken widely on the need for legal culture to transform itself to address the social alienation — those distortions in human relationship resulting from living in an isolated, individualistic, and materialistic culture blind to the communal longings of the human soul. The Project was founded at New College of California, where its leader, Peter Gabel, teaches in its public interest law school as well as its program on culture, ecology, and sustainable community. Gabel is a founder of the Critical Legal Studies movement. For more information on the Project, call Coordinator Wendy Ervin at (415) 437-3496 or email **wervin@newcollege.edu**.

Therapeutic Jurisprudence

An interdisciplinary perspective that focuses on the law's impact on the emotional and psychological health of the participants, mostly the clients. Known as TJ, the goal is to bring sensitivity into law practice by listening to clients with an awareness of psychological and emotional issues including stress, confidence, and trust. TJ also looks at the court system and how it impacts society. For more information, visit the International Network on Therapeutic Jurisprudence at **www.therapeuticjurisprudence.org**.

Transformative Approaches to Mediation

As mediation has become more accepted and institutionalized, new approaches have arisen, many tailored to the organization or system in which they are employed. While the success of a typical mediation process is measured by whether settlement is reached, transformative mediation often has broader goals. At least three distinct approaches to transformative mediation are in wide use. For information and online links go to www.mediate.com. We suggest reading *The Promise of Mediation: Responding to Conflict Through Empowerment and Recognition*, by Robert A. Baruch Bush and Joseph P. Folger and *The Mediation Field Guide*, by attorney Barbara Ashley Phillips. For information on additional mediation models, visit the Institute for the Study of Conflict Transformation at Hofstra School of Law, at **www.hofstra.edu/Law/isct**, The Center for Mediation in Law, at **www.mediationinlaw.org** and **www.crtraining.org**, a resource for materials on forgiveness.

J. Kim Wright, JD; Dolly M. Garlo, JD — Wright and Garlo are principals at Renaissance Lawyer Society, a non-profit organization that serves as a clearinghouse and resource center for innovative approaches to law practice that are based on connecting people, solving problems and resolving conflict. Contact — www.RenaissanceLawyer.com.

INDEX TO

LEGAL ORGANIZATIONS

ONLINE

ATTORNEYS

American Academy of Appellate Lawyers (www.amappacad.org).

American Academy of Matrimonial Lawyers (www.aaml.org).

American Association of Attorney-CPAs (www.attorney-cpa.com) — To join, must be licensed both as a lawyer and a CPA, or be licensed in one and in the process of obtaining a license for the other.

American Association of Nurse Attorneys (www.taana.org) — Acts as an employment network and assists new nurse attorneys.

American College of Real Estate Lawyers (www.acrel.org) — An organization of real estate lawyers invited to be members because of their reputation for high quality legal work.

American College of Trust & Estate Counsel (www.actec.org) — Lawyers invited to be members due to their high standards of practice.

American Corporate Counsel Association (www.acca.com) — An organization of attorneys employed in corporate law departments, with nationwide chapters.

American Health Lawyers Association (www.healthlawyers.org) — Health lawyers and their clients consolidated in a merger of the National Health Lawyers Association and the American Academy of Healthcare Attorneys.

American Immigration Lawyers Association (www.aila.org) — Lawyers who specialize in assisting families and businesses with immigration issues.

American Intellectual Property Association (www.aipla.org) — Lawyers specializing in the practice of intellectual property law.

Association of Federal Defense Attorneys (www.afda.org).

Association of Professional Responsibility Lawyers (www.aprl.net) — Consultants, teachers and practitioners in attorney discipline, ethics and risk management.

American Society of International Law (www.asil.org) — Information on international careers in human rights, international trade, environment, telecommunications, finance & banking, international development and dispute resolution.

Association of Trial Lawyers of America (www.atlanet.org) — Lawyers, judges, law professors and law students interested in civil plaintiff and criminal defense advocacy.

Christian Legal Society (www.clsnet.org) — Lawyers, judges, law professors, students and non-lawyers.

Computer Law Association (www.cla.org) — An international organization of technology lawyers.

Defense Research Institute (www.dri.org) — Insurance defense lawyers.

Federal Bar Association (www.fedbar.org).

International Alliance of Holistic Lawyers (www.iahl.org) — Lawyers interested in supporting each other in practicing law from a whole systems approach.

International Trademark Association (www.inta.org) — Members include trademark holding companies and intellectual property lawyers, among others.

Lawyer-Pilots Bar Association (www.lpba.org) — For lawyers who are licensed pilots or engaged in aviation law.

Minority Corporate Counsel Association (www.mcca.net) — A national organization committed to furthering minority representation in the ranks of corporate counsel. Online job bank and articles.

National Academy of Elder Law Attorneys (www.naela.org) — Lawyers nationwide with practices involving estate planning, probate and guardianship, and other legal services to the elderly and disabled.

National Asian Pacific American Bar Association (www.napaba.org) — The only national association of Asian Pacific American attorneys, judges, law professors and law students. Established 1988; 4000 members in 45 local APA bar associations in the US. Quarterly online newsletter.

National Association of Bond Lawyers (www.nabl.org) — Lawyers involved with state and municipal bond work.

National Association of Criminal Defense Lawyers (www.criminaljustice.org).

National Association of Hearing Officials (www.naho.org) — Members include attorney and non-attorney hearing officials, ALJ's and managers in the resolution of human services-related administrative matters.

National Association of Patent Practitioners (www.napp.org) — Online job bank, newsletter; has regional chapters.

National Association of Women Lawyers (www.abanet.org/nawl) — Established in 1899, NAWL serves as an educational forum for the concerns of women in the legal profession worldwide. Online job bank, networking directory, members-only page.

National Criminal Justice Association (www.ncja.org).

National Directory of Prosecuting Attorneys (www.ndaa-apri.org) — Identifies prosecuting attorneys and assistant prosecuting attorneys nationwide, as well as providing a guide to each state's prosecution system.

National District Attorneys Association (www.ndaa-apri.org) — Online newsletters and members-only page.

National Employment Lawyers Association (www.nela.org) — Established in 1985 to provide assistance to lawyers in protecting the rights of employees against employers and the defense bar. Online job bank, newsletter.

National Lawyers Association (www.nla.org).

National Lawyers Guild (www.nlg.org/committees/labor/newsletter_index.htm) — The AFL-CIO Lawyers Coordinating

Committee puts online a state-by-state listing of AFL-CIO counsel.

National Legal Aid & Defender Association (www.nlada.org) — Public defense organizations.

National Lesbian and Gay Law Association (www.nlgla.org).

National Organization of Bar Counsel (www.nobc.org) — Disciplinary counsel to state and federal courts, and bar associations.

NSBA Council of School Attorneys (www.nsba.org/cosa) — Primarily private practitioners representing school districts nationwide.

Sports Lawyers Association (www.sportslaw.org/sla) — An international educational nonprofit devoted to the understanding, advancement and ethical practice of sports law.

Transportation Lawyers Association (www.translaw.org).

Volunteer Lawyers for the Arts (www.vlany.org).

BAR ASSOCIATIONS

American Bar Association (www.abanet.org).

Directory of Lawyer Disciplinary Agencies & Client Protection Funds (www.abanet.org/cpr/disciplinary.html).

National Association of Bar Executives (www.abanet.org/nabe) — Managing directors, public information officers, CLE directors, counsel and other professional staff of state, county and city bar associations.

National Conference of Bar Foundations (www.abanet.org/barserv/ncbf/home.html) — You'll find a list of member foundations online.

Compliance Officers

Health Care Compliance Association (www.hcca-info.org).

National Society of Compliance Professionals (www.nscp.org).

Consulting

Altman Weil Pensa (www.altmanweil.com) — Management consulting.

Hildebrandt Law Firm Consulting Services (www.hildebrandt.com) — Management consulting services exclusively for law firms, corporate law departments and others in the legal profession.

Technical Advisory Services for Attorneys (www.tasanet.com) — An expert referral service for lawyers.

Counseling

American Counseling Association (www.counseling.org).

National Board for Certified Counselors (www.nbcc.org) — National organization of vocational counselors.

Education

Academy of Legal Studies in Business (www.alsb.org) — Teachers and scholars who work in the field of business law, legal environment and law-related courses outside of professional law schools.

Environment

American Association of Professional Landmen, www.landman.org — Law school graduates and others who negotiate mineral rights and exploration agreements for energy companies.

Judiciary

American Judges Association (http://aja.ncsc.dni.us).

American Judicature Society (www.ajs.org).

Federal Administrative Law Judges Conference (www.faljc.org).

National Association of Administrative Law Judges (www.aalj.org) — Nonprofit group dedicated to promoting the legal education, training and professional standing of social security administrative law judges. Members

include anyone appointed to the position of administrative law judge.

National Association for Court Management (www.nacmnet.org) — Addresses court management issues in federal, state and local courts; online newsletter.

National Association of Women Judges (www.nawj.org).

National Conference of Administrative Law Judges (www.abanet.org/jd/ncalj/home.html).

National Conference of Bankruptcy Judges (www.ncbj.org/ncbjhomepage/index.htm).

National Council of Juvenile and Family Court Judges (www.ncjfcj.unr.edu).

Judicial Law Clerks

Judicial Clerkships (www.bu.edu/law/careers/clerkships.html).

National Conference of Appellate Court Clerks (http://ncacc.ncsconline.org) — An organization of court administrators.

World of Judicial Clerkships (www.judicialclerkships.com).

Law schools

American Association of Law Schools (www.aals.org) — Web site lists faculty, administrative and law library job openings at US law schools.

Equal Justice Works (formerly National Association for Public Interest Law) www.napil.org — A national coalition of student groups mostly from ABA-approved law schools.

Law School Admission Council (www.lsac.org).

Pre-Law Advisors National Council (www.planc.org).

Society of American Law Teachers (www.scu.edu/law/salt).

Teachlaw (http://teachlaw.law.us.edu).

Lawyer education/training

ALI-ABA Committee on Continuing Professional Education (www.ali-aba.org) — Assists in the development, organization and implementation of educational tools for lawyers.

American Institute for Law Training Within the Office (www.aliaba.org/aliaba/ailto.htm) — A project of ALI-ABA in cooperation with the ABA Standing Committee on Continuing Education of the Bar. Assists law firms in establishing in-firm training programs for lawyers.

Association of Continuing Legal Education (www.aclea.org) — Coordinating group for CLE providers across the country. Open to bar associations, law schools, legal publishers, adult ed specialists, editors, publishers, marketing and media specialists and in-house educators that present a minimum number of CLE-accredited programs annually. Publishes a quarterly newsletter and holds annual and mid-year conferences.

Legal Support Personnel

American Association for Paralegal Education (www.aafpe.org) — Paralegal educators and institutions of higher learning offering paralegal programs.

Association of Legal Administrators (www.alanet.org).

Association of Support Professionals (www.asponline.com).

Legal Marketing Association (formerly National Law Firm Marketing Association) www.legalmarketing.org.

National Association of Legal Assistants (www.nalanet.org).

National Association of Legal Search Consultants (www.nalsc.org).

National Career Development Association (www.ncda.org).

National Paralegal Association (www.NationalParalegal.org). Offers benefits and services to individuals, law firms, corporate legal departments, independent paralegals and colleges.

Paralegal Associations (www.paralegals.org).

Libraries

American Association of Law Libraries (www.aallnet.org) — Librarians for courts, bar associations, law schools, private law firms, corporations and government.

Special Libraries Association, Legal Division (www.slalegal.org).

Mediation

American Arbitration Association (www.adr.org) — Branch offices maintain panels of arbitration and mediation attorneys available for referral.

American Bar Association Section of Dispute Resolution (www.abanet.org/dispute)

Association for Attorney-Mediators (www.attorney-mediators.org)

Association for Conflict Resolution (formerly Academy of Family Mediators), www.mediators.org — A national membership organization for lawyers and mental health professionals involved in the resolution of domestic relations issues.

Association of Family and Conciliation Courts (www.afccnet.org) — Judges, counselors, lawyers, mediators and others interested in the resolution of family disputes as they affect children.

CPR Institute for Dispute Resolution (www.cpradr.org) — General counsel from major corporations, senior partners in leading law firms and legal scholars interested in installing ADR into the mainstream of corporate law departments and law firms.

Martindale-Hubbell Dispute Resolution Directory (www.martindale.com) — State-by-state listing of over 45,000 professionals participating in alternative dispute resolution.

National Academy of Arbitrators (www.naarb.org).

Military

Air Force Attorney Recruiting Office (www.jagusaf.hq.af.mil).

Army Civilian Attorney Program

(www.jagnet.army.mil/ppto).

Army JAG Corps Recruiting & Placement Office (www.jagcnet.army.mil/recruit.nsf).

Judge Advocate Association (www.jaa.org).

Navy JAG Recruiting Office (www.jag.navy.mi) — Information about both law student recruitment and direct commissions for experienced lawyers.

US Coast Guard Direct Commission Lawyer Program (www.uscg.mil/legal/recruit/dclinterinfo.htm).

US Marine Corps JAG (www.mcrc.usmc.mil/section/o/index(ol).htm).

Publishing, Legal

Aspen Publishers (www.aspenpub.com).

Bureau of National Affairs, Inc. (www.bna.com).

Commerce Clearinghouse (www.cch.com).

James Publishing (www.jamespublishing.com).

Lexis Law Publishing (www.lexislawpublishing.com).

Martindale-Hubbell (www.martindale.com).

Matthew Bender & Co. (www.bender.com).

Nolo Press (www.nolo.com).

Reed Elsevier (www.reed-elsevier.com).

Research Institute of America (www.riahome.com).

Shepard's/McGraw-Hill, Inc. (www.shepards.com).

Thomson Corporation (www.thomcorp.com).

VersusLaw (www.versuslaw.com).

West Information Publishing Group (www.westgroup.com).

More Career Resources

for a Life in the Law

Order Now from DecisionBooks.com*

■ ■ ■

What Can You Do With a Law Degree?
A Lawyer Guide to Career Alternatives Inside, Outside & Around the Law
By Deborah Arron, JD
$29.95, 360 pages/5th edition Companion workbook due Spring 2004; $21.95

Should You Marry a Lawyer?
A Couple's Guide to Balancing Work, Love & Ambition
By Fiona Travis, Ph.D.
$18.95, 160 pages

Should You Really Become a Lawyer?
A Guide to the Biggest (and Most Expensive) Career Decision You'll Ever Make
By Deborah Schneider, JD & Gary Belsky
$21.95, 224 pages (due Spring 2004)

Should You Become a Freelance Lawyer?
What Every Lawyer & Law Firm Needs to Know About Temporary Legal Services.
By Deborah Arron, JD & Deborah Guyol, JD
$29.95, 288 pages/3rd edition

Running From the Law
Why Good Lawyers Are Getting Out of the Legal Profession
By Deborah Arron, JD
$16.95, 192 pages/3rd edition

■ ■ ■

To order, call **1-800-359-9629**. Or order online from **www.DecisionBooks.com**.

AMERICA

AMERICA

A NARRATIVE HISTORY

Brief Seventh Edition

GEORGE BROWN TINDALL

DAVID EMORY SHI

W · W · NORTON & COMPANY · NEW YORK · LONDON

FOR BRUCE AND SUSAN
AND FOR BLAIR

FOR
JASON AND JESSICA

Copyright © 2007, 2004, 2000, 1999, 1997, 1996, 1993, 1992, 1989, 1988, 1984
by W. W. Norton & Company, Inc.

Composition: TechBooks
Manufacturing: Quebecor, Taunton
Book design: Jo Anne Metsch
Editor: Karl Bakeman
Editorial assistant: Rebecca Arata
Manuscript editor: Abigail Winograd
Project editor: Carla L. Talmadge
Associate managing editor, College: Lory A. Frenkel
Director of Manufacturing, College: Roy Tedoff
Cartographer: CARTO-GRAPHICS/Alice Thiede and William Thiede

Acknowledgments and copyrights continue on page A104,
which serves as a continuation of the copyright page.

Library of Congress Cataloging-in-Publication Data

Tindall, George Brown.
    America : a narrative history / George Brown Tindall,
David E. Shi.—Brief 7th ed.
        p.   cm.
    Includes bibliographical references and index.
    ISBN 13: 978-0-393-92734-4 (pbk.)
    ISBN 10: 0-393-92734-2 (pbk.)
    I. Shi, David E.   II. Title.
    E178.1.T55 2007   2006046845
    973—dc22

W. W. Norton & Company, Inc., 500 Fifth Avenue, New York, NY 10110
www.wwnorton.com

W. W. Norton & Company Ltd., Castle House, 75/76 Wells Street, London W1T 3QT

1 2 3 4 5 6 7 8 9 0

*W. W. Norton & Company has been independent since its founding in 1923,
when William Warder Norton and Mary D. Herter Norton first published
lectures delivered at the People's Institute, the adult education division of
New York City's Cooper Union. The Nortons soon expanded their program
beyond the Institute, publishing books by celebrated academics from America
and abroad. By mid-century, the two major pillars of Norton's publishing
program—trade books and college texts—were firmly established. In the 1950s,
the Norton family transferred control of the company to its employees, and
today—with a staff of four hundred and a comparable number of trade, college, and professional titles published each year—W. W. Norton & Company
stands as the largest and oldest publishing house owned wholly by its employees.*

CONTENTS

Part Two | BUILDING A NATION

Part Three / A N   E X P A N S I V E   N A T I O N

Part Four | A HOUSE DIVIDED
AND REBUILT

Part Six / M O D E R N   A M E R I C A

MAPS

PREFACE

Just as history is never complete, neither is a historical textbook. We have learned much from the responses of readers and instructors to the first six editions of *America: A Narrative History*. Perhaps the most important and reassuring lesson is that our original intention has proved valid: to provide a compelling narrative history of the American experience, a narrative animated by human characters, informed by analysis and social texture, and guided by the unfolding of events. Readers have also endorsed the book's distinctive size and format. *America* is designed to be read and to carry a moderate price. While the book retains its classic look, *America* sports a new color design for the Seventh Edition. We have added new eye-catching maps and included new art in full color. Despite these changes, we have not raised the price between the Sixth and the Seventh Editions.

As in previous revisions of *America,* we have adopted an overarching theme that informs many of the new sections we introduce throughout the Seventh Edition. In previous editions we have traced such broad-ranging themes as immigration, the frontier and the West, popular culture, and work. In each case we blend our discussions of the selected theme into the narrative, where they reside through succeeding editions.

The Seventh Edition of *America* highlights environmental history, a relatively new field that examines how people have shaped—and been shaped by—the natural world. Geographic features, weather, plants, animals, and diseases are important elements of environmental history. Environmental historians study how environments have changed as a result of natural processes such as volcanic eruptions, earthquakes, hurricanes, wildfires, droughts, floods, and climatic changes. They also study how societies have used and abused their natural environment through economic activities such as hunting, farming, logging and mining, manufacturing, building dams, and irrigation. Equally interesting is how different societies over time have perceived nature, as reflected in their religion, art, literature, and popular culture, and how they have reshaped nature according to those perceptions through the creation of parks, preserves, and designed landscapes. Finally, another major area of inquiry among environmental historians centers on the development of laws and regulations to govern the use of nature and maintain the quality of the natural environment.

Some of the new additions to the Seventh Edition related to environmental history are listed below.

- Chapter 1 includes discussions of the transmission of deadly infectious diseases from Europe to the New World and the ecological and social impact of the arrival of horses on the Great Plains.
- Chapter 3 examines the ways in which European livestock reshaped the New World environment and complicated relations with Native Americans.
- Chapters 5 and 6 describe the effects of smallpox on the American armies during the Revolution.
- Chapter 12 details the impact of early industrialization on the environment.
- Chapter 19 includes new material related to the environmental impact of the sharecrop-tenant farm system in the South after the Civil War, industrial mining in the Far West, and the demise of the buffalo on the Great Plains.
- Chapter 21 describes the dramatic rise of large cities after the Civil War and the distinctive aspects of the urban environment.
- Chapter 24 surveys the key role played by sportsmen in the emergence of the conservation movement during the late nineteenth century and details Theodore Roosevelt's efforts to preserve the nation's natural resources.
- Chapter 37 discusses President George W. Bush's controversial environmental policies and describes the devastation in Mississippi and Louisiana wrought by Hurricane Katrina.

Beyond these explorations of environmental history we have introduced other new material throughout the Seventh Edition. Fresh insights from important new scholarly works have been incorporated, and we feel confident that the book provides students with an excellent introduction to the American experience.

To enhance the pedagogical features of the text, we have added Focus Questions at the beginning of each chapter. Students can use these review tools to remind themselves of the key themes and central issues in the chapters. These questions are also available online as quizzes, the results of which students can e-mail to their instructors. In addition, the maps feature new enhanced captions designed to encourage students to think analytically about the relationship between geography and American history.

We have also revised the outstanding ancillary package that supplements the text. *For the Record: A Documentary History of America,* Third Edition, by David E. Shi and Holly A. Mayer (Duquesne University), is a rich resource with over 300 primary source readings from diaries, journals, newspaper articles, speeches, government documents, and novels. The *Study Guide,* by Charles Eagles (University of Mississippi), is another valuable resource. This edition contains chapter outlines, learning objectives, timelines, expanded vocabulary exercises, and many new short-answer and essay questions. *America: A Narrative History* Study Space is an online collection of tools for review and research. It includes chapter summaries, review questions and quizzes, interactive map exercises, timelines, and research modules, many new to this edition. *Norton Media Library* is a CD-ROM slide and text resource that includes images from the text, four-color maps, additional images from the Library of Congress archives, and audio files of significant historical speeches. Finally, the *Instructor's Manual and Test Bank,* by Mark Goldman (Tallahassee Community College) and Stephen Davis (Kingwood College) includes a test bank of short-answer and essay questions, as well as detailed chapter outlines, lecture suggestions, and bibliographies.

In preparing the Seventh Edition, we have benefited from the insights and suggestions of many people. Some of these insights have come from student readers of the text and we encourage such feedback. Among the scholars and survey instructors who offered us their comments and suggestions are: James Lindgren (SUNY Plattsburgh), Joe Kudless (Raritan Valley Community College), Anthony Quiroz (Texas A&M University – Corpus Christi), Steve Davis (Kingwood College), Mark Fiege (Colorado State University), David Head (John Tyler Community College), Hutch Johnson (Gordon College), Charles Eagles (University of Mississippi), Christina White and Eddie Weller at the South campus of San Jacinto College, Blanche Brick, Cathy Lively, Stephen Kirkpatrick, Patrick Johnson, Thomas Stephens, and others at the Bryan Campus of Blinn College, Evelyn Mangie (University of South Florida), Michael McConnell (University of Alabama – Birmingham), Alan Lessoff (Illinois State University), Joseph Cullon (Dartmouth University), Keith Bohannon (University of West Georgia), Tim Heinrichs (Bellevue Community

College), Mary Ann Heiss (Kent State University), Edmund Wehrle (Eastern Illinois University), Adam Howard (University of Florida), David Parker (Kennesaw State University), Barrett Esworthy (Jamestown Community College), Samantha Barbas (Chapman University), Jason Newman (Cosumnes River College), Paul Cimbala (Fordham University), Dean Fafoutis (Salisbury University), Thomas Schilz (Miramar Community College), Richard Frucht (Northwest Missouri State University), James Vlasich (Southern Utah University), Michael Egan (Washington State University), Robert Goldberg (University of Utah), Jason Lantzer (Indiana University), and Beth Kreydatus (College of William & Mary). Our special thanks go Tom Pearcy (Slippery Rock University) for all of his work on the timelines. Once again, we thank our friends at W. W. Norton, especially Steve Forman, Steve Hoge, Karl Bakeman, Neil Hoos, Lory Frenkel, Roy Tedoff, Dan Jost, Rebecca Arata, and Matt Arnold, for their care and attention along the way.

—George B. Tindall
—David E. Shi

Part One

A
NEW
WORLD

900	Classical Mayan civilization collapses (A.D. 900)	Viking Leif Eriksson sails along the coast of North America (1001)

Aztecs found capital city of Tenochtitlán (1325)

Italian city-states begin to trade with Asia (1050–1300)

Crusades further open up West to knowledge and trade with the East (1095–1270)

Marco Polo travels to China (1275)

Europeans seek westward sea route to Far East (1290s–1520s)

1400 Aztec Empire flourishes (1400–1519)
Inca Empire flourishes (1438–1538)

Spanish expel Moors; Christopher Columbus undertakes his first voyage (1492)

John Cabot, sailing for England, reaches North America (1497)

Vasco da Gama reaches port of Calicut, India, in search of spices (1498)

1500 Juan Ponce de León explores Florida (1513)
Hernando Cortés conquers Aztecs for Spain (1519)
Francisco Pizarro conquers Incas for Spain (1531)

Spanish establish St. Augustine (1565)

Martin Luther protests Catholic practice of selling indulgences (1517)

Ferdinand Magellan's crew circumnavigates the earth in pursuit of Asian riches (1519–1522)

John Calvin establishes Calvinism (1536)

Nicolaus Copernicus describes heliocentric universe (1543)

1600 James I charters Virginia Company (1606)
English establish Jamestown (1607)
French establish Quebec (1608)

House of Burgesses meets in Virginia, becoming the first representative assembly in the English colonies (1619)

Pilgrims land at Plymouth, draft and sign the Mayflower Compact (1620)

Virginia becomes a royal colony (1624)

Dutch found New Amsterdam (1625)

Massachusetts Bay Company is founded (1629)

English East India Company is chartered (1600); Dutch East India Company is chartered (1602)

Dutch send Henry Hudson to find northwest passage to China (1609)

Galileo Galilei describes planets revolving around sun (1610)

Thirty Years' War is fought in Europe (1618–1648)

Dutch West India Company is chartered (1623)

Charles I grants Maryland to Lord Baltimore as a proprietary colony (1634)

Roger Williams establishes the town of Providence, Rhode Island (1636)

Settlers from Massachusetts Bay Colony organize the self-governing colony of Connecticut (1637)

Massachusetts Bay Company charter evolves into two-house legislature (1644)

English Civil War (1642–1649) culminates in the execution of King Charles I (1649)

Colonies are left to themselves and practice home rule during the Commonwealth (1653–1658)

Oliver Cromwell governs the Commonwealth of England as lord protector (1653–1659)

European exploitation of Native Americans begins centuries of unrest between colonists and natives (1490s–1500s)

Native Americans die by the thousands, devastated by smallpox and other diseases brought from Europe (1500s–1600s)

Export of American agricultural goods (such as maize, potatoes, and cocoa) to Europe fundamentally alters Europeans' diet (1490s–1600s)

Spanish *encomienda* extracts tribute from natives (1500s)

Proprietors and chartered companies seek wealth by establishing colonies in America (1580s–1600)

Population of English settlers in America increases from 105 to more than 2 million (1607–1770)

Iroquois Confederacy serves as buffer between French and English (1609–1770s)

First Africans are brought to English America as slaves (1619)

First Thanksgiving is celebrated (1621)

John Winthrop calls the Massachusetts Bay Colony the "city upon a hill" (1630)

Great Migration to America results from enclosure movement and religious persecution in England (1630s)

Maryland becomes refuge for English Catholics (1634)

Rhode Island legislates freedom of religion (1636)

Harvard College is founded (1636)

Colonists kill hundreds of natives in the Pequot War (1637)

Anne Hutchinson is tried (1637) and banished (1638)

Colonists continue the English practice of coverture, which requires married women to surrender their right to own property (1600s–1700s)

Mercantilism, based on state-supported manufacturing and trade, is dominant economic system (1600s–1750)

French begin trading fur pelts with various Indian nations (1607)

"Starving time" takes place as Jamestown falls into ruin (1609–1610)

John Rolfe begins experimenting with tobacco in Virginia (1612)

Iroquois League completely depletes its hunting grounds and expands into neighboring areas (1630s–1640s)

Triangular trade begins between Europe, Africa, and the Americas (1643)

Massachusetts Bay Colony mandates public education (1647)

Navigation Act excludes foreign shipping from English and colonial trade (1651)

| 1660 | Carolina is established as a proprietary colony (1663) | England's monarchy is restored under Charles II (1660) |

1660 Carolina is established as a proprietary colony (1663)

Dutch surrender New York to British (1664)

Duke of York establishes New Jersey as a proprietary colony (1664)

Bacon's Rebellion is suppressed by royal officials (1675–1676)

Charles II gives Pennsylvania and Delaware to William Penn as proprietary colonies (1681)

Dominion of New England reestablishes royal control by merging Connecticut, Rhode Island, Massachusetts Bay, and Plymouth colonies into a royal province (1686)

Dominion colonies revert to self-government (1688)

King William's War (1689–1697)

Vice-admiralty courts established by the crown (1696)

1700 Queen Anne's War (1702–1713)

French establish New Orleans (1718)

Georgia is set up as philanthropic experiment and military buffer (1732)

Trial of John Peter Zenger confirms the right of the press to criticize the government (1735)

King George's War (1744–1748)

1750 Albany Congress enacts the Plan of Union (1754)

French and Indian War (Seven Years' War in Europe) (1754–1763)

Royal Proclamation limits expansion beyond the Appalachians (1763)

Boston Massacre (1770)

First Continental Congress meets (1774)

King George III of England declares colonists "open and avowed enemies" (1775)

Battles of Lexington and Concord (1775)

Second Continental Congress meets (1775)

Battle of Bunker Hill (1775)

1776 Congress adopts the Declaration of Independence (1776)

England's monarchy is restored under Charles II (1660)

French explore along the Mississippi River (1673–1682)

Germans migrate to America as a result of incessant wars (1680s–1690s)

Revocation of Edict of Nantes in France leads to Huguenot migration to Holland and America (1685)

Isaac Newton theorizes that natural law governs all things (1687)

England's Glorious Revolution establishes a constitutional monarchy (1688)

War of the League of Augsburg (1689–1697)

John Locke sets forth his contract theory of government (1690)

Bank of England is founded (1694)

French begin to settle Louisiana (1699)

War of the Spanish Succession (1701–1714)

Treaty of Utrecht (1713)

Many Ulster Scots fleeing Anglican persecution come to America (1717–1775)

War of the Austrian Succession (1740–1748)

Population of Europe begins to increase (ca. 1750)

Many areas of Europe are devastated by resumed fighting in the Seven Years' War (1756–1763)

King Philip's War is fought between colonists and natives (1675–1676)

Pueblos under Popé revolt against the Spanish in New Mexico (1680)

Pennsylvania becomes a haven for Quakers and other persecuted religious groups (1681)

Salem witch trials take place (1692)

College of William and Mary is founded (1693)

The Wonders of the Invisible World:

Being an Account of the

TRYALS

OF

Several Witches,

Lately Executed in

NEW-ENGLAND:

And of several remarkable Curiosities therein Occurring.

Together with,

I. Observations upon the Nature, the Number, and the Operations of the Devils.
II. A short Narrative of a late outrage committed by a knot of Witches in Swede-Land, very much resembling, and so far explaining, that under which New-England has laboured.
III. Some Councils directing a due Improvement of the Terrible things lately done by the unusual and amazing Range of Evil-Spirits in New-England.
IV. A brief Discourse upon those Temptations which are the more ordinary Devices of Satan.

By COTTON MATHER.

Published first at the Special Command of his EXCELLENCY the Governor of the Province of the Massachusetts-Bay in New-England.

Printed first, at Boston in New-England, and Reprinted at London, for John Dunton, at the Raven in the Poultry. 1693.

Enlightenment thinkers challenge monarchical abuses of power (1700s)

Non-native colonial population grows from 250,000 (1700) to 2.5 million (1775)

Iroquois tribes negotiate peace with French (1701)

Florida Indians are on the verge of extinction (1710)

Creek and Choctaw tribes revolt in the massive Yamasee War (1715)

Great Awakening leads to religious revival and widespread evangelism (1730s–1740s)

Benjamin Franklin establishes the American Philosophical Society (1743)

Iroquois, Cherokees, and Shawnees are pushed to give up land to white settlers (1760s–1770s)

American nationalism reaches its zenith as Revolution approaches (1760s–1770s)

Thomas Paine publishes *Common Sense*, directly attacking allegiance to British monarchy (1776)

Navigation Act requires three quarters of the crews of ships trading with England and its colonies to be English subjects (1660)

Navigation Act requires colonial governors to enforce Navigation Acts of 1651 and 1660 (1696)

Carolinas trade with Cherokees, Creeks, and Chickasaws and export an average of 54,000 deerskins annually (1699–1715)

South Carolina exports 100,000 pounds of rice annually (1700)

English Molasses Act prevents colonies from trading with the French sugar islands (1733)

To raise tax revenues, Lord Grenville enacts the Sugar Act and Currency Act (1764), and the Stamp Act and Quartering Act (1765)

Townshend Acts provoke a boycott of British goods (1767)

South Carolina and Georgia export 65 million pounds of rice annually (1770s)

In response to Boston Tea Party (1773), British pass Coercive Acts (1774)

Adam Smith's *The Wealth of Nations* promotes free-market competition (1776)

1660

1700

1750

1776

Long before Christopher Columbus accidentally discovered the New World in his effort to find a passage to Asia, the tribal peoples he mislabeled Indians had occupied and shaped the lands of the Western Hemisphere. By the end of the fifteenth century, when Columbus began his voyage west from Europe, there were millions of natives living in the "New World." Over the centuries they had developed diverse and often highly sophisticated societies, some rooted in agriculture, others in trade or imperial conquest.

The indigenous cultures were, of course, profoundly affected by the arrival of people from Europe and Africa. The Indians were exploited, enslaved, displaced, and exterminated. Yet this conventional tale of conquest oversimplifies the complex process by which Indians, Europeans, and Africans interacted. The Indians were more than passive victims; they were also trading partners and rivals of the transatlantic newcomers. They became enemies and allies, neighbors and advisers, converts and spouses. As such they fully participated in the creation of the new society known as America.

The Europeans who risked their lives to settle in the New World were themselves quite varied. Young and old, men and women, they came from Spain, Portugal, France, Great Britain, the Netherlands, Italy, and the various German states. A variety of motives inspired them to undertake the harrowing transatlantic voyage. Some were adventurers and fortune seekers eager to find gold and spices. Others were fervent Christians determined to create kingdoms of God in the New World. Still others were convicts, debtors, indentured servants, or political or religious exiles. Many were simply seeking a plot of land, higher wages, and greater economic opportunity. A settler in Pennsylvania noted that "poor people (both men and women) of all kinds can here get three times the wages for their labour than they can in England or Wales."

Yet such enticements did not attract enough workers to keep up with the rapidly expanding colonial economies. So the Europeans began to force Indians to work for them, but there were never enough laborers to meet the unceasing demand. Moreover, the captive Indians often escaped or were so rebellious that their use was banned. The Massachusetts legislature instituted such a ban because Indians were of "a malicious, surly and revengeful spirit; rude and insolent in their behavior, and very ungovernable."

Beginning early in the seventeenth century, more and more colonists turned to the African slave trade for their labor needs. In 1619 white traders began transporting captured Africans to the English colonies. This development would transform American society in ways that no one at the time envisioned. Few Europeans during the colonial era saw the contradiction between the New World's promise of individual freedom and the expanding institution of race-based slavery. Nor did they imagine the problems associated with introducing into the new society a race of people they considered alien and unassimilable.

The intermingling of people, cultures, plants and animals from the continents of Africa, Europe, and North America gave colonial American society its distinctive vitality and variety. In turn, the diversity of the environment and the climate led to the creation of quite different economies and patterns of living in the various regions of North America. As the original settlements grew into prosperous and populous colonies, the transplanted Europeans had to fashion social institutions and political systems to manage growth and control tensions.

At the same time, imperial rivalries among the Spanish, French, English, and Dutch produced numerous clashes and costly wars. The monarchs of Europe struggled to manage and exploit this fluid and often volatile colonial society. Many of the colonists, they discovered, had brought with them to the New World a feisty independence that led them to resent government interference in their affairs. A British official in North Carolina reported that the residents of the Piedmont region were "without any Law or Order. Impudence is so very high, as to be past bearing." As long as the reins of imperial control were loosely applied, mother countries and their colonists parties maintained an uneasy partnership. But as the British authorities tightened their control during the mid–eighteenth century, they met resistance, which escalated into revolt and culminated in revolution.

1

THE COLLISION
OF CULTURES

FOCUS QUESTIONS

· What were the reasons for the founding of the colonies?
· How did Europeans and Native Americans adapt to each other's presence?
· What was the Spanish influence in North America?

To answer these questions and access additional review material, please visit
www.wwnorton.com/studyspace.

The "New World" discovered by Christopher Columbus was in fact home to civilizations thousands of years old. Until recently archaeologists had long assumed that the first human residents were Siberians who some 12,000 to 15,000 years ago crossed the Bering Strait on a land bridge to Alaska made accessible by receding waters during the last Ice Age. Over the next 500 years the Asian migrants fanned out in small bands from the Arctic Circle to the tip of South America. Recent archaeological discoveries in Pennsylvania, Virginia, and Chile, however, suggest that humans may have arrived by sea much earlier (perhaps 18,000 to 40,000 years ago) from various parts of Asia—and some of them may even have crossed the Atlantic Ocean from southwestern Europe.

PRE-COLUMBIAN INDIAN CIVILIZATIONS

Whatever their place of origin and time of arrival, the first peoples in the Western Hemisphere spread across North and South America, establishing new communities and cultures. In the high altitudes of Mexico and Peru, Mayas, Aztecs, Incas, and others built great empires and a monumental architecture, supported by large-scale agriculture and far-flung commerce.

INDIAN CULTURES OF NORTH AMERICA Of the hundreds of Indian tribes inhabiting the present-day United States, the ancestors of only a few, such as the Pueblos, Creeks, and Iroquois, ever approached the level of social organization or cultural sophistication achieved by the Mayas and Aztecs in Central America and Mexico. North American tribes tended to be smaller, more scattered, and less settled. Most of them migrated with the seasons in search of food and temperate locales. They built few permanent structures and tended to own land communally, although individuals were allowed to own the food they produced or gathered.

In the Ohio and Mississippi River valleys many tribes developed a thriving village culture. While still primarily dependent upon hunting and gathering for subsistence, they also cultivated squash, beans, and maize. But even the most developed Indian societies of the sixteenth century were ill equipped to resist the dynamic European cultures invading their world. There were fatal gaps in Indian knowledge and technology. The Indians of Mexico, for example, had copper and bronze but no iron, except a few specimens of meteorites. They had domesticated dogs, turkeys, and llamas, but horses were unknown until the Spaniards arrived. When fighting erupted, arrows and tomahawks were seldom a match for guns. And the new diseases contracted from European invaders proved to be catastrophic for the Native Americans.

Yet against the odds the Indians resisted European invaders for centuries. They displayed an amazing capacity for adapting to changing circumstances, incorporating European technology and weaponry, forging new alliances, changing their community structures, and often converting whites to their way of life. Many Spanish, English, and French settlers voluntarily joined Indian society or chose to stay after being captured.

FIRST CONTACTS

The discovery of the New World coincided with the spread of European power and culture around the world. The expansion of Europe derived from, and in turn affected, the peculiar patterns and institutions that distinguished modern times from the medieval: the revival of learning and the rise of the inquiring spirit; the explosive growth of trade, towns, and modern corporations; the decline of feudalism and the rise of national states; the religious zeal generated by the Protestant Reformation and the Catholic Reformation; and on the darker side some old sins—greed, conquest, racism, and slavery.

By the fifteenth century these forces had combined to focus European eyes on new lands to conquer or settle and on new peoples to convert, civilize, or exploit. Europeans were especially attracted by the lure of Asia, a near-mythical land of silks, jewels, and millions of "heathens" to be Christianized. Equally valued were the spices—pepper, nutmeg, clove—so essential to the preservation of food, especially in southern Europe, where the warm and humid climate accelerated spoilage.

THE VOYAGES OF COLUMBUS Asia's wealth tantalized Christopher Columbus, a gold-loving adventurer. Born in 1451, the son of an Italian weaver, Columbus took to the sea at an early age. During the 1480s he hatched a scheme to reach Asia by sailing west. After years of disappointment and disgrace, he finally won the financial support of Ferdinand and Isabella, the Spanish monarchs.

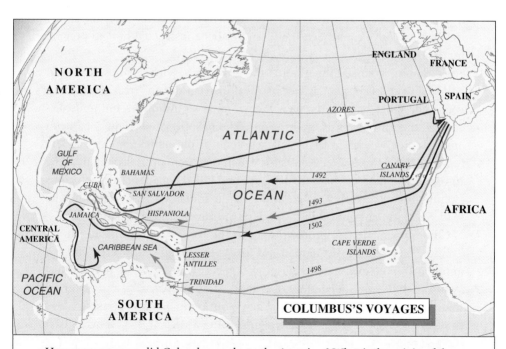

How many voyages did Columbus make to the Americas? What is the origin of the name for the Caribbean Sea? What happened to the colony that Columbus left on Hispaniola in 1493?

Columbus chartered one small ship, the *Santa María,* and the Spanish city of Palos supplied two smaller caravels, the *Pinta* and the *Niña.* From Palos this little squadron, with eighty-seven men, set sail on August 3, 1492. Early on October 12, 1492, a lookout called out, "*Tierra! Tierra!*" (Land! Land!) It was an island in the Bahamas that Columbus named San Salvador (Blessed Savior). Columbus assumed they were near the Pacific "East Indies," so he called the islanders *Indios,* Indians. Their docile temperament led him to write in his journal that "with fifty men they could all be subjugated and compelled to do anything one wishes."

At the moment, however, Columbus was not interested in enslaving "noble savages"; he was seeking the East Indies and their fabled gold. He therefore continued to search through the Bahamas down to Cuba, a place-name that suggested Cipangu (Japan), and then eastward to the island he named Española (or Hispaniola), where he first found significant amounts of gold jewelry. On the night before Christmas in 1492, the *Santa María* ran aground off Hispaniola. Columbus, still believing he had reached Asia, decided to return home. He left about forty men behind and seized a dozen natives to present as gifts to Spain's royal couple. After Columbus reached Palos, he received a hero's welcome. The news of his discovery spread rapidly throughout Europe, and Ferdinand and Isabella instructed him to prepare for a second voyage.

Columbus recrossed the Atlantic in 1493 with seventeen ships, livestock, and well over 1,000 men, as well as royal instructions to "treat the Indians very well." Once back in the New World, however, Admiral Columbus discovered the Europeans' camp in chaos. The unsupervised soldiers had run amok, raping women, robbing villages, and as Columbus's son later added, "committing a thousand excesses for which they were mortally hated by the Indians." The natives finally struck back and killed ten Spaniards. A furious Columbus launched a wholesale attack on the Indian villages, after which he loaded 550 Indians onto ships bound for the slave market in Spain.

Columbus made two more voyages to the New World. Ironically, however, the New World was named not for its European "discoverer" but for another Italian explorer, Amerigo Vespucci, who traveled to the New World in 1499. He sailed along the coast of South America and reported that it was so large it must be a new continent. European mapmakers thereafter began to label the new world using a variant of Vespucci's first name: America.

THE GREAT BIOLOGICAL EXCHANGE European contact with the New World produced a worldwide biological exchange that had profound consequences. If anything, the plants and animals of the two worlds were more different from each other than were the peoples and their ways of life. Europeans had never seen such creatures as the iguana, the flying squirrel, the catfish, and the rattlesnake, nor had they seen anything quite like several other species native to America: bison, cougars, armadillos, opossums, sloths, anacondas, toucans, condors, and hummingbirds. Among the Native Americans' few domesticated animals they could recognize the dog and the duck, but turkeys, guinea pigs, llamas, and alpacas were all new. Nor did the Native Americans know of horses, cattle, pigs, sheep, and goats, which soon arrived from Europe in abundance.

The transfer of plant life transformed the diets of both hemispheres. Before 1492 maize (corn), potatoes (sweet and white), and many kinds of beans (snap, kidney, lima, and others) were unknown in the Old World. Columbus returned to Spain with a handful of corn kernels, and within a few years corn had become a staple crop throughout Europe. The white potato, although commonly called Irish, actually migrated from South America to Europe and reached North America only with the Scotch-Irish immigrants of the 1700s. Other New World food plants include peanuts, squash, peppers, tomatoes, pumpkins, pineapples, papayas, avocados, cacao (the source of chocolate), and chicle (for chewing gum). Europeans in turn soon introduced into the New World rice, wheat, barley, oats, wine grapes, melons, coffee, olives, bananas, "Kentucky" bluegrass, daisies, dandelions, and clover.

The beauty of the ecological exchange between Old and New Worlds was that the food plants were more complementary than competitive. Indian corn spread quickly throughout the world. Before the end of the 1500s, American maize and sweet potatoes were staple crops in China. Plants initially domesticated by Native Americans now make up about one third of the world's food crops.

Europeans also adopted many Native American devices, such as canoes, snowshoes, moccasins, hammocks, kayaks, ponchos, dogsleds, toboggans, and parkas. The rubber ball and the game of lacrosse have Indian origins as well. Still other New World contributions include tobacco and several other drugs, among them coca (for cocaine), curare (a muscle relaxant), and cinchona bark (for quinine).

A land Sort of the Savages welcome aboue all other Torts

Unfamiliar Wildlife

A box tortoise drawn by John White, one of the earliest English settlers in America.

By far the most significant aspect of the biological exchange, however, was the transmission of infectious diseases from Europe and Africa to the New World. European colonists and enslaved Africans brought with them deadly pathogens that Native Americans had never experienced: smallpox, typhus, diphtheria, bubonic plague, malaria, yellow fever, and cholera. In dealing with such diseases over the centuries, people in the Old World had developed antibodies that enabled most of them to survive infection. Disease-toughened adventurers, colonists, and Africans invading the New World thus carried viruses and bacteria that consumed Indians, who lacked the immunity that forms from experience with the diseases.

The results were catastrophic. Epidemics are one of the most powerful forces shaping history, and disease played a profound role in decimating the indigenous peoples of the Western Hemisphere. Far more Indians died from contagions than from combat. Major diseases such as typhus and smallpox produced pandemics in the New World on a scale never witnessed in history. The social chaos caused by the arrival of European invaders contributed to the devastation of native communities. In the face of such terrible and mysterious diseases, panic-stricken and often malnourished Indians fled to neighboring villages, unwittingly spreading the diseases in the process. Unable to explain or cure the contagions, Indian chiefs and religious leaders often lost their stature. As a consequence, tribal cohesion and cultural life disintegrated, and efforts to resist European assaults collapsed. Over time, Native Americans adapted to the presence of the diseases and better managed their effects. They began to quarantine victims and infected villages to confine the spread of germs, and they developed elaborate rituals to sanctify such practices.

Smallpox was an especially ghastly and highly contagious disease in the New World. Santo Domingo boasted almost 4 million inhabitants in 1496; by 1570 the number of natives had plummeted to 125. In central Mexico alone, some 8 million people, perhaps one third of the entire Indian population, died of smallpox within a decade of the arrival of the Spanish. Smallpox brought horrific suffering. The virus passes through the air on moisture droplets or dust particles that enter the lungs of its victims. After incubating for twelve days, the virus causes headaches, backache, fever, and nausea. Victims then develop sores in the mouth, nose, and throat. Within a few days gruesome skin eruptions cover the body. Death usually results from massive internal bleeding.

In colonial America, as Indians died by the thousands, disease became the most powerful weapon of the European invaders. A Spanish explorer noted that "half the natives" died from smallpox and "blamed us." Many Europeans, however, interpreted such epidemics as diseases sent by God to punish Indians who resisted conversion to Christianity.

EXPLORATION AND CONQUEST OF THE NEW WORLD

Excited by Columbus's discoveries, professional explorers, mostly Italians, probed the shorelines of America during the early sixteenth century and greatly increased European knowledge of the New World. The first to sight the North American continent was John Cabot, a Venetian sponsored by King Henry VII of England. Cabot sailed across the North Atlantic in 1497. His landfall at what the king called "the newe founde lande" gave England the basis for a later claim to all of North America. During the early sixteenth century, however, the British became so preoccupied with internal divisions and conflicts with France that for several decades they failed to follow up Cabot's discoveries.

The New World thus was a Spanish preserve, except for Brazil, which was a Portuguese colony. The Caribbean Sea served as the funnel through which Spanish power entered the New World. After establishing colonies on Hispaniola and at Santo Domingo, which became the capital of the West Indies, the Spaniards proceeded eastward to Puerto Rico (1508) and westward to Cuba (1511–1514). Their motives were explicit. Said one soldier, "We came here to serve God and the king, and also to get rich."

A CLASH OF CULTURES The encounter between Spaniards and Indians in North America brought together quite different forms of technological development. Whereas Indians used dugout canoes for transportation, Europeans sailed oceangoing warships and brought steel swords, firearms, explosives, and armor, as well as greyhounds, which the Spaniards used to guard their camps. The advanced military tools and attack dogs help explain why the Europeans were able to defeat far superior numbers of Indians.

The Europeans also enjoyed other cultural advantages. For example, the only domesticated four-legged animals in North America were dogs and llamas. The Spaniards, on the other hand, brought horses, pigs, and cattle, all of which served as sources of food and leather. Horses provided greater speed in battle and introduced a decided psychological advantage.

The first European conquest of a major Indian civilization began in 1519, when the Spaniard Hernando Cortés and 600 men landed at the site of Vera

Cortés in Mexico

Page from the Tlaxcala Lienzo, a historical narrative from the sixteenth century. The scene, in which Cortés is shown seated on a throne, depicts the arrival of the Spaniards in Tlaxcala.

Cruz, in Mexico. Cortés then set about a daring conquest of the Aztec Empire. The 200-mile march from Vera Cruz through difficult mountain passes to the magnificent Aztec capital of Tenochtitlán (near present-day Mexico City) and the subjugation of the Aztecs, who thought themselves "masters of the world," were two of the most remarkable feats in human history. Tenochtitlán, with some 200,000 inhabitants, was by far the largest city in North America, much larger than Seville, the most populous city in Spain. Graced by wide canals and featuring beautiful stone pyramids and buildings, the fabled capital seemed impregnable to invasion.

Cortés, however, made the most of his assets. His invasion force had landed in a region where the natives were still resisting the spread of Aztec power and were ready to embrace new allies, especially those who possessed powerful weapons. By a combination of threats and deception, Cortés entered Tenochtitlán peacefully and made the emperor, Montezuma II, his puppet. This state of affairs lasted until the spring of 1520, when the Aztecs rebelled, took over the city, and stoned Montezuma to death. The Spaniards' Indian allies remained loyal, however, and Cortés gradually regrouped his forces; in 1521 he took the city again.

Within twenty years the Spanish soldiers had established a sprawling empire in the New World. Between 1522 and 1528 various lieutenants of Cortés's conquered the remnants of Indian culture in the Yucatán Peninsula and Guatemala. Then, in 1531, Francisco Pizarro led a band of soldiers down the Pacific coast from Panama toward Peru, where they brutally subdued the Inca Empire. From Peru, conquistadores extended Spanish authority south through Chile and north to present-day Colombia.

SPANISH AMERICA The Spanish conquistadores transferred to America a system known as the *encomienda*, whereby favored officers became privileged landowners (*encomenderos*) who controlled Indian villages or groups of villages. They were called upon to protect and care for the villages and support missionary priests. In turn they could require tribute from the native villagers in the form of goods and labor. Spanish America therefore developed from the start a society of extremes: wealthy European conquistadores at one end of the spectrum and native peoples held in poverty at the other end.

Yet by the mid-1500s Indians were nearly extinct in the West Indies, killed more often by European diseases than by Spanish exploitation. To take their place, the colonizers as early as 1503 began to import Africans to work as slaves. In all of Spain's New World empire, the Indian population dropped from about 50 million at the outset to 4 million in the seventeenth century and slowly rose again to 7.5 million by the end of the eighteenth century. Whites, who totaled no more than 100,000 in the mid–sixteenth century, numbered over 3 million by the end of the colonial period.

The Indians, however, did not always lack advocates. Many Catholic missionaries offered a sharp contrast to the conquistadores. They ventured into remote areas, often without weapons or protection, to spread the gospel—sometimes risking their lives. Where conquistadores sought to wrest gold, land, and labor from the Indians, the Spanish missionaries wanted their souls, and they had a tremendous impact upon Native American culture. At their worst the missionaries were bigots determined to rid "heathen" people of their native religion and many of their cultural practices. At their best, however, missionaries were impassioned defenders of the Indians.

THE SPANISH HERITAGE Throughout the sixteenth century much of what is now the United States belonged to Spain, and Spanish culture has left a lasting imprint upon American ways of life. Spain's colonial presence lasted more than three centuries, much longer than either England's or France's, and its possessions were much more far-reaching. The vice royalty of New Spain was centered in Mexico, but its frontiers extended from the Florida Keys to Alaska and included areas not currently thought of as formerly Spanish, such as the Deep South and the lower Midwest. Spanish place-names—San Francisco, Santa Barbara, Los Angeles, San Diego, Tucson, Santa Fe, San Antonio, Pensacola, and St. Augustine—survive to this day, as do Spanish influences in art, architecture, literature, music, law, and cuisine.

Although Spain's influence was strongest from Mexico southward, the "Spanish borderlands" of the southern United States, from Florida to California, preserve many reminders of the Spanish presence. The earliest known exploration of Florida was made in 1513 by Juan Ponce de León, then governor of Puerto Rico. He sought the mythic fountain of youth but instead found alligators, swamps, and abundant wildlife. Meanwhile, other Spanish explorers skirted the Gulf coast from Florida to Vera Cruz, scouted the Atlantic coast from Key West to Newfoundland, established a town at St. Augustine, Florida, and a mission at Santa Fe, New Mexico, and planted a short-lived colony on the Carolina coast.

Spain established provinces in North America not so much as commercial enterprises but as defensive buffers protecting its more lucrative trading empire in Mexico and South America. The Spaniards were concerned about French traders infiltrating from Louisiana, English settlers crossing into Florida, and Russian seal hunters wandering down the California coast. Yet the Spanish settlements in what is today the United States never flourished. England and France surpassed Spain in America because Spain failed to embrace what the other imperial powers decided early on: that developing a thriving Indian trade in goods was more important than the conversion of "heathens" and the often fruitless search for gold and silver.

THE SPANISH SOUTHWEST Spain eventually founded other permanent settlements in present-day New Mexico, Texas, and California. Eager to pacify rather than fight the far more numerous Indians of the region, the Spanish used religion as an instrument of colonial control. Missionaries, particularly Franciscans and Jesuits, established isolated Catholic missions where they imposed Christianity upon the Indians. The soldiers who were sent to protect the missions were housed in presidios, or forts, while their families and the merchants accompanying the soldiers lived in adjacent villages.

The land that would later be called New Mexico was the first center of mission activity in the American Southwest. In 1598 Juan de Oñate, the

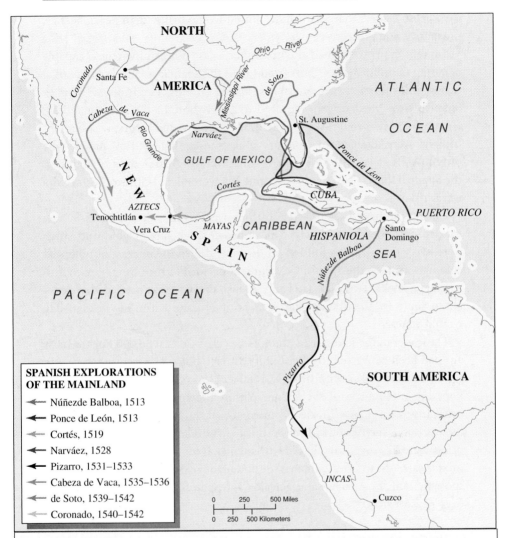

SPANISH EXPLORATIONS OF THE MAINLAND

← Núñezde Balboa, 1513
← Ponce de León, 1513
← Cortés, 1519
← Narváez, 1528
← Pizarro, 1531–1533
← Cabeza de Vaca, 1535–1536
← de Soto, 1539–1542
← Coronado, 1540–1542

0   250   500 Miles
0   250 500 Kilometers

What were the Spanish conquistadores' goals for exploring the Americas? How did Cortés conquer the Aztecs? Why did the Spanish first explore North America, and why did they establish St. Augustine, the first European settlement in what would become the United States?

wealthy son of a Spanish family in Mexico, received a patent for the territory north of Mexico above the Rio Grande. With an expeditionary military force made up of Mexican Indians and mestizos (sons of Spanish fathers and native mothers), he took possession of New Mexico, established a capital at San Gabriel, and dispatched expeditions to look for gold and silver. He promised the Pueblo leaders that Spanish dominion would bring them peace, justice, prosperity, and protection.

Some Indians welcomed the missionaries as "powerful witches" capable of easing their burdens. Others tried to use the Spanish as allies against rival tribes. Still others saw no alternative but to submit. The Indians living in Spanish New Mexico were required to pay tribute to their *encomenderos* and perform personal tasks for them, including sexual favors. Disobedient Indians were flogged by soldiers and priests. Before the end of the province's first year, the Indians revolted. During three days of fighting, the Spanish killed 500 Pueblo men and 300 women and children. Survivors were enslaved.

During the first three quarters of the seventeenth century, Spanish New Mexico expanded very slowly. The hoped-for deposits of gold and silver were never found, and a limited food supply dulled the interest of potential colonists. In 1608 the Spanish government decided to turn New Mexico into a royal province. Two years later the Spanish moved the capital of New Mexico to Santa Fe, the first permanent seat of government in the present-day United States.

The leader of the Franciscan missionaries claimed that 86,000 Pueblo Indians had been converted to Christianity. In fact, however, resentment among the Indians increased with time. In 1680 a charismatic Indian leader named Popé organized a massive rebellion. Within a few weeks the Spaniards had been driven from New Mexico. Almost 400 of the Europeans were killed in the uprising. The outraged Indians burned churches, tortured and executed priests, and destroyed all relics of Christianity. It took fourteen years and four military assaults for the Spaniards to subdue the region. Thereafter, except for sporadic raids by Apaches and Navajos, the Spanish exercised stable control over New Mexico.

HORSES AND THE GREAT PLAINS Another major consequence of the Pueblo Revolt was the opportunity it afforded Indian rebels to acquire hundreds of coveted Spanish horses (Spanish authorities had made it illegal for Indians to own horses). The Pueblos in turn established a thriving horse trade with the Navajos, Apaches, and other tribes. By 1690 horses were evident in Texas, and they soon spread across the Great Plains, the vast rolling grasslands extending from the Missouri River valley in the east to the base of the Rocky Mountains in the west.

Horses were a disruptive ecological force in North America. Prior to the arrival of horses, Indians hunted on foot and used dogs as their beasts of burden, hauling their supplies on travois, devices made from two long poles connected by leather straps. But dogs are carnivores, and it was often difficult to find enough meat to feed them. Horses thus changed everything, providing the pedestrian Plains Indians with a transforming source of mobility and power. They are grazing animals, and the endless grasslands of the Great Plains offered plenty of forage. Horses could also haul up to seven times as much weight as dogs, and their speed and endurance made the Indians much more effective hunters and warriors. In addition, horses enabled Indians to travel farther to trade and fight.

The ready availability of large numbers of horses thus worked a revolution in the economy and ecology of the Great Plains. Such tribes as the Arapaho, Cheyenne, Comanche, Kiowa, and Sioux reinvented themselves as equestrian societies. They left their traditional woodland villages on the fringes of the plains and became nomadic bison (buffalo) hunters. Using horses, they could haul larger tepees and more meat and hides with them, building temporary camps as they migrated year-round with the immense bison herds, wintering in sheltered glades along rivers. The once-deserted plains soon were a crossroads of activity.

Plains Indians

The horse-stealing raid depicted in this hide painting demonstrates the essential role horses played in Plains life.

Indians used virtually every part of the bison they killed: meat for food; hides for clothing, shoes, bedding, and shelter; muscles and tendons for thread and bowstrings; intestines for containers; bones for tools; horns for eating utensils; hair for headdresses; and dung for fuel. One scholar has referred to the bison as the "tribal department store." The Plains Indians supplemented bison meat with roots and berries they gathered along the way. In the fall the nomadic tribes would travel south to exchange hides and robes for food or to raid Indian farming villages.

In the short run the horse brought prosperity and mobility to the Plains Indians. Horses became the center and symbol of Indian life on the plains. Yet the noble animal also brought insecurity, instability, and conflict. Indians began to kill more bison than the herds could replace. In addition, the herds of horses competed with the bison for food, depleting the grass and compacting the soil in the river valleys during the winter. As tribes traveled greater distances and encountered more people, infectious diseases spread more widely.

Horses became so valuable that they provoked thievery and intensified intertribal competition and warfare. Within tribes a family's status was determined by the number of horses it possessed. Horses eased some of the physical burdens on women but imposed new demands. Women and girls were assigned the responsibility of tending to the horses. They also had to butcher and dry the buffalo meat and tan the hides. As the value of the hides grew, male hunters began to indulge in polygamy: more wives could process more buffalo. The rising economic value of wives eventually led Plains Indians to raid farming tribes in search of captive brides as well as horses. The introduction of horses into the Great Plains, then, was a decidedly mixed blessing. By 1800 a plains trader could observe that "this is a delightful country, and were it not for perpetual wars, the natives might be the happiest people on earth."

CHALLENGES TO THE SPANISH EMPIRE The Spanish monopoly on the New World colonies did not go unchallenged. The French were the first to pose a serious threat. In 1524 the French king sent the Italian Giovanni da Verrazano in search of a passage to Asia. Sighting land (probably at Cape Fear, North Carolina), he ranged along the coast as far north as Maine, but it would be another seventeen years before the French made their first effort at colonization. Jacques Cartier explored the Gulf of St. Lawrence and ventured up the St. Lawrence River as far as present-day Montreal. Near Quebec he established a short-lived colony in 1541.

Thereafter, however, French interest in Canada waned, as the French were preoccupied with the religious civil wars racking their country. Not until the early seventeenth century, when Samuel de Champlain established settlements in Acadia (Nova Scotia) and at Quebec, did French colonization in America begin in earnest. Enterprising French traders negotiated with Indians for their fur pelts, and French Jesuit missionaries cultivated their souls.

Acquiring furs and ministering to "heathens" took the French southward as well. In 1673 Louis Jolliet and Père Jacques Marquette, a Jesuit priest, explored the Mississippi River, but fearing an encounter with the Spaniards, they turned back before reaching the Gulf of Mexico. Nine years later René-Robert Cavelier, sieur de La Salle, did the same, but he ventured all the way to the Gulf of Mexico. There, near the river's delta, the French in the early eighteenth century would establish a settlement called New Orleans. The French thereby came to control not only Canada but also the major inland waterway in North America, the Mississippi River. But because the French monarchy never emphasized permanent settlement, French America remained only sparsely populated.

From the mid-1500s greater threats to Spanish power in the New World arose from the growing strength of the Dutch and the English. The prosperous provinces of the Netherlands, which had passed by inheritance to the Spanish king and had become largely Protestant, rebelled against Spanish Catholic rule in 1567. A bloody struggle for independence was interrupted by a twelve-year truce, but Spain did not accept the independence of the Dutch republic until 1648.

Almost from the beginning of the Dutch revolt against Spain, Dutch privateers plundered Spanish ships. The Dutch raiders soon had their counterpart in England's sea dogges: John Hawkins, Francis Drake, and others. While Queen Elizabeth of England steered a tortuous course to avoid open war with Catholic Spain, she encouraged both Dutch and English sea captains to attack Spanish vessels. In 1577 Francis Drake set out on his famous adventure around South America to raid Spanish towns along the Pacific coast. Three years later he returned in triumph.

Sporadic British piracy against the Spanish continued until 1587, when Queen Elizabeth had her Catholic cousin, Mary, Queen of Scots, beheaded for her involvement in a plot to kill the English queen and elevate herself to the throne. In revenge for Mary's execution, Spain's King Philip II decided to crush Protestant England and began to gather his ill-fated invasion fleet, called the Armada. The ambitious enterprise quickly became a case of incompetence and mismanagement accompanied by bad luck. The heavy Spanish galleons could not cope with the smaller, faster English vessels. Defeat of the Spanish Armada convinced the English that the Spanish navy was

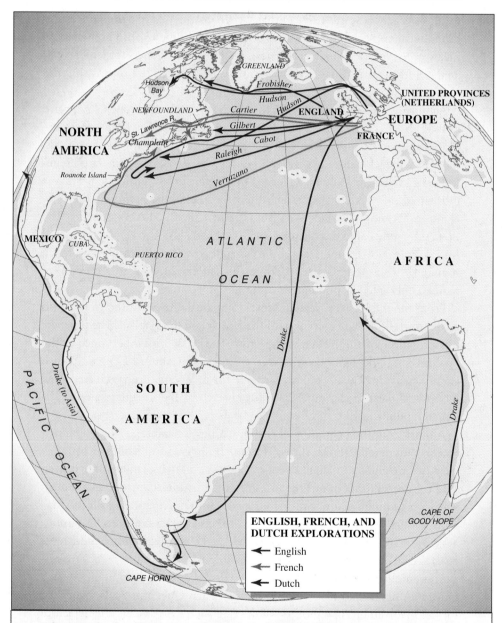

Who were the first European explorers to rival Spanish dominance in the New World, and why did they cross the Atlantic? Why was the defeat of the Spanish Armada important to the history of English exploration? What was the significance of the voyages of Gilbert and Raleigh?

no longer invincible and cleared the way for English colonization of the Americas. England at the end of the sixteenth century entered the springtime of its power, filled with a youthful zest for the new worlds and their wonders.

MAKING CONNECTIONS

- The funding of the voyages of discovery by various European nations had implications for the settlement and control of the New World, as will be discussed in later chapters.

- The settlement pattern of the Spanish in the New World and the wealth they plundered will be contrasted in the next chapter with the patterns of English settlement and the English sources of wealth in the New World.

- The next chapter describes how the Reformation and religious controversies in Europe led various groups to found their own settlements in the New World, where they did not face religious discrimination and persecution.

FURTHER READING

A fascinating study of pre-Columbian migration is Brian M. Fagan's *The Great Journey: The Peopling of Ancient America*, rev. ed. (2004). Alice B. Kehoe's *North American Indians: A Comprehensive Account*, 2nd ed. (1992) provides an encyclopedic treatment of Native Americans. An evocative portrait of the Aztecs can be found in Michael E. Smith's *The Aztecs*, 2nd ed. (2003). An excellent introduction to the prehistory of the American Southwest, its people, and its archaeology is Stephen Plog's *Ancient Peoples of the American Southwest* (1997).

The most comprehensive overviews of European exploration are two volumes by Samuel Eliot Morison, *The European Discovery of America: The Northern Voyages, A.D. 500–1600* (1971) and *The Southern Voyages, A.D. 1492–1616* (1974).

The voyages of Columbus are surveyed in William D. Phillips Jr. and Carla Rahn Phillips's *The Worlds of Christopher Columbus* (1992). For sweeping overviews of Spain's creation of a global empire, see Henry Kamen's *Empire: How Spain Became a World Power, 1492–1763* (2003) and Hugh Thomas's *Rivers of Gold: The Rise of the Spanish Empire, from Columbus to Magellan* (2004). David J. Weber examines Spanish colonization in *The Spanish Frontier in North America* (1992). For the French experience, see William J. Eccles's *France in America,* rev. ed. (1990).

The conflict between Native Americans and Europeans is treated well in James Axtell's *The Invasion Within: The Contest of Cultures in Colonial North America* (1986) and *Beyond 1492: Encounters in Colonial North America* (1992). Karen Ordahl Kupperman's *Settling with the Indians: The Meeting of English and Indian Cultures in America, 1580–1640* (1980) stresses the racist nature of the conflict.

2

BRITAIN AND
ITS COLONIES

FOCUS QUESTIONS

· What were the reasons for the founding of the colonies in
  North America?

· How did the British colonists and the Native Americans adapt
  to each other's presence?

· What were the factors making for England's success in North
  America?

To answer these questions and access additional review material, please visit
www.wwnorton.com/studyspace.

nglish colonization of North America began in 1584,
when Sir Walter Raleigh led an expedition that explored
the Outer Banks of North Carolina and discovered
Roanoke Island. Three years later about 100 settlers arrived, including
women and children, under the leadership of Governor John White. After a
month in Roanoke, White returned to England to get supplies, leaving
behind the other colonists, including his daughter Elinor, her husband, and
her baby, Virginia Dare, the first English child born in the New World.
White, however, was long delayed because of the war with Spain. When he
finally returned, in 1590, he found the village of "Ralegh" abandoned and
pillaged, possibly by hostile Indians or by Spaniards. No trace of the "lost
colonists" was ever found, and there were no English settlers in North
America when Queen Elizabeth died in 1603.

SETTLING THE CHESAPEAKE

With the death of Queen Elizabeth, the Tudor family line ended, and the throne fell to Elizabeth's cousin James VI of Scotland, the son of the ill-fated Mary, Queen of Scots. The first of the Stuarts, he ruled England as James I. The Stuart dynasty spanned most of the seventeenth century, a turbulent time of religious and political tensions, civil war, and foreign intrigues. During those eventful years in English history, all but one of the thirteen North American colonies had their start. They were quite diverse in geography, motives, and composition, a diversity that has since been a trademark and a strength of American society.

In 1606, having made peace with Spain, thereby freeing up resources and men for colonization, James I chartered what was called the Virginia Company, with two divisions, the First Colony of London and the Second Colony of Plymouth. The stockholders expected a potential return from gold and products such as wine, citrus fruits, olive oil, and forest products needed for naval use. Many also still hoped to discover a passage to India. Few if any investors foresaw what the first English colony would become: a fertile place to grow tobacco.

From the outset the pattern of English colonization diverged significantly from the Spanish activities in the New World. The autocratic Spaniards conquered people and regulated all aspects of colonial life. The English had a different model, based on their settlements, or "plantations," in Ireland, which the English had conquered by military force under Queen Elizabeth. Within their own pale (or limit) of settlement in Ireland, the English had set about transplanting their familiar way of life insofar as possible. Thus the English subjugated the Indians of North America much as they had the Irish in Ireland. In America the English settled along the Atlantic seaboard, where the native populations were relatively sparse. There was no Aztec or Inca Empire to conquer.

VIRGINIA   The London group of the Virginia Company planted the first permanent colony in Virginia, named after Elizabeth I, "the Virgin Queen." On May 6, 1607, three tiny ships loaded with 105 men reached Chesapeake Bay after four storm-tossed months at sea. They chose a river with a northwest bend—in the hope of finding a passage to Asia—and settled about forty miles inland to hide from marauding Spaniards.

The river they called the James and the colony, Jamestown. After building a fort, thatched huts, a storehouse, and a church, the colonists began planting, but most were either townsmen unfamiliar with farming or "gentlemen" adventurers who scorned manual labor. They had come to find gold, not to live as homesteaders. Ignorant of woodlore, they did not know how to exploit the area's abundant game and fish. Supplies from England were undependable, and only firm leadership and trade with the Indians, who taught the colonists to grow maize, enabled them to survive.

The Indians of the region were loosely organized. Powhatan was the charismatic chief of some thirty Algonquian-speaking tribes in eastern Virginia. The Indians making up the so-called Powhatan Confederacy were largely an agricultural people; corn was their primary crop. Despite occasional clashes with the colonists, the Indians initially adopted a stance of cautious assistance and watchful waiting. Powhatan hoped to develop a lucrative trade and military alliance with the newcomers; he realized too late that the newcomers intended to expropriate his lands and subjugate his people.

Ould Virginia

A 1624 map of Virginia by John Smith, showing Chief Powhatan in the upper left.

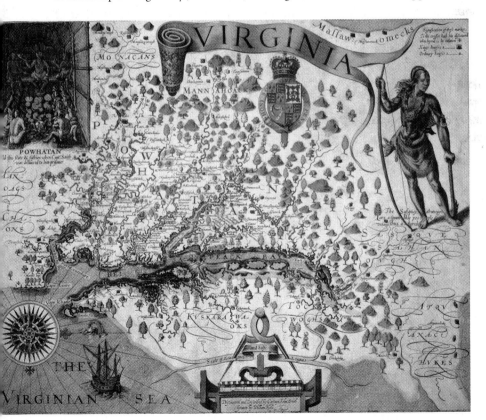

The colonists, as it happened, had more than a match for Powhatan in Captain John Smith, a soldier of fortune with rare powers of leadership and self-promotion. With the colonists on the verge of starvation, Smith imposed strict discipline and forced all to labor, declaring that "he that will not work shall not eat." Smith also bargained with the Indians and mapped the Chesapeake region. Despite his efforts, only 38 of the original 105 colonists survived the first nine months.

John Smith's efforts to save the struggling colony abruptly ended when he suffered a gunpowder burn and sailed back to England in 1609. More colonists were dispatched, including several women. The colony lapsed into anarchy and suffered the "starving time," the winter of 1609–1610, during which most of the colonists, weakened by hunger, fell prey to disease. A relief party found only about sixty settlers still alive in 1610.

For the next seven years the colony limped along until it gradually found a reason for being: tobacco. In 1612 John Rolfe had begun to experiment with the harsh-tasting Virginia tobacco, and by 1616 a smoother-tasting variety of the weed had become a valuable export. As Virginia's tobacco production soared, planters purchased indentured servants, thus increasing the flow of immigrants to the colony. Meanwhile John Rolfe had made another contribution to stability by marrying Pocahontas, the daughter of Powhatan. Their marriage helped ease deteriorating relations between the Indians and the English settlers.

In 1618 officials in London initiated a series of reforms intended to shore up their struggling American colony. They first inaugurated a new "head-right" policy. Anyone who bought a share in the company or could transport himself to Virginia could have fifty acres and fifty more for any servants he might send or bring. The following year the company relaxed its tight legal code and promised that the settlers would have the "rights of Englishmen," including a representative assembly. On July 30, 1619, the first General Assembly of Virginia met in the Jamestown church and deliberated for five days, "sweating and stewing, and battling flies and mosquitoes." It was an eventful year in two other respects. During 1619 a ship arrived with ninety "young maidens" to be sold to husbands of their own choice for the cost of transportation (about 125 pounds of tobacco). And a Dutch warship dropped off "20 Negars," the first Africans known to have been brought to English America.

Yet the English foothold in Virginia remained tenuous. Some 14,000 people had migrated to the colony since 1607, but the population in 1624 stood at a precarious 1,132. The king appointed a commission to investigate the running of the struggling colony by the Virginia Company, and on the commission's recommendation a court dissolved the company. In 1624 Virginia became a royal colony.

Relations with the Indians continued in a state of what the governor's council called "perpetual enmity" until the Indians staged a major attack in 1644. The English suffered as many casualties as they had twenty-two years before, but they put down the uprising with such ferocity that nothing quite like it happened again. The combination of warfare and disease decimated the Indians of Virginia. The 24,000 Algonquians who inhabited the colony in 1607 were reduced to 2,000 by 1669.

MARYLAND   In 1634, ten years after Virginia became a royal colony, a neighboring settlement, named Maryland, appeared on the northern shores of Chesapeake Bay. It was the first so-called proprietary colony, granted not

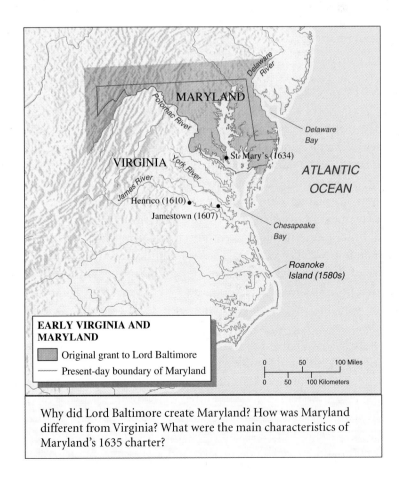

EARLY VIRGINIA AND MARYLAND

▨ Original grant to Lord Baltimore

— Present-day boundary of Maryland

Why did Lord Baltimore create Maryland? How was Maryland different from Virginia? What were the main characteristics of Maryland's 1635 charter?

to a joint-stock company but to an individual, Lord Baltimore. Sir George Calvert, the first Lord Baltimore, had announced in 1625 his conversion to Catholicism and sought the colony as a refuge for English Catholics, who were subjected to discrimination at home. The charter for such a colony was finally issued in 1632, after his death.

His son, Cecilius Calvert, the second Lord Baltimore, founded the colony in 1634 at St. Marys, on a small stream near the mouth of the Potomac River. Calvert brought along Catholic gentlemen as landholders, but a majority of the servants were Protestants. The charter gave Calvert power to make laws with the consent of the freemen (all property holders). The first legislative assembly met in 1635 and later divided into two houses, with governor and council sitting separately. The charter also empowered the proprietor to grant huge manorial estates, and Maryland had some sixty before 1676. But the Lords Baltimore soon found that to draw large numbers of settlers they had to offer small farms. The colony was meant to rely upon mixed farming, but its fortunes, like those of Virginia, soon came to depend upon tobacco.

SETTLING NEW ENGLAND

Meanwhile, far to the north of the Chesapeake Bay, quite different colonies were emerging. The New England colonists were generally made up of middle-class families who could pay their own way across the Atlantic. In the Northeast there were relatively few indentured servants, and there was no planter elite. Most male settlers were small farmers, merchants, seamen, or fishermen. New England also attracted more women than did the southern colonies. Although its soil was not as fertile and its farmers not as wealthy, New England was a much healthier place to settle. Because of its colder climate, the region did not foster the infectious diseases that ravaged the southern colonies. Life expectancy was much longer. By 1700 New England's white population exceeded that of Maryland and Virginia.

Most early New Englanders were devout Puritans, who embraced a much more rigorous faith and simpler rituals than the Anglicans of Virginia and Maryland. The zealous Puritans believed themselves to be on a divine mission to create a model society committed to the proper worship of God. In the New World these self-described "saints" could purify their churches of all Catholic and Anglican rituals, supervise one another in practicing a communal faith, and enact a code of laws and a government structure based upon biblical principles. Such a holy settlement, they hoped, would provide a beacon of righteousness for a wicked England to emulate.

PLYMOUTH   The Pilgrims who established Plymouth Colony were bent not on finding gold or making a fortune but on building a Christian commonwealth. They belonged to the most uncompromising sect of Puritans, the Separatists, who had severed all ties with the Church of England. Persecuted by King James I and Anglican officials, they had fled to Holland in 1607.

The Separatists grew uneasy with Dutch folkways, however, and decided to move to America. These "Pilgrims" secured a land patent from the Virginia Company, and in 1620, 102 men, women, and children, led by William Bradford, crammed into the *Mayflower* for the transatlantic voyage. Only half the voyagers were Pilgrim "saints," Christians recognized as having been elected by God for salvation; the rest were non-Pilgrim "strangers": ordinary settlers, hired hands, and indentured servants.

A stormy voyage led them to Cape Cod, off the coast of Massachusetts, far north of Virginia. Exploring parties hit upon a place called Plymouth for their settlement. Since they were outside the jurisdiction of any organized government, forty-one of the Pilgrims entered into a formal agreement to abide by laws made by leaders of their own choosing—the Mayflower Compact of November 21, 1620. Used later as a model by other New England settlers, the compact helped establish the distinctive American tradition of consensual government.

Throughout its separate existence, until it was absorbed into Massachusetts in 1691, the Plymouth colony's government grew out of the Mayflower Compact, which was not a formal constitution but an agreement among members of a religious group who believed that God had made a covenant (or agreement) with them to provide a way to salvation. Thus the civil government evolved naturally out of the church government, and the members of each were initially identical.

Nearly half the Pilgrims died of exposure and disease, but friendly relations with the neighboring Wampanoag Indians proved their salvation. In the spring of 1621, the colonists met Squanto, who showed them how to grow maize. By autumn the Pilgrims had a bumper crop of corn, a flourishing fur trade, and a supply of lumber for shipment. To celebrate, they held a harvest feast with the Wampanoags, an annual ritual that would later be dubbed Thanksgiving.

MASSACHUSETTS BAY   The Plymouth colony's population never rose above 7,000, and after ten years it was overshadowed by its larger neighbor,

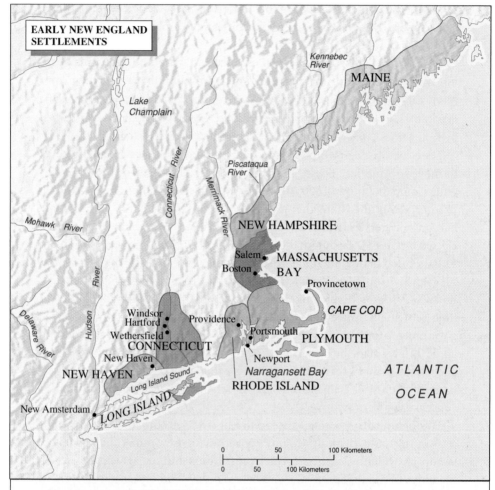

EARLY NEW ENGLAND SETTLEMENTS

Why did European settlers first populate the Plymouth colony? How were the settlers of the Massachusetts Bay Colony different from those of Plymouth's? What was the origin of the Rhode Island colony?

the Massachusetts Bay Colony. It, too, was intended to be a holy common-wealth made up of religious settlers bound together in the harmonious wor-ship of God and the pursuit of their "callings." The colony got its start in 1629, when a group of Puritans and merchants convinced King Charles I (son of James I) to grant their newly formed Massachusetts Bay Company an area north of the Plymouth colony for settlement. Leaders of the company at first looked upon it mainly as a business venture, but a majority faction, led by

John Winthrop, a respected lawyer animated by intense religious convictions, resolved to use the colony as a refuge for persecuted Puritans and as an instrument for building a "wilderness Zion" in America.

Winthrop was a courageous leader who reflected the strengths and weaknesses of the Puritan movement. In 1629 he was forty years of age, had a large family, and found himself managing a floundering English estate that could not support his seven sons. Even more unsettling was the government's heightened persecution of Puritans and other dissenters. Hence he eagerly supported the idea of establishing a spiritual plantation in the New World, and he agreed to head up the enterprise. Winthrop shrewdly took advantage of a fateful omission in the royal charter for the Massachusetts Bay Company: the usual proviso that the company maintain its home office in England. Winthrop's group took its charter with them, thereby transferring government authority to Massachusetts Bay, where they hoped to ensure Puritan control.

In 1630 the *Arbella*, with John Winthrop and the charter aboard, embarked with six other ships for Massachusetts. In "A Modell of Christian Charity," a speech delivered on board, Winthrop told his fellow Puritans that "we must consider that we shall be a city upon a hill"—a shining example of what a truly godly community could be. By the end of 1630, seventeen ships bearing 1,000 more colonists had arrived in Massachusetts. As settlers—Puritan and non-Puritan—poured into the region, Boston became the chief city and capital.

The transfer of the Massachusetts charter, whereby an English trading company evolved into a provincial government, was a unique venture in colonization. Under this royal charter, power rested with the Massachusetts General Court, which elected the governor and his assistants and consisted of shareholders, called freemen (those who had the "freedom of the company"), but of those who came, few besides Winthrop and his assistants had such status. That suited Winthrop and his friends, but soon other settlers demanded a share of political power. Rather than risk trouble, the inner group invited applications and finally admitted 118 additional freemen in 1631. The

John Winthrop

The first governor of Massachusetts Bay Colony, in whose vision the colony would be as "a city upon a hill."

inner group also stipulated that only official church members, a limited category, could become freemen.

At first the freemen had no power except to choose "assistants," who in turn elected the governor and deputy governor. The procedure violated provisions of the charter, but Winthrop kept the document hidden, and few knew of its exact provisions. Controversy simmered until 1634, when each town sent two delegates to Boston to confer on matters coming before the Massachusetts General Court. There they demanded to see the charter, which Winthrop reluctantly produced, and they read that the power to pass laws and levy taxes rested in the General Court. Winthrop argued that the body of freemen had grown too large, but when it met, the General Court responded by turning itself into a representative body with two or three deputies to represent each town. A final stage in the evolution of the government, a two-house legislature, came in 1644, with the deputies and assistants sitting apart and all decisions requiring a majority in each house.

Thus over a period of fourteen years, the Massachusetts Bay Company, a trading corporation, evolved into the governing body of a commonwealth. Membership in a Puritan church replaced the purchase of stock as a means of becoming a freeman, which was to say a voter. The General Court, like Parliament, became a representative body of two houses, with the House of Assistants corresponding roughly to the House of Lords and the House of Deputies corresponding to the House of Commons. The charter remained unchanged, but practice under the charter differed considerably from the original expectation.

RHODE ISLAND   More by accident than design, Massachusetts became the staging area for the rest of New England as new colonies grew out of religious quarrels. Puritanism created a volatile mixture: on the one hand, the search for God's will could lead to a rigid orthodoxy; on the other hand, it could lead troubled consciences to diverse, radical, or even bizarre convictions.

Young Roger Williams, who had arrived from England in 1631, was among the first to cause problems, precisely because he was the purest of Puritans, a Separatist troubled by the failure of the Massachusetts Nonconformists to repudiate the Church of England entirely. Williams held a brief pastorate in Salem, then moved to Plymouth. Governor Bradford found him gentle and kind in his personal relations and a charismatic speaker, but noted that he "began to fall into strange opinions." A quarrel with the authorities over their treatment of Indians led Williams to return to Salem. There he continued to challenge social and religious norms. Williams's belief that a true church must have no relations with the English government, the

Anglican establishment, or the unregenerate eventually led him to the conclusion that no true church was possible, unless perhaps one consisting of his wife and himself.

In Williams's view the purity of the church required complete separation of church and state and freedom from all coercion in matters of faith. "Forced worship," he declared, "stinks in God's nostrils." Such radical views were too advanced even for the progressive church of Salem, which finally removed him, whereupon Williams charged that the churches were "ulcered and gangrened." In 1635 the General Court banished him to England. Aided by Narragansett Indian friends, however, Williams and a few followers headed into the wilderness in the dead of winter and were eventually taken in by the Narragansetts. In the spring of 1636, he bought land from the Indians and established the town of Providence at the head of Narragansett Bay, the first permanent settlement in Rhode Island and the first in America to legislate freedom of religion.

Thus the colony of Rhode Island, the smallest in America, grew up in Narragansett Bay as a refuge for dissenters who believed that the state had no right to coerce religious belief. In 1640 they formed a confederation and in 1643 secured their first charter of incorporation as Providence Plantations. Roger Williams lived until 1683, an active and beloved citizen of the commonwealth he founded. During his lifetime at least, Rhode Island lived up to his principles of religious freedom and a government based on the consent of the people.

Anne Hutchinson quarreled with the Puritan leaders for different reasons. She was married to a prominent merchant and had given birth to thirteen children. Strong-willed and articulate, she also worked as a healer and midwife and hosted meetings in her Boston home to discuss sermons. Soon, however, those discussions turned into large forums for Hutchinson's commentaries on religious matters. She claimed to have had direct revelations from the Holy Spirit that convinced her that only two or three Puritan ministers actually preached the appropriate "covenant of grace." The others, she charged, were godless hypocrites, deluded and incompetent. They were promoting a "covenant of works" that led people to believe that good conduct would ensure their salvation.

Hutchinson's beliefs were provocative for several reasons. Puritan theology presumed that people could be saved only by God's grace rather than through their own willful actions. But Puritanism in practice also insisted that ministers were necessary to interpret God's will for the people so as to "prepare" them for the possibility of their being selected for salvation. In challenging the very legitimacy of the ministerial community as well as the hard-earned assurances of salvation enjoyed by current church members, Hutchinson was undermining the stability of an already fragile social system and theological order. What made the situation worse in such a male-dominated society, of course, was that a *woman* had the audacity to make such charges and assertions. Anne Hutchinson had both offended authority and sanctioned a disruptive self-righteousness.

A pregnant Hutchinson was hauled before the General Court in 1637, and for two days she verbally sparred with the presiding magistrates and testifying ministers. Her skillful deflections of the charges and her ability to cite biblical chapter-and-verse defenses of her actions led an exasperated Governor Winthrop to explode, "We do not mean to discourse with those of your sex." He found Hutchinson to be "a woman of haughty and fierce carriage, of a nimble wit and active spirit, and a very voluble tongue."

As the trial continued, an overwrought Hutchinson was eventually lured into convicting herself by claiming direct divine inspiration. Banished in 1638 as "a woman not fit for our society," she walked through the wilderness and settled with her family and a few followers on an island south of Providence, near what is now Portsmouth, Rhode Island. The arduous journey had taken a toll, however. Hutchinson grew sick, and her baby was stillborn, leading her critics in Massachusetts to assert that the "monstrous birth" was God's way of punishing her for her sins. Hutchinson's spirits never recovered. After her husband's death in 1642, she moved to what is now New York, then under Dutch jurisdiction, and the following year she and five of her children were massacred during an Indian attack.

CONNECTICUT, NEW HAMPSHIRE, AND MAINE   Connecticut had a more orthodox beginning than Rhode Island. It was founded by groups of Massachusetts Puritans seeking better land and access to the fur trade farther west. In 1636 three entire church congregations trekked westward by the "Great Road," driving their hogs and cattle before them, and settled the Connecticut River towns of Wethersfield, Windsor, and Hartford.

Led by Thomas Hooker, they organized the self-governing colony of Connecticut in 1637 as a response to the danger of attack from the Pequot Indians, who lived nearby. In 1639 the Connecticut General Court adopted the Fundamental Orders, a series of laws providing for a government like that of Massachusetts. In the Connecticut colony, however, voting was not limited to church members.

Although it would later become part of Connecticut, a separate colony was initially established in New Haven. A group of English Puritans led by their minister, John Davenport, had migrated first to Massachusetts and then, seeking a place to establish themselves in commerce, had settled in

New Haven, on Long Island Sound, in 1638. Like all the other offshoots of Massachusetts, the New Haven colony lacked a charter and maintained its independence. In 1662 it was absorbed into Connecticut.

To the north of Massachusetts, most of what are now the states of New Hampshire and Maine was granted in 1622 by the Council for New England to Sir Ferdinando Gorges and Captain John Mason. In 1629 Gorges and Mason divided their territory at the Piscataqua River, Mason taking the southern part, which he named New Hampshire, and Gorges taking the northern part, which became the province of Maine. In the 1630s Puritan immigrants began filtering in, and in 1638 the Reverend John Wheelwright, one of Anne Hutchinson's followers, founded Exeter, New Hampshire. Maine consisted of a few small, scattered settlements, mostly fishing stations, the chief of them being York.

INDIANS IN NEW ENGLAND

The English settlers who poured into New England found not a "virgin land" of uninhabited wilderness but a developed region populated by over 100,000 Indians. The white colonists viewed the Native Americans as an alien race and an impediment to their economic and spiritual goals. To the Indians the newcomers seemed like magical monsters, and they coped with their changing circumstances in different ways. Many resisted, others sought accommodation, and still others grew dependent upon European culture. The interactions of the two cultures involved misunderstandings, the mutual need for trade and adaptation, and sporadic outbreaks of epidemics and warfare.

In general, the English colonists adopted a strategy for dealing with the Native Americans quite different that was from that of the French and the Dutch. Merchants from France and the Netherlands were preoccupied with exploiting the fur trade. Thus they established permanent trading outposts, which led them to nurture amicable relations with the Indians, who were far more numerous than they. In contrast, the English colonists were more interested in pursuing their "God-given" right to fish and farm. They were quite willing, therefore, to manipulate and exploit the Indians they encountered rather than deal with them on an equal footing. Their goal was subordination rather than reciprocity.

Initially the coastal Indians helped the white settlers develop a subsistence economy. They taught the Europeans how to plant corn and use fish for fertilizer. They also developed a flourishing trade with the newcomers, exchanging furs for manufactured goods and "trinkets." The various Indian

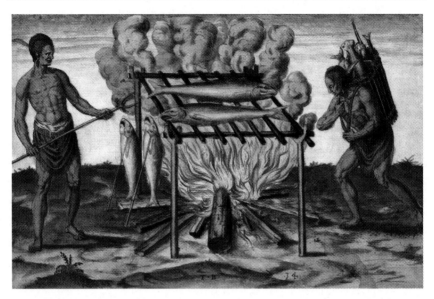

The Broiling of Their Fish Over the Flame

In this drawing by John White, reproduced in an engraving by Theodor de Bry, Algonquian men in North Carolina broil fish, a dietary staple of coastal societies.

tribes of New England fought among themselves, usually over disputed land. Had they been able to forge a solid alliance, they would have been better able to resist the encroachments of white settlers. As it was, they were not only fragmented but also vulnerable to the infectious diseases carried on board the ships transporting European settlers to the New World. Epidemics of smallpox soon devastated the Indian population, leaving the coastal areas "a widowed land." Between 1610 and 1675 the Abenakis, a tribe in Maine, declined from 12,000 to 3,000 and the southern New England tribes from 65,000 to 10,000.

THE PEQUOT WAR   Indians who survived the epidemics and refused to yield their lands were dislodged by force. In 1636 settlers in Massachusetts accused a Pequot of murdering a colonist. Joined by Connecticut colonists, they exacted their revenge by setting fire to a Pequot village on the Mystic River. As the Indians fled their burning huts, the Puritans shot and killed them—men, women, and children. In less than an hour, all but seven of the Pequot villagers were dead.

Sassacus, the Pequot chief, organized the survivors among his followers and attacked the whites. During the Pequot War of 1637, the colonists and their Narragansett allies indiscriminately killed hundreds of Pequots. The colonists captured most of the surviving Pequots and sold them into slavery in Bermuda. Under the terms of the Treaty of Hartford (1638), the Pequot Nation was declared dissolved.

Renewed Settlement

By 1640 English settlers in New England and around Chesapeake Bay had established two great beachheads on the Atlantic coast, with the Dutch colony of New Netherland in between. After 1640, however, the power struggle between king and Parliament, which erupted into civil war in 1642 between those who backed Parliament and those who supported the king, distracted attention from colonization. As a result, migration to America dwindled to a trickle for more than twenty years. During the time of the English Civil War and Oliver Cromwell's Puritan dictatorship, the struggling colonies were left pretty much alone. Virginia and Maryland remained almost as independent from British authority as New England did.

The Restoration of King Charles II in 1660 involved scarcely any changes in colonial governments. Immigration rapidly expanded the populations of Virginia and Maryland. Fears of reprisals against Puritan New England on account of the reestablishment of the Anglican Church as the official church of England proved unfounded, at least for the time being. The charter of Massachusetts was reconfirmed in 1662, and Connecticut and Rhode Island received their first royal charters in 1662 and 1663. All three colonies retained their status as self-governing corporations.

The Restoration also opened a new season of enthusiasm for colonial expansion. Within twelve years the English would conquer New Netherland, settle Carolina, and nearly fill out the shape of the American colonies. In the middle region, formerly claimed by the Dutch, four new colonies sprang into being: New York, New Jersey, Pennsylvania, and Delaware. Without exception, the new colonies were proprietary, awarded by the king to "proprietors," men who had remained loyal during the civil war.

THE CAROLINAS   Carolina from the start comprised two widely separated areas of settlement. The northernmost part, long called Albemarle, remained a remote scattering of settlers along the shores of Albemarle Sound, isolated from Virginia by the Dismal Swamp and lacking easy access to ocean-going vessels. The eight lords proprietors to whom the king had given Carolina neglected Albemarle from the outset and focused on more promising sites to the south. Eager to find settlers who had already been seasoned in the colonies, they looked first to Barbados. In 1669 three ships left London with

EARLY
SETTLEMENTS
IN THE SOUTH

VIRGINIA

James River

Roanoke River

Albemarle
Sound

*Occaneechi
Trading
Path*

Bath

Roanoke
Island

Cape Fear River

NORTH
CAROLINA

SOUTH
CAROLINA

APPALACHIAN MOUNTAINS

PIEDMONT

Oconee R.

Savannah River

GEORGIA

Ashley
River

Cooper River

Charles Town

*Altamaha
River*

Savannah

Added to Georgia,
1763

St. Mary's River

ATLANTIC

OCEAN

FLORIDA
(Spanish)

St. Augustine
(Spanish)

GULF
OF
MEXICO

0   100   200 Miles

0   100   200 Kilometers

How were the Carolina colonies created? What were the impedi-
ments to settling North Carolina? How did the lord proprietors
settle South Carolina? What were the major items traded by settlers in South Carolina?

about 100 settlers recruited in England; they sailed first to Barbados to pick
up more settlers and then north to Bermuda. The expedition landed in
America at a place several miles up the Ashley River, which they named
Charles Town (later known as Charleston).

The government of South Carolina rested upon one of the most curious
documents of colonial history, the Fundamental Constitutions of Carolina,
drawn up by one of the proprietors, Lord Anthony Ashley Cooper, with the
help of his secretary, the philosopher John Locke. Its cumbersome form of
government and its provisions for an almost feudal social system and an
elaborate nobility had little effect in the colony except to encourage a practice of large land grants. From the beginning, however, smaller headrights
were given to immigrants who could afford the cost of transit. The provision
that had greatest effect was a grant of religious toleration, designed to
encourage immigration, which gave South Carolina a distinctive degree of
indulgence (extending even to Jews and "heathens") and ethnic pluralism.

Ambitious English planters from Barbados dominated South Carolina and soon organized a major trade in Indian slaves. The first major export other than furs and slaves was cattle, and a true staple crop was not developed until the introduction of rice in the 1690s. South Carolina became a separate royal colony in 1719. North Carolina remained under the proprietors' rule for ten more years, when they surrendered their governing rights to the crown.

THE SOUTHERN INDIANS The English proprietors of South Carolina wanted the colony to focus on producing commercial crops for profit (staples). Such production took time to develop, however. Land had to be cleared, and crops planted and harvested. These activities required laborers. Some of the South Carolina planters from Barbados brought enslaved Africans and British indentured servants with them. But many more workers were needed, and slaves and servants were expensive. The quickest way to raise capital in the early years of South Carolina's development was through trade with the Indians.

Beginning in the late seventeenth century the Creeks developed a flourishing trade with the British settlers, exchanging deerskins and slaves from rival tribes for manufactured goods. By 1690 traders from Charleston, South Carolina, made their way up the Savannah River to arrange deals with the Indians.

The trade with the English not only exposed the Indians to contagious diseases but also entwined them in a dependent relationship that would prove disastrous to their way of life. Eager to receive more finished goods, weapons, and ammunition, the Indians became pliable trading partners, easily manipulated by wily English entrepreneurs and government officials. The English traders began providing the Indians with firearms and rum as incentives to persuade them to capture members of rival tribes to be sold as slaves.

While colonists themselves captured and enslaved Indians, the Westos, Creeks, and most other tribes willingly captured other Indians and drove them to the coast to be exchanged for British trade goods, guns, and rum. Colonists, in turn, put some of the Indian

A War Dance

The Westo Indians of Georgia, pictured here doing a war dance, were among the first Native Americans to obtain firearms and used this advantage to enslave natives throughout Georgia, Florida, and the Carolinas.

captives to work on their plantations. But because Indian captives often ran away, the traders preferred to ship the enslaved Indians to New York, Boston, and the West Indies and import Africans to work in the Carolinas.

The complex profitability of Indian captives prompted a frenzy of slaving activity. Slave traders turned Indian tribes against one another in order to ensure a continuous supply of captives. As many as 50,000 Indians, most of them women and children, were sold as slaves in Charles Town between 1670 and 1715. More Indians were exported during that period than Africans were imported. Thousands more captured Indians circulated through such New England ports as Boston and Salem. Although the South Carolina proprietors in England expressly prohibited the enslavement of Indians, the traders paid no attention. The burgeoning trade in Indian slaves caused bitter struggles between tribes, gave rise to unprecedented colonial warfare, and spawned massive internal migrations across the southern colonies.

During the last quarter of the seventeenth century, the trade in Indian slaves spread across the entire Southeast. Slave raiding became the region's single most important economic activity and a powerful weapon in Britain's global conflict with France and Spain. During the early eighteenth century, Indians equipped with British weapons and led by English soldiers crossed into Spanish territory in south Georgia and north Florida. They destroyed thirteen Spanish missions, killed hundreds of Indians and Spaniards, and enslaved over 300 Indians. By 1710 the Florida tribes were on the verge of extinction. In 1708, when the total population of South Carolina was 9,580, including 2,900 Africans, there were 1,400 enslaved Indians in the colony.

SETTLING THE MIDDLE COLONIES AND GEORGIA

NEW NETHERLAND BECOMES NEW YORK   In London, King Charles II resolved to pluck out that old thorn in the side of the English colonies: New Netherland. The Dutch colony was older than New England, having been started when the two Protestant powers, England and the Netherlands, allied in opposition to Catholic Spain. The Dutch East India Company (organized in 1602) had hired an English captain, Henry Hudson, to seek the elusive passage to China. In 1609 Hudson had discovered Delaware Bay and had explored the river named for him to a point probably beyond Albany, where he helped initiate a lasting trade between the Dutch and the Iroquois Nations. In 1610 the Dutch established fur-trading posts on Manhattan Island and upriver at Fort Orange (later Albany). In the 1620s a newly organized Dutch

West India Company began to establish permanent settlements. In 1626 Governor Peter Minuit purchased Manhattan from the Indians, and the new village of New Amsterdam became the capital of New Netherland.

The colony's government was under the almost absolute control of a governor sent out by the West India Company. The governors depended upon a small army garrison for defense, and the inhabitants (including a number of English on Long Island) showed almost total indifference in 1664 when Governor Peter Stuyvesant called them to arms against a threatening British fleet. Almost defenseless, the old soldier Stuyvesant blustered and stomped about on his wooden leg, but he finally surrendered to the English without firing a shot.

The plan of conquest had been hatched by Charles II's brother, the duke of York, later King James II. When he and his advisers counseled that New Netherland could easily be conquered, Charles II simply granted the region to his brother. The English transformed New Amsterdam into New York and Fort Orange into Albany, and they held the country thereafter, except for a brief Dutch reoccupation in 1673–1674. Nonetheless, the Dutch left a permanent imprint on the land and the language. Whereas the Dutch vernacular faded away, place-names like Wall Street (named for the original wall that provided protection against the Indians) and Broadway (Breede Wegh) remained, along with family names like Rensselaer, Roosevelt, and Van Buren.

THE IROQUOIS LEAGUE   One of the most significant effects of European settlement in North America during the seventeenth century was the intensification of warfare among Indian peoples. The same combination of forces that weakened the Indian populations of New England and the Carolinas befell the tribes around New York City and the lower Hudson Valley. Dissension among the Indians and susceptibility to infectious disease left them vulnerable to exploitation by whites and other Indians.

In the interior of New York, however, a different situation arose. There the tribes of the Iroquois (an Algonquian term signifying "Snake" or "Terrifying Man") forged an alliance so strong that the outnumbered Dutch and, later, English traders were forced to work with the Indians in exploiting the lucrative fur trade. The Iroquois League represented a federation of five tribes that spoke related languages: the Mohawk, Oneida, Onondaga, Cayuga, and Seneca (a sixth tribe, the Tuscaroras who lived in the Carolinas, joined them in 1712). When the Iroquois began to deplete the local game during the 1640s, they used firearms supplied by their Dutch trading partners to seize the Canadian hunting grounds of the neighboring Hurons and Eries. During the so-called Beaver Wars the Iroquois defeated the western tribes and thereafter hunted the region to extinction.

During the second half of the seventeenth century, the relentless search for furs led Iroquois war parties to range across eastern North America. They gained control over a huge area from the St. Lawrence River to Tennessee and from Maine to Michigan. The Iroquois's wars helped reorient the political relationships in the whole eastern half of the continent. Besieged by the Iroquois League, the western tribes forged defensive alliances with the French.

In the 1690s the French and their Indian allies gained the advantage over the Iroquois. They destroyed crops and villages and infected the Iroquois with smallpox. Facing extermination, the Iroquois made peace with the French in 1701. During the first half of the eighteenth century, the Iroquois maintained a shrewd neutrality in the struggle between the two rival European powers, which enabled them to play the British off against the French while creating a thriving fur trade for themselves.

NEW JERSEY   Shortly after the English conquest of New Netherland, the duke of York granted his lands between the Hudson and Delaware rivers to Sir George Carteret and Lord John Berkeley and named the territory for Carteret's native island of Jersey. In East Jersey, peopled first by perhaps 200 Dutch, new settlements gradually arose: disaffected Puritans from New Haven founded Newark, and a group of Scots founded Perth Amboy. In the west, facing the Delaware River, a scattering of Swedes, Finns, and Dutch remained, soon to be overwhelmed by swarms of English Quakers. In 1702 East and West Jersey were united as a royal colony.

PENNSYLVANIA AND DELAWARE   The Quaker sect, as the Society of Friends was called in ridicule (because they were supposed to "tremble at the word of the Lord"), became the most influential of many radical groups that sprang from the turbulence of the English Civil War. Founded in Great Britain by George Fox in about 1647, the Quakers carried further than any other group the doctrine of individual spiritual inspiration and interpretation—the "inner light," they called it. They discarded all formal sacraments and formal ministry, refused deference to persons of rank, used the familiar *thee* and *thou* in addressing everyone, declined to take oaths, claiming they were contrary to Scripture, and embraced simple living and pacifism. Quakers experienced intense persecution—often in their zeal they seemed to invite it—but never inflicted it on others. Their tolerance extended to complete religious freedom for everyone and to the equality of the sexes, including the full participation of women in religious affairs.

The settling of Quakers in New Jersey encouraged others to migrate, especially to the Delaware River side of the colony. And soon across the river arose the Quaker commonwealth, the colony of Pennsylvania. William Penn, the

The Quakers Meeting

A Quaker meeting, at which the presence of women is evidence of Quaker views on the equality of the sexes.

colony's founder, was raised as a proper English gentleman but in 1667 became a Quaker. In 1681 King Charles II gave Penn proprietary rights to a huge tract of land in America and named it Pennsylvania (literally, "Penn's Woods"). William Penn vigorously recruited settlers to his new colony, and religious dissenters from England and the Continent—Quakers, Mennonites, Amish, Moravians, Baptists—flocked to the region. Indian relations were good from the beginning because of the Quakers' friendliness and Penn's careful policy of purchasing land titles from the Indians.

Pennsylvania's government resembled that of other proprietary colonies except that the councilors as well as the assembly were elected by the freemen (taxpayers and property owners) and the governor had no veto—although Penn, as proprietor, did. "Any government is free . . . where the laws rule and the people are a party to the laws," Penn wrote in the 1682 Frames of Government.

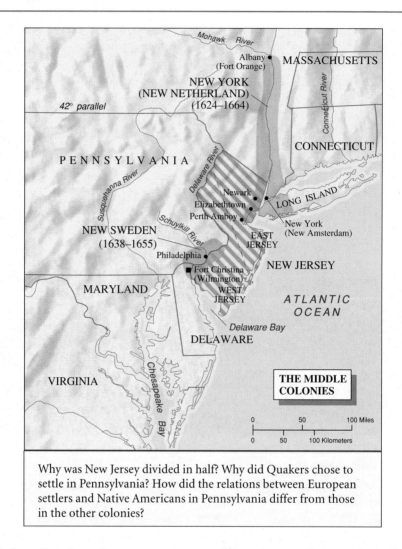

THE MIDDLE COLONIES

Why was New Jersey divided in half? Why did Quakers chose to settle in Pennsylvania? How did the relations between European settlers and Native Americans in Pennsylvania differ from those in the other colonies?

He hoped to show that a government could run in accordance with Quaker principles, that it could maintain peace and order without oaths or wars, that religion could flourish without an established church and with absolute freedom of belief.

In 1682 the duke of York also granted Penn the area of Delaware, another part of the former Dutch territory. At first, Delaware became part of Pennsylvania, but after 1704 the settlers were granted the right to choose their own assembly. From then until the American Revolution, Delaware had a separate assembly but shared Pennsylvania's governor.

GEORGIA   Georgia was the last of the British colonies to be established in North America—half a century after Pennsylvania. In 1732 King George II gave the land between the Savannah and Altamaha rivers to the twenty-one trustees of Georgia. In two respects, Georgia was unique among the colonies: it was set up both as a philanthropic experiment and as a military buffer against Spanish Florida. General James E. Oglethorpe, who accompanied the first colonists as resident trustee, represented both concerns: he served as a soldier who organized the colony's defenses and as a philanthropist who championed prison reform and sought a colonial refuge for the poor and the religiously persecuted.

In 1733 General Oglethorpe and about 120 colonists founded Savannah near the mouth of the Savannah River. Soon thereafter they were joined by Protestant refugees from central Europe, who made the colony for a time more German than English. The addition of Welsh, Highland Scots, Portuguese (Sephardic) Jews, and others gave the early colony a cosmopolitan character much like that of Charleston, South Carolina.

As a buffer against Spanish Florida, the colony succeeded, but as a philanthropic experiment it failed. Efforts to develop silk and wine production foundered. Landholdings were limited to 500 acres, rum was prohibited, and the importation of slaves forbidden, partly to leave room for servants brought on charity, partly to ensure security. But the utopian rules soon collapsed. The regulations against rum and slavery were widely disregarded and finally abandoned. By 1759 all restrictions on landholding had been removed.

In 1754 the trustees' charter expired, and the province reverted to the crown. As a royal colony, Georgia acquired an effective government for the first time. The province developed slowly over the next decade and grew rapidly in population and wealth after 1763. Instead of wine and silk, Georgians exported rice, indigo, lumber, naval stores, beef, and pork and carried on a lively trade with the West Indies. The colony had become a commercial success.

THRIVING COLONIES

After a late start and with little design, the English had outstripped both the French and the Spanish in the New World. British America had become the most populous, prosperous, and powerful region on the continent. By the mid–seventeenth century, American colonists on average were better fed, clothed, and housed than their counterparts in Europe, where a majority of the people lived in destitution. But the English colonization of North America included many failures as well as successes. Lots of settlers found only hard labor and an early death in the New World. Others flourished only at the expense of Indians, indentured servants, or African slaves.

The British succeeded in creating a lasting American empire because of crucial advantages they had over their European rivals. The lack of plan

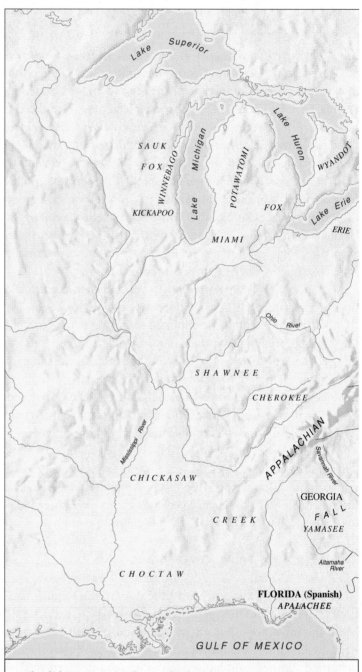

Why did European settlement lead to the expansion of hostilities among Indian peoples? What were the consequences of the trade and commerce between the English settlers and the southern Indian tribes? How were the relationships between the settlers and the members of the Iroquois League different from those between settlers and tribes in other regions?

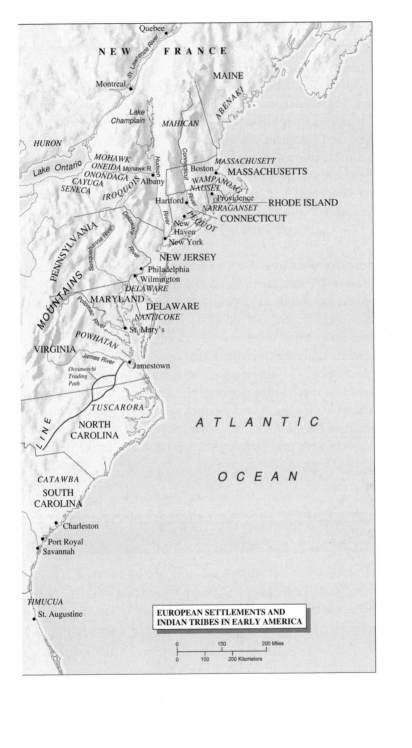

EUROPEAN SETTLEMENTS AND
INDIAN TRIBES IN EARLY AMERICA

0	100	200 Miles
0	100	200 Kilometers

marked the genius of English colonization, for it gave free rein to a variety of human impulses. The centralized control imposed by the monarchs of Spain and France got their colonies off the mark more quickly but eventually caused their downfall because it hobbled innovation in response to new circumstances. The British preferred private investment with minimal royal control. Not a single colony was begun at the direct initiative of the crown. In the English colonies poor immigrants had a much greater chance of getting at least a small parcel of land, and a greater degree of self-government made the English colonies more responsive to new challenges—though they were sometimes hobbled by controversy.

Moreover, the compact model of English settlement contrasted sharply with the pattern of Spain's far-flung conquests and France's far-reaching trade routes to the interior by way of the St. Lawrence and Mississippi rivers. Geography reinforced England's bent for the concentrated settlement of its colonies. The rivers and bays indenting the Atlantic seaboard served as veins of communication along which colonies first sprang up, but no great river offered a highway to the far interior. For 150 years the western outreach of British settlement stopped at the slopes of the Appalachian Mountains. To the east lay the wide expanse of ocean, which served not only as a highway for the transport of European culture to America but also as a barrier that separated old ideas from new, allowing the new to evolve in the new environment.

MAKING CONNECTIONS

- What we now know about the early settlements sets the stage for the regional differences in social patterns that will be discussed in the next chapter.

- This chapter concluded with the observation that "the lack of plan marked the genius of English colonization." In Chapter 4 we will see how that situation changes, as England begins to take control of the American colonies.

- Later relations between colonists and Native Americans, described in Chapter 4, had their roots in the history of these early settlements.

FURTHER READING

Bernard Bailyn's Voyagers to the West: *A Passage in the Peopling of America on the Eve of the Revolution* (1986) provides a comprehensive view of European migration. Carl Bridenbaugh's *Vexed and Troubled Englishmen, 1590–1642* (1968) helps explain why so many sought a new home in a strange land. English constitutional traditions and their effect on the colonists are examined in Edmund S. Morgan's *Inventing the People: The Rise of Popular Sovereignty in England and America* (1988). Jack P. Greene provides a brilliant synthesis of British colonization in *Pursuits of Happiness: The Social Development of Early Modern British Colonies and the Formation of American Culture* (1988). Alfred W. Crosby's *Ecological Imperialism: The Biological Expansion of Europe, 900–1900,* rev. ed. (2004) explores the ecological effects of European settlement. Alfred A. Cave's *The Pequot War* (1996) and Jill Lepore's *The Name of War: King Philip's War and the Origins of American Identity* (1998) describe the conditions leading to the wars between settlers and Indians.

A succinct overview of Puritanism can be found in Alan Simpson's *Puritanism in Old and New England* (1955). Andrew Delbanco's *The Puritan Ordeal* (1989) is a powerful study of the tensions inherent in the Puritan outlook. The best biography of John Winthrop is Francis Bremer's *John Winthrop: America's Forgotten Founding Father* (2004). Useful works on the problem of dissent in a theocracy include Edmund S. Morgan's *Roger Williams: The Church and the State* (1967) and Emery John Battis's *Saints and Sectaries: Anne Hutchinson and the Antinomian Controversy in Massachusetts Bay Colony* (1962).

The pattern of settlement in the middle Atlantic colonies is illuminated in Barry Levy's *Quakers and the American Family: British Settlement in the Delaware Valley* (1988). Randall Balmer's *A Perfect Babel of Confusion: Dutch Religion and English Culture in the Middle Colonies* (1989) describes how the English conquest of New Netherland intensified the cultural complexity of the middle colonies. On the early history of New York, see Russell Short's *The Island at the Center of the World: The Epic Story of Dutch Manhattan and the Forgotten Colony That Shaped America* (2004). The influence of Quakers can be studied in Gary B. Nash's *Quakers and Politics: Pennsylvania, 1681–1726* (1968).

Settlement of the areas along the southern Atlantic coast is traced in Wesley F. Craven's *The Southern Colonies in the Seventeenth Century, 1607–1689* (1949) and Clarence Lester Ver Steeg's *Origins of a Southern*

Mosaic (1975). Robert M. Weir's *Colonial South Carolina: A History* (1983) covers the activities of the lords proprietors. On the flourishing trade in captive Indians, see Allan Gallay's *The Indian Slave Trade: The Rise of the American South, 1670–1717* (2003). Those interested in the colonization of Georgia should consult *Oglethorpe in Perspective: Georgia's Founder after Two Hundred Years* (1989), edited by Phinizy Spalding and Harvey H. Jackson.

3

COLONIAL WAYS OF LIFE

FOCUS QUESTIONS

· What were the social and economic differences among the southern, middle, and New England colonies?

· How did various groups of people of different genders, races, and classes fit into colonial society?

· What was the impact of the Enlightenment and the Great Awakening on the American colonies?

To answer these questions and access additional review material, please visit www.wwnorton.com/studyspace.

Those who colonized America during the seventeenth and eighteenth centuries were part of a massive social migration occurring throughout Europe and Africa. They moved for different reasons. Most were responding to powerful social and economic forces: rapid population growth, the rise of commercial agriculture, and the early stages of the Industrial Revolution. Others sought political security or religious freedom. An exception was the Africans, who were captured and moved to new lands against their will.

THE SHAPE OF EARLY AMERICA

Most of the new Americans were young (over half were under twenty-five), and most were male. Almost half were indentured servants or slaves.

England also transported some 50,000 convicted felons to the North American colonies. Only one third of the newcomers journeyed with their families. Most immigrants were of the "middling sort," neither very rich nor very poor. Whatever their status or ambition, however, this extraordinary mosaic of ordinary yet adventurous people created America's enduring institutions and values.

SEABOARD ECOLOGY   America's ecosystem was shaped by both Native Americans and European settlers. For thousands of years, Indian hunting practices produced what one scholar has called the "greatest known loss of wild species" in American history. In addition, the Indians burned woods and undergrowth to provide cropland, ease travel through hardwood forests, and nourish the grasses, berries, and other forage for the animals they hunted. This "slash-and-burn" agriculture halted the normal forest succession and, especially in the Southeast, created large stands of longleaf pine, still the most common source of timber in the region.

Equally important in shaping the ecosystem of America was the European attitude toward the environment. Whereas the Native Americans tended to be migratory, considering land and animals communal resources to be shared and consumed only as necessary, many European colonizers viewed natural resources as privately owned commodities. Settlers thus looked with disdain upon the subsistence level of Indian agriculture and quickly set about evicting Indians; clearing, fencing, improving, and selling land; growing surpluses; and trapping game for furs to be sold or traded.

European ships brought to America domesticated animals—cattle, oxen, sheep, goats, horses, and pigs—that were unknown in the New World. By 1650 English farm animals outnumbered the colonists. Rapidly multiplying livestock reshaped the American environment and affected Indian life in unexpected ways. British settlers discovered that they did not have time to feed and care for livestock in pens, as they had in the Old World. Chesapeake farmers, for example, were too busy tending profitable tobacco plants to devote time to animal husbandry. So from late spring to harvest time in New England and year-round in Maryland and Virginia, hard-pressed farmers allowed their cows, horses, and pigs to roam freely through the woods, clipping their ears to identify them. Such free-range husbandry made sense in the short run, since the labor shortage made it too expensive to pen the animals in barnyards or fence them in pastures. In the longer term, however, the failure to constrain farm animals denied the planted fields dung for use as a valuable fertilizer. The fertility of the soil declined with each passing year. The Virginia planter Robert Beverley chastised his neighbors for engaging in such "exceeding ill-husbandry" and for making their hogs "find their own support in the woods."

Hogs, in particular, thrived in the New World. The animals eat virtually anything and breed frequently. A sow can give birth three times a year to as many as sixteen piglets at a time. In a few years a dozen transplanted English pigs had spawned thousands of hogs throughout the colonies. In 1700 a visitor to Virginia observed that the pigs "swarm like vermin upon the earth. . . . The hogs run where they want and find their own support in the woods without any care of the owners."

Many of the farm animals turned wild (feral), ran amok in Indian cornfields, and devastated native flora and fauna. In New England, rooting pigs devoured the shellfish that local Indians depended upon for subsistence. Colonists often had trouble finding their wandering herds. One Marylander spent three days hunting for stray hogs. Others hired Indians to track them down. As livestock herds grew, settlers felt the need to acquire more land from the Indians. A single cow needed five acres of woodland to subsist. Trespassing livestock and expanding colonial settlements caused friction with the Indians, which occasionally helped ignite violent confrontations. One historian, in fact, has referred to roaming English livestock as four-legged "agents of empire" invading Indian land. As a frustrated Maryland Indian charged in 1666, "Your hogs & cattle injure us. You come too near us to live & drive us from place to place. We can fly no farther. Let us know where to live & how to be secured for the future from the hogs & cattle."

Roaming livestock exacerbated other environmental problems. European ships brought weeds as well as animals. Native weeds, such as ragweed, goldenrod, and milkweed, were not nearly as tenacious as the weeds that arrived from Europe: dandelion, thistle, plantain, and sedge. Their seeds were transported in the hay and grain brought from abroad. As pigs, cattle, and horses ate the hay, the weed seeds passed through their digestive tracts and were deposited in manure wherever the animals roamed. In 1672 a British naturalist reported that he had identified twenty-two English weeds that were flourishing in America. The

Colonial Farm

This plan of a newly cleared American farm shows how trees were cut down and the stumps left to rot.

Indians nicknamed plantain Englishman's foot because it seemed to sprout wherever the colonists walked. Today biologists estimate that half the weeds in the United States originated in Europe or Africa.

In time a denser population of humans and their domestic animals created a landscape of fields, meadows, fences, barns, and houses. Such innovations radically altered the ecology of the New World. Foraging cattle, sheep, horses, and pigs gradually changed the distribution of trees, shrubs, and grasses. Because cleared and grazed land is warmer and drier, it floods and erodes more easily. Indians, far from being passive observers, contributed to the process of environmental change by trading furs for metal or glass trinkets. The increased hunting decimated the populations of large mammals that had earlier been central to Indian culture—and to the ecological balance. By 1800 such unintended consequences had markedly changed the physical environment. New England, for example, had become a commercial success but was essentially an agricultural wasteland.

POPULATION GROWTH   England's first footholds in America were bought at a fearsome price. Many settlers died in the first years. But once the brutal seasoning was past and the colonies were on their feet, Virginia and its successors grew at a prodigious rate. After the last major Indian uprising in 1644, Virginia's population quadrupled, from about 8,000 to 32,000 over the next thirty years, then more than doubled, to 75,000, by 1704. In 1700 the English at home outnumbered the colonists by about twenty to one; by 1775, on the eve of the American Revolution, the ratio had fallen to three to one.

America's plentiful land beckoned immigrants and induced them to replenish the earth with large families. Where labor was scarce, children could lend a hand and, once grown, find new land for themselves if need be. Colonists tended, as a result, to marry and start families at an earlier age than their European counterparts.

BIRTHRATES AND DEATH RATES   The initial scarcity of women in the colonies had significant social effects. Whereas in England the average age of women at marriage was twenty-five or twenty-six, in America it dropped to twenty or twenty-one. Men also married younger in the colonies than in the Old World. The birthrate rose accordingly, because women who married earlier had time for about two additional pregnancies during the childbearing years. Given the better economic prospects in the colonies, a greater proportion of American women married, and the birthrate remained much higher than in Europe.

Equally important in explaining rapid population growth in the New World was its much lower death rate, at least in the New England colonies (in the South, death rates remained higher due to malaria, dysentery, and other warm-climate diseases). After the difficult first years of settlement, infants generally had a better chance of reaching maturity, and adults had a better chance of reaching old age than their counterparts in Europe. This greater longevity resulted less from a more temperate climate than from the character of the settlements themselves. Since the land was initially bountiful, famine seldom occurred after a settlement's first year. Although the winters were more severe than those in England, firewood was plentiful. Being younger on the whole—the average age in the colonies in 1790 was sixteen!—American adults were less susceptible to disease than were Europeans. More widely scattered, they were also less exposed to disease. That began to change, of course, as cities grew and trade and travel increased. By the mid–eighteenth century the colonies were beginning to experience levels of contagion much like those in Europe.

WOMEN IN THE COLONIES Colonists brought to America deeply rooted convictions about the inferiority of women. God and nature, it was widely assumed, had stained women with original sin and made these "weaker vessels" smaller in stature, feebler in mind, and prone to both excited emotions and psychological dependency. Women were expected to be meek and model housewives. Their role in life was clear: to obey and serve their husbands, nurture their children, and maintain their households. John Winthrop insisted that a "true wife accounts her subjection [as] her honor and freedom" and would find true contentment only "in subjection to her husband's authority."

Such commonly held attitudes meant that most women were conditioned to accept their subordinate status in a male-dominated society. A Virginia woman explained that "one of my first resolutions I made after marriage was never to hold disputes with my husband." Both social custom and legal codes ensured that women remained deferential and powerless. They could not vote, preach, hold office, attend public schools or colleges, bring lawsuits, make contracts, or own property except under extraordinary conditions. In the eighteenth century, "women's work" typically involved activities in the house, garden, and yard. Despite the conventions that limited women, the scarcity of labor in the colonies opened social opportunities. Quite a few women, either by necessity or choice, worked in traditionally male vocations. In the towns, women commonly served as tavern hostesses and shopkeepers, and some worked as doctors, printers, upholsterers, painters, silversmiths, or shipwrights. They often, but not always, were widows who carried on their husbands' trades. Some women in the South managed plantations.

The First, Second, and Last Scene of Mortality

Prudence Punderson's needlework (ca. 1776) shows the domestic path, from cradle to coffin, followed by most colonial women.

The acute shortage of women in the early years of colonial settlement made them more highly valued than in Europe, and the Puritan emphasis on well-ordered family life led to laws protecting wives from physical abuse and allowing for divorce. In addition, colonial laws gave wives greater control over property that they contributed to a marriage or that was left after a husband's death. But the traditional notion of female subordination and domesticity remained firmly entrenched in the New World. As a Massachusetts boy maintained in 1662, the superior aspect of life was "masculine and eternal; the feminine inferior and mortal."

SOCIETY AND ECONOMY IN THE SOUTHERN COLONIES

CROPS   The southern climate enabled colonists to grow exotic staples (market crops) prized by the mother country. In Virginia by 1619, annual tobacco production had reached 20,000 pounds, and by 1688 it was up to 18 million

Virginia Plantation

Southern colonial plantations were constructed with easy access for oceangoing vessels, as shown on this 1730 tobacco label.

pounds. Tobacco, however, was only one of many cash crops being grown in the southern colonies. After 1690 rice became the staple crop in South Carolina. The southern woods also provided for the production of lumber and naval stores (tar, pitch, and turpentine). From their early leadership in the latter trade, North Carolinians would later derive the nickname of Tar Heels.

The economy of the southern colonies centered on a fundamental fact: land was plentiful, and laborers were scarce. The low cost of land lured most colonists. In 1614 each of the Virginia Company's colonists received three acres, and this policy marked the beginning of a "headright" system that provided every settler in the colony with a plot of land. In 1618 the company increased the land grants, giving 100 acres each to those already in the colonies and 50 acres each to new settlers or anyone paying the passage of immigrants (for example, indentured servants) to Virginia.

If one distinctive feature of the South's commercial agriculture was a ready market in England, another was a trend toward large-scale production. Those who planted tobacco discovered that it quickly exhausted the soil, thereby giving an advantage to the planter who had extra fields in which to plant beans and corn or to leave fallow. With the increase of the tobacco crop, moreover, a fall in prices meant that economies of scale might come into play—the large planter with the lower cost per unit might still make a profit. Gradually he would extend his holdings along the riverfronts and thereby secure the advantage of direct access to the oceangoing vessels that moved freely up and down the waterways of the Chesapeake. So easy was the access, in fact, that the Chesapeake colonies never required a city of any size as a center of commerce.

INDENTURED SERVANTS AND SLAVES   The plantation economy depended upon manual labor, and voluntary indentured servitude accounted for probably half the white settlers in all the colonies outside New England. The name derived from the indenture, or contract, by which a person agreed to work for a fixed number of years in return for transportation to the New World.

Although many servants saw the opportunity to go to the New World as a chance to better themselves, not all went voluntarily. The London underworld developed a flourishing trade in "kids," who were "spirited" into servitude. On occasion, orphans were bound off to the New World, and from time to time the mother country sent convicts into colonial servitude. Once an indenture had run its course, usually after four to seven years, a servant claimed the freedom dues set by law—some money, tools, clothing, food—and often took up land-owning.

Slavery, long a dying institution in Europe, evolved in the Chesapeake after 1619, when a Dutch vessel dropped off twenty Africans in Jamestown. Some of the first slaves were treated as indentured servants. Those who worked out their term of indenture gained freedom and a fifty-acre parcel of land. They themselves sometimes acquired slaves and white indentured servants. But gradually the practice of perpetual black slavery became the custom and the law of the land.

AFRICAN ROOTS AND BLACK CULTURE   Enslaved Africans came from lands as remote from one another as the Congo is from Senegal, and they spoke Mandingo, Ibo, Kongo, and countless other languages. For all their differences, however, the many peoples of Africa did share similar kinship and political systems. African societies were often matrilineal: property and political status descended through the mother rather than the father. Priests and the nobility lorded over the masses of farmers and craftspeople. Below the masses were the slaves, typically war captives, criminals, or debtors.

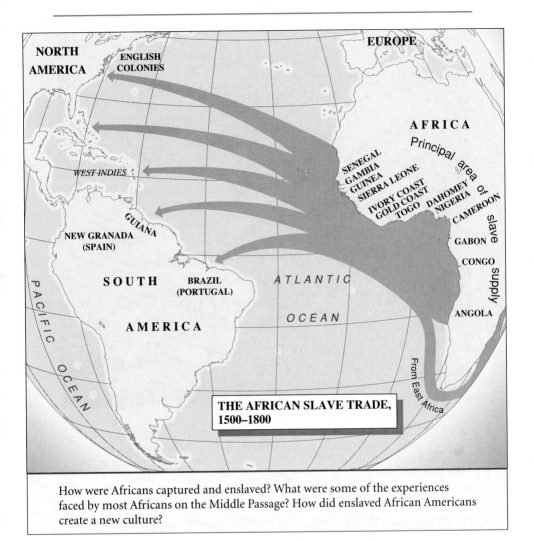

NORTH AMERICA

ENGLISH COLONIES

EUROPE

WEST INDIES

AFRICA

Principal area of slave supply

SENEGAL
GAMBIA
GUINEA
SIERRA LEONE
IVORY COAST
GOLD COAST
TOGO DAHOMEY
NIGERIA
CAMEROON

GUIANA

NEW GRANADA (SPAIN)

GABON

CONGO

SOUTH

BRAZIL (PORTUGAL)

ATLANTIC

ANGOLA

AMERICA

OCEAN

PACIFIC OCEAN

From East Africa

THE AFRICAN SLAVE TRADE, 1500–1800

How were Africans captured and enslaved? What were some of the experiences faced by most Africans on the Middle Passage? How did enslaved African Americans create a new culture?

Most of the Africans who arrived in British North America during the seventeenth century did not come directly from Africa, however. Instead, they had first been brought to the sugar-producing colonies in Brazil and the Caribbean. Once in North America, they often worked alongside white indentured servants, and personal relations between the two groups tended to be more open and casual than they would be a century later. A surprising number of the early slaves were able to earn money on the side and buy their freedom. Thus, the enslaved Africans of the seventeenth century had a more fluid and independent existence than their successors.

African Heritage

The survival of African culture among enslaved Americans is evident in this late-eighteenth-century painting of a South Carolina plantation. The musical instruments, pottery, and clothing are of African (probably Yoruban) origin.

During the eighteenth century, with the rapid development of a plantation economy in the Chesapeake Bay region and coastal South Carolina, the demand for slaves grew so quickly that a much higher proportion came directly from the African interior. Captured by ruthless traders, many of them Africans, the people destined for slavery were packed together in slave ships and subjected to a grueling transatlantic voyage that killed one in seven of them. Planters wanted field hands, so most of these newer slaves were young males who had had no exposure to European culture or languages, a factor that discouraged relations between the races.

Some of the enslaved blacks rebelled against their new masters, resisting work orders, sabotaging crops and tools, or running away to the frontier. In a few cases they organized rebellions, which were ruthlessly suppressed. "You would be surprised at their perseverance," noted one white planter. "They often die before they can be conquered." Those still alive when recaptured frequently faced ghastly retribution. After capturing slaves who participated in the Stono Uprising in South Carolina in 1739, enraged planters "cutt off their heads and set them up at every Mile Post."

In the process of being forced into bondage, blacks from diverse home-lands forged a new identity as African Americans while entwining in the fabric of American culture more strands of African heritage than historians and anthropologists can ever disentangle. Most important are African influences in music, folklore, and religious practices. On one level, slaves used songs, stories, and sermons to distract themselves from their toil; on another level these compositions conveyed coded messages of distaste for masters or overseers. Slave religion, a unique blend of African and Christian beliefs, centered on the theme of deliverance: God, slaves believed, would eventually free them and open up the gates to the promised land. The planters, how-ever, sought to strip slave religion of its liberationist hopes. In 1667 the Vir-ginia legislature declared that "the conferring of baptism does not alter the condition of the person as to his bondage or freedom."

Africans brought to America powerful kinship ties. Although most colonies outlawed slave marriages, many masters realized that slaves would work harder and more reliably if allowed to form families. Though many couples were broken up when one partner was sold, slave culture was remark-able for its powerful domestic ties. It was also remarkable for developing sex roles distinct from those of white society. Most enslaved women were by ne-cessity field workers as well as wives and mothers responsible for household affairs. They worked in proximity to enslaved men and in the process were treated more equally than were most of their white counterparts.

SOCIETY AND ECONOMY IN NEW ENGLAND

TOWNSHIPS   In contrast to the seaboard planters, who transformed the English manor into the southern plantation, the Puritans transformed the English village into the New England town, although there were many vari-eties. Land policy in New England had a stronger social and religious pur-pose than elsewhere. The headright system of the Chesapeake never took root in New England. There were cases of large individual grants, but the standard practice was one of township grants to organized groups. A group of settlers, often already gathered into a congregation, would petition the general court for a town and then divide the parcel according to a rough principle of equity—those who invested more or had larger families or greater status might receive more land—retaining some pasture and wood-land in common and holding some for later arrivals. In some early cases the towns arranged each settler's land in separate strips after the medieval prac-tice, but with time land was commonly divided into separate farms away from the central village, to which landholders would move.

ENTERPRISE   New England farmers and their families led hard lives. The growing season was short, and the harsh climate precluded profitable cash crops. The crops and livestock were those familiar to the English coun-tryside: wheat, barley, oats, some cattle, swine, and sheep. With abundant fishing grounds that stretched northward to Newfoundland, it is little won-der that New Englanders turned to the sea for their livelihood. New Eng-land's proximity to waters rich in cod, mackerel, halibut, and other varieties of fish made it America's most important maritime center. Whales, too, abounded in New England waters and supplied oil for lighting and lubrica-tion, as well as ambergris, a secretion used in perfumes.

New England's fisheries, unlike its farms, supplied a product that could be profitably exported to Europe, with lesser grades of fish going to the West Indies as food for slaves. Fisheries encouraged the development of shipbuilding, and experience at seafaring spurred commerce. This in turn led to wider contacts in the Atlantic world and a degree of materialism and cosmopolitanism that clashed with the Puritan credo of plain living and high thinking. In 1714 a worried Puritan deplored the "great extravagance that people are fallen into, far beyond their circumstances, in their purchases, buildings, families, expenses, apparel, generally in the whole way of living." But such laments failed to stop the material growth of the New England colonies.

NEW ENGLAND SHIPBUILDING   The abundant forests of New Eng-land represented a source of enormous wealth. Old-growth trees were espe-cially prized by the British government for use as ships' masts and spars. At the same time, British officials encouraged the colonists to develop their own shipbuilding industry. The New England economy was utterly depen-dent upon fishing and maritime commerce, and this placed a premium on the availability of boats and ships—and shipbuilders. American seaports ag-gressively sought to entice shipwrights to emigrate, and American-built ships quickly became prized by European traders for their quality and price. It was much less expensive to purchase American-built ships than to trans-port American timber to Britain for ship construction, especially since a large ship might require the timber from as many as 2,000 trees.

Profitable Fisheries

Fishing for, curing, and drying codfish in Newfoundland in the early 1700s. For centuries the rich fishing grounds of the North Atlantic provided New Englanders with a prosperous industry.

Nearly one third of all British ships were made in the colonies. By the mid–seventeenth century bustling shipyards had appeared in many New England towns where rivers flowed into the ocean. By the eighteenth century, Massachusetts was second only to London in the number of ships produced. Shipbuilding was one of colonial America's first big industries, and it in turn nurtured many other businesses: timber, sawmills, iron foundries, sail lofts, fisheries, and taverns.

TRADE   By the end of the seventeenth century, America had become part of a great North Atlantic commercial network, trading not only with the British Isles and the British West Indies but also—and often illegally—with Spain, France, Portugal, Holland, and their colonies. Since the colonists lacked the means to produce goods themselves, they imported manufactured goods from Europe. Their central economic problem was finding the means to pay for those imports—the eternal problem of the balance of trade.

The mechanism of trade in New England and the middle Atlantic colonies differed from that in the South in two respects: the northern colonies were at a disadvantage in their lack of cash crops to exchange for English goods, but the abundance of their shipping and mercantile enterprise worked in their

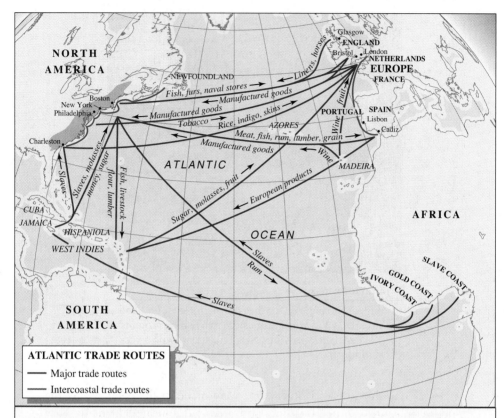

ATLANTIC TRADE ROUTES
— Major trade routes
— Intercoastal trade routes

How was overseas trade in the South different from that in New England and the middle Atlantic colonies? What was the "triangular trade"? What were North America's most important exports?

favor. After 1660, in order to protect England's agriculture and fisheries, the English government placed prohibitive duties (taxes) on certain major products exported by the northern colonies—fish, flour, wheat, and meat—while leaving the door open to timber, furs, and whale oil. As a consequence, in the early eighteenth century New York and New England bought more from England than they sold there, incurring an unfavorable trade balance.

The northern colonies solved the problem in two ways: they used their own ships and merchants, thus avoiding the "invisible" charges for trade and transport, and they found other markets for the staples excluded from England, thus acquiring goods or bullion to pay for imports from the mother country. These circumstances gave rise to the famous "triangular trade" (more a descriptive convenience than a rigid pattern), in which New Englanders shipped rum to the west coast of Africa, where they bartered for slaves; took the slaves on the "Middle Passage" to the West Indies; and returned home with various commodities, including molasses, from which they manufactured rum. In another version they shipped provisions to the West Indies, carried sugar and molasses to England, and returned with goods manufactured in Europe.

The generally unfavorable balance of trade left the colonies with a chronic shortage of hard currency, which drifted away to pay for imports and invisible charges. Various expedients met the money shortage. Most of the colonies at one time or another issued bills of credit, on promise of payment in hard currency later (hence the dollar "bill"), and most set up land banks that issued paper money for loans to farmers on the security of their land, which was mortgaged to the banks. Colonial farmers, recognizing that an inflation of paper money led to an inflation of crop prices, asked for more and more paper. Thus began in colonial politics what was to become a recurrent issue in later times: currency inflation. Wherever the issue arose, debtors commonly favored growth in the money supply, which would make it easier for them to settle accounts, whereas creditors favored a limited money supply, which would increase the value of their capital.

RELIGION   New England was settled by religious fundamentalists. The Puritans were God-fearing colonists who looked to the Bible for authority and inspiration.They read the Bible daily and memorized its passages and stories. They read it silently alone and aloud as families and in church services, which lasted from eight until noon on Sunday mornings. The Christian faith was a living source of daily inspiration and obligation for most New Englanders. The Puritans who settled Massachusetts, unlike the Separatists of Plymouth, proposed only to form a purified version of the Anglican Church. They believed that they could remain loyal to the Church of England. But their remoteness from England led them very quickly to a congregational form of church government identical with that of the Pilgrim Separatists.

In the Puritan version of Genevan John Calvin's theology, God had voluntarily entered into a covenant, or contract, with worshippers through which they could secure salvation. By analogy, therefore, an assembly of true Christians could enter into a church covenant, a voluntary union for the common worship of God. From this it was a fairly short step to the idea of a voluntary union for the purpose of government.

The covenant theory contained certain kernels of democracy in both church and state, but democracy was no part of Puritan political thought, which like so much else in Puritan belief began with original sin. Innate human depravity made governments necessary. The Puritan was dedicated to seeking not the will of the people but the will of God. The ultimate source of authority resided in the Bible, but the Bible had to be explained by "right reason." Hence, most Puritans deferred to an intellectual elite for a true knowledge of God's will. Church and state were but two aspects of the same unity, the purpose of which was to carry out God's will on earth. Although Puritan New England has often been called a theocracy, the church in theory was entirely separate from the state. By law, however, each town had to support a church through taxes levied on every household. And every resident was required to attend midweek and Sunday religious services. The average New Englander heard over 7,000 sermons in a lifetime.

DIVERSITY AND SOCIAL STRAINS   The harmony sought by Puritans settling New England was elusive. Increasing diversity and powerful disruptive forces combined to erode the consensual society envisioned by the founding settlers. Social strains and worldly pursuits increased as time passed, a consequence primarily of population pressure on the land and increasing disparities of wealth. Initially fathers exercised strong patriarchal authority over their sons through their control of the land. They kept the sons in town, not letting them set up their own households or get title to their farmland until they reached middle age. In New England as elsewhere, the tendency was to subdivide the land among all the children. But by the eighteenth century, with land scarcer, the younger sons were either getting control of the property early or moving on. Often the younger male children were forced, with family help and blessings, to seek land elsewhere, or find new kinds of work in the commercial cities along the coast or inland rivers. With the growing pressure on land in the settled regions, poverty and social tension increased in what had once seemed a country of unlimited opportunity.

Sectarian disputes and religious indifference also fractured many communities. The emphasis on a direct accountability to God, which forms the base of all Protestant theology, led believers to challenge authority in the name of private conscience. Massachusetts repressed such heresy in the 1630s, but it resurfaced during the 1650s among Quakers and Baptists, and in 1659–1660 the colony hanged four Quakers who persisted in returning after they had been expelled. These acts caused such revulsion—and an investigation by the crown—that they were not repeated, although heretics continued to face harassment and persecution.

More damaging to the Puritan utopia was the growing materialism of New England, which strained church discipline. More and more children of the "visible saints" found themselves unable to testify that they had received the gift of God's grace. In 1662 an assembly of ministers at Boston accepted the "Half-Way Covenant," whereby baptized children of church members could be admitted to a "halfway" membership. Their own children could be baptized, but such "halfway" members could neither vote nor take communion. A further blow to Puritan convention and control came with the Massachusetts royal charter of 1691, which required toleration of dissenters and based the right to vote on property rather than church membership.

NEW ENGLAND WITCHCRAFT   The strains accompanying Massachusetts's transition from Puritan utopia to royal colony reached an unhappy climax in the witchcraft hysteria at Salem Village (now the town of Danvers) in 1692. Belief in witchcraft pervaded European and New England society in the seventeenth century. Prior to the dramatic episode in Salem, almost 300 New Englanders (mostly lower-class, middle-aged spinsters or widows) had been accused of being witches, and more than 30 had been hanged.

Still, the Salem outbreak exceeded all precedents in its scope and intensity. The episode began when a few teenage girls became entranced by African tales told by Tituba, a West Indian slave, and began acting strangely—shouting, barking, groveling, and twitching for no apparent reason. The town doctor concluded that they had been bewitched, and the girls pointed to Tituba and two older white women as the culprits. Town dwellers were seized with panic as word spread that the devil was in their midst. At a hearing before the magistrates, the "afflicted" girls rolled on the floor in convulsive fits as the three women were questioned by the magistrates. In the midst of this hysterical carnival, Tituba shocked her listeners by not only confessing to the charge but also divulging that many others in the community were performing the devil's work.

With that the crazed girls began pointing accusing fingers at dozens of residents, including several of the most respected members of the community. Within a few months the Salem jail overflowed with townspeople—men, women, and children—accused of practicing witchcraft. Before the hysteria ran its course ten months later, nineteen people (including some men) had been hanged, one man—stubborn Giles Corey, who refused to plead either guilty or not guilty—was pressed to death by heavy stones, and more than 100 others were jailed.

But as the net of accusation spread wider, extending far beyond the confines of Salem, colonial leaders feared that the witch hunts were out of control. When the afflicted girls charged Samuel Willard, the distinguished pastor of Boston's First Church and president of Harvard College, the stunned magistrates had seen enough. Shortly thereafter the governor intervened when his own wife was accused of serving the devil. He disbanded the special court and ordered the remaining suspects released. Nearly everybody responsible for the

Salem executions later recanted, and nothing quite like it happened in the colonies again.

What explains the witchcraft hysteria at Salem? Some historians have argued that it represented nothing more than a contagious exercise in adolescent imagination intended to enliven the dreary routine of everyday life. Yet adults pressed the formal charges against the accused and provided most of the testimony. This fact has led some scholars to speculate that long-festering local feuds and property disputes may have triggered the prosecutions. One of the leaders of the young girls, for instance, was twelve-year-old Anne Putnam, whose older male kinfolk pressed many of the complaints. The Putnam clan were landowners whose power was declining, and their frenetic pursuit of witches might have served as a psychic weapon to restore their prestige.

More recently historians have focused on the most salient fact about the accused witches: almost all of them were women. Many of the accused women, it turns out, had in some way defied the traditional roles assigned to females. Some had engaged in business transactions outside the home; others did not attend church; some were curmudgeons; many were worried about Indian attacks. Most of them were middle-aged or older, beyond child-bearing age, and without sons or brothers. They thus stood to inherit property and live as independent women. The notion of autonomous spinsters flew in the face of prevailing social conventions. Whatever the precise cause, there is little doubt that the witchcraft hysteria reflected the peculiar social dynamics of the Salem community.

SOCIETY AND ECONOMY IN THE MIDDLE COLONIES

AN ECONOMIC MIX   Both geographically and culturally the middle Atlantic colonies stood between New England and the South, blending their own influences with elements derived from the older regions on either side. In so doing, they more completely reflected the diversity of colonial life and more fully foreshadowed the pluralism of the American nation than did the other regions. Their crops were those of New England but more bountiful, owing to better land and a longer growing season, and they developed surpluses of foodstuffs for export to the plantations of the South and the West Indies: wheat, barley, and livestock. The region's commerce rivaled that of New England, and indeed Philadelphia in time supplanted Boston as the largest city in the colonies.

Land policies in the middle colonies followed the headright system of the South. In New York the early royal governors carried forward, in practice

Quebec

QUEBEC

MAINE
(Mass.)

Augusta

Montreal

NEW
HAMPSHIRE

Lake
Champlain

MASSACHUSETTS

NEW YORK

Boston   Cape
          Cod
F

St. Lawrence River

Mohawk River

F

Lake Ontario

Hudson River

Connecticut River

J

Newport

RHODE ISLAND

CONNECTICUT

Lake Erie

APPALACHIAN MOUNTAINS

Susquehanna
River

Delaware River

F

W
F J New York

PENNSYLVANIA   NEW JERSEY

W Philadelphia
S S

ATLANTIC
OCEAN

Baltimore   DELAWARE

MARYLAND

Potomac
River

Ohio River

VIRGINIA
Shenandoah River
Richmond F

James River

Chesapeake
Bay

Williamsburg

NORTH
CAROLINA

New Bern
F

Charlotte

Fayetteville

W

SOUTH
CAROLINA

Savannah River

F F
J Charleston

GEORGIA   J Savannah

FLORIDA (Spanish)

**MAJOR IMMIGRANT
GROUPS IN COLONIAL
AMERICA**

	English
	Africans
	Scotch-Irish
	German
	Dutch
	Highland Scots
	French
J	Jews
S	Swedes
W	Welsh
F	French Huguenots

0   100   200 Miles
0 100 200 Kilometers

N

What attracted German immigrants to the middle colonies? Why did the
Scotch-Irish spread across the Appalachian backcountry? What major
population changes were reflected in the 1790 census?

if not in name, the Dutch device of the patroonship, granting influential friends vast estates on Long Island and up the Hudson and Mohawk valleys. These realms most nearly approached the medieval manor. They were self-contained domains farmed by tenants who paid fees to use the landlords' mills, warehouses, smokehouses, and wharves. But with free land elsewhere, new waves of immigrants avoided these autocratic patroonships in favor of broader opportunities in the promised land of Pennsylvania.

AN ETHNIC MIX   In the makeup of their population, the middle colonies stood apart from both the mostly English Puritan settlements of New England and the biracial plantation colonies to the south. In New York and New Jersey, for instance, Dutch culture and language lingered, along with the Dutch Reformed Church. Up and down the Delaware River, the few Swedes and Finns, the first settlers, were overwhelmed by the influx of English and Welsh Quakers, followed in turn by Germans and Scotch-Irish.

The Germans came mainly from regions devastated by incessant war. The promise of religious freedom in the New World appealed to persecuted sects, especially the Mennonites, whose beliefs resembled those of the Quakers. West of Philadelphia thrifty immigrant farmers and artisans created a belt of settlement in which the "Pennsylvania Dutch" (a corruption of *Deutsch*, meaning "German") predominated. The Scotch-Irish began to arrive later and moved still farther out into the backcountry throughout the eighteenth century. (*Scotch-Irish* is an enduring misnomer for Ulster Scots, Presbyterians transplanted from Scotland to confiscated lands in northern Ireland to give that country a more Protestant tone.) The Scotch-Irish, mostly Presbyterians, fled from economic disaster and Anglican persecution. They settled first in Pennsylvania and then fanned out across the fertile valleys stretching southwestward into Virginia and Carolina. With the Germans they became the most numerous of the non-English groups in the colonies, but others also enriched the diversity of the population in New York and the Quaker colonies: Huguenots (French Protestants), Irish, Welsh, Swiss, Jews, and others. By 1790 barely half the populace could trace their origins to England.

COLONIAL CITIES

Since commerce was their chief reason for being, colonial cities hugged the coastline or, like Philadelphia, sprang up on rivers where oceangoing vessels could reach them. Never having more than 10 percent of the colonial population, they exerted an influence in commerce, politics, and culture out of proportion to their size. Five port cities outdistanced the rest. By the end of the colonial period, Philadelphia had some 30,000 people and was the largest city in the colonies, second only to London in the British Empire; New York, with about 25,000, ranked second; Boston numbered 16,000; Charleston, South Carolina, 12,000; and Newport, Rhode Island, 11,000.

THE SOCIAL AND POLITICAL ORDER   Merchants formed the upper crust of urban society, and below them came a middle class of craftspeople, retailers, innkeepers, and artisans. Almost two thirds of the adult male workers were artisans, people who made their living at handicrafts. They included carpenters, shoemakers, tailors, blacksmiths, weavers, and potters. At the bottom of the pecking order were sailors and unskilled workers. Such class stratification in the cities became more pronounced during the eighteenth century and thereafter.

Problems created by urban growth are nothing new. Colonial cities were busy, crowded, and dangerous. They required not only paved roads and street lights but regulations to protect children and animals from reckless riders. Other regulations restrained citizens from tossing their garbage into the street. Devastating fires led to building codes, restrictions on burning rubbish, and the organization of fire companies. Rising crime and violence required more police protection. And in cities the poor became more visible than they were in the countryside. Colonists responded according to the English principle of public responsibility for the needy. Most of the aid went to "outdoor" relief in the form of money, food, clothing, and fuel, but almshouses also appeared to house the destitute.

THE URBAN WEB   Transit within and between early-American cities was initially difficult. The first roads were Indian trails, which themselves often followed the tracks of bison through the forests. Those trails widened with travel, then were made into roads by order of provincial and local authorities. Land travel was initially by horse or by foot. The first stagecoach line for the public opened in 1732. From the main ports good roads might reach thirty or forty miles inland, but all were dirt roads subject to washouts and mud holes. Aside from city streets, there was not a single hard-surfaced road constructed during the entire colonial period.

Taverns were an important aspect of colonial travel, since movement by night was risky. By the end of the seventeenth century, there were more taverns in America than any other business, and they became the most important social institution in the colonies—and the most democratic. By 1690 there were fifty-four taverns in Boston alone, half of them operated by women.

Taverns

A tobacconist's business card from 1770 captures the atmosphere of late-eighteenth-century taverns. Here men in a Philadelphia tavern share conversation while they drink ale and smoke pipes.

Colonial taverns and inns were places to drink, relax, read the newspaper, play cards or billiards, gossip about people or politics, learn news from travelers, or conduct business. Local ordinances regulated them, setting prices and usually prohibiting them from serving liquor to African Americans, Indians, servants, or apprentices.

Taverns served as a collective form of social discourse; long-distance communication, however, was more complicated. Postal service in the seventeenth century was almost nonexistent—people entrusted letters to travelers or sea captains. Massachusetts set up a provincial postal system in 1677 and Pennsylvania in 1683. Under a parliamentary law of 1710, the postmaster of London named a deputy in charge of the colonies, and a postal system eventually extended the length of the Atlantic seaboard. Benjamin Franklin, who served as deputy postmaster for the colonies from 1753 to 1774, sped up the service with shorter routes and night-traveling post riders, and he increased the volume by inaugurating lower rates.

More reliable mail delivery gave rise to newspapers in the eighteenth century. Before 1745 twenty-two newspapers had been started: seven in New England, ten in the middle colonies, and five in the South. An important landmark in the progress of freedom of the press was John Peter Zenger's trial for seditious libel, for publishing criticisms of New York's governor in his newspaper, the *New York Weekly Journal.* Zenger was imprisoned for ten months and brought to trial in 1735. English common law held that one might be punished for criticism that fostered "an ill opinion of the government." The jury's function was only to determine whether the defendant had published the opinion. Zenger's lawyer startled the court with his claim that the editor had published the truth—which the judge ruled an unacceptable defense. The jury, however, agreed with the assertion and held the editor not guilty. The libel law remained standing as before, but editors thereafter were emboldened to criticize officials more freely.

THE ENLIGHTENMENT

Through their commercial contacts, newspapers, libraries, and other channels, cities became the centers for the discussion of new ideas. In the world of ideas a new development dazzled minds: the Enlightenment. During the seventeenth century, Europe experienced a scientific revolution in which the prevailing notion of an earth-centered universe was overthrown by the sun-centered system discovered by the sixteenth-century Polish astronomer Nicolaus Copernicus. The scientific revolution climaxed in 1687 when England's Sir Isaac Newton set forth his theory of gravitation. Newton had, in short, proposed a design of a mechanistic universe moving in accordance with natural laws that could be grasped by human reason and explained by mathematics.

By analogy to Newton's view of the world as a machine, one could reason that natural laws govern all things—the orbits of the planets and the orbits of human relations: politics, economics, and society. Reason could make people aware, for instance, that the natural law of supply and demand governs economics or that the natural rights to life, liberty, and property determine the limits and functions of government.

Much of enlightened thought could be reconciled with established beliefs: the idea of natural law existed in Christian theology, and religious people could reason that the worldview of Copernicus and Newton simply showed the glory of God. Yet Deists carried the idea to its ultimate conclusion, reducing God to a remote Creator, a master clockmaker who planned the universe and set it in motion. Evil in the world, one might reason further, resulted not from original sin so much as from an imperfect understanding of the laws of nature. People, the English philosopher John Locke argued in his *Essay Concerning Human Understanding* (1690), reflect the impact of their environment, the human mind being a blank tablet at birth that gains knowledge through experience. Corrupt society therefore might corrupt the mind. The way to improve both society and human nature was by the application and improvement of Reason—which was the highest Virtue (Enlightenment thinkers often capitalized both words).

THE AMERICAN ENLIGHTENMENT   However interpreted, such "enlightened" ideas profoundly affected the climate of thought in the eighteenth century. The premises of Newtonian science and the Enlightenment, moreover, fitted the American experience, which placed a premium on observation, experiment, and the need to think anew. America was therefore especially receptive to the new science.

Benjamin Franklin epitomized the Enlightenment. He rose from the ranks of the common folk and never lost the common touch, a gift that accounted for his success as a publisher. Born in Boston in 1706, Franklin was the son of a maker of candles and soap. Apprenticed to his older brother, a printer, Franklin left home at the age of seventeen and relocated to Philadelphia. There, before he was twenty-four, he owned a print shop, where he edited and published the *Pennsylvania Gazette.* When he was twenty-six, he brought out *Poor Richard's Almanack,* a collection of homely teachings on success and happiness. Before he retired from business, at the age of forty-two, Franklin, among other achievements, had founded a library, set up a fire company, helped start the academy that became the University of Pennsylvania, and organized a debating club that grew into the American Philosophical Society. After his early retirement, he intended to devote himself to public affairs and the sciences.

The course of events allowed Franklin less and less time for science, but that remained his passion. His speculations extended widely to the fields of medicine, meteorology, geology, astronomy, and physics. He invented the Franklin stove, the lightning rod, and a glass harmonica for which Mozart and Beethoven wrote works. The triumph of this untutored genius further confirmed the Enlightenment trust in the powers of Nature and Reason.

Benjamin Franklin

Shown here as a young man in a portrait by Robert Feke.

EDUCATION IN THE COLONIES   The heights of abstract reasoning, of course, were remote from the everyday concerns of most colonists. For the colonists at large, education in the traditional ideas and manners of society—even literacy itself—remained primarily the responsibility of family and church.

Conditions in New England, however, proved most favorable for the establishment of schools. The Puritan emphasis on Scripture reading, which all Protestants shared to some degree, implied an obligation to ensure literacy. In 1647 the Massachusetts Bay Colony required every town of fifty or more families to set up a grammar school (a "Latin school" that could prepare a student for college). Although the act was widely evaded, it set an example that the rest of New England emulated.

In Pennsylvania the Quakers never heeded William Penn's instructions to establish public schools, but they did respect the usefulness of education and financed a number of private schools, where practical as well as academic subjects were taught. In the southern colonies, efforts to establish schools were hampered by the more scattered population and in parts of the backcountry by indifference and neglect. Some of the wealthiest planters and merchants of the Tidewater sent their children to England or hired tutors, who in some cases would also serve the children of neighbors. In some places wealthy patrons or the people collectively managed to raise some kind of support for academies.

THE GREAT AWAKENING

The new currents of learning and the questioning outlook spawned by the Enlightenment led many people to drift away from the moorings of orthodox religion during the eighteenth century. Many of those in the educated classes were attracted to Deism (which denied that God interfered with the laws and working of the universe) and skepticism (which questioned accepted assumptions and religious beliefs). The pious feared that the great Puritan and Quaker merchants of Boston and Philadelphia were prospering because the devil had lured them into the vain pursuit of worldly gain. Meanwhile, out along the fringes of settlement there grew up a great backwater of the unchurched, people who had no minister to preach or administer sacraments or perform marriages. By the 1730s the sense of spiritual decline had prepared the time for a revival of faith, the Great Awakening, a wave of evangelism that within a few years swept the colonies from one end to the other, America's first mass movement.

EDWARDS AND WHITEFIELD   In 1734–1735 a remarkable spiritual revival occurred in the congregation of Jonathan Edwards, a Congregationalist minister in Northampton, in western Massachusetts. One of America's most brilliant philosophers and theologians, Edwards had entered Yale in 1716, at age thirteen, and graduated as valedictorian four years later. In 1727 Edwards took charge of the Congregational church in Northampton and found the congregation's spirituality at a low ebb. He was convinced that Christians had become preoccupied with making and spending money and that religion had become too intellectual and in the process had lost its animating force. "Our people," he said, "do not so much need to have their heads stored [with education] as to have their hearts touched." He added that he considered it a "reasonable thing to endeavor to fright persons away from hell." His own vivid descriptions of the torments of hell and the delights of heaven helped rekindle spiritual fervor among his congregants. By 1735 Edwards could report that "the town seemed to be full of the presence of God; it never was so full of love, nor of joy."

The true catalyst of the Great Awakening, however, was a young English minister, George Whitefield, whose reputation as a spellbinding evangelist preceded him to the colonies. Congregations were lifeless, he claimed, "because dead men preach to them." Too many ministers were "slothful shepherds and dumb dogs." To restore the fires of religious fervor to American congregations, Whitefield reawakened the notion of individual salvation. In the autumn of 1739, Whitefield arrived in Philadelphia and late in that year preached to huge crowds. After visiting Georgia, he made a triumphal procession northward to New England, drawing great crowds and releasing "Gales of Heavenly Wind" that dispersed sparks throughout the colonies.

Whitefield enthralled audiences with his unparalleled eloquence. The English revivalist stressed the need for individuals to experience a "new birth," a sudden and emotional moment of conversion and salvation. By the end of his sermon, one listener

George Whitefield

The English minister's dramatic eloquence roused American congregants, inspiring many to experience a religious rebirth.

reported, the entire congregation was "in utmost Confusion, some crying out, some laughing, and Bliss still roaring to them to come to Christ, as they answered, *I will, I will, I'm coming, I'm coming.*"

Jonathan Edwards heard Whitefield preach and wept through most of the sermon. Thereafter he spread his own revival gospel throughout New England. The Great Awakening in New England reached its peak in 1741 when Edwards delivered his most famous sermon. Titled "Sinners in the Hands of an Angry God," it represented a devout appeal to repentance. Edwards reminded the congregation of the reality of hell, the omnipotence of God's vision, and the certainty of his judgment. He warned that God "holds you over the pit of hell, much as one holds a spider, or some loathsome insect, over the fire, abhors you, and is dreadfully provoked . . . he looks upon you as worthy of nothing else, but to be cast into the fire."

The message and technique of Edwards and Whitefield were infectious, and imitators sprang up everywhere. Once unleashed, however, spiritual enthusiasm was hard to control, and in many ways the Great Awakening backfired on those who had intended it to bolster church discipline and social order. Some revivalists began to court those at the bottom of society—laborers, seamen, servants, and farmers. The Reverend James Davenport, for instance, a fiery New England Congregationalist, set about shouting, raging, and stomping on the devil and beseeching his listeners to renounce the established clergy, whom he branded unconverted, and become the agents of their own salvation. The radical revivalists, said one worried conservative, were breeding "anarchy, levelling, and dissolution."

PIETY AND REASON   Whatever their motive or method, the revivalists succeeded in awakening the piety of many Americans. Between 1740 and 1742 some 25,000 to 50,000 New Englanders, out of a total population of 300,000, joined churches. The Great Awakening also helped fragment spiritual life. It spawned a proliferation of new religious groups and sects that helped undermine the notion of state-supported churches. Everywhere the revivals induced splits, especially in the more Calvinist churches. Traditional clergymen found their position undermined as church members chose sides and either dismissed their old ministers or deserted them.

By the middle of the eighteenth century, New England Puritanism had finally fragmented. The precarious balance in which the founders had held the elements of piety and reason was shattered, and more and more Baptists, Presbyterians, Anglicans, and members of other denominations began establishing footholds in formerly Congregationalist Puritan communities. Yet the revival frenzy scored its most lasting victories along the chaotic frontiers of the middle and southern colonies. In contrast, in the more sedate churches of Boston, rational religion ultimately got the upper hand in a reaction against the excesses of revival emotion. The rationality of Newton and Locke, the idea of natural law, crept more and more into the sermons of Boston ministers, and they embarked on the road to Unitarianism and Universalism.

In reaction to taunts that the "born-again" revivalist ministers lacked learning, the Great Awakening gave rise to the denominational colleges that became characteristic of American higher education. The three colleges already in existence had their origins in religious motives: Harvard College, founded in 1636 because the Puritans dreaded "to leave an illiterate ministry to the church when our present ministers shall lie in the dust"; the College of William and Mary, created in 1693 to strengthen the Anglican ministry; and Yale College, set up in 1701 to serve the Puritans of Connecticut, who believed that Harvard was drifting from the strictest orthodoxy. The College of New Jersey, later Princeton University, was founded by Presbyterians in 1746 as the successor to William Tennent's Log College. In close succession came King's College (1754) in New York, later Columbia University, an Anglican institution; the College of Rhode Island (1764), later Brown University, which was Baptist; Queens College (1766), later Rutgers, which was Dutch Reformed; and the Congregationalist Dartmouth College (1769), the outgrowth of an earlier school for Indians. Among the colonial colleges only the University of Pennsylvania, founded as the Academy of Philadelphia in 1751, arose from a secular impulse.

The Great Awakening, like the Enlightenment, set in motion powerful currents that still flow in American life. It implanted permanently in American culture evangelical energies and the appeal of revivalism. The movement weakened the status of the established clergy, encouraged believers to exercise their own judgment, and thereby weakened habits of deference generally. The proliferation of denominations heightened the need for toleration of dissent. In some respects the Great Awakening, characterized by piety and emotion, and the Enlightenment, dominated by reason and rationality, led by different roads to similar ends. Both movements emphasized the power and right of individual choice and popular resistance to established authority, and both aroused millennial hopes that America would become the promised land in which people might approach the perfection of piety or reason, if not both. Such hopes had both social and political, as well as religious, implications. As the eighteenth century advanced, fewer and fewer people were willing to defer to the ruling social and political elite, and many such rebellious if pious folk would be transformed into revolutionaries.

MAKING CONNECTIONS

- This chapter reveals social and racial tensions in colonial Virginia society; in the next chapter, these tensions will come to a head with Bacon's Rebellion.

- During the imperial crisis of the 1760s and 1770s, the ideas of the Great Awakening and especially the Enlightenment helped shape the American response to British actions and thereby contributed to a revolutionary mentality.

FURTHER READING

The diversity of colonial societies may be seen in David Hackett Fischer's *Albion's Seed: Four British Folkways in America* (1989). Other useful works include Richard Hofstadter's *America at 1750: A Social Portrait* (1971) and James A. Henretta's *The Evolution of American Society, 1700–1815* (1973). For a fascinating account of the impact of livestock on colonial history, see Virginia DeJohn Anderson's *Creatures of Empire: How Domestic Animals Transformed Early America* (2004).

Bernard Rosenthal challenges many myths concerning the Salem witch trials in *Salem Story: Reading the Witch Trials of 1692* (1993). Mary Beth Norton's *In the Devil's Snare: The Salem Witchcraft Crisis of 1692* (2002) emphasizes the role of Indian violence. Discussions of women in the New England colonies can be found in Laurel Thatcher Ulrich's *Good Wives: Image and Reality in the Lives of Women in Northern New England, 1650–1750* (1980), Joy Day Buel and Richard Buel Jr.'s *The Way of Duty: A woman and Her Family in Revolutionary America* (1984), and Carol F. Karlsen's *The Devil in the Shape of a Woman: Witchcraft in Colonial New England* (1987). John Demos describes family life in *A Little Commonwealth: Family Life in Plymouth Colony,* new ed. (2000).

For the social history of the southern colonies, see Allan Kulikoff's *Tobacco and Slaves: The Development of Southern Cultures in the Chesapeake, 1680–1800* (1986) and *Colonial Chesapeake Society* (1988), edited by Lois Green Carr, Philip D. Morgan, and Jean B. Russo. Edmund S. Morgan's *American Slavery, American Freedom: The Ordeal of Colonial Virginia* (1975) examines Virginia's social structure, environment, and labor patterns in a biracial context. On the interaction of the cultures of blacks and whites, see Mechal Sobel's *The World They Made Together: Black and White Values in Eighteenth-Century Virginia* (1987). African-American viewpoints are presented in Timothy H. Breen and Stephen Innes's *"Myne Owne Ground": Race and Freedom on Virginia's Eastern Shore, 1640–1676*, new ed. (2004). David W. Galenson's *White Servitude in Colonial America: An Economic Analysis* (1981) looks at the indentured labor force.

Henry F. May's *The Enlightenment in America* (1976) examines intellectual trends in eighteenth-century America. Lawrence A. Cremin's *American Education: The Colonial Experience, 1607–1783* (1970) surveys educational developments.

On the Great Awakening, see Edwin S. Gaustad's *The Great Awakening in New England* (1957), Patricia U. Bonomi's *Under the Cope of Heaven: Religion, Society, and Politics in Colonial America* (1986), and Timothy D. Hall's *Contested Americn Boundaries: Itinerancy and the Reshaping of the Colonial American Religious World* (1994). The political impact of the new religious enthusiasm is shown in Rhys Issac's *The Transformation of Virginia, 1740–1790* (1982). Patricia J. Tracy's *Jonathan Edwards, Pastor* (1980) stresses the Northampton minister's relations to his community.

4

THE IMPERIAL
PERSPECTIVE

FOCUS QUESTIONS

· How did England's political and economic administration of
  the colonies change?

· How were the colonial governments structured?

· What were relations like between the English colonists and
  their neighbors in North America: the French, the Spanish,
  and the Indians?

To answer these questions and access additional review material, please visit
www.wwnorton.com/studyspace.

For the better part of the seventeenth century, England remained too distracted by the struggle between Parliament
and the Stuart kings to perfect either a systematic colonial
policy or effective agencies of imperial control. The English Civil War, which
lasted from 1642 to 1649, ushered in Oliver Cromwell's Puritan Commonwealth and Protectorate, during which the colonies were given a respite from
royal control. After the Restoration of King Charles II and the Stuart dynasty
in 1660, the British government slowly developed a new plan of colonial
administration. By the end of the seventeenth century, however, it still lacked
coherence and efficiency, leaving Americans accustomed to rather loose
colonial reins.

ENGLISH ADMINISTRATION
OF THE COLONIES

Throughout the colonial period the British king exercised legal authority in America, and land titles derived ultimately from royal grants to individuals and groups. All important colonial officials held office at the pleasure of the monarch. Before the English Civil War the king supervised colonial officials through the Privy Council, a body of thirty to forty advisers, eleven of whom in 1634 were made responsible for colonial administration. After the Restoration the king tried to reassert his control over the colonies, but administration by the mother country continued to be inconsistent and inefficient. The British government regarded English colonists as citizens, but it refused to grant them the privileges of citizenship. It insisted that the settlers contribute to the expense of maintaining the colonies, but it refused to allow them a voice in the shaping of administrative policies. Such inconsistencies bred tension that festered over time. By the mid–eighteenth century, when the British tried to impose on their colonies in America the kinds of controls that were reaping such profits in India, it was too late. British Americans had developed a far more powerful sense of their rights than had any other colonial people, and they were determined to assert and defend those rights.

THE MERCANTILE SYSTEM   In developing national economic policy, Restoration England under Charles II adopted the mercantile system, or mercantilism, which was based on the assumption that the world's supply of gold and silver remained essentially fixed, with only a nation's share in that wealth subject to change. Thus one nation could gain wealth only at the expense of another—by seizing its gold and silver and dominating its trade. To acquire gold and silver, a government had to control all economic activities, limiting foreign imports and preserving a favorable balance of trade. Thus a mercantilist government had to encourage manufacturing, through subsidies and monopolies if need be, to develop and protect its own shipping and to exploit colonies as sources of raw materials and markets for its finished goods.

During the English Civil War, Dutch shipping companies had taken over the trade with England's colonies. To win it back, Oliver Cromwell persuaded Parliament in 1651 to adopt the Navigation Act, which required that all goods imported by England or the colonies arrive on English ships and that the majority of the crew be English.

With the Restoration, Parliament passed the Navigation Act of 1660, which added a twist to Cromwell's act; ships' crews had to be three-quarters English, and "enumerated" products not produced by the mother country, such as tobacco, cotton, and sugar, were to be shipped from the colonies only to England or other English colonies. Not only did England (and its colonies) become the sole outlet for these colonial exports, but the Navigation Act of 1663 required that all ships carrying goods from Europe to America dock in England, be offloaded, and pay a duty before proceeding. A third major act rounded out the trade system. The Navigation Act of 1673 (sometimes called the Plantation Duty Act) required that every captain loading enumerated articles in the colonies pay a duty, or tax, on them.

ENFORCING THE NAVIGATION ACTS   The Navigation Acts supplied a convenient rationale for a colonial system: to serve the economic needs of the mother country. Their enforcement in far-flung colonies, however, was another matter. In 1675 Charles II designated certain members of his Privy Council the Lords of Trade. These officials were to make the colonies abide by the mercantile system and make them more profitable for the crown. To these ends the Lords of Trade served as the clearinghouse for all colonial affairs, building up a staff of colonial experts. They also named colonial governors,

Boston from the Southeast

This view of eighteenth-century Boston shows the importance of shipping and its regulation in the colonies, especially in Massachusetts Bay.

wrote or reviewed the governors' instructions, and handled all reports and correspondence dealing with colonial affairs.

Between 1673 and 1679 British collectors of customs duties arrived in all the colonies, and with them appeared the first seeds of colonial resentment. New England's Puritan leaders in particular harbored a persistent distrust of royal intentions. The Massachusetts Bay Colony not only ignored royal wishes; it also tolerated violations of the Navigation Acts. This led the Lords of Trade to begin legal proceedings against the colonial charter in 1678. The issue remained in legal snarls for another six years; in 1684 the Lords of Trade won a court decision annulling the Massachusetts charter.

THE DOMINION OF NEW ENGLAND   Temporarily the Massachusetts Bay government fell under the control of a special royal commission. Then, in 1685, King Charles II died and was succeeded by his brother the duke of York, as King James II, the first Catholic sovereign since Queen Mary (r. 1553–1558). Plans long maturing in the Lords of Trade for a general reorganization of colonial government coincided with the autocratic notions of James II, who asserted power more forcefully than his brother had. The new king therefore readily approved a proposal to create a Dominion of New England that included all the colonies south through New Jersey.

The Dominion was to have a government named by royal authority; a governor and council would rule without any colonial assembly. The royal governor, Sir Edmund Andros, appeared in Boston in 1686 to establish his rule, which he soon extended over Connecticut and Rhode Island and, in 1688, over New York and East and West Jersey. Not surprisingly, a rising resentment greeted Governor Andros's measures, especially in Massachusetts. Andros levied taxes without the consent of the General Court, suppressed town governments, enforced the trade laws, and clamped down on smuggling. Most ominous of all, he and his lieutenants took over one of Boston's Puritan churches for Anglican worship. Puritan leaders believed, with good reason, that he proposed to break their power and authority.

But the Dominion was scarcely established before word arrived that the Glorious Revolution of 1688 had erupted in England. King James II, like Andros, had aroused resentment by instituting arbitrary measures and openly parading his Catholic faith. The birth of a son who was sure to be reared a Catholic put the Anglican opposition on notice that James's pro-Catholic system would survive him. In 1688, therefore, parliamentary leaders, their patience exhausted, invited James's Protestant daughter Mary and her husband, the Dutch leader William III, to assume the throne as joint monarchs. James II, his support dwindling, fled to France.

THE GLORIOUS REVOLUTION IN AMERICA   When news reached Boston that William and Mary had landed in England, the city staged its own Glorious Revolution. Andros and his councilors were arrested, and Massachusetts reverted to its former government, as did the other colonies that had been absorbed into the Dominion. All were permitted to retain their former status except Massachusetts Bay and Plymouth, which after some delay were united under a new charter in 1691 as the royal colony of Massachusetts Bay.

The Glorious Revolution in England had significant long-term effects on American history. The Bill of Rights and the Toleration Act, passed in England in 1689, limited the powers of the country's monarchs and affirmed a degree of freedom of worship for all Christians, thereby influencing attitudes—and the course of events—in the colonies. And what was more significant for the future, the overthrow of James II set a precedent for revolution against the monarch. In defense of that action, the English philosopher John Locke published his *Two Treatises on Government* (1690), which had an enormous impact on political thought in the colonies. Whereas the first treatise refuted theories of the divine right of kings, the more important second treatise set forth Locke's contract theory of government, which argued that people were endowed with natural rights to life, liberty, and property. When a ruler violated these rights, the people had the right—in extreme cases—to overthrow the monarch and change their government.

In the American experience colonial governments had actually grown out of contractual arrangements such as John Locke had described; a good example is the Mayflower Compact. The royal charters themselves also constituted a sort of contract between the crown and the settlers. Such precedents made John Locke's writings especially appealing to colonial readers, and his philosophy probably had more influence in America than in England.

AN EMERGING COLONIAL SYSTEM   William and Mary oversaw a refinement of the Navigation Acts and the administrative system for regulating the American colonies. The Navigation Act of 1696, officially called the Act to Prevent Frauds and Abuses, required colonial governors to enforce the Navigation Acts, allowed customs officials to use "writs of assistance" (general search warrants that did not have to specify the place to be searched), and ordered that accused violators be tried in admiralty courts, because colonial juries habitually refused to convict their peers. Admiralty cases were decided by judges whom the royal governors appointed.

Also in 1696 King William III created a Lords Commissioners of Trade and Plantations to take the place of the Lords of Trade. Intended to ensure that the colonies served England's economy, the new Board of Trade oversaw the enforcement of the Navigation Acts and recommended ways to limit manufacturing in the colonies and encourage their production of raw materials.

From 1696 to 1725, the Board of Trade sought to bring more efficient royal control to the administration of the colonies. After 1725, however, its energies and activities waned. The Board of Trade became chiefly an agency of political patronage, studded with officials whose main interest was their salaries.

THE HABIT OF SELF-GOVERNMENT

Government within the American colonies, like colonial policy, evolved essentially without plan. In broad outline the governor, council, and assembly in each colony corresponded to the king, lords, and commons of the mother country. At the outset all the colonies except Georgia had begun as projects of trading companies or feudal proprietors holding charters from the crown, but eight colonies eventually relinquished or forfeited their charters and became royal provinces. In these the crown named the governor. Connecticut and Rhode Island were the last of the corporate colonies; they elected their own governors to the end of the colonial period. In the corporate and proprietary colonies and in Massachusetts, the charter served as a rough equivalent to a written constitution. Over the years certain anomalies appeared as colonial governments diverged from trends in England. On the one hand, the governors retained powers and prerogatives that the king had lost in the course of the seventeenth century. On the other hand, the assemblies acquired powers, particularly with respect to government appointments, that Parliament had yet to gain.

POWERS OF THE GOVERNORS   The crown never vetoed acts of Parliament after 1707, but the colonial governors, most of whom were mediocre or incompetent, still held an absolute veto over the assemblies, and the crown could disallow (in effect, veto) colonial legislation on advice of the Board of Trade. With respect to the assembly, the governor still had the power to determine when and where it would meet, prorogue (adjourn or recess) legislative sessions, and dissolve the assembly for new elections or postpone elections indefinitely. In contrast, in the mother country the crown had pledged to summon Parliament every three years and call elections at least every seven and could not prorogue sessions. The royal or proprietary governor, moreover, nominated for life appointment the members of his council (except in Massachusetts, where they were chosen by the lower house), and the council functioned as both the upper house of the legislature and the highest court of appeal within the colony.

With respect to the judiciary, in all but the charter colonies the governor still held the prerogative of creating courts and naming and dismissing judges, powers explicitly denied the king in England. Over time, however, the colonial assemblies generally made good their claim that courts should be created only by legislative authority, although the crown repeatedly disallowed acts to grant judges life tenure in order to make them more independent.

As chief executive, the governor could appoint and remove officials, command the militia and naval forces, grant pardons, and as his commission often put it, "execute everything which doth and of right ought to belong to the governor," which might cover a multitude of powers. In these respects, his authority resembled the crown's, for the king still exercised executive authority and had the power to name administrative officials.

POWERS OF THE ASSEMBLIES   Unlike the governor and members of the council, who were appointed by either king or proprietor, the colonial assembly was elected. Whether called the House of Burgesses (Virginia), or Delegates (Maryland), or Representatives (Massachusetts), or simply the assembly, the lower houses were chosen by popular vote in counties, towns, or, in South Carolina, parishes. Religious tests for voting were abandoned during the seventeenth century, and the chief restriction remaining was a property qualification, based upon the notion that only men who held a "stake in society" could vote responsibly. Yet the property qualifications generally set low hurdles in the way of potential voters. Property holding was widespread, and a greater proportion of the population could vote in the colonies than anywhere else in the world of the eighteenth century. Women, Indians, and African Americans were excluded—few then questioned this—and continued to be excluded for the most part into the twentieth century.

By the early eighteenth century the colonial assemblies, like Parliament, held two important strands of power. First, they controlled the budget by their right to vote on taxes and expenditures. Second, they held the power to initiate legislation. They used these powers to pull other strands of power into their hands when the chance presented itself. For example, they held governors on a tight leash by their control of political salaries. Throughout the eighteenth century the assemblies expanded their power and influence, sometimes in conflict with the governors and sometimes in harmony with them. Often in the course of routine business, the assemblies passed laws and set precedents the collective significance of which neither

The Boston Statehouse

Built in 1713.

they nor the imperial authorities fully recognized. Once established, however, these laws and practices became fixed principles, part of the "constitution" of the colonies. Self-government in the colonies became first a habit, then a "right."

TROUBLED NEIGHBORS

Self-government was not the only institution that began as a habit during the colonial period. The claims of white settlers on Indian lands had their roots in the first English settlements, where relations between the colonists and the Indians were at times cooperative and at times hostile. Indian-white relations transformed the human and ecological landscape of colonial North America, stirred up colonial politics, and disrupted or destroyed the fabric of Indian culture. Relations between European settlers and North American Indians were themselves agitated by the fluctuating balance of power in Europe. The French and the English each sought to use Indians to their advantage in fighting each other for control of New World territory.

DISPLACING THE INDIANS   The English invasion of North America would have been a different story had the English encountered greater resistance. Instead, in the coastal regions they found scattered and mutually hostile Indian tribes, whom they subjected to a policy of divide and conquer. Whether tempted by trade goods or the promise of alliances or intimidated by a show of force, most of the Native Americans let matters drift until the English were too entrenched to be pushed back into the sea.

During the first half of the seventeenth century, the most severe tests of the colonists' will to prevail came with the Virginia troubles in 1644 and Connecticut's Pequot War of 1637. In both colonies, Indian leaders engaged in last-chance efforts to save their lands; in both instances they failed. For the Pequots the result was virtual extermination—Puritans killed Pequots with such savagery that they offended their allies, the Narragansetts, who had never seen such total war. In Virginia, according to a census taken in 1669, only eleven of twenty-eight tribes described by John Smith in 1608, and only about 2,000 of some 30,000 Indians, remained in the colony. Indian resistance had been broken for the time.

Then, in the mid-1670s, both New England and Virginia went through another time of troubles: an Indian war in New England and a civil war masquerading as an Indian war in Virginia. The spark that set New England ablaze was the murder of John Sassamon, a "praying Indian" who had attended Harvard, strayed from the faith while serving King Philip (Metacom) of the Wampanoag tribe, and then returned to the Christian fold. When Plymouth tried and executed three Wampanoags for Sassamon's murder, King Philip's tribesmen attacked.

Thus began King Philip's War, which the land-hungry leaders of Connecticut and Massachusetts quickly enlarged by assaulting the peaceful Narragansetts at their chief refuge in Rhode Island, a massacre the Rhode Island authorities were helpless to prevent. From June to December 1675, Indian attacks ravaged the interior of Massachusetts Bay and Plymouth, and guerrilla war continued through 1676. Finally, depleted supplies and the casualty toll wore down Indian resistance. Philip's wife and son were captured and sold into slavery. In August 1676 Philip himself was tracked down and killed. Sporadic fighting continued until 1678 in New Hampshire and Maine. Indians who survived the slaughter had to submit to colonial authority and accept confinement to ever-dwindling plots of land.

BACON'S REBELLION   The news from New England heightened tensions among colonists in the sparsely settled Virginia interior and contributed to the tangled events thereafter known as Bacon's Rebellion. The roots of the revolt grew out of a festering hatred for the domineering colonial governor, William Berkeley. Appointed by the king in 1641, he served as Virginia's governor for most of the next thirty-five years. Berkeley was an unapologetic elitist who limited his circle of friends to the wealthiest and most ambitious planters. He granted them most of the frontier land and public offices, and he rarely allowed new elections to the assembly for fear that his cronies might be defeated. The large planters who dominated the assembly levied high taxes to finance Berkeley's regime, which in turn supported their interests at the expense of the small farmers and servants. With little nearby land available, newly freed indentured servants were forced to migrate westward in their quest for farms. Their lust for land led them to displace the Indians. When Governor Berkeley failed to support the aspiring farmers, they rebelled.

The discontent turned to violence in 1675 when a petty squabble between a frontier planter and the Doeg Indians on the Potomac River led to the murder of the planter's herdsman. Frontier militiamen retaliated by killing ten or more Doegs and, by mistake, fourteen Susquehannocks. Soon a force of Virginia and Maryland militiamen laid siege to the Susquehannocks and murdered five chieftains. The enraged Indian survivors took their revenge on frontier settlements. Scattered attacks continued down to the James River, where Nathaniel Bacon's overseer was killed.

In 1676 Bacon defied Governor Berkeley's authority by assuming command of a group of frontier vigilantes. The vain, ambitious, and hot-tempered Bacon had a talent for trouble and an enthusiasm for terrorizing peaceful Indians. After threatening to kill the governor and the assemblymen if they tried to intervene, Bacon began preparing for a total war against all Indians. Berkeley opposed Bacon's genocidal plan not because he liked Indians but because he wanted to protect his lucrative monopoly over the deerskin trade with them. To prevent any government interference, Bacon ordered the governor arrested, thus pitting his own followers (who were largely servants, small farmers, and even slaves) against Virginia's wealthy planters and political leaders. Berkeley's forces resisted—but only feebly—and Bacon's men burned Jamestown in 1676. But Bacon could not savor the victory long; he fell ill and died of dysentery a month later.

Governor Berkeley quickly regained control and subdued the leaderless rebels. In the process he hanged twenty-three men and confiscated several estates. For such severity the king recalled Berkeley to England. A royal commission then made treaties of pacification with the remaining Indians, some of whose descendants still live on tiny reservations guaranteed them in 1677. For the colonists the fighting had opened new lands and confirmed the power of an inner group of established landholders who sat on the Virginia council.

SPANISH AMERICA IN DECLINE   By the start of the eighteenth century, the Spanish were ruling over a huge colonial empire spanning North America. Yet their settlements in the borderlands north of Mexico were a colossal failure when compared with Spanish Mexico and the colonies of the other European powers. The Spanish failed to create thriving colonies in the American Southwest for several reasons. Perhaps the most obvious was that the region lacked the gold and silver, as well as the large native populations, that attracted Spain to Mexico and Peru. In addition, the Spanish were distracted by their need to control the perennial unrest in Mexico among the natives and the mestizos (people of mixed Indian and European ancestry). Moreover, those Spaniards who led the colonization effort in the borderlands were so preoccupied with military and religious control that they never produced viable settlements with self-sustaining economies. Only rarely, for example, did the Spanish send many women to their colonies in North America. Even more important, they never understood that the main

Champlain in New France

Samuel de Champlain firing at a group of Iroquois, killing two chiefs (1609).

factor in creating a successful community was a thriving market economy. Instead, they concentrated on building missions and forts and looking—in vain—for gold. Whereas the French and the English based their Indian policies on trade (that included providing Indians with firearms), Spain emphasized conversion to Catholicism and stubbornly adhered to an outdated mercantilism that forbade manufacturing within the colonies and strictly limited trade with the natives.

NEW FRANCE AND LOUISIANA   Permanent French settlements in the New World began in 1608, when the French explorer Samuel de Champlain founded a settlement at Quebec. From there he pushed his explorations into the Great Lakes as far as Lake Huron and southward to the lake that still bears his name. There, in 1609, he joined a band of Indian allies in a fateful encounter, fired his gun into the ranks of their Iroquois foes, and thereby kindled a hatred that pursued New France to the end. Thenceforth the Iroquois stood as a buffer against any French designs to move toward the English of the middle Atlantic colonies and as a constant menace on the flank of the French waterways to the interior.

From the Great Lakes, French explorers moved southward down the Mississippi River. The French thus enjoyed access to the great water routes that led to the heartland of the continent. Yet French involvement in North America never approached that of the British. In part this was because the French-held areas were less enticing than the English seaboard settlements. Few Frenchmen were willing to challenge the interior's rugged terrain, fierce winters, and hostile Indians. In addition, the French government impeded colonization by refusing to allow Huguenots to migrate. New France was to remain Roman Catholic. It was also to remain a howling wilderness, home to a mobile population of traders, trappers, missionaries—and, mainly, Indians. In 1750, when the English colonists in America numbered about 1.5 million, the French population was no more than 80,000.

In some ways, however, the French had the edge on the British. Their relatively small numbers forced them to develop cooperative relationships with the Indians. Unlike the English settlers, the French established trading outposts (to trade European goods for furs) rather than farms, mostly along the St. Lawrence River, on lands not claimed by Indians. Thus they did not have to confront initial hostility. The heavily outnumbered and disproportionately male French settlers sought to integrate themselves with Indian culture rather than displace it. Many French traders married Indians and raised families, in the process exchanging languages and customs. They also encouraged the Indians to embrace Catholicism and to hate the English. This more fraternal bond between the French and the Indians proved to be a source of strength in the wars with the English. French governors could mobilize for action without any worry about quarreling assemblies or ethnic and religious diversity. New France was thus able to survive until 1760, despite the lopsided disparity in numbers between the colonies of the two powers.

THE COLONIAL WARS

For most of the seventeenth century, the French and the British Empires in America developed in relative isolation from each other; for most of that century, the homelands remained at peace. After the Restoration in 1660, Charles II and then James II pursued a policy of friendship with Louis XIV. The Glorious Revolution of 1688 abruptly reversed English diplomacy, however. William III, the new British king from the Dutch republic, had engaged in a running conflict with the ambitions of Louis XIV in Europe. His ascent to the throne brought England almost immediately into a Grand Alliance against the French in the War of the League of Augsburg, known in the colonies simply as King William's War (1689–1697). This was the first of four great European and intercolonial wars to be fought over the next seventy-four years.

Thereafter the major European wars of the period were the War of the Spanish Succession (known in the colonies as Queen Anne's War, 1702–1713); the War of the Austrian Succession (known in the colonies as King George's War, 1744–1748); and the Seven Years' War (known in the colonies as the French and Indian War, which lasted nine years in America, from 1754 to 1763). In all except the last, the battles in America were but a sideshow accompanying greater battles in Europe, where British policy aimed to keep a balance of power with the French. The multinational alliances shifted from one fight to the next, but Britain and France were pitted against each other every time.

So for much of the century after the great Indian conflicts of 1676, the colonies were embroiled in global wars and rumors of war. The effect on much of the population was devastating. The New England colonies, especially Massachusetts, suffered more than the rest, for they were closest to the centers of French population. It is estimated that 900 Boston men (about 2.5 percent of the men eligible for service) died in the fighting. One result of such carnage was that Boston's population stagnated through the eighteenth century while the population of Philadelphia and New York continued to grow, and Boston had to struggle to support a large population of widows and orphans. Eventually the economic impact of the four imperial wars left increasing numbers of poor people in New England, and many of them would participate in the popular unrest leading to the Revolutionary movement. Moreover, these prolonged conflicts led the English government to incur an enormous debt, establish a huge navy and standing army, and excite a militant sense of nationalism. These changes would ultimately lead to a reshaping of the relationship between the mother country and its American colonies.

THE FRENCH AND INDIAN WAR   Of the four major wars involving the European powers and their New World colonies, the climactic conflict between Britain and France in North America was the French and Indian War. It began in 1754, after enterprising Virginians during the early 1750s had crossed the Allegheny Mountains into the upper Ohio River valley in order to trade with Indians and survey 200,000 acres granted them by King George. The incursion by the Virginians infuriated the French, and they set about building a string of forts in the disputed area.

The Virginia governor sent an emissary to warn off the French. An ambitious young officer in the Virginia militia, Major George Washington, having volunteered for the mission, received a polite but firm French refusal. In the spring of 1754 the Virginia governor sent Washington back to the disputed region with a small force to erect a fort at the strategic fork where the Allegheny and Monongahela rivers meet to form the Ohio River in southwestern Pennsylvania. The twenty-two-year-old Washington, hungry for combat and yearning for military glory, led his 150 volunteers and Iroquois allies across the Alleghenies, only to learn that French soldiers had beaten them to the strategic site and erected Fort Duquesne, named for the French governor of Canada. Washington decided to make camp about forty miles from the fort and await reinforcements. The next day the Virginians ambushed a French detachment. Ten French soliders were killed, one escaped, and twenty-one were captured. The Indians then scalped several of the wounded soldiers as a stunned Washington looked on. Washington was unaware that the French had been on a peaceful mission to discuss the disputed fort. The mutilated soliders were the first fatalities in what would become the French and Indian War.

Washington and his troops retreated and hastily constructed a crude stockade at Great Meadows, dubbed Fort Necessity, which a large force of vengeful French soliders attacked a month later, on July 3, 1754. After a daylong battle, George Wahington surrendered, having seen all his horses and cattle killed and one third of his 300 men killed or wounded. The French permitted

The First American Political Cartoon

Benjamin Franklin's exhortation to the colonies to unite
against the French in 1754 would become popular again
twenty years later, when the colonies faced a different threat.

the surviving Virginians to withdraw after stripping them of their weapons.
After the regiment limped home, Washington decided to resign rather than
accept a demotion. His blundering expedition triggered a series of events
that would ignite a protracted world war. As a prominent British politician
exclaimed, "The volley fired by a young Virginian in the backwoods of America
set the world on fire."

Back in London the Board of Trade had already taken notice of the growing conflict in the American backwoods. The British government decided to
force a showdown with the French in America, but things went badly at first.
In 1755 the British fleet failed to halt the landing of French reinforcements
in Canada. The British buttressed their hold on Nova Scotia by expelling
most of its French population. Some 5,000 to 7,000 Acadians who refused to
take an oath of allegiance were scattered through the colonies, from Maine
to Georgia. Impoverished and homeless, many of them desperately found
their way to French Louisiana, where they became the Cajuns (a corruption
of the term *Acadians*) whose descendants still preserve elements of the
French language along the remote bayous and in many urban centers.

A WORLD WAR   For two years, war raged along the American-Canadian
frontier without igniting war in Europe. In 1756, however, the colonial war
merged with what became the Seven Years' War in Europe. In the final alignment of European powers, France, Austria, Russia, Saxony, Sweden, and Spain

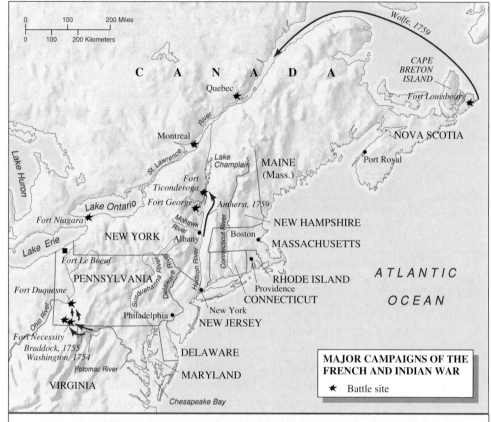

What was the significance of the siege of Fort Necessity? What was the Plan of Union? How did the three-pronged offensive of 1759 lead to a British victory in North America?

fought against Britain, Prussia, and Hanover. The onset of world war brought into office a new British government, with the popular, eloquent William Pitt as head of the ministry. Pitt's ability and assurance ("I know that I can save England and no one else can") instilled confidence at home and abroad.

British sea power cut off French reinforcements and supplies to the New World—and the goods with which they bought Indian allies. In 1758 the tide began to turn. Fort Louisbourg in Canada fell to the British. When a new expedition marched against Fort Duquesne, the outnumbered French burned the fort and fled the scene. On the site arose the British Fort Pitt and, later, the city of Pittsburgh.

In 1759 the decisive battle occurred at Quebec, in Canada. Commanding the British expedition up the St. Lawrence River was General James Wolfe, a dedicated professional soldier who, at the age of thirty-two, had already spent more than half his life in military service. For two months, Wolfe probed the French defenses of Quebec, seemingly impregnable on its fortified heights and manned by alert forces under General Louis-Joseph de Montcalm. Finally Wolfe's troops found a path up the cliffs behind Quebec. During the night of September 12–13, they scrambled up the sheer walls and emerged on the Plains of Abraham, athwart the main roads to the city. There, in a battle more like conventional European warfare than a frontier skirmish, the British forces allowed the French to advance within close range and then fired two devastating volleys that ended French power in North America for all time. News of the victory was clouded by word of Wolfe's—and Montcalm's—deaths in the battle.

The war in North America dragged on until 1763, but the rest was a process of mopping up. In the South, where little significant action had occurred, the Cherokee Nation flared into belated hostility, but a force of British regulars and provincials broke their resistance in 1761.

Just six weeks after the capture of Montreal in 1760, King George II died, and his twenty-two-year-old grandson ascended the throne as George III. The new king took a more active role in colonial affairs than his Hanoverian predecessors had. The new king yearned for peace, which entailed forcing his chief minister, William Pitt, out of office. Pitt had wanted to declare war on Spain before the French could bring that other Bourbon monarchy into the conflict. He was forestalled, but Spain belatedly entered the war, in 1761. During the next year the Spanish met the same fate as the French: in 1762 British forces took Manila in the Philippines and Havana in Cuba. By 1763 the French and the Spanish were ready to negotiate a surrender. Britain ruled the world.

THE PEACE OF PARIS The war culminated in the Treaty of Paris of 1763. It ended French power in North America, and Britain took all of France's North American possessions east of the Mississippi River (except New Orleans), several islands in the West Indies, and all of Spanish Florida. The English invited the Spanish settlers to remain and practice their Catholic religion, but few accepted the offer. The Spanish king ordered them to evacuate the colony and provided free transportation to Spanish possessions in the Caribbean Sea. Within a year most of the Spaniards sold their property at bargain prices to English speculators and began an exodus to Cuba and Mexico. When the Indian tribes that had been allied with the French learned of the 1763 peace settlement, they were despondent. Their lands were being given over to the British without any consultation. The Shawnees, for instance,

NORTH AMERICA, 1713

- England
- France
- Spain

HUDSON BAY

HUDSON BAY COMPANY

UNEXPLORED

NEWFOUNDLAND

NEW FRANCE

NOVA SCOTIA

NEW ENGLAND

Mississippi River

LOUISIANA

ENGLISH COLONIES

VIRGINIA

PACIFIC OCEAN

ATLANTIC OCEAN

CAROLINAS

NEW SPAIN

FLORIDA

GULF OF MEXICO

CUBA

HISPANIOLA

CARIBBEAN SEA

NEW GRANADA

What events led to the first clashes between the French and the British in the late seventeenth century? Why did New England suffer more than other regions of North America during the wars of the eighteenth century? What were the long-term financial, military, and political consequences of the wars between France and Britain?

demanded to know "by what right the French could pretend" to transfer Indian territory to the British. The Indians also worried that a victorious Britain had "grown too powerful & seemed as if they would be too strong for God itself." The Indians had hoped that the departure of the French from the Ohio Valley would mean that the area would revert to their control. Instead, the British cut off the trade and gift-giving practices that had bound the

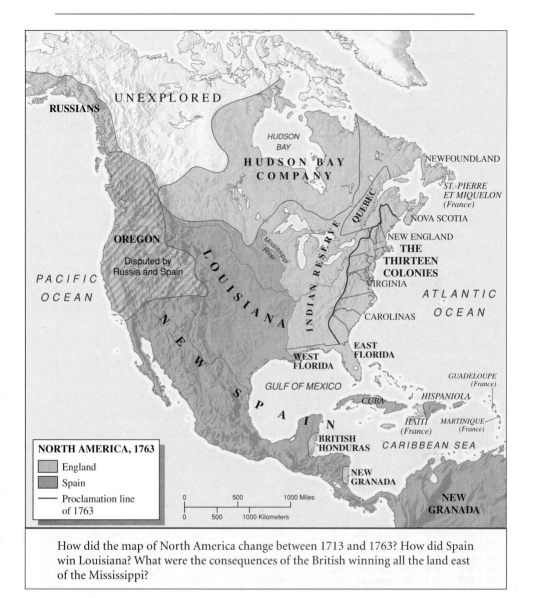

NORTH AMERICA, 1763

- England
- Spain
- Proclamation line of 1763

How did the map of North America change between 1713 and 1763? How did Spain win Louisiana? What were the consequences of the British winning all the land east of the Mississippi?

Indians to the French. General Jeffrey Amherst, the British military governor for the western region, demanded that the Indians learn to live without "charity." British forces also moved into the French frontier forts. In a desperate effort to recover their autonomy, tribes struck back in the spring of 1763, capturing most of the British forts around the Great Lakes and in the Ohio Valley. They also raided colonial settlements in Pennsylvania, Maryland, and Virginia, destroying hundreds of homesteads and killing several thousand people. In the midst of the Indian attack on Fort Pitt (formerly Fort Duquesne), General Amherst approved the distribution of smallpox-infested blankets and handkerchiefs, from the fort's hospital, to the Indians besieging the garrison. His efforts at germ warfare were intended to "extirpate this execrable race" of Indians.

Called Pontiac's Rebellion because of the prominent role played by the Ottawa chief, the far-flung attacks on the frontier forts convinced most colonists that all Indians must be removed. The British government, meanwhile, negotiated an agreement with the Indians that allowed redcoats to reoccupy the frontier forts in exchange for a renewal of trade and gift giving. Still, as Pontiac stressed, the Indians asserted their independence and denied the legitimacy of the British claim to their territory under the terms of the Treaty of Paris. He told a British official that the "French never conquered us, neither did they purchase a foot of our Country, nor have they a right to give it to you." The British may have won a global empire as a result of the Seven Years' War, but their grip on the American colonies grew ever weaker.

In compensation for the loss of Florida, Spain received Louisiana (New Orleans and all French land west of the Mississippi River) from France. Unlike the Spanish in Florida, however, few of the French settlers left Louisiana after 1763. The French government encouraged them to stay and work with their new Spanish governors to create a bulwark against further English expansion. Spain would hold title to Louisiana for nearly four decades but would never succeed in erasing the region's French roots. The French-born settlers always outnumbered the Spanish.

The loss of Louisiana left France with no territory on the continent of North America. After 1763 British power reigned supreme over North America east of the Mississippi River. In gaining Canada, however, the British government put in motion a train of events that would end twenty years later with the loss of the rest of British North America. Britain's success against France threatened the Indian tribes of the interior because they had long depended upon playing the two European powers off against each other. Now, with the British dominant on the continent, American settlers were emboldened to encroach even more upon Indian land. In addition, victory on the battlefields encouraged the British to tighten their imperial control over the Americans and demand more financial contributions from the colonists to defray the cost of British army troops. Meanwhile, humiliated France thirsted for revenge. In London, Benjamin Franklin, agent for the colony of Pennsylvania from 1764 to 1775, found the French minister inordinately curious about America and suspected him of wanting to ignite the coals of controversy. Less than three years after Franklin left London and only fifteen years after the conquest of New France, he would be in Paris arranging an alliance on behalf of Britain's rebellious colonists.

MAKING CONNECTIONS

- Although the British victory in the French and Indian War brought the colonies and England closer together in some ways, it was also an important factor in the approach of the American Revolution, as will be demonstrated in Chapter 5.

- One of the great struggles of the Revolution would be transforming the dependent British colonies, as described in this chapter, into independent American states, as described in Chapter 6.

FURTHER READING

The economics motivating colonial policies are covered in John J. McCusker and Russell R. Menard's *The Economy of British America, 1607–1789*, rev. ed. (1991). The problems of colonial customs administration are explored in Micheal Kammen's *Empire and Interest: The American Colonies and the Politics of Mercantilism* (1970).

Jack P. Greene's *The Quest for Power: The Lower Houses of Assembly in the Southern Royal Colonies, 1689–1776* (1963) describes the politics of the southern colonies, and Richard P. Johnson's *Adjustment to Empire: The New England Colonies, 1675–1715* (1981) examines New England. The Andros crisis and related topics are treated in Jack M. Sosin's *English America and the Revolution of 1688: Royal Administration and the Structure of Provincial Government* (1982). Stephen Saunders Webb's *The Governors-General: The English Army and the Definition of the Empire, 1569–1681* (1979) argues that the crown was more concerned with military administration than with commercial regulation, and Webb's *1676: The End of American Independence* (1984) shows how the Indian wars undermined the autonomy of the colonial governments.

The early Indian wars are treated in Jill Lepore's *The Name of War: King Philip's War and the Origins of American Identity* (1998) and in Francis

Jennings's *The Invasion of America: Indians, Colonialism, and the Cant of Conquest* (1975). See also Jennings's *The Ambiguous Iroquois Empire: The Covenant Chain Confederation of Indian Tribes with English Colonies* (1984) and *Empire of Fortune: Crowns, Colonies, and Tribes in the Seven Years War in America* (1988) and Richard Aquila's *The Iroquois Restoration: Iroquois Diplomacy on the Colonial Frontier, 1701–1754* (1983).

A good introduction to the imperial phase of the colonial conflicts is Howard H. Peckham's *The Colonial Wars, 1689–1762* (1964). More analytical is Douglas Edward Leach's *Arms for Empire: A Military History of the British Colonies in North America, 1607–1763* (1973). Fred Anderson's *Crucible of War: The Seven Years' War and the Fate of Empire in British North America, 1754–1766* (2000) is the best history of the Seven Years' War.

5

FROM EMPIRE TO
INDEPENDENCE

FOCUS QUESTIONS

- What were the changes in British colonial policy after 1763?
- How did Whig ideology shape the colonial response to changes in British policy?
- What was the role of Revolutionary leaders, including Samuel Adams, John Dickinson, Thomas Paine, and Thomas Jefferson?

To answer these questions and access additional review material, please visit www.wwnorton.com/studyspace.

Seldom if ever since the days of Queen Elizabeth had England thrilled with such pride as it did in the closing years of the Seven Years' War. The military victories of 1759 had delivered Canada and India to British control. In 1760 young George III had ascended the throne. And in 1763 the Treaty of Paris confirmed a new global empire. The end of the French imperial domain in North America opened the prospect of British development of the sprawling region between the Appalachian Mountains and the Mississippi River, from the Gulf of Mexico north to Hudson Bay in Canada.

The American colonists shared in the euphoria of victory over the French, but the celebration masked festering resentments and new problems. Underneath the pride in the sprawling British Empire, a sense of an American nationalism was maturing. For over a generation the colonists had essentially been

George III

At age thirty-three, the young king of a victorious empire.

allowed to govern themselves and were beginning to think and speak of themselves more as American than as English or British. With vast new western lands to exploit, they could look to the future with confidence.

THE HERITAGE OF WAR

The colonists had a new sense of importance after fighting a major war with such success. Many in the early stages of the war had lost their awe of the British soldiers, who were vigorously inept at frontier fighting. American colonists were also dismayed by the sharp social distinctions between officers and men in the British army. The provincials, by contrast, presumed that by volunteering, they had formed a contract with a particular American officer from their community.

During the war many Americans became convinced of their moral superiority to their British allies. Although they admired the courage and discipline of British redcoats under fire, New Englanders abhorred the carefree cursing, whoring, and Sabbath breaking they observed among the British troops. Most upsetting were the brutal punishments imposed by British officers on their wayward men. Minor offenses might earn hundreds of lashes. The war thus heightened the New Englanders' sense of their separate identity and of their greater worthiness to be God's chosen people.

In the aftermath of victory, the British government faced massive new problems. How should it manage the defense and governance of the new territories acquired from France? How were they to pay an unprecedented debt built up during the war and bear the new financial and administrative burdens of greater colonial administration and more far-flung global defense? And— the thorniest problem of all, as it turned out—what role should the colonies play in all this? The problems were of a magnitude and complexity to challenge men of the greatest statesmanship and vision, but those qualities were rare among the ministers of George III. The king himself, while a conscientious and deeply religious man, was obstinate, unimaginative, and overly dependent upon his advisers and ministers.

In the English government of the eighteenth century, nearly every politician called himself a Whig, as did the king. *Whig* had been the name given to those who opposed James II, led the Glorious Revolution of 1688, and secured the Protestant Hanoverian succession in 1714. The Whigs were the champions of liberty and parliamentary supremacy, but with the passage of time Whiggism had drifted into complacency, and leadership settled upon an aristocratic elite of the Whig gentry. In the absence of party organization, parliamentary politics hinged upon factions bound together by personal loyalties, family connections, local interests, and the pursuit of royal patronage in the form of government appointments. Throughout the 1760s the king turned first to one and then to another mediocre prime minister, and the government grew more unstable just as the new problems of colonial administration required forceful solutions. Colonial policy remained marginal to the chief concerns of British politics. The result was inconsistency and vacillation followed by stubborn inflexibility.

WESTERN LANDS

No sooner was peace arranged in 1763 than the problem of America's western lands provoked a crisis in the British government. The Indians of the Ohio River valley, fearing the arrival of English settlers, joined Ottawa chief Pontiac's attempt to renew frontier warfare. Within a few months, Indians had wiped out every British post in the Ohio Valley region except Forts Detroit and Pitt.

To secure peace on the frontier, the ministers in London postponed further settlement of the western lands. The immediate need was to stop Pontiac's warriors and pacify the Indians. The king had signed the Royal Proclamation of 1763, which drew an imaginary line along the crest of the Appalachians, beyond which settlers were forbidden to go and colonial governors were forbidden to authorize surveys or issue land grants. It also established the new British colonies of Quebec and East and West Florida.

But Pontiac did not agree to peace until 1766, and Britain's proclamation line did not remain intact for long. Hardy pioneers ignored the line and pushed over the Appalachian ridges. By 1770 the town of Pittsburgh had twenty log houses, and four years later Daniel Boone and a party of settlers cut the Wilderness Road through the Cumberland Gap, in southwestern Virginia, to the Kentucky River.

GRENVILLE'S COLONIAL POLICY

As the Royal Proclamation of 1763 was being drafted, a new ministry in London began to grapple with the problems of imperial finances. The new chief minister, George Grenville, first lord of the Treasury, wanted to keep a large army (10,000 men) in America to avoid a rapid demobilization that would force many influential officers to retire and thereby spark political criticism at home. On top of an already staggering government debt, however, he faced sharply rising costs for defense of the American colonies.

CUSTOMS AND CURRENCY   Because there was a heavy tax burden at home and a much lighter one in the colonies, Grenville reasoned that the prosperous Americans should share the cost of their own defense. He also learned that the royal customs service in America was amazingly inefficient. Evasion and corruption were rampant. Grenville thus issued stern orders to colonial officials and dispatched the navy to patrol the coast in search of smugglers evading royal duties. Parliament agreed to set up a new maritime court in Halifax, Nova Scotia, granting it jurisdiction over all the colonies. Decisions would be made by judges appointed by the crown rather than by

The Great Financier, or British Economy for the Years 1763, 1764, 1765

This cartoon, critical of Grenville's tax policies, shows America, depicted as an Indian (at left), groaning under the burden of new taxes.

juries of colonists sympathetic to smugglers. The old habits of "salutary neglect" in the enforcement of the Navigation Acts were coming to an end, to the growing annoyance of American shippers.

The Molasses Act of 1733 had set a sixpence-per-gallon customs duty on molasses in order to prevent trade with the French sugar islands. New England merchants evaded this tax, smuggling in French molasses to make rum. Recognizing that the duty, if enforced, would ruin the rum distillers, Grenville put through the Sugar Act (1764), which cut the duty in half. This, he believed, would reduce the temptation to smuggle or to bribe customs officers. In addition, the Sugar Act levied new duties (taxes) on imports of foreign textiles, wine, coffee, indigo, and sugar. The act, Grenville estimated, would bring in enough revenue to help defray "the necessary expenses of defending, protecting, and securing" the colonies. For the first time, Parliament had adopted taxes on trade explicitly designed to raise revenues in the colonies rather than just regulate trade.

Another key element in Grenville's colonial program was the Currency Act of 1764. The colonies faced a chronic shortage of hard currency, which kept going out to pay debts in England. To meet the shortage, they issued their own paper money. British creditors feared receiving payment in such a depreciated paper currency, however. To alleviate their fears, Grenville prohibited the colonies from printing money. The value of existing paper money soon plummeted, since nobody was obligated to accept it in payment of debts, even in the colonies. The deflationary impact of the Currency Act, combined with new duties on commodities and stricter enforcement, jolted a colonial economy already suffering a postwar slump.

THE STAMP ACT   Grenville's strategy to raise revenue from the colonies entailed one more key provision. Because the Sugar Act would defray only part of the cost of maintaining British troops along the western frontier, he proposed another measure to raise money in America, a stamp tax. Enacted on February 13, 1765, the Stamp Act created revenue stamps that were to be purchased and attached to printed matter and legal documents of all kinds: newspapers, pamphlets, almanacs, bonds, leases, deeds, licenses, insurance policies, ship clearances, college diplomas, even playing cards. The requirement was to go into effect on November 1.

In March 1765 Grenville put through the final measure of his new program, the Quartering Act. It required the colonies to supply British troops with provisions and provide them barracks or submit to their use of inns and vacant buildings owned by colonists. The Quartering Act applied to all colonies but affected mainly New York, headquarters of the British forces.

THE IDEOLOGICAL RESPONSE   The cumulative effect of Grenville's measures outraged colonists. Unwittingly he stirred up a storm of protest and set in motion a profound exploration of English traditions and imperial relations. By this time the radical ideas of the so-called Real Whig minority in England had slowly begun to take hold in the colonies. The Real Whigs sought to safeguard citizens against government abuse of power.

Whig radicals charged that Grenville had loosed upon the colonies the very engines of tyranny from which Parliament had rescued England in the seventeenth century. A standing army, Whigs believed, encouraged despots, and now, with the French gone and Chief Pontiac subdued, several thousand British soldiers remained in the colonies. Among the fundamental English rights were trial by jury and the presumption of innocence, but the new vice-admiralty courts excluded juries and put the burden of proof on the defendant. Most important, the English had the right to be taxed only by their elected representatives. Parliament claimed that privilege in England, and the colonial assemblies had long exercised it in America. Now, with the Stamp Act, Parliament sought to usurp the assemblies' power of the purse strings. This could only lead to tyranny and enslavement.

PROTEST IN THE COLONIES   In a flood of colonial pamphlets, speeches, and resolutions, critics of the Stamp Act repeated a slogan familiar to all Americans: "No taxation without representation." The Stamp Act became the chief target of colonial protest because it burdened all colonists who did any kind of business. And it affected most of all the articulate elements in the community: merchants, planters, lawyers, printer-editors—all strategically placed to influence public opinion.

Through the spring and summer of 1765, popular resentment against Grenville boiled over in meetings, parades, bonfires, and other demonstrations. Calling themselves Sons of Liberty, colonial militants met underneath "liberty trees"—in Boston a great elm, in Charleston a live oak. One day in mid-August 1765, nearly three months before the effective date of the Stamp Act, an effigy of Boston's royal stamp agent swung from the city's liberty tree. In the evening a mob carried it through the streets, destroyed the stamp office, and used the wood to burn the effigy. Somewhat later another mob sacked the homes of the lieutenant governor and the local customs officer. The stamp agent in Boston, thoroughly shaken, resigned his commission, and stamp agents throughout the colonies felt impelled to follow his example.

The widespread protests encouraged colonial unity, as rebellious Americans discovered that they had more in common with each other than with

London. In May 1765 the Virginia House of Burgesses struck the first blow against the Stamp Act with the Virginia Resolves, a series of resolutions inspired by the young Patrick Henry. Virginians, the burgesses declared, were entitled to all English rights, and the English could be taxed only by their own representatives. Virginians, moreover, had always been governed by laws passed with their own consent. Newspapers spread the resolutions throughout the colonies, and other assemblies hastened to copy Virginia's example. In June 1765 the Massachusetts House of Representatives invited the various colonial assemblies to send delegates to confer in New York on appeals for relief from the king and Parliament.

Nine responded, and on October 7 the twenty-seven delegates of the Stamp Act Congress issued a Declaration of the Rights and Grievances of the Colonies, a petition to the king for relief, and a petition to Parliament for repeal of the Stamp Act. The delegates argued that Parliament might have powers to legislate for the regulation of colonial trade, but it had no right to levy taxes, which were a gift granted by the people through their elected representatives.

By November 1, its effective date, the Stamp Act was a dead letter. Business activities were conducted without the revenue stamps. Newspapers appeared with the skull and crossbones where the stamp belonged. Colonial rebels were beginning to sense their power. After passage of the Sugar Act, rebels began to boycott British goods rather than pay the new import duties. Now colonists adopted nonimportation agreements to exert pressure on British merchants. Americans knew they had become a major market for British products. By shutting off imports from the home country, they could exercise real leverage. Sage and sassafras took the place of British tea, and homespun garments became the fashion as symbols of colonial defiance.

REPEAL OF THE STAMP ACT   The storm had scarcely broken before Grenville's ministry was out of office, dismissed not because of the colonial turmoil but because of tensions with the king over the distribution of lucrative government appointments. In July 1765 the king installed a new minister, the marquis of Rockingham, leader of the "Rockingham Whigs," who sympathized with the colonists' views. Rockingham resolved to end the quarrel with America by repealing the Stamp Act, but he needed to move carefully in order to win a majority. Simple repeal was politically impossible without some affirmation of parliamentary authority over the colonies. When Parliament assembled early in 1766, the powerful parliamentary leader William Pitt demanded that the Stamp Act be repealed "absolutely, totally, and immediately,"

The Repeal, or the Funeral Procession of Miss America-Stamp

This 1766 cartoon shows Grenville carrying the dead Stamp Act in its coffin. In the background, trade with America starts up again.

but he urged that Britain's authority over the colonies "be asserted in as strong terms as possible," except on the point of taxation.

In March 1766 Parliament repealed the Stamp Tax but passed the Declaratory Act, which asserted the full power of Parliament to make laws binding the colonies "in all cases whatsoever." It was a cunning evasion that made no concession with regard to taxes but made no mention of them either. It reinforced a distinction between "external" taxes on trade and "internal" taxes within the colonies, a distinction that would have fateful consequences. To be sure, the Sugar Act remained on the books, but Rockingham reduced the molasses tax from threepence to onepence a gallon, less than the cost of a bribe.

FANNING THE FLAMES

Meanwhile, King George continued to play musical chairs with his ministers. After Rockingham lost the king's confidence, William Pitt formed a ministry that included the major factions of Parliament. Soon thereafter, however, Pitt slipped over the fine line between genius and madness, and he resigned in 1768. For a time in 1767 the guiding force in the ministry was Charles Townshend, chancellor of the Exchequer (Treasury). The witty but erratic Townshend took advantage of Pitt's mental confusion to reopen the question of colonial taxation. He asserted that "external" taxes were tolerable to the colonies—not that he believed it for a moment.

THE TOWNSHEND ACTS   In 1767 Townshend put his plan through the House of Commons, and in September he died, leaving a bitter legacy: the Townshend Acts. With this legislation, Townshend had sought to bring the New York assembly to its senses. That body had defied the Quartering Act and refused to provide beds or supplies for the king's troops. Parliament, at Townshend's behest, had suspended all acts of the New York assembly until it would yield. New York finally caved in, inadvertently confirming the British suspicion that too much indulgence had encouraged colonial bad manners. Townshend had followed up with the Revenue Act of 1767, which levied duties ("external taxes") on colonial imports of glass, lead, paints, paper, and tea. Next, he had set up a Board of Customs Commissioners at Boston, the hotbed of colonial smuggling. Finally, he had reorganized the vice-admiralty courts, providing four in the continental colonies: at Halifax, Boston, Philadelphia, and Charleston.

The Townshend duties increased government revenues, but the intangible costs were greater. The duties taxed goods exported from England, indirectly hurting British manufacturers, and they had to be collected in colonial ports, increasing collection costs. More important, the new taxes accelerated colonial resentment and resistance. The Revenue Act of 1767 posed a more severe threat to colonial assemblies than Grenville's taxes had, for Townshend proposed to apply the revenues to pay the salaries of royal governors and other officers and thereby release them from financial dependence on the colonial assemblies.

DICKINSON'S "LETTERS"   The Townshend Acts inspired the colonists to boycott British goods and to develop their own manufactures. Once again the colonial press spewed out protests, most notably the essays of John Dickinson, a Philadelphia lawyer who hoped to resolve the dispute by persuasion. Late in 1767 his twelve "Letters from a Farmer in Pennsylvania" (as he chose to style himself) began to appear in the *Pennsylvania Chronicle*, from which they were copied in other newspapers. He argued that Parliament might regulate American commerce and collect duties incidental to that purpose, but it had no right to levy taxes for revenue, whether they were internal or external.

SAMUEL ADAMS AND THE SONS OF LIBERTY   But British officials could neither conciliate moderates like Dickinson nor cope with firebrands like Boston's Samuel Adams, who was now emerging as the supreme genius of revolutionary agitation. Born in 1722, Adams graduated from Harvard and soon thereafter inherited the family brewery, which he proceeded to run into bankruptcy. His distant cousin John Adams described Sam as a "universal good character," a "plain, simple, decent citizen, of middling stature, dress, and manners" who prided himself on his frugality and his distaste for ceremony and display. Politics, not profit, excited his passion, and he spent most of his time debating political issues with sailors, roustabouts, and stevedores at local taverns. Adams insisted that Parliament had no right to legislate for the colonies, that Massachusetts must return to the spirit of its Puritan founders and defend itself from a new royal conspiracy against its liberties.

Adams was a relentless rebel. He whipped up the Sons of Liberty, writing incendiary newspaper articles and letters and organizing protests at the Boston town meeting and in the provincial assembly. The royal governor called him "the most dangerous man in Massachusetts." Early in 1768 Adams and Boston lawyer James Otis formulated a letter that the Massachusetts assembly dispatched to the other colonies. It restated the illegality of parliamentary taxation, warned that the new duties would be used to pay colonial officials, and invited the other colonies to join in a boycott of British goods.

In mid-May 1769 the Virginia assembly reasserted its exclusive right to tax Virginians and called upon the colonies to unite in protest. Virginia's royal governor promptly dissolved the assembly, but the members met independently and adopted a new set of nonimportation agreements. Once again, as with the Virginia Resolves against the Stamp Act, most of the other colonial assemblies followed suit.

THE BOSTON MASSACRE   In Boston roving gangs enforced the boycott of goods from England, intimidating Loyalist merchants and their customers. This led the governor to appeal for military support, and two British regiments arrived from Canada. The presence of British soldiers in Boston had always been a source of provocation, but now tensions heightened. On March 5, 1770, in the square before the custom house, a mob began heaving taunts, icicles, and oyster shells at the British sentry, whose call for help brought reinforcements. Then somebody rang the town fire bell, drawing a larger crowd to the scene. Among the mob was Crispus Attucks, a runaway mulatto slave who had worked for some years on ships out of Boston. The riotous crowd began striking at the troops with sticks, and it knocked one soldier down. He rose to his feet and fired into the crowd. Others fired, too, and when the smoke cleared, five people lay dead or dying, and eight more were wounded.

The cause of colonial resistance now had its first martyrs, and the first to die was Crispus Attucks. News of the Boston Massacre sent shock waves through the colonies. The incident, remembered one Bostonian, "created a resentment which emboldened the timid" and "determined the wavering." But late in April 1770 news arrived that Parliament had repealed all the Townshend duties save one. The cabinet, by a vote of five to four, had advised keeping the tea tax as a token of parliamentary authority. Colonial diehards insisted that pressure should be kept on British merchants until

The Bloody Massacre

Paul Revere's partisan engraving of the Boston Massacre.

Parliament gave in altogether, but the nonimportation movement soon faded. Parliament, after all, had given up most of the taxes, and much of the colonists' tea was smuggled from Holland anyway.

For two years thereafter colonial discontent simmered down. The Stamp Act was gone, as were all the Townshend duties except that on tea. Yet most of the hated regulations remained in effect: the Sugar Act, the Currency Act, the Quartering Act, the vice-admiralty courts, the Board of Customs Commissioners. The redcoats had left Boston, but they remained nearby, and the British navy still patrolled the coast, looking for smugglers. Each remained a source of irritation and the cause of occasional incidents. As Sam Adams stressed, "Where there is a Spark of patriotick fire, we will enkindle it."

Discontent on the Frontier

Many colonists showed no interest in the disputes over British regulatory policies raging along the seaboard. Parts of the backcountry had stirred with quarrels that had nothing to do with the Stamp and Townshend Acts. Rival land claims to the east of Lake Champlain pitted New York against New Hampshire and the Green Mountain Boys, led by Ethan Allen, against both. Eventually the residents of the area would simply create their own state, Vermont, in 1777, although it was not recognized as a member of the Union until 1791.

In Pennsylvania a group of frontier ruffians took the law into their own hands. Outraged at the lack of frontier protection provided by the Quaker-influenced assembly during Chief Pontiac's Rebellion, a group called the Paxton Boys took revenge by massacring peaceful Susquehannock Indians in Lancaster County, then threatened the so-called Moravian Indians, a group of Moravian converts near Bethlehem. When the Moravian Indians took refuge in Philadelphia, some 1,500 Paxton Boys marched on the capital, where Benjamin Franklin talked them into returning home by promising more protection along the frontier.

Farther south settlers along the South Carolina backcountry complained about the lack of protection from horse thieves, cattle rustlers, and Indians. They organized societies called Regulators to administer vigilante justice in the region and refused to pay taxes until they gained effective government. In 1769 the assembly finally set up six new circuit courts in the region and revised the taxes, but it still did not respond to the backcountry's demand for representation in the legislature.

In North Carolina the protest was less over the lack of government than over the abuses and extortion by government appointees from the eastern part of the colony. In 1766 farmers organized to resist, but their efforts were more pitiful than potent. In the spring of 1771, the royal governor and 1,200 militiamen defeated some 2,000 ill-organized Regulators in the Battle of Alamance. The pitched battle illustrated the growing tensions between back-country settlers and the wealthy planters in the eastern part of the colony, tensions that would erupt again during and after the Revolution.

These disputes and revolts within the colonies illustrate the fractious diversity of opinion and outlook evident among Americans on the eve of the Revolution. Colonists were of many minds about many things, including British rule. Frontier conflicts in colonial America also helped convince British authorities that the colonies were inherently unstable and that they required firmer oversight, including the use of military force to ensure civil stability.

A WORSENING CRISIS

Two events in June 1772 shattered the period of calm in the quarrels with the mother country. Near Providence, Rhode Island, a British schooner, the *Gaspee,* patrolling for smugglers, ran aground. Under cover of darkness, colonial rebels boarded the ship, removed the crew, and set fire to the vessel. Three days after the burning, Massachusetts's angry royal governor, Thomas Hutchinson, told the provincial assembly that his salary thenceforth would come out of the customs revenues. Massachusetts Superior Court judges would be paid from the same source and would no longer be dependent upon the assembly for their income. The assembly feared that this portended "a despotic administration of government."

To keep the pot simmering, in November 1772 Sam Adams convinced the Boston town meeting to form the Committee of Correspondence, which issued a statement of rights and grievances and invited other towns to do the same. Committees of Correspondence soon sprang up in other colonies. In March 1773 the Virginia assembly proposed the formation of such committees on an intercolonial basis, and a network of the committees spread across the colonies, maintaining contact, mobilizing public opinion, and keeping colonial resentments at a simmer.

THE BOSTON TEA PARTY   Frederick, Lord North, who had replaced Townshend as chancellor of the Exchequer, soon brought colonial resentment to a boil. In May 1773 he contrived a scheme to bail out the foundering East

India Company. The company had in its British warehouses some 17 million pounds of unsold tea. Under the Tea Act of 1773, the government would refund the British duty of twelvepence per pound on all tea shipped to the colonies and collect only the existing threepence duty payable at the colonial port. By this arrangement, colonists could get tea more cheaply than the English could. North miscalculated, however, in assuming that price alone would govern colonial reaction.

The Committees of Correspondence, backed by colonial merchants, alerted colonists to the British conspiracy to purchase their loyalty and passivity with cheap tea. Before the end of the year, large shipments of tea had gone out to major colonial ports. In Charleston it was unloaded into warehouses—and later sold to finance the Revolution. In Boston, however, Governor Hutchinson and Sam Adams engaged in a test of will. The ships' captains, alarmed by the rebel opposition, proposed to turn back, but Hutchinson refused permission until the tea was unloaded and the duty paid. Then, on December 16, 1773, a group of colonial Patriots, disguised as Mohawk Indians, boarded the three ships and threw the 342 chests of tea overboard—cheered on by a crowd along the shore. One participant later testified that Sam Adams and John Hancock were there.

Given a more tactful response from London, the Boston Tea Party might easily have undermined the radicals' credibility. Many people, especially merchants, abhorred the wanton destruction of property. British authorities, however, had reached the end of their patience. They were now convinced that the very existence of the empire was at stake. The rebels in Boston were inspiring what could become a widespread effort to evade royal authority and imperial regulations. A firm response was required. "The colonists must either submit or triumph," George III wrote to Lord North, and North hastened to make the king's judgment a self-fulfilling prophecy.

THE COERCIVE ACTS   In April 1774 Parliament enacted four harsh measures designed by Lord North to discipline Boston. The Boston Port Act closed the harbor from June 1, 1774, until the lost tea was paid for. An Act for the Impartial Administration of Justice let the governor transfer to England the trial of any official accused of committing an offense in the line of duty. A new Quartering Act directed local authorities to provide lodging for British soldiers, in private homes if necessary. Finally, the Massachusetts Government Act made the colony's governing council and law-enforcement officers all appointive, rather than elective, declared that sheriffs would select jurors, and stipulated that no town meeting could be held without the governor's consent, except for the annual election of town officers. In May,

The Able Doctor, or America Swallowing the Bitter Draught

This 1774 engraving shows Lord North, the Boston Port Act in his pocket, pouring tea down America's throat and America spitting it back.

General Thomas Gage replaced Hutchinson as governor of Massachusetts and assumed command of the British forces in the colonies.

Designed to isolate Boston and make an example of the colony, the Coercive Acts of 1774 instead cemented colonial unity and emboldened resistance. At last, it seemed to the colonists, their worst fears were being confirmed. If these "Intolerable Acts," as the colonists labeled the Coercive Acts, were not resisted, they would eventually be applied to the other colonies.

Further confirmation of British "tyranny" came with news of the Quebec Act, passed in June 1774. That act provided that the government in Canada would not have a representative assembly and would be led by an appointed governor and council. It also gave a privileged position to the Catholic Church. Americans viewed the measure as another indicator of British authoritarianism. In addition, colonists pointed out that they had lost many lives in an effort to liberate the trans-Appalachian West from the control of French Catholics. Now the British seemed to be protecting papists at the expense of their own Protestant colonists. What was more, the act placed within the boundaries of Quebec the western lands north of the Ohio River, lands that Pennsylvania, Virginia, and Connecticut had long claimed.

Meanwhile, colonists rallied to the cause of besieged Boston, taking up collections and sending provisions. When the Virginia assembly met in

May 1774, a young member of the Committee of Correspondence, Thomas Jefferson, proposed to set aside June 1, the effective date of the Boston Port Act, as a day of fasting and prayer in Virginia. The irate British governor thereupon dissolved the Virginia assembly, whose members then retired to a nearby tavern and resolved to create a "Continental Congress" to represent all the colonies. Similar calls were coming from Providence, New York, Philadelphia, and elsewhere, and in June the Massachusetts assembly suggested a September meeting in Philadelphia. Shortly before George Washington left to represent Virginia at the meeting, he wrote to a friend that "the crisis is arrived when we must assert our rights, or submit to every imposition that can be heaped upon us, till custom and use shall make us as tame and abject slaves, as the blacks we rule over with such arbitrary sway."

THE CONTINENTAL CONGRESS   On September 5, 1774, the First Continental Congress assembled in Philadelphia. The fifty-five delegates represented twelve continental colonies, all but Georgia, Quebec, Nova Scotia, and the Floridas. Peyton Randolph of Virginia was elected president, and Charles Thomson, "the Sam Adams of Philadelphia," became secretary. In effect, the delegates functioned as a congress of ambassadors, gathered to join forces on common policies, neither to govern nor to rebel but to adopt and issue a series of resolutions and protests.

The Congress endorsed the radical Suffolk Resolves, resolutions that declared null and void the recent acts of Parliament intended to coerce the colonies, urged Massachusetts to arm for defense, and called for economic sanctions against British commerce. The Congress also adopted a Declaration of American Rights, which conceded only Parliament's right to regulate commerce and those matters that were strictly imperial affairs. It denied Parliament's authority with respect to internal colonial affairs and proclaimed the right of each assembly to determine the need for troops within its own province.

Finally, the Congress adopted the Continental Association of 1774, which recommended that every county, town, and city form committees to enforce a boycott of all British goods. These committees would become the organizational and communications network for the Revolutionary movement, connecting every locality to the leadership. The Continental Association also included provisions for the nonimportation of British goods (implemented in December 1774) and the nonexportation of American goods to Britain (to be implemented in September 1775 unless colonial grievances were addressed).

In London the king fumed. In late 1774 he wrote his prime minister that the "New England colonies are in a state of rebellion," and "blows must decide whether they are to be subject to this country or independent." British critics of the American actions reminded the colonists that Parliament had absolute sovereignty. Power could not be shared.

Parliament declared Massachusetts in rebellion and prohibited the New England colonies from trading with any nation outside the empire. Lord North's Conciliatory Resolution, adopted on February 27, 1775, was as far as they would go to avert a crisis. Under its terms, Parliament would levy taxes only to regulate trade and would grant to each colony the duties collected within its boundaries, provided the colonies would contribute voluntarily to a quota for defense of the empire. It was a formula not for peace but for new quarrels.

SHIFTING AUTHORITY

Events were already moving beyond conciliation. All through late 1774 and early 1775 the defenders of American rights were seizing the initiative. The unorganized Loyalists (or Tories), if they did not submit to nonimportation agreements, found themselves confronted with tar and feathers. The Continental Congress urged each colony to mobilize its militia. The militia organized special units of "Minutemen" to be ready for quick mobilization. Royal and proprietary officials were losing control as provincial congresses assumed authority and colonial militias organized and gathered arms and gunpowder. Still, British military officials remained smugly confident. Major John Pitcairn wrote home from Boston in March, "I am satisfied that one active campaign, a smart action, and burning two or three of their towns, will set everything to rights."

LEXINGTON AND CONCORD   Pitcairn soon had his chance. On April 14, 1775, General Thomas Gage, the British commander, received orders to suppress the "open rebellion." Gage decided to seize Sam Adams and John Hancock in Lexington and destroy the militia's supply depot at Concord, about twenty miles northwest of Boston. But local Patriots got wind of the plan, and on April 18 Boston's Committee of Safety sent silversmith Paul Revere and tanner William Dawes by separate routes on their famous ride to spread the alarm. Revere reached Lexington about midnight and alerted John Hancock and Samuel Adams. Joined by Dawes and Samuel Prescott, who had been visiting in Lexington, Revere rode on toward Concord. A British patrol intercepted the trio, but Prescott slipped through and continued to deliver the warning.

The Battle of Lexington

Amos Doolittle's impression of the Battle of Lexington as combat begins.

At dawn on April 19, the British advance guard found Captain John Parker and about seventy "Minutemen" lined up on the Lexington village green. Parker apparently intended only a silent protest, but Major Pitcairn rode onto the green, swung his sword, and brusquely yelled, "Disperse, you damned rebels! You dogs, run!" The Americans had already begun backing away when someone fired a pistol shot, whereupon the British soldiers loosed a volley into the Minutemen and then charged them with bayonets, leaving eight dead and ten wounded.

The British officers hastily reformed their men and proceeded to Concord. There the Americans had already carried off most of their valuable supplies, but the British destroyed what they could. In the meantime, American Patriots were swarming over the countryside, eager to wreak vengeance on the hated British troops. At Concord's North Bridge the growing American militia inflicted fourteen casualties on a British platoon, and by about noon the exhausted redcoats had begun marching back to Boston.

By then, however, the road back had turned into a gauntlet of death as the rebels from "every Middlesex village and farm" sniped at the redcoats from behind stone walls, trees, barns, and farmhouses all the way back to the Charlestown peninsula. By nightfall the redcoat survivors were under the protection of the fleet and army at Boston, having suffered over 250 killed or wounded; the Americans had lost less than 100. A British general reported to

London that the rebels, though untrained, had earned his respect: "Whoever looks upon them as an irregular mob will find himself much mistaken."

THE SPREADING CONFLICT   The Revolutionary War had begun. When the Second Continental Congress convened at Philadelphia on May 10, 1775, British-held Boston was under siege by Massachusetts militia units. On the very day that Congress met, a force of Green Mountain Boys under Ethan Allen of Vermont and Massachusetts volunteers under Benedict Arnold of Connecticut captured the strategic Fort Ticonderoga in upstate New York. In a prodigious feat of daring energy, the Americans then transported sixty captured British cannons down rivers and over ridges to support the siege of Boston.

The Continental Congress, with no legal authority and no resources, met amid reports of spreading warfare; it had little choice but to assume the role of Revolutionary government. The Congress accepted a request that it "adopt" the motley army gathered around Boston and on June 15 named George Washington to be general and commander in chief of a Continental army. He accepted on the condition that he receive no pay. The Congress fastened on the charismatic Washington because his service in the French and Indian War had made him one of the most experienced officers in America. The fact that he was from influential Virginia, the most populous province, heightened his qualifications.

On June 17, the very day that George Washington was commissioned, the colonial rebels and British troops engaged in their first major fight, the Battle of Bunker Hill. While the Continental Congress deliberated, both American and British forces around Boston had increased. Militiamen from Rhode Island, Connecticut, and New Hampshire joined in the siege. British reinforcements included three major generals: William Howe, Sir Henry Clinton, and John Burgoyne. On the day before the battle, Americans began to fortify the high ground of Charlestown peninsula, overlooking Boston. Breed's Hill was the battle location, nearer to Boston than Bunker Hill, the site first chosen (and the source of the battle's erroneous name).

With civilians looking on from rooftops and church steeples, the British attacked in the blistering heat, with 2,400 troops moving in tight formation through tall grass. The Americans, pounded by naval guns, watched from behind hastily built earthworks as the waves of brightly uniformed British troops advanced up the hill. Ordered not to fire until they could see "the whites of their eyes," the militiamen waited until the attackers had come within fifteen to twenty paces, then loosed a shattering volley. Through the cloud of oily smoke, the Americans could see fallen bodies "as thick as sheep

View of the Attack on Bunker's Hill

The Battle of Bunker Hill and the burning of Charlestown peninsula.

in a fold." The militiamen cheered as they watched the greatest soldiers in the world retreating in panic.

Within a half hour, however, the British had re-formed and attacked again. Another sheet of flames and lead greeted them, and the vaunted redcoats retreated a second time. Still, the proud British generals were determined not to be humiliated by the ragtag rustics. On the third attempt, when the colonials began to run out of gunpowder and were forced to throw stones, a bayonet charge ousted them. The British took the high ground, but at the cost of 1,054 casualties. Colonial losses were about 400. "A dear bought victory," recorded General Clinton, "another such would have ruined us."

The Battle of Bunker Hill had two profound effects. First, the high number of British casualties made the English generals more cautious in subsequent encounters with the Continental army. Second, Congress recommended that all able-bodied men enlist in a militia. This tended to divide the male population into Patriot and Loyalist camps. A middle ground was no longer tenable.

While Boston remained under siege, the Continental Congress held to the dimming hope of a compromise. On July 5 and 6, 1775, the delegates issued two major documents: an appeal to the king, thereafter known as the Olive Branch Petition, and a Declaration of the Causes and Necessity of

Taking Up Arms. The Olive Branch Petition, written by John Dickinson, professed continued loyalty to George III and begged him to restrain further hostilities pending a reconciliation. The declaration, also largely Dickinson's work, traced the history of the controversy, denounced the British for the unprovoked assault at Lexington, and rejected independence but affirmed the colonists' purpose to fight for their rights rather than submit to slavery. "Our cause is just," he declared. "Our Union is perfect." Such impassioned rhetoric failed to impress George III. On August 22 he declared the defiant colonists "open and avowed enemies." The next day he issued a proclamation of rebellion.

Before the end of July 1775, the Congress had authorized an ill-fated attack against British troops in the walled Canadian city of Quebec. One force, under General Richard Montgomery, advanced toward Quebec by way of Lake Champlain; another, under General Benedict Arnold, struggled through the Maine woods. The American units arrived outside Quebec in September, exhausted and hungry. Then they were ambushed by a silent killer: smallpox. "The small pox [is] very much among us," wrote one soldier. As the deadly virus raced through the American camp, General Montgomery faced a brutal dilemma. Most of his soldiers had signed up for short tours of duty, many of which were scheduled to expire at the end of the year. He could not afford to wait until spring for the smallpox to subside. Seeing little choice but to fight, Montgomery ordered a desperate attack on the British forces at Quebec during a blizzard, on December 31, 1775. The assault was a disaster. Montgomery was killed early in the battle and Benedict Arnold wounded. Over 400 Americans were taken prisoner. The rest of the Patriot force retreated to its camp outside the walled city and appealed to the Continental Congress for reinforcements.

The smallpox virus continued attacking both the Americans in the camp and their comrades taken captive by the British. As fresh troops arrived, they, too, fell victim to the deadly virus. Benedict Arnold warned George Washington in February 1776 that the runaway disease would soon lead to "the entire ruin of the Army." By May there were only 1,900 American soldiers left outside Quebec, and 900 of them were infected with smallpox. Sensing the weakness of the American force, the British attacked and sent the ragtag Patriots on a frantic retreat up the St. Lawrence River to the American-held city of Montreal and eventually back to New York and New England. The sick were left behind, but the smallpox virus traveled with the fleeing soldiers. Major General Horatio Gates later remarked that "every thing about this Army is infected with the Pestilence; The Clothes, The Blankets, the Air & the Ground they Walk on."

Quebec was the first military setback for the Revolutionaries. It would not be the last. And smallpox would continue to bedevil the American war effort. The veterans of the failed Canadian campaign brought home both smallpox and demoralizing stories about the disease, thus spreading the epidemic to civilians and making the recruitment of new soldiers more difficult. Men who might risk British gunfire balked at the more terrifying thought of contracting smallpox in a military camp.

As the fighting spread north into Canada and south into Virginia and the Carolinas, the Continental Congress appointed commissioners to negotiate peace treaties with Indian tribes, organized a Post Office Department, and formed a navy and marine corps.

When George Washington arrived outside Boston to take charge of the American forces after the Battle of Bunker Hill, the military situation was stalemated, and so it remained through the winter, until early March 1776. At that time American forces occupied Dorchester Heights, to the south of Boston, bringing the city under threat of bombardment with cannon and mortars. General William Howe, who had long since replaced Gage as British commander, reasoned that discretion was the better part of valor and retreated with his forces by water to Halifax. The last British troops, along with fearful American Loyalists, embarked from Boston on March 17, 1776. By that time British power had collapsed nearly everywhere, and the British faced not the suppression of a rebellion but the reconquest of a continent.

COMMON SENSE   In early 1776 Thomas Paine's pamphlet *Common Sense* was published anonymously in Philadelphia, transforming the revolutionary controversy. Born of Quaker parents, Paine had distinguished himself in England chiefly as a drifter, a failure in marriage and business. At age thirty-seven he had sailed for America with a letter of introduction from Benjamin Franklin and the purpose of setting up a school for young ladies. When the school did not work out, he moved into the political controversy as a freelance writer and, with *Common Sense,* proved himself the consummate Revolutionary rhetorician. Until his pamphlet appeared, the squabble had been mainly with Parliament, but Paine directly attacked allegiance to the monarchy, the last frayed connection to Britain. The common sense of the matter, to Paine, was that King George III and his advisers bore the responsibility for the malevolence toward the colonies. Americans should consult their own interests, abandon George III, and declare their independence: "The blood of the slain, the weeping voice of nature cries, 'TIS TIME TO PART."

INDEPENDENCE

Within three months more than 100,000 copies of Thomas Paine's pamphlet were in circulation across the colonies. "*Common Sense* is working a powerful change in the minds of men," George Washington noted. One by one the provincial governments authorized their delegates in the Continental Congress to take the final step. On June 7, 1776, Richard Henry Lee of Virginia moved "that these United Colonies are, and of right ought to be, free and independent states." South Carolina and Pennsylvania, however, initially opposed severing ties with England. After feverish lobbying by radical Patriots, the dissenters changed their minds and the resolution passed on July 2, a date that "will be the most memorable epoch in the history of America," John Adams wrote to his wife, Abigail. The memorable date, however, became July 4, 1776, when Congress adopted the Declaration of Independence, an eloquent statement of political philosophy that still retains its dynamic force.

JEFFERSON'S DECLARATION   Although Thomas Jefferson is often called the author of the Declaration of Independence, he is more accurately termed its draftsman. In June 1776 the Continental Congress appointed a committee of five men—Jefferson, Benjamin Franklin, John Adams, Robert Livingston of New York, and Roger Sherman of Connecticut—to develop a public explanation of the reasons for colonial discontent and to provide a rationale for independence. John Adams convened the committee on June 11. The group asked Adams and Jefferson to produce a first draft, whereupon Adams deferred to Jefferson because of the thirty-three-year-old Virginian's reputation as a superb writer.

During two days in mid-June 1776, in his rented lodgings in Philadelphia, Jefferson wrote the first statement of American grievances and principles. He drew primarily upon two sources: his own draft preamble to the Virginia Constitution, written a few weeks earlier, and George Mason's draft of Virginia's Declaration of Rights, which had appeared in Philadelphia newspapers in mid-June.

Jefferson shared his draft with the committee members, and they made several minor revisions to the opening paragraphs and to his listing of the charges against King George III. They submitted the document to the entire Congress on June 28, whereupon it was tabled until July 1. Over the next three days the legislators made eighty-six changes in Jefferson's declaration, including shortening its overall length by one fourth. Jefferson regretted many of the changes, but the legislative editing improved the declaration,

The Coming Revolution

The Continental Congress votes for independence on July 2, 1776.

making it more concise, accurate, and coherent—and, as a result, more powerful.

The Declaration of Independence is grounded in John Locke's contract theory of government—the theory, in Jefferson's words, that governments derived "their just Powers from the consent of the people," who were entitled to "alter or abolish" those that denied their "unalienable rights" to "life, Liberty, and the pursuit of Happiness." The appeal was no longer simply to "the rights of Englishmen" but to the broader "laws of Nature and Nature's God." The document set forth "a history of repeated injuries and usurpations, all having in direct object the establishment of an absolute Tyranny over these States." The "Representatives of the United States of America," therefore, declared the thirteen "United Colonies" to be "Free and Independent States."

"WE ALWAYS HAD GOVERNED OURSELVES"　　So it had come to this, thirteen years after Britain had won domination of North America. Historians have advanced numerous explanations of what caused the Revolutionary controversy: "unfair" regulation of trade, the restrictions on settling western lands, the tax controversy, the debts to British merchants, the growth of a national consciousness, the lack of representation in Parliament, ideologies of Whiggery and the Enlightenment, and the abrupt shift from a mercantile to an "imperial" policy after 1763.

Each factor contributed something to the collective colonial grievances that rose to a climax in a gigantic failure of British statesmanship. A conflict between British sovereignty and American rights had come to a point of confrontation that adroit statesmanship might have avoided, sidestepped, or outflanked. Irresolution and vacillation in the British ministry finally gave way to the stubborn determination to force an issue long permitted to drift. The colonists saw these developments as the conspiracy of a corrupted oligarchy—and finally, they decided, of a despotic king—to impose an "absolute Tyranny."

Perhaps the last word on how the Revolution came about should belong to an obscure participant, Levi Preston, a Minuteman from Danvers, Massachusetts. Asked sixty-seven years after Lexington and Concord about British oppressions, the ninety-one-year-old veteran responded: "What were they? Oppressions? I didn't feel them." When asked about the hated Stamp Act, he claimed that he "never saw one of those stamps" and was "certain I never paid a penny for one of them." Nor had he ever heard of John Locke or his theories. "We read only the Bible, the Catechism, Watts's Psalms and Hymns, and the Almanack." When his exasperated interviewer asked why, then, he had support the Revolution, Preston replied, "Young man, what we meant in going for those redcoats was this: we always had governed ourselves, and we always meant to. They didn't mean we should."

MAKING CONNECTIONS

- The American Revolutionary rhetoric was important not only for fighting the Revolution: it also provided the framework for the creation of state and national governments after independence was won. This framework will be discussed in the next two chapters.

- The discussion of "Discontent on the Frontier" showed the tension between colonists in the more urban eastern areas of several states and those on the western frontier. These tensions will reappear in several chapters—for example, in the Federalist–anti-Federalist debate over ratification of the Constitution (in Chapter 7).

FURTHER READING

For a narrative survey of the events leading to the Revolution, see Edward Countryman's *The American Revolution,* rev. ed. (2003). For Great Britain's perspective on the imperial conflict, see Sir Lewis Bernstein Namier's *England in the Age of the American Revolution,* 2nd ed. (1961) and Ian R. Christie, *Crisis of Empire* (1966).

The intellectual foundations of revolt are traced in Bernard Bailyn's *The Ideological Origins of the American Revolution,* enlarged ed. (1992) and in John Phillip Reid's *Constitutional History of the American Revolution: The Authority of Rights* (1987). To understand how these views were connected to organized protest, see Pauline Maier's *From Resistance to Revolution: Colonial Radicals and the Development of American Opposition to Britain, 1765–1776* (1972).

A number of books deal with specific events in the crisis. Oliver M. Dickerson's *The Navigation Acts and the American Revolution* (1951) stresses the change from trade regulation to taxation in 1764. Edmund S. Morgan and Helen M. Morgan's *The Stamp Act Crisis: Prologue to Revolution,* rev. ed. (1962) gives the colonial perspective on that crucial event. Also valuable are Hiller B. Zobel's *The Boston Massacre* (1970), Benjamin Woods Labaree's *The Boston Tea Party, 1773: Catalyst for Revolution* (1964), and David Ammerman's *In the Common Cause: American Response to the Coercive Acts of 1774* (1974).

Events west of the Appalachian Mountains are chronicled concisely by Jack M. Sosin in *The Revolutionary Frontier, 1763–1783* (1967). Pauline Maier's *American Scripture: Making the Declaration of Independence* (1997) is the best analysis of the framing of that crucial document.

Part Two

BUILDING A NATION

1776

States initiate their own constitutions (1776–1787)
Battle of Saratoga (1777)
British occupy Philadelphia; George Washington's troops winter at Valley Forge, Pennsylvania (1777–1778)
Americans sign the Treaty of Alliance with France (1778)

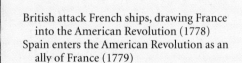

British attack French ships, drawing France into the American Revolution (1778)
Spain enters the American Revolution as an ally of France (1779)

1780

Federalists and anti-Federalists debate the role of the federal government (1780s–1790s)
Americans and French defeat British at Yorktown (1781)
U.S. operates under the Articles of Confederation (1781–1789)
Treaty of Paris ends the American Revolution (1783)
Constitutional Convention (1787)
Shays's Rebellion pits a debtor army against the republic's elite, leading to a victory for conservatism (1787)
Alexander Hamilton, John Jay, and James Madison publish The Federalist, defending the idea of a strong central government (1787–1788)
George Washington serves as the first U.S. president (1789–1797)

Industrial Revolution begins in England (ea. 1780)
James Watt installs a steam engine powered loom in an English cotton-spinning factory (1785)
British iron production increases from 17,000 tons (1740) to 68,000 tons (1788)
British prisoners are first transported to Australia (1788)
French Revolution begins (1789)

1790

Debate over national bank spawns the first national political parties, the Federalists and the Republicans (1790s)
Bill of Rights is adopted (1791)
Jay's Treaty settles most major issues between U.S. and England (1795)
Pinckney's Treaty challenges Spain's presence in North America (1795)
Treaty of Greenville opens up white settlement in the Northwest Territory (1795)
George Washington's farewell address advises against permanent foreign entanglements (1796)
John Adams serves as U.S. president (1797–1801)
Congress creates the Department of the Navy and a new army (1798)
Alien and Sedition Acts limit freedom of speech and the press (1798)

French national convention declares France a republic (1792)
French Revolution results in the execution of King Louis XVI (1793)
England and France fight a prolonged war (1793–1815)
England announces its orders in council, allowing the British navy to seize the cargo of ships bound for, or coming from, French Caribbean possessions (1793)
XYZ affair brings U.S. and France to the brink of war (1797–1798)

1776

100,000 colonists (more than 3 percent of the population) remain loyal to the crown and flee America during the Revolutionary War (1770s–1780s)

The war disrupts life in the colonies, destroying crops and livestock and making family life more difficult (1770s–1780s)

55,000 slaves flee to freedom during the war (1770s–1780s)

John Trumbull, Charles Willson Peale, and other American artists depict events of the war and its leaders (1770s–1780s)

17 colleges are established in the colonies (1770s–1780s)

British occupy major colonial ports, disrupting trade (1776–1781)

Continental Congress has difficulty financing and supplying the Continental army (1776–1781)

Price for a bushel of wheat in the colonies rises from less than $1 (1777) to $80 (1779) as a result of the war

1780

Independence Day becomes the most important public ritual in the U.S. (1780s)

Indian tribes lose huge parcels of land to U.S. expansion (1780s)

Women emerge from the Revolution with no political rights (1783)

Congress reserves income from land sales for support of schools (1785)

Virginia Statute of Religious Freedom (1786)

Delegates to the Constitutional Convention make no formal mention of women's rights, nor do they use the word *slavery* in the Constitution (1787)

U.S. extends from the Atlantic Ocean to the Mississippi River and has a population of nearly 4 million (1789)

Land reforms and new political rights establish the basis for greater social and political equality and for a middle class (1780s–1800s)

U.S. suffers acute economic downturn (1770s–1790s)

U.S. resumes trade with England (1783)

Trade with China begins (1784–1785)

Land Ordinance of 1785 outlines procedures for land surveys and sale (1785)

Seven states issue paper currency to increase available credit (1785–1786)

Agricultural crisis leads to a revolt against high taxes and a demand for debt and tax relief (1787)

Northwest Ordinance sets a precedent for future U.S. expansion (1787)

Congress grants land as payment to Revolutionary War veterans (1787)

U.S. has heavy federal debt and almost no federal revenue (1789)

1790

Women's rights activist Judith Sargent Murray calls for "mutuality in marriage," reflecting a new sense of women's role in society (1790)

Free Slave Act protects freed slaves from kidnapping or seizure (1793)

Shawnee, Ottawa, Chippewa, and Potawatomi warriors are defeated at the Battle of Fallen Timbers (1794)

Naturalization Act lengthens the residency requirement for citizenship (1798)

Alien Act and Alien Enemies Act empower the president to deport or imprison dangerous aliens (1798)

U.S. commerce and exports far surpass colonial trade (1790)

Hamilton's "Report on Manufactures" recommends protective tariffs to foster and protect U.S. industries (1791)

Bank of the United States is established (1791)

Vigilantes in Pennsylvania lead the Whiskey Rebellion in opposition to Hamilton's 1791 excise tax (1794)

Land Act doubles the price of land, benefiting speculators (1796)

1800

Thomas Jefferson and Aaron Burr are tied in vote for the president; the election is thrown into the House of Representatives (1800)

Judiciary Act is passed by lame-duck Congress to ensure Federalist control of the judiciary (1801)

Thomas Jefferson serves as U.S. president (1801–1809)

Marbury v. Madison establishes that the Supreme Court can invalidate federal laws (1803)

U.S. purchases Louisiana Territory from France; Lewis and Clark depart St. Louis to explore the West (1803)

Jefferson claims executive privilege and withholds documents from the Burr conspiracy trial (1807)

James Madison serves as U.S. president (1809–1817)

1810

War of 1812 (1812–1815)

U.S. troops occupy West Florida (1813)

British burn the White House and the Capitol (1814)

Treaty of Ghent ends War of 1812 (1814)

U.S. defeats England at the Battle of New Orleans (1815)

Barbary pirates hold U.S. ships for ransom; Jefferson blockades Tripoli (1801–1805)

Slave rebellion overturns French rule in Haiti (1801)

Napoleonic Empire (1804–1815)

Napoléon defeats Russia and Austria and controls western Europe (1805)

England defeats French and Spanish fleets in the Battle of Trafalgar, securing British control of the high seas (1805)

England sets up a "paper blockade" of European ports (1806)

British steel production reaches 260,000 tons (1806)

England again begins to interfere with U.S. shipping and resumes the practice of impressment (1807)

French enact the continental system and blockade English ports (1806–1807)

Latin America gains independence from Europe (1810–1824)

George Stephenson invents the first locomotive (1814)

Congress of Vienna establishes the diplomatic principle of the balance of power (1814–1815)

Foreign slave trade is outlawed (1808)
300,000 slaves are illegally smuggled into
the U.S. (1808–1861)

U.S. shipping and Treasury revenues increase as a result of wars in Europe
(early 1800s)

Land Act reduces minimum sale of land,
allowing purchases by ordinary settlers
(1800)

Jefferson repeals the whiskey tax and other
Federalist excises (1802)

Enticed by the Lewis and Clark expedition,
trappers and traders travel west of the
Mississippi River to exploit the region's
abundance of pelts (1806 and after)

Embargo Act (1807) causes exports to
plummet from $108 million in 1806 to
$22 million in 1808

Nonintercourse Act reopens trade with all
countries except France and Great
Britain (1809)

Tecumseh attempts to unite natives in an
Indian confederacy, loses the Battle of
Tippecanoe, and flees to Canada (1811)

Francis Scott Key pens "The Star-Spangled
Banner" (1814)

Macon's bill reopens trade with Britain and
France (1810)

Improved transportation and more readily
available credit spawn industrialization,
expressed in a shift to commercial farming and manufacturing (1810–1840s)

Construction of the National Road (Cumberland Road) begins (1811)

Charter of the Bank of the United States
expires (1811)

First fully mechanized U.S. factory opens at
Waltham, Massachusetts (1813)

While it was one thing for Patriot leaders to declare American independence from British authority, it was quite another to win it on the battlefield. Barely one third of the colonists actively supported the Revolution, the political stability of the new nation was uncertain, and George Washington found himself in command of a poorly supplied, untested army.

But the Revolutionary movement would persevere and prevail. The skill and fortitude of Washington and his lieutenants enabled the Americans to exploit their geographic advantages. Equally important was the intervention of the French on behalf of the Revolutionary cause. The Franco-American alliance proved decisive. In 1783, after eight years of sporadic fighting and heavy human and financial losses, the British gave up the fight and their American colonies.

Amid the Revolutionary turmoil the Patriots faced the daunting task of forming new governments for themselves. Their deeply engrained resentment of British imperial rule led them to grant considerable powers to the individual states. As Thomas Jefferson declared, "Virginia, Sir, is my country." Such powerful local ties help explain why the colonists focused their attention on creating new state constitutions rather than a national government. The Articles of Confederation, ratified in 1781, provided only the semblance of national authority. All power to make and execute laws remained with the states.

After the end of the Revolutionary War, the flimsy government authorized by the Articles of Confederation proved inadequate to the needs of the new—and expanding—nation. This realization led to the Constitutional Convention of 1787. The process of drafting and ratifying the new constitution prompted a debate on the relative significance of national power, local control, and individual freedom that has provided the central theme of American political thought ever since.

The American Revolution involved much more than the apportionment of political power, however. It also unleashed social forces and posed social questions that would help reshape the very fabric of American culture. What would be the role of women African Americans, and Native Americans in the new republic? How would the contrasting economies of the various regions of the new United States be developed? Who would control the vast territories to the west of the original thirteen states? How would the new republic relate to the other nations of the world?

These controversial questions helped foster the first national political parties in the United States. During the 1790s Federalists, led by Alexander Hamilton, and Republicans, led by Thomas Jefferson and James Madison, engaged in a heated debate about the political and economic future of the new nation. With Jefferson's election as president in 1800, the Republicans gained the upper hand in national politics for the next quarter century. In the process they presided over a maturing society that aggressively expanded westward at the expense of the Native Americans, ambivalently embraced industrial development, fitfully engaged in a second war with Great Britain, and ominously witnessed a growing sectional controversy over slavery.

6

THE AMERICAN REVOLUTION

FOCUS QUESTIONS

- What were the American and British military strategies and the Revolutionary War's major turning points?
- What was the effect of the war on the home front?
- Why is the American Revolution considered a "social revolution" in matters of social equality, slavery, the rights of women, and religious freedom?
- How did the Revolution mark the beginnings of a distinctive American culture?

To answer these questions and access additional review material, please visit www.wwnorton.com/studyspace.

Few foreign observers thought the upstart American Revolutionaries could win a war against the world's greatest empire. The Americans lost most of the battles in the Revolutionary War but eventually forced the British to sue for peace and grant the colonists their independence. The surprising result testified to the tenacity of the Patriots, to the importance of the French alliance, and to the peculiar difficulties facing the British as they tried to conduct a demanding military campaign thousands of miles from home.

The American Revolution had unexpected consequences affecting political, economic, and social life. While securing American independence, it generated a new sense of nationalism and created a unique system of self-governance; it also began a process of societal definition and change that has yet to run its course. The turmoil of revolution upset traditional class and social relationships and helped transform the lives of people who had long been relegated to the periphery of historical concern—African Americans, women, and Indians. In important ways, then, the Revolution was much more than simply a war for independence. It was an engine for political experimentation and social transformation.

1776: WASHINGTON'S NARROW ESCAPE

On July 2, 1776, the day that Congress voted for independence, British redcoats landed on Staten Island, across New York Harbor from Manhattan. By mid-August, Major General William Howe had some 32,000 men at his disposal, including 9,000 Hessians (German soldiers hired by the British), the largest force mustered by the British in the eighteenth century. General Washington transferred most of his men from New York to Boston, but he could muster only about 19,000 poorly trained soldiers and militiamen. Such a force could not defend New York, but Congress wanted it held. This meant that Washington had to expose his men to entrapments from which they escaped more by luck and Howe's caution than by any strategic genius of the American commander. The inexperienced George Washington was still learning the art of generalship, and the New York campaign afforded some costly lessons.

FIGHTING IN NEW YORK AND NEW JERSEY By invading and occupying New York, the British sought to sever New England from the rest of the rebellious colonies. In late August the British inflicted heavy losses and forced Washington to evacuate Long Island in order to reunite his divided forces. Only a timely rainstorm kept the British fleet out of the East River and made possible a nighttime withdrawal of American forces to Manhattan.

Had the British moved quickly, they could have trapped Washington's army in lower Manhattan. But the main American force of 6,000 men withdrew northward to the mainland of New York, crossed the Hudson River, and retreated across New Jersey and over the Delaware River into Pennsylvania. In the retreating army marched a volunteer from England, Thomas Paine. Having opened an eventful year with his inspiring pamphlet *Common Sense,* he would now compose *The American Crisis,* in which he exhorted Americans with the immortal line "These are the times that try men's souls." The eloquent pamphlet, ordered read in the American army camps, helped restore shaken morale—as events would soon do more decisively.

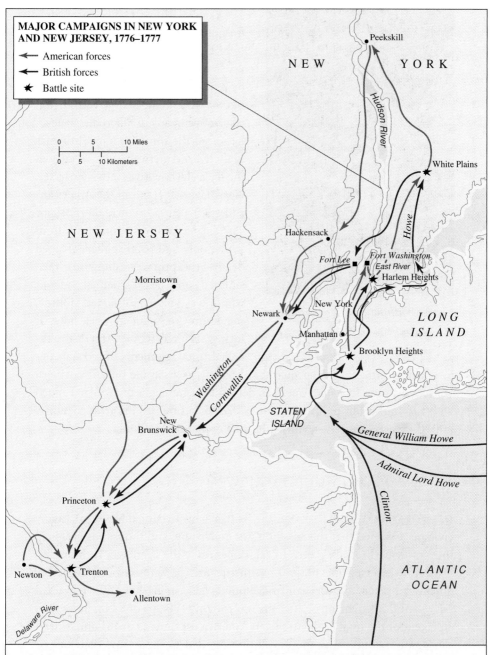

MAJOR CAMPAIGNS IN NEW YORK AND NEW JERSEY, 1776–1777

← American forces

← British forces

★ Battle site

0   5   10 Miles

0   5   10 Kilometers

NEW YORK

Peekskill

Hudson River

White Plains

Howe

NEW JERSEY

Hackensack

Fort Lee

Fort Washington

East River

Harlem Heights

Morristown

New York

Newark

Manhattan

LONG ISLAND

Washington

Cornwallis

Brooklyn Heights

New Brunswick

STATEN ISLAND

General William Howe

Admiral Lord Howe

Princeton

Clinton

Newton

Trenton

ATLANTIC OCEAN

Allentown

Delaware River

Why did Washington lead his army from Brooklyn Heights to Manhattan and from there to New Jersey? How could Howe have ended the rebellion in New York? What is the significance of the battle at Trenton?

George Washington at Princeton

By Charles Willson Peale.

General Howe, firmly—and comfortably—based in New York City (which the British held throughout the war), followed conventional practice by settling down with his army to wait out the winter. But George Washington was not yet ready to hibernate; instead, he seized the initiative. On Christmas night 1776 American soldiers crossed the icy Delaware River into New Jersey. Near dawn at Trenton, the Americans surprised a garrison of 1,500 Hessians. The daring raid was a total rout, from which only 500 royal soldiers escaped death or capture. Washington's men suffered only six casualties, one of whom was Lieutenant James Monroe, the future president. A week later, at nearby Princeton, the Americans repelled three regiments of redcoats before taking refuge in winter quarters at Morristown, in the hills of northern New Jersey. After repeated American defeats the campaigns of 1776 had ended with two minor but uplifting victories. Howe had missed his great chance—indeed, several chances—to bring the rebellion to a speedy end.

AMERICAN SOCIETY AT WAR

DIVIDED LOYALTIES After the British army occupied New York, many civilians assumed that the rebellion was collapsing, and thousands hastened to sign an oath of allegiance to the crown. But the events at Trenton and Princeton reversed the outlook. With the British withdrawal, New Jersey quickly reverted to rebel control. Nonetheleas, many colonists remained Tory in outlook. During or after the war roughly 100,000 of them, more than 3 percent of the total population, left America for Canada or Britain. American opinion concerning the Revolution divided in three ways: Patriots, or Whigs (as the Revolutionaries called themselves), Tories, and an indifferent middle group swayed by the better organized and more energetic radicals.

Tories were concentrated mainly in the seaport cities, but they came from all walks of life. Almost all governors, judges, and other royal officials were loyal to Britain; most Anglican ministers also preferred the mother country. Where planter aristocrats tended to be Whigs, as in North Carolina, back-country farmers (many of them recently Regulators) leaned toward the Tories. When Patriots took control of an area, Loyalists faced a difficult choice: accompany the British and leave behind their property, or stay behind and face the wrath of the Patriots. In this sense the War for Independence was also very much a civil war that divided families and communities. The fratricidal hatred that often goes with civil war gave rise to bloodcurdling atrocities in the backcountry of New York and Pennsylvania and in Georgia, where Tory militiamen and their Indian allies went marauding against frontier Whigs. Whigs responded in kind against the Loyalists.

MILITIA AND ARMY Since the end of the French and Indian War, the colonies had required all adult males between the ages of fifteen and sixty to enroll in their local militia company, attend monthly drills, and turn out on short notice for emergencies. When fighting erupted between the British and the Revolutionaries, members of community militias had to choose sides.

American militiamen served two purposes. They were a home guard, defending their community, and they augmented the Continental army. Dressed in hunting shirts and armed with muskets, they preferred to ambush their opponents or engage them in hand-to-hand combat rather than fight in

American Militia

This sketch of the militiamen by a French soldier at Yorktown shows "one of those ubiquitous American frontiersman-turned-soldier" (second from right).

traditional formations. They also tended to kill unnecessarily and to torture prisoners. To repel an attack, the militia somehow materialized; the danger past, it evaporated, for there were chores to do at home.

The Continental army was on the whole better trained and more motivated than the militias. Although many soldiers were attracted by bounties of land or cash and some deserted, most of those who persevered were animated by genuine patriotic fervor and a thirst for adventure that enabled them to survive the horrors of combat and the tedium of camp life. Unlike the full-time professional soldiers in the British army, George Washington's Continental army, which fluctuated in size from 5,000 to 20,000, was populated mostly by citizen-soldiers, poor native-born Americans or immigrants who had been indentured servants or convicts.

FINANCIAL STRAINS AND SMALLPOX The new Continental Congress struggled to provide the army with adequate supplies. None of the states contributed more than a part of its share, and Congress reluctantly let army agents take supplies directly from farmers in return for certificates promising future payment. To pay for the war, Congress and the states printed paper money. With goods scarce, prices in terms of paper dollars, or "Continentals," rose sharply.

During the harsh winter at Morristown, New Jersey (1776–1777), George Washington's army nearly disintegrated as terms of enlistment expired and deserters fled the hardships of brutally cold weather, inadequate food, and widespread disease. Smallpox continued to wreak havoc among the American armies. "The small Pox! The small Pox!" John Adams wrote to his wife, Abigail. "What shall We do with it?" By 1777 George Washington had come to view the virus with greater dread than "the Sword of the Enemy." On any given day, one fourth of the American troops were deemed unfit for duty, usually because of smallpox. Some Americans suspected that the British were practicing biological warfare by sending infected civilians and clothing behind the American lines.

The threat of smallpox to the war effort was so great that in early 1777 Washington ordered a mass inoculation, which he managed to keep secret from British intelligence. Inoculating an entire army was an enormous and risky undertaking. Each soldier had to be interviewed to determine whether he had ever had smallpox. Then those who believed they had never been infected were inoculated. The virus was implanted in an incision, usually on the arm or hand. For unknown reasons the resulting smallpox produced less severe symptoms than natural infections—fewer pustules, less scarring, and far fewer deaths. Inoculated soldiers had to be quarantined while the virus ran its course, but the infected soldiers were thereafter immune to the disease. Washington's daring gamble paid off. One of the 400 Connecticut soldiers who was inoculated in the summer of 1777 reported its success: "We lost none. I had the smallpox favorably as did the rest." The successful inoculation of the American army marks one of Washington's greatest strategic accomplishments of the war.

Only about 1,000 soldiers stuck out the winter in New Jersey. With the spring thaw, however, recruits began arriving to claim the bounty of $20 and 100 acres of land offered by Congress to those who would enlist for three years or for the duration of the conflict, if less. With some 9,000 regular troops, George Washington began sparring and feinting with British forces in northern New Jersey.

BEHIND THE LINES Civilians saw their lives profoundly changed by the Revolutionary War. British forces occupied the major cities (Boston, New York, Philadelphia, Charleston, Savannah), towns and villages were destroyed, crops and livestock confiscated, families disrupted, and husbands and fathers killed or maimed.

While some civilians viewed the hardships as a patriotic duty, others saw in the Revolution a means of self-aggrandizement rather than self-sacrifice. The inflation in prices for basic foods and products created new opportunities for quick profits and entrepreneurial chicanery. Robert Morris, a prominent Philadelphia merchant who became treasurer of the Congress upon the condition that he continue his private ventures, told a colleague that "there never has been so fair an opportunity for making a large fortune since I have been conversant in the world."

The poor suffered most amid the disruptions and skyrocketing prices. A bushel of wheat that sold for less than $1 in 1777 brought $80 two years later. Many consumers appealed to authorities to institute price controls so they could afford basic necessities. Others took more direct action. In Boston, women paraded through the streets a merchant accused of hoarding while "a large concourse of men stood amazed." The poor saw themselves as victims of gouging merchants and retailers. No longer willing to defer quietly to the discrimination, they grabbed the opportunity afforded by the Revolution to claim new economic and political rights. To Revolutionary leaders such as John Adams, the "democratical" demands put forward by the laboring classes were as odious as British regulatory measures. The specter of mechanics and laborers exercising political power horrified him. The American people, he and others insisted, must accept social inequality as a fact of human existence and defer to the leadership of their betters. The "one thing" absolutely required of a new republic was "a decency, and respect, and veneration introduced for persons of authority."

1777: SETBACKS FOR THE BRITISH

Indecision, overconfidence, and poor communications plagued British military planning in the campaigns of 1777. The profoundly confident "Gentleman Johnny" Burgoyne proposed to bisect the colonies. His men would advance southward from Canada to the Hudson River while another force moved eastward from Fort Oswego, on Lake Ontario, down the Mohawk Valley. The British general Howe decided to move against the Patriot capital, Philadelphia, expecting the Pennsylvania Tories to rally to the crown and secure the colony.

Washington, sensing Howe's purpose, withdrew most of his men from New Jersey to meet the new threat. At Brandywine Creek, south of Philadelphia, the British outmaneuvered and routed Washington's forces on September 11, and fifteen days later British troops occupied Philadelphia. Washington counterattacked in a dense fog at Germantown on October 4, but British reinforcements from Philadelphia under General Lord Charles Cornwallis arrived in time to repulse the Americans. Washington's army retired to winter quarters at Valley Forge, Pennsylvania, while Howe and his men remained for the winter in the relative comfort of Philadelphia, twenty miles away. Howe's plan had succeeded, up to a point. He had taken Philadelphia—or as Benjamin Franklin put it, Philadelphia had taken him. But the Tories there proved fewer than Howe had expected, and his decision to move on Philadelphia from the south, by way of Chesapeake Bay, put his forces even farther from Burgoyne's army in the north. Meanwhile, Burgoyne was stumbling into disaster in northern New York.

SARATOGA   General Burgoyne moved south toward Lake Champlain in 1777 with about 7,000 men, his mistress, and a baggage train that included some thirty carts carrying his personal trappings and a large supply of champagne. A powerful force on paper, the expedition was in fact much too cumbersome to be effective in the dense forests and rugged terrain of upstate New York. Burgoyne sent part of his army down the St. Lawrence River with Lieutenant Colonel Barry St. Leger, and at Fort Oswego they were joined by a force of Iroquois allies. The combined group headed east toward Albany. When they met the more mobile Americans, the British suffered two serious reversals.

At Oriskany, New York, on August 6, 1777, a band of militiamen thwarted an ambush by Tories and Indians and gained time for Benedict Arnold to bring 1,000 soldiers to the relief of Fort Stanwix, which had been under siege by St. Leger. Convinced they faced an even greater force than they actually did, the Indians deserted, and the Mohawk Valley was secured for the Patriot forces. To the east, at Bennington, Vermont, on August 16, New England militiamen

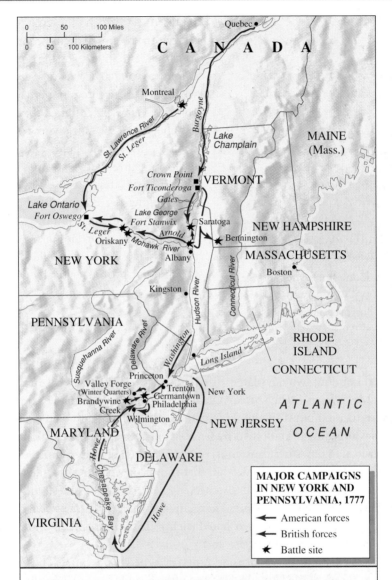

What were the consequences of Burgoyne's strategy of dividing the colonies with two British forces? How did life in Washington's camp at Valley Forge transform the American army? Why was Saratoga a turning point in the American Revolution?

General John Burgoyne

Commander of England's northern forces. Burgoyne and most of his British troops surrendered to the Americans at Saratoga on October 17, 1777.

repulsed a British foraging party. American reinforcements continued to gather, and after two sharp clashes Burgoyne pulled back to Saratoga, where American forces under General Horatio Gates surrounded him. On October 17, 1777, Burgoyne, resplendent in his scarlet, gold, and white uniform, surrendered to the plain-blue-coated Gates. Most of Burgoyne's 5,700 soldiers were imprisoned in Virginia, but Gentleman Johnny himself was permitted to go home, where he received an icy reception. The victory at Saratoga proved critically important to the American cause.

ALLIANCE WITH FRANCE On December 2, 1777, news of the surprising American triumph at Saratoga reached London; two days later it reached Paris, where it was celebrated almost as if it were a French victory. Its impact on the French made Saratoga a decisive turning point of the war. In 1776 the French had taken their first step toward aiding the colonists by sending fourteen ships with military supplies crucial to the Americans; most of the Continental army's gunpowder in the first years of the war came from that source. Besides arms, artillery, and ammunition, the French had also secretly sent clothing, shoes, and other supplies to help the Americans. After Saratoga the French saw their chance to strike a sharper blow at their hated enemy, Britain, and entered into serious negotiations with the Americans.

On February 6, 1778, France and America signed two treaties. The first officially recognized the United States and offered trade concessions, including important privileges to American shipping. The second agreed, first, that if France entered the war, both countries would fight until American independence was won; second, that neither would conclude a "truce or peace" without the consent of the other; and third, that each guaranteed the other's possessions in America "from the present time and forever against all other powers." France further bound itself to seek neither Canada nor other British possessions on the mainland of North America.

By June 1778 British vessels had fired on French ships, and the two nations were at war. In 1779, after extracting promises from the French to help it regain territories taken by the British in the previous war, including Gibraltar, Spain entered the war as an ally of France but not of the United States. The following year, Britain declared war on the Dutch, who persisted in carrying on a profitable trade with the French and shot Americans. The rebel farmers at Concord had indeed fired a shot "heard round the world." The American fight for independence had expanded into a world war, and the fighting now spread to the Mediterranean, Africa, India, the West Indies, and the high seas.

1778: BOTH SIDES REGROUP

THE REVOLUTIONARY ARMY AT VALLEY FORGE   For George Washington's army, bivouacked at Valley Forge, near Philadelphia, the winter of 1777–1778 was a season of intense suffering. The American force, encamped in crowded, lice-infested huts, endured cold, hunger, and disease. Some troops lacked shoes and blankets. Their makeshift log-and-mud huts offered little protection from the howling winds and bitter cold. Most of the army's horses died of exposure or starvation. By February 7,000 troops were too ill for duty. More than 2,500 soldiers died at Valley Forge; another 1,000 deserted. Fifty officers resigned on one December day. Several hundred more left before winter's end. By March the once-gaunt troops at Valley Forge saw their strength restored. Their improved health enabled Washington to begin a rigorous training program designed to bring unity and order to his motley force. By the end of March 1778, the ragtag soldiers were beginning to resemble a professional army. Moreover, as winter drew to an end, the army's morale gained strength from congressional promises of extra pay and bonuses after the war and from the news of the French alliance.

PEACE OVERTURES AND THE EVACUATION OF PHILADELPHIA After Saratoga, Lord North, the British prime minister, knew that winning the war was unlikely, but the king refused to let him either resign or make peace. On March 16, 1778, the House of Commons adopted a program that in effect granted all the American demands prior to independence. Parliament repealed the Townshend tea duty, the Massachusetts Government Act, and the Prohibitory Act, which had closed the colonies to commerce. It then dispatched a peace commission to negotiate an end to the war, but its members did not reach Philadelphia until after Congress had ratified the French treaties. Congress refused to begin any negotiations until American independence was recognized or British forces withdrawn, neither of which the royal commissioners could promise.

Unbeknownst to the British negotiators, the crown had already authorized the evacuation of British troops from Philadelphia, a withdrawal that further weakened what little bargaining power the commissioners had. After Saratoga, General Howe resigned his command, and Sir Henry Clinton replaced him. Fearing a blockade by the French fleet that had sailed from France in June 1778, Clinton pulled his troops out of Philadelphia and sent them to New York.

As General Clinton's forces marched eastward toward New York, Washington pursued them across New Jersey. On June 28 he engaged the British in an indecisive battle at Monmouth Court House. Clinton's forces then slipped away to New York City while Washington's army took up a position at White Plains, north of the city. From that time on, the northern theater, scene of the major campaigns and battles in the first years of the war, settled into a long stalemate.

ACTIONS ON THE FRONTIER The one major American success of 1778 occurred far from the New Jersey battlefields. Out to the west, at Forts Niagara and Detroit, the British under Colonel William Hamilton had incited frontier Tories and Indians to raid western settlements and had offered to pay for American scalps. To end the attacks, young George Rogers Clark took 175 frontiersmen on flatboats down the Ohio River in early 1778. They marched through the woods and on the evening of July 4 surprised the British at Kaskaskia (in present-day Illinois). At the end of the year, Clark marched his men (almost half of them French volunteers) through icy rivers and flooded prairies, sometimes in water neck deep, and captured an astonished British garrison at Vincennes (in present-day Indiana).

Meanwhile, Tories and Iroquois in western Pennsylvania continued to terrorize frontier settlements through the summer of 1778. In response, General Washington dispatched an expedition of 4,000 men to the area. At Newton, New York (near Elmira), the American force defeated the only serious opposition on August 29, 1779, and proceeded to carry out Washington's instruction that the Iroquois country be not "merely overrun but destroyed." The American troops burned about forty Indian villages, together with their orchards and food stores. The destruction broke the power of the Iroquois federation for all time, but sporadic encounters with various tribes of the region continued to the end of the war.

In the Kentucky territory, Daniel Boone and his small band of settlers risked constant attack by the Shawnees and their British and Tory allies. During the Revolution they survived frequent ambushes, at least seven skirmishes, and three pitched battles. In 1778 Boone and some thirty men, aided by their wives and children, held off an assault by more than 400 Indians at Boonesborough.

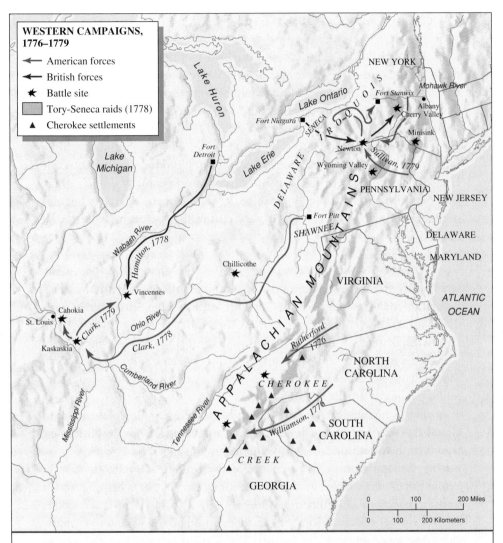

How did George Rogers Clark secure Cahokia and Vincennes? Why did the American army destroy Iroquois villages in 1779? Why were the skirmishes between settlers and Indian tribes significant for the future of the trans-Appalachian frontier?

Despite such ferocious fighting and dangerous circumstances, the white settlers refused to leave Kentucky. By thus weakening the major Indian tribes along the frontier, the American Revolution cleared the way for rapid settlement of the trans-Appalachian West after the war ended.

THE WAR IN THE SOUTH

At the end of 1778, the focus of the British military action shifted suddenly to the South. The whole region from Virginia southward had been free of major action since 1776. Now it would become the focus of the war as the British tested King George's belief that a sleeping Tory power in the South needed only the presence of a few redcoats to be awakened. From the point of view of British imperial goals, the southern colonies were ultimately more important than the northern ones because they produced valuable staple crops such as tobacco, indigo, tar, and turpentine. Eventually the war in the Carolinas not only involved opposing British and American armies but also degenerated into brutal guerrilla-style civil conflicts between Loyalists and Patriots.

THE CAROLINAS   In November 1778 British forces took Savannah, Georgia, and then headed toward Charleston, South Carolina, plundering plantation manors along the way. Outside Charleston the British awaited additional naval and land forces from New York and New Jersey. After their arrival with Generals Clinton and Cornwallis in February 1780, the British launched a massive assault against the Patriot defenders, and on May 12, in the single greatest American loss of the war. General Benjamin Lincoln surrendered the city and its 5,500 soldiers.

At that point, against Washington's advice, Congress turned to Horatio Gates, the victor of Saratoga, giving him command of the Revolutionary troops in the South. Meanwhile, General Clinton sailed back to New York, leaving General Cornwallis in charge of the British troops in the South. While Cornwallis was subduing the Carolina interior, Gates began a march on Camden, South Carolina, then held by the British. Cornwallis's troops clashed with Gates's forces outside Camden in August 1780, and the American army was routed by the British. The Patriots retreated all the way to Hillsborough, North Carolina, 160 miles away.

Cornwallis had South Carolina just about under British control, but his cavalry leaders, Sir Banastre Tarleton and Patrick Ferguson, who mobilized Tory militiamen, overreached themselves in their effort to subdue the Whigs. "Bloody Tarleton" ordered rebels killed after they surrendered. Ferguson sealed his doom when he threatened to march over the mountains and hang the Revolutionary leaders there. Instead, the feisty "overmountain men" went after Ferguson. They caught him and his Tories on Kings Mountain, along the border between North Carolina and South Carolina. There, on October 7, 1780, they routed his force. Kings Mountain was the turning point of the war in the South. By proving that the British were not invincible, the American victory emboldened small farmers to join guerrilla bands under such partisan leaders as Francis Marion, "the Swamp Fox," and Thomas Sumter, "the Carolina Gamecock."

While the overmountain men were closing in on Ferguson, Congress chose a new commander for the southern theater, General Nathanael Greene, "the fighting Quaker" of Rhode Island. Greene shrewdly lured Cornwallis and his troops, making them chase the Americans across the Carolinas, thus taxing British energy and supplies. Splitting his army, Greene sent out about 700 men under General Daniel Morgan to engage Tarleton's 1,000 men at Cowpens, South Carolina, on January 17, 1781. The Americans routed the British; Tarleton and a handful of cavalry escaped, but more than 100 of his men were killed, and more than 700 were taken prisoner. Morgan and his men then linked up with Greene's main force, and the combined army offered battle at Guilford Courthouse, North Carolina (near what became Greensboro), on March 15, 1781. After inflicting heavy losses, Greene withdrew, and Cornwallis was left in possession of the field, but at a cost of nearly 100 men killed and more than 400 wounded.

Cornwallis's army marched off toward Wilmington, on the North Carolina coast, to take on supplies. Greene returned to South Carolina in the hope of drawing Cornwallis after him or forcing the British to give up the state. There he joined forces with the local guerrillas and in a series of brilliant actions kept losing battles while winning the war. By September 1781 he had narrowed British control in the Deep South to Charleston and Savannah, although for more than a year longer Whigs and Tories slashed at each other "with savage fury" in the backcountry.

Meanwhile, Cornwallis's army had headed north, away from Greene's forces, reasoning that Virginia must be eliminated as a source of reinforcement before the Carolinas could be subdued. In 1781 Cornwallis met up with the traitor Benedict Arnold, now a *British* general, who had been engaged in a war of maneuver against the American forces. Arnold, from July until September 1780, had been the American commander at West Point, New York. Overweening in ambition, lacking in moral scruples, and a reckless spender on his fashionable wife, he had nursed a grudge against Washington over an official reprimand for his extravagances as commander of reoccupied Philadelphia. Arnold crassly plotted to sell out the American garrison at West Point to the British, even suggesting how they might capture George Washington himself. The American seizure of the British go-between, Major John André, ended Arnold's plot. Forewarned that his plan had been discovered, Arnold joined the British in New York, and the Americans hanged André as a spy.

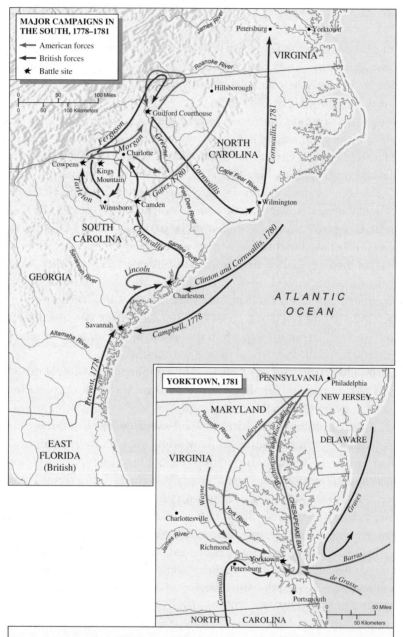

Why did the British suddenly shift their campaign to the South? Why
were the battles at Savannah and Charleston major victories for the
British? How did Nathaniel Greene undermine British control of the
Deep South? Why did Cornwallis march to Virginia and camp at
Yorktown? How was the French navy crucial to the American victory?
Why was Cornwallis forced to surrender?

YORKTOWN   When Lord Cornwallis linked up with Benedict Arnold at Petersburg, Virginia, their combined forces totaled 7,200, far more than the small American army they faced. The arrival of American reinforcements led Cornwallis to pick Yorktown, Virginia, as a defensible site. There appeared to be little reason to worry about a siege, since General Washington's main land force seemed preoccupied with attacking New York, and the British navy controlled American waters.

To be sure, there was a small American navy, but it was no match for the British fleet. The American fleet was little more than a nuisance to the British. But at a critical point, thanks to the French navy, the British lost control of the Chesapeake waters. Indeed, it is impossible to imagine an American victory in the Revolution without the assistance of the French. As long as the British navy maintained supremacy at sea, the Americans could not hope to force a settlement to their advantage.

Then, in 1781, the elements for a combined American-French action suddenly fell into place. As General Cornwallis moved his British army into Virginia in May, Washington persuaded the commander of the French army to join forces for an attack on New York. The two armies linked up in July, but before they could strike at New York, word came from the West Indies that an entire French fleet and some 3,000 soldiers under Admiral de Grasse were bound for Chesapeake Bay. Washington and his troops secretly slipped out of New York and met up with the French in Philadelphia; the combined American-French forces immediately set out toward Yorktown. Meanwhile, a French fleet that had been blockaded by the British at Newport evaded the barricade and sailed south toward Chesapeake Bay.

On August 30 Admiral de Grasse's fleet reached Yorktown, where his troops joined the American force already watching Cornwallis. On September 6, the day after a British fleet under Admiral Thomas Graves appeared, de Grasse gave battle and forced the British to abandon the effort to relieve Cornwallis, whose fate was quickly sealed. When the siege of Yorktown began, on September 28, the situation already looked bleak for Cornwallis. Washington commanded 16,000 soldiers, double the size of the British army. Unable to break the siege or escape, Cornwallis was forced to surrender. On October 17, 1781, four years to the day after Saratoga, a red-coated drummer boy climbed atop the British parapet and began beating the call for a truce. Cornwallis sued for peace, and on October 19, their colors cased (that is, sheathed in a cloth covering), the British force marched out to the tune of "The World Turned Upside Down." Cornwallis himself claimed to be too "ill" to appear.

Surrender of Lord Cornwallis

The pivotal British surrender at Yorktown in 1794.

NEGOTIATIONS

Whatever lingering hopes of victory the British may have harbored vanished at Yorktown. "Oh God, it is all over," Lord North groaned at news of the surrender. On February 27, 1782, the House of Commons voted against continuing the war and on March 5 authorized the crown to make peace. Peace negotiations between the American diplomats—Ben Franklin, John Jay, and John Adams—and the British began in Paris, but their difficult task was immediately complicated by the French commitment to Spain. Both the United States and Spain were allied with France but not with each other. America was bound by its French alliance to fight on until the French made peace, and the French were bound to help the Spanish recover Gibraltar from England. Unable to deliver Gibraltar, or so the tough-minded Jay reasoned, the French might try to bargain off American land west of the Appalachians in its place. Fearful that the French were angling for a separate peace with the British, Jay persuaded Franklin to play the same game. Ignoring their instructions to consult fully with the French, they agreed to further talks with the British. On November 30, 1782, the talks produced a preliminary treaty with

Great Britain. If it violated the spirit of the alliance, it did not violate the strict letter of the treaty with France, for the French minister was notified the day before it was signed, and final agreement still depended on a Franco-British settlement.

THE TREATY OF PARIS   Early in 1783 France and Spain gave up trying to acquire Gibraltar and reached an armistice with Britain. The Treaty of Paris was finally signed on September 3, 1783. In accord with the bargain already struck, Great Britain recognized the independence of the United States and agreed to a Mississippi River boundary to the west. Both the northern and the southern borders left ambiguities that would require further definition. Florida, as it turned out, passed back to Spain. The British further granted the Americans the "liberty" of fishing off Newfoundland and in the Gulf of St. Lawrence and the right to dry their catch on the unsettled coast of Canada. On the matter of pre–Revolutionary War debts owed by Americans, the best the British could get was a promise that British merchants should "meet with no legal impediment" in seeking to collect them. And on the tender point of Loyalists whose property had been confiscated, the negotiators agreed that Congress would "earnestly recommend" to the states the restoration of confiscated property. Each of the last two points was little more than a face-saving gesture to the British.

THE POLITICAL REVOLUTION

REPUBLICAN IDEOLOGY   The Americans had won their War of Independence. Had they undergone a political revolution as well? John Adams offered an answer: "The Revolution was effected before the war commenced. The Revolution was in the minds and hearts of the people. . . . This radical change in the principles, opinions, sentiments, and affections of the people, was the real American Revolution."

Yet Adams's observation ignores the fact that the Revolutionary War itself served as the catalyst for a prolonged debate about what forms of government would best serve the new American republic. The conventional British model of mixed government sought to balance the monarchy, the aristocracy, and the common people so as to protect individual liberty. Because of the more fluid and democratic nature of their new society, however, Americans knew that they must develop new political assumptions and institutions. They had no monarchy or aristocracy. Yet how could sovereignty reside in the common people? How could Americans ensure the survival of a

NORTH AMERICA, 1783

- England
- United States
- Spain

How did France's treaties with Spain complicate the peace-treaty negotiations with the British? What were the terms of the Peace of Paris? Why might the ambiguities in the treaty have led to conflicts among the Americans, the Spanish, and the English?

republican form of government, long assumed to be the most fragile? The war thus provoked a flurry of state constitution making that remains unique in history. Ideas such as the contract theory of government, the sovereignty of the people, the separation of powers, and natural rights found their way quickly, almost automatically, into the frames of government that were devised while the fight went on—amid other urgent business.

The very idea of republican government—a balanced polity animated by civic virtue—was a far more radical departure in that day than it would seem to later generations. Through the lens of republican thinking, Americans began to see themselves in a new light. As free citizens of a republic, Americans would cast off the aristocratic corruptions of the Old World and usher in a new reign of individual liberty and public virtue. The new American republic, in other words, would endure as long as the majority of the people were virtuous and willingly placed the good of society above the self-interest of individuals. Herein lay the hope and the danger of the American experiment in popular government: even as leaders enthusiastically fashioned new state constitutions, they feared that their experiments in republicanism would fail because of a lack of civic virtue among the people.

STATE CONSTITUTIONS Most political experimentation between 1776 and 1787 occurred at the state level. At the onset of the fighting, every colony experienced the departure of its governor and other officials and usually the expulsion of Loyalists from its assembly, which then assumed power as a provincial "congress" or "convention." But those legislatures were acting as revolutionary bodies without any legal basis for the exercise of authority. In two states this presented little difficulty. Connecticut and Rhode Island, which as corporate colonies had been virtually little republics, simply purged their charters of any reference to colonial ties. Massachusetts followed their example until 1780.

In the other states the prevailing notions of social contract and popular sovereignty led to written constitutions that specified the framework and powers of government. Constitution making began even before independence. In May 1776 Congress advised the colonies to set up new governments "under the authority of the people." The first state constitutions varied mainly in detail. They formed governments much like the colonial administrations, but with elected governors and senates instead of appointed governors and councils. Generally they embodied, sometimes explicitly, a separation of powers as a safeguard against abuses. Most of them also included a bill of rights that protected the time-honored rights of petition, freedom of speech, trial by jury, freedom from self-incrimination, and the like. Most tended to limit the powers of governors and increase the powers of the legislatures, which had led the people in their quarrels with the colonial governors.

THE ARTICLES OF CONFEDERATION The new central American government, like the state governments, grew out of an extralegal revolutionary body. The Continental Congress exercised government powers without any constitutional sanction before 1781. Plans for a permanent national government emerged very early, however, when a committee headed by John Dickinson produced a draft constitution, the Articles of Confederation and Perpetual Union, which was adopted in November 1777.

The central government envisaged by the Articles of Confederation had little authority. Congress was intended not as a legislature, nor as a sovereign entity unto itself, but as a collective substitute for the monarch. In essence it was to be a plural executive rather than a parliamentary body. For all the weaknesses of the central government proposed by the Articles of Confederation, it represented the most appropriate structure for the new nation. After all, the Revolution on the battlefields had yet to be won, and the statesmen did not have the luxury of engaging in prolonged and perhaps fratricidal debates over the distribution of power that proposals for other systems would have provoked. There would be time later for modifications.

THE SOCIAL REVOLUTION

Political revolutions often spawn social revolutions, and the turmoil of the Revolution allowed outlets for long-festering frustrations among the lower ranks. What did the Revolution mean to those workers, servants, farmers, and freed slaves who participated in the Stamp Act demonstrations, supported the boycotts, idolized Tom Paine, and fought with Washington and Greene? The more conservative Patriots would have been content to replace royal officials with the rich, the wellborn, and the able and let it go at that. But more radical revolutionaries, in the apt phrase of one historian, raised the question not only of home rule but also of who shall rule at home.

EQUALITY AND ITS LIMITS   This spirit of equality weakened old habits of deference. Participation in the army or militia activated men who had taken little interest in politics. The new political opportunities afforded by the creation of state governments thus led more ordinary citizens to participate than ever before. The social base of the new legislatures was much broader than that of the old assemblies.

Men fighting for their liberty found it difficult to justify denying other white men the rights of suffrage and representation. The property qualifications for voting, which already admitted an overwhelming majority of white men, were lowered still further in some states. In Pennsylvania, Delaware, North Carolina, and Georgia, any male taxpayer could vote, although officeholders had to meet

Social Democracy

In this watercolor by Benjamin Latrobe, a gentleman plays billiards with artisans, suggesting that "the spirit of independence was converted into equality."

more stringent property requirements. In the state legislatures younger men often replaced older men, some of whom had been Loyalists. More often than not, the newcomers were men with less property and little education. Some states concentrated much power in a legislature chosen by a wide suffrage, but not even Pennsylvania, which adopted the most radical state constitution, went quite so far as to grant universal male suffrage.

New developments in land tenure that grew out of the Revolution extended the democratic trends of suffrage requirements. The state legislatures seized Tory estates. This land was of small consequence, however, in comparison to the unsettled land that had been at the disposal of the crown and proprietors. Now in the hands of state assemblies, much of this land was distributed as bonuses to veterans of the war. Western lands, formerly closed by the Royal Proclamation of 1763 and the Quebec Act of 1774, were soon thrown open to settlers.

THE PARADOX OF SLAVERY   The Revolutionary generation of leaders was the first to confront slavery and consider abolishing it. The principles of liberty and equality so crucial to the rebellion against England had clear implications for America's enslaved blacks. Thomas Jefferson's draft of the Declaration of Independence had indicted the king for having violated the "most sacred rights of life and liberty of a distant people" by encouraging the slave trade in the colonies, but Jefferson had deleted the clause "in complaisance to

South Carolina and Georgia." After independence all the states except Georgia stopped the importation of African slaves, although South Carolina later reopened it.

African-American soldiers or sailors were present at most major Revolutionary battles, from Lexington to Yorktown, most of them serving on the Loyalist side. Slaves who served in the cause of independence got their freedom and in some cases land bounties. But the British army, which freed tens of thousands of slaves during the war, was a greater instrument of emancipation than the American forces. Most of the freed blacks found their way to Canada or to British colonies in the Caribbean. American Whigs showed no mercy to blacks caught aiding or abetting the British cause. A Charleston mob hanged and then burned Thomas Jeremiah, a free black man who was convicted of telling slaves that the British "were come to help the poor Negroes."

In the northern states, which had fewer slaves than the southern states, the doctrines of liberty led swiftly to emancipation for all, either during the fighting or shortly afterward. South of Pennsylvania the potential consequences of emancipation were so staggering—South Carolina had a black majority—that whites refused to extend the principle of liberty to their slaves. Although some southern slaveholders were troubled, most could not bring themselves to free their own slaves. Anti-slavery sentiment in the southern states went only so far as to relax the manumission laws under which owners might voluntarily free their slaves. Some 10,000 enslaved Virginians were manumitted during the 1780s. By the outbreak of the Civil War, in 1861, approximately half the blacks living in Maryland were free.

Slaves, especially in the upper South, also earned their freedom through their own actions during the Revolutionary era, frequently by running away. They often gravitated to the growing number of African-American communities in the North. Because of emancipation laws in the northern states, and with the formation of free black neighborhoods in the North and in several southern cities, runaways found refuge and the opportunities for new lives. It is estimated that 55,000 slaves fled to freedom during the Revolution.

THE STATUS OF WOMEN   The logic of liberty applied to the status of women as much as to that of African Americans. Women had remained essentially confined to the domestic sphere during the eighteenth century. They could not vote or preach or hold office. Few had access to formal education. Although in some colonies women could own property and execute contracts, in other colonies they could not legally own even their own clothes, and they had no legal rights over their children. Divorces were extremely difficult to obtain.

The Revolution offered women new opportunities and engendered in many a new outlook. The war also drew women at least temporarily into new roles. They plowed fields and melted down pots and pans to make shot. Women also served the armies in various roles—by handling supplies and serving as spies or couriers. Wives often followed their husbands to army camps, where they nursed the wounded and sick, cooked and washed for the able, and frequently buried the dead. On occasion, women took their place in the firing line.

To be sure, most women retained the domestic outlook that had long been imposed upon them, but a few free-spirited reformers demanded equal treatment. In an essay titled "On the Equality of the Sexes," written in 1779 and published in 1790, Judith Sargent Murray of Gloucester, Massachusetts, stressed that women were perfectly capable of excelling outside the domestic sphere.

Elizabeth Freeman

Also known as Mum Bett, was born around 1742 and sold as a slave to a Massachusetts family. She won her freedom by claiming in court that the Bill of Rights and the new state constitution gave liberty to all, and her case contributed to the eventual abolition of slavery in Massachusetts. One of Freeman's great-grandchildren was scholar and civil rights leader W.E.B. Du Bois.

Early in the Revolutionary struggle, Abigail Adams, one of the most learned women of the time, wrote her husband, John: "In the new Code of Laws which I suppose it will be necessary for you to make I desire you would remember the Ladies. . . . Do not put such unlimited power into the hands of the Husbands." Since men were "Naturally Tyrannical," she stressed, "why then, not put it out of the power of the vicious and the Lawless to use us with cruelty and indignity." Otherwise, "the Ladies" would "foment a Rebellion, and will not hold ourselves bound by any Laws in which we have no voice, or Representation."

John Adams expressed surprise that women might be discontented, but he clearly knew the privileges enjoyed by males and was determined to retain them: "Depend upon it, we know better than to repeal our Masculine systems." The supposedly more liberal Thomas Jefferson agreed with John Adams on the matter. When asked about women's voting rights, he replied

that "the tender breasts of ladies were not formed for political convulsion."
The legal status of women thus did not benefit dramatically from the egalitarian doctrine unleashed by the Revolution. Married women in most states
still forfeited control of their own property to their husbands, and women
gained no political rights.

FREEDOM OF RELIGION   The Revolution also set in motion a transition from the toleration of religious dissent to a complete freedom of religion in the separation of church and state. The Anglican Church, established
as the official state religion in five colonies and parts of two others, was especially vulnerable because of its association with the crown and because non-
Anglicans outnumbered Anglicans in all states except Virginia. And all but
Virginia eliminated tax support for the church before the fighting was over.
In 1776 the Virginia Declaration of Rights (a bill of rights) guaranteed the
free exercise of religion, and in 1786 the Virginia Statute of Religious Freedom (written by Thomas Jefferson) declared that "no man shall be compelled to frequent or support any religious worship, place or ministry whatsoever" and "that all men shall be free to profess and by argument to maintain,

Religious Development

The Congregational Church developed a national presence in the early nineteenth
century, and Lemuel Haynes, depicted here, was its first African-American preacher.

their opinions in matters of religion." These statutes and the Revolutionary ideology that justified them helped shape the course that religion would take in the new United States: pluralistic and voluntary rather than monolithic and state supported.

In churches as in government, the Revolution set off a period of constitution making as some of the first national church bodies emerged. In 1784 the Methodists, who at first were an offshoot of the Anglicans, came together in a general conference at Baltimore. The Anglican Church, rechristened Episcopal, gathered in a series of meetings that by 1789 had united the various dioceses in a federal union; in 1789 the Presbyterians also held their first general assembly, in Philadelphia. That same year the Catholic Church got its first higher official in the United States when John Carroll was named bishop of Baltimore.

The Emergence of an American Culture

The Revolution generated among some Americans a sense of common nationality. One of the first ways in which to forge a national consciousness was through the annual celebration of the new nation's independence from Great Britain. On July 2, 1776, when the Second Continental Congress had resolved "that these United Colonies are, and of right ought to be, free and independent states," John Adams had written his wife, Abigail, that future generations would remember that date as their "day of deliverance."

As it turned out, however, Americans fastened not upon July 2 but upon July 4 as their Independence Day. To be sure, it was on the Fourth that Congress formally adopted the Declaration of Independence and ordered it to be printed and distributed throughout the states, but America by then had been officially independent for two days. Independence Day quickly became the most popular and most important public ritual in the United States. Huge numbers of people from all walks of life suspended their normal routine in order to devote a day to parades, formal orations, and fireworks displays. In the process the infant republic began to create its own myth of national identity that transcended local or regional concerns and forged a feeling of national unity.

AMERICA'S "DESTINY"   In a special sense, American nationalism embodied an idea of divine mission. Many people, at least since the time of the Pilgrims, had thought of America as singled out by God for a special identity, a special mission. John Winthrop referred to the Puritan commonwealth as representing a "city upon a hill," and Jonathan Edwards believed that God had singled out America as "the glorious renovator of the world." This sense of mission was neither limited to New England nor rooted solely in Calvinism. From the democratic rhetoric of Thomas Jefferson to the pragmatism of George Washington to heady toasts bellowed in South Carolina taverns, patriots everywhere articulated a special role for American leadership in history. The mission was now a call to lead the way toward liberty and equality. Meanwhile, however, Americans had to address more immediate problems created by their new nationhood. The Philadelphia patriot, doctor, and scientist Benjamin Rush issued a prophetic statement in 1787: "The American war is over: but this is far from being the case with the American Revolution. On the contrary, but the first act of the great drama is closed."

MAKING CONNECTIONS

- The American Revolution was the starting point for the foreign policy of the United States. Many of the specific foreign concerns that will be discussed in Chapters 8 and 9 sprang from issues directly relating to the Revolution.

- Much of what became Jacksonian democracy (introduced in Chapter 10) can be traced to social and political movements associated with the American Revolution.

- The innovations set forth in the new state constitutions during the Revolution created a reservoir of ideas and experience that formed the basis for the creation of the federal Constitution in 1787, as we will see in Chapter 7.

FURTHER READING

The Revolutionary War is the subject of Colin Bonwick's *The American Revolution* (1991), Theodore Draper's *A Struggle for Power: The American Revolution* (1996), Gordon S. Wood's *The Radicalism of the American Revolution* (1991), Benson Bobrick's *Angel in the Whirlwind: The Triumph of the American Revolution* (1997), and Jeremy Black's *War for America: The Fight for Independence, 1775–1783* (1991).

On the social history of the Revolutionary War, see John W. Shy's *A People Numerous and Armed: Reflections on the Military Struggle for American Independence,* rev. ed. (1990), Charles Royster's *A Revolutionary People at War: The Continental Army and American Character, 1775–1783* (1979), Lawrence Delbe Cress's *Citizens in Arms: The Army and the Militia in American Society to the War of 1812* (1982), and E. Wayne Carp's *To Starve the Army at Pleasure: Continental Army Administration and American Political Culture, 1775–1783* (1984). Colin G. Calloway tells the neglected story of the Indian experiences in the Revolution in *The American Revolution in Indian Country: Crisis and Diversity in Native American Communities* (1995).

Why some Americans remained loyal to the crown is the subject of Bernard Bailyn's *The Ordeal of Thomas Hutchinson* (1974), Robert M. Calhoon's *The Loyalists in Revolutionary America, 1760–1781* (1973), and Mary Beth Norton's *The British-Americans: The Loyalist Exiles in England, 1774–1789* (1972).

The definitive study of African Americans during the Revolutionary era remains Benjamin Quarles's *The Negro in the American Revolution* (1961). Mary Beth Norton's *Liberty's Daughters: The Revolutionary Experience of American Women, 1750–1800,* new ed. (1996) and Linda K. Kerber's *Women of the Republic: Intellect and Ideology in Revolutionary America* (1980) document the role women played in securing independence. Joy Day Buel and Richard Buel Jr.'s *The Way of Duty: A Woman and Her Family in Revolutionary America* (1984) shows the impact of the Revolution on one New England family.

The standard introduction to the diplomacy of the Revolutionary era is Jonathan R. Dull's *A Diplomatic History of the American Revolution* (1985).

7

SHAPING A
FEDERAL UNION

FOCUS QUESTIONS

- What were the achievements and weaknesses of the Confederation government?
- What were the issues involved in writing the Constitution?
- What were the debates surrounding the ratification of the Constitution?

To answer these questions and access additional review material, please visit www.wwnorton.com/studyspace.

In an address to fellow graduates at the Harvard commencement ceremony in 1787, young John Quincy Adams, the son of John and Abigail Adams, lamented "this critical period" when the United States was struggling to establish itself as a new nation. Historians thereafter used his phrase to designate the years when the infant republic operated under the Articles of Confederation, 1781 to 1787. Fear of centralized government power dominated the period and limited the scope and effectiveness of the new government. Yet while there were weaknesses of the Confederation, there were also major achievements during the so-called critical period. Moreover, lessons learned under the Confederation would prompt the formulation of a national constitution intended to balance central and local authority.

THE CONFEDERATION

The Confederation Congress had little authority. It could only request money from the states; it could make treaties with foreign countries but could not enforce them; it could borrow money but lacked the means to ensure repayment. Congress was virtually helpless to cope with the postwar problems of diplomacy and economic depression, problems that would have challenged the resources of a much stronger government. Yet in spite of its handicaps, the Confederation Congress somehow managed to keep afloat and to lay important foundations. It concluded the Treaty of Paris in 1783, created the first federal executive departments, and formulated principles of land distribution and territorial government that guided westward expansion all the way to the Pacific coast.

THE ARTICLES OF CONFEDERATION   When the Articles of Confederation took effect, in 1781, they did little more than legalize the status quo. Congress had full power over foreign affairs and questions of war and peace; it could decide disputes between the states; it had authority over coinage, the postal service, and Indian affairs and responsibility for the government of the western territories. But it had no courts and no power to enforce its resolutions and ordinances. It also had no power to levy taxes, but had to rely on requests submitted to the states, which state legislatures could ignore—and usually did.

The states, after their battles with Parliament, were in no mood for a strong central government. Congress could not regulate interstate and foreign commerce and for certain important acts a "special majority" was required. Nine states had to approve measures dealing with war, privateering, treaties, coinage, finances, or the army and navy. Unanimous approval by the states was needed to levy tariffs (often called duties) on imports. Amendments to the articles also required unanimous ratification by the states.

The Confederation had neither an executive nor a judicial branch; there were no administrative head of government (only the president of the Congress, chosen annually) and no federal courts. In 1781, however, anticipating ratification of the Articles of Confederation, Congress set up three government departments: Foreign Affairs, Finance, and War. Each was to have a single head responsible to Congress. Given time and stability, Congress and the department heads might have evolved into something like the parliamentary cabinet system. As it turned out, these agencies were the forerunners of the government departments to be established under the Constitution.

FINANCE   Since there was neither president nor prime minister, but only the presiding officer of Congress and its secretary, the closest thing to an executive head of the Confederation was Robert Morris, who was superintendent of finance in the final years of the war. Morris wanted to make both himself and the Confederation more powerful. He envisioned a coherent program of taxation and debt management to make the government financially stable.

As the foundation of his plan, Morris secured in 1781 a congressional charter for the Bank of North America, which would hold government cash, lend money to the government, and issue currency. But his program depended ultimately upon a secure income for the Confederation government, and it proved impossible to win the unanimous approval of the states for the necessary amendments to the Articles of Confederation. As a consequence the Confederation never did put its finances in order. The Continental currency quickly proved worthless and was never redeemed. The government debt, domestic and foreign, grew from $11 million to $28 million as Congress paid off citizens' and soldiers' claims. Each year, Congress ran a deficit in its operating expenses.

LAND POLICY   Congress might ultimately have hoped to draw an independent income from the sale of western lands, but throughout the Confederation period little acreage was sold. The Confederation nevertheless dealt more effectively with the western lands than with anything else. There Congress had direct authority, at least on paper. Thinly populated by Indians, French settlers, and a growing number of American squatters, the region north of the Ohio River and west of the Appalachian Mountains had long been the site of overlapping claims by colonies and speculators.

Between 1784 and 1787 policies for western development emerged in three major ordinances of the Confederation Congress. These documents, which rank among its greatest achievements —and among the most important in American history—set precedents that the United States would follow in its future expansion. Thomas Jefferson's inclination was to grant self-government to western territories at an early stage, allowing settlers to meet and choose their own officials. Under Jefferson's proposed ordinance of 1784, when a territory's population equaled that of the smallest existing state, the territory would achieve full statehood.

In the Land Ordinance of 1785, the delegates outlined a plan of surveys and sales that eventually stamped a rectangular pattern on much of the nation's surface. Wherever Indian titles had been extinguished, the Northwest was to be surveyed and six-mile-square townships established along east-west and north-south lines. Each township was in turn to be divided into thirty-six sections, each one mile square (or 640 acres). The 640-acre sections were to be auctioned for no less than $640. Such terms favored land speculators, of course, since few common folk had that much money or were able to work that much land. In later years new land laws would make smaller lots available at lower prices, but in 1785 Congress confronted an empty Treasury, and delegates believed this system would raise the needed funds.

Spurred by the plans for land sales and settlement, Congress drafted the Northwest Ordinance of 1787. The new plan abandoned the commitment to early self-government in the territories. Because of the trouble that might be expected from squatters who were clamoring for free land, the Northwest Ordinance transition required a period of colonial. At first the territory fell subject to a governor, a secretary, and three judges, all chosen by Congress. When any territory in the region had a population of 5,000 free male adults, it could choose an assembly, and Congress would name a governing council. The governor would have a veto, and so would Congress.

The resemblance of these territorial governments to the old royal colonies is clear, but there were three significant differences. For one, the Northwest Ordinance anticipated statehood when any territory's population reached 60,000 "free inhabitants." At that point a convention could be called to draft a state constitution and apply to Congress for statehood. For another, it included a bill of rights that guaranteed religious freedom, proportional representation, trial by jury, habeas corpus, and the application of common law. Finally, the ordinance excluded slavery permanently from the Northwest. This decision proved fateful. As the progress of emancipation in the existing states gradually freed all slaves in the North, the Ohio River boundary of the Old Northwest extended the line between freedom and slavery all the way to the Mississippi River, encompassing what would become the states of Ohio, Indiana, Illinois, Michigan, and Wisconsin.

The Northwest Ordinance had an importance larger than establishing a formal procedure for transforming territories into states. It represented a sharp break with the imperialistic assumption behind European expansion into the Western Hemisphere. The new states were to be admitted to the American republic as equals rather than be treated as subordinate colonies.

The lands south of the Ohio River followed a different process of development. Title to the western lands remained with Georgia, North Carolina, and Virginia for the time being, but settlement proceeded at a far more rapid pace during and after the Revolution with substantial population centers growing up in Kentucky and Tennessee.

The Iroquois and Cherokees, battered during the Revolution, were in no position to resist encroachments. During the mid-1780s the Iroquois were forced to cede land in western New York and Pennsylvania, and the Cherokees gave up all claims in South Carolina, much of western North Carolina, and large portions of present-day Kentucky and Tennessee. At the same time the major Ohio tribes dropped their claim to most of Ohio, except for a segment bordering the western part of Lake Erie. The Creeks, pressed by Georgia to cede portions of their lands in 1784–1785, went to war in the summer of 1786 with covert aid from Spanish Florida. When Spanish support lapsed, however, the Creek chief struck a bargain in 1791 that gave the Creeks favorable trade arrangements with the United States but did not restore the lost land.

TRADE AND THE ECONOMY   The American economy after the Revolution went through a turbulent transition. Although farmers enmeshed in local markets maintained their livelihood during the Revolutionary era, commercial agriculture dependent upon trade with foreign markets suffered a severe downturn. In New England and much of the backcountry, fighting seldom interrupted the tempo of farming, and the producers of foodstuffs for local markets benefited in particular from rising prices and wartime demands. Virginia suffered a loss of enslaved workers, most of them carried off by the British. The British decision to close its West Indian colonies to American trade devastated what had been a thriving commerce in timber, wheat, and other foodstuffs.

Merchants suffered far more wrenching adjustments during the Revolution than farmers. Cut out of the British mercantile system, they had to find new markets. Circumstances that impoverished some enriched those who financed privateers, supplied the armies on both sides, and hoarded precious goods while demand and prices soared. By the end of the war, a strong sentiment for free trade had developed in both Britain and America. In the memorable year 1776 the Scottish economist Adam Smith published *The Wealth of Nations,* a classic manifesto against mercantilism. Some British statesmen embraced the new gospel of free trade, but the public and Parliament would cling to mercantilism for years to come.

British trade with the United States resumed after 1783. American ships were allowed to deliver American products and return to the United States with British goods, but they could not carry British goods anywhere else. The pent-up demand for consumer goods created a vigorous market in exports to America, fueled by British credit and the hard money that had come into the new nation with foreign aid, the expenditures of foreign armies, and

Merchants' Counting House

Americans involved in overseas trade, such as the merchants depicted here, had been sharply affected by the dislocations of war.

wartime trade and privateering. The result was a quick cycle of postwar boom and bust, a buying spree followed by a money shortage and economic troubles that lasted several years.

In colonial days the chronic trade deficit with Britain had been offset by the influx of coins from trade with the West Indies. Now American ships found themselves legally excluded from the British West Indies. But the islands still demanded wheat, fish, lumber, and other products from the mainland, and American shippers had not lost their talent for smuggling. By 1787 Americans were also trading with the Dutch, the Swedes, the Prussians, the Moroccans, and the Chinese, and American seaports were flourishing more than ever. By 1790 the value of American commerce and exports had far exceeded the trade of the colonies. Although most of the exports were the products of American forests, fields, and fisheries, during and after the war more workers had turned to small-scale manufacturing—shoes, textiles, soap—mainly for domestic markets.

DIPLOMACY   The achievements of the energetic young nation are more visible in hindsight than they were at the time. Until 1787 the shortcomings and failures of the Confederation government remained far more apparent— and the advocates of a stronger central government were extremely vocal on the subject. In diplomacy there remained the nagging problems of relations with Great Britain and Spain, both of which still kept military posts on American soil and conspired with Indians and white settlers in the West. The British, despite the peace treaty of 1783, held on to a string of forts along the Canadian border. From these outposts they kept a hand in the lucrative fur trade and maintained a degree of influence with the Indian tribes, whom they were suspected of stirring up to make sporadic attacks on American settlers.

Another major irritant was the confiscation of Loyalist property. The peace treaty with Britain had obligated Congress to end confiscations of Tory property, to guarantee immunity to Loyalists for twelve months, during which they could return and wind up their affairs, and to recommend that the states return confiscated property. Persecutions, even lynchings, of Loyalists occurred even after the end of the war. After 1783 some Loyalists returned unmolested, however, and resumed their lives in their former homes. By the end of 1787, moreover, all the states had rescinded laws discriminating against former Tories.

With Spain the chief issues were the southern boundary and the right to navigate the Mississippi River. According to the preliminary treaty with Britain, the United States claimed as its boundary a line running eastward from the mouth of the Yazoo River in what is now Mississippi. The treaty ending the war with Britain had also given Americans the right to navigate the Mississippi River to its mouth, near New Orleans, but the river was entirely within Spanish Louisiana in its lower reaches. The right to navigate the Mississippi River was crucial because of the growing American settlements upriver in Kentucky and Tennessee, but in 1784 Louisiana's Spanish governor closed the river to American commerce. In 1785 the Spanish government sent to America an ambassador who entered into long but fruitless negotiations with John Jay, the secretary for foreign affairs, over navigation of the Mississippi River and the southern border of the United States. The issue of American access to the lower Mississippi would remain unsettled for nearly another decade.

THE CONFEDERATION'S PROBLEMS   Of greatest concern to most Americans after the Revolution were protection of infant American industries from foreign competition and the currency shortage. Merchants and artisans were frustrated by British policies excluding them from British markets, and in retaliation they sought from the states tariffs on foreign goods (taxes on imports) that competed with theirs. The country would be on its way to economic independence, they argued, if only the money that flowed into the country were invested in domestic manufactures instead of being paid out for foreign goods. Nearly all the states gave some preference to American goods, but the lack of consistency in their laws put them at cross purposes, and so urban mechanics, along with merchants, were drawn into the movement for a stronger central government in the interest of uniform regulation of trade.

Domestic Industry

American craftsmen, such as this cabinet-maker, favored tariffs against foreign goods that competed with theirs.

The shortage of cash and other economic difficulties gave rise to more immediate demands for paper currency as legal tender, for postponement of tax and debt payments, and for laws to "stay" the foreclosure of mortgages. Farmers who had profited during the war found themselves squeezed afterward by depressed crop prices and mounting debts while merchants sorted out and opened up new trade routes. Creditors demanded hard money, but it was in short supply—and paper money was both scarce and virtually worthless after the depreciation of the Continental currency. The result was an outcry among debtor groups for relief, and around 1785 the demand for new paper money became the most divisive issue in state politics. In 1785–1786 seven states (Pennsylvania, New York, New Jersey, South Carolina, Rhode Island, Georgia, and North Carolina) issued paper money. In spite of the cries of calamity, the money served positively as a means of extending credit to hard-pressed farmers through state loans on farm mortgages. It was also used to fund state debts and to pay off the claims of veterans.

SHAYS'S REBELLION   But many Americans—especially bankers and merchants—were horrified by such inflationary policies. An event in Massachusetts provided the final proof (some said) that the country was on the brink of anarchy: Shays's Rebellion. After 1780 Massachusetts had remained in the grip of a rigidly conservative regime. The state levied high poll and land taxes to pay off a heavy war debt, held mainly by wealthy creditors in Boston. The taxes fell most heavily upon beleaguered farmers and the poor in general.

When the legislature adjourned in 1786 without providing paper money or any other relief from taxes and debts, three western agricultural counties revolted. Armed bands closed the courts and prevented foreclosures, and a ragtag "army" of some 1,200 disgruntled farmers led by Captain Daniel Shays, a destitute farmer and war veteran, advanced upon the federal arsenal at Springfield in 1787. Shays and his followers sought a more flexible monetary policy, laws allowing them to use corn and wheat as money, and the right to postpone paying taxes until the depression lifted.

A small militia scattered Shays's men with a single volley that left four dead. The rebels nevertheless had a victory of sorts. The new state legislature included members sympathetic to the agricultural crisis. The legislators omitted direct taxes the following year, lowered court fees, and exempted clothing, household goods, and tools from the debt process. But a more important consequence was the impetus the rebellion gave to conservatism and nationalism.

CALLS FOR A STRONGER GOVERNMENT   Shays's Rebellion convinced many political leaders that the Articles of Confederation were inadequate. Self-interest led many bankers, merchants, and mechanics to promote a stronger central government as the only alternative to anarchy. Gradually Americans were losing the ingrained fear of a powerful central authority as they saw evidence that tyranny might come from other quarters, including the common people themselves.

Such developments led many of the Revolutionary leaders to revise their assessment of the American character. "We have, probably," concluded George Washington in 1786, "had too good an opinion of human nature in forming our confederation." People were stretching the meaning of liberty far beyond what he and others had envisioned. He found a "spirit of *locality*" rampant in the state legislatures that was destroying the "aggregate interests of the community." Even worse, he saw people taking the law and other people's property into their own hands. James Madison and other so-called Federalists concluded that the new republic must now depend for its success upon the constant virtue of the few rather than the public-spiritedness of the many.

ADOPTING THE CONSTITUTION

For these reasons, well before Shays's Rebellion nationalists were demanding a convention to revise the Articles of Confederation. After stalling for several months, Congress in 1787 passed a resolution endorsing a convention "for the sole and express purpose of revising the Articles of Confederation." By then five states had already named delegates; before the meeting six more states had acted. Rhode Island kept aloof throughout, leading critics to label it Rogue Island.

THE CONSTITUTIONAL CONVENTION Twenty-nine delegates began work in Philadelphia on May 25. Altogether fifty-five attended at one time or another, and after four months thirty-nine signed the Constitution. The document's durability and flexibility testify to the remarkable qualities of its creators. The delegates were surprisingly young: forty-two was the average age. Most were planters, merchants, lawyers, judges, bankers, many of them widely read in history, law, and political philosophy. At the same time they were practical, experienced, and tested in the fires of the Revolution. Twenty-one had fought in the conflict, seven had been state governors, most had served in the Continental Congress, and eight had signed the Declaration of Independence.

The magisterial George Washington served as presiding officer but participated little in the debates. Eighty-one-year-old Benjamin Franklin, the oldest delegate, also said little from the floor but provided a wealth of experience, wit, and common sense. More active in the debates were the thirty-six-year-old James Madison, the ablest political philosopher in the group;

Drafting the Constitution

George Washington presides over a session of the Constitutional Convention.

George Mason, the prickly author of the Virginia Declaration of Rights and a slaveholding planter who was burdened by gout, chronic indigestion, and a deep-rooted suspicion of all government; the witty, eloquent, and arrogant New York aristocrat Gouverneur Morris; James Wilson of Pennsylvania, one of the shrewdest lawyers in the new nation and next in importance at the convention only to Washington and Madison; and Roger Sherman of Connecticut, a self-trained lawyer adept at negotiating compromises. John Adams, like Jefferson, was serving abroad on a diplomatic mission. Also conspicuously absent during most of the convention was Alexander Hamilton, who regretfully went home when the two other New York delegates walked out to protest the loss of states' rights.

The delegates spent four sweltering months fighting flies, the humidity, and one another. However, on certain fundamentals they generally agreed: that government derives its just powers from the consent of the people but that society must be protected from the tyranny of the majority; that the people at large must have a voice in their government but that checks and balances must be provided to keep any one group from dominating; that a stronger central authority was essential but that all power is subject to abuse. Even the best of people are naturally selfish, they believed, and therefore government could not be founded upon a trust in goodwill and virtue. Yet by carefully checking power with countervailing power, the Founding Fathers hoped to devise institutions that could somehow constrain individual sinfulness and channel individual self-interest on behalf of the public good. Madison proved to be the energizing force at the convention, persuading others by the convincing eloquence of his arguments.

THE VIRGINIA AND NEW JERSEY PLANS   James Madison drafted the proposals that came to be called the Virginia Plan, presented on May 29, 1787. This plan called for separate legislative, executive, and judicial branches and a truly national government whose laws would be binding upon individual citizens as well as states. Congress would be divided into two houses: a lower house to be chosen by popular vote and an upper house of senators elected by the state legislatures. Congress could disallow state laws under the plan and would itself define the extent of its and the states' authority.

On June 15 William Paterson submitted the "New Jersey Plan," which kept the existing equal representation of the states in a unicameral Congress but gave the Congress power to levy taxes, regulate commerce, and name a plural executive (with no veto) and a supreme court. The plans presented the convention with two major issues: whether to amend the Articles of Confederation or draft an entirely new document and whether to apportion congressional representation by population or by state.

On the first point the convention voted to design a national government as envisioned by the Virginians. Experience had persuaded the delegates that an effective central government, as distinguished from a loose confederation of states needed the power to levy taxes, regulate commerce, raise an army and navy, and make laws binding upon individual citizens. The lessons of the 1780s suggested to them, moreover, that in the interest of order and uniformity the states must be denied certain powers: to issue money, void contracts, make treaties or wage war, and levy tariffs.

But other issues sparked furious disagreements. The first clash in the

James Madison

Madison was only thirty-six when he assumed a major role in the drafting of the Constitution. This miniature (ca. 1783) is by Charles Willson Peale.

convention involved the issue of representation, and it was solved by the Great Compromise, (sometimes called the Connecticut Compromise, as it was proposed by Roger Sherman). In the House of Representatives, apportionment would be by population, which pleased the more populous states; in the Senate there would be equal representation of each state (although the vote would be by individuals, not by states), which appeased the smaller states.

An equally contentious struggle ensued between northern and southern delegates over slavery. Few if any of the framers considered the possibility of abolishing slavery in those states—mostly southern—where it was still legal. In this respect they reflected the prevailing attitude of their time. Most agreed with South Carolina's John Rutledge when he asserted, "Religion and humanity [have] nothing to do with this [slavery] question. Interest alone is the governing principle of nations."

The "interest" of southern delegates, with enslaved African Americans so numerous in their states, dictated that slaves be counted as part of the population in determining the number of a state's representatives. Northerners were willing to count slaves when deciding each state's share of direct taxes but not for purposes of representation in Congress. The delegates, with little dissent, agreed in a compromise to count three fifths of the slaves as a basis for apportioning both representatives and direct taxes.

A more sensitive issue involved an effort to prevent the new central government from stopping the slave trade with Africa. Some state governments had already outlawed the practice, and several delegates demanded that the national government do the same. Southern delegates quickly protested. Eventually a compromise was reached whereby Congress could not prohibit the traffic until 1808 but could levy a tax of $10 a head on imported slaves. In drafting both provisions, a sense of delicacy—and hypocrisy—dictated the use of euphemisms. The Constitution thus spoke of "free persons" and "all other persons." The odious word *slavery* did not appear in the Constitution until the Thirteenth Amendment (1865) abolished the practice.

If the delegates found the slavery issue distracting, they considered irrelevant any discussion of the legal or political role of women under the new constitution. The Revolutionary rhetoric of liberty prompted a few women to demand political equality. "The men say we have no business [with politics]," Eliza Wilkinson of South Carolina observed, "but I won't have it thought that because we are the weaker sex as to bodily strength we are capable of nothing more than domestic concerns. They won't even allow us liberty of thought, and that is all I want." Her complaint, however, fell on deaf ears. There was never any formal discussion of women's rights at the convention. The new political framework still defined politics and government as outside the realm of female endeavor.

THE SEPARATION OF POWERS   The details of the government structure generated less debate in Philadelphia than the basic issues pitting the large states against the small and the northern states against the southern. Existing state constitutions, several of which already separated powers among legislative, executive, and judicial branches, set an example that reinforced the convention's resolve to disperse power with checks and balances. Some delegates displayed a thumping disdain for any democratizing of the political system. Hamilton called the people "a great beast," and Elbridge Gerry asserted that most of the nation's problems "flow from an excess of democracy."

Those elitist views were incorporated into the Constitution's mixed legislative system, which allowed the direct popular choice of just one chamber of Congress. The lower house was designed to be closest to the voters, who elected its delegates every two years. The upper house, or Senate, was elected by the state legislatures rather than directly by the voters. Staggered six-year terms prevent the choice of a majority in any given year and thereby further isolate senators from the passing fancies of public passion.

The decision that a single person be made the chief executive caused the delegates "considerable pause," according to James Madison. George Mason protested that this would create a "fetus of monarchy." Indeed, although subject to election every four years, the chief executive would wield powers that would exceed those of the British king. The president could veto acts of Congress, subject to being overridden by a two-thirds vote in each house, was commander in chief of the armed forces, and was responsible for the execution of the laws. The chief executive could make treaties with the advice and consent of two thirds of the Senate and appoint diplomats, judges, and other officers with the consent of a majority of the Senate. The president was instructed to report annually on the state of the nation and was authorized to recommend legislation.

But the president's powers were limited in certain key areas. The chief executive could neither declare war nor make peace; those powers were reserved for Congress. Unlike the British monarch, moreover, the president could be removed from office. The House could impeach (indict) the chief executive—and other civil officers—on charges of treason, bribery, or "other high crimes and misdemeanors"; the president could then be removed by the Senate with a two-thirds vote to convict. The presiding officer at the trial of a president would be the chief justice, since the usual presiding officer of the Senate (the vice president) would have a personal stake in the outcome.

The leading nationalists—men like James Madison, James Wilson, and Alexander Hamilton—wanted to strengthen the independence of the president by entrusting the choice to popular election. But an elected executive was still too far beyond the American experience. Besides, a national election would have created enormous problems of organization and voter qualification. James Wilson suggested instead that the people of each state choose presidential electors equal to the number of their senators and representatives. Others proposed that the legislators make the choice. Finally the convention voted to let the legislature decide the method in each state. Before long nearly all the states were choosing their electors by popular vote, and the electors were acting as agents of the party will, casting their votes as they had pledged them before the election. This method diverged from the original expectation that the electors would deliberate and make their own choices.

The third branch of government, the judiciary, caused surprisingly little debate. Both the Virginia and the New Jersey Plans had called for a supreme court, which the Constitution established, providing specifically for a chief justice of the United States and leaving up to Congress the number of other justices. Although the Constitution nowhere authorizes the courts to declare laws void when they conflict with the Constitution, the power of judicial review is implied and was soon exercised in cases involving both state and federal laws. Article VI declares the federal constitution, federal laws, and treaties to be the "supreme Law of the Land," state laws or constitutions "to the Contrary notwithstanding."

Although the Constitution extended vast new powers to the national government, the delegates' mistrust of unchecked power is apparent in repeated examples of countervailing forces: the separation of the three branches of government, the president's veto, the congressional power of impeachment and removal, the Senate's power to approve treaties and appointments, and the courts' implied right of judicial review. In addition, the new form of government specifically forbade Congress to pass ex post facto laws (laws adopted after an event to criminalize deeds already committed). It also reserved to the states large areas of sovereignty—a reservation soon made explicit by the Tenth Amendment. By dividing sovereignty between the people and the government, the framers of the Constitution provided a distinctive contribution to political theory. That is, by vesting ultimate authority in the people, they divided sovereignty *within* the government. This constituted a dramatic break with the colonial tradition. The British had always insisted that the sovereignty of the king-in-Parliament was indivisible.

The most glaring defect of the Articles of Confederation, the rule of state unanimity that defeated every effort to amend them, led the delegates to

Signing the Constitution, September 17, 1787

Thomas Pritchard Rossiter's painting shows George Washington presiding over what Thomas Jefferson called an assembly of demigods.

provide a less forbidding though still difficult method of amending the new constitution. Amendments can be proposed either by a two-thirds vote of each house or by a national convention specially called by two thirds of the state legislatures. Amendments can be ratified by approval of three fourths of the states acting through their legislatures or in special conventions.

THE FIGHT FOR RATIFICATION   The final article of the Constitution provided that it would become effective upon ratification by nine states (not quite the three-fourths majority required for amendment). The Congress submitted the convention's work to the states on September 28, 1787. In the ensuing political debate, advocates of the Constitution, who might properly have been called Nationalists because they preferred a strong central government, assumed the more reassuring name of Federalists. Opponents, who favored a more decentralized federal system, became anti-Federalists.

The Federalists were better prepared and better organized. They were usually clustered in or near cities and tended to be more cosmopolitan, urbane, and well educated. Anti-Federalists tended to be small farmers and frontiersmen who saw little to gain from the promotion of interstate commerce and much to lose from prohibitions on paper money and "stay" laws, which prevented foreclosure proceedings against farmers. Many of them also feared that an expansive land policy was likely to favor speculators.

THE FEDERALIST   Among the supreme legacies of the debate over the Constitution was a collection of essays called *The Federalist,* originally published in New York newspapers between 1787 and 1788. Initiated by Alexander Hamilton, the eighty-five articles published under the name Publius included about thirty by James Madison, nearly fifty by Hamilton, and five by John Jay. Written to promote state ratification of the Constitution, the essays defended the principle of a supreme national authority but sought to reassure doubters that there was little reason to fear tyranny by the new government.

In perhaps the most famous essay, Number 10, Madison argued that the country's very size and diversity would make it impossible for any single faction to form a majority that could dominate the government. This contradicted the prevailing notion that republics could work only in small countries like Switzerland and the Netherlands. In larger countries republican government would descend into anarchy and tyranny through the influence of factions. Quite the contrary, Madison argued. A republic with a balanced federal government could survive in a large and diverse country better than in a smaller country. "Extend the sphere," he wrote, "and you take in a greater variety of parties and interests; you make it less probable that a majority of the whole will have a common motive to invade the rights of other citizens."

The Federalists insisted that the new union would contribute to prosperity. The anti-Federalists, however, highlighted the dangers of power. They noted the absence of a bill of rights to protect individuals and states, and they found the ratification process highly irregular, which it was—indeed, it was illegal under the Articles of Confederation. Maryland's Luther Martin, who had walked out of the Constitutional Convention, urged his state not to ratify the Constitution by rejecting "those chains which are forged for it." The Anti-Federalist leaders—Martin, Patrick Henry, Richard Henry Lee of Virginia, George Clinton of New York, and Samuel Adams and Elbridge Gerry of Massachusetts—were often men whose careers and reputations had been established well before the Revolution. The Federalist leaders, on the other hand, were more likely to be younger men whose careers had begun in the Revolution and who had been "nationalized" in the fires of battle—men like Hamilton, Madison, and Jay.

The two groups disagreed more over means than ends, however. Both sides for the most part agreed that a stronger national government was needed and that it required an independent income to function properly. Both were convinced that the people must erect safeguards against tyranny, even the tyranny of the majority. Once the new government had become an accomplished fact, few diehards were left who wanted to undo the work of the Philadelphia convention.

THE DECISION OF THE STATES Ratification of the new federal Constitution gained momentum before the end of 1787, and several of the smaller states were among the first to act, apparently satisfied that they had gained all the safeguards they could hope for in equality of representation in the Senate. New Hampshire was the ninth state to ratify the Constitution, on June 21, 1788, enabling it to be put into effect, but the Union could hardly succeed without the approval of Virginia, the most populous state, or New York, which had the third highest population and occupied a key position geographically.

There was strong opposition in both states. In Virginia, Patrick Henry became the chief spokesman for backcountry farmers who feared the powers of the new government, but wavering delegates were won over by a proposal that the convention should recommend a bill of rights. Virginia's convention voted for ratification on June 25, 1788. In New York, Alexander Hamilton and the other Federalists delayed a vote in the hope that action by Virginia would persuade the delegates that the new framework would go into effect

RATIFICATION OF THE CONSTITUTION

Order of Ratification	State	Date of Ratification
1	Delaware	December 7, 1787
2	Pennsylvania	December 12, 1787
3	New Jersey	December 18, 1787
4	Georgia	January 2, 1788
5	Connecticut	January 9, 1788
6	Massachusetts	February 6, 1788
7	Maryland	April 28, 1788
8	South Carolina	May 23, 1788
9	New Hampshire	June 21, 1788
10	Virginia	June 25, 1788
11	New York	July 26, 1788
12	North Carolina	November 21, 1789
13	Rhode Island	May 29, 1790

with or without New York. On July 26, 1788, they carried the day by the closest margin thus far, thirty to twenty-seven. North Carolina stubbornly withheld action until November 1789, when amendments comprising a bill of rights were submitted by Congress. Rhode Island, true to form, did not relent until May 29, 1790, by the closest margin of all—two votes.

Upon notification that New Hampshire had become the ninth state to ratify the Constitution, the Confederation Congress began to draft plans for an orderly transfer of power. On September 13, 1788, it selected New York City as the seat of the new government and fixed the date for elections. On October 10, 1788, the Confederation Congress transacted its last business and passed into history. "Our constitution is in actual operation," the elderly Benjamin Franklin wrote to a friend; "everything appears to promise that it will last; but in this world nothing is certain but death and taxes." George Washington was even more uncertain about the future under the new plan of government. He had told a fellow delegate as the convention adjourned, "I do not expect the Constitution to last for more than twenty years."

"A MORE PERFECT UNION"

The Constitution has lasted much longer, of course, and in the process it has provided a model of republican government whose features have been repeatedly borrowed by other nations through the years. Yet what makes the

U.S. Constitution so distinctive is not its specific provisions but its remarkable harmony with the particular "genius of the people" it governs. The Constitution has provided a flexible system of government that presidents, legislators, judges, and the people have modified to accord with a fallible human nature and changing social, economic, and political circumstances. In this sense the Founding Fathers not only created "a more perfect Union" in 1787; they also engineered a form of government whose resilience has enabled later generations to continue to perfect their republican experiment. But the framers of the Constitution failed in one significant respect: in skirting the issue of slavery so as to cement the new Union, they unknowingly allowed tensions over the "peculiar institution" to reach the point where there would be no political solution—only civil war.

MAKING CONNECTIONS

- The Founding Fathers might have created "a more perfect Union," but from time to time Americans have debated the nature of the national government and its relation to the people and the states. Examples include the Kentucky and Virginia Resolutions (Chapter 8), the Hartford Convention (Chapter 9), and the nullification crisis (Chapter 11).

- Slavery, viewed by the delegates to the Constitutional Convention as little more than a "distracting question," soon became a major political problem—especially after the 1820 Missouri Compromise (see Chapter 10).

FURTHER READING

A good overview of the Confederation period is Richard B. Morris's *The Forging of the Union, 1781–1789* (1987). Another useful analysis of this period is Richard Buel Jr.'s *Securing the Revolution: Ideology in American Politics, 1789–1815* (1972).

David P. Szatmary's *Shays's Rebellion: The Making of an Agrarian Insurrection* (1980) covers that fateful incident. For a fine account of cultural change during the period, see Joseph J. Ellis's *After the Revolution: Profiles of Early American Culture* (1979).

Excellent treatments of the post-Revolutionary era include Edmund S. Morgan's *Inventing the People: The Rise of Popular Sovereignty in England and America* (1988), Michael Kammen's *Sovereignty and Liberty: Constitutional Discourse in American Culture* (1988), and Joyce Appleby's *Inheriting the Revolution: The First Generation of Americans* (2000). Among the better collections of essays on the Constitution are *Toward a More Perfect Union: Six Essays on the Constitution* (1988), edited by Neil L. York, and *The Framing and Ratification of the Constitution* (1987), edited by Leonard W. Levy and Dennis J. Mahoney.

Bruce Ackerman's *We the People,* vol. 1, *Foundations* (1991) examines Federalist political principles. For the Bill of Rights that emerged from the ratification struggles, see Robert A. Rutland's *The Birth of the Bill of Rights, 1776–1791* (1955).

8

THE FEDERALIST ERA

FOCUS QUESTIONS

· How did the new government operate?

· What was Alexander Hamilton's Federalist program?

· What characterized the beginnings of the first party system (composed of Federalists and Republicans)?

· What were the elements of the Federalists' foreign policy?

To answer these questions and access additional review material, please visit www.wwnorton.com/studyspace.

T he new American republic was a sprawling nation of energetic individuals eager to test the limits of their freedom and exploit the nation's vast natural resources and economic opportunities. The new Constitution created a more powerful central government to deal with the problems of the vast new nation, but several foreign and domestic crises did not allow for an easy transition.

A NEW NATION

In 1789 the United States and the western territories reached from the Atlantic Ocean to the Mississippi River and was inhabited by almost 4 million people. The new nation harbored distinct regional differences. Although still characterized by small farms and bustling seaports, New

CW.Peale del.^t   Thackara & Vallance Sculp.^t

A New Society

An engraving from the title page of *The Universal Asylum and Columbian Magazine*, (published in Philadelphia in 1790). America is represented as a woman laying down her shield to engage in education, art, commerce, and agriculture.

England was on the verge of developing a small-scale manufacturing sector. The middle Atlantic states boasted the most well-balanced economy, the largest cities, and the most diverse collection of ethnic and religious groups. The South, a more ethnically homogeneous agricultural region, was increasingly dependent upon slave labor. By 1790 the southern states were exporting as much tobacco as they had been before the Revolution. Most important, however, was the surge in cotton production. Between 1790 and 1815 the annual production of cotton rose from less than 3 million pounds to 93 million pounds.

The United States in 1790 was predominantly a rural society. Eighty percent of households were involved in agricultural production. Only a few cities had more than 5,000 residents. The first national census, taken in 1790, counted 750,000 African Americans, almost one fifth of the population. Most of them lived in the five southernmost states; less than 10 percent lived outside the South. Most African Americans, of course, were enslaved, but there were many free blacks as a result of the Revolutionary turmoil. In fact, the proportion of free to enslaved blacks was never higher than in 1790.

The 1790 census did not even count the many Indians still living east of the Mississippi River. It is estimated that there were over eighty tribes numbering perhaps as many as 150,000 persons in 1790. In the Old Northwest along the Great Lakes, the British continued to arm the Indians and encouraged them to resist American encroachments. Between 1784 and 1790 Indians killed or captured some 1,500 settlers in Kentucky alone. Such bloodshed generated a ferocious reaction among settlers eager to eradicate the Indians. In the South the five most powerful tribes—the Cherokees, Chickasaws, Choctaws, Creeks, and Seminoles—numbered between 50,000 and 100,000. They steadfastly refused to recognize U.S. authority and used Spanish-supplied weapons to thwart white settlement.

Only about 125,000 whites and blacks lived west of the Appalachian Mountains in 1790. But that was soon to change. Rapid population growth, cheap land, and new economic opportunities fueled the westward migration. The average white woman gave birth to eight children, and the white population doubled approximately every twenty-two years. This made for a very young population on average. In 1790 almost half of all white Americans were under sixteen.

A NEW GOVERNMENT   The new Congress of the United States opened with a whimper rather than a bang. On March 4, 1789, the appointed date of its first session in bustling New York City, only eight senators and thirteen representatives took their seats. A month passed before both chambers gathered a quorum. Only then could the temporary presiding officer of the Senate count the ballots and certify the foregone conclusion that George Washington, with sixty-nine votes, was the unanimous choice of the Electoral College for president. John Adams, with thirty-four votes, the second-highest number, became vice president. Washington was a reluctant president. Yet he felt compelled to serve because he had been "summoned by my country." A self-made man with little formal education, Washington had a remarkable capacity for moderation and mediation that helped keep the infant republic from disintegrating.

THE GOVERNMENT'S STRUCTURE   The president and the Congress had to create a government anew. During the summer of 1789, Congress created executive departments corresponding to those already formed under the Confederation. To head the Department of State, Washington named Thomas Jefferson, recently back from his diplomatic duties in France. Leadership of the Department of the Treasury went to Washington's wartime aide, Alexander Hamilton, who had since become a prominent lawyer in

New York. Tall, graceful Edmund Randolph, former governor of Virginia and owner of a 7,000-acre debt-ridden plantation worked by 200 slaves, assumed the new position of attorney general. Almost from the beginning, Washington routinely called these men to sit as a group to discuss and advise on policy matters. This was the origin of the president's cabinet, an advisory body for which the Constitution made no formal provision.

Washington named John Jay as the first chief justice of the Supreme Court, and Jay served until 1795. Born in New York City in 1745, Jay had graduated from King's College (now Columbia University). His distinction as a lawyer led New York to send him as its representative to the First and Second Continental Congresses. After serving as president of the Continental Congress in 1778–1779, Jay became the American minister in Spain. While in Europe he helped John Adams and Benjamin Franklin negotiate the Treaty of Paris in 1783. After the Revolution, Jay served as secretary of foreign affairs. He joined Madison and Hamilton as co-author of *The Federalist* and became one of the most effective champions of the Constitution.

THE BILL OF RIGHTS   In the new House of Representatives, James Madison made a bill of rights one of the first items of business. The lack of provisions protecting individuals' and states' rights had been one of the anti-Federalists' major objections to the Constitution. In May 1789 Madison drew the first eight amendments to the Constitution from the Virginia Declaration of Rights, which George Mason had written in 1776. They provided safeguards for certain fundamental individual rights: freedom of religion, press, speech, and assembly; the right to keep and bear firearms; the right to refuse to house soldiers in private homes; protection from unreasonable searches and seizures; the right to refuse to testify against oneself; the right to a speedy public trial, with legal counsel present before an impartial jury; and protection against cruel and unusual punishment. The Ninth and Tenth Amendments declared that the enumeration of rights in the Constitution "shall not be construed to deny or disparage others retained by the people" and that "powers not delegated to the United States by the Constitution . . . are reserved to the States respectively, or to the people." The states voted separately on each proposed amendment, and the Bill of Rights became effective on December 15, 1791.

Madison viewed the Bill of Rights as "the most dramatic single gesture of conciliation that could be offered the remaining opponents of the government." Those "opponents" included prominent Virginians George Mason and Richard Henry Lee as well as artisans, small traders, and backcountry farmers who expressed a profound egalitarianism. These "poor and middling" folk were skeptical that even the "best men" were capable of subordinating self-interest to the good of the republic. They believed that all people were prone to corruption; no one could be trusted. Therefore, a bill of rights was necessary to protect the liberties of all against the encroachments of a few. Yet the Bill of Rights provided no rights or legal protection to African Americans or Indians.

Hamilton's Vision

Revenue was the new federal government's most critical need, and Congress quickly enacted a tariff intended to raise money and protect America's new manufacturers from foreign competition by raising prices on imported goods. Yet tariffs resulted in higher prices on imported goods bought by Americans, most of whom were tied to the farm economy. This circumstance raised a basic and perennial question: should rural consumers be forced to subsidize the nation's infant manufacturing sector?

The tariff launched the effort to get the country on a sound financial footing. In finance, with all its broad implications for policy in general, it was the thirty-four-year-old Alexander Hamilton who seized the initiative in 1789.

Alexander Hamilton

Secretary of the Treasury from 1789 to 1795.

The first secretary of the Treasury was born out of wedlock on a Caribbean island, deserted by his ne'er-do-well Scottish father, and left an orphan at thirteen by the death of his mother. With the help of friends and relatives, he found his way, at seventeen, to New York, attended King's College, and entered the Continental army, where he became a favorite of George Washington's. Hamilton distinguished himself at the siege of Yorktown, and he remained a frustrated military genius, hungry for greater glory on the field of battle. He studied law, passed the bar examination, established a legal practice in New York, and became a self-made aristocrat, serving as a collector of revenues and as a member of the Confederation Congress. An early convert to nationalism, he played a crucial part in promoting the Constitutional Convention and defending its work in *The Federalist.*

During the Revolutionary War, Colonel Hamilton had witnessed the near-fatal weaknesses of the Confederation Congress. Its lack of authority and money almost lost the war. Now, as the nation's first secretary of the Treasury, he was determined to transform an economically weak and fractious nation. To flourish in a warring world, Hamilton believed, the United States needed to unleash the energy and ambition of its citizens so as to create a vibrant economy driven by the engines of capitalism. He wanted to nurture the hustling, bustling, aspiring spirit that he believed distinguished Americans from others. Just as he had risen from poverty and shame to become immensely successful, he wanted to ensure that Americans would always have such opportunities. To do so, he envisioned a limited but assertive government that encouraged new fields of enterprise and fostered investment and entrepreneurship. Thriving markets and new industries would best ensure the fate of the republic, and a secure federal debt would give investors a stake in the success of the new national government. The young Hamilton was supremely confident in his ability to shape fiscal policies that would provide economic opportunity and ensure government stability. His success in minting a budget, a funded debt, a federal tax system, a national bank, a customs service, and a coast guard provided the foundations for American capitalism and American government.

The new government needed Hamilton's ambition and brilliance. In a series of reports submitted to Congress in 1790 and 1791, he outlined his program for government finances and the economic development of the United States.

ESTABLISHING THE PUBLIC CREDIT   Hamilton's first of two "Reports on Public Credit" dealt with the vexing issue of war-generated debt. Both the federal government and the individual states had emerged from the Revolution with substantial debts. France, Spain, and Holland had lent the United States money and supplies to fight the war, and Congress had incurred more debt by printing paper money and selling government bonds. State governments had also accumulated huge obligations. After the war some states had set about paying off their debts, but the efforts were uneven. Only the federal government could wipe the slate clean. Hamilton insisted that the debts from the Revolution were a *national* responsibility because all Americans had benefited from independence. He also knew that federal assumption of state debts would enhance a sense of nationalism by helping the people see the benefits of a strong central government. Finally, the Treasury secretary was determined to shore up the federal government's finances because he believed that preserving individual freedom and the sanctity of property went hand in hand.

Hamilton's controversial report on public credit made two key recommendations: first, it called for funding the federal debt at face value, which meant that citizens holding government securities could exchange them for new interest-bearing bonds of the same face value; second, it declared that the federal government should assume state debts from the Revolution. Holders of state bonds would exchange them for new national bonds. The funding scheme was controversial because many farmers and ex-soldiers in need of immediate money had sold their securities for a fraction of their value to speculators. Spokesmen for the sellers argued that they should be reimbursed for their losses; otherwise, the speculators would gain a windfall. Hamilton sternly resisted. The speculators, he argued, had "paid what the commodity was worth in the market, and took the risks." Therefore, they should reap the benefits. In fact, Hamilton insisted, the government should favor the financial community because it represented the bedrock of a successful nation.

Payment of the national debt, Hamilton believed, would be not only a point of national honor and sound finance, ensuring the country's credit for the future; it would also be an occasion to assert the federal power of taxation and thus instill respect for the authority of the national government. It was on this point, however, that Madison, who had been Hamilton's close ally in the movement for a stronger government, broke with him. Madison did not question whether the debt should be paid, but he was troubled that speculators would become the chief beneficiaries. Also disturbing was the fact that northerners held most of the debt. Madison's opposition touched off a vigorous debate that deadlocked the question of debt funding and assumption through much of 1790.

The stalemate finally ended in the summer of 1790, when Hamilton, Jefferson, and Madison reached a compromise. In return for northern votes in favor of locating the permanent national capital on the Potomac River along the Virginia border, Madison pledged to seek enough southern votes to pass the debt-assumption bill, with the further arrangement that those states with smaller debts would get in effect outright grants from the federal government to equalize the difference. These arrangements secured enough votes to carry Hamilton's funding and assumption plans. The national capital would be moved from New York City to Philadelphia for ten years, after which it would be located in a new federal city bordering northern Virginia. In August 1790 Congress finally passed the legislation for Hamilton's plan. Jefferson later claimed to have been "duped" by Hamilton into agreeing to the "Compromise of 1790" because he did not fully understand the implications of the debt-assumption plan. It is more likely that Jefferson had been outsmarted. He only later realized how relatively insignificant the location of the national capital was when compared with the far-reaching effects of Hamilton's economic program.

A NATIONAL BANK   Alexander Hamilton's vast program of funding federal and state debts generated, as if by magic, a great sum of capital for the new nation. Having established the federal government's creditworthiness, the relentless Hamilton moved on to a related measure essential to his vision of national greatness: a national bank, which by issuance of bank notes (paper money) might provide a uniform national currency as well as a source of expanding capital for the developing economy. Government bonds held by the bank would back up the currency. The Bank of the United States, chartered by Congress, would remain under government oversight, but private investors would supply four fifths of the $10 million capital and name twenty of the twenty-five directors; the government would purchase the other one fifth of the capital and name five directors. Government bonds would be received in payment for three fourths of the stock in the bank, and the other fourth would be payable in gold and silver.

Once again James Madison rose to lead the opposition, arguing that he could find no basis in the Constitution for a national bank. That was enough to raise in President Washington's mind serious doubts as to the constitutionality of the measure, which Congress passed over Madison's objections.

The vote in Congress revealed the growing sectional division in the young United States. Representatives from the northern states voted thirty-three to one in favor of the national bank; southern congressmen opposed the bank nineteen to six. Before signing the bill into law, President Washington sought the advice of his cabinet and found an equal division of opinion. This resulted in the first great debate on constitutional interpretation. Should there be a strict or a broad construction of the Constitution? Were the powers of Congress only those explicitly stated in the document, or were others implied? The argument turned chiefly on Article I, Section 8, which authorizes Congress to "make all Laws which shall be necessary and proper for carrying into execution the foregoing Powers."

Such language left room for disagreement and led to a colossal confrontation between Jefferson and Hamilton. Secretary of State Jefferson pointed to the Tenth Amendment, which reserves to the states and the people powers not delegated to Congress. A bank might be a convenient aid to Congress in collecting taxes and regulating the currency, but it was not, as Article I,

Section 8, specified, *necessary*. Hamilton insisted that the power to charter corporations was included in the sovereignty of any government, whether or not expressly stated. George Washington accepted Hamilton's argument and signed the bill. By doing so, in Jefferson's words, the president had opened up "a boundless field of power," which in coming years would lead to a further broadening of implied powers with the approval of the Supreme Court.

ENCOURAGING MANUFACTURES Alexander Hamilton's fertile imagination and his audacious ambitions for the new country were not yet exhausted. At the end of 1790, he submitted the second of his "Reports on Public Credit," which included a proposal for an excise tax on alcoholic beverages to help raise federal revenue to cover the nation's debts. Six weeks later Hamilton proposed a national mint, which was established in 1792 to provide money for the new nation. And on December 5, 1791, as the culmination of his financial program, he proposed, in his "Report on Manufactures," an extensive program of federal aid to promote the development of manufacturing enterprises.

Certificate of the New York Mechanick Society

An illustration of the growing diversification of labor, by Abraham Godwin (ca. 1785).

In the "Report on Manufactures," Hamilton argued for active government encouragement of manufacturing to provide productive uses for the new capital he had created by his funding, assumption, and banking schemes. Multiple advantages would flow from the aggressive development of manufactures: the diversification of labor in a country given over too exclusively to farming; improved productivity through the greater use of machinery; work for those not ordinarily employed, such as women and children; the promotion of immigration; a greater scope for the diversity of talents in business; and a better domestic market for agricultural products.

To secure his ends, Hamilton advocated protective tariffs, some of which were enacted in 1792, to protect young American industries from foreign competitors. Tariffs were, in essence, taxes on imported goods. The rest of Hamilton's manufacturing program was filed away—but not forgotten: it provided an arsenal of arguments for the manufacturing sector in years to come. Hamilton denied that his scheme favored the northern states. If, as seemed likely, the northern and middle Atlantic states should become the chief sites for manufacturing, he claimed, they would create robust markets for agricultural products, some of which the southern states were peculiarly qualified to produce. The nation as a whole would benefit, he argued, as commerce between North and South increased, supplanting the trade across the Atlantic Ocean with Britain and Europe.

HAMILTON'S ACHIEVEMENT   Largely because of the skillful Hamilton, the Treasury Department during the 1790s began retiring the Revolutionary War debt, enhanced the value of the Continental paper dollar, secured the government's credit, and attracted foreign capital. Prosperity, so elusive in the 1780s, began to flourish at the end of the century.

Hamilton professed a truly nationalist outlook, and he focused his energies on the rising power of commercial capitalism. Tying the government closely to the rich and the wellborn, Hamilton believed, promoted the government's financial stability and guarded the public order against the potential social turbulence that he feared would emerge in a republic.

But many Americans then and since have interpreted such views as elitist and self-serving. To be sure, Hamilton never understood the people of the villages and farms, the people of the frontier. They were foreign to his world, despite his own humble beginnings. And they, along with the planters of the South, would be at best only indirect beneficiaries of his programs. There were, in short, vast numbers of people who saw little gain from the Hamiltonian economic program and thus were drawn into opposition against it. Indeed, Jefferson claimed that he and Hamilton were "pitted against each other every day in the cabinet like two fighting-cocks."

THE REPUBLICAN ALTERNATIVE

Opposition to the Hamiltonian economic program spawned the first national political parties. Alexander Hamilton emerged as the embodiment of the Federalists; James Madison and Thomas Jefferson led those who took the name Republicans (also called the Democratic Republicans) and thereby implied that the Federalists aimed at a monarchy. Neither side in the disagreement over national policy deliberately set out to create formal political parties. But there were growing differences of both philosophy and self-interest that simply would not subside.

The crux of the debate centered on the relative power of the federal government and the states. At the outset, Madison assumed leadership of Hamilton's opponents in Congress, and he argued that Hamilton was trampling upon states' rights in forging a powerful central government. After the Compromise of 1790, which assured the funding of state debts, Jefferson and Madison resolutely opposed Hamilton's policies. They opposed his move to place an excise tax on whiskey, which would especially burden the trans-Appalachian farmers whose livelihood depended upon the sale of the beverage, and they opposed his proposal for a national bank and his "Report on Manufactures." As these differences developed, the personal hostility between Jefferson and Hamilton festered within the cabinet, much to the distress of President Washington.

Thomas Jefferson

A portrait by Charles Willson Peale (1791).

JEFFERSON'S AGRARIAN VIEW Thomas Jefferson, twelve years Hamilton's senior, was in most respects his opposite. In contrast to the self-made Hamilton, Jefferson was an agrarian aristocrat, the son of a successful surveyor and land speculator. Jefferson read or spoke seven languages. He was an architect of some distinction (Monticello, the Virginia state capitol, and the University of Virginia are monuments to his talent), a man who understood mathematics and engineering, an inventor, and an agronomist.

Hamilton and Jefferson had contrasting perspectives on America's future. Hamilton was a hardheaded realist who foresaw a diversified capitalist economy, with agriculture balanced by commerce and industry, and was thus the better prophet. Jefferson was an agrarian idealist who feared that the growth of crowded cities would divide society into a capitalist aristocracy on the one hand and a deprived working class on the other. Hamilton feared anarchy and loved order; Jefferson feared tyranny and loved liberty.

Hamilton championed a strong central government run by a wealthy elite actively engaged in encouraging capitalist enterprise. Jefferson desired a decentralized agrarian republic. Jefferson's ideal America was one in which small farmers predominated. He did not oppose all forms of manufacturing; he feared that the unlimited expansion of commerce and industry would produce a large class of propertyless wage laborers dependent upon others for their livelihood and therefore subject to political manipulation and economic exploitation.

CRISES FOREIGN AND DOMESTIC

As the disputes between Jefferson and Hamilton intensified, George Washington proved ever more adept at transcending party differences and holding things together with his unmatched prestige. In 1792 he won unanimous reelection, and no sooner had his second term begun than problems of foreign relations leaped to center stage, delivered by the consequences of the French Revolution, which had begun in 1789, during the first months of his presidency. Americans supported the popular revolt against the French monarchy, up to a point. By the spring of 1792, the idealistic experiment in liberty, equality, and fraternity had turned into a monster that plunged France into war with Austria and Prussia and began devouring its own children, along with its enemies, in the Terror of 1793–1794.

After the execution of King Louis XVI, early in 1793, Great Britain joined with the monarchies of Spain and Holland in a war against the French republic. For the next twenty-two years, Britain and France were at war, with only a brief respite, until the final defeat of the French forces under Napoléon in 1815. The war presented George Washington, just beginning his second term, with an awkward problem. By the 1778 Treaty of Alliance, the United States was a perpetual ally of France, obligated to defend her possessions in the West Indies.

Americans, however, wanted no part of the European war. They were determined to maintain their lucrative trade with both sides. For their part, Hamilton and Jefferson found in the neutrality policy one issue on which they could agree. Where they differed was in how best to implement it. President Washington issued a neutrality proclamation on April 22, 1793, that declared the United States "friendly and impartial toward the belligerent powers."

CITIZEN GENET   At the same time, President Washington had accepted Thomas Jefferson's argument that the United States should recognize the new French government (becoming the first country to do so) and receive its new ambassador, Edmond-Charles Édouard Genet. Early in 1793, Genet landed at Charleston, South Carolina, where he received a hero's welcome, and made his way northward to Philadelphia. En route he brazenly engaged in quite nonneutral activities. He outfitted privateers to capture British ships, and he conspired with frontiersmen and land speculators to launch an attack on Spanish Florida and Louisiana in retaliation for Spain's opposition to the French Revolution.

After arriving in Philadelphia, Genet quickly became an embarrassment even to his Republican friends. The cabinet finally agreed unanimously that he had to go, and George Washington demanded his recall. The behavior of the French made it hard even for Republicans to retain sympathy for the French Revolution, but Jefferson and others maintained their support. Jefferson was so disgusted by Washington's refusal to support the French Revolution and by his own ideological warfare with Alexander Hamilton that he would resign as secretary of state at the end of 1793. Nor did the British make it easy for Federalists to rally to their side. Near the end of 1793, they announced orders in council allowing them to seize the cargo of American ships with provisions for or exports from French islands in the Caribbean. By 1794 a prolonged foreign-policy crisis between the United States and Great Britain threatened to renew warfare between the two old enemies.

JAY'S TREATY   Early in 1794 Republican leaders in Congress were gaining support for commercial retaliation to end British trade abuses when the British gave George Washington a timely opening for a settlement. They stopped seizing American ships, and on April 16, 1794, Washington named Chief Justice John Jay as a special envoy to Great Britain. Jay left with instructions to settle all major issues: to get the British out of their forts along the northwestern frontier, win reparations for the losses of American shippers, secure compensation to planters for southern slaves carried away in 1783, and negotiate a commercial treaty that would legalize American commerce with the British West Indies.

The pro-British Jay had little leverage with which to wring concessions from the British, however, and after seven months of negotiations he won only two pledges: the British promised to evacuate the northwestern posts by 1796 and to pay damages for the seizure of American ships and cargo in 1793–1794. In exchange for those concessions, Jay agreed to the British definition of neutral rights. He accepted the principles that naval stores (tar, pitch, and turpentine), food, and war supplies headed to enemy ports on neutral ships were contraband and that trade with enemy colonies prohibited in peacetime could not be opened in wartime (the "rule of 1756"). Britain also gained most-favored-nation treatment in American commerce and a promise that French privateers would not be outfitted in American ports. Finally, Jay conceded that the British need not compensate U.S. citizens for the enslaved people who had escaped during the war, and he promised that the pre-Revolutionary American debts to British merchants would be paid by the U.S. government. Perhaps most important, he failed to gain unrestricted access for American commerce to the British West Indies.

Public outrage greeted the terms of Jay's Treaty. The public debate was so intense that some Americans feared civil war might erupt. Even Federalist shippers, ready for a settlement with the British on almost any terms, criticized Jay's failure to fully open up the British West Indies to American commerce. Much of the outcry, however, came from disappointed Republican partisans who had sought an escalation of the conflict with the hated England. In the end, moderation prevailed. George Washington worried that his opponents were prepared to separate "the Union into Northern & Southern." Once he endorsed Jay's Treaty, there were even calls for his impeachment. Yet the president, while acknowledging that the proposed agreement was imperfect, concluded that adopting it was the only way to avoid war with Britain. Without a single vote to spare, Jay's Treaty won the necessary two-thirds majority on June 24, 1795. Washington hesitated but signed the treaty as the best he was likely to get. The major votes in Congress were again aligned by region; 80 percent of the votes for the treaty came from New England or the middle Atlantic states; 74 percent of those voting against the treaty were cast by southerners.

THE FRONTIER   Other events also had an important bearing on Jay's Treaty, adding force to the importance of its settlement of the Canadian frontier. While Jay was haggling in London, frontier conflict with Indians escalated, with U.S. troops twice crushed by northwestern Indians. At last, General Wayne, known as Mad Anthony, led an expedition into the Northwest Territory in the fall of 1793. The following year, on August 4, Indians representing eight tribes and reinforced by some Canadian militias, attacked

General Wayne's force south of Detroit at the Battle of Fallen Timbers. The Americans repulsed them, and the Indian's suffered substantial losses. Dispersed and decimated, the Indians finally agreed to the Treaty of Greenville, signed in 1795. According to the terms of the treaty, the United States bought from twelve tribes, at the cost of a $10,000 annuity, the rights to the southeastern quarter of the Northwest Territory (now Ohio and Indiana) and enclaves at the sites of Detroit, Chicago, and Vincennes Indiana.

THE WHISKEY REBELLION   General Wayne's forces were still mopping up after the Battle of Fallen Timbers when the administration decided on another show of strength in the backcountry, against the so-called Whiskey Rebellion. Treasury Secretary Hamilton's excise tax on liquor, levied in 1791, had angered frontier farmers because it taxed their most profitable commodity. In the areas west of the Appalachian Mountains, the primary cash crop was liquor distilled from grain or fruit. Such emphasis on distilling reflected a practical problem. Many farmers could not afford to transport bulky crops of corn and rye across the mountains or down the Mississippi River to the seaboard markets. Instead, it was much more profitable to distill liquor from corn and rye or apples and peaches. Unlike grain crops, distilled spirits could be easily stored, shipped, or sold—and at higher profits. Western farmers were also suspicious of the new federal government in Philadelphia and considered the whiskey tax another part of Hamilton's scheme to pick the pockets of the poor to enrich the pockets of urban speculators. All through the backcountry, from Georgia to Pennsylvania and beyond, the tax aroused resistance and evasion.

In the summer of 1794, discontent over liquor taxes exploded into open rebellion in western Pennsylvania, where vigilantes, mostly of Scottish or Irish descent, terrorized revenue officers and taxpayers. Rebels robbed the mails, stopped court proceedings, and threatened an assault on Pittsburgh. On August 7, 1794, President Washington issued a proclamation ordering the rebels to disperse and go home and calling out militiamen from Virginia, Maryland, Pennsylvania, and New Jersey. Getting no response from the "Whiskey boys," he ordered the army to suppress the rebellion.

Under the command of General Henry Lee, 13,000 soldiers marched out from Harrisburg, Pennsylvania, across the Allegheny Mountains with Alexander Hamilton in their midst, itching to smite the insurgents. The tax-defying rebels, however, disappeared into the woods. The troops finally captured twenty barefoot, ragged rebels, whom they paraded down Market Street in Philadelphia and clapped into prison. Some of the soldiers regretted not having cornered more of the rebels. As one of the militiamen

Whiskey Rebellion

George Washington as commander in chief reviews the troops mobilized to quell the Whiskey Rebellion in 1794.

explained, "We all lament that so few of the insurgents fell—such disorders can only be cured by copious bleedings."

There was, in fact, little bleeding of any kind. One of the captured rebels died in prison. Two were convicted of treason and sentenced to be hanged, but Washington pardoned them on the grounds that one was a "simpleton" and the other "insane." Although President Washington had overreacted, the government had made its point in defense of the rule of law and federal authority. It thereby gained "reputation and strength," according to Alexamder Hamilton, by suppressing a rebellion that, in Thomas Jefferson's words, "could never be found." The use of such excessive federal force led many who sympathized with the frontiersmen to become

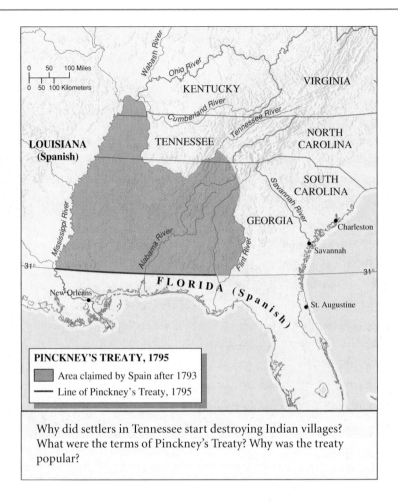

PINCKNEY'S TREATY, 1795

Area claimed by Spain after 1793
— Line of Pinckney's Treaty, 1795

Why did settlers in Tennessee start destroying Indian villages?
What were the terms of Pinckney's Treaty? Why was the treaty
popular?

Republicans, however, and Jefferson's party scored heavily in the next
Pennsylvania elections.

PINCKNEY'S TREATY   While these stirring events were transpiring in
Pennsylvania, Spain was suffering setbacks to its schemes to consolidate its
control over Florida and the Louisiana territory. Spain had refused to recognize the legitimacy of America's southern boundary established by the Treaty
of Paris in 1783, and its agents thereafter sought to thwart American expansion southward. Spanish intrigues among the Creeks, Choctaws, Chickasaws,
and Cherokees were keeping up the same sort of turmoil the British had fomented along the Ohio River.

In the mid-1790s, however, the shifting balance of power in Europe led Spain to end its designs on America. This change of heart resulted in Pinckney's Treaty, by which the U.S. ambassador, Thomas Pinckney, pulled off a diplomatic triumph in 1795 when he won Spanish acceptance of an American boundary at the 31st parallel, free navigation of the Mississippi River, the right to deposit goods at New Orleans without having to pay customs duties for a period of three years (with promise of renewal), a commission to settle American claims against Spain, and a promise on each side to refrain from inciting Indian attacks on the other. Ratification of Pinckney's Treaty was immensely popular, especially among westerners eager to use the Mississippi River to transport crops to market.

Settlement of New Land

Now that John Jay and Thomas Pinckney had settled matters with Britain and Spain and General Anthony Wayne in the Northwest had suppressed Indian resistance, a renewed surge of settlers headed for the West. New lands, ceded by the Indians in the Treaty of Greenville, revealed a Congress once again divided on the issue of federal land policy. There were two basic viewpoints on the matter: that the public domain should serve mainly as a source of revenue and that it was more important to get the country settled, an endeavor that required low land prices. Policy would evolve from the first to the second viewpoint, but for the time being the federal government's need for revenue took priority.

LAND POLICY   Opinions on land policy, like opinions on other issues, separated Federalists from Republicans. Federalists involved in real-estate speculation might prefer lower land prices, but the more influential Federalists, like Hamilton and Jay, preferred to build the population of the eastern states first, lest the East lose political influence and a labor force important to the growth of manufactures. Men of their persuasion favored high federal land prices to enrich the Treasury and the sale of relatively large parcels of land to speculators rather than small tracts to settlers. Jefferson and Madison were reluctantly prepared to go along with such a land policy for the sake of reducing the national debt, but Jefferson yearned for a plan by which the land could be settled more readily. In any case, he suggested, frontiersmen would do as they had done before: "They will settle the lands in spite of everybody." The pioneers of the West, always moving out beyond the settlers and the surveyors, were already proving him right.

The Federalist land policy prevailed in the Land Act of 1796, which retained the 640-acre minimum size mandated by the Northwest Ordinance of 1787 while doubling the price per acre to $2 and requiring that the full amount be paid within a year. Such terms were well beyond the means of most settlers and even many speculators. As a result, by 1800 federal land offices had sold fewer than 50,000 acres. Continuing demands for cheaper land led to the Land Act of 1800, which reduced the minimum unit to 320 acres and spread payments over four years. The Land Act of 1804 further reduced the minimum parcel to 160 acres, which became the traditional homestead, and the price per acre went down to $1.64.

THE WILDERNESS ROAD   The lure of western lands led thousands of settlers to follow Daniel Boone into the territory known as Kentucky or Kaintuck, from the Cherokee name Ken-Ta-Ke (Great Meadow). In the late eighteenth century, Kentucky was a farmer's fantasy and a hunter's paradise, with its fertile soil and abundant forests teeming with buffalo, deer, and wild turkeys.

Boone himself was the product of a pioneer background. Born on a small farm in 1734 in central Pennsylvania, the son of hardworking Quakers, he moved with his family to western North Carolina in 1750. There Daniel emerged as the region's greatest hunter, trading animal skins for salt and other household goods. After hearing numerous reports about the territory over the mountains, Boone set out alone in 1769 to find a trail into Kentucky. Armed with a long rifle, tomahawk, and hunting knife and dressed in a hunting shirt, deerskin leggings, and moccasins, he found what was called the Warriors' Path, a narrow foot trail that buffalo, deer, and Indians had worn along the steep ridges. It took him through the Cumberland Gap, in southwestern Virginia. For two years thereafter, Boone explored the region, living off the plentiful game. He returned to North Carolina with exciting stories about the riches of Kentucky.

In 1773 Boone led the first group of settlers through the Appalachian Mountains at the Cumberland Gap. Two years later Boone and thirty woodsmen used axes to widen the Warriors' Path into what became known as the Wilderness Road, a passage that more than 300,000 settlers would use over the next twenty-five years. At a point where a branch of the Wilderness Road intersected with the Kentucky River, near what is now Lexington, Boone built a settlement that was named Boonesborough.

A steady stream of settlers, mostly Scotch-Irish from Pennsylvania, Virginia, and North Carolina, poured into Kentucky during the last quarter of the eighteenth century. The backcountry settlers came on foot or horseback, often leading a mule or a cow that carried their few tools and other possessions. On a good day they might cover fifteen miles. Near a creek or spring they would buy a parcel or stake out a claim and mark its boundaries by chopping notches into "witness trees." They would then build a lean-to for temporary shelter and clear the land for planting. The pioneers grew melons, beans, turnips, and other vegetables, but corn was the preferred crop because it kept well and had so many uses. Pigs provided pork, and cows supplied milk, butter, and cheese. Many of the frontier families also built crude stills to manufacture a potent whiskey they called corn likker.

The Wilderness Trail

Daniel Boone Escorting Settlers through the Cumberland Gap by George Caleb Bingham.

TRANSFER OF POWER

By 1796 President Washington had decided that two terms in office were enough. Weary of increasingly bitter political quarrels and the venom of the partisan press, he was ready to retire to Mount Vernon. He would leave behind a formidable record of achievement: the organization of a national government with demonstrated power, the establishment of the national credit and a growing economy, the settlement of territory previously held by Britain and Spain, the stabilization of the northwestern frontier, and the admission of three new states: Vermont (1791), Kentucky (1792), and Tennessee (1796).

WASHINGTON'S FAREWELL   President George Washington's farewell address to the nation focused on domestic policy and, in particular, on the need for unity among Americans in backing their new government. Washington decried the "baneful effects" of sectionalism and partisanship while acknowledging that parties were "useful checks upon the administration of the government, and serve to keep alive the spirit of liberty."

In foreign relations, he asserted, the United States should display "good faith and justice toward all nations" and avoid either "an habitual hatred or an habitual fondness" for other countries. The young nation should also "steer clear of permanent alliances with any portion of the foreign world." This statement drew little notice at the time, but it proved profoundly important in shaping American attitudes toward foreign policy for generations thereafter. Later spokesmen for such an isolationist policy would distort Washington's position by claiming that he had opposed any "entangling alliances." On the contrary, Washington was not preaching isolationism; he was instead warning against any further permanent arrangements like the one with France, still technically in effect. Washington recognized that "we may safely trust to temporary alliances for extraordinary emergencies." Washington's warning against permanent foreign entanglements served as a fundamental principle in U.S. foreign policy until the early twentieth century.

THE ELECTION OF 1796   With George Washington out of the race, the United States in 1796 held its first partisan election for president. The logical choice of the Federalists would have been Washington's protégé, Alexander Hamilton, the chief architect of their programs. But Hamilton's policies had left scars and made enemies. In Philadelphia a caucus of Federalist congressmen chose John Adams as their heir apparent, with Thomas Pinckney of South Carolina, fresh from his treaty negotiations in Spain, as the nominee for vice president. As expected, the Republicans drafted Thomas Jefferson and added geographic balance to the ticket with Aaron Burr of New York.

The growing strength of the Republicans, fueled by the smoldering resentment of Jay's Treaty, very nearly swept Jefferson into office and perhaps would have but for the public appeals of the French ambassador for Jefferson's election—an action that backfired. The Federalists won a majority among the electors, but Alexander Hamilton hatched an impulsive scheme that nearly threw the election away after all. Thomas Pinckney, Hamilton thought, would be easier to influence than the strong-minded Adams. He therefore sought to have the South Carolina Federalists withhold a few votes for Adams and bring Pinckney in first. The Carolinians cooperated, but New Englanders got wind of the scheme and dropped Pinckney. The upshot of Hamilton's failed scheme was to cut Pinckney out of both the presidency and the vice presidency and elect Jefferson vice president with sixty-eight electoral votes, to Adams's seventy-one.

THE ADAMS YEARS

Vain and cantankerous, short and paunchy, John Adams had crafted a distinguished career as a Massachusetts lawyer; a leader in the Revolutionary movement and the hardest-working member of the Continental Congress; a diplomat in France, Holland, and Britain; and George Washington's vice president. His political philosophy fell somewhere between Jefferson's and Hamilton's. He shared neither the one's faith in the common people nor the other's fondness for an aristocracy of "paper wealth." He favored the classic republican balance of aristocratic, democratic, and monarchical elements in government. A man of powerful intellect and forthright convictions, Adams was haunted by the feeling that he was never properly appreciated—and he may have been right. On the overriding issue of his administration, war and peace, he kept his head when others about him were losing theirs—probably at the cost of his reelection.

WAR WITH FRANCE   John Adams faced the daunting task of succeeding the most popular man in America. He inherited from George Washington his divided cabinet—there was as yet no precedent for changing personnel at the start of each new administration. Adams also inherited a menacing quarrel with France, a byproduct of Jay's Treaty. When John Jay had accepted the British position that food and naval stores, as well as war supplies, bound for enemy ports were contraband subject to seizure, the French reasoned that American cargo headed for British ports was subject to the same interpretation. The French loosed their corsairs with even more devastating effect than the British had in 1793–1794. By the time of Adams's inauguration, in 1797, the French had plundered some 300 American ships and broken diplomatic relations with the United States.

John Adams

Political philosopher and politician. Adams was the first president to take up residence in the White House, in 1800.

President Adams immediately acted to restore relations with France. In 1797 Charles Cotesworth Pinckney (brother of Thomas) sailed for

Paris with John Marshall, a Virginia Federalist, and Elbridge Gerry, a Massachusetts Republican, for further negotiations. After long, nagging delays the three commissioners were accosted by three French counterparts (whom Adams labeled X, Y, and Z in his report to Congress), agents of the French foreign minister, Charles-Maurice de Talleyrand. The French diplomats said that negotiations could begin only if the Americans paid a bribe of $250,000 to the French government.

Such bribes were common eighteenth-century diplomatic practice, but Talleyrand's price was high for a mere promise to negotiate. The American answer, according to the commissioners' report, was "no, no, not a sixpence." When the XYZ affair was reported in Congress and the press, the response was translated into the more stirring slogan "millions for defense but not one cent for tribute." Even the most partisan Republicans, except for Thomas Jefferson, were hard put to make any more excuses for the French, and many of them joined the chorus for war. An undeclared naval war in fact raged from 1798 to 1800, but Adams resisted a formal declaration of war.

Conflict with France

A cartoon indicating the anti-French sentiment generated by the XYZ affair. The three American ministers (at left) reject the "Paris Monster's" demand for money.

Congress, however, authorized the capture of armed French ships, suspended commerce with France, and renounced the 1778 Treaty of Alliance, which was already defunct.

Adams used the French crisis to strengthen American defenses. In 1798 Congress created a Department of the Navy, and by the end of 1799 the number of naval ships had increased from three to thirty-three. By then American ships had captured eight French vessels and secured America's overseas commerce.

By the fall of 1798, even before the naval war was fully under way, Talleyrand began to make peace overtures. Adams named three peace commissioners, who arrived in Paris to find themselves confronting a new government under First Consul Napoléon Bonaparte. They sought two objectives: $20 million to pay for the American ships seized by the French and the formal cancellation of the 1778 Treaty of Alliance. By the Convention of 1800, ratified in 1801, the French agreed only to terminate the alliance and the quasi war.

THE WAR AT HOME   The simmering naval conflict with France mirrored an ideological war at home between Federalists and Republicans. Already-heated partisan politics had begun boiling over during the latter years of Washington's administration. The rhetoric grew so personal that opponents commonly resorted to duels. Federalists and Republicans saw each other as traitors to the principles of the American Revolution. Thomas Jefferson, for example, decided that Alexander Hamilton, George Washington, John Adams, and other Federalists were suppressing individual liberty in order to promote selfish interests. He adamantly opposed Jay's Treaty because it was pro-British and anti-French, and he was disgusted by the army's suppression of the Whiskey Rebellion.

Such volatile issues forced Americans to take sides, and the Revolutionary generation of leaders, a group that John Adams had called the band of brothers, began to fragment into die-hard factions. Long-standing political friendships disintegrated amid the venomous partisan attacks and sectional divisions between North and South. Jefferson observed that a "wall of separation" had come to divide the nation's political leaders. "Politics and party hatreds," he wrote his daughter from the nation's capital, "destroy the happiness of every being here."

Jefferson was no innocent in the matter; his no-holds-barred tactics contributed directly to the partisan tensions. As vice president under Adams, he displayed a gracious deviousness. He led the Republican faction opposed to Adams and schemed to embarrass him. In 1797 Jefferson secretly hired a rogue journalist, James Callender, to produce a scurrilous pamphlet that described President Adams as a deranged monarchist intent upon naming himself king.

For his part the combative Adams refused to align himself completely with the Federalists, preferring instead to mimic George Washington and retain his independence as chief executive. He was too principled and too prickly to toe a party line. Soon after his election he invited Jefferson to join with him in creating a bipartisan administration. After all, they had worked well together in the Continental Congress and in France, and they harbored great respect for each other. After consulting with James Madison, however, Jefferson refused to accept the new president's offer. Within a year he and Adams were at each other's throats.

The conflict with France deepened the partisan divide emerging in the young United States. The real purpose of the French crisis all along, the more ardent Republicans suspected, was to provide Federalists with an excuse to put down domestic political opposition. The infamous Alien and Sedition Acts of 1798 lent credence to their suspicions. These and two other measures, passed amid the wave of patriotic war fever, limited freedom of speech and the press and the liberty of aliens. Proposed by extreme Federalists in Congress, the legislation did not originate with John Adams but had his blessing. Goaded by his wife, Abigail, his primary counselor, Adams signed the controversial statutes and in doing so made the greatest mistake of his presidency. By succumbing to the partisan hysteria and enacting the vindictive acts, Adams bore out what Benjamin Franklin had said about him years before: he "means well for his country, is always an honest man, often a wise one, but sometimes and in some things, absolutely out of his senses."

Three of the four repressive acts reflected native hostility to foreigners, especially the French and the Irish, a large number of whom had become active Republicans and were suspected of revolutionary intent. The Naturalization Act extended from five to fourteen years the residency requirement for citizenship. The Alien Act empowered the president to deport "dangerous" aliens at his discretion. The Alien Enemies Act authorized the president in time of declared war to expel or imprison enemy aliens at will. Finally, the Sedition Act defined as a high misdemeanor any conspiracy against legal measures of the government, including interference with federal officers and insurrection or rioting. What is more, the law forbade writing, publishing, or speaking anything of "a false, scandalous and malicious" nature against the government.

The purpose of such laws was transparently partisan, designed to punish Republicans. Of the ten convictions under the act, all were directed at Republicans, some for trivial matters. In the very first case a drunk Republican was fined $100 for wishing out loud that the wad of a salute cannon might hit President Adams in his rear. The few convictions under the act only created martyrs to the cause of freedom of speech and the press and exposed the vindictiveness of Federalist judges.

To offset the "reign of witches" unleashed by the Alien and Sedition Acts, Jefferson and Madison drafted the Kentucky and Virginia Resolutions. These passed the legislatures of their respective states in late 1798. The resolutions, much alike in their arguments, denounced the Alien and Sedition Acts as "alarming infractions" of constitutional rights and advanced the state-compact theory. Since the Constitution arose as a compact among the states, the resolutions argued, it followed logically that the states retained the right to say when Congress had exceeded its powers. The states could "interpose" their judgment on acts of Congress and "nullify" them if necessary.

These doctrines of interposition and nullification, reworked by later theorists, were destined to be used for causes unforeseen by their authors. At the time, it seems, both Jefferson and Madison intended the resolutions to serve chiefly as propaganda, the opening guns in the presidential campaign of 1800. Neither Kentucky nor Virginia took steps to nullify or interpose its authority in the enforcement of the Alien and Sedition Acts. Instead, both called upon the other states to help them win a repeal in Congress. In Virginia, citizens talked of armed resistance to the federal government.

REPUBLICAN VICTORY   As the presidential election of 1800 approached, civil unrest boiled over. Grievances were mounting against Federalist policies: taxation to support an unneeded army, the Alien and Sedition Acts, the lingering fears of John Adams's affinity for "monarchism," the hostilities aroused by Alexander Hamilton's economic programs, the suppression of the Whiskey Rebellion, and Jay's Treaty. When Adams opted for peace with France in 1800, he probably doomed his one chance for reelection. Only a wave of patriotic war fever with a united party behind him could have gained him victory at the polls. His decision for peace gained him much goodwill among Americans but left the Hamiltonians angry and his party divided.

In 1800 the Federalists summoned enough unity to name Adams and Charles Cotesworth Pinckney as their candidates. But the Hamiltonian Federalists continued to snipe at the president and his policies, and soon after his renomination Adams removed two of them from his cabinet. A furious Hamilton struck back with a pamphlet questioning Adams's fitness to be president, citing his "disgusting egotism." Intended for private distribution among Federalist leaders, the pamphlet reached the hands of Aaron Burr, who circulated it widely.

Jefferson and Burr, as the Republican presidential candidates, once again represented the alliance of Virginia and New York. Jefferson, perhaps even more than Adams, became the target of vitriolic abuse. Opponents labeled him an atheist and a supporter of the excesses of the French Revolution. Jefferson refused to answer the attacks and directed the campaign from his Virginia home at Monticello. He was portrayed as a friend to farmers and a champion of states' rights, frugal government, liberty, and peace.

John Adams proved more popular than his party, whose candidates generally fared worse than the president, but the Republicans edged him out by seventy-three electoral votes to sixty-five. The decisive states were New York and South Carolina, either of which might have given the victory to Adams. But in New York former senator Aaron Burr's organization won control of the legislature, which cast the electoral votes. In South Carolina, Charles Pinckney (cousin of the Federalist Pinckneys) won over the legislature with well-placed promises of Republican patronage. Still, the result was not final, for Jefferson and Burr had tied with seventy-three votes each, and the choice of the president was thrown into the House of Representatives, where Federalist diehards tried vainly to give the election to Burr. This was too much for Hamilton, who opposed Jefferson but held a much lower opinion of Burr. The stalemate in the House continued for thirty-five ballots. The deadlock was broken only when a Jefferson supporter assured a Federalist congressman from Delaware that Jefferson would refrain from the wholesale removal of Federalists appointed to federal offices and would uphold Hamilton's financial policies. The representative resolved to vote for Jefferson, and several other Federalists agreed simply to cast blank ballots, permitting Jefferson to win without any of them having to vote for him.

Before the Federalists relinquished power to the Jeffersonian Republicans on March 4, 1801, their lame-duck Congress passed the Judiciary Act of 1801. Intended to ensure Federalist control of the judicial system, this act created sixteen circuit courts with a new judge for each and increased the number of federal attorneys, clerks, and marshals. Before he left office, Adams named John Marshall to the vacant office of chief justice of the Supreme Court and appointed Federalists to all the new positions in the federal judiciary, including forty-two justices of the peace for the new District of Columbia. The Federalists, defeated and destined never to regain national power, had in the words of Jefferson "retired into the judiciary as a stronghold."

The election of 1800 marked a major turning point in American political history. It was the first time that one political party, however ungracefully, relinquished power to the opposition party. Jefferson's victory signaled the

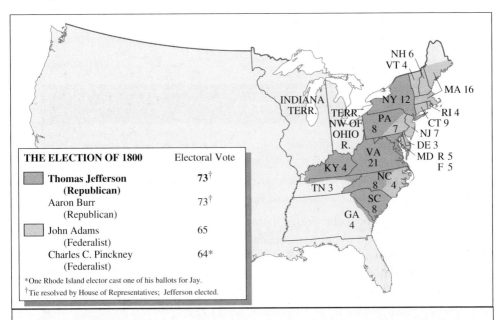

THE ELECTION OF 1800	Electoral Vote
Thomas Jefferson (Republican)	73[†]
Aaron Burr (Republican)	73[†]
John Adams (Federalist)	65
Charles C. Pinckney (Federalist)	64*

*One Rhode Island elector cast one of his ballots for Jay.
[†]Tie resolved by House of Representatives; Jefferson elected.

Why was the election of 1800 a key moment in American history? How did the Republicans win New York and South Carolina? How did Congress break the tie between Jefferson and Burr?

emergence of a new, more democratic political system, dominated by parties, partisanship, and wider public participation—at least among white men. Before and immediately after independence, politics was a popular but undemocratic activity: people took a keen interest in public affairs, but socially prominent families, the "rich, the able, and the wellborn," dominated political life. However, the fierce political battles of the late 1790s, culminating in 1800 with Jefferson's election, wrested control of politics from the governing elite and established the right of more people to play an active role in governing the young republic. With the gradual elimination of property qualifications for voting and the proliferation of newspapers, pamphlets, and other publications, the "public sphere" in which political issues were debated and decided expanded enormously in the early nineteenth century.

John Adams regretted the democratization of politics and the rise of fractious partisanship. "Jefferson had a party, Hamilton had a party, but the commonwealth had none," he sighed. The defeated president was so distraught at the turn of events that he decided not to participate in Jefferson's inauguration in the new capital of Washington, D.C. Instead, he boarded a stagecoach for the 500-mile trip to his home in Quincy, Massachusetts. He and Jefferson would not communicate for the next twelve years.

MAKING CONNECTIONS

- Thomas Jefferson's Republican philosophy offered a strong alternative to Alexander Hamilton's Federalism. As the next chapter shows, however, once the Republicans got into power, they adopted a number of Federalist principles and positions.

- The Bank of the United States and the protective tariff continued to be controversial. The bank's charter was renewed for another twenty years in 1816, the same year in which the first truly protective tariff was passed (Chapter 10), but in the 1830s the bank was eliminated, and the tariff became a major source of sectional conflict (Chapter 11).

- The foreign-policy crises with England and France described in this chapter will lead to the War of 1812, discussed in Chapter 9.

FURTHER READING

The best introduction to the early Federalists remains John C. Miller's *The Federalist Era, 1789–1801* (1960). Other works analyze the ideological debates among the nation's first leaders. Richard Buel Jr.'s *Securing the Revolution: Ideology in American Politics, 1789–1815* (1972), Joyce Appleby's *Capitalism and a New Social Order: The Republican Vision of the 1790s* (1984), Drew R. McCoy's *The Last of the Fathers: James Madison and the Republican Legacy* (1989), and Stanley Elkins and Eric McKitrick's *The Age of Federalism: The Early American Republic, 1788–1800* (1993) trace the persistence and transformation of ideas first fostered during the Revolutionary crisis. John F. Hoadley's *Origins of American Political Parties, 1789–1803* (1986) is superb.

Federalist foreign policy is explored in Jerald A. Comb's *The Jay Treaty: Political Battleground of the Founding Fathers* (1970), William Stinchcombe's *The XYZ Affair* (1980), and Felix Gilbert's *To the Farewell Address: Ideas of Early American Foreign Policy* (1961).

For specific domestic issues, see Thomas P. Slaughter's *The Whiskey Rebellion: Frontier Epilogue to the American Revolution* (1986) and Harry Ammon's *The Genet Mission* (1973). Patricia Watlington's *The Partisan Spirit: Kentucky Politics, 1779–1792* (1972) examines the Kentucky Resolutions. The treatment of Indians in the Old Northwest is explored in Richard H. Kohn's *Eagle and Sword: The Federalists and the Creation of the Military Establishment in America, 1783–1802* (1975). For the Alien and Sedition Acts, consult James Morton Smith's *Freedom's Fetters: The Alien and Sedition Laws and American Civil Liberties* (1956). Daniel Sisson's *The American Revolution of 1800* (1974) is useful for its treatment of that important election.

Several books focus on social issues of the post-Revolutionary period, including *Keepers of the Revolution: New Yorkers at Work in the Early Republic* (1992), edited by Paul A. Gilje and Howard B. Rock; Ronald Schultz's *The Republic of Labor: Philadelphia Artisans and the Politics of Class, 1720–1830* (1993); and Peter Way's *Common Labour: Workers and the Digging of North American Canals, 1780–1860* (1993).

The African-American experience in the Revolutionary era is detailed in Mechal Sobel's *The World They Made Together: Black and White Values in Eighteenth-Century Virginia* (1987) and Gary B. Nash's *Forging Freedom: The Formation of Philadelphia's Black Community, 1720–1840* (1988).

9

THE EARLY REPUBLIC

FOCUS QUESTIONS

· What were the domestic policies of the Republicans once they were in power?

· How did politics divide the early republic?

· What were the causes and effects of the War of 1812?

To answer these questions and access additional review material, please visit www.wwnorton.com/studyspace

The early years of the new republic laid the foundation for the nation's development as the first society in the world organized around the promise of equal opportunity for all—except African-American slaves, Indians, and women. White American men in the fifty years after independence were on the move and on the make. Their prospects seemed unlimited, their optimism unrestrained. Land sales west of the Appalachian Mountains soared in the early nineteenth century as aspiring farmers shoved Indians aside in order to establish homesteads of their own. Enterprising, mobile, and increasingly diverse in religion and national origin, thousands of ordinary folk uprooted themselves from settled communities and went in search of personal advancement, occupying more territory in a single generation than had been settled in the 150 years of colonial history. Between 1800 and 1820 the trans-Appalachian population soared from 300,000 to 2 million. By 1840 over 40 percent of Americans lived west of the mountains in eight new states.

The migrants flowed westward in three streams between 1780 and 1830. One ran from the Old South—Virginia, Maryland, and the Carolinas—through Georgia into the newer states of Alabama and Mississippi. Another wave traversed the Blue Ridge Mountains from Maryland and Virginia, crossing into Kentucky and Tennessee. The third route was in the North, taking New Englanders westward across the Berkshires into New York, Pennsylvania, Ohio, and Michigan. Many of the pioneers stayed only a few years before continuing westward in search of cheaper and more fertile land.

The spirit of opportunistic independence affected free blacks as well as whites, Indians as well as immigrants. Free blacks were the fastest growing segment of the population during the early nineteenth century. Many slaves had gained their freedom during the Revolutionary War, by escaping, joining British forces, or serving in American units. Every state except South Carolina promised freedom to slaves who fought the British. Afterward state after state in the North outlawed slavery, and anti-slavery societies blossomed, exerting increasing pressure on the South to end the degrading practice.

The westward migration of whites brought incessant conflict with Native Americans. Indians fiercely resisted but ultimately succumbed to a federal government and a federal army determined to displace them. Most white Americans, however, were less concerned about Indians and slavery than they were about seizing their own opportunities. Politicians suppressed the volatile issue of slavery; their priorities were elsewhere. Westward expansion, economic growth, urban development, and the democratization of politics fostered a pervasive entrepreneurial spirit among the generation of Americans born after 1776—especially outside the South. In 1790 nine out of ten Americans lived on the land and engaged in what is called household production; their sphere of activity was local. But with each passing year, farmers increasingly focused on producing surplus crops and livestock to be sold in regional markets. Cotton prices soared, and in the process the Deep South grew ever more committed to a plantation economy dependent upon slave labor, world markets, and New England shippers and merchants. The burgeoning market economy produced boom-and-bust cycles, but overall the years from 1790 to 1830 were quite prosperous, with young Americans experiencing a "widening scope of opportunity."

While most Americans after the Revolution continued to work as farmers, a growing number of young adults found employment in new or greatly expanded enterprises: textiles, banking, transportation, publishing, retailing, teaching, preaching, medicine, law, construction, and engineering.

Technological innovations (steam power, power tools, and new modes of transportation) and their social applications (mass communication turn-pikes, the postal service, banks, and corporations) fostered an array of new industries and businesses. The emergence of a factory system transformed the nature of work for many Americans. Proud apprentices, journeymen, and master craftsmen, who controlled their labor and invested their work with an emphasis on quality rather than quantity, resented the prolifera-tion of mills and factories populated by "half-trained" workers dependent upon an hourly wage and subject to the sharp fluctuations of the larger economy.

Young America was rapidly changing. The decentralized agrarian republic of 1776, nestled along the Atlantic seaboard, had become by 1830 a sprawl-ing commercial nation connected by networks of roads and canals and ce-mented by economic relationships—all animated by a restless spirit of en-terprise, experimentation, and expansion.

JEFFERSONIAN SIMPLICITY

On March 4, 1801, the soft-spoken, brilliant, and charming Thomas Jefferson became the first president to be inaugurated in the new federal city. Washington, District of Columbia, was then an array of undistinguished buildings clustered around two centers, Capitol Hill and the executive man-sion. Congress, having met in eight towns since 1774, had at last found a permanent home but enjoyed few amenities. There were two places of amusement, a racetrack and a theater thick with "tobacco smoke, whiskey breaths, and other stenches." Practically deserted much of the year, the na-tion's new capital came to life only when Congress assembled.

Jefferson's inauguration befitted the simple surroundings. The new presi-dent walked two blocks from his lodgings to the unfinished Capitol, entered the Senate chamber, took the oath administered by the recently appointed chief justice John Marshall, read his address in a barely audible voice, and re-turned to his boardinghouse for dinner. A tone of simplicity and concilia-tion ran through Jefferson's inaugural address. "We are all Republicans—we are all Federalists," he assured the nation. He then presented a ringing affir-mation of republican government: "I know, indeed, that some honest men fear that a republican government cannot be strong; that this government is not strong enough. I believe this, on the contrary, the strongest government on earth. I believe it is the only one where every man . . . would meet inva-sions of the public order as his own personal concern."

JEFFERSON IN OFFICE

The deliberate display of republican simplicity at Jefferson's inauguration set the style of his administration. Although a man of expensive personal tastes, he took pains to avoid the monarchical trappings of his Federalist predecessors. Jefferson, a widower, discarded the coach and six in which Washington and Adams had traveled to state occasions and rode about the city on horseback, often by himself. He continued to wear plain clothes. White House dinners were held at a circular table so that no one should take precedence. This practice infuriated several European diplomats accustomed to aristocratic formalities, and they boycotted White House affairs.

Jefferson liked to think of his election as the "revolution of 1800," but the electoral margin had been razor thin, and the policies that he followed were more conciliatory than revolutionary. Jefferson placed in policy-making positions men of his own party, and he was the first president to pursue the role of party leader, cultivating congressional support at his dinner parties and elsewhere. In the cabinet the leading figures were Secretary of State James Madison, a longtime neighbor and political ally, and Swiss-born secretary of the Treasury Albert Gallatin, a Pennsylvania Republican whose financial skills had won him the respect of the Federalists. In an effort to cultivate Federalist New England, Jefferson chose men from that region for the positions of attorney general, secretary of war, and postmaster general.

The Executive Mansion

A watercolor of the president's house during Jefferson's term in office. Jefferson called it "big enough for two emperors, one pope, and the grand lama in the bargain."

In lesser offices, Jefferson resisted the wholesale removal of Federalists, preferring to wait until vacancies appeared. But pressure from Republicans often forced him to remove the Federalists. In one area, however, he managed to remove the offices rather than the appointees. In 1802 Congress repealed the Judiciary Act of 1801 and so abolished the circuit judgeships and other offices to which John Adams had made his "midnight appointments" before leaving office. A new judiciary act restored to six the number of Supreme Court justices and set up six circuit courts, each headed by a justice.

MARBURY V. MADISON The "midnight appointments" that President Adams made just before he left office sparked the important case of *Marbury v. Madison* (1803), the first in which the Supreme Court asserted its right to declare an act of Congress unconstitutional. The case involved the appointment of the Maryland Fedaralist William Marbury as justice of the peace in the District of Columbia. Marbury's official letter of appointment, or commission, signed by President Adams just two days before he left office, remained undelivered when James Madison became secretary of state, and President Jefferson directed him to withhold it. Marbury then sued for a court order (a writ of mandamus) directing Madison to deliver his commission. Chief Justice John Marshall, a distant Virginia cousin of Jefferson's, wrote the Court's opinion. He held that Marbury deserved his commission but denied that the Court had jurisdiction in the case. Marshall and the court ruled that Section 13 of the Federal Judiciary Act of 1789, which gave the Court original jurisdiction in mandamus proceedings, was unconstitutional because the Constitution specified that the Court should have original jurisdiction only in cases involving ambassadors or states. The Court, therefore, could issue no order in the case. With one bold stroke, the Federalist Marshall had chastised the Jeffersonians while avoiding an awkward confrontation with an administration that might have defied his order. At the same time he established the stunning precedent of the Court's declaring a federal law invalid on the grounds that it violated provisions of the Constitution.

DOMESTIC REFORMS Jefferson's first term was a succession of triumphs in both domestic and foreign affairs. The president did not set out to discard Alexander Hamilton's Federalist economic program. Under the tutelage of Treasury Secretary Gallatin, he learned to accept the national bank as an essential convenience. It was too late, of course, to undo Hamilton's funding and debt-assumption operations but none too soon, in the opinion of both Jefferson and Gallatin, to begin retiring the resultant federal debt. Jefferson detested

Hamilton's belief that a regulated federal debt was a national "blessing" because it gave the bankers and investors who lent money to the U.S. government a direct stake in the success of the new republic. Jefferson believed that a large federal debt would bring only high taxes and government corruption, so he set about reducing government expenses and paying down the debt. In 1802 Jefferson won the repeal of the whiskey tax and other Federalist excises, much to the relief of backwoods distillers, drinkers, and grain farmers.

Without the revenue from excise taxes, frugality was all the more necessary to a federal government chiefly dependent upon its tariffs and the sale of western lands for revenue. Happily for the Treasury, both trade and land sales flourished. The European war continually increased American shipping traffic, and thus tariff revenues padded the Treasury. At the same time, settlers flocked to the western land purchased from the federal government. Ohio's admission to the Union in 1803 increased the number of states to seventeen.

By the "wise and frugal government" that the president promised in his inaugural address, Jefferson and Gallatin reasoned, the United States could live within its income, like a prudent farmer. The basic formula was simple: cut back on military expenses. A standing army menaced a free society anyway. It therefore should be kept to a minimum, with defense left primarily to state militias. The navy, which the Federalists had already reduced, ought to be reduced further. Coastal defense, Jefferson argued, should rely upon land-based fortifications and a "mosquito fleet" of small gunboats.

In 1807 Jefferson crowned his reforms by signing an act that outlawed the foreign slave trade as of January 1, 1808, the earliest date possible under the Constitution. At the time, South Carolina was the only state that still permitted the trade, but for years to come an illegal traffic in Africans would continue. By one informal estimate perhaps 300,000 enslaved blacks were smuggled into southern states between 1808 and 1861.

THE LOUISIANA PURCHASE   In 1803 events produced the greatest single achievement of Jefferson's administration. The Louisiana Purchase of 1803 more than doubled the territory of the United States by bringing into its borders the entire Mississippi River valley west of the river itself.

The French had settled Louisiana in the early eighteenth century, but after their defeat by England in the Seven Years' War they had ceded the territory to Spain in exchange for West Florida. Soon after taking power in France in 1799, however, Napoléon had forced the Spanish to return the territory and expressed his intention of creating a North American empire. When word of the deal reached Washington, D.C. in 1801, Jefferson dispatched the New Yorker Robert R. Livingston, as the new American minister to France. Spain

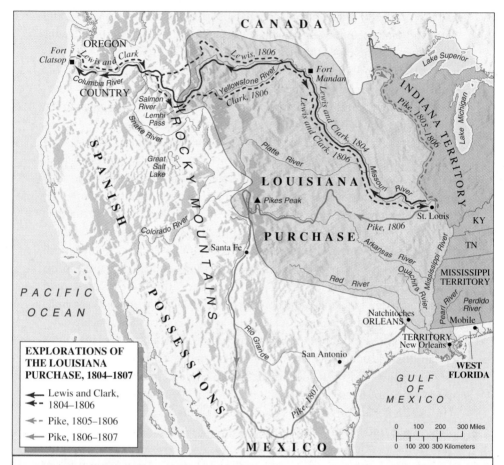

How did the United States acquire the Louisiana Purchase? What was the mission of Lewis and Clark's expedition? What were the consequences of Lewis and Clark's reports about the Western territory?

in control of the Mississippi River outlet was bad enough, but Napoléon in control could mean serious trouble.

Livingston engaged the French in a series of long and frustrating negotiations. In April 1803 Napoléon's foreign minister, Talleyrand, suddenly asked if the United States would like to buy the whole of Louisiana. Livingston, once he regained his composure, snapped up the offer. Disease again played an important role in shaping history. Napoléon was willing to sell the territory because his French army on Hispaniola had been decimated not only by a slave revolt but also by yellow fever. Having failed to conquer the sugar-rich island and eager to renew his struggle against England, Napoléon had apparently decided simply to cut his losses in the New World, turn a quick profit, please the Americans, and go back to reshaping the map of Europe.

By the treaty of cession, dated April 30, 1803, the United States paid about $15 million for the huge territory. The treaty was vague in defining the boundaries of Louisiana. Its language could be stretched to provide a tenuous claim on Texas and a much stronger claim on West Florida, from Baton Rouge on the Mississippi River past Mobile to the Perdido River on the east. When Livingston asked about the boundaries, Talleyrand responded: "I can give you no direction. You have made a noble bargain for yourselves, and I suppose you will make the most of it."

The surprising turn of events presented Jefferson with a great new "empire of liberty"—and a constitutional dilemma. Nowhere did the Constitution mention the purchase of territory. Jefferson at first suggested a constitutional amendment, but his advisers argued against delay lest Napoléon change his mind. The power to purchase territory, they reasoned, resided in the power to make treaties. In the end, Jefferson relented, trusting, he said, "that the good sense of our country will correct the evil of loose construction when it shall produce ill effects." New England Federalists boggled at the prospect of new western states that would probably strengthen the Jeffersonian party. In a reversal that foreshadowed many similar reversals on constitutional issues, Federalists found themselves arguing for strict construction of the Constitution while Republicans brushed aside such scruples. Gaining over 800,000 square miles trumped any legal concerns. The Senate ratified the treaty by an overwhelming vote of twenty-six to six, and on December 20, 1803, U.S. representatives took formal possession of the vast Louisiana Territory.

The Spanish kept West Florida, but within a decade it would be ripe for the plucking. American settlers in 1810 staged a rebellion in Baton Rouge and proclaimed the republic of West Florida, which was quickly annexed and occupied by the United States as far east as the Pearl River. In 1812 the state of Louisiana absorbed the region. The following year, with Spain itself a battlefield for French and British forces, U.S. troops took over the rest of West Florida, now the Gulf coast of the states of Mississippi and Alabama. The United States had truly made the most of a shrewd bargain.

THE LEWIS AND CLARK EXPEDITION   An amateur scientist long before he became president, Thomas Jefferson asked Congress to finance a mapping and scientific expedition to explore the far Northwest in 1803, beyond the Mississippi, in what was still foreign territory. Congress approved, and Jefferson assigned as commanders the twenty-nine-year-old Meriwether Lewis, his former private secretary, and another Virginian, a former army officer, William Clark.

In 1804 the "Corps of Discovery," numbering nearly fifty, set out from the small village of St. Louis to ascend the muddy Missouri River. Local Indians introduced them to clothes made from deer hides and taught them hunting techniques. Lewis and Clark kept detailed journals of their travels and drew maps of the unexplored regions. As they moved up the Missouri, the landscape changed from forest to prairie grass. They saw huge herds of bison and other large game animals, which had become more abundant after a smallpox epidemic had wiped out most of the Indian villages in the area. The expedition passed trappers and traders headed south with rafts and boats laden with furs. Six months after leaving St. Louis, near the Mandan Sioux villages in what is now North Dakota, they built a fort and wintered in relative comfort, sending back a barge loaded with maps, soil samples, and plant and animal specimens. In the spring they added to their main party a French guide and his remarkable Shoshone wife, Sacagawea, and they set out once again upstream. At the head of the Missouri River, they took the north fork, thenceforth named the Jefferson River, crossed the rugged Rocky Mountains, braved attacks by grizzly bears, and in dugout canoes descended the Snake and Columbia rivers to the Pacific. The following spring they split

Exploring the Far Northwest

Captain Clark and his men shooting bears, from a book of engravings of the Lewis and Clark expedition (ca. 1810).

into two parties, with Lewis heading back east by almost the same route and Clark going by way of the Yellowstone River. They reunited at the juncture of the Missouri and Yellowstone rivers, returning together to St. Louis in 1806, having been gone nearly two and a half years and having traversed over 8,000 miles. No longer was the Far West unknown country. Their reports of friendly Indians and abundant beaver pelts attracted traders and trappers to the region and gave the United States a claim to the Oregon Country by right of discovery and exploration.

POLITICAL SCHEMES   President Jefferson's policies, including the Louisiana Purchase, brought him solid support in the South and the West. Even New Englanders were moving to his side. By 1809 John Quincy Adams, the son of the second president, would become a Republican. Die-hard Federalists read the handwriting on the wall. The acquisition of vast new territories in the West would reduce New England and the Federalist party to insignificance in political affairs. Under the leadership of Timothy Pickering, secretary of state under Washington and Adams and now a U.S. senator, a group of bitter Massachusetts Federalists called the Essex Junto considered seceding from the Union, an idea that would simmer in New England for another decade.

Timothy Pickering and other Federalists also hatched a scheme that involved Vice President Aaron Burr, who had been on the outs with the Jeffersonians. Their plan, which would link New York with New England and depended upon Burr's election as governor of New York, could not win the support of even the extreme Federalists: Alexander Hamilton bitterly opposed it on the grounds that Burr was "a dangerous man, and one who ought not to be trusted with the reins of government."

Those remarks led to a duel between Hamilton and Burr in July 1804 at Weehawken, New Jersey, across the Hudson River from New York City. Hamilton personally opposed dueling, but his romantic streak and sense of manly honor compelled him to meet the vice president's challenge and demonstrate his courage—he was determined not to kill his opponent. Burr had no such scruples. On a grassy ledge above the Hudson River, he shot Hamilton through the heart. Hamilton went to his death, as his son had gone to his in a similar duel, also settled in Weehawken, the previous year. Hamilton's death ended both Pickering's scheme and Burr's political career—but not Burr's intrigues.

Burr would lose the gubernatorial election. In the meantime, the presidential campaign of 1804 began when a Republican congressional caucus renominated Jefferson. Opposed by the Federalist Charles C. Pinckney, Jefferson won 162 of the 176 electoral votes. It was the first landslide election in American history.

DIVISIONS IN THE REPUBLICAN PARTY

JOHN RANDOLPH AND THE OLD REPUBLICANS   Freed from a strong opposition—Federalists made up only one quarter of the new Congress—the Republican majority began to lose its cohesion as the nineteenth century progressed. The Virginia congressman known as John Randolph of Roanoke, initially a Jefferson supporter, became the most conspicuous of the dissidents. A brilliant, witty, but erratic and unyielding Virginia planter-philosopher, he was a powerful combination of principle, intelligence, wit, arrogance, and rancor.

Randolph became the crusty spokesman for a shifting group of "Old Republicans," whose adherence to party principles had rendered them more Jeffersonian than Jefferson himself. The Old Republicans were mostly southerners who defended states' rights and strict construction of the Constitution. They opposed any compromise with the Federalists and promoted an agrarian way of life. The Jeffersonian, or moderate, Republicans tended to be more pragmatic and nationalist in their orientation. As Thomas Jefferson himself demonstrated, they were willing to go along with tariffs and national banks. Randolph broke with Jefferson in 1806, when the president sought an appropriation of $2 million for a thinly disguised bribe to win French influence in persuading Spain to give up the Floridas. Thereafter he resisted Jefferson's initiatives almost reflexively. Randolph and his colleagues were sometimes called Quids, or the Tertium Quid (Third Something), and their dissent gave rise to talk of a third party, neither Republican nor Federalist. But they never got together, and their failure would typify the experience of almost all third-party movements thereafter.

THE BURR CONSPIRACY   Sheer brilliance and shrewdness had carried Aaron Burr to the vice presidency, and he might have become Jefferson's heir apparent but for his taste for intrigue. Caught up in the dubious schemes of Federalist diehards in 1800 and again in 1804, he ended his political career when he killed Alexander Hamilton. Indicted in New York and New Jersey for murder and heavily in debt, Burr fled first to Spanish-held Florida. Once the furor subsided, the vice president boldly returned to Washington in November to preside over the Senate. As long as he stayed out of New York and New Jersey, he was safe.

But Burr focused his attention less on the Senate than on a cockeyed scheme to carve out a personal empire for himself in the West. The so-called Burr conspiracy originated when Burr met with General James Wilkinson, an old friend with a tainted Revolutionary War record who was a spy for the

Spanish and had a penchant for easy money, a taste for rum, and an eye for intrigue. Just what Wilkinson and Burr were up to will probably never be known. The most likely explanation is that they sought to organize a secession of the Louisiana territory and set up an independent republic. Wilkinson developed cold feet, however, and sent a letter to President Jefferson warning of "a deep, dark, wicked and wide-spread conspiracy." Traveling south to recruit adventurers, Burr was apprehended and taken to Richmond, Virginia, for a trial that, like the conspiracy, had a stellar cast. Charged with treason, Burr was brought before Chief Justice John Marshall.

The case established two major constitutional precedents. The first came about when Jefferson, on the grounds of executive privilege, ignored a subpoena requiring him to appear in court with certain papers. He believed that the independence of the executive branch would be compromised if the president were subject to a court writ. The second was Marshall's rigid definition of treason. Treason under the Constitution, Marshall concluded, consisted of "levying war against the United States or adhering to their enemies" and required "two witnesses to the same overt act." Since the prosecution failed to produce two witnesses to an overt act of treason by Burr, the jury found him not guilty. To avoid further legal entanglements, Burr left the country for France. He returned unmolested in 1812 to practice law in New York and died at the age of eighty.

WAR IN EUROPE

Oppositionists of whatever stripe were more an annoyance than a threat to Jefferson. The more intractable problems of his second term involved the renewal of the European war in 1803, which helped resolve the problem of Louisiana but put more strains on Jefferson's desire to avoid "entangling alliances" and the quarrels of Europe. In 1805 Napoléon's defeat of Russian and Austrian forces gave him control of western Europe. That same year the British

Preparation for War to Defend Commerce

In 1806 and 1807 American shipping was caught in the crossfire of the war between Britain and France.

defeat of the French and Spanish fleets in the Battle of Trafalgar secured Britain's control of the seas. The war turned into a battle of elephant and whale, Napoléon dominant on land, the British dominant on the water, neither able to strike a decisive blow at the other, and neither restrained by concerns over neutral rights or international law.

HARASSMENT BY BRITAIN AND FRANCE   For two years after the renewal of European warfare, American shippers reaped the benefits, taking over trade with the French and Spanish West Indies. But in the case of the *Essex* (1805), a British court ruled that the practice of shipping French and Spanish goods through U.S. ports on their way elsewhere did not neutralize enemy goods. The practice violated the British rule of 1756, under which trade closed in time of peace remained closed in time of war. Goods shipped in violation of the rule, the British held, could be seized at any point under the doctrine of continuous voyage. After 1807 British interference with American shipping increased, not just to keep supplies from Napoléon's continent but also to hobble competition with British merchant ships.

In 1806 the British ministry adopted orders in council, which set up a paper blockade of Europe. Vessels headed for European ports had to get British licenses and accept British inspection or be liable to seizure. It was a paper blockade because even the powerful British navy was not large enough to monitor every European port. Napoléon retaliated with his "Continental System," proclaimed in the Berlin Decree of 1806 and the Milan Decree of 1807. In the first he declared his own paper blockade of the British Isles; in the second he ruled that neutral ships that complied with British regulations were subject to seizure when they reached Continental ports. The situation presented American shippers with a dilemma: if they complied with the demands of one side, they were subject to seizure by the other.

The risks were daunting, but the prospects for profits were so great that American shippers ran the risk. Seamen faced a more dangerous risk: a renewal of the practice of impressment. The use of press-gangs to kidnap men in British (and colonial) ports was a long-standing method of recruitment used by the British navy. The seizure of British subjects from American vessels became a new source of recruits, justified on the principle that British subjects remained British subjects for life: "Once an Englishman, always an Englishman."

In the summer of 1807, the British frigate, *Leopard* accosted a U.S. vessel, the *Chesapeake,* just outside territorial waters off the coast of Virginia. After the *Chesapeake*'s captain refused to allow his ship to be searched, the *Leopard* opened fire, killing three and wounding eighteen. The *Chesapeake,* unready for battle, was forced to strike its colors (that is, to lower its flag as a sign of surrender). A British search party seized four men, one of whom was later hanged for desertion from the British navy. Public wrath was so aroused that Jefferson could have had war on the spot. Like Adams before him, however, he resisted war fever and suffered politically as a result.

THE EMBARGO   Jefferson resolved to use public indignation at the British to promote "peaceable coercion." In December 1807, in response to his request, Congress passed the Embargo Act, which stopped all exports of American goods and prohibited American ships from leaving for foreign ports. It also effectively ended imports, since it was unprofitable for foreign ships to return from America empty. The constitutional basis of the embargo was the power to regulate commerce, which in this case Republicans interpreted broadly as the power to prohibit commerce.

Jefferson's embargo failed from the beginning, however, because few Americans were willing to make the necessary sacrifices. Trade remained profitable despite the risks, and violating the embargo was almost laughably easy. While American ships sat idle in ports, their crews laid off and unpaid, smugglers flourished and the British enjoyed a near monopoly of legitimate trade. Neither France nor Great Britain was significantly hurt by Jefferson's policy.

But Jefferson was injured. The unpopular embargo revived the languishing Federalist party in New England, which renewed the charge that Jefferson was in league with the French. At the same time, agriculture in the South and the West suffered for want of foreign outlets for grain, cotton, and tobacco. After fifteen months, Jefferson accepted failure, and on March 1, 1809, he signed a repeal of the embargo shortly before he relinquished the "splendid misery" of the presidency. In the election of 1808, the presidency passed to another Virginian, Secretary of State James Madison.

THE DRIFT TO WAR   Madison was entangled in foreign affairs from the beginning of his presidency. Still insisting on neutral rights and freedom of the seas, he pursued Jefferson's policy of "peaceful coercion" by different but equally ineffective means. In place of the embargo, Congress had substituted the Nonintercourse Act, which reopened trade with all countries except France and Great Britain and authorized the president to reopen trade with whichever nation gave up its restrictions. Nonintercourse proved as impotent as the embargo. In the vain search for an alternative, Congress in 1810, reversed itself and adopted a measure introduced by Nathaniel Macon of North Carolina. Macon's bill reopened trade with the warring powers but provided that if either dropped its restrictions, nonintercourse would be restored with the other.

Napoléon's foreign minister, the duke de Cadore, informed the U.S. minister in Paris that he had withdrawn the Berlin and Milan Decrees, but the carefully worded Cadore letter had strings attached: revocation of the decrees depended upon withdrawal of the British orders in council. The strings were plain to see, but Madison either misunderstood or, more likely, went along in the hope of putting pressure on the British. The British initially refused to give in, and on June 1, 1812, Madison reluctantly asked Congress for a declaration of war. On June 16, 1812, however, the British foreign minister, facing economic crisis, revoked the orders in council. Britain preferred not to risk war with the United States on top of its war with Napoléon. But it was too late. On June 18, 1812, Congress, unaware of the British repeal, granted Madison's request for war. With more time, more patience, or a transatlantic cable, Madison's policy would have been vindicated without resort to war.

THE WAR OF 1812

CAUSES   The main cause of the war—the violation of neutral shipping rights—seems clear enough. Neutral rights dominated Madison's war message and provided the salient reason for mounting public hostility toward the British. Yet the geographic distribution of the congressional vote raised a troubling question. Most votes for war came from the farm regions that stretched from Pennsylvania southward and westward. The maritime states of New York and New England, the region that bore the brunt of British attacks on U.S. trade, voted against the declaration. One explanation for this seeming anomaly is simple enough. The farming regions suffered damage to their markets for grain, cotton, and tobacco while New England shippers made profits from smuggling in spite of the British restrictions.

Other plausible explanations for the sectional vote, however, include frontier Indian attacks that were blamed on the British, western land hunger, and the American desire for territory in British Canada and Spanish Florida. The constant pressure to open new lands repeatedly forced or persuaded Indians to sign treaties they did not always understand, causing stronger resentment among tribes that were losing more and more of their land. It was an old story, dating from the Jamestown settlement, but one that took a new turn with the rise of a powerful Shawnee leader, Tecumseh.

Tecumseh recognized the consequences of Indian disunity and set out to form a confederation of tribes to defend Indian hunting grounds, insisting that no land cession was valid without the consent of all tribes, since they held the land in common. By 1811 Tecumseh had matured his plans and headed south from the Indiana Territory to win the Creeks, Cherokees, Choctaws, and Chickasaws to his cause. His speeches were filled with emotion and anger. "The white race is a wicked race," he declared. "They seize your land; they corrupt your women." Only by driving them out "upon a trail of blood" would the Indians survive.

General William Henry Harrison, governor of the Indiana Territory, learned of Tecumseh's plans and met with him twice. In the fall of 1811, however, Harrison decided that Tecumseh must be stopped. He gathered 1,000 troops near the Shawnees' capital on the Tippecanoe River while the Indian leader was away. Although Tecumseh had warned the Shawnees against fighting in his absence, they attacked Harrison's encampment. One quarter of Harrison's men died or were wounded, yet the Shawnees lost the Battle of Tippecanoe; their town was burned, their supplies destroyed.

Tecumseh's dreams of an Indian confederacy went up in smoke, and the Shawnee leader sought British protection in Canada.

The Battle of Tippecanoe reinforced suspicions that the British were inciting the Indians. Frontier settlers believed that a U.S. conquest of Canada would end British influence among the Indians and open a new empire for land-hungry Americans. It was also one place where the British, in case of war, were vulnerable to an American attack. Madison and others acted on the mistaken assumption that the Canadians were eager to be liberated from British control. Thomas Jefferson had told Madison that the U.S. "acquisition of Canada" was "[a] matter of marching [north with a military force]." The British were vulnerable in Florida as well. East Florida, still under Spanish

Tecumseh

The Shawnee leader who tried to unite Indian tribes in defense of their land. He was killed in 1813 at the Battle of the Thames.

control, also posed a threat to the Americans, since Spain allowed sporadic Indian attacks across the frontier. Moreover, the British were suspected of smuggling goods through Florida and intriguing with the Indians on the southwestern border.

Such concerns helped generate war fever. In the Congress that assembled in 1811, several new members from southern and western districts clamored for war in defense of "national honor" and demanded an invasion of Canada. Among them were Henry Clay and Richard Mantor Johnson of Kentucky, Felix Grundy of Tennessee, and John C. Calhoun of South Carolina. John Randolph of Roanoke christened these "new boys" the "war hawks." The young senator Henry Clay, a tall, rawboned westerner know for his combative temperament and propensity for dueling, yearned for war. "I am for resistance by the *sword*," he vowed. He promised that the Kentucky militia stood ready to march on Canada and acquire its lucrative fur trade.

PREPARATIONS   As it turned out, the war hawks would get neither Canada nor Florida, for in 1812 James Madison had carried into war a nation that was ill prepared both financially and militarily. The Republican program of small federal budgets and military cutbacks was not an effective way to win a war. And Madison, a studious, soft-spoken man, lacked anything resembling martial qualities. He was no George Washington.

The year before, despite urgent pleas from Treasury Secretary Albert Gallatin, Congress had let the twenty-year charter of the Bank of the United States expire. A combination of strict-constructionist Republicans and Anglophobes, who feared the large British interest in the bank, caused its demise. Meanwhile, trade had collapsed, and tariff revenues had declined. Loans were needed to cover about two thirds of the war costs, but northeastern opponents of the war were reluctant to lend money.

The military situation was almost as bad. War had been likely for nearly a decade, but Republican budgetary constraints had prevented preparations. When the War of 1812 began, the army numbered only 6,700 men, ill trained, poorly equipped, and led by aging officers. The navy, on the other hand, was in comparatively good shape, with able officers and trained men. Its ships were well outfitted and seaworthy—all sixteen of them. In the first year of the war, the navy produced the only U.S. victories in isolated duels with British vessels, but their effect was mainly an occasional boost to morale. Within a year the British had blockaded the U.S. coast, except for New England, where they hoped to cultivate anti-war feeling, and most of the little American fleet was bottled up in port.

THE WAR IN THE NORTH   The only place where the United States could effectively strike at the British was Canada. Madison's best hope was a quick attack on Quebec or Montreal to cut Canada's lifeline, the St. Lawrence River. The Madison administration opted for a three-pronged drive against Canada: along the Lake Champlain route toward Montreal, with General Henry Dearborn in command; along the Niagara River, with forces under General Stephen Van Rensselaer; and into Upper Canada (north of Lake Erie and Lake Ontario) from Detroit, with General William Hull and some 2,000 men. In Detroit the sickly and senile Hull procrastinated while his position worsened and the news arrived that an American fort isolated at the head of Lake Huron had surrendered. The British commander cleverly played upon Hull's worst fears. Gathering what redcoats he could to parade in view of Detroit's defenders, he announced that thousands of Indian allies were at the rear and he would be unable to control them once fighting began. Fearing a massacre, Hull, without consulting his officers and without a shot being fired, surrendered his entire force.

Along the Niagara River front, General Van Rensselaer was more aggressive. An advance party of 600 Americans crossed the river and worked their way up the bluffs on the Canadian side to occupy Queenstown Heights. The stage was set for a major victory, but the New York militia refused to reinforce Van Rensselaer's men, claiming that their military service did not obligate them to leave the country. They complacently remained on the New York side and watched their outnumbered countrymen fall to a superior force across the river.

On the third front, the old invasion route via Lake Champlain, the incompetent General Dearborn led his army north from Plattsburgh toward Montreal. He marched his men up to the border, where the state militia once again stood on its alleged constitutional rights and refused to cross, and then marched them back to Plattsburgh.

Madison's navy secretary now pushed vigorously for American control of inland waters. At Presque Isle (near Erie), Pennsylvania, in 1813, the twenty-eight-year-old Oliver Hazard Perry, already a fourteen-year veteran who had seen action against Tripoli, was busy building ships from green timber. At the end of the summer, Commodore Perry set out in search of the British, whom he found at Lake Erie's Put-in-Bay on September 10. After completing the preparations for battle, Perry told an aide, "This is the most important day of my life."

Two British warships used their superior weapons to pummel the *Lawrence*, Perry's flagship, from a distance. Blood flowed on the deck so

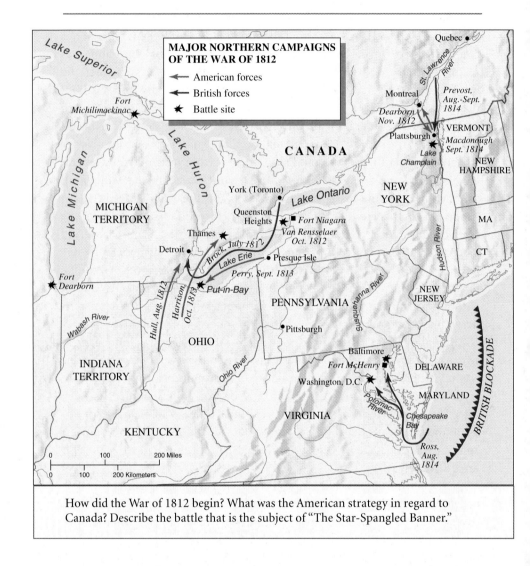

MAJOR NORTHERN CAMPAIGNS OF THE WAR OF 1812

← American forces
← British forces
★ Battle site

How did the War of 1812 begin? What was the American strategy in regard to Canada? Describe the battle that is the subject of "The Star-Spangled Banner."

freely that the sailors slipped and fell as they wrestled with the cannon. After four hours of intense shelling, none of the *Lawrence's* guns was working, and most crew members were dead or wounded. The British expected the Americans to turn tail, but Perry refused to quit. He had himself rowed to another vessel, carried the battle to the enemy, and finally accepted surrender of the entire British squadron. Hatless, begrimed, and bloodied, Perry sent General William Henry Harrison the long-awaited message: "We have met the enemy and they are ours."

More good news followed. At the Battle of the Thames, on October 5, in Canadian territory east of Detroit, General Harrison eliminated British

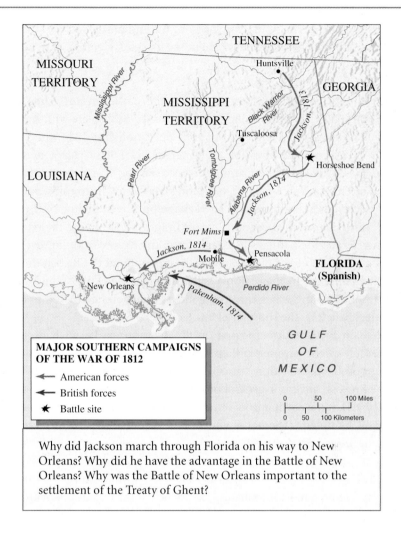

Why did Jackson march through Florida on his way to New Orleans? Why did he have the advantage in the Battle of New Orleans? Why was the Battle of New Orleans important to the settlement of the Treaty of Ghent?

power in Upper Canada and released the Northwest from any further threat. In the course of the battle, the great Indian leader Tecumseh was killed, his dream of Indian unity dying with him.

THE WAR IN THE SOUTH   In the South, too, the war flared up in 1813. On August 30 Creeks allied with the British attacked Fort Mims, on the Alabama River above Mobile, killing almost half the people in the fort. As major general of the Tennessee militia, Andrew Jackson summoned about 2,000 volunteers and set out on a vengeful campaign that crushed Creek resistance. The decisive battle occurred in eastern Alabama on March 27, 1814, at Horseshoe Bend, on the Tallapoosa River, in the heart of the Upper Creek country. With the Treaty of Fort Jackson, the Indians ceded two thirds of their land to the United States, including part of Georgia and most of Alabama.

BRITISH STRATEGY   Four days after the Battle of Horseshoe Bend, Napoléon's French Empire collapsed. Now free to deal solely with America, the British developed a threefold plan of operations for 1814: they would launch a two-pronged invasion of America via Fort Niagara and Lake Champlain to increase the clamor for peace in the Northeast; extend the naval blockade to New England, subjecting coastal towns to raids; and seize New Orleans and take control of the Mississippi River, lifeline of the West. Uncertainties about the peace settlement in Europe prevented the release of British veterans for a full-scale assault upon the New World, however. And after a generation of conflict, war-weariness countered the British thirst for revenge against the former colonials. British plans were also stymied by the more resolute young American commanders Madison had placed in charge of strategic areas by the summer of 1814.

The main British effort focused on the invasion via Lake Champlain. A land assault might have taken Plattsburgh and forced American troops out of their protected positions nearby, but England's army, led by General George Prevost, governor general of Canada, bogged down while its flotilla engaged a U.S. naval squadron, led by Commodore Thomas Macdonough, on Lake Champlain. The battle ended in September 1814 with the British flotilla destroyed or captured.

FIGHTING IN THE CHESAPEAKE   Meanwhile however, American forces suffered the most humiliating experience of the war, as the British captured and burned Washington, D.C. With attention focused on the Canadian front, the Chesapeake Bay offered the British several inviting targets, including Baltimore, then the fourth-largest city in America. On the evening of August 24, 1814, the British marched unopposed into Washington and straight to the White House, where officers ate a meal that had been prepared for President and Mrs. Madison, who had hastily joined other refugees in Virginia. The British then burned the White House, the Capitol, and all other government buildings except the Patent Office. A tornado the next day compounded the damage, but a violent thunderstorm dampened both the fires and the enthusiasm of the British forces, who left to prepare a new assault on Baltimore.

That attack was a different story. With some 13,000 men, chiefly militia, American units fortified the heights behind the city. About 1,000 men held Fort McHenry, on an island in the harbor. The British fleet bombarded the fort to no avail, and the invaders abandoned their attack. Francis Scott Key, a Washington lawyer, watched the siege from a vessel in the harbor. The sight of the flag still in place at dawn inspired him to draft the verses of what come to be called "The Star-Spangled Banner." Later revised and set to the tune of an English drinking song, it was immediately popular and eventually became America's national anthem.

THE BATTLE OF NEW ORLEANS The British failure at Baltimore followed by three days their failure on Lake Champlain; their offensive against New Orleans, however, had yet to run its course. Along the Gulf coast, General Andrew Jackson had been shoring up the defenses of Mobile and New Orleans. In late 1814, without authorization, he invaded Spanish Florida and took Pensacola, putting an end to British intrigues there. Back in Louisiana by the end of November, he began to erect defenses on the approaches to New Orleans. But the British fleet, with some 8,000 soldiers under General Sir Edward Pakenham, cautiously took up positions on a plain near the Mississippi River just south of the city.

Pakenham's painfully careful approach—he waited until all his artillery was available—gave Jackson time to build earthworks bolstered by cotton bales. It was an almost invulnerable position, but Pakenham, contemptuous of Jackson's motley array of frontier militiamen, Creole aristocrats, free blacks, and pirates, ordered a frontal assault at dawn on January 8, 1815. His redcoats emerged out of the morning fog and ran into a murderous hail of artillery shells and deadly rifle fire. Before the British withdrew, about 2,000 had been killed or wounded, including Pakenham himself, whose body, pickled in a barrel of rum, was returned to the ship where his wife awaited news of the battle.

The slow pace of communication during the early nineteenth century meant that the Battle of New Orleans occurred after a peace treaty had been signed in Europe. But this is not to say that it was an anticlimax or that it had no effect on the outcome of the war, for the treaty was yet to be ratified, and the British might have exploited to advantage the possession of New Orleans had they won it. The battle ensured ratification of the treaty as it stood, and both governments acted quickly.

THE TREATY OF GHENT Peace efforts had begun in 1812, even before hostilities commenced, but negotiations bogged down after the fighting started. The British were stalling, awaiting news of smashing victories to strengthen their hand. Word of the U.S. victory on Lake Champlain weakened the British resolve. The British will to fight was further eroded by a continuing power struggle in Europe, by the eagerness of British merchants to renew trade with America, and by the war-weariness of a tax-burdened public. The British finally decided that the war was not worth the cost. Envoys from both sides eventually agreed to end the fighting, return prisoners, restore previous boundaries, and settle nothing else. The Treaty of Ghent was signed on Christmas Eve of 1814.

THE HARTFORD CONVENTION   While the diplomats converged on a peace settlement, in Europe, an entirely different kind of meeting was taking place in Hartford, Connecticut. An ill-fated affair, the Hartford Convention represented the climax of New England's disaffection with "Mr. Madison's war." New England had managed to keep aloof from the war and extract a profit from illegal trading and privateering. After the fall of Napoléon, however, the British extended their blockade to New England, occupied part of Maine, and conducted several raids along the coast. Even Boston seemed threatened. Instead of rallying to the American flag, however, Federalists in the Massachusetts legislature voted to convene a meeting of New England states to plan independent action.

On December 15, 1814, the Hartford Convention assembled with delegates from Massachusetts, Rhode Island, Connecticut, Vermont, and New Hampshire. The convention proposed seven constitutional amendments designed to limit Republican influence, including the requirement of a two-thirds vote to declare war or admit new states, a prohibition on embargoes lasting more than sixty days, a one-term limit on the presidency, and a ban on successive presidents from the same state.

The Hartford Convention carried the unmistakable threat of secession if its demands were ignored. Yet the threat quickly evaporated. When messengers from Hartford reached Washington, D.C., they found the battered capital celebrating the good news from Ghent and New Orleans. The consequence was a fatal blow to the Federalist party, which never recovered from the stigma of disloyalty stamped on it by the Hartford Convention.

THE AFTERMATH   For all the ineptitude with which the War of 1812 was fought, it generated an intense patriotic feeling. Despite the standoff with which it ended at Ghent, the American public felt victorious, thanks to Andrew Jackson and his men at New Orleans, as well as to the heroic exploits of U.S. frigates in their duels with British ships. However, the war revealed America's desperate need for a more efficient system of internal transportation—roads, bridges, canals. Even more important, the conflict launched the United States toward economic independence, as the interruption of trade encouraged the birth of American manufactures. This was a profound development, for the emergence of a factory system would generate far-reaching social effects as well as economic growth. After forty years of fragile independence, it dawned on the world that the new republic might not only survive but flourish.

One of the strangest results of the War of 1812 was a reversal of roles by the Republicans and the Federalists. Out of the wartime experience the Republicans had learned some lessons in nationalism. The necessities of war had "Federalized" Madison or "re-Federalized" the Father of the Constitution. Perhaps, he reasoned, a peacetime army and navy were necessary. He also had come to see the value of a national bank and of higher tariffs to protect infant American industries from foreign competition. But while Madison was embracing such nationalistic measures, the Federalists were borrowing the Jeffersonian theory of states' rights and strict construction. It was yet another reversal of roles in constitutional interpretation. It would not be the last.

We Owe Allegiance to No Crown

The War of 1812 generated a renewed spirit of nationalism.

MAKING CONNECTIONS

- Jefferson's embargo and the War of 1812 encouraged the beginnings of manufacturing in the United States, an important subject to be discussed in Chapter 12.

- The Federalist party collapsed because of its opposition to the War of 1812. But as the next chapter shows, Republicans did not prosper as much as might have been expected in the absence of political opposition.

- The American success in the War of 1812 (a moral victory at best) led to a tremendous sense of national pride and unity, a spirit analyzed in the next chapter.

FURTHER READING

Marshall Smelser's *The Democratic Republic, 1801–1815* (1968) presents an overview of the Republican administrations. The standard biography of Jefferson is Joseph J. Ellis's *American Sphinx: The Character of Thomas Jefferson* (1996). On the life of Jefferson's friend and successor, see Drew R. McCoy's *The Last of the Fathers: James Madison and the Republican Legacy* (1989). Joyce Appleby's *Capitalism and a New Social Order: The Republican Vision of the 1790s* (1984) minimizes the impact of republican ideology.

Linda K. Kerber's *Federalists in Dissent: Imagery and Ideology in Jeffersonian America* (1970) explores the Federalists while out of power. The concept of judicial review and the courts can be studied in Richard E. Ellis's *The Jeffersonian Crisis: Courts and Politics in the Young Republic* (1971). On John Marshall, see G. Edward White's *The Marshall Court and Cultural Change, 1815–1835* (1988). Milton Lomask's two-volume *Aaron Burr: The Years from Princeton to Vice President, 1756–1805* (1979) and *The Conspiracy and the Years of Exile, 1805–1836* (1982) trace the career of that remarkable American.

For the Louisiana Purchase, consult Alexander De Conde's *This Affair of Louisiana* (1976). For a captivating account of the Lewis and Clark expedition, see Stephen Ambrose's *Undaunted Courage: Meriwether Lewis, Thomas Jefferson, and the Opening of the American West* (1996). Bernard W. Sheehan's *Seeds of Extinction: Jeffersonian Philanthropy and the American Indian* (1973) is more analytical in its treatment of the Jeffersonians' Indian policy and the opening of the West.

Burton Spivak's *Jefferson's English Crisis: Commerce, Embargo, and the Republican Revolution* (1979) discusses Anglo-American relations during Jefferson's administration; Clifford L. Egan's *Neither Peace Nor War: Franco-American Relations, 1803–1812* (1983) covers French-American relations. An excellent revisionist treatment of the events that brought on war in 1812 is J.C.A. Stagg's *Mr. Madison's War: Politics, Diplomacy, and Warfare in the Early American Republic, 1783–1830* (1983). The war itself is the focus of Donald R. Hickey's *The War of 1812: A Forgotten Conflict* (1989). See also David Curtis Skaggs and Gerard T. Altoff's *A Signal Victory: The Lake Erie Campaign, 1812–1813* (1997).

Part Three

AN EXPANSIVE NATION

James Monroe serves as U.S. president (1817–1825)

McCulloch v. Maryland decision declares the federal government "supreme within its sphere of action" (1819)

1820 Missouri Compromise defuses sectional crisis over slavery (1820)

Election of 1824 is thrown into the House of Representatives; John Quincy Adams serves as U.S. president (1825–1829)

1828 Widespread labor organization leads to the formation of the Workingmen's party (1828)

John Calhoun writes *South Carolina Exposition and Protest,* which declares that states can nullify federal law (1828)

Andrew Jackson is elected U.S. president (1828)

Andrew Jackson serves as U.S. president (1829–1837)

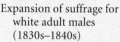

1830

Expansion of suffrage for white adult males (1830s–1840s)

Webster-Hayne debate regarding states' rights (1830)

Indian Removal Act begins forced federal acquisition of tribal lands (1830)

In *Cherokee Nation v. Georgia,* the Supreme Court denies Cherokees the right to self-government (1831)

Jackson's entire cabinet resigns (1831)

The first national party conventions (1831)

A South Carolina state convention adopts a nullification ordinance declaring unconstitutional the tariff acts of 1828 and 1832 (1832)

Calhoun resigns as vice president to defend nullification in Senate (1832)

Jackson issues his Nullification Proclamation (1832)

The Anti-Masonic party is the first third party to run a candidate for president (1832)

The passage of the compromise tariff and the force bill averts crisis in the Union (1833)

A new two-party system pits Democrats against the Whig coalition (1836)

English defeat Napoléon at the Battle of Waterloo (1815)

Reactionaries take control of France (1815)

Spain cedes all of Florida to the U.S. (1819)

Peterloo Massacre of workers in England (1819)

Liberal revolts occur in Naples, northern Italy, Spain, and Brazil (1820)

French put down revolution in Spain (1822–1823)

Monroe Doctrine reaffirms U.S. hegemony in the Americas (1823)

Decembrist revolt of liberal army officers in Russia fails (1825)

Trade unionism in England promotes the interests of laborers (1820s–1830s)

Mexico controls former Spanish holdings in the American West and welcomes American merchants (1820s–1840s)

Greek independence from the Ottoman Empire (1829)

20,000 white settlers and 1,000 black slaves reside in the coastal region of East Texas, outnumbering the 5,000 Mexicans residing in the area (1830)

Revolution in France overthrows Restoration monarchy and brings Louis-Philippe and bourgeoisie to power (1830)

Revolutions in Belgium, the Rhineland, Italy, and Brazil (1830)

George Stephenson's locomotive speeds along the Liverpool-Manchester railway at sixteen miles per hour (1830)

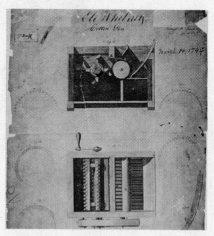

Mechanized cotton mills account for 22 percent of England's entire industrial production (1831)

Revolutions in Poland, Spain, and Italy are put down by conservatives (1831–1834)

The Reform Bill of 1832 expands suffrage in England by 50 percent and prevents revolution in Britain (1832)

American patriotism is greatly intensified by war with Great Britain (1815)

Andrew Jackson attacks Seminoles in Florida (1817)

American Colonization Society is founded to return blacks to Africa (1817)

Congressional report concludes that Indians should be "moralized or exterminated" (1818)

First free public secondary school opens (1821)

First freed slaves are returned to Africa (1822)

Over 200,000 people flee a drought in South Carolina (1820s–1830s)

U.S. population is nearly 13 million (1828)

Social and economic inequality abound, with 4 percent of New York City's population controlling 76 percent of its wealth (1828)

The Second Great Awakening occurs as religious revivals combine emotional fervor with a spirit of social equality (1820s–1830s)

The number of city dwellers doubles (1820s–1840)

The number of churches in New England increases by one third in one year (1830–1831)

The founding of the Mormon Church (1830)

Nativism surges as the immigration of Irish and German Catholics increases (1830s)

"Oregon Fever" draws thousands of migrants to the Oregon Trail in search of land to settle (1830s–1840s)

Nat Turner leads a slave uprising in Virginia (1831)

Roger B. Taney calls blacks "a separate but degraded people" (1831)

Technology improves diet, clothing, housing, and transportation (1830s–1840s)

Samuel Morse invents the telegraph machine, leading to a communications revolution (1832)

U.S. merchants resume trade with England (1815)

Congress reestablishes the Bank of the United States (1816)

Tariff protects U.S. industry but jeopardizes agriculture (1816)

Collapse of cotton prices in England triggers panic in U.S. (1819)

Trappers, traders, and Indians gather annually in Rocky Mountains to trade (1820s–1830s) **1820**

Tariff favors manufacturing interests (1824)

Henry Clay's American System is defined (1824)

Erie Canal opens (1825)

Tariff further promotes manufacturing at the expense of agricultural interests (1828) **1828**

The Industrial Revolution is in full bloom as textile mills and other factories sprout up around much of New England; the beginnings of labor organization (1820s–1840s)

State and private building of roads, canals, and railroads promotes growth of cities, further settlement, and commercial farming (1820s–1850s)

Jackson vetoes the Maysville Road bill and sets a precedent for limiting federal assistance for internal improvements (1830) **1830**

The Preemption Acts allow squatters to stake out land claims prior to surveys and later to purchase that land at $1.25 per acre (1830, 1841)

American shipping companies set up trading offices and warehouses on the California coast to tap into that region's rich supply of animal hides (1830s)

Jackson vetoes the early renewal of Second Bank's charter, and his use of "pet banks" fuels a bank war (1832)

Cyrus Hall McCormick builds the first grain reaper, transforming the scale of American agriculture (1834)

National trade and craft unions are established (1834)

Sale of public land rises from 4 million acres to 20 million acres, an increase fueled by speculative investment spawned by state banks (1834–1836)

The Distribution Act and Specie Circular promote Jackson's hard currency theories and strain the economy (1836)

Jackson sets ten-hour workday at a Philadelphia naval yard (1836)

Charter expires on the Second Bank of the U.S.; Jackson wins bank war (1836)

1840

Martin Van Buren serves as U.S. president (1837–1841)

Van Buren calls a special session of Congress to deal with financial panic (1837)

Congress debates petitions to abolish slavery and slave trade in Washington, D.C. (1837–1841)

Parties organize down to the precinct level; the proportion of white male voters increases from 20 percent (1824) to 78 percent (1840)

William Henry Harrison is elected president (1840)

John Tyler serves as president when Harrison dies (1841–1845)

Tyler vetoes Henry Clay's bill for a new national bank; his entire cabinet (except for Daniel Webster) resigns (1842)

Congressional Whigs expel Tyler from their party (1842)

James Polk serves as president (1845–1849)

John L. O'Sullivan refers to U.S. expansion as "our manifest destiny" (1845)

Texas is formally annexed (1845)

The Mexican War with the United States heightens American nationalism (1845–1848)

The United States acquires Oregon (1846)

American troops capture Mexico City (1847)

1848

The Treaty of Guadalupe Hidalgo ends the Mexican War; the United States is awarded Texas north of the Rio Grande, California, and New Mexico (1848)

England's Factory Act limits the workday for children to eight hours (1833)

Abolition of slavery in the British Empire (1833)

Poor-law reform in England (1834)

Santa Anna's Mexican army defeats American forces at the Alamo (1836)

Santa Anna signs a treaty recognizing the independence of Texas (1836)

Depression in England (1837)

Canadian insurrection (1837)

The Chartist Movement in England seeks radical political reforms, including universal male suffrage (1838–1848)

The Opium War between China and Britain over trade in opium (1839–1842)

Lower and Upper Canada are united by an act of Parliament (1840)

The beginnings of socialism in Europe (1840s)

England claims the right to patrol the coast of Africa and to search American ships sailing there to see if they carry slaves (1841)

The Webster-Ashburton Treaty settles contested boundaries with British Canada and calls for joint British-American patrols of the African coast (1842)

China is forced to cede Hong Kong to Britain and to open up five ports to trade with the West (1842)

Railroad construction fuels the consumption of iron and coal (1840s)

Friedrich Engels publishes *The Condition of the Working Class* (1844)

The Irish potato famine (1845); similar crop failures in 1846, 1848, and 1851 in Ireland and Europe force 1 million people to flee, many to the United States

Approximately 800 Americans live in Mexican-controlled California (1846)

England repeals its Corn Laws, which had regulated the price of imported wheat (1846)

Ten Hours Act passed in England, limiting the workday to ten hours per day (1848)

John Stuart Mill publishes *Principles of Political Economy* (1848)

Karl Marx publishes *The Communist Manifesto* (1848)

The British complete the conquest of India (1848)

Revolutions in France, Prussia, Italy, and Austria; many refugees flee to America (1848–1849)

The American Temperance Union is founded (1833)

12,000 Cherokees are forced to migrate westward along the Trail of Tears (1835–1838)

Prosperity enables the urban middle class to hire maids and cooks, which creates additional free time (1830s–1860s)

Daily newspapers such as the *New York Herald* and *New York Tribune* make reading a form of popular entertainment (1830s–1860s)

One third of the labor force is jobless as a result of the depression (1837)

Mississippi becomes the first state to grant married women control over their own property (1839); by 1860, eleven other states do likewise

325,000 Indians (200 tribes) inhabit lands west of the Mississippi River (1840)

78 percent of total population, 91 percent of whites are literate (1840)

America has seventy-eight colleges and universities (1840)

Catharine Beecher publishes *A Treatise on Domestic Economy,* which becomes the "leading handbook for the cult of domesticity" (1841)

350,000 persons travel to California and Oregon, leading to tensions between settlers and Indians (1841–1867)

American writers including Dickinson, Hawthorne, Poe, Melville, and Whitman reexamine life in nineteenth-century America (1840s–1870s)

Urbanization leads to new forms of entertainment, including circuses, boxing, fraternal societies, theater, concerts, dances, lectures, etc. (mid-1800s)

Knickerbocker Base Ball Club becomes the first professional baseball team in America (1845)

2.4 million immigrants arrive in America (1845–1854)

The first professional baseball game is played (1846)

The Mormon Trek to Utah (1846–1851)

The Seneca Falls Convention promotes women's rights (1848)

Mass migration of young, unmarried men from every social class, state, territory, and from abroad, to disorderly mining shantytowns occurs (1848–1850)

The panic of 1837 leads to unemployment, wage cuts, and soaring prices (1837)

John Deere introduces the steel plow (1837)

3,000 miles of waterways link much of the nation to New York City (1837)

Port of New Orleans exports more than any other U.S. port (1830s–1840s)

Cotton accounts for more than half of the U.S.'s exports (1830s–1860)

The United States produces 60 percent of the world's cotton (1840)

The United States has 3,328 miles of railroads (1840), which soon increase to 30,626 (1860)

Independent Treasury Act (1840)

Van Buren extends the ten-hour workday to all government offices (1840)

Thirty-two mills and factories operate in Lowell, Massachusetts (1840)

Independent Treasury is repealed (1841)

The Supreme Court rules that labor unions are not illegal (1842)

Samuel Morse inaugurates the first telegraph line (1844)

Charles Goodyear patents stronger, improved (vulcanized) rubber (1844)

Fifty-two transatlantic shipping lines operate between New York and Europe (1845)

The advent of clipper ships doubles the speed of older merchant ships (1845)

Elias Howe invents the sewing machine (1846)

Independent Treasury is restored (1846)

1840

1848

Gold is discovered at Sutter's Mill in California (1848)

americans during the early nineteenth century formed a relentless migratory stream that spilled over the Appalachian Mountains, spanned the Mississippi River, and in the 1840s reached the Pacific Ocean. Wagons, canals, flatboats, steamboats, and eventually railroads helped transport them. The feverish expansion of the United States into new western territories brought Americans into conflict with Native Americans, Mexicans, the British, and the Spanish. Only a few people, however, expressed moral reservations about displacing others. Most Americans believed it was the "manifest destiny" of the United States to spread across the entire continent—at whatever cost and at whomever's expense. Americans generally felt that they enjoyed the blessing of Providence in their efforts to consolidate the entire continent under their control.

While most people continued to earn their living from the soil, textile mills and manufacturing plants began to dot the landscape and transform the nature of work and the pace of life. By midcentury the United States was emerging as one of the world's major industrial powers. In addition, the lure of cheap land and plentiful jobs, as well as the promise of political equality and religious freedom, attracted millions of immigrants from Europe. The newcomers, mostly from Germany and Ireland, faced ethnic prejudices, religious persecution, and language barriers that made assimilation into American culture difficult.

These developments gave social life in the second quarter of the nineteenth century a dynamic and fluid quality. The United States, said the philosopher-poet Ralph Waldo Emerson, was "a country of beginnings, of projects, of designs, of expectations." A restless optimism characterized the period. People of a lowly social status who heretofore had accepted their lot in life now strove to climb the social ladder and enter the political arena. The patrician republic espoused by Jefferson and Madison gave way to the frontier democracy promoted by Andrew Jackson and his supporters. Americans were no longer content to be governed by a small, benevolent aristocracy of talent and wealth. They began to demand—and obtain—government of, by, and for the people.

The fertile economic environment during the antebellum era helped foster the egalitarian idea that individuals (except African Americans, Native Americans, and women) should have an equal opportunity to better themselves and should be granted political rights and privileges.

In America, observed a journalist in 1844, "one has as good a chance as another according to his talents, prudence, and personal exertions."

The exuberant individualism embodied in such mythic expressions of economic equality and political democracy spilled over into the cultural arena during the first half of the century. The so-called Romantic movement applied democratic ideals to philosophy, religion, literature, and the fine arts. In New England, Ralph Waldo Emerson and Henry David Thoreau joined other transcendentalists in espousing a radical individualism. Other reformers were motivated more by a sense of spiritual mission than by democratic individualism. Reformers sought to introduce public schools, abolish slavery, promote temperance, and improve the lot of the disabled, the insane, and the imprisoned. Their efforts ameliorated some of the problems created by the frenetic economic growth and territorial expansion. But the reformers made little headway against slavery. It would take a brutal civil war to dislodge America's "peculiar institution."

10

NATIONALISM AND SECTIONALISM

FOCUS QUESTIONS

- What were the characteristics of the "Era of Good Feelings"?
- How did economic policies, diplomacy, and judicial decisions reflect the nationalism of those years?
- What were the various issues that promoted sectionalism?
- What was the fate of the Republican party after the collapse of the Federalists?

To answer these questions and access additional review material, please visit www.wwnorton.com/studyspace.

Amid the jubilation that followed the War of 1812, Americans began to transform their young republic into a sprawling nation. Hundreds of thousands of people began to stream westward at the same time that the largely local economy was maturing into a national market. The spread of plantation slavery and the cotton culture into the Old Southwest—Georgia, Alabama, Mississippi, Louisiana, Arkansas, and Texas—disrupted family ties and changed social life. In the North and the West, meanwhile, a dynamic urban middle class began to emerge. Such dramatic changes prompted vigorous political debates over economic policies, transportation improvements, and the extension of slavery into the new territories. In the process the nation began to divide into three powerful regional blocs—North, South, and West—whose shifting coalitions would shape the political landscape until the Civil War.

ECONOMIC NATIONALISM

After the War of 1812, a new surge of economic prosperity generated a widespread sense of well-being and enhanced the prestige of the national government. The idea spread that the country needed a more balanced "national" economy of farming, commerce, and manufacturing, as well as a more muscular military. President James Madison, in his first annual message to Congress after the war, recommended several steps to strengthen the nation: better fortifications, a permanent national army and a strong navy, a new national bank, effective protection of the new industries against foreign competition through the use of tariffs, a system of canals and roads for commercial and military use, and to top it off, a great national university. "The Republicans have out-Federalized Federalism," one observer remarked.

THE BANK OF THE UNITED STATES   The trinity of economic nationalism—proposals for a second national bank, protective tariffs, and internal improvements—ignited the greatest controversies. After the national bank's charter expired in 1811, the country fell into a financial muddle. State-chartered banks mushroomed with little or no regulation, and their bank notes (paper money) flooded the channels of commerce with currency of uncertain value. Because hard money (coins) had been in such short supply during the war, many state banks had suspended specie (gold or silver) payments in exchange for paper notes, thereby further depressing their value.

To remedy this situation, Congress in 1816 created a new Bank of the United States, to be located in Philadelphia. Modeled on Alexander Hamilton's first national bank, its charter again ran for twenty years, and the government owned one fifth of the stock and named five of the twenty-five directors. The bank served as the depository for government funds, and its bank notes were accepted in payments to the government. In return for its privileges, the Bank of the United States had to keep the government's funds without charge, lend the government up to $5 million upon demand, and pay the government a cash bonus of $1.5 million.

The bitter debate over the bank set a pattern of regional alignment for most other economic issues. Missouri senator Thomas Hart Benton predicted that the currency-short western towns would be at the mercy of a centralized eastern bank. "They may be devoured by it any moment! They are in the jaws of the monster! A lump of butter in the mouth of a dog! One gulp, one swallow, and all is gone!"

The debate over the national bank was also noteworthy because of the leading roles played by the era's greatest statesmen: John C. Calhoun of South

Carolina, Henry Clay of Kentucky, and Daniel Webster of New Hampshire. Calhoun, as an economic nationalist, introduced the bank measure and pushed it through, justifying its constitutionality by citing the congressional power to regulate the currency. Clay, who had long opposed a central national bank, now asserted that new circumstances had made one indispensable. Webster, on the other hand, led the opposition of the New Englanders, who did not want Philadelphia to displace Boston as the nation's banking center. Later, after he had moved from New Hampshire to Massachusetts, Webster would return to Congress as the champion of a much stronger national government, whereas events would steer Calhoun toward a defiant embrace of states' rights.

A PROTECTIVE TARIFF   The shift of capital from commerce to manufactures, begun during Thomas Jefferson's embargo of 1807, had accelerated during the war. Peace in 1815 brought a sudden renewal of cheap British imports and generated pleas for tariffs (taxes on imports) to protect young American industries. The self-interest of the manufacturers, who as yet had little political power, was reinforced by a patriotic desire for economic independence from Britain.

The Tariff of 1816, the first intended more to protect industry against foreign competition than to raise revenue, easily passed in Congress. Both the South and New England split their votes, with New England supporting the tariff and the South opposing the bill, while the middle Atlantic states and the Old Northwest cast only five negative votes altogether. Led by John Calhoun, the minority of southerners who voted for the tariff had hoped that the South might itself become a manufacturing center. Although in 1810 the southern states had almost as many mills and factories as New England, within a few years New England would move ahead of the South in manufacturing, and Calhoun would turn against tariffs. The tariff would then become a sectional issue, with manufacturers and food growers favoring higher tariffs while cotton and tobacco planters and shipping interests favored lower duties.

INTERNAL IMPROVEMENTS   The third major economic issue of the time involved goverment financing of internal improvements: the building of roads and the development of water transportation. The war had highlighted the shortcomings of existing arteries. Troop movements through the western wilderness had proved very difficult, and settlers found that unless they located themselves near navigable waters, they were cut off from trade and limited to a frontier subsistence.

The Union Manufactories of Maryland in Patapsco Falls, Baltimore County (ca. 1815)

A textile mill established during the embargo of 1807, the Union Manufactories would employ over 600 people by 1825.

The federal government had entered the field of internal improvements under Thomas Jefferson. In 1803, when Ohio became a state, Congress decreed that 5 percent of the proceeds from state land sales would go to building a National Road from the Atlantic coast into Ohio and beyond as the territory developed. Construction of the National Road began in 1815. Originally called the Cumberland Road, it was the first federally financed interstate roadway. By 1818 it ran from Cumberland, Maryland, to Wheeling, Virginia, on the Ohio River. By 1838 it extended all the way to Vandalia, Illinois. By reducing transportation costs and opening up western markets, the National Road and privately financed turnpikes accelerated the commercialization of agriculture.

In 1817 John Calhoun put through the House a bill to place in a fund for internal improvements the $1.5 million bonus that the Bank of the United States had paid for its charter, as well as all future dividends on the government's bank stock. Opposition to federal spending on transportation projects centered in New England and the South, regions that expected to gain the least from western development. Support came largely from the West, which urgently needed good roads. On his last day in office, President Madison, bothered by questions about the bill's constitutionality, vetoed the proposed legislation. Internal improvements remained for another hundred years, with few exceptions, the responsibility of states and private enterprise.

Nonetheless, despite disagreements about who would pay for internal improvements, improved transportation and communication (daily newspapers, express mail service, and the telegraph) during the second quarter of the nineteenth century helped create a national market for goods and services. No longer limited to local or regional markets, farmers and manufacturers rapidly expanded production. Banks offered easy access to capital, and enterprising Americans rushed to take advantage of unprecedented entrepreneurial opportunities. Commercial agriculture and the factory system began to displace subsistence farming and household production during the second quarter of the nineteenth century. Mills and factories sprouted across the countryside. New technologies greatly increased productivity and in the process changed the rhythms of work and the relationships between laborers and employers. These first stirrings of an industrial revolution spawned a sustained economic expansion that would transform society and politics.

"GOOD FEELINGS"

JAMES MONROE   As James Madison approached the end of a turbulent presidency, he, like Jefferson, turned to a fellow Virginian, another secretary of state, to be his successor. For Madison that man would be James Monroe. At the outbreak of the Revolution, Monroe was just beginning his studies at the College of William and Mary. He joined the army at sixteen, was wounded at Trenton, and had been made a lieutenant colonel by the time the war ended. Later he studied law with Thomas Jefferson, absorbing Jeffersonian principles in the process.

Monroe had served in the Virginia assembly, as governor of Virginia, in the Confederation Congress and the U.S. Senate, and as minister (ambassador) to France, England, and Spain. Under Madison he had been secretary of state and secretary of war. In the 1816 presidential election he overwhelmed his Federalist opponent, Rufus King of New York. Monroe, with his powdered wig, cocked hat, and knee breeches, was the last of the Revolutionary generation to serve in the White House and the last president to dress in the old style.

Firmly grounded in Republican principles, Monroe was never able to keep up with the onrush of the "new nationalism," which advocated federal economic policies such as a central national bank and a tariff on imports so as to promote industrial growth and enhance economic independence from Europe. Monroe accepted as an accomplished fact the Bank of the United States and the protective tariff, but during his tenure there was no further extension of economic nationalism. Indeed, there was a minor setback: he permitted the National Road to be carried forward, but in his veto of the 1822 Cumberland Road bill, he denied the authority of Congress to collect tolls for its repair and maintenance. Instead, he urged a constitutional amendment, as had Jefferson and Madison, to remove all doubt about federal authority in the field of internal improvements.

Monroe surrounded himself with some of the ablest young Republican leaders: John Quincy Adams became secretary of state, William H. Crawford of Georgia continued as secretary of the Treasury, and John C. Calhoun headed the War Department. The new administration took power with America at peace and the economy flourishing. Soon after his inauguration, Monroe embarked on a goodwill tour of New England. In Boston, lately a hotbed of wartime dissent, a Federalist newspaper commented on the president's visit under the heading "Era of Good Feelings." The label became a popular catchphrase for Monroe's administration, one that historians would later seize upon. Yet the Era of Good Feeling was brief. The collapse of the Federalist party did not mean that the Republicans would grow more unified. They continued to suffer from rancorous internal tensions. Moreover, the social order began to show signs of increasing stratification as the nation experienced dramatic economic growth and rapid westward migration. A resurgence of sectionalism erupted just as the postwar prosperity collapsed in the panic of 1819.

For two years, however, general harmony in national politics reigned, and even when troubles arose, little of the blame fell on Monroe. In 1820 he was re-elected without opposition, as the Federalists were too weak to put up a candidate. Monroe won all the electoral votes except three abstentions and one vote from New Hampshire for John Quincy Adams.

RELATIONS WITH BRITAIN   Fueling the contentment after the war was a growing rapprochement with England. American shippers resumed trade with Britain in 1815. The Treaty of Ghent had left unsettled a number of minor disputes, but two important compacts—the Rush-Bagot Agreement of 1817 and the Convention of 1818—removed several potential causes of irritation. In the first, resulting from an exchange of notes between Acting Secretary of State Richard Rush and the British minister to the United States, Charles Bagot, the threat of naval competition on the Great Lakes vanished with an arrangement to limit forces there to several federal ships collecting customs duties. Although the exchange made no reference to the disputed land boundary between the United States and Canada, its spirit gave rise to the tradition of an unfortified border, the longest in the world.

The Convention of 1818 covered three major points. The northern limit of the Louisiana Purchase was settled by extending the national boundary along the 49th parallel west from Lake of the Woods in what would become Minnesota to the crest of the Rocky Mountains. West of that point the Oregon Country would be open to joint U.S.-British occupation, but the boundary remained unsettled. The right of Americans to fish off Canada's Newfoundland and Labrador, granted in 1783, was acknowledged once again. The chief remaining problem was Britain's continuing exclusion of U.S. ships from the West Indies in order to reserve that lucrative trade for British ships. The rapprochement with Britain therefore fell short of perfection.

THE EXTENSION OF BOUNDARIES   The year 1819 was one of the more fateful in American history, a time when a whole sequence of developments came into focus. Controversial efforts to expand U.S. territory, an intense financial panic, a combative debate over the extension of slavery, and several landmark Supreme Court cases combined to bring an unsettling end to the Era of Good Feelings.

The aggressive new nationalism reached a climax with the acquisition of Florida. Spanish sovereignty over Florida was more a technicality than an actuality. The tenuously held province had been a thorn in the side of the United States during the War of 1812, when it had served as a center of British intrigue; a haven for Creek refugees, who were beginning to take the name Seminole (Runaway or Separatist); and a harbor for runaway slaves and criminals.

Spain, once the dominant power of the Americas, was now a nation in rapid decline, suffering from both internal decay and colonial revolts and unable to enforce its obligations under Pinckney's Treaty of 1795 to pacify the Florida frontier. In 1816 U. S. forces clashed with a group of escaped slaves who had taken over a British fort on the Appalachicola River. Seminoles were soon fighting white settlers in the area, and in 1817 Secretary of War Calhoun authorized a military campaign against the Seminoles and summoned General Andrew Jackson from Nashville to take command.

Jackson's orders allowed him to pursue Indians into Spanish territory but not to attack any Spanish post. A man of Jackson's tenacity naturally felt hobbled by such a restriction, since when it came to Spaniards or Indians, few white Tennesseans—certainly not Andrew Jackson—were likely to bother with technicalities. Jackson pushed his troops eastward through Florida, reinforced by Tennessee volunteers and friendly Creeks, taking a Spanish post and skirmishing with the Seminoles. He hanged two of their leaders without a trial. For two British agents in the area, he convened a court-martial, during

BOUNDARY TREATIES, 1818–1819

What territorial terms did the Convention of 1818 settle? How did Jackson's actions in Florida help Adams claim the territory from Spain? What were the terms of the treaty with Spain?

which it was revealed that they had befriended the Seminoles and offered them military training. Jackson had one hanged and the other shot. The Florida Panhandle was in American hands by the end of May 1818.

Jackson's exploits aroused anger in Madrid and concern in Washington. Spain demanded the return of its territory and the punishment of Jackson, but Spain's impotence was plain for all to see. Monroe's cabinet at first prepared to disavow Jackson's actions, especially his direct attack on Spanish posts. Calhoun, as secretary of war, wanted to discipline Jackson for disregard of orders—a stand that would later cause bad blood between the two men—but privately confessed a certain pleasure at the outcome. In any case a man as popular as Jackson was almost invulnerable. And he had one important friend in Washington, Secretary of State John Quincy Adams, who realized that Jackson's military actions had strengthened his own hand in negotiations already under way with the Spanish. U.S. forces withdrew from

Florida, but negotiations resumed with the knowledge that the United States could retake Florida at any time.

With Florida's fate a foregone conclusion, John Quincy Adams cast his eye toward a larger purpose, a final definition of the ambiguous western boundary of the Louisiana Purchase and—his boldest stroke—extension of its boundary to the Pacific coast. In lengthy negotiations, Adams gradually gave ground on claims to Texas but stuck to his demand for a transcontinental line. Agreement came early in 1819. With the Transcontinental Treaty, Spain ceded all of Florida to the United States in return for the U.S. government assumption of Spanish debts owed to U.S. merchants. The western boundary of the Louisiana Purchase would run along the Sabine River in Texas and then, in stair-step fashion, up to the Red River, along the Red, and up to the Arkansas River. From the source of the Arkansas, it would go north to the 42nd parallel and thence west to the Pacific coast. Florida became a U.S. territory, and its first governor was Andrew Jackson. In 1845 Florida finally achieved statehood.

CRISES AND COMPROMISES

THE PANIC OF 1819   John Quincy Adams's Transcontinental Treaty of 1819 was a diplomatic triumph and the climactic event of America's postwar nationalism. Even before it was signed, however, two thunderclaps signaled the end of the brief Era of Good Feelings and warned of stormy weather ahead: the financial panic of 1819 and the controversy over Missouri statehood. The panic resulted from a sudden collapse of cotton prices in the English market as British textile mills turned from American cotton to cheaper East Indian sources. The price collapse set off a decline in the demand for other American goods and revealed the fragility of the prosperity that had begun after the War of 1812.

Since 1815 much of the economic boom had been built upon a shaky foundation. Businessmen, bankers, farmers, and land speculators had caused a volatile expansion of credit, succumbing to the contagion of get-rich-quick fever that was sweeping the country. Even the directors of the second Bank of the United States engaged in the same reckless extension of loans that the state banks had pursued. In 1819, just as alert businessmen began to take alarm, a case of extensive fraud and embezzlement in the Baltimore branch of the Bank of the United States came to light. The disclosure led to the resignation of the director of the bank. His replacement, Langdon Cheves, a former congressman from South Carolina, established sounder policies.

Cheves reduced salaries and other costs, postponed the payment of dividends, restrained the extension of credit, and presented for redemption the state bank notes that came in, thereby forcing the state-chartered banks to keep specie (gold and silver) reserves. Cheves rescued the bank from near ruin, but only by putting pressure on the state banks. They in turn put pressure on their debtors, who found it harder to renew old loans or get new ones. In 1822, his job completed, Cheves retired and was succeeded in the following year by Nicholas Biddle of Philadelphia. The Cheves policies were the result rather than the cause of the panic, but they pinched debtors. Hard times lasted about three years, and in the popular mind the federal bank deserved much of the blame. The panic passed, but resentment of the national bank lingered in the South and the West.

THE MISSOURI COMPROMISE   Just as the financial panic was breaking over the country, another cloud appeared on the horizon: the onset of a fierce sectional controversy over slavery. By 1819 the country had an equal number of slave and free states—eleven of each. The line between them was defined by the southern and western boundaries of Pennsylvania and the Ohio River. Although slavery lingered in some places north of the line, it was on the way to extinction there. West of the Mississippi River, however, no move had been made to extend the dividing line across the Louisiana Territory, where slavery had existed from the days when France and Spain had colonized the area. At the time the Missouri Territory embraced all of the Louisiana Purchase except the state of Louisiana, which entered the Union in 1812, and the Arkansas Territory, organized in 1819. The old French town of St. Louis became the funnel through which settlers, largely southerners who brought their slaves with them, rushed westward beyond the Mississippi River.

In early 1819 the House of Representatives was asked to approve legislation enabling Missouri to draft a state constitution, its population having passed the minimum of 60,000. At that point, Representative James Tallmadge Jr., a New York congressman, proposed a resolution prohibiting the further introduction of slaves into Missouri, which already had some 10,000, and providing freedom at age twenty-five to those born after the territory's admission as a state. The House passed the amendment on an almost strictly sectional vote, and the Senate rejected it by a similar tally, but with several northerners joining in the opposition. With population growing faster in the North, a political balance between the free states and the slave states could be held only in the Senate.

Maine's application for statehood made it easier to arrive at an agreement. Since colonial times, Maine had been the northern province of Massachusetts.

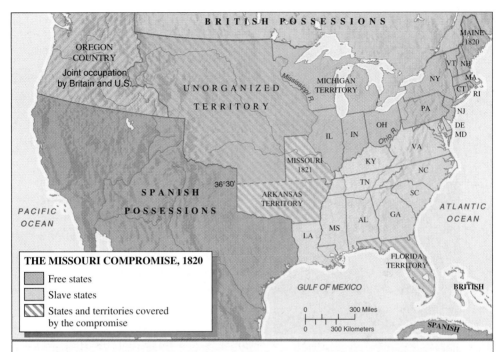

THE MISSOURI COMPROMISE, 1820

- Free states
- Slave states
- States and territories covered by the compromise

What caused the sectional controversy over slavery in 1819? What were the terms of the Missouri Compromise? What was Henry Clay's solution to the Missouri constitution's ban on free blacks in that state?

The Senate linked its request for separate statehood with Missouri's and voted to admit Maine as a free state and Missouri as a slave state, thus maintaining the balance between free and slave states in the Senate. An Illinois senator further extended the compromise by an amendment to exclude slavery from the rest of the Louisiana Purchase north of 36°30′, Missouri's southern border. Slavery thus would continue in the Arkansas Territory and in Missouri but would be excluded from the remainder of the area. People at that time presumed that what remained was the Great American Desert, unlikely ever to be settled. Thus the arrangement seemed to be a victory for the slave states. On August 10, 1821, President Monroe proclaimed the admission of Missouri as the twenty-fourth state. For the moment the controversy was settled. "But this momentous question," the aging Thomas Jefferson wrote to a friend, "like a firebell in the night awakened and filled me with terror. I considered it at once as the knell of the Union."

JUDICIAL NATIONALISM

JOHN MARSHALL   During the early nineteenth century many of the nation's leading attorneys and judges were nationalists. They believed that an expanding nation needed a central government with enough

John Marshall

Chief justice and pillar of judicial nationalism.

power and responsibility to override state and local interests. And they argued that an independent judiciary should have the authority to settle disputes between the states and the federal government. The leader among these judicial nationalists was John Marshall. A Virginia veteran of the Revolution, Marshall had served as secretary of state for John Adams. He had never been a judge before becoming chief justice in 1801. Yet he established the power of the Supreme Court by his force of mind and determination. During Marshall's early years on the Court (he served thirty-four years altogether), he affirmed the principle of judicial review of legislative acts. In *Marbury v. Madison* (1803) and *Fletcher v. Peck* (1810) the Court struck down first a federal law and then a state law as unconstitutional.

EXPANDING THE POWER OF THE FEDERAL GOVERNMENT In the fateful year of 1819, John Marshall and the Court made two decisions of major importance in checking the power of the states and expanding the power of the federal government: *Dartmouth College v. Woodward* and *McCulloch v. Maryland.*

The *Dartmouth College* case involved an attempt by the New Hampshire legislature to alter a charter granted the college by King George III in 1769, under which the governing body of trustees became a self-perpetuating board. In 1816 the state's Republican legislature, irritated by this residue of monarchical rule as well as by the fact that Federalists dominated the board of trustees, placed Dartmouth under the control of a board named by the governor. The original trustees sued and lost in the state courts but with Daniel Webster as their counsel gained a hearing before the Supreme Court.

The charter, declared Marshall, was a valid contract that the legislature had violated, an action expressly forbidden by the Constitution. This decision implied an enlarged definition of *contract* that seemed to put private corporations beyond the reach of the states that chartered them. "If business is to prosper," Marshall explained, "men must have the assurance that contracts will be enforced."

John Marshall's single most important interpretation of the constitutional system appeared in *McCulloch v. Maryland* (1819). In the unanimous decision the Court upheld the "implied powers" of Congress to charter the Bank of the United States and denied the state of Maryland's attempt to tax it. In a lengthy opinion, Marshall rejected Maryland's argument that the federal government was the creature of sovereign states. Instead, he insisted, it arose directly from the people acting through the conventions that had ratified the Constitution ("We, the people of the United States, . . . do ordain and establish"). Whereas sovereignty was divided between the states and the national government, the latter, "though limited in its powers, is supreme within its sphere of action."

The state's effort to tax the national bank conflicted with the supreme law of the land. One great principle that "entirely pervades the Constitution," Marshall wrote, was "that the Constitution and the laws made in pursuance thereof are supreme: . . . they control the Constitution and laws of the respective states, and cannot be controlled by them." Maryland's effort to tax a national bank was therefore unconstitutional, for "the power to tax involves the power to destroy"—which was precisely what the legislatures of Maryland and several other states had in mind with respect to the bank.

John Marshall's last great decision, *Gibbons v. Ogden* (1824), established national supremacy in regulating interstate commerce and thereby dealt another blow to proponents of states' rights. In 1808 the New York legislature had granted Aaron Ogden the exclusive ferry rights across the Hudson River between New York and New Jersey. A competitor, Thomas Gibbons, protested the state's right to grant such a monopoly. On behalf of a unanimous Court, Marshall ruled that the state's action conflicted with the federal Coasting Act, under which Gibbons operated. Congressional power to regulate commerce among the states, the Court said, "like all others vested in Congress, is complete in itself, may be exercised to its utmost extent, and acknowledges no limitations other than are prescribed in the Constitution." In striking down the monopoly created by the state, the nationalist Marshall had opened the way to extensive development of steamboat navigation and, soon afterward, railroads. Such judicial nationalism provided a crucial support for economic expansion.

NATIONALIST DIPLOMACY

THE PACIFIC NORTHWEST   In foreign affairs, too, nationalism continued to be an effective force. Within two years of final approval of John Quincy Adams's Transcontinental Treaty, the secretary of state was able to draw another important transcontinental line. In 1819 Spain had abandoned its claim to the Oregon Country above the 42nd parallel. Russia, however, had claims along the Pacific coast as well, including trading outposts from Alaska as far south as California. In 1823 Secretary of State Adams contested "the right of Russia to any territorial establishment on this continent." The U.S. government, he informed the Russian minister, assumed the principle "that the American continents are no longer subjects for any new European colonial establishments." The upshot of his protest was a treaty signed in 1824, whereby Russia, which had more pressing concerns in Europe, accepted the latitude line of 54°40′ as the southern boundary of its claim. The Oregon Territory, to the south of the line, remained subject to joint occupation by the United States and Great Britain under their agreement of 1818.

THE MONROE DOCTRINE   Secretary of State Adams's disapproval of further European colonization in the Western Hemisphere had clear implications for Latin America as well. One consequence of the Napoleonic Wars and the French occupation of Spain and Portugal was a series of wars of liberation in Latin America. Within little more than a decade after the flag of rebellion was first raised in 1811, Spain had lost almost its entire empire in the Americas. All that was left were the islands of Cuba and Puerto Rico and the colony of Santo Domingo on the island of Hispaniola.

That Spain could not regain her empire seems clear enough in retrospect. The British navy would not have permitted it because Britain's trade with the area was too important. For a time after Napoléon's defeat, however, European rulers were determined to restore monarchical "legitimacy" everywhere. In 1822, when the major European powers met in the Congress of Verona, they authorized France to suppress the constitutionalist movement in Spain and restore the authority of the monarchy. In 1823 French troops crossed the Spanish border, put down the rebels, and restored King Ferdinand VII to absolute authority. Rumors began to circulate that France would also try to restore Ferdinand's "legitimate" power over Spain's American empire. President Monroe and Secretary of War Calhoun were alarmed at the possibility, although John Quincy Adams took the more realistic view that any such action was unlikely. The British foreign minister, George Canning, was also worried about French and Spanish intentions, and he urged the

United States to protect Latin America. Monroe at first agreed, with the support of his sage advisers Jefferson and Madison.

Adams urged upon Monroe and the cabinet the independent course of proclaiming a unilateral policy against the restoration of Spain's colonies. "It would be more candid," Adams said, "as well as more dignified, to avow our principles explicitly to Russia and France, than to come in as a cockboat in the wake of the British man-of-war." Adams knew that the British navy would stop any action by a European power in Latin America. The British wanted the United States to agree not to acquire any more Spanish territory, including Cuba, Texas, and California, but Adams preferred to avoid such a commitment.

Monroe incorporated the substance of Adams's views into his annual message to Congress in 1823. The Monroe Doctrine, as it was later called, comprised four major points: (1) that "the American continents . . . are henceforth not to be considered as subjects for future colonization by any European powers"; (2) that the political system of European powers was different from that of the United States, which would "consider any attempt on their part to extend their system to any portion of this hemisphere as dangerous to our peace and safety"; (3) that the United States would not interfere with existing European colonies; and (4) that the United States would keep out of the internal affairs of European nations and their wars.

At the time the statement drew little attention either in the United States or abroad. Over the years, however, the Monroe Doctrine, not even so called until 1852, became one of the cherished principles of U.S. foreign policy. For the time being, however, it slipped into obscurity for want of any occasion to invoke it. In spite of Adams's affirmation, the United States came in as a cockboat in the wake of the British man-of-war after all, for the effectiveness of the doctrine depended upon British naval supremacy. The doctrine had no standing in international law. It was merely a statement of intent by an American president to Congress and did not even draw enough interest for the European powers to renounce it.

ONE-PARTY POLITICS

Almost from the start of Monroe's second term, in 1821, jockeying for the presidential succession in 1824 began. Three members of Monroe's cabinet were active candidates: Secretary of War John Calhoun, Secretary of the Treasury William H. Crawford, and Secretary of State John Quincy Adams.

Henry Clay

Clay entered the Senate at age twenty-eight despite the requirement that senators be at least thirty years old.

Henry Clay, longtime Speaker of the House, and an outspoken economic nationalist, also thirsted for the office. And on the fringes of the Washington scene, a new force appeared in the person of Andrew Jackson, the scourge of the British, Spanish, and Seminoles, who had became a senator from Tennessee in 1823. All were Republicans, for again no Federalist stood a chance, but they were competing in a new political world, complicated by the cross-currents of nationalism and sectionalism. With only one party there was in effect no party, for there existed no generally accepted method for choosing a "regular" candidate.

State legislatures were free to nominate presidential candidates Tennessee and Pennsylvania supported Jackson, and Calhoun agreed to serve as his running mate. (The 1824 election was the first to feature paired presidential and vice-presidential candidates.) Kentucky named Clay, Massachusetts named Adams, and the amiable, hulking Crawford was selected by a poorly attended congressional caucus. Of the four candidates only two articulated defined programs, and the outcome was an early lesson in the danger of committing oneself on the issues too soon. Crawford's friends emphasized his devotion to states' rights and strict constitutional construction. Clay, on the other hand, took his stand for the "American System": the national bank, the protective tariff, and a national program of internal improvements to bind the country together and strengthen its economy. Adams was close to Clay, openly dedicated to internal improvements but less strongly committed to the tariff. Jackson, where issues were concerned, carefully avoided commitment. His managers hoped that by being all things to all voters, Jackson could capitalize on his popularity as the hero of New Orleans at the end of the War of 1812.

THE "CORRUPT BARGAIN" The election of 1824 turned on personalities and sectional allegiance more than issues. Adams, the only northern candidate, carried New England, the former bastion of the Federalist party, and won most of New York's electoral votes. Clay took Kentucky, Ohio, and Missouri, while Crawford carried Virginia, Georgia, and Delaware.

Jackson swept the Southeast plus Illinois and Indiana and, with Calhoun's support, the Carolinas, Pennsylvania, Maryland, and New Jersey.

The result was inconclusive in both the electoral vote and the popular vote. In the Electoral College, Jackson had ninety-nine votes, Adams eighty-four, Crawford forty-one, and Clay thirty-seven; in the popular vote the proportion ran about the same. Whatever else might have been said about the outcome, it was clearly a defeat for Clay's American System: New England and New York opposed him on internal improvements, the South and the Southwest on the protective tariff. Sectionalism had defeated the national economic program, yet the advocate of the American System now assumed the role of president maker, since the election was thrown into the House of Representatives, where Clay's influence as Speaker of the House was decisive. Clay had little trouble choosing, since he regarded Jackson as unfit for the office. "I cannot believe," he muttered, "that killing 2,500 Englishmen at New Orleans qualifies for the various, difficult and complicated duties of the Chief Magistracy." He eventually threw his support to Adams. The final vote in the House, which was by state, carried Adams to victory with thirteen votes to Jackson's seven and Crawford's four.

It was a costly and controversial victory, for it united Adams's foes and crippled his administration before it got under way. There is no evidence that Adams entered into any secret bargain with Clay to win his support, but the charge was widely believed after Adams made Clay his secretary of state, the office from which three successive presidents had risen. A campaign to elect Jackson next time was launched almost immediately after the 1824 decision. "The people have been cheated," Jackson growled. William Crawford's supporters, including Martin Van Buren, "the Little Magician" of New York politics, soon moved into the Jackson camp.

JOHN QUINCY ADAMS   Short, plump, peppery John Quincy Adams was one of the ablest men, one of the hardest workers, and one of the finest intellects ever to enter the White House, but he lacked the common touch and the politician's gift for maneuver. A stubborn man who saw two brothers and two sons die from alcoholism, he suffered from chronic bouts of depression that spawned a grim self-righteousness and self-pity, qualities that did not endear him to fellow politicians.

Adams's first annual message to Congress provided a grandiose blueprint for national development, set forth so bluntly that it became a political disaster. The central government, the president asserted, should finance internal improvements, set up a national university, fund scientific explorations, build

John Quincy Adams

A brilliant man but an ineffective leader.

astronomical observatories, and create a department of the interior. To refrain from using broad federal powers, Adams maintained, "would be treachery to the most sacred of trusts." In leading the nation, officers of the government should not be "palsied by the will of our constituents."

Such provocative language obscured whatever grandeur of conception the message to Congress had. For a minority president to demean the sovereignty of the voter was tactless enough, but for the son of John Adams to cite the example "of the nations of Europe and of their rulers" was downright suicidal. At one fell swoop he had revived all the Republican suspicions of the Adamses as closet monarchists.

Adams's presidential message hastened the emergence of a new party system. The minority who cast their lot with Adams and Clay were turning into National Republicans; the opposition, the growing party of Jacksonians, were the Democratic Republicans, who would eventually drop the name Republican and become Democrats.

Adams's headstrong plunge into nationalism and his refusal to play the game of politics condemned his administration to utter frustration. The popular mood was turning against federal authority. Congress ignored most of Adams's domestic proposals, and in foreign affairs the triumphs he had scored as secretary of state had no sequels.

The central political issue during Adams's presidency was a complex debate over tariff policy. The panic of 1819 had provoked calls in 1820 for a higher tariff, but the effort failed by one vote in the Senate. In 1824 those determined to protect American industry from foreign competition renewed the effort, with greater success. The Tariff of 1824 favored the middle Atlantic and New England manufacturers with higher duties on woolens, cotton, iron, and other finished goods. Henry Clay's Kentucky won a tariff on hemp, a fiber used for making rope, and a tariff on raw wool brought the wool-growing interests to the support of the measure. Additional federal revenues were provided by duties on sugar, molasses, coffee, and salt.

Four years later Andrew Jackson's supporters sought to advance their presidential candidate through an awkward scheme hatched by John Calhoun.

The plan was to present a bill with such outrageously high tariffs on imported raw materials that the eastern manufacturers would join the commercial interests there and, with the votes of the agricultural South and Southwest, combine to defeat the measure. In the process, Jacksonians in the Northeast could take credit for supporting the tariff, and other Jacksonians, wherever it fit their interests, could take credit for opposing it—while Jackson himself remained in the background. Virginia's John Randolph saw through the ruse. The tariff bill, he asserted, "referred to manufactures of no sort of kind, but the manufacture of a President of the United States."

The complicated scheme did help elect Jackson in 1828, but in the process John Calhoun became a victim of his own machinations. His tariff bill, to his chagrin, passed, thanks to the growing strength of manufacturing interests in New England and several crucial amendments that exempted certain raw materials needed by American industry. Daniel Webster, now a senator from Massachusetts, explained that he was ready to deny all he had said before against the tariff because New England had built up her manufactures on the understanding that the protective tariff was a settled policy.

When the tariff bill passed in May 1828, it was Calhoun's turn to explain his newfound opposition to the gospel of protection, and nothing so well illustrates the flexibility of constitutional principles as the switch in positions by Webster and Calhoun. Back in South Carolina, Calhoun prepared the *South Carolina Exposition and Protest* (1828), which was issued anonymously along with a series of resolutions by the state legislature. In that document, Calhoun set forth the right of a state to nullify an act of Congress that it found unconstitutional.

THE ELECTION OF JACKSON   Thus far the stage was set for the election of 1828, which might more truly be called a political revolution than that of 1800. But if the issues of the day had anything to do with the election, they were hardly visible in the campaign, in which politicians on both sides reached depths of scurrilousness that had not been plumbed since 1800. Those campaigning for Adams denounced Jackson as a hot-tempered, ignorant barbarian, a participant in repeated duels and frontier brawls, a man whose fame rested upon his reputation as a killer. In addition, Jackson's enemies dredged up the story that he had lived in adultery with his wife, Rachel, before they were married. In fact they had been married for two years before discovering that her divorce from her former husband had not been finalized. As soon as the divorce was official, Andrew and Rachel had remarried.

The Jacksonians, however, were also not averse to mudslinging. They lambasted Adams, condemning him as a man corrupted by foreigners in the courts of Europe. They called him a gambler and a spendthrift for having bought a billiard table and a chess set for the White House and a puritanical hypocrite for despising the common people and warning Congress to ignore the will of the people. The Jacksonians also attacked Adams for signing the Tariff of 1828 and for winning the 1824 election by backroom deals. Adams had gained the presidency, the Jacksonians claimed, by a "corrupt bargain" with Henry Clay.

In the campaign of 1828, Jackson held most of the advantages. As a military victor he stirred the patriotism of voters. As a son of the West and an Indian fighter, he was a hero to voters in the new states along the frontier. As a planter and slaveholder he had the trust of southern planters. Debtors and local bankers who hated the national bank also turned to Jackson. In addition, his vagueness on the issues protected him from attack by interest groups. Not least of all, Jackson benefited from a spirit of democracy in which the common folk were no longer satisfied to look to elites for leadership, as they had done in the past.

Since the Revolution and especially since 1800, more people were voting as more and more states expanded the suffrage from only those men with property to taxpaying white men and even, in some states, to universal male suffrage. After 1815 the new states of the West entered the Union with either white male suffrage or a low taxpaying requirement, and older states such as Connecticut (in 1818), Massachusetts (in 1821), and New York (in 1821) abolished their property requirements for voting. As more men voted and participated in political activities, the ideal of social equality took on more importance in the political culture.

Jackson embodied this new, more democratic political world. A tall, sinewy frontiersman born in South Carolina, he grew to be proud, gritty, and short-tempered. During the Revolution, when he was a young boy, his mother died, two of his brothers were killed by redcoats, and Jackson himself was wounded by a British officer's saber. He would carry this scar for life, along with the conviction that it was not enough for a man to be right; he had to be tough as well. His toughness inspired his soldiers to nickname him Old Hickory. During a duel with a man reputed to be the best shot in Tennessee, Jackson nevertheless let his opponent fire first. For his gallantry he received a bullet that lodged next to his heart. Unfazed, he straightened himself, patiently took aim, and killed his foe. "I should have hit him," Jackson claimed, "if he had shot me through the brain." As a fighter, horse

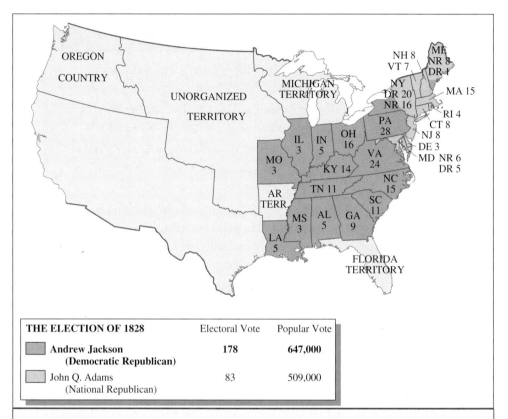

THE ELECTION OF 1828	Electoral Vote	Popular Vote
Andrew Jackson (Democratic Republican)	178	647,000
John Q. Adams (National Republican)	83	509,000

How did the two presidential candidates, Adams and Jackson, portray each other? Why did Jackson seem to have the advantage in the election of 1828? How did the broadening of suffrage affect the presidential campaign?

trader, land speculator, and frontier lawyer, Jackson symbolized the rugged western temperament. A fellow law student described him as a "most roaring, rollicking, game-cocking, horse-racing, card-playing, mischievous fellow." One of his campaign slogans announced, "Adams can write, Jackson can fight."

The 1828 election returns revealed that Jackson had won by a comfortable margin. The electoral vote was 178 to 83. Adams had won all of New England (except one of Maine's nine electoral votes) and a scattering of votes in New York and Maryland. All the rest belonged to Jackson. A convulsive new era in American politics was about to begin.

MAKING CONNECTIONS

- Thomas Jefferson referred to the Missouri Compromise as "a firebell in the night." He was right. The controversy over the expansion of slavery, introduced here, will reappear in Chapter 14, in the discussion of Texas and the Mexican War.

- John Quincy Adams's National Republicans, who could trace some of their ideology to the Federalists, will be at the core of the Whig coalition that opposes Jackson in Chapter 11.

- Several of the issues on which the nation united during the Era of Good Feelings—the bank and the protective tariff, for example—will become much more divisive, as will be discussed in the next chapter.

FURTHER READING

The standard overview of the Era of Good Feelings remains George Dangerfield's *The Awakening of American Nationalism, 1815–1828* (1965). The gathering sense of a national spirit can be traced in Daniel J. Boorstin's *The Americans: The National Experience* (1965).

For discussions of the American System, see Bray Hammond's *Banks and Politics in America from the Revolution to the Civil War* (1957) and George Rogers Taylor's *The Transportation Revolution, 1815–1860* (1951). A classic overview of the economic trends of the period is Douglass C. North's *The Economic Growth of the United States, 1790–1860* (1961).

A stimulating synthesis of economic, social, and political developments is Sean Wilentz's *Chants Democratic: New York City and the Rise of the American Working Class, 1788–1850* (1984). The emergence of slavery as the most divisive sectional issue is treated in Donald L. Robinson's *Slavery in the Structure of American Politics, 1765–1820* (1970).

On diplomatic relations during James Monroe's presidency, see William Earl Weeks's *John Quincy Adams and American Global Empire* (1992). For relations after 1812, see Ernest R. May's *The Making of the Monroe Doctrine* (1975).

Background on Andrew Jackson can be obtained from works cited in Chapter 11. The campaign that brought Jackson to the White House is analyzed in Robert Vincent Remini's *The Election of Andrew Jackson* (1963).

11

THE JACKSONIAN IMPULSE

FOCUS QUESTIONS

· What was the social and political context of the Jackson and Van Buren administrations?

· What were Andrew Jackson's attitudes and actions concerning the tariff (and nullification), Indian policy, and the Bank of the United States?

· Why did a new party system (of Democrats versus Whigs) arise?

To answer these questions and access additional review material, please visit www.wwnorton.com/studyspace.

The election of Andrew Jackson coincided with a distinctive new era in politics, economic development, and social change. Jackson was the first president not to come from a prominent colonial family. As a self-made soldier, politician, and land speculator from the backcountry, he symbolized a transformation in the nation's social structure and political temper.

Profound economic and social transformations were reshaping the young United States. In 1828 there were twenty-four states and almost 13 million people, many of them recent arrivals from Germany and Ireland. The national population was growing rapidly, doubling every twenty-three years. Surging foreign demand for cotton and other goods helped fuel a transportation revolution and an economic boom. Textile mills and shoe factories sprouted across the New England countryside, their spinning looms fed by cotton grown in the newly cultivated lands of Alabama and Mississippi.

Cities increasingly became the centers of the nation's commerce, industry, finance, and political activity. The urban population grew twice as fast as the rural population during the second quarter of the nineteenth century. A more urban society and a more specialized and speculative economy created more instability as people took greater risks to make money. A more stratified social order also emerged, with some people acquiring great wealth while most others worked for wages.

An agrarian economy that earlier had produced crops and goods for household use or local exchange expanded into a market-oriented economy engaged in national and international commerce. New canals and roads opened up eastern markets to western farmers in the Ohio River valley. The new economic order brought with it regional specialization and increasing division of labor. As more land was put into cultivation and commercial farmers came to rely upon banks for credit to buy land and seed, they were subject to greater risks and the volatility of the market. In the midst of periodic financial panics and sharp business depressions, farmers unable to pay their debts lost their farms to "corrupt" banks, which they believed had engaged in reckless speculative ventures and had benefited from government favoritism.

For many people the transition to cash-crop agriculture and capitalist manufacturing was painful and unsettling. A traditional economy of independent artisans and subsistence farmers was giving way to a system of centralized workshops, mills, and factories based on wage labor. Chartered corporations and commercial banks began to dominate local economies. With the onset of the factory system and urban commerce, people left farms and shops and became dependent upon others for their food, clothing, and livelihood. This transformation called into question the traditional assumption of Thomas Jefferson and others that a republic could survive only if most of its citizens were independent, self-reliant property owners, neither too rich to dominate other people nor too poor to become dependent and subservient.

A NEW POLITICAL CULTURE

At the same time that the urban population was increasing and more people were engaging in wage labor rather than agriculture, many states, especially those west of the Appalachian Mountains, were reducing or eliminating the property requirement for voting. This enabled white men with little or no property to participate in the political process. The easing of voting restrictions reflected the feeling on the parts of workers, artisans, and small merchants, as well as farmers, that a more democratic ballot would help combat the rising influence of commercial and manufacturing interests. By 1830 only six states continued to require voters to own a certain amount of property. The easing of such restrictions meant that four times as many men voted in the 1828 presidential election as had voted in the 1824 election.

By gaining access to the political process as voters, propertyless men encouraged a new type of politician, one who identified with the values and desires of the masses. To have been born in a log cabin and to be a "common man" wearing a coonskin cap rather than a powdered wig became great political advantages during the Jacksonian era. As Andrew Jackson himself declared, he governed on behalf of "the humble members of society—the farmers, mechanics, and laborers."

The mass-based Democratic party that ushered Jackson into the White House in early 1829 reflected the emergence of a new political culture during the 1820s. Up to that time well-organized national political parties had been virtually nonexistent. The Jacksonian era witnessed the crystallization of formal parties (the Democratic party and the Whig party), which took

Verdict of the People

George Caleb Bingham's painting depicts the increasingly democratic politics of the mid–nineteenth century.

particular stands on issues, held formal nominating conventions to select presidential and vice-presidential candidates, and had as members congressmen and senators who voted with their party on the issues.

The second quarter of the nineteenth century also witnessed a new style of politicking. It featured fierce polemics, colorful politicians, expensive campaigns, tightly controlled local party "machines," and intense partisan loyalties. Politics during the Jacksonian era was a vibrant public phenomenon that involved mass marches, vigorous debates, and high voter turnout. The local party machines used a partisan network of employers and landlords to help party members find jobs and housing; in return they could expect their members to vote without question for the candidates they designated. Citizens turned to local, state, and federal politicians to help relieve their distress and promote their prosperity. For example, they expected the government to settle the Indian "problem," open up new and cheaper land, and build roads and canals along which they could send their produce and goods.

The new Democratic party was an unstable coalition of northern workers (many of them Irish and German immigrants), owners of small farms, landless laborers, and aspiring entrepreneurs from all sections of the country. Their shared concern was the preservation of a "just" and "virtuous" society in which most people were small property holders jealous of their freedom from monopolists or corrupt politicians. Democrats therefore opposed tariffs and the central national bank, as well as any other efforts to centralize government power. At the same time frontier folk settling in the new states of the Old Northwest (Ohio, Indiana, and Illinois) and the Old Southwest were no longer willing to defer to traditional political and social elites.

Yet to call the Jacksonian era the age of the common man, as many historians have done, is misleading. While political participation increased during the Jacksonian era, the period never produced true economic and social equality. Power and privilege, for the most part, remained in the hands of an "uncommon" elite. Moreover, many Jacksonians in power proved to be as opportunistic and manipulative as the "corrupt" patrician politicians they displaced. And for all their egalitarian rhetoric, Jacksonian Democrats never embraced the principle of economic equality. "Distinctions in society will always exist under every just government," Andrew Jackson observed. "Equality of talents, or education, or of wealth cannot be produced by human institutions." He and his supporters wanted people to have an equal chance to compete in the economic marketplace and in the political arena, but they never sanctioned equality of income or status. "True republicanism," one commentator declared, "requires that every man shall have an equal chance—that every man shall be free to become as unequal as he can."

In the afterglow of Jackson's electoral victory, however, few observers troubled with such distinctions. It was time to celebrate the commoner's ascension to the presidency.

JACKSON TAKES OFFICE

APPOINTMENTS AND RIVALRIES   Andrew Jackson believed that government workers who stayed too long in office became corrupt. So he set about replacing John Quincy Adams's appointees with his own supporters. But his use of the "spoils system" has been exaggerated. During his first year in office, Jackson replaced only about 9 percent of the appointed officials in the federal government, and during his entire term he replaced fewer than 20 percent.

Jackson's administration was from the outset divided between the partisans of Secretary of State Martin Van Buren and those of Vice President John

All Creation Going to the White House

The scene following Jackson's inauguration as president, according to the satirist Robert Cruikshank.

C. Calhoun. Much of the political history of the next few years would turn upon the rivalry between the two statesmen as each jockeyed for position as Jackson's successor. Van Buren held most of the advantages, foremost among them his skill at timing and tactics. Jackson, new to political administration, leaned heavily upon him for advice and for help in soothing the ruffled feathers of rejected office seekers. Calhoun, a man of towering intellect, humorless outlook, and apostolic zeal, possessed a demonic sense of duty and a keen interest in political theory. As vice president he was determined to defend southern interests against the advance of northern industrialism and abolitionism.

THE EATON AFFAIR   In his battle for political power with Calhoun, Van Buren had luck as well as political skill on his side. Fate handed him a trump card: the succulent scandal known as the Peggy Eaton affair. The daughter of an Irish tavern owner, Margaret Eaton was a vivacious widow whose husband supposedly had committed suicide upon learning of her affair with Tennessee senator John Eaton. Her marriage to Eaton, three months before he entered Jackson's cabinet as secretary of war, had scarcely made a virtuous woman of her in the eyes of the proper ladies of Washington. Floride Calhoun, the vice president's wife, especially objected to Peggy Eaton's lowly origins and unsavory past. She pointedly snubbed her, and the cabinet wives followed suit.

Peggy's plight reminded Jackson of the gossip that had pursued his wife, Rachel, and he pronounced Peggy "chaste as a virgin." The cabinet members, however, were unable to cure their wives of what Van Buren dubbed "the Eaton Malaria." Van Buren was a widower, free to lavish on poor Peggy all the attention that Jackson thought was her due. Mrs. Eaton herself finally gave in to the chill and withdrew from society. The outraged Jackson came to link Calhoun with what he called a conspiracy against her and drew even closer to Van Buren.

INTERNAL IMPROVEMENTS   While Washington social life weathered the winter of 1829–1830, Van Buren delivered some additional blows to Calhoun. It was easy to bring Jackson into opposition to federally financed internal improvements and thus to programs with which Calhoun had long been identified. In 1830 the Maysville Road bill, passed by Congress, offered Jackson a happy chance for a dual thrust at his rivals John Calhoun and Henry Clay. The bill authorized the government to buy stock in a road from Maysville to Clay's hometown of Lexington. The road lay entirely within the state of Kentucky, and though part of a larger scheme to link up with the

National Road via Cincinnati it could be viewed as a purely local undertaking. On that ground, Jackson vetoed the bill, prompting widespread acclaim. Yet while Jackson continued to oppose federal aid to local projects, he supported such projects as the National Road, as well as road building in the territories and river and harbor bills, the "pork barrels" from which every congressman tried to pluck a morsel for his district. Even so, Jackson's attitude toward the Maysville Road set an important precedent, on the eve of the railroad age, for limiting federal initiative in internal improvements. Railroads would be built altogether by state funds and private capital at least until 1850.

NULLIFICATION

CALHOUN'S THEORY   There is a fine irony to John Calhoun's plight in the Jackson administration, for the South Carolinian was now midway between his early phase as an economic nationalist and his later phase as a states' rights sectionalist. Conditions in his home state had brought on the change. Suffering from agricultural depression, South Carolina lost almost 70,000 residents to emigration during the 1820s and would lose nearly twice that number in the 1830s. Most South Carolinians blamed the protective tariff, which tended to raise the prices of manufactured goods. Insofar as tariffs discouraged the sale of foreign goods in the United States, they reduced the ability of British and French traders to buy southern cotton. This situation worsened already existing problems of low cotton prices and exhausted land. The South Carolinians' malaise was compounded by the increasing criticism of slavery. Hardly had the nation emerged from the Missouri controversy when the city of Charleston, South Carolina, was thrown into panic by the thwarted Denmark Vesey slave insurrection of 1822.

The unexpected passage of the Tariff of 1828, called the tariff of abominations by its critics, left Calhoun no choice but to join the opposition or give up his home base. Calhoun's *South Carolina Exposition and Protest* (1828), written in opposition to the new tariff, contained a finespun theory of nullification, whereby a state could in effect repeal a federal law. This theory stopped just short of justifying secession from the Union. The unsigned statement accompanied resolutions of the South Carolina legislature protesting the tariff. Calhoun, however, had not entirely abandoned his earlier nationalism. He wanted to preserve the Union by protecting the minority rights that the agricultural and slaveholding South claimed. The fine balance he struck between states' rights and central authority was actually not far removed from Andrew Jackson's own philosophy, but growing tensions between the two men would complicate

John C. Calhoun

During the Civil War the Confederate government printed, but never issued, a one-cent postage stamp bearing Calhoun's likeness.

the issue. The flinty Jackson, in addition, was determined to prevent any state defiance of federal law.

THE WEBSTER-HAYNE DEBATE

South Carolina's leaders hated the tariff, but they had postponed any action against its enforcement, hoping for a new tariff policy from the Jackson administration. There the issue stood until 1830, when the great Webster-Hayne debate sharpened the lines between states' rights and the Union. The immediate occasion for the debate, however, was the question of federally-owned land.

The federal government still owned immense tracts of land, and the question of how to dispose of the acreage dominated the sectional debate. Late in 1829 a Connecticut senator, fearing the continued drain of residents from New England, sought to restrict land sales in the West. When the resolution came before the Senate in 1830, Missouri's Thomas Hart Benton, who for years had been calling for lower land prices, denounced it as a sectional attack designed to impede the settlement of the West so that the East might maintain its supply of cheap factory labor.

Robert Y. Hayne of South Carolina took Benton's side. Senator Hayne saw in the public land issue a chance to strengthen the alliance of South and West reflected in the 1828 presidential vote for Jackson. Perhaps by endorsing a policy of cheap land in the West, southerners could win western support for lower tariffs. The government, said Hayne, endangered the Union by imposing a hardship upon one section to the benefit of another. The sale of public land as a source of revenue for the central government would create "a fund for corruption—fatal to the sovereignty and independence of the states."

Daniel Webster of Massachusetts rose to offer a dramatic defense of the East. Possessed of a thunderous voice and a theatrical flair, Webster was widely recognized as the nation's foremost orator. With the gallery hushed, the "God-like Daniel" denied that the East had ever sought to restrict development of the West. He then rebuked those southerners who "habitually speak of the Union in terms of indifference, or even of disparagement." Webster sought to lure Hayne into defending states' rights and upholding the doctrine of nullification instead of pursuing coalition with the West.

Hayne took the bait. Young, handsome, and himself an accomplished speaker, he defended Calhoun's *South Carolina Exposition*, arguing that the Union was a compact of the states, and that the federal government, which was their agent, could not be the judge of its own powers, else its powers would be unlimited. Rather, the states remained free to judge when the national government had overstepped the bounds of its constitutional authority. The right of state interposition, whereby a state could interpose its authority over a federal law in order to thwart an unjust federal statute, was "as full and complete as it was before the Constitution was formed."

In rebutting the idea that a state could thwart a federal law, Webster offered a nationalistic view of the Constitution. From the beginning, he asserted, the American Revolution had been a crusade of the united colonies rather than one of each separately. True sovereignty resided in the people as a whole, for whom both federal and state governments acted as agents in their respective spheres. If a single state could nullify a law of the federal government, then the Union would be a "rope of sand," a practical absurdity. A state could neither nullify a federal law nor secede from the Union. The practical outcome of nullification would be a confrontation leading to civil war.

Those sitting in the Senate galleries and much of the nation at large thrilled to Webster's eloquence. His closing statement has become justly famous: "Liberty and Union, now and forever, one and inseparable." In the practical world of coalition politics, Webster also had the better argument, for the Union and majority rule meant more to westerners, including Jackson, than the abstractions of state sovereignty and nullification promoted by Calhoun and other southerners. As for the public lands, the disputed resolution to restrict land sales was soon defeated anyway. And whatever one might argue about the origins of the Union, its evolution would more and more validate Webster's position.

THE RIFT WITH CALHOUN   As yet, however, Jackson had not spoken out on the issue. Like Calhoun he was a slaveholder, albeit a westerner, and he might be expected to sympathize with South Carolina, his native state. Soon all doubt was removed, at least on the point of nullification. On April 13, 1830, a Jefferson Day dinner, honoring the birthday of the former president, was held in Washington. Jackson and Van Buren agreed that the president should present a dinner toast that would indicate his opposition to nullification. When his turn came, Jackson rose, stood erect as a poplar, raised his glass, pointedly stared at Calhoun, and announced, "Our Union— it must be preserved!" Calhoun tried quickly to retrieve the situation with a toast to "the Union, next to our liberty most dear!" But Jackson had set off a bombshell that exploded the plans of the states' righters.

Nearly a month afterward, the final nail was driven into the coffin of Calhoun's presidential ambitions. On May 12, 1830, Jackson saw a letter confirming reports that in 1818 Calhoun, as secretary of war, had proposed disciplining him for his reckless behavior during the Florida invasion. This discovery prompted a tense correspondence between President Jackson and Calhoun and ended with a curt note from the president cutting off further communication.

The growing rift prompted Jackson to remove all Calhoun partisans from the cabinet. He then named Van Buren the U. S. minister to London, pending Senate approval. In the fall of 1831, Jackson announced his readiness for one more term as president, with the idea of returning Van Buren from London in time for the New Yorker to succeed him in 1836. But in 1832, when the Senate reconvened, Van Buren's enemies opposed his appointment as minister to England and gave Calhoun, as vice president, a chance to reject the nomination with a tie-breaking vote. "It will kill him, sir, kill him dead," Calhoun told Senator Thomas Hart Benton. Benton disagreed: "You have broken a minister, and elected a Vice-President." So, it turned out, he had. Calhoun's vote against Van Buren aroused popular sympathy for the New Yorker, who would soon be nominated to succeed Calhoun as vice president.

The Rats Leaving a Falling House

During his first term, Jackson was beset by dissension within his administration. Here "public confidence in the stability and harmony of this administration" is toppling.

His own presidential hopes blasted, Calhoun eagerly became the public leader of the South Carolina nullificationists, who believed that despite reductions supported by Jackson, tariff rates remained too high. By the end of 1831, Jackson was calling for further tariff reductions to take the wind out of the nullificationists' sails, and the Tariff of 1832 did cut revenues another $5 million, but mainly on unprotected items. Average tariff rates were about 25 percent, but rates on cottons, woolens, and iron remained around 50 percent. South Carolinians labeled such high rates an "abomination."

THE SOUTH CAROLINA ORDINANCE South Carolinians, living in the only state where slaves were a majority, feared that the federal authority to impose tariffs might eventually be used to end slavery. In the state elections of 1832, the advocates of nullification took the initiative in organization and agitation. A special legislative session called for the election of a state convention, which overwhelmingly adopted a nullification ordinance repudiating the tariff acts of 1828 and 1832 as unconstitutional and forbidding collection of the duties in the state after February 1, 1833. The legislature chose Robert Hayne as governor and elected Calhoun to succeed him as senator. Calhoun promptly resigned as vice president in order to defend nullification on the Senate floor.

In the crisis, South Carolina found itself standing alone. Other southern states expressed sympathy, but none endorsed nullification. Jackson's response was measured and firm—at least in public. In private he threatened to hang Calhoun and all other traitors—and later expressed regret that he had failed to hang at least Calhoun. In his annual message on December 4, 1832, Jackson announced his firm intention to enforce the tariff, but once again he urged Congress to lower the rates. On December 10 he followed up with his Nullification Proclamation, a document that characterized the doctrine of nullification as an "impractical absurdity." Jackson appealed to the people of his native state not to follow false leaders: "The laws of the United States must be executed. . . . Those who told you that you might peaceably prevent their execution, deceived you. . . . Their object is disunion. But be not deceived by names. Disunion by armed force is treason."

CLAY'S COMPROMISE Jackson then sent federal soldiers and ships to Charleston to enforce the tariff in South Carolina. The nullifiers mobilized the state militia while their local opponents, called Unionists, organized a volunteer force. In 1833 the president requested from Congress a "force bill" authorizing him to use the army to compel compliance with federal law in South Carolina. At the same time he endorsed a bill in Congress that would have lowered tariff duties.

When the force bill was introduced, Calhoun immediately rose in opposition, denying that either he or his state favored disunion. Calhoun claimed that he did not want the South to leave the Union; he wanted the region to regain its political dominance of the Union. Passage of the bill eventually came to depend upon the support of Kentucky senator Henry Clay, who finally yielded to those urging him to save the day. On February 12, 1833, he introduced a plan to reduce the tariff gradually until 1842, by which time no rate would be more than 20 percent. South Carolina would have preferred a greater reduction, but Clay's plan got the nullifiers out of the corner into which they had painted themselves.

On March 1, 1833, Congress passed the compromise tariff and the force bill, and Jackson signed both. The South Carolina convention then met and rescinded its nullification ordinance. In a face-saving gesture it nullified the force bill, for which Jackson no longer had any need. Both sides were able to claim victory. The president had upheld the supremacy of the Union, and South Carolina had secured a reduction of the tariff. Calhoun, worn out by the controversy, returned to his plantation. "The struggle, so far from being over," he ominously wrote, "is not more than fairly commenced."

RACIAL PREJUDICE IN THE JACKSONIAN ERA

The Jacksonian era was rife with contradictions. Many of the same social factors and economic forces that promoted the democratization of the political process during the 1820s also led Democrats, North and South, to justify white supremacy, slavery, and the removal of Indians from their ancestral lands. The same Democrats who demanded political equality for themselves denied social equality and political rights to African Americans, Indians, and women.

What explains such contradictory behavior? By emphasizing the racial inferiority of Indians and blacks, white wage earners could, in a tortuous sense, enhance their own self-esteem and justify their own economic interests. In addition, many northern workers feared for their own jobs if runaway slaves continued to stream northward or if all the enslaved workers in the South were freed.

ATTITUDES TOWARD BLACKS   Roger B. Taney, Andrew Jackson's attorney general, declared in 1831 that blacks were a "separate and degraded people" and therefore could be discriminated against by local and state governments. Free blacks in most northern states during the Jacksonian era were denied basic civil rights and forced to live under segregated conditions. In 1829 government officials in Cincinnati, a haven for runaway southern slaves, ordered all African Americans out of the city within thirty days. A mob of whites decided to hurry them on, destroying most of the city's black neighborhood in their fury.

Anti-black riots occurred in other northern cities as well. Whites who participated in an 1834 riot against African Americans in Philadelphia explained that they were simply defending themselves against the efforts of blacks and abolitionists "to break down the distinctive barrier between the colors [so] that the poor whites may gradually sink into the degraded condition of the Negroes—that, like them, they may be slaves and tools" of economic elites. Four years later, the state of Pennsylvania officially disenfranchised blacks. By 1860 almost every state, old and new, had disenfranchised free blacks while easing voting qualifications for white men.

The Democratic coalition that elected Jackson thus depended for its survival on a widely shared "white racism" and the ability to avoid potentially divisive discussions of slavery. In the South the majority of farmers who supported the slaveholding Jackson and identified with the Democrats did not own slaves, but they still embraced theories of racial superiority.

JACKSON'S INDIAN POLICY   During the 1820s and 1830s the United States was fast becoming a multicultural nation of people from many countries. Most whites, however, were as racist in their treatment of Indians as they were in their treatment of blacks. "Next to the case of the black race within our bosom," declared former president James Madison, "that of the red [race] on our borders is the problem most baffling to the policy of our country."

Andrew Jackson, however, saw nothing baffling about Indian policy. His attitude toward Indians was typically western: Native Americans were barbarians and better off out of the way. At the Battle of Horseshoe Bend in Alabama in 1814, General Jackson's federal troops had massacred nearly 900 Creeks. Jackson and most Americans on the frontier despised and feared Indians—and vice versa. Jackson believed that a "just, humane, liberal policy toward Indians" dictated moving all of them onto the plains west of the Mississippi River, to the Great American Desert, which white settlers would never covet since it was believed to be fit mainly for horned toads and rattlesnakes.

Most of the northern tribes were too weak to resist the offers of Indian commissioners who, if necessary, used bribery and alcohol to woo the chiefs. Only rarely did the tribes rebel. In Illinois and the Wisconsin Territory an armed clash known as the Black Hawk War erupted in 1832. Under Chief Black Hawk, bands of Sauk and Fox sought to reoccupy land they had abandoned the previous year. Facing famine and hostile Sioux west of the Mississippi River, they were simply seeking a place to raise a crop of corn. The Illinois militia mobilized to expel them, chased them into the Wisconsin Territory, and massacred women and children as they tried to escape across the Mississippi River. When Black Hawk surrendered, he confessed that his "heart is dead, and no longer beats quick in his bosom. He is now a prisoner to the white men; they will do with him as they wish. But he can stand torture and is not afraid of death. He is no coward. Black Hawk is an Indian." The Black Hawk War came to be remembered, however, less because of the atrocities inflicted on the Indians than because among the participants were two native Kentuckians later to be pitted against each other: Lieutenant Jefferson Davis of the regular army and Captain Abraham Lincoln of the Illinois volunteers.

In the South two proud Indian nations, the Seminoles and the Cherokees, put up a stubborn resistance to white encroachments. The Seminoles were in fact a group of different tribes that had gravitated to Florida in the eighteenth century. They fought a protracted guerrilla war in the Everglades from 1835 to 1842, but most of the vigor went out of their resistance after 1837, when their leader, Osceola, was seized by treachery under a flag of truce, imprisoned, and left to die. After 1842 only a few hundred Seminoles remained, hiding out in the swamps. Most of the rest had been banished to the West.

THE TRAIL OF TEARS   The Cherokees had, by the end of the eighteenth century, fallen back into the mountains of northern Georgia and western North Carolina, settling on land guaranteed them in 1791 by a treaty with the U. S. government. In 1827 the Cherokees, relying upon their treaty rights, adopted a constitution in which they pointedly declared that they were not subject to any other state or nation. The next year, Georgia declared that after June 1, 1830, the authority of state law would extend over the Cherokees living within the boundaries of the state.

The discovery of gold in 1829 brought bands of rough white prospectors onto Cherokee land. The Cherokees sought relief in the Supreme Court, but in *Cherokee Nation v. Georgia* (1831) John Marshall ruled that the Court lacked jurisdiction because the Cherokees were a "domestic dependent nation" rather than a foreign state in the meaning of the Constitution. Marshall added, however, that the Cherokees had "an unquestionable right" to their land until they wished to cede it to the United States.

In 1830 a Georgia law had required whites in the Cherokee territory to obtain licenses authorizing their residence there and to take an oath of allegiance to the state. Two New England missionaries among the Indians refused to abide by the law and were sentenced to four years at hard labor. On appeal their case reached the Supreme Court as *Worcester v. Georgia* (1832), and the court held that the Cherokee Nation was "a distinct political community" within which Georgia law had no force. The Georgia law was

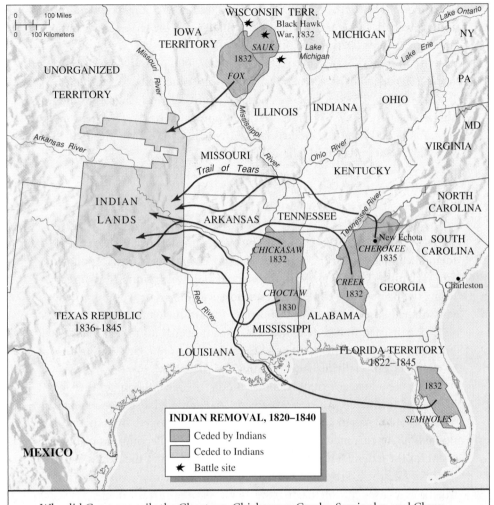

Why did Congress exile the Choctaws, Chickasaws, Creeks, Seminoles, and Cherokees to the territory west of Arkansas and Missouri? How far did the tribes have to travel, and what were the conditions on the trip? Why were the Indians not forced to move earlier than the 1830s?

therefore unconstitutional. Now Georgia faced down the Supreme Court with the tacit consent of the president. Andrew Jackson is supposed to have said privately, "[Chief Justice John]Marshall has made his decision, now let him enforce it!" Whether or not he spoke so bluntly, Jackson did nothing to implement the Court's decision. Under the circumstances there was nothing for the Cherokees to do but give in and sign a treaty, which they did in

1835. They gave up their land in the Southeast in exchange for land in the Indian Territory west of Arkansas, $5 million from the federal government, and expenses for transportation.

By 1838 some 17,000 Cherokees, and some 2,000 African Americans they had enslaved, had departed westward, following other tribes on the 800-mile "Trail of Tears." It was a grueling journey. Four thousand Cherokees did not survive the trip. A few who never left their homeland held out in their native mountains and acquired title to land in North Carolina; thenceforth they were the "Eastern Band" of Cherokees.

THE BANK CONTROVERSY

THE BANK'S OPPONENTS   The overriding national issue in the presidential campaign of 1832 was neither Andrew Jackson's Indian policy nor South Carolina's obsession with the high tariff. It was the question of rechartering the Bank of the United States, whose legal mandate would soon lapse. Jackson had absorbed the West's hostility toward the bank after the panic of 1819. He insisted that the bank was unconstitutional no matter what Chief Justice John Marshall had said in *McCulloch v. Maryland*. Jackson, suspicious of all banks, especially disliked a central national bank.

Under the management of Nicholas Biddle, the second Bank of the United States had facilitated business expansion and supplied a stable currency by forcing state banks to keep a specie (gold or silver) reserve on hand to back up their paper currency. The bank also acted as the collecting and disbursing agent for the federal government, which held one fifth of the bank's $35 million capital stock. From the start this combination of private and public functions caused problems for the bank. As the government's revenues soared, the bank became the most powerful lending institution in the country, a central bank, in effect, whose huge size enabled it to determine the amount of available credit for the nation. Moreover, by issuing paper money of its own, the bank provided a stable, uniform currency for the expanding economy as well as a mechanism for regulating the pace of growth.

Arrayed against the bank were powerful enemies: some of the state and local banks that had been forced to reduce their volume of paper money, groups of debtors who had suffered from the reduction, and businessmen and speculators on the make, who disliked the bank's tight credit policies. States' rights groups questioned the bank's constitutionality. Financiers on New York's Wall Street resented the supremacy of the bank on Philadelphia's Chestnut Street. Like Jackson many westerners and workingmen believed that the bank was a powerful monopoly controlled by the wealthy few and was irreconcilable with a democracy. Biddle, born to wealth and social prestige, cultured, witty, and supremely self-confident, was an excellent banker but also a convenient symbol for those who saw the bank as the cozy friend of capitalists.

THE RECHARTER EFFORT   The bank's twenty-year charter would run through 1836, but Biddle could not afford the uncertainty of waiting until then for a renewal. He pondered whether to force the issue of recharter before the election of 1832 or after. On this point, leaders of the National Republicans, especially Henry Clay and Daniel Webster, argued that the time to move was before the election. Clay, already the candidate of the National Republicans, proposed making the bank the central issue of the presidential election. Friends of the bank held a majority in Congress, and Jackson would risk loss of support in the election if he vetoed renewal. But they failed to grasp the depth of public distaste for the bank and succeeded mainly in handing Jackson a charged issue on the eve of the election. "The Bank," Jackson told Martin Van Buren in May 1832, "is trying to kill me. But I will kill it."

Rechartering the Bank

Jackson Battling the Hydra-headed Bank of the United States

Both houses passed the recharter by a comfortable margin but without the two-thirds majority needed to override a presidential veto. On July 10, 1832, Jackson vetoed the bill, sending it back to Congress with a ringing denunciation of monopoly and special privilege. An effort to overrule the veto failed in the Senate. The stage was set for a nationwide financial crisis.

CAMPAIGN INNOVATIONS   In the 1832 presidential campaign a third party entered the field for the first time. The Anti-Masonic party had grown out of popular hostility toward the Masonic order, a fraternal organization whose members were suspected of having kidnapped and murdered a New Yorker for revealing the "secrets" of his lodge. Opposition to a fraternal order was hardly the foundation on which to build a lasting national political organization, but the Anti-Masonic party made three important contributions to national politics: in addition to being the first third party, it was the first party to hold a national nominating convention and the first to announce an official platform, all of which it accomplished in 1831 when it nominated William Wirt of Maryland for president.

The major parties followed its example by holding national conventions of their own. In 1831 delegates of the National Republican party assembled in Baltimore to nominate Henry Clay. Andrew Jackson endorsed the idea of a nominating convention for the Democratic party (the name Republican was now formally dropped) to demonstrate popular support for its candidates. To that purpose the convention first adopted the two-thirds rule for nomination (which prevailed until 1936) and then named Martin Van Buren as Jackson's running mate. The Democrats, unlike the other two parties, adopted no formal platform at their first convention and relied substantially upon hoopla and the president's popularity to carry the election.

The outcome was an overwhelming endorsement of Jackson in the Electoral College, with 219 votes to 49 for Clay, and a less overwhelming but solid victory in the popular vote, 688,000 to 530,000. William Wirt carried only Vermont. South Carolina, preparing for nullification and unable to stomach either Jackson or Clay, delivered its eleven votes to the governor of Virginia.

THE REMOVAL OF GOVERNMENT DEPOSITS   Andrew Jackson viewed the 1832 election as a mandate to further weaken the Bank of the United States, and he decided to remove all government deposits and distribute them to state banks. When Secretary of the Treasury Louis McLane opposed removal of the federal deposits and suggested a modified version of the bank, Jackson shook up his cabinet. In the reshuffling, Attorney General

Roger Taney moved to the Treasury, where he complied with the president's wishes.

Taney continued to draw on government accounts with the national bank, but deposited new government receipts in state banks. By the end of 1833, twenty-three state banks—"pet banks," as they came to be called—had the benefit of federal deposits. Transferring the government's deposits was a highly questionable action under the law, and the Senate voted to censure Jackson.

Biddle also rejected Jackson's efforts to cripple the bank. "This worthy President," he declared, "thinks that because he has scalped Indians and imprisoned judges, he is to have his way with the bank. He is mistaken." Biddle ordered that the bank curtail loans throughout the nation and demand the redemption of state bank notes in specie as quickly as possible. By tightening the nation's money supply, he sought to bring the economy to a halt, create a sharp depression, and reveal to the nation the importance of maintaining the bank. By 1834 the tightness of credit was creating widespread complaints of business distress.

The financial contraction resulting from the bank war quickly gave way to a speculative binge encouraged by the deposit of federal funds in state banks. With the restraint of the Bank of the United States removed, the state banks issued paper money without keeping sufficient gold reserves on hand. New banks proliferated, blissfully printing bank notes to lend to speculators. Sales of public land rose from 4 million acres in 1834 to 15 million in 1835 and 20 million in 1836. At the same time the states plunged heavily into debt to finance the building of roads and canals, inspired by the success of New York's Erie Canal in opening up the entire state's economy to the markets of the eastern seaboard and Europe. By 1837 the total indebtedness of the states had soared to $170 million, a very large sum for the time.

FISCAL MEASURES   Still, the federal surplus continued to mount as the widespread purchases of public land continued. Many westerners proposed simply to lower the price of land; southerners preferred to lower the tariff, but such action would upset the compromise achieved in the Tariff of 1833. Finally, in 1836, the Distribution Act was passed, a compromise that allowed the government to distribute most of the surplus as loans to the states. To satisfy Jackson's concerns, the funds were technically deposits, but they were never demanded. Distribution of the federal surplus was to be in proportion to each state's representation in Congress.

About a month after passage of the Distribution Act, Jackson's Treasury secretary issued the Specie Circular of July 11, 1836. With that document the president belatedly applied his hard-money convictions to the sale of public land. According to his order, the government after August 15 would accept only gold and silver in payment for land. Doing so would supposedly "repress frauds," withhold support "from the monopoly of the public lands in the hands of speculators and capitalists," and discourage the "ruinous extension" of bank notes and credit.

Irony dogged Jackson to the end on this matter. Since few settlers could get their hands on hard money, they were now left all the more at the mercy of speculators for land purchases. Both the Distribution Act and the Specie Circular put many state banks in jeopardy. The distribution of the federal surplus to the state governments entailed the removal of large deposits from state banks. In turn the state banks had to call in many of their loans in order to accumulate enough money to be able to transfer federal funds to the state governments. This situation caused greater dismay in the already chaotic state banking community. At the same time the new requirement that only hard money be accepted for federal land purchases put an added strain on the local supplies of gold and silver.

BOOM AND BUST   The boom-and-bust cycle of the 1830s had causes larger even than Andrew Jackson, causes that were beyond his control. The inflation of middecade was rooted not solely in a sudden expansion of bank notes, as it seemed at the time, but also in an increase of gold and silver flowing into the country from England and France and, especially, Mexico, for investment and for the purchase of American cotton and other products.

Contrary to appearances the gold and silver reserves in U. S. banks actually kept pace with the increase of bank notes, despite reckless behavior by some banks. By 1836, however, a tighter economy had caused a decline in both British investments abroad and British demand for American cotton just when the new western lands were creating a rapid increase in the cotton supply. Fortunately for Jackson the panic of 1837 did not erupt until he was out of the White House. His successor would serve as the scapegoat.

Van Buren and the New Party System

THE WHIG COALITION   Before the depression set in, the Jacksonian Democrats reaped a political bonanza. Jackson had defeated nullification in South Carolina and eliminated the national bank, and the people loved him for it. The hard times following the contraction of the economy turned Americans against Nicholas Biddle and the national bank, but not against Jackson, the professed friend of "the people" and foe of the "selfish" interests of financiers and speculators.

By 1834 Jackson's opponents had begun to pull together a new coalition of diverse elements, united chiefly by their hostility to him. The imperious demeanor of the so-called champion of democracy had given rise to the name King Andrew I. Jackson's followers therefore were labeled Tories, supporters of the king, and his opponents Whigs, a name that linked them to the Patriots of the American Revolution. The diverse coalition of Whigs clustered around the National Republican party of John Quincy Adams, Henry Clay, and Daniel Webster. Into the combination streamed remnants of the Anti-Masons and the Democrats, who for one reason or another were alienated by Jackson's stand on the bank, Indian removal, hard money, or internal improvements. Of the forty-one Democrats in Congress who had voted to recharter the bank, twenty-eight had joined the Whigs by 1836.

Whiggery always had about it an atmosphere of social conservatism and elitism. The core Whigs were the supporters of Henry Clay, men who promoted a national economic policy. In the South the Whigs enjoyed the support of the urban banking and commercial interests, as well as their planter associates, holders of most of the slaves in the region. In the West, farmers who valued internal improvements joined the Whig ranks. Most states' rights supporters eventually dropped away, and by the early 1840s the Whigs were becoming the party of economic nationalism, even in the South. Unlike the Democrats, who attracted Catholic immigrants from Germany and Ireland, Whig voters tended to be native-born or British-American Protestants—Presbyterians, Baptists, and Congregationalists—who were active in promoting social reforms such as abolition and temperance.

THE ELECTION OF 1836 By 1836, a new two-party system was emerging from the Jackson and anti-Jackson forces, a system that would remain in fairly even balance for twenty years. In 1835, eighteen months before the election, the Democrats held their second national convention, nominating Jackson's handpicked successor, Vice President Martin Van Buren. The Whig coalition, united chiefly in its opposition to Jackson, held no convention but adopted a strategy of multiple candidacies, hoping to throw the election into the House of Representatives. The result was a free-for-all reminiscent of 1824, except that this time one candidate stood apart from the rest. It was Van Buren against the field. The Whigs put up three favorite sons: Daniel Webster, named by the Massachusetts legislature; Hugh Lawson White, chosen by anti-Jackson Democrats in the Tennessee legislature; and William Henry Harrison of Indiana, nominated by a predominantly Anti-Masonic convention in Harrisburg, Pennsylvania. In the popular vote, Van Buren outdistanced the entire Whig

Martin Van Buren

"The Little Magician."

field, with 765,000 votes to 740,000 votes for the Whigs, most of which were cast for Harrison.

Martin Van Buren, the eighth president, was the first of Dutch ancestry. The son of a tavern keeper in Kinderhook, New York, he had attended a local academy, read law, and entered politics. Although he kept up a limited legal practice, he had been primarily a professional politician, so skilled in the arts of organization and manipulation that he was dubbed the Little Magician. In 1824 he supported Crawford, then switched his allegiance to Jackson in 1828 but continued to look to the Old Republicans of Virginia as the southern anchor of his support. Elected governor of New York, Van Buren quickly resigned to join Jackson's cabinet and, because of Jackson's support, became minister to London and then vice president. Short and trim, Van Buren was also called the Red Fox for his long reddish sideburns, dominant forehead, and long, striking nose. His elegant attire, engaging personality, and constant political scheming gave further credence to his nicknames.

THE PANIC OF 1837   President Van Buren inherited a financial panic. An already precarious economy was tipped over by a depression in England, which resulted in a drop in the price of cotton and caused English banks and investors to contract their activities in the United States and refuse extensions of loans. This was a particularly hard blow since much of America's economic expansion depended upon European—and mainly English—investment capital. As creditors hastened to foreclose, the inflationary spiral went into reverse. States curtailed ambitious plans for roads and canals and in many cases felt impelled to repudiate their debts. In the crunch many of the state banks collapsed, and the federal government itself lost some $9 million it had deposited in pet banks.

The common folk, as always, were particularly hard hit during the economic slump and largely had to fend for themselves. By the fall of 1837, one third of the workforce was jobless. Those still fortunate enough to have jobs saw their wages cut by 30 to 50 percent within two years. At the same time, prices for food and clothing skyrocketed. As the winter of 1837 approached, a journalist reported that in New York City 200,000 people were "in utter and hopeless distress with no means of surviving the winter but those provided by charity." There was no government aid, only that provided by churches and voluntary societies.

Van Buren's advisers and supporters were inclined to blame speculators and bankers for the hard times. At the same time they expected the evildoers to get what they deserved in a healthy shakeout that would restore the economy. Van Buren did not believe that he or the government had any responsibility to rescue hard-pressed farmers or businessmen or to provide public welfare. But he did feel obliged to keep the government itself in a healthy financial situation. To that end he called a special session of Congress in 1837, which quickly voted to postpone indefinitely the distribution of the surplus because of a probable upcoming deficit and approved an issue of Treasury notes to cover immediate expenses.

AN INDEPENDENT TREASURY   Van Buren proposed that the federal government cease risking its deposits in shaky state banks and set up an independent Treasury. Under this plan the federal government would keep its funds in its own vaults and do business entirely in hard money. The Whigs preferred that the federal government promote economic development, perhaps in the form of tariff or currency legislation.

Van Buren's Independent Treasury Act aroused stiff opposition from a combination of Whigs and conservative Democrats who feared deflation, and it took the Red Fox several years of maneuvering to get what he wanted. John Calhoun signaled a return to the Democratic fold, after several years of flirting with the Whigs, when he came out in favor of the independent Treasury. Van Buren gained western support for the plan by backing a more liberal policy of federal land sales. Congress finally passed the Independent Treasury Act on July 4, 1840. Although the Whigs repealed it in 1841, it would be restored in 1846.

The protracted struggle over the Treasury was only one of several issues that occupied politicians' attention during the late 1830s. Petitions asking Congress to abolish slavery and the slave trade in the District of Columbia provoked tumultuous debate, especially in the House of Representatives. A dispute over the Maine boundary kept British-American animosity at a simmer. But basic to the spreading malaise was the depressed condition of the economy, which lasted through Van Buren's term. Fairly or not, the administration became the target of growing discontent. The president won renomination by the Democrats easily enough, but the general election was another matter.

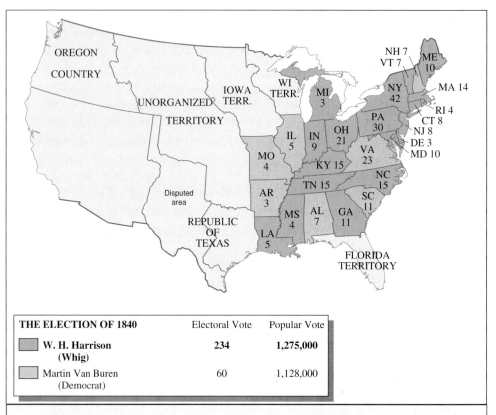

THE ELECTION OF 1840	Electoral Vote	Popular Vote
W. H. Harrison (Whig)	234	1,275,000
Martin Van Buren (Democrat)	60	1,128,000

Why did Van Buren carry several western states but few others? How did the Whigs achieve a decisive electoral victory over the Democrats? How was their strategy in 1840 different from their campaign in 1836?

THE "LOG CABIN AND HARD CIDER" CAMPAIGN   The Whigs got an early start on their election campaign when they met at Harrisburg, Pennsylvania, on December 4, 1839, to choose a candidate. Henry Clay, the legislative veteran who coupled the ideas of a visionary with shrewd political savvy, expected 1840 to be his year. He was wrong. Although Clay led on the first ballot, the Whig convention preferred a military hero who could enter the race with few known political convictions or enemies. So the delegates turned to William Henry Harrison, victor at the Battle of Tippecanoe against the Shawnees in 1811 while governor of the Indiana Territory and briefly a congressman and a senator from Ohio. To rally their states' rights wing, the Whigs chose for vice president John Tyler of Virginia, Clay's close friend.

The Whigs had no platform. A detailed platform would have risked dividing a coalition united chiefly by opposition to the Democrats. But they had a catchy slogan, "Tippecanoe and Tyler Too," and they soon had a rousing campaign theme, which a Democratic newspaper unwittingly supplied: it declared sardonically "that upon condition of his receiving a pension of $2,000 and a barrel of cider, General Harrison would no doubt consent to withdraw his pretensions, and spend his days in a log cabin on the banks of the Ohio." The Whigs seized upon the cider and log-cabin symbols to depict Harrison as a simple man sprung from the people. Actually, he sprang from one of the first families of Virginia, was a college graduate, and lived in an Ohio farmhouse.

The presidential campaign of 1840 produced the largest turnout of any election up to that time. To the Whigs, Van Buren symbolized the economic slump as well as aristocratic snobbery. "Van! Van! Is a Used-Up Man!" went one of their campaign slogans, and down he went by the thumping margin of 234 electoral votes to 60.

Assessing the Jackson Years

The Whigs may have won in 1840, but the Jacksonian movement had permanently altered American politics. Long-standing ambivalence about political parties had been purged in the fires of political conflict, and mass political parties had arrived to stay. They were now widely justified as a "positive good." By 1840 both parties were tightly organized down to the precinct level, and the proportion of adult white males who voted in the presidential election had nearly tripled, from 27 percent in 1824 to 78 percent in 1840. That much is beyond dispute, but the phenomenon of Andrew Jackson, the great symbol for an age, has inspired conflicts of interpretation as spirited as those among his supporters and opponents at the time. Was he the leader of a vast democratic movement that welled up in the West and mobilized a farmer-laborer alliance to sweep the "monster" bank into the dustbin of history? Or was he essentially a frontier tycoon, an opportunist for whom the ideal of democracy provided effective political rhetoric?

In the Jacksonian view the alliance of government and business always invited special favors and made for an eternal source of corruption. The central bank epitomized such evil. Good government policy, at the national level in particular, avoided the granting of special privileges and let free competition regulate the economy.

In the bustling world of the nineteenth century, Jackson's laissez-faire policies actually opened the way for a host of aspiring entrepreneurs eager to replace the established economic elite with a new order of free-enter-prise capitalism. And in fact there was no great conflict in the Jacksonian mentality between the farmer or planter who delved in the soil and the independent speculator and entrepreneur who grew wealthy by other means. Jackson himself was both. The Jacksonian mentality did not fore-see the degree to which, in a growing country, unrestrained enterprise could lead to new economic combinations, centers of economic power largely independent of government regulation. But history is forever producing unintended consequences. Here the ultimate irony would be that the laissez-faire rationale for preserving an agrarian republic even-tually became the justification for the growth of unregulated corporate powers far greater than any ever wielded by Nicholas Biddle's hated cen-tral bank.

MAKING CONNECTIONS

- This chapter analyzed the political side of "Jacksonian democracy." Chapter 12 concludes with an assessment of the accuracy of that term from social and economic perspectives.

- John C. Calhoun, Henry Clay, and Daniel Webster, three of the statesmen considered in this chapter, continued for many years to be the major spokesmen for their positions. Their last great debate, over the Compromise of 1850, is discussed in Chapter 16.

FURTHER READING

A fine survey of events covered in this chapter is Daniel Feller's *The Jacksonian Promise: America, 1815–1840* (1995). A more political focus can be found in Harry L. Watson's *Liberty and Power: The Politics of Jacksonian America* (1990).

A still-valuable standard introduction to the development of the political parties of the 1830s is Richard Patrick McCormick's *The Second Party System: Party Formation in the Jacksonian Era* (1966). For an outstanding analy-sis of women in New York City during the Jacksonian period, see Christine Stansell's *City of Women: Sex and Class in New York, 1789–1860* (1986). John

F. Marszalek's *The Petticoat Affair: Manners, Mutiny, and Sex in Andrew Jackson's White House* (1997) assesses the Peggy Eaton controversy.

The best biography of Jackson remains Robert Vincent Remini's three-volume work: *Andrew Jackson: The Course of American Empire, 1767–1821* (1977), *Andrew Jackson: The Course of American Freedom, 1822–1832* (1981), and *Andrew Jackson: The Course of American Democracy, 1833–1845* (1984). On Jackson's successor, consult John Niven's *Martin Van Buren: The Romantic Age of American Politics* (1983).

The political philosophies of Jackson's opponents are treated in Daniel Walker Howe's *The Political Culture of the American Whigs* (1979) and William P. Vaughn's *The Antimasonic Party in the United States, 1826–1843* (1983).

Two studies of the impact of the bank controversy are William G. Shade's *Banks or No Banks: The Money Issue in Western Politics, 1832–1865* (1972) and James Roger Sharp's *The Jacksonians versus the Banks: Politics in the States after the Panic of 1837* (1970). Daniel Feller's *The Public Lands in Jacksonian Politics* (1984) is a good introduction to that important topic.

The outstanding book on the nullification issue remains William W. Freehling's *Prelude to Civil War: The Nullification Controversy in South Carolina, 1816–1836* (1965). John M. Belohlavek's *"Let the Eagle Soar!": The Foreign Policy of Andrew Jackson* (1985) is a thorough study of Jacksonian diplomacy. Ronald N. Satz's *American Indian Policy in the Jacksonian Era* (1974) surveys Jackson's Indian policy.

12

THE DYNAMICS
OF GROWTH

FOCUS QUESTIONS

- What caused the expansion of agriculture, industry, and transportation?
- How had patterns of immigration changed by the middle of the nineteenth century?
- What was the status of labor unions?

To answer these questions and access additional review material, please visit www.wwnorton.com/studyspace.

The Jacksonian-era political debate between democratic ideals and elitist traditions was rooted in a profound transformation of social and economic life. Between 1815 and 1850 the United States expanded all the way to the Pacific coast. An industrial revolution in the Northeast began to reshape the economy and propel an unrelenting process of urbanization. In the West an agricultural empire began to emerge, focused on corn, wheat, and cattle. In the South, cotton became king, and its reign came to depend upon the expanding institution of slavery. At the same time, innovations in transportation—canals, steamboats, and railroads—conquered time and space and knit together a transcontinental market. In sum, an eighteenth-century economy based upon small-scale farming and local commerce matured into a far-flung capitalist marketplace entwined with world trade. These economic developments in turn generated changes in every other area of life, from politics to the legal system, from the family to social values.

AGRICULTURE AND THE NATIONAL ECONOMY

The first stage of industrialization brought with it an expansive commercial and urban outlook that by the end of the century would supplant the agrarian philosophy espoused by Thomas Jefferson and many others. "We are greatly, I was about to say fearfully, growing," South Carolina's John Calhoun told his congressional colleagues in 1816, and many other statesmen shared his ambivalent outlook. Would the republic retain its virtue and cohesion amid the turmoil of chaotic commercial development? In the brief Era of Good Feelings after the War of 1812, such a troublesome question was easily brushed aside as economic opportunities seemed available to free Americans everywhere.

COTTON   A major source of economic opportunity in the South was provided by the cultivation of cotton, the profitable staple crop that was spreading from South Carolina and Georgia into the new lands of Mississippi and Alabama. Cotton had been cultivated since ancient times, but the proliferation of English textile mills during the late eighteenth century created a rapidly growing market for the fluffy fiber. For many years, cotton had remained rare and expensive because of the need for hand labor to separate the lint from the tenacious green seeds. But that problem was solved in 1793 when Eli Whitney, a Yale graduate who had gone south to teach, devised a mechanism for removing the sticky seeds. The cotton gin (short for "engine") enabled a person to separate fifty times as much cotton as could be done by hand.

By inventing the cotton gin, Eli Whitney had spurred a revolution. Cotton production soared during the first half of the nineteenth century, and planters found a profitable new use for slavery. Planters and their enslaved workers migrated westward into Kentucky, Tennessee, Alabama, Mississippi, Louisiana, and Texas, and the cotton culture became a way of life that tied the Old Southwest to the coastal Southeast in a common interest.

Not the least of the cotton gin's revolutionary consequences was that cotton became a major export commodity for the United States. After Napoléon's defeat in 1815, European demand for cotton skyrocketed. From 1815 to 1819, cotton exports averaged 39 percent of the value of all exports, and from the mid-1830s to 1860 they accounted for more than half the total. Cotton precipitated a phenomenal expansion of the national economy. The South supplied the North with both raw materials and markets for manufactures. Income from the North's role in handling the cotton trade then provided surpluses for capital investment.

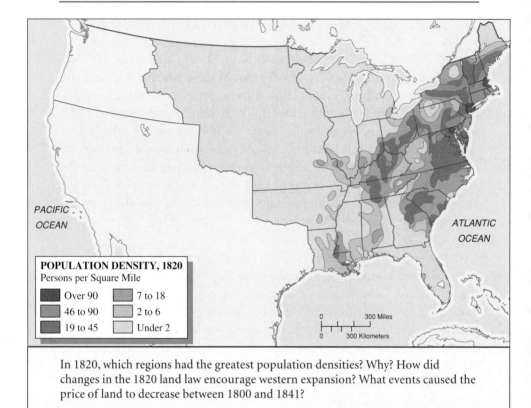

POPULATION DENSITY, 1820
Persons per Square Mile

Over 90
46 to 90
19 to 45
7 to 18
2 to 6
Under 2

PACIFIC OCEAN

ATLANTIC OCEAN

0   300 Miles
0   300 Kilometers

In 1820, which regions had the greatest population densities? Why? How did changes in the 1820 land law encourage western expansion? What events caused the price of land to decrease between 1800 and 1841?

FARMING THE WEST The westward flow of planters and their slaves to Alabama and Mississippi during these flush times mirrored another migration: through the Ohio River valley and the Great Lakes region, where the Indians had been steadily pushed westward. By 1860 more than half the nation's expanded population resided west of the Appalachians, and the restless movement had long since spilled across the Mississippi River and touched the shores of the Pacific. North of the expanding cotton belt in the Gulf states, the fertile woodland soil, riverside bottomlands, and black loam of the prairies drew farmers from the rocky lands of New England and the exhausted soils of the Southeast. The development of effective iron plows greatly eased the grueling job of breaking the soil.

A new federal land law passed in 1820 reduced the minimum price per acre and reduced the minimum plot from 160 acres to 80. A settler could

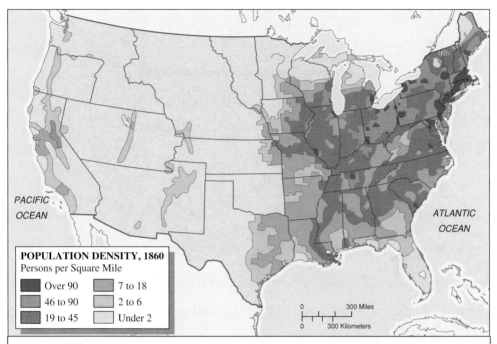

POPULATION DENSITY, 1860
Persons per Square Mile

- Over 90
- 46 to 90
- 19 to 45
- 7 to 18
- 2 to 6
- Under 2

In 1860, which regions had the greatest population densities? Why? How did new technologies allow farmers to grow more crops on larger pieces of land? What regions benefited most from the new technologies?

now buy a farm for as little as $100, and over the years the proliferation of state banks made it possible to continue buying land on credit. Even that was not enough for westerners, however, who began a long—and eventually victorious—agitation for further relaxation of the land laws. They favored "preemption," the right of squatters to purchase land at the minimum price, and graduation, the progressive reduction of the price on land that did not sell.

Congress eventually responded with two bills. Under the Preemption Act of 1830, squatters could stake out claims ahead of the land surveys and later get 160 acres at the minimum price of $1.25 per acre. In effect the law recognized a practice enforced more often than not by frontier vigilantes. Under the Graduation Act of 1854, the price of unsold land was to go down in stages until the land could sell for $1.25 per acre after thirty years.

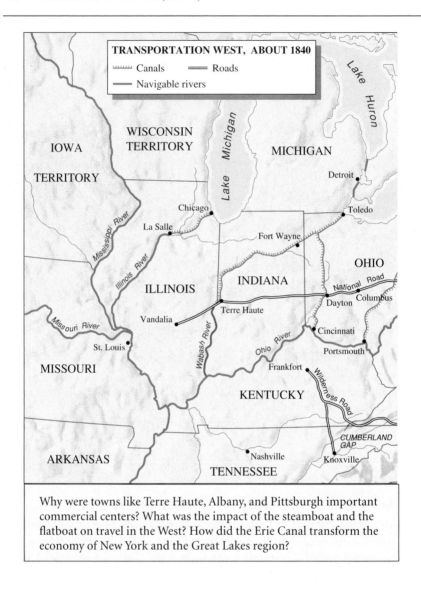

TRANSPORTATION WEST, ABOUT 1840

~~~~~ Canals   === Roads
——— Navigable rivers

Why were towns like Terre Haute, Albany, and Pittsburgh important commercial centers? What was the impact of the steamboat and the flatboat on travel in the West? How did the Erie Canal transform the economy of New York and the Great Lakes region?

TRANSPORTATION, COMMUNICATION, AND THE NATIONAL ECONOMY

NEW ROADS Transportation improvements helped spur the development of a national market for goods and services. In 1795 the Wilderness Road, which followed the trail blazed by Daniel Boone twenty years before,

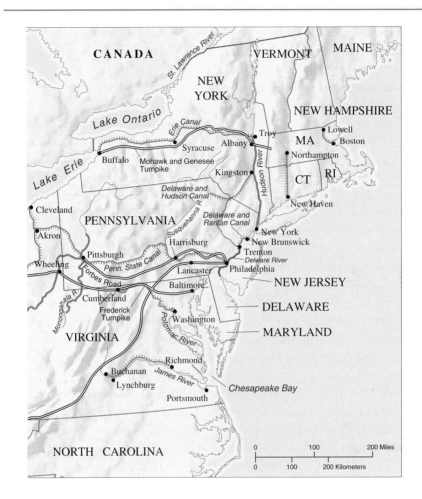

was opened to wagon and stagecoach traffic, thereby easing the route through the Cumberland Gap in Kentucky. In the Deep South there were no such major highways. South Carolinians and Georgians pushed westward on whatever trails or rutted roads had appeared.

To the northeast, public demand for graded and paved roads packed with crushed stones gathered momentum after completion of the Philadelphia-Lancaster Turnpike in 1794 (the term *turnpike*, derives from a pole, or pike, at the tollgate, which was turned to admit the traffic). By 1821 there were some 4,000 miles of turnpikes, mainly connecting eastern cities, but western traffic could move along the Frederick Turnpike to Cumberland and thence along the National Road to Wheeling, Virginia, on the Ohio River, in 1818, then to Columbus in the Northwest Territory and by about midcentury on to Vandalia, Illinois.

WATER TRANSPORTATION Once turnpike travelers had reached the Ohio River, they could float westward on flatboats. In the early 1820s an estimated 3,000 flatboats went down the Ohio River every year, and for many years thereafter the flatboat remained the chief means for conveying freight and people downstream.

By the early 1820s the turnpike boom was giving way to new developments in water transportation: the river steamboat and the canal barge, which carried goods far more cheaply than did Conestoga wagons on the National Road. The first commercially successful steamboat appeared when Robert Fulton and Robert R. Livingston sent the *Clermont* up the Hudson River to Albany in 1807. After that the use of steamboats spread rapidly to other eastern and western rivers. By 1836, 361 steamboats were navigating the western waters. During the next decade, the shallow-draft, steam-powered ships ventured into far reaches of the Mississippi River valley.

The durable flatboat still carried to market most of the western wheat, corn, flour, meal, port, whiskey, and soap and candles (byproducts of slaughterhouses), lead from Missouri, copper from Michigan, lumber from the Rockies, and ironwork from Pittsburgh. But the steamboat, by bringing cheaper and faster two-way traffic to the Mississippi River valley, created a continental market and an agricultural empire that became the new bread-basket of America. Along with the new farmers came promoters, speculators, and retailers. Villages at strategic trading points along the streams evolved into centers of commerce and urban life. The port of New Orleans grew in the 1830s and 1840s to lead all others in exports.

By then, however, the Erie Canal was drawing eastward much of the trade that had once gone down the Mississippi to the Gulf of Mexico. In 1817 the New York legislature had endorsed Governor DeWitt Clinton's dream of a canal connecting the Hudson River with Lake Erie. Eight years later, in 1825, the canal, forty feet wide and four feet deep, was open for the entire 363 miles from Albany west to Buffalo; branches soon put most of the state within its reach. The Erie Canal was an engineering marvel. The longest canal in the world, it traversed rivers and valleys, forests and marshes. It reduced travel time from New York City to Buffalo from twenty days to six, and the cost of moving a ton of freight plummeted from $100 to $5.

The speedy success of the New York waterways inspired a mania for canals in other states that lasted more than a decade. But no other canal ever matched the spectacular success of the Erie. It rendered the entire Great Lakes region an economic tributary to New York City and had major economic and political consequences, tying together West and East while further isolating the Deep South. With the addition of new canals spanning

The Erie Canal

Junction of the Northern and Western Canals (1825), an aquatint by John Hill.

Ohio and Indiana from north to south, much of the upper Ohio River valley was also drawn into New York's economic sphere.

RAILROADS The financial panic of 1837 and the subsequent depression cooled the canal fever. Meanwhile, a more versatile form of transportation was gaining on the canal: the railroad. In 1825, the year the Erie Canal was completed, the world's first commercial steam railway began operation in England, and soon the port cities of Baltimore, Charleston, and Boston were alive with schemes to penetrate the hinterlands by rail. By 1840 American railroads, with a total of 3,328 miles, had outdistanced the canals by just two miles. Over the next twenty years, though, railroads grew nearly tenfold, covering 30,626 miles; more than two thirds of that total was built in the 1850s. But it was still not until the eve of the Civil War that railroads surpassed canals in total haulage.

Travel on the early railroads tested the courage of passengers. Wood was used for fuel, and sparks often caused fires or damaged passengers' clothing. Invention of the "spark arrester" and the use of coal for fuel alleviated those problems. Yet land travel, whether by stagecoach or train, remained a jerky, bumpy, wearying ordeal.

Water travel, where available, offered far more comfort, but the railroad gained supremacy over other forms of transportation because of its economy, speed, and reliability. Trains averaged ten miles an hour, doubling the speed of stagecoaches. Railroads also provided indirect benefits, by encouraging frontier settlement and making farming more profitable. During the antebellum period the reduced shipping costs resulting from the growth of railroads aided the expansion of farming more than manufacturing, since manufacturers in the Northeast, especially in New England, had better access to water transportation. The railroads' demand for iron and equipment of various kinds did provide an enormous market for the industries that made those capital goods, however. And the ability of railroads to operate year-round in all kinds of weather gave them an advantage in carrying freight.

But the epic railroad boom had negative effects as well. By opening up possibilities for quick and often shady profits, it helped corrupt political life, and by opening up access to the trans-Appalachian West, it helped accelerate the decline of Indian culture. In addition, the railroad dramatically quickened the tempo and mobility of life. The writer Nathaniel Hawthorne spoke for many Americans when he charged that the locomotive "comes down upon you like fate, swift and inevitable." With its unsettling whistle it brought "the noisy world into the midst of our slumbrous peace."

OCEAN TRANSPORTATION For oceangoing traffic the start of regularly scheduled service was the most important change of the early 1800s. In the first week of 1818, ships of the New York–based Black Ball Line inaugurated weekly transatlantic service between New York and Liverpool, England. By 1845 some fifty-two transatlantic lines ran square-riggers on schedule from New York, with three regular sailings per week. Many other lines ran in the coastwise trade, to Charleston, Savannah, New Orleans, and elsewhere.

The same year, 1845, witnessed a great innovation with the launching of the first clipper ship, the *Rainbow*. Built for speed, the sleek clippers doubled the speed of the older merchant vessels, and trading companies rushed to purchase them. Long and lean, with tall masts and many sails, they cut dashing figures during their brief but colorful career, which lasted less than two decades. What prompted the clipper boom was the lure of Chinese tea, a drink long coveted in America but in scarce supply. Tea leaves were a perishable commodity that had to reach the market quickly, and the new clippers

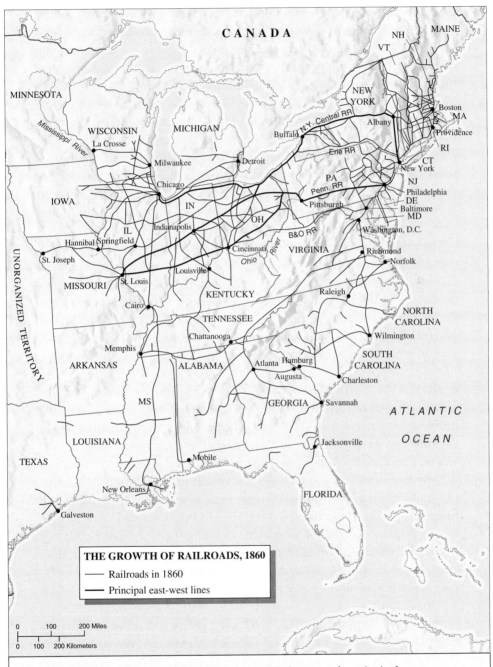

THE GROWTH OF RAILROADS, 1860
— Railroads in 1860
— Principal east-west lines

Why did railroads expand rapidly in the 1850s? What were the principal east-west lines? Why did many lines terminate in places like St. Louis and Chicago?

made this possible. Even more important, the discovery of California gold in 1848 lured thousands of prospectors and entrepreneurs from the Atlantic seaboard. The new settlers generated an urgent demand for goods, and the clippers met it. But clippers, while fast, lacked ample cargo space, and after the Civil War they would give way to the larger steamship.

THE ROLE OF THE GOVERNMENT The massive internal improvements of the antebellum era were the product of initiatives by both state governments and private ventures, undertaken sometimes jointly and sometimes separately. After the panic of 1837, however, the states left railroad development mainly to private corporations, the source of most investment capital. Still, several southern and western states built their own lines, and most states granted generous tax concessions.

The federal government helped, too, despite the belief of some politicians that direct involvement in internal improvements was unconstitutional. The federal government bought stock in turnpike and canal companies and after the success of the Erie Canal extended land grants to several western states for the support of canal projects. Congress provided for railroad surveys by government engineers, granted tracts of land, and reduced the tariff duties on iron used in railroad construction.

A COMMUNICATIONS REVOLUTION During the first half of the nineteenth century, the transportation revolution helped spark dramatic improvements in communications. At the beginning of the century, it took days or often weeks for news to travel along the Atlantic seaboard. For example, after George Washington died in 1799 at his Mount Vernon estate, the announcement of his death did not appear in New York City newspapers until a week later. Naturally news took even longer to travel to and from Europe. On December 24, 1814, the United States and Great Britain met in Belgium to sign the peace treaty ending the War of 1812. Yet two weeks later, on January 8, 1815, the Battle of New Orleans was fought. Both armies were oblivious to the cease-fire that had been declared. It took forty-nine days for news of the peace treaty ending the War of 1812 to reach New York from Europe.

The speed of communications accelerated greatly as the nineteenth century unfolded. The construction of turnpikes, canals, and railroads and the development of steamships and the telegraph generated a communications revolution. By 1830 Andrew Jackson's inaugural address could be "conveyed" from Washington, D.C., to New York City in sixteen hours, but it reached New Orleans in six days. Mail began to be delivered by "express," a system in which riders could mount fresh horses at relay stations. Still, even with such advances the states and territories west of the Appalachian Mountains struggled to get timely deliveries and news.

THE INDUSTRIAL REVOLUTION

While the South and the West developed the agricultural basis for a national economy, the Northeast was laying the foundation for an industrial revolution. Technology in the form of the cotton gin and the mechanical grain harvester and improvements in transportation had quickened agricultural development. But technology altered the economic landscape even more profoundly, by giving rise to the factory system.

EARLY TEXTILE MANUFACTURES   At the end of the colonial period, manufacturing remained at the household, or handicraft, stage of development or, at most, at the "putting-out" stage, in which a merchant capitalist would distribute raw material (say, leather patterns for shoes) to be worked up at a laborer's home, collected, and sold. Eighteenth-century farm families had to produce much of what they needed in the way of crude implements, shoes, and clothing. The transition from home production to the factory was slow, but one for which a base had been laid before 1815.

In the eighteenth century, Great Britain had gotten a long head start in industrial production. Britain led the way in the development of iron smelting by coke (refined coal), the invention of the steam engine in 1705, its improvement by James Watt in 1765, and a series of inventions that mechanized textile production. Britain carefully guarded its hard-won secrets, forbidding the export of machines or even publication of descriptions of them, even preventing informed mechanics from leaving the country. But the secrets could not be kept. In 1789 Samuel Slater arrived in Rhode Island from England with the plan of a water-powered spinning machine in his head. He contracted with an enterprising merchant-manufacturer to build a mill in Pawtucket, and in that little mill, completed in 1790, nine children turned out a satisfactory cotton yarn.

Still, the progress of textile production faltered until Thomas Jefferson's embargo in 1807 and the War of 1812 restricted imports and encouraged New England merchant capitalists to transfer their resources to manufacturing. New England, it happened, had one distinct advantage: ample rivers near the coast, where water transportation was readily available. By 1815 New England textile mills numbered in the hundreds. The foundations of textile manufacture were laid, and they spurred the growth of garment trades and a machine-tool industry that built and serviced the mills.

AMERICAN TECHNOLOGY Meanwhile, Americans became famous for their "practical" inventiveness. In 1804 Oliver Evans developed a high-pressure steam engine that was adapted to a variety of uses in ships and factories. Among the other outstanding American originals was Cyrus Hall McCormick of Virginia. McCormick invented a primitive grain reaper in 1831, a development as significant to the agricultural economy of the Old Northwest as the cotton gin was to the South.

After tinkering with his machine for almost a decade, McCormick applied for a patent in 1841. Six years later he moved to Chicago and built a plant for manufacturing his reapers and mowers. Within just a few years, he had sold thousands of new machines, transforming the scale of agriculture. With a sickle a farmer could harvest half an acre of wheat a day; with a McCormick reaper two people could work twelve acres a day. McCormick's success attracted other manufacturers and inventors, and soon there were mechanical threshers to separate the grains of wheat from the straw. As the volume of agricultural products soared, prices dropped, income rose, and for many farm families in the Old Northwest the standard of living improved.

A spate of inventions in the 1840s generated profound changes. In 1844 Charles Goodyear patented a process for vulcanizing rubber, which made the product stronger and more elastic, and in the process created the fabric for rainproof coats. In the same year the first intercity telegraph message was transmitted, from Baltimore to Washington, D.C., on the device Samuel F. B. Morse had invented back in 1832. The telegraph was slow to catch on, but seventeen years after that demonstration, with the completion of connections to San Francisco, an entire continent had been wired for instant communication. In 1846 Elias Howe patented his design of the sewing machine, soon improved upon by Isaac Merrit Singer. The sewing machine, incidentally, was one invention that slowed the progress of the factory. Since it was adapted to use in the home, it gave the putting-out system a new life in the clothing industry.

It is hard to exaggerate the importance of science and technology in changing the way people were living by midcentury. For examples, improved transportation and a spreading market economy combined with innovations in canning and refrigeration allowed for a more healthful diet. Fruit and vegetables, heretofore available only during harvest season, could be shipped during much of the year. At the same time, the scientific breeding of cattle helped make meat and milk more abundant.

Technological advances also improved living conditions: houses could be larger, better heated, and better illuminated. Although working-class residences had few creature comforts, the affluent were able to afford indoor plumbing, central heating, gas lighting, bathtubs, iceboxes, and sewing machines. Even the lower classes were able to afford new coal-burning cast-iron cooking stoves, which facilitated more varied meals and improved heating. The first sewer systems helped cities begin to rid streets of human and animal waste, while underground water lines enabled fire companies to use hydrants rather than bucket brigades. Machine-made clothes fit better and were cheaper than clothes sewed by hand from homespun cloth; newspapers and magazines were more abundant and affordable, as were clocks and watches. Technology changed not only how people lived but also how they worked. The factory system would have profound effects on the nineteenth-century economic landscape, particularly in the Northeast.

THE LOWELL SYSTEM Modern industrialism appeared first in New England. At Lowell, Massachusetts, along the Merrimack River, the Merrimack Manufacturing Company in 1822 developed a water-powered plant similar to one in Waltham, Massachusetts, in which spinning and weaving by power machinery had been brought together under one roof for the first time in 1813. Lowell grew dramatically, and it soon provided the model for other mill towns in Massachusetts, New Hampshire, and Maine.

The chief features of the "Lowell system" were a large capital investment, the concentration of all production processes in one plant under unified management, and specialization in a relatively coarse cloth requiring minimum skill by workers. In the public mind, however, the system was associated above all with the conscious attempt by its founders to establish an industrial center compatible with republican virtues. Lowell's founders insisted that they could design model factory centers that would enhance rather than corrupt the social fabric. They would avoid the drab, crowded, and wretched life of the English mill villages by locating their mill in the countryside and then establishing an ambitious program of paternal supervision of the workers. The employees were mostly young women from New England farm families whose prospects for finding gainful employment or a husband were diminishing. With so many men migrating westward, New England had been left with a surplus of women. Employers also preferred to hire women because of their manual dexterity and their willingness to work for wages lower than those demanded by men. Many women were drawn to the mills by the chance to escape the wearying routine of farm life and earn money to help the family or improve their own circumstances. As one female mill

Merrimack Mills and Boarding Houses (1848)

Just one of the milling companies in Lowell, Massachusetts.

worker explained, she was working because of "a father's debts . . . to be paid, an aged mother to be supported, a brother's ambition to be aided."

Single girls flocked to Lowell. To reassure concerned parents, the mill owners promised to provide the "Lowell girls" with good wages, tolerable work, comfortable housing, moral discipline, and a variety of educational and cultural opportunities, such as lectures and evening classes. The carefully planned and supervised factory system was designed bring together the benefits of industrial capitalism and republican simplicity.

Initially visitors to Lowell praised the well-designed red-brick mills. The laborers appeared "healthy and happy." The female workers lived in dormitories staffed by matronly supervisors, church attendance was mandatory, and temperance regulations and curfews were rigidly enforced. Despite thirteen-hour days and six-day workweeks, one worker described Lowell's community life as approaching "almost Arcadian simplicity." But with mushrooming growth, Lowell lost its innocence. By 1840 Lowell had thirty-two mills and factories in operation, and the blissful rural town had become a bleak industrial city.

Other factory centers sprouted up across New England, displacing forests and farms and engulfing villages, filling the air with smoke, noise, and stench. Between 1820 and 1840 the number of Americans engaged in manufacturing increased eightfold, and the number of city dwellers more than doubled. During the 1830s, as textile prices and wages dropped, relations between workers and managers deteriorated. A new generation of owners and foremen stressed efficiency and profit margins over community values. The machines were worked at a faster pace, and workers organized strikes to protest conditions.

The "Lowell girls" drew attention less because they were typical than because they were special. Increasingly common was the family system, sometimes called the Rhode Island system or the Fall River system, which prevailed in textile companies outside northern New England. Factories that relied upon waterpower often appeared in unpopulated areas, along with tenements or mill villages that increasingly housed newly arrived foreign immigrants. Whole families might be hired, the men for heavy labor, the women and children for the lighter work. The system also promoted paternalism. Employers dominated the life of the mill villages. Employees worked from sunup to sunset and longer in winter. Such long hours were common on the farms of the time, but in factories the work was more intense and less varied and offered no seasonal letup.

Mill Girls

Massachusetts mill workers of the mid–nineteenth century, photographed holding shuttles. Although mill work initially provided women with an opportunity for independence and education, conditions soon deteriorated as profits took precedence.

INDUSTRIALIZATION AND THE ENVIRONMENT Textile mills along New England's rivers provided new jobs but in the process transformed the environment. The mills, fed by waterpower, led to deforestation,

Milling and the Environment

A mill dam on the Appomattox River near Petersburg, Virginia, in 1865.

air pollution, and a decline in the spring fish runs throughout New England's network of river valleys. They also provoked violent conflicts between farmers and mill owners.

Between 1820 and 1850 some forty textile and flour mills were built along the Merrimack River, which runs from New Hampshire through northeastern Massachusetts. In pre-industrial England and America the common-law tradition required that water be permitted to flow as it had always flowed; the right to use it was reserved to those who owned land adjoining streams and rivers. In other words, running water, by nature, could not be converted into private property. People living along rivers could divert water for domestic use or to water livestock but could not use naturally flowing water to irrigate land or drive machinery.

The rise of the water-powered textile industry challenged those long-standing assumptions. Entrepreneurs acquired water rights by purchasing land adjoining rivers and buying the acquiescence of nearby landowners; then, in the 1820s, they began renting the water that flowed to the textile mills. Water suddenly became a commodity independent of the land. It was then fully incorporated into the industrial process. Canals, locks, and dams were built to facilitate the needs of the proliferating mills. Flowing water was transformed from a societal resource to a private commodity.

The changing uses of water transformed the region's ecology. Rivers shape regions far beyond their banks, and the changing patterns of streams now affected marshlands, meadows, vegetation, and the game and other wildlife that depended upon those habitats. The dams built to harness water to turn the mill wheels that ground corn and wheat flooded pastures and decimated fish populations, spawned urban growth that in turn polluted the rivers, and aroused intense local resentment, particularly among the New Hampshire residents far upstream of the big Massachusetts textile factories. In 1859 angry farmers, loggers, and fishermen tried to destroy a massive dam in Lake Village, New Hampshire. But their axes and crowbars caused little damage. By then the Industrial Revolution could not be stopped. It was not only transforming lives and property; it was reshaping nature as well.

INDUSTRY AND CITIES In 1855 a journalist exclaimed that "the great phenomenon of the Age is the growth of cities." In terms of the census definition of *urban* as a place with 8,000 inhabitants or more, the proportion of urban to rural populations grew from 3 percent in 1790 to 16 percent in 1860. Because of their strategic locations and their importance as centers of trade and transportation, the Atlantic seaports of New York, Philadelphia, Baltimore, and Boston were the four largest U.S. cities throughout the pre–Civil War period. New York outpaced all its competitors. By 1860 it was the first American city to boast a population of more than 1 million, largely because of its superior harbor and its unique access to commerce afforded by the Erie Canal.

Pittsburgh, at the head of the Ohio River, was already a center of iron production by 1800, and Cincinnati, at the mouth of the Little Miami River, soon surpassed all other meatpacking centers. Louisville, because it stood at the falls of the Ohio River, became an important trade center. On the Great Lakes the leading cities—Buffalo, Cleveland, Detroit, Chicago, and Milwaukee—also stood at important breaking points in water transportation. Chicago was especially well located to become a hub of both water and rail transportation, connecting the Northeast, the South, and the trans-Mississippi West. During the 1830s St. Louis tripled in size, mainly because most of the trans-Mississippi grain and fur trade was funneled down the Missouri River. By 1860 St. Louis and Chicago were positioned to challenge Baltimore and Boston for third and fourth places on the list of the nation's largest cities.

The Popular Culture

During the colonial era working Americans had little time for play or amusement. Their priority was sheer survival, and most adults worked from dawn to dusk six days a week. In rural areas, people participated in barn raisings and corn-husking parties, shooting matches and footraces, while residents of the seacoast sailed and fished. In colonial cities, people attended balls, went on sleigh rides and picnics, and played "parlor games" at home—billiards, cards, and chess. By the early nineteenth century, however, a more urban society could indulge in more diverse forms of recreation. As more people moved to cities in the first half of the nineteenth century, they began to create a distinctive urban culture. Laborers and shopkeepers sought new forms of leisure and entertainment as pleasant diversions from their long workdays.

URBAN RECREATION In working-class neighborhoods at midcentury, young men formed volunteer fire companies and fraternal societies whose primary activities were drinking and gambling. Social drinking was pervasive during the first half of the nineteenth century. Barn raisings, corn huskings, quilting parties, militia musters, church socials, court sessions, holidays, and political gatherings—all featured liquor, hard cider, or beer. In Mississippi, recalled Senator Henry Foote, heavy drinking on such social occasions had become so fashionable that "a man of strict sobriety" was considered "a cold-blooded and uncongenial wretch."

The more affluent and educated people viewed leisure time as an opportunity for self-improvement and so attended lectures by prominent figures such as Ralph Waldo Emerson and the minister Henry Ward Beecher. Circuses began touring the country. Footraces, horse races, and boat races began attracting thousands of spectators. Nearly 100,000 people attended a horse race at Union Track on Long Island.

So-called blood sports were also a popular form of amusement. Cockfighting and dogfighting at saloons attracted excited crowds and frenzied betting. Prizefighting, also known as boxing, eventually displaced the animal contests. Imported from Britain, boxing surged into prominence at midcentury and then, as now, proved popular with all social classes. The early contestants tended to be Irish or English immigrants, often sponsored by a neighborhood fire company, fraternal association, or street gang.

THE PERFORMING ARTS Theaters were the most popular form of indoor entertainment at midcentury. People flocked to opera houses and

Bare Knuckles

Blood sports emerged as popular urban entertainment for men of all social classes.

theaters to watch a wide spectrum of performances: Shakespeare's tragedies, "blood and thunder" melodramas, comedies, minstrel shows, operas, magic shows, acrobatics, and pageants. Audiences were predominantly young and middle-aged men. "Respectable" women rarely attended. Behavior in antebellum theaters was raucous and at times disorderly. Patrons were participants as well as spectators: audiences cheered the heroes and heroines and hissed at the villains. If an actor did not meet expectations, audiences hurled epithets, nuts, eggs, fruit, shoes, or chairs.

The 1830s witnessed the emergence of the first uniquely American form of mass entertainment: the blackface minstrel show. Rooted in a tradition of folk theatricals, minstrel shows featured white performers made up as blacks. "Minstrelsy" drew upon African-American subjects and reinforced prevailing racial stereotypes. It featured banjo and fiddle music, "shuffle" dances, and lowbrow humor. Between the 1830s and the 1870s minstrel shows were immensely popular throughout the nation, especially among northern working-class ethnic groups and southern whites.

Although antebellum minstrel shows usually portrayed slaves as loyal and happy and caricatured northern free blacks as superstitious buffoons who preferred slavery to freedom, minstrelsy represented more than an expression of virulent racism and white exploitation of black culture; it also

THE

C R O W
QUADRILLES

Consisting of

Jim Crow   Virgo Crow
Sich a gitting up stairs   I'm dream
A Longtime ago   Weasel in Luff
Sittin on a Rail   My long tail blue
Clare de kitchen

Arranged with FIGURES for the

Piano Forte.

JOHN. H. HEWITT.

The Crow Quadrilles

This sheet-music cover, printed in 1837, shows eight vignettes caricaturing African Americans. Minstrel shows enjoyed nationwide popularity while reinforcing racial stereotypes.

provided a medium for the expression of authentic African-American dance and music.

IMMIGRATION

Throughout the nineteenth century, land in America remained plentiful and relatively cheap, while labor was scarce and relatively expensive. The United States in the nineteenth century thus remained a strong magnet for immigrants, offering them chances to take up farming or urban employment. Glowing reports from early arrivals who made good reinforced romantic views of American economic opportunity and political and religious freedom.

During the forty years from the outbreak of the Revolution to the end of the War of 1812, immigration had slowed to a trickle. Wars in Europe restricted travel from Europe until 1815. Within a few years, however, passenger ships had begun to cross the North Atlantic in large numbers. The years from 1845 to 1854 saw the greatest proportional influx of immigrants in U.S. history, 2.4 million, or about 14.5 percent of the total population in 1845. In 1860 the population was 31 million, with more than one of every eight resident foreign-born. The largest groups were the Irish (1.6 million), the Germans (1.2 million), and the British (588,000), mostly English.

THE IRISH What caused so many Irish to flee their homeland in the nineteenth century was the onset of a prolonged depression that brought immense social hardship. The most densely populated country in Europe, Ireland was so ravaged by its economic collapse that in rural areas the average age at death declined to nineteen. By the 1830s the number of Irish immigrants leaving for America was growing quickly, and after an epidemic of potato rot in 1845 brought to rural Ireland a famine that killed upward of 1 million peasants, the flow of Irish immigrants to Canada and the United States became a flood.

By 1850 the Irish constituted 43 percent of the foreign-born population of the United States. Unlike the German immigrants, who were predominantly male, the Irish newcomers were relatively evenly apportioned by sex; in fact a slight majority of them were women, most of whom were single young adults.

Most of the Irish arrivals had been tenant farmers, but their rural sufferings left them with little taste for farmwork and little money with which to buy land in America. Many Irish men hired on with the construction gangs building canals and railways—about 3,000 went to work on the Erie Canal as early as 1818. Others labored in iron foundries, steel mills, warehouses, and shipyards. Many

Irish Immigration

In 1847 nearly 214,000 Irish immigrated to the United States and Canada aboard ships of the White Star Line and other companies. Despite promises of spacious, well-lit, well-ventilated, and heated accommodations in steerage, 30 percent of these immigrants died on board.

Irish women found jobs as domestic servants, laundresses, or workers in New England textile mills. In 1845 the Irish constituted only 8 percent of the workforce in the Lowell mills; by 1860 they made up 50 percent. Relatively few immigrants during the Jacksonian era found their way to the South, where land was expensive and industries scarce. The widespread use of slavery also left few opportunities in the region for free manual laborers.

Too poor to move inland, most of the destitute Irish congregated in the eastern cities. By the 1850s the Irish made up over half the population of Boston and New York City and were almost as prominent in Philadelphia. Irish newcomers crowded into filthy, poorly ventilated buildings plagued by high rates of crime, infectious disease, prostitution, alcoholism, and infant mortality. The archbishop of New York at midcentury described the Irish as "the poorest and most wretched population that can be found in the world."

Many enterprising Irish immigrants forged remarkable careers, however. Twenty years after arriving in New York, Alexander T. Stewart became the owner of the nation's largest department store and thereafter accumulated vast real estate holdings in Manhattan. Michael Cudahy, who began work in a Milwaukee meatpacking business at age fourteen, became head of the Cudahy Packing Company and developed a process for the curing of meats using refrigeration. Dublin-born Victor Herbert emerged as one of America's most revered composers, and Irish dancers and playwrights came to dominate the stage.

These accomplishments did little to quell the anti-Irish sentiments prevalent in nineteenth-century America. Irish immigrants confronted demeaning stereotypes and violent anti-Catholic prejudices. It was commonly assumed that the Irish were ignorant, filthy, clannish folk incapable of assimilation. Many employers posted signs saying "No Irish Need Apply." But the Irish could be equally contemptuous of other groups, such as free blacks, who competed with them for low-status jobs. In 1850 the *New York Tribune* expressed concern that the Irish, having themselves escaped from "a galling, degrading bondage" in their homeland, typically voted against any proposal for equal rights for African Americans. For their part, many blacks viewed the Irish with equal disdain.

The Irish, after becoming citizens, formed powerful voting blocs. Drawn mainly to the party of Andrew Jackson, they set a crucial example of identification with the Democrats, one that other ethnic groups by and large followed. In Jackson the Irish immigrants found a hero. Himself the son of Irish colonists, he was also popular for having defeated the hated English at New Orleans. In addition, the Irish immigrants' loathing of aristocracy, which they associated with English rule, attracted them to the party claiming to represent "the common man."

Although property requirements initially kept most Irish Americans from voting, a New York State law extended the franchise in 1821, and five years later the state removed the property qualification altogether. In the 1828 election, Irish voters made the difference between Jackson and John Quincy Adams. With African Americans, women, and Native Americans still years away from gaining voting rights, Irish men became the first "minority group" to exert a remarkable political influence.

Perhaps the greatest collective achievement of the Irish immigrants was their stimulating the growth of the Catholic Church in the United States. Years of persecution had instilled in Irish Catholics a fierce loyalty to the doctrines of the church as the supreme authority over all the affairs of the world. Such passionate attachment to Catholicism generated both community cohesion among Irish Americans and fear among American Protestants.

GERMAN AND OTHER IMMIGRANTS During the eighteenth century, Germans had responded to William Penn's offer of religious freedom and cheap, fertile land by coming in large numbers to America. As a consequence, when a new wave of German migration formed in the 1830s, there were still many Germans in Pennsylvania and Ohio who had preserved their language and rural culture.

The new wave of German migration took on a markedly different cast. It peaked in 1854, just a few years after the crest of Irish arrivals, when 215,000 Germans disembarked in U.S. ports. These immigrants included a large number of learned, cultured professional people—doctors, lawyers, teachers, engineers—some of them refugees from the failed German revolution of 1848. In addition to an array of political opinions ranging from laissez-faire conservatism to Marxism, the Germans brought with them a variety of religious preferences. One third of the new arrivals were Catholic, most were Protestants (usually Lutherans), and a significant number were Jews, free thinking atheists, or agnostics.

Unlike the Irish many Germans were independent farmers, skilled workers, or shopkeepers who arrived with enough money to establish themselves as skilled laborers or in farm jobs. They often migrated in families and groups rather than individually, and this clannish quality helped them sustain elements of their language and culture in the New World.

Among those who prospered in America were Ferdinand Schumacher, who began peddling flaked oatmeal in Ohio and whose company became eventually the Quaker Oats Company; Heinrich Steinweg, a piano maker who changed his name to Steinway and became famous for the quality of his pianos; and Levi Strauss, a Jewish tailor who followed the gold rushers to California and began making durable work pants that were later dubbed blue jeans, or Levi's. Major centers of German settlement developed in southwestern Illinois and Missouri (around St. Louis), Texas (near San Antonio), Ohio, and Wisconsin (especially around Milwaukee). The larger German communities developed traditions of bounteous food, beer, and music along with German turnvereins (gymnastic societies), sharpshooter clubs, fire-engine companies, and kindergartens.

Two other groups that began to arrive during the 1840s and 1850s were but the vanguard for greater numbers to come later. Annual arrivals from Scandinavia, most of them religious dissenters, did not exceed 1,000 until 1843, but by 1860 a total of 72,600 Scandinavians were living in the United States. The Norwegians and Swedes gravitated, usually in family groups, to Wisconsin and Minnesota, where the climate and woodlands reminded them of home.

By the 1850s the rapid development of California after the discovery of gold had attracted Chinese, who, like the Irish in the East, did the heavy work of construction. Most of the Chinese immigrants came from Kwang-tung (Guangdong)* Province, a region noted for its political turmoil, social violence, and economic hardship. The immigrants to the United States were mostly married, illiterate men desperate for work. Single women did not travel abroad, and married women usually stayed behind to raise their children. During the mid–nineteenth century a laborer in southern China might earn $5 a month; in California he could work for a railroad or a mine and make six times as much. After three or four years of such work, an immigrant could return to China with his savings and become a "big, very big gentleman."

NATIVISM Many native-born Americans resented those newcomers who brought with them alien languages, mysterious customs, and perhaps worst of all, feared religions. The flood of Irish and German Catholics aroused Protestant hostility to "popery." A militant Protestantism growing out of the early nineteenth-century revivals heated up the climate of suspicion. There were also fears that German communities were fomenting political radicalism and that the Irish were forming voting blocs, but above all hovered the menace of unfamiliar religious practices. Catholic authoritarianism was widely perceived as a threat to hard-won American liberties, religious and political.

By the 1830s nativism was conspicuously on the rise. In 1834 a series of anti-Catholic sermons by the leading New England minister of the era, revivalist and later abolitionist Lyman Beecher, incited a mob to burn a convent in Charlestown, Massachusetts. In 1844 armed clashes between Protestants and Catholics in Philadelphia caused numerous deaths and injuries. Sporadically the nativist spirit took organized form in groups that proved their patriotism by hating foreigners and Catholics.

In 1855 delegates from thirteen states gathered to form the American party, which had the trappings of a secret fraternal order. Members pledged never to vote for any foreign-born or Catholic candidate. When asked about the organization, they were to say "I know nothing," and in popular parlance the American party thus became the Know-Nothing party. In state and local campaigns during 1854, Know-Nothings had carried one election after another. They swept the Massachusetts legislature, winning all but two seats in the lower house. That fall they elected more than forty congressmen. For a while the Know-Nothings threatened to control New England, New York,

*Wade-Giles transliterations are used in this text with Pinyin transliterations, adopted by the Chinese government after the death of Mao Tse-tung (Mao Zedong) in 1976, in parentheses.

A Know-Nothing Cartoon

The Catholic Church attempts to control American religious and political life through Irish immigration.

and Maryland and showed strength elsewhere, but the movement subsided when slavery became the focal issue of the 1850s.

The Know-Nothings demanded the exclusion of immigrants and Catholics from public office and the extension of the period for naturalization (citizenship) from five to twenty-one years, but the American party never gathered the political strength to effect such legislation. Nor did Congress act during the period to restrict immigration in any way.

IMMIGRANT LABOR By meeting the need for cheap, unskilled labor, immigrants made a twofold contribution to economic growth: they moved into jobs vacated or bypassed by those who went to work in the factories, and they made up a pool of labor from which factory workers were eventually drawn.

In New England the large number of Irish workers, accustomed to harsh treatment and willing to work for what natives considered low wages, spelled the end of the "Lowell girls." By 1860 immigrants made up more than half the labor force in New England's mills. Even so their pay was generally higher than that of the women and children who worked to supplement family incomes. The flood of immigration never rose fast enough to stem the long-term rise in wages. Factory labor thus continued to draw laborers from the countryside. Work in the cities offered higher real wages than work on the farm. Labor costs encouraged factory owners to seek ever more efficient machines in order to increase production without hiring more workers. In addition, the owners' desire to control the upward pressure on wage rates accelerated the emphasis on mass production. By stressing high production and low prices, owners made it easier for workers to buy the items they made.

LABOR

Skilled workers in cities before and after the Revolution were called artisans, craftsmen, or mechanics. They made or repaired shoes, hats, saddles, ironware, silverware, jewelry, glass, ropes, furniture, tools, weapons, and an array of wooden products; printers published books, pamphlets, and newspapers. These skilled workers operated within a guild system, a centuries-old economic and social structure developed in medieval Europe.

The Shoemaker, from The Book of Trades (1807)

When Philadelphia boot makers and shoemakers went on strike in 1806, a court found them guilty of a "conspiracy to raise their wages."

The daily routine of urban workers engaged in the "finishing trades" was a mixture of labor, recreation, and fellowship. Their workday began at around six in the morning. At eight-thirty they would take a break to eat pastries. At eleven another break would feature a dram of beer or sugared rum. The workers ate lunch around one o'clock and took another break in late afternoon. During their breaks they would engage in animated discussions of political issues, social trends, and an array of other topics and ideas. Workers in several of the skilled trades, especially shoemaking and printing, formed their own professional associations. Like medieval guilds, which were organized by particular trades, these trade associations were local societies that promoted the interests of their members. The trade groups pressured politicians for tariffs to protect them from foreign imports, provided insurance benefits, and drafted regulations to improve working conditions, ensure quality control, and provide equitable treatment of apprentices and journeymen. They also sought to control the total number or tradesmen in their profession so as to maintain wage levels. The New York shoemakers, for instance, complained about employers taking on too many apprentices, insisting that "two was as many as one man can do justice by."

The use of slaves as skilled workers also caused controversy among tradesmen. White journeymen in the South objected to competing with enslaved laborers. Other artisans refused to take advantage of slave labor. The Baltimore Carpenters' Society, for example, admitted as members only those employers who refused to use forced labor.

EARLY UNIONS Early labor unions faced serious legal obstacles—they were prosecuted as unlawful conspiracies. In 1806, for instance, Philadelphia shoemakers were found guilty of a "combination to raise their wages." The decision broke the union. Such precedents were used for many years to hamstring labor organizations until the Massachusetts Supreme Judicial Court made a landmark ruling in *Commonwealth v. Hunt* (1842). In that case the court ruled that forming a trade union was not in itself illegal, nor was a demand that employers hire only members of the union.

Until the 1820s labor organizations took the form of local trade unions, confined to one city and one craft. From 1827 to 1837, however, organization on a larger scale began to take hold. In 1834 the National Trades' Union was set up to federate the city societies. At the same time, national craft unions were established by the shoemakers, printers, combmakers, carpenters, and handloom weavers, but all the national groups and most of the local ones vanished in the economic collapse of 1837.

LABOR POLITICS With the widespread removal of property qualifications for voting, labor politics flourished briefly in the 1830s. Workingmen's parties appeared in New York, Boston, Philadelphia, and about fifteen states. They admitted many who were not workers by any strict definition, and their leaders were mainly reformers and small businessmen. These labor parties faded quickly, for a variety of reasons: the inexperience of labor politicians left the parties prey to manipulation by political professionals; some of their issues were also espoused by the major parties; and they were vulnerable to attack on the grounds of extreme radicalism. In addition, they often splintered into warring factions, which limited their effectiveness.

Once the labor parties had faded, many of their supporters found their way into a radical wing of the Jacksonian Democrats, which acquired the name Locofocos in 1835 when their opponents from New York City's regular Democratic organization, Tammany Hall, turned off the gaslights at one of their meetings and they produced candles, lighting them with the new friction matches known as locofocos. The Locofocos soon faded as a separate group but endured as a radical faction within the Democratic party.

Though the labor parties elected few candidates, they did succeed in drawing notice to their demands, many of which attracted the support of middle-class reformers. Above all they called for free public education for all children and the abolition of imprisonment for debt, causes that won widespread popular support. The labor parties and unions also actively promoted the ten-hour workday. In 1836 President Jackson established the ten-hour workday at the Naval Shipyard in Philadelphia in response to a strike, and in 1840 President Van Buren extended the limit to all government offices and projects. In private jobs the ten-hour workday became increasingly common, although by no means universal, before 1860.

THE REVIVAL OF UNIONS During the first half of the nineteenth century, labor unions remained local and weak. Often they came and went with a single strike. The greatest single labor dispute before the Civil War occurred on February 22, 1860, when shoemakers at Lynn and Natick, Massachusetts, walked out after their requests for higher wages were denied. Before the strike ended, it had spread through New England, involving perhaps twenty-five towns and 20,000 workers. The strike stood out not just for its size but also because the workers won. Most of the employers agreed to wage increases, and some also agreed to recognize the union as a bargaining agent.

By the mid–nineteenth century the union movement was maturing. Workers sought union recognition and regular collective-bargaining agreements. They also shared a growing sense of solidarity. In 1852 the National Typographical Union revived the effort to organize skilled crafts on a national scale. Others followed, and by 1860 about twenty such organizations had appeared, although none was strong enough as yet to do much more than hold national conventions and pass resolutions.

THE RISE OF THE PROFESSIONS The dramatic social changes of the first half of the nineteenth century opened up an array of new professions. Bustling new towns required new services—retail stores, printing shops, post offices, newspapers, schools, banks, lawyers, doctors, and others—that created more high-status jobs than had ever existed before. By definition professional workers are those who have specialized knowledge and skills that ordinary people lack. To be a professional in Jacksonian America, to be a self-governing individual exercising trained judgment in an open society, was the epitome of the democratic ideal, an ideal that rewarded hard work, ambition, and merit.

The rise of the professions resulted in large measure from the expansion of education and the circulation of knowledge. In the half century after the Revolution, Americans became a distinctively literate people. The nation's passion for reading fueled a thirst for education. Teaching was one of the fastest growing vocations in the antebellum period. Public schools initially preferred men over women as teachers, usually hiring them at age seventeen or eighteen. The pay was so low that few stayed in the profession their entire career, but for many educated, restless young adults, teaching was a convenient first job that offered independence and stature, as well as an alternative to the rural isolation of farming. The New Englander Bronson Alcott remembered being attracted to teaching by "a curiosity to see beyond the limits of my paternal home and become acquainted with the great world."

Teaching was a common stepping-stone for men who became lawyers. In the decades after the Revolution, young men, often hastily or superficially trained, swelled the ranks of the legal profession. They typically would teach for a year or two before clerking for a veteran attorney, who would train them in the law in exchange for their labors. The absence of formal standards for legal training and the scarcity of law schools help explain why there were so many attorneys in the antebellum period. In 1820 eleven of the twenty-three states required no specific length or type of study for aspiring lawyers.

Like attorneys, physicians in the early nineteenth century often had little formal academic training. Healers of every stripe and motivation established a medical practice without regulation. Most of them were self-taught or had learned their profession by assisting a doctor for several years, occasionally supplementing such internships with a few classes at the handful of new medical schools, which in 1817 graduated a total of only 225 students. That same year there were almost 10,000 physicians in the nation. By 1860 there were 60,000 self-styled physicians, and quackery was abundant. As a result, the medical profession lost its social stature and the public's confidence. Yet despite the lack of the first-rate medical education, American physicians were responsible for many breakthroughs in the treatment of a variety of illnesses.

The physical and industrial expansion of the United States during the first half of the nineteenth century gave rise to the profession of engineering, a field that has since become the single largest professional occupation for men in the United States. Building canals and railroads, developing machine tools and steam engines, constructing roads and bridges—all required specialized expertise. Beginning in the 1820s, Americans gained access to technical knowledge in mechanics' institutes, scientific libraries, and special schools that sprouted up across the young nation. Rensselaer Polytechnic Institute was founded in Troy, New York, in 1824 to teach the "applications of science to the common purposes of life." The already existing Franklin Institute of Philadelphia shifted its emphasis in the 1830s to mechanical engineering. By the outbreak of the Civil War, engineering had become one of the largest professions in the nation.

WOMEN'S WORK Women during the first half of the nineteenth century still worked primarily in the home. The prevailing assumption was that women by nature were most suited to marriage, maternal duties, and household management. The only professions readily available to women were nursing (often midwifery, the delivery of babies) and teaching, both of which were extensions of the domestic roles of health care and child care. Teaching and nursing commanded lower status and pay than did the male-dominated professions.

Most middle-class or affluent women focused their time outside the home on religious and benevolent work. They were unstinting volunteers in churches and reform societies. A very few women, however, courageously pursued careers in male-dominated professions. Harriet Hunt of Boston was a teacher who, after nursing her sister through a serious illness, set up shop in 1835 as a self-taught physician and persisted in medical practice although she was twice rejected for admission by the Harvard Medical School. Elizabeth Blackwell of Ohio managed to gain admission to the Geneva Medical College of Western New York, despite the disapproval of the faculty. When she walked in to her first class, "a hush fell upon the class as if each member had been struck with paralysis." Blackwell had the last laugh when she finished at the head of her class in 1849, but thereafter the medical school refused to admit any more women. Blackwell went on to found the New York Infirmary for Women and Children and later had a long career as a professor of gynecology at the London School of Medicine for Women.

JACKSONIAN INEQUALITY

During the years before the Civil War, the American myth of rags to riches endured. The legend had just enough basis in fact to make it plausible. John Jacob Astor, the wealthiest man in America (worth more than $20 million at his death in 1848), came of humble if not exactly destitute origins. But his and similar cases were more exceptional than common. Those who started with the handicaps of poverty and ignorance seldom made it to the top. In 1828 the top 1 percent of New York's families (worth $34,000 or more) held 40 percent of the wealth, and the top 4 percent held 76 percent. Similar circumstances prevailed in Philadelphia, Boston, and other cities.

A supreme irony of the times was that the so-called age of the common man, the age of Jacksonian democracy, seems actually to have been an age of growing social and economic inequality. Years before, in the late eighteenth century, slavery aside, American society probably approached equality more closely than any other population of its size anywhere else in the world. During the last half of the 1700s, social mobility was higher than before or since. By the time popular egalitarianism caught up with reality, reality was moving back toward greater inequality.

Why that happened is difficult to say, except that the boundless wealth of the untapped frontier narrowed as the land was occupied and claims on various opportunities were staked out. Such developments took place in New England towns even before the end of the seventeenth century. But despite growing social distinctions, it seems likely that the white population of America, at least, was better off than the general run of Europeans. New frontiers, both geographic and technological, raised the level of material well-being for all. And religious as well as political freedoms continued to attract people eager for liberty in a new land.

MAKING CONNECTIONS

- Eli Whitney's invention of the cotton gin had a profound effect on southern economic and social development. Chapter 15 describes the economy and society of the Old South in greater detail.

- The westward migration traced in this chapter increased tremendously in the 1840s, a trend discussed in Chapter 14.

- As this chapter demonstrated, the birth and expansion of railroads in the first half of the nineteenth century was an important part of "the dynamics of growth." Chapter 16 shows how a proposal for the first transcontinental railroad had an unexpected side effect: it intensified the debate over the spread of slavery westward.

FURTHER READING

On economic development in the nation's early decades, see Stuart Bruchey's *Enterprise: The Dynamic Economy of a Free People* (1990). The classic study of transportation and economic growth is George Roger Taylor's *The Transportation Revolution, 1815–1860* (1951). A fresh view is provided in Sarah H. Gordon's *Passage to Union: How the Railroads Transformed American Life, 1829–1929* (1996). On the Erie Canal, see Carol Sheriff's *The Artificial River: The Erie Canal and the Paradox of Progress, 1817–1862* (1996).

The impact of technology is traced in David J. Jeremy's *Transatlantic Industrial Revolution: The Diffusion of Textile Technologies between Britain and America, 1790–1830s* (1981) and John Lauritz Larson's *Internal Improvement: National Public Works and the Promise of Popular Government in the Early United States* (2001). On the invention of the telegraph, see Kenneth Silverman's *Lightning Man: The Accursed Life of Samuel F. B. Morse* (2003). For the story of steamboats, see Andrea Sutcliffe's *Steam: The Untold Story of America's First Great Invention* (2004).

Paul E. Johnson's *A Shopkeeper's Millennium: Society and Revivals in Rochester, New York, 1815–1837* (1978) studies the role religion played in the emerging industrial order. The attitude of the worker during this time of transition is surveyed in Edward E. Pessen's *Most Uncommon Jacksonians: The Radical Leaders of the Early Labor Movement* (1967). Detailed case studies of working communities include Anthony F. C. Wallace's *Rockdale: The Growth of an American Village in the Early Industrial Revolution* (1978), Thomas Dublin's *Women at Work: The Transformation of Work and Community in Lowell, Massachusetts, 1826–1860* (1979), and Sean Wilentz's *Chants Democratic: New York and the Rise of the American Working Class* (1984). Walter Licht's *Working for the Railroad: The Organization of Work in the Nineteenth Century* (1983) is rich in detail.

For a fine treatment of urbanization, see Charles N. Glaab and A. Theodore Brown's *A History of Urban America* (1967). On immigration, see *The Irish in America,* edited by Michael Coffey with text by Terry Golway (1997).

13

AN AMERICAN RENAISSANCE: RELIGION, ROMANTICISM, AND REFORM

FOCUS QUESTIONS

· Why did new religious movements emerge during the early nineteenth century?

· How did a distinctive American literary culture develop?

· What were the goals of the different reform movements during the second quarter of the nineteenth century?

To answer these questions and access additional review material, please visit www.wwnorton.com/studyspace.

American thought and culture in the early nineteenth century remained rooted in two contrasting perspectives: Puritan piety and Enlightenment rationalism. America, it was widely believed, had a mission to stand as an example of republican virtue to the world. The concept of America's unique mission still carried spiritual overtones, for the religious fervor that quickened in the Great Awakening had reinforced the idea of a providential national destiny and had infused American idealism with an element of perfectionism. The combination of widespread religious belief and fervent social idealism brought major reforms and advances in human rights.

RATIONAL RELIGION

DEISM   The currents of the Enlightenment and the Great Awakening, now mingling, now parting, flowed on into the nineteenth century and in different ways eroded the remnants of Calvinist orthodoxy. As time passed, the image of a stern God promising predestined hellfire and damnation gave way to a more optimistic religious outlook. Enlightenment rationalism increasingly stressed humanity's inherent goodness rather than its depravity and encouraged a belief in social progress and the promise of individual perfectibility.

Many leaders of the Revolutionary War era, such as Thomas Jefferson and Benjamin Franklin, became Deists even while nominally attached to churches. Deism, which arose in eighteenth-century Europe, embraced Sir Isaac Newton's image of the world as a smoothly operating machine. The God of the Deist had planned the universe, built it, set it in motion, and then left it to its own fate. By the use of reason, people might grasp the natural laws governing the universe. Deists rejected the belief that every statement in the Bible was literally true. They were skeptical of miracles and questioned the divinity of Jesus. Deists also supported freedom from religious coercion of all sorts.

Orthodox Christians could hardly distinguish such a doctrine from atheism, but Enlightenment rationalism soon began to make deep inroads into American Protestantism. The Congregational churches around Boston proved most vulnerable. A strain of rationalism had run through Puritan belief in its stress on literacy and the need for "right reason" to interpret the Scriptures. Moreover, Boston's progress—some would say its degeneration—from Puritanism to prosperity had persuaded many affluent families that they were anything but sinners in the hands of an angry God. Drawn to more consoling and less strenuous religious doctrines, some went back to the traditional rites of the Episcopal Church. Others simply dropped or qualified their adherence to Calvinist theology while remaining in the Congregational churches.

UNITARIANISM AND UNIVERSALISM By the end of the eighteenth century, many well-educated New Englanders were drifting into Unitarianism, a belief emphasizing the oneness and benevolence of God, the inherent goodness of people, and the primacy of the individual's reason and conscience over established creeds and scriptural literalism. Humans were not inherently depraved, Unitarianism stressed; people were capable of doing tremendous good, and all were eligible for salvation. Boston was very much the center of the Unitarian movement, and its notion of "rational religion" flourished chiefly within Congregational churches. During the early nineteenth century more and more of these "liberal" churches adopted the name *Unitarian*.

A parallel anti-Calvinist movement, Universalism, attracted a different social group: wage laborers and people of more humble means. Universalists stressed the salvation of all men and women, not just the predestined elect of the Calvinist doctrine. God, they taught, was too merciful to condemn anyone to eternal punishment; eventually all souls would come into harmony with God. "Thus, the Unitarians and Universalists were in fundamental agreement," wrote one historian of religion, "the Universalists holding that God was too good to damn man; the Unitarians insisting that man was too good to be damned." Although both religious groups remained relatively small in number, they exercised a powerful influence over intellectual life, especially in New England.

THE SECOND GREAT AWAKENING

Despite the inroads of rationalism, nineteenth-century Americans remained a profoundly religious people—as they have been ever since. There was, the perceptive French visitor Alexis de Tocqueville observed in the 1830s, "no country in the world where the Christian religion retains a greater influence over the souls of men than in America." Around 1800, however, fears that secularism was on the march sparked an intense revival that soon grew into the Second Great Awakening, sometimes called the Great Revival. The new wave of evangelical fervor fed upon the spreading notion of social equality. Methodists and Baptists, neither of whom featured an educated clergy, sought to democratize religious practices and congregational structures. Such "populist" tendencies were reinforced by the growing popularity of the concept of free will. Salvation was available to everyone.

FRONTIER REVIVALS   In its frontier phase the Second Great Awakening, like the first, generated great excitement and strange manifestations. It gave birth, moreover, to a new ritual, the camp meeting, in which the fires of faith were repeatedly rekindled. Preachers on horseback found ready audiences among lonely frontier folk hungry for spiritual meaning and a sense of community. In the backwoods and in small rural hamlets, the traveling revival was as welcome an event as the traveling circus.

The Baptists embraced a simplicity of doctrine and organization that appealed especially to the common people of the frontier. Their theology was grounded in the authority of the Bible and the recognition of a person's innate depravity. But they replaced the Calvinist notion of predestination with the concept of universal redemption and highlighted the ritual of adult baptism. They also stressed the equality of all before God, regardless of wealth, social standing, or education. Since each congregation was its own highest authority, a frontier church would choose a Baptist minister on its own. Sometimes whole congregations moved across the mountains as a body.

The Methodists, who shared with the Baptists an emphasis on salvation by free will, established a much more centralized organization. They also developed the most effective recruiting method of all: the minister on horseback, who sought out people in the most remote areas with the message of salvation as a gift free for the taking. The "circuit rider" system began with Francis Asbury, a tireless British-born revivalist who scoured the trans-Appalachian frontier for lost souls, preaching some 25,000 sermons while defying hostile Indians and suffering through harsh winters. Asbury's mobile evangelism perfectly suited the frontier environment and the new democratic age. By the 1840s the Methodists had grown into the largest Protestant denomination in the country.

During the early nineteenth century, the Great Revival spread through the West and into more settled regions back East. Camp meetings were held in late summer or fall, when farmwork slackened. People converged from far and wide, camping in wagons, tents, or crude shacks. The crowds often numbered in the thousands, and the unrestrained atmosphere made for chaos. If a particular hymn or sermon excited someone, he or she would cry, shout, dance, or repeat the phrase. Mass excitement swept up even the most skeptical onlookers, and infusions of the spirit elicited strange manifestations. Some participants went into cataleptic trances; others contracted the "jerks," laughed the "holy laugh," babbled in unknown tongues, or got down on all fours and barked like dogs to "tree the devil," as a hound might tree a raccoon.

But dwelling on the bizarre aspects of the camp meetings distorts a social institution that offered a meaningful outlet to isolated rural folk. For women the camp meetings provided an alternative to the rigors and isolation of frontier domesticity. Camp meetings also brought a more settled community life through the churches they spawned and helped spread a more democratic faith among the frontier people.

CHARLES FINNEY AND THE BURNED-OVER DISTRICT Regions swept by revival fevers have been compared to forests devastated by fire. In 1830–1831 alone the number of churches in New England grew by one third. Western New York from Lake Ontario to the Adirondacks experienced such intense levels of fiery evangelical activity that it was labeled the burned-over district.

The most successful northern evangelist was a lawyer named Charles Grandison Finney. In the winter of 1830–1831, he preached for six months in

Religious Revival

An aquatint of a Methodist camp meeting in 1819.

upstate New York and helped generate 100,000 conversions. Finney wrestled with an age-old question that had plagued Protestantism: What role can the individual play in earning salvation? Orthodox Calvinists had long argued that grace was a gift of God, a predetermined decision apart from human understanding or control. In contrast, Finney insisted that the individual could choose to be saved. Finney thus transformed revivals into collective conversions.

THE MORMONS   The burned-over district gave rise to several religious movements, of which the most important was the Church of Jesus Christ of Latter-day Saints, or the Mormons. The founder, Joseph Smith, was the child of wandering parents who finally settled in the village of Palmyra, New York. In 1820 young Smith, then fourteen, had a vision of "two Personages, whose brightness and glory defy all description." They identified themselves as the Savior and God the Father and cautioned him that all existing religious denominations were false. About three years later. Smith claimed, an angel named Moroni led him to a hill near his father's farm in upstate New York, where Smith claimed to have found the *Book of Mormon*, a lost section of the Bible. It told the story of ancient Hebrews who inhabited the New World and to whom Jesus had made an appearance.

On the basis of this revelation, the charismatic Smith began forming his own church in 1830, and after a few years he was gathering converts by the thousands. Mostly poor New England farmers who had migrated to western New York, these religious seekers found in Mormonism the promise of a pure kingdom of Christ in America and an alternative to the era's social turmoil and degrading materialism. From the outset the Mormon "saints" upset the "gentiles" with their close-knit sense of community and their assurance of righteousness. Mormons rejected the notion of original sin staining the human race. They instead professed an optimistic creed stressing human goodness.

In their search for a refuge from persecution, the Mormons moved from New York to Ohio, then to several places in Missouri and finally, in 1839, to Nauvoo, Illinois, where they settled for some five years. Nauvoo became a bustling city of 12,000, and Joseph Smith, "the Prophet," became the community's leading entrepreneur: he owned the hotel and general store, served as mayor and as general of the city's militia, and was the trustee for the church.

Smith practiced "plural marriage," and in 1844 a crisis arose when dissidents accused him of justifying polygamy. The upshot was a schism in the church, efforts by non-Mormons in the neighboring counties to attack

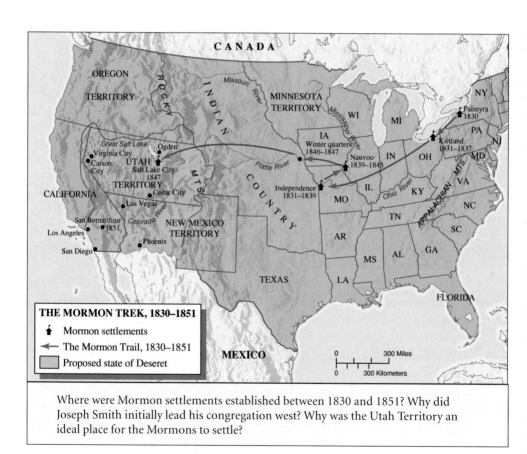

THE MORMON TREK, 1830–1851

⛏ Mormon settlements

⟵ The Mormon Trail, 1830–1851

▢ Proposed state of Deseret

Where were Mormon settlements established between 1830 and 1851? Why did Joseph Smith initially lead his congregation west? Why was the Utah Territory an ideal place for the Mormons to settle?

Nauvoo, and the arrest of Smith and his brother Hyrum. On June 27, 1844, an anti-Mormon lynch mob stormed the feebly defended Nauvoo jail and killed Joseph and Hyrum Smith.

In Brigham Young, the remarkable successor to Joseph Smith, the Mormons found a leader who was strong-minded, intelligent, and authoritarian. After the murder of Smith, Young patched up an unsure peace with the neighbors by promising that he and the Mormons would leave Illinois. Before the year was out, Young had chosen a new destination, near the Great Salt Lake in Utah, guarded by mountains to the east and north, deserts to the west and south, yet fed by mountain streams of melted snow. Despite its isolation, the Utah site was close enough to the Oregon Trail for the "saints" to prosper by trade with passing "gentiles."

The epic Mormon trek to Utah was better organized and less arduous than most of the overland migrations of the time. By the fall of 1846, in wagons and on foot, 15,000 migrants had reached winter quarters on the Missouri River, where they paused until the first bands set out the next spring for "the Promised Land." The first arrivals at Salt Lake in July 1847 found only "a broad and barren plain hemmed in by mountains . . . the paradise of the lizard, the cricket and the rattlesnake." By the end of 1848, however, the Mormons had developed an efficient irrigation system, and over the next decade, by cooperative labor, they brought about a spectacular greening of the desert. At first they organized their own state of Deseret (meaning "Land of the Honeybee," according to Young), but their independence was short-lived. In 1849 Congress incorporated the Utah Territory, including the Mormons' Salt Lake settlement, into the United States. Nevertheless, with Brigham Young named the territorial governor, the new arrangement afforded the Mormons virtual independence. By 1869 some 80,000 Mormons had settled in Utah.

ROMANTICISM IN AMERICA

The revival of emotional piety and the founding of new religions during the early 1800s represented a widespread tendency in the Western world to accentuate the stirrings of the spirit rather than the dry logic of reason. Another great victory of heart over head was the Romantic movement in thought, literature, and the arts. By the 1780s a revolt was brewing in Europe against the well-ordered world of Enlightenment thinkers. Were there not, many wondered, more activities that reason and logic could explain: moods, impressions, feelings; mysterious, unknown, and half-seen things? Americans took readily to the Romantics' emphasis on a realm beyond reason, individual freedom, and the inspiring beauties of nature.

TRANSCENDENTALISM   The most intense expression of such Romantic ideals in America was the transcendentalist movement of New England, which drew its name from its emphasis on transcending (or rising above) the limits of reason. American transcendentalism was largely inspired by the German philosopher Immanuel Kant and the British poet Samuel Taylor Coleridge, but it was rooted in New England Puritanism, to which it owed a pervasive moralism and profound spirituality. It also had a close affinity with the Quaker doctrine of the inner light. The inner light, a gift from God's grace, was transformed by transcendentalists into intuition, a faculty of the mind capable of perceiving things inaccessible to reason.

In 1836 an informal discussion group known as the Transcendental Club began to meet in Boston and Concord, Massachusetts. It was a loose association of freethinkers. The club included liberal clergymen such as Theodore Parker and George Ripley; writers such as Henry David Thoreau, Bronson Alcott, and Orestes Brownson; and learned women such as Margaret Fuller and Elizabeth Peabody and her sister Sophia, who married Nathaniel Hawthorne in 1842. Fuller edited the group's quarterly review, the *Dial* (1840–1844), before the duty fell to Ralph Waldo Emerson, soon to become the acknowledged high priest of transcendentalism.

EMERSON AND THOREAU   More than any other person, Emerson spread the transcendentalist gospel. Sprung from a line of New England ministers, he set out to be a Unitarian parson but quit the "cold and cheerless" denomination because of growing doubts about its emotional vitality. After travel to Europe, where he met England's great literary romantics, Emerson settled in Concord to take up the life of an essayist, poet, and popular speaker on the lecture circuit, preaching the good news of optimism, self-reliance, and the individual's unlimited potential. Having found reason "cold as a cucumber," he was determined to *transcend* the limitations of inherited conventions and rationalism in order to penetrate the inner recesses of the self.

Ralph Waldo Emerson

Transcendental poet and essayist.

Emerson's young friend and Concord neighbor Henry David Thoreau practiced the introspective self-reliance that Emerson preached. "I like people who can do things," Emerson stressed, and Thoreau, fourteen years his junior, could do many things well: carpentry, masonry, painting, surveying, sailing, and gardening. Thoreau, Emerson noted, was "as ugly as sin, long-nosed, queer-mouthed" and possessed of "uncouth and somewhat rustic manners." But he displayed a sense of uncompromising integrity, outdoor vigor, and tart individuality that Emerson found captivating.

Thoreau was also a thoroughgoing individualist. "If a man does not keep pace with his companion," he wrote, "perhaps it is because he hears a different drummer." After graduating from Harvard, Thoreau settled down in Concord to eke out a living as a part-time surveyor and maker of pencils. But he yearned to be a writer and a philosophical naturalist, and he took daily saunters in the woods and fields to drink in the beauties of nature and reflect upon the mysteries of life. The scramble for wealth among his neighbors disgusted rather than tempted him. "The mass of men," he wrote, "lead lives of quiet desperation."

Determined to practice "plain living and high thinking," Thoreau embarked on an experiment in self-reliant simplicity. On July 4, 1845, he took to the woods to live in a cabin he had built on Emerson's land beside Walden Pond, about a mile outside Concord. He wanted to free himself from the complexities and hypocrisies of society so as to devote his time to reflection and writing. His purpose was not to lead a hermit's life. He frequently walked the mile or so to town to dine with his friends and often welcomed guests at his cabin. "I went to the woods because I wished to live deliberately," he wrote in *Walden, or Life in the Woods* (1854), ". . . and not, when I came to die, discover that I had not lived."

Thoreau saw the Mexican War, which erupted while he was at Walden Pond, as a corrupt attempt to advance the cause of slavery. He refused to pay his poll tax as a gesture of opposition, for which he was put in jail (for only one night; an aunt paid the tax). Out of the incident grew the classic essay "Civil Disobedience" (1849), which

Henry David Thoreau

Author of the American classics *Walden* and "Civil Disobedience."

would influence the passive-resistance movements of Mahatma Gandhi in India and Martin Luther King Jr., in the American South. "If the law is of such a nature that it requires you to be an agent of injustice to another," Thoreau wrote, "then, I say, break the law."

The influence of Thoreau's ideas more than a century after his death shows the impact a contemplative individual can have on the world of action. For the most part, Thoreau and the transcendentalists avoided organized reform or political activities. They prized their individual freedom and distrusted all institutions—even those promoting causes they deemed worthy. The transcendentalists taught a powerful lesson: people must follow their conscience. In doing so, they inspired reform movements and were the quickening force for a generation of writers who produced the first age of classic American literature.

The Flowering of American Literature

Ever since gaining independence, the United States had suffered from a cultural inferiority complex. The Old World continued to set the standards in philosophy, literature, and the fine arts. As a British literary critic sneered in 1819, "Americans have no national literature." That may have been true, but during the early nineteenth century American culture began to flower.

A New England renaissance featured four poets who shaped the American imagination in a day when poetry was still read by a wide public: Henry Wadsworth Longfellow, John Greenleaf Whittier, Oliver Wendell Holmes Sr., and James Russell Lowell. Emily Dickinson was probably the most original of the writers contributing to this renaissance, but few of her poems were published at the time. Two New York writers, Washington Irving and James Fenimore Cooper, began to draw wide notice in Britain as well as in America. Irving's *The Sketch Book* (1819–1820) introduced such captivating stories as "Rip Van Winkle" and "The Legend of Sleepy Hollow." Cooper wrote about the frontiersman Natty Bumppo (also known as Hawkeye) in *The Pioneers* (1823), the first of the five *Leather-Stocking Tales*, novels of people pitted against nature in the backwoods. Virginian Edgar Allan Poe emerged as the master of horrifying stories and profound poetry. Then in the half decade of 1850–1855 came the publication of such works as *The Scarlet Letter* and *The House of the Seven Gables* by Nathaniel Hawthorne, *Moby-Dick* by Herman Melville, and *Leaves of Grass* by Walt Whitman. The literary historian F.O. Mathiessen wrote in his book *American Renaissance*, "You might search all the rest of American literature without being able to collect a group of books equal to these in imaginative quality."

The most provocative writer during the antebellum period was Walt Whitman, a remarkably vibrant personality who disdained inherited social conventions and artistic traditions. There was something elemental in Whitman's character, something bountiful and generous and compelling—even his faults and inconsistencies were ample. Born on a Long Island farm, he moved with his family to Brooklyn and from the age of twelve worked mainly as a handyman and journalist, frequently taking the ferry across the harbor to booming, bustling Manhattan.

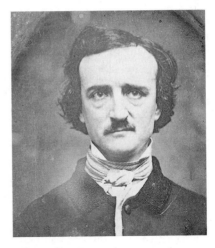

Edgar Allan Poe

Perhaps the most inventive American writer of the period.

Whitman remained relatively obscure until the first edition of his poems, *Leaves of Grass* (1855), caught the eye and aroused the ire of readers. Emerson found it "the most extraordinary piece of wit and wisdom that America has yet contributed," but more conventional critics shuddered at Whitman's explicit sexual references and groused at his indifference to rhyme and meter as well as his buoyant egotism. The jaunty Whitman refused to conform to genteel notions of art, however, and he spent most of his career working on *Leaves of Grass*, enlarging and reshaping it in successive editions. He identified the growth of his gargantuan collection of poems with the growth of the country, which he celebrated in all its variety. Thoreau described Whitman as the "greatest democrat the world has seen."

Politics in an Oyster House **(1848) by Richard Caton Woodville**

A newspaper reader engages in eager discussion.

NEWSPAPERS The flowering of American literature during

the first half of the nineteenth century came at a time of massive expansion in newspaper readership. In 1847 Richard Hoe of New York invented the rotary press, which printed 20,000 sheets an hour. Like many technological advances this one was a mixed blessing. The high cost of the press made it harder for someone of small means to break into publishing. On the other hand, it expedited production of cheap newspapers as well as magazines and books. The availability of newspapers costing only a penny apiece transformed daily reading into a form of popular entertainment. Newspaper circulation soared in every city. The "penny dailies," explained one editor, "are to be found in every street, lane, and alley; in every hotel, tavern, counting-house, [and] shop." The United States had more newspapers than any other nation in the world. As readership grew, the content of the papers expanded beyond political news and commentary to include society gossip, sports, and reports of sensational crimes and accidents.

EDUCATION

Literacy in nineteenth-century America was surprisingly widespread, given the condition of public education. In 1840, according to census data, some 78 percent of the total population and 91 percent of the white population could read and write. Since the colonial period, in fact, Americans had enjoyed the highest literacy rate in the Western world. Most children learned to read in church or private schools, from formal tutors, or from their families.

EARLY PUBLIC SCHOOLS   During the 1830s the demand for government-supported public schools peaked. Workers wanted free public schools to give their children an equal chance at economic and social success. Education, it was also argued, would be a means of social reformeled, by improving manners and reducing crime and poverty.

Horace Mann of Massachusetts led the drive for statewide school systems. Trained as a lawyer, he shepherded through the legislature in 1837 a bill that created a state board of education, then served as head of the new agency. Mann went on to sponsor many reforms in Massachusetts, including the first state-supported training for teachers, a state association of teachers, and a minimum school year of six months. Mann defended the public- school system as the best conduit to social stability and equal economic opportunity: "Education then, beyond all other devices of human origin, is a great equalizer of the conditions of men—the balance wheel of the social machinery."

While the North had made great strides in public education by 1850, the educational pattern in the South continued to reflect the region's aristocratic pretensions and rural isolation: the South had a higher percentage of college students than any other region but a lower percentage of public-school students. And the South had some 500,000 white illiterates, more than half the total number in the young nation.

Nationwide, most students going beyond the elementary grades went to private academies, often subsidized by church and public funds. Such schools, begun in colonial days, multiplied until there were more than 6,000 of them in 1850. Public high schools became well established in school systems only after the Civil War; in 1860 there were barely 300 in the whole country.

HIGHER EDUCATION   The post-Revolutionary proliferation of colleges continued after 1800 with the spread of small denominational colleges and state universities. Nine colleges had been founded in the colonial

The George Barrell Emerson School, Boston (ca. 1850)

Although higher education for women initially met with some resistance, seminaries like this one, started in the 1820s and 1830s, taught women mathematics, physics, and history, as well as music, art, and the social graces.

period, all of which survived; but not many of the fifty that sprang up between 1776 and 1800 lasted. Of the seventy-eight colleges and universities in 1840, fully thirty-five had been founded after 1830, almost all affiliated with a Christian denomination. A post-Revolutionary movement for state-supported universities flourished in those southern states that had had no colonial university. Federal policy abetted the spread of universities in the West. When Congress granted statehood to Ohio in 1803, it set aside two townships for the support of a state university and kept up that policy in other new states.

Colleges and universities during the nineteenth century were tiny when compared with today's institutions of higher learning. Most enrolled 100 students or fewer, and the largest rarely had more than 600. Virtually all of those students were men. Elementary education for girls was generally accepted, but training beyond that level was not. Progress began with the academies, some of which taught boys and girls alike. Good "female seminaries," like those founded by Emma Willard at Troy, New York (1821), and Mary Lyon at South Hadley, Massachusetts (1837), paved the way for women's colleges.

The curricula in female seminaries usually differed from the courses in men's schools, giving more attention to the social amenities and such "embellishments" as music and art. Vassar, opened at Poughkeepsie, New York, in 1861, is usually credited with being the first women's college to give priority to conventional academic subjects and standards. In general the West gave the greatest impetus to coeducation, with state universities in the lead. But once admitted, female students remained in a subordinate status. At Oberlin College in Ohio, for instance, women were expected to clean male students' rooms and were not allowed to speak in class or recite at graduation exercises. Coeducation did not mean equality.

Antebellum Reform

The United States in the antebellum period was awash in reform movements. The urge to eradicate evil had its roots in the American sense of spiritual zeal and moral mission, which in turn drew upon increasing faith in the perfectibility of humankind. The revival fever of the Second Great Awakening helped generate a widespread belief that people could eradicate many of the evils afflicting society. Transcendentalism, the spirit of which infected even those unfamiliar with its philosophical roots, offered a romantic faith in the individual and the belief that human intuition led to right thinking.

Such a perfectionist bent found outlet in diverse reform movements and activities during the first half of the nineteenth century. Few areas of life escaped the concerns of the reformers: observance of the Sabbath, dueling, crime and punishment, the hours and conditions of work, poverty, vice, care of the handicapped, pacifism, foreign missions, temperance, women's rights, and the abolition of slavery. Some crusaders challenged a host of evils; others focused on pet causes. One Massachusetts reformer, for example, insisted that "a vegetable diet lies at the basis of all reforms."

While a perfectionist impulse helped excite the reform movements of the Jacksonian era, social and economic changes helped supply the reformers themselves, most of whom were women. The rise of an urban middle class offered affluent women greater time to devote to social concerns. Material prosperity enabled them to hire maids and cooks, often Irish immigrants, who in turn freed them from household chores. Many women joined charitable organizations, most of which were led by men. Some reformers proposed legislative remedies for social ills; others stressed personal conversion or private philanthropy. Whatever the method or approach, social reformers mobilized in great numbers during the second quarter of the nineteenth century.

TEMPERANCE   The temperance crusade was perhaps the most widespread of the reform movements. The census of 1810 reported some 14,000 distilleries producing 25 million gallons of alcoholic beverages each year. William Cobbett, an English reformer who traveled in the United States, noted in 1819 that one could "go into hardly any man's house without being asked to drink wine or spirits, even *in the morning.*"

The temperance movement during the first half of the nineteenth century rested on a number of arguments. Foremost was the religious demand that "soldiers of the cross" lead blameless lives. Others stressed the economic implications of sottish workers. The dynamic new economy, with factories and railroads moving on strict schedules, made tippling by the labor force a far greater problem than it had been in a simpler agrarian economy. Humanitarians also emphasized the relations between drinking and poverty. Much of the movement's propaganda focused on the sufferings of innocent mothers and children. "Drink," said a pamphlet from the Sons of Temperance, "is the prolific source (directly or indirectly) of nearly all the ills that afflict the human family."

In 1826 a group of Boston ministers organized the American Society for the Promotion of Temperance. The society pursued its objectives through lectures, press campaigns, an essay contest, and the formation of local and state societies. A favorite device was to ask each person who took the pledge to put by his signature a *T* for "total abstinence." With that a new word entered the language: *teetotaler.*

In 1833 the society called a national convention in Philadelphia, where the American Temperance Union was formed. It passed a resolution that the sale of liquor was morally wrong and ought to be prohibited by law. The Temperance Union, at its spring convention in 1836, called for abstinence from all alcoholic beverages, a decision that caused moderates to abstain from the movement instead. Still, between 1830 and 1860 the temperance agitation drastically reduced per capita consumption of alcohol.

PRISONS AND ASYLUMS   The Romantic era's belief that people are innately good and capable of improvement brought about major changes in the treatment of prisoners, the disabled, and dependent children. If removed from society, it was believed, the needy and deviant could be made whole again. Unhappily, this ideal kept running up against the dictates of convenience and economy. The institutions for people with problems had a way of turning into breeding grounds of brutality and neglect.

In the colonial period, prisons were usually places for brief confinement before punishment, which was either death or some kind of pain or humiliation: whipping, mutilation, confinement in stocks, branding, and the like. A new attitude began to emerge after the Revolution, and gradually the idea of the penitentiary developed. It would be a place where the guilty experienced penitence and underwent rehabilitation, not just punishment.

An early model of the new system, widely copied, was the Auburn Penitentiary, commissioned by New York in 1816. The prisoners at Auburn had separate cells and gathered for meals and group labor. Discipline was severe. The men were marched out in lockstep and never put face-to-face or allowed to talk. But prisoners were at least reasonably secure from abuse by other prisoners. The system, its advocates argued, had a beneficial effect on the prisoners and saved money, since the workshops supplied prison needs and produced goods for sale at a profit. By 1840 there were twelve prisons of the Auburn type scattered across the nation.

The reform impulse also found an outlet in the care of the insane. The Pennsylvania Hospital (1751), one of the first in the country, had a provision in its charter that it should care for "lunaticks," but before 1800 few other hospitals provided care for the mentally ill. There were in fact few hospitals of any kind. The insane were usually confined at home with hired keepers or in jails and almshouses. After 1815, however, public asylums that separated the disturbed from criminals began to appear.

The most important figure in arousing public concern about the plight of the mentally ill was Dorothea Dix. A pious Boston schoolteacher, she was called upon to instruct a Sunday-school class at the East Cambridge House of Correction in 1841. She found there a roomful of insane persons completely neglected, fed slop, and left without heat on a cold March day. In a report to the state legislature in 1843, Dix told of persons confined "*in cages, closets, cellars, stalls, pens! Chained, naked, beaten with rods, and lashed into obedience.*" Wardens charged Dix with "slanderous lies," but she won the support of leading reformers as well as a large state appropriation for improving the treatment of the insane. From Massachusetts she carried her campaign throughout the country and abroad. By 1860 she had persuaded twenty states to heed her advice to develop programs to improve the conditions in prisons and asylums.

WOMEN'S RIGHTS Whereas Dorothea Dix stood out as an example of the opportunity that reform activities gave middle-class women to enter public life, Catharine Beecher, a founder of women's schools in Connecticut and Ohio, published a guide prescribing the domestic sphere for women. *A Treatise on Domestic Economy* (1841) became the leading handbook of what historians have labeled the cult of domesticity. While Beecher upheld high standards in women's education, she also accepted the prevailing view that a "woman's sphere" was the home and argued that young women should be primarily trained in the domestic arts of housework and child rearing.

The official status of women during this period remained much as it had been in the colonial era. Legally a woman was unable to vote, and after marriage she was denied legal control of her property and even of her children. Women could not be ministers or pursue most other professions. Higher education was rarely an option. A wife could not make a will, sign a contract, or bring suit in court without her husband's permission. Gradually, however, more and more women began to complain about their status. The organized movement for women's rights in the United States had its origins in 1840, when the anti-slavery movement split over the question of women's right to participate. Women decided then that they needed to organize on behalf of their own emancipation, too.

In 1848 two prominent moral reformers and advocates of women's rights, Lucretia Mott, a Philadelphia Quaker, and Elizabeth Cady Stanton, a graduate of Troy Female Seminary who refused to be merely "a household drudge," called a convention to discuss "the social, civil, and religious condition and rights of women." The hastily organized Seneca Falls Convention, the first of its kind, issued on July 19, 1848, the Declaration of Sentiments.

The document proclaimed the self-evident truth that "all men and women are created equal," and the attendant resolutions said that all laws placing women "in a position inferior to that of men, are contrary to the great precept of nature, and therefore of no force or authority." Such language was too strong for most of the 1,000 delegates, and only about one third of them signed the document. Yet the Seneca Falls gathering represented an important first step in the evolving campaign for women's rights.

From 1850 until the Civil War, the women's rights leaders held annual conventions and carried on a program of organizing, lecturing, and petitioning. The movement had to struggle in the face of meager funds and anti-feminist women and men. The movement owed its success to the work of a few courageous women who refused to be intimidated by the odds against them. Susan B. Anthony, an ardent Quaker already active in temperance and anti-slavery groups, joined the crusade in the 1850s. Unlike Stanton and Mott, she was unmarried and therefore able to devote most of her attention to the women's crusade. As one observer put it, Stanton "forged the thunderbolts and Miss Anthony hurled them." Both were young when the movement started, and both lived into the twentieth century, focusing after the Civil War on demands for women's suffrage. Although women did not win voting rights until much later, they did make some legal gains. The state of Mississippi, seldom regarded as a hotbed of reform, was the first to grant married women control over their property, in 1839; by the 1860s eleven more states had such laws.

Elizabeth Cady Stanton and Susan B. Anthony

Stanton (*left*) "forged the thunderbolts and Miss Anthony hurled them."

UTOPIAN COMMUNITIES

The pervasive climate of reform during and after the Jacksonian era also excited a quest for utopia. Plans for ideal communities had long been an American passion, at least since the Puritans set out to build a wilderness Zion. Over 100 utopian communities sprang up between 1800 and 1900. Among the most durable were the Shakers, officially the United Society of Believers in Christ's Second Appearing, founded by Ann Lee (Mother Ann Lee). She arrived in New York State from England with eight followers in 1774. Believing religious fervor to be a sign of inspiration from the Holy Ghost, they had strange fits in which they saw visions and prophesied. These manifestations later evolved into a ritual dance—hence the name Shakers. Mother Ann claimed that God was genderless and that she was the female incarnation, as Jesus had been the male. She preached celibacy to prepare Shakers for the perfection that was promised them in Heaven.

Mother Ann died in 1784, but the group found new leaders. From the first community at New Lebanon, New York, the movement spread into New England, Ohio, and Kentucky. By 1830 about twenty groups of Shakers were flourishing. In these communities all property was held in common, and strict celibacy was practiced. Men and women not only slept separately but also worked and ate separately. Governance of the colonies was concentrated in the hands of select elders chosen by the ministry. To outsiders this might seem almost despotic, but the Shakers emphasized equality of labor and reward, and members were free to leave at will. The superbly managed Shaker farms yielded a surplus for the market. They were among the nation's leading sources of garden seed and medicinal herbs, and many of their manufactures, including clothing, household items, and especially furniture, were prized for their simple beauty. By the mid–twentieth century, however, few members remained alive; the Shakers reached the peak of activity between 1830 and 1860.

John Humphrey Noyes, founder of the Oneida Community, developed a quite different ideal community. Educated at Dartmouth and Yale Divinity School, he was converted at one of Charles G. Finney's revivals and entered the ministry. He was forced out, however, when he declared that with true conversion came perfection and a complete release from sin. In 1836 he gathered a group of a dozen or so "Perfectionists" around his home in Putney, Vermont. Ten years later Noyes announced a new doctrine of "complex marriage," which meant that every man in the community was married to every woman and vice versa. "In a holy community," he claimed, "there is no more reason why sexual intercourse should be restrained by law, than why eating and drinking should be." To outsiders such theology smacked of "free love," and Noyes was arrested. He fled to New York State and in 1848 established the Oneida Community, which numbered more than 200 by 1851.

The communal group at Oneida eked out a living with farming and logging until the mid-1850s, when the inventor of a new steel animal trap joined the community. Oneida traps were soon known as the best in the country. The community then branched out into sewing silk, canning fruit, and making silver spoons. The spoons were so popular that, with the addition of knives and forks, tableware became the Oneida specialty. In 1879, however, the community faced a crisis when Noyes fled to Canada to avoid prosecution for adultery. The members then abandoned the practice of universal marriage, and in 1881 they converted the community to a joint-stock company, the Oneida Community, Ltd., which today remains a successful flatware company.

In contrast to these religious-based communities, Robert Owen's New Harmony was based upon a secular principle. A British capitalist who worried about the degrading social effects of the factory system, Owen bought the town of Harmonie, Indiana, promptly christening it New Harmony. In 1825 a varied group of about 900 colonists gathered in New Harmony for a period of transition from Owen's ownership to the new system of cooperation. The high proportion of learned participants generated a certain intellectual electricity about the place. There were frequent lectures and social gatherings with music and dancing. For a time, New Harmony looked like a brilliant success, but it soon fell into discord. The problem, it seems, was one common to most reform groups: every idealist wanted his own patented plan put into practice. In 1827 Owen returned from a visit to England to find New Harmony insolvent. The following year he dissolved the project and sold or leased the land.

Brook Farm was the most celebrated of all the utopian communities, because it had the support of Ralph Waldo Emerson and other well-known literary figures of New England. George Ripley, a Unitarian minister and transcendentalist, conceived of Brook Farm as a combination of high thinking and plain living. Most Brook Farmers found considerable fulfillment in the new community. Said one, "We were happy, contented, well-off and care-free; doing a great work in the world, enthusiastic and faithful, we enjoyed every moment of every day." The place survived financially, however, mainly because of an excellent community school that drew tuition-paying students from outside. But when a new central building burned down on the day of its dedication in 1846, the community spirit expired in the embers.

Like Brook Farm most of the utopian communities were short-lived. While such experiments had little effect on the larger society, they did express the deeply ingrained desire for perfectionism inherent in the American character, a desire that would continue to spawn such noble, if frequently naive, experiments thereafter. Among all the targets of the reformers' wrath, however, one great evil would finally take precedence over the others: human bondage. The paradox of American slavery coupled with American freedom, of "the world's fairest hope linked with man's foulest crime," in the novelist

Herman Melville's words, would inspire the climactic crusade of the age, abolitionism, one that would ultimately move to the center of the political stage and sweep the nation into an epic—and tragic—civil war.

MAKING CONNECTIONS

- The anti-slavery campaign, especially its abolitionist aspect, was related to the reform movements discussed in this chapter. It is discussed again in Chapter 15.

- Chapter 17 will show how the Civil War had a significant impact on the status of women in society, a continuation of a theme discussed here.

FURTHER READING

Russel Blaine Nye's *Society and Culture in America, 1830–1860* (1974) provides a wide-ranging survey. On the reform impulse, consult Ronald G. Walter's *American Reformers, 1815–1860,* rev. ed. (1997). Revivalist religion is treated in Nathan O. Hatch's *The Democratization of American Christianity* (1989) and Christine Leigh Heyrman's *Southern Cross: The Beginnings of the Bible Belt* (1997). On the Mormons, see Leonard Arrington's *Brigham Young: American Moses* (1985).

The best introduction to transcendentalist thought is Paul F. Boller's *American Transcendentalism, 1830–1860: An Intellectual Inquiry.* (1974). A more recent treatment is Carlos Baker's *Emerson among the Eccentrics: A Group Portrait* (1996). Several books describe various aspects of the antebellum reform movement. For temperance, see W. J. Rorabaugh's *The Alcoholic Republic: An American Tradition* (1979) and Barbara Leslie Epstein's *The Politics of Domesticity: Women, Evangelism, and Temperance in Nineteenth-Century America* (1981). Stephen Nissenbaum's *Sex, Diet, and Debility in Jacksonian America: Sylvester Graham and Heath Reform* (1980) looks at a pioneering reformer concerned with diet and lifestyle. On prison reform and other humanitarian projects, see David J. Rothman's *The Discovery of the Asylum: Social Order and Disorder in the New Republic,* rev. ed. (2002), Gerald N. Grob's *Mental Institutions in America: Social Policy to 1875* (1973), Charles E. Rosenberg's *The Care of Strangers: The Rise of America's Hospital*

System (1987), and Thomas J. Brown's biography *Dorothea Dix: New England Reformer* (1998).

Lawrence A. Cremin's *American Education: The National Experience, 1783–1876* (1980) traces early school reform. For other views, see Stanley K. Schultz's *The Culture Factory: Boston Public Schools, 1789–1860* (1973) and Carl F. Kaestle and Eric Foner's *Pillars of the Republic: Common Schools and American Society, 1780–1860* (1983).

On women during the antebellum period, see Nancy F. Cott's *The Bonds of Womanhood: "Woman's Sphere" in New England, 1780–1835*, 2nd ed. (1997) and Ellen C. DuBois's *Feminism and Suffrage: The Emergence of an Independent Women's Movement in America, 1848–1869* (1978). Also valuable are Shirley Samuels's *The Culture of Sentiment: Race, Gender, and Sentimentality in Nineteenth-Century America* (1992), Jeanne Boydston, Mary Kelley, and Anne Margolis's *The Limits of Sisterhood: The Beecher Sisters on Women's Rights and Woman's Sphere* (1988), and Mary P. Ryan's *Women in Public: Between Banners and Ballots, 1825–1880* (1989).

Michael Fellman's *The Unbounded Frame: Freedom and Community in Nineteenth-Century American Utopianism* (1973) surveys the utopian movements.

14

MANIFEST DESTINY

FOCUS QUESTIONS

- What were the main issues in national politics in the 1840s?
- Why did settlers migrate west, and what conditions did they face?
- What were the causes and consequences of the Mexican War?

To answer these questions and access additional review material, please visit www.wwnorton.com/studyspace.

During the 1840s the quest for better economic opportunities and more space in the West continued to excite the American imagination. People frustrated by the growing congestion and rising cost of living along the Atlantic seaboard saw in the West a bountiful source of personal freedom, business potential, social democracy, and adventure. "If hell lay to the west," one pioneer declared, "Americans would cross heaven to get there."

Millions of Americans in the nineteenth century crossed the Mississippi River and endured unrelenting hardships in order to fulfill their "providential destiny" to subdue and settle the entire continent. Economic depressions in 1837 and 1841 intensified the appeal of starting anew out West. Texas, Oregon, and Utah were the favored destinations until the discovery of gold in California in 1848 sparked a stampede that threatened to depopulate New England of its young men. Trappers and farmers, miners and merchants, hunters, ranchers, teachers, house servants, and prostitutes, among others, also headed west seeking their fortune. Others sought religious freedom or new converts to Christianity. Whatever the reason, the pioneers formed an unceasing migratory stream flowing across the Great Plains and the Rocky Mountains. The Indian and Mexican inhabitants of the region soon found themselves swept aside by successive waves of American settlers.

THE TYLER YEARS

When President William Henry Harrison took office in 1841, elected, like Andrew Jackson, mainly on the strength of his military record and his lack of a public stand on major issues, observers expected him to be a tool in the hands of Whig leaders Daniel Webster and Henry Clay. Webster became secretary of state, and although Clay preferred to stay in the Senate, his friends filled the cabinet. As it turned out, however, Harrison's administration would never prove itself, for Harrison served the shortest term of any president. At the inauguration, held on a chilly, rainy day, he caught cold. On April 4, 1841, exactly one month after the inauguration, he died of pneumonia at age sixty-eight.

John Tyler, the first vice president to succeed upon the death of a president, served practically all of Harrison's term. At age fifty-one, the Virginia slaveholder was the youngest president to date. He already had a long career behind him as legislator, governor, congressman, and senator, and his positions on all the important issues had been forcefully stated. Although a Whig, he favored a strict construction of the Constitution and was a stubborn defender of states' rights. When someone asked if he was a nationalist, Tyler retorted that he had "no such word in my political vocabulary." He opposed Henry Clay's American system—protective tariffs, a national bank, and internal improvements at national expense. Originally a Democrat, Tyler had broken with the party over Andrew Jackson's condemnation of South Carolina's effort to nullify a federal law and Jackson's imperious use of executive authority. Thus Tyler, the states' rights Whig, had been chosen to "balance" the ticket by party leaders in 1840; no one expected that he would actually wield power. After Tyler become president, some critics called him His Accidency.

DOMESTIC AFFAIRS   Given more finesse by Henry Clay, the powerful senator might have bridged the policy divisions between him and the president. But for once, driven by his own presidential ambition, the Great Compromiser lost his instinct for compromise. When Congress met in a special session in 1841, Clay introduced a series of resolutions designed to supply the platform that the party had evaded in the previous election. The chief points were repeal of the Independent Treasury Act, establishment of a third

Bank of the United States, distribution to the states of money from federal land sales, and higher tariffs. The imperious Clay then set out to push his program through Congress. "Tyler dares not resist. I will drive him before me," Clay predicted.

Tyler, it turned out, was not easily driven. Although he agreed to the repeal of the Independent Treasury Act and signed a higher tariff bill in 1842, Tyler vetoed Clay's bill for a new national bank. This prompted his entire cabinet to resign with the exception of Secretary of State Daniel Webster, an unprecedented action. Tyler replaced the defectors with anti-Jackson Democrats who, like him, had become Whigs. Irate congressional Whigs expelled Tyler from the party, and Democrats viewed him as an untrustworthy renegade. Henry Clay assumed leadership of the Whig party, and the stubborn Tyler became a president without a party.

FOREIGN AFFAIRS   In foreign relations, tensions with Great Britain captured Tyler's attention. A major issue involved the suppression of the African slave trade, which both countries had outlawed in 1808. In 1841 the British prime minister asserted the right to patrol off the coast of Africa and search American vessels for slaves. But the U.S. government refused to accept such intrusions. Relations were further strained late in 1841 when enslaved Africans on the *Creole*, bound from Hampton Roads, Virginia, to New Orleans, mutinied and sailed to the Bahamas, where the British set them free. Secretary of State Webster demanded that the slaves be returned as American property, but the British refused.

At this point a new British government accepted Webster's overtures for negotiations and sent Lord Ashburton to Washington, D.C. Ashburton was widely known to be friendly to Americans, and the talks proceeded smoothly. The negotiations settled the disputed Maine boundary as well as other border disputes with Great Britain by accepting the existing line between the Connecticut and St. Lawrence rivers and compromising on the line between Lake Superior and Lake of the Woods along the border between the future state of Minnesota and Canada. The Webster-Ashburton Treaty (1842) also provided for joint naval patrols off the African coast to suppress the slave trade.

THE WESTERN FRONTIER

In the 1840s most Americans were no more stirred by the quarrels of John Tyler and Henry Clay over such issues as the banking system and tariffs than students of history would be at a later date. What aroused public interest was the contining migration westward across the Great American Desert and the Rocky Mountains to the Pacific coast. In 1845 a magazine editor labeled this bumptious spirit of expansion. "Our manifest destiny," he wrote, "is to overspread the continent allotted by Providence for the free development of our yearly multiplying millions." God, in other words, felt that the United States should extend itself from the Atlantic to the Pacific—and beyond. At its best this much-trumpeted notion of Manifest Destiny offered a moral justification for American expansion, a prescription for what an enlarged United States could and should be. At its worst it was a cluster of flimsy rationalizations for naked greed and imperial ambition. Whatever the case, settlers began streaming into the Far West during the 1840s in the aftermath of the panic of 1837 and the prolonged economic depression.

As they crossed the Mississippi River and made their way westward, pioneers entered not only a new environment but a new culture as well. The Great Plains and the Far West were already occupied by Indians and Mexicans, who had lived in the region for centuries and had established their own distinctive customs and ways of life. Now they were joined by Americans of diverse ethnic origins and religious persuasions. It made for a volatile mix.

WESTERN INDIANS   Historians estimate that over 325,000 Indians inhabited the Southwest, the Great Plains, California, and the Pacific Northwest in 1840, when the flood of white settlers began to pour into the region. The Native Americans often warred against one another. They were divided into more than 200 tribes, each with its own language, religion, economic base, kinship practices, and system of governance. Some were primarily farmers; others were nomadic hunters who preyed upon game animals.

Some twenty-three tribes resided on the Great Plains, a vast grassland stretching from the Mississippi River west to the Rocky Mountains and from Canada south to Mexico. Plains Indians such as the Arapaho, Blackfoot, Cheyenne, Kiowa, and Sioux were horse-borne nomads; they migrated across the grasslands with the buffalo herds, carrying their tepees with them. Disputes over buffalo and hunting grounds sparked clashes between rival tribes, events that help explain the cult of the warrior among the Plains Indians. Scalping or killing an enemy would earn praise from elders and feathers for ceremonial headdresses.

Quite different Indian tribes lived to the south and west of the Plains Indians. In the arid region including what is today Arizona, New Mexico, and southern Utah were the peaceful Pueblo tribes: Acoma, Hopi, Laguna, Taos, Zia, Zuni. They were sophisticated farmers who lived in adobe villages along rivers that irrigated their crops of corn, beans, and squash. Their rivals were the Apache and the Navajo, war-loving hunters who roamed the countryside in small bands and preyed upon the Pueblos. They, in turn, were periodically harassed by their powerful enemies, the Comanches.

To the north, in the Great Basin between the Rocky Mountains and the Sierra Nevadas, Paiutes and Gosiutes struggled to survive in the harsh, arid region of what is today Nevada, Utah, and eastern California. They traveled in family groups and subsisted on berries, pine nuts, insects, and rodents. West of the mountains, along the California coast, Indians lived in small villages. They gathered wild plants and acorns and were adept at fishing in the rivers and bays. The Indian tribes living in the Northwest—the Nisqually, Spokane, Yakama, Chinook, Klamath, and Nez Perce (Pierced Nose)— enjoyed the most abundant natural resources and the most temperate climate.

All the Indian tribes eventually felt the unrelenting pressure of white expansion. Because Indian life on the plains depended upon the buffalo, the influx of white settlers and buffalo hunters posed a dirct threat to the Indians' cultural survival. In an 1846 petition to President James Polk, the Sioux protested that "for several years past the Emigrants going over the Mountains from the United States have been the cause that Buffalo in great measure left our hunting grounds, thereby causing us to go into the Country of Our Enemies to hunt, exposing our lives daily for the necessary subsistence of our wives and children and getting killed on several occasions." But the

Buffalo Hunt, Chasing Back (1860s)

This painting by George Catlin shows a hunter outrunning a buffalo.

federal government turned a deaf ear to such pleas for assistance. It continued to build a string of frontier forts to protect the advancing settlers, and it sought to use treaties to gain control of more Indian land. When officials of the Bureau of Indian Affair could not coerce, cajole, or confuse Indian leaders into selling the title to their tribal land, fighting ensued. And after the discovery of gold in California in 1848, the tidal wave of white expansion flowed all the way to the West Coast.

THE SPANISH WEST AND MEXICAN INDEPENDENCE   As American settlers moved westward, they also encountered Spanish-speaking peoples. Many whites were as contemptuous of Latinos as they were of Indians. Senator Lewis Cass, an expansionist from Michigan, expressed the sentiment of many Americans during a debate over the annexation of New Mexico. "We do not want the people of Mexico," he declared, "either as citizens or as subjects. All we want is a portion of territory." The vast majority of the Spanish-speaking people in what is today called the American Southwest resided in New Mexico. Most of them were mestizos (of mixed Indian and Spanish blood), and they were usually poor ranch hands or small farmers and herders.

The Spanish efforts at colonization had been less successful in Arizona and Texas than in New Mexico and Florida. The Yuma and Apache Indians in Arizona and the Comanches and Apaches in Texas had thwarted their efforts to establish Catholic missions. In eastern Texas during the first half of the eighteenth century, French traders from Louisiana undermined the authority and influence of the Spanish missions that were established. The French supplied the Indians with guns, ammunition, and promises of protection. Several of the Texas missions were abandoned and reestablished near San Antonio in 1731. By 1750 the Pawnees, Wichitas, Comanches, and Apaches were using Spanish horses and French rifles to raid Spanish settlements in Texas. By 1790 the Latino population in Texas numbered only 2,510, while in New Mexico it exceeded 20,000.

In 1807 French forces had occupied Spain and imprisoned the king, creating chaos throughout Spain's colonial possessions, including Mexico. Miguel Hidalgo y Costilla, a creole priest (born in the New World of European ancestry), took advantage of the fluid situation to organize a revolt of Indians and mestizos against Spanish rule in Mexico. The poorly organized uprising failed miserably. In 1811 Spanish troops captured Hidalgo and executed him. Other Mexicans, however, continued to yearn for independence. In 1820 Mexican creoles again tried to liberate themselves from Spanish authority. By then the Spanish forces in Mexico had lost much of their cohesion and

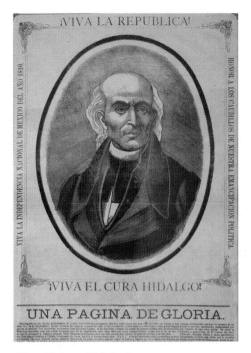

¡VIVA LA REPUBLICA!

HONOR A LOS CAUDILLOS DE NUESTRA EMANCIPACION POLITICA.

VIVA LA INDEPENDENCIA NACIONAL DE MEXICO DEL AÑO 1810.

¡VIVA EL CURA HIDALGO!

UNA PAGINA DE GLORIA.

¡Viva El Cura Hidalgo!

This patriotic broadside celebrating Mexican independence shows Father Miguel Hidalgo in an oval medallion.

dedication. Facing a growing revolt, the last Spanish officials withdrew in 1821, and Mexico became an independent nation.

Mexican independence from Spain unleashed tremors throughout the Southwest. American fur traders streamed into New Mexico and Arizona and developed a lucrative commerce in beaver pelts. Soon thereafter wagon trains carrying American settlers were leaving Missouri and heading west to Santa Fe. American entrepreneurs flooded into the western Mexican province of California and soon became a powerful force for change; by 1848 Americans made up half the non-Indian population. In Texas, American adventurers decided to promote their own independence from a newly independent—and chaotic—Mexican government. Suddenly, it seemed, the Southwest was a frontier ripe for American exploitation and settlement.

THE ROCKY MOUNTAINS AND OREGON COUNTRY During the early nineteenth century, the Northwest frontier consisted of the Nebraska, Washington, and Oregon territories. Fur traders especially were drawn to the Missouri River, with its many tributaries. During the 1820s and 1830s the fur trade had inspired a uniquely reckless breed of "mountain men" who relished life in the wilderness. They were the first whites to find their way around the Rocky Mountains, and they pioneered the trails that settlers by the 1840s were beginning to traverse as they flooded the Oregon Country and trickled across the border into California.

Beyond the mountains the Oregon Country stretched from the 42nd parallel north to 54°40. Between those parallels, Spain and Russia had given up their right of settlement, leaving Great Britain and the United States as the only claimants. By the Convention of 1818, the two countries had agreed to "joint occupation" of the region. Until the 1830s, however, joint occupation had been a legal technicality because the only American presence was the occasional mountain man who wandered across the Sierra Nevadas or the infrequent trading vessel from Boston or New York City. Word of Oregon's fertile soil, plentiful rain, and magnificent forests gradually spread eastward. By the late 1830s a stream of emigrants began flowing along the Oregon Trail. Soon "Oregon fever" swept the nation. By 1845 there were about 5,000 settlers in Oregon's Willamette Valley.

THE SETTLEMENT OF CALIFORNIA   California was also an alluring attraction for new settlers and entrepreneurs. It first felt the influence of European culture in 1769, when Spain grew concerned about Russian fur traders moving south along the Pacific coast from their base in Alaska. To thwart Russian intentions, Spain sent a naval expedition to explore and settle the region. The Spanish discovered San Francisco Bay and constructed presidios (military garrisons) at San Diego and Monterey. Even more important, Franciscan friars, led by Junípero Serra, established a Catholic mission at San Diego.

Over the next fifty years, Franciscans built twenty more California missions, spaced a day's journey apart along the coast from San Diego to San Francisco. There they converted Indians and established thriving agricultural estates. As in Mexico the Spanish monarchy awarded huge land grants in California to a few ex-soldiers and colonists, who turned the grants into profitable cattle ranches. The Indians were left with the least valuable land, and most of them subsisted as farmers or artisans serving the missions. The mission-centered culture created by the Hispanic settlers who migrated to California from Mexico was quite different from the patterns of conquest and settlement in Texas and New Mexico. In those more settled regions the original missions were converted into secular parishes and the property divided among the Indians. In California the missions were much larger, more influential, and longer lasting.

Franciscan missionaries, aided by Spanish soldiers, gathered most of the coastal Indian population in California under their control: the number of "mission Indians" more than doubled between 1776 and 1784. The Spanish saw the Indians as ignorant and indolent heathens who must be converted to Catholicism and made useful members of the Spanish Empire. Viewing the missions as crucial imperial outposts, the Spanish government provided military support, annual cash grants, and supplies from Mexico. The Franciscan friars enticed the local Indians into the adobe-walled, tile-roofed missions by offering them gifts or impressing them with their "magical" religious rituals. Once inside the missions, the Indians were baptized as Catholics, taught the Spanish language, and stripped of their Indian heritage. They were forced to wear Spanish clothes, abandon their native rituals, and obey the friars. Soldiers living in the missions enforced the will of the friars.

The California mission served multiple roles. It was church, fortress, home, town, farm, and imperial agent. The missions were economic as well as religious and cultural institutions; they quickly became substantial agricultural enterprises. Missions produced crops, livestock, clothing, and household goods, both for profit and to supply the neighboring presidios. Indians provided the labor.

The Franciscans used overwhelming force to maintain the labor system in the missions. Rebellious Indians were whipped or imprisoned; soldiers hunted down runaways. Mission Indians died at an alarming rate. One Franciscan friar reported that "of every four Indian children born, three die in their first or second year, while those who survive do not reach the age of twenty-five." Infectious disease was the primary threat, but the intensive labor regimen took a high toll as well. The Indian population along the California coast declined from 72,000 in 1769 to 18,000 by 1821. Saving souls cost many lives.

EARLY DEVELOPMENT IN CALIFORNIA   For all of its rich natural resources, California remained thinly populated by Indians and mission friars well into the nineteenth century. It was a simple, almost feudal agrarian society without schools, industry, or defenses. In 1821, when Mexico wrested its independence from Spain, Californians took comfort in the fact that Mexico City was so far away that it would exercise little effective control over its most distant state. During the next two decades, Californians, including many recent American arrivals, staged ten revolts against the Mexican governors dispatched to lord over them.

Yet Mexican rule did produce a dramatic change in California history. In 1824 Mexico passed a colonization act that granted hundreds of huge "rancho" estates to Mexican settlers. With free labor extracted from Indians, who were treated like slaves, the rancheros lived a life of self-indulgent luxury, gambling, horse racing, bull baiting, and dancing. They soon cast covetous eyes on the vast estates controlled by the Franciscan missions. In 1833–1834 they persuaded the Mexican government to confiscate the missions, exile the friars, release the Indians from Church control, and make the mission lands available to new settlement. Within a few years some 700 new rancho grants of 4,500 to 50,000 acres were issued along the coast from San Diego to San Francisco. Organized like feudal estates, these California ranches resembled southern cotton plantations, but the death rate among Indian workers was twice as high as that of enslaved blacks in the Deep South.

Few accounts of life in California took note of the brutalities inflicted upon the Indians, however. Instead, they portrayed the region as a proverbial land of milk and honey, ripe for development. Such a natural paradise could not long remain a secret, and already Americans had been visiting the Pacific coast in search of profits and land. By the mid-1830s shippers had begun setting up agents to buy cowhides and store them until a company ship arrived. One of the traders, John A. Sutter, had tried the Santa Fe trade first, then found his way to California. At the juncture of the Sacramento and American rivers (later the site of Sacramento), he built an enormous enclosure that guarded an entire village of settlers and shops. Completed in 1843, the enclosure became the mecca for Americans bent on settling the Sacramento country. It stood at the end of what became the most traveled route through the Sierra Navadas, the California Trail, which forked off from the Oregon Trail and ran through the mountains near Lake Tahoe. By 1846 there were perhaps 800 Americans in California, along with some 8,000 to 12,000 Californians of Mexican descent.

MOVING WEST

Most of the western pioneers during the second quarter of the nineteenth century were American-born whites from the upper South and the Midwest. Only a few African Americans joined in the migration. Although some emigrants traveled by sea to California, most went overland. Between 1841 and 1867 some 350,000 men, women, and children made the arduous trek to California or Oregon, while hundreds of thousands of others settled along the way in Colorado, Texas, Arkansas, and other areas.

THE SANTA FE TRAIL   After gaining its independence from Spain in 1821, the government of Mexico was much more interested in trade with the United States than Spain had been. In Spanish-controlled Santa Fe, in fact, all commerce with the United States had been banned. After 1821, however, trade flourished. Hundreds of entrepreneurs made the 1,000-mile trek from St. Louis to Santa Fe, forging a route that became known as the Santa Fe Trail. Soon Mexican traders began leading caravans east to Missouri. By the 1830s there was so much commercial activity between Mexico and St. Louis that the Mexican silver peso had become the primary medium of exchange in Missouri. The traders pioneered more than a new territory. They also showed that heavy wagons could cross the plains and the mountains, and they developed the technique of organized caravans for common protection.

THE OVERLAND TRAILS   Like travelers on the Santa Fe Trail, people bound for Oregon and California rode in wagon caravans. But on the Overland Trails to the West Coast, most of them were settlers rather than traders. They traveled mostly in family groups and came from all over the United States. The wagon trains followed the trail west from Independence, Missouri, along the North Platte River into what is now Wyoming, through South Pass down to Fort Bridger, then down the Snake River to the Columbia River, and along the Columbia to their goal in Oregon's fertile Willamette Valley. They usually left Missouri in late spring, completing the grueling 2,000-mile trek in six months. Traveling in ox-drawn canvas-covered wagons nicknamed prairie schooners, they jostled their way across the dusty or muddy trails and traversed rugged mountains. By 1845 some 5,000 people were making the arduous journey annually. The discovery of gold in California in 1848 brought some 30,000 pioneers along the Oregon Trail in 1849. By 1850, the peak year of travel along the trail, the annual count had risen to 55,000.

The journey west was extraordinarily difficult. Cholera claimed many lives. On average there was one grave every eighty yards along the trail between the Missouri River and the Willamette Valley. The trail's grinding routine of chores and physical labor took its toll on once-buoyant spirits. This was especially true for women, who worked throughout the day and into the night. Women cooked, washed, sewed, and monitored the children while men drove the wagons, tended the horses and cattle, and did the heavy labor. But the unique demands of the trail soon dissolved such neat distinctions and posed new tasks. Women found themselves gathering buffalo dung for fuel, pitching in to dislodge a wagon mired in mud, helping to construct an impromptu bridge, or performing a variety of other "unlady-like" tasks.

THE INDIANS AND THE WAGON TRAINS   Contrary to the mythology, Indians rarely attacked wagon trains. Less than 4 percent of the fatalities associated with the Overland Trails experience resulted from Indian raids. More often Indians either allowed the settlers to pass through their tribal lands

Wagon-wheel Ruts near Guernsey, Wyoming

The wheels of thousands of wagons traveling to Oregon cut into solid rock as oxen strained up hillsides, leaving indentations that are still visible today.

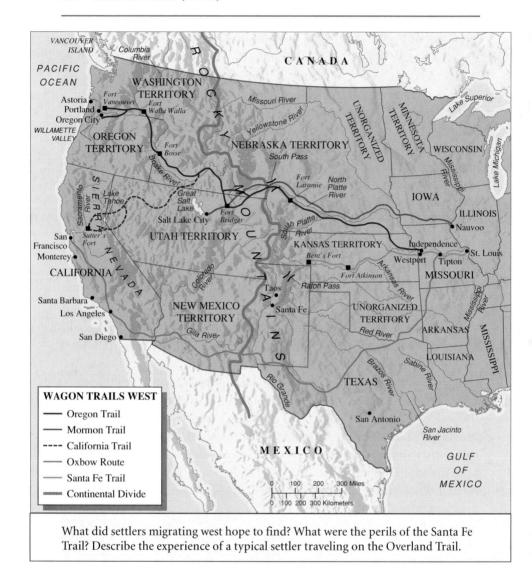

WAGON TRAILS WEST

— Oregon Trail
— Mormon Trail
---- California Trail
— Oxbow Route
— Santa Fe Trail
▓▓▓ Continental Divide

What did settlers migrating west hope to find? What were the perils of the Santa Fe Trail? Describe the experience of a typical settler traveling on the Overland Trail.

unmolested or demanded payment. Many wagon trains never encountered a single Indian, and others received generous aid from Indians who served as guides, advisers, or traders. The Indians, one woman pioneer noted, "proved better than represented." To be sure, as the number of pioneers increased dramatically during the 1850s, clashes between overlanders and Indians over water and land increased, but never to the degree portrayed in Western novels and films.

In 1851 U.S. officials invited the Indian tribes from the northern plains to a conference in the grassy valley, along the North Platte River, near Fort Laramie in what is now southeastern Wyoming. Almost 10,000 Indians—men, women, and children—attended the treaty council. What made the huge gathering even more remarkable is that so many of the tribes were at war with one another. After nearly three weeks of heated discussions, during which the chiefs were presented with a mountain of gifts, federal negotiators and tribal leaders agreed to the Fort Laramie Treaty. The government promised to provide an annual cash payment to the Indians as compensation for the damage caused by wagon trains traversing their hunting grounds. In exchange the Indians agreed to stop harassing white caravans, to allow federal forts to be built, and to confine themselves to a specified area "of limited extent and well-defined boundaries." Specifically, the Indians were restricted to land north and south of a corridor through which the Overland Trails passed.

Several tribes, however, refused to accept the provisions. The most powerful, the Lakota Sioux, reluctantly signed the agreement but thereafter failed to abide by its restrictions. "You have split my lands and I don't like it," declared Black Hawk, a Sioux chief at Fort Laramie. "These lands once belonged to the Kiowas and Crows, but we whipped these nations out of them, and in this we did what the white men do when they want the lands of the Indians." Despite the dissension the agreement was significant, in part because it foreshadowed the "reservation" concept of Indian management that would be instituted after the Civil War.

GREAT PLAINS ECOLOGY The massive migrations along the Santa Fe and Overland trails wreaked havoc on the environment of the Great Plains. Hundreds of thousands of settlers and traders brought with them millions of animals—horses, cattle, oxen, and sheep—all of which consumed huge amounts of prairie grass. The wagons and herds trampled vegetation and gouged ruts in the landscape that survive to this day. With the onset of the California gold rush in 1849, Plains Indians, led by Cheyennes, seized the opportunity to supply buffalo meat and skins to the white pioneers. Tracking and killing buffalo required a great many horses, and the four-legged creatures added to the strain on the prairie grasslands and river bottoms. A major climatic change coincided with the mass migrations sparked by the discovery of gold in California. In 1849 a prolonged drought struck the region west of the Mississippi River and produced widespread suffering. Starving Indians demanded or begged for food from passing wagon trains. Tensions between Native Americans and white travelers brought additional federal cavalry units to the plains, exacerbating the shortage of forage grasses.

THE PATHFINDER: JOHN FRÉMONT   The most aggressive champion of American settlement in Mexican California and the Far West was John Charles Frémont, "the Pathfinder." Frémont, born in Savannah, Georgia, and raised in the South, became the consummate explorer and romantic adventurer. Possessed of boundless energy and reckless courage, a robust love of the outdoors, and an exuberant, self-promoting personality, he inspired both respect and awe.

Frémont was commissioned a second lieutenant in the U.S. Topographical Corps in 1838. In 1842 he mapped the Oregon Trail beyond South Pass—and met Christopher "Kit" Carson, one of the most knowledgeable of the mountain men. Carson became Frémont's frequent associate and the most famous frontiersman after Daniel Boone. In 1843–1844 Frémont, typically clad in a deerskin shirt, blue army trousers, and moccasins, launched a second expedition. He moved on to Oregon, then swept down the eastern slopes of the Sierra Nevadas, headed southward through the central valley of California, bypassed the mountains in the south, and returned via the Great Salt Lake. His excited reports on both expeditions, published together in the 1845, gained a wide national circulation and helped arouse the interest of easterners.

ANNEXING TEXAS

AMERICAN SETTLEMENTS   America's lust for new land focused on the most accessible of all the Mexican borderlands, Texas. By the 1830s Texas was rapidly turning into a province of the United States, for Mexico in 1823 had begun welcoming American settlers into the region as a means of stabilizing the border.

Foremost among the promoters of the American colonization of Texas was Stephen F. Austin, a Missouri resident who gained from Mexico a huge land grant originally given to his father by Spanish authorities. Before Spain finally granted Mexican independence, Austin had started a colony on the lower Brazos River in central Texas, and by 1824 more than 2,000 hardy souls had settled on his land. Most of the newcomers were southern farmers drawn to rich new cotton land selling for only a few cents an acre. By 1830 the coastal region of Texas had approximately 20,000 white settlers and 1,000 African-American slaves brought in to work the cotton. The newcomers quickly outnumbered the Mexicans in the area and showed little interest in Catholicism or other aspects of Mexican culture.

The Mexican government, opposed to slavery, grew alarmed at the flood of strangers engulfing the Texas province and in 1830 forbade further immigration. But illegal immigrants from the United States crossed the long border as easily as illegal Mexican immigrants would later cross in the opposite direction. By 1835 the American population in Texas had mushroomed to around 30,000, about ten times the Mexican population. Friction mounted in 1832 and 1833 as Americans demanded greater representation and power from the Mexican government. Instead of granting the request, General Antonio López de Santa Anna, who had seized power in Mexico, dissolved the national congress late in 1834, abolished the federal system of government, and became dictator.

In the fall of 1835, Texans rebelled against Santa Anna's "despotism." Delegates from all the towns and settlements met in November and drafted a Declaration of Causes explaining the rebellion. It forcefully expressed their grievances against the Mexican government but stopped short of declaring independence. A furious Santa Anna ordered all Americans expelled, all Texans disarmed, and all rebels arrested. As fighting erupted, volunteers from southern states rushed to assist the 30,000 Texans in their revolution against a Mexican nation of 7 million people. On March 2, 1836, as Santa Anna approached with an army to oust them, the Texans declared their independence.

TEXAS INDEPENDENCE   At San Antonio the Mexican army assaulted a small garrison of Texans and American volunteers holed up in an abandoned mission, the Alamo. Among the most celebrated of the volunteers was Davy Crockett, the Tennessee frontiersman who had fought Indians under Andrew Jackson and served as a congressman. He was indeed a colorful character, full of spunk and brag and thoroughly expert at killing with his trusty rifle, Old Betsy.

On February 23, 1836, General Santa Anna demanded that the Alamo's defenders surrender, only to be answered with a cannon shot. Thousands of Mexican soldiers then launched a series of frontal assaults. For twelve days the Mexicans were repulsed and suffered fearful losses. Then, on March 6, the defenders of the Alamo, fewer than 200, were awakened by the sound of Mexican bugles playing the dreaded "Deguello" ("No Mercy to the Defenders"). Soon thereafter Santa Anna's men attacked from every side. They were twice repulsed, but on the third try, as the defenders ran low on ammunition, the Mexicans broke through the battered north wall and swarmed through the breach.

The frontiersmen used their muskets as clubs, but soon most were slain. Santa Anna ordered the wounded Americans killed and their bodies burned with the rest. The only survivors were sixteen women, children, and servants. It was a complete victory for Santa Anna, but a costly one. The defenders of the Alamo gave their lives at the price of 1,544 Mexicans, and their heroic stand inspired the rest of Texas to fanatic resistance. While Santa Anna dictated a "glorious" victory declaration, his aide wrote in his diary, "One more such 'glorious victory' and we are finished."

On March 2, 1836, while the siege of the Alamo continued, delegates from all fifty-nine Texas towns met at the village of Washington-on-the-Brazos and signed a declaration of independence. Over the next seventeen days the delegates drafted a constitution for the Republic of Texas and established an interim government. The delegates then hastily adjourned as Santa Anna's troops, fresh from their victory at the Alamo, bore down upon them.

The commander in chief of the gathering Texas forces was Sam Houston, a flamboyant Tennessee frontiersman. Houston was born into a military family in Virginia in 1793. His father died when Sam was fourteen, and his mother took the children to live on a farm in eastern Tennessee. As a youth, Houston befriended the Cherokee Indians and developed close ties with them, learning their customs and language. He joined the army in 1813, serving under Andrew Jackson in the Creek War. After receiving three near-mortal wounds, Houston rose to the rank of first lieutenant before resigning in 1818 to practice law. He later served two terms in Congress and in 1827 was elected governor of Tennessee. In 1835 Houston moved to Texas and soon thereafter was named commanding general of the revolutionary army.

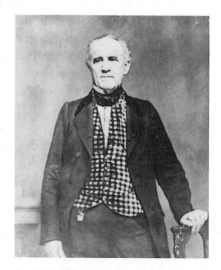

After the Mexican victory at the Alamo, Sam Houston beat a strategic retreat eastward from Gonzales, gathering reinforcements as he went, including volunteers from the United States. Just west of the San Jacinto River he paused near the site of the city that would later bear his name and on April 21, 1836, surprised a Mexican encampment there. The 800 Texans and American volunteers charged, yelling "Remember the Alamo," and overwhelmed the panic-stricken Mexican force. They killed 630 Mexican soldiers while losing only 9 of their own, and they took

Sam Houston

Commander in chief of the Texas forces.

Santa Anna prisoner. The Mexican dictator bought his freedom by signing a treaty recognizing the independence of Texas. The Mexican Congress repudiated the treaty and refused to recognize the loss of its northern province, but the war was at an end.

NEGOTIATIONS FOR ANNEXATION Residents of the Lone Star Republic drafted a constitution that legalized slavery and banned free blacks. They made Sam Houston their first president and voted for annexation to the United States as soon as the opportunity arose. The U.S. president then was Houston's old friend Andrew Jackson, but even Old Hickory could put politics ahead of friendship and be discreet when delicacy demanded it. The addition of Texas as a new slave state in 1836 threatened to ignite a fractious sectional quarrel that might endanger Martin Van Buren's election as Jackson's successor. Worse than that, it raised the specter of war with Mexico. Concerned about such repercussions, Jackson delayed official recognition of the Republic of Texas until his last day in office, and his successor, Van Buren, avoided the issue of annexation during his term as president.

Rebuffed in Washington, Texans focused on building their separate republic. They began to talk of expanding Texas to the Pacific, creating a new nation rivaling the United States. France and Britain extended official recognition to the nation of Texas and began to develop trade relations with the republic. Meanwhile, thousands of Americans poured into the new republic. The population grew from 40,000 in 1836 to 150,000 in 1845. Many settlers were attracted by low land prices. And most were eager to see Texas join the Union.

Reports of growing British influence in Texas during the early 1840s created anxieties in the U.S. government and among southern slaveholders, who became the chief advocates of annexation. The United States began secret negotiations with Texas in 1843, and in April, John C. Calhoun, President Tyler's secretary of state, completed an annexation treaty that went to the Senate for ratification.

Calhoun chose this moment to send the British minister (ambassador) to the United States a letter instructing him on the blessings of slavery and stating that the annexation of Texas was needed to foil the British abolitionists. Publication of the note fostered the claim that Calhoun and Tyler wanted Texas as a means to promote the expansion of slavery. It was so worded, one newspaper editor wrote Andrew Jackson, as to "drive off every northern man from the support of the measure." Sectional division, plus fear of a war with Mexico, contributed to the Senate's overwhelming rejection of Calhoun's Texas annexation treaty. Solid Whig opposition contributed more than anything else to its defeat.

POLK'S PRESIDENCY

THE ELECTION OF 1844   Although adding Texas to the Union was a popular idea among the citizenry, prudent leaders in both political parties had hoped to keep the divisive issue out of the 1844 presidential campaign. Whig Henry Clay and Democrat Martin Van Buren, the leading candidates, opposed annexation of pro-slavery Texas on the grounds that it might spark civil war. Whigs embraced Clay's stance, and the convention nominated him unanimously. The Whig platform omitted any reference to Texas.

The Democratic Convention was a different story. Former President Van Buren's southern supporters, including Andrew Jackson, abandoned his effort to gain the nomination because of his opposition to Texas annexation. With the convention deadlocked, expansionist forces nominated James Knox Polk of Tennessee. The party platform promoted territorial expansion, and to win support in the North and the West as well as in the South, it called for "the re-occupation of Oregon and the re-annexation of Texas."

The Democratic combination of southern and western expansionism constituted a winning strategy that forced Whig nominee Henry Clay to hedge his statement on Texas. While he still believed the integrity of the Union to be the chief consideration, he had "no personal objection to the annexation" if it could be achieved "without dishonor, without war, with the common consent of the Union, and upon just and fair terms." His explanation seemed clear enough, but prudence was no match for spread-eagle oratory and the emotional pull of Manifest Destiny. Clay's divisive stand turned more Whig votes to the new Liberty party, an anti-slavery party begun by a group of abolitionists in 1840. In the western counties of New York, the Liberty party drew enough votes away from the Whigs to give the state to Polk. Had he carried New York, the overconfident Clay would have won the election by seven electoral votes. Instead, Polk won a narrow plurality of 38,000 popular votes nationwide but a clear majority of the Electoral College, 170 to 105. At forty-nine, Polk was the youngest president the nation had seen.

POLK AND HIS PROGRAM   Born near Charlotte, North Carolina, James Polk moved to Tennessee as a young man. After studying at the University of North Carolina, he had become a successful lawyer and planter and entered politics early, serving fourteen years in Congress (four as Speaker of the House) and two as governor of Tennessee. Young Hickory, as his partisans liked to call him, was a short, slender man with a shock of grizzled hair, probing gray eyes, and a seemingly permanent grimace. Humorless and dogmatic, he had none of Andrew Jackson's charisma but

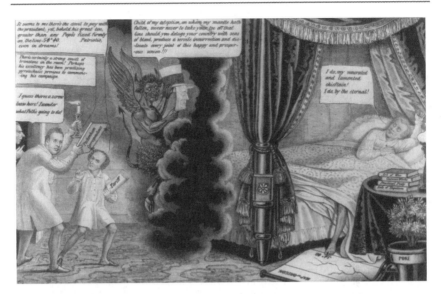

Polk's Dream (1846)

The devil advises Polk to claim all of disputed Oregon even if "you deluge your country with seas of blood, produce a servile insurrection, and dislocate every joint of this happy and prosperous union."

shared Jackson's strong prejudices and his stubborn determination. Polk had a penchant for eighteen-hour workdays, which destroyed his health during his four years in the White House. He would die just three months after leaving office.

On domestic policies, Polk adhered to Jackson's principles, but he and the new Jacksonians subtly reflected the growing influence of the slaveholding South on the Democratic party. Abolitionism, Polk warned, could destroy the Union, but his pro-slavery stance further fragmented public opinion. Anti-slavery northerners had already begun to drift away from the Democratic party, which was increasingly perceived as representing the slaveholding interest in the South.

Single-mindedly committed to the tasks at hand, Polk was a poor diplomat but a formidable leader. His major objectives were reduction of the tariff, reestablishment of the federal independent Treasury, settlement of the Oregon boundary dispute with Britain, and the acquisition of California from Mexico. He got them all. The Walker Tariff of 1846, in keeping with Democratic tradition, lowered the tariff, and in the same year, Polk persuaded Congress to restore the independent Treasury, which the Whigs had eliminated. Twice Polk vetoed internal-improvement bills, leading critics to charge that he was determined to further the South's interests at the expense of the national interest.

Polk's chief concern remained geographic expansion. The acquisition of slaveholding Texas was already under way before he took office. President Tyler, taking Polk's election as a mandate to act, had asked Congress to accomplish annexation by joint resolution, which required only a simple majority in each house and avoided the two-thirds Senate vote needed to ratify a treaty. Congress had read the election returns, too, and after a bitter debate over slavery, the resolution passed by votes of 27 to 25 in the Senate and 120 to 98 in the House. Tyler signed the resolution on March 1, 1845, offering to admit Texas to the Union, just three days before Polk was inaugurated. Texas voters ratified the action in October, and the new state formally entered the Union on December 29, 1845. A furious Mexico dispatched troops to the Texas border.

OREGON   Meanwhile, the Oregon boundary issue heated up as American expansionists insisted that the newly elected president abandon previous offers to settle with Britain on the 49th parallel and stand by the Democrats' platform pledge to take all of Oregon. In his inaugural address, President Polk claimed that the American title to Oregon was "clear and unquestionable," but privately he favored a prudent compromise. The British, however, refused his offer to extend the boundary along the 49th parallel. Polk then withdrew the offer and renewed his demand for all of Oregon. In the annual message to Congress at the end of 1845, he asked permission to give Britain notice that joint occupation of Oregon would end in one year. After a long and bitter debate, Congress adopted the provocative resolution.

Fortunately for Polk the British government had no enthusiasm for war over a distant territory at the cost of profitable trade relations with the United States. In early June 1846 the British government submitted a draft treaty to extend the Canadian-American border along the 49th parallel and through the main channel south of Vancouver Island. On June 18 the Senate ratified the treaty. Most of the country was satisfied. Southerners cared less about Oregon than Texas, and northern business interests valued British trade more than Oregon. Besides, the country was by then at war with Mexico.

THE MEXICAN WAR

THE OUTBREAK OF WAR   On March 6, 1845, two days after Polk took office, the Mexican government broke off relations with the United States. When an effort at negotiation failed, Polk ordered troops under General

Zachary Taylor to take up positions along the Rio Grande. These positions lay in territory that was doubly disputed: Mexico recognized neither the U.S. annexation of Texas nor the Rio Grande boundary between itself and Texas. Polk's intention was clear: he wanted to goad the Mexicans into a conflict in order to secure Texas and also obtain California and New Mexico. Ulysses S. Grant, then a young officer serving under Taylor, later admitted, "We were sent to provoke a fight, but it was essential that Mexico commence it."

Polk resolved that he could achieve his purposes only by force, and he won the cabinet's approval of a war message to Congress. That very evening, May 9, 1846, the news arrived that Mexicans had attacked U.S. soldiers north of the Rio Grande. Eleven Americans were killed, five wounded, and the remainder taken prisoner. Polk's provocative scheme had worked. In his war message the president seized the high ground, declaring that the use of force was a response to Mexican aggression, a recognition that war had been forced upon the United States. Mexico, he claimed, "has invaded our territory, and shed American blood upon the American soil." The House and Senate quickly passed the resolution, and Polk signed the declaration of war on May 13, 1846.

OPPOSITION TO THE WAR   In the Mississippi River valley, where expansion fever ran high, the war with Mexico was immensely popular. Whig opinion in the North, however, ranged from lukewarm to hostile. Massachusetts congressman John Quincy Adams, who voted against participation, called it "a most unrighteous war." An obscure congressman from Illinois named Abraham Lincoln, upon taking his seat in 1847, began introducing "spot resolutions," calling upon President Polk to name the spot where American blood had been shed on American soil, implying that the troops may in fact have been in Mexico when fired upon. Once again, as in 1812, New England was a hotbed of opposition. Some New Englanders were ready to separate from the slave states, and the Massachusetts legislature called the conflict a war of conquest.

PREPARING FOR BATTLE   However flimsy the justification for conflict, both the United States and Mexico were ill prepared for war. The U.S. military was small and inexperienced. At the outset of war, the regular army numbered barely over 7,000, in contrast to the Mexican force of 32,000. Many of the Mexicans, however, had been pressed into service or recruited from prisons and thus made less than enthusiastic fighters. Before the war ended, the American force had grown to 104,000, of whom about 31,000 were regular army troops and marines. The rest were six- and twelve-month volunteers.

Among the volunteers were sons of Henry Clay and Daniel Webster, but most of the soldiers came from coarser backgrounds. Volunteer militia companies, often filled with frontier toughs, lacked uniforms, standard equipment, and discipline. Repeatedly, despite the best efforts of the commanding generals, these undisciplined forces engaged in plunder, rape, and murder. Nevertheless, these rough-and-tumble Americans consistently defeated the larger Mexican forces, which had their own problems with training, discipline, and munitions.

The United States entered the war without even a tentative plan of action, and politics complicated the task of devising one. President Polk sought to manage every detail of the conflict. What Polk wanted, Senator Thomas Hart Benton wrote later, was "a small war, just large enough to require a treaty of peace, and not large enough to make military reputations, dangerous for the presidency." Winfield Scott, general in chief of the army, was both a Whig and a politically ambitious officer. Polk nevertheless put him in charge of the Rio Grande front, but when Scott quarreled with Polk's secretary of war, the exasperated president withdrew the appointment.

There now seemed a better choice for commander. General Zachary Taylor's men had scored two victories over Mexican forces north of the Rio Grande, and on May 18, 1846, they crossed the river border and occupied Matamoros, which a demoralized and bloodied Mexican army had abandoned. These quick victories brought Taylor instant popularity, and the president responded willingly to the public demand that he be made overall commander for the conquest of Mexico. "Old Rough and Ready" Taylor, a bowlegged and none-too-handsome man of sixty-one, seemed unlikely stuff from which to fashion a hero, but he had achieved Polk's main objective, the conquest of Mexico's northern provinces. Taylor became an immediate folk hero to his troops and to Americans back home, so much so that Polk began to see him as a political threat.

THE ANNEXATION OF CALIFORNIA   President Polk had long coveted the valuable Mexican territory along the Pacific coast and had tried buying it, but to no avail. He then sought to engineer a Texas-style revolt against Mexican rule among the American settlers in California. To that purpose, near the end of 1845, John C. Frémont brought out a band of sixty frontiersmen, including Kit Carson, ostensibly on another exploration of California and Oregon. In 1846 Frémont and his men moved into the Sacramento Valley in northern California. Soon thereafter, Americans in the area fell upon Sonoma on June 14, proclaimed the independent Republic of California, and hoisted the hastily designed Bear flag, a California grizzly bear and star painted on white cloth, a version of which would become the state flag.

By the end of June, Frémont had endorsed the Bear Flag Republic and set out for Monterey on the coast. Before he arrived, the commander of the Pacific Fleet, having heard of the outbreak of hostilities, sent a party ashore to raise the U.S. flag and proclaim California part of the United States. The Republic of California had lasted less than a month, and most Californians of whatever origin welcomed a change that promised order instead of the confusion of the unruly Bear Flaggers. Sporadic clashes with Mexicans continued until 1847, when they finally capitulated. Meanwhile, Colonel Stephen Kearny's army, having earlier captured Santa Fe, ousted the Mexican forces from southern California and occupied Los Angeles.

TAYLOR'S BATTLES   Both California and New Mexico had been taken before General Zachary Taylor fought his first major battle in northern Mexico. Having waited for more men and munitions, Taylor and his troops finally headed southward, in September 1846, toward the heart of Mexico. His first goal was the fortified city of Monterrey, which he took after a five-day siege. President Polk was growing increasingly unhappy with Taylor's popularity, however, and with what he considered Taylor's excessive passivity.

But Polk's grand strategy was itself flawed. Having never seen the Mexican desert, the president wrongly assumed that Taylor's men could live off the land and need not depend upon resupply. Polk therefore misunderstood the general's reluctance to strike out across several hundred miles of barren desert north of Mexico City. On another point the president was simply duped. The old Mexican General Santa Anna, forced out of power in 1845, got word to Polk from his exile in Cuba that in return for the right considerations he would bring about a settlement of the war. Polk in turn assured the Mexican leader that Washington would pay well for any territory taken through such a settlement. In 1846 U.S. forces allowed Santa Anna to return to his homeland. Soon he was again in command of the Mexican army and was named president once more. But instead of carrying out his pledge to Polk to negotiate an end to the war, Santa Anna prepared to fight Taylor's army. Polk's blundering intrigue had put the ablest Mexican general back in command of the enemy army.

In October 1846, Polk and his cabinet decided to order an assault of Mexico City from the south by way of Vera Cruz, which left General Taylor's forces idle. Polk would have preferred a Democratic general to lead the new offensive, but for want of a better choice he named Winfield Scott to the field command. Zachary Taylor, miffed at his reduction to a minor role and harboring a "violent disregard" for Scott's abilities, disobeyed orders and took the offensive himself.

Near the hacienda of Buena Vista, Santa Anna's large but ill-trained army met Taylor's untested volunteers. The Mexican general invited the vastly outnumbered Americans to surrender. "Tell him to go to hell," Taylor replied. In the hard-fought Battle of Buena Vista (February 22–23, 1847), Taylor's son-in-law, Colonel Jefferson Davis, the future president of the Confederacy, led a regiment that broke up a Mexican cavalry charge. Neither side could claim victory. Buena Vista was the last major action on the northern front, and Taylor was granted leave to return home.

SCOTT'S TRIUMPH   Meanwhile, the long-planned southern assault on Mexico City began on March 9, 1847, when Winfield Scott's army landed on the beaches south of Vera Cruz. It was the first major amphibious operation by U.S. forces and was carried out without loss. The Mexican commander at Vera Cruz surrendered on March 27 after a week-long siege. Scott and some 14,000 soldiers then retraced the 260-mile route to Mexico City taken by Cortés and the Spanish more than 300 years earlier. Santa Anna tried to set a trap for the Americans at the mountain pass of Cerro Gordo, but Scott's men did the trapping, taking more than 3,000 Mexican prisoners.

Scott then waited until reinforcements and new supplies arrived from the coast. After three months, with his numbers almost doubled, Scott and his army set out on August 7 through the mountain passes into the valley of Mexico. The general directed a brilliant flanking operation around the lakes and marshes that guard the eastern approaches to Mexico City, then another around the Mexican defenses at San Antonio. On September 13, 1847, U.S. forces entered Mexico City. At the national palace a battalion of marines raised the flag and occupied the "halls of Montezuma."

After the fall of the Mexican capital, Santa Anna resigned and fled the country. By the Treaty of Guadalupe Hidalgo, signed on February 2, 1848, Mexico gave up all claims to Texas above the Rio Grande and ceded California and New Mexico to the United States. In return the United States agreed to pay Mexico $15 million and assume the claims of U.S. citizens against Mexico up to $3.25 million. The Senate ratified the treaty on March 10, 1848. By the end of July, the last remaining U.S. soldiers had boarded ship for home.

THE WAR'S LEGACIES   The seventeen-month-long war cost the United States 1,733 killed, 4,152 wounded, and far more—11,550—dead of disease, mostly dysentery and chronic diarrhea ("Montezuma's revenge"). It remains the deadliest war in American history in terms of the percentage of combatants killed. Out of every 1,000 U.S. soldiers in Mexico, some 110 died. The

MAJOR CAMPAIGNS OF THE MEXICAN WAR

← U.S. forces ← Mexican forces

★ Battle site

--- Line set by Treaty of Guadalupe Hidalgo, 1848

Why did Frémont initially settle in the Salinas Valley before marching north, only to march south to San Francisco? How did Polk's fear of Taylor's popularity undermine the Americans' military strategy? What was the significance of Scott's assault on Mexico City?

next highest death rate would be in the Civil War, with 65 killed out of every 1,000 participants.

The military and naval expenditures were $98 million. For that price, and payments made under the treaty, the United States acquired more than 500,000 square miles of territory (more than 1 million, counting Texas), including the great Pacific harbors of San Diego, Monterey, and San Francisco.

Except for a small addition made by the Gadsden Purchase in 1853, these annexations rounded out the continental United States.

Several important firsts are associated with the Mexican War: the first successful offensive American war, the first major amphibious military operation, and the nation's first war covered by correspondents. It was also the first significant combat experience for a group of junior officers who would serve as leading generals during the Civil War: Robert E. Lee, Ulysses S. Grant, Thomas "Stonewall" Jackson, George B. McClellan, George Pickett, Braxton Bragg, George Meade, and others.

Initially the victory in Mexico unleashed a surge of national pride, but as the years passed, the Mexican War was increasingly seen as a war of conquest. The acquisition of Oregon, Texas, California, and the new Southwest made the United States a transcontinental nation. Extending authority over this vast new land greatly expanded the scope of the federal government. In 1849, for example, Congress created the Department of the Interior to supervise the distribution of land, the creation of new territories and states, and the "protection" of the Indians and their land. President Polk naively assumed that the dramatic expansion of American territory to the Pacific would strengthen "the bonds of Union." He was wrong. No sooner was Texas annexed than a violent debate erupted over the extension of slavery into the new territories. That debate would culminate in a war that would nearly destroy the Union.

MAKING CONNECTIONS

- This chapter opened with an account of the brief administration of William Henry Harrison, the first Whig president. The collapse of the Whig party is detailed in Chapter 16.

- The West developed quickly after the expansionist policies of the 1840s. Chapter 19 takes the story to the 1890s.

- This chapter ended by noting that the debate over slavery "would culminate in a war that would nearly destroy the union." Chapter 16's discussion of "The Crisis of Union" traces the relationship between the Mexican War and the Civil War more explicitly.

FURTHER READING

For background on Whig programs and ideas, see Richard Patrick McCormick's *The Second American Party System: Party Formation in the Jacksonian Era* (1966). Frederick Merk's *Manifest Destiny and Mission in American History* (1963) remains a classic. Another treatment of expansionist ideology is Thomas R. Hietala's *Manifest Design: Anxious Aggrandizement in Late Jacksonian America* (1985).

The best survey of western expansion is Richard White's *"It's Your Misfortune and None of My Own": A New History of the American West* (1991). Robert M. Utley's *A Life Wild and Perilous: Mountain Men and the Paths to the Pacific* (1997) tells the dramatic story of the rugged frontiersmen who discovered corridors over the Rocky Mountains. The movement of settlers to the West is ably documented in John Mack Faragher's *Women and Men on the Overland Trail*, 2nd ed. (2001) and David Dary's *The Santa Fe Trail: Its History, Legends, and Lore* (2000). The best account of the California gold rush is Malcolm J. Rohrbough's *Days of Gold: The California Gold Rush and the American Nation* (1997).

Gene M. Brack's *Mexico Views Manifest Destiny, 1821–1846: An Essay on the Origins of the Mexican War* (1975) describes Mexico's viewpoint on U.S. designs on the West. On the siege of the Alamo, see William C. Davis's *Three Roads to the Alamo: The Lives and Fortunes of David Crockett, James Bowie, and William Barret Travis* (1998). An excellent biography related to the emergence of Texas is Gregg Cantrell's *Stephen F. Austin: Empresario of Texas* (1999). On James K. Polk and the war, see John H. Schroeder's *Mr. Polk's War: American Opposition and Dissent, 1846–1848* (1973). The best survey of the military conflict is John S. D. Eisenhower's *So Far from God: The U.S. War with Mexico, 1846–1848* (1989). An excellent analysis of the diplomatic aspects of Mexican-American relations is David M. Pletcher's *The Diplomacy of Annexation: Texas, Oregon, and the Mexican War* (1973).

Part Four

A HOUSE
DIVIDED
AND REBUILT

1846	Wilmot Proviso attempts to ban slavery in former Mexican lands (1846)	Liberals demand reforms in Britain, Austria, Hungary, the German states, and the Italian states (1848)
	The Calhoun resolutions counter the Wilmot Proviso (1847)	Revolutions erupt in France, Prussia, Italy, and Austria (1848–1849)
	"Free soil" becomes focus of the 1848 presidential campaign (1848)	Counterrevolutions take place in France, Prussia, Italy, and Austria (1849)
	Zachary Taylor serves as president (1849–1850)	
1850	California (1849) and New Mexico (1850) adopt free-state governments	
	Compromise of 1850 temporarily defuses the slavery issue	Taiping Rebellion in China (1850–1864)
	Fugitive Slave Act heightens racial tensions in the North (1850)	Expansion of European banking system promotes investment in railroads, industry, and commerce (1850s–1870s)
	Millard Fillmore serves as president following Taylor's death (1850–1853)	Industry fuels growth of middle class in Britain, France, and Germany (1850s–1870s)
	Franklin Pierce serves as president (1853–1857)	French acquire Indochina (1850–1890s)
	Gadsden Purchase renews debate regarding slavery in the territories (1853)	Louis Napoléon assumes the throne in France, taking the name Napoléon III (1852–1870)
1854	Kansas-Nebraska Act repeals portions of the Missouri Compromise and allows settlers to determine whether new territories will be slave or free (1854)	France is governed by the Second Republic (1852–1870)
	Republican party is formed (1854)	Commodore Matthew Perry arrives in Japan (1853)
	Dred Scott ruling declares that slaves, even if freed, cannot be citizens (1857)	Crimean War (1853–1856)
	James Buchanan serves as president (1857–1861)	Panama Railroad is completed, shortening the water route from New York to California by 8,000 nautical miles (1855)
	Lincoln-Douglas debates highlight the issue of slavery (1858)	Following the Indian Mutiny, power in India is transferred from the East India Company to the British government (1857–1858)
1860	South Carolina secedes from Union after election of Abraham Lincoln (1860)	Harris Convention opens Japan to American trade (1858)
	Abraham Lincoln serves as president (1861–1865)	Treaty of Tientsin ends the Anglo-Chinese War and opens some Chinese ports to U.S. commerce (1858)
	Mississippi, Florida, Alabama, Georgia, Louisiana, and Texas secede from the Union (1861)	Italy is unified (1859–1870)
	The seceded states form the Confederate States of America and name Jefferson Davis its president (1861)	England receives shipment of 23 billion pounds of southern cotton, resulting in 50 percent oversupply (1861)
	Confederates attack Fort Sumter; Lincoln blockades southern ports, and both sides call up armies (1861)	British allow Confederate agents to acquire British gunships for use against northern vessels (1861–1865)
	Battle of Bull Run becomes first major land battle of the war (1861)	Serfs in Russia are emancipated (1861)
1862	Robert E. Lee takes command of the Army of Northern Virginia (1862)	
	Battles of Shiloh, Antietam, and Fredericksburg (1862)	England's cotton surplus runs out, closing mills and leaving tens of thousands of mill workers unemployed; many emigrate to the U.S. (1862)
	Lincoln issues a preliminary Emancipation Proclamation (1862)	French install Austrian archduke Maximilian as emperor of Mexico (1862)

Frederick Douglass, a former slave, provides focused leadership for the abolition campaign in the North (1840s–1850s)

U.S. population is 23 million, including 3.2 million enslaved African Americans (1850)

Most of southern society consists of yeoman farmers (1850s–1860s)

Plains tribes agree to tribal borders in the Fort Laramie Treaty (1851)

Harriet Beecher Stowe's *Uncle Tom's Cabin* is published (1852)

Henry David Thoreau writes *Walden, or Life in the Woods* in response to the complexities of modern life (1854)

Pottawatomie Massacre pits pro- and anti-slavery factions against each other in "bleeding" Kansas (1856)

John Brown leads a raid on Harpers Ferry, Virginia, to protest slavery (1859)

25 percent of southerners hold slaves (1860)

Wealthy planters owning considerable land and 100 or more slaves are the elite of southern society (1860)

U.S. population reaches 31 million, of which 16 percent is urban (1860)

New York City becomes the first U.S. city with a population of 1 million (1860)

The Union has a population of 23 million, the Confederacy, 9 million (1860)

180,000–200,000 African Americans serve in the Union army (1861–1865)

All southern white men aged 18 to 35 are conscripted into the Confederate army (1862)

Thousands of women assume roles previously filled by men (1861–1865)

South continues to use slaves to grow staple crops, such as cotton, for export (1840s–1850s)

Mining camps crowded with prospectors dot the California landscape (1850s)

"Prime field hands" are sold for $1,500 to $2,000 (1850s)

Democratic tariff decreases rates to their lowest levels since 1816 (1857)

Financial panic leads to depression (1857)

Edwin Drake drills America's first oil well near Titusville, Pennsylvania (1859)

Record cotton crops are harvested (1859–1860)

Union states produce 97 percent of firearms and 96 percent of railroad equipment in the U.S. (1860)

Confederacy produces just 7 percent of manufactured goods (1860)

Union has 20,000 miles of railroad; the Confederacy has 10,000 miles (1860)

The South produces 4 million bales of cotton (1860)

The South has 60 percent of the nation's pigs and half its cattle (1860)

The Confederacy prints $1 billion in currency, causing runaway inflation (1861–1865)

Wheat replaces cotton as the nation's chief export (1861–1865)

First U.S. paper currency is issued (1862)

Congress approves Homestead Act, transcontinental railroad project, and Morrill Land Grant Act to expand the economy (1862)

1846

1850

1854

1860

1862

Battles of Chancellorsville, Vicksburg, Gettysburg, and Chattanooga (1863)

Lincoln issues a Proclamation of Amnesty and Reconstruction (1863)

Ulysses S. Grant becomes supreme commander of the Union armies (1864)

Wade-Davis bill outlines a radical plan for Reconstruction (1864)

1865 Robert E. Lee surrenders to Ulysses S. Grant at Appomattox Court House (1865)

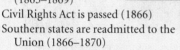

Bureau of Refugees, Freedmen, and Abandoned Lands is established (1865)

Andrew Johnson serves as president after Lincoln is assassinated (1865–1869)

Civil Rights Act is passed (1866)

Southern states are readmitted to the Union (1866–1870)

With "Seward's folly," Alaska formally becomes a U.S. possession (1867)

Congress enacts Military Reconstruction Act, Command of the Army Act, and Tenure of Office Act (1867)

Johnson violates Tenure of Office Act by firing the secretary of war (1867)

House votes to impeach Johnson; Senate votes not to convict (1868)

Fourteenth Amendment grants citizenship to all persons born or naturalized in the U.S. (1868)

1870 Ulysses S. Grant serves as president (1869–1877)

Fifteenth Amendment forbids governments to deny vote to any person based on race, color, or previous condition of servitude (1870)

Department of Justice is created (1870)

Crédit Mobilier scandal breaks, rocking the Grant administration (1872)

Civil Rights Act prohibits discrimination in public places (1875)

1877 Compromise of 1877 gives election to Ohioan Rutherford B. Hayes

Reconstruction ends (1877)

Forced to find other sources of raw cotton, English manufacturers turn to Egypt, India, and Brazil (1862–1864)

International Workingmen's Association (First International) is founded (1864)

Prussia and Austria declare war on Denmark (1864)

Otto von Bismarck unites Germany under Prussian leadership (1866–1871)

Prussian-Italian alliance forms against Austria, leading to war (1866–1867)

French withdraw from Mexico (1866–1867)

British North America Act makes Canada a united confederation with its own government (1867)

Karl Marx publishes *Das Kapital* (1867)

Reform Act expands suffrage in England (1867)

Japanese shogunate is abolished; Meiji restoration begins (1867–1868)

Suez Canal opens (1869)

Prussia wins decisive victory in Franco-Prussian War (1870–1871)

Defeat of the Paris Commune leads to declaration of the Third Republic in France (1871)

England legalizes labor unions (1871)

German Empire is declared at Versailles (1871)

All northern men aged 20 to 45 are conscripted into the Union army; announcement of draft lottery causes rioting and $2 million in damages in New York (1863)

Thirteenth Amendment frees 4 million slaves (1865)

White women's roles are redefined in the South as women do tasks previously assigned to slaves (1865)

600 blacks serve in state legislatures and U.S. Congress (1865–1870)

"Black codes" establish a distinct set of laws for African Americans in the South (1865–1866)

Freed slaves reaffirm their families and establish schools and communities (1865–1870)

Ku Klux Klan is established in Pulaski, Tennessee (1866)

Enforcement Acts are passed to protect southern blacks (1870–1871)

Terrorism of Molly Maguires reaches its peak (1874–1875)

Higher taxes, new currency, and sale of bonds help North finance its war effort, providing over $2 billion (1862–1865)

National Banking Act provides uniform system of banking (1863)

Severe food shortages leave the Confederate army competing with civilians for the few surviving crops (1863)

Contract Labor Act allows employers to bind immigrant laborers by paying for their passage to the U.S. (1864)

Sherman's troops leave the southern economy in ruins (1864–1865)

Emancipation results in widespread unemployment and $4 billion in lost revenue (1865)

Wartime changes enable northern industrialists to further develop the North's economy (1865)

Congress begins trying to retire paper currency issued during the war (1866)

National Labor Union (NLU) convenes in Baltimore (1866)

Freed blacks take up sharecropping, become wage laborers, and otherwise integrate themselves into the postwar economy (1865–1870)

Knights of Labor is formed (1869)

Financial panic sets off depression (1873)

U.S. Treasury reissues $26 million to offset deflationary spiral (1874)

1865

1870

600,000 African-American students attend southern schools (1877)

Repression of southern blacks escalates with the Compromise of 1877

Specie Resumption Act allows paper currency to be exchanged for gold (1875)

Great Railroad Strike of 1877

1877

O f all the regions of the United States during the first half of the nineteenth century, the South was the most distinctive. Southern society remained fundamentally rural and agricultural long after the rest of the nation embraced urban-industrial development. Likewise, the planter elite's tenacious desire to preserve and expand the institution of slavery muted social-reform impulses in the South and ignited a prolonged political controversy that would end in civil war.

The relentless settlement of the western territories set in motion a ferocious competition between North and South for political influence in the burgeoning West. Would the new western states be "slave" or "free"? The issue of allowing slavery into the new territories involved more than humanitarian concern for the plight of enslaved blacks. By the 1840s the North and the South had developed quite different economic interests. The North wanted high tariffs on imported products to "protect" its industries from foreign competition. Southerners, on the other hand, favored free trade because they wanted to import British goods in exchange for the cotton they provided British textile mills.

A series of political compromises glossed over the fundamental differences between the regions during the first half of the nineteenth century. But abolitionists refused to give up their crusade against slavery. Moreover, a new generation of politicians emerged in the 1850s, leaders from both North and South who were less willing to seek political compromises. The continuing debate over allowing slavery into the western territories kept sectional tensions at a fever pitch. By the time Abraham Lincoln was elected president in 1860, many people had decided that the nation could not survive half-slave and half-free; something had to give.

In a last-ditch effort to preserve the institution of slavery, eleven southern states seceded from the Union and created a separate Confederate nation. That, in turn, prompted northerners such as Lincoln to support a civil war to preserve the Union. No one realized in 1861 how prolonged and costly the War between the States would become. Over 630,000 soldiers and sailors would die of wounds or disease. The colossal carnage caused even the most seasoned observers to blanch in disbelief. As President Lincoln confessed in his second inaugural address, no one expected the war to become so "fundamental and astonishing."

Nor did anyone envision how sweeping the war's effects would be on the future of the country. The northern victory in 1865 restored the Union and in the process helped accelerate America's transformation into a modern nation-state. National power and a national consciousness began to displace the sectional emphases of the antebellum era. A Republican-led Congress enacted federal legislation to foster industrial and commercial development and western expansion. In the process the United States began to leave behind the Jeffersonian dream of a decentralized agrarian republic.

The Civil War also ended slavery, yet the status of the freed African Americans remained precarious. The former slaves found themselves legally free, but most were without property, homes, education, or training. Although the Fourteenth Amendment (1868) set forth guarantees for the civil rights of African Americans and the Fifteenth Amendment (1870) provided that black men could vote, local authorities found ingenious—and often violent—ways to avoid the spirit and letter of the new laws.

The restoration of the former Confederate states to the Union did not come easily. Much bitterness and resistance remained among the vanquished. Although Confederate leaders were initially disenfranchised, they continued to exercise considerable authority in political and economic matters. Indeed, in 1877 the last federal troops were removed from the occupied South, and former Confederates declared themselves "redeemed" from the stain of occupation. By the end of the nineteenth century, most states of the former Confederacy had devised a system of legal discrimination that re-created many aspects of slavery.

15

THE OLD SOUTH

FOCUS QUESTIONS

- What were the dominant industries and forms of agriculture in the Old South?
- How did the dependence upon agriculture and slavery shape southern society?
- How did the anti-slavery movement emerge, and how did the South respond to it?

To answer these questions and access additional review material, please visit www.wwnorton.com/studyspace.

Southerners, a North Carolina newspaper editor once wrote, are "a mythological people, created half out of dream and half out of slander, who live in a still legendary land." Most Americans, including southerners themselves, harbor a cluster of myths and stereotypes about the South. Perhaps the most enduring myths come from novels and movies such as *Gone with the Wind* (1939). The South portrayed in romanticized Hollywood productions is a stable agrarian society led by paternalistic white planters and their families, who live in white-columned mansions and represent a "natural" aristocracy of virtue and talent within their community. In these accounts, southerners are kind to their slaves and devoted to the rural values of independence and chivalric honor, values celebrated by Thomas Jefferson.

By contrast, a much darker image of the Old South emerged from abolitionist pamphlets and Harriet Beecher Stowe's best-selling novel, *Uncle*

Tom's Cabin (1852). Those exposés of southern culture portrayed planters as arrogant aristocrats who raped enslaved women, brutalized enslaved workers, and lorded over their community with haughty disdain for the rights and needs of others. They bred slaves like cattle, broke up slave families, and sold slaves "down the river" to certain death in the Louisiana sugar mills and rice plantations.

Such contrasting images die hard, in large part because each one is rooted in reality. Nonetheless, efforts to determine what really set the Old South apart from the rest of the nation generally pivot on two lines of thought: the impact of the environment (climate and geography) and the effects of human decisions and actions. The South's warm, humid climate was ideal for the cultivation of commercial crops such as tobacco, cotton, rice, and sugarcane. The growth of those lucrative cash crops helped foster the plantation system and the expansion of slavery. In the end those developments brought about the civil war that shook the foundations of a republic rooted in the principles of freedom and equality.

THE DISTINCTIVE FEATURES OF THE OLD SOUTH

While geography was a key determinant of the South's economy and culture, many observers have located the origins of southern distinctiveness in the institution of racial slavery. The resolve of whites to maintain and expand such a labor system in turn led to a sense of racial unity that muted class conflict among whites. Yet the biracial character of the population exercised an even greater influence over southern culture, as it has since that time. In shaping patterns of speech, folklore, music, and literature, black southerners immeasurably influenced and enriched the region's culture.

The South differed from other sections of the country in its high proportion of native-born Americans in its population, both white and black. Unlike the North, the South drew few European immigrants after the Revolution. One reason was that the main shipping lines went from Britain to northern ports; another, that the prospect of competing with slave labor deterred immigrants. After the Missouri controversy of 1819–1821, the South increasingly became a consciously minority region, its population growth lagging behind that of other sections of the country, and its defiant dependence upon slavery more and more an isolated and odious anachronism.

AGRICULTURAL DIVERSITY   The preponderance of farming also remained a distinctive southern characteristic, whether pictured as the Jeffersonian yeoman living by the sweat of his brow or the lordly planter

Southern Agriculture

Planting sweet potatoes on James Hopkinson's plantation, Edisto Island, South Carolina, April 1862.

dispatching his slave gangs. The focus on King Cotton and other cash crops such as rice and sugarcane has obscured the degree to which the South fed itself from its own fields. The upper South in many areas practiced general farming in much the same way as the Old Northwest. Corn grew everywhere, but it went less to the market than for local consumption, as feed for herds and food for people. Livestock added to the diversity of the farm economy. In 1860 the South had half the nation's cattle, over 60 percent of the hogs, nearly 45 percent of the horses, 52 percent of the oxen, nearly 90 percent of the mules, and about 33 percent of the sheep, the last mostly in the upper South.

Yet the story of the antebellum southern economy was hardly one of unbroken prosperity. The South's cash crops quickly exhausted the soil. Planting cotton or tobacco year after year leached the fertility from the fields. By 1860 much of eastern Virginia had long ago abandoned tobacco and in some places had turned to growing wheat for the northern market. The older farming lands had trouble competing with the newer soil farther west, in Alabama, Mississippi, and Louisiana, but these lands, too, began to show wear and tear. So first the Southeast and then the Old Southwest faced a growing sense of economic crisis as the nineteenth century advanced.

MANUFACTURING AND TRADE By 1840 many thoughtful southerners had concluded that the agrarian region desperately needed to develop its own manufacturing and trade. After the War of 1812, as cotton growing swept everything before it, the South became increasingly dependent upon the northern economy. Cotton and tobacco were exported mainly in northern vessels, and southerners also relied upon connections in the North for goods imported from Europe. The South became a kind of colonial dependency of the North.

Two major explanations were given for the lag in southern industrial development. First, blacks were presumed unsuited to factory work, perhaps because they supposedly could not adjust to the discipline of work by the clock. Second, the ruling elites of the Old South were said to have developed a lordly disdain for industrial activity, because a certain aristocratic prestige derived from owning plantations and holding slaves. But any argument that black labor was incompatible with industry flew in the face of the evidence, since factory owners bought or hired enslaved workers for just about every kind of manufacture.

Nor should one take at face value the legendary indifference of aristocratic planters to profits and losses. More often than not by the second quarter of the nineteenth century the successful planter was an acquisitive entrepreneur bent on maximizing profits. Economic historians have concluded that enslaved workers on the average supplied a hefty 10 percent return on their cost. By a strictly economic calculation, investment in slaves and land was the most profitable investment available in the antebellum South.

WHITE SOCIETY IN THE SOUTH

If an understanding of the Old South must begin with a knowledge of potent social myths, it must end with a sense of tragedy. White southerners had won short-term economic gains at the cost of both lagging social development and moral isolation in the eyes of the world. The concentration on slave-based agriculture as well as the paucity of cities and immigrants deprived the South of dynamic sources of economic growth and social innovation. The slaveholding South hitched its wagon not to a star but to the growing British demand for cotton. During the late 1850s southern agricultural prosperity seemed endless. Yet end it did. The heyday of expansion in British textiles was over by 1860, but by then the Deep South had become locked into large-scale cotton production that would endure for generations to come.

PLANTERS AND PLANTATION MISTRESSES During the first half of the nineteenth century, wealth in the South was increasingly concentrated

King Cotton Captured

An engraving showing cotton being trafficked in Louisiana.

in the hands of the planter elite. Although great plantations were relatively few in number, they set the tone for economic and social life. What distinguished the plantation from the farm, in addition to its size, was the use of a large enslaved labor force, managed by overseers, to grow primarily staple crops (cotton, rice, tobacco, and sugarcane) for profit.

If to be called a planter one had to hold twenty slaves, only 1 out of every 30 whites in the South in 1860 was a planter. Fewer than 11,000 planters held 50 or more slaves, and the owners of over 100 slaves numbered only 2,300. The census listed just 11 planters with 500 slaves and only 1 with as many as 1,000 slaves. Yet this privileged elite tended to think of its class interests as synonymous with the interests of the entire South and to perceive of its members as "natural aristocrats."

The planter group, making up under 4 percent of the adult white men in the South, held more than half the slaves and produced most of the cotton and tobacco and all of the sugar and rice. In a white population numbering just over 8 million in the states and territories that allowed slavery in 1860, the total number of slaveholders was only 383,637. But assuming that each family numbered five people, then whites with some proprietary interest in slavery constituted 1.9 million, or roughly one fourth of the South's white population. While most southern whites belonged to the small-farmer class, they often deferred to the planter elite. In part such deference reflected the desire of many small farmers to become planters themselves. Over time, however, land and slave prices soared, thereby narrowing prospects for upward social mobility. Between 1830 and 1860 the cotton belt witnessed a growing concentration of wealth in the hands of a slaveholding elite.

The mistress of the plantation supervised the domestic household in much the same way that the planter took care of the business outdoors. She oversaw the preparation of food and linens, the housecleaning, the care of the sick, and a hundred other details. While plantation wives enjoyed entertaining and being entertained, they owed their genteel circumstances to the domestic services provided by enslaved blacks, often women and girls.

One of the most frustrating realities for the plantation mistress was the lack of personal freedom occasioned by the complex demands of her "separate sphere" of genteel domesticity. White women living in a slaveholding culture confronted a double standard in terms of moral and sexual behavior. While they were expected to be models of Christian piety and sexual discretion, their husbands, brothers, and sons enjoyed greater latitude. Many white planters and their sons viewed slave women not only as sources of labor but also as sources of sexual satisfaction. They often rationalized the rape of a slave woman as no crime at all, for slaves had no rights in their eyes.

THE MIDDLE CLASS Overseers on the largest plantations generally came from the middle class of small farmers or skilled workers (artisans) or were younger sons of planters. Most wanted to become slaveholders themselves, but others were constantly on the move in search of more lucrative opportunities. Occasionally there were black overseers, but the highest management position to which a slave could aspire was usually that of "driver," or leader, placed in charge of a small group of slaves with the duty of getting them to work without creating dissension.

The most numerous white southerners were the yeoman farm families, who lived in modest two-room cabins rather than columned mansions. They raised a few hogs and chickens, grew some corn and cotton, and traded with neighbors more than they bought from stores. The men in the family focused their energies on outdoor labors. Women and children worked in the fields during harvest time but spent most of their days attending to domestic chores. Many of these "middling" farmers held a handful of slaves, but most had none. Most of the South's small farms were located in the midst of the plantation economy.

Southern farmers were typically mobile folk, willing to pull up stakes and move west or southwest in pursuit of better land. They tended to be fiercely independent and suspicious of government authority, and they overwhelmingly embraced the Democratic party and evangelical Protestantism. Even though only a minority of the middle-class farmers held slaves, most of them supported the slave system. They feared that the slaves, if freed, would compete with them for land, and they enjoyed the social status that racially based slavery afforded them. Such sentiments pervaded the border states as well as the Deep South. Kentucky, for example, held a referendum on the issue of slavery in 1849, and the voters, most of whom owned no slaves, resoundingly endorsed the slave system.

"POOR WHITES" Stereotyped views of southern society had prepared many visitors to the Old South to see only planters and "poor whites," and many a yeoman farmer living in crude comfort, his wealth concealed in cattle and swine off foraging in the woods, was mistaken for "white trash," a degraded class relegated to the least desirable land and given over to hunting and fishing, hound dogs and moonshine whiskey. Speculation had it that the "poor whites" were descended from indentured servants or convicts transported to the colonies from Britain. The problem, however, was less heredity than environment, the consequence of a trilogy of "lazy diseases": hookworm, malaria, and pellagra, all of which produced an overpowering lethargy. Around 1900 modern medicine discovered cures for these diseases. By 1930 the regional diseases had practically disappeared, taking with them many of the stereotypes about "poor whites."

HONOR AND VIOLENCE From colonial times most southern white men had prided themselves on adhering to a moral code centered on a prickly sense of honor that included a combative sensitivity to slights; loyalty to family, locality, state, and region; deference to elders and social "betters"; and an almost theatrical hospitality. Duels constituted the ultimate public expression of personal honor and manly courage. Although not confined to the South, dueling was much more common there than in the rest of the young nation, a fact that gave rise to the observation that southerners will be polite until they are angry enough to kill you. Dueling was outlawed in the northern states after Aaron Burr killed Alexander Hamilton in 1804, and a number of southern states and counties banned the practice as well—but the prohibition was rarely enforced. Many of the most prominent southern leaders engaged in duels—congressmen, senators, governors, newspaper editors, and planters. The roster of participants included Andrew Jackson, Henry Clay, Sam Houston, and Jefferson Davis.

BLACK SOCIETY IN THE SOUTH

Slavery was one of the fastest growing elements of American life during the first half of the nineteenth century. In 1790 there were less than 700,000 enslaved blacks in the United States. By 1830 there were more than 2 million, and by 1860 there were almost 4 million.

"FREE PERSONS OF COLOR" African Americans had diverse experiences in the United States, depending upon their geographic location and the nature of their working and living conditions. In the Old South "free persons of color" occupied an uncertain status, balanced somewhere between slavery and freedom, subject to racist legal restrictions not imposed upon whites. Free blacks gained liberty in several ways. Over the years some slaves were able to purchase their freedom, and some gained it as a reward for wartime military service. Others were freed by conscientious masters.

By 1830 there were 319,000 free blacks in the United States, about 150,000 of whom lived in the South. The free persons of color included a large number of mulattoes, people of mixed racial ancestry. The census of 1860 reported 412,000 such persons in the United States, or about 10 percent of the black population, probably a drastic undercount. In urban centers like Charleston and especially New Orleans, "colored" society became virtually a third caste, made up of people who occupied a status somewhere between that of blacks and that of whites. Some of them built substantial fortunes and even became slaveholders.

Black slaveholders were a tiny minority, however. The 1830 census revealed that 3,775 free blacks held 12,760 slaves. Most often black slaveholders were free blacks who bought their own family members with the express purpose of freeing them. But some African Americans engaged in slavery for purely selfish reasons.

Free Blacks

This badge, issued in Charleston, South Carolina, was worn by a free black so that he would not be mistaken for someone's "property."

Free blacks were often skilled artisans (blacksmiths, carpenters, cobblers), farmers, or common laborers. The increase in their numbers slowed as legislatures put more and more restrictions on the right to free slaves, but by 1860 there were 262,000 free blacks in the slave states, a little over half the national total of 488,000. They were most numerous in the upper South and tended to live in urban areas.

Free blacks suffered widespread discrimination. All southern states required them to carry a pass. Whites often fraudulently claimed that a free black was in fact one of their runaway slaves, and if the African American did not have an official certificate of freedom, he could be enslaved. In many other ways as well, free blacks were not truly free. In North Carolina, blacks could not travel farther than one county away from their home. Most southern states prohibited them from voting. Blacks were not allowed to testify in court against whites, nor could they hold church services without the presence of a white minister.

PLANTATION SLAVERY Most slaves worked on plantations. The preferred jobs were as household servants and skilled workers, such as blacksmiths and carpenters. Field hands were usually housed in one- or two-room wooden shacks with dirt floors, some without windows. Based upon detailed records from eleven plantations in the lower South, scholars have calculated that more than half of all slave babies died in the first year of life, a mortality rate more than twice that of white infants.

Field hands worked from dawn to dusk. The slave codes adopted by the southern states subjected slaves not only to the slaveholder's governance but to surveillance by patrols of county militiamen, who abused slaves found at large. A majority of both planters and small farmers whipped slaves, at least occasionally. The difference between a good owner and a bad one, according to one ex-slave, was the difference between one who did not "whip too much" and one who "whipped till he bloodied you and blistered you."

Organized slave revolts were rare in the face of overwhelming white authority and firepower. In the nineteenth century only three major slave insurrections were attemped, two of which were betrayed before they got under way. Only the Nat Turner insurrection of August 1831, in rural Virginia, got beyond the planning stage. Turner, a black overseer, was also a religious exhorter who professed a divine mission in leading the movement. The revolt began when a small group of slaves killed Turner's master's family and set off down the road, repeating the process at other farmhouses, where other slaves joined in. Before it ended, at least fifty-five whites had been killed. Eventually trials resulted in seventeen hangings and seven deportations. The Virginia militia, for its part, killed large numbers of slaves indiscriminately in the process of putting down the rebels.

There were very few Nat Turners, however. Slaves more often retaliated against oppression by malingering or engaging in outright sabotage. Yet slaves

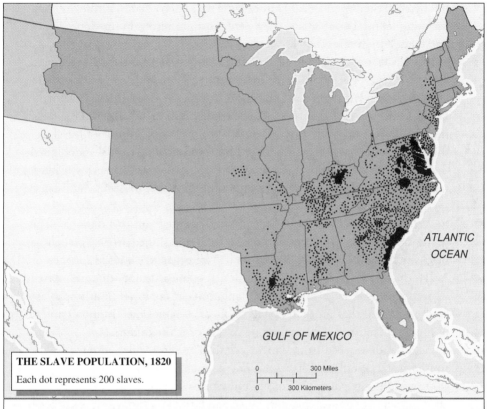

THE SLAVE POPULATION, 1820

Each dot represents 200 slaves.

ATLANTIC OCEAN

GULF OF MEXICO

0   300 Miles

0   300 Kilometers

Consider where the largest populations of slaves were clustered in the South in 1820. Why were most slaves clustered in these regions of the South and not in others? What were the limitations on the spread of slavery? How was the experience of plantation slavery different for men and women?

also knew that they would likely eat better on a prosperous plantation than on one they had reduced to poverty, and the shrewdest slaveholders knew that they would more likely benefit by holding out rewards than by inflicting pain. Plantations based upon the profit motive fostered mutual dependency between slaves and slaveholders, as well as natural antagonism. And in an agrarian society in which personal relations counted for much, blacks could win concessions that moderated the harshness of slavery, permitting them a certain degree of individual and community development.

THE EXPERIENCE OF SLAVE WOMEN Although black men and women often performed similar labors, they did not experience slavery in the same way. Slaveholders had different expectations for the men and women they

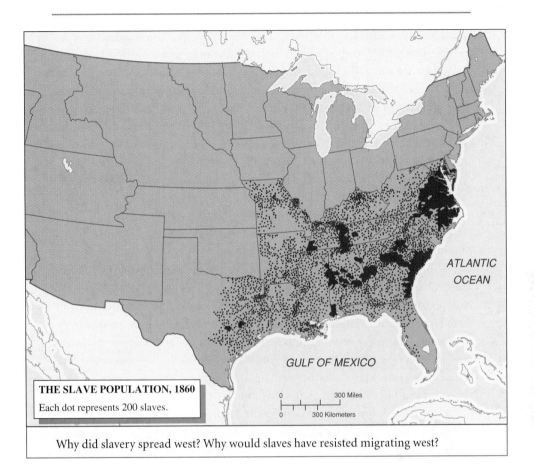

THE SLAVE POPULATION, 1860

Each dot represents 200 slaves.

0   300 Miles

0   300 Kilometers

ATLANTIC OCEAN

GULF OF MEXICO

Why did slavery spread west? Why would slaves have resisted migrating west?

controlled. During the colonial period male slaves vastly outnumbered females. By the mid–eighteenth century, however, the gender ratio had come into balance. Once slaveholders owners realized how profitable a fertile female slave could be over time, giving birth every two and a half years to a child who eventually could be sold, they began to encourage reproduction through a variety of incentives. Pregnant slaves were given less work to do and more food. Owners on some plantations rewarded new mothers with dresses and silver dollars.

But if motherhood endowed enslaved women with stature and benefits, it also entailed exhausting demands. Within days after childbirth the mother was put to work spinning, weaving, or sewing. A few weeks thereafter mothers were sent back to the fields; breast-feeding mothers were often forced to take their babies to the fields with them. On larger plantations elderly women, called grannies, kept the children during the day while their mothers worked outside. Once slave women passed their childbearing years, around the age of forty, their workload increased. Slaveholders put middle-aged women to work full-time in the fields or performing other outdoor labor. Enslaved women were expected to do "man's work" outside. They cut trees, hauled logs, plowed fields with mules, dug ditches, spread fertilizer, slaughtered and dressed animals, hoed corn, and picked cotton. Slave women of all ages usually worked in sex-segregated gangs, which enabled them to form close bonds with one another. To enslaved African Americans, developing a sense of community and camaraderie meant emotional and psychological survival.

Enslaved women faced the constant threat of sexual abuse. Sometimes a white master or overseer would rape a woman in the fields or cabins. Sometimes the owner would lock a woman in a cabin with a male slave whose task was to impregnate her. Female slaves responded to the sexual abuse in different ways. Often they fiercely resisted the sexual advances—and were usually whipped or even killed for their disobedience. Some seduced their master away from his wife. Others killed their babies rather than see them grow up in slavery.

Women had fewer opportunities than men to escape. Women tended to lack the physical strength and endurance required to run away and stay ahead of relentless pursuers. An even greater impediment was a mother's responsibility to her children. A few enslaved women did escape, but most of them learned to cope and resist within the confines of captivity. For them resistance to slavery took forms other than flight. Some engaged in truancy, hiding for days at a time. Many feigned illness to avoid work. Others sabotaged food or crops or stole from their master. Several slave women started fires. A few killed their masters, most often by poison.

FORGING A SLAVE COMMUNITY To generalize about slavery is to miss elements of diversity from place to place and time to time. The experience was as varied as people are. Enslaved African Americans were victims, but to stop at so obvious a perception would be to miss an important story of endurance and achievement. If ever there was an effective melting pot in American history, it may have been that in which Africans with a variety of ethnic, linguistic, and tribal origins fused to form a new community and a new culture as African Americans. Slave culture incorporated many African customs, especially in areas with few whites. Among the Gullah of the South Carolina and Georgia coast, for example, a researcher found as late as the 1940s more than 4,000 words still in use from the languages of twenty-one African tribes. Elements of African culture not only have survived but have interacted with those of the other cultures with which they came in contact.

SLAVE RELIGION Among the most important manifestations of slave culture was its dynamic religion, a mixture of African and Christian elements. Most Africans brought with them to the Americas a concept of a Creator, or Supreme God, whom they could recognize in the Christian Jehovah, and lesser gods, whom they might identify with Christ, the Holy Ghost, and the saints, thereby reconciling their African beliefs with Christianity. Alongside the church they retained beliefs in spirits, magic spells and herbs, and conjuring (the practice of healing by warding off evil spirits). Belief in magic is in fact a common response to conditions of danger or helplessness. Masters sought to instill lessons of Christian humility and obedience, but African Americans identified their plight with that of the Israelites in Egypt. And the ultimate hope of a better world gave solace in this one.

THE SLAVE FAMILY Slave marriages had no legal status, but slaveholders generally accepted marriage as a stabilizing influence on the plantation.

Plantation of J. J. Smith, Beaufort, South Carolina, 1862

Several generations of a family raised in slavery.

Sometimes they performed the marriages themselves or had a minister celebrate a formal wedding with all the trimmings. But whatever the formalities,
the norm for the slave community, as for the white, was the nuclear family,
with the father regarded as head of the household. Most slave children were
socialized by means of the nuclear family, a process that afforded some degree
of independence from white influence.

Childhood was short for slaves. At five or six years of age, children were
given work assignments: they collected trash and kindling, picked cotton,
scared away crows, weeded, and ran errands. By age ten they were full-time
field hands. Children were often sold to new masters. In Missouri an enslaved woman saw six of her seven children, aged one to eleven, sold to six
separate masters.

THE CULTURE OF THE SOUTHERN FRONTIER

There was substantial social and cultural diversity in the South during
the three decades before the Civil War. The region known as the Old Southwest, for example, is perhaps the least well known. It included the states and
territories west of the Georgia-Alabama border—Alabama, Mississippi, and
Texas, Arkansas, Louisiana—as well as the frontier areas of Tennessee, Kentucky, and Florida.

Largely unsettled until the 1820s, this region bridged the South and the
West, exhibiting characteristics of both areas. Raw and dynamic, marked by
dangers, uncertainties, and opportunities, it served as a powerful magnet,
luring thousands of settlers from Virginia and the Carolinas. By the 1830s
most cotton production was centered in the lower South. The migrating
southerners carved out farms, built churches, established towns, and eventually brought culture and order to a raw frontier. As they took up new lives
and occupations, the southern pioneers transplanted many practices and institutions from the coastal states. But they also fashioned a distinctly new set
of values and customs.

THE DECISION TO MIGRATE During the 1820s the agricultural
economy of the upper South suffered from depressed commodity prices and
soil exhaustion. Hard times in the Carolinas and Virginia led many to migrate to the Old Southwest. Women were underrepresented among these migrants. Most dreaded the thought of taking up life in such a disease-ridden,
violent, and primitive region, one that offered them neither independence

nor adventure. They would remain part of a patriarchal culture in either area. Many women feared that life on the frontier would produce a "dissipation" of morals. They heard vivid stories of frontier lawlessness, drunkenness, gambling, and miscegenation.

Enslaved blacks had many of the same reservations about moving west. Almost 1 million captive African Americans were taken to the Old Southwest during the antebellum era, most of them in the 1830s. Like white women, they feared the region's harsh working conditions and torpid heat and humidity. They were also despondent at the breakup of their family ties. As the former slave turned abolitionist Frederick Douglass observed, the "removal" of a slave to the Southwest was considered a form of psychological "death."

THE JOURNEY AND SETTLEMENT Once in the Old Southwest, the pioneers bought land that had been appropriated from Indians. Parcels of 640 acres sold for as little as $2 an acre; land in Alabama's fertile black belt (named for the color of the soil) brought higher prices. As cotton prices soared in the 1830s, aspiring planters invested in as much land and as many slaves as possible. As a result, the average size of farms and plantations in the Old Southwest was larger than that in the Carolinas and Virginia.

But the Old Southwest was much more unhealthy than the Carolina Piedmont. The hot climate, contaminated water, and poor sanitation combined to unleash an epidemic of disease. Malaria was especially common. Life in tents and crude log cabins made many newcomers yearn for the material comforts they had left behind. A male settler reported that "all the men is very well pleased but the women is not very satisfied."

A MASCULINE CULTURE The southern frontier prompted important changes in sex roles, and relations between men and women became uncreasingly inequitable. Young men in the Old Southwest indulged in activities that would have generated disapproval in the Carolinas and Virginia. They drank, gambled, fought, and indulged their sexual desires. Alcohol consumption reached new heights along the southwestern frontier. Most plantations had their own stills for manufacturing whiskey, and alcoholism ravaged frontier families. Violence was also commonplace. The frequency of fights, stabbings, shootings, and murders shocked visitors. Equally disturbing was the propensity of white men to take sexual advantage of slave women. An Alabama woman married to a lawyer-politician was outraged by the "beastly passions" of the white men who fathered slave children and then sold them like livestock. She also recorded in her diary instances of men regularly beating their wives with whips and drinking to excess. Wives, it seems, had little choice but to endure the mistreatment because, as one woman wrote about a friend whose husband abused her, she was "wholly dependent upon his care."

Anti-slavery Movements

EARLY OPPOSITION TO SLAVERY Scattered criticism of slavery developed in the North and the South in the decades after the Revolution, but the emancipation movement accelerated with the formation, in 1817, of the American Colonization Society, which proposed to resettle freed slaves in Africa. Its supporters included such prominent figures as James Madison, James Monroe, Henry Clay, John Marshall, and Daniel Webster, and its appeal was broad. Some backed it because of their opposition to slavery, while others saw it as a way to uphold slavery, by ridding the country of potentially troublesome free blacks. Articulate elements of the free African-American community denounced it from the start. A group of free blacks in Philadelphia, for example, stressed that they had "no wish to separate from our present homes for any purpose whatever." America, they insisted, was their native land.

Nevertheless, in 1821 agents of the Colonization Society acquired a parcel of land in West Africa that became the nucleus of a new country. In 1822 the first freed slaves arrived there from the United States, and twenty-five years later the society relinquished control to the Free and the Independent Republic of Liberia. But given its uncertain purpose, the colonization movement received only meager support from either anti-slavery or pro-slavery elements. By 1860 only about 15,000 blacks had emigrated, approximately 12,000 with the help of the Colonization Society. The number was infinitesimal compared with the number of slave births in the United States.

FROM GRADUALISM TO ABOLITION Meanwhile, in the early 1830s the anti-slavery movement went in a new direction. In Boston in 1831, William Lloyd Garrison began publication of an anti-slavery newspaper, the *Liberator*. Garrison, who rose from poverty in Newburyport, Massachusetts, had been apprenticed to a newspaperman and had edited several anti-slavery newspapers, but he had grown impatient with the strategy of moderation. In the first issue of his new paper, he renounced "the popular but pernicious doctrine of gradual emancipation" and vowed: "I *will be* as harsh as truth, and as uncompromising as justice. On this subject, I do not wish to think, to speak, or write, with moderation."

Garrison's combative language provoked outraged retorts from slaveholders. Their anger at abolitionists soared after the Nat Turner insurrection in 1831. Garrison, they assumed, bore a large part of the responsibility for the affair, but there is no evidence that Nat Turner had ever heard of him, and Garrison said that his newspaper had not a single subscriber in the South at the time. However violent his language, Garrison was in fact a pacifist, opposed to the use of force.

William Lloyd Garrison

Vocal abolitionist and advocate for immediate emancipation.

During the 1830s Garrison became the nation's most fervent foe of slavery. In 1831 he and his followers set up the New England Anti-Slavery Society. Two years later, with the help of Garrison and other abolitionists, two wealthy New York merchants, Arthur and Lewis Tappan, founded the American Anti-Slavery Society. They hoped to build on the publicity gained by the British anti-slavery movement, which had just induced Parliament to end slavery throughout the British Empire.

The American Anti-Slavery Society sought to convince people "that Slaveholding is a heinous crime in the sight of God, and that the duty, safety, and best interests of all concerned, require its *immediate abandonment*, without expatriation." The society went beyond the issue of emancipation to argue that blacks should "share an equality with the whites, of civil and religious privileges." The group issued a barrage of propaganda for its cause, including periodicals, tracts, lecturers, organizers, and fund-raisers.

FRACTIOUS TENSIONS As the anti-slavery movement spread, debates over tactics intensified. The Garrisonians, mainly New Englanders, were radicals who believed that American society had been corrupted from top to bottom and needed universal reform. Garrison embraced just about every important reform movement of the day: abolition, temperance, pacifism, and women's rights. He broke with the organized church, which to his mind was in league with slavery. The federal government was all the more so. The Constitution, he said, was "a covenant with death and an agreement with hell." Garrison therefore refused to vote.

Other reformers were less dogmatic. They saw American society as fundamentally sound and concentrated on purging it of slavery. Most of these abolitionists were evangelical Christians, and they promoted pragmatic political organization as the best instrument to end slavery. Garrison struck them as an impractical fanatic.

A showdown came in 1840 on the issue of women's rights. Women had joined the abolition movement from the start, but the activities of the Grimké sisters brought the issue of women's rights to center stage. Sarah and Angelina Grimké, daughters of a prominent slaveholding family in South Carolina, had broken with their parents and moved north to embrace Quakerism, abolitionism, and feminism. They set out speaking first to women in New England and eventually to audiences of both men and women.

Male leaders chastised the Grimkés and other female activists for engaging in "unfeminine" activity. The chairman of the Connecticut Anti-Slavery Society declared, "No woman will speak or vote where I am a moderator. It is enough for women to rule at home." He refused to "submit to PETTICOAT GOVERNMENT." Angelina Grimké stoutly rejected the conventional arguments. "It is a woman's right," she insisted, "to have a voice in all laws and regulations by which she is to be governed, whether in church or in state."

The debate over the role of women in the anti-slavery movement crackled and simmered until it finally exploded in 1840. At the American Anti-Slavery Society's annual meeting, the Garrisonians insisted upon the right of women to participate equally in the organization, and they carried their point. They did not commit the group to women's rights in any other way, however. Contrary opinion, mainly from the Tappans' New York group, ranged from outright anti-feminism to the simple fear of scattering their energies over too many reforms. The New Yorkers thus broke away to form the American and Foreign Anti-Slavery Society.

BLACK ANTI-SLAVERY ACTIVITY White male abolitionists also balked at granting full recognition to black abolitionists of either sex. Often blindly patronizing, white abolitionists expected free blacks to take a backseat in the movement. Despite the invitation to form separate black groups, black leaders were active in the white societies from the beginning. Three attended the organizational meeting of the American Anti-slavery Society in 1833, and some, notably former slaves, who could speak from firsthand experience, became outstanding agents for the movement.

One of the most effective black abolitionists was Sojourner Truth. Born to slaves in New York in 1797, she was given the name Isabella, but she renamed herself in 1843 after experiencing a mystical conversation with God, who told her "to travel up and down the land" preaching against the sins of slavery. She did just that, crisscrossing the country during the 1840s and 1850s, exhorting

Frederick Douglass (left) and Sojourner Truth (right)

Leading abolitionists.

audiences to support abolition and women's rights. Having been a slave until she fled to freedom in 1827, Sojourner Truth spoke with conviction and knowledge about the evils of the "peculiar institution" and the inequality of women. As she reportedly told a gathering of the Women's Rights Convention in Ohio in 1851, "I have plowed, and planted, and gathered into barns, and no man could head me—and ar'n't I a woman? I have borne thirteen children, and seen 'em mos' all sold off into slavery, and when I cried out with a mother's grief, none but Jesus heard—and ar'n't I a woman?" Through such compelling testimony, Sojourner Truth demonstrated the powerful intersection of abolitionism and women's rights agitation, and in the process she tapped the distinctive energies that women brought to reformist causes.

An equally gifted black abolitionist was Frederick Douglass, originally of Maryland. Blessed with an imposing appearance and a simple eloquence, he became the best-known black man in America. "I appear before the immense assembly this evening as a thief and a robber," he told a Massachusetts group in 1842. "I stole this head, these limbs, this body from my master, and ran off with them." Fearful of capture after publishing his influential

Narrative of the Life of Frederick Douglass (1845), he left for an extended lecture tour of the British Isles and returned two years later with enough money to purchase his freedom. He then started an abolitionist newspaper for blacks, the *North Star,* in Rochester, New York.

Douglass's *Narrative* was the best known of hundreds of accounts of enslavement and the escape to freedom, many of which described the Underground Railroad, a network of people who helped runaways escape and start new lives, often over the Canadian border. A few intrepid black refugees ventured back into slave states to organize additional escapes. Harriet Tubman, the most celebrated liberator, returned nineteen times. Born a slave on a Maryland plantation in about 1820, Tubman escaped when her master died. She fled north, eventually arriving in Philadelphia. There she met William Still, an African-American clerk for the Pennsylvania Anti-Slavery Society who served as a "conductor" on the Underground Railroad. Tubman soon became a conductor herself. Slipping back into the slave states, she would shepherd runaways northward, traveling at night and sleeping by day in the barns or attics of sympathizers along the way. A feisty, determined woman, she threatened to kill any slave who wanted to turn back. Among the 300 slaves Tubman helped liberate were her parents, her sister, and her two children.

REACTIONS TO ABOLITION Even in the North, blacks encountered widespread racial discrimination and segregation. Garrison, Douglass, and other abolitionists often confronted hostile white crowds who disliked blacks or found anti-slavery agitation bad for business. In 1837 an Illinois mob killed the anti-slavery newspaper editor Elijah P. Lovejoy, giving the movement a martyr to the causes of both abolition and freedom of the press.

In the 1830s abolition took a political turn, focusing at first on Congress. One shrewd strategy was to deluge Congress with petitions calling for the abolition of slavery in the nation's capital, the District of Columbia. Most such petitions were presented by former president John Quincy Adams, elected to the House from Massachusetts in 1830. In 1836, however, the House adopted a rule to lay abolition petitions automatically on the table, in effect ignoring them. Adams, "Old Man Eloquent," stubbornly fought this "gag rule" as a violation of the First Amendment and hounded its supporters until the rule was repealed in 1844.

Meanwhile, in 1840, the year of the schism in the anti-slavery movement, a small group of abolitionists called a national convention in Albany, New York, and launched the Liberty party, with James G. Birney, a one-time slaveholder from Alabama and Kentucky, as its candidate for president. In the 1840 presidential election, Birney polled only 7,000 votes, but in 1844 he won 60,000, and from that time forth an anti-slavery party contested every national election until Abraham Lincoln won the presidency in 1860.

THE DEFENSE OF SLAVERY James Birney was but one among a number of southerners propelled north during the 1830s by the South's growing hostility to emancipationist ideas. The anti-slavery movement in the upper South had its last stand in 1831–1832, when the Virginia legislature rejected a plan of gradual emancipation and African colonization. Thereafter southern partisans worked out an elaborate intellectual defense of slavery, presenting it in a positive light.

The evangelical Christian churches, which had widely condemned slavery at one time, gradually turned pro-slavery, at least in the South. Ministers of all denominations joined in the argument. Had not the patriarchs of the Hebrew Bible held bondsmen? Had not Saint Paul advised servants to obey their masters and told a fugitive servant to return to his master? And had not Jesus remained silent on the subject, at least insofar as the Gospels reported his words? In 1845 disputes over slavery split two great denominations along sectional lines and led to the formation of the Southern Baptist Convention and the Methodist Episcopal Church, South. Presbyterians, the only other major denomination to split, did not do so until the Civil War.

A more fundamental feature of the pro-slavery argument stressed the racial inferiority of blacks. Other arguments took a more "practical" view. Not only was slavery profitable, one argument went, but it was also a matter of social necessity. Thomas Jefferson, for instance, in his *Notes on the State of Virginia* (1785), had argued that emancipated slaves and whites could not live together without the risk of a race war growing out of the recollection of past injustices. What is more, it seemed clear to some defenders of slavery that blacks could not be expected to work if freed. They were too shiftless and improvident, the argument went. White workers, on the other hand, feared the competition in the job market if slaves were freed.

In his books *Sociology for the South; or, The Failure of Free Society* (1854) and *Cannibals All! or, Slaves without Masters* (1857), George Fitzhugh of Virginia argued that slavery provided security for African Americans in sickness and old age, whereas workers in the North were exploited for profit and then cast aside. People were not born equal, he insisted. Fitzhugh argued for an organic, hierarchical society, much like the family, in which each member had a place with both rights and obligations.

Within one generation such ideas had triumphed in the white South. Opponents of the faith in slavery as a "positive good" were either silenced or exiled. Freedom of thought in the Old South had become a victim of the region's growing obsession with the preservation and expansion of slavery.

MAKING CONNECTIONS

- The abolition movement never represented the majority of northerners. As Chapter 16 shows, however, by the end of the 1850s most voters in the North supported the idea of limiting the expansion of slavery westward, if not the abolition of it in the southern states.

- The Civil War brought great changes to southerners, both black and white. Chapter 17 describes the effect of the war on southern society.

- There are striking contrasts between the Old South of this chapter and the New South of Chapter 19.

FURTHER READING

Those interested in the problem of distinguishing myth and reality in the southern experience should consult William R. Taylor's *Cavalier and Yankee: The Old South and American National Character* (1961). Two assessments of the mind of the Old South and its defense of slavery are Eugene D. Genovese's *The Slaveholders' Dilemma: Freedom and Progress in Southern Conservative Thought, 1820–1860* (1992) and Eric H. Walther's *The Fire-Eaters* (1992).

Contrasting analyses of the plantation system are Eugene D. Genovese's *The World the Slaveholders Made: Two Essays in Interpretation* (1988) and Gavin Wright's *The Political Economy of the Cotton South: Households, Markets, and Wealth in the Nineteenth Century* (1978). Stephanie McCurry's *Masters of Small Worlds: Yeoman Households, Gender Relations, and the Political Culture of the Antebellum South Carolina Low Country* (1995) greatly enriches our understanding of southern households, religion, and political culture.

Other essential works on southern culture and society include Bertram Wyatt-Brown's *Honor and Violence in the Old South* (1986), Elizabeth Fox-Genovese's *Within the Plantation Household: Black and White Women of the Old South* (1988), Catherine Clinton's *Plantation Mistress: Woman's World in the Old South* (1982), Joan E. Cashin's *A Family Venture: Men and Women on the Southern Frontier* (1991), and Theodore Rosengarten's *Tombee: Portrait of a Cotton Planter* (1986).

A provocative discussion of the psychology of African-American slavery can be found in Stanley M. Elkins's *Slavery: A Problem in American Institutional and Intellectual Life,* 3rd ed. (1976). John W. Blassingame's *The Slave Community: Plantation Life in the Antebellum South,* rev. and enlarged ed. (1979); Eugene D. Genovese's *Roll, Jordan, Roll: The World the Slaves Made* (1974), and Herbert G. Gutman's *The Black Family in Slavery and Freedom, 1750–1925* (1976) all stress the theme of a persisting slave culture. On the question of slavery's profitability, see Robert William Fogel and Stanley L. Engerman's *Time on the Cross: The Economics of American Negro Slavery* (1974).

Other works on slavery include Lawrence W. Levine's *Black Culture and Black Consciousness: Afro-American Folk Thought from Slavery to Freedom* (1977); Albert J. Raboteau's *Slave Religion: The "Invisible Institution" in the Antebellum South* (1978); *We Are Your Sisters,* edited by Dorothy Sterling (1984); Deborah Gray White's *Ar'n't I a Woman? Female Slaves in the Plantation South,* rev. ed., (1999); and Joel Williamson's *The Crucible of Race: Black-White Relations in the American South since Emancipation* (1984). Charles Joyner's *Down by the Riverside: A South Carolina Slave Community* (1984) offers a vivid reconstruction of one community.

Useful surveys of abolitionism include James Brewer Stewart's *Holy Warriors: The Abolitionists and American Slavery,* rev. ed. (1997) and Julie Roy Jeffrey's *The Great Silent Army of Abolitionism: Ordinary Women in the Antislavery Movement* (1998). On William Lloyd Garrison, see Henry Mayer's *All on Fire: William Lloyd Garrison and the Abolition of Slavery* (1998). For the pro-slavery argument as it developed in the South, see Larry E. Tise's *Proslavery: A History of the Defense of Slavery in America, 1701–1840* (1987) and James Oakes's *The Ruling Race: A History of American Slaveholders* (1982). The problems southerners had in justifying slavery are explored in Kenneth S. Greenberg's *Masters and Statesmen: The Political Culture of American Slavery* (1985).

16

THE CRISIS OF UNION

FOCUS QUESTIONS

· How was slavery politicized?

· How did the Compromise of 1850 and the Kansas-Nebraska Act reflect sectional tensions?

· What led to the rise of a third-generation party system, dominated by Republicans and Democrats?

· What were the specific events that led to the secession of the southern states?

To answer these questions and access additional review material, please visit www.wwnorton.com/studyspace.

Wars have a way of corrupting ideals and breeding new wars, often in unforeseen ways. America's victory over Mexico in 1848 and its acquisition of vast new territories gave rise to quarrels over the newly acquired land. Those quarrels set in motion a series of disputes that would culminate in a crisis of union.

SLAVERY IN THE TERRITORIES

THE WILMOT PROVISO   The Mexican War was less than three months old when the seeds of a new conflict began to sprout. On August 8, 1846, a freshman Democrat from Pennsylvania, David Wilmot, stood up in the House of Representatives to discuss President Polk's request for $2 million to support the war effort against Mexico. Wilmot favored expansion, he explained, even the annexation of Texas as a slave state. But slavery had come to an end in Mexico, and if the United States should acquire Mexican territory, "God forbid that we should be the means of planting this institution upon it." Drawing upon the words of the Northwest Ordinance, he proposed that in land acquired from Mexico, "neither slavery nor involuntary servitude shall ever exist in any part of said territory."

The Wilmot Proviso politicized slavery finally and definitively. For a generation, since the Missouri controversy of 1819–1821, the issue had been lurking in the wings, kept there most of the time by politicians who feared its disruptive force. For the two decades following Wilmot's proposal, however, the question of extending slavery into new territories would never be far from center stage.

The House adopted the Wilmot Proviso, but the Senate balked. When Congress reconvened in December 1846, Polk persuaded Wilmot to withhold his amendment, but by then others were ready to take up the cause of prohibiting slavery in the new territories. When a New York congressman revived the proviso, the House again approved the amendment; again the Senate refused to endorse it. The House finally gave up, but in one form or another Wilmot's idea kept being revived.

John C. Calhoun devised a thesis to counter the proviso, which he set before the Senate in four resolutions on February 19, 1847. The Calhoun resolutions, which never came to a vote, argued that since the territories were the common possession of the states, Congress had no right to prevent any citizen from taking slaves into them. To do so would violate the Fifth Amendment, which forbids Congress to deprive any person of life, liberty, or property without due process of law, and slaves were property. By this clever stroke of logic, Calhoun took the basic guarantee of liberty, the Bill of Rights, and turned it into a basic guarantee of slavery. Calhoun's logic became established southern dogma, echoed by his colleagues and formally endorsed by the Virginia legislature.

POPULAR SOVEREIGNTY To bypass the brewing conflict, President Polk suggested extending the Missouri Compromise, dividing free and slave territory at the latitude of 36°30′ all the way to the Pacific. Senator Lewis Cass of Michigan, an ardent Whig expansionist, offered a different solution. He argued that the citizens of a territory "regulate their own internal concerns," like the citizens of a state. Such an approach would combine the merits of expediency and democracy. It would take the issue of slavery in the territories out of the national arena and put it in the hands of those directly affected.

Popular sovereignty, or "squatter sovereignty," as Cass's idea was also called, had much to commend it. Without directly challenging the slaveholders' access to the new territories, it promised to open them quickly to nonslaveholding farmers, who would almost surely become the majority. With this tacit understanding the idea prospered in Cass's Old Northwest, where Stephen A. Douglas of Illinois and other prominent Democrats soon endorsed it.

When the Mexican War ended in 1848, the question of slavery in the new territories was no longer hypothetical. Nobody doubted that Oregon would become "free soil," but it, too, was drawn into the growing controversy. Territorial status for Oregon, pending since 1846, was delayed because its provisional government had excluded slavery. To concede that provision would imply an authority drawn from the powers of Congress, since a territory was created by Congress. After much wrangling, an exhausted Congress let Oregon settlers organize their territorial status without slavery but postponed a decision on the Southwest territories. Polk signed the bill on the principle that Oregon was north of 36°30′, the Missouri Compromise line of latitude.

Polk had promised to serve only one term, and having accomplished his major goals, he refused to run again. At the 1848 Democratic Convention, Lewis Cass, the author of "squatter sovereignty," won the presidential nomination, but the platform simply denied the power of Congress to interfere with slavery in the states and criticized all efforts to bring the question before Congress. The Democrats hoped that the voters would reward their party for winning the war against Mexico. The Whigs devised an even more artful shift. Once again, as in 1840, they passed over Henry Clay, their party leader, for a general, Zachary Taylor, whose popularity had grown since the Battle of Buena Vista. A resident of Louisiana and holder of more than 100 slaves, Taylor was an apolitical figure who had never voted in a national election. Once again, as in 1840, the party adopted no platform at all.

THE FREE-SOIL COALITION   The anti-slavery impulse was not easily squelched, however. David Wilmot had raised a standard to which a broad coalition could rally. People who shied away from the militant abolitionism of William Lloyd Garrison could more readily endorse the exclusion of slavery from all the territories. By doing so, moreover, they could strike a blow for liberty without caring about slavery itself, or about the slaves. One might simply want free soil for white farmers while keeping the unwelcome blacks far away in the South, where they supposedly belonged. Free soil in the new territories, therefore, rather than abolition in the South itself, became the rallying point for many Americans—and also the name of a new party.

Three major groups entered the new free-soil coalition: rebellious Democrats, anti-slavery Whigs, and members of the anti-slavery Liberty party. In 1848 they organized the Free-Soil party at a convention in Buffalo, New York. Its presidential nomination went to the former Democratic president,

Martin Van Buren. The party platform pledged the government to abolish slavery whenever such action became constitutional, but its main principle was the Wilmot Proviso, and it entered the campaign with the catchy slogan of "free soil, free speech, free labor, and free men."

The impact of the new party on the 1848 election was mixed. The Free-Soilers split the Democratic vote enough to throw New York's thirty-six electoral votes to Taylor and split the Whig vote enough to give Ohio to Lewis Cass, but Van Buren's total of 291,000 votes was far below the totals of 1,361,000 for Taylor and 1,222,000 for Cass. Taylor won with 163 to 127 electoral votes for Cass, and both major parties retained a national following.

THE CALIFORNIA GOLD RUSH   Meanwhile, a new dimension had been introduced into the vexing question of slavery in the territories. On January 24, 1848, gold was discovered in California. The word spread quickly, and gold fever became a worldwide epidemic. During 1849 more than 80,000 gold-seeking adventures reached California, with 55,000 traveling overland and the rest going by ship. The influx quickly reduced the Mexicans there to a minority, and sporadic conflicts with the Indians of the Sierra Nevada foothills decimated California's Native Americans.

Of all the frontiers in the American experience, the mining frontier was perhaps the most unstable. Unlike the land-hungry pioneers who traversed the overland trails, the miners were mostly unmarried young men with greatly diverse ethnic and cultural backgrounds. Few miners were interested in permanent settlement. They wanted to strike it rich quickly and return home. The mining camps in California's valleys and canyons and along its creek beds thus sprang up like mushrooms and disappeared almost as rapidly.

After touring the gold region, the territorial governor reported that the surge of newcomers had "entirely changed the character of Upper California." The mining shantytowns were disorderly, unsanitary, and often lawless communities where vigilante justice prevailed and leisure time revolved around saloons. One newcomer reported that "in the short space of twenty-four days, we have had murders, fearful accidents, bloody deaths, a mob, whippings, a hanging, an attempt at suicide, and a fatal duel." Within six months of arriving in California in 1849, one in every five gold seekers was dead. The gold fields and mining towns were so dangerous that nearly everyone carried a weapon—usually a pistol or bowie knife. Suicides were common, and disease was rampant.

Women were as rare in the mining camps as liquor was abundant. In 1850 less than 8 percent of California's total population was female, and even fewer women hazarded life in the camps. Racial and ethnic prejudice

Gold Miners, ca. 1850

Daguerreotype of miners panning for gold at their claim.

abounded in the mining camps. White Americans in the camps often looked with disdain upon the Latinos and Chinese, who were most often employed as wage laborers to help in the panning process, separating gold from sand and gravel. But the white Americans focused their contempt on the Indians. In the mining culture it was not a crime to kill Indians or to work them to death. American miners tried several times to outlaw foreigners in the mining country but had to settle for a tax on foreign miners, which was applied to Mexicans in express violation of the treaty ending the Mexican War.

CALIFORNIA STATEHOOD   California's civic leaders grew frustrated by the inability of military authorities to maintain law and order in the mining communities. In this context the new president, Zachary Taylor, thought he saw an ideal opportunity to use California statehood as a lever to end the stalemate in Congress brought about by the slavery issue.

Born in Virginia and raised in Kentucky, Taylor had been a soldier most of his adult life. Constantly on the move, he had acquired a home in Louisiana and a plantation in Mississippi. Southern Whigs had rallied to his support, expecting him to uphold the cause of slavery. Instead, he turned out to be a southern man who upheld Union principles and had no more use for John Calhoun's pro-slavery abstractions than Jackson had for his nullification doctrine. Slavery should be upheld where it existed, Taylor believed, but he had little patience with abstract theories about slavery in territories where it probably could not exist. Why not make the California and New Mexico territories, acquired from Mexico, into free states immediately, Taylor reasoned, and bypass the whole issue?

But the Californians, in desperate need of organized government, were ahead of him. In December 1849, without consulting Congress, California organized a free-state government. New Mexico responded more slowly, but by 1850 Americans there had adopted a free-state constitution. In his annual message on December 4, 1849, Taylor endorsed immediate statehood for California and enjoined Congress to avoid injecting slavery into the issue.

THE COMPROMISE OF 1850

The spotlight fell on the Senate, where the Compromise of 1850, one of the great dramas of American politics, was enacted by a stellar cast: the great triumvirate of Henry Clay, John C. Calhoun, and Daniel Webster. Seventy-three-year-old Henry Clay once again took the role of the Great Compromiser.

THE GREAT DEBATE   In January 1850 Clay presented a package of eight resolutions designed to solve all the disputed issues. He proposed to (1) admit California as a free state, (2) organize the remainder of the Southwest territories without restrictions on slavery, (3) deny Texas its extreme claim to much of New Mexico, (4) compensate Texas by assuming its debt, (5) uphold slavery in the District of Columbia, but (6) abolish the slave trade across its boundaries, (7) adopt a more effective fugitive slave act, and (8) deny congressional authority to interfere with the interstate slave trade. His proposals, in substance, became the Compromise of 1850, but only after a prolonged debate, the most celebrated, if not the greatest, in the annals of Congress—and the final great debate for Calhoun, Clay, and Webster.

On February 5–6 Clay summoned all his eloquence in defending his proposed settlement. In the interest of "peace, concord and harmony," he called for an end to "passion, passion—party, party—and intemperance." Otherwise, continued sectional bickering would lead to a "furious, bloody, implacable, exterminating" civil war. To avoid that catastrophe, he stressed, California should be admitted on the terms that its own citizens had approved.

The debate continued sporadically through February, with the Texan Sam Houston rising to support Clay's compromise, Mississippi's Jefferson

Davis defending the slavery cause on every point, and none endorsing President Taylor's straightforward plan. Taylor believed that slavery in the South could best be protected if southerners avoided injecting the issue into the dispute over new territories. Unlike Calhoun, he did not believe the new western territories were suitable for slave-based agriculture. Because Taylor believed the issue of bringing slaves into the territories was moot, he continued to urge Congress to admit California and New Mexico without reference to slavery. But few others embraced such a simple solution. In fact, a rising chorus of southern leaders threatened to secede from the Union if slavery were not allowed in California.

Then, in a dramatic move on March 4, Calhoun, desperately ill with tuberculosis, from which he would die in a few weeks, left his sickbed to sit in the Senate chamber. A colleague read his defiant remarks. "I have, Senators, believed from the first that the agitation on the subject of slavery would, if not prevented by some timely and effective measure, end in disunion," wrote Calhoun. Neither Clay's compromise nor Taylor's efforts, he declared, would serve the Union. The South needed simply an acceptance of its rights: to take slaves into the territories, to receive federal assistance in capturing and returning fugitive slaves, and to receive some guarantee of "an equilibrium between the sections."

Three days later Calhoun returned to hear Daniel Webster. The "godlike Daniel" no longer possessed the thunderous voice of his youth, nor did his shrinking frame project its once magisterial aura, but he remained a formidable presence. For his address to the Senate, he chose as his central theme the preservation of the Union: "I wish to speak today, not as a Massachusetts man, not as a Northern man, but as an American . . . I speak today for the preservation of the Union." The extent of slavery was already determined, he insisted, by the Northwest Ordinance, by the Missouri Compromise, and in the new lands by the law of nature. Both sections, to be sure, had legitimate grievances: on the one hand the excesses of "infernal fanatics and abolitionists" in the North and on the other hand southern efforts to expand slavery. But instead of threatening secession, he declared, let everyone "enjoy the fresh air of liberty and union."

Webster's March 7 speech was a supreme gesture of conciliation, but the famed senator had knowingly brought down a storm upon his head. New England abolitionists lambasted this "Benedict Arnold" for not aggressively supporting the free-soil cause and for endorsing the new fugitive slave law. On March 11 William H. Seward, a freshman Whig senator from New York, gave the anti-slavery reply to Webster. Compromise with slavery, he argued, was "radically wrong and essentially vicious." Seward insisted that a "higher law than the Constitution" demanded the abolition of slavery.

In mid-April a select committee of thirteen senators bundled Clay's suggestions into one comprehensive bill. Taylor continued to oppose Clay's compromise, and their feud threatened to split the Whig party. Another crisis loomed when word came that a convention in New Mexico was applying for statehood, with Taylor's support and on the basis of boundaries that conflicted with the Texas claim to the east bank of the Rio Grande.

TOWARD A COMPROMISE On July 4, 1850, supporters of the Union staged a rally at the base of the unfinished Washington Monument. President Taylor attended the ceremonies in the hot sun. Five days later he died of a gastrointestinal affliction caused by tainted food or water. Taylor's sudden death strengthened the chances of compromise. The soldier in the White House was followed by a politician, Millard Fillmore. The son of a poor farmer in upstate New York, Fillmore had made his way as a lawyer and then as a candidate in the rough-and-tumble world of New York politics. Experience had taught him caution, which some interpreted as indecision, but he had made up his mind to support Henry Clay's compromise and had so informed Taylor. It was a strange switch. Taylor, the Louisiana slaveholder, had stoutly opposed the expansion of slavery and was ready to make war on his native region if it pressed the issue; Fillmore, whom southerners thought was anti-slavery, was ready to make peace.

At this point the young Senator Stephen A. Douglas of Illinois, a rising star of the Democratic party, rescued Clay's faltering compromise. Short and stocky, brash and brilliant, Douglas adopted the same strategy that Clay had used to pass the Missouri Compromise thirty years before. Reasoning that nearly everybody objected to one or another provision of Clay's proposal, Douglas worked on the principle of breaking it up into six (later five) separate measures. Few members were prepared to vote for all of them, but from different elements Douglas hoped to mobilize a majority for each.

Millard Fillmore

His support of the Compromise of 1850 helped the Union muddle through the crisis.

The plan worked. By September 1850 President Fillmore had signed the last of the five measures into law. The Union had muddled through, and the settlement went down in history as the Compromise of 1850. For a time it defused an explosive situation and settled each of the major points at issue.

First, California entered the Union as a free state, ending forever the old balance of free and slave states. Second, the Texas–New Mexico Act made New Mexico a territory and set the Texas boundary at its present location. In return for giving up its claims east of the Rio Grande, Texas was paid $10 million. Third, the Utah Act set up that future state's territory. The territorial act in each case omitted reference to slavery except to give the territorial legislature authority over "all rightful subjects of legislation" with provision for appeal to federal courts. For the sake of agreement, the deliberate ambiguity of the statement was its merit. Northern congressmen could assume that territorial legislatures might act to exclude slavery on the unstated principle of popular sovereignty. Southern congressmen assumed that they could not do so.

Fourth, a new Fugitive Slave Act put the matter of retrieving runaways wholly under federal jurisdiction and stacked the cards in favor of slave catchers. Fifth, as a gesture to anti-slavery forces, the slave trade, but not slavery itself, was abolished in the District of Columbia. Millard Fillmore pronounced the five measures making up the Compromise of 1850 "a final settlement" of the issues dividing the nation. Events would soon prove him wrong.

THE FUGITIVE SLAVE ACT Northern abolitionists were determined to keep the issue of slavery's evils in the forefront of public concerns. Southern intransigence in demanding the Fugitive Slave Act had presented abolitionists with an emotional new focus for agitation. The law offered a strong temptation to kidnap free blacks by denying alleged fugitives a jury trial and by providing a reward of $10 for each fugitive delivered to federal authorities. In addition, federal marshals could require citizens to help in its enforcement; violators could be imprisoned for up to six months and fined $1,000. Trouble followed. In Detroit, for example, authorities used military force to stop the rescue of an alleged fugitive slave by an outraged mob in October 1850.

There were relatively few such incidents, however. In the first six years of the Fugitive Slave Act, only three runaways were forcibly rescued from slave catchers. On the other hand, probably fewer than 200 were returned to bondage during those years. More than that were rescued by stealth. Still, the Fugitive Slave Act excited the anti-slavery impulse in the North.

UNCLE TOM'S CABIN Antislavery forces found their most persuasive appeal not in opposition to the Fugitive Slave Act but in the fictional drama of Harriet Beecher Stowe's *Uncle Tom's Cabin* (1852). The novel depicts a combination of unlikely saints and sinners, social stereotypes, and melodramatic escapades, and it was a smashing commercial success. Slavery, seen through Stowe's eyes, subjected its victims to callous brutality or, at the hands of indulgent masters, to the indignity of extravagant ineptitude and bankruptcy. Stowe poignantly portrayed the evils of the interstate slave trade, especially the breaking up of slave families, and she highlighted the

"The Greatest Book of the Age"

Uncle Tom's Cabin, as this advertisement indicates, was a tremendous commercial success.

horrors of the Fugitive Slave Act. It took time for the novel to work its effect on public opinion, however. The country was enjoying a surge of prosperity, and the course of the presidential campaign in 1852 reflected a common desire to lay sectional quarrels to rest.

THE ELECTION OF 1852 The Democrats chose as their presidential candidate Franklin Pierce of New Hampshire, a personable veteran of the Mexican War with little political experience. Soon they had a catchy slogan to aim at the Whigs: "We Polked you in 1844, we shall Pierce you in 1852." The platform pledged the Democrats to "abide by and adhere to a faithful execution of the acts known as the Compromise measures." Pierce rallied both the southern rights' partisans and the Van Burenite Democrats. The Free-Soilers, as a consequence, mustered only half as many votes as they had won in 1848.

The Whigs were less fortunate. They repudiated the lackluster Fillmore, who had faithfully supported the compromise, and tried to exploit martial glory by finally choosing General Winfield Scott, the hero of Mexico City, a native of Virginia backed mainly by northern Whigs. The Whig convention dutifully endorsed the Compromise of 1850, but with some opposition from the North. Scott, an able field commander but an inept politician, had gained a reputation for anti-slavery and nativist sentiments, alienating German-American and Irish-American voters. In the end, Scott carried only four states. The popular vote was closer: 1.6 million to 1.4 million.

Pierce, an undistinguished but sincere, boyishly handsome figure, a former congressman, senator, and soldier, was, like Polk, touted as another Young Hickory. But the youngest president yet was unable to unite the warring factions of his party. By the end of President Pierce's first year in office, Democratic leaders had decided he was a failure. By trying to be all things to all people, Pierce looked more and more like a "Northern man with Southern principles."

FOREIGN ADVENTURES

CUBA   Foreign diversions now distracted attention from domestic quarrels. Cuba, one of Spain's earliest possessions in the New World, had long been an object of U.S. desire, especially to southerners determined to expand slavery into new areas. In 1854 the Pierce administration offered Spain $130 million for the island, which Spain spurned. The U.S. ministers to Spain, France, and Britain then drafted the Ostend Manifesto, which declared that if Spain, "actuated by stubborn pride and a false sense of honor refused to sell," the United States must ask itself, "Does Cuba, in the possession of Spain, seriously endanger our internal peace and existence of our cherished Union?" If so, "we shall be justified in wresting it from Spain." Publication of the supposedly confidential dispatch left the administration no choice but to disavow what northern opinion widely regarded as a slaveholders' plot to acquire Cuba.

DIPLOMATIC GAINS IN ASIA   In Asia, American diplomacy scored some important achievements. In 1844 China signed an agreement with the United States that opened four ports, including Shanghai, to U.S. trade. A later treaty opened eleven more ports and granted Americans the right to travel and trade throughout China. About fifty American Protestant missionaries were in China by 1855, and for nearly a century China remained the most active field for missionaries.

Japan, meanwhile, had remained closed to U.S. trade for two centuries. Moreover, American whalers wrecked on the shores of Japan had been forbidden to leave the country. Mainly in their interest, President Fillmore entrusted a special Japanese expedition to Commodore Matthew Perry, who arrived in Tokyo in 1853. Perry sought to impress—and intimidate—the Japanese with U.S. military and technological superiority. He demonstrated the cannons on his steamships and presented the Japanese with gifts of rifles, pistols, telegraph instruments, and a working miniature locomotive. For their part the Japanese presented Perry with silk and ornate furnishings. Negotiations followed, and Japan eventually agreed to allow a U.S. consulate, treat castaways cordially, and permit American ships to visit certain ports to take on supplies and make repairs. Broad commercial relations began after the first American envoy, Townsend Harris, negotiated the Harris Convention of 1858, which opened five Japanese ports to U.S. trade. Japan continued to ban emigration but found the law increasingly difficult to enforce, and by the 1880s the Japanese government had abandoned its efforts to prevent Japanese from seeking work abroad.

THE KANSAS-NEBRASKA CRISIS

American commercial interests in Asia helped spark a growing interest in constructing a transcontinental railroad that would link the eastern seaboard to the Pacific coast. Railroad developers and land speculators also promoted this link, as did slaveholders who were eager to see the reach of slavery extended. During the 1850s the idea of building a transcontinental railroad, though a great national goal, reignited sectional rivalries and reopened the slavery issue.

Stephen Douglas, ca. 1852

Initiator of the Kansas-Nebraska Act.

DOUGLAS'S PROPOSAL   In 1852 and 1853 Congress debated and dropped several likely proposals for the route of the transcontinental rail line. For various reasons, including terrain, climate, and sectional interests, Secretary of War Jefferson Davis favored a southern route and encouraged what became known as the Gadsden Purchase, a barren stretch of

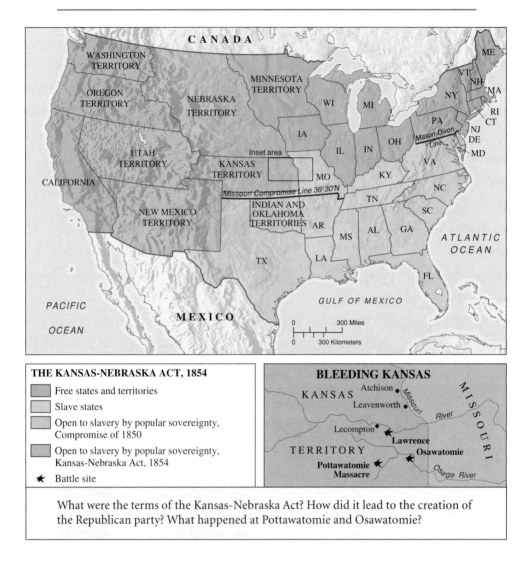

THE KANSAS-NEBRASKA ACT, 1854

- Free states and territories
- Slave states
- Open to slavery by popular sovereignty, Compromise of 1850
- Open to slavery by popular sovereignty, Kansas-Nebraska Act, 1854
- ★ Battle site

BLEEDING KANSAS

What were the terms of the Kansas-Nebraska Act? How did it lead to the creation of the Republican party? What happened at Pottawatomie and Osawatomie?

land in present-day New Mexico and Arizona. In 1853, at a cost of $10 million, the United States acquired the area from Mexico as a likely route for a Pacific railroad.

But midwestern spokesmen had other ideas concerning the path of the railroad. Since 1845 Illinois senator Stephen A. Douglas and others had been pushing for a route through a new territory west of Missouri and Iowa, bearing the Indian name Nebraska. In 1854, as chairman of the Committee on Territories, Douglas put forward a bill dealing with the entire unorganized portion of the Louisiana Purchase to the Canadian border. To carry his point, Douglas needed the support of southerners, and to win that support he needed to make some concession on slavery in the new territories. This he did by writing the concept of popular sovereignty into the bill, allowing voters in each territory to decide the issue themselves.

It was a clever dodge since the Missouri Compromise would exclude slaves until a territorial government had made a decision, thereby preventing slaveholders from getting established before the decision was reached. Southerners quickly spotted the barrier, and Douglas just as quickly made two more concessions. He supported an amendment for repeal of the Missouri Compromise insofar as it excluded slavery north of 36°30', and he agreed to organize two territories: Kansas, west of Missouri, and Nebraska, west of Iowa and Minnesota.

Douglas's motives remain unclear. Railroads were surely foremost in his mind, but he may also have been influenced by the desire to win support for his bill in the South, by the hope that the principle of popular sovereignty would quiet the slavery issue and open the Great Plains, or by a chance to split the Whigs. But he had blundered by failing to appreciate the depth of anti-slavery feelings, thus damaging his presidential chances and setting the country on the road to civil war. Douglas himself preferred that the territories become free. Their climate and geography excluded plantation agriculture, he reasoned, and he could not comprehend how people could get so wrought up over abstract rights to take slaves into the territories. Yet he had in fact opened the possibility that slavery might gain a foothold in Kansas.

Douglas's proposal to repeal the Missouri Compromise was less than a week old when six anti-slavery congressmen published a protest, the "Appeal of the Independent Democrats." Their moral indignation quickly spread among those who opposed Douglas. Across the North, editorials, sermons, speeches, and petitions denounced Douglas's bill as a conspiracy to extend slavery. But Douglas had the votes in Congress for his Kansas-Nebraska Act and, once committed, he forced the issue with tireless energy. President Pierce impulsively added his support, and the bill passed in May 1854 by a vote of 37 to 14 in the Senate and 113 to 100 in the House.

Very well, many in the North reasoned, if the Missouri Compromise was not a sacred pledge and could be scrapped, then neither was the Fugitive Slave Act. On June 2, 1854, Boston witnessed the most dramatic demonstration against the act. After several attempts had failed to rescue a slave named Anthony Burns from being returned south, soldiers dispatched by President

Pierce marched him to a waiting ship through streets lined with people shouting "Kidnappers!" Burns was the last fugitive slave to be returned from Boston and was soon freed through purchase by Boston's African-American community.

THE EMERGENCE OF THE REPUBLICAN PARTY   The cords that John C. Calhoun had said were holding the Union together were beginning to fray. The national church organizations of Baptists and Methodists, for instance, had split over slavery by 1845. The national political parties, which had mutual interests transcending sectional issues, were beginning to unravel under the strain of slavery. The Democrats managed to postpone disruption for yet a while, but their congressional delegation lost heavily in the North, enhancing the influence of the southern wing.

The strain of the Kansas-Nebraska Act soon destroyed the Whig party, however. Southern Whigs now tended to abstain from voting, while northern Whigs gravitated toward two new parties. One was the new American (Know-Nothing) party, which had raised the banner of nativism and the hope of serving the patriotic cause of Union. More northern Whigs joined with independent Democrats and Free-Soilers in spontaneous anti-slavery coalitions with a confusing array of names, including Anti-Nebraska, Fusion, and People's party. These coalitions finally converged in 1854, choosing the name Republican.

BLEEDING KANSAS   After passage of the Kansas-Nebraska Act, attention swung to the plains of Kansas, where opposing elements gathered to stage what would turn out to be a dress rehearsal for civil war. All agreed that Nebraska would be a free state, but Kansas soon exposed the potential for mischief in Douglas's concept of popular sovereignty. The ambiguity of the law, useful to Douglas in getting it passed, only added to the chaos. The people of Kansas were "perfectly free to form and regulate their domestic institutions in their own way, subject only to the Constitution." That in itself invited conflicting interpretations, but the law failed to specify the time of any decision, adding to each side's sense of urgency in getting control of the territory.

The settlement of Kansas therefore differed from the typical pioneering efforts. Groups sprang up in North and South to hurry right-minded settlers westward, mostly from Missouri and the surrounding states. Although few of them held slaves, they were not sympathetic to militant abolitionism; racism was prevalent even among nonslaveholding whites. Many of the

Kansas settlers wanted to keep all blacks, enslaved or free, out of the territory. By 1860 there were only 627 African Americans in the territory.

When Kansas's first territorial governor arrived, in 1854, he found several thousand settlers already in place. He ordered that a census be taken and scheduled an election for a territorial legislature in 1855. On election day several thousand "border ruffians" crossed over from Missouri, illegally cast pro-slavery votes, and pledged to kill every "God-damned abolitionist in the Territory." The governor denounced the vote as a fraud but did nothing to alter the results, for fear of being killed. The new legislature expelled the few anti-slavery members, adopted a drastic slave code, and made it a capital offense to aid a fugitive slave.

Free-state advocates rejected this "bogus" government and quickly formed their own. In 1855 a constitutional convention, the product of an election of dubious legality, met in Topeka, drafted a state constitution excluding both slavery and free blacks from Kansas, and applied for admission to the Union. By 1856 a free-state "governor" and "legislature" were functioning in Topeka. Thus the territory had two illegal governments vying for recognition and control. The prospect of getting any government to command authority in Kansas seemed dim, and both sides began to arm. Once armed, they began to fight. In May 1856, 700 pro-slavery thugs entered the free-state town of Lawrence and smashed newspaper presses, set fire to the free-state governor's home, stole property, and destroyed the Free-State Hotel.

The "sack of Lawrence" resulted in just one casualty, but the incident aroused a fanatic Kansas Free-Soiler named John Brown, who had a history of mental instability. Two days after the sack of Lawrence, Brown, the father of twenty children, set out with four of his sons and three other men toward Pottawatomie, site of a pro-slavery settlement. There they dragged five men from their houses and hacked them to death in front of their screaming wives and children, ostensibly as revenge for the deaths of free-state men.

The Pottawatomie Massacre (May 24–25, 1856) set off a guerrilla war in the Kansas Territory that lasted through the fall. On August 30 Missouri ruffians raided the free-state settlement at Osawatomie. They looted the houses, burned them to the ground, and shot John Brown's son Frederick through the heart. The elder Brown, who barely escaped, swore to his surviving sons and followers, "I have only a short time to live—only one death to die, and I will die fighting for this cause." Altogether, by the end of 1856, about 200 settlers had been killed in Kansas and $2 million in property destroyed during the territorial civil war.

VIOLENCE IN THE SENATE   The violence in Kansas spilled over into Congress itself. On May 22, 1856, the day after the sack of Lawrence and two days before Brown's Pottawatomie Massacre, a flash of savagery on the Senate floor electrified the country. Just two days earlier Senator Charles Sumner of Massachusetts had finished an inflammatory speech in which he described the treatment of Kansas as "the rape of a virgin territory" and blamed it on the South's "depraved longing for a new slave State." Sumner made the elderly senator Andrew Pickens Butler of South Carolina a special target of his censure. He called Butler a liar and implied that he kept a slave mistress. Sumner also teased him about a speech impediment, the result of a stroke.

Sumner's rudeness might well have backfired had it not been for Butler's kinsman Preston S. Brooks, a fiery-tempered South Carolina congressman. For two days Brooks brooded over the insults to his relative, knowing that Sumner would refuse a challenge to a duel. On May 22 a vengeful Brooks confronted Sumner at his Senate desk, accused him of libel against South Carolina and Butler, and began beating him about the head with a cane. Sumner, struggling to rise, wrenched the desk from the floor and collapsed.

Brooks had satisfied his rage but in the process had created a martyr for the anti-slavery cause. Like so many other men in those years, he betrayed the zealot's gift for snatching defeat from the jaws of victory. For two and a half years, Sumner's empty Senate seat was a solemn reminder of the violence done to him. When the House censured Brooks, he resigned, but he was triumphantly reelected. His admirers presented him with new canes. The *Richmond Enquirer* urged Brooks to cane Sumner again: "These vulgar abolitionists in the Senate—must be lashed into submission."

SECTIONAL POLITICS   Within the span of five days in May of 1856, "Bleeding Kansas," "Bleeding Sumner," and "Bully Brooks" had fragmented the political landscape. The major parties could no longer evade the slavery issue. Already it had split the hopeful American party wide open. Southern delegates, with help from New York, killed a resolution to restore the Missouri Compromise and nominated Millard Fillmore for president. Later what was left of the Whig party endorsed him as well.

At its first national convention the new Republican party followed the Whig tradition by seeking out a military hero, John C. Frémont, "the Pathfinder" and leader in the conquest of California. The Republican platform also owed much to the Whigs. It favored a transcontinental railroad and, in general, more internal improvements. It condemned the repeal of the Missouri Compromise and the Democratic policy of territorial expansion.

The campaign slogan echoed that of the Free-Soilers: "Free soil, free speech, and Frémont." It was the first time a major-party platform had taken a stand against slavery.

The Democrats, meeting two weeks earlier, had rejected Pierce, the hapless victim of so much turmoil. They also spurned Douglas, because of the damage done by his Kansas-Nebraska Act. The party therefore turned to James Buchanan of Pennsylvania, who had long sought the nomination. The Democratic platform endorsed the Kansas-Nebraska Act and urged Congress not to interfere with slavery in either states or territories. The party reached out to its newly acquired Irish Catholic and German Catholic voters by condemning nativism and endorsing religious liberty.

The campaign of 1856 resolved itself into a contest in which the parties vied for northern or southern votes. The Republicans had few southern supporters and only a handful in the border states, where fear of disunion held many Whigs in line. Buchanan thus went into the campaign as the candidate of the only remaining national party. Frémont swept the northernmost states with 114 electoral votes, but Buchanan added five free states to his southern majority for a total of 174.

Buchanan, the only unmarried president then or since, brought to the White House a portfolio of impressive achievements in politics and diplomacy. He had been in Congress, had served as minister to Russia and Britain, and had been Polk's secretary of state in between. His long quest for the presidency had been built upon a southern alliance, and his political debts reinforced his belief that saving the Union depended upon concessions to the South. Republicans charged that he lacked the backbone to stand up to the southerners who dominated the Democratic majorities in Congress. To them his choice of four slave-state and only three free-state men for his cabinet seemed a bad omen.

THE DEEPENING SECTIONAL CRISIS

During James Buchanan's first six months in office, he encountered three crises in succession: the *Dred Scott* decision, new troubles in Kansas, and a business panic. These and other challenges proved his undoing.

THE *DRED SCOTT* CASE On March 6, 1857, two days after Buchanan's inauguration, the Supreme Court rendered a decision in the long-pending case of *Dred Scott v. Sandford*. Dred Scott, born a slave in Virginia in about 1800, had been taken to St. Louis in 1830 and sold to an

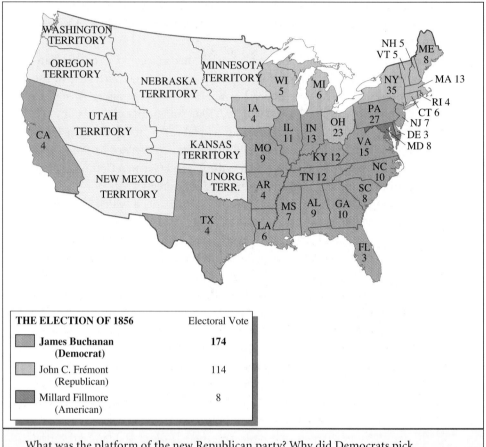

THE ELECTION OF 1856 — Electoral Vote

James Buchanan (Democrat) — **174**

John C. Frémont (Republican) — 114

Millard Fillmore (American) — 8

What was the platform of the new Republican party? Why did Democrats pick Buchanan? What were the key factors that decided the election?

army surgeon, who took him as his servant to Illinois, then to the Wisconsin Territory (later Minnesota), where slavery was prohibited, and finally returned him to St. Louis in 1842. While in the Wisconsin Territory, Scott had met and married Harriet Robinson, and they eventually had two daughters.

After his master's death, in 1843, Scott apparently tried unsuccessfully to buy his freedom. In 1846 Harriet Scott persuaded her husband to file suit in the Missouri courts, claiming that residence in Illinois and the Wisconsin Territory had made them free. A jury decided in their favor, reaffirming the widespread notion that "once free, forever free." But the state supreme court ruled against the Scotts, arguing that a slave state did not have to honor freedom granted to slaves by free states. When the case rose on appeal to the Supreme Court, the country anxiously awaited its opinion on the issue of whether freedom once granted could be lost by returning to a slave state.

Eight of the justices filed a separate opinion, and one concurred with Chief Justice Roger B. Taney. By different lines of reasoning, seven justices ruled that Scott had reverted to slave status upon his return to Missouri. Taney ruled that Scott lacked standing in the courts because he lacked citizenship. At the time the Constitution was adopted, Taney added, blacks "had for more than a century been regarded as . . . so far inferior, that they had no rights which the white man was bound to respect."

To clarify the definition of Scott's status, Taney moved to a second major question. He argued that the Missouri Compromise, by ruling that certain new territories were to exclude slaves, had deprived citizens of property by prohibiting slavery, an action "not warranted by the Constitution." The Supreme Court had declared an act of Congress unconstitutional for the first time since *Marbury v. Madison* (1803). Congress had repealed the Missouri Compromise in the Kansas-Nebraska Act three years earlier, but the decision now challenged the concept of popular sovereignty. If Congress itself could not exclude slavery from a territory, then presumably neither could a territorial government created by an act of Congress.

Pro-slavery elements, of course, greeted the court's opinion with glee. Many northerners denounced Taney's ruling, however. Little wonder that Republicans protested: the Court had declared their free-soil program unconstitutional. It had also reinforced the suspicion that the slavocracy was hatching a conspiracy. Were not all but one of the justices who joined Taney southerners? And had not Buchanan chatted with the chief justice at the inauguration and then urged the people to accept the decision as a final settlement?

And what of Dred Scott? Ironically his owner, now a widow, married a prominent Massachusetts abolitionist, who saw to it that Scott and his family were freed in 1857. A year later Dred Scott died of tuberculosis.

THE LECOMPTON CONSTITUTION   Out in Kansas, meanwhile, the struggle over slavery continued through 1857. The contested politics in the territory now resulted in an anti-slavery legislature and a pro-slavery constitutional convention. The convention, meeting at Lecompton, drew up a constitution under which Kansas would become a slave state. A referendum on the document was set for December 21, 1857, with rules and officials chosen by the convention.

Although Kansas had only about 200 slaves at the time, free-state men boycotted the election, claiming that it was rigged. At that point, President Buchanan took a fateful step. Influenced by southern advisers and politically dependent upon southern congressmen, he supported the pro-slavery Lecompton Convention. The election went according to form: 6,226 votes for the constitution with slavery, 569 for the constitution without slavery. Meanwhile, the acting governor had convened the anti-slavery legislature, which called for another election to vote on the Lecompton Constitution. Most of the pro-slavery settlers boycotted this election, and the result, on January 4, 1858, was overwhelming: 10,226 against the constitution, 138 for the constitution with slavery, 24 for the constitution without slavery.

The results suggested a clear majority against slavery, but Buchanan stuck to his support of the Lecompton Constitution, driving another wedge into the Democratic party. Senator Douglas, up for reelection in Illinois, could not afford to run as a champion of Lecompton. He broke dramatically with the president in a tense confrontation, but Buchanan persisted in trying to drive Lecompton "naked" through Congress. In the Senate, administration forces held firm, and in 1858 Lecompton was passed. In the House enough anti-Lecompton Democrats combined to put through an amendment for a new and carefully supervised popular vote in Kansas. Enough senators went along to pass the House bill. Southerners were confident the vote in Kansas would favor slavery, because to reject it the voters would have to reject the constitution, an action that would postpone statehood until the population reached 90,000. On August 2, 1858, Kansas voters nevertheless rejected Lecompton, 11,300 to 1,788. With that vote, Kansas, now firmly in the hands of its anti-slavery legislature, largely ended its role in the sectional controversy.

THE PANIC OF 1857   The third crisis of Buchanan's first half year in office, a financial panic, occurred in August 1857. It was brought on by a reduction in Europe's demand for American grain, a surge in manufacturing that outran the growth of markets, and the continued weakness and confusion of the state bank-note system. Failure of the Ohio Life Insurance and Trust Company precipitated the panic, which brought on a depression from which the country did not emerge until 1859.

Everything in those years seemed to get drawn into the vortex of sectional conflict, and business troubles were no exception. Northern businessmen tended to blame the depression on the Democratic tariff of 1857, which had put rates at their lowest level since 1816. The agricultural South weathered the crisis better than the North. Cotton prices fell, but slowly, and world markets for cotton quickly recovered. The result was an exalted notion of King Cotton's importance to the world and apparent confirmation of the growing argument that the southern system of slave-based agriculture was superior to the free-labor system of the North.

DOUGLAS VERSUS LINCOLN   Amid the recriminations over the *Dred Scott* decision, Kansas, and the depression, the center could not hold. The Lecompton battle put severe strains on the most substantial cord of Union that was left, the Democratic party. To many, Douglas seemed the best hope for unity and union, one of the few remaining Democratic leaders with support in both the North and the South. But now Douglas was being whipsawed by the extremes. The Kansas-Nebraska Act had cast him in the role of a doughface, a southern sympathizer. Yet his opposition to Lecompton, the fraudulent fruit of popular sovereignty, had alienated him from Buchanan's southern junta. For all his flexibility and opportunism, however, Douglas had convinced himself that popular sovereignty was a point of principle, a bulwark of democracy and local self-government. In 1858 he faced reelection to the Senate against the opposition of both Buchanan Democrats and Republicans. The year 1860 would give him a chance for the presidency, but first he had to secure his home base in Illinois.

To oppose him, Illinois Republicans named Abraham Lincoln of Springfield, a former Whig state legislator, one-term congressman, and small-town lawyer. Born in a Kentucky log cabin in 1809 and raised on farms in Indiana and Illinois, the young Lincoln had the wit and will to rise above his coarse beginnings. With less than twelve months of sporadic schooling, he learned to read, studied such books as came to hand, and eventually developed a prose style as lean and muscular as the man himself. He worked at various farm tasks, operated a ferry, and made two trips down to New Orleans as a flatboatman. Striking out on his own, he managed a general store in New Salem, Illinois, learned

Abraham Lincoln

Republican candidate for president, June 1860.

surveying, served in the Black Hawk War in 1832, won election to the legislature in 1834 (at the age of twenty-five), read law, and was admitted to the
bar in 1836.

Lincoln abhorred slavery but was no abolitionist. He did not believe the
two races could coexist as equals. But he did oppose any further extension of
slavery into new territories, assuming that over time it would die a "natural
death." Slavery, he said in the 1840s, was a vexing but "minor question on its
way to extinction." Lincoln stayed in the Illinois legislature until 1842 and in
1846 won a seat in Congress. After a single term he retired from active politics to cultivate his law practice in Springfield.

In 1854 the Kansas-Nebraska debate drew Lincoln back into the political
arena. At first he held back from the rapidly growing Republicans, but in 1856
he joined the new party, and by 1858 he was the obvious Republican choice to
oppose Douglas for the Senate. Candidate Lincoln resorted to the classic ploy
of the underdog: he challenged the favorite to a debate. Douglas knew he was
up against a formidable foe and had little relish for drawing attention to his
opponent, but he agreed to meet Lincoln in seven sites around the state. The
legendary Lincoln-Douglas debates took place that summer and fall.

The two men could not have presented a more striking contrast. Lincoln
was well over six feet tall, sinewy and craggy featured with a long neck and
deep-set, brooding eyes. Unassuming in manner, dressed in homely, well-
worn clothes and walking with a shambling gait, he lightened his essentially
serious demeanor with a refreshing sense of humor. To sympathetic observers, Lincoln conveyed an air of simplicity, sincerity, and common sense.
Douglas, on the other hand, was short, rotund, stern, and cocky, attired in
the finest custom-tailored suits. A man of considerable abilities and even
greater ambition, he strutted to the platform with the pugnacious air of a
predestined champion.

At the time and since, much attention focused on the second debate, at
Freeport, where Lincoln asked Douglas how he could reconcile popular sovereignty with the *Dred Scott* ruling that citizens had the right to carry slaves
into any territory. Douglas's answer, thenceforth known as the Freeport
Doctrine, was to state the obvious: whatever the Supreme Court might say
about slavery, it could not exist anywhere unless supported by local police
regulations. Thus, if settlers did not want slavery, they should simply refuse
to adopt a local code protecting it.

Douglas then tried to set some traps of his own. He accused Lincoln of ad-
vocating racial equality. Lincoln countered by affirming white supremacy.
There was, he asserted, a "physical difference between the white and black
races," and it would "forever forbid the two races living together on terms of

social and political equality." Lincoln did insist that blacks had an "equal" right to their freedom and the fruits of their labor. But the basic difference between the two men, Lincoln insisted, lay in Douglas's professed indifference to the moral question of slavery.

If Lincoln had the better of the argument, at least in the long view, Douglas had the better of the election, which he won in a vote by the Illinois legislature. Across the nation the elections recorded one loss after another for Buchanan Democrats. The administration had lost control of the House.

JOHN BROWN'S RAID   The gradual return of prosperity in 1859 offered hope that the political storms of the 1850s might yet pass. But the sectional issue of slavery still haunted the nation, and like lightning on the horizon it warned that a storm was brewing. In 1859 John Brown surfaced again, this time in the East. Since the Pottawatomie Massacre in 1856, he had led a furtive existence, engaging in fund-raising, recruiting, and occasional bushwhacking. His commitment to abolish the "wicked curse of slavery" had intensified, meanwhile, to a fever pitch.

On October 16, 1859, Brown launched his supreme gesture. From a Maryland farm he crossed the Potomac River with about twenty men, including five blacks, and occupied the federal arsenal in Harpers Ferry, Virginia (now West Virginia). He intended to arm the Maryland slaves he assumed would flock to his cause, set up a black stronghold in the mountains of western Virginia, and provide a nucleus of support for slave insurrections across the South.

What Brown actually did was to take the arsenal by surprise, seize a few hostages, and hole up in the fire-engine house. There he and his band were quickly surrounded by militiamen and town residents. The next morning, Brown sent his son Watson and another supporter out under a white flag, but the enraged crowd shot them both. Intermittent shooting broke out, and another Brown son was wounded.

John Brown

Although his anti-abolition efforts were based in Kansas, Brown was a native of Connecticut.

That night Lieutenant Colonel Robert E. Lee arrived with his aide, Lieutenant J.E.B. Stuart, and a force of marines. The following morning, October 18, Stuart and his troops broke down the barricaded doors and rushed into the fire-engine house. A young lieutenant found Brown kneeling with his rifle cocked. Before Brown could fire, however, the marine used the hilt of his sword to beat him unconscious. By then the siege was over. Altogether Brown's men had killed four people (including one marine) and wounded nine. Of their own force, ten died (including two of Brown's sons), five escaped, and seven were captured.

Brown, who survived his wounds, was quickly tried for treason, convicted, and sentenced to be hanged. "Let them hang me," he exulted. "I am worth inconceivably more to hang than for any other purpose." He was never more right. If Brown had failed in his purpose—whatever it was—he had become a martyr for the anti-slavery cause, and he had set off a panic throughout the slaveholding South. At his sentencing he delivered one of America's classic speeches: "Now, if it is deemed necessary that I should forfeit my life for the furtherance of the ends of justice, and mingle my blood further with the blood of my children and with the blood of millions in this slave country whose rights are disregarded by wicked, cruel, and unjust enactments, I say, let it be done."

When Brown, still unflinching, met his end, northern sympathizers held solemn observances. "That new saint," Ralph Waldo Emerson predicted, ". . . will make the gallows glorious like the Cross." William Lloyd Garrison, the lifelong pacifist, now wished "success to every slave insurrection at the South and in every slave country." By far the gravest effect of Brown's raid was to leave pro-slavery southerners in no mood to distinguish between John Brown and the Republican party. All through the fall and winter of 1859–1860, rumors of conspiracy and insurrection swept the region. Every northern visitor, commercial traveler, or schoolteacher came under suspicion, and many were driven out. "We regard every man in our midst an enemy to the institutions of the South," said an Atlanta newspaper editor, "who does not boldly declare that he believes African slavery to be a social, moral, and political blessing."

THE CENTER COMES APART

THE DEMOCRATS DIVIDE   Amid such hysteria unleashed by John Brown's assault at Harper's Ferry, the nation approached a presidential election destined to be the most fateful in its history. The Democrats gathered in Charleston, South Carolina, for their 1860 convention. Douglas's supporters

PROGRESSIVE DEMOCRACY—PROSPECT OF A SMASH UP.

Prospect of a Smash Up (1860)

This cartoon shows the Democratic Party—the last remaining national party—about to be split by sectional differences and the onrush of Republicans, led by Lincoln.

reaffirmed the platform of 1856, which simply promised congressional non-interference with slavery. Southern firebrands, however, now demanded a federal law protecting slavery in the territories. Buchanan supporters, hoping to stop Douglas, encouraged the strategy. When the southern planks lost in the ensuing debate, Alabama's delegation walked out of the convention, followed by delegates from the other Gulf states. The convention then decided to leave the overwrought atmosphere of Charleston and reassemble in Baltimore on June 18. The Baltimore convention finally nominated Douglas. The Charleston seceders met first in Richmond and then in Baltimore, where they adopted the slave-code platform defeated in Charleston and named Vice President John C. Breckinridge of Kentucky for president. Another cord of union had snapped: the last remaining national party.

LINCOLN'S ELECTION   The Republicans, meanwhile, gathered in Chicago in the summer of 1860. There everything suddenly came together for "Honest Abe" Lincoln, the uncommon common man. Lincoln had emerged on the national scene during his unsuccessful senatorial campaign two years before and had since taken a stance on the containment of slavery strong enough to satisfy the abolitionists yet moderate enough to seem less threatening than they were.

Lincoln won the Republican nomination on the third ballot. The party platform denounced John Brown's raid as "among the gravest of crimes" and affirmed that each state should "control its own domestic institutions." The party repeated its resistance to the extension of slavery and, in an effort to gain broader support, endorsed a higher protective tariff for manufacturers, free homesteads for farmers, a more liberal naturalization law for immigrants, and internal improvements, including a Pacific railroad. With this platform, Republicans made a strong appeal to eastern businessmen, western farmers, and the large immigrant population.

Both major conventions revealed that opinions about slavery tended to become more radical in the upper North and the Deep South. Attitude seemed to follow latitude. In the border states between North and South—Missouri, Kentucky, Delaware, and Maryland—a sense of moderation aroused the diehard Whigs there to make one more try at reconciliation. Meeting in Baltimore a week before the Republicans met in Chicago, they organized the Constitutional Union party and named John Bell of Tennessee for president. Their platform simply called for the preservation of the Constitution and the Union.

Of the four candidates not one generated a national following, and the campaign devolved into a choice between Lincoln and Douglas in the North, Breckinridge and Bell in the South. One consequence of these campaigns was that each section gained a false impression of the other. The South never learned to distinguish Lincoln from the radicals; the North failed to gauge the force of southern intransigence. Lincoln stubbornly refused to offer the South assurances or to explain his position on slavery, which he insisted was a matter of public record.

The one man who tried to break through the barrier that was falling between the North and the South was Douglas, who attempted to mount a national campaign. Only forty-seven but already weakened by excessive drink, ill health, and disappointments, he wore himself out in one final glorious campaign. Down through the hostile areas of Tennessee, Georgia, and Alabama, he carried appeals on behalf of the Union.

By midnight on November 6, however, Lincoln's victory was clear. In the final count he had about 39 percent of the total popular vote but a clear electoral majority, with 180 votes in the Electoral College. He carried all eighteen free states by a wide margin. Among all the candidates only Douglas had electoral votes from both slave and free states, but his total of 12 was but a pitiful remnant of Democratic unionism. Bell took Virginia, Kentucky, and Tennessee, and Breckinridge swept the other slave states to come in second with 72 electoral votes.

SECESSION OF THE DEEP SOUTH   Lincoln's election panicked Southerners. Soon after the election, South Carolina set a special election for December 6 to choose delegates to a state convention. In Charleston

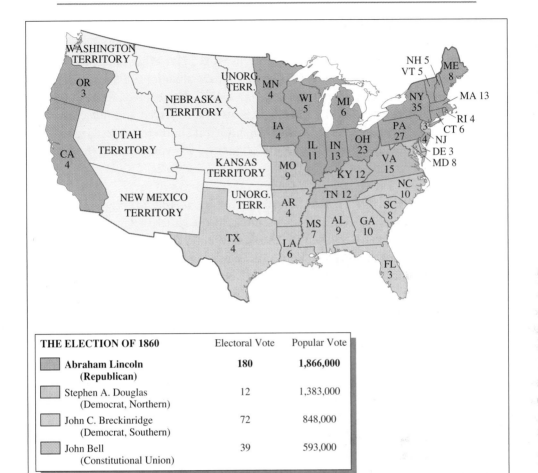

THE ELECTION OF 1860	Electoral Vote	Popular Vote
Abraham Lincoln (**Republican**)	**180**	**1,866,000**
Stephen A. Douglas (Democrat, Northern)	12	1,383,000
John C. Breckinridge (Democrat, Southern)	72	848,000
John Bell (Constitutional Union)	39	593,000

What caused the division in the Democratic party? How did Lincoln position himself to win the Republican nomination? What were the major factors that led to Lincoln's electoral victory?

on December 20, 1860, the convention unanimously endorsed an Ordinance of Secession, repealed the state's ratification of the Constitution, and severed its ties to the Union. By February 1, 1861, Mississippi, Florida, Alabama, Georgia, Louisiana, and Texas had declared themselves out of the Union. On February 4 a convention of those seven states met in Montgomery, Alabama, and on February 7 it adopted a provisional constitution for a new nation, the Confederate States of America. Two days later the delegates elected Jefferson Davis as its president. He was inaugurated February 18, with Alexander Stephens of Georgia as vice president.

In all seven states of the southernmost tier, a solid majority had voted for secessionist convention delegates, but their combined vote would not have been a majority of the presidential vote in November. What happened, it seemed, was what often happens in revolutionary situations: a determined and decisive minority acted quickly in an emotionally charged climate and carried its program over the weak objections of a confused and indecisive opposition. Trying to decide whether a majority of southern whites favored secession is probably beside the point—a majority was vulnerable to the decisive action of the secessionists.

BUCHANAN'S WAITING GAME   History is full of might-have-beens. A bold stroke, even a bold statement, by the lame-duck president at this point might have defused the crisis, but James Buchanan waffled. As Ulysses S. Grant recognized, Buchanan was a "granny of an Executive." Besides, a bold stroke might simply have hastened the conflict. No bold stroke came from president-elect Lincoln either, nor would he consult with the Buchanan administration during the long months before his inauguration on March 4, 1861. He inclined all too strongly to the belief that secession was just another bluff and kept his silence.

In his annual message on December 3, 1860, President Buchanan declared that secession was illegal but that he lacked authority to coerce a state to rejoin the Union. "Seldom have we known so strong an argument come to so lame and impotent a conclusion," the *Cincinnati Enquirer* editorialized. There was, however, a hidden weapon in the president's reaffirmation of a duty to "take care that the laws be faithfully executed" insofar as he was able. If the president could enforce the law upon all citizens, he would have no need to "coerce" a state. Indeed, Buchanan's position became the policy of the Lincoln administration, which fought a war on the theory that individuals, but not states, were in rebellion.

Buchanan held firm to his resolve, with some slight stiffening by the end of 1860, when secession became a fact, but he refrained from forceful action. On the day after Christmas, the small federal garrison at Charleston's Fort Moultrie had been moved into the nearly completed Fort Sumter by Major Robert Anderson, a Kentucky Unionist. South Carolina authorities exploded at this provocative act. Commissioners of the newly "independent" state demanded withdrawal of all federal forces, but they had overplayed their hand. Buchanan sharply rejected the South Carolina ultimatum to withdraw and dispatched a steamer, *Star of the West*, to Fort Sumter with reinforcements and provisions. On January 9, as the ship approached Charleston Harbor, Confederate batteries at Fort Moultrie and Morris Island opened fire and drove it away. It was in fact an act of war, but Buchanan chose to ignore the challenge. He decided instead to hunker down and ride out the remaining weeks of his term, hoping against hope that one of several compromise efforts would yet prove fruitful.

FINAL EFFORTS AT COMPROMISE   Desparate efforts at compromise continued in Congress until dawn on the day of Lincoln's inauguration. On December 18 Senator John J. Crittenden of Kentucky had proposed a series of resolutions that recognized slavery in the territories south of 36°30′ and guaranteed to maintain it where it already existed. The fight for a compromise was carried to the floor of each house of Congress and subjected to intensive but inconclusive debate during January and February.

Meanwhile, a peace conference met in a Washington hotel in February 1861. Twenty-one states sent delegates, and former president John Tyler presided, but the convention's proposal, substantially the same as the Crittenden Compromise, failed to win the support of either house of Congress. The only compromise proposal that met with any success was an amendment guaranteeing slavery where it existed. Many Republicans, including Lincoln, were prepared to go that far to save the Union, but they were unwilling to repudiate their stand against slavery in the territories. As it happened, after passing the House, the amendment passed the Senate without a vote to spare, twenty-four to twelve, on the dawn of inauguration day. It would have become the Thirteenth Amendment, with the first use of the word *slavery* in the Constitution, but the states never ratified it. When a Thirteenth Amendment was ratified in 1865, it did not guarantee slavery—it abolished it.

MAKING CONNECTIONS

- Through the 1850s most of the debate over slavery concerned its expansion into the territories; with Lincoln's Emancipation Proclamation, discussed in the next chapter, the issue would shift to slavery itself.

- Many of the Radical Republicans who designed Reconstruction (Chapter 18) had been anti-slavery Republicans before the war.

- The proposed transcontinental railroad that had brought about the Kansas-Nebraska crisis would finally be completed in 1869 (Chapter 20).

FURTHER READING

The best surveys of the forces and events leading to the Civil War include James M. McPherson's *Battle Cry of Freedom: The Civil War Era* (1988), Stephen B. Oates's *The Approaching Fury: Voices of the Storm, 1820–1861* (1997), and Bruce Levine's *Half Slave and Half Free: The Roots of Civil War* (1992). An excellent narrative of the political debate leading to secession is Michael A. Morrison's *Slavery and the American West: The Eclipse of Manifest Destiny and the Coming of the Civil War* (1997).

Mark J. Stegmaier's *Texas, New Mexico, and the Compromise of 1850: Boundary Dispute and Sectional Crisis* (1996) probes that crucial dispute while Michael F. Holt's *The Political Crisis of the 1850s* (1978) traces the demise of the Whigs. Eric Foner, in *Free Soil, Free Labor, Free Men: The Ideology of the Republican Party before the Civil War* (1970), shows how events and ideas combined in the formation of a new political party. A more straightforward study of the rise of the Republicans is William E. Gienapp's *The Origins of the Republican Party, 1852–1856* (1987). The economic, social, and political crises of 1857 are examined in Kenneth M. Stampp's *America in 1857: A Nation on the Brink* (1990).

Robert W. Johannsen's *Stephen A. Douglas* (1973) analyzes the issue of popular sovereignty. A more national perspective is provided in James A. Rawley's *Race and Politics: "Bleeding Kansas" and the Coming of the Civil War* (1969). On the role of John Brown in the sectional crisis, see Stephen B. Oates's *To Purge This Land with Blood: A Biography of John Brown* (1970). An excellent study on the South's journey to secession is William W. Freehling's *The Road to Disunion: Secessionists at Bay, 1776–1854,* (1990).

On Lincoln's role in the coming crisis of war, see Don E. Fehrenbacher's *Prelude to Greatness: Lincoln in the 1850s* (1962). Harry V. Jaffa's *Crisis of the House Divided: An Interpretation of the Issues in the Lincoln-Douglas Debate* (1959) details the debates, and Maury Klein's *Days of Defiance: Sumter, Secession, and the Coming of the Civil War* (1997) treats the Fort Sumter controversy.

17

THE WAR OF THE UNION

FOCUS QUESTIONS

· What were the major miltary strategies of the Civil War?

· How did the war affect the home front in the North and the South?

· What were the reasons for, and the results of, Lincoln's Emancipation Proclamation?

To answer these questions and access additional review material, please visit www.wwnorton.com/studyspace.

In mid-February 1861 Abraham Lincoln left Springfield, Illinois, and began a long, roundabout rail trip to Washington, D.C. At the end of the journey, reluctantly yielding to warnings of a plot to assassinate him, he secretly passed through Baltimore in the middle of the night and slipped into Washington before daybreak. As Lincoln prepared to take office and the possibility of civil war captured the attention of a divided nation, no one imagined the horrendous scope and intensity of the conflict that was to come. On both sides, people believed that any fighting would be over in little more than a month and that their daily lives would go on as usual.

END OF THE WAITING GAME

LINCOLN AND SECESSION   In his inaugural address on March 4, 1861, Lincoln reassured southerners that he had no intention of interfering with "slavery in the States where it exists." But secession was another matter. He insisted that the "Union of these States is perpetual," and he promised to "hold, occupy, and possess" areas belonging to the federal government. He pledged that the federal government would use force only if attacked, and he concluded with an appeal for harmony, saying: "We are not enemies, but friends. We must not be enemies. Though passion may have strained, it must not break our bonds of affection."

The momentum of secession took control of events, however. The day after the inauguration, word arrived from Charleston that time was running out at the federal garrison at Fort Sumter. The commander, Major Robert Anderson, had enough supplies for only a month, and the fort was surrounded by a Confederate "ring of fire." On April 4 Lincoln decided to resupply Anderson's garrison. Hoping to avoid a confrontation, he informed the governor of South Carolina that he was sending provisions but no guns, ammunition, or soldiers. The Confederate government was not willing to avoid a showdown, however, and it ordered the Confederate general Pierre G. T. Beauregard to demand that his former West Point professor surrender Fort Sumter. Anderson refused, and just before dawn on April 12 Confederate batteries opened fire. After thirty-three hours, Anderson, his ammunition exhausted, surrendered.

The attack on Fort Sumter signaled the end of the tense waiting game. On April 15 Lincoln issued a war proclamation calling upon the loyal states to supply 75,000 militiamen to put down the rebellion. Volunteers in both the North and the South crowded into recruiting stations, and huge new armies began to take shape. On April 19 Lincoln proclaimed a blockade of southern ports, which, as the Supreme Court later ruled, confirmed the existence of a state of war.

TAKING SIDES   Lincoln's war proclamation led four states of the upper South to join the Confederacy: Virginia, Arkansas, Tennessee, and North Carolina. Each had areas (mainly in the mountains) where both slaves and secessionists were scarce and Union sentiment ran strong. In fact, Unionists in western Virginia, bolstered by a Union army from Ohio under General George B. McClellan, formed a new state. In 1863 Congress admitted West Virginia with a state constitution that provided for emancipation of the few slaves there.

Of the other slave states, Delaware remained firmly in the Union, but Maryland, Kentucky, and Missouri went through bitter struggles to decide which side to support. The secession of Maryland would have encircled Washington, D.C., with Confederate states. To hold on to the state, Lincoln took drastic measures: he suspended the writ of habeas corpus (under which judges can require arresting officers to produce their prisoners and justify their arrest) and jailed pro-Confederate leaders. The fall elections ended the threat of Maryland's secession by returning a solidly Unionist majority in the state.

Kentucky, native state of both Abraham Lincoln and Jefferson Davis, harbored divided loyalties. Its fragile neutrality lasted until September 3, 1861, when a Confederate force captured several towns. General Ulysses S. Grant then moved Union troops into Paducah. Thereafter, Kentucky for the most part remained with the Union. It joined the Confederacy, some have said, only after the war.

Robert E. Lee's decision to join the confederacy epitomized the agonizing choice facing many Americans in 1861. Son of a Revolutionary War hero, Lee had graduated second in his class from West Point, had fought with distinction during the Mexican War, and had served in the U.S. Army for thirty years. When Fort Sumter was attacked, he was summoned by Lincoln's seventy-five-year-old general in chief, Winfield Scott, another Virginian, and offered command of the Union forces. After a sleepless night spent pacing the floor, he told Scott he could not go against his "country," meaning Virginia. Although Lee failed to "see the good of secession," he could not "raise my hand against my birthplace, my home, my children." Lee resigned his commission, retired to his estate, and soon answered a call to command the Virginia—later the Confederate—military forces.

On the other hand many southerners made great sacrifices to remain loyal to the Union. Some left their native region once the fighting began. Others who remained in the South found ways to support the Union. In every Confederate state except South Carolina, whole regiments were organized to fight for the Union, and at least 100,000 men from the southern states fought against the Confederacy. Many of the southern loyalists were Irish or German immigrants who had no love for slavery or the planter elite. Whatever their motives, they and other southern loyalists played a significant role in helping the Union cause.

NORTHERN AND SOUTHERN ADVANTAGES   The South seceded in part out of a growing awareness of its minority status in the nation: a balance sheet of the sections in 1861 shows the accuracy of that perception.

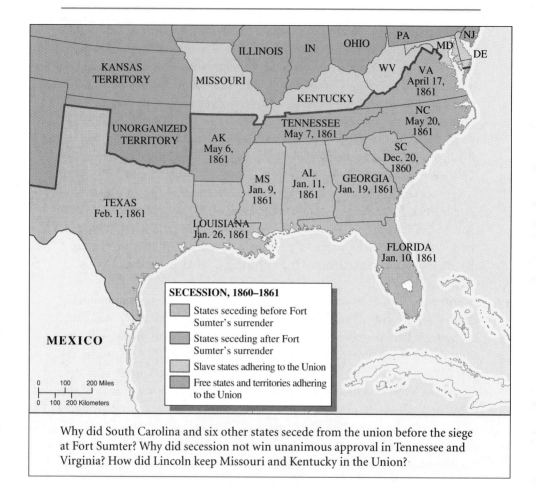

KANSAS TERRITORY

ILLINOIS IN OHIO PA NJ

MISSOURI MD DE

WV VA
April 17,
1861

KENTUCKY

NC
May 20,
1861

UNORGANIZED
TERRITORY

AK
May 6,
1861

TENNESSEE
May 7, 1861

SC
Dec. 20,
1860

MS
Jan. 9,
1861

AL
Jan. 11,
1861

GEORGIA
Jan. 19, 1861

TEXAS
Feb. 1, 1861

LOUISIANA
Jan. 26, 1861

FLORIDA
Jan. 10, 1861

SECESSION, 1860–1861

States seceding before Fort Sumter's surrender

States seceding after Fort Sumter's surrender

Slave states adhering to the Union

Free states and territories adhering to the Union

MEXICO

0   100   200 Miles
0 100 200 Kilometers

Why did South Carolina and six other states secede from the union before the siege at Fort Sumter? Why did secession not win unanimous approval in Tennessee and Virginia? How did Lincoln keep Missouri and Kentucky in the Union?

The Union held twenty-three states, including four border slave states, while the Confederacy had eleven. The population count was about 22 million in the Union to 9 million in the Confederacy, and about 4 million of the latter were enslaved. The Union therefore had an edge of about four to one in potential human resources. To help redress the imbalance, the Confederacy mobilized 80 percent or more of its military-age white, men, one third of whom would die during the prolonged war.

An even greater advantage for the North was its industry. The states that joined the Confederacy produced just 7 percent of the nation's manufactures on the eve of the war. The Union states produced 97 percent of the firearms and 96 percent of the railroad equipment. They had most of the trained mechanics and engineers, most of the shipping and mercantile firms, and the bulk of the banking and financial resources. The North's advantage in transportation weighed heavily as the war went on. The Union had more wagons, horses, and ships than the Confederacy and an impressive edge in railroads.

The South had the advantage of geography: the Confederates could fight a defensive war on their own territory. In addition, the South initially had more experienced military leaders. A number of circumstances had given rise to a strong military tradition in the South: the frequent skirmishes with Indians, the fear of slave insurrection, and a history of territorial expansion. Military careers had prestige, and military schools multiplied in the antebellum years, the most notable West Points of the South being the Citadel and Virginia Military Institute. West Point itself had drawn many southerners, producing a cadre of officers dominated by men from the region. By the end of the war, however, the Union had developed the better commanders.

BULL RUN   Caught up in the frothy excitement of military preparation, both sides predicted quick victory. Nowhere was this naive optimism more clearly displayed than at the First Battle of Bull Run (or Manassas).*An impatient public pressured both sides to strike quickly. Jefferson Davis allowed the battle-hungry General Pierre G. T. Beauregard to hurry the main Confederate army to Manassas Junction, Virginia, about twenty-five miles west of Washington. Lincoln decided that General Irvin McDowell's hastily assembled Union army of some 37,000 might overrun the outnumbered Confederates and quickly march on to Richmond, Virginia, the Confederate capital. With buoyant assumptions of victory, Johnny Reb and Billy Yank breezily stumbled into an entangling web of horror. The mood was so breezy, in fact, that hundreds of civilians had ridden out from Washington to picnic and watch the entertaining spectacle of what they thought would be a one-battle war. Instead, they witnessed a chaotic defeat.

It was a dry summer day on July 21, 1861, when General McDowell's raw recruits encountered Beauregard's army dug in behind a meandering, log-strewn little stream called Bull Run. The two generals, former classmates at West Point, adopted markedly similar plans: each would try to turn the other's left flank. The Union forces almost achieved their purpose early in the afternoon, but Confederate reinforcements, led by General Joseph E. Johnston, poured in to check the Union offensive. Amid the fury a South Carolina general rallied his men by pointing to Thomas Jackson's brigade of

---

*The Union most often named battles for natural features; the Confederacy, for nearby towns—thus Bull Run (Manassas), Antietam (Sharpburg), Stons River (Murfresboro), and the like.

Union Soldiers at Harpers Ferry, Virginia, in 1862

Neither side in the Civil War was prepared for the magnitude of this first "modern" war.

Virginians: "Look at Jackson standing there like a damned stone wall." The analogy captured Jackson's fortitude, and the general was called Stonewall thereafter.

Their attack blunted, the exhausted northern troops eventually broke, and their frantic retreat turned into a panic as fleeing soldiers and terrified civilians clogged the Washington road. Lincoln read a gloomy dispatch from the front: "The day is lost. Save Washington and the remnants of this army. The routed troops will not re-form." Stonewall Jackson had hoped to pursue the fleeing Union troops into Washington. But the Confederates were almost as disorganized and exhausted as the Yankees, and they failed to give chase. It would have been futile anyway, for the next day a summer downpour turned roads into quagmires. The Battle of Bull Run was a sobering experience for both sides. Much of the romance—the splendid uniforms, bright flags, fervent songs— gave way to the agonizing realization that this would be a long, costly struggle.

THE WAR'S EARLY PHASE

The Battle of Bull Run demonstrated that the war would not be decided with one sudden stroke. General Winfield Scott had predicted as much, and now Lincoln fell back upon the three-pronged "anaconda" strategy that Scott had proposed. It called first for the Army of the Potomac to defend Washington D.C., and exert constant pressure on the Confederate capital at Richmond. At the same time the navy would blockade the southern coast and dry up the Confederacy's access to foreign goods and weapons. The final component of the plan would divide the Confederacy by sending navy gunboats and transports to invade the South along the main water routes: the Mississippi, Tennessee, and Cumberland rivers. While newspapers derided the anaconda strategy as far too slow, indicative of General Scott's old age and caution, it was intended to entwine and crush the southern resistance.

The Confederate strategy was simpler. If the Union forces could be stalemated, Jefferson Davis and others hoped, then the British or the French might be persuaded to join their cause, or perhaps public sentiment in the North would force Lincoln to seek a negotiated settlement. So at the same time that armies were forming in the South, Confederate diplomats were seeking assistance in London and Paris, and Confederate sympathizers in the North were urging an end to the North's war effort.

NAVAL ACTIONS   After the Battle of Bull Run and for the rest of 1861 and early 1862, the most important military actions involved naval war and a Union blockade of key southern ports. The Union navy never completely sealed off the South, but it greatly constricted the flow of goods and supplies into the region. The one great threat to the Union navy proved to be short-lived. The Confederates in Norfolk, Virginia, had fashioned an ironclad ship from an abandoned Union steam frigate, the *Merrimack*. Rechristened the *Virginia*, it ventured out on March 8, 1862, and wrought havoc among the Union ships at the entrance to Chesapeake Bay. But as luck would have it, a new Union ironclad, the *Monitor*, arrived from New York in time to engage the *Virginia* on the next day. They fought to a draw, and the *Virginia* returned to port, where the Confederates destroyed it when they had to give up Norfolk soon afterward. Thereafter the North tightened its grip on the South. The navy extended its bases down the Carolina coast in the late summer and fall of 1862. In the spring of 1862, Admiral David Farragut's ships forced open the lower Mississippi River and captured New Orleans and took Baton Rouge upriver.

FORMING ARMIES   While the Union navy was blockading southern ports and building new ships, the armies on both sides were recruiting men to form regiments to fight the land battles of the war. After Lincoln's initial

The U.S. Army Recruiting Office in City Hall Park, New York City

The sign advertises the money offered those willing to serve: $677 to new recruits, $777 to veteran soldiers, and $15 to anyone who brought in a recruit.

call for 75,000 ninety-day militiamen, Congress enlisted 500,000 more men, and after the Battle of Bull Run it added another 500,000. The typical nineteenth-century army often organized its units along community and ethnic lines. The Union army, for example, included a Scandinavian regiment (the 15th Wisconsin Infantry), a Highland Scots unit (the 79th New York Infantry), a French regiment (the 55th New York Infantry), and a mixed unit of Poles, Hungarians, Germans, Spaniards, and Italians (the 39th New York Infantry).

In the Confederacy, Jefferson Davis initially requested 100,000 twelve-month volunteers. Once the fighting started, he was authorized to raise up to 400,000 three-year volunteers. By early 1862 most of the veteran Confederate soldiers were nearing the end of their enlistment without having encountered much significant action. They were also resisting the incentives of bonuses and furloughs for reenlistment. The Confederate government then turned to conscription. On April 16, 1862, all white male citizens aged eighteen to thirty-five were declared members of the army for three years, and those already in service were required to serve out three years. In 1862 the upper age was raised to forty-five, and in 1864 the age limit was further extended from seventeen to fifty, with those under eighteen and over forty-five reserved for state defense.

The conscription law included two loopholes, however. First, a draftee might escape service either by providing an able-bodied substitute not of draft age or by paying $500 in cash. Second, exemptions, designed to protect key civilian work, were subject to abuse by men seeking "bombproof" jobs. The exemption of one white man for each plantation with twenty or more slaves led to bitter complaints about "a rich man's war and a poor man's fight."

The Union took nearly another year to begin drafting men into service. In 1863 the government began to draft men aged twenty to forty-five. Exemptions were granted to specified federal and state officeholders and to others on medical or compassionate grounds. By paying $300 one could avoid service. Conscription spurred men to volunteer, either to collect bounties or to avoid the disgrace of being drafted.

The Civil War draft flouted an American tradition of voluntary service and was widely held to be arbitrary and unconstitutional. Widespread public opposition impeded its enforcement in the North and the South. In New York City the announcement of a draft lottery on July 11, 1863, incited a week of rioting in which roving bands of working-class toughs took control of the streets. Although provoked by opposition to the draft, the riots exposed racial and ethnic tensions. The mobs, mostly Irish Catholic immigrants, set upon conscription offices, factories, docks, and the homes of prominent Republicans. But they directed their wrath most furiously at African Americans. They blamed blacks for causing the war and for threatening to take their own unskilled jobs. Over 100 people died before soldiers brought from Gettysburg restored order.

CONFEDERATE DIPLOMACY   While the Union and Confederate armies mobilized, Confederated diplomacy focused on gaining help from foreign governments in the form of supplies, formal recognition, and perhaps even armed intervention. The Confederates indulged the unrealistic hope that official foreign recognition would prove decisive, when in fact it more likely would have followed a decisive victory in the field, which never came.

The first Confederate emissaries to England and France took hope when the British foreign minister received them informally after their arrival in London in 1861. In Paris, Napoléon III even promised them that he would recognize the Confederacy if Britain would lead the way. When the agents returned to London, however, the government refused to see them, partly because of Union pressure and partly out of British self-interest.

Confederate negotiators were far more successful at getting European supplies than gaining official recognition as a new nation. The most spectacular feat was the procurement of raiding ships. Although British law prohibited the sale of warships to belligerents, a southern agent was able to have ships built in Britain and then, on trial runs, escape to be outfitted with guns. In all, eighteen such ships were activated and saw action in the Atlantic, Pacific, and Indian oceans, where they sank hundreds of Union ships and instilled terror in the rest.

THE WEST AND THE CIVIL WAR   During the Civil War western settlement continued. New discoveries of gold and silver along the eastern slopes of the Sierra Nevadas and in Montana and Colorado lured thousands of prospectors and their suppliers. Dakota, Colorado, and Nevada gained territorial status in 1861, Idaho and Arizona in 1863, and Montana in 1864. Silver-rich Nevada gained its statehood in 1864.

With the firing on Fort Sumter, many of the regular army units assigned to frontier outposts in the West began to head east to meet the Confederate threat. In Texas, the Indian Territory (Oklahoma), and southern New Mexico, Union soldiers left altogether. Elsewhere they left behind skeleton units. Texas was the only western state to join the Confederacy. For the most part, the federal government maintained its control of the other western territories during the war.

The most intense fighting in the West during the war occurred along the Kansas-Missouri border. There the disputes between the pro-slavery and anti-slavery settlers of the 1850s turned into brutal guerrilla warfare. The most prominent pro-Confederate leader in the area was William Quantrill. He and his pro-slavery followers, mostly teenagers, fought under a black flag, meaning that they gave no quarter. In destroying Lawrence, Kansas, in 1863, Quantrill ordered his forces to "kill every male and burn every house." By the end of the day, 182 boys and men had been killed. Their opponents, the Jayhawkers, responded in kind. They tortured and hanged pro-Confederate prisoners, burned houses, and destroyed livestock.

Many Indian tribes found themselves caught up in the war. Indian regiments fought on both sides, and in the Indian Territory they fought against each other. Indians among the "Five Civilized Tribes" held African-American slaves and felt a natural bond with southern whites. Oklahoma's proximity to Texas influenced the Choctaws and Chickasaws to support the Confederacy. The Cherokees, Creeks, and Seminoles were more divided in their loyalties.

ACTIONS IN THE WESTERN THEATER   Little military activity happened in the eastern theater (east of the Appalachian Mountains) before

May 1862. The western theater (from the mountains to the Mississippi River), on the other hand, flared up with several clashes and an important penetration of the Confederate states. In western Kentucky the Confederate general Albert Sidney Johnston, a strapping Texan whom Davis considered the South's best general, had perhaps 40,000 men stretched over some 150 miles.

Early in 1862 General Ulysses S. Grant made the first Union thrust against the weak center of Johnston's overextended lines. Grant had graduated from West Point in the lower half of his class and in 1854 had resigned from the army in disgrace for drunkenness. Volunteering to serve in the Union army in 1861, he was assigned as an officer in the western theater. Moving out of Cairo, Illinois, and Paducah, Kentucky, with a gunboat flotilla, Grant swung southward up the Tennessee River and captured Fort Henry on February 6. He then moved overland to attack Fort Donelson and on February 16 captured its 12,000 men. Grant's blunt demand of "immediate and unconditional surrender" and his quick success sent a thrill through the dispirited North. The short, slouching, disheveled Grant was now a national hero—but not for long.

SHILOH After defeats in Kentucky and Tennessee, General Johnston regrouped the Confederate forces in Corinth, Mississippi, in hopes of retaking control of the Mississippi River valley. As Grant moved his forces southward along the Tennessee River during the early spring of 1862, he made a costly mistake. While planning his attack on Corinth, he clumsily placed his troops on a rolling plateau between two creeks and failed to dig defensive trenches. Johnston shrewdly recognized Grant's oversight, and on the morning of April 6 the Confederate leader ordered an attack on the vulnerable Union soldiers.

The 44,000 Confederates struck suddenly at Shiloh, the site of a log church in the center of the Union camp in southwestern Tennessee. They found most of Grant's troops still sleeping or eating breakfast. Some died in their bedrolls. After a day of bloody carnage and confusion, Grant's men were pinned against the river. They may well have been annihilated had General Johnston not been mortally wounded at the peak of the battle; his second in command called off the attack. Grant and a brilliant general from Ohio, William Tecumseh Sherman, rallied their troops. Reinforcements arrived that night during a torrential rainstorm, and the next day Grant took the offensive. The Confederates glumly withdrew to Corinth, leaving the Union army too battered to pursue. Throughout the Civil War winning armies would fail to pursue their retreating foe, thus allowing the wounded opponent to slip away and fight again.

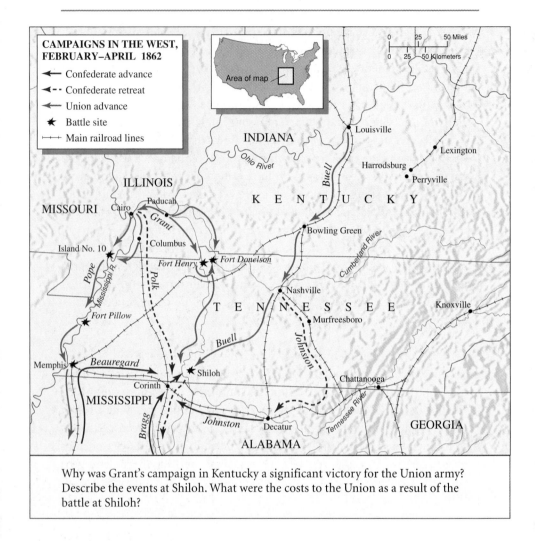

CAMPAIGNS IN THE WEST,
FEBRUARY–APRIL 1862

← Confederate advance
◄-- Confederate retreat
← Union advance
★ Battle site
+--+ Main railroad lines

Why was Grant's campaign in Kentucky a significant victory for the Union army?
Describe the events at Shiloh. What were the costs to the Union as a result of the
battle at Shiloh?

Shiloh, a Hebrew word meaning "Place of Peace," was the costliest battle
in American history up to that point, although worse was to come. Combined casualties of nearly 20,000 exceeded the total dead and wounded of
the Revolution, the War of 1812, and the Mexican War. After Shiloh, Confederate and Union leaders realized there would not be a quick end to the war.
Moreover, after this battle the Union lost for a while the leadership of its
finest general. Grant had blundered badly. Some critics charged that he had
been drinking and called upon Lincoln to replace him. But the president,
faced with the dithering of his other generals (especially George McClellan

in the eastern theater), declined: "I can't spare this man; he fights." Grant's superior, General Henry Halleck, was not as forgiving, however. He relieved Grant of his command for several months, and as a result the Union thrust southward ground to a halt.

MCCLELLAN'S PENINSULAR CAMPAIGN   The eastern theater remained fairly quiet for nine months after Bull Run. After the Union defeat, Lincoln had replaced McDowell with the brilliant if theatrical and hesitant general George B. McClellan, Stonewall Jackson's classmate at West Point. As head of the Army of the Potomac, McClellan instituted a rigid training regimen, determined to build a powerful force that would be ready for its next battle. When General Winfield Scott retired in November 1861, McClellan became general in chief. On the surface, McClellan exuded confidence and poise, but his innate caution would prove crippling. Fearing failure, McClellan procrastinated as long as possible to avoid meeting the enemy in battle. After nine months of agonizing preparation, Lincoln and much of the public had grown impatient. The exasperated president finally ordered McClellan to begin moving by Washington's Birthday, February 22, 1862. McClellan brashly predicted, "I will be in Richmond in ten days."

In mid-March 1862, McClellan's army finally embarked, and before the end of May his advance units sighted the church steeples in Richmond. Thousands fled the city in panic, and President Jefferson Davis sent his family to a safe haven. But McClellan failed to capitalize on his situation. On May 31 the Confederate general Joseph E. Johnston struck at the Union forces, which were isolated by floodwaters on the south bank of the Chickahominy River. In the Battle of Seven Pines (Fair Oaks), only the arrival of reinforcements prevented a disastrous Union defeat. Both sides took heavy casualties, and Johnston was severely wounded.

At this point the fifty-five-year-old Robert E. Lee assumed command of the Army of Northern Virginia, changing the course of the war. Tall, erect, and broad shouldered, Lee was a slashing, daring leader. Unlike Johnston he enjoyed Jefferson Davis's trust and assembled a galaxy of superb field commanders: Stonewall Jackson, James Longstreet, D. H. Hill, Ambrose P. Hill, and J.E.B. Stuart.

Once in command, Lee assaulted the Union forces east of Richmond on June 26, 1862. But heavy losses prevented the Confederates from sustaining their momentum. Lee launched a final desperate attack at Malvern Hill (July 1), where the Confederates were riddled by artillery. As D. H. Hill observed, "It was not war, it was murder." This week of intense fighting, lumped together as the Seven Days Battles, failed to dislodge the Union forces.

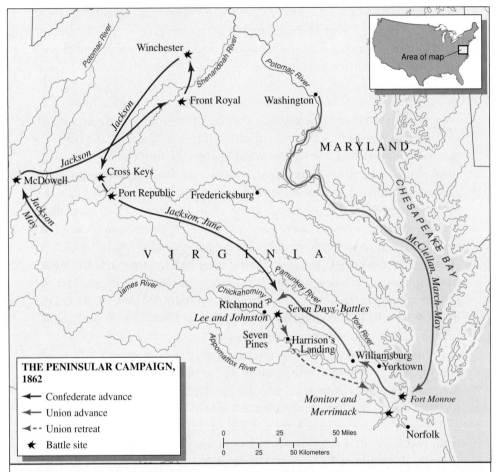

THE PENINSULAR CAMPAIGN, 1862

← Confederate advance
← Union advance
◄-- Union retreat
✹ Battle site

What was McClellan's strategy for attacking Richmond? How did Jackson divert the attention of the Union army? Why did Lincoln demote McClellan after the Peninsular campaigns?

On July 9 Lincoln visited the front, where McClellan lectured him on the correct strategy. Such insubordination was ample reason to remove the cocky general, but Lincoln recognized that doing so would demoralize the soldiers, who were still intensely loyal to McClellan. Instead, Lincoln returned to Washington and on July 11 called Henry Halleck from the west to take charge as general in chief, a post that McClellan had temporarily vacated. Thus began what would become Lincoln's frustrating search for a capable and consistent military leader.

SECOND BULL RUN   Lincoln and Halleck ordered McClellan to join forces with the bombastic John Pope for a new assault against Richmond from the north. Lee decided to attack Pope's army before the Union forces could be joined. At Cedar Mountain, Stonewall Jackson pushed back an advance party of Union troops and then seized supplies and destroyed the Union supply base at Manassas Junction.

At the Second Battle of Bull Run (or Manassas), fought on almost the same site as the earlier battle, the Confederates thoroughly confused Pope. J.E.B. Stuart's horsemen raided his headquarters, taking Pope's dress uniform and strategy book, which outlined the position of his units. Pope then exhausted his own men as he frantically tried to find the elusive Jackson. By the time they made contact with what they thought were only Jackson's forces, Lee's main army had joined in.

The trap was baited, and the Union army was lured in. On August 30, 1862, as Pope's troops engaged Jackson's line, James Longstreet's corps of 30,000 Confederates, screaming the Rebel yell "like demons emerging from the earth," drove the Union forces from the field. One New York regiment lost 124 of its 490 men, the highest percentage of deaths in any battle of the war. In the next few days the whipped Union forces pulled back to the fortifications around Washington, where McClellan once again took command and reorganized. He displayed his unflagging egotism in a letter to his wife: "Again I have been called upon to save the country." The disgraced Pope was dispatched to Minnesota to fight in the Indian wars.

ANTIETAM   Still on the offensive, Lee determined to move the battlefield out of the South and perhaps thereby gain foreign recognition of the Confederacy as a new nation. In September 1862 he led his troops into western Maryland and headed for Pennsylvania. As luck would have it, however, Lee's bold strategy was uncovered when a Union soldier picked up a bundle of cigars and discovered a secret order from Lee wrapped around them. The paper revealed that Lee had again divided his army, sending Jackson off to take Harpers Ferry, West Virginia.

McClellan boasted upon seeing the captured document, "Here is a paper with which, if I cannot whip Bobby Lee, I will be willing to go home." But instead of leaping at his unexpected opportunity, he delayed for sixteen crucial hours, still worried—as always—about enemy strength, and Lee was thereby able to reassemble most of his tired army behind Antietam Creek. Still, McClellan was optimistic, and Lincoln, too, relished the chance for a truly decisive blow. "God bless you and all with you," he wired McClellan. "Destroy the rebel army if possible."

On September 17, 1862, McClellan's army attacked Confederate forces near Sharpsburg, Maryland, along Antietam Creek, and the furious Battle of Antietam (Sharpsburg) began. Just as the Confederate lines seemed ready to break, Ambrose P. Hill's division arrived from Harpers Ferry, having marched sixteen miles to the battlefield. Bone weary and foot sore, they nevertheless plunged immediately into the fray, battering the Union's left flank. Still outnumbered more than two to one, the Confederates forced a standoff in the most costly day of the Civil War, a day participants thought would never end.

In the late afternoon, McClellan backed off, letting Lee's army slip south across the Potomac River. Lincoln was disgusted by McClellan's failure to follow up and gain a truly decisive victory, and he fired off a tart message to the general: "I have just read your dispatch about sore-tongued and fatigued horses. Will you pardon me for asking what the horses of your army have done . . . that fatigues anything?" Later the president sent his commander a one-sentence letter: "If you don't want to use the army, I should like to borrow it for a while." Failing to receive a satisfactory answer, Lincoln removed McClellan from command and assigned him to recruiting duty in New Jersey. Never again would he command troops.

FREDERICKSBURG   The Battle of Antietam was the turning point in the war. It revived sagging northern morale, emboldened Abraham Lincoln to issue the Emancipation Proclamation, freeing all slaves in the Confederate states, and dashed the Confederacy's hopes of foreign recognition and aid. But the war was far from over. In his search for a fighting general, Lincoln now made the worst choice of all. He turned to Ambrose E. Burnside, a handsome, personable, modest figure who had twice before turned down the job on the grounds that he felt unfit for so large a command.

Yet if the White House wanted him to fight, Burnside would fight, even in the face of the oncoming winter. On a cold December 13, 1862, he sent his men across the icy Rappahannock River to face Lee's forces who were well entrenched behind a stone wall and on high ground just west of Fredericksburg, Virginia. Blessed with a clear field of fire, Confederate artillery and muskets chewed up the valorous blue ranks as they crossed a mile of open bottomland outside the town. Six times the courageous but suicidal Union assaults melted under the murderous fire coming from protected Confederate positions above and below them. It was, as a Union general said, "a great slaughter pen." The scene was both awful and awe inspiring, prompting Lee to remark, "It is well that war is so terrible—we should grow too fond of it." After seeing his men suffer more than 12,000 casualties, twice as many as the Confederates, Burnside wept as he gave the order to withdraw.

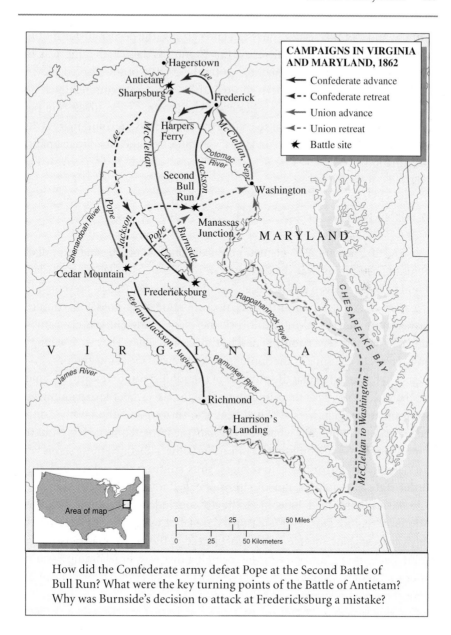

CAMPAIGNS IN VIRGINIA AND MARYLAND, 1862

◀—— Confederate advance
◀- - Confederate retreat
◀—— Union advance
◀- - Union retreat
★ Battle site

How did the Confederate army defeat Pope at the Second Battle of Bull Run? What were the key turning points of the Battle of Antietam? Why was Burnside's decision to attack at Fredericksburg a mistake?

The year 1862 ended with forces in the East deadlocked and the Union advance in the West stalled since midyear. Union morale plummeted: northern Democrats were calling for a negotiated peace, while the so-called Radical Republicans were pushing Lincoln to prosecute the war even more forcefully. Several questioned the president's competence.

In the midst of this second-guessing and carping, the deeper currents of the war were in fact turning in favor of the Union: in the lengthening war the Union's superior resources began to tell on the morale of the Confederacy. In both the eastern and the western theaters the Confederate counterattack had been repulsed. And while the armies clashed, Lincoln, by the stroke of a pen, changed the conflict from a war to restore the Union into a revolutionary struggle for the abolition of slavery: on January 1, 1863, he signed the Emancipation Proclamation.

EMANCIPATION

The Emancipation Proclamation was the product of long and painful deliberation, as opinion was divided even in the North as to whether all slaves should be freed. A deep-seated racial prejudice in the North had prevented the formation of a unified position. While most abolitionists favored both complete emancipation and social integration of the races, many anti-slavery activists wanted to prohibit slavery only in new territories and states. They were willing to allow slavery to continue in the South in order to avoid racial integration.

Lincoln had insisted that the purpose of the conflict was to restore the Union and that he did not have the authority to free the slaves. Yet the expanding war forced the issue. Fugitive slaves had begun to turn up in Union army camps, and generals did not know whether to declare them free. Some generals put the "contrabands" to work building fortifications; others liberated those slaves who had been held by Confederate owners, thus running the risk of upsetting border-state slaveholders. Lincoln himself edged toward emancipation.

As the war continued, Lincoln eventually concluded that complete emancipation was required for several reasons: slave labor was bolstering the Confederate cause, sagging morale in the North needed the boost of a transcendent moral ideal, and public opinion was swinging that way. Proclaiming a war on slavery, moreover, would end forever any chance that France or Britain would support the Confederacy.

The time to act came after the Battle of Antietam. On September 22, 1862, Lincoln issued a preliminary Emancipation Proclamation, warning that on January 1, 1863, all slaves in Confederate states or in areas still under active rebellion would be "thenceforward and forever free." The Emancipation Proclamation, with few exceptions, freed only those slaves still under Confederate control, as cynics noted then and later. But critics missed a point that slaves readily grasped. "In a document proclaiming liberty," wrote an African-Americans historian, "the unfree never bother to read the fine print."

Two Views of the Emancipation Proclamation

The Union view (top) shows a thoughtful Lincoln composing the proclamation, the Constitution and the Holy Bible in his lap. The Confederate view (bottom) shows a demented Lincoln, his foot on the Constitution and his inkwell held by the devil.

BLACKS IN THE MILITARY Lincoln's Emancipation Proclamation reaffirmed the policy that African Americans could enroll in the armed services and sparked efforts to organize all-black military units. The War Department authorized general recruitment of blacks all over the country, thus making more concrete Lincoln's transformation of a war to preserve the Union into a revolution to overthrow the social, economic, and racial status quo in the South. The first challenge for black troops, however, was to overcome embedded racial fears of northern whites and to prove themselves in battle. By mid-1863 African-American soldiers were finally involved in significant combat in both the eastern and western theaters. Lincoln reported that several of his commanders believed that "the use of colored troops constitutes the heaviest blow yet dealt to the rebels."

Altogether almost 180,000 African Americans served in the Union army, around 10 percent of the total. Some 38,000 gave their lives. Blacks accounted for about one fourth of all enlistments in the navy, and of those almost 3,000 died. As the war entered its final months, freedom emerged more fully as a legal reality. The Thirteenth Amendment, which abolished slavery, was ratified by three fourths of the reunited states and became part of the Constitution on December 18, 1865, thus removing any lingering doubts about the legality of emancipation. By then, in fact, slavery remained only in the border states of Kentucky and Delaware.

WOMEN AND THE WAR

While breaking the bonds of slavery, the Civil War also loosened traditional restraints on female activity. Women on both sides played prominent roles in the conflict. Initially the call to arms revived heroic images of female self-sacrifice and domesticity. Women in the North and the South sewed uniforms, composed uplifting poems and songs, and raised money and supplies. Thousands of northern women worked with the U.S. Sanitary Commission, which organized medical relief and other services for soldiers. Others supported the freedmen's aid movement to help impoverished freed slaves.

In the North alone some 20,000 women served as nurses or other health-related volunteers. The most famous nurses were Dorothea Dix and Clara Barton, both untiring volunteers in service to the wounded and dying. Dix, the veteran reformer of the nation's insane asylums, became the Union army's first superintendent of women nurses. Barton was a schoolteacher and then one of the nation's first female patent clerks, but she remained frustrated by her desire to find "something to do that *was* something." She discovered fulfilling work at last as a nurse in the Civil War. Instead of accepting an assignment to a general hospital, she followed the troops on her own, working in makeshift field hospitals. At Antietam she came so close to the fighting that as she worked on a wounded soldier, a Confederate bullet ripped through the sleeve of her dress and killed the man.

The departure of hundreds of thousands of men for the battlefield forced women to assume the public and private roles the men left behind. In many southern towns and counties the home front became a world of white women, children, and slaves. But not all women willingly accepted the new roles required by the war. Many among the slaveholding elite found themselves woefully unprepared: they could not cook, sew, or knit, and they balked at the idea of daily chores.

Women in the North and the South found themselves farmers or plantation managers, clerks, munitions-plant workers, and schoolteachers. Some 400 women disguised themselves as men and fought in the war; dozens served as spies; others traveled with the armies, cooking meals and writing letters, and assisting with amputations. The number of widows, spinsters, and orphans mushroomed. Many bereaved women on both sides came to look on the war with what the poet Emily Dickinson called a "chastened stare."

GOVERNMENT DURING THE WAR

Freeing 4 million slaves and loosening the restraints on female activity constituted a monumental social and economic revolution. But an even broader revolution developed as political power shifted from South to North. Before the war southern congressmen exercised a great deal of influence. Once the secessionists had abandoned Congress to the Republicans, however, dramatic change occurred. Without congressional opposition from the South, Republicans were able to pass a new protective tariff, approve a transcontinental railroad that would run through Omaha, Nebraska, to Sacramento, California, and enact a homestead act, which granted free homesteads of 160 acres to settlers who occupied the land for five years—all acts that had been stalled by sectional controversy and were adopted before the end of 1862. That year also saw the passage of the Morrill Land Grant

Act, which provided federal aid to state colleges focused on the "agricultural and mechanic arts." The National Banking Act, which created a uniform system of banking and bank-note currency, followed in 1863 and helped the Union address a critical problem: how to finance the war.

UNION FINANCES   Congress had three options for solving the problem of financing the war: raising taxes, printing paper money, and borrowing. The taxes came chiefly in the form of the Morrill Tariff and excise taxes on manufacturers and nearly every profession. A butcher, for example, had to pay 30¢ for every head of beef he slaughtered, 10¢ for every hog, 5¢ for every sheep. An income tax rounded out the revenue measures.

But federal tax revenues trickled in so slowly that Congress in 1862 ordered the printing of paper money. Eventually $450 million in greenbacks was printed, enough to pay the bills without unleashing the kind of runaway inflation that burdened the Confederacy after Jefferson Davis allowed the unlimited issue of paper money. The congressional decision to allow the Treasury to print paper money was a profoundly important development for the U.S. economy, then and since. Unlike previous paper currencies issued by local banks, the federal greenbacks could not be exchanged for gold or silver. Instead, their value relied upon public trust in the government. Many bankers were outraged by the advent of the greenbacks. "Gold and silver are the only true measure of value," one financier declared. "These metals were prepared by the Almighty." But the crisis of the Union and the desperate need to finance the expanding war demanded such a solution.

Still, paper money and taxes provided only about two thirds of the money that financed the war. The rest came chiefly from the sale of bonds. A Philadelphia banker named Jay Cooke mobilized a nationwide network of agents and propaganda for the sale of government war bonds. It worked well, and over $2 billion was raised in the process.

CONFEDERATE FINANCES   Confederate finances were a disaster from the start. Tariffs were tried, but imports were low and therefore raised little revenue. In 1863 the Confederate Congress passed a measure that, like the Union's excises, taxed nearly everything. A 10 percent tax on all agricultural products did more to outrage farmers and planters than to supply the army. Enforcement was so lax and evasion so easy that the taxes produced only negligible income. The last resort, printing paper money, was in fact resorted to early. Beginning in 1861, the new Confederate government began an extended inflationary binge. Altogether the Confederacy turned out more than $1 billion in paper money, creating a dramatic spike in prices. By 1864 a wild turkey sold in a Richmond market for $100, flour went for $425 a barrel, and bacon for $10 a pound. Those living on a fixed income were caught in a merciless inflationary squeeze.

UNION POLITICS AND CIVIL LIBERTIES   On the home fronts during the Civil War, there was no moratorium on partisan politics, northern or southern. Within his own party, Lincoln faced a Radical wing composed mainly of prewar abolitionists. The so-called Radical Republicans formed a Joint Committee on the Conduct of the War, which increasingly pressured Lincoln to emancipate the slaves, confiscate southern plantations, and prosecute the war more vigorously. The majority of Republicans, however, supported the president, and the party was virtually united on economic matters.

The Democratic party suffered the loss of its southern wing as well as the death of its leader, Stephen A. Douglas, in June 1861. By and large northern Democrats supported a war for the Union "as it was" before 1860, giving reluctant support to Lincoln's policies but opposing wartime constraints on civil liberties and the new economic legislation. "War Democrats," such as Senator Andrew Johnson from Tennessee and Secretary of War Edwin Stanton, fully supported Lincoln's policies, while a peace wing of the party preferred a negotiated end to the fighting, even if that meant risking the Union. An extreme fringe among the peace Democrats flirted with outright disloyalty. The Copperheads, as they were called, were strongest in Ohio, Indiana, and Illinois, states with many transplanted southerners, some of whom were pro-Confederate.

Such open sympathy for the enemy spurred Lincoln to crack down hard. Early in the war he assumed certain emergency powers, such as the suspension of the writ of habeas corpus, which guarantees arrested citizens a speedy hearing. When critics charged that this violated the Constitution, Lincoln's congressional supporters pushed through the Habeas Corpus Act of 1863, which authorized the suspension of the writ. Some 14,000 Confederate sympathizers were arrested under the terms of the act.

In the midterm elections of 1862, the Democrats exploited growing warweariness and resentment of Lincoln's war measures to gain a startling recovery, though not control of Congress. When asked his reaction to the election results, Lincoln replied that he felt somewhat "like the boy in Kentucky who stubbed his toe while running to see his sweetheart. The boy said he was too big to cry, and far too badly hurt to laugh." In fact the political climate left Lincoln increasingly perplexed as time passed.

At their 1864 national convention the Democrats called for an immediate armistice and named General George McClellan as their candidate, but he distanced himself from the peace platform by declaring that the two sides must agree on the terms of reunion before the fighting could stop. Radical Republicans, who still regarded Lincoln as too soft on the traitorous southerners, tried to thwart his renomination, but Lincoln outmaneuvered them at every turn. In a shrewd move he named as his vice-presidential running mate Andrew Johnson, a "war Democrat" from Tennessee, and called the two of them the National Union ticket to minimize partisanship. As the war ground on through 1864, with Grant's army taking heavy losses in Virginia, Lincoln fully expected to lose the election, but key military victories in August and September turned the tide. McClellan carried only New Jersey, Delaware, and Kentucky.

Abraham's Dream

This cartoon depicts Lincoln having a nightmare about the election of 1864. Lady Liberty brandishes the severed head of a black man at the door of the White House as General McClellan walks up the steps and Lincoln runs away.

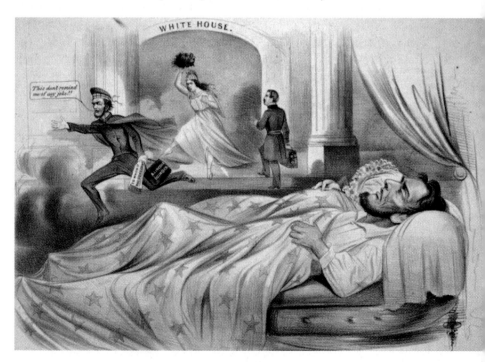

CONFEDERATE POLITICS   Unlike Lincoln, Jefferson Davis never had to face a presidential contest. He and his vice president, Alexander Stephens, were elected for a six-year term. But discontent flourished in the South as food grew scarce and prices skyrocketed. Starving women set off riots from Richmond to Mobile. A bread riot in Richmond in 1863, for example, ended only when Jefferson Davis threatened to shoot the demonstrators. After the Confederate congressional elections of 1863, about one third of the legislators were openly hostile toward the Davis administration. Although parties as such did not figure in the elections, it was noteworthy that many ex-Whigs and other opponents of secession were chosen.

Davis, like Lincoln, had to contend with dissenters. Especially troublesome were supporters of states' rights and secession who steadfastly opposed the centralizing tendencies of the Confederate government in Richmond. Georgia and North Carolina were strongholds of such sentiment. The states' rights champions challenged, among other things, the legality of conscription, taxes on farm produce, and above all the suspension of habeas corpus. Vice President Alexander Stephens himself carried on a running battle with Davis, accusing the president of trying to establish a "military despotism."

The internal bickering did not alone cause the Confederacy's defeat, but it certainly contributed to it. Whereas Lincoln was the consummate pragmatist, Davis was a brittle dogmatist with a waspish temper. Once he made a decision, nothing could change his mind. Nor could Davis ever admit a mistake. Such a personality was ill suited to serve as the chief executive of an infant nation.

THE CIVIL WAR AND THE ENVIRONMENT   Wars not only kill and maim people; they also transform the environment. While almost 750,000 soldiers died of wounds, disease, or accidents, equally appalling numbers of animals, especially horses and mules but also cattle and pigs, were killed in battle or for food. During the final year of the war, nearly 500 horses a day died of shell fire, starvation, overwork, or disease. Pork was the staple of the southern diet before the Civil War, and the region produced enough hogs to feed itself. After the war, however, the southern hog population was so devastated that the region had to import pigs and pork from the Midwest. Because midwestern hogs were bred for weight, their high fat content contributed to higher rates of heart disease and stroke in the postwar South.

Fighting during the Civil War also destroyed much of the Southern landscape. In 1864 a Confederate major wrote that near Chickamauga, Georgia,

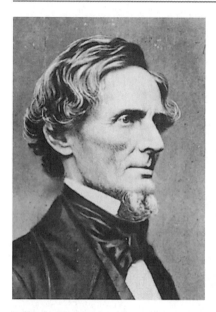

Jefferson Davis

President of the Confederacy.

just south of Chattanooga, Tennessee, the road was "covered with the skeletons of horses, and every tree bears the mark of battle. Many strong trunks were broken down by artillery fire." Hundreds of bridges and levees were also destroyed during the war, as were endless miles of fences, which foraging soldiers used for firewood. The loss of levees caused massive flooding; the loss of fencing meant that much of the postwar South would revert to open-range grazing. Craters gouged out by cannonballs pockmarked the landscape and provided breeding grounds for mosquitoes. The loss of so many animals meant that the mosquitoes focused on humans for their blood meal, thus increasing the spread of malaria. Hundreds of miles of trenches dug for military defense scarred the land and accelerated erosion. All told, the environment was as much a victim of the warfare as were the soldiers, and it would take years to heal nature's wounds across the South.

THE FALTERING CONFEDERACY

After the Union disaster at Fredericksburg, Lincoln's frustrating search for a capable general turned to one of Burnside's disgruntled lieutenants, Joseph Hooker, a handsome, ruddy-faced, hard-drinking character whose pugnacity had earned him the nickname Fighting Joe. But he was no more able to deliver the goods than Burnside.

CHANCELLORSVILLE   With a force of 130,000 men, the largest Union army yet gathered, and a brilliant plan, Hooker failed his leadership test at Chancellorsville, Virginia, on May 1–5, 1863. Robert E. Lee, with perhaps half that number of troops, staged a textbook classic of daring and maneuver. Hooker's plan was to leave his base, opposite Fredericksburg, on a sweeping movement upstream across the Rappahannock and Rapidan rivers and flank Lee's position. A large diversionary force was to cross the Rappahannock below the town. Initially all went well, but Lee sniffed out the ruse. He moved his main force to meet Hooker and dispatched J.E.B. Stuart's cavalry to disrupt the Union lines of communication. Hooker suddenly lost sight of his opponent and panicked when rebel skirmishers fired on his advance columns. He then ordered his troops to pull back to the Chancellorsville crossroads. Lee quickly took advantage of Hooker's failure of nerve. He divided his army again, sending Stonewall Jackson with more than half the men on a long march to hit the enemy's exposed right flank.

On May 2 Jackson surprised Hooker's right flank at the edge of a densely wooded area called the Wilderness. The Confederates slammed into the Union lines with such furor that the defenders panicked and ran. The thick undergrowth made troop movements more chaotic than usual, and the fighting died out in confusion as darkness fell. The next day was Lee's, however, as his troops forced Hooker's army to recross the Rappahannock. It was the peak of Lee's career, but Chancellorsville was his last significant victory—and his costliest: the South lost 1,600 soldiers, among them Stonewall Jackson, mistakenly shot by his own men in the confused fighting. "I have lost my right arm," lamented Lee.

VICKSBURG   While Lee's army held the Union forces at bay in the East, Ulysses Grant, his command now restored, had been groping his way down the Mississippi River toward the Confederate stronghold at Vicksburg, in western Mississippi. If Union forces could gain control of the Mississippi River, they could split the Confederacy in two. For months, Grant tried to discover a way to penetrate Vicksburg's heavily fortified defenses. The terrain complicated his task: Vicksburg was surrounded by bayous and marshes that made travel and resupply almost impossible. Torrential rains and widespread disease also hampered the army's movements. So in the spring of 1863, Grant finally decided to leave his supply base and live off the land. His soldiers crossed over to Louisiana, took a roundabout route to Jackson, Mississippi, where they routed the Confederates, and headed back to Vicksburg. The Union army pinned down 30,000 Confederates in Vicksburg, and Grant resolved to starve them out.

GETTYSBURG   The plight of besieged Vicksburg put the Confederate high command in a quandary, in response to which Lee proposed a diversion. If he could win a great victory on northern soil, he might do more than just relieve the pressure on Vicksburg; he might bring an end to the war. In June 1863, therefore, he moved his forces into the Shenandoah Valley and again headed north across Maryland. Neither side chose Gettysburg, Pennsylvania,

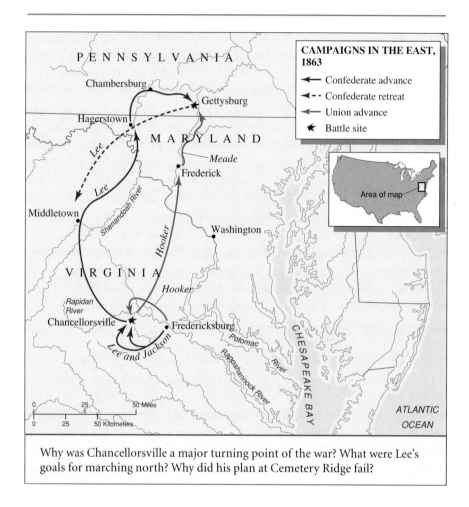

CAMPAIGNS IN THE EAST, 1863

← Confederate advance
◄- - Confederate retreat
← Union advance
★ Battle site

Area of map

Why was Chancellorsville a major turning point of the war? What were Lee's goals for marching north? Why did his plan at Cemetery Ridge fail?

as the site for the war's climactic battle. A Confederate foraging party entered the town in search of shoes and encountered units of Union cavalry on June 30, 1863. The main forces then quickly converged there.

On July 1, a hot, steamy day, the Confederates pushed the Union soldiers out of the town, but into stronger positions on high ground to the south. The new Union commander, George Meade, hastened reinforcements to the new lines along the heights. On July 2 Confederates launched furious assaults at the extreme flanks of Meade's army. The Union forces, who outnumbered their attackers almost two to one, fought just as bravely—and the assaults were repulsed.

The next day, Lee staked everything on a final attack on the Union center at Cemetery Ridge. At about two in the afternoon, General George Pickett's

15,000 Confederate troops emerged from the woods west of Cemetery Ridge and began their advance across rising open ground commanded by Union artillery. "Pickett's charge" was hopeless. At a distance of 700 yards, the Union artillery homed in on the advancing Virginians. Those who avoided the canister and grapeshot were devastated by a wall of musket fire. At the head of Pickett's division were the University Greys, thirty-one college students from Mississippi. Within an hour of their assault, every one of them was killed or wounded. As he watched the few survivers returning from the bloody field, General Lee muttered, "All this has been my fault."

With nothing left to do but retreat, Lee's dejected and mangled army began to slog south in a driving rain that "washed the blood from the grass." They left one third of their number behind on the ground, having had failed in all their purposes, not the least being to relieve the pressure on Vicksburg. On that same day, July 4, the entire Confederate garrison at Vicksburg surrendered after a forty-seven-day siege. The Confederacy was now irrevocably split. Had Meade aggressively pursued Lee, he might have delivered the final blow before the Rebels could get back across the flooded Potomac River, but again an army failed to capitalize on its advantage.

After the furious fighting at Gettysburg had ended, a group of northern states funded a military cemetery for the 6,000 soldiers killed in the battle. On

Harvest of Death

Timothy H. O'Sullivan's grim photograph of the dead at Gettysburg.

November 19,1863, the new cemetery was officially dedicated. In his brief remarks, since known as the Gettysburg Address, President Lincoln eloquently expressed the pain and sorrow of the brutal civil war. The prolonged conflict was testing whether a nation "dedicated to the proposition that all men are created equal . . . can long endure." Lincoln declared that all Americans must ensure that the "honored dead" had not "died in vain." In stirring words that continue to inspire, Lincoln predicted that "this nation, under God, shall have a new birth of freedom—and that government of the people, by the people, and for the people, shall not perish from the earth."

CHATTANOOGA   The third great Union victory of 1863 occurred in fighting around Chattanooga, the railhead of eastern Tennessee and gateway to northern Georgia. On September 9 a Union army led by General William Rosecrans took Chattanooga and then rashly pursued General Braxton Bragg's forces into Georgia, where the two sides clashed at Chickamauga (an old Cherokee word ironically meaning "River of Death"). The battle (September 19–20) had the makings of a Union disaster because it was one of the few times the Confederates had a numerical advantage (about 70,000 to 56,000). On the second day, Bragg smashed the Union's right flank, and only the stubborn stand on the left under the Virginia Unionist George H. Thomas (thenceforth known as the Rock of Chickamauga) prevented a rout. The battered Union forces fell back to Chattanooga while Bragg cut the railroad and held the city virtually under siege.

Rosecrans seemed stunned and immobilized, but Lincoln urged him to hang on: "If we can hold Chattanooga, and East Tennessee, I think rebellion must dwindle and die." The president then dispatched reinforcements. General Grant, given overall command of the western theater on October 16, replaced Rosecrans with George Thomas. On November 24 the Union forces broke out of the city and captured Lookout Mountain in what was mainly a feat of mountaineering. The next day, Grant ordered Thomas's troops forward to positions at the foot of Missionary Ridge. But the men did not stop there. Still fuming because the Confederates had jeered them at Chickamauga, they charged toward the crest without orders. One of Thomas's aides explained to Grant, "When those fellows get started all hell can't stop them." The attackers could have been decimated, but the Confederates were unable to lower their big guns enough to hit the scrambling Yankees, and despite Bragg's "cursing like a sailor," his men fled as Thomas's troops reached the summit.

After the Confederate defeat, as the Union forces consolidated their control of East Tennessee, already full of Unionist sympathizers, Jefferson Davis reluctantly replaced Bragg with Joseph Johnston. Lincoln, on the other hand, had finally found the general for whom he had been searching for almost three years. In March 1864 Ulysses S. Grant was brought to Washington and made general in chief.

THE CONFEDERACY'S DEFEAT

During the winter of 1863–1864, Confederates began to despair of victory. A War Department official in Richmond reported in his diary a spreading "sense of hopelessness." At the same time, Mary Chesnut of South Carolina reported that "gloom and despondency hang like a pall everywhere." Union leaders, sensing the momentum swinging their way, stepped up their pressure on Confederate forces.

The Union's main targets now were Lee's army in Virginia and General Joseph Johnston's forces in Georgia. Grant personally would accompany George Meade, who retained direct command over the Army of the Potomac; operations in the West were entrusted to Grant's longtime lieutenant, William T. Sherman. Grant brought with him a new strategy against Lee. Where his predecessors had hoped for the climactic single battle, he opted for a war of attrition. He would attack, attack, attack, keeping the pressure on the Confederates, grinding down their numbers and taking away their initiative and their will to fight. Victory, he had decided, would come to the side "which never counted its dead." Grant ordered his commanders to wage total war, confiscating or destroying civilian property of use to the Confederate war effort. It was a brutal, costly, but effective plan.

GRANT'S PURSUIT OF LEE   In May 1864 Grant's Army of the Potomac, numbering about 115,000 to Lee's 65,000, moved south across the Rappahannock River into the Wilderness of eastern Virginia, where Hooker had come to grief in the Battle of Chancellorsville. In the nightmarish Battle of the Wilderness (May 5–6), the armies fought blindly through the tangled brush and vines, the horror and agony of the wounded heightened by crackling brushfires. Grant's men suffered heavier casualties than Lee's, but the Confederates were running out of replacements.

Many of the officers in the Army of the Potomac were in awe of Lee. They especially feared another decisive counterattack on their flanks. When one of Grant's officers expressed concern about what Lee might do, Grant exploded:

Oh, I am heartily tired of hearing what Lee is going to do. Some of you always seem to think he is suddenly going to turn a double somersault, and

Ulysses S. Grant

At his headquarters in City Point (now Hopewell), Virginia.

land in our rear and on both our flanks at the same time. Go back to your command, and try to think what we are going to do ourselves, instead of what Lee is going to do.

Always before, Lee's adversaries had retreated to lick their wounds, but Grant slid off to the left and continued his relentless advance southward, now toward Spotsylvania Court House. "Whatever happens," he assured Lincoln, "we will not retreat."

Along the Chickahominy River the two sides clashed at Cold Harbor (June 1–3). In twenty minutes 7,000 attacking Union soldiers were killed or wounded. Many of them had predicted as much. After the failed assault, Confederates retrieved a diary from a dead Massachusetts soldier. The final entry read: "June 3, 1864, Cold Harbor, Virginia. I was killed." Battered and again repulsed, Grant soon had his men moving again, headed for Petersburg, the junction of railroads running into Richmond from the south. "I shall take no backward steps," he declared.

Lee's army dug in around the town while Grant's forces laid siege. For nine months the two armies faced each other down while Grant kept trying to break the railroad arteries that were Lee's lifeline. Grant's men were generously supplied by vessels moving up the James River, while Lee's forces, beset by hunger, cold, and desertion, wasted away in their muddy trenches. Petersburg had become Lee's prison while disasters piled up elsewhere in the Confederacy. "From the summer of 1862," wrote a Confederate veteran, "the war became a war of wholesale devastation. From the spring of 1864, it seemed to have become nearly a war of extermination."

SHERMAN'S MARCH While Grant was besieging Lee in Virginia, the battle-hardened General William T. Sherman was doggedly pursuing Joseph Johnston's army through northern Georgia, toward Atlanta. Tightly strung, profane, and plagued by fits of depression, Sherman was one of the few generals to appreciate the concept of total war. He wanted to destroy Confederate

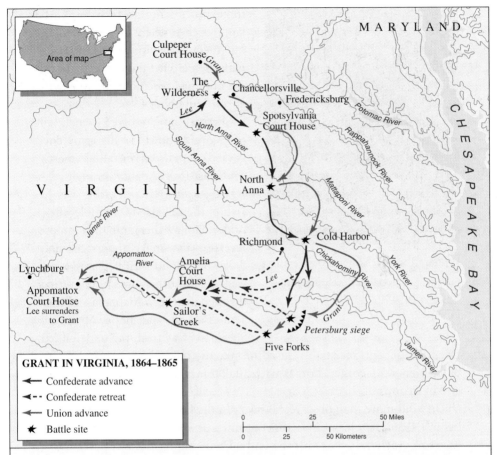

GRANT IN VIRGINIA, 1864–1865
← Confederate advance
◄-- Confederate retreat
← Union advance
★ Battle site

How were Grant's tactics in the Battle of the Wilderness different from the Union's previous encounters with Lee's army? Why did Grant have the advantage at Petersburg? How did Grant eventually force Lee to surrender?

morale as well as Confederate armies. Where Sherman loved a toe-to-toe fight, Johnston preferred retreat and evasion, determined not to risk a single life until the perfect conditions for fighting were obtained.

An impatient Jefferson Davis finally exploded at Johnston and replaced him with the towering, blond-bearded Texan John B. Hood, who did not know the meaning of retreat or evasion. As Lee once noted, Hood was "all lion, none of the fox." Having had an arm crippled by a bullet at Gettysburg and most of one leg shot off at Chickamauga, Hood had to be strapped to his horse. He was one of the most tenacious—and impetuous—fighters in the war, and during late July 1864 the army led by "the gallant Hood" struck

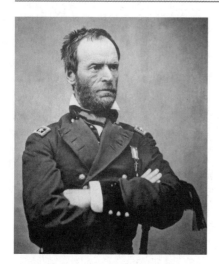

William Tecumseh Sherman

Sherman's campaign developed into a war of maneuver, but without the pitched battles of Grant's campaign.

three times from their base at Atlanta, each time fighting desperately but meeting a bloody rebuff. Sherman then circled the city and cut off the rail lines, forcing Hood to evacuate on September 1.

Sherman now resolved to make all of Georgia "howl" as his army embarked on its devastating march southeast from Atlanta through central Georgia. His intention was to "whip the rebels, to humble their pride, to follow them into their inmost recesses, and make them fear and dread us." Hood's Confederate army went in the other direction, cutting through northern Alabama and into Tennessee in the hope of luring Sherman away from the undefended Deep South. But Sherman refused to take the bait, although he did dispatch General George Thomas with 30,000 men to keep watch on Hood and his troops.

They did more than observe, however. In the Battle of Franklin (November 30), Hood sent his army across two miles of open Tennessee ground. Six waves of gray crashed against the entrenched Union lines but never broke through. A month later, on December 27, Hood suffered another devastating defeat, at Nashville, that effectively ended Confederate activity in Tennessee.

During all this Sherman and the main Union force were marching triumphantly through Georgia, waging war against the enemy's resources and will to resist. "War is war," Sherman bluntly declared, "not a popularity contest." On November 15, 1864, his men burned much of Atlanta and then spread out over a front twenty to sixty miles wide and headed southeast living off the land and destroying any crops, livestock, or supplies that might serve Confederate forces. Bands of stragglers and deserters from both armies joined in looting along the flanks.

When Sherman's army approached Savannah, Georgia, a month later, a swath of desolation 250 miles long lay behind them. Sherman's purpose was clear: he would keep the pressure on the Confederates "until they are not only ruined, exhausted, but humbled in pride and spirit." On December 21 Sherman rode into Savannah, and three days later he offered the city as a

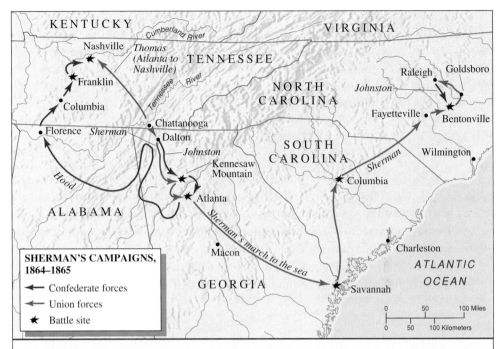

SHERMAN'S CAMPAIGNS, 1864–1865

← Confederate forces

← Union forces

★ Battle site

What was Sherman's goal as he marched across Georgia? How much damage did Sherman do in Georgia and South Carolina? How did this affect the Confederate war effort?

Christmas gift to Lincoln. But Sherman paused only long enough to resupply his forces, who then moved on that "hell-hole of secession," South Carolina. There his men wrought even greater destruction. More than a dozen towns were torched, including the state capital of Columbia, which was captured on February 17, 1865. That same day the Confederates abandoned Charleston and headed north to join an army that Joseph Johnston was desperately trying to form.

During the late winter and early spring of 1865, the Confederacy found itself besieged. Defeat was in the air. Some Rebel leaders argued that it was time to negotiate a peace settlement. Confederate secretary of war John C. Breckinridge, the Kentuckian who had served as vice president under James Buchanan and had run for president in 1860, urged Robert E. Lee to negotiate an honorable end to the war. "This has been a magnificent epic," he said. "In God's name, let it not terminate in a farce." But Jefferson Davis dismissed any talk of surrender. If the Confederate armies should be defeated, he wanted the soldiers to disperse and fight a guerrilla war. "The war came and now it must go on," he stubbornly insisted, "till the last man of this generation falls in his tracks, and his children seize his musket and fight our battle."

While Confederate forces made their last stands, Abraham Lincoln prepared for his second term as president. He was the first president since Andrew Jackson to have been reelected. The weary commander in chief had weathered constant criticism during his first term, but with the war nearing its end, Lincoln now garnered deserved praise. The *Chicago Tribune* observed that the president "has slowly and steadily risen in the respect, confidence, and admiration of the people."

On March 4, 1865, amid rumors of a Confederate attempt to abduct or assassinate the president, the six-foot-four-inch, rawboned Lincoln, dressed in a black suit and stovepipe hat, his face weathered by prairie wind and political worry, delivered his brief but eloquent second inaugural address on the East Portico of the Capitol. Not 100 feet away, looking down on Lincoln from the Capitol porch, was a twenty-six-year-old actor named John Wilkes Booth, who five weeks later would kill the president in a desperate attempt to do something "heroic" for his beloved South.

The nation's capital had long before become an armed camp and a massive military hospital. Sick and wounded soldiers were scattered everywhere: in hotels, warehouses, schools, businesses, and private homes. Thousands of Confederate deserters roamed the streets. After a morning of torrential rains, the sun broke through the clouds just as Lincoln began to speak to the mud-spattered audience of some 35,000, half of whom were African Americans. While managing a terrible civil war, the president had experienced personal tragedy (the loss of a second child, a wife plagued by mental instability) and chronic depression. What kept him from unraveling was a principled pragmatism and godly foundation that endowed his life with purpose.

Lincoln's address was more sermon than speech, the reflections of a somber statesman still struggling to understand the relation between divine will and human endeavor. Rather than detailing the progress of the war effort or indulging in self-congratulatory celebration, Lincoln focused on the origins and paradoxes of the war. Slavery, he said, had "somehow" caused the war, and everyone bore some guilt for the national shame of racial injustice and its bloody expiation. Both sides had known before the fighting began that war was to be avoided at all costs, but "one of them would *make* war rather than let the nation survive; and the other would *accept* war rather than let it perish."

The weary but resolute commander in chief longed for peace. "Fondly do we hope—fervently do we pray—that this mighty scourge of war may speedily pass away." He wondered aloud why the war had lasted so long and been so brutal. "The Almighty," he acknowledged, "has His own purposes." Lincoln noted the paradoxical irony of both sides in this civil war reading the same Bible, praying to the same God, and appealing for divine support in its fight against the other. The God of Judgment, however, would not be misled or denied. If God willed that the war continue until "every drop of blood drawn with the lash, shall be paid with another drawn by the sword, as was said three thousand years ago, so still it must be said 'the judgments of the Lord are true and righteous altogether.'" After four years of escalating combat, the war had grown "incomprehensible" in its scope and horrors. Now the president, looking gaunt and tired, urged the Union forces "to finish the work we are in," bolstered with "firmness in the right insofar as God gives us to see the right."

As Lincoln looked ahead to the end of the fighting and a "just and lasting peace," he stressed the need to "bind up the nation's wounds" by exercising the Christian virtues of forgiveness and mercy. Vengeance must be avoided at all costs. Reconciliation must be pursued "with malice toward none; with charity for all." Those eight words marvelously captured Lincoln's hopes for a restored Union. His simple but powerful and profound second inaugural speech, only 700 words long, endures because it manifests the extraordinary humility and complex faith of a president too humane to be vengeful or partisan. Redemption was his goal; victory was less important than peace. The sublime majesty of Lincoln's brief speech revealed how the rigors of war had transformed and elevated him from the obscure congressman who had entered the White House in 1861. The abolitionist leader Frederick Douglass proclaimed Lincoln's second inaugural address "a sacred effort."

APPOMATTOX   During this final season of the Confederacy, Ulysses Grant kept pushing, probing, and battering General Lee's defenses around Petersburg, twenty miles south of Richmond. The Confederates were slowly starving, their trenches filled with rats and lice. Scurvy and dysentery were rampant. News of Sherman's devastating sweep through Dixie only added to the Confederates' gloom and the impulse to desert.

Under siege for almost ten months, the Confederate lines around Petersburg were becoming woefully thin, and Lee decided to sneak away to join Johnston's forces in North Carolina. In Richmond, President Davis, exhausted but still defiant, gathered what valuables he could carry and escaped by train. Torching everything of military and industrial value in Richmond, the retreating Confederate forces left the city on April 2, and the Union army entered, accompanied by Abraham Lincoln himself. Jefferson Davis would be captured in Georgia on May 10 by Union cavalry, but by then the Confederacy was already dead.

Robert E. Lee

Mathew Brady took this photograph in Richmond eleven days after Lee's surrender at Appomattox.

As Richmond lay burning, Lee pulled his shrunken army out of the trenches around nearby Petersburg with Grant's men in hot pursuit. Lee soon found his escape route cut by Union cavalry. Outnumbered six to one, surrounded, and out of food, Lee dismissed proposals to scatter his forces to wage guerrilla warfare. He instead told Grant he was prepared to surrender. Although his men shouted their willingness to keep fighting, Lee decided it was senseless to waste any more lives.

On April 9 (Palm Sunday), 1865, Lee donned a dress uniform and met the mud-spattered Grant in the parlor of Wilmer McLean's home at Appomattox Court House to tender his surrender. Grant, at Lee's request, let the Confederate officers keep their sidearms and permitted soldiers to keep their own horses and mules. Three days later the Confederate troops formed ranks for the last time as they prepared for the formal surrender. Deeply moved by the solemn splendor, Joshua Chamberlain, the Union general in charge, ordered his men to salute their foes as they paraded past. His Confederate counterpart signaled his troops to do likewise. General Chamberlain remembered that there was not a sound—no trumpets or drums, no cheers or jeers, simply "an awed stillness . . . as if it were the passing of the dead." On April 18 Johnston surrendered his forces to Sherman near Durham, North Carolina. The remaining Confederate forces surrendered during May.

A MODERN WAR

The Civil War was in many respects the first modern war. Its scope was unprecedented. One out of every twelve men served in the war, and few families were unaffected by the event. Over 630,000 men died in the conflict from wounds or disease, 50 percent more than in World War II. Because battlefield surgeons were constantly overworked and frequently lacked equipment, supplies, and knowledge, almost any stomach or head wound proved fatal, and gangrene was rampant. Of the survivors, 50,000 returned home with one or more limbs amputated. Disease, however, was the greatest threat to soldiers, killing twice as many as were lost in battle.

The Civil War was also modern in that much of the killing was distant, impersonal, and mechanical. The opposing forces used an array of new weapons and instruments of war: artillery with "rifled," or grooved, barrels for geater accuracy, repeating rifles, ironclad ships, observation balloons, and wire entanglements. Men were killed without knowing who had fired the shot that felled them.

Historians have provided conflicting assessments of the reasons for the Union victory. Some have focused on the inherent weaknesses of the Confederacy: its lack of industry, the fractious relations between the states and the central government in Richmond, poor political and military leadership, faulty coordination and communication, the burden of slavery, and the disparities in population and resources compared with those of the North. Still others have highlighted the erosion of Confederate morale in the face of chronic food shortages and horrific human losses. The debate over why the North won and the South lost the Civil War will probably never end, but as in other modern wars, firepower and manpower were essential factors. Robert E. Lee's own explanation of the Confederate defeat retains an enduring legitimacy: "After four years of arduous service marked by unsurpassed courage and fortitude, the Army of Northern Virginia has been compelled to yield to overwhelming numbers and resources."

MAKING CONNECTIONS

- Certain fiscal measures enacted during the Civil War (when southerners were not in Congress to block them) helped fuel the postwar economic growth (discussed in Chapter 20).

- The Confederacy's defeat had a tremendous impact on all dimensions of life in the South, as Chapter 19 (on the New South) demonstrates.

FURTHER READING

The best one-volume overview of the Civil War period is James M. McPherson's *Battle Cry of Freedom: The Civil War Era* (1988). A good introduction to the military events is Herman Hattaway's *Shades of Blue and Gray* (1997). The outlook and experiences of the common soldier are explored in James M. McPherson's *For Cause and Comrades: Why Men Fought in the Civil War* (1997) and Earl J. Hess's *The Union Soldier in Battle: Enduring the Ordeal of Combat* (1997).

For emphasis on the South, turn first to Gary W. Gallagher's *The Confederate War* (1997). For a sparkling account of the birth of the Rebel nation, see William C. Davis's *"A Government of Our Own": The Making of the Confederacy* (1994). The same author provides a fine biography of the Confederate president in *Jefferson Davis: The Man and His Hour* (1991). On the best Confederate commander, see John M. Taylor's *Duty Faithfully Performed: Robert E. Lee and His Critics* (2000). On the key Union generals, see Lee Kennett's *Sherman: A Soldier's Life* (2001) and Josiah Bunting III's *Ulysses S. Grant* (2004).

Analytical scholarship on the military conflict includes Joseph L. Harsh's *Confederate Tide Rising: Robert E. Lee and the Making of Southern Strategy, 1861–1862* (1998), Steven E. Woodworth's *Jefferson Davis and His Generals: The Failure of Confederate Command in the West* (1990), and Paul D. Casdorph's *Lee and Jackson: Confederate Chieftains* (1992). Lonnie R. Speer's *Portals to Hell: Military Prisons of the Civil War* (1977) details the ghastly experience of prisoners of war.

The history of the North during the war is surveyed in Philip Sphaur Paludan's *A People's Contest: The Union and Civil War, 1861–1865,* 2nd ed. (1996) and J. Matthew Gallman's *The North Fights the Civil War: The Home Front* (1994).

The central northern political figure, Abraham Lincoln, is the subject of many books. See Harry V. Jaffa's *A New Birth of Freedom: Abraham Lincoln and the Coming of the Civil War* (2000). On Lincoln's great speeches, see Ronald C. White Jr.'s *The Eloquent President: A Portrait of Lincoln through His Words* (2005). The election of 1864 is treated in John C. Waugh's *Reelecting Lincoln: The Battle of the 1864 Presidency* (1997). On Lincoln's assassination, see William Hanchett's *The Lincoln Murder Conspiracies* (1983).

Concerning specific military campaigns, see Larry J. Daniel's *Shiloh: The Battle That Changed the Civil War* (1997), Thomas Goodrich's *Black Flag: Guerrilla Warfare on the Western Border, 1861–1865* (1995), Stephen W. Sears's

To the Gates of Richmond: The Peninsula Campaign (1992), James M. McPherson's *Crossroads of Freedom: Antietam* (2002), James Lee McDonough and James Pickett Jones's *War So Terrible: Sherman and Atlanta* (1988), Robert Garth Scott's *Into the Wilderness with the Army of the Potomac* (1985), Albert Castel's *Decision in the West: The Atlanta Campaign of 1864* (1992) and Ernest B. Furgurson's *Not War but Murder: Cold Harbor, 1864* (2000). On the final weeks of the war, see William C. Davis's *An Honorable Defeat: The Last Days of the Confederate Government* (2001).

The experience of the African-American soldier is surveyed in Joseph T. Glatthaar's *Forged in Battle: The Civil War Alliance of Black Soldiers and White Officers* (1990) and Ira Berlin, Joseph P. Reidy, and Leslie S. Rowland's *Freedom's Soldiers: The Black Military Experience in the Civil War* (1998). For the African-American woman's experience, see Jacqueline Jones's *Labor of Love, Labor of Sorrow: Black Women, Work, and the Family from Slavery to the Present* (1985).

Recent gender and ethnic studies include *Divided Houses: Gender and the Civil War,* edited by Catherine Clinton and Nina Silber (1992), Drew Gilpin Faust's *Mothers of Invention: Women of the Slaveholding South in the American Civil War* (1996), George C. Rable's *Civil Wars: Women and the Crisis of Southern Nationalism* (1989), and William L. Burton's *Melting Pot Soldiers: The Union's Ethnic Regiments,* 2nd ed. (1998).

18

RECONSTRUCTION: NORTH AND SOUTH

FOCUS QUESTIONS

- What were the different approaches to Reconstruction?
- How did Congress try to reshape southern society?
- What was the role of African Americans in the early postwar years?
- What were the main issues in national politics in the 1870s?

To answer these questions and access additional review material, please visit www.wwnorton.com/studyspace.

In the spring of 1865, the wearying war was over. At a frightful cost of over 600,000 lives and the destruction of the southern economy and much of its landscape, American nationalism had emerged triumphant, and some 4 million enslaved African-Americans were freed. Now the nation faced the imposing task of reuniting, providing for the freed slaves, and "reconstructing" a ravaged and resentful South.

THE WAR'S AFTERMATH

In the war's aftermath the victors faced important questions: Should the Confederate leaders be tried for treason? How should new governments be formed? How and at whose expense was the South's economy to be rebuilt? Should debts incurred by the Confederate state governments be honored?

Who should pay to rebuild the South's railroads and public buildings, dredge the clogged southern harbors, and restore damaged levees? What was to be done for the freed slaves? Were they to be given land? social equality? education? voting rights? Such complex questions required sober reflection and careful planning, but policy makers did not have the luxury of time or the benefit of consensus. Some wanted the former Confederate states returned to the Union with little or no changes in the region's social, political, and economic life. Others wanted southern society punished and transformed. At the end of 1865, the editors of the nation's foremost magazine, *Harper's Weekly,* expressed this vengeful attitude when they declared that "the forgive-and-forget policy . . . is mere political insanity and suicide."

ECONOMIC DEVELOPMENT IN THE NORTH   The Civil War was more truly a social revolution than the War of Independence, for it reduced the once-dominant power of the South's planter elite in national politics and elevated that of the northern "captains of industry." Government, both federal and state, grew more friendly to business leaders and more unfriendly to those who would probe into their activities. The wartime Congress had delivered on the major platform promises of the 1860 campaign, which had cemented the allegiance of northeastern businessmen and western farmers to the Republican party.

In the absence of southern members, Congress during the war had centralized national power and enacted the Republican economic agenda. It passed the Morrill Tariff, which doubled the average level of import duties. The National Banking Act created a uniform system of banking and banknote currency and helped finance the war. Congress also passed legislation confirming that the first transcontinental railroad would run along a north-central route, from Omaha to Sacramento, and donated public land and public bonds to ensure its financing. In the Homestead Act of 1862, moreover, Congress voted free federal homesteads of 160 acres to settlers, who had only to occupy the land for five years to gain title. The Morrill Land Grant Act of the same year conveyed to each state 30,000 acres of federal land per member of Congress from the state, the proceeds from the sale of which went to create colleges of "agriculture and mechanic arts." Such measures helped stimulate the North's economy in the years after the Civil War.

DEVASTATION IN THE SOUTH   The postwar South offered a sharp contrast to the victorious North. Along the path of General William T. Sherman's army, one observer reported in 1866, the countryside of Georgia and

A Street in the "Burned District"

Richmond, Virginia, Spring 1865.

South Carolina "looked for many miles like a broad black streak of ruin and desolation." Columbia, South Carolina, said another witness, was "a wilderness of ruins," Charleston a place of "vacant houses, of widowed women, of rotting wharves, of deserted warehouses, of weed-wild gardens, of miles of grass-grown streets, of acres of pitiful and voiceless barrenness."

Throughout the South, property values had collapsed. Confederate bonds and paper money were worthless; most railroads were damaged or destroyed. Cotton that had escaped destruction was seized as Confederate property or in forfeit of federal taxes. Emancipation wiped out $4 billion invested in human flesh and left the labor system in disarray. The great age of expansion in the cotton market was over. Not until 1879 would the cotton crop again equal the record harvest of 1860; tobacco production did not regain its prewar level until 1880; the sugar crop of Louisiana not until 1893; and the old rice industry of the Tidewater and the hemp industry of the Kentucky Bluegrass never regained their prewar status.

A TRANSFORMED SOUTH   The defeat of the Confederacy transformed much of southern society. The liberation of slaves, the destruction of property, and the free fall in land values left many planters destitute and homeless. After the Civil War many former Confederates were so embittered that they abandoned their native region rather than submit to "Yankee rule." Some migrated to Canada, Europe, Mexico, South America, or Asia. Others preferred the western territories and states. Still others moved to northern and midwestern cities on the assumption that their educational and economic opportunities would be better among the victors.

Most of those who remained in the South found their farms, homes, and communities transformed. One Confederate army captain reported that on his father's plantation "our negroes are living in great comfort. They were delighted to see me with overflowing affection. They waited on me as before, gave me breakfast, splendid dinners, etc. But they firmly and respectfully informed me: 'We own this land now. Put it out of your head that it will ever be yours again.'"

LEGALLY FREE, SOCIALLY BOUND   In the former Confederate states the newly freed slaves suffered most of all. According to the African-American abolitionist Frederick Douglass, the former slave remained dependent: "He had neither money, property, nor friends. He was free from the old plantation, but he had nothing but the dusty road under his feet. . . . He was turned loose, naked, hungry, and destitute to the open sky."

A few northerners argued that what the ex-slaves needed most was their own land. In 1865 Representative George Washington Julian of Indiana and Senator Charles Sumner of Massachusetts proposed to give freed slaves forty-acre homesteads carved out of Confederate lands taken under the Confiscation Act of 1862. But their plan for outright grants was replaced by a program of rentals, since under the law confiscation was effective only for the lifetime of the Confederate property owner. Discussions of land distribution, however, fueled rumors that freed slaves would get "forty acres and a mule," a slogan that swept the South at the end of the war. But even dedicated abolitionists shrank from taking land from whites to give to the freed slaves. Citizenship and legal rights were one thing, wholesale confiscation of property and land redistribution quite another.

Freedmen in Richmond, Virginia

According to a former Confederate general, freed blacks had "nothing but freedom."

Instead of land or material help, the freed slaves more often got advice about proper behavior.

THE FREEDMEN'S BUREAU   On March 3, 1865, while the war was still raging, Congress set up within the War Department the Bureau of Refugees, Freedmen, and Abandoned Lands to provide "provisions, clothing, and fuel" to relieve "destitute and suffering refugees and freedmen and their wives and children." Agents of the Freedmen's Bureau were entrusted with negotiating labor contracts (a new practice for both African Americans and planters), providing medical care, and setting up schools, often in cooperation with such northern agencies as the American Missionary Association and the Freedmen's Aid Society. The bureau had its own courts to deal with labor disputes and land titles, and its agents were authorized to supervise trials involving blacks in other courts.

The failure to grasp the intensity of white intransigence and racial prejudice thwarted the efforts of Freedmen's Bureau agents to protect and assist the former slaves, however. Congress was not willing to strengthen the powers of the bureau to deal with such problems. Beyond temporary relief measures, no program of Reconstruction ever incorporated much more than constitutional and legal rights for freedmen. These were important in themselves, of course, but the extent to which even they should go was very uncertain, to be settled more by the course of events than by any clear-cut commitment to social and economic equality.

THE BATTLE OVER RECONSTRUCTION

The problem of reconstructing the South centered on deciding what governments would constitute authority in the defeated states. This problem arose first in Virginia at the very beginning of the Civil War, when the state's thirty-five western counties refused to go along with secession. In 1861 a loyal state government of Virginia was proclaimed at Wheeling, and that government in turn formed a new state, called West Virginia, which was admitted to the Union in 1863. As Union forces advanced into the South, President Lincoln in 1862 named military governors for Tennessee, Arkansas, and Louisiana. By the end of the following year, he had formulated a plan for regular civilian governments in those states and any others that might be liberated from Confederate rule.

LINCOLN'S PLAN AND CONGRESS'S RESPONSE In late 1863 President Lincoln had issued a Proclamation of Amnesty and Reconstruction, under which any Confederate state could form a Union government whenever a number equal to 10 percent of those who had voted in 1860 took an oath of allegiance to the Constitution and Union and received a presidential pardon. Participants also had to swear support for laws and proclamations dealing with emancipation. Excluded from the pardon, however, were certain groups: civil, diplomatic, and high military officers of the Confederacy; judges, congressmen, and military officers of the United States who had left their federal posts to aid the rebellion; and those accused of failure to treat captured black soldiers and their officers as prisoners of war.

Under this plan, governments loyal to the Union appeared in Tennessee, Arkansas, and Louisiana, but Congress refused to recognize them. In the absence of specific provisions for Reconstruction in the Constitution, politicians disagreed as to where authority properly rested. A few conservative and most moderate Republicans supported Lincoln's program of immediate restoration. A small but influential group, known as Radical Republicans, demanded a sweeping transformation of southern society that would include making the freed slaves full-fledged citizens. The Radicals hoped to reconstruct southern society so as to dismantle the planter elite and the Democratic Party.

The Radical Republicans were talented, earnest leaders who maintained that Congress, not the president, should supervise the Reconstruction program. To this end in 1864 they helped pass the Wade-Davis bill, sponsored by Senator Benjamin Franklin Wade of Ohio and Representative Henry Winter Davis of Maryland. In contrast to Lincoln's 10 percent plan, the Wade-Davis bill required that a *majority* of white male citizens declare their allegiance and that only those who swore an "ironclad" oath that they had always remained loyal to the Union could vote or serve in the state constitutional conventions. The conventions, moreover, would have to abolish slavery, deny political rights to high-ranking civil and military officers of the Confederacy, and repudiate Confederate war debts. Passed during the closing days of the 1864 session, the bill went unsigned by Lincoln, and that "pocket veto" led the bill's sponsors to issue the Wade-Davis Manifesto, a blistering statement accusing the president of usurping power and attempting to use readmitted states to ensure his reelection.

Lincoln issued his final statement on Reconstruction in his last public address, on April 11, 1865. Speaking from the White House balcony, he dismissed the theoretical question of whether the Confederate states had technically remained in the Union as "good for nothing at all—a mere pernicious abstraction." Those states were simply "out of their proper practical relation with the Union," and the object was to get them "into their proper practical relation" as quickly as possible. Lincoln hoped to get new southern state governments in operation before Congress met in December. He worried that Congress might push through a harsher Reconstruction program. Lincoln wanted "no persecution, no bloody work," no dramatic restructuring of southern social and economic life.

On the evening of April 14, Lincoln went to Ford's Theater and his rendezvous with death. Shot in the head by John Wilkes Booth, a crazed actor and Confederate zealot, the president died the next morning. Pursued into Virginia, Booth was trapped and shot in a burning barn. His last words were "Tell mother I die for my country. I thought I did for the best." Three collaborators were tried and hanged, along with Mary Surratt, at whose boardinghouse they had plotted. Three other conspirators received life sentences, including a Maryland doctor who set the leg Booth had broken when he jumped from Lincoln's box onto the stage.

JOHNSON'S PLAN Lincoln's death elevated to the White House Vice President Andrew Johnson of Tennessee, a man who lacked most presidential virtues. When General Ulysses Grant learned that Lincoln had died and Johnson was president, he said that he "dreaded the change" because the new commander in chief was vindictive toward his native South. Essentially illiterate, Johnson was provincial and bigoted. He was also short-tempered and lacking in self-control. At the inaugural ceremonies in early 1865, he had drunkenly slurred his address, embarrasing Lincoln and the nation. Johnson was a War (pro-Union) Democrat who had been put on the National Union ticket in 1864 as a gesture of unity. Of origins as humble as Lincoln's, Johnson had moved as a youth from his birthplace in Raleigh, North Carolina, to Greeneville, Tennessee, where he became the proprietor of a tailor shop. Self-educated with the help of his wife, Johnson grew prosperous, acquiring several slaves in the process.

Beginning in the 1830s, Johnson emerged as a leading Jacksonian Democrat. A bitter critic of the "swaggering" planter aristocracy "who are too lazy and proud to work," he promoted free land for the poor, defended slavery, and championed white supremacy. A notoriously stubborn man, he became a self-righteous, hot-tempered orator who enjoyed strong drink and employed abusive language to belittle his opponents. His fiery speeches and firm principles helped him win election as mayor, congressman, governor, and senator.

Like many other whites living in mountainous eastern Tennessee, Johnson ardently believed in the Union. In 1861 he was the only southern senator from a Confederate state to vote against secession, leading critics to denounce him as a "traitor" to the region. Yet his devotion to the Union did not include opposition to slavery. He hated the Confederacy because he hated the planter elite. "Damn the Negroes," Johnson bellowed to a friend during the war, "I am fighting those traitorous aristocrats, their masters."

Some of the Radical Republicans at first thought President Johnson, unlike Lincoln, was one of them. Johnson had, for example, asserted that treason "must be made infamous and traitors must be impoverished." But the Radicals would soon find Johnson to be as unsympathetic as Lincoln had been to their sweeping agenda, if for different reasons. Johnson's loyalty to the Union sprang from a strict adherence to the Constitution and a fervent belief in

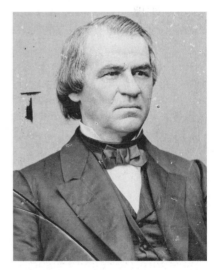

Andrew Johnson

A pro-Union Democrat from Tennessee.

limited government. He held that the rebellious states should be quickly brought back into their proper relation to the Union because the states and the Union were indestructible. In 1865 Johnson declared that "there is no such thing as Reconstruction. Those states have not gone out of the Union. Therefore Reconstruction is unnecessary."

Johnson's plan to restore the Union thus closely resembled Lincoln's. A new Proclamation of Amnesty, issued on May 29, 1865, excluded from pardon not only those Lincoln had excluded but also everybody with taxable property worth more than $20,000. Those wealthy planters and merchants were the people Johnson believed had led the South to secede. Those in the excluded groups might make special applications for presidential pardon, and before the year was out Johnson had issued some 13,000 pardons.

In each of the Rebel states not already organized by Lincoln, Johnson named a native Unionist provisional governor with authority to call a convention of men elected by loyal voters. Lincoln's 10 percent requirement was omitted. Johnson called upon the conventions to invalidate the secession ordinances, abolish slavery, and repudiate all debts incurred to aid the Confederacy. Each state, moreover, was to ratify the Thirteenth Amendment, which ended slavery. Like Lincoln, Johnson also endorsed limited voting rights for blacks. The state conventions for the most part met Johnson's requirements. Emboldened by the president's indulgence, however, southern whites ignored his advice to move cautiously in restoring their political and social traditions. Suggestions of black suffrage were scarcely raised in the state conventions and promptly squelched when they were.

SOUTHERN INTRANSIGENCE   When Congress met in December 1865, for the first time since the end of the war, it faced the fact that the new state governments in the former Confederacy were remarkably like the old ones. Among the new members presenting themselves to Congress were Georgia's Alexander Stephens, former vice president of the Confederacy, four Confederate generals, eight colonels, and six cabinet members. The Congress forthwith denied seats to all members from the eleven former Confederate states. It was too much to expect, after four bloody years, that the Unionists in Congress would welcome back ex-Confederates.

Furthermore, the new southern state legislatures, in passing repressive "black codes" restricting the freedom of blacks, baldly revealed that they intended to preserve the trappings of slavery as nearly as possible. As one southerner stressed, the "ex-slave was not a free man; he was a free Negro," and the black codes were intended to highlight the distinction.

The black codes varied from state to state, but some provisions were common. Existing black marriages, including common-law marriages, were recognized (although interracial marriages were prohibited), and testimony by blacks was accepted in legal cases involving them—in six states in all cases. Blacks could own property. They could sue and be sued in the courts. On the other hand, in Mississippi they could not own farmland, and in South Carolina they could not own city lots. They were required to enter into labor contracts with white employers, renewable annually, with provision for punishment in case of violation. Their dependent children were subject to compulsory apprenticeship and corporal punishment by the employer. "Vagrant" (unemployed) blacks were punished with severe fines, and if unable to pay, they were forced to work in the fields for whites who paid the courts for cheap labor. Slavery was thus revived in another guise.

THE RADICAL REPUBLICANS   Faced with such evidence of southern intransigence, moderate Republicans drifted more and more toward the Radical camp. The new Congress set up a Joint Committee on Reconstruction, with nine members from the House and six from the Senate, to gather evidence and submit proposals for reconstructing the Southern states. As a parade of witnesses testified to the Rebels' impenitence, initiative on the committee fell to determined Radicals: Benjamin Wade of Ohio, George Julian of Indiana, Henry Wilson of Massachusetts, and most conspicuously of all, Thaddeus Stevens of Pennsylvania and Charles Sumner of Massachusetts.

Stevens, a crusty old bachelor with a chiseled face, thin, stern lips, and brooding eyes, was the domineering floor leader in the House. Driven by a genuine if at times fanatical idealism, he angrily insisted that the "whole fabric of southern society *must* be changed." Sumner, Stevens's counterpart in the Senate, agreed. Now recovered from "Bully" Brooks's 1856 assault, Sumner strove to see the South *reconstructed* rather than simply restored. This put him at odds with President Johnson. After visiting the White House, Sumner found the president "harsh, petulant, and unreasonable." He was especially disheartened by President Johnson's "prejudice, ignorance, and perversity" regarding the treatment of African Americans. Sumner and other Radicals now grew determined to take matters into their own hands. He argued that "Massachusetts could govern Georgia better than Georgia could govern herself." The southern plantations, seedbeds of aristocratic pretension and secession, he later added, "must be broken up, and the freedmen must have the pieces."

Most of the Radical Republicans had long been connected with the anti-slavery cause, and they approached the question of African-American rights with a sincere humanitarian impulse. Yet the Republicans also had political reasons for promoting civil rights. The Republicans needed black votes to maintain their control of Congress and the White House. They also needed to disenfranchise former Confederates to keep them from helping to elect Democrats who would restore the old ruling class to power. In public, however, the Radical Republicans rarely disclosed such partisan self-interest. Instead, they asserted that the Republicans, the party of Union and freedom, could best guarantee the fruits of victory and that extending voting rights to African Americans would be the best way to promote their welfare.

The growing conflict of opinion over Reconstruction policy brought about an inversion in constitutional reasoning. Secessionists—and Andrew Johnson—were now arguing that the Confederate states had in fact technically remained in the Union, and some Radical Republicans were contriving arguments that they had left the Union after all. Thaddeus Stevens argued that the Confederate states had indeed seceded and were now conquered provinces, subject to the absolute will of the victors. He added that the "whole fabric of southern society must be changed." Charles Sumner maintained that the southern states, by their acts of secession, had in effect committed suicide and reverted to the status of unorganized territories and thus were subject to the will of Congress. Most congressmen, however, embraced the "forfeited-rights theory," which held that the states continued to exist but by the acts of secession and war had forfeited "all civil and political rights under the Constitution." And Congress, not the president, was the proper authority to determine how and when such rights might be restored.

JOHNSON'S BATTLE WITH CONGRESS   A long year of political battling remained, however, before this idea triumphed. By the end of 1865, the Radical Republicans' views had gained only a slight majority in Congress, insufficient to override presidential vetoes. The critical year of 1866 saw the gradual waning of Andrew Johnson's power, much of which was self-induced. Johnson first challenged Congress in February, when he vetoed a bill to extend the life of the Freedmen's Bureau. The measure, he said, assumed that wartime conditions still existed, whereas the country had returned "to a state of peace and industry." Since the Bureau was no longer valid as a war measure, Johnson believed it violated the Constitution. For the moment, Johnson's prestige remained sufficiently intact that the Senate upheld his veto.

Three days after the veto, however, on George Washington's Birthday, Johnson undermined his authority by launching an intemperate assault upon the Radical Republican leaders during an impromptu speech. From that point, moderate Republicans backed away from the president, and Radical Republicans went on the offensive.

In mid-March 1866 the Radical-led Congress passed the Civil Rights Act. A direct response to the black codes created by unrepentant state legislatures in the South, it declared that "all persons born in the United States . . . excluding Indians not taxed" were citizens entitled to "full and equal benefit of all laws." The granting of citizenship to native-born blacks, Johnson claimed, exceeded the scope of federal power. It would, moreover, "foment discord among the races." He vetoed the

The Cruel Uncle

A cartoon depicting Andrew Johnson leading two children, "Civil Rights" and "the Freedmen's Bureau," into the "Veto Wood."

measure, but this time, in April, Congress overrode the presidential veto. Then in July it enacted a revised Freedmen's Bureau bill, again overturning a veto. From that point on, Johnson's public and political support steadily eroded.

THE FOURTEENTH AMENDMENT   To remove all doubt about the validity of the new Civil Rights Act, the joint committee recommended a new constitutional amendment, which passed Congress in 1866 and was ratified by the states in 1868. The Fourteenth Amendment went far beyond the Civil Rights Act, however. The first section asserts four principles: it reaffirms the state and federal citizenship of all persons—regardless of race—born or naturalized in the United States, and it forbids any state (the word *state* would be important in later litigation) to "abridge the privileges and immunities of citizens," to deprive any *person* (again an important term) "of life, liberty, or property without due process of law," or to "deny any person . . . the equal protection of the laws."

These clauses have been the subject of lawsuits resulting in applications not foreseen at the time. The "due-process clause" has come to mean that state as well as federal power is subject to the Bill of Rights, and it has been used to protect corporations, as legal "persons," from "unreasonable" regulation by the states. Other provisions of the amendment had less far-reaching effects. One section specified that the debt of the United States "shall not be questioned" but declared "illegal and void" all debts contracted in aid of the Confederate rebellion. The final sentence specified the power of Congress to pass laws enforcing the amendment.

Johnson's home state was among the first to ratify the Fourteenth Amendment. In Tennessee, which had harbored more Unionists than any other Confederate state, the government had fallen under Radical Republican control. The rest of the South, however, steadfastly resisted the Radical challenge to Johnson's program. In 1866 bloody race riots in Memphis and New Orleans added fuel to the flames. Both incidents sparked indiscriminate massacres of blacks by local police and white mobs. The rioting, Radical Republicans argued, was the natural fruit of Johnson's foolish policy.

RECONSTRUCTING THE SOUTH

THE TRIUMPH OF CONGRESSIONAL RECONSTRUCTION   As 1866 drew to an end, the November congressional elections promised to be a referendum on the growing split between Johnson and the Radical Republicans. The president embarked on a speaking tour of the Midwest, a "swing around the circle," which provoked undignified shouting contests between the president and his audiences. In Cleveland he described the Radical Republicans as "factious, domineering, tyrannical" men. Various incidents tended to confirm his image as a "ludicrous boor," which Radical Republican newspapers eagerly promoted. When the election returns came in, the Republicans had more than a two-thirds majority in each house, a comfortable margin with which to override presidential vetoes.

Congress actually enacted a new reconstruction program even before the new members took office. On March 2, 1867, two days before the old Congress expired, it passed three basic laws of congressional Reconstruction over Johnson's vetoes: the Military Reconstruction Act, the Command of the Army Act, and the Tenure of Office Act.

The first of these acts prescribed conditions under which new southern state governments should be formed. The other two sought to block any effort by the president to obstruct the process. The Command of the Army Act required that all orders from the president as commander in chief go through the headquarters of the general of the army, then Ulysses Grant. The Tenure of Office Act required the Senate's permission for the president to remove any officeholder whose appointment the Senate had confirmed.

In large measure it was intended to retain Secretary of War Edwin Stanton, the one Radical Republican sympathizer in Johnson's cabinet. But an ambiguity crept into the wording of the act. Cabinet officers, it said, should serve during the term of the president who appointed them—and Lincoln had appointed Stanton, although, to be sure, Johnson was serving out Lincoln's term.

The Military Reconstruction Act was hailed—or denounced—as the triumphant victory of "Radical" Reconstruction. Originally intended by the Radical Republicans to give military commanders in the South ultimate control over law enforcement and to leave open indefinitely the terms of restoration, it was diluted by moderate Republicans until it boiled down to little more than a requirement that southern states accept African-American suffrage and ratify the Fourteenth Amendment.

Tennessee, which had already ratified the Fourteenth Amendment, was exempted from the application of the act. The other ten states were divided into five military districts, and the commanding officer of each was authorized to keep order and protect the "rights of persons and property." The Johnson governments remained intact for the time being, but new constitutions were to be framed "in conformity with the Constitution of the United States," in conventions elected by male citizens aged twenty-one and older "of whatever race, color, or previous condition." Each state constitution had to provide the same universal male suffrage. Then, once the constitution was ratified by a majority of voters and accepted by Congress, the state legislature had ratified the Fourteenth Amendment, and the amendment had become part of the Constitution, any given state would be entitled to renewed representation in Congress. Persons excluded from officeholding by the proposed amendment were also excluded from participation in the process. Before the end of 1867, new elections had been held in all the states but Texas.

Having clipped the president's wings, the Republican Congress moved a year later to safeguard its southern program from possible interference by the Supreme Court. On March 27, 1868, Congress simply removed the power of the Supreme Court to review cases arising under the Military Reconstruction Act, which Congress clearly had the constitutional right to do under its power to define the Court's appellate jurisdiction. The Court accepted this curtailment of its authority on the same day it affirmed the notion of an "indestructible Union" in *Texas v. White* (1869). In that case the Court also acknowledged the right of Congress to reframe state governments, thus endorsing the Radical Republican point of view.

THE IMPEACHMENT AND TRIAL OF JOHNSON   By 1868 Radical Republicans were convinced not only that the power of the Supreme Court and the president needed to be curtailed but also that Andrew Johnson himself had to be removed from office. Johnson, though hostile to the congressional Reconstruction program, had gone through the motions required of him. He continued to pardon former Confederates, however, and transferred several of the district military commanders who had displayed Radical Republican sympathies. Johnson lacked Lincoln's resilience and pragmatism, and he allowed his temper to get the better of his judgment. He castigated the Radical Republicans as "a gang of cormorants and bloodsuckers who have been fattening upon the country." During 1867 newspapers reported that the differences between Johnson and the Republicans had grown irreconcilable.

The Radical Republicans unsuccessfully tried to impeach Johnson early in 1867, alleging a variety of flimsy charges, none of which represented an indictable crime. Then Johnson himself provided the occasion for impeachment when he deliberately violated the Tenure of Office Act in order to test its constitutionality. Secretary of War Edwin Stanton had become a thorn in Johnson's side, refusing to resign despite his disagreements with the president's Reconstruction policy. On August 12, 1867, during a congressional recess, Johnson suspended Stanton and named General Ulysses Grant in his place. When the Senate refused to confirm Johnson's action, however, Grant returned the office to Stanton.

The Radical Republicans now saw their chance to remove the president, and they were explicit about their political purpose. As Charles Sumner declared, "Impeachment is a political proceeding before a political body with a political purpose." The debate in the House was clamorous and vicious. On February 24, 1868, the House passed eleven articles of impeachment by a party-line vote of 126 to 47.

Eight of the articles focused on the charge that Johnson had unlawfully removed Stanton. Article 9 accused the president of issuing orders in violation of the Command of the Army Act. The last two articles in effect charged him with criticizing Congress by "inflammatory and scandalous harangues." Article 11 also accused him of "unlawfully devising and contriving" to violate the Reconstruction Acts, contrary to his obligation to execute the laws. At the very least, it stated, Johnson had tried to obstruct Congress's will while observing the letter of the law.

The Senate trial began on March 5, 1868, and continued until May 26, with Chief Justice Salmon P. Chase presiding. Debate eventually focused on

Stanton's removal, the most substantive impeachment charge. Johnson's lawyers argued that Lincoln, not Johnson, had appointed Stanton, so the Tenure of Office Act did not apply to him. At the same time they claimed (correctly, as it turned out) that the law was unconstitutional.

As the five-week trial ended and the voting began in May 1868, the Senate Republicans could afford only six defections from their ranks to ensure the two-thirds majority needed to convict. In the end seven moderate Republicans and all twelve Democrats voted to acquit. The final tally was thirty-five to nineteen for conviction, one vote short of the two thirds needed for removal from office. The renegade Republicans offered two primary reasons for their controversial votes: they feared damage to the separation of powers among the branches of government if Johnson were removed, and they were assured by Johnson's attorneys that the president would stop obstructing congressional policy in the South.

Although the Senate failed to remove Johnson, the trial crippled his already weak presidency. During the remaining ten months of his term, he initiated no other clashes with Congress. In 1868 Johnson sought the Democratic presidential nomination but lost to New York governor Horatio Seymour, who then lost to the Republican, Ulysses Grant, in the general election. A bitter Johnson refused to attend Grant's inauguration. His final act as president was to issue a pardon to former Confederate president Jefferson Davis. In 1874, after failed bids for the Senate and the House, Johnson won a measure of vindication with election to the Senate, the only former president ever to do so, but he died a few months later. He was buried with a copy of the Constitution placed under his head.

As for the impeachment trial, only two weeks after it ended, a Boston newspaper reported that Americans were amazed at how quickly "the whole subject of impeachment seems to have been thrown into the background and dwarfed in importance" by other events. Moreover, impeachment of Johnson was in the end a great political mistake, for the failure to remove the president damaged Radical Republican morale and support. Nevertheless, the Radical cause did gain something: Johnson's agreement not to obstruct the process of Reconstruction. Thereafter Radical Reconstruction began in earnest.

RADICAL RULE IN THE SOUTH   In June 1868 Congress agreed that seven southern states had met the conditions for readmission to the Union, all but Virginia, Mississippi, and Texas. Congress rescinded Georgia's admission, however, when the state legislature expelled twenty-eight African-American members and seated former Confederate leaders. The federal military commander in Georgia then forced the legislature to reseat the black members and remove the Confederates, and the state was compelled to ratify the Fifteenth Amendment before being readmitted in July 1870. Mississippi, Texas, and Virginia had returned earlier in 1870, under the added requirement that they, too, ratify the Fifteenth Amendment. That amendment, ratified in 1870, forbade the states to deny any citizen the right to vote on grounds of "race, color, or previous condition of servitude."

Long before the new governments had been established, partisan Republican groups began to spring up in the South, promoted by the Union League, an organization founded in 1862 to rally support for the federal government. Its representatives enrolled blacks and loyal whites as members, initiated them into the secrets and rituals of the order, and instructed them "in their rights and duties." These Union Leagues became a powerful source of Republican political strength in the South and as a result drew the ire of unreconstructed whites.

THE RECONSTRUCTED SOUTH

Throughout the South during Reconstruction, many former Confederates continued to harbor deeply ingrained racial prejudices. They adopted a militant stance against federally imposed changes in southern society. Whites used terror, intimidation, and violence to suppress black efforts to gain social and economic equality. In July 1866, for instance, a black woman in Clinch County, Georgia, was arrested and given sixty-five lashes for "using abusive language" in an encounter with a white woman. A month later another black woman suffered the same punishment. The Civil War had brought freedom to the enslaved, but it did not bring protection against exploitation or abuse.

THE FREED SLAVES   To focus solely on what white Republicans did to reconstruct the defeated South creates the false impression that the freed slaves were simply pawns in the hands of others. In fact, southern blacks were active agents in affecting the course of Reconstruction. Many former slaves found themselves liberated but destitute after the fighting ended. The mere promise of freedom, however, had raised their hopes for biracial democracy, equal justice, and economic opportunity. "Most anyone ought to know that a man is better off free than as a slave, even if he did not have anything," said the Reverend E. P. Holmes, a black Georgia preacher and former domestic servant. "I would rather be free and have my liberty."

Participation in the Union army or navy had provided many freedmen with training in leadership. Black military veterans would form the core of the first generation of African-American political leaders in the postwar South. Military service provided many former slaves with the first opportunities to learn to read and write. Army life also alerted them to alternative social choices and to new opportunities for economic advancement and social respectability. Fighting for the Union cause also instilled a fervent sense of nationalism. A Virginia freedman explained that the United States was "now *our* country—made emphatically so by the blood of our brethren."

Former slaves established independent churches after the war, churches that quickly formed the foundation of African-American community life. Blacks preferred Baptist churches over other denominations, in part because the decentralized structure allowed each congregation to worship in its own way. By 1890 over 1.3 million African Americans were worshipping in Baptist churches in the South, nearly three times as many as had joined any other denomination. In addition to forming viable new congregations, freed blacks organized thousands of fraternal, benevolent, and mutual-aid societies, clubs, lodges, and associations. Memphis, for example, had over 200 such organizations; Richmond boasted twice that number.

Freed slaves also hastened to reestablish and reaffirm their families. Marriages that had been prohibited were now legitimized through the assistance of the Freedmen's Bureau. By 1870 most former slaves were living in two-parent households.

Former slaves had little money or technical training and were thus faced with the prospect of becoming wage laborers to support themselves. To avoid this and retain as much autonomy as possible over their productive energies and those of their children, many freed slaves chose to become sharecroppers, tenant farmers who gained access to separate plots of land owned by whites. In payment for the use of the land and cabin, and sometimes even the tools, seed, and fertilizer needed to farm the land, they were required to give between one half and two thirds of the harvested crops to the white landowner. This arrangement gave them higher status than they would have had as wage laborers. It also gave them the freedom to set their own hours and work as much or as little as they pleased, and it enabled mothers and wives to devote time to domestic responsibilities while contributing to the family's income.

African-American communities in the postwar South also sought to establish schools. The antebellum planter elite had denied education to blacks because they feared that literate slaves would organize uprisings. After the war the white elite worried that formal education would encourage poor

whites and poor blacks to leave the South in search of better social and economic opportunities. Economic leaders wanted to protect the competitive
advantage afforded by the region's low-wage labor market. Yet white opposition to education for blacks made it all the more important to African Americans. South Carolina's Mary McLeod Bethune, the seventeenth child of former slaves and one of the first children in the household born after the
Civil War, reveled in the opportunity to gain an education: "The whole
world opened to me when I learned to read." She walked five miles to
school as a child, earned a scholarship to college, and went on to become
the first black woman to found a school that became a four-year college,
Bethune-Cookman, in Daytona Beach, Florida.

The general resistance among the former slaveholding class to initiatives
involving education forced the freed slaves to rely upon northern assistance
or take their own initiative. African-American churches and individuals
helped raise the money and often built the schools and paid the teachers.
Soldiers who had acquired some literacy skills often served as the first teachers, and the classes included adults.

BLACKS IN SOUTHERN POLITICS In the postwar South the new
role of African Americans in politics caused the most controversy. If largely
illiterate and inexperienced in the rudiments of politics, southern blacks
were little different from the millions of whites enfranchised in the age of
Jackson or immigrants herded to the polls by political bosses in New York
and other cities after the war. Some freedmen frankly confessed their disadvantages. Beverly Nash, a black delegate to the South Carolina convention
of 1868, told his colleagues: "I believe, my friends and fellow-citizens, we
are not prepared for this suffrage. But we can learn. Give a man tools and let
him commence to use them, and in time he will learn a trade. So it is with
voting."

Several hundred African-American delegates participated in the statewide
political conventions. Most had been selected by local political meetings or
by churches, fraternal societies, Union Leagues, or black Federal army units,
although a few simply appointed themselves. The African-American delegates "ranged all colors and apparently all conditions," but free mulattoes
from the cities played the most prominent roles. At Louisiana's Republican
state convention, for instance, nineteen of the twenty black delegates had
been born free.

By 1867 former slaves had begun to gain political influence and vote in
large numbers, and this development revealed emerging tensions within the
African-American community. Some southern blacks resented the presence

of northern brethren who moved south after the war, while others complained that few ex-slaves were represented in leadership positions. Northern blacks and the southern black elite, most of whom were urban dwellers, opposed efforts to redistribute land to the rural freedmen, and many insisted that political equality did not mean social equality. As an Alabama black leader stressed, "We do not ask that the ignorant and degraded shall be put on a social equality with the refined and intelligent." In general, however, unity rather than dissension prevailed, and African Americans focused on common concerns such as full equality under the law.

Brought suddenly into politics in times that tried the most skilled of statesmen, many African Americans served with distinction. Nonetheless, the derisive label "black Reconstruction" used by later critics exaggerates African-American political influence, which was limited mainly to voting, and overlooks the political clout of the large number of white Republicans, especially in the mountain areas of the upper South, who supported the congressional plan for Reconstruction. Only one of the new conventions, South

Freedmen Voting in New Orleans

The Fifteenth Amendment, passed in 1870, guaranteed at the federal level the right of citizens to vote regardless of "race, color, or previous condition of servitude." But former slaves had been registering to vote—and voting in large numbers—in state elections since 1867, as in this scene.

Carolina's, had a black majority, seventy-six to forty-one. Louisiana's was evenly divided racially, and in only two other conventions were more than 20 percent of the members black: Florida's, with 40 percent, and Virginia's, with 24 percent.

In the new state governments, any African-American participation was a novelty. Although some 600 blacks—most of them former slaves—served as state legislators, no black man was ever elected governor, and few served as judges. In Louisiana, however, Pinckney Pinchback, a northern black and former Union soldier, won the office of lieutenant governor and served as acting governor when the white governor was indicted for corruption. Several blacks were elected lieutenant governor, state treasurer, or secretary of state. There were two black senators in Congress during Reconstruction, Hiram Revels and Blanche K. Bruce, both from Mississippi, and fourteen black members of the House. Among them were some of the ablest congressmen of the time.

CARPETBAGGERS AND SCALAWAGS   The top positions in southern state governments went for the most part to white Republicans whom the opposition soon labeled carpetbaggers and scalawags, depending upon their place of birth. Northern opportunists who allegedly came south with all their belongings in carpetbags to reap political spoils were more often than not Union veterans who had arrived as early as 1865 or 1866, drawn south by the hope of economic opportunity. Others were lawyers, businessmen, editors, teachers, social workers, or preachers who came on missionary endeavors.

The scalawags, or southern white Republicans, were even more reviled and misrepresented. A Nashville newspaper editor called them the "merest trash that could be collected in a civilized community, of no personal credit or social responsibility." Most scalawags had opposed secession, forming a Unionist majority in mountain counties as far south as Georgia and Alabama and especially in the hills of eastern Tennessee. Though many were indeed crass opportunists who indulged in corruption at the public's expense, several were distinguished figures. They included the former Confederate general James Longstreet, who decided after Appomattox that the Old South must change its ways. To that end he became a successful cotton broker in New Orleans, joined the Republican party, and supported the Radical Reconstruction program. Others were former Whigs who found the Republican party's expansive industrial and commercial program in keeping with Henry Clay's earlier efforts to use the government to promote economic growth and industrial development.

THE RADICAL RECORD   Former Confederates not only resented carpetbaggers and scalawags, but they also objected to the new state constitutions, primarily because of their provisions allowing for black suffrage and civil rights. Nonetheless, most of the state constitutions remained in effect for some years after the end of Radical Republican control, and later constitutions incorporated many of their features. Conspicuous among the Radical innovations were steps toward greater democracy, such as requiring universal male suffrage, reapportioning legislatures more nearly according to population, and making more state offices elective.

Given the hostile circumstances in which the Radical Republican governments operated, their achievements were remarkable. They established the first state school systems, in which some 600,000 black pupils were enrolled by 1877. State governments under the Radical Republicans also paid more attention to the poor and to orphanages, asylums, and institutions for the disabled of both races. Public roads, bridges, railroads, and buildings were repaired or rebuilt. African Americans achieved new rights and opportunities that would never again be taken away, at least in principle: equality before the law and the right to own property, carry on business, enter professions, attend schools, and learn to read and write.

Yet several of the Republican state regimes also engaged on systematic corruption. Public money and public credit were often awarded to privately owned corporations, notably railroads, under conditions that invited influence peddling. Still, corruption was not invented by the Radical Republican regimes, nor did it die with them. In Mississippi the Republican Reconstruction governments were quite honest compared with those of their Democratic successors.

The Grant Years

THE ELECTION OF 1868   Ulysses S. Grant, who served as president during the collapse of Republican rule in the South, brought to the White House little political experience. But in 1868 northern voters supported the Lion of Vicksburg because of his brilliant record as a war leader. Both parties wooed Grant, but his falling-out with President Johnson pushed him toward the Republicans and built trust in him among the Radicals.

The Republican platform of 1868 endorsed Radical Reconstruction, cautiously defending black suffrage as a necessity in the South but a matter that each northern state should settle for itself. It also urged payment of the nation's war debt in gold rather than in the new "greenback" paper currency printed during the war. More important than the platform were the great expectations of a soldier-president, whose slogan was "Let us have peace."

The Democrats opposed the Republicans on both Reconstruction and the debt. The Republican Congress, the Democratic platform charged, had subjected ten states, "in the time of profound peace, to military despotism and Negro supremacy." As for the public debt the party endorsed the "Ohio idea" of Representative George H. Pendleton: since most war bonds had been bought with depreciated greenbacks, they should be paid off in greenbacks. With no conspicuously available candidate in sight, the convention turned to Horatio Seymour, wartime governor of New York and chairman of the convention. The Democrats ran a closer race than expected, attesting to the strength of traditional party loyalties. Although Grant swept the Electoral College by 214 to 80, his popular majority was only 307,000 out of 5.7 million votes. Over 500,000 African-American voters accounted for Grant's margin of victory.

Grant had proved himself a great leader in the war, but in the White House he was often blind to the political forces and influence peddlers around him. Shy and withdrawn, he was uncomfortable around intellectuals and impatient with idealists. Grant preferred watching horse races to reading about complex issues. Although personally honest, he was dazzled by men of wealth and unaccountably loyal to greedy subordinates who betrayed his trust. In the formulation of policy, he passively followed the lead of Congress. This approach initially endeared him to Republican party leaders, but it left him ineffective and caused others to grow disillusioned with his leadership. At the outset, Grant consulted nobody on his cabinet appointments. Some of his choices indulged personal whims; others simply reflected bad judgment. Secretary of State Hamilton Fish of New York turned out to be a fortunate exception; he masterfully guided foreign policy throughout the Grant presidency. Other than Fish, however, Grant's cabinet overflowed with incompetents.

THE GOVERNMENT DEBT   Financial issues dominated Grant's presidency. After the war the Treasury had assumed that the $432 million in greenbacks issued during the conflict would be retired from circulation and that the nation would revert to a "hard-money" currency—gold coins. Congress in 1866 granted the Treasury discretion to do so gradually. Many agrarian and debtor groups resisted this contraction of the money supply, believing that it would mean lower farm prices and harder-to-pay debts. They were joined by a large number of Radical Republicans who thought a combination of high tariffs and inflation would generate more rapid economic growth. In 1868 "soft-money" supporters in Congress halted the retirement of greenbacks, leaving $356 million outstanding. There matters stood when Grant took office.

The "sound-money" (or hard-money) advocates, mostly bankers, merchants, and other creditors, claimed that Grant's election was a mandate to save the country from the Democrats' "Ohio idea" of using greenbacks to repay government bonds. Quite influential in Republican circles, the sound-money advocates also had the benefit of agreeing with the deeply ingrained popular assumption that hard money was morally preferable to paper currency. Grant agreed as well, and in his inaugural address he endorsed payment of the national debt in gold as a point of national honor.

SCANDALS Within less than a year of his election, Grant had fallen into a cesspool of scandal. In the summer of 1869, two railroad entrepreneurs, the crafty Jay Gould and the flamboyant con man James Fisk, connived with the president's brother-in-law to corner the nation's gold market. That is, they would create a public craze for gold by purchasing massive quantities and convincing traders that the price would keep climbing. As more buyers joined the frenzy, the value of gold would soar. The only danger was the federal Treasury's selling large amounts of gold. Gould concocted an argument that the government should refrain from selling gold on the market because the resulting rise in gold prices would raise temporarily depressed farm prices. Grant apparently smelled a rat from the start, but he was seen in public with the speculators. As the rumor spread on Wall Street, gold rose from $132 to $163 an ounce. Finally, on Black Friday, September 24, 1869, Grant ordered the Treasury to sell a large quantity of gold, and the bubble burst. Fisk got out by repudiating his agreements and hiring thugs to intimidate his creditors. "Nothing is lost save honor," he said.

The plot to corner the gold market was only the first of several scandals that rocked the Grant administration. In 1872 the public learned about the financial crookery of the Crédit Mobilier, a construction company that had milked the Union Pacific Railroad for exorbitant fees to line the pockets of insiders who controlled both firms. Union Pacific shareholders were left holding the bag. This chicanery had transpired before Grant's election in 1868, but it now touched a number of prominent Republicans who had been given shares of Crédit Mobilier stock in exchange for favorable votes. Of the thirteen congressmen involved, only two were censured.

Even more odious disclosures soon followed, some involving the president's cabinet. Grant's secretary of war, it turned out, had accepted bribes from merchants who traded with Indians at army posts in the West. He was impeached, but he resigned in time to elude trial. Post-office contracts, it was revealed, went to carriers who offered the highest kickbacks. In St. Louis a "whiskey ring" bribed tax collectors to bilk the government of millions of dollars in revenue. Grant's private secretary was enmeshed in that scheme, taking large sums of money and other valuables in return for inside information. There is no evidence that Grant himself participated in any of the scandals, but his poor choice of associates and his gullibility earned him widespread censure.

WHITE TERROR   President Grant initially fought hard to enforce the federal efforts to reconstruct the postwar South. By the time he became president, southern resistance had turned violent, as unrepentant whites organized vigilante groups to terrorize blacks. Most white southerners remained so conditioned by the social prejudices embedded in the institution of slavery that they were unable to conceive of blacks as citizens. In some places, hostility to the new regimes turned violent. Said one unreconstructed Mississippian in 1875, "Carry the election peaceably if we can, forcibly if we must."

The prototype of all the terrorist groups was the Ku Klux Klan (KKK), first organized in 1866 by some young men of Pulaski, Tennessee, as a social club, with the costumes and secret rituals common to fraternal groups. At first a group of pranksters, its members soon began to intimidate blacks and white Republicans, and the KKK spread rapidly across the South in answer to the Republican party's Union League. Klansmen rode about the countryside, hiding behind masks and under robes, spreading horrendous rumors, harassing blacks, and wreaking violence and destruction.

Worse Than Slavery

This Thomas Nast cartoon chides the Ku Klux Klan and the White League for promoting conditions "worse than slavery" for southern blacks after the Civil War.

At the urging of President Grant, Congress struck back with three Enforcement Acts (1870-1871) to protect black voters. The first of these measures levied penalties on persons who interfered with any citizen's right to vote. A second placed the election of congressmen under surveillance by federal election supervisors and marshals. The third (the Ku Klux Klan Act) outlawed the characteristic activities of the Klan—forming conspiracies, wearing disguises, resisting law officers, and intimidating government officials. In 1871 the federal government singled out nine counties in up-country South Carolina and pursued mass prosecutions that brought an abrupt halt to Klan terrorism. In general, however, the federal acts designed to protect African Americans suffered from weak and inconsistent enforcement. Moreover, the South's strong tradition of states' rights and local autonomy resisted federal force.

CONSERVATIVE RESURGENCE   The Klan in fact could not take credit for the overthrow of Republican control in any state. Perhaps its most important effect was to weaken the morale of African Americans and Republicans in the South and strengthen in the North a growing weariness with the whole "southern question." Republican control in the South gradually loosened as "Conservative" parties—a name used by Democrats to mollify former Whigs—mobilized the white vote. Scalawags and many carpetbaggers drifted away from the Radical Republican ranks under pressure from their white neighbors. Few of them had joined the Republicans out of concern for black rights in the first place. And where persuasion failed to work, Democrats were willing to use chicanery. As one enthusiastic Democrat boasted, "The white and black Republicans may outvote us, but we can outcount them."

Such factors led to the collapse of Republican control in Virginia and Tennessee as early as 1869 and in Georgia and North Carolina in 1870. Reconstruction lasted longest in states with the largest black population, where whites abandoned Klan hoods for barefaced intimidation in paramilitary groups like the Mississippi Rifle Club and the South Carolina Red Shirts. In the 1873 elections in Yazoo County, Mississippi, the Republicans cast 2,449 votes and the Democrats 638; two years later the Democrats polled 4,049 votes, the Republicans 7. By 1876 Radical Republican regimes survived only in Louisiana, South Carolina, and Florida, and those collapsed after the elections of that year.

The erosion of northern interest in promoting civil rights in the postwar South reflected weariness as well as interest in other activities. Western expansion, Indian wars, new economic opportunities, and political debates over the tariff and the currency distracted attention from southern outrages. In addition, a business panic in 1873 led to a sharp depression and created both social problems and new racial tensions in the North and the South

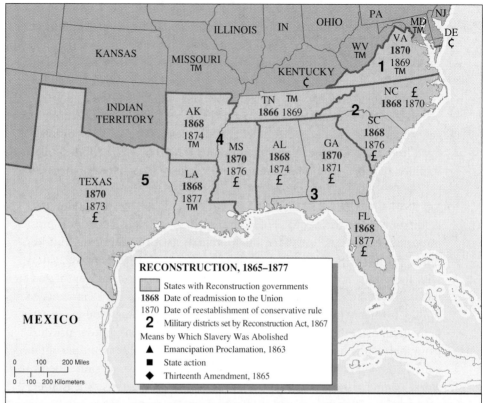

RECONSTRUCTION, 1865–1877

☐ States with Reconstruction governments
1868 Date of readmission to the Union
1870 Date of reestablishment of conservative rule
2 Military districts set by Reconstruction Act, 1867
Means by Which Slavery Was Abolished
▲ Emancipation Proclamation, 1863
■ State action
◆ Thirteenth Amendment, 1865

How did the Military Reconstruction Act reorganize government in the South in the late 1860s and 1870s? What did the former Confederate states have to do to be readmitted to the Union? How did "Conservative" parties gradually regain control of the South from the Republicans in the 1870s?

that helped undermine already inconsistent federal efforts to promote racial justice in the former Confederacy.

REFORM AND THE ELECTION OF 1872   Long before Grant's first term ended, Republicans broke ranks with the administration. Their alienation was a reaction to Radical Reconstruction and the incompetence and corruption in the administration. A new faction, called Liberal Republicans, favored free trade, the redemption of greenbacks with gold, the removal federal troops from the South, the restoration of the rights of former Confederates, and civil service reform. Open revolt first broke out in Missouri, where Carl Schurz, a German immigrant and war hero, led a group of Liberal

What I Know about Raising the Devil

With the tail and cloven hoof of the devil, Horace Greeley (center) leads a small band of Liberal Republicans in pursuit of incumbent president Ulysses S. Grant and his supporters in this 1872 cartoon.

Republicans who, with Democratic help, elected a governor in 1870 and sent Schurz to the Senate.

In 1872 the Liberal Republicans held their own national convention, which produced a compromise platform condemning the Republican party's "vindictive" southern policy and favoring civil service reform but remaining silent on the protective tariff. The delegates stampeded to endorse an anomalous presidential candidate: Horace Greeley, editor of the *New York Tribune* and an enthusiastic reformer. During his long journalistic career, Greeley had promoted vegetarianism, brown bread, free thinking, socialism, and spiritualism. His image as a visionary eccentric was complemented by his open hostility to the Democrats, whose support the Liberals needed. The Democrats gave the nomination to Greeley as the only hope of beating Grant and the Radical Republicans. Greeley's promise to end Radical Reconstruction and restore "self government" to the South won over Democrats who otherwise despised the man and his beliefs.

The 1872 election result surprised no one. Republican regulars duly endorsed Radical Reconstruction and the protective tariff. Grant still had seven southern states in his pocket, generous aid from business and banking interests, and the stalwart support of the Radical Republicans. Above all he still evoked the glory of military heroism. Greeley carried only six southern and border states, none in the North. Devastated by his crushing defeat and the death of his wife, Greeley entered a saniatorium and died three weeks later.

PANIC AND REDEMPTION   A paralyzing economic panic followed closely upon the public scandals besetting the Grant administration. A contraction of the nation's money supply resulting from the Treasury's postwar withdrawal of greenbacks and the reckless overexpansion of the railroads into sparsely settled areas helped precipitate a financial panic. During 1873 some twenty-five strapped railroads defaulted on their interest payments. A financial panic in Europe forced many financiers to unload American stocks and bonds. Caught short of cash, the prominent investment bank of Jay Cooke and Company went bankrupt on September 18, 1873. The event so frightened investors that the New York Stock Exchange had to close for ten days. The panic of 1873 set off a depression that lasted six years. It was the longest and most severe depression that Americans had yet suffered, marked by widespread bankruptcies, chronic unemployment, and a drastic slowdown in railroad building.

Hard times and political scandals hurt Republicans in the midterm elections of 1874, allowing the Democrats to win control of the House of Representatives and gain seats in the Senate. The new Democratic House immediately launched inquiries into the Grant scandals and unearthed further evidence of corruption in high places. The financial panic, meanwhile, focused attention once more on greenback currency. Since the value of greenbacks was lower than that of gold, paper money had become the chief circulating medium. Most people spent greenbacks first and held their gold or used it to settle foreign accounts, thereby draining much gold out of the country. To relieve this deflationary spiral and stimulate business expansion, the Treasury reissued $26 million in greenbacks that had previously been withdrawn.

For a time the advocates of paper money were riding high. But Grant vetoed an attempt to issue more greenbacks in 1874, and in his annual message he called for their gradual withdrawal and resumption of specie—redeeming greenbacks in gold. Congress obliged the president by passing the specie Resumption Act of 1875. The resumption of payments in gold to customers who turned in greenbacks began on January 1, 1879, after the Treasury had built a gold reserve for the purpose and reduced the value of the greenbacks in circulation. This act infuriated those promoting an inflationary monetary policy and led to the formation of the National Greenback party. The much debated and very complex "money question" would remain one of the most divisive issues in American politics until the end of the century.

THE COMPROMISE OF 1877   Grant yearned to run for president again in 1876, but his scandal-ridden administration cost him Republican support. James Gillespie Blaine of Maine, a former Speaker of the House, emerged as the Republican front-runner, but he, too, bore the taint of scandal. Letters in the possession of James Mulligan of Boston linked Blaine to dubious railroad dealings. Newspapers soon published the "Mulligan letters," and Blaine's candidacy was dealt a hefty blow.

The Republican Convention therefore eliminated Blaine and several other hopefuls in favor of Ohio's favorite son, Rutherford B. Hayes. Three times governor of Ohio and an advocate of hard money, Hayes had a sterling reputation and had been a civil service reformer. But his chief virtue, as a journalist put it, was that "he is obnoxious to no one."

The Democratic Convention was abnormally harmonious from the start. The nomination went on the second ballot to Samuel J. Tilden, a millionaire corporation lawyer and reform governor of New York who had directed a campaign to overthrow first the corrupt Tweed ring that controlled New York City politics and then the canal ring in Albany, which had bilked New York State of millions.

The 1876 election campaign generated no burning issues. Both candidates favored the trend toward relaxing federal authority and restoring white conservative rule in the South. In the absence of strong differences, Democrats waved the Republicans' dirty linen. In response, Republicans waved "the bloody shirt," which is to say that they engaged in verbal assaults on former Confederates and the spirit of rebellion, linking the Democratic party to secession and the outrages committed against Republicans in the South.

Early election returns pointed to a Tilden victory. Tilden had a 254,000-vote edge in the popular vote and won 184 electoral votes, just one short of a majority. Hayes had 165 electoral votes, but Republicans also claimed 19 disputed votes from Florida, Louisiana, and South Carolina. The Democrats laid a counterclaim to 1 of Oregon's 3 votes. The Republicans had clearly carried Oregon, but the outcome in the South was less certain, and given the fraud and intimidation perpetrated on both sides, nobody will ever know the truth of the matter. In all three of the disputed southern states, rival canvassing boards sent in different returns. The Constitution offered no guidance in this unprecedented situation. Even if Congress were empowered to sort things out, the Democratic House and the Republican Senate proved unable to reach an agreement.

The impasse dragged on for months, and there was even talk of partisan violence. Finally, on January 29, 1877, the two houses set up a special Electoral Commission that would investigate and report its findings. It had fifteen members, five each from the House, the Senate, and the Supreme Court. Members were chosen such that there were seven from each major party, with Justice David Davis of Illinois as the swing vote. Davis, though appointed to the Court by Lincoln, was no party regular and in fact was thought to be leaning toward the Democrats. Thus the panel appeared to be stacked in favor of Tilden.

As it turned out, however, the panel got restacked the other way. Short-sighted Democrats in the Illinois legislature teamed up with minority Greenbackers to name Davis their senator. Davis accepted, no doubt with a sense of relief. From the remaining justices, all Republicans, the panel chose Joseph P. Bradley to fill the vacancy. The decision on each state went by a vote of eight to seven along party lines, in favor of Hayes. After much bluster and the threat of a filibuster by the Democrats, the House voted on March 2 to accept the report and declared Hayes elected by an electoral vote of 185 to 184.

Critical to this outcome was the defection of southern Democrats who had made several informal agreements with the Republicans. On February 26, 1877, a bargain was struck at Wormley's Hotel in Washington, D.C., between prominent Ohio Republicans (including James A. Garfield) and powerful southern Democrats. The Republicans promised that if elected, Hayes would withdraw federal troops from Louisiana and South Carolina, letting the Republican governments there collapse. In return, the Democrats pledged to withdraw their opposition to Hayes, accept in good faith the Reconstruction amendments, and refrain from partisan reprisals against Republicans in the South.

Southern Democrats could now justify deserting Tilden. This so-called Compromise of 1877 brought a final "redemption" from the Radicals and a return to "home rule," which meant rule by white Democrats. As a former slave observed in 1877, "The whole South—every state in the south—has got [back] into the hands of the very men that held us as slaves." Other, more informal promises, bolstered the secret agreement. Hayes's friends pledged more support for rebuilding Mississippi River levees and other internal improvements, including a federal subsidy for a transcontinental railroad along a southern route. Southerners extracted a further promise that Hayes would name a white southerner as postmaster general, the cabinet position with the most patronage jobs to distribute. In return, southerners would let the Republicans make James Garfield the Speaker of the new House. Such a deal illustrates the relative weakness of the presidency compared with Congress during the postwar era.

THE END OF RECONSTRUCTION   In 1877 President Hayes withdrew federal troops from Louisiana and South Carolina, and the Republican governments there soon collapsed—along with Hayes's claim to legitimacy. Hayes chose a Tennessean as postmaster general. But after southern Democrats failed to permit the choice of James Garfield as Speaker of the House, Hayes expressed doubt about any further subsidy for railroad building, and none was voted. Most of the other promises made at Wormley's Hotel were renounced or forgotten.

As for southern promises regarding the civil rights of blacks, only a few Democratic leaders remembered them for long. Over the next three decades the federal protection of civil rights crumbled under the pressure of restored white rule in the South and the force of Supreme Court decisions narrowing the application of the Fourteenth and Fifteenth Amendments. Radical Reconstruction never offered more than an uncertain commitment to racial equality. Yet it left an enduring legacy, the Thirteenth, Fourteenth, and Fifteenth Amendments—not dead but dormant, waiting to be revived. If Reconstruction did not provide social equality or substantial economic opportunities for African Americans, it did create the opportunity for future transformation. It was a revolution, sighed former North Carolina governor Jonathan Worth, and "nobody can anticipate the action of revolutions."

MAKING CONNECTIONS

- The political, economic, and racial policies of the conservatives who overthrew the Republican governments in the southern states are described in Chapter 19.

- Several of the political scandals mentioned in this chapter were related to the railroads, a topic discussed in greater detail in Chapter 20.

- This chapter ended with the election of Rutherford B. Hayes; for a discussion of Hayes's administration, see Chapter 22.

FURTHER READING

The most comprehensive treatment of Reconstruction is Eric Foner's *Reconstruction: America's Unfinished Revolution, 1863-1877* (1988). On Andrew Johnson, see Hans L. Trefousse's *Andrew Johnson: A Biography* (1989). An excellent brief biography of Grant is Josiah Bunting III's *Ulysses S. Grant* (2004).

Scholars have been fairly sympathetic to the aims and motives of the Radical Republicans. See, for instance, Herman Belz's *Reconstructing the Union: Theory and Policy during the Civil War* (1969) and Richard Nelson Current's *Those Terrible Carpetbaggers: A Reinterpretation* (1988). The ideology of the Radical Republicans is explored in Michael Les Benedict's *A Compromise of Principle: Congressional Republicans and Reconstruction, 1863–1869* (1974).

The intransigence of southern white attitudes is examined in Michael Perman's *Reunion without Compromise* (1973) and Dan T. Carter's *When the War Was Over: The Failure of Self-Reconstruction in the South, 1865–1867* (1985). Allen W. Trelease's *White Terror: The Ku Klux and Southern Reconstruction* (1971) covers the various organizations that practiced vigilante tactics. The difficulties former laborers had in adjusting to the new labor system are documented in James L. Roark's *Masters without Slaves: Southern Planters to the Civil War and Reconstruction* (1977). Books on southern politics during Reconstruction include Michael Perman's *The Road to Redemption: Southern Politics, 1869–1879* (1984), Terry L. Seip's *The South Returns to Congress: Men, Economic Measures, and Intersectional Relationships, 1868–1879* (1983), and Mark W. Summer's *Railroads, Reconstruction, and the Gospel of Prosperity: Aid under Radical Republicans, 1865–1877* (1984).

Numerous works feature the freed blacks' experience in the South. Start with Leon F. Litwack's *Been in the Storm So Long: The Aftermath of Slavery* (1979), which covers the transition from slavery to freedom. Joel Williamson's *After Slavery: The Negro in South Carolina during Reconstruction, 1861–1877* (1965) argues that South Carolina blacks took an active role in pursuing their political and economic rights. The Freedmen's Bureau is explored in William S. McFeely's *Yankee Stepfather: General O. O. Howard and the Freedmen* (1968). The situation of freed slave women is discussed in Jacqueline Jones's *Labor of Love, Labor of Sorrow: Black Women, Work, and the Family, from Slavery to the Present* (1985).

The politics of corruption outside the South is depicted in William S. McFeely's *Grant: A Biography* (1981). The political maneuvers of the election of 1876 and the resultant crisis and compromise are explained in C. Vann Woodward's *Reunion and Reaction: The Compromise of 1877 and the End of Reconstruction* (1951) and in William Gillette's *Retreat from Reconstruction, 1869–1879* (1979).

Part Five

GROWING

PAINS

| 1876 | Granger movement brings about passage of Granger laws to help farmers (1870s) | Large numbers of Irish, British, and Germans immigrate to the U.S., including anarchists (1870s–1880s) |

1876

Granger movement brings about passage of Granger laws to help farmers (1870s)

No president wins a majority of the popular vote (1876–1896)

Rutherford B. Hayes serves as president after disputed election (1877–1881)

Bourbons (planter-merchant elite) dominate southern politics and use poll taxes, literacy tests, and the grandfather clause to disenfranchise blacks (1877–1890s)

Large numbers of Irish, British, and Germans immigrate to the U.S., including anarchists (1870s–1880s)

Japan industrializes and rises to world-power status (1870s–1890s)

Queen Victoria of England is proclaimed empress of India (1876)

Famine in China leads many Chinese men to immigrate to America (1877–1878)

First shipments of frozen meats arrive in Europe from Argentina and Australia (late 1870s)

Congress of Berlin gives Austria the right to "occupy and administer" the Ottoman provinces of Bosnia and Herzegovina (1878)

Socialist Labor party is organized in America (1877)

Greenback party, which favors expansion of currency through additional paper money, elects 15 congressmen (1878)

1880

Government services—such as water, sewers, street lighting, and fire and police protection—expand (1880s–1900)

Urban political machines help provide food, coal, money, and food for the poor (1880s–1910s)

James A. Garfield becomes president (1881)

European drive for raw materials and markets leads to scramble for colonies in Africa (1880s–1890s)

French company begins to dig a canal through Panama (1881–1887)

Pro-imperialist German colonial League established; British occupy Egypt (1882)

Austria, Germany, and Italy form the Triple Alliance (1882)

Germany enacts social security reform laws (1883–1889)

England's Reform Act gives vote to nearly all men (1884)

Berlin Conference meets to consider issues of imperialism (1884–1885)

Canadian Pacific, a transcontinental railroad, is completed (1885)

Indian National Congress is formed to foster Indian participation in government (1885)

Three Emperors' League (Germany, Russia, and Austria) collapses (1887)

Japan adopts a constitution (1889)

Second (Socialist) International attempts to strengthen the socialist movement (1889–1914)

Chester A. Arthur serves as president after Garfield is assassinated (1881–1885)

Civil Rights Act of 1875 is declared unconstitutional (1883)

Congress passes Pendleton Civil Service Reform Act to ensure distribution of government jobs based on merit (1883)

Grover Cleveland serves as president (1885–1889)

Greenback party disintegrates (1885)

African-American Exodusters move from the South to Kansas (1870s–1880s)

"Flood tide" of pioneers goes west; harsh life results in greater equality between men and women (1870s–1890s)

Vaudeville houses are established in cities across the U.S. (1870s–1890s)

Colleges and high schools organize football teams (1870s–1900s)

Andrew Carnegie invests $120 million in public libraries and education (1870s–1910s)

Indians defeat George A. Custer's forces in the Battle of Little Bighorn (1876)

Alexander Graham Bell patents the telephone, making possible unprecedented rapid communication over long distances (1876)

Thomas Edison's inventions of the phonograph (1877) and the first successful incandescent lightbulb drastically affect leisure and work (1879)

Atlanta Constitution heralds the advent of a "New South" (1880s)

Proponents of the New South espouse idea of "separate but equal" (1880s–1960s)

Baseball becomes national pastime (1880s)

Construction of taller buildings, made possible by iron and steel frames and electric elevators, allows more people to live and work in cities (1880s–1890s)

Immigrants from Europe and Asia settle in large numbers in the largest U.S. cities, providing much-needed labor; ethnic and racial tensions increase (1880s–1890s)

States hold referenda on the prohibition of alcoholic beverages (1880s–1890s)

Amusement parks appear in many major cities (1880s–1900s)

Number of employed women increases (1880s–1890s)

Chinese Exclusion Act prohibits immigration of Chinese for ten years (1882)

John D. Rockefeller consolidates oil-refining industry into Standard Oil Company of Ohio, which comes to control 90–95 percent of U.S. oil (1870s)

Second Industrial Revolution connects national transportation and communications networks, expanding the international market for U.S. goods (1870s)

Grangers promote farmer-owned cooperatives for buying and selling farm products (1870s)

Building of transcontinental railways and trunk lines extends miles of railways from 35,000 to 200,000 (1870s–1890s)

Mining, dry farming, and irrigation further open the West for settlement (1870s–1890s)

"Bonanza" farms, for mass production of crops and livestock, are established in the West (1870s–1890s)

Southern coal production increases from 5 million tons to 49 million tons (1875–1900)

Great Railroad Strike erupts when workers oppose wage cuts (1877)

Knights of Labor becomes a national movement (1878)

Andrew Carnegie consolidates steel industry in Pittsburgh (1880s)

George Westinghouse's improvements of the alternating-current motor enables factories to locate wherever they wish (1880s)

Textile production expands in the South; the number of mills increases from 161 to 400 (1880s–1900)

Sagging crop prices make it increasingly difficult to own land (1880s–1890s)

Rise of sheepherding and barbed-wire fencing disrupts cattle grazing, causing "barbed-wire wars" between small farmers and cattle barons (1880s)

Edison Electric Illuminating Company, the world's first public utilities company, is established in New York City (1882)

Foran Act is passed, penalizing employers who import contract labor from abroad (1885)

Strike at Chicago's International Harvester plant leads to the Haymarket bombing (1886)

American Federation of Labor is founded (1886)

1876

1880

In *Wabash Railroad v. Illinois*, U.S.
Supreme Court denies states the right to
regulate interstate commerce (1886)

Cleveland administration creates Interstate
Commerce Commission (1887)

Dawes Severalty Act disrupts Indian culture by privatizing Indians' land (1887)

Farmers' Alliances turn to politics but fail
to achieve significant gains for rural
America (1880s–1890)

Benjamin Harrison serves as president
(1889–1893)

1890 Mississippi constitutional convention effectively disenfranchises African Americans (1890)

National American Woman Suffrage Association is established, with Elizabeth
Cady Stanton as its first president (1890)

People's party is established, otherwise
known as the Populist party (1892)

Grover Cleveland serves as president for
the second time (1893–1897)

Populists poll 1.5 million votes for congressional candidates (1894)

Supreme Court rules in *In re Debs* that
force may be used to enforce federal law
(1895)

Plessy v. Ferguson sanctions "separate but
equal" segregation (1896)

Bismarck is dismissed as prime minister of
Germany (1890)

Doctrine of Social Darwinism fuels imperialism (1890s)

Large numbers of eastern and southern
Europeans immigrate to in the U.S.
(1890s–1900s)

France and Russia form the Dual Alliance
(1894)

Sino-Japanese War furthers Japan's imperialism (1894–1895)

William Jennings Bryan runs for president
as Democratic-Populist-Silverite candidate on a free-silver platform (1896)

Struggle between urban and rural America
culminates in 1896 election; collapse of
the Populist party signals the failure of

1900 agrarian activism (1896)

South Carolina becomes the first southern
state to adopt a statewide primary, effectively excluding black voters (1896)

Eugene Debs organizes the Social Democratic party (1897)

William McKinley serves as president
(1897–1901)

Spanish-American War (1898)

Hawaii is annexed by U.S.; Puerto Rico,
Guam, and the Philippines become U.S.
territories (1898)

Fashoda crisis in the Sudan brings British
and French to brink of war (1898)

U.S. appoints military governor of Cuba
(1898)

Beginning of Open Door trade policy in
China (1899)

Boer War in South Africa (1899–1902)

Boxer Rebellion occurs in reaction to Western presence in China (1900)

Britain agrees to establishment of the
Commonwealth of Australia (1900)

Foraker Act establishes a civil government
in Puerto Rico (1900)

William Howard Taft is sent to the Philippines by McKinley to set up a civil government (1901)

Mark Twain publishes *The Adventures of Huckleberry Finn* (1884)

Depletion of buffalo and capture of Geronimo (1886) lead to collapse of Indian resistance movement (1880s)

Black players are banned from minor-league baseball teams (1887)

Andrew Carnegie's "Gospel of Wealth" is published (1889)

College enrollment increases from 52,000 (1870) to 157,000 (1890); professors increasingly have doctorates (1890s)

12 percent of whites and 50 percent of blacks are illiterate (1890)

Ghost Dance movement leads to bloodbath at Wounded Knee (1890)

"Streetcar suburbs" spring up as a result of transportation revolution, leading to exodus of middle and upper classes from city centers (1890s)

Annual lynchings average 187 with 82 percent occurring in the South (1890–1899)

Ongoing nativism leads to further immigration restrictions (1890s–1950s)

James Naismith invents basketball (1891)

Chinese Exclusion Act of 1882 is renewed for another 10 years (1892)

Ellis Island is opened as a reception center for new immigrants (1892)

Frederick Jackson Turner presents "The Significance of the Frontier in American History" (1893)

Stephen Crane publishes *The Red Badge of Courage* (1895)

Booker T. Washington's "Atlanta Compromise" urges blacks to accommodate white racism and domination (1895)

W.E.B. Du Bois calls for "ceaseless agitation" by blacks (1897)

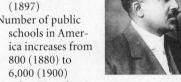

Number of public schools in America increases from 800 (1880) to 6,000 (1900)

Nearly 100 settlement houses dot urban America (1900)

30 percent of residents of major cities are foreign-born (1900)

Texas Farmers' Alliance unsuccessfully promotes Alliance Exchange to free farmers from dependence on food processors and banks (1887)

Severe winters decimate the open range (1886, 1887), followed by 10 years of drought in the West (1890s)

Congress defeats the Farmers' Alliance sub-treasury plan for storage of crops and loans to farmers (1890)

Dependent Pension Act provides funds to veterans who cannot work (1890)

1890

Five vertically integrated companies produce 90 percent of all meat shipped in interstate commerce (1890)

Tenant farmers and sharecroppers constitute a majority of farmworkers in the Deep South (1890)

Sherman Silver Purchase Act (1890)

McKinley Tariff raises duties on manufactured goods 49.5 percent (1890)

Sherman Anti-Trust Act prohibits businesses from monopolizing trade (1890)

U.S. surpasses Britain in iron and steel production (1890s)

Sears, Roebuck comes to dominate the mail-order industry (1890s)

Pittsburgh steelworkers stage Homestead strike (1892)

Ohio Supreme Court orders dissolution of Standard Oil Company (1892)

Depression destroys many small businesses (1893)

President Cleveland rescinds Sherman Silver Purchase Act, sharpening the debate regarding silver coinage (1893)

American Railway Union is founded by Eugene Debs (1893)

Employees of Pullman Palace Car Company in Illinois stage a major strike (1894)

J. P. Morgan and other financiers supply gold to buy up government bonds and stop demands on Treasury (1895)

Dingley Tariff raises duty to 57 percent of the value of imported goods, the highest in U.S. history (1897)

1900

Gold Standard Act ends the silver movement (1900)

he Federal victory in 1865 restored the Union and in the process helped accelerate America's transformation into a modern nation-state. A distinctly national consciousness began to displace the sectional emphases of the antebellum era. During and after the Civil War the Republican-led Congress pushed through legislation to foster industrial and commercial development and western expansion. In the process the United States abandoned the Jeffersonian dream of a decentralized agrarian republic and began to forge a dynamic new industrial economy generated by an increasingly national market.

After 1865 many Americans turned their attention to the unfinished business of settling a continent and completing an urban-industrial revolution begun before the war. Huge national corporations based upon mass production and mass marketing began to dominate the economy. As the prominent sociologist William Graham Sumner remarked, the process of industrial development "controls us all because we are all in it. It creates the conditions of our own existence, sets the limits of our social activity, and regulates the bonds of our social relations."

The Industrial Revolution was not only an urban phenomenon; it transformed rural life as well. Those who got in the way of the new emphasis on large-scale, highly mechanized commercial agriculture and ranching were brusquely pushed aside. The friction between new market forces and traditional folkways generated political revolts and social unrest during the last quarter of the nineteenth century.

The clash between tradition and modernity peaked during the 1890s, one of the most strife-ridden decades in American history. A deep depression, agrarian unrest, and labor violence provoked fears of class warfare. This turbulent situation transformed the presidential election campaign of 1896 into a clash between rival visions of America's future. The Republican candidate, William McKinley, campaigned on behalf of modern urban-industrial values. By contrast, William Jennings Bryan, the nominee of the Democratic and Populist parties, was an eloquent defender of America's rural past. McKinley's victory proved to be a watershed in political and social history. By 1900 the United States would emerge as one of the world's greatest industrial powers, and it would thereafter assume a new leadership role in world affairs.

19

THE SOUTH AND THE WEST TRANSFORMED

FOCUS QUESTIONS

· What were the economic and political policies of the states in the post-Reconstruction South?

· How did segregation and disenfranchisement shape race relations in the New South?

· What were the experiences of the farmers, miners, and cowboys in the West?

· What were the consequences of late-nineteenth-century Indian policy?

To answer these questions and access additional review material, please visit www.wwnorton.com/studyspace.

After the Civil War the South and the West provided enticing opportunities for pioneers and entrepreneurs. Before 1860 most Americans had viewed the region between the Mississippi River and California as a barren landscape unfit for human habitation or cultivation, an uninviting land suitable only for Indians and animals. Half the state of Texas, for instance, was still not settled at the end of the Civil War. After 1865, however, the federal government encouraged western settlement and economic development. The construction of transcontinental railroads, the military conquest of the Indians, and a liberal land-distribution policy combined to help lure thousands of pioneers and expectant capitalists westward.

Although the first great wave of railroad building occurred in the 1850s, the most spectacular growth took place during the quarter century after the Civil War. From about 35,000 miles of track in 1865, the national rail network grew to nearly 200,000 miles by 1897. The transcontinental rail lines led the way, and they helped populate the plains and the Far West. Meanwhile, southern rail lines were rebuilt and supplemented with new branches. The defeated South, although not a frontier in the literal sense of the term, offered a fertile new ground for investment and industrial development. After 1865 proponents of a "New South" argued that the region must abandon its single-minded preoccupation with agriculture and pursue industrial and commercial development. As a result, the South as well as the West experienced dramatic social and economic changes during the last third of the nineteenth century. By 1900 the South and the West had been transformed in ways that few could have predicted, and fourteen new states were created out of the western territories.

THE NEW SOUTH

A FRESH VISION   After the Civil War many southerners looked wistfully to the plantation life that had characterized their region before the firing on Fort Sumter in 1861. A few prominent leaders, however, insisted that the postwar South must liberate itself from nostalgia and create a new society of small farms, thriving industries, and bustling cities. The major prophet of this New South was Henry W. Grady, the young editor of the *Atlanta Constitution*. Grady's compelling vision of a New South attracted many supporters, who preached the gospel of industry with evangelical fervor. The Confederacy, they reasoned, had lost because it had relied too much upon King Cotton. In the future the South must follow the North's example and industrialize. From that central belief flowed certain implications: that a more diversified and a more efficient agriculture would be a foundation for economic growth and that more widespread education, especially vocational training, would promote material success. By the late 1870s, with Reconstruction over and the panic of 1873 forgotten, a mood of progress permeated the editorials and speeches of the day.

ECONOMIC GROWTH   The chief accomplishment of the New South movement was an expansion of the region's textile production. From 1880 to 1900, the number of cotton mills in the South grew from 161 to 400, and the number of mill workers (among whom women and children outnumbered men) increased fivefold.

Tobacco growing also increased significantly after the Civil War. Essential to the rise of the tobacco industry was the Duke family of Durham, North Carolina. At the end of the Civil War, the story goes, Washington Duke took a load of tobacco and, with the help of his three sons, beat it out with hickory sticks, stuffed it into bags, hitched two mules to his wagon, and set out across the state, selling tobacco as he went. By 1872 the Dukes had a factory producing 125,000 pounds of tobacco annually, and Washington Duke prepared to settle down and enjoy success.

His son Buck (James Buchanan Duke), wanted even greater success, however. He recognized that the tobacco industry was "half smoke and half ballyhoo," so he poured large sums into advertising schemes. Duke also undersold competitors in their own market and cornered the supply of ingredients. In 1890 Duke brought most of his competitors into the American Tobacco Company, which controlled nine tenths of the nation's cigarette production. In 1911 the Supreme Court ruled that the company was in violation of the anti-trust laws and ordered it broken up, but by then Duke had found new worlds to conquer, in hydroelectric power and aluminum.

Systematic use of other natural resources helped revitalize the region along the Appalachian Mountain chain from West Virginia to Alabama. Coal production in the South grew from 5 million tons in 1875 to 49 million tons by 1900. At the southern end of the mountains, Birmingham, Alabama, sprang up during the 1870s as a major steel-producing center and soon tagged itself the Pittsburgh of the South.

Industrial growth created a need for wood-framed housing, and after 1870 lumbering became a thriving industry in the South. By the turn of the century, it had surpassed textiles in value. Tree cutting seemed to know no bounds, despite the resulting ecological devastation. In time the industry would be saved only by the warm climate, which fostered quick growth of replanted forests, and the rise of scientific forestry.

Two forces that would impel an even greater industrial revolution were already on the southern horizon at the turn of the century: petroleum in the Southwest and hydroelectric power in the Southeast. In 1901 the Spindletop oil gusher in Texas brought a huge bonanza. Electrical power proved equally profitable, and local power plants dotted the South by the 1890s. Richmond, Virginia, developed the nation's first electric streetcar system in 1888, and Columbia, South Carolina, boasted the first electrically powered cotton mill in 1894. The greatest advance would begin in 1905 when Buck Duke's Southern Power Company set out to electrify entire river valleys in the Carolinas.

AGRICULTURE OLD AND NEW   At the start of the twentieth century, however, most of the South remained undeveloped, at least by northeastern standards. Despite the optimistic rhetoric of Henry Grady and other New South spokesmen, the typical southerner was less apt to be tending a textile loom than, as the saying went, facing the eastern end of a westbound mule. King Cotton survived the Civil War and expanded over new acreage even as its export markets leveled off. Louisiana cane sugar, probably the most war-devastated of all crops, was flourishing again by the 1890s.

The majority of southern farmers were not flourishing, however. A prolonged deflation in crop prices affected the entire Western world during the last third of the nineteenth century. Sagging prices for farm crops made it more difficult than ever to own land. Sharecropping and tenancy among poor blacks and whites became the norm. By 1890 most southern farms were worked by people who did not own the land.

How did the system work? Sharecroppers, who had nothing to offer the landowner but their labor, worked the owner's land in return for supplies and a share of the crop, generally about half. Tenant farmers, hardly better off, might have their own mule, a plow, and credit with the country store. They were entitled to claim a larger share of the crops. The sharecropper-tenant system was horribly inefficient; it was essentially a form of land slavery, and tenants and owners developed an intense suspicion of each other. The folklore of the rural South was replete with tales of tenants who remained stubbornly shiftless and scheming landlords who swindled farmworkers by not giving them a fair share of the crops.

The postwar South suffered an acute shortage of capital; people had to devise ways to operate without cash. One innovation was the crop-lien system: merchants furnished supplies in return for liens (or mortgages) on farmers' crops. To a few tenants and small farmers who seized the chance, such credit offered a way out of dependency, but to most it offered only a hopeless cycle of perennial debt. The merchant, who assumed great risks, generally charged interest that ranged, according to one journalist, "from 24 percent to grand larceny." The merchant required his farmer clients to grow a cash crop that could be readily sold at harvest time. Thus the routines of tenancy and sharecropping were geared to a staple crop, usually cotton. The resulting stagnation of rural life held millions, white and black, in bondage to privation and ignorance.

TENANCY AND THE ENVIRONMENT   The pervasive use of tenancy and sharecropping unwittingly caused profound environmental damage. Growing commercial row crops like cotton on the same land year after year

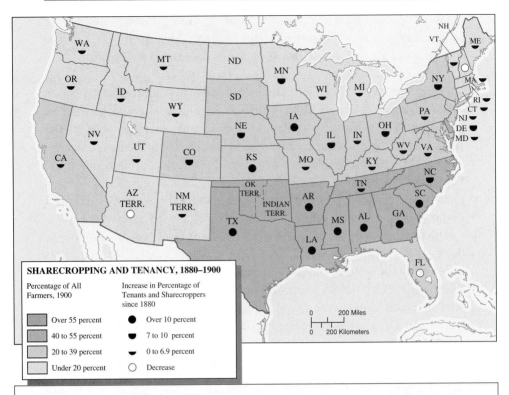

SHARECROPPING AND TENANCY, 1880–1900

Percentage of All Farmers, 1900
- Over 55 percent
- 40 to 55 percent
- 20 to 39 percent
- Under 20 percent

Increase in Percentage of Tenants and Sharecroppers since 1880
- ● Over 10 percent
- ◗ 7 to 10 percent
- ◡ 0 to 6.9 percent
- ○ Decrease

Why was there a dramatic increase in sharecropping and tenancy in the late nineteenth century? Why did the South have more sharecroppers than other parts of the country? Why do you think the rate of sharecropping was lowest in western states like New Mexico and Arizona?

leached the nutrients from the soil. Tenants had no incentive to take care of farmland by manuring fields or rotating crops because it was not their own. They used fertilizer to accelerate the growing cycle, but the extensive use of phosphate fertilizers only accelerated soil depletion, by enabling multiple plantings each year. Fertilizer, said an observer, seduced southern farmers into believing that there was a "short cut to prosperity, a royal road to good crops of cotton year after year. The result has been that their lands have been cultivated clean year after year, and their fertility has been exhausted."

Once the soil had lost its fertility, the tenants moved on to another farm, leaving behind rutted fields whose topsoil washed away with each rain. The silt and mud flowed into creeks and rivers, swamping many lowland fields and filling millponds and lakes. By the early twentieth century much of the rural South resembled a ravaged land: deep gullies sliced through bare eroded hillsides, and streams and deep lakes were clogged with silt. As far as the eye could see, red clay devoid of nutrients dominated the landscape.

THE BOURBON REDEEMERS   In post–Civil War southern politics, habits of social deference and elitism still prevailed. After Reconstruction ended, in 1877, a planter-merchant elite dominated southern politics. The supporters of these postwar Democratic leaders referred to them as redeemers because they supposedly redeemed, or saved, the South from Yankee domination as well as from the limitations of a purely rural economy. The redeemers included a rising class of entrepreneurs eager to promote a more diversified economy based upon industrial development and railroad expansion.

The opponents of the redeemers labeled them Bourbons in an effort to depict them as reactionaries. Like the French royal family that, Napoléon had said, forgot nothing and learned nothing in the ordeal of revolution, the Bourbons of the postwar South were said to have forgotten nothing and to have learned nothing in the ordeal of the Civil War.

The Bourbons of the New South perfected a political alliance with northeastern conservatives and an economic alliance with northeastern capitalists. They generally pursued a government policy of frugality, except for the tax exemptions and other favors they offered business. They slashed expenditures and avoided political initiatives, making the transition from Republican rule to Bourbon rule less abrupt than is often assumed. The Bourbons' favorable disposition toward the railroads was not unlike that of the Radical Republicans. And despite their reputation for honesty, Bourbon officeholders were occasionally caught with their fingers in the till.

The Bourbons focused on cutting back the size and cost of government. This policy spelled austerity for public services, including the school systems started during Reconstruction. In 1871 the southern Atlantic states were spending $10.27 per pupil; by 1880 the figure was down to $6, and in 1890 it stood at only $7.63. In South Carolina in 1882, there were 3,183 schools but only 3,413 teachers. Illiteracy rates at the time were at about 12 percent among whites and 50 percent among blacks.

The Bourbons' urge to economize led them to adopt the degrading system of convict leasing. The destruction of prisons during the Civil War and the poverty of state treasuries afterward combined with the demand for cheap labor to make the leasing of convict workers a way for southern states to avoid penitentiary expenses and generate revenue. Convict leasing, in the absence of state supervision, allowed inefficiency, neglect, and disregard for human life to proliferate.

The Bourbons reduced not only state expenditures but also a vast amount of government debt. The corruption and extravagance of Radical Republican rule were commonly advanced as justification for the process, but repudiation of debts was not limited to debt incurred during Reconstruction. Altogether nine states repudiated more than half of what they owed bondholders and other creditors.

The penny-pinching Bourbon regimes did respond to the demand for commissions to regulate the rates charged by railroads for commercial transport. They also established boards of agriculture and public health, agricultural and mechanical colleges, teacher-training schools and women's colleges, and even state colleges for African Americans. Nor can any simplistic interpretation encompass the variety of Bourbon leaders. The Democratic party was then a mongrel coalition that threw old Whigs, Unionists, secessionists, businessmen, small farmers, hillbillies, planters, and even some Republicans together in an alliance against the Reconstruction Radicals. Democrats, therefore, even those who bore the Bourbon label, often marched to different drummers, and the Bourbon regimes never achieved complete unity in philosophy or government.

The Effects of Radical and Bourbon Rule in the South

This 1880 cartoon shows the South staggering under the oppressive weight of military Reconstruction (left) and flourishing under the "Let 'Em Alone Policy" of President Rutherford B. Hayes and the Bourbons (right).

Perhaps the ultimate paradox of the Bourbons' rule was that these paragons of white supremacy tolerated a lingering black voice in politics and showed no haste to raise legal barriers of racial separation. African Americans sat in Virginia's state legislature until 1890, in South Carolina's until 1900, and in Georgia's until 1908; some of them were Democrats. The South sent black congressmen to Washington in every election except one, until 1900, though they always represented gerrymandered districts into which most of a state's black voters had been thrown. Under the Bourbons the disenfranchisement of black voters remained inconsistent, a local matter brought about mainly by fraud and intimidation, although it occurred often enough to ensure white control of the southern states.

A like flexibility applied in other aspects of race relations. The color line was drawn less strictly immediately after the Civil War than it would be in the twentieth-century South. In some places, to be sure, racial segregation appeared before the end of Reconstruction, especially in schools, churches, hotels and rooming houses, and private social relations. In other public places, such as trains, depots, theaters, and soda fountains, however, segregation was more sporadic.

DISENFRANCHISING AFRICAN AMERICANS   During the 1890s the attitudes that permitted moderation in race relations evaporated. A violent "Negrophobia" swept across the South and much of the nation at the end of the century. Many whites had come to resent signs of black success and social influence. An Alabama newspaper editor declared that "our blood boils when the educated Negro asserts himself politically. We regard each assertion as an unfriendly encroachment upon our native superior rights, and a dare-devil menace to our control of the affairs of the state."

Education did bring enlightenment—as it was supposed to do. In 1889 the student newspaper at all-black Fisk University in Nashville predicted a profound change in race relations at the end of the century. It stressed that a new generation of young African Americans born since the end of the Civil War and educated in schools and colleges were determined to gain true equality. They were more assertive and less patient than their parents. A growing number of young white adults, however, were equally determined to keep "Negroes in their place."

Racial violence and repression surged to the fore during the last decade of the nineteenth century and the first two decades of the twentieth. By the end of the nineteenth century, the so-called New South had come to resemble the Old South. Ruling whites ruthlessly imposed their will over all areas of

African-American life. They prevented blacks from voting and enacted "Jim Crow" laws mandating public separation of the races. This development was not the logical culmination of the Civil War and emancipation but rather the result of a calculated campaign by white elites and thugs to limit African-American political, economic, and social life.

The political dynamics of the 1890s exacerbated racial tensions. The rise of Populism, a farm-based protest movement that culminated in the creation of a third political party in the 1890s, divided the white vote to such an extent that in some places the African-American vote became the balance of power. Some Populists courted black votes. In response the Bourbons revived the race issue, which they exploited with seasoned finesse, all the while controlling for their ticket a good part of the black vote in plantation areas. Nevertheless, during the 1890s the Bourbons began to insist that the black vote be eliminated completely from southern elections. Some farm leaders hoped that the disenfranchisement of African Americans would make it possible for whites to divide politically without raising the specter of "Negro domination."

But since the Fifteenth Amendment made it illegal simply to deny blacks the vote, racists accomplished their purpose indirectly, through such devices as poll taxes (or head taxes) and literacy tests. Mississippi led the way to near-total disenfranchisement of blacks—and many poor whites as well. The state called a constitutional convention in 1890 to change the suffrage provisions of the Radical Republican constitution of 1868. The resulting Mississippi plan set the pattern that seven more states would follow over the next twenty years. First, a residence requirement—two years in the state, one year in an election district—struck at those black tenant farmers who were in the habit of moving yearly in search of better opportunities. Second, voters were disqualified if convicted of certain crimes, many of them petty. Third, all taxes, including a poll tax, had to be paid by February 1 of each year. This proviso fell most heavily on the poor, most of whom were black. Finally, all voters had to be literate. The alternative, designed as a loophole for otherwise-disqualified whites, was an "understanding" clause. The voter, if unable to read the Constitution, could qualify by "understanding" it—to the satisfaction of the registrar. Fraud was thus institutionalized by "legal" disenfranchisement.

Other states added variations on the Mississippi plan. In 1898 Louisiana invented the "grandfather clause," which allowed illiterates to register to vote if their fathers or grandfathers had been eligible to vote on January 1, 1867, when African Americans were still disenfranchised. By 1910 Georgia, North

Carolina, Virginia, Alabama, and Oklahoma had adopted the grandfather clause. Every southern state, moreover, adopted a statewide Democratic primary, which became the only meaningful election outside isolated areas of Republican strength. With minor exceptions the Democratic primaries excluded African-American voters altogether. The effectiveness of these measures can be seen in a few sample figures: Louisiana in 1896 had 130,000 black voters registered and in 1900, 5,320. Alabama in 1900 had 121,159 literate black men over twenty-one, according to the census; only 3,742 were registered to vote.

THE SPREAD OF SEGREGATION   What came to be called Jim Crow social segregation followed disenfranchisement and in some states came first. From 1875 to 1883, in fact, any racial segregation violated a federal Civil Rights Act, which forbade discrimination in places of public accommodation. But in 1883 the Supreme Court ruled on seven civil rights cases involving discrimination against blacks by corporations or individuals. The Court held, with only one dissent, that the force of federal law could not extend to individual action because the Fourteenth Amendment, which provided that "no State" could deny citizens equal protection of the law, stood as a prohibition only against state action, not against individual action.

This interpretation left as an open question the validity of state laws *requiring* separate public facilities under the rubric of "separate but equal," a slogan popular with the New South prophets. In 1888 Mississippi required railway passengers to occupy the car set aside for their race. When Louisiana followed suit in 1890, the law was challenged in the case of *Plessy v. Ferguson,* which the Supreme Court decided in 1896.

The test case originated in New Orleans when Homer Plessy, an octoroon (a person of one-eighth African ancestry), refused to leave a whites-only railroad car when asked to do so. He was convicted of violating the segregation statute, and the case rose on appeal to the Supreme Court. The Court ruled that segregation laws "have been generally, if not universally recognized as within the competency of state legislatures in the exercise of their police power." Soon the principle of statutory racial segregation extended to every area of southern life, including streetcars, hotels, restaurants, hospitals, sports, and employment.

Violence accompanied the Jim Crow laws. From 1890 to 1899, lynchings in the United States averaged 188 per year, 82 percent of which occurred in the South; from 1900 to 1909, they averaged 93 per year, of which 92 percent occurred in the South. Whites constituted 32 percent of the victims during the former period but only 11 percent in the latter. A young Episcopal priest in Montgomery, Alabama, remarked that extremists had proceeded "from an undiscriminating attack upon the Negro's ballot to a like attack upon his schools, his labor, his life."

By the end of the nineteenth century, legalized racial discrimination—segregation of public facilities, political disenfranchisement, and vigilante justice punctuated by brutal public lynchings and race riots—had elevated government-sanctioned bigotry to an official way of life in the South. South Carolina senator Benjamin Tillman declared in 1892 that blacks "must remain subordinate or be exterminated."

How did African Americans respond to the resurgence of racism and statutory segregation? Some left the South in search of equality and opportunity, but the vast majority stayed in their native region. In the face of overwhelming force and prejudicial justice, survival in the South required blacks to wear a mask of deference and apply discretion. "Had to walk a quiet life," explained James Plunkett, a Virginia black. "The least little thing you would do, they [whites] would kill ya."

Yet accommodation did not mean total submission. Excluded from the dominant white world and eager to avoid confrontations, black southerners after the 1890s increasingly turned inward and constructed their own culture and nurtured their own pride. A young white visitor to Mississippi in 1910 noticed that nearly every black person he met had "two distinct social selves, the one he reveals to his own people, the other he assumes among the whites."

African-American churches continued to provide the hub for black community life. Often the only public buildings available for blacks, churches were used not only for worship but also for activities that had nothing to do with religion: social gatherings, club meetings, and political activities. For men especially, churches offered leadership roles and political status. Serving as a deacon was one of the most prestigious roles an African-American man could achieve. Churches enabled African Americans of all classes to interact and exercise roles denied them in the larger society. Religious life provided great comfort to people worn down by the daily hardships and abuses associated with segregation.

One irony of state-enforced segregation is that it opened up new economic opportunities for blacks. A new class of African-American entrepreneurs emerged to provide services—insurance, banking, funerals, barbering, hair salons—to the black community in the segregated South. At the same time, African Americans formed their own social and fraternal clubs and organizations, all of which helped bolster black pride and provide fellowship and opportunities for service. For example, the Independent Order of Odd Fellows, the largest of the African-American fraternal orders, had over 400,000 members in 1904.

Middle-class black women formed a network of thousands of racial-uplift organizations across the South and around the nation. The women's clubs were engines of social service in their communities. They cared for the aged and the infirm, the orphaned and the abandoned. They created homes for single mothers and provided nurseries for working mothers. They sponsored health clinics and classes in home economics for women. In 1896 the leaders of such women's clubs from around the country converged to form the National Association of Colored Women, an organization meant to combat racism and segregation. Its first president, Mary Church Terrell, told members that they had an obligation to serve the "lowly, the illiterate, and even the vicious to whom we are bound by the ties of race and sex, and put forth every effort to uplift and reclaim them."

WELLS   One of the most outspoken African-American activists of the time was Ida B. Wells. Born into slavery in 1862 in Mississippi, she attended a school staffed by white missionaries. In 1878 an epidemic of yellow fever killed both her parents as well as an infant brother. At age sixteen, Wells assumed responsibility for her five younger siblings and secured a job as a country schoolteacher. In search of greater economic security and opportunity, Wells moved to nearby Memphis, then fast emerging as a commercial hub and cultural center.

In 1883 Wells confronted the power of white supremacy. After being denied a seat on a railroad car because she was black, she became the first African American to file suit against such discrimination. The circuit court decided in her favor and fined the railroad, but the Tennessee Supreme Court overturned the ruling. Wells thereafter discovered her "first and [it] might be said, my only love"—journalism—and, through it, a weapon with which to promote civil rights. Writing under the pen name Iola, she became a prominent editor of *Memphis Free Speech,* a newspaper focusing on African-American issues.

In 1892, when three of her friends were lynched by a white mob, Wells launched a lifelong crusade against lynching. Angry whites responded by destroying her newspaper office and threatening to lynch her. She moved to New York and continued to use her fiery journalistic talent to criticize Jim Crow laws and demand that African Americans have their voting rights restored. Wells helped found the National Association for the Advancement of Colored People (NAACP) in 1909 and promoted women's suffrage. In demanding full equality, Wells often found herself in direct opposition to the accommodationist views of Booker T. Washington.

WASHINGTON AND DU BOIS

Booker T. Washington, born in Virginia of a slave mother and a white father, fought extreme adversity to get an education at Hampton Institute, one of the postwar missionary schools, and went on to build at Tuskegee, Alabama, a leading college for African Americans. By 1890 Washington had become the nation's foremost black educator.

Booker T. Washington

Founder of the Tuskegee Institute.

Washington argued that blacks should not antagonize whites by demanding social or political equality; instead, they should concentrate on establishing an economic base for their advancement. In a speech at the Atlanta Cotton States and International Exposition in 1895 that propelled him to fame, Washington advised African Americans: "Cast down your bucket where you are—cast it down in making friends . . . of the people of all races by whom we are surrounded. Cast it down in agriculture, mechanics, in commerce, in domestic service, and in the professions." He conspicuously omitted politics from that list and implied an endorsement of segregation: "In all things that are purely social we can be as separate as the five fingers, yet one as the hand in all things essential to mutual progress."

Some people bitterly criticized Washington, in his lifetime and after, for making a bad bargain: the sacrifice of broad education and civil rights for the dubious acceptance of white conservatives and the creation of economic opportunities for blacks. W.E.B. Du Bois led African Americans in this criticism. A native of Great Barrington, Massachusetts, and the son of free blacks, Du Bois first experienced southern racial practices as an undergraduate at Fisk University in Nashville. Later he earned a doctoral degree in history from Harvard and afterward attended the University of Berlin. In addition to an active career in racial protest, he left a distinguished record as a teacher and scholar. Trim and dapper in appearance, sporting a goatee, cane, and gloves, he possessed a combative, fiery spirit. Not long after he began his teaching career at Atlanta University in 1897, he began to assault

W.E.B. Du Bois

A fierce advocate for black education.

Booker T. Washington's accommodationist philosophy and put forward his own program of "ceaseless agitation."

Washington, Du Bois argued, preached "a gospel of Work and Money to such an extent" that it overshadowed "the higher aims of life." The education of African Americans, Du Bois maintained, should not be merely vocational but should nurture bold leaders willing to challenge segregation and discrimination through political action. He demanded that disenfranchisement and legalized segregation cease and that the laws of the land be enforced. Du Bois minced no words in criticizing Washington's "Atlanta Compromise" philosophy: "We refuse to surrender the leadership of this race to cowards."

The New West

Like the South the region west of the Mississippi River has become wrapped in myths and constricting stereotypes. It is a land of extremes—majestic mountains, roaring rivers, searing deserts, dense forests, and fertile plains. For vast reaches of western America, the great epics of the Civil War and Reconstruction were remote events hardly touching the lives of Indians, Mexicans, Asians, and white trappers, miners, cowboys, traders, and Mormons scattered through the plains and mountains. There the march of settlement and exploitation continued, propelled by a lust for land and a passion for profit. On one level the settlement of the West beyond the Mississippi River constitutes a colorful drama of determined pioneers and cowboys overcoming all obstacles to secure their vision of freedom and opportunity amid the region's awesome vastness. On another level, however, the colonization of the Far West involved short-sighted greed and irresponsible behavior, a story of reckless exploitation that scarred the land, decimated its wildlife, and nearly exterminated the culture of Native Americans.

In the second tier of trans-Mississippi states—Iowa, Kansas, Nebraska—and in western Minnesota, farmers began spreading out onto the Great

Plains after the Civil War. From California, miners spread east through the mountains as scattered enclaves sprang up at one new strike after another. From Texas nomadic cowboys migrated northward onto the plains and across the Rocky Mountains into the Great Basin. As settlers moved west, they encountered a markedly different climate and landscape. The scarcity of water and timber on the Great Plains rendered obsolete the ax, the log cabin, the rail fence, and the usual methods of tilling the soil. For a long time the region had been called the Great American Desert; it was a barren barrier to cross on the way to the Pacific, unfit for human habitation and therefore, to white Americans, the perfect refuge for Indians. But that pattern changed in the last half of the nineteenth century as a result of newly discovered gold, silver, and other minerals, the completion of the transcontinental railroads, the destruction of the buffalo, the rise of the range-cattle industry, and the dawning realization that the arid region need not be a sterile desert. With the use of what water was available, techniques of dry farming and irrigation could make the land fruitful after all.

THE MIGRATORY STREAM   During the second half of the nineteenth century, an unrelenting stream of migrants flowed into the largely Indian and Latino West. Millions of Anglo-Americans, African Americans, Mexicans, and European and Chinese immigrants transformed the patterns of western society and culture. Most of the settlers were relatively prosperous white, native-born farming families. Because of the expense of transportation, land, and supplies, the very poor could not afford to relocate. Three quarters of the western migrants were men. The largest number of foreign immigrants came from northern Europe and Canada. In the northern plains, Germans, Scandinavians, and Irish were especially numerous.

AFRICAN-AMERICAN MIGRATION   In the aftermath of the collapse of Radical Republican rule in the South, thousands of African Americans began migrating west from Kentucky, Tennessee, Louisiana, Arkansas, Mississippi, and Texas. Some 6,000 southern blacks arrived in Kansas in 1879 alone, and as many as 20,000 may have come the following year. They came to be known as Exodusters, making their exodus from the South in search of a haven from racism and poverty.

The foremost promoter of African-American migration to the West was Benjamin "Pap" Singleton. Born a slave in Tennessee in 1809, he escaped and settled in Detroit. After the Civil War he returned to Tennessee, convinced that God was calling him to rescue his brethren. When Singleton learned that land in Kansas could be had for $1.25 an acre, he began distributing a

Nicodemus, Kansas

A colony founded by southern blacks in the 1860s.

recruiting pamphlet, *The Advantage of Living in a Free State,* to former slaves. In 1878 Singleton led his first party of 200 colonists to Kansas, bought 7,500 acres that had been an Indian reservation, and established the Dunlop community. Over the next several years, thousands of African Americans followed Singleton into Kansas, causing many southern leaders to worry about the loss of laborers. In 1879 white Mississippians closed access to the river and threatened to sink all boats carrying black colonists to the West.

The African-American exodus to the West died out by the early 1880s. Many of the settlers were unprepared for life on the plains. Their homesteads were not large enough to allow them to be self-sufficient, and most of the farmers were forced to supplement their income by hiring themselves out to white ranchers. Drought, grasshoppers, prairie fires, and dust storms led to crop failures. The sudden influx of so many people taxed resources and patience. Many of the black pioneers in Kansas soon abandoned their land and moved to the few cities in the state. Life on the frontier was not always the "promised land" that setters had been led to expect. Nonetheless, by 1890, some 520,000 African-Americans lived west of the Mississippi River. As many as 25 percent of the cowboys who participated in the Texas cattle drives were African Americans.

In 1866 Congress passed legislation establishing two "colored" cavalry units and dispatched them to the western frontier. Nicknamed buffalo soldiers by the Indians, they were mostly Civil War veterans from Louisiana and Kentucky. They built and maintained forts, mapped vast areas of the

Southwest, strung hundreds of miles of telegraph lines, protected railroad construction crews, subdued hostile Indians, and captured outlaws and rustlers. For this they were paid $13 a month. Eighteen of the buffalo soldiers won Congressional Medals of Honor for their service.

MINING THE WEST   Valuable mineral deposits continued to lure people to the West after the Civil War. The mass migration of miners to California in 1849 (the forty-niners) set the typical pattern, in which the disorderly rush of prospectors was quickly joined by camp followers, a motley array of saloon keepers, prostitutes, cardsharps, hustlers, and assorted desperadoes out to mine the miners. An era of lawlessness eventually gave way to vigilante rule and, finally, to a stable community.

The drama of the 1849 gold rush was reenacted time and again in the following three decades. While nearly 100,000 early rushers were crowding around Pikes Peak in Colorado in 1859, miners discovered the Comstock Lode at Gold Hill, Nevada. The lode produced gold and silver and within twenty years had yielded more than $300 million from shafts that reached hundreds of feet into the mountainside. Yet in Arizona and Montana the most important mineral proved to be neither gold nor silver but copper.

The growing demand for orderly government in the West led to the hasty creation of new territories and eventually the admission of a host of new states. In 1861 Nevada became a territory, and in 1864 it was admitted to the Union in time to give its three electoral votes to Abraham Lincoln. After Colorado's admission in 1876, however, no new states entered the union for over a decade because of party divisions in Congress: Democrats were reluctant to create states out of territories that were heavily Republican. After the sweeping Republican victory of 1888, however, Congress admitted the Dakotas, Montana, and Washington in 1889 and Idaho and Wyoming in 1890, completing a tier of states from coast to coast. Utah entered the union in 1896 (after the Mormons abandoned the practice of polygamy) and Oklahoma in 1907, and in 1912 Arizona and New Mexico rounded out the forty-eight continental states.

MINING AND THE ENVIRONMENT   During the second half of the nineteenth century, the nature of mining changed drastically. It became a mass-production industry as individual prospectors gave way to large companies. The first wave of miners who rushed to California in 1849 sifted gold dust and nuggets out of riverbeds by means of "placer" mining, or "panning." But once the placer deposits were exhausted, efficient mining required large-scale operations and huge investments. Companies shifted from surface digging to hydraulic mining, dredging, or deep-shaft "hard-rock" mining. Hydraulic mining used a powerful jet of water to excavate whole hillsides, washing the gravel through sluices that caught gold nuggets and disposed of the tailings (dirt and gravel debris). Dredging carved out whole riverbeds in order to sift gold from the surrounding sand and gravel.

Hydraulicking, dredging, and shaft mining transformed vast areas of vegetation and landscape. Huge hydraulic cannons shot enormous streams of water under high pressure, stripping the topsoil and gravel from the bedrock and creating steep-sloped barren canyons that could not sustain plant life. The tons of dirt and debris unearthed by the water cannons covered rich farmland downstream and created sandbars that clogged rivers and killed fish. In 1880 alone some 40,000 acres of farmland and orchards were destroyed by the effects of hydraulic mining while another 270,000 acres were severely damaged. All told, some 12 billion tons of earth were blasted out of the Sierra Nevadas and washed into local rivers. At the massive Malakoff Diggings in northeastern California, hydraulic mining removed an estimated 41 million cubic yards of soil and rock and left a lifeless canyon over a mile long and up to 350 feet deep. The mine used three huge nozzles and 30.5 million gallons of water, twice as much water as was used by the entire city of San Francisco. The sprawling complex had over 150 miles of ditches, dams, and associated reservoirs to supply its gigantic operations.

Irate California farmers in the fertile Central Valley bitterly protested the damage done downstream by the industrial mining operations. In 1878 they formed the Anti-Debris Association, with its own militia, to challenge the powerful mining companies. Efforts to pass state legislation restricting hydraulic mining repeatedly failed because mining companies controlled the votes. The Anti-Debris Association then turned to the courts. On January 7, 1884, the farmers won their case when federal judge Lorenzo Sawyer, a former miner, outlawed the dumping of mining debris where it could reach farmland or navigable rivers. Thus *Woodruff v. North Bloomfield Gravel Mining Company* became the first major environmental ruling in the nation. The town of Marysville, California, which in 1875 had been completely buried in silt and debris unleashed by upstream mines, threw a huge celebration upon learning of Judge Sawyer's decision. Similar parties occurred in farming communities across the state. As a result of the ruling, hydraulic mining dried up, leaving a legacy of abandoned equipment, ugly ravines, ditches, gullies, and mountains of discarded rock and gravel.

THE INDIAN WARS   As settlers pressed in from east and west, the Indians were forced into what was supposed to be their last refuge. Perhaps

What was the Great Sioux War? What happened at Little Bighorn, and what were the consequences? Why were hundreds of Indians killed at Wounded Knee?

250,000 Indians on the Great Plains and in the mountain regions lived mainly off the buffalo herds that provided food and, from their hides, clothing and shelter. In 1851 the chiefs of the Plains tribes had gathered at Fort Laramie in what would become Wyoming Territory, where they had agreed to accept definite tribal borders and leave settlers on their trails unmolested. The treaty worked for a while, with wagon trains passing safely through Indian lands and the army building roads and forts without resistance. Fighting resumed, however, as the emigrants began to encroach upon Indian land rather than merely pass through it. From 1850 to 1860, for example, 150,000 whites moved into Sioux territory in violation of treaty agreements.

From the early 1860s until the late 1870s, the frontier raged with Indian wars. In 1864 Colonel John Chivington's poorly trained militia assaulted an Indian camp along Sand Creek in Colorado Territory. Although the Indian camp displayed a white flag of truce, the soldiers slaughtered 200 Indians— men, women, and children. One general called the Sand Creek Massacre the "foulest and most unjustifiable crime in the annals of America."

With other scattered battles erupting, a congressional committee began to gather evidence on the grisly Indian wars and massacres. Its 1867 "Report on the Condition of the Indian Tribes" led to an act to establish an Indian Peace Commission charged with removing the causes of Indian wars in general. Congress decided that this would be best accomplished at the expense of the Indians, by persuading them to take up life on out-of-the-way reservations, a solution that perpetuated the encroachment on Indian hunting grounds.

In 1867 a conference at Medicine Lodge, Kansas, ended with the Kiowas, Comanches, Arapahos, and Cheyennes reluctantly accepting land in western Oklahoma. The following spring the Sioux agreed to settle within the Black Hills reservation in Dakota Territory. But Indian resistance on the southern plains continued until the Red River War of 1874–1875, when soldiers led by General Philip Sheridan, a hard-charging Civil War cavalryman, forced the Indians to disband in the spring of 1875. Seventy-two Indian chiefs were imprisoned for three years.

Meanwhile, trouble was brewing again in the north. In 1874 Lieutenant Colonel George A. Custer, a reckless, glory-seeking officer, led an exploratory expedition into the Black Hills, accompanied by gold seekers. Miners were soon filtering into the Sioux hunting grounds despite promises that the army would keep them out. The army had done little to protect Indian land, but when ordered to move against wandering bands of Sioux hunting on the range according to their treaty rights, it moved vigorously.

What became the Great Sioux War was the largest military event since the end of the Civil War. It lasted fifteen months and entailed some fifteen battles in a vast area of present-day Wyoming, Montana, South Dakota, and Nebraska. After several indecisive encounters, Custer found the main encampment of Sioux and their Northern Cheyenne allies on the Little Bighorn River. Separated from the main body of his men and surrounded by 2,500 warriors, Custer and 210 soldiers were annihilated.

Instead of following up their victory, the Indians threw away their advantage in celebration and renewed hunting. The army soon regained the offensive, and the Sioux were forced to give up their hunting grounds and the goldfields in return for payments. Forced onto reservations situated on the

The Battle of Little Bighorn

A painting by Amos Bad Heart Bull, an Oglala Sioux, 1876.

least valuable lands in the region, the Indians soon found themselves struggling to subsist under harsh conditions. Many died of starvation or disease.

In the Rocky Mountains and to the west, the same story of hopeless resistance was repeated. In Idaho the peaceful Nez Perces refused to surrender land along the Salmon River. Chief Joseph tried to avoid war, but when some unruly warriors started a fight, he directed a masterful campaign against overwhelming odds, one of the most spectacular feats in the history of Indian warfare. After a 1,500-mile retreat he was caught thirty miles short of the Canadian border and exiled to Oklahoma. In 1886 a generation of Indian wars virtually ended with the capture of Geronimo, a chief of the Chiricahua Apaches who had fought encroachments in the Southwest for fifteen years.

The epilogue, too, would be tragic. Late in 1888 Wovoka (or Jack Wilson), a Paiute in western Nevada, fell ill and in a delirium imagined he had visited the spirit world, where he learned of a deliverer coming to rescue the Indians and restore their lands. To hasten the day, he said, they had to take up a ceremonial dance at each new moon. The Ghost Dance craze fed upon old legends of a coming messiah and spread rapidly. In 1890 the Lakota Sioux took it up with such fervor that it alarmed white authorities. They banned the Ghost Dance on Lakota reservations, but the Indians defied the order, and a crisis erupted. On December 29, 1890, a bloodbath occurred at Wounded Knee, South Dakota. An accidental rifle discharge led nervous soldiers to fire into a group of Indians who had come to surrender. Nearly 200 Indians and 25 soldiers died in the Battle of Wounded Knee. The Indian wars had ended with characteristic brutality and misunderstanding.

THE DEMISE OF THE BUFFALO   Over the long run the collapse of Indian resistance in the face of white settlement on the Great Plains resulted as much from the decimation of the buffalo herds as from the actions of federal troops. In 1750 there were an estimated 30 million buffalo on the plains; by 1850 there were less than 10 million; by 1900 only a few hundred were left. What happened to them? The conventional story focuses on intensive harvesting of buffalo by white hunters after the Civil War. Americans east of the Mississippi River developed a voracious demand for buffalo robes and buffalo leather. The average white hunter killed 100 animals a day, and the hides and bones (to be ground into fertilizer) were shipped east on railroad cars. Some army officers encouraged the slaughter. "Kill every buffalo you can!" Colonel Richard Dodge told a sport hunter in 1867. "Every buffalo dead is an Indian gone."

This conventional explanation tells only part of a more complicated story, however. The buffalo disappeared from the western plains for a variety of environmental reasons, including a significant change in climate; competition with other grazing animals; and cattle-borne disease. A prolonged drought on the Great Plains during the late 1880s and 1890s, the same drought that would help spur the agrarian revolt and the rise of populism, also devastated the buffalo herds by reducing the grasslands upon which the animals depended. At the same time the buffalo had to compete for forage with an ever increasing number of horses, cattle, and sheep. By the 1880s over 2 million horses were grazing on buffalo lands. In addition, the Plains Indians themselves, empowered by horses and guns and spurred by the profits reaped from selling hides and meat to white traders, accounted for much of the devastation of the buffalo herds after 1840. White hunters who killed buffaloes by the millions in the 1870s and 1880s played a major role in the animal's demise, but only as the final catalyst. If there had been no white hunters, the buffalo would probably have lasted only another thirty years because their numbers had been so greatly reduced by other factors.

INDIAN POLICY   Most white westerners had little tolerance for moralizing on the Indian question, but many easterners decried the slaughter and mistreatment of Indians. Well-intentioned reformers sought to "Americanize" Indians by dealing with them as individuals rather than tribes. The

Dawes Severalty Act of 1887 proposed to introduce the communal Indians to individual land ownership and agriculture. Sponsored by Senator Henry Dawes of Massachusetts, the act permitted the president to divide the land of any tribe and grant 160 acres to each head of a family and lesser amounts to others. To protect the Indians' property, the government held it in trust for twenty-five years, after which the owner won full title and became a U.S. citizen. In 1901 citizenship was extended to the Five Civilized Tribes of Oklahoma and, in 1924, to all Indians.

But the more it changed, the more Indian policy remained the same. Although well-intended, the Dawes Act created new chances for more plundering of Indian land and disrupted what remained of the traditional culture. The Dawes Act broke up reservations and often led to the loss of Indian land to whites. Land not distributed to Indian families was sold, and some of the land the Indians did receive was lost to land speculators because of the Indians' inexperience with private ownership or simply because of their powerlessness in the face of fraud. Between 1887 and 1934 Indians lost an estimated 86 million of their 130 million acres. Most of what remained was unsuited for agriculture.

CATTLE AND COWBOYS   While the West was being taken from the Indians, cattle entered the grasslands where the buffalo had roamed. The cowboy enjoyed his brief heyday before fading into the folklore of the Wild West. From colonial times, especially in the South, cattle raising had been a common enterprise just beyond the fringe of settlement. In many cases, slaves took care of the livestock. Later, in the West, African-American cowboys were common.

Much of the romance of the open-range cattle industry derived from its Mexican roots. The Texas longhorns and the cowboys' horses had in large part descended from stock brought to America by the Spaniards, and many of the industry's trappings had been worked out in Mexico first: the cowboy's saddle, chaps (*chaparreras*) to protect the legs, spurs, and lariat.

For many years wild cattle competed with the buffalo in the Spanish borderlands. Natural selection and contact with Anglo-American scrub cattle produced the Texas longhorns: lean and rangy, they were noted more for speed and endurance than for yielding a choice steak. They had little value, moreover, because the largest markets for beef were too far away. At the end of the Civil War, as many as 5 million longhorns roamed the grasslands of Texas, still neglected—but not for long. In the upper Mississippi River valley, where herds had been depleted by the war, cattle were in great demand, and the Texas cattle could be had just for the effort of rounding them up.

The Cowboy Era

Cowboys herd cattle near Cimarron, Colorado, 1905.

New opportunities arose as railroads pushed farther west, where cattle could be driven through relatively vacant lands. Joseph G. McCoy, an Illinois livestock dealer, encouraged railroad executives to run a line from the prairies to Chicago, the meatpacking center. The Kansas-Pacific Railroad liked McCoy's vision, and with its help he made Abilene, Kansas, the western terminus of a new line. In 1867 the first shipment of Texas cattle went to Chicago.

During the twenty years after the Civil War, some 40,000 cowboys roamed the Great Plains. They were young—the average age was twenty-four—and from diverse backgrounds. Some 30 percent were either Mexican or African American, and hundreds were Indians. Many others were Civil War veterans from the North and the South, and still others were immigrants from Europe. The life of a cowboy, for the most part, was rarely as exciting as has been depicted by motion pictures and television shows. Working as a ranch hand involved grueling wage labor interspersed with drudgery and boredom.

The thriving cattle industry spurred rapid growth, however. The population of Kansas increased from 107,000 in 1860 to 365,000 ten years later and reached almost 1 million by 1880. Nebraska witnessed similar increases. During the 1860s cattle would be delivered to rail depots, loaded onto freight cars, and shipped east. By the time the animals arrived in New York or Massachusetts, some would be dead or dying, and all would have lost significant weight. The secret to higher profits for the cattle industry was to devise a way to slaughter the cattle in the Midwest and ship the dressed carcasses east and west. That process required refrigeration to keep the meat from spoiling. In 1869 G. H. Hammond, a Chicago meat packer, shipped the first refrigerated beef in an air-cooled car from Chicago to Boston. Eight years later Gustavus Swift developed a more efficient system of mechanical refrigeration, an innovation that earned him a fortune and provided the cattle industry with a major stimulus.

The flush times of the cowtowns soon faded, however. The long cattle drives played out because they were economically unsound. The dangers of the trail, the wear and tear on men and cattle, the charges levied on drives that crossed Indian territory, and the advance of farms across the trails combined to persuade cattlemen that they could function best near railroads. As railroads spread out into Texas and across the plains, the cattle business spread with them as far as Montana and on into Canada.

In the absence of laws governing the open range, cattle ranchers at first worked out their own arrangements when rights and uses conflicted. As cattle wandered onto other ranchers' property, cowboys would "ride the line" to keep the strays off the adjoining ranches. In the spring they would "round up" the herds and sort out ownership by identifying the distinctive mark "branded" into the cattle. All that changed in 1873, when Joseph Glidden, an Illinois farmer, invented the first effective barbed wire, which ranchers used to fence off their claims at relatively low cost. Orders for the new fence poured in, and soon the open range was no more.

THE END OF THE OPEN RANGE   Yet a combination of factors put an end to the open range. Farmers kept crowding in and laying out homesteads. The boundless range was being overstocked by 1883, and expenses mounted as stock breeders formed associations to keep intruders off overstocked ranges, to establish and protect land titles, deal with railroads and buyers, to fight prairie fires, and cope with rustlers and wolves. The rise of sheepherding by 1880 caused still another conflict with the ranchers. A final blow to the open-range industry came with two unusually severe winters in 1886 and 1887, followed by ten long years of drought.

Surviving the hazards of the range required establishing legal title, fencing in the land, limiting the herds to a reasonable size, and providing shelter and hay during the rigors of winter. Moreover, as the long cattle drives gave way to more rail lines and refrigerated railcars, the cowboy settled into a more sedentary existence. Within merely two decades, from 1866 to 1886, the era of the cowboy had come and gone.

RANGE WARS   Conflicting claims over land and water rights ignited violent disputes between ranchers and farmers. Ranchers often tried to drive off neighboring farmers, and farmers in turn tried to sabotage the cattle barons, cutting their fences and spooking their herds. The cattle ranchers also clashed with sheepherders over access to grassland. A strain of ethnic and religious prejudice heightened the tension between ranchers and herders. In the Southwest, shepherds were typically Mexican Americans; in Idaho and Nevada, they were from the Basque region of Spain or Mormons. Many Anglo-American cattlemen and cowboys viewed those ethnic and religious groups as un-American and inferior, an attitude that helped them rationalize the use of violence against the sheepherders. Conflict faded, however, as the sheep for the most part found refuge in the high pastures of the mountains, leaving the grasslands of the plains to the ranchers.

Yet there also developed a perennial tension between large and small cattle ranchers. The large ranchers fenced in huge tracts of public land, leaving the smaller ranchers with too little pasture. To survive, the smaller ranchers cut the fences. In central Texas this practice sparked the Fence-Cutters' War of 1883–1884. Several ranchers were killed and dozens wounded before the state ended the conflict by passing legislation outlawing fence cutting.

FARMERS AND THE LAND   Among the legendary figures of the West, farmers projected an unromantic image in contrast to that of the cowboys, cavalrymen, and Indians. After 1865, on paper at least, the federal land laws offered farmers favorable terms. Under the Homestead Act of 1862, a farmer could realize the old dream of free land either by simply staking out a claim and living on it for five years or by buying the land at $1.25 an acre after six months.

As so often happens, however, environmental forces shaped development. The unchangeable fact of aridity, rather than land laws, influenced institutions in the West after the Civil War. Where farming was impossible, ranchers simply established dominance by control of the water, regardless of the law. Belated legislative efforts to develop irrigable land finally achieved a major success when the 1901 Newlands Reclamation Act (after the aptly named Senator Francis G. Newlands of Nevada) set up the Bureau of Reclamation. The proceeds of public land sales in sixteen states created a fund for irrigation works, and the Reclamation Bureau set about building such major projects as the Boulder (later the Hoover) Dam on the Nevada-Arizona line, the Roosevelt Dam in Arizona, and the Elephant Butte Dam in New Mexico.

The lands of the New West, like those on previous frontiers, passed to their ultimate owners more often from private hands than directly from the government. Many of the 274 million acres claimed under the Homestead Act passed quickly to cattle ranchers or speculators and thence to settlers. The land-grant railroads got some 200 million acres of the public domain between 1851 and 1871 and sold much of it to build towns along the lines. The West of ranchers and farmers was in fact largely the product of the railroads.

The first arrivals on the sod-house frontier of the Plains faced a grim struggle against danger, adversity, and monotony. Though land was relatively cheap, horses, livestock, wagons, wells, fencing, seed, and fertilizer were not. Freight rates and interest rates on loans seemed criminally high. As in the South, declining crop prices produced chronic indebtedness, leading strapped western farmers to embrace virtually any plan to inflate the money supply. The land itself, although fertile, resisted planting; the heavy sod broke many a plow. Since wood was almost nonexistent on the prairie, pioneer families used buffalo chips (dried dung) for fuel.

Farmers and their families also fought a constant battle with the elements: tornadoes, hailstorms, droughts, prairie fires, blizzards, and pests. Swarms of locusts would often cloud the horizon, occasionally covering the ground six inches deep and consuming everything in their path. A Wichita newspaper reported in 1878 that the grasshoppers devoured "everything green, stripping the foliage off the bark and from the tender twigs of the fruit trees, destroying every plant that is good for food or pleasant to the eyes, that man has planted."

As time passed and farmers were able to lay aside some money from their labor, farm families could leave their sod-houses and build frame houses with lumber carried from Chicago by the railroads. New machinery also provided fresh opportunities for farmers. In 1868 James Oliver, a Scottish immigrant living in Indiana, made a successful chilled-iron plow. With further improvements his "sodbuster" plow greatly eased the task of breaking the shallow but tough grass roots of the Plains. Improvements and new inventions lightened the burden of labor but added to the farmers' capital outlay.

To get a start on a family homestead required a minimum investment of $1,000. And while the overall value of farmland and farm products increased in the late nineteenth century, small farmers did not keep up with the march of progress. Their numbers grew but decreased in proportion to the population at large. The wheat produced on the eastern plains from Minnesota and North Dakota down to Texas, like cotton in the antebellum period, was the great export crop that evened America's balance of payments and spurred economic growth. For a variety of reasons, however, few small farmers prospered. And by the 1890s many were in open revolt against "greedy" bankers, railroads, and grain processors who seemed to thwart their efforts and deny their dreams.

PIONEER WOMEN   The West remained a largely male society throughout the nineteenth century. In Texas, for example, the ratio of men to women in 1890 was 110 to 1. Women continued to face traditional legal barriers and social prejudice. A wife could not sell property without her husband's approval. Texas women could not sue except for divorce, nor could they serve on juries, act as lawyers, or witness a will. But the fight for survival in the West often made husbands and wives more equal partners in everyday life than their eastern counterparts. Prairie life also allowed women more independence than could be had by leading domestic life back East.

"THE END OF THE FRONTIER HAS GONE"   American life reached an important juncture in the last decade of the nineteenth century. After the

Women of the Frontier

A woman and her family in front of their sod house. The difficult life on the prairie led to more egalitarian marriages than were found in most other regions of the country.

1890 population count, the superintendent of the national census noted that he could no longer locate a continuous frontier line beyond which population thinned out to fewer than two people per square mile. This fact inspired the historian Frederick Jackson Turner to develop the influential frontier thesis, first outlined in "The Significance of the Frontier in American History," a paper delivered to the American Historical Association in 1893. "The existence of an area of free land," Turner wrote, "its continuous recession, and the advance of American settlement westward, explain American development." The frontier, he added, had shaped the national character in striking ways. It was

> to the frontier [that] the American intellect owes its striking characteristics. That coarseness and strength combined with acuteness and acquisitiveness; that practical, inventive turn of mind, quick to find expedients; that masterful grasp of material things, lacking in the artistic but powerful to effect great ends; that restless, nervous energy; that dominant individualism, working for good and for evil, and with all that buoyancy and exuberance which comes with freedom—these are traits of the frontier, or traits called out elsewhere because of the existence of the frontier.

But, Turner ominously concluded in 1893, "the frontier has gone and with its going has closed the first period of American history."

Turner's "frontier thesis" guided several generations of scholars and students in their understanding of the distinctive characteristics of American history. His view of the frontier as the westward-moving source of the nation's democratic politics, open society, unfettered economy, and rugged individualism, far removed from the corruptions of urban life, gripped the popular imagination as well. But it left out much of the story. Turner's description of the frontier experience exaggerated the homogenizing effect of the environment and virtually ignored the role of women, African Americans, Indians, Mormons, Latinos, and Asians in shaping the diverse human geography of the western United States. Turner also implied that the West would be fundamentally different after 1890 because the frontier experience was essentially over. In many respects, however, that region has retained the qualities associated with the rush for land, gold, timber, and water rights during the post–Civil War decades. The mining frontier, as one historian has recently written, "set a mood that has never disappeared from the West: the attitude of extractive industry—get in, get rich, get out."

MAKING CONNECTIONS

- The problems of southern and western farmers described in this chapter set the stage for the rise of the Populists, as discussed in Chapter 22.

- The late nineteenth century was a crucial period in the evolution of race relations in the South, bridging the antebellum period and the twentieth century.

- This chapter closes with the observation that as of 1890, according to the superintendent of the census and the historian Frederick Jackson Turner, "the frontier has gone." Where would Americans now look to fulfill their expansionist urges?

FURTHER READING

The classic study of the emergence of the New South remains C. Vann Woodward's *Origins of the New South, 1877–1913* (1951). A more recent treatment of southern society after the end of Reconstruction is Edward L. Ayers's *Southern Crossing: A History of the American South, 1877–1906* (1995). A good survey of industrialization in the South is James C. Cobb's *Industrialization and Southern Society, 1877–1984* (1984).

C. Vann Woodward's *The Strange Career of Jim Crow*, 3rd ed. (2002), re- mains the standard on southern race relations at the end of the nineteenth century. Some of Woodward's points are challenged in Howard N. Rabi- nowitz's *Race Relations in the Urban South, 1865–1890* (1978). Leon Litwack's *Trouble in Mind: Black Southerners in the Age of Jim Crow* (1998) treats the rise of legal segregation, while Michael Perman's *Struggle for Mastery: Disfranchise- ment in the South, 1888–1908* (2001) surveys efforts to keep African Americans from voting. J. Morgan Kousser's *The Shaping of Southern Politics: Suffrage Re- striction and the Establishment of the One-Party South, 1880–1910* (1974) han- dles disenfranchisement. An award-winning study of white women and the race issue is Glenda Elizabeth Gilmore's *Gender and Jim Crow: Women and the Politics of White Supremacy in North Carolina, 1896–1920* (1996).

For stimulating reinterpretations of the frontier and the development of the West, see William Cronon's *Nature's Metropolis: Chicago and the Great West* (1991), Patricia Nelson Limerick's *The Legacy of Conquest: The Unbro-*

ken *Past of the American West* (1987), Richard White's *"It's Your Misfortune and None of My Own": A New History of the American West* (1991), and Walter Nugent's *Into the West: The Story of Its People* (1999).

The role of African Americans in western settlement is the focus of William Laren Katz's *The Black West: A Documentary and Pictorial History of the African-American Role in the Westward Expansion of the United States* (1996) and Nell Irvin Painter's *Exodusters: Black Migration to Kansas after Reconstruction* (1977). The best account of the conflicts between Indians and whites is Robert Utley's *The Indian Frontier of the American West, 1846–1890* (1984). For a presentation of the Native American side of the story, see Peter Nabokov's *Native American Testimony: A Chronicle of Indian-White Relations from Prophecy to the Present, 1492–2000*, rev. ed. (1999).

On the demise of the buffalo herds, see Andrew C. Isenberg's *The Destruction of the Bison: An Environmental History, 1750–1920* (2000).

20

BIG BUSINESS AND ORGANIZED LABOR

FOCUS QUESTIONS

- What factors fueled the growth of the post–Civil War economy?
- What were the methods and achievements of major entrepreneurs?
- What led to the rise of large labor unions?

To answer these questions and access additional review material, please visit www.wwnorton.com/studyspace.

America emerged as an industrial and agricultural giant in the late nineteenth century. Between 1869 and 1899 the nation's population nearly tripled, farm production more than doubled, and the value of manufactures grew sixfold. Within three generations after the Civil War, the predominantly rural nation had became an urban-industrial society buffeted by the imperatives of mass production, mass consumption, and time-clock efficiency. Bigness became the prevailing standard of corporate life, and social tensions worsened with the rising scale of business enterprise.

THE RISE OF BIG BUSINESS

The Industrial Revolution created huge corporations that came to dominate the economy—as well as political and social life—during the late nineteenth century. As businesses grew, their owners sought to integrate all the processes of production and distribution into single companies, thus producing even larger firms. Others joined forces with their competitors in "pools" or "trusts" in an effort to dominate entire industries. This process of industrial combination and concentration transformed the nation's social order. It also aroused widespread dissent and the emergence of an organized labor movement.

Many factors converged to help launch the dramatic business growth after the Civil War. A nationwide shortage of labor served as a powerful incentive, motivating inventors and business owners to develop more efficient, labor-saving machinery. Technological innovations not only created new products but also brought about improved machinery and equipment, spurring dramatic advances in productivity. As the volume of production increased, the larger businesses and industries expanded into numerous states and in the process developed standardized machinery and parts, which became available nationwide. A group of shrewd, determined, and energetic entrepreneurs took advantage of fertile business opportunities to create huge enterprises. Federal and state officials after the Civil War actively encouraged the growth of big business by imposing high tariffs on foreign manufacturers as a means of blunting foreign competition and by providing government land and cash to finance railroads and other internal improvements.

The American agricultural sector, by 1870 the world's leader, fueled the rest of the economy by providing wheat and corn to be milled into flour and meal. With the advent of the cattle industry, the processes of slaughtering and packing meat themselves became major industries. So the farm sector directly stimulated the industrial sector of the economy. A national government-subsidized network of railroads connecting the East and West coasts played a crucial role in the development of related industries and in the evolution of a national market for goods and services. Industry in the United States also benefited from an abundance of power sources—water, wood, coal, oil, and electricity—that were inexpensive compared with those of the other nations of the world.

THE SECOND INDUSTRIAL REVOLUTION The Industrial Revolution "controls us all," said Yale sociologist William Graham Sumner, "because we are all in it." Sumner and other Americans living during the second half of the nineteenth century experienced what economic historians have termed the Second Industrial Revolution. The First Industrial Revolution began in Britain during the late eighteenth century. It was propelled by the convergence of three new technologies: the coal-powered steam engine, textile machines for spinning thread and weaving cloth, and blast furnaces to produce iron.

The Second Industrial Revolution began in the mid–nineteenth century and was centered in the United States and Germany. It was sparked by an array of innovations and inventions in the production of metals, machinery, chemicals, and foodstuffs. While the First Industrial Revolution helped accelerate the growth of the early American economy, the second transformed the economy and the society into their modern urban-industrial form.

The Second Industrial Revolution involved three related developments. The first was the creation of an interconnected national transportation and communication network, which facilitated the emergence of new national and even international markets for American goods and services. Contributing to this development were the completion of the national telegraph and railroad systems, the emergence of steamships, and the laying of the undersea telegraph cable, which spanned the Atlantic Ocean and connected the United States with Europe.

During the 1880s a second major breakthrough—the use of electric power—accelerated the pace of change. Electricity created dramatic advances in the power and efficiency of industrial machinery. It also spurred urban growth through the addition of electric trolleys and subways, and it greatly enhanced the production of steel and chemicals.

The third major aspect of the Second Industrial Revolution was the systematic application of scientific research to industrial processes. Laboratories

The Hand of Man (1902)

Photogravure by Alfred Stieglitz.

staffed by graduates of new research universities sprouted up across the country, and scientists and engineers discovered dramatic new ways in which to improve industrial processes. Researchers figured out, for example, how to refine kerosene and gasoline from crude oil. They also improved techniques for refining steel from iron and spawned new products—telephones, typewriters, adding machines, sewing machines, cameras, elevators, and farm machinery—and lower consumer prices. These advances in turn expanded the scope and scale of industrial organizations. Capital-intensive industries such as steel and oil, as well as processed food and tobacco, took advantage of new technologies to gain economies of scale that emphasized maximum production and national as well as international marketing and distribution.

BUILDING THE TRANSCONTINENTAL RAILROADS   Railroads were the first big business, the first magnet for the great financial markets, and the first industry to develop a large-scale management bureaucracy. The railroads opened the trans-Mississippi West to economic development, connected raw materials to factories, and in so doing created an interconnected national market for the country's goods and produce. At the same time, the railroads were themselves gigantic consumers of iron, steel, lumber, and other capital goods.

The renewal of railroad building after the Civil War filled out the railway network east of the Mississippi River, but the most spectacular exploits were the transcontinental lines built across the Great Plains and the Rocky Mountains. Running through sparsely settled land, they served the purpose of binding the country together. The buccaneering executives and financiers directing the transcontinental railroads were shrewd entrepreneurs so driven by dreams of great wealth that they often cut corners and bribed legislators. They also ruthlessly used federal troops to suppress the Plains Indians. But their shenanigans do not diminish the heroic efforts of the workers and engineers who built the rail lines, erected the bridges, and gouged out the tunnels under terrible weather conditions. Building the transcontinental railroads was an epic feat of daring engineering that tied a nation together, changed the economic and political landscape, and enabled the United States to emerge as a world power.

Before the Civil War, sectional differences over routes had delayed the start of a transcontinental line. Secession and the departure of southerners from Congress finally permitted passage of the Pacific Railroads Act, which Abraham Lincoln signed into law in 1862, authorizing a line along a north-central route, to be built jointly by the Union Pacific Railroad westward from Omaha, Nebraska, and by the Central Pacific Railroad eastward from Sacramento, California.

Both railroads began construction during the war, but most of the work was done after 1865. The Union Pacific pushed across the plains at a rapid pace, avoiding the Rocky Mountains by going through Evans Pass in Wyoming. The work crews, including large numbers of ex-soldiers and Irish immigrants, had to cope with bad roads, water shortages, rugged weather, and Indian attacks.

The Central Pacific construction crews were mainly composed of Chinese workers lured to America first by the California gold rush and then by railroad jobs. Thousands of Chinese had emigrated, raising their numbers in the United States from 7,500 in 1850 to 105,000 in 1880. Most of these "coolie" laborers were single men intent upon accumulating money and returning to their homeland, where they could then afford to marry and buy a parcel of land. Their temporary status and dream of a good life back in China apparently made them more willing than American laborers to endure the dangerous working conditions and low pay of railroad work, as well as

The Union Pacific Meets the Central Pacific

The celebration of the completion of the first transcontinental railroad, Promontory, Utah, May 10, 1869.

the blatant racism. By 1867 the Central Pacific Railroad's 12,000 Chinese laborers represented 90 percent of its workforce.

Clearing trees, handling explosives, operating power drills, and working in snowdrifts were dangerous activities, and many Chinese died on the job. Fifty-seven miles east of Sacramento the construction crews encountered the towering Sierra Nevadas, through which they had to cut before reaching more level country in Nevada. The Union Pacific had built 1,086 miles to the Central Pacific's 689 when the race ended on the salt plains of Promontory, Utah, near Ogden. There, on May 10, 1869, Leland Stanford, former governor of California and one of the organizers of the Central Pacific, drove a gold spike symbolizing the railroad's completion.

The next transcontinental line, completed in 1881, linked the Atchison, Topeka, and Santa Fe Railroad with the Southern Pacific Railroad in southern California. The transcontinentals soon sprouted numerous trunk lines, which in turn encouraged the building of other transcontinentals. The result was a massive railroad-building boom that lasted into the 1890s and stimulated the rest of the economy.

FINANCING THE RAILROADS   The railroads were built by private companies that raised money for construction primarily by selling bonds to U.S. and foreign investors. While constitutional scruples over state sovereignty initially constrained the granting of federal aid for internal improvements, many states had subsidized the building of railroads within their borders. Finally, in 1850, Senator Stephen Douglas secured from Congress a federal grant of public lands to subsidize a north-south railroad connecting Chicago and Mobile, Alabama. Over the next twenty years transcontinental railroad companies received generous government aid in the form of federal land grants, as well as loans and tax breaks from federal, state, and local governments.

In the long run the federal government recovered much if not all of its investment. As farms, ranches, and towns sprouted around the rail lines, the value of the government land along the tracks skyrocketed. The railroads also hauled government freight, military personnel and equipment, and the mail. Moreover, by helping to accelerate the creation of a national market, the railroads spurred economic growth and thereby increased government revenues.

But that is only part of the story. The vast sums of money used to finance the building of the transcontinental lines generated shameless profiteering. Prince of the railroad robber barons was Jay Gould, a secretive trickster who mastered the art of buying rundown railroads, making cosmetic improvements, and

TRANSCONTINENTAL
RAILROAD LINES, 1880s

What was the route of the first transcontinental railroad, and why was it not in the South? Who built the railroads? How were they financed?

selling out at a profit while using corporate funds for personal gain and political bribes. Nearly every enterprise he touched was compromised or ruined; Gould, meanwhile, built a fortune that amounted to $100 million upon his death.

Few railroad fortunes were built in those freewheeling times by purely ethical methods, but compared with opportunists such as Gould most railroad entrepreneurs were giants of honesty. They at least took some interest in the welfare of their companies, if not always in that of the public. Cornelius Vanderbilt, called Commodore by virtue of his early exploits in steamboating, stands out among the railroad barons. Already rich before the Civil War, he decided to give up the hazards of wartime shipping and move his money into land transport. His great achievement was consolidating separate trunk lines into a single powerful rail network led by the New York Central. After the Commodore's death, in 1877, his son William Henry extended the Vanderbilt lines to include more than 13,000 miles in the Northeast. The consolidation trend was nationwide: about two thirds of the nation's railroad mileage were under the control of only seven major groups by 1900.

INVENTIONS SPUR MANUFACTURING   Like the railroad industry, the story of manufacturing after the Civil War shows much the same pattern of expansion and merger in old and new industries. The U.S. Patent Office, which had recorded only 276 inventions during its first decade of existence, the 1790s, registered 234,956 in the 1890s. The list of innovations after the Civil War can be extended nearly indefinitely: barbed wire, farm implements, the air brake for trains, steam turbines, gas distribution and electrical devices, the typewriter (1867), the vacuum cleaner (1869), and countless others. Before the end of the century, the internal-combustion engine and the motion picture were spawning new industries that would blossom in the twentieth century.

These technological advances altered the lives of ordinary people far more than politics or intellectual developments. In no field was this truer than in the application of electricity to communications and power. Few if any inventions of the time could rival the importance of the telephone, which Alexander Graham Bell patented in 1876. To promote the new device, the inventor and his supporters formed the Bell Telephone Association, out of which grew in 1877 the Bell Telephone Company. In 1885 the Bell interests organized the American Telephone and Telegraph Company, which by 1899 was a huge holding company controlling forty-nine licensed subsidiaries and an operating company for long-distance lines.

In the development of electrical industries, the name Thomas Alva Edison stands above those of other inventors. Edison invented the phonograph in 1877 and the first successful incandescent lightbulb in 1879. At his laboratories in Menlo Park, New Jersey, he created or perfected hundreds of new devices and processes, including the storage battery, Dictaphone, mimeograph, electric motor, electric transmission, and the motion picture. In the process, Edison and his assistants demonstrated the significance of "research and development" activities.

In 1882, with the backing of the financier J. P. Morgan, the Edison Electric Illuminating Company began to supply current to eighty-five customers in New York City, beginning the great electric utility industry. A number of companies making lightbulbs merged into the Edison General Electric

Company in 1888. But the use of direct current limited Edison's lighting system to a radius of about two miles. To cover greater distances required an alternating current, which could be transmitted at high voltage and then stepped down by transformers. George Westinghouse, inventor of the air brake for railroads, developed the first alternating-current electric system in 1886 and set up the Westinghouse Electric Company to manufacture the equipment. Edison considered the new method too dangerous, but just as Edison's instrument supplanted Bell's first telephone, the Westinghouse system won the "battle of the currents," and the Edison companies had to switch over. After the invention of the alternating-current motor in 1888, Westinghouse improved upon it. This invention enabled factories to locate wherever they wished. Capable now of using electricity as a power source, they no longer had to cluster around waterfalls and coal deposits for a ready supply of energy.

ENTREPRENEURS

Thomas Edison and George Westinghouse were rare examples of inventors with the luck and foresight to get rich from the industries they created. Most of the architects of industrial growth—the great captains of industry—were not inventors but pure entrepreneurs, men skilled mainly in organizing and promoting industry. Called robber barons by critics because of their greed and ruthlessness, they helped create thousands of new jobs and supplied the nation with an array of new goods and services. Three post–Civil War business titans stand out for their enterprise: John D. Rockefeller, Andrew Carnegie, and J. Pierpont Morgan. Each of them in different ways replaced the small-scale economy of the early republic with vast new industries that forever altered the size and scope of the nation's business. Two other entrepreneurs, Richard Sears and Alvah Roebuck, perfected mail-order retailing.

ROCKEFELLER AND THE OIL TRUST   Born in New York State, the son of a flamboyant con man and a devout Baptist, John D. Rockefeller moved as a youth to Cleveland. Soon thereafter his father abandoned the family and started a new life under an assumed name with a second wife. Raised by his mother, John Rockefeller developed a passion for systematic organization and self-discipline. He was obsessed with precision, order, and tidiness. And early on he decided to bring order and rationality to the chaotic oil industry.

Cleveland's railroad and shipping connections made it a strategic location for servicing the oil fields of western Pennsylvania. In economic importance the Pennsylvania oil rush of the 1860s far outweighed the California gold rush of just ten years earlier. Well before the end of the Civil War, derricks checkered the area around Titusville, Pennsylvania, where the first oil well had been struck, and refineries sprang up in Pittsburgh and Cleveland.

John D. Rockefeller

His Standard Oil Company dominated the oil industry.

Of the two cities, Cleveland had the edge in transportation, and John Rockefeller made the most of the fast-growing commercial city's advantages. A man of icy efficiency and tenacious daring, Rockefeller moved aggressively into the oil business. In 1870 he incorporated his various interests, naming his enterprise the Standard Oil Company of Ohio. His goal was to eliminate all of his competitors. To do that, he hatched an ingenious scheme. In the early 1870s Rockefeller created the South Improvement Company, which he made the marketing agent for a large percentage of his oil shipments. By controlling this traffic, he gained clout with the railroads, which in turn gave him large rebates (or secret refunds) on the standard freight rates in order to keep his high-volume business. In some cases they even gave him information on competitors' shipments. Rockefeller then approached his Cleveland competitors and pressured them to sell out at his price. Most of them complied. Those who resisted were forced out. In less than six weeks, Rockefeller had taken over twenty-two of his twenty-six competitors. By 1879 Standard Oil was controlling 90 to 95 percent of the oil refined throughout the country.

Much of Rockefeller's success reflected his determination to "pay nobody a profit." Instead of depending upon the products or services of other firms, known as middlemen, Standard Oil started making its own barrels, cans, and whatever else it needed—in economic terms this is called vertical integration. The company kept large cash reserves to make it independent of banks in case of a crisis. Rockefeller also set out to control his transportation needs. With Standard Oil owning most of the pipelines leading to railroads, as well as the railroad tank cars and the oil-storage facilities, it was able to dissuade the railroads from serving its eastern competitors. Those rivals that insisted on holding out then faced a giant marketing organization capable of driving them to the wall with price wars.

Eventually, in order to consolidate scattered business interests under more efficient control, Rockefeller and his advisers resorted to the legal device of the trust. Long established in law to enable one or more persons to manage property belonging to others, such as children or the mentally incompetent, the trust was now used for another purpose: centralized control of business across state lines. Thus in 1882 Rockefeller organized the Standard Oil Trust. All thirty-seven stockholders in various Standard Oil enterprises conveyed their stock to nine trustees, getting "trust certificates" in return. The nine trustees were thus empowered to give central direction to the scattered Standard Oil companies.

But the trust device, widely copied in the 1880s, proved legally vulnerable to prosecution under state laws against monopoly or restraint of trade. In 1892 Ohio's supreme court ordered the Standard Oil Trust dissolved. For a while the company managed to unify control by the simple device of interlocking directorates, through which the board of directors of one company was made identical or nearly so to the boards of the others. Gradually, however, Rockefeller perfected the idea of the holding company, a company that controlled other companies by holding all or at least a majority of their stock. In 1899, Rockefeller brought his empire under the direction of the Standard Oil Company of New Jersey, a holding company. Though less vulnerable to prosecution under state law, some holding companies were broken up by the Sherman Anti-Trust Act of 1890.

Rockefeller not only made a colossal fortune, but he also gave much of it away, mainly to support advances in education and medicine. A man of simple tastes, who opposed the use of tobacco and alcohol and believed his fortune was a public trust awarded by God, Rockefeller became the world's leading philanthropist. He donated more than $500 million during his ninety-eight-year lifetime. "I have always regarded it as a religious duty," Rockefeller said late in life, "to get all I could honorably and to give all I could."

CARNEGIE AND THE STEEL INDUSTRY   Andrew Carnegie, like Rockefeller, experienced the atypical rise from poverty to riches that came to be known in those days as the typical American success story. Born in Scotland, he migrated with his family to Allegheny County, Pennsylvania, in 1848. Then thirteen, he started work in a textile mill at wages of $1.20 per week. At fourteen he was getting $2.50 per week as a telegraph messenger. Quick-witted, shrewd, and brilliant, he worked hard, and in 1853 he became personal secretary and telegrapher to the district superintendent of the Pennsylvania Railroad. When the superintendent became president of the line, Carnegie took his place, and the pace of his career accelerated. During the Civil War, Carnegie went to Washington, D.C., where he developed a military telegraph system.

Carnegie kept on moving—from telegraphy to railroading to bridge building, then to iron- and steel-making and investments. In 1872 he netted $150,000 on a trip to Great Britain, during which he met Sir Henry Bessemer, inventor of a new process of steelmaking. The next year, Carnegie resolved to concentrate on steel, the miracle material of the post–Civil War era, not because it was new but because it was suddenly cheap. Until the mid–nineteenth century, steel could be made only from wrought iron—itself expensive—and only in small quantities. Then, in 1855, Henry Bessemer invented what became known as the Bessemer converter, a process by which steel could be produced directly and quickly from pig iron (crude iron made in a blast furnace) by using forced air to heat the metal. As more steel was produced, its price dropped and use soared. In 1860 the United States had produced only 13,000 tons of steel. By 1880 production had reached 1.4 million tons.

Carnegie was never a technical expert on steel. He was a promoter, salesman, and organizer with a gift for hiring men of expert ability. Fiercely competitive and obsessed with efficiency and innovation, he insisted on up-to-date machinery and equipment. Carnegie retained a large portion of his annual profits during good times. During business depressions, when construction costs were low and competitors were forced to the wall, he used his surplus capital to buy out competitors and expand. He preached to his employees a philosophy of continual innovation in order to reduce operating costs.

Carnegie stood out from other business titans as a thinker who publicized a philosophy of big business, a conservative rationale that became deeply ingrained in the conventional wisdom of some Americans. Carnegie argued that the captains of industry were on the whole public benefactors. He believed that the best way to

Andrew Carnegie

Steel magnate and business icon.

dispense a fortune was to donate it during one's lifetime to causes promoting the public good: "The man who dies rich dies disgraced." Carnegie insisted that the wealthy should provide means for the less fortunate to help themselves by supporting universities, libraries, hospitals, parks, halls for meetings and concerts, and church buildings. Carnegie spent some $60 million on public libraries and another $60 million on higher education.

J. P. MORGAN, FINANCIER Unlike Carnegie and Rockefeller, J. Pierpont Morgan was born to wealth, in Hartford, Connecticut, and increased it enormously through his bold financial innovations. Morgan's father was a partner in a London banking house, and his wealth enabled him to send young Pierpont to schools in Switzerland and Germany. After a brief apprenticeship, Morgan in 1857 began work in a New York firm that represented his father's London bank, and in 1860 he set himself up as its New York agent under the name J. Pierpont Morgan and Company. This firm, under various names, channeled European capital into the United States and grew into a financial power in its own right.

As an investment banker, Morgan bought corporate stocks and bonds wholesale and sold them at a profit. The growth of large corporations put investment firms such as Morgan's in an increasingly strategic position in the economy. Since the investment business depended upon the health of client companies, investment bankers became involved in the operation of their clients' firms, demanding seats on boards of directors so as to influence company policies.

Like John Rockefeller, J. P. Morgan viewed competition as wasteful and chaotic. The solution was to consolidate rival firms into giant trusts. Morgan realized that railroads were the key to the times, so he bought and reorganized one rail line after another. After the panic of 1893, when hard times gutted the net worth of many railroads, Morgan bought many of them. By the 1890s he controlled one sixth of America's railway system.

J. Pierpont Morgan

A famous portrait by Edward Steichen (1903).

Yet Morgan's crowning triumph was the consolidation of the steel industry. In 1901 he bought out Andrew Carnegie's huge steel and iron holdings. Carnegie set the price, nearly $500 million, of which Carnegie's personal share was nearly $300 million. After closing the deal, Morgan told the steel king, "Mr. Carnegie, I want to congratulate you on being the richest man in the world." Morgan's new United States Steel Corporation, a holding company for various steel interests, was a marvel of the new century, the first billion-dollar corporation, the climactic event in the age of corporate consolidation.

SEARS AND ROEBUCK   American inventors helped manufacturers after the Civil War produce a vast number of new products, but the most important challenge was extending the reach of modern commerce to the millions of people who lived on isolated farms and in small towns. In the aftermath of the Civil War, a traveling salesman from Chicago named Aaron Montgomery Ward decided that he could reach more people by mail than on foot and in the process could eliminate the middlemen whose services increased the retail price of goods. Beginning in the early 1870s, Montgomery Ward and Company began selling goods at a 40 percent discount through mail-order catalogs.

By the end of the century, a new retailer had come to dominate the mail-order industry: Sears, Roebuck and Company, founded by two young midwestern entrepreneurs, Richard Sears and Alvah Roebuck, who began offering a cornucopia of goods by mail in the early 1890s. The Sears, Roebuck catalog in 1897 was 786 pages long and was published in German and Swedish as well as English. It included groceries, drugs, tools, bells, furniture, iceboxes, stoves and household utensils, musical instruments, farm implements, boots and shoes, clothes, books, and sporting goods.

Cover of the 1897 Sears, Roebuck and Company Catalog

Sears's extensive mail-order business and discounted prices allowed its many products to reach customers in cities and the backcountry.

The Sears catalog helped create a truly national market and in the process transformed the lives of millions of people. With the advent of free rural mail delivery in 1898 and the widespread distribution of Sears catalogs, families on farms and in small towns and villages could purchase by mail the products that heretofore were either prohibitively expensive or available only to city dwellers. By the turn of the century, 6 million Sears catalogs were being distributed each year, and the catalog had become the single most widely read book in the nation after the Bible.

LABOR CONDITIONS AND ORGANIZATION

SOCIAL TRENDS   Accompanying the spread of giant corporations during the Gilded Age was a rising standard of living for most people. If the rich were still getting richer, a lot of other people were at least better off. The continuing demand for workers, meanwhile, was filled by new groups entering the workforce at the bottom: immigrants above all, but also growing numbers of women and children. Because of a long-term decline in prices and the cost of living, real wages and earnings in manufacturing went up about 50 percent between 1860 and 1890 and another 37 percent from 1890 to 1914. By latter-day standards, however, working conditions were dreary. At the turn of the century, the average hourly wage in manufacturing was about $3.50 in 2006 dollars. The average workweek was fifty-nine hours, which amounted to nearly six ten-hour workdays, but that was only an average. Most steelworkers put in a twelve-hour workday, and as late as the 1920s a great many worked a seven-day, eighty-four-hour workweek.

CHILD LABOR   A growing number of wage laborers in the late nineteenth century were children—boys and girls who worked full-time for meager wages amid unhealthy conditions. Young people had always worked in America: farms required everyone to pitch in. After the Civil War, however, many children took up work outside the home, operating machines, digging coal, stitching clothes, shucking oysters, peeling shrimp, canning food, blowing glass, and tending looms. Parents desperate for income believed they had no choice but to put their children to work. By 1880 one out of every six children was working full-time. By 1900 there were almost 2 million child laborers in the United States. In southern cotton mills, where few African Americans were hired, one fourth of the employees were below the age of fifteen, with half of the children below age twelve. Children as young as eight were laboring alongside adults twelve hours a day, six days a week. This meant they received little or no education and had little time for play or parental nurturance.

Factories, mills, mines, and canneries were dangerous places, especially for children. Throughout Appalachia, thousands of soot-smeared boys worked deep in the coal mines. In New England and the South, thousands of young girls worked in dusty textile mills. Foremen kept children awake by dousing them with water. Children suffered three times as many on-the-job accidents as adult workers, and respiratory diseases were common in the un-ventilated buildings. A child working in a textile mill was only half as likely to reach age twenty as a child outside a mill. Although some states passed laws limiting the number of hours children could work and establishing minimum-age requirements, they were rarely enforced and often ignored. By 1881 only seven states, mostly in New England, had laws requiring children to be at least twelve before they worked for wages. Yet the only proof required by employers in such states was a statement from a child's parents. Working-class and immigrant parents were often so desperate for income that they forged work permits for their children or taught their children to lie about their age to keep a job.

DISORGANIZED PROTEST   Under these circumstances it was difficult for workers to organize unions. Civic officials and business leaders respected property rights more than the rights of labor. Among workers recently removed from an agrarian world, the idea of permanent labor unions was slow to take hold. And much of the workforce was made up of immigrant workers from a variety of cultures. They spoke different languages and har-bored ethnic animosities. Many, if not most, saw their jobs as transient, the first rung on the ladder to success. They hoped to move on to a homestead or return with their earnings to the old farms of their European homeland. Nonetheless, with or without unions, workers often staged impromptu strikes protesting long working hours and wage cuts. Such action often led to violent incidents during the 1870s, however, that colored much of the public's view of labor unions thereafter.

The decade's early years saw a reign of terror in the eastern Pennsylvania coalfields, attributed to an Irish group called the Molly Maguires. The Mollies took their name from an Irish patriot who had directed violent resistance against the British. They were motivated by the dangerous working conditions in the mines and the owners' brutal efforts to sup-press union activity. Convinced of the justness of their cause, the Mollies aimed to right perceived wrongs against Irish workers by such methods as intimidation, beatings, and killings. Their terrorism reached its peak in 1874–1875. At trials in 1876, twenty-four of the Molly Maguires were convicted, and ten of them were hanged. The trials also resulted in a wage reduction in the mines.

THE RAILROAD STRIKE OF 1877   A more widespread labor incident was the Great Railroad Strike of 1877, the first major interstate strike in American history. After the panic of 1873 and the ensuing depression, the major rail lines in the East had cut wages. In 1877 they made another 10 percent cut, which provoked most of the railroad workers at Martinsburg, West Virginia, to walk off the job and block the tracks. Without organized direction, however, the group of picketers degenerated into a mob that burned and plundered railroad property.

Walkouts and sympathy demonstrations spread spontaneously from Maryland to San Francisco. The strike engulfed hundreds of cities and towns, leaving in its wake over 100 people dead and millions of dollars in property destroyed. Public sympathy for the strikers was so great at first that local militiamen, called out to suppress them, joined the workers instead. Militiamen from Philadelphia managed to disperse one crowd at the cost of twenty-six lives but then found themselves besieged in the railroad's round-house, where they disbanded and shot their way out.

Federal troops finally quelled the violence, but the looting, rioting, and burning went on for another day until the frenzy wore itself out. A reporter described the scene as "the most horrible ever witnessed, except in the carnage of war." Public opinion, sympathetic at first, began to blame the workers for the looting and violence. Eventually the strikers, lacking organized bargaining power, had no choice but to drift back to work. Everywhere the strikes failed.

For many Americans the Great Railroad Strike raised the specter of a worker-based social revolution. As a Pittsburgh newspaper warned, "This may be the beginning of a great civil war in this country between labor and capital." From the point of view of organized labor, however, the Great Railroad Strike demonstrated potential union strength and the need for tighter organization.

THE SAND-LOT INCIDENT   In California the railroad strike indirectly gave rise to a working-class political movement. At a San Francisco sand lot, a meeting to express sympathy for the strikers ended with attacks on some passing Chinese. Within a few days sporadic anti-Chinese riots had led to a mob attack on Chinatown. The depression of the 1870s had hit the

West Coast especially hard, and the Chinese were handy scapegoats for white laborers' frustrations.

Soon an Irish immigrant, Denis Kearney, had organized the Workingmen's Party of California, whose platform called for an end to further Chinese immigration. A gifted agitator, himself only recently naturalized, Kearney harangued the "sand lotters" about the "foreign peril" and assaulted the rich railroad barons for exploiting the poor—sometimes at gatherings outside their mansions on Nob Hill. In 1878 his new party won a hefty number of seats to a state constitutional convention but managed to incorporate into the state's basic law little more than ineffective attempts to regulate the railroads. The workingmen's movement peaked in 1879, when it elected many members to the state legislature and the mayor of San Francisco. Kearney lacked the gift for building a durable movement, but as his party went to pieces, his anti-Chinese theme became a national issue—in 1882 Congress voted to prohibit Chinese immigration for ten years.

TOWARD PERMANENT UNIONS   Meanwhile, efforts to build a permanent labor-union movement had begun to bear fruit. Earlier efforts, in the 1830s and 1840s, had largely been dominated by reformers with schemes that ranged from free homesteads to utopian socialism. But the 1850s witnessed the beginning of "job-conscious" unions in selected skilled trades. By 1860 there were about twenty such unions, and during the Civil War, because of the demand for labor, those craft unions grew in strength and number.

There was no overall federation of these groups until 1866, when the National Labor Union (NLU) convened in Baltimore. The NLU was composed of delegates from labor and reform groups more interested in political and social change than in bargaining with employers. The groups espoused such ideas as the eight-hour workday, workers' cooperatives, paper money, and equal rights for women and African Americans. But the organization lost momentum after the death of its president in 1869, and by 1872 it had entirely collapsed. The NLU was not a total failure, however. It was influential in persuading Congress to enact an eight-hour workday for federal employees and to repeal the 1864 Contract Labor Act, which allowed employers to bind immigrant (contract) laborers by paying for their passage from Europe. That immigrants were willing to work for low wages made them unpopular with American workers.

THE KNIGHTS OF LABOR   Before the National Labor Union collapsed, another labor group of national standing had emerged: the Noble

Order of the Knights of Labor, a name that evoked the aura of medieval guilds. The founder of the Knights of Labor, Uriah S. Stephens, a Philadelphia tailor, was a habitual "joiner" involved with several secret orders, including the Masons. Secrecy, he felt, along with a semireligious ritual, would protect members from retaliation by employers and create a sense of solidarity.

The Knights of Labor, started in 1869, grew slowly, but during the years of depression after 1873, as other unions collapsed it spread more rapidly. Throughout its existence the Knights emphasized reform measures and preferred boycotts to strikes as a way to put pressure on employers. It also had a liberal membership policy, welcoming all who had ever worked for wages, except lawyers, doctors, bankers, and those who sold liquor. Theoretically it was one big union of all workers, skilled and unskilled, regardless of race, color, creed, or sex. In the 1880s membership in the Knights grew rapidly, from about 100,000 to more than 700,000 in 1886. But the organization peaked in 1886 and went into rapid decline after the failure of a railroad strike.

ANARCHISM   The tensions between labor and management during the late nineteenth century in the United States and Europe helped generate

Members of the Knights of Labor

This national union was more egalitarian than most of its contemporaries.

interest in the doctrine of anarchism. Anarchists believed that government—any government—was in itself an abusive device used by the rich and powerful to oppress and exploit the working poor. Anarchists dreamed of the eventual disappearance of government altogether, and many of them believed that the transition to this stateless society could be hurried along by promoting revolutionary action among the masses. One favored tactic was the use of dramatic acts of violence against representatives of the government. A number of European anarchists emigrated to the United States during the last quarter of the nineteenth century, bringing with them their belief in the impact of "propaganda of the deed."

THE HAYMARKET AFFAIR   Labor-related violence increased during the 1880s. On May 3, 1886, Chicago's International Harvester plant was the site of an unfortunate clash between strikers and policemen in which one striker was killed. Leaders of a minuscule anarchist movement in Chicago scheduled an open meeting the following night at Haymarket Square to protest the killing. Under a light drizzle the crowd listened to long speeches promoting socialism and anarchism and was beginning to break up when a group of policemen arrived and called upon the activists to disperse. At that point someone threw a bomb at the police, killing one officer and wounding others. The police fired on the demonstrators, killing four. Six more policemen were also killed. Subsequently, in a trial marked by prejudice and hysteria, seven anarchist leaders were sentenced to death despite the lack of any evidence linking them to the bomb thrower, whose identity was never established. Of the seven, two were reprieved, one committed suicide in prison, and four were hanged. All but one of the group were German speaking, and that one held a membership card in the Knights of Labor.

By the turn of the century, the Knights were but a memory. Several problems accounted for their decline: a leadership devoted more to ideas than to pragmatic organization, the failure of the Knights' cooperative enterprises, and a preoccupation with politics rather than negotiations with management. The Knights nevertheless attained some lasting achievements, among them the creation of the federal Bureau of Labor Statistics and the Foran Act of 1885, which penalized employers who imported contract laborers from abroad. The Knights also spread the idea of unionism and initiated a new type of union organization: the industrial union, an industrywide union of skilled and unskilled workers.

GOMPERS AND THE AFL   The craft unions opposed the industrial unionism of the Knights. They organized workers who shared special skills, such as typographers or cigar makers. Leaders of the crafts unions feared that joining with unskilled laborers would mean a loss of their craft's identity and a loss of the skilled workers' bargaining power. In the summer of 1886, delegates from craft unions met at Columbus, Ohio, and organized the American Federation of Labor (AFL). In structure it differed from the Knights in that it was a federation of national craft organizations, each of which retained a large degree of autonomy and exercised greater leverage against management.

Samuel Gompers served as president of the AFL from its start until his death in 1924, with only one year's interruption. Born in London of Dutch Jewish ancestry, Gompers came to the United States as a teenager, joined the Cigarmakers' Union in 1864, and became president of his New York local in 1877. Gompers and other leaders of the union focused on concrete economic gains—higher wages, shorter hours, better working conditions—and avoided involvement with utopian ideas or politics.

Gompers had a thick hide, liked to talk and drink with workers in the back room, and advocated using the strike to achieve labor's objectives. His preference, though, was to achieve those objectives through agreements with management that included provisos for union recognition in the form of closed shops (which could hire only union members) or union-preference shops (which could hire others only if no union members were available).

The AFL at first grew slowly, but by 1890 it had already surpassed the Knights of Labor in membership. By the turn of the century, it claimed 500,000 members in affiliated unions; in 1914, on the eve of World War I, it had 2 million; and in 1920 it reached a peak of 4 million. But even then the AFL embraced less than 15 percent of the nation's non-agricultural workers. All unions, including the unaffiliated railroad brotherhoods, accounted for little more than 18 percent of those workers. Organized labor's strongholds were in transportation and the building trades. Most of the larger manufacturing industries—including textiles, tobacco, and packinghouses—remained almost untouched.

THE HOMESTEAD STRIKE   Two violent labor incidents in the 1890s scarred the emerging industrial-union movement and set it back for forty years: the Homestead steel strike of 1892 and the Pullman strike of 1894. The Amalgamated Association of Iron and Steel Workers, founded in 1876, had by 1891 a membership of more than 24,000 and was probably the largest craft union at the time. But it excluded unskilled steelworkers and had failed to organize the larger steel plants. The Homestead Works near Pittsburgh was an important exception. There the union had enjoyed friendly relations with Andrew Carnegie's company until Henry Clay Frick became its president in 1889. A showdown was delayed until 1892, however, when the union contract came up for renewal. Carnegie, who had expressed sympathy for unions in the past, had gone to Scotland and left matters in Frick's hands. Carnegie, however, knew what was afoot: a cost-cutting reduction in the number of workers and a deliberate attempt to smash the union. "Am with you to the end," he wrote to Frick.

As negotiations dragged on, the company announced it would deal with workers as individuals unless an agreement with the union was reached by June 29. A strike—or, more properly, a lockout of unionists—began on that date. Even before the negotiations ended, Frick had begun barricading the plant and had hired as plant guards 300 Pinkerton detectives whose specialty was union busting. On July 6, 1892, a battle erupted, in which nine workers and seven Pinkertons died. In the end the Pinkertons surrendered and marched away, taunted by crowds in the street. Six days later 8,000 state militiamen appeared at the plant to protect the strikebreakers hired to restore production. The strike dragged on until November, but by then the union was dead at Homestead. Its cause was not helped when an anarchist, a Lithuanian immigrant, tried to assassinate Frick. Much of the local sympathy for the strikers evaporated.

THE PULLMAN STRIKE   The Pullman strike of 1894 was perhaps the most notable walkout in American history. It paralyzed the economies of twenty-seven states and territories making up the western half of the nation. It grew out of a dispute at Pullman, Illinois, a model corporate town built on 4,000 acres outside Chicago, where workers of the Pullman Palace Car Company were housed in neat brick homes nestled on grassy lots along shaded streets. The town's idyllic appearance was deceptive, however. Employees were required to live there, pay rents and utility costs that were higher than those in nearby towns, and buy their goods from company stores. With the onset of the depression in 1893, George Pullman laid off 3,000 of 5,800 employees and cut wages 25 to 40 percent, but not his rents and other charges. After Pullman fired three members of a workers' grievance committee, a strike began on May 11, 1894.

During this tense period, Pullman workers had been joining the American Railway Union, founded the previous year by Eugene V. Debs. A charismatic man who led by example and the electric force of his convictions, Debs was a tireless spokesman for labor radicalism who launched a crusade to organize *all* railway workers—skilled and unskilled—into the American Railway Union. His earnest appeal generated a tremendous response, and soon he

Eugene V. Debs

Founder of the American Railway Union and later candidate for president as head of the Socialist Party of America.

was in charge of a powerful new labor organization. He quickly turned his attention to the Pullman controversy.

After George Pullman refused Debs's plea for arbitration, the union workers in June 1894 stopped handling Pullman railcars and by the end of July had tied up most of the railroads in the Midwest. The rail owners brought strikebreakers to connect mail cars to Pullman cars so that interference with Pullman cars would entail interference with the federal mail. U.S. attorney general Richard Olney, a former railroad attorney, swore in 3,400 special deputies to keep the trains running. When clashes occurred between the deputies and some of the strikers, lawless elements ignored Debs's plea for an orderly boycott and repeated some of the violent scenes of the 1877 strike.

Finally, on July 3, 1894, President Grover Cleveland answered an appeal from the railroads to send federal troops into the Chicago area, where the strike was centered. Illinois governor John Peter Altgeld issued a vigorous protest, insisting that the state could keep order, but Cleveland claimed authority and a duty to ensure delivery of the mail. "If it takes every dollar in the Treasury and every soldier in the United States to deliver a postal card in Chicago," he vowed, "that postal card should be delivered."

As strikers clashed with troops and burned hundreds of railcars, the federal district court granted an injunction forbidding any interference with the mail or any effort to restrain interstate commerce. On July 13 the union called off the strike, and a few days later the district court cited Debs for violating the injunction, and he served six months in jail. The Supreme Court upheld the decree in the case of *In re Debs* (1895) on broad grounds of national sovereignty. Debs served his term, during which he read deeply in socialist literature, and he emerged to devote the rest of his life to socialism.

SOCIALISM AND THE UNIONS   The major American unions, for the most part, never allied themselves with the socialists, as many European labor movements did. Although socialist ideas had been circulating in the country at least since the 1820s, the movement gained little notice before the rise of Daniel De Leon in the 1890s as the dominant figure in the Socialist Labor party. De Leon proposed to organize industrial unions with a socialist purpose and to build a political party that would abolish the state once it gained power. His ideas seem to have influenced Vladimir Lenin, leader of Russia's Bolshevik revolution of 1917, but De Leon preached revolution at the ballot box, not by violence.

To many, De Leon seemed doctrinaire and inflexible. Eugene Debs was therefore more successful at building a socialist movement in America. In 1897 Debs announced that he was a socialist and organized the Social Democratic party from the remnants of the American Railway Union; he received over 96,000 votes as its candidate for president in 1900. In 1901 his followers joined a number of secessionists from De Leon's party, led by Morris Hillquit of New York, to set up the Socialist Party of America. In 1904 Debs polled over 400,000 votes as the party's candidate for president and in 1912, more than doubled that, to more than 900,000 votes, or 6 percent of the popular vote.

By 1912 the Socialist party seemed well on the way to becoming a permanent fixture in American politics. Thirty-three cities had Socialist mayors. The Socialist party sponsored five English-language daily newspapers, eight foreign-language dailies, and a number of weeklies and monthlies. In the Southwest the party built a sizable grassroots following among farmers and tenants. But it reached its peak in 1912. It would be wracked by disagreements over America's participation in World War I and was split thereafter.

THE WOBBLIES   During the years of Socialist party growth, a parallel effort to revive industrial unionism emerged, led by the Industrial Workers of the World (IWW), nicknamed the Wobblies. The chief base for this group was the Western Federation of Miners, organized at Butte, Montana, in 1893. Like the Knights of Labor, it was designed to include all workers, skilled or unskilled. Its roots were in the mining and lumber camps of the West, where unstable conditions of employment created a large number of nomadic workers, to whom neither the AFL's pragmatic approach nor the socialists' political appeal held much attraction. The revolutionary goal of the Wobblies was an idea labeled syndicalism by its French supporters: the ultimate destruction of the state and its replacement by one big union. How that union would govern remained vague.

The Wobblies reached out to the fringe elements with the least power and influence, chiefly the migratory workers of the West and the ethnic groups of the East. Always ambivalent about diluting their revolutionary principles, Wobblies scorned the usual labor agreements even when they participated in them. They engaged in spectacular battles with employers but scored few victories. The largest was a textile strike at Lawrence, Massachusetts, in 1912; the strikers won wage raises, overtime pay, and other benefits. But the next year a strike of silk workers at Paterson, New Jersey, ended in disaster, and the IWW entered a rapid decline.

The fading of the movement was accelerated by the hysterical opposition it engendered. Its members branded as anarchists, bums, and criminals, the IWW was effectively destroyed during World War I, when most of its leaders were jailed for their militant opposition to the war. Nonetheless, the Wobblies left behind a rich folklore of nomadic working folk and a gallery of heroic agitators.

A Nation Transformed

By the end of the nineteenth century, the accelerating Industrial Revolution had transformed the nature of work and social life, generated a new urban consciousness and culture, and unleashed rising class tensions. With each passing year, more and more people jettisoned traditional rural folkways in favor of urban environs and enticing economic and social opportunities. As centers of production and consumption, the new industrial cities controlled the pace of national life.

The Industrial Revolution occurred at different rates and produced different effects across the expanding nation. Despite the energetic efforts of New South boosters, the states of the former Confederacy, burdened by a chronic shortage of capital and a poorly educated populace, lagged well behind the rest of the nation in industrial development, urban expansion, and per capita income.

The recurring theme of American life after the Civil War was an acute sense of accelerated social and intellectual change. The velocity and scope of change at midcentury and after was bewildering. Some believed that the United States had lost much of its stability and cohesion as a result of urban-industrial development and western expansion. It had become a loose aggregate of competing individuals, separated from one another by economic differences and ethnic, racial, and class prejudices. How to restore a sense of community and cohesion would become the collective challenge of all Americans.

MAKING CONNECTIONS

- The Darwinian ideas implicit in the attitudes of many leading entrepreneurs, especially Andrew Carnegie, are described in greater detail in the next chapter.

- In response to the growth of the railroads, reformers in the 1880s and 1890s began to push for government regulation of industry, a trend explored in Chapter 22.

- The economic and industrial growth described in this chapter was an important factor in America's "new imperialism" of the late nineteenth century, as shown in Chapter 23.

- The socialist approach to reform was a significant influence on the Progressive movement, covered in Chapter 24.

FURTHER READING

For a masterful synthesis of post–Civil War industrial development, see Walter Licht's *Industrializing America: The Nineteenth Century* (1995). On the growth of railroads, see Albro Martin's *Railroads Triumphant: The Growth, Rejection, and Rebirth of a Vital American Force* (1992). A monumental study of the transcontinental railroad is David Haward Bain's *Empire Express: Building the First Transcontinental Railroad* (1999). On the 1877 railroad strike, see David O. Stowell's *Streets, Railroads, and the Great Strike of 1877* (1999).

On entrepreneurship in the iron and steel sector, see Thomas J. Misa's *A Nation of Steel: The Making of Modern America, 1865–1925* (1995). The best biographies of the leading business tycoons are Ron Chernow's *Titan: The Life of John D. Rockefeller, Sr.* (1998) and Jean Strouse's *Morgan, American Financier* (1999). Nathan Rosenberg's *Technology and American Economic Growth* (1972) documents the growth of invention during the period.

Much of the scholarship on labor stresses the traditional values and the culture of work that people brought to the factory. Herbert G, Gutman's *Work, Culture, and Society in Industrializing America: Essays in American Working-Class History* (1975) best introduces these themes. Also see David Montgomery's *The Fall of the House of Labor: The Workplace, the State, and American Labor Activism, 1865–1925* (1987).

For the role of women in the changing workplace, see Alice Kessler-Harris's *Out to Work: A History of Wage-Earning Women in the United States* (1982) and Susan E. Kennedy's *If All We Did Was to Weep at Home: A History of White Working-Class Women in America* (1979).

As for the labor unions, Gerald N. Grob's *Workers and Utopia: A Study of Ideological Conflict in the American Labor Movement, 1865–1900* (1961) examines the difference in outlook between the Knights of Labor and the American Federation of Labor. For the Knights, see Leon Fink's *Workingmen's Democracy: The Knights of Labor and American Politics* (1983). Also useful is Susan Levine's *Labor's True Woman: Carpet Weavers, Industrialization, and Labor Reform in the Gilded Age* (1984), on the role of women in the Knights. To trace the rise of socialism among organized workers, see Nick Salvatore's *Eugene V. Debs: Citizen and Socialist* (1982). Strikes are discussed in Paul Avrich's *The Haymarket Tragedy* (1984) and Paul Krause's *The Battle for Homestead, 1880–1892: Politics, Culture, and Steel* (1992).

21

THE EMERGENCE OF
URBAN AMERICA

FOCUS QUESTIONS

· How did immigration affect the growth of the modern city?
· What led to the rise of powerful reform movements?
· What was the impact of Darwinian thought on the social sciences?
· What were the literary and philosophical trends of the late nineteenth century?

To answer these questions and access additional review material, please visit www.wwnorton.com/studyspace.

During the second half of the nineteenth century, the United States experienced an urban transformation unparalleled in world history. The late nineteenth century, declared an economist in 1899, was "not only the age of cities, but the age of great cities." Between 1860 and 1910 the urban population of the United States mushroomed from 6 million to 44 million. By 1920 more than half the population lived in urban areas.

The rise of big cities during the nineteenth century created a distinctive urban culture. People from different ethnic and religious backgrounds and representing every walk of life poured into the high-rise apartment buildings and congested tenements springing up in every major city. They came in search of jobs, wealth, and excitement.

Not surprisingly, the rise of metropolitan America created an array of social problems. Rapid urban development produced widespread poverty and political corruption. It also produced dirt and disease, crowded housing, and unsafe working conditions in factories, mines, mills, and slaughterhouses. People needed basic services, such as education, transportation, sewers, fresh water, inoculations against disease, and factory inspections to prevent unsafe working conditions. Broadened access to public education and to public health services would eventually improve literacy and lower infant mortality rates. Breakthroughs in medical science would bring cures for tuberculosis, typhoid, and diphtheria—although those infectious diseases would remain the century's leading killers. But in the meantime, the question of how to feed, clothe, shelter, and educate the new arrivals taxed the imagination and patience of many urban leaders.

America's Move to Town

The prospect of good jobs and social excitement lured people to the cities from the countryside and overseas. City people and laborers became recognizably urban in demeanor and outlook. The contrasts between farm and city life grew more vivid with each passing year.

EXPLOSIVE URBAN GROWTH   The frontier was a safety valve for urban unrest, the historian Frederick Jackson Turner said in his influential thesis on American development. Its cheap lands afforded a release for the population pressures mounting in the cities. If there were such a thing as a safety valve in his own time, however, he had it exactly backward. The flow of population toward cities was greater than the flow toward the West.

Much of the westward migration in fact was itself an urban movement, spawning new towns near the mining digs or at the railheads. The Pacific coast boasted a greater urban proportion of the population in the West than anywhere else; its major concentrations were first around San Francisco Bay and then in Los Angeles, which became a boomtown after the arrival of the Southern Pacific and Santa Fe Railroads in the 1880s. In the Northwest, Seattle also grew quickly, first as the terminus of three transcontinental railroad lines and, by the end of the century, as the staging area for the Yukon gold rush. Minneapolis, St. Paul, Omaha, Kansas City, and Denver were no longer the mere villages they had been in 1860. The South, too, produced new cities: Durham, North Carolina, and Birmingham, Alabama, which were centers of tobacco and iron manufactures, and Houston, Texas, which handled cotton and cattle and, later, oil. The industrial explosion powered the growth of new cities during this period.

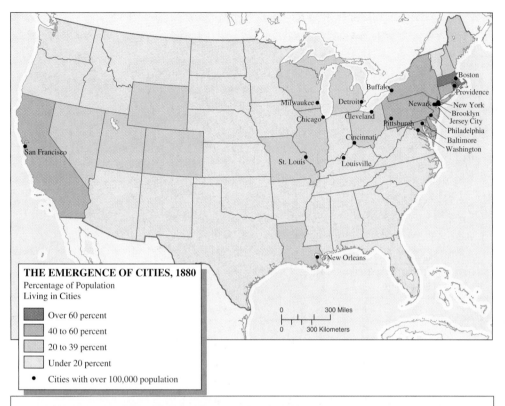

THE EMERGENCE OF CITIES, 1880

Percentage of Population
Living in Cities

- Over 60 percent
- 40 to 60 percent
- 20 to 39 percent
- Under 20 percent
- • Cities with over 100,000 population

Which states had the largest population in 1880? What drove the growth of western cities? How were western cities different from eastern cities?

Several technological innovations enabled cities to expand vertically to accommodate their surging populations. In the 1870s innovations in heating, such as steam circulating through pipes and radiators, contributed to the building of multiple-apartment dwellings, since fireplaces were no longer needed. In 1889 the Otis Elevator Company installed the first electric elevator, which made possible the erection of taller buildings—before the Civil War few structures had risen higher than three or four stories. During the 1880s engineers developed cast-iron and steel-frame construction, which was stronger than brick and thereby enabled the construction of "skyscrapers," which depend on steel frames and girders.

Cities also expanded horizontally after the introduction of important transportation innovations. Before the 1890s the chief power sources of urban transport were either animals or steam. Horse- and mule-drawn streetcars had

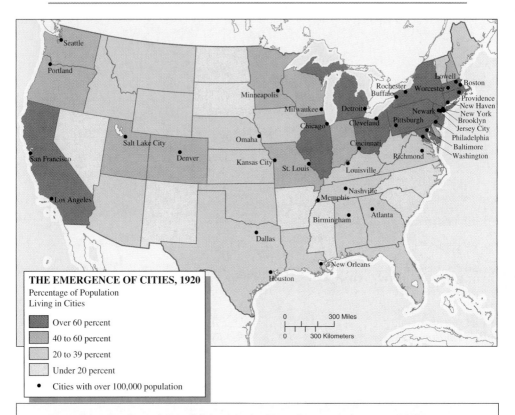

THE EMERGENCE OF CITIES, 1920

Percentage of Population
Living in Cities

Over 60 percent

40 to 60 percent

20 to 39 percent

Under 20 percent

• Cities with over 100,000 population

How did technology change life in cities in the early twentieth century? What was the role of mass transit in expanding the urban population? How did the demographics of these new cities change between 1880 and 1920?

appeared in antebellum cities, but they were slow and cumbersome, and cleaning up manure from the streets added to their cost. In 1873 San Francisco became the first city to use cars pulled by steam-driven cables. Some cities used steam-powered commuter trains on elevated tracks, but by the 1890s electric trolleys were preferred. Mass transportation received an added boost around the turn of the century, when subway systems began to operate in Boston, New York, and Philadelphia.

The spread of mass transit allowed large numbers of people to become commuters, and a growing middle class retreated to quieter, tree-lined "streetcar suburbs," whence they could travel into the central city for business or entertainment (though laborers generally stayed put, unable to afford even the nickel fare). Urban growth often became a sprawl, since it

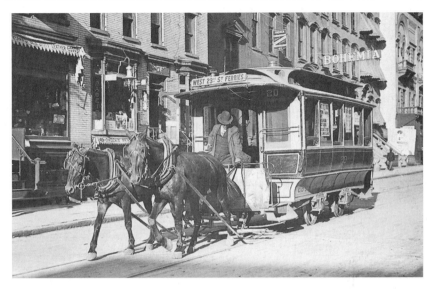

Urban Mass Transit

A horse-drawn streetcar moving along rails in New York City.

usually took place without plan, in the interest of a fast buck, and without thought to the need for parks and public services.

THE ALLURE AND PROBLEMS OF THE CITIES   The wonder of the cities—their glittering new electric lights, their streetcars, telephones, department stores, vaudeville shows and other amusements, newspapers and magazines, and a thousand other attractions—cast a magnetic lure on rural youth. The new cities threw into stark contrast the frustration of unending toil and the isolation of country life. In times of rural depression, thousands left farms for the cities in search of opportunity and personal freedom.

Yet those who moved to the city often traded one set of problems for another. Workers in the big cities often had no choice but to live in crowded apartments, most of which were poorly designed. In 1900 Manhattan's 42,700 tenements housed almost 1.6 million people. Such unregulated urban growth created immense problems of health and morale.

During the last quarter of the nineteenth century, cities became so cramped and land so scarce that architects were forced to build upward. In New York City this resulted in "dumbbell" tenement houses. These structures, usually six to eight stories tall and jammed tightly against one another,

Urbanization and the Environment

A garbage cart retrieves trash in New York City, ca. 1890

derived their name from the fact that housing codes required a two-foot-wide air shaft between buildings. The fronts and the backs of adjoining buildings abutted each other, but the midsections were narrower, giving the structures the appearance of dumbbells when viewed from overhead. Twenty-four to thirty-two families would cram into each building. Some city blocks housed almost 4,000 people. The tiny air shaft provided little ventilation; instead, it proved to be a fire hazard, fueling and conveying flames from building to building.

The early tenements were poorly heated and had communal toilets outside in a yard or alley. Shoehorned into their quarters, families had no privacy, free space, or sunshine; children had few places to play except in the streets; infectious diseases and noxious odors were rampant. Not surprisingly, the mortality rate among the urban poor was much higher than that of the general population. In one poor Chicago district at the end of the century, three out of five babies died before their first birthday.

CITY POLITICS   The sheer size of the cities helped create a new form of politics. Because local government was often fragmented and beset by parochial rivalries, a need grew for a central organization to coordinate citywide services such as public transportation, sanitation, and utilities. Urban political machines developed, consisting of local committeemen, district captains, and culminating in a political boss. While the bosses granted patronage favors and engaged in graft, buying votes and taking kickbacks, they also provided needed services. They distributed food, coal, and money to the poor; found jobs for those who were out of work; sponsored English-language classes for immigrants; organized sports teams, social clubs, and neighborhood gatherings; fixed problems at city hall; and generally helped newcomers adjust to their new life. In return the political professionals felt entitled to some reward for having done the grubby work of the local organization.

CITIES AND THE ENVIRONMENT Nineteenth-century urban communities were filthy and disease ridden, noisy and smelly. They overflowed with garbage, contaminated water, horse manure, roaming pigs, and untreated sewage. Providing clean water was a chronic problem, and raw sewage was dumped into streets and waterways. Epidemics of water-related diseases such as cholera, typhoid fever, and yellow fever ravaged populations. Animal waste was pervasive. In 1900, for example, there were over 3.5 million horses in American cities, each of which generated 20 pounds of manure and several gallons of urine daily. In Chicago alone, 82,000 horses produced 300,000 tons of manure each year. The life expectancy of urban draft horses was only two years, which meant that thousands of horse carcasses had to be disposed of each year. In New York City alone, 15,000 dead horses were removed annually.

During the late nineteenth century, municipal reformers organized to clean up the cities. Their goal was not only to improve the appearance of metropolises but also to remove the environmental causes of disease. The "sanitary reformers"—public health officials and municipal engineers—persuaded city governments to banish hogs and cattle, mount cleanup campaigns, establish water and sewage systems, institute trash collection, and replace horses with electric streetcars. By 1900, 94 percent of American cities had developed regular trash-collection services.

Yet such improvements in public health had important social and ecological trade-offs and caused unanticipated problems. Waste that once had been put into the land was now dumped into waterways. Urban populations had to deal with the waste dumped upstream; rural populations had to deal with the urban waste sent downstream.

Similarly, solving the horse-manure problem involved trade-offs. The manure dropped on city streets did cause stench and bred countless flies, many of which carried diseases such as typhoid fever. But urban horse manure also had benefits. Farmers living on the outskirts of cities used it to fertilize hay and vegetable crops. City-generated manure was the agricultural lifeblood of the vegetable farms outside New York, Baltimore, Philadelphia, and Boston. Likewise, human waste was used on farm fields. In the nineteenth century most cities converted the "night soil" from outhouses into agricultural fertilizer.

Ultimately, however, the development of public water and sewer systems and flush toilets separated urban dwellers and their waste from the agricultural cycle at the same time that the emergence of refrigerated railcars and massive meatpacking plants separated most people from their sources of food. While the advances provided great benefits, a flush-and-forget-it mentality emerged. Well into the twentieth century, people presumed that running water purified itself, and consequently they dumped massive amounts of untreated waste into rivers and bays. What they failed to calculate was the carrying capacity of the waterways. And the high phosphorous content of bodily waste dumped into streams led to algae blooms that sucked the oxygen out of the water and unleashed a string of environmental reactions that suffocated fish and affected marine ecology. By the 1930s, Lake Erie was coated with algae; the fish population had plummeted.

THE NEW IMMIGRATION

The Industrial Revolution during the second half of the nineteenth century brought to American shores waves of immigrants from every part of the globe. By 1900 nearly 30 percent of the residents of major cities were foreign-born. These newcomers provided much-needed labor, but their arrival also generated ugly racial and ethnic tensions.

AMERICA'S PULL   The migration of foreigners to the United States has been one of the most powerful forces shaping American history, and this was especially true after the Civil War. The tide of immigration rose from just under 3 million in the 1870s to more than 5 million in the 1880s then fell to a little over 3.5 million in the depression decade of the 1890s and rose to its high-water mark of 8.8 million in the first decade of the new century. European immigrants moved from the great agricultural areas of eastern and southern Europe directly to the foremost cities of America. They wanted to live with others of like language, customs, and religion, and they lacked the means to go west and settle on farms.

This nation of immigrants continued to draw new inhabitants for much the same reasons as always and from much the same segments of society. Immigrants took flight from famine, cholera, or the lack of economic opportunity in their native lands. They fled racial, religious, and political persecution and compulsory military service.

Yet more immigrants were probably pulled by America's opportunities than were pushed out by conditions at home. American industries, seeking cheap labor, sent recruiters abroad. Railroads, eager to sell land and build up the traffic on their lines, distributed tempting propaganda in a medley of languages. Many of the western and southern states set up official bureaus and agents to attract immigrants. Under the Contract Labor Act of 1864, the federal government itself encouraged immigration: it allowed companies to recruit foreign workers by paying for their passage and then recouping the money from the immigrants' wages. The law was repealed in 1868, but not until 1885 did the government forbid companies to import contract labor, a practice that put immigrants under the control of their employers.

A NEW WAVE   Before 1880 immigrants were mainly from northern and western Europe. By the 1870s, however, that pattern had begun to change. The proportion of people from southern and eastern Europe rose sharply. After 1890 they made up a majority of the newcomers, and by the first decade of the new century they formed 70 percent of the immigrants to the United States. Among these new immigrants were Italians, Hungarians, Czechs, Slovaks, Poles, Serbs, Croats, Russians, Romanians, and Greeks—all people whose culture and language were markedly different from those of western Europe and whose religion for the most part was Judaism or Catholicism.

ELLIS ISLAND   As the number of immigrants passing through the port of New York soared during the late nineteenth century, the state-run Castle Garden receiving center overflowed with corruption. With reports of abuses filling the newspapers, Congress ordered an investigation, which resulted in the closure of Castle Garden, in 1890. Thereafter the federal government's new Bureau of Immigration took responsibility for admitting newcomers to New York City.

To launch this effort, Congress funded the construction of a new reception center on a tiny island off the New Jersey coast, a mile south of Manhattan, near the Statue of Liberty. In 1892 Ellis Island opened its doors to the "huddled masses" of the world. In 1907, the reception center's busiest year, more than 1 million new arrivals passed through the receiving center, an average of about 5,000 per day; in one day alone, immigration officials processed some 11,750.

Steerage Deck of the S.S. *Pennland*, 1893

These immigrants are about to arrive at Ellis Island in New York Harbor. Many newcomers to America settled in cities because they lacked the means to take up farming.

MAKING THEIR WAY   Once on American soil, immigrants felt exhilaration, exhaustion, and usually a desperate need for work. Many were greeted by family and friends who had arrived earlier, others by representatives of the many immigrant-aid societies or by agents offering the men jobs in mines, mills, or sweatshops. Since most immigrants knew little if any English and nothing about American employment practices, they were easy subjects for exploitation.

In exchange for some whiskey and a job, obliging recruiters claimed a healthy percentage of their wages. Among Italians and Greeks these agents were known as padrones, and they came to dominate the labor market in New York. Other contractors provided train tickets to cities such as Buffalo, Pittsburgh, Cleveland, Chicago, Milwaukee, Cincinnati, and St. Louis.

Strangers in a new land, most of the immigrants gravitated to neighborhoods populated by their own kind. The immigrant enclaves—nicknamed Little Italy, Little Hungary, Chinatown, and so on—served as crucial transitional communities between the newcomers' Old World past and their New World future. In such kinship communities, immigrants practiced

The Registry Room at Ellis Island

Inspectors asked arriving passengers twenty-nine probing questions, including "Are you a polygamist?"

their religion and clung to their native customs, conversed in their native tongue, and filled an aching loneliness. But they paid a price for such community solidarity. When the "new immigrants" moved into an area, older residents typically moved out, taking with them whatever social prestige and political influence they had achieved. The quality of living quickly deteriorated as housing and sanitation codes then went unenforced.

THE NATIVIST RESPONSE Many native-born Americans saw the new immigration as a threat, and the undercurrent of nativism so often present in American culture surfaced during the late nineteenth century, mainly expressed in anti-Catholic and anti-Semitic sentiments. But more than religious prejudice underlay hostility toward the latest newcomers. Cultural differences confirmed in the minds of nativists the assumption that the Nordic peoples of the old immigration were superior to the Slavic and Latin peoples of the new immigration. Many of the new immigrants were illiterate, and more appeared so because they could not speak English. Some resorted to crime, and political and social radicals turned up in sufficient numbers to encourage nativists to blame labor disputes on alien elements.

Nativism led to a movement to restrict immigration, but it had mixed success beyond the exclusion of certain individuals deemed undesirable. In 1891 Representative Henry Cabot Lodge of Massachusetts took up the cause of excluding illiterates, a measure that would have affected much of the new wave of immigrants even though literacy in English was not required. Bills embodying the restriction passed Congress several times during the next twenty-five years but were vetoed by Presidents Grover Cleveland, William H. Taft, and Woodrow Wilson. In 1917, however, Congress overrode Wilson's veto.

Advocates of immigration restriction during the late nineteenth century did succeed in excluding the Chinese, who were victims of every act of discrimination that the new European immigrants suffered and color prejudice as well. By 1880 there were some 75,000 Chinese in California, about one ninth of the state's population. Railroad owners found them hardworking. Many white workers, however, resented them for accepting lower wages, but their greater sin, a New York newspaper editor stressed, was perpetuating "those disgusting habits of thrift, industry, and self-denial."

Exclusion of the Chinese began in 1880, when the urgent need for railway labor had ebbed. A new treaty with China permitted the United States to "regulate, limit, and suspend" Chinese immigration, and in 1882 Congress passed a bill authorizing a ten-year suspension of Chinese immigration. The legislation closing the doors to Chinese immigrants received overwhelming support. The Chinese Exclusion Act was periodically renewed before being extended indefinitely in 1902. Not until 1943 were barriers to Chinese immigration finally removed.

The West Coast counterpart to Ellis Island was the Immigration Station on rugged Angel Island, six miles offshore from San Francisco. Opened in 1910, it served as a processing center for tens of thousands of Asian immigrants, most of them Chinese. Although the Chinese Exclusion Act had sharply reduced the flow of Chinese immigrants, it did not stop the influx completely. Those arrivals who could claim a Chinese-American parent were allowed to enter, as were certain officials, teachers, merchants, and students. The powerful prejudice the Chinese immigrants encountered helps explain why over 30 percent of the arrivals at Angel Island were denied entry.

POPULAR CULTURE

The sprawling new cities created new patterns of recreation and leisure. Popular culture took on new or greatly expanded dimensions that endowed life with a more cosmopolitan quality. For example, traveling circuses brought entertainment to large cities and small towns. Creative promoters such as Phineas T. Barnum and James A. Bailey made the circus the most eclectic form of entertainment. In the congested metropolitan areas, politics became as much a form of public entertainment as it was a means of providing civic representation and public services. People flocked to hear visiting candidates give speeches in cavernous halls, on outdoor plazas, or from railway cars. In cities such as New York, Philadelphia, Boston, and Chicago, membership in a political party was akin to belonging to a social club. In addition, labor unions provided activities that were more social than economic in nature, and members often visited the union hall as much to socialize as to discuss working conditions. The sheer number of people congregated in cities also helped generate a market for new forms of mass entertainment, such as traveling Wild West shows, vaudeville shows, and spectator sports.

VAUDEVILLE   Growing family incomes and innovations in urban transportation—cable cars, subways, electric streetcars and streetlights—enabled more people to take advantage of urban cultural life. By far the most popular—and most diverse—form of theatrical entertainment in the late nineteenth century was vaudeville. The term derives from a French word for a play accompanied by music. It emerged in the United States in saloons whose owners sought to attract more customers by offering a free show.

Early "variety" shows were held in seedy beer halls and featured comedians, singers, musicians, blackface minstrels, farcical plays, animal acts, jugglers, gymnasts, dancers, mimes, and magicians. Vaudeville houses became popular gathering places for all social classes and types—men, women, and children—all of whom were expected to behave according to middle-class standards of gentility and decorum.

OUTDOOR RECREATION   The congestion and disease associated with city life led many people to participate in forms of outdoor recreation intended to restore their vitality and improve their health. People sought places within the city to escape the tenements and the factories and offices. New York City in the 1850s set up a park commission, which hired Frederick Law Olmsted to design and plan Central Park. Olmsted viewed city parks as much more than recreational centers; he sought to create oases of culture that would promote social stability and cohesion. He was convinced that Central Park would exercise "a distinctly harmonizing and refining influence upon the most unfortunate and lawless classes of the city—an influence favorable to courtesy, self-control, and temperance." Olmsted went on to design parks for Boston, Brooklyn, Chicago, Philadelphia, and San Francisco.

Although originally intended as places where people could walk and commune with nature, parks soon offered more vigorous forms of exercise and recreation. Croquet lawns and tennis courts were among the first additions to city parks because they took up little space and required little maintenance. Because croquet could be played by both sexes, it combined the virtues of sport with the opportunities of courtship. Croquet as a public sport suffered a setback in the 1890s, however, when Boston clergymen lambasted the drinking, gambling, and licentious behavior associated with it.

Even more popular than croquet or tennis was cycling, or "wheeling." In the 1870s bicycles began to be manufactured in the United States, and by the end of the century a bicycle craze had swept the country. Bicycles were especially popular with women who chafed at the restricting conventions of the

Tandem Tricycle

In spite of the danger and discomfort of early bicycles, "wheeling" became a popular form of recreation and mode of transportation.

Victorian era. The new vehicles offered exercise, freedom, and access to the countryside. Female cyclists were able to discard their cumbersome corsets and full dresses in favor of "bloomers" and split skirts.

The urban working poor could not afford to acquire a bicycle or join a croquet club, however. Nor did they have as much free time as the affluent. They toiled long hours six days a week, and at the end of their long days and on Sundays they eagerly sought recreation and fellowship on street corners or on the front stoops of their apartment buildings. Organ grinders and musicians would perform on the sidewalks among the food vendors. Many ethnic groups, especially the Germans and the Irish, formed male singing, drinking, or gymnastic clubs. Working folk also attended bare-knuckle boxing matches or baseball games and on Sundays would gather for picnics. By the end of the century, large-scale amusement parks such as Brooklyn's Coney Island provided entertainment for the entire family. Yet many inner-city youth could not afford the trolley fare, so the crowded streets and dangerous alleys remained their playgrounds.

SALOON CULTURE   The most popular destinations for working-class Americans with free time were saloons and dance halls. The saloon was the poor-man's social club during the late nineteenth century. By 1900 there were more saloons in the United States than there were grocery stores and meat markets. New York City alone had 10,000, or one for every 500 residents. Chicago had one saloon for every 335 people; Houston, one for every 300; San Francisco, one for every 215. Often sponsored by beer brewers and frequented by local politicians, saloons offered a free lunch to encourage patrons to visit and buy 5¢ beer or 15¢ whiskey.

Saloons provided much more than food and drink, however; they were in effect public homes, offering haven and fellowship to people who often worked ten hours a day, six days a week. Saloons were especially popular among male immigrants seeking friends and companionship in a new land. Saloons served as busy social hubs and were often aligned with local political machines. In New York City in the 1880s, most of the primary elections and local political caucuses were conducted in saloons.

Saloons were defiantly male enclaves. Although women and children occasionally entered a saloon—through a side door—in order to carry home a pail of beer (called "rushing the growler") or to drink at a backroom party, the main bar at the front of the saloon was for men only. Some saloons provided "snugs," small separate rooms for female patrons.

Saloons aroused intense criticism. Anti-liquor societies such as the Women's Christian Temperance Union and the Anti-Saloon League charged that saloons contributed to alcoholism, divorce, crime, and absenteeism from work. The reformers demanded that saloons be closed down. Yet drunkenness in saloons was the exception rather than the rule. Most patrons of working-class saloons had little money to waste, and recent studies have revealed that the average amount of money spent on liquor was no more than 5 percent of a man's annual income. Saloons were the primary locus of the workingman's leisure time and political activity. As a journalist observed, "The saloon is, in short, the social and intellectual center of the neighborhood."

WORKINGWOMEN AND LEISURE   In contrast to the male public culture centered in saloons, the leisure activities of working-class women, many of them immigrants, were more limited at the end of the nineteenth century. Married women were so encumbered by housework and maternal responsibilities that they had little free time. Married working-class women could not afford domestic help or sitters for their children, so they tended to combine entertainment with their work and often used the streets as their public space. Washing clothes, supervising children, or shopping at the local market provided opportunities for fellowship with other women.

Single women had more opportunities for leisure and recreation than did working mothers. As the average workday gradually declined from twelve hours in the 1880s to nine or ten hours in 1914, all working people had more free time. In the cities young factory hands, domestic servants, office workers, and retail clerks eagerly sought access to urban pleasures. City amusements enticed women from their congested and drab tenements. Women flocked to dance halls, theaters, amusement parks, and picnic grounds. On hot summer days many working-class folk went to public beaches. For young workingwomen in and around New York City, for example, an excursion to Coney Island was a special treat. Not only could they swim, but they could also experience the sideshow attractions, vaudeville shows, dance pavilions, restaurants, and boardwalk. By 1900 as many as 500,000 people converged on Coney Island on Saturdays and Sundays.

With the advent of movie theaters during the second decade of the twentieth century, the cinema became the most popular form of entertainment for women. As a promotional flyer for a movie theater promised, "If you are tired of life, go to the movies. If you are sick of troubles rife, go to the picture show. You will forget your unpaid bills, rheumatism and other ills, if you stow your pills and go to the picture show." Although some parents and social reformers tried to restrict young single women's freedom to engage in urban recreation and entertainment, many young women followed their own wishes and in so doing helped carve out their own social sphere.

Pool in Steeplechase
Coney Island, N. Y.

STEEPLECHASE POOL

Steeplechase Park, Coney Island, Brooklyn, New York
Members of the working class could afford the inexpensive rides at this popular amusement park.

SPECTATOR SPORTS   In the last quarter of the nineteenth century, new spectator sports such as college football and basketball and professional baseball gained mass popularity, reflecting the growing urbanization of life. People could gather easily for sporting events in the large cities. And news of the games could be conveyed quickly by newspapers and specialized sports magazines that relied upon telegraph reports. Saloons also posted the scores. Athletic rivalries between distant cities were made possible by the network of railroads spanning the continent. Spectator sports became urban extravaganzas, unifying the diverse ethnic groups in the large cities and attracting people with the leisure time and ready cash to spend on watching others perform—or bet on the outcome.

Football emerged as a modified form of soccer and rugby. The College of New Jersey (Princeton) and Rutgers played the first college football game in 1869. Some 200 students and other spectators saw Rutgers win, six to four. By the end of the century, dozens of colleges and high schools had football teams, and some college games attracted more than 50,000 spectators.

Basketball was invented in 1891, when Dr. James Naismith, a physical-education instructor, nailed two peach baskets to the walls of the Young Men's Christian Association training school in Springfield, Massachusetts. Naismith wanted to create an indoor winter game that could be played between the fall football and spring baseball seasons. Basketball quickly grew in popularity among boys and girls. All-female Vassar and Smith Colleges added the sport in 1892. In 1893, Vanderbilt University in Tennessee became the first college to field a men's team.

Baseball laid claim to being America's national pastime at midcentury. Contrary to popular opinion, Abner Doubleday did not invent the game. Instead, Alexander Cartwright, a New York bank clerk and sportsman, is recognized as the father of organized baseball. In 1845 he gathered a group of merchants, stockbrokers, and physicians to form the Knickerbocker Base Ball Club of New York.

The first professional baseball team was the Cincinnati Red Stockings, which made its appearance in 1869. In 1900 the American League was organized, and two years later the first World Series was held. Baseball became the national pastime and the most democratic sport in America. People from all social classes (mostly men) attended the games, and ethnic immigrants were among the most faithful fans. Cheering for a city baseball team gave uprooted people a common loyalty and a sense of belonging. Only white players were allowed in the major leagues, however. African Americans played on "minor-league" teams or in all-black Negro leagues.

Baseball Card, 1887

The excitement of rooting for the home team united all classes.

By the end of the nineteenth century, sports of all kinds had become a major cultural phenomenon in the United States. A writer for *Harper's Weekly* announced in 1895 that "ball matches, football games, tennis tournaments, bicycle races, [and] regattas, have become part of our national life." They "are watched with eagerness and discussed with enthusiasm and understanding by all manner of people, from the day-laborer to the millionaire."

EDUCATION AND THE PROFESSIONS

THE SPREAD OF PUBLIC EDUCATION   The growth of public education, spurred partly by the determination to "Americanize" immigrant children, helped quicken the emergence of a new urban society after the Civil War. In 1870 there were 7 million pupils in public schools; by 1920 the number had more than tripled. Despite such progress, leaders in education struggled to overcome a pattern of political appointments, corruption, and incompetence in the public schools.

The spread of secondary schools accounted for much of the increased enrollment. In antebellum America private academies had prepared those who intended to enter college. At the beginning of the Civil War, there were only about 100 public high schools in the whole country, but their number grew to about 800 in 1880 and to 6,000 at the turn of the century.

HIGHER EDUCATION   Colleges at this time sought to instill discipline and morality, with a curriculum heavy on mathematics and the classics (and, in church-related schools, theology), along with ethics and rhetoric. History, modern languages and literature, and some science courses were tolerated, although laboratory work was usually limited to a professor's demonstration in class.

The college-student population rose from 52,000 in 1870 to 157,000 in 1890 and 600,000 in 1920. During those years the number of institutions rose from 563 to about 1,000. To accommodate the diverse needs of these growing numbers, colleges moved from rigidly prescribed courses toward an elective system. The new approach allowed students to favor their strong points and colleges to expand their scope. But as Senator Henry Cabot Lodge complained, it also allowed students to "escape without learning anything at all by a judicious selection of unrelated subjects taken up only because they were easy or because the burden imposed by those who taught them was light."

Colleges remained largely male enclaves, but women's access to higher education did improve markedly in the late nineteenth century. Before the Civil War a few colleges had already become coeducational, and state universities in the West were commonly open to women from the start. But colleges in the South and the East fell in line very slowly. Vassar, opened in 1865, was the first women's college to teach by the same standards as the best of the men's colleges. In the 1870s two more excellent women's schools appeared in Massachusetts: Wellesley and Smith, the latter being the first to set the same admission requirements as men's colleges. Thereafter the older women's colleges rushed to upgrade their standards in the same way.

The dominant new trend in American higher education after the Civil War was the rise of the graduate school. Heretofore most professors had a knowledge more broad than deep. With some notable exceptions they engaged in little research, nor were they expected to advance the frontiers of knowledge. Gradually, however, more and more American scholars studied at German universities, where training was more systematic and focused. After the Civil War the German system became the basis for the modern American graduate university. By the 1890s the doctorate degree was fast becoming a requirement to become a professor.

Realism in Thought, Culture, and Literature

Much as popular culture was transformed as a result of the urban-industrial revolution, intellectual life adapted to new social realities. Before the Civil War various forms of idealism dominated American thought. Although quite diverse in motive and method, idealists shared a basic conviction that fundamental truths rested in the unseen world of ideas and spirit or in the distant past rather than in the tangible world of fact and contemporary experience. The most prominent writers, artists, and philosophers were more concerned with Romantic or biblical themes than with common aspects of "real" life.

At midcentury and after, however, a more realistic sensibility began to challenge this idealistic tradition. This realistic movement matured into a full-fledged cultural force during the second half of the nineteenth century. More and more thinkers, writers, and artists focused on the emerging realities of scientific research and technology, factories and railroads, cities and immigrants, wage labor and social tensions.

The rise of realism resulted from a transformed social, intellectual, and moral landscape. The horrors of the Civil War led many people to adopt a more realistic outlook, as did the growing influence of a modern scientific belief that empirical evidence constituted the only admissible basis for knowledge.

The prestige of empirical science increased enormously during the second half of the nineteenth century as researchers explored electromagnetic induction, the conservation of matter, the laws of thermodynamics, and the relationship between heat and energy. Breakthroughs in chemistry led to new understandings of the formation of compounds and the nature of reactions. Discoveries of fossils opened up new horizons in geology and paleontology, and greatly improved microscopes enabled zoologists to decipher cell structures.

DARWINISM AND SOCIAL DARWINISM   Every field of thought in the post–Civil War years felt the impact of Charles Darwin's *On the Origin of Species* (1859). In that seminal work Darwin argued that existing species, including humanity itself, had evolved through a long process of "natural selection" from less complex forms of life: those species that adapted to survival by reason of quickness, shrewdness, or other advantages reproduced their kind, while others died away. This idea of evolution shocked people who held conventional religious views in that it contradicted a literal interpretation of the creation stories in the biblical Book of Genesis. Heated arguments arose between scientists and clergymen. Some of the faithful rejected Darwin's doctrine while others found their faith severely shaken. Many people, however, eventually came to reconcile science and religion, viewing evolution as a natural process created by God.

The temptation to apply evolutionary theory to the social (human) world proved irresistible. Darwin's fellow Englishman Herbert Spencer became the first major prophet of what came to be called social Darwinism, and he exerted an important influence on American thought. Spencer argued that human society and institutions, like plant and animal species, passed through the process of natural selection, which resulted in what he called the "survival of the fittest."

If, as Spencer believed, society naturally evolved for the better, then individual freedom was inviolable, and any government interference with the competitive process of social evolution was a serious mistake. Social Darwinism thus endorsed a hands-off government policy, then known as laissez-faire; it decried the government regulation of business, the proposals for a graduated income tax, sanitation and housing regulations, and even protection of consumers against medical quacks. Such initiatives, no matter how well intended, would only help the "unfit" survive and thereby impede progress. The only acceptable charity for social Darwinists was voluntary, and even that was of dubious value. Spencer warned that "fostering the good-for-nothing at the expense of the good, is an extreme cruelty."

For Spencer and his many supporters, successful businessmen and corporations were the engines of social progress. If small businesses were crowded out by trusts and monopolies, that, too, was part of the evolutionary process.

Corporate titan John D. Rockefeller told his Baptist Sunday-school class that the "growth of a large business is merely a survival of the fittest."

REFORM DARWINISM   Herbert Spencer's use of Darwin to promote "rugged individualism" did not go without challenge. Reform found its major philosopher in an obscure civil servant, Lester Frank Ward, who fought his way up from poverty and never lost his empathy for the underdog. Ward's book *Dynamic Sociology* (1883) singled out one product of evolution that Spencer and others had neglected: the human brain. Humans, unlike animals, had a mind that could plan for and shape the future. Far from being the helpless pawn of powerful evolutionary forces, Ward argued, humanity could actively shape the process of societal improvement. The competition extolled by Spencer and other social Darwinists was in fact highly wasteful, as was the natural competitive process: plant or cattle breeding, for instance, could actually improve on the results of natural selection.

Ward's so-called reform Darwinism held that cooperation, not competition, would better promote progress. Government could become the agency of progress by striving to ameliorate poverty, which impeded the development of the mind, and to promote the education of the masses. "Intelligence, far more than necessity," Ward wrote, "is the mother of invention," and "the influence of knowledge as a social factor, like that of wealth, is proportional to the extent of its distribution." Intellect, rightly informed by science, could plan successfully. In the benevolent "sociocracy" of the future, Ward argued, legislatures would function mainly to sanction decisions worked out in the sociological laboratory.

PRAGMATISM   Around the turn of the century, the concept of evolutionary human and social development found expression in a philosophical principle set forth in mature form by Harvard professor William James in his book *Pragmatism: A New Name for Some Old Ways of Thinking* (1907). James shared Lester Frank Ward's concern with the role of ideas in the process of evolution. Pragmatists, said James, believed that ideas gain their validity not from their inherent truth but from their social consequences and practical applications. Thus, scientists could test the validity of their ideas in the laboratory and judge their import by their applications. Pragmatism reflected a quality often looked upon as genuinely American: the inventive, experimental spirit, which recognized that science—and society—are characterized by change rather than fixity.

John Dewey, who would become the chief philosopher of pragmatism after James, preferred the term *instrumentalism*, by which he meant that ideas were instruments for action, especially for promoting social reform. Dewey, unlike James, threw himself into movements for the rights of labor and women, the promotion of peace, and the reform of education. He believed that education was the process through which society would gradually progress toward greater social equality and harmony.

REALISM IN FICTION AND NONFICTION

Literature also felt the impact of new scientific ideas and the modern urban scene. A rebellious group of young writers discarded the Romanticism and sentimentalism of antebellum culture in favor of fiction and poetry that depicted contemporary reality without moralizing.

CLEMENS   Samuel Langhorne Clemens (Mark Twain) was a transitional figure between Romanticism and Realism. A native of Missouri, he was impelled to work at age twelve, becoming first a printer and then a Mississippi riverboat pilot. When the Civil War shut down the river traffic, he briefly joined a Confederate militia company, then left with his brother for Nevada, where he wrote for a local newspaper. He moved on to California in 1864 and first gained widespread notice with his tall tale of the gold country, "The Celebrated Jumping Frog of Calaveras County" (1865). With the success of *Roughing It* (1872), an account of his western years, he moved to Hartford, Connecticut, and was able to set himself up as a full-time author and hilarious lecturer.

Clemens was the first significant writer born and raised west of the Appalachian Mountains. His early writings accentuated his western background, but for his greatest books he drew heavily upon his boyhood in the border slave state of Missouri and the tall-tale tradition of southwestern humor. In *The Adventures of Tom Sawyer* (1876), he evoked the prewar Hannibal, Missouri, where his own boyhood was cut so short. Clemens's masterpiece, *The Adventures of Huckleberry Finn* (1884), created unforgettable characters in Huck Finn, his shiftless father, the runaway slave Jim, the Widow Douglas, "the King," and "the Duke." Huck Finn embodied the instinct of every red-blooded boy to "light out for the territory" whenever polite society set out to civilize him. Huck's effort to help his friend Jim escape bondage expressed well the moral dilemmas imposed by slavery on everyone.

LITERARY NATURALISM   Realism grew into a powerful literary movement during the 1880s, but during the 1890s it took on a new character in the writings of the so-called naturalists. This group of young literary rebels imported scientific determinism into literature, viewing people as prey to natural forces and internal drives without control or full understanding of them. Frank Norris thus pictured in *McTeague* (1899) the descent into madness of a San Francisco dentist and his wife, driven by greed, violence, and lust. Stephen Crane in *Maggie: A Girl of the Streets* (1893) and *The Red Badge of Courage* (1895) portrayed people caught up in environments that were beyond their control. *Maggie* depicts a tenement girl driven to prostitution and death amid scenes so grim and sordid that Crane had to finance the book's publication himself. *The Red Badge of Courage,* his masterpiece, evokes fear, nobility, and courage amid the carnage of the Civil War.

Two naturalists, Jack London and Theodore Dreiser, achieved a degree of popular success. London was both a professed socialist and a believer in the German philosopher Friedrich Nietzsche's doctrine of the superman. In adventure stories such as *The Call of the Wild* (1903) and *The Sea Wolf* (1904), London celebrated the triumph of brute force and the will to survive.

Theodore Dreiser did not celebrate the overwhelming power of social and biological forces; he dissected them for the reader. The result was powerfully disturbing to readers accustomed to more genteel fare. Dreiser shocked the public probably more than the others with protagonists who sinned without remorse and without punishment. *Sister Carrie* (1900), for example, shows Carrie Meeber surviving illicit loves and going on to success on the stage.

SOCIAL CRITICISM   Behind their dogma of determinism, several of the naturalists harbored intense outrage at human misery and social injustice. Their indignation was shared by an increasing number of journalists and social critics who addressed themselves more directly to protest and reform. One of the most influential of these reformers was Henry George, a journalist who vowed to seek out the cause of poverty in the midst of the industrial progress he saw around him. The basic social problem, George reasoned, was the "unearned increment" in wealth that came to those who owned land. He published the fruit of his thought in *Progress and Poverty* (1879), a thick, rambling, and difficult book whose earnest moralism and sympathetic tone helped it sell 2 million copies in several languages.

George held that everyone had a basic right to the use of the land, since it was provided by nature to all. Nobody had a right to the increasing value that accrued from it, however, since that was created by the community, not by its owner. He proposed simply to tax the "unearned" increment in the value of the land, or the rent. George's "single-tax" idea generated much discussion, but his influence centered on the paradox he posed in his title, *Progress and Poverty*, and his plea for social cooperation and equality.

Another social critic, Thorstein Veblen, brought to his work a background of formal training in economics and the purpose of making that subject into an evolutionary or historical science. In his best-known work, *The Theory of the Leisure Class* (1899), he examined the pecuniary values of the affluent and introduced phrases that have since become commonplace in our language: *conspicuous consumption* and *conspicuous leisure*. With the advent of industrial society, Veblen argued, the showy display of money and property became the conventional basis of social status. For the upper classes, moreover, it became necessary to spend time nonproductively as evidence of the ability to afford a life of leisure.

THE SOCIAL GOSPEL

While novelists, journalists, and commentators were writing about the rising social tensions and injustices of late-nineteenth-century America, more and more people were addressing these problems through social action. Some reformers focused on legislative solutions to social problems; others stressed philanthropy or organized charity. A few militants promoted socialism or anarchism. Whatever the method or approach, however, social reformers were on the march at the turn of the century, and their activities gave American life a new urgency and energy.

THE RISE OF THE INSTITUTIONAL CHURCH   Churches responded slowly to the mounting social concerns, for American Protestantism had become one of the main props of the established order. The Reverend Henry Ward Beecher, for instance, pastor of the fashionable Plymouth Congregational Church in Brooklyn, preached material success, social Darwinism, and the unworthiness of the poor.

As the middle classes moved out to the streetcar suburbs, their churches followed. From 1868 to 1888, for instance, seventeen Protestant churches abandoned the area south of Fourteenth Street in Manhattan. In the center of Chicago, 60,000 residents had no church, Protestant or Catholic. Where churches became prosperous, they fell under the spell of complacent respectability and do-nothing social Darwinism. Some prominent clergymen expressed open disdain for the lower classes. Not surprisingly, more and more working-class people felt out of place in churches where affluence was both worshipped and flaunted.

A Salvation Army Group

In Flint, Michigan, 1894.

Gradually, however, some religious leaders realized that Protestantism was in danger of losing its working-class constituency unless it reached out to the urban poor. Two organizations were created expressly for that purpose. The Young Men's Christian Association (YMCA) entered the United States from England in the 1850s and grew rapidly after 1870; the Salvation Army, founded in London in 1878, entered the United States a year later. Individual urban churches also began to develop institutional features that were more social than strictly religious in function. Church leaders acquired gymnasiums, libraries, lecture rooms, and other facilities in an effort to attract working-class people back to organized religion.

RELIGIOUS REFORMERS   Church reformers who feared that Christianity was becoming irrelevant to the needs and aspirations of the working poor began preaching what came to be called the social gospel. Washington Gladden of Columbus, Ohio, professed the social gospel from the pulpit of a middle-class Congregational church. The new gospel in fact expressed the social conscience of the middle class. Gladden maintained that true Christianity resided not in rituals, dogmas, or even the mystical experience of God, but in the principle that "thou shalt love thy neighbor as thyself." Christian law should therefore govern the workplace, with laborer and employer united in serving each other's interests. The "law of greed and strife," he insisted, "is not a natural law; it is unnatural; it is a crime against nature; the law of brotherhood is the only natural law." In attacking the premises of social Darwinism, Gladden thus argued for labor's right to organize, supported maximum-hours laws and factory inspections, and endorsed antitrust legislation.

EARLY EFFORTS AT URBAN REFORM

THE SETTLEMENT-HOUSE MOVEMENT   While preachers of the social gospel dispensed inspiration, other dedicated reformers attacked the problems of the slums from community centers called settlement houses. By 1900 perhaps 100 settlement houses existed in America, some of the best known being Jane Addams and Ellen Starr's Hull-House in Chicago and Lillian Wald's Henry Street Settlement in New York City.

The settlement houses were staffed mainly by idealistic middle-class young people, a majority of them college-trained women who had few other outlets for meaningful work. Settlement workers sought to broaden the horizons and improve the lives of slum dwellers in diverse ways. At Hull-House, for instance, staff members recruited the neighborhood children into clubs and kindergartens and set up a nursery for the infant children of working mothers. Settlement houses were also meant to provide workingmen with an alternative to the saloon as a place of recreation and an alternative to the neighborhood political boss as a source of social services. Their programs gradually expanded to include health clinics, lectures, music and art studios, employment bureaus, men's clubs, gymnasiums, and savings banks.

Settlement-house leaders realized, however, that the spreading slums made their work as effective as bailing out the ocean with a teaspoon. They therefore organized political support for tenement laws, public playgrounds, juvenile courts, mothers' pensions, workers' compensation laws, and legislation prohibiting child labor.

Jane Addams

One of the heroic leaders of the settlement house movement.

WOMEN'S SUFFRAGE   Settlement-house workers, insofar as they were paid, made up but a fraction of all gainfully employed women. With rapid population growth in the late nineteenth century, the number of employed women steadily increased, as did the percentage of women in the labor force. These changes in occupational status had little connection with the women's rights movement, however, which increasingly focused on the issue of suffrage. Immediately after the Civil War, Susan B. Anthony, a seasoned veteran of the movement, demanded that the Fifteenth Amendment guarantee the vote for women as well as black men. But she made little impression on those who insisted that women belonged solely in the home.

In 1869 the unity of the women's movement disintegrated in a manner reminiscent of the anti-slavery rift three decades before. The question once again was whether the movement should concentrate on one overriding issue or broaden its focus. Susan B. Anthony and Elizabeth Cady Stanton founded the National Woman Suffrage Association to promote a women's suffrage amendment to the Constitution, but they looked upon suffrage as but one among many feminist causes to be promoted. Later that same year, Lucy Stone, Julia Ward Howe, and other leaders formed the American Woman Suffrage Association, which focused single-mindedly on the vote as the first and most basic reform.

In 1890, after three years of negotiation, the rival groups united as the National American Woman Suffrage Association, with Elizabeth Cady Stanton as president for two years, followed by Susan B. Anthony until 1900. The work thereafter was carried on by a new generation of activists led by Anna Howard Shaw and Carrie Chapman Catt. Over the years the movement achieved some local and partial victories as a few states granted women suffrage in school-board or municipal elections. In 1869 the territory of Wyoming provided full suffrage to women and after 1890 retained women's suffrage when it became a state. Three other western states soon followed suit, but not until New York acted in 1917 did a state east of the Mississippi River adopt universal suffrage.

Despite the focus on the vote, women did not confine their public activism to that issue. In 1866 the Young Women's Christian Association, a parallel to the YMCA, appeared in Boston and spread elsewhere. The New England Women's Club, started in 1868 by Julia Ward Howe and others, was an early example of the women's clubs that proliferated to the extent that a General Federation of Women's Clubs tied them together nationally in 1890. Many women's clubs confined themselves to "literary" and social activities, but others became deeply involved in charities and reform. The New York Consumers' League, formed in 1890, and the National Consumers' League,

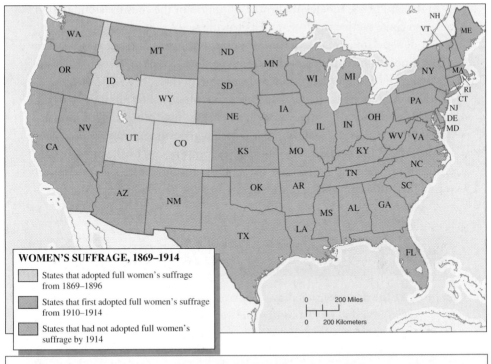

WOMEN'S SUFFRAGE, 1869–1914

States that adopted full women's suffrage from 1869–1896

States that first adopted full women's suffrage from 1910–1914

States that had not adopted full women's suffrage by 1914

Which states first gave women the right to vote? Why did it take fifty-one years, from Wyoming's grant of full suffrage to women until Congress's ratification of the Nineteenth Amendment, for women to receive the right to vote? How was suffrage part of a larger women's reform movement?

established nine years later, sought to make the buying public, chiefly women, more aware of degrading labor conditions.

TOWARD A WELFARE STATE Even without the support of voting women in most places, the states adopted rudimentary measures to regulate big business and labor conditions in the public interest. They passed laws to regulate railroads and working conditions, but the laws were generally poorly enforced or overturned by the courts. In the meantime, it was often the local political machines that stepped in to help those who were suffering. While local and federal governments lacked a bureaucracy to assist those who had fallen on hard times, the political machines in the cities supplied temporary jobs, food, or other necessities. The machines, then, were the precursor to the modern welfare state.

At the end of the nineteenth century, opinion in the country stood poised between conservative rigidities and a growing sense that new conditions imposed new personal and government responsibilities. The last two decades of the nineteenth century had already seen a slow erosion of free-market values, which had found their most secure home in the courts. There emerged instead a concept of the general-welfare state, which called upon the government to act on behalf of the whole society rather than allow rugged individualism to run rampant. The conflict between government intervention and laissez-faire values spilled over into the new century, but by the mid–twentieth century, after the Progressive movement and the New Deal, the nation would be firmly committed to the premises of the general-welfare state.

MAKING CONNECTIONS

- As the next chapter shows, the presidential election of 1896 was in many ways a contest between the new urban values discussed in this chapter and those of a more traditional rural society.

- The reform impulse discussed in this chapter finds voice again in the discussion of the Progressive movement in Chapter 24.

- The nativist thinking discussed in this chapter fueled the restrictive immigration laws of the 1920s, discussed in Chapter 26.

FURTHER READING

For a survey of urbanization, see David, R. Goldfield's *Urban America: A History*, 2nd ed. (1989) Gunther Barth discusses the emergence of a new urban culture in *City People: The Rise of Modern City Culture in Nineteenth-Century America* (1980). John Bodnar offers a synthesis of the urban immigrant experience in *The Transplanted: A History of Immigrants in Urban America* (1985). See also Roger Daniels's *Guarding the Golden Door: American Immigration Policy and Immigrants since 1882* (2004). Walter Nugent's *Crossings: The Great Transatlantic Migrations, 1870–1914* (1992) provides a wealth of demographic information and insight.

On urban environments and sanitary reforms, see Martin v. Melosi's *The Sanitary City: Urban Infrastructure in America from Colonial Times to the Present* (2000), Joel A. Tarr's *The Search for the Ultimate Sink: Urban Pollution in Historical Perspective* (1996), and Suellen Hoy's *Chasing Dirt: The American Pursuit of Cleanliness* (1995).

For the growth of urban leisure and sports, see Roy Rosenzweig's *Eight Hours for What We Will: Workers and Leisure in an Industrial City, 1870–1920* (1983) and Steven A. Riess's *City Games: The Evolution of American Urban Society and the Rise of Sports* (1989). Saloon culture is examined in Medelon Powers's *Faces along the Bar: Lore and Order in the Workingman's Saloon, 1870–1920* (1998).

Richard Hofstadter's *Social Darwinism in American Thought*, rev. ed. (1969) and Cynthia Eagle Russett's *Darwin in America: The Intellectual Response, 1865–1912* (1976) examine the impact of evolutionary theory on thought and culture. On the rise of realism in thought and the arts during the second half of the nineteenth century, see David E. Shi's *Facing Facts: Realism in American Thought and Culture, 1850–1920* (1995).

Eleanor Flexner and Ellen Fitzpatrick's *Century of Struggle: The Woman's Rights Movement in the United States* (1996) surveys the condition of women in the late nineteenth century. The best study of the settlement-house movement is Jean Bethke Elshtain's *Jane Addams and the Dream of American Democracy: A Life* (2002).

22

GILDED AGE POLITICS AND AGRARIAN REVOLT

FOCUS QUESTIONS

· What were the political developments of the Gilded Age?

· What problems, real and perceived, affected farmers of the era?

· What factors precipitated the agrarian revolt and the rise of the Populists?

· What was significant about the election of 1896?

To answer these questions and access additional review material, please visit www.wwnorton.com/studyspace.

I n 1873 the writers Mark Twain and Charles Dudley Warner created an enduring label for the post-Civil War era when they collaborated on a novel titled *The Gilded Age*. The book depicts an age of widespread political corruption, personal greed, and social vulgarity. Perspectives on the times would eventually change, but generations of political scientists and historians have since reinforced the two novelists' judgment. As a young college graduate in 1879, Woodrow Wilson described the state of the post-Civil War political system: "No leaders, no principles; no principles, no parties."

PARADOXICAL POLITICS

Throughout the last third of the nineteenth century, political inertia reigned at the national level. A close balance between Republicans and Democrats in Congress created a sense of stalemate. Neither party was willing to embrace controversial issues or take bold initiatives because neither had a commanding advantage with the electorate. Timidity prevailed. The Gilded Age has long been viewed as a time of political mediocrity, in which the parties refused to confront "real issues" such as the runaway growth of an unregulated economy and its attendant social injustices.

Voters of the time nonetheless thought politics was very important. Voter turnout during the Gilded Age was commonly about 70 to 80 percent, even in the South, where the disenfranchisement of African Americans was not yet complete. (By contrast, the turnout for the 2004 presidential election was 56 percent.) The paradox of such a high rate of voter participation in the face of the inertia at the national political level raises an obvious question: How was it that leaders who failed to address the "real issues" of the day presided over the most highly organized and politically active electorate in U.S. history?

The answer is partly that the politicians and the voters believed that they *were* dealing with crucial issues: tariff rates, the initial efforts to regulate corporations, monetary policy, Indian disputes, civil service reform, and immigration. But the answer also reflects the extreme partisanship of the times and the essentially local nature of political culture during the Gilded Age.

PARTISAN POLITICS Most Americans after the Civil War were intensely loyal to the Democratic or Republican party. Political parties gave people an anchor for their activity and loyalty in an unstable world. Local party officials took care of those who voted their way and distributed appointive public offices and other favors to party loyalists. These "city machines" used patronage and favoritism to retain the loyalty of business supporters while providing jobs, food, or fuel to working-class voters who had fallen on hard times. The party faithful eagerly took part in rallies and picnics, deriving a sense of camaraderie as well as an opportunity for recreation that offered a welcome relief from their usual workday routine.

Party loyalties and voter turnout in the late nineteenth century reflected religious and ethnic divisions as well as geographic differences. The Republican party attracted mainly Protestants of British descent. Their base was New England, and their other strongholds were New York and the upper Midwest, both of which were populated with Yankee stock. The Republicans, the party of Abraham Lincoln, could rely upon the votes of African Americans and Union veterans of the Civil War.

The Democrats, by contrast, tended to be a heterogeneous, often unruly coalition embracing southern whites, immigrants and Catholics of any origin, Jews, freethinkers, skeptics, and all those repelled by the "party of morality." As one Chicago Democrat explained, "A Republican is a man who wants you t' go t' church every Sunday. A Democrat says if a man wants to have a glass of beer on Sunday he can have it."

Republicans pressed nativist causes, calling for restrictions on both immigration and the employment of foreigners and greater emphasis on the teaching of the "American" language in the schools. Prohibitionism revived along with nativism in the 1880s. Among the immigrants who crowded into the growing cities were many Irish, Germans, and Italians who enjoyed alcoholic beverages. Republicans increasingly saw saloons as the central social evil around which all others revolved, including vice, crime, political corruption, and neglect of families, and they associated these problems with the ethnic groups that frequented saloons.

POLITICAL STALEMATE AT THE NATIONAL LEVEL   Between 1869 and 1913, from the presidency of Ulysses S. Grant through that of William Howard Taft, Republicans monopolized the White House except for the two nonconsecutive terms of Democrat Grover Cleveland, but Republican domination was more apparent than real. Between 1872 and 1896 no president won a majority of the popular vote. In each of those presidential elections, sixteen states invariably voted Republican and fourteen voted Democratic, leaving a pivotal six states whose results might change. The important swing-vote role played by two of those states, New York and Ohio, helps explain the election of eight presidents from those states from 1872 to 1912.

Lackluster presidents also contributed to the political stalemate. No chief executive between Abraham Lincoln and Theodore Roosevelt could be described as a "strong" president. None challenged the prevailing view that Congress, not the White House, should formulate policy. Senator John Sherman of Ohio expressed the widely held notion that the legislative branch should take initiative in a republic: "The President should merely obey and enforce the law."

Republicans controlled the Senate and Democrats controlled the House during the Gilded Age. Only during 1881–1883 and 1889–1891 did a Republican president coincide with a Republican Congress, and only between 1893 and 1895 did a Democratic president enjoy a Democratic majority in Congress.

The counterbalancing strength of the parties in Congress and the fear in each party of alienating key factions deterred any vigorous initiatives in Congress. Because most bills required bipartisan support to pass both houses and because legislators tended to vote along party lines, the Democrats and the Republicans pursued a policy of evasion on the national issues of the day. Only the tariff provoked clear-cut divisions between protectionist

Republicans and low-tariff Democrats, but there were individual exceptions even on that. On the important questions of the money supply, regulation of big business, farm problems, civil service reform, and immigration, the parties differed very little. As a result, they primarily became vehicles for seeking office and dispensing patronage in the form of government jobs and contracts.

STATE AND LOCAL INITIATIVES   Unlike today, Americans during the Gilded Age expected little direct support from the federal government; most significant political activity occurred at the state and local levels. Residents of the western territories were largely forced to fend for themselves rather than rely upon federal authorities. They formed towns, practiced vigilante justice, and made laws on their own. Once incorporated into the Union, the former territories retained much of their autonomy.

Thus state governments after the Civil War were the primary centers of political activity and innovation. Over 60 percent of the nation's spending and taxing were exercised by state and local authorities. Then, unlike today, the large cities spent far more on local services than did the federal government. And three fourths of all public employees worked for state and local governments. Local issues such as prohibition, Sunday closing laws, and parochial-school funding often generated more excitement than complex debates over tariffs and monetary policies. It was the state and local governments that first sought to curb the power and restrain the abuses of corporate interests.

CORRUPTION AND REFORM

During the Gilded Age, states attempted to regulate big business; most of those efforts were overturned by the courts, however. A close alliance developed between business owners and political leaders. Railroad passes, free entertainment, and a host of other favors were freely provided to politicians, newspaper editors, and other leaders in positions to influence public opinion or affect legislation.

On the local level the exchange of favors for votes was not perceived as improper either. People voted for their party out of intense partisan loyalty. Although they looked to their parties to supply them with favors and even jobs, they did not see themselves as "selling their vote." This was simply the age-old practice of patronage democracy, in which local officials awarded party loyalists with contracts and public jobs, such as heading custom houses and post offices.

The Bosses of the Senate

This 1875 cartoon bitingly portrays the period's alliance between big business and politics.

Both Republican and Democratic leaders squabbled over the "spoils" of office, the appointive offices at the local and national levels. After each election it was expected that the victorious party would throw out the defeated party's appointees and appoint their own men to office. Each party had its share of corrupt officials willing to buy and sell government appointments or congressional votes, yet each also witnessed the emergence of factions promoting honesty in government. The struggle for cleaner government soon became one of the foremost issues of the day.

HAYES AND CIVIL SERVICE REFORM   In the aftermath of Reconstruction, President Rutherford B. Hayes admirably embodied the "party of morality." Hayes brought to the White House in 1877 a new style of uprightness, in sharp contrast to the corruption of the Grant administration. The son of an Ohio farmer, Hayes was wounded four times in the Civil War and was promoted to the rank of major general. Elected governor of Ohio in 1867, he served three terms. Honest and respectable, competent and dignified, he lived in a modest style with his wife, who was nicknamed Lemonade Lucy because of her refusal to serve alcohol at White House functions.

Yet Hayes's presidency suffered from the supposedly secret deal that awarded him victory over the Democrat Samuel Tilden in the 1876 election. Snide references to Hayes as "His Fraudulence" denied him any chance at a second term, which he renounced from the beginning. Hayes's Republican party was split between so-called Stalwarts and Half-Breeds, led respectively by senators Roscoe Conkling of New York and James G. Blaine of Maine. The difference between these Republican factions was even murkier than that between the parties. The Stalwarts had been stalwart in their support of President Grant during the furor over the misbehavior of his cabinet members. They also promoted Radical Reconstruction of the South and the "spoils system" of distributing federal political jobs to party loyalists. The Half-Breeds acquired their name because they were only half loyal to Grant and half committed to reform of the spoils system.

Hayes aligned himself with the growing public discontent over the corruption that had undermined the Grant administration. In promoting civil service reform, he issued an executive order in 1877 declaring that those already in office (for the most part Grant's appointees) would be dismissed only for the good of the government and not for political reasons. His cabinet tried to carry out the new policy. Secretary of the Treasury John Sherman revealed that both New York customs collector Chester A. Arthur and naval officer Alonzo Cornell were guilty of "laxity" and of using the customhouse to reward political favors on behalf of Conkling's organization. Hayes removed Arthur and Cornell and thereby won Conkling's lasting hatred.

For all of Hayes's efforts to clean house, he retained a limited vision of government's role in society. On the economic issues of the day, he held to a conservative line that would guide his successors for the rest of the century. His solution to labor troubles, demonstrated during the Great Railroad Strike of 1877, was to send in federal troops and break the strike. His answer to the demands of farmers and debtors that he expand the currency was to veto the Bland-Allison Act, which provided for a limited expansion of silver currency through the government's purchase of $2 million to $4 million in silver coins per month. (The bill was passed when Congress overrode Hayes's veto.)

GARFIELD AND ARTHUR   With Hayes out of the running for a second term, the Republicans were forced to look elsewhere in 1880. The Stalwarts, led by Conkling, brought Ulysses S. Grant forward for a third time, still a strong contender despite the tarnish of his administration's scandals. For two days the Republican Convention in Chicago was deadlocked, with Grant holding a slight lead over James G. Blaine and John Sherman. When

Wisconsin's delegates suddenly switched their votes to former House Speaker (now Senator-elect) James A. Garfield, the convention stampeded to the dark-horse candidate. As a sop to the Stalwarts, the convention tapped Chester A. Arthur, of customhouse notoriety, for vice president.

The Democrats named Winfield Scott Hancock, a Union general during the Civil War, to counterbalance the Republicans' "bloody-shirt" attacks on their party as the vehicle of secession. In the close election, Garfield eked out a plurality of only 39,000 votes, or 48.5 percent of the vote, but with a comfortable margin of 214 to 155 in the Electoral College.

On July 2, 1881, after only four months in office, President Garfield was walking through the Washington, D.C., railroad station when a deranged man, Charles Guiteau, shot him in the back. "I am a Stalwart," Guiteau shouted to the arresting officers. "Arthur is now President of the United States." Two months later, Garfield died of complications resulting from the shooting.

Chester Arthur, one of the chief henchmen of Stalwart leader Roscoe Conkling, was now president. Little in his past suggested that he would rise above spoils politics. But Arthur, a wealthy, handsome widower who loved fine wines and sported a lavish wardrobe and billowing sideburns, demonstrated surprising leadership qualities as president. He distanced himself from Conkling and the Stalwarts and established a genuine independence. As Arthur noted, "For the vice-presidency I was indebted to Mr. Conkling, but for the presidency of the United States my debt is to the Almighty."

Most startling of all was Arthur's emergence as something of a civil service and tariff reformer, despite the Stalwarts' expectations that he would oppose such changes. The assassin Guiteau had unwittingly galvanized public support of political reform. A civil service reform bill sponsored by "Gentleman George" Pendleton, a Democratic senator from Ohio, passed in 1883, setting up a three-member federal Civil Service Commission independent of the cabinet departments, the first such agency established on a permanent basis. About 14 percent of all government jobs would now be filled on the basis of competitive examinations rather than political connections. What was more, the president could enlarge the class of jobs based on merit at his discretion, as many presidents later did.

Meanwhile, the tariff continued to be the most controversial national political issue. The high tariff, a heritage of the Civil War, had by the early 1880s raised federal revenues to a point where the government was enjoying a surplus that drew money into the Treasury and out of circulation, thus impeding economic growth. Some argued that lower tariff rates would reduce consumer prices by enabling foreign competition, and at the same time leave more money in circulation. In 1882 Arthur named a special tariff commission, which recommended a 20 to 25 percent rate reduction, but Congress's effort to enact the proposal was marred by logrolling (the trading of votes to benefit different legislators' local interests). The result was the "mongrel tariff" of 1883, so called because of its different rates for different commodities. Overall the new tariff provided for a slight rate reduction, but it also raised the duty on some articles.

THE SCURRILOUS CAMPAIGN As the 1884 presidential election neared, Chester Arthur's record as an unexpected reformer might have commended him to the voters, but it did not please the leaders of his party. The Republicans dumped Arthur and turned to the majestic senator James G. Blaine of Maine, leader of the Half-Breeds. Blaine was the consummate politician. He never forgot a name or a face, he inspired the party faithful with his oratory, and at the same time he knew how to wheel and deal in the back rooms.

During the campaign, however, letters surfaced that linked Blaine to efforts to exchange his influence for selfish gain. For the reform element of the Republican party, this was too much, and many bolted the ticket. Party regulars scorned the idealists as goo-goos—the good-government crowd who ignored partisan realities—and one newspaper editor jokingly tagged them mugwumps, after an Algonquian word for a self-important chieftain. To the party regulars, in what soon became a stale joke, mugwumps were unreliable Republicans who had their mugs on one side of the fence and their "wumps" on the other.

The rise of the mugwumps influenced the Democrats to nominate the New Yorker Stephen Grover Cleveland as a reform candidate. Elected mayor of Buffalo in 1881, Cleveland first attracted national attention for battling corruption in that city. In 1882 he was elected governor of New York, and he continued to build a reform record by fighting New York City's corrupt Tammany Hall organization. As mayor and as governor, he repeatedly vetoed what he considered special-privilege bills serving selfish interests. Cleveland possessed little charisma but impressed the public with his stubborn integrity. He was a crusader against corruption, and as such he drew many of those making up the growing chorus of political reformers.

Senator James G. Blaine of Maine

The Republican candidate in 1884.

But a scandal erupted when the *Buffalo Evening Telegraph* revealed that as a bachelor Cleveland had had an affair with an attractive Buffalo widow, Maria Halpin. Mrs. Halpin had named Cleveland as the father of a boy born to her in 1874. Cleveland had responded by providing financial support when the child was placed in an orphanage. The respective personal escapades of Blaine and Cleveland provided the 1884 campaign with some of the most colorful battle cries in political history: "Blaine, Blaine, James G. Blaine, the continental liar from the state of Maine," Democrats chanted; Republicans countered with "Ma, ma, where's my pa? Gone to the White House, ha, ha, ha!"

Near the end of the mudslinging campaign, Blaine and his supporters committed two fateful blunders. The first occurred at New York's fashionable Delmonico's restaurant, where Blaine attended a lavish fund-raising dinner with a clutch of millionaire bigwigs. Cartoons and accounts of this "Belshazzar's feast" festooned the opposition press for days.

The second fiasco occurred when a Protestant minister visiting the Republican headquarters in New York City insolently referred to the Democrats as the party of "rum, Romanism, and rebellion." Blaine let pass the implied insult to Irish Catholics—a fatal oversight, since he had always cultivated Irish-American support with his anti-British talk and public reminders that his mother was Catholic. Democrats spread the word that Blaine was anti-Irish and anti-Catholic. The two incidents may have tipped the election. The electoral vote, in Cleveland's favor, stood at 219 to 182, although the popular vote ran far closer: Cleveland's plurality nationwide was fewer than 30,000 votes.

CLEVELAND AND THE SPECIAL INTERESTS   For all of Cleveland's hostility to the spoils system and politics as usual, he represented no sharp break with the conservative public policies of his Republican predecessors, except in opposing government favors to business. He held to a strictly limited view of government's role in both economic and social matters, a rigid philosophy illustrated by his 1887 veto of a bill to aid drought-stricken farmers. Back to Congress it went with a lecture on the need to limit the powers and functions of government. "Though the people support the government, the government should not support the people," Cleveland asserted.

Despite his strong convictions, Cleveland had a mixed record on civil service. He harbored good intentions, but as the first Democratic president since James Buchanan's term from 1856 to 1860, he also led a party hungry for partisan appointments. Before his inauguration he repeated his support for the Pendleton Civil Service Reform Act: he pledged not to remove able government workers simply on partisan grounds. Yet party pressures gradually forced Cleveland's hand. When he left office, about two thirds of federal officeholders were Democrats, but he had almost doubled the number of jobs subject to civil service regulation. Cleveland thereby satisfied neither mugwumps nor spoilsmen; indeed, he managed to antagonize both.

Cleveland also incurred the wrath of many Union war veterans by his firm stand against expanded pensions. Congress had passed the first Civil War pension law in 1862 to provide for Union veterans disabled in service and for the widows, orphans, and dependents of veterans. By 1882 the Grand Army of the Republic, an organization of Union veterans and a powerful pressure group, was trying to get pensions paid for any disability, no matter how it was incurred. Meanwhile, many veterans succeeded in getting legislators to pass private pension bills. Insofar as time permitted, Cleveland examined the bills critically and vetoed the dubious ones. Although he signed more pension bills than any of his predecessors, he also vetoed more. The issue reached a climax in 1887 when Cleveland vetoed a new dependent pension bill containing more liberal benefits to veterans and their families. Cleveland argued that it would become a refuge for frauds rather than a "roll of honor."

In about the middle of his term, Cleveland advocated an important new policy: railroad regulation. Since the late 1860s states had adopted laws regulating railroads and from the early 1870s Congress had debated federal legislation. In 1886 a Supreme Court decision spurred action. Reacting to the case of *Wabash, St. Louis, and Pacific Railroad Company v. Illinois,* in which the Court had ruled that a state could not regulate rates on interstate traffic, Cleveland urged that since this "important field of control and regulation [has] thus been left entirely unoccupied," Congress should act.

It did, and in 1887 Cleveland signed into law an act creating the Interstate Commerce Commission (ICC), the first independent federal regulatory commission. The law required that all freight and passenger railroad rates be "reasonable and just," and it empowered the ICC to investigate railroads and prosecute violators. Railroads were also forbidden to grant secret rebates to preferred shippers; discriminate against persons, places, and commodities; or enter into pools (agreements among competing companies to fix rates). The commission's actual powers proved to be weak, however, when first tested in the courts. Though creating the ICC seemed to conflict with Cleveland's fear of big government, it accorded with his wariness of the growing influence of big business. The Interstate Commerce Act, to his mind, was a legitimate exercise of sovereign power.

THE TARIFF   Cleveland's most dramatic challenge to special interests focused on tariff reform. Why was the tariff such an important and controversial issue? By the late nineteenth century, Republican party officials and business leaders had come to assume that national prosperity and high tariffs were closely linked. Others disagreed. Many observers concluded that the formation of huge corporate "trusts" was not a natural development of a maturing capitalist system. Instead, critics charged that government tariff policies had fostered big business at the expense of small producers and retailers by effectively shutting out foreign imports, thereby enabling American corporations to dominate their markets and charge higher prices for their products.

Grover Cleveland

As president, he made the issue of tariff reform central to the politics of the late 1880s.

By shielding manufacturers from foreign competition, critics argued, the tariff made it easier for them to combine into ever-larger entities.

Cleveland agreed. Having decided that the rates were too high and too often inequitable, he devoted his entire annual message in 1887 to the subject. He did so with the full knowledge that he was walking onto a political minefield on the eve of an election year. "What is the use of being elected if you don't stand for something?" he asked skeptical advisers.

Cleveland's annual message noted that tariff revenues had bolstered the federal surplus, making the Treasury "a hoarding place for money needlessly withdrawn from trade and the people's use." The high tariff, he added, pushed up prices for everybody and benefited only a few politically powerful manufacturing interests. The wise solution was to spur Congress to look at the items on the tariff list, more than 4,000 of them, with an eye to eliminating as many as possible and lowering all the remaining duties.

The House soon passed a bill calling for modest tariff reductions, from an average of about 47 percent of the value of imported goods to about 40 percent. But the bill stalled in the Republican Senate and finally died a lingering death, the victim of committee debate. If Cleveland's tariff proposal accomplished his purpose of drawing party lines more firmly, it also confirmed the fears of his advisers. A presidential election, for the first time in years, highlighted a sharp difference between the major parties on an issue of substance.

THE ELECTION OF 1888   In 1888 Cleveland was the nominee of his party. The Republicans, now calling themselves the GOP (Grand Old Party), turned to the obscure Benjamin Harrison. Grandson of a former president, Harrison was a lawyer in Indiana, a pivotal state in national elections. He also boasted a good war record, and little in his political record would offend any voter. The Republican platform accepted Cleveland's challenge to make the protective tariff the chief issue; it also promised generous pensions to Civil War veterans.

The campaign thus became the first one waged mainly on the tariff issue. To ensure against tariff reduction, manufacturers obligingly filled up Harrison's campaign fund, which was used to denounce Cleveland's un-American "free-trade" stance and his vetoes of veterans' pension bills.

On the eve of the election, Cleveland suffered a devastating blow from a dirty campaign trick. Posing as an English immigrant and using the false name Charles F. Murchison, a California Republican had written the British ambassador, Sir Lionel Sackville-West, asking his advice on how to vote. Sackville-West hinted in reply that the man should vote for Cleveland. Published two weeks before the election, the "Murchison letter" aroused a storm of protest against foreign intervention and suggested a link between Cleveland and British free traders.

Still, the outcome in the 1888 election was very close. Cleveland won the popular vote by 5,538,000 to 5,447,000, but that was little comfort. The distribution of votes was such that Harrison, with the key states of Indiana and New York on his side, carried the Electoral College by 233 to 168.

REPUBLICAN REFORM UNDER HARRISON   As president, Benjamin Harrison was a competent and earnest figurehead overshadowed by his flamboyant secretary of state, James G. Blaine. Harrison's first step was to reward those responsible for his victory. He owed a heavy debt to the Union war veterans, which he discharged by naming the head of the veterans' group to the office of federal pension commissioner. The new commissioner proceeded to approve veterans' pensions with such abandon that the secretary of the interior removed him from office six months later. In 1890 Congress passed, and Harrison signed, the Dependent Pension Act, substantially the same measure that Cleveland had vetoed three years earlier. Any war veteran unable to make a living by manual labor for whatever reason was granted a monthly pension. The pension rolls almost doubled by 1893.

During the first two years of Harrison's term, the Republicans controlled the presidency and both houses of Congress for the first time between 1875 and 1895. They made the most of their clout. During 1890 several significant pieces of legislation made their way to the White House for Harrison's signature. In addition to the Dependent Pension Act, Congress and the president approved the Sherman Anti-Trust Act, the Sherman Silver Purchase Act, the

McKinley Tariff Act, and the admission of Idaho and Wyoming as new states, following the admission of the Dakotas, Montana, and Washington in 1889.

Both parties had pledged during the campaign to address the growing power of trusts and monopolies. The Sherman Anti-Trust Act, named for Ohio senator John Sherman, chairman of the committee that drafted it, forbade contracts, combinations, or conspiracies in restraint of trade or in the effort to establish monopolies in interstate or foreign commerce. A broad consensus put the vague law through, but its passage turned out to be largely symbolic. During the next decade successive administrations rarely enforced the new law, in part because of confusion about what constituted "restraint of trade." From 1890 to 1901, the Justice Department instituted only eighteen anti-trust suits, and four of those were against labor unions.

Congress, meanwhile, debated currency legislation against the backdrop of growing distress in the farm regions of the West and the South. Hard-pressed farmers demanded increased coinage of silver to inflate the currency supply and raise commodity prices, making it easier for them to earn the money with which to pay their debts. The silverite forces were also strengthened, especially in the Senate, by members from new western states with silver-mining interests. Congress thus passed the Sherman Silver Purchase Act replacing the Bland-Allison Act of 1878. It required the Treasury to purchase 4.5 million ounces of silver each month and to issue in payment paper money redeemable in gold or silver. Although it doubled the amount of silver purchased, that was still too little to inflate the nation's overall money supply. The stage was thus set for the currency issue to eclipse all others during the financial panic that would sweap the country three years later.

Republicans viewed their victory over Cleveland in 1888 as a mandate not just to maintain the protective tariff but to raise it. Piloted through Congress by the prominent Ohio representative William McKinley, the McKinley Tariff of 1890 raised duties on manufactured goods to the highest level ever. The absence of a public consensus for higher tariffs became clearly visible in the 1890 midterm elections. The voters repudiated the Republican-sponsored McKinley Tariff with a landslide of Democratic votes. In the new House, Democrats outnumbered Republicans by almost three to one; in the Senate the Republican majority was reduced to eight. One of the election casualties was Congressman William McKinley himself. But there was more to the election than the tariff. Voters also reacted to the baldly partisan measures of the Harrison administration and its extravagant expenditures on military pensions and other programs.

The large Democratic vote in 1890 may also have been a reaction to Republican efforts to legislate on a local level against government-supported

Catholic (parochial) schools. In many districts with a high percentage of Catholic constituents, Democratic legislators had defied the principle of separation of church and state by allocating local tax revenues to help support parochial schools. In 1889 Wisconsin Republicans pushed through a law that struck at parochial schools and turned large numbers of outraged Catholic immigrants into Democratic activists. Protestant Republicans also sought to prohibit alcoholic beverages. Between 1880 and 1890 sixteen out of twenty-one states outside the South held referenda on a constitutional prohibition of alcoholic beverages, although only six states actually voted for prohibition. With this assault on drinking, Republicans were playing a losing game, arousing anti-prohibitionists on the Democratic side. In 1890 the Democrats swept state after state.

AGRARIAN PROTEST MOVEMENTS

The 1890 election reflected more than a reaction against the Republican tariff, patronage politics, extravagant spending, and moralizing. The Democratic victory revealed a deep-seated unrest in the farming communities of the South and the West. As the congressional Democrats took power, the beginnings of an economic crisis appeared on the horizon. Farmers' debts mounted as crop prices plummeted.

Frustrated by the unwillingness of Congress to meet their demands and ease their plight, disgruntled farmers began to organize their political efforts. Like so many of their counterparts laboring in urban factories, they realized that social change required demonstrations of power, and power lay in numbers—and organization. Unlike labor unions, however, the farm organizations faced a complex array of economic variables affecting their livelihood. They had to deal with more than just management. Bankers, food processors, railroad and grain-elevator operators, as well as the world commodities market, all affected the agricultural sector. So, too, did the unpredictable forces of nature: droughts, blizzards, insects, and erosion.

There were also important obstacles to collective action by farmers. Farmers' rugged individualism and physical isolation made communication and organization especially difficult. Another hurdle was the fact that after the Civil War agricultural interests had diverged and in some cases conflicted with one another. On the Great Plains, for example, the railroads were the largest landowners. In addition, there were large absentee landowners, some foreign, who leased out vast tracts of land. There were also huge "bonanza" farms that employed hundreds of seasonal workers.

Yet the majority of farmers were simple rural folk in the South and West who were small landowners, tenant farmers, and hourly wage workers. It was the middle-size landowners who were most affected by rapidly rising land values and rising indebtedness. Those farmers were concerned with land values and crop prices, while tenants, sharecroppers, and farmhands supported land-distribution schemes that would give them access to their own land.

Given such a diversity of interests within the agricultural sector, farm activists discovered that it was often difficult to develop and maintain a cohesive political organization. Yet for all the difficulties, they persevered, and the results were dramatic, if not completely successful. Thus, for example, the deep-seated unrest in the farming communities of the South and the West began to find voice in the Granger movement, the Farmers' Alliances, and the new People's party (also known as the Populist party), agrarian movements of considerable political and social significance.

ECONOMIC CONDITIONS   For some time, farmers in the South and Midwest had been subject to worsening economic and social conditions. The source of their problems was a long decline in commodity prices, from 1870 to 1898, the product of domestic increases in production and growing international competition for world markets. Considerations of abstract economic forces puzzled many farmers, however. How could one speak of overproduction when so many remained in need? Instead, many farmers assumed, there must be a screw loose somewhere in the system.

The railroads and the food processors who handled the farmers' products were seen as the villains. Farmers resented the high railroad freight rates that prevailed in farm regions with no alternative forms of transportation. High tariffs operated to the farmers' disadvantage because they protected manufacturers from foreign competition, allowing them to raise the prices of factory goods upon which farmers depended. Farmers, however, had to sell their wheat, cotton, and other staples in foreign markets, where competition lowered prices. Tariffs inflicted a double blow on farmers because insofar as they hampered imports, they indirectly hampered exports by making it harder for foreign buyers to get the currency or exchange necessary to purchase American crops.

Debt, too, had been a perennial agricultural problem. After the Civil War, farmers grew ever more enmeshed in debt: western farmers incurred mortgages to cover the costs of land and machinery, while southern farmers were forced to pledge their crops to the local merchant in exchange for food and supplies. As commodity prices dropped, the debt burden grew because

"I Feed You All!"

This 1875 poster shows the farmer at the center of society.

farmers had to cultivate more wheat or cotton to raise the same amount of money. By growing more, they furthered the vicious cycle of surpluses and price declines.

THE GRANGER MOVEMENT   When the Department of Agriculture sent Oliver H. Kelley, a former Minnesota farmer and post-office clerk, on a tour of the South in 1866, it was the farmers' isolation that most impressed him. Resolving to do something about it, Kelley in 1867 founded the National Grange of the Patrons of Husbandry, better known as the Grange (an old word for granary). In the next few years the Grange mushroomed, reaching a membership as high as 1.5 million by 1874. While the Grange started out as a social and educational response to the isolation of farm folk, as it grew, it began to promote farmer-owned cooperatives for the buying and selling of crops. The Grangers' goal was to free farmers from the conventional "middlemen" to whom they were forced to pay high fees.

The Grange soon became indirectly involved in politics, through independent third parties, especially in the Midwest during the early 1870s. The Grangers' chief political goal was state regulation of the rates charged by railroads and crop warehouses. In five states they brought about the passage of "Granger laws," which were challenged in the courts. In a key case involving warehouse regulation, *Munn v. Illinois* (1877), the Supreme Court affirmed that the state, according to its "police powers," had the right to regulate property when that property was clothed in a public interest.

Although such legal victories bolstered the Granger cause, the movement gradually declined as members' energies were drawn off into cooperatives, whereby farmers would make collective agreements about the storage and sale of their crops. Other former Grange members focused on political action. Out of the independent political movements of the time, there grew in 1875 the Greenback party, which favored expansion of the money supply with more paper money. In the 1878 midterm elections it polled over 1 million votes and elected fifteen congressmen. But in 1880 the party's fortunes declined, and it disintegrated after 1884.

FARMERS' ALLIANCES   As the Grange lost energy, another consortium of farm organizations grew in size and significance: the Farmers' Alliances. Like the Grange, the Farmers' Alliances offered social and recreational opportunities for their members, but they also emphasized political action. Farmers throughout the South and Midwest, where tenancy rates were highest, rushed to join the Alliance movement. They saw in collective action a way to seek relief from the hardships created by chronic indebtedness, declining crop prices, and devastating droughts. Yet unlike the Grange, which was a national organization that tended to attract larger and more prosperous farmers, the Alliance was a grassroots local organization representing marginal farmers.

The Alliance movement swept across the Southern cotton belt and established strong positions in Kansas and the Dakotas. In 1886 a white minister in Texas, which had one of the largest and most influential Alliance movements, responded to the appeals of African-American farmers by organizing the Colored Farmers' National Alliance. The white leadership of the Alliance movement in Texas endorsed this development because the Colored Alliance stressed that its objective was economic justice, not social equality. By 1890 the Alliance movement had members from New York to California, numbering about 1.5 million, and the Colored Farmers' National Alliance claimed over 1 million members.

A powerful attraction for many isolated, struggling farmers and their families was the sense of community provided by the Alliance network. The Alliance movement welcomed rural women and men over sixteen years of age who displayed a "good moral character," believed in God, and demonstrated "industrious habits." Women eagerly embraced the opportunity to engage in economic and political issues. An Alliance publication made the point explicitly: "The Alliance has come to redeem woman from her enslaved condition, and place her in her proper sphere." The number of women in the movement grew rapidly, and many assumed key leadership roles in the "grand army of reform."

The Alliance movement sponsored an ambitious social and educational program and about 1,000 affiliated newspapers. Unlike the Grange, however, the Alliance proposed an elaborate economic program. In 1890 Alliance agencies and exchanges in some eighteen states claimed a business of $10 million, but they soon went the way of the Granger cooperatives, victims of both discrimination by wholesalers, manufacturers, railroads, and bankers and their own inexperienced management and overextended credit.

In 1887 Charles W. Macune, the new Alliance president, proposed that Texas farmers create their own Alliance Exchange in an effort to free themselves from their dependence upon grain processors and banks. Members of the exchange would sign joint notes (to be used to get cash), borrow money from banks, and purchase their goods and supplies from a new corporation created by the Alliance in Dallas. The exchange would also build its own warehouses to store and market members crops. While their crops were being stored, member farmers would be able to obtain credit from the warehouse cooperative so that they could buy household goods and supplies.

This grand cooperative scheme collapsed when Texas banks refused to accept the joint notes from Alliance members. Macune and others then focused their energies on what Macune called a "subtreasury plan." Under this scheme, farmers would be able to store their crops in new government warehouses and obtain government loans for up to 80 percent of the value of their crops at 1 percent interest. Besides providing immediate credit, the plan would allow the farmer the leeway to hold a crop for a better price later, since he would not have to sell it immediately at harvest time to pay off debts. The plan would also promote inflation because the loans to farmers would be made in new legal-tender notes.

The subtreasury plan went before Congress in 1890 but was never adopted. Its defeat as well as setbacks to other Alliance proposals convinced many farm leaders that they needed more political power in order to secure railroad regulation, currency inflation, state departments of agriculture, anti-trust laws, and farm credit.

FARM POLITICS   In the West, where hard times had descended after the blizzards of 1887, farmers demanded third-party political action. In the South, however, white Alliance members hesitated to bolt the Democratic party, seeking instead to influence or control it. Both approaches gained startling success. Independent parties under various names upset the political balance in western states. In the South, the Alliance forced the Democrats to nominate candidates pledged to their program. In 1890 the southern states elected four pro-Alliance governors, seven pro-Alliance legislatures, forty-four pro-Alliance congressmen,

Mary Elizabeth Lease, 1890

A charismatic leader in the farm protest movement.

and several senators. Among the most respected of the southern Alliance leaders was Thomas E. Watson of Georgia. The son of prosperous slaveholders who had lost everything during and after the Civil War, Watson became a successful lawyer and colorful orator on behalf of the Alliance cause. He took the lead in urging African-American tenant farmers and sharecroppers to join with their white counterparts in ousting the white political elite. "You are kept apart," he told black and white farmers, "that you may be separately fleeced of your earnings."

THE POPULIST PARTY AND THE ELECTION OF 1892   As economic conditions worsened, many agrarian activists began promoting the formation of a new national political party. In 1891 delegates from farm, labor, and reform organizations met in Cincinnati to discuss the creation of the People's party. Few southerners attended, but many delegates endorsed the third-party idea after their failure to win over the Democratic party to the subtreasury plan. In 1891 William Peffer of Kansas and Tom Watson of Georgia were the first People's party candidates elected to the Senate. In 1892 a larger meeting in St. Louis proposed a national convention of the People's party at Omaha to adopt a platform and choose national candidates.

The 1892 Populist platform focused on issues of finance, transportation, and land. Its financial program demanded implementation of the subtreasury plan, unlimited coinage of silver, an increase in the amount of money in circulation, and a graduated income tax, whose rates would rise with personal levels of income. As for transportation, the party called for the government to nationalize the railroads, as well as the telephone and telegraph systems. It also called for the government to reclaim from railroads and other corporations lands "in excess of their actual needs" and forbid land ownership by immigrants who were not citizens. Finally, the platform endorsed the eight-hour workday and laws restricting immigration, taking these positions to win support from urban workers, whom Populists looked upon as fellow "producers." The party's platform turned out to be more exciting than its candidate, Iowa's James B. Weaver. Though an able, prudent man, Weaver carried the stigma of his defeat on the Greenback ticket twelve years before. To attract southern voters who might be distracted by Weaver's service as a Union general, the party named a former Confederate general for vice president.

The Populist party was the startling new feature of the 1892 campaign. The Democrats renominated Grover Cleveland, and Republicans turned again to Benjamin Harrison. The tariff remained the chief issue between them. The outcome, however, was different. Both major candidates polled over 5 million votes, but Cleveland carried a plurality of the popular vote and a majority of the Electoral College. Weaver gained over 1 million votes, 10 percent of the total, and carried Colorado, Kansas, Nevada, and Idaho, for a total of twenty-two electoral votes. In Kansas the Populists won the governor's office, four congressional seats, and control of the state senate. In neighboring Nebraska the Populists won control of both statehouses.

THE ECONOMY AND THE SILVER SOLUTION

INADEQUATE CURRENCY   While agitated farmers were funneling their discontent into politics and businessmen were consolidating their holdings, a fundamental weakness in the economy was about to manifest itself in a major economic collapse. The nation's money supply in the late nineteenth century lacked the flexibility to grow along with the expanding economy. From 1865 to 1890, the amount of currency in circulation per capita decreased about 10 percent. Currency deflation raised the cost of borrowing money, as a tight money supply caused bankers to hike interest rates on loans.

Metallic currency dated from the Mint Act of 1792, which authorized free and unlimited coinage of silver and gold at a ratio of 15 to 1, meaning that the amount of precious metal in a silver dollar weighed fifteen times as much as that in a gold dollar, a reflection of the relative value of gold and silver at the time. "Free and unlimited coinage" simply meant that owners of precious metals could have any quantity of their gold or silver coined free, except for a nominal fee to cover costs.

A fixed ratio of the values of gold and silver did not reflect fluctuations in the market value of the metals, however. When gold rose to a market value higher than that reflected in the official ratio, owners ceased to present it for coinage. The country was actually on a silver standard until 1837, when Congress changed the ratio to 16 to 1, which soon reversed the situation. Silver became more valuable in the open market than in coinage, and the country drifted to a gold standard. This state of affairs prevailed until 1873, when Congress passed a general revision of the coinage laws and dropped the then-unused provision for the coinage of silver.

This occurred just when silver production in the western states began to increase, however, reducing its market value through the growth in supply. Under the old laws that development would have induced owners of silver to present it at the mint for coinage. Soon advocates of currency inflation began to denounce the "crime of '73," which they had scarcely noticed at the time. Gradually suspicion grew that bankers and merchants had conspired in 1873 to ensure a scarcity of money. But the pro-silver forces had little more legislative success than the advocates of greenback inflation. The Bland-Allison Act of 1878 and the Sherman Silver Purchase Act of 1890 provided for some silver coinage, but too little in each case to offset the overall contraction of the nation's money supply.

THE DEPRESSION OF 1893   Just before Grover Cleveland started his second presidential term in 1893 (the only non-consecutive second term of a president in U.S. history), one of the most devastating business panics in history erupted when the Philadelphia and Reading Railroad declared bankruptcy, setting off a national financial panic. Not only was business affected, but entire farm regions were also devastated by the spreading depression. One quarter of the cities' unskilled workers lost their jobs, and by the fall of 1893 over 600 banks had closed. By 1894 the economy had reached bottom. That year some 750,000 workers went on strike, millions found themselves unemployed, and railroad construction workers, laid off in the West, began tramping east and talked of marching on Washington, D.C.

Few of them, however, made it to the capital. One protest group that did reach Washington was "Coxey's Army," led by Jacob S. Coxey, a wealthy Ohio quarry owner turned Populist who demanded that the federal government provide the unemployed with meaningful work. Coxey, his wife, and their son, Legal Tender Coxey, rode in a carriage ahead of some 400 hardy protesters who finally straggled into Washington. There Coxey was arrested for walking on the grass. Although his ragtag army dispersed peacefully, the march on Washington, as well as the growing political strength of Populism, struck fear into the hearts of many Americans. Critics portrayed Populists as "hayseed socialists" whose election would endanger property rights and the entire capitalist system.

The 1894 congressional elections taking place amid this climate of anxiety represented a severe setback for the Democrats, who paid politically for the economic downturn, and the Republicans were the chief beneficiaries. The third-party Populists emerged with six senators and seven representatives. They had polled 1.5 million votes for their congressional candidates and expected the festering discontent to carry them to national power in 1896.

SILVERITES VERSUS GOLDBUGS   The course of events would dash that hope, however. In the mid-1890s national attention focused on the currency issue. One of the causes of the 1893 depression was the failure of a major British bank, which had led many British investors to unload their American stocks and bonds in return for gold. Soon after Grover Cleveland's inauguration the U.S. gold reserve had fallen below $100 million. To plug the drain on the Treasury, by stopping the issuance of silver notes redeemable in gold, the president sought repeal of the Sherman Silver Purchase Act. Cleveland won the repeal in 1893, but at the cost of irreparable division in his own party. One embittered pro-silver Democrat labeled the president a traitor.

Western silver interests now escalated their demands for silver coinage, presenting a strategic dilemma for Populists: Should the party promote the long list of varied reforms it had originally advocated, or should it try to ride the silver issue into power? The latter seemed the practical choice. As a consequence, the Populist leaders decided, over the protests of more radical members, to hold their 1896 nominating convention last, confident that the two major parties would at best straddle the silver issue, and they would then reap a harvest of bolting silverite Republicans and Democrats.

THE ELECTION OF 1896   Contrary to those expectations, the major parties took opposing positions on the currency issue. The Republicans, as expected, chose Ohioan William McKinley on a gold-standard platform. On the Democratic side the pro-silver forces gathered to wrest control of the party from Cleveland and the fiscal conservatives. In William Jennings Bryan the silver Democrats found a crusading, charismatic leader. A fervent Baptist and advocate of the free coinage of silver, Bryan was a two-term congressman from Nebraska who had been defeated in the senate race in 1894. At the 1896 convention the self-assured Bryan delivered a galvanizing speech that had most of the 20,000 delegates on their feet and many in tears. Like a revivalist at a camp meeting, he galvanized the audience with the emotion of his appeal. Bryan spoke for silver and the new West, for the "hardy pioneers" and against the "financial magnates" of the urban East as well as Cleveland's "do-nothing" response to the depression. He directly challenged Republicans as well as Cleveland and the gold Democrats with a compelling metaphor:

William Jennings Bryan

His "cross of gold" speech at the 1896 Democratic Convention roused the delegates and secured him the party's presidential nomination.

"You shall not press down upon the brow of labor this crown of thorns. You shall not crucify mankind upon a cross of gold!"

The next day the heroic Bryan was nominated on the fifth ballot, and in the process the Democratic party was fractured beyond repair. Disappointed pro-gold Cleveland Democrats were so disgusted by Bryan's inflationary program and Populist rhetoric that they walked out of the convention and nominated their own candidate, who then announced, "Fellow Democrats, I will not consider it any great fault if you decide to cast your vote for [the Republican] William McKinley."

When the Populists met in St. Louis two weeks later, they faced an impossible choice. "If we fuse [with the Democrats]," one Populist admitted, "all the silver men we have will leave us for the more powerful Democrats." But if the Populists named their own candidate, they would divide the silver vote with Bryan and give the election to McKinley. In the end the delegates backed Bryan but chose their own vice presidential candidate, Georgia's Thomas Watson, and invited the Democrats to drop their vice-presidential nominee, an action Bryan refused to countenance.

During the 1896 campaign, the thirty-six-year-old Bryan crisscrossed the country, using his spellbinding eloquence to support "the struggling masses" of workers, farmers, and small-business owners and promising the panacea of the unlimited coinage of silver. McKinley, meanwhile, conducted a "front-porch campaign," receiving selected delegations of supporters at his home in Canton, Ohio, and giving only prepared responses. His campaign manager, Mark Hanna, shrewdly portrayed Bryan as a radical whose "communistic spirit" would ruin the capitalist system. Many observers agreed with the portrait.

By preying upon such fears, the McKinley campaign raised vast sums of money to finance an army of Republican speakers who stumped the country in his support. In the end the Democratic-Populist-Silverite candidates were overwhelmed. McKinley won the popular vote by 7.1 million to 6.5 million and the Electoral College vote by 271 to 176.

Bryan carried most of the West and the South but garnered little support in the metropolitan centers east of the Mississippi and north of the Ohio and

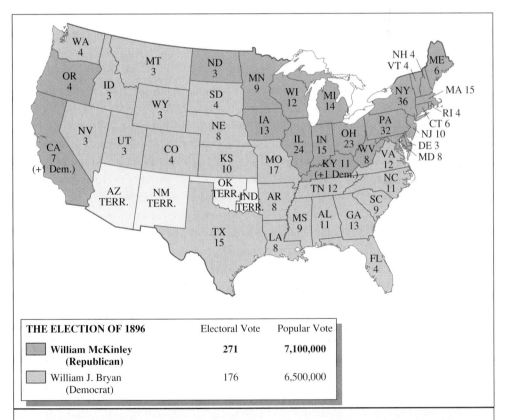

THE ELECTION OF 1896	Electoral Vote	Popular Vote
William McKinley (Republican)	**271**	**7,100,000**
William J. Bryan (Democrat)	176	6,500,000

How did Bryan's "cross of gold" speech divide the Democratic party? How was McKinley's strategy different from Bryan's? Why was Bryan able to carry the West and the South but unable to win in cities and the North?

Potomac rivers. Urban workers saw little to gain from the inflation promoted by Bryan and the silverites. Factory workers in the cities found it easier to identify with McKinley's "full dinner pail" campaign slogan than with Bryan's free silver. Moreover, in the critical midwestern battleground, from Minnesota and Iowa eastward to Ohio, Bryan carried not a single state. Many ethnic voters, normally drawn to the Democrats, were repelled by Bryan's evangelical style. Farmers in the East and the Midwest, moreover, were hurting less than those in the wheat and cotton belts. With less tenancy and a greater diversity of crops in those farm regions, prospering farmers saw little attraction in agrarian radicalism.

A NEW ERA

The election of 1896 was a climactic political struggle between rural and metropolitan America, and metropolitan America won. As its first important act the McKinley administration called a special session of Congress to raise the tariff again. The Dingley Tariff of 1897 became the highest ever. By 1897 prosperity was returning, helped along by inflation of the currency, which bore out the arguments of the greenbackers and silverites. But the inflation came, in one of history's many ironies, not from silver but from a new flood of gold onto the market and into the mints. During the 1880s and 1890s discoveries of gold in South Africa, Canada, and Alaska led to spectacular new gold rushes, a return to the gold standard, and an end to the free-silver movement.

At the close of the nineteenth century, the old issues of tariff and currency policy, which had dominated national politics since the Civil War, gave way to global concerns: the outbreak of the Spanish-American War and the acquisition of territories outside the Western Hemisphere. At the same time, the advent of a new century brought new social and political developments. Although the Populist movement faded with William Jennings Bryan's defeat, most of the policies promoted by Bryan Democrats and Populists, dismissed as too radical and controversial in 1896, would be implemented over the next two decades. Bryan's impassioned candidacy helped transform the Democratic party into a vigorous instrument of "progressive" reform during the early twentieth century. Democrats began to promote anti-trust prosecutions, state laws to limit the working hours of women and children, the establishment of a minimum wage, and measures to support farmers and protect labor-union organizers. As the United States looked ahead to a new century, it began to place more emphasis on the role of national government in society and the economy.

MAKING CONNECTIONS

- The laissez-faire policies of the Gilded Age were challenged by progressive reform activists, as will be discussed in Chapter 24.

- William Jennings Bryan was one of the most prominent figures in American politics and political culture over some thirty years. He will be discussed again in Chapters 24 and 26.

FURTHER READING

A good overview of the Gilded Age is Vincent P. De Santis's *The Shaping of Modern America, 1877–1920* (1973). Nell Irvin Painter's *Standing at Armageddon: The United States, 1877–1919* (1987) focuses on the experience of the working class.

Excellent presidential biographies include Hans L. Trefousse's *Rutherford B. Hayes* (2002), Zachary Karabell's *Chester Alan Arthur* (2004), Henry F. Graff's *Grover Cleveland* (2002), and Kevin Phillips's *William McKinley* (2003).

Scholars have also examined various Gilded Age issues and interest groups. Gerald W. McFarland's *Mugwumps, Morals, and Politics, 1884–1920* (1975) explores the issue of reforming the civil service. Tom E. Terrill's *The Tariff, Politics, and American Foreign Policy, 1874–1901* (1973) lends clarity to that complex issue. The complex finances of the Gilded Age are covered in Walter T. K. Nugent's *Money and American Society, 1865–1880* (1968).

One of the most controversial works on populism is Lawrence Goodwyn's *The Populist Movement: A Short History of the Agrarian Revolt in America* (1978). A more balanced account in Robert C. McMath Jr.'s *American Populism: A Social History, 1877–1898* (1992).

Part Six

MODERN AMERICA

1900

William McKinley is reelected president (1900)

Progressives promote efficiency, regulation, and reform legislation (1900–1917)

Commission system of municipal government is implemented for the first time (1901)

McKinley is assassinated; Theodore Roosevelt serves as president (1901–1909)

Government reforms continue as more states adopt direct primaries and direct elections (1900s–1920s)

City-manager plan of municipal government is implemented (1908)

William Howard Taft serves as president (1909–1913)

1910

Ballinger-Pinchot controversy over conservation leads to reform of committee system in the House (1910)

Roosevelt forms "Bull Moose" party after split with Taft (1912)

Seventeenth Amendment is ratified, establishing direct election of senators (1913)

Woodrow Wilson serves as president (1913–1921)

U.S. enters World War I on side of Britain, France, and Russia (1917)

Espionage and Sedition Acts outlaw criticism of government leaders and war policies (1917, 1918)

Wilson delivers his Fourteen Point peace plan to Congress (1918)

Congress rejects Wilson's Fourteen Points and the League of Nations (1919)

Secretary of State A. Mitchell Palmer leads witch hunts against suspected liberals, launching the first Red Scare in the U.S. (1919)

1920

Nineteenth Amendment grants women the right to vote (1920)

Warren G. Harding serves as president (1921–1923)

Hay-Pauncefote Treaty establishes mutual consent of Britain and U.S. to construction of Central American canal (1901)

Panama wins independence from Colombia with support of U.S. troops (1903); U.S. constructs Panama Canal (1904–1914)

Roosevelt Corollary to the Monroe Doctrine aims to curtail European interference in the Americas (1904)

Russo-Japanese War (1904–1905)

U.S. accepts Japanese control of Korea with Taft-Katsura Agreement (1905)

Bloody Sunday Massacre leads to revolt in Russia (1905)

Great White Fleet circles the globe, brandishing U.S. naval might (1907–1909)

U.S. troops intervene in Honduras (1907, 1911, 1912, 1919, 1924)

Root-Takahira Agreement reaffirms Open Door policy in China (1908)

Revolution takes place in China (1911)

U.S. troops occupy Nicaragua (1912–1925; 1926–1933)

Panama Canal opens (1914)

Wilson sends troops to Mexico, Haiti, and Dominican Republic (1914–1916)

Serbian nationalist murders Austrian archduke Franz Ferdinand, precipitating World War I (1914)

German U-boat sinks the British liner *Lusitania* (1915)

Albert Einstein publishes *The Foundations of the General Theory of Relativity* (1916)

Bolsheviks seize power in Russia (1917)

Russians withdraw from war after separate peace with Germany in Treaty of Brest-Litovsk (1918)

Treaty of Versailles ends World War I (1919)

League of Nations is in effect (1920–1946)

Washington Conference attempts to ward off conflicts in the Pacific (1921)

Benito Mussolini seizes power in Italy (1922)

Muckrakers use the press to arouse America's social conscience (1900s)

Baseball's first World Series is played (1903)

National Child Labor Committee is founded to combat employment of young children (1904)

Upton Sinclair's *The Jungle* depicts horrors of meatpacking industry (1906)

Gentlemen's Agreement halts influx of Japanese laborers to U.S. (1907)

Angel Island is established as West Coast reception center for immigrants, mainly Asians (1910)

Civil rights activists establish NAACP (1910)

Triangle Shirtwaist Company fire leads to increased regulation of the workplace (1911)

Frederick W. Taylor publishes *The Principles of Scientific Management* (1911)

U.S. drafts 4 million men; women, blacks, and other ethnic minorities are employed in munitions factories (1916–1919)

Great Migration of southern blacks to northern cities takes place (1916–1920s)

Influenza epidemic kills 500,000 Americans (1918–1919)

Nationwide race riots result in hundreds of dead and injured (1919)

Eighteenth Amendment launches Prohibition (1919)

Marcus Garvey promotes Negro nationalism (1920s)

Gangsters make fortunes illegally producing and distributing alcohol (1920s)

KKK leads nativist campaign (1920s)

Jazz music becomes popular (1920s)

Discovery of Spindletop gusher in Texas brings oil rush to Southwest (1901)

Roosevelt's intervention (1902) leads to settlement of coal strike (1903)

Congress creates Department of Commerce and Labor (1903)

Northern Securities Company is broken up in the first of 25 successful Roosevelt-administration anti-trust suits (1904)

Industrial Workers of the World (Wobblies) is established (1905)

Swift and Company v. U.S. establishes "stream-of-commerce" doctrine, making meat packers subject to federal legislation (1905)

Hepburn Act, Meat Inspection Act, and Pure Food and Drug Act increase federal regulatory authority over the economy (1906)

Mann-Elkins Act extends federal regulation to telephone and telegraph industries (1910)

Supreme Court dissolves Standard Oil and the American Tobacco Company (1911)

AFL membership increases 37 percent (1913–1918)

Sixteenth Amendment creates income tax (1913)

Federal Reserve Act creates regional reserve banks (1913)

Underwood-Simmons Tariff reduces average duty from 37 percent to 29 percent (1913)

Federal Trade Commission is created to prevent unfair trade practices (1914)

Clayton Anti-Trust Act tightens 1890 Sherman Anti-Trust Act (1914)

War in Europe causes economic boom in U.S. (1915)

War mobilization results in widespread civilian rationing (1916–1919)

Federal Highways Act provides funds for national road network (1916)

War Industries Board sets priorities and plans industrial production (1917)

Widespread strikes partially paralyze U.S. economy (1919)

1900

1910

1920

National Woman's party proposes equal rights amendment (1923)

Harding administration is plagued with corruption; Teapot Dome scandal unfolds (1923–1924)

Calvin Coolidge serves as president after Harding dies in office (1923–1929)

Progressive party is organized and nominates Robert La Follette for president (1924)

1930

Herbert Hoover serves as president (1929–1933)

Hoover signs Emergency Relief Act to provide funds to states to relieve suffering (1932)

Franklin D. Roosevelt serves as president (1933–1945)

FDR pushes through New Deal relief measures to combat Great Depression (1933)

FDR's stalemate with Congress brings New Deal legislation to a halt (1935)

FDR launches his Second New Deal to break stalemate with Congress and radicals (1935)

1940

FDR proposes lend-lease bill to Congress, pledging to make America the "arsenal for democracy" (1941)

U.S. funds Manhattan Project, which builds the atomic bomb (1942–1945)

1945

FDR is elected to a fourth term (1944)

Harry S. Truman serves as president after FDR dies in office (1945–1953)

Kellogg-Briand Pact renounces war as "an instrument of national policy" (1928)

Nationalists rule in China under Chiang Kai-shek (1928–1949)

Japanese occupy Manchuria (1931)

U.S. annouces formal diplomatic recognition of Soviet Union (1933)

Hitler becomes chancellor of Germany (1933)

U.S. troops are withdrawn from Nicaragua, Haiti, and Cuba as part of the "Good Neighbor" policy (1934)

Spanish Civil War (1936–1939)

Chinese and Japanese troops begin full-scale war in the Pacific (1937)

Germany annexes Austria (1938)

France and Britain abandon Czechoslovakia with the Munich Pact (1938)

Germany invades Czechoslovakia (1939)

Germany signs nonaggression pact with Soviets, then invades Poland, leading to World War II in Europe (1939)

Japan, Italy, and Germany sign the Tripartite Pact, a defensive alliance (1940)

Nazi troops begin blitzkrieg (1940)

Germany invades Russia (1941)

Atlantic Charter sets forth Allied war aims (1941)

Japanese attack Pearl Harbor; U.S. enters the war (1941)

Allies take control of North Africa, then attack Italy (1943)

D-day invasion is launched (1944)

Allies "leapfrog" toward Japan (1944–1945)

Soviets set up puppet regimes in Eastern Europe (1944–1945)

Big Three meet at Yalta to discuss the postwar world (1945)

Germany surrenders (1945)

U.S. drops atomic bombs on Hiroshima and Nagasaki, ending the war (1945)

50 million people die in World War II (1939–1945)

Modernist literary movement includes
F. Scott Fitzgerald, Ernest Hemingway,
Thomas Wolfe, William Faulkner
(1920s–1930s)

Harlem Renaissance epitomizes black cultural movement (1920s–1930s)

Scopes "monkey trial" debates teaching of
evolution in public schools (1925)

95 million people attend 23,000 movie theaters weekly (1930)

Unemployed veterans demonstrate in
Washington, D.C. (1932)

800,000 dust-bowl migrants flee to California (1932–1935)

Twenty-first Amendment ends Prohibition
(1933)

Poverty delays 800,000 marriages in the
1930s; marriages decline by one fourth
(1930s)

John Steinbeck and Richard Wright write
about displacement and racism during
the Great Depression (1930s–1940s)

NAACP membership rises from 50,000 to
450,000 during the war (1941–1945)

FDR orders internment of Japanese Americans (1942)

Bracero program brings over 200,000
Mexican farmworkers to U.S.
(1942–1945)

One third of eligible Native American men
(25,000) serve in the war (1941–1945)

6 million women enter the labor force during the war (1941–1945)

15 million Americans serve in World War II
(1941–1945)

Nonfarm wages increase 20 percent; wages
for farmers increase only 10 percent
(1921–1928)

Membership in labor unions declines from
5 million to 3.5 million (1920–1929)

McNary-Haugen bill calls for tariffs to protect farmers (1924)

Speculative investment in stocks and real
estate sets stage for depression
(1925–1929)

Stock market crashes (1929)

1930

Great Depression causes personal income
to plummet, unemployment rises from
3 percent to 25 percent, 9,000 banks
close, and runs on banks occur
(1929–1933)

Hawley-Smoot Tariff establishes high rates
on imports (1930)

Roosevelt declares a 4-day banking holiday
and establishes the Emergency Banking
Relief Act (1933)

FERA, AAA, NIRA, and CCC are some of
the Hundred Days measures enacted under the New Deal (1933)

Johnson Debt Default Act prohibits private
loans to countries that have defaulted on
World War I debts (1934)

1940

Wagner Act legalizes collective bargaining
for labor (1935)

AFL expels CIO unions (1936)

Social Security Act (1935)

Office of Price Administration enacts
wartime rationing (1942)

Servicemen's Readjustment Act (G.I. Bill)
earmarks $13 billion for veterans (1944)

1945

National Security Industrial Association
forges permanent peacetime alliance between industry and military (1944)

National debt reaches $260 billion, 6 times
what it was in 1941 (1945)

The United States entered the twentieth century on a wave of unrelenting change. In 1800 the nation was a rural, agrarian society largely detached from the concerns of international affairs. By 1900 the United States had become a highly industrialized urban culture with a growing involvement in world politics and commerce. In other words, the nation was on the threshold of modernity.

The prospect of modernity both excited and scared Americans. Old truths and beliefs clashed with unsettling scientific discoveries and social practices. People debated the legitimacy of Darwinism, the existence of God, the dangers of jazz, and the federal effort to prohibit the sale of alcoholic beverages. The automobile and airplane helped shrink distances, and communications innovations such as radio and film contributed to a national consciousness. In the process the United States began to emerge from its isolationist shell.

Noninvolvement in foreign wars and nonintervention in the internal affairs of foreign governments formed the pillars of foreign policy until the end of the century. During the 1890s, however, expanding commercial interests around the world led Americans to extend the horizons of their concerns. Imperialism was the order of the day among the great European powers, and a growing number of American expansionists demanded that the United States also adopt a global ambition and join in the hunt for new territories and markets. Such motives helped spark the Spanish-American War of 1898 and helped justify the resulting acquisition of colonies outside the continental United States. Entangling alliances with European powers soon followed.

The outbreak of the Great War in Europe in 1914 posed an even greater challenge to the American tradition of isolation and nonintervention. The prospect of a German victory over the French and the British threatened the European balance of power, which had long ensured the security of the United States. By 1917 it appeared that Germany might emerge triumphant and begin to menace the Western Hemisphere. Woodrow Wilson's crusade to use American intervention in World War I to transform the world order in accordance with his idealistic principles severed U.S. foreign policy from its isolationist moorings. It also spawned a prolonged debate about the role of the United States in world affairs, a debate that World War II would resolve for a time on the side of internationalism.

While the United States was entering the world stage as a formidable military power, it was also settling into its role as a great industrial power. Cities and factories sprouted across the landscape. An abundance of new jobs served as a magnet attracting millions of immigrants. They were not always welcomed, nor were they readily assimilated. Ethnic and racial strife, as well as labor agitation, increased after 1900. In the midst of such social turmoil and unparalleled economic development, reformers made their first sustained attempt to adapt their political and social institutions to the realities of the industrial age. The worst excesses and injustices of urban-industrial development—corporate monopolies, child labor, political corruption, hazardous working conditions, urban ghettos—were finally addressed in a comprehensive way. During the Progressive Era (1900–1917) local, state, and federal governments sought to rein in the excesses of industrial capitalism and develop a more efficient public policy.

A conservative Republican resurgence challenged the notion of the new regulatory state during the 1920s. Free enterprise and corporate capitalism witnessed a dramatic revival. But the stock market crash of 1929 helped propel the United States and the world into the worst economic downturn in history. The unprecedented severity of the Great Depression renewed public demands for federal programs to protect the general welfare. "This nation asks for action," declared President Franklin D. Roosevelt in his 1933 inaugural address. The many New Deal initiatives and agencies instituted by Roosevelt and his Democratic administration created the framework for a welfare state that has since served as the basis for American public policy.

The New Deal helped revive public confidence and put people back to work, but it did not end the Great Depression. It took a world war to restore full employment. The necessity of mobilizing the nation in support of the Second World War also served to accelerate the growth of the federal government. And the incredible scope of the war helped catapult the United States into a leadership role in world politics. The creation and use of nuclear bombs ushered in a new era of atomic diplomacy that held the fate of the world in the balance.
For all of the new creature comforts associated with modern life, Americans in 1945 found themselves living amid an array of new anxieties, not the least of which was a global "cold war" against Communism.

23

AN AMERICAN EMPIRE

FOCUS QUESTIONS

· What were the circumstances that led to America's "new imperialism"?
· What were the causes of the Spanish-American War?
· What were the main tenets of Theodore Roosevelt's foreign policy in Asia and Latin America?

To answer these questions and access additional review material, please visit www.wwnorton.com/studyspace.

Throughout the nineteenth century most Americans displayed what one senator called "only a languid interest" in foreign affairs. The overriding priorities of the time were industrial development, western settlement, and domestic politics. Foreign relations simply were not important to the vast majority of people. After the Civil War an isolationist mood swept across the United States as the country basked in its geographic advantages: wide oceans as buffers, the British navy situated between America and the powers of Europe, and militarily weak neighbors in the Western Hemisphere.

Yet the notion of America's having a Manifest Destiny ordained by God to expand its territory and its influence remained alive in the decades after the Civil War. Several prominent political and business leaders argued that the rapid industrial development of the United States required the acquisition of foreign territories to gain easier access to vital raw materials. In addition, as their exports grew, American companies and farmers became increasingly intertwined in the world economy. This, in turn, required an expanded naval presence to protect the global shipping lanes. And a modern steam-powered navy needed bases where its ships could replenish their supplies of coal and water. For these reasons and others the United States during the last quarter of the nineteenth century began to expand its military presence beyond the Western Hemisphere.

TOWARD THE NEW IMPERIALISM

By the late nineteenth century, European powers had already unleashed a new surge of imperialism in Africa and Asia, where they had seized territory, established colonies, and promoted economic exploitation and Christian evangelism. Writing in 1902, the British economist J. A. Hobson declared that imperialism was "the most powerful factor in the current politics of the Western world."

IMPERIALISM IN A GLOBAL CONTEXT   Western imperialism had economic roots; it was above all a quest for markets and raw materials. The Second Industrial Revolution generated such dramatic increases in production that business leaders felt compelled to find new markets for their burgeoning supply of goods and new sources of investment for their growing supply of capital. Manufacturers, on the other hand, were eager to find new sources of raw materials to supply their expanding needs. At the same time, the aggressive nationalism and bitter rivalries of the European powers made all of them compete with one another as they expanded their farflung empires.

The result was a widespread process of imperial expansion into Africa and Asia. Beginning in the 1880s, the British, French, Belgians, Italians, Dutch, Spanish, and Germans used military force and political guile to conquer those continents. Each of the imperial nations, including the United States, dispatched Christian missionaries to convert native peoples. By 1900 some 18,000 Christian missionaries were scattered around the world. Often the conversion to Christianity was the first step in the loss of a culture's indigenous traditions. The Western religious activities also influenced the colonial power structure. As a British nationalist explained such global ambitions, "Today, power and domination rather than freedom and independence are the ideas that appeal to the imagination of the masses—and the national ideal has given way to the imperial." This imperial outlook set in motion clashes among the Western powers that would lead to unprecedented conflict in the twentieth century.

AMERICAN IMPERIALISM   As the European nations expanded their control over much of the rest of the world, the United States also began to acquire territories outside the North American continent. Most Americans became increasingly aware of world markets as developments in transportation and communication quickened the pace of commerce and diplomacy. From the first, agricultural exports had been the basis of economic growth. Now the conviction grew that American manufacturers had matured to the point where they could outsell foreign competitors in the world market. But should the expansion of markets lead to territorial expansion as well? or to intervention in the internal affairs of other countries? On such points, Americans disagreed, but a small yet influential group of public officials embraced the idea of overseas possessions, regardless of the implications. These expansionists included Senators Albert J. Beveridge of Indiana and Henry Cabot Lodge of Massachusetts, Theodore Roosevelt, and not least of all, naval captain Alfred Thayer Mahan.

During the 1880s Captain Mahan had become a leading advocate of sea power and Western imperialism. In 1890 he published *The Influence of Sea Power upon History, 1660–1783,* in which he argued that national greatness and prosperity flowed from sea power. Modern economic development called for a powerful navy, a strong merchant marine, foreign commerce, colonies, and naval bases. Mahan championed America's "destiny" to control the Caribbean, build an isthmian canal, and spread Western civilization in the Pacific. His ideas were widely circulated in popular journals and within the U.S. government.

Yet even before Mahan's writings became influential, a gradual expansion of the navy had begun. In 1880 the nation had fewer than 100 seagoing vessels, many of them rusting or rotting at the docks. By 1896 eleven powerful new battleships had been built or authorized.

IMPERIALIST THEORY   Claims of racial superiority bolstered the new imperialist spirit. Spokesmen in each Western country, including the United States, used the arguments of social Darwinism to justify economic exploitation and territorial conquest. Among nations as among individuals, expansionists claimed, the fittest survive and prevail. John Fiske, a historian and popular lecturer on Darwinism, developed racial corollaries from Darwin's ideas. In *American Political Ideas Viewed from the Standpoint of Universal History* (1885), he stressed the superior character of "Anglo-Saxon" institutions and peoples. The English "race," he argued, was destined to dominate the globe in the institutions, traditions, language—even in the blood—of the world's peoples. Josiah Strong, a Congregationalist minister, added the sanction of religion to theories of racial and national superiority. In his book *Our Country: Its Possible Future and Its Present Crisis* (1885), Strong asserted that "Anglo-Saxons" embodied two great ideas: civil liberty and "a pure spiritual Christianity." The Anglo-Saxon was "divinely commissioned to be, in a peculiar sense, his brother's keeper."

EXPANSION IN THE PACIFIC

For Josiah Strong and other expansionists, Asia offered an especially alluring temptation. President Andrew Johnson's secretary of state, William H. Seward, believed that the United States must inevitably exercise commercial domination "on the Pacific Ocean, and its islands and continents." Eager for American manufacturers to exploit Asian markets, Seward believed the United States first had to remove all foreign interests from the northern Pacific coast and gain access to that region's valuable ports. To that end, Seward cast covetous eyes on the British crown colony of British Columbia, sandwiched between Russia's possessions in Alaska and the Washington Territory.

Late in 1866, while encouraging British Columbians to consider making their colony a U.S. territory, Seward learned of Russia's desire to sell Alaska. He leaped at the opportunity, and in 1867 the United States bought Alaska for $7.2 million, less than 2¢ an acre. "Seward's folly" of buying the Alaskan "icebox" proved in time to be the biggest bargain since the Louisiana Purchase.

SAMOA AND HAWAII   Seward's successors at the State Department sustained his expansionist vision. During the post–Civil War years the United States sought coaling stations and trading posts in the Pacific Ocean, and it laid claim to various small islands and atolls. Two of those island groups were especially strategic: Samoa and Hawaii (also known as the Sandwich Islands). In 1878 the Samoans signed a treaty granting the United States a naval base on one of its islands. The following year the German and British governments worked out similar arrangements on other Samoan islands. In Hawaii the Americans had a clearer field to exploit. The islands, a united kingdom since 1795, hosted a sizable settlement of American missionaries and planters. The Hawaiian Islands were strategically more important to the United States than

Samoa was, since their occupation by another major power might have posed a threat to American sugar interests and even to defense of the continent.

In 1875 the Hawaiians signed a reciprocal trade agreement, according to which their sugar entered the United States duty-free. Twelve years later they granted the United States a naval base at Pearl Harbor, near Honolulu. These agreements prompted a boom in sugar growing, and American settlers in Hawaii came to dominate the economy. In 1887 the Americans forced Hawaii's king to create a constitutional government, which they controlled.

Queen Liliuokalani

The Hawaiian queen sought to preserve her nation's independence.

Hawaii's political climate changed sharply when the king's sister, Queen Liliuokalani, ascended the throne in 1891 and tried to reclaim power. Shortly before that the McKinley Tariff had destroyed Hawaii's favored position in the sugar trade by putting the sugar of all countries on the duty-free list and granting growers in the United States a 2¢ subsidy per pound of sugar. The resultant economic crisis and discontent in Hawaii led the white population to revolt early in 1893 and seize power. U.S. marines supported the coup. Within a month the new American-dominated government sent a delegation to Washington and signed a treaty annexing Hawaii to the United States.

These events occurred just weeks before President Benjamin Harrison left office, however, and Democratic senators blocked the treaty's ratification. President Cleveland withdrew the treaty and sent a special commissioner to Hawaii to investigate the situation. The commissioner ordered the marines home and reported that Americans on the islands had acted improperly. Most Hawaiians opposed annexation, said the commissioner, who thought the revolution had been engineered mainly by U.S. sugar planters hoping for annexation in order to be eligible for the new subsidy for sugar grown in the United States. Cleveland therefore proposed to restore the queen in return for amnesty to the revolutionists. The provisional government refused to step down, however, and on July 4, 1894, it proclaimed the islands the Republic of Hawaii, which included in its constitution a standing provision for annexation to the United States.

When William McKinley became president in 1897, he was looking for an excuse to annex the Hawaiian Islands. This excuse was found when the Japanese, also hoping to take over the islands, sent warships to Hawaii. McKinley responded by sending U.S. warships and asking the Senate to annex the territory. When the Senate could not muster the two-thirds majority needed to approve the treaty, McKinley used a joint resolution of the House and the Senate to achieve his aims. The resolution passed by simple majorities in both houses, and the United States annexed Hawaii in the summer of 1898.

The Spanish-American War

Until the 1890s a nagging ambivalence about acquiring overseas territories had checked America's drive to expand. Suddenly, in 1898 and 1899, the inhibitions collapsed, but not in a quest for bases and trade. Rather, the chief motive was a sense of outrage at another country's imperialism.

"CUBA LIBRE" Throughout the second half of the nineteenth century, Cubans had repeatedly revolted against Spanish rule, only to be ruthlessly put down. Cuba was one of Spain's oldest colonies and had become a major export market for the mother country. Yet American investments in Cuba, mainly in sugar and mining, were steadily increasing. The United States in fact traded more with Cuba than Spain did. The growing economic interest in their island neighbor made Americans sympathetic to the idea of Cuban independence. So when Cubans revolted against Spanish rule on February 24, 1895, public feeling in the United States was with the rebels.

Events in Cuba supplied exciting copy for the press. William Randolph Hearst's *New York Journal* and Joseph Pulitzer's *New York World* were at the time locked in a monumental competition for readers. "It was a battle of gigantic proportions," one journalist wrote, "in which the sufferings of Cuba merely chanced to furnish some of the most convenient ammunition." The sensationalism in covering events in Cuba came to be called yellow journalism, and Hearst emerged as the undisputed champion.

PRESSURE FOR WAR American neutrality in the Cuban struggle for independence changed sharply when William McKinley entered office in 1897. His platform had endorsed Cuban independence as well as U.S. control of Hawaii and the construction of an isthmian canal. Knowing that the Cuban rebels enjoyed American support, Spain offered autonomy (self-government without formal independence) in return for peace: The Cubans rejected the offer. Spain was impaled on the horns of a dilemma, unable to end the rebellion and unready to give up Cuba.

Early in 1898 events moved rapidly to arouse American opinion against Spain. On February 9 Hearst's *New York Journal* released the text of a letter from a Spanish official, Depuy de Lôme, to a friend in Havana. In the letter, which had been stolen from the post office by a Cuban spy, de Lôme called President McKinley "weak and a bidder for the admiration of the crowd." The breach in diplomatic etiquette was such that de Lôme resigned to prevent further embarrassment to his government.

Six days later, during the night of February 15, 1898, the U.S. battleship *Maine* exploded and sank in Havana Harbor with a loss of 260 men. The ship's captain, one of only 84 survivors, scribbled a telegram to Washington: "*Maine* blown up in Havana Harbor at nine forty tonight and destroyed. Many wounded and doubtless more killed or drowned. . . . Public opinion should be suspended until further report." But those eager for a war with Spain saw no need to withhold judgment; they demanded an immediate declaration of war. Theodore Roosevelt, assistant secretary of the navy, called the sinking "an act of dirty treachery on the part of the Spaniards." The United States, he declared, "needs a war."

A naval court of inquiry reported that an external mine had sunk the ship. Lacking hard evidence, the court made no effort to fix the blame, but the yellow press had no need of evidence. The *New York Journal* gleefully reported: "The Whole Country Thrills with War Fever." The outcry against Spain rose in a crescendo with the words "Remember the *Maine!* To Hell with Spain!" Few of those promoting war wrestled with the obvious fact that the Spanish government was determined to avoid a confrontation with the United States and therefore had nothing to gain from sinking the *Maine.* A comprehensive study in 1976 concluded that the sinking of the *Maine* was an accident, the result of an internal explosion triggered by a fire in its coal bunker.

The weight of outraged public opinion and the influence of militant Republicans such as Theodore Roosevelt and Henry Cabot Lodge eroded President McKinley's neutrality. On March 9, 1898, the president pushed through Congress a $50-million defense appropriation. The Spanish government, sensing the growing militancy in the United States, announced a unilateral cease-fire in early April. On April 10 the Spanish ambassador gave the U.S. State Department a message that amounted to a surrender. But the message came too late. The following day, McKinley sent Congress his war message. He asked for the power to use armed forces in Cuba to protect U.S. property and trade. On April 20 a joint resolution of Congress declared

The Sinking of the *Maine* in Havana Harbor

The uproar created by the incident and its coverage in the "yellow press" pushed President William McKinley to declare war.

Cuba independent and demanded withdrawal of Spanish forces. The Teller Amendment, added on the Senate floor, disclaimed any American designs on Cuban territory. McKinley signed the resolution and sent a copy to the Spanish government. On April 22 the president announced a blockade of Cuba, an act of war under international law. Rather than give in to an ultimatum, the Spanish government declared war on April 24. Determined to be first, Congress declared war the next day, making the declaration retroactive to April 21, 1898.

Why such a rush to war after the message from Spain had indicated that it was ready for an armistice? No one knows for sure, but it seems apparent that too much momentum and popular pressure had built up for a confidential message to change the course of events. Also, leaders of the business community were demanding a quick resolution of the problem. Many of them lacked faith in the willingness or ability of the Spanish government to resolve the crisis. Still, it is fair to ask why McKinley did not take a stronger stand for peace. He might have defied Congress and public opinion, but in the end he deemed the political risk too high. The ultimate blame for war, if blame must be levied, belongs to the American people for letting themselves be whipped into such a hostile frenzy.

MANILA   The war itself lasted only 114 days. The American victory marked the end of Spain's once-great New World empire and the emergence of the United States as a world power. But if war with Spain saved many lives by ending the insurrection in Cuba, it also led to U.S. involvement in another insurrection, in the Philippines, and it created a host of commitments in the Caribbean and the Pacific that would haunt American policy makers during the twentieth century.

The Spanish-American War was barely under way before the U.S. navy produced a spectacular victory in an unexpected quarter: Manila Bay. While public attention centered on Cuba, young Theodore Roosevelt focused on the Spanish-controlled Philippines. As assistant secretary of the navy, he ordered Commodore George Dewey to engage Spain's ships in the Philippines in case of war. President McKinley approved the orders. Arriving late on April 30, 1898, Dewey's squadron destroyed or captured all the Spanish warships in Manila Bay. Dewey, without an occupation force, was now in awkward possession of the bay. Once reinforcements arrived, the American forces, with the help of Filipino insurrectionists under Emilio Aguinaldo, liberated Manila from Spanish control on August 13.

THE CUBAN CAMPAIGN   While these events transpired halfway around the world, the fighting in Cuba reached a surprisingly quick climax. The U.S. Navy blockaded the Spanish fleet at Santiago while an invasion force of some 17,000 American troops was hastily assembled at Tampa, Florida. One significant unit was the First Volunteer Cavalry, better known as the Rough Riders and best remembered because Lieutenant Colonel Theodore Roosevelt was second in command. Eager to get "in on the fun" and "act up to my preachings," Roosevelt had quit the Navy Department after war was declared. He ordered a custom-fitted uniform with yellow trim, grabbed a dozen pairs of spectacles, and rushed to help organize a colorful volunteer regiment of Ivy League athletes, leathery ex-convicts, Indians, and southwestern sharpshooters.

The major land action of the Cuban campaign occurred on July 1. While a much larger American force attacked Spanish positions at San Juan Hill, a smaller unit, including the dismounted Rough Riders—most of whose horses were still in Florida—and two African-American regiments, seized the enemy position atop nearby Kettle Hill. Theodore Roosevelt later claimed that he "would rather have led that charge than serve . . . three terms in the U.S. Senate." A friend wrote to Roosevelt's wife that her husband was "revelling in victory and gore."

The two battles put U.S. forces atop heights from which they could bring Santiago and the Spanish fleet under siege. On July 3 the Spanish ships made a gallant run for it, but the aging vessels were little match for the newer American fleet. The casualties were one-sided: 474 Spanish were killed or wounded and 1,750 were taken prisoner, while only one American was killed and one wounded. Santiago surrendered on July 17. On July 25 an American force moved onto the Spanish-held island of Puerto Rico.

The next day the Spanish government sued for peace. After discussions lasting two weeks, negotiators signed an armistice on August 12, 1898, less than four months after the war's start and the day before American troops entered Manila. The peace protocol specified that Spain should give up Cuba and that the United States should annex Puerto Rico and occupy the city, bay, and harbor of Manila pending the transfer of power in the Philippines.

And so the "splendid little war," as the future secretary of state John Hay called it in a letter to Roosevelt, officially ended. It was splendid only in the sense that its cost was relatively slight. Of the more than 274,000 Americans who served during the war and the ensuing demobilization, 5,462 died, but only 379 in battle. Most succumbed to malaria, typhoid, dysentery, or yellow fever. At such a cost the United States was launched onto the world stage as a great power, with all the benefits—and burdens—of that new status.

THE DEBATE OVER ANNEXATION The United States and Spain signed the Treaty of Paris on December 10, 1898, but the status of the Philippines remained in limbo. President McKinley, who claimed that at first he could not locate the Philippines on a map, gave ambiguous signals to the peace commission, which itself was divided. There had been no demand for annexation of the Philippines or other Spanish possessions before the war, but Commodore Dewey's victory at Manila Bay quickly kindled expansionist fever. Business leaders began thinking of the commercial possibilities in the nearby continent of Asia, such as oil for the lamps of China and textiles for its millions of people. Missionary societies yearned to convert "the little brown brother" to Christianity. Although most of these Filipino candidates for conversion were already Catholic, the word went forth that the Philippines should be taken for the sake of their souls. Spanish negotiators raised

"Well, I Hardly Know Which to Take First."

At the end of the nineteenth century, it seemed that Uncle Sam had developed a considerable appetite for foreign territory.

the delicate point that U.S. forces had no claim by right of conquest and had even taken Manila after the armistice. American negotiators finally offered the Spanish $20 million as compensation for possession of the Philippines, as well as Puerto Rico in the Caribbean and Guam in the Pacific.

Meanwhile, Americans had taken other giant steps in the Pacific. Hawaii had been annexed in the midst of the war. In 1899, after another outbreak of fighting over the royal succession in Samoa, Germany and the United States agreed to partition the Samoa Islands. The United States annexed the easternmost islands; Germany took the rest.

The Treaty of Paris was opposed by most Democrats and Populists and some Republicans. Anti-imperialists argued that the unprecedented acquisition of the Philippines would undermine democracy. They appealed to traditional isolationism, American principles of self-government, the inconsistency of liberating Cuba and annexing the Philippines, the involvement in foreign entanglements that would undermine the logic of the Monroe Doctrine, and the danger that the Philippines would be expensive if not impossible to defend. The prospect of incorporating so many alien peoples was also troubling. "Bananas and self-government cannot grow on the same piece of land," one senator claimed.

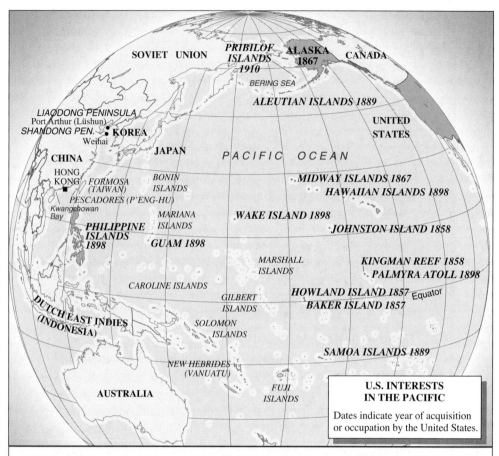

SOVIET UNION
PRIBILOF ISLANDS 1910
ALASKA 1867
CANADA
BERING SEA
ALEUTIAN ISLANDS 1889
LIAODONG PENINSULA
Port Arthur (Lüshun)
SHANDONG PEN.
Weihai
KOREA
UNITED STATES
CHINA
JAPAN
PACIFIC OCEAN
HONG KONG
FORMOSA (TAIWAN)
BONIN ISLANDS
PESCADORES (P'ENG-HU)
Kwangchowan Bay
MARIANA ISLANDS
MIDWAY ISLANDS 1867
HAWAIIAN ISLANDS 1898
WAKE ISLAND 1898
JOHNSTON ISLAND 1858
PHILIPPINE ISLANDS 1898
GUAM 1898
KINGMAN REEF 1858
PALMYRA ATOLL 1898
MARSHALL ISLANDS
CAROLINE ISLANDS
GILBERT ISLANDS
HOWLAND ISLAND 1857
BAKER ISLAND 1857
Equator
DUTCH EAST INDIES (INDONESIA)
SOLOMON ISLANDS
NEW HEBRIDES (VANUATU)
SAMOA ISLANDS 1889
AUSTRALIA
FUJI ISLANDS

U.S. INTERESTS IN THE PACIFIC

Dates indicate year of acquisition or occupation by the United States.

Why was McKinley eager to acquire territory in the Pacific and the Caribbean?
What kind of political system did the U.S. government create in Hawaii and in the
Philippines? How did Filipinos and Hawaiians resist the Americans?

The opposition may have been strong enough to kill the treaty had not the
populist Democrat William Jennings Bryan influenced the vote for approval.
A formal end to the war, he argued, would open the way for the future independence of Cuba and the Philippines. Ratification finally came on February
6, 1899.

By that time U.S. troops had already clashed with Filipino insurrectionists
near Manila. The Filipino rebel leader, Emilio Aguinaldo, had been in exile
until Commodore Dewey brought him back to Luzon to make trouble for the
Spanish. Since Aguinaldo's forces were more or less in control of the islands

Turmoil in the Philippines

Emilio Aguinaldo (seated third from right) and other leaders of the Filipino insurgence.

outside Manila, what followed over the next two years was largely an American war of conquest. It was a sordid conflict, with massacres and torture on both sides. In the end it took 63,000 U.S. troops, 4,300 American deaths, and almost three years to suppress the revolt. Organized Filipino resistance collapsed by the end of 1899, but even after the American capture of Aguinaldo in 1901, sporadic guerrilla action lasted until mid-1902.

Against the backdrop of this nasty guerrilla war, the great debate over annexation continued in the United States. The treaty debates inspired a number of anti-imperialist groups, which united in 1899 as the American Anti-Imperialist League. The league attracted members representing many shades of opinion; the main characteristic they had in common was that most belonged to an older generation. Andrew Carnegie footed the bills; on imperialism, at least, the union leader Samuel Gompers agreed with him. The usually soft-spoken philosopher William James exploded in voicing his opposition to the expansionists: "God damn the United States for its vile conduct in the Philippine Isles!" The selfish proponents of imperialism, he declared, had caused the nation to "puke up its ancient soul."

ORGANIZING THE ACQUISITIONS   Such criticism, however, did not faze the expansionists. McKinley quickly moved to set up a civil government in the Philippines. On July 4, 1901, the U.S. military government came to an end, and under an act of Congress, Judge William Howard Taft became the civil governor. The Philippine Government Act, passed by Congress on July 1, 1902, declared the Philippine Islands an "unorganized territory." In 1934 the Tydings-McDuffie Act offered independence after ten more years. Independence finally took effect on July 4, 1946.

Closer to home, Puerto Rico had been acquired in part to serve as a U.S. outpost guarding the approach to the Caribbean and any future isthmian canal. In 1900 the Foraker Act established a civil government on the island. Residents of the island were declared citizens of Puerto Rico; they were not made citizens of the United States until 1917. In 1952 Puerto Rico became a commonwealth with its own constitution and elected officials, a unique status. Like a state, Puerto Rico is free to change its constitution insofar as it does not conflict with the U.S. Constitution.

Liberated Cuba, American authorities soon learned, posed problems at least as irksome as those in the new possessions. After the American occupation forces had restored order, started schools, and improved sanitary conditions, they began handing the reins of power to the Cubans. The Platt Amendment to the army-appropriations bill passed by Congress in 1901 sharply restricted the new government's independence, however. The amendment required that Cuba never impair its independence by signing a treaty with a third power, that it keep its debt within the government's power to repay it out of ordinary revenues, and that it acknowledge the right of the United States to intervene in Cuba for the preservation of Cuban independence and the maintenance of "a government adequate for the protection of life, property, and individual liberty." Finally, Cuba was called upon to sell or lease to the United States lands to be used for coaling or naval stations, a proviso that led to a U.S. naval base at Guantánamo Bay, which is still in operation.

Imperial Rivalries in East Asia

THE "OPEN DOOR" During the 1890s not only the United States but also Japan emerged as a world power. Commodore Matthew Perry's voyage of 1853–1854 had opened Japan to Western ways, and the island nation had begun modernization in earnest after the 1860s. Flexing its new muscles, Japan defeated China's stagnant empire in the First Sino-Japanese War (1894–1895) and as a result acquired the island of Formosa (modern-day Taiwan). China's weakness, demonstrated in the war, led Russia, England, France, and Germany to renew their scramble for "spheres of influence" on that remaining frontier of imperialist expansion.

The possibility that those competing powers would carve up China and erect tariff barriers in their own spheres of influence dimmed the bright prospect of American trade with China. The British had much to lose in a tariff war, for they already enjoyed substantial trade with China. Fearful of such a development, the British suggested in 1899 that the United States join them in preserving China's commercial and territorial integrity. The State Department agreed that something must be done, but Secretary of State John Hay preferred to act alone rather than in concert with the British.

In its origins and content, what came to be known as the Open Door policy resembled the Monroe Doctrine. In both cases the United States unilaterally proclaimed a hands-off policy that the British had earlier proposed as a joint statement. The policy outlined in Hay's Open Door Note, dispatched in 1899 to London, Berlin, and St. Petersburg and a little later to Tokyo, Rome, and Paris, proposed to keep China open to trade with all countries on an equal basis. None except Britain accepted Hay's principles, but none rejected them either, so Hay simply announced that all powers had accepted the policy.

The Open Door policy was rooted in the self-interest of American businesses eager to exploit Chinese markets. Yet it also tapped the deep-seated sympathies of those who opposed imperialism, especially as it endorsed China's territorial integrity. But it had little legal standing. When the Japanese, concerned about Russian pressure in Manchuria, asked how the United States intended to enforce the Open Door policy, Hay replied that the United States was "not prepared" to do so. So it would remain for forty years, a hollow but dangerous commitment, until continued Japanese expansion would bring about war with America in 1941.

THE BOXER REBELLION   A new Asian crisis arose in 1900 when a group of Chinese nationalists known to the Western world as Boxers ("Fists of Righteous Harmony") rebelled against foreign involvement in China, surrounding the foreign embassies in Peking (Beijing). The British, Germans, Russians, Japanese, and Americans quickly mounted a military expedition to relieve the embassy compound. Hay, fearful that the intervention might become an excuse to dismember China, seized the chance to further refine his Open Door policy. The United States, he declared in a circular letter of July 3, 1900, sought a solution that would "preserve Chinese territorial and administrative integrity" as well as "equal and impartial trade with all parts of the Chinese Empire." Six weeks later the expedition reached Peking and broke the Boxer Rebellion.

Big-Stick Diplomacy

More than any other American political leader of his time, Theodore Roosevelt transformed the role of the United States in world affairs. The nation had emerged from the Spanish-American War a world power, and he insisted that this status entailed major new responsibilities. To ensure that the country accepted its international obligations, Roosevelt stretched both the Constitution and executive power to the limit. In the process he pushed a reluctant nation onto the center stage of world affairs.

ROOSEVELT'S RISE   In the fall elections of 1898, Republicans benefited from the euphoria of military victory, increasing their majority in Congress. That hardly amounted to a mandate for imperialism, however, since the election preceded most of the debates on the issue. But in 1900 the Democrats turned once again to William Jennings Bryan, who sought to make imperialism the "paramount issue" of the campaign. The Democratic platform condemned the Philippine conflict as "an unnecessary war" that had "placed the United States, previously known . . . throughout the world as the champion of freedom, in the false and un-American position of crushing with military force the efforts of our former allies to achieve liberty and self-government." The Republicans welcomed the opportunity to disagree. They renominated William McKinley and named as his running mate Theodore Roosevelt, who had been elected governor of New York after his self-inflated role in the Spanish-American War.

The trouble with Bryan's idea of a solemn referendum on imperialism was the near impossibility of making any presidential contest so simple. Bryan himself complicated his message by insisting once again on the free coinage of silver, and the tariff became an issue again as well. The Republicans' biggest advantage was probably the return to national prosperity, which they were fully ready to take credit for. Those who opposed imperialism but also opposed free silver or tariff reduction faced a bewildering choice.

The outcome was a victory for McKinley greater than his last, 7.2 million to 6.4 million popular votes and 292 to 155 electoral votes. There had been no clear-cut referendum on annexations, but the question was settled nonetheless, although it would take another year and a half to subdue the Filipino rebels. The job would be finished under the direction of another president, however.

On September 6, 1901, at a reception at the Pan-American Exposition in Buffalo, an anarchist named Leon Czolgosz (pronounced chole-gosh) approached McKinley, a pistol concealed in his bandaged hand, and fired at point-blank range. McKinley died six days later, thereby elevating Theodore Roosevelt to the White House. "Now look," Republican senator Mark Hanna erupted. "That damned cowboy is President of the United States!"

Six weeks short of his forty-third birthday, Roosevelt was the youngest man ever to take charge of the White House, but he had more experience in public affairs than most and more vitality than any. Born in 1858, the son of a wealthy New York merchant and a Georgia belle, Roosevelt had grown up in Manhattan in cultured comfort, had visited Europe as a child, spoke German fluently, and had graduated from Harvard Phi Beta Kappa in 1880. Rigorous exercise and outdoor adventure were two of his many passions. Boxer, wrestler, and outdoorsman, he was also an omnivorous reader, a renowned historian and essayist, and a zealous moralist.

Roosevelt studied law briefly and within two years of graduation from college won election to the New York legislature. That same year he published *The Naval War of 1812,* the first of numerous historical, biographical, and other works to flow from his pen. He seemingly had the world at his feet—and then disaster struck. In 1884 his beloved mother, only forty-eight years old, died. Eleven hours later, in the same house, his twenty-two-year-old wife struggled with kidney failure before dying in his arms, having recently given birth to their only child. Roosevelt was distraught and bewildered. "The light has gone out of my life," he wrote in his diary. The double funeral was so wrenching that the officiating minister wept throughout his prayer. In an attempt to recover from this "strange and terrible fate," Roosevelt turned his baby daughter over to his sister, quit his political career, sold the family house, and moved west to take up the cattle business in the Dakota Territory. The blue-blooded New Yorker relished hunting, leading roundups, capturing outlaws, fighting Indians—and reading novels by the campfire. Although his western career lasted only two years, he never quite got over being a cowboy.

Back in New York City, Roosevelt remarried and ran unsuccessfully for mayor; and he later served six years as civil service commissioner in Washington, D.C., and two years as New York City's police commissioner. After President McKinley appointed him assistant secretary of the navy in 1897, Roosevelt did all he could to promote the war with Spain over Cuba. "A just war," he insisted, "is in the long run far better for a man's soul than the most prosperous peace."

Roosevelt combined his boundless energy with an unshakable righteousness that led him to cast every issue in moral and patriotic terms. He saw the presidency as his "bully pulpit," and he was eager to preach fist-smacking

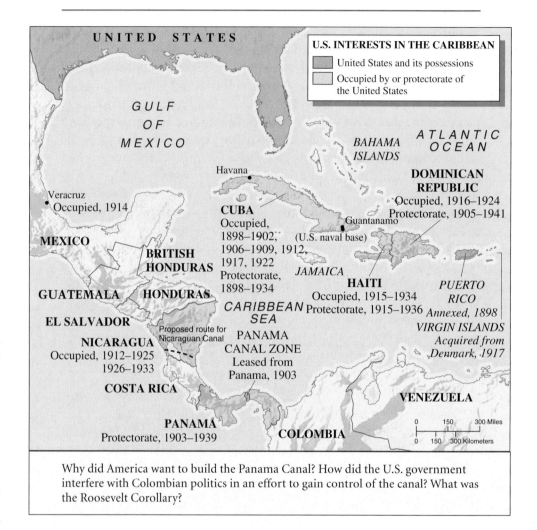

U.S. INTERESTS IN THE CARIBBEAN

United States and its possessions

Occupied by or protectorate of the United States

UNITED STATES

GULF OF MEXICO

ATLANTIC OCEAN

BAHAMA ISLANDS

Havana

DOMINICAN REPUBLIC
Occupied, 1916–1924
Protectorate, 1905–1941

Veracruz
Occupied, 1914

CUBA
Occupied,
1898–1902,
1906–1909, 1912,
1917, 1922
Protectorate,
1898–1934

Guantanamo
(U.S. naval base)

MEXICO

BRITISH HONDURAS

JAMAICA

GUATEMALA   HONDURAS

HAITI
Occupied, 1915–1934
Protectorate, 1915–1936

PUERTO RICO
Annexed, 1898

CARIBBEAN SEA

EL SALVADOR

VIRGIN ISLANDS
Acquired from
Denmark, 1917

NICARAGUA
Occupied, 1912–1925
1926–1933

Proposed route for
Nicaraguan Canal

PANAMA
CANAL ZONE
Leased from
Panama, 1903

COSTA RICA

VENEZUELA

PANAMA
Protectorate, 1903–1939

COLOMBIA

0   150   300 Miles
0   150   300 Kilometers

Why did America want to build the Panama Canal? How did the U.S. government interfere with Colombian politics in an effort to gain control of the canal? What was the Roosevelt Corollary?

sermons on the virtues of honesty, civic duty, and the strenuous life to his national flock. But appearances were deceiving. His energy left a false impression of impulsiveness, and the talk of morality cloaked a cautious pragmatism. Roosevelt could get carried away, but as he said of his foreign-policy actions, this was likely to happen only when "I am assured that I shall be able eventually to carry out my will by force."

THE PANAMA CANAL   After the Spanish-American War the United States became more deeply involved than ever in the Caribbean, where one issue overshadowed every other: the Panama Canal. The narrow isthmus of Panama, a part of Colombia, had long excited dreams of an interoceanic canal. After America's victory over Spain, Secretary of State John Hay commenced talks with the British ambassador to revise the Clayton-Bulwer Treaty of 1850, which prohibited either nation from constructing a transoceanic canal. The negotiations led to the Hay-Pauncefote Treaty of 1901, in which Britain gave its consent to the American plan for a canal across Panama.

Other obstacles remained, however. From 1881 to 1887, a French company had spent nearly $300 million and sacrificed some 20,000 lives to dig less than one third of a canal

Digging the Canal

President Theodore Roosevelt operating a steam shovel during his 1906 visit to the Panama Canal.

through Panama. The company now offered to sell its holdings to the United States. Meanwhile, Secretary of State Hay had opened negotiations with Ambassador Tomás Herrán of Colombia to build a canal across Panama, which was then a reluctant province of Colombia. In return for a Canal Zone six miles wide, the United States agreed to pay $10 million in cash and a rental fee of $250,000 a year. The United States Senate ratified the Hay-Herrán Treaty in 1903, but the Colombian senate held out for $25 million in cash.

Colombia's rejection of the treaty heightened the desire of Panamanian rebels for independence. An employee of the French canal company then hatched a plot in collusion with the company's representative, Philippe Bunau-Varilla. Bunau-Varilla visited Roosevelt and Hay and then, apparently with inside information, informed the Panamanian rebels that the U.S.S. *Nashville* would arrive at Colón, Panama, on November 2, 1903.

An army of some 500 Panamanians revolted against Colombian rule the next day. Colombian troops, who could not penetrate the overland jungle, found U.S. ships blocking the sea-lanes. On November 7 the Roosevelt administration made good on its collusion with the revolutionaries by recognizing Panama's independence, and on November 18 Roosevelt and the new Panamanian ambassador, who happened to be Bunau-Varilla, signed a treaty extending the Canal Zone from six to ten miles in width. For $10 million down and $250,000 a year, the United States received "in perpetuity the use, occupation and control" of the Canal Zone. Colombia eventually got its $25 million, in 1921, but only after America's interest in Colombian oil had lubricated the wheels of diplomacy. There was no apology, but the payment was made to remove "all misunderstandings growing out of the political events in Panama, November, 1903." The canal opened on August 15, 1914, two weeks after the outbreak of World War I in Europe. It was a tribute to American engineering and a boon to American commerce and the Panamanian economy.

THE ROOSEVELT COROLLARY   Even without the canal the United States would have been concerned with the stability of the Caribbean region, and particularly with the activities of any hostile power there. A prime excuse for intervention in those days was to force the collection of debts owed to foreigners. In 1904 a crisis over the Dominican Republic's debts gave Roosevelt an opportunity to formulate U.S. policy. In his annual address to Congress in 1904, he set forth what came to be known as the Roosevelt Corollary to the Monroe Doctrine: the principle, in short, that since the Monroe Doctrine prohibited European intervention in the region, the United States was justified in intervening first to forestall the actions of outsiders. Roosevelt suggested that the United States could exercise an "international police power" in its own sphere of influence. As put into practice by mutual agreement with the Dominican Republic in 1905, the Roosevelt Corollary called for the United States to install and protect a collector of customs, who would apply a portion of the nation's revenues to debt payments owed

The World's Constable

President Theodore Roosevelt wields "the big stick," symbolizing his approach to diplomacy.

foreign nations. The principle, applied peaceably in 1905, became the basis for military interventions later on.

THE RUSSO-JAPANESE WAR   In east Asia, meanwhile, the principle of equal trading rights embodied in the Open Door policy received a serious challenge when tensions between Russia and Japan flared into a fight over China and Korea. On February 8, 1904, war broke out when the Japanese launched a surprise attack that devastated the Russian fleet. The Japanese then occupied Korea and drove the Russians back across the Yalu River into Manchuria. But neither side could score a knockout blow, and neither relished a prolonged war. When the Japanese signaled President Roosevelt that they would welcome a negotiated settlement, he agreed to sponsor a peace conference, held in Portsmouth, New Hampshire. In the Treaty of Portsmouth (1905), the concessions all went to the Japanese. Russia acknowledged Japan's "predominant political, military, and economic interests in Korea" (Japan would annex the kingdom in 1910), and both powers agreed to evacuate Manchuria.

RELATIONS WITH JAPAN   Japan's show of strength in the war with Russia raised doubts about the security of the Philippines. During the Portsmouth talks, Roosevelt sent Secretary of War William Howard Taft to meet with the Japanese foreign minister in Tokyo. The two men arrived at the Taft-Katsura Agreement of July 29, 1905, in which the United States accepted Japanese control of Korea and Japan disavowed any designs on the Philippines. Three years later the Root-Takahira Agreement, negotiated by Secretary of State Elihu Root and the Japanese ambassador, promised to respect the other's possessions and reinforced the Open Door policy by supporting "the independence and integrity of China" and "the principle of equal opportunity for commerce and industry in China."

Behind the diplomatic facade of goodwill, however, lay simmering mutual distrust. For many Americans the Russian threat in east Asia now gave way to distrust of Japan's "yellow peril" (a term apparently coined by Germany's kaiser Wilhelm II). Racial animosities on the West Coast helped sour relations with Japan. In 1906 San Francisco's school board ordered students of Chinese, Japanese, and Korean descent to attend a separate public school. The Japanese government sharply protested the show of ethnic prejudice, and President Roosevelt managed to talk the school board into changing its policy. For its part, Japan agreed to limit sharply its issuance of visas to the United States. This "Gentleman's Agreement" of

1907, the precise terms of which have never been revealed, halted the influx of Japanese immigrants and brought some respite to racial agitation in California.

THE UNITED STATES AND EUROPE   During these years of expansionism the United States cast its gaze mainly westward and southward. But events in Europe also required attention. While Roosevelt was mediating the Russo-Japanese War in 1905, another crisis was brewing in Morocco, where the Germans and French fought for control. Roosevelt felt that the United States had something at stake in preventing the outbreak of a major war. At the kaiser's behest he talked the French and the British into attending an international conference at Algeciras, Spain, with American delegates present. Roosevelt then maneuvered the Germans into accepting his lead. The Act of Algeciras, signed in 1906, affirmed the independence of Morocco and guaranteed an open door for trade there. Roosevelt received the Nobel Peace Prize in 1906 for his work at Portsmouth and Algeciras. For all his bellicosity on other occasions, he had earned it.

Before Roosevelt left the White House in March 1909, he celebrated America's rise to the status of a world power with one great flourish. In late 1907 he sent the entire U.S. Navy, by then second in strength only to the British fleet, on a grand tour around the world. It was the first such display of American naval might in the Pacific, and many feared the reaction of the Japanese, for whose benefit Roosevelt had in fact staged the show. They need not have worried, for in Japan the flotilla got the greatest welcome of all. Thousands of schoolchildren turned out, waving tiny American flags and singing "The Star-Spangled Banner" in English. The triumphal procession continued home by way of the Mediterranean and steamed back into American waters in 1909, just in time to close out Roosevelt's presidency on a note of success.

Yet it was a success that would have mixed consequences. Roosevelt's ability to project American power abroad was burdened by a racist ideology shared by many prominent political figures of the time. He once told the graduates of the Naval War College that all "the great masterful races have been fighting races, and the minute that a race loses the hard fighting virtues . . . it has lost the right to stand as equal to the best." On another occasion he called war the best way to promote "the clear instinct for race selfishness" and insisted that "the most ultimately righteous of all wars is a war with savages." Such a belligerent and bigoted attitude would come back to haunt the United States in world affairs—and at home.

MAKING CONNECTIONS

- The Spanish-American War marked a turning point in U.S. foreign policy. America's emergence as a global power is a central theme of the twentieth century.

- Theodore Roosevelt's foreign policy displayed an activist approach to the presidency. The next chapter describes connections between his foreign policies and his approach to domestic affairs.

FURTHER READING

An excellent survey of the diplomacy of the era is Charles Soutter Campbell's *The Transformation of American Foreign Relations, 1865–1900* (1976). For background on the events of the 1890s, see Walter LaFeber's *The American Search for Opportunity, 1865–1913* (1993) and D. Healy's *U.S. Expansionism: The Imperialist Urge in the 1890s* (1970). The dispute over American policy in Hawaii is covered in Thomas J. Osborne's *"Empire Can Wait": American Opposition to Hawaiian Annexation, 1893–1898* (1981).

Ivan Musicant's *Empire by Default: The Spanish-American War and the Dawn of the American Century* (1998) is the most comprehensive volume on the conflict. For the war's aftermath in the Philippines, see Stuart Creighton Miller's *"Benevolent Assimilation": The American Conquest of the Philippines, 1899–1903* (1982). Robert L. Beisner's *Twelve against Empire: The Anti-Imperialists, 1898–1900* (1968) handles the debate over annexation.

A good introduction to American interest in China is Michael H. Hunt's *The Making of a Special Relationship: The United States and China to 1914* (1983). Kenton J. Clymer's *John Hay: The Gentleman as Diplomat* (1975) examines the role of this key secretary of state in forming policy.

For U.S. policy in the Caribbean and Central America, see Walter LaFeber's *Inevitable Revolutions: The United States in Central America*, 2nd ed. (1993). David McCullough's *The Path between the Seas: The Creation of the Panama Canal, 1870–1914* (1977) presents the fullest account of how the United States secured the Panama Canal.

24

THE PROGRESSIVE ERA

FOCUS QUESTIONS

- What were the basic elements of Progressive reform?
- What were the central issues confronting the presidencies of Theodore Roosevelt, William H. Taft, and Woodrow Wilson?
- What was the significance of the election of 1912?

To answer these questions and access additional review material, please visit www.wwnorton.com/studyspace.

Theodore Roosevelt's emergence as a national leader coincided with the onset of what historians have labeled the Progressive Era (1900–1917). The Progressive movement arose in response to many societal changes, the most powerful of which were the devastating depression of the 1890s and its attendant social unrest. The depression brought hard times to the cities, deepened distress in rural areas, and provoked both the fears and the conscience of the rapidly growing middle and upper-middle classes. By the turn of the century, so many outraged activists were at work seeking to improve social conditions and political abuses that people began to speak of a Progressive Era, a time of fermenting idealism, moral and religious fervor, and constructive social, economic, and political change.

ELEMENTS OF REFORM

Progressivism was a reform movement so varied and comprehensive in its goals and motives that it almost defies definition. Political Progressives crusaded against the abuses of urban political bosses and corporate robber barons. Their goals were greater democracy, honest and efficient government, more effective regulation of big business and "special interests," and greater social justice for working people.

The Progressive movement represented the animating spirit of the times rather than a single organized group or party. What reformers shared was a common assumption that the complex social ills and tensions generated by the urban-industrial revolution required expanding the scope of local, state, and federal government authority so as to elevate the public interest over private greed. Many Progressives were motivated by religious beliefs that led some of them to concentrate on moral reforms such as the prohibition of alcoholic beverages and Sunday closing laws.

The "real heart of the movement," declared one reformer, was "to use the government as an agency of human welfare." Governments were now called upon to extend a broad range of direct services: schools, good roads (a movement propelled first by cyclists and then by automobilists), conservation of natural resources, public health and welfare, care of the disabled, and farm loans and farm demonstration agents (county workers who visited farms to demonstrate new technology), among others. Such initiatives represented the first tentative steps toward what would become known during the 1930s and thereafter as the welfare state.

THE ANTECEDENTS OF PROGRESSIVISM The Progressive impulse began at the local level in the 1880s as a response to problems caused by industrialization and urbanization and only gradually emerged on the national level. Beginning in the large cities of the East and the Midwest, private citizens worked to improve basic public services such as sewerage, housing, and transportation. Reformers of local government believed in greater efficiency, less favoritism, and more expertise. They wanted to reorder government itself through detailed budgets, audits, and a more rationalized structure of government offices. Early efforts to improve public health, education, and factory conditions grew out of a desire to improve the administration and enforcement of local and state laws.

Another significant force in fostering the spirit of Progressivism was the growing prominence of socialist critiques of living and working conditions. The Socialist party of the time, small but earnest and vocal, served as the left wing of Progressivism. Most Progressives found socialist remedies unacceptable, and the main Progressive reform impulse grew in part from a desire to counter the growing appeal of socialist doctrines.

THE MUCKRAKERS Poverty, unsafe working conditions, infectious diseases, and child labor in unhealthy factories were complex social issues; remedying them would take more than an idealistic desire to effect change in government, public health, and working conditions. Public consciousness needed to be raised, a process that required publicizing both scandals and festering social ills. A group of journalists dubbed muckrakers rose to the challenge. These writers, who thrived on exposing corruption and social injustice, got their name when Theodore Roosevelt compared them to a character in John Bunyan's *Pilgrim's Progress:* "A man that could look no way but downwards with a muckrake in his hands." "Muckrakers are often indispensable to . . . society," Roosevelt said, "but only if they know when to stop raking the muck."

Henry Demarest Lloyd is sometimes cited as the first of the muckrakers, for his critical examination of the Standard Oil Company and other monopolies in his book *Wealth against Commonwealth* (1894). Lloyd exposed the growth of corporate giants responsible to none but themselves, able to corrupt if not control governments. Lincoln Steffens likewise revealed the prevalence of municipal corruption in a series of articles later collected into a book, *The Shame of the Cities* (1904).

Another early muckraker was Jacob Riis, a Danish immigrant who exposed slum conditions in *How the Other Half Lives* (1890). The chief outlets for social critics were the popular middle-class magazines that began to flourish in the 1890s, such as the *Arena* and *McClure's.*

Without the muckrakers, Progressivism would never have achieved widespread popular support. In feeding a growing public appetite for facts about modern social problems, the muckrakers demonstrated one of the salient features of the Progressive movement, and one of its central failures. The Progressives were stronger on diagnosis than on remedy. They harbored a naive faith in the power of democracy. Reveal the facts, expose corruption, arouse public indignation, and bring government closer to the people, they assumed, and the correction of evils would follow automatically. The cure for the ills of democracy was, to Progressive reformers, simply a more enlightened and more engaged democracy.

FEATURES OF PROGRESSIVISM

DEMOCRACY   The most important Progressive reform intended to democratize government was the direct primary, in which candidates would be nominated by the vote of all party members rather than by a few political bosses who selected candidates for the parties. After South Carolina adopted the first statewide primary in 1896, the concept spread within two decades to nearly every other state.

The primary was but one expression of a broad movement for greater public participation in the political process. In 1898 South Dakota became the first state to adopt the initiative and referendum, procedures that allow voters to enact laws directly. If a designated number of voters petitioned to have a measure put on the ballot (the initiative), the electorate could then vote it up or down (the referendum). Oregon also adopted a spectrum of reform measures, including a voter-registration law (1899), the initiative and referendum (1902), the direct primary (1904), a sweeping corrupt-practices act (1908), and the recall (1910), whereby public officials could be removed by a public petition and vote. By 1920 nearly twenty states had adopted the initiative and referendum, and nearly a dozen had adopted the recall. The direct election of U.S. senators by the people, rather than by the state legislatures, was another Progressive political reform. The popular election of senators required a constitutional amendment, and by 1912 the Senate finally agreed to the Seventeenth Amendment, which was ratified by the states in 1913.

EFFICIENCY   A second major theme of Progressivism was the "gospel of efficiency." In the business world at the turn of the century and after, Frederick W. Taylor, the original "efficiency expert," developed an array of scientific management techniques designed to cut manufacturing costs and enhance productivity. Taylorism, as scientific management came to be known, promised to reduce waste through the careful analysis of labor processes. By meticulously studying the time it took each worker to perform a task, Taylor prescribed the optimal technique for the average worker and established detailed performance standards for each job classification. The promise of higher wages, he believed, would motivate workers to exceed the "average" expectations.

Instead, many workers resented Taylor's innovations. They saw in scientific management a tool to make employees work faster than was healthy or fair. Yet Taylor's controversial efficiency system brought concrete improvements in productivity, especially among those industries whose production processes

Robert M. La Follette

A proponent of expertise in government.

were highly standardized and whose jobs were precisely defined.

In government the efficiency movement called for nonpartisan "experts" to replace bureaucrats and demanded the reorganization of agencies to prevent redundancy, establish clear lines of authority, and assign accountability to specific officials. The most ardent disciple of the principle of government by experts was Wisconsin governor Robert M. La Follette, "Fighting Bob," who established a Legislative Reference Bureau staffed by professors and specialists to provide research, advice, and help in the drafting of legislation designed to curb the power of special interests and promote social justice. This "Wisconsin idea" of efficient government was widely publicized and copied by other states.

Two ideas for making municipal government more efficient gained headway in the first decade of the new century. The commission system was first adopted by Galveston, Texas, in 1901, when local government collapsed in the aftermath of a devastating hurricane that killed 6,000 people and destroyed half the town. It placed ultimate authority in a board composed of elected administrative heads of city departments, commissioners of sanitation, police, utilities, and so on. By 1914 more than 400 towns and small cities across the country had adopted the commission system. The more durable idea, however, was the city-manager plan, under which a professional administrator ran the municipal government in accordance with policies set by the elected council and mayor. Staunton, Virginia, first adopted the plan in 1908. By 1914 the National Association of City Managers had heralded the arrival of a new profession.

REGULATION   Of all the problems facing American society at the turn of the century, one engaged a greater diversity of reformers and elicited more solutions than any other: the regulation of giant corporations, which became a third major theme of Progressivism. Beginning in the 1870s, states had tried to regulate the freight rates of railroads and the working conditions in other businesses, only to be thwarted by Supreme Court rulings. The judges declared that only the federal government could regulate companies involved in interstate commerce. By the 1890s the growth of monopolistic corporations had spurred reformers to act on a national level. While some Progressives believed that the problems of concentrated economic power and its abuses should be left to business to work out for itself, a policy known as laissez-faire, others advocated an active government policy of trust-busting in the belief that restoring old-fashioned competition was the best way to prevent economic abuses.

Efforts to restore the competitiveness of small firms proved unworkable, however, in part because breaking up large corporations was fraught with difficulty. As a consequence, the main thrust of Progressive reform over the years was toward regulation, rather than dissolution, of big businesses. To some extent, regulation and "stabilization" won acceptance among business leaders because whatever respect they paid to competition in principle, they preferred not to face it in practice. As time passed, however, regulatory agencies often came under the influence or control of those they were supposed to regulate.

SOCIAL JUSTICE   A fourth important feature of the Progressive spirit was the impulse toward social justice, which motivated diverse actions, from the promotion of private charities to campaigns against child labor and liquor. Led by women, the settlement-house movement of the late nineteenth century had spawned a corps of social workers and genteel reformers animated by religious ideals and devoted to the uplift of slum dwellers. But with time it became apparent that social evils extended beyond the reach of private charities and demanded government intervention.

Labor legislation was perhaps the most significant reform to emerge from the drive for social justice. It emerged first at the state level. The National Child Labor Committee, organized in 1904, led a movement for state laws banning the still-widespread employment of young children. Within ten years the committee

Child Labor

A young girl working as a spinner in a cotton mill in Vermont, 1910.

helped foster in most states new laws banning the labor of underage children (the minimum age varying from twelve to sixteen) and limiting the hours older children might work.

Closely linked to the child-labor reform movement was a concerted effort to regulate the hours of work for women. Spearheaded by Florence Kelley, the head of the National Consumers' League, this Progressive crusade promoted the passage of state laws addressing the distinctive hardships that long working hours imposed on women who were wives and mothers.

The Supreme Court pursued a curiously erratic course in ruling on new state labor laws. In *Lochner v. New York* (1905), the Court voided a ten-hour workday law because it violated workers' "liberty of contract" to accept any terms they chose. Then in *Muller v. Oregon* (1908), the high court upheld a ten-hour-workday law for women. The justices relied largely on sociological data that attorney Louis D. Brandeis presented regarding the adverse effects of long hours on the health and morals of women. In *Bunting v. Oregon* (1917), the Court accepted a ten-hour workday for both men and women but for twenty more years held out against state minimum-wage laws.

Legislation to protect workers against avoidable accidents gained momentum from disasters such as the 1911 fire at the Triangle Shirtwaist Company in New York City, in which 146 people, mostly young women, died because the owner kept the stairway doors locked to prevent theft. Workers trapped on the three upper floors of the ten-story building died in the fire or leaped to their death. Stricter building codes and factory-inspection acts followed.

PROHIBITION   For many Progressive activists with strong religious convictions, the cause of liquor prohibition was the foremost societal concern. The Women's Christian Temperance Union had been battling the sale of alcoholic beverages since 1874, but the most successful political action followed the formation in 1893 of the Anti-Saloon League, an organization that pioneered the strategy of the single-issue pressure group. In 1913 the league endorsed an amendment to the Constitution prohibiting the sale of all alcoholic beverages, which was adopted by Congress in 1917. By the time it was ratified two years later, state and local action had already dried up areas occupied by nearly three fourths of the nation's population.

ROOSEVELT'S PROGRESSIVISM

While most Progressive initiatives originated at the state and local levels, calls for national Progressive efforts began to appear around 1900. Theodore

Roosevelt brought to the White House in 1901 an expansive vision of the presidency that well suited the cause of Progressive reform. In one of his first addresses to Congress, he stressed the need for a new political approach. When the Constitution was first drafted, he explained, the nation's social and economic conditions were quite unlike those at the dawn of the twentieth century. Modern urban-industrial society required more active government involvement.

More than any other president since Lincoln, Roosevelt possessed an activist bent. Still, his initial approach to reform was cautious. He sought to avoid the extremes of socialism on the one hand and laissez-faire individualism on the other. A skilled political maneuverer, he broke the tradition of the Gilded Age presidents by serving as a very active chief executive. Roosevelt greatly expanded the role and visibility of the presidency, as well as the authority and scope of the federal government. His capacity for hard work was boundless; his boyish energy was infectious. He thrived on crises and took the leadership role in negotiating major legislation and labor disputes. Always a self-promoter, he effectively managed publicity and news about the White House. Roosevelt craved the spotlight. As one of his sons explained, "Father always wanted to be the bride at every wedding and the corpse at every funeral." He also cultivated party leaders in Congress and steered away from such divisive issues as the tariff and regulation of the banks. And when he did approach the explosive issue of the trusts, he took care to reassure the business community. For him politics was the art of the possible. Unlike the more radical Progressives and the doctrinaire "lunatic fringe," as he called it, he would take half a loaf rather than none at all.

THE TRUSTS   On the issue of huge business trusts, Roosevelt endorsed the "sincere conviction that combination and concentration should be, not prohibited, but supervised and within reasonable limits controlled." In 1902 he proposed a "square deal" for all, calling for enforcement of existing antitrust laws and stricter controls on big business. Effective regulation, he insisted, was better than a futile effort to restore small business by breaking up all giant corporations, which might be achieved only at a cost to the efficiencies of scale gained in larger operations.

Because Congress balked at regulatory legislation, Roosevelt forced the issue by a more vigorous federal prosecution of the Sherman Anti-Trust Act of 1890. He chose his target carefully. In the case against the sugar trust (*United States v. E. C. Knight and Company,* 1895), the Supreme Court had declared manufacturing strictly an *intrastate* activity. Most railroads, however, were beyond question engaged in *interstate* commerce and thus subject to federal authority. Consequently, in 1902 Roosevelt moved against the Northern

Roosevelt's Duality

Theodore Roosevelt as an "apostle of prosperity" (top) and as a Roman tyrant (bottom). Roosevelt's energy, spirit, self-righteousness, and impulsiveness elicited sharp reactions.

Securities Company, a holding company merging the competing Great Northern and Northern Pacific Railroads. Roosevelt attacked the trust for essentially forming a monopoly, and in 1904, in *United States v. Northern Securities Company*, the Supreme Court ordered the combination dissolved. Roosevelt continued to use his executive powers to enforce the Sherman Anti-Trust Act, but he avoided conflict in Congress by proposing no further anti-trust legislation. Altogether, his administration brought about twenty-five anti-trust suits.

THE 1902 COAL STRIKE   Support for Roosevelt's use of the "big stick" against corporations was strengthened by the stubbornness of mine owners in the anthracite coal strike of 1902. On May 12 some 150,000 members of the United Mine Workers (UMW) walked off the job in West Virginia and Pennsylvania. They demanded a 20 percent wage increase, a reduction in daily working hours from ten to nine, and formal recognition of their union by management. The operators dug in their heels and shut down the mines in an effort to starve out the miners, many of whom were immigrants from eastern Europe. One mine owner revealed the social prejudices of the era when he asserted, "The miners don't suffer—why, they can't even speak English."

Presidents such as Hayes and Cleveland had responded to labor unrest by dispatching federal troops. But the coal strike had not become violent when Roosevelt aggressively intervened. He was concerned about the approach of winter amid a nationwide coal shortage and the effects of the strike on the fall congressional elections—he told a friend that the public would blame the Republicans if coal were in short supply. By October 1902 the price of coal had soared, and hospitals and schools reported empty coal bins. Roosevelt thus decided upon a bold move: he invited leaders of both sides to a conference in Washington, where he appealed to their "patriotism, to the spirit that sinks personal considerations and makes individual sacrifices for the public good." The mine owners attended the conference but refused even to speak to the UMW leaders. The "extraordinary stupidity and temper" of the "wooden-headed" owners infuriated Roosevelt. With the conference deadlocked, the president threatened to take over the mines and send in the army to run them. Militarizing the mines would have been an act of dubious legality, but the owners feared that Roosevelt might do it and that public opinion would support him.

The coal strike ended on October 23, 1902, with an agreement to submit the issues to an arbitration commission named by the president. The agreement enhanced the prestige of both Roosevelt and the union's leader, although it produced only a partial victory for the miners. By the arbitrators' decision in 1903, the miners won a nine-hour workday but only a 10 percent wage increase and no union recognition.

AN EXPANDING GOVERNMENT   In 1903 Congress strengthened both anti-trust enforcement and government regulation by creating a new federal agency, the Department of Commerce and Labor, and passing the Elkins Act, which made it illegal for corporations to take, as well as to give, secret rebates to their preferred customers. The Bureau of Corporations had no direct regulatory powers, but it did have a mandate to report on the activities of interstate corporations. Its findings could lead to anti-trust suits, but its purpose was rather to help corporations correct malpractices and avoid the need for lawsuits. Many companies cooperated, but others held back. When Standard Oil refused to turn over its records, the government brought an anti-trust suit that resulted in the campany's dissolution in 1911. The Supreme Court ordered the American Tobacco Company broken up at the same time.

ROOSEVELT'S SECOND TERM

Roosevelt's energy and policies built a coalition of Progressive- and conservative-minded voters who assured his election in his own right in 1904. The Democrats, having twice lost with William Jennings Bryan, turned to Alton B. Parker, who as chief justice of New York's supreme court, had upheld labor's right to the closed shop (requiring that all employees be union members) and the state's right to limit hours of work. Despite Parker's liberal record, party leaders presented him as a safe conservative. Yet the effort to portray their Democratic candidate as more conservative than Roosevelt proved a futile gesture for the party that had twice nominated Bryan. Despite Roosevelt's trust-busting, most business leaders, according to the *New York Sun,* preferred the "impulsive candidate of the party of conservatism to the conservative candidate of the party which the business interests regard as permanently and dangerously impulsive."

An invincible popularity and the sheer force of his personality swept Roosevelt to an impressive victory of 7.6 million votes to Parker's 5.1 million, with 336 electoral votes for Roosevelt and 140 for Parker. Parker carried only the Solid South of the former Confederacy and two border states, Kentucky and Maryland. On election night, Roosevelt announced that he would not run again, a statement he later would regret.

LEGISLATIVE LEADERSHIP   Elected in his own right, Roosevelt approached his second term with heightened confidence and a stronger commitment to Progressive reform. In 1905 he devoted most of his annual message to the need for greater regulation and control of big business. The independent Roosevelt took aim at the railroads first.

Roosevelt asked Congress to extend the authority of the Interstate Commerce Commission to give it more effective control over railroad rates. He had to mobilize all the pressure and influence at his disposal to push through the bill introduced by Representative Peter Hepburn of Iowa. Enacted in 1906, the Hepburn Act gave the ICC power to set maximum freight rates. The commission no longer had to go to court to enforce its decisions. The Hepburn Act also extended the ICC's regulatory reach beyond railroads, to pipelines, freight companies, sleeping-car companies, bridges, and ferries.

On the very day after passage of the Hepburn Act, a growing movement for the regulation of meat packers, food processors, and makers of drugs and patent medicines reached fruition. Discontent with abuses in the processing of food and drugs had grown rapidly as a result of the muckrakers' disclosures. The chief chemist of the Agriculture Department, for example, supplied telling evidence of harmful additives used in the preparation of "embalmed meat" and other food products. Others reported on dangerous ingredients in some patent medicines.

Perhaps the most telling blow against such abuses was struck by Upton Sinclair's novel *The Jungle* (1906), which graphically portrayed the filthy conditions in Chicago's meatpacking industry. Roosevelt read *The Jungle*—and reacted quickly. He sent two federal agents to Chicago to investigate, and their report confirmed all that Sinclair had said. Soon Roosevelt and Congress were hammering out a bill to address the problems.

The Meat Industry

Pigs strung up along the hog-scraping rail at Armour's packing plant in Chicago, ca. 1909.

The Meat Inspection Act of 1906 required federal inspection of meats destined for interstate commerce and empowered officials in the Agriculture Department to impose sanitary standards. The Pure Food and Drug Act, enacted the same day, placed restrictions on the makers of prepared foods and patent medicines and forbade the manufacture, sale, or transportation of adulterated, misbranded, or harmful foods, drugs, and liquors.

With the achievements of 1903 and 1906, Theodore Roosevelt's campaign for regulatory legislation reached its chief goals and in the process moved the federal government a great distance from the laissez-faire policies that had prevailed before the turn of the century.

CONSERVATION   One of the most enduring legacies of Roosevelt's leadership was his energetic support for the emerging conservation movement. Roosevelt was the first president to challenge the long-standing myth of America's having inexhaustible natural resources. In fact, Roosevelt came to believe that conservation of natural resources was the "great material question of the day." He and other early conservationists were convinced that the tradition of freewheeling individual and corporate exploitation of the environment must be supplanted by the scientific management of the nation's natural resources for the *long-term* public benefit. "The things that will destroy America," he said, "are prosperity at any price, peace at any price, safety first instead of duty first, the love of soft living and the get-rich-quick theory of life."

After the Civil War a growing number of organizations and individuals had begun to oppose the unregulated exploitation of natural resources and sought to preserve wilderness areas. Timber companies stripped forests and moved on, leaving debris and erosion behind. Ranchers abused the native grasslands by overgrazing their herds, and farmers depleted the soil by excessive planting. Commercial hunters, trappers, and fishermen decimated game animals. Industries polluted streams, rivers, and air.

Such reckless abuse of the environment eventually generated intense concern and organized opposition. George Perkins Marsh, a Vermont diplomat and one of the first advocates of government conservation efforts, published a best-selling book, *Man and Nature* (1864), in which he observed that man was "everywhere a disturbing agent. Wherever he plants his foot, the harmonies of nature are turned to discords." Marsh urged Americans to intervene to protect the long-term health of the environment.

By the end of the nineteenth century, many Americans were heeding Marsh's warning. Just as reformers promoted the regulation of business and industry for the public welfare, activists championed efforts to manage and preserve the natural environment for future generations. Among the first promoters of resource conservation were ardent sport hunters and fishermen among the social elite (including Theodore Roosevelt), who worried that rapacious commercial hunters and trappers were killing game animals to the point of extermination. In 1886, for example, the sportsman-naturalist George Bird Grinnell, editor of *Forest and Stream,* founded the Audubon Society to protect wild birds from being decimated for their plumage. Two years later Grinnell, Roosevelt, and a dozen other recreational hunters formed the Boone and Crockett Club, named in honor of Daniel Boone and Davy Crockett, the legendary frontiersmen. The club's goal was to ensure that big-game animals and fish were protected for posterity, a goal shared by national monthly newspapers such as *American Sportsman, Forest and Stream,* and *Field and Stream.* By 1900 most states had enacted laws regulating game hunting and had created game refuges and wardens to enforce the new rules, much to the chagrin of local hunters, including Indians, who now were forced to abide by state laws designed to protect the interests of wealthy recreational hunters.

Along with industrialists concerned about water quality, Roosevelt and the sportsmen conservationists formed a powerful coalition promoting the rational government management of natural resources: rivers and streams, forests, minerals, and natural wonders. Those concerns, as well as the desire of railroad companies to transport tourists to destinations featuring majestic scenery, led the federal government to displace Indians in order to establish the 2-million-acre Yellowstone National Park in 1872 at the junction of the Montana, Wyoming, and Idaho territories (the National Park Service would be created in 1916 after other parks had been established). In 1881 Congress created a Division of Forestry (now the U.S. Forest Service) within the Department of the Interior. At the same time, New York State officials established a Forest Commission in 1885 to manage timber in the vast state-owned acreage of the Adirondack Mountains. Seven years later the legislature created the 5-million-acre Adirondack Park. The legislature also imposed restrictions on hunting in state forests and created a "forest police" to enforce the new regulations. As president, Theodore Roosevelt created fifty federal wildlife refuges, approved five new national parks, and designated as national monuments unfit for economic use such natural treasures as the Grand Canyon.

In 1898 Roosevelt, while serving as vice president, had endorsed the appointment of Gifford Pinchot, a close friend and the nation's first professional forester, as the head of the Division of Forestry. Pinchot and Roosevelt believed that conservation entailed the scientific management of natural resources to serve the public interest. In his first State of the Union address, delivered in 1901, Roosevelt explained that conservationists were concerned not simply with protecting national forests for their beauty; their foremost objective was utilitarian: to ensure that there would always be forests to "increase and sustain the resources of our country and the industries which depend upon them." Pinchot explained that the conservation movement sought to promote the "greatest good for the greatest number for the longest time."

Roosevelt and Pinchot championed the Progressive notion of efficiency and government regulation. They were not romantics about nature, nor were they ecologists; they did not understand the complex interdependence of trees, plants, insects, and animals, nor did they appreciate the environmental benefits of natural fires. Instead, they were utilitarian Progressives determined to ensure that entrepreneurs and industrialists exploited nature in appropriate ways. As Pinchot insisted, "The first principle of conservation is development." He sought to ensure the wisest "use of the natural resources now existing on this continent for the benefit of the people who live here now."

The president and Pinchot were especially concerned about the millions of acres of public land still owned by the government. Over the years vast tracts of federal land had been given away or sold at discount prices to large business enterprises. Roosevelt and Pinchot were determined to end such carelessness. They championed the systematic management of natural resources by government experts trained to promote the most efficient public use of the environment. This meant, for example, that commercial loggers must abide by Forestry regulations; otherwise there would be no trees for future generations to exploit. "Forestry," Pinchot explained, "is handling trees so that one crop follows another." He and Roosevelt opposed the mindless clear-cutting of entire forests for short-term profit and sought to restrict particular forests from any economic development. In fact, Roosevelt as president used the Forest Reserve Act (1891) to exclude from settlement or harvest some 172 million acres of federal timberland. Lumber companies were furious, but Roosevelt held firm. As he bristled, "I hate a man who skins the land."

FROM ROOSEVELT TO TAFT

Toward the end of his second term, Roosevelt crowed: "I have had a great time as president." But he was ready to move on, and he held to his 1904 decision not to run again. Instead he sought to have his secretary of war, William Howard Taft, replace him, and the Republican Convention ratified the choice on its first ballot in 1908. The Democrats, whose conservative strategy had backfired in 1904, decided to give William Jennings Bryan one more chance. Still vigorous at forty-eight, Bryan retained a faithful following, but once again it was not enough. In the end, voters opted for Roosevelt's chosen successor, leaving Bryan only the southern states plus Nebraska, Colorado, and Nevada. The real surprise of the election was the strong showing of the Socialist party candidate, labor hero Eugene V. Debs, who attracted over 400,000 votes, illustrating the mounting intensity of working-class unrest.

Born to a prominent Cincinnati family, Taft boasted more experience in public service than any other president since Martin Van Buren. After graduating second in his class at Yale, he had progressed through appointive offices, from assistant prosecutor, tax collector, and judge in Ohio to solicitor in the Justice Department, federal judge, governor general in the Philippines, and secretary of war. The presidency was the only elective office he ever held. Later he would be appointed chief justice of the Supreme Court (1921–1930), a job more suited to his temperament.

Taft never felt comfortable in the White House. He once observed that whenever someone said "Mr. President," he looked around for Roosevelt. The political dynamo in the family was his wife, Helen, who had wanted the presidency more than he. One of the major tragedies of Taft's presidency was

William Howard Taft

Speaking at Manassas, Virginia, in 1911.

that Helen Taft suffered a debilitating stroke soon after they entered the White House, and for most of his term she remained unable to serve as his political adviser.

TARIFF REFORM   A former student of the social Darwinist William Graham Sumner, Taft had absorbed the laissez-faire views of his mentor and therefore differed with orthodox Republican protectionism. Against Roosevelt's advice he had promised a tariff reduction during the campaign, and true to his word he called a special session of Congress to consider his proposal eleven days after his inauguration. But if Taft seemed bolder in pressing an issue that Roosevelt had skirted, he proved less adroit in shepherding legislation through Congress.

A reduced tariff passed the House with surprising ease. Before the Senate passed the bill, however, it made more than 800 changes, most of which raised tariff rates. Outraged by the obvious catering to special state and local interests, a group of ten Progressive Republicans joined the Democrats in an unsuccessful effort to defeat the bill. Taft at first agreed with them but then, fearful of a party split, backed the Republican majority and agreed to an imperfect bill. Temperamentally conservative, inhibited by scruples about interfering too much with the legislative process, Taft drifted into the orbit of the Republican Old Guard and quickly alienated the Progressive wing of his party, whom he tagged "assistant Democrats."

BALLINGER AND PINCHOT   In 1910 Taft's policies drove the wedge deeper between the conservative and Progressive Republican factions. What came to be known as the Ballinger-Pinchot controversy made Taft appear to be a less reliable custodian of Roosevelt's conservation policies than he actually was. The controversy arose after Taft's secretary of the interior, Richard A. Ballinger, turned over coal-rich federal lands in Alaska to a group of investor friends. Apparently without Ballinger's knowledge, this group had already agreed to sell part of the land to a mining syndicate. When Gifford Pinchot, chief of forestry, revealed the scam, Taft fired Pinchot for insubordination. A joint congressional investigation later exonerated Ballinger from all charges of fraud or corruption, but conservationist suspicions created such pressure that he resigned in 1911.

In firing Pinchot, Taft had acted according to the strictly legal view that his training had taught him to value. But the unsavory circumstances surrounding the incident tarnished Taft's public image. Events had conspired to cast the president in a conservative role at a time when Progressive sentiment was riding high. The result was a sharp setback in the congressional elections of 1910, first by the widespread defeat of pro-Taft candidates in the Republican primaries, then by the election of a Democratic majority in the House and enough Democrats in the Senate to allow Progressive Republicans to wield the balance of power.

TAFT AND ROOSEVELT   In 1910 Theodore Roosevelt returned from his extended travels abroad. With news accounts highlighting the Taft "betrayal" of Roosevelt's programs, the former president's followers urged him to take action. After hesitating for several months, Roosevelt again entered the political arena. At a speech in Kansas, he issued a stirring call for an array of new federal regulatory laws, a federal social-welfare program, and new measures of direct democracy, including the old Populist demands for the initiative, recall, and referendum on a nationwide basis. Thereafter, Roosevelt intensified his criticism of the Taft administration.

Equally critical of Taft was Senator Robert La Follette of Wisconsin, who in 1911 helped organize the National Progressive Republican League and soon became its leading candidate for the Republican party nomination. A militant reformer fiercely committed to greater government regulation of business and civil rights for all Americans, La Follette was more of a crusader than a politician. Complicating matters for the Republicans, Roosevelt officially threw his hat into the ring in 1912. Even though many of La Follette's supporters rushed to embrace the ex-president, the Wisconsin idealist stubbornly refused to give way. He felt that Roosevelt was not genuinely committed to the sweeping reforms necessary for a truly progressive America.

The rebuke implicit in Roosevelt's decision to run against Taft, his chosen successor, was in many ways undeserved. During Taft's first year in office, one political tempest after another had left his image irreparably damaged. The three years of solid achievement that followed could not restore its luster or reunite his divided party. Taft had at least attempted tariff reform, which

The Bull Moose Candidate in 1912

A skeptical view of Theodore Roosevelt.

Roosevelt had never dared. And in the end his administration set aside more public land for conservation in four years than Roosevelt's had in nearly eight and brought more anti-trust suits, by a score of eighty to twenty-five. Taft also established the Bureau of Mines and the federal Children's Bureau (1912). He supported both the Sixteenth Amendment (1913), which authorized a federal income tax, and the Seventeenth Amendment (1913), which provided for the popular election of senators instead of state legislatures appointing them.

Despite Taft's Progressive record, Roosevelt now hastened the demise of his former friend and lieutenant. Brusquely pushing aside La Follette's claim to the Progressive Republican mantle, Roosevelt won most of the Republican primaries in 1912, even in Taft's Ohio. But such popular support was no match for Taft's advantages as president and party leader. The Taft forces nominated their man at the national convention by the same steamroller tactics that had nominated Roosevelt in 1904. Outraged at such "naked theft," the Roosevelt delegates issued a call for a Progressive party convention, which assembled in Chicago on August 5. The new third-party supporters were a curious mixture of social-gospel clergymen and laymen, college presidents, professors, journalists, liberal businessmen, and social workers. Roosevelt told the group he felt "fit as a bull moose" in accepting their nomination. Now it was the Democrats' turn.

WOODROW WILSON'S PROGRESSIVISM

WILSON'S RISE   The emergence of Thomas Woodrow Wilson as the Democratic nominee in 1912 climaxed a political rise even more rapid than that of Grover Cleveland. In 1910, before his entering the race for election as governor of New Jersey, Wilson had been president of Princeton University but had never run for public office. Born in Staunton, Virginia, in 1856, the son of a stern Presbyterian minister, he had grown up in Georgia and the Carolinas during the Civil War and Reconstruction.

Driven by a sense of destiny and duty, Wilson was resolute, humane, rigid, and self-exacting to a fault. He nurtured a righteous commitment to principle, and his fits of tenacious inflexibility would prove to be his greatest weakness. Running as a reform candidate, Wilson was elected governor of New Jersey. After his election he pressured New Jersey lawmakers to enact a workers' compensation law, a corrupt-practices law, measures to regulate public utilities, and ballot reforms. Such strong leadership in a state known as the home of the trusts because of its lenient in-corporation laws brought Wilson to national attention.

In the spring of 1911, a group of southern Democrats in New York opened a Wilson presidential-campaign headquarters, and Wilson set forth on strenuous tours to all regions of the country, denouncing special privilege and political bossism. Wilson believed that the president of the country should be as active in directing legislation as in the administration and enforcement of laws. In calling for a strong presidency, Wilson expressed views closer to Roosevelt's than to Taft's. He likewise shared Roosevelt's belief that politicians should promote the general welfare rather than narrow special interests. And like Roosevelt he was critical of big business, organized labor, socialism, and agrarian radicalism.

Despite a fast start the Wilson campaign seemed headed for defeat by convention time, and House Speaker Champ Clark of Missouri seemed destined to win the nomination. On the fourteenth ballot, however, William Jennings Bryan, having decided that party conservatives were behind Clark, went over to Wilson; others followed, and Wilson captured the nomination.

THE ELECTION OF 1912   The 1912 presidential election involved four candidates: Wilson and Taft represented the two major parties, while Eugene Debs ran as a Socialist, and Roosevelt headed the Progressive party ticket. No sooner did the campaign open than Roosevelt's candidacy almost ended. While stepping into a car in Milwaukee, he was shot by a crazed man. The bullet went through his overcoat, spectacles case, and fifty-page speech, then fractured a rib before lodging just below his right lung. Roosevelt demanded that he be driven to the auditorium to deliver his speech. In a dramatic gesture he showed the audience his bloodstained shirt and punctured text and vowed, "It takes more than this to kill a bull moose."

With Taft and Debs trailing, the campaign settled down to a debate over the competing ideologies of the two front-runners: Roosevelt's New Nationalism and Wilson's New Freedom. The fuzzy ideas that Roosevelt fashioned into his New Nationalism had first been presented systematically in *The Promise of American Life* (1909), a widely influential book by Herbert Croly, a New York journalist. Its central point was that Progressives must give up Jeffersonian prejudices against big government and use the power of government to achieve democratic ends in the public interest.

Roosevelt's New Nationalism would enable government to promote social justice and enact such reforms as graduated income and inheritance taxes, workers' compensation for disabling injuries or illnesses, regulation of the labor of women and children, and a stronger Bureau of Corporations. These ideas and more went into the platform of his Progressive party, which called for a federal trade commission with sweeping authority over business and a tariff commission to set rates on a "scientific basis."

Before the end of his administration, Wilson would be swept into the current of such New Nationalism, too, but initially he adhered to the decentralizing anti-trust traditions of his party. Wilson relied heavily for his political stances on Louis D. Brandeis, a Progressive lawyer from Boston who focused Wilson's thought much as Croly had focused Roosevelt's. Brandeis's design for Wilson's New Freedom differed from Roosevelt's New Nationalism in its belief that the federal government should restore competition rather than regulate monopolies. This required eliminating all trusts, lowering tariffs, and breaking up the concentration of financial power on Wall Street. Brandeis and Wilson also dreamed of turning over most federal social programs to the states and cities. In this sense they saw the vigorous expansion of federal power as only a temporary necessity, not a permanent condition. Having restored competition and the diffusion of power and programs, the national government would revert to its aloof heritage. Roosevelt, who was convinced that both corporate concentration and an expanding federal government were permanent developments, dismissed the New Freedom as mere nostalgia.

The Republican schism between Taft and Roosevelt opened the way for Woodrow Wilson to win by 435 electoral votes to 88 for Roosevelt and 8 for Taft. The 1912 election was significant in a number of respects. First, it was a high-water mark for Progressivism. The candidates debated the basic issues in a campaign unique in its focus on vital alternatives and its highly philosophical tone. And the Socialist party, the left wing of Progressivism, polled over 900,000 votes for Eugene V. Debs, about 6 percent of the total vote, its highest proportion ever.

Second, the election gave the Democrats effective national power for the first time since the Civil War. For two years during the second administration of Grover Cleveland, 1893–1895, they had held the White House and majorities in both houses of Congress, but they had quickly fallen out of power during the severe depression of the 1890s. Now, under Wilson, the Democrats again held the presidency and enjoyed majorities in the House and Senate.

Wilson's Reforms

Woodrow Wilson campaigning from a railroad car.

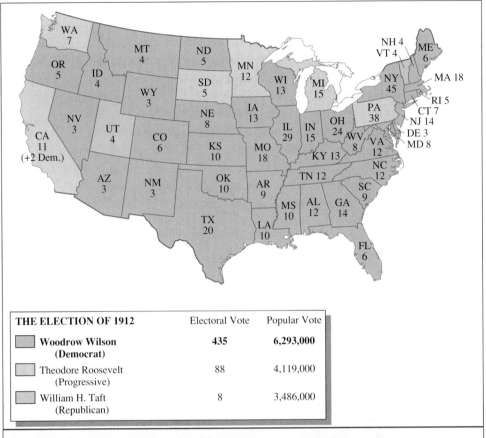

THE ELECTION OF 1912	Electoral Vote	Popular Vote
Woodrow Wilson (Democrat)	435	6,293,000
Theodore Roosevelt (Progressive)	88	4,119,000
William H. Taft (Republican)	8	3,486,000

Why was Taft so unpopular? How did the division between Roosevelt and Taft give Wilson the victory? Why was Wilson's victory in 1912 significant?

Third, Wilson's election brought southerners back into the orbit of national and international affairs in a significant way for the first time since the Civil War. Five of Wilson's ten cabinet members were born in the South, and William Jennings Bryan, the secretary of state, was an idol of the southern masses. At the president's right hand, and one of the most influential members of the Wilson circle, was "Colonel" Edward M. House of Texas. Wilson described House as "my second personality." Southern legislators, by virtue of their seniority, held most committee chairmanships. As a result, much of the Progressive legislation of the Wilson era would bear the names of the southerners who guided the bills through Congress.

WILSONIAN REFORM   Wilson's 1913 inaugural address vividly expressed the ideals of economic reform that inspired many Progressives. "We have been proud of our industrial achievements," he observed, "but we have not hitherto stopped thoughtfully enough to count the human cost." He promised specifically a lower tariff and a new banking system.

Whereas Roosevelt had been a strong president by force of personality, Wilson became a strong president by force of conviction. The president, he argued, must become the dynamic voice in national affairs. Wilson courted popular support, but he also courted members of Congress through personal contacts, invitations to the White House, and speeches to Congress. He used patronage power to reward friends and punish enemies. Though he might have acted through a bipartisan Progressive coalition, he chose instead to rely upon party loyalty.

THE TARIFF   The new president's leadership met its first test on the issue of tariff reform. Tariffs were originally needed to protect infant American industries from foreign competition. Now, however, Wilson believed, tariffs were being abused by corporations to suppress foreign competition and keep consumer prices high. He often claimed that the "tariff made the trusts," believing that tariffs had encouraged the growth of monopolies and degraded the political process by spawning armies of paid lobbyists who invaded Congress each year. In attacking high tariffs, Wilson sought to strike a blow for consumers and honest government. He acted quickly and boldly, summoning Congress to a special session and addressing it in person—the first president to do so since John Adams. In response to Wilson's request for lower tariff duties to promote competition, Congress voted for tariff reductions, with only four Democrats crossing the party line, and the bill passed the House easily. The opposition centered in the Senate, the traditional graveyard of tariff reform. In the end, Louisiana's two "sugar senators" were the only Democrats to vote against the bill. The Underwood-Simmons Tariff of 1913 reduced the overall average duty from about 37 percent to about 29 percent. The Wilson administration lowered tariff rates but raised revenues with the first federal income tax levied under the newly ratified Sixteenth Amendment.

THE FEDERAL RESERVE ACT   Before the new tariff had cleared the Senate, the administration proposed the first major banking and currency reform since the Civil War. Ever since Andrew Jackson had killed the second Bank of the United States in the 1830s, the nation had been without a central bank. Instead, the country's money supply was provided by hundreds of private banks. Such a decentralized system fostered instability and inefficiency. It also gave disproportionate influence to banks centered in New York City. By 1913 virtually everyone agreed that the banking system needed restructuring. Wilson told Congress that a federal banking system was needed to ensure that "the banks may be the instruments, not the masters, of business and of individual enterprise and initiative."

The Federal Reserve Act of 1913 created a new national banking system with twelve regional Federal Reserve banks, each owned by member banks in its district. All national banks became members of the new Federal Reserve system; state banks could join if they wished. Each member bank had to subscribe 6 percent of its capital to the Federal Reserve bank and deposit a portion of its reserve there.

This arrangement made it possible to expand both the money supply and bank credit in times of high business activity or as the level of borrowing increased. A Federal Reserve Board exercised general supervision over the activities of the member banks and adjusted interest rates to fight inflation or stimulate business. It is hard to exaggerate the significance of the passage of the Federal Reserve Act. Through Wilson's skillful leadership, Congress took a major step in providing the nation with a sound yet flexible currency system and at the same time helped decentralize the money supply.

ANTI-TRUST LAWS Wilson made trust-busting the central focus of the New Freedom because the concentration of economic power had continued to grow despite the Sherman Anti-Trust Act and the federal watchdog agency, the Bureau of Corporations. During the summer of 1914, Wilson decided to make a strong Federal Trade Commission (FTC) the cornerstone of his anti-trust program. Created in 1914, the five-member commission replaced Roosevelt's Bureau of Corporations and assumed new powers to

Reading the Death Warrant

Woodrow Wilson's plan for banking and currency reform spells the death of the "money trust," according to this cartoon.

define "unfair trade practices" and issue "cease-and-desist" orders when it found evidence of unfair competition.

Henry D. Clayton, an Alabama Democrat, drafted an Anti-trust Act, passed in 1914, that outlawed practices such as price discrimination (charging different customers different prices for the same goods); "tying" agreements, which limited the right of dealers to handle the products of competing manufacturers; and corporations' acquisition of stock in competing corporations. In every case, however, conservative forces in the Senate qualified these provisions by tacking on the weakening phrase "where the effect may be to substantially lessen competition" or words of similar effect. And conservative southern Democrats and northern Republicans amended the Clayton Anti-Trust Act to allow for broad judicial review of the FTC's decisions, further weakening its freedom of action. In accordance with the president's recommendation, however, corporate officials were made personally responsible for any violations.

Agrarian reformers, allied with organized labor won a stipulation in the Clayton Act declaring that farm and labor organizations were not per se unlawful combinations in restraint of trade. Injunctions in labor disputes, moreover, were not to be handed down by federal courts unless "necessary to prevent irreparable injury to property." President Wilson himself admitted that the act did little more than affirm the right of unions to exist by forbidding their dissolution for being in restraint of trade.

Administration of the anti-trust laws generally proved disappointing to the more vehement Progressives under Wilson. The Justice Department offered advice to business owners interested in arranging matters so as to avoid anti-trust prosecutions. The appointment of conservatives to the Interstate Commerce Commission and the Federal Reserve Board won plaudits from the business world and profoundly disappointed Progressives.

SOCIAL JUSTICE   Wilson had in fact never been a strong Progressive of the social-justice persuasion. He had carried out his promises to lower the tariff, reorganize the banking system, and strengthen the anti-trust laws, but he was not inclined to go much further. The New Freedom was now complete, he wrote late in 1914; the future would be "a time of healing because [it would be] a time of just dealing."

The sweep of events and the pressures of more far-reaching Progressives pushed Wilson beyond where he intended to go on some points. Yet Wilson retained several social blind spots. Although he endorsed state action for women's suffrage, he declined to support a federal suffrage amendment because his party platform had not done so. He withheld support from federal child-labor legislation because he regarded it as a state matter, and he opposed a bill providing federal loans for strapped farmers on the grounds that it was "unwise and unjustifiable to extend the credit of the government to a single class of the community."

PROGRESSIVISM FOR WHITES ONLY   Like many other Progressives, Woodrow Wilson showed little interest in the plight of African Americans. In fact, he shared many of the racist attitudes prevalent at the time. Although Wilson never joined the Ku Klux Klan and he denounced its "reign of terror," he sympathized with its motives of restoring white rule in the postwar South and relieving whites of the "ignorant and hostile" power of the black vote. As a student at Princeton, Wilson had detested the enfranchisement of blacks, arguing that Americans of Anglo-Saxon origin would always resist domination by "an ignorant and inferior race."

Later, as a politician, Wilson courted black voters, but he rarely consulted African-American leaders and repeatedly avoided opportunities to associate with them in public. Many of the southerners he appointed to his cabinet were uncompromising racists who systematically segregated the employees in their agencies. When black leaders protested these actions, Wilson replied that such racial segregation was intended to eliminate "the possibility of friction" in the federal workplace.

PROGRESSIVE RESURGENCE   The need to weld a winning coalition in 1916 pushed Wilson back on the road of reform. Progressive Democrats were restless, and after war broke out in Europe in 1914, further divisions in the party arose over defense and foreign policy. At the same time the Republicans were repairing their own rift. The Progressive party showed little staying power in the 1914 midterm election, and Roosevelt showed little will to preserve it. Most observers recognized that Wilson could gain reelection only by courting Progressives of all parties. In 1916 Wilson scored points with them when he nominated Louis D. Brandeis to the Supreme Court. Conservatives waged a vigorous battle against Brandeis, but Senate Progressives rallied to win confirmation of the social-justice champion as the first Jewish member of the Supreme Court.

Wilson, meanwhile, began to embrace the broad program of farm and labor reforms he had earlier spurned. The agricultural sector continued to suffer from a shortage of capital. To address the problem, Wilson supported a proposal to set up land banks to sponsor farm loans. With this boost the Federal Farm Loan Act became law in 1916. It created twelve Federal Land banks that paralleled the Federal Reserve banks and offered low-interest loans to farmers.

Farmers with automobiles had more than a passing interest as well in the Federal Highways Act of 1916, which provided dollar-matching contributions to states with highway departments that met certain federal standards. The measure authorized distribution of $75 million over five years and marked a sharp departure from Jacksonian opposition to internal improvements at federal expense, just as the Federal Reserve System departed from Jacksonian banking principles. Although the argument that highways were one of the nation's defense needs had weakened constitutional scruples against the act, the Highways Act still restricted support to "post roads" used for the delivery of mail. A renewal act in 1921 would mark the beginning of a systematic network of numbered U.S. highways.

The Progressive resurgence of 1916 broke the logjam on labor reforms as well. Advocates of child-labor legislation persuaded Wilson to overcome doubts about its constitutionality and sign the Keating-Owen Act, which excluded from interstate commerce goods manufactured by children under the age of fourteen. But the Supreme Court soon ruled it unconstitutional on the grounds that regulation of interstate commerce could not extend to the conditions of labor. On the other hand, the Supreme Court upheld the Adamson Act of 1916, which mandated the eight-hour workday for railroad workers.

In Wilson's first term, Progressive government reached its zenith. Progressivism had conquered the old premise that the government is best that governs least. Progressivism, a loose amalgam of agrarian, business, government, and social reform, amounted in the end to a movement for active government on behalf of the public interest.

LIMITS OF PROGRESSIVISM

Like all great historic movements, Progressivism contained elements of paradox and irony. Despite all the talk of greater democracy at the turn of the century, it was also the age of disenfranchisement of African Americans in the South and xenophobic reactions to "new" immigrants. The initiative and referendum, supposedly democratic reforms, proved subject to manipulation by well-financed publicity campaigns. And much of the public policy of the time came to be formulated by experts and members of appointed boards, not by broad segments of the population. There is a fine irony in the fact that the drive to increase the political role of ordinary people paralleled efforts to strengthen executive leadership and exalt professional expertise.

This age of much-ballyhooed efficiency and expertise, in business as well as government, generated a situation in which more and more key decisions were made by faceless policy makers.

Progressivism was largely a middle-class movement in which the poor and unorganized had little influence. It is surprising that a movement so dedicated to democratic rhetoric should experience so steady a decline in voter participation. In 1912, the year of the Bull Moose campaign, voting dropped off by almost 7 percent. The new politics of issues and charismatic leaders proved to be less effective in turning out voters than traditional party organizations and bosses had been. And by 1916 the optimism of an age that looked to infinite progress was already confronted by a vast slaughter. Europe had stumbled into war, and America would soon be drawn in. The twentieth century, which had dawned with such bright hopes, held in store episodes of unparalleled horror.

MAKING CONNECTIONS

- Many of the Progressive reforms described in this chapter—particularly business regulation and the growth of the welfare state—provided the seeds for the New Deal reforms of the 1930s, the focus of Chapter 28.

- After World War I, the Progressive impulse manifested itself in reforms such as Prohibition and women's suffrage, but the moralistic strain in Progressivism would take an ugly turn in the Red Scare and immigration restriction.

- The next chapter shows how Wilson's foreign policy in Latin America and Europe reflected the same moralism that guided his domestic policy.

FURTHER READING

A splendid analysis of Progressivism is John Whiteclay Chambers II's *The Tyranny of Change: America in the Progressive Era, 1890–1920* (1992). The evolution of government policy toward business is examined in Martin J. Sklar's *The Corporate Reconstruction of American Capitalism, 1890–1916: The Market, the Law, and Politics* (1988). Mina Carson's *Settlement Folk:*

Social Thought and the American Settlement Movement, 1885–1930 (1990) and Jack M. Holl's *Juvenile Reform in the Progressive Era: William R. George and the Junior Republic Movement* (1971) examine social problems in the cities. An excellent study of the role of women in Progressivism's emphasis on social justice is Kathryn Kish Sklar's *Florence Kelley and the Nation's Work: The Rise of Women's Political Culture, 1830–1900* (1995). On the tragic fire at the Triangle Shirtwaist Company, see David Von Drehle's *Triangle: The Fire That Changed America* (2003).

There is a rich body of scholarship focused on the conservation movement. See especially Rebecca Conard's *Places of Quiet Beauty: Parks, Preserves, and Environmentalism* (1997), Samuel P Hays's *Canservation and the Gospel of Efficiency: The Progressive Conservation Movement, 1890–1920* (1959), Karl Jacoby's *Crimes against Nature: Squatters, Poachers, Thieves, and the Hidden History of American Conservation* (2001), John F. Reiger's *American Sportsmen and the Origins of Conservation* (1975), and Ted Steinberg's *Down to Earth: Nature's Role in American History* (2002). Robert Kanigel's *The One Best Way: Frederick Winslow Taylor and the Enigma of Efficiency* (1997) highlights the role of efficiency in the Progressive Era.

On the pivotal election of 1912, see James Chace's *1912: Wilson, Roosevelt, Taft, and Debs—The Election That Changed the Country* (2004) Excellent biographies include Kathleen Dalton's *Theodore Roosevelt: A Strenuous Life* (2002) and H. W. Brands's *Woodrow Wilson* (2003). For banking developments, see Allan H. Meltzer's *A History of the Federal Reserve, vol. 1, 1913–1951* (2003).

25

AMERICA AND
THE GREAT WAR

FOCUS QUESTIONS

· How did Wilson's foreign policy lead to American involvement in Latin America?

· What were the causes of the Great War in Europe?

· Why did the United States enter the Great War, and what was its role?

· How did Wilson promote his peace plan?

· What were the consequences of the war?

To answer these questions and access additional review material, please visit www.wwnorton.com/studyspace.

Throughout the nineteenth century the United States reaped the benefits of its geographic distance from the wars that plagued Britain and Europe. The Atlantic Ocean provided a welcome buffer. During the early twentieth century, however, events combined to end the nation's comfortable isolation. Expanding world trade entwined American interests with the fate of Europe. In addition, the development of steam-powered ships and submarines meant that foreign navies could threaten American security. At the same time the election of Woodrow Wilson in 1912 brought to the White House a stern moralist determined to impose his standards for right conduct on renegade nations. This combination of circumstances made the outbreak of war in Europe in 1914 a profound crisis for the United States, a crisis that would transform the nation's role in international affairs.

Wilson and Foreign Affairs

Woodrow Wilson brought to the presidency little background in foreign relations. The former college professor admitted before taking office that "it would be an irony of fate if my administration had to deal chiefly with foreign affairs." But events in Latin America and Europe were to make the irony all too real. From the summer of 1914, when a catastrophic world war erupted in Europe, foreign relations increasingly preoccupied Wilson's attention.

Although lacking in international experience, Wilson did not lack ideas or convictions about global issues. He saw himself as a man of destiny who would help create a new world order governed by morality and idealism rather than crass national interests. Both he and Secretary of State William Jennings Bryan believed that America had a religious duty to promote democracy and moral progress in the world. How to foster such democratic idealism and self-determination abroad, however, remained a thorny issue, as Wilson soon discovered in responding to rapidly changing events on his own continent.

INTERVENTION IN MEXICO   Between 1876 and 1910, Porfirio Díaz had dominated Mexico. As military dictator he had suppressed opposition and showered favors upon wealthy allies and foreign investors, who piled up holdings in Mexican mines, petroleum, railroads, and agriculture. Eventually, however, the dictator's grip slipped, and in 1910 popular resentment boiled over in revolt. Revolutionary armies occupied Mexico City, and in 1911 Díaz fled.

The leader of the rebellion, Francisco Madero, a charismatic dreamer, proved unable to manage the tough customers attracted to the revolt by the scramble for power. In 1913 Madero's chief of staff, General Victoriano Huerta, assumed power, and Madero was murdered soon afterward. Confronted with a military dictatorship across the nation's southern border, Wilson challenged the legitimacy of Huerta's violent coup but expressed sympathy with a revolutionary faction led by Venustiano Carranza and began to put diplomatic pressure on Huerta. "I am going to teach the South American republics to elect good men," he vowed to a British diplomat.

Early in 1914 Wilson removed an embargo on arms to Mexico in order to help Carranza's forces, and he stationed warships off Veracruz (formerly Vera Cruz)

Pancho Villa (center)

Villa and his followers rebelled against the president of Mexico and antagonized the United States with violent attacks against "gringos."

to halt foreign arms shipments to Huerta. On April 9, 1914, several American sailors gathering supplies at Tampico strayed into a restricted area and were arrested. The Mexican officials quickly released them and sent an apology to the U.S. naval commander. There the incident might have ended, but the naval officer demanded that the Mexicans salute the American flag. Wilson backed him up and won from Congress authority to use force to bring Huerta to terms. Before the Tampico incident could be resolved, Wilson sent a naval force to Veracruz. U.S. marines and sailors went ashore on April 21, 1914, occupying the city at a cost of 19 American lives. At least 200 Mexicans were killed.

In Mexico the U.S. occupation aroused the opposition of all factions, and Huerta tried to rally support against a foreign invasion. At this juncture, Wilson accepted a mediation offer by the ABC powers (Argentina, Brazil, and Chile). In 1914 they proposed a withdrawal of U.S. forces, the removal of Huerta, and the installation of a provisional government. Huerta refused to step down, but the moral effect of the proposal, his isolation abroad, and the growing strength of his foes soon forced him to leave office. The Carranzistas entered Mexico City, and the Americans left Veracruz. Wilson's "missionary diplomacy" seemed to have worked. In 1915 the United States and several Latin American governments recognized Carranza as president of Mexico.

But no sooner had the Carranzistas taken power than they began to squabble among themselves for the spoils of office. The most incendiary confrontation occurred between Carranza and his foremost general, the popular Pancho Villa, a violent former bandit who shrewdly claimed to represent "the people" behind the revolution. Enraged by America's recognition of Carranza as the de facto leader of Mexico, Villa, in early 1916, led an attack that murdered sixteen American mining engineers. It was a deliberate attempt to provoke U.S. intervention, discredit Carranza, and build up Villa as an opponent of the "gringos." Two months later Villa's band of renegades entered Columbus, New Mexico, burned the town, and killed seventeen Americans.

A furious Woodrow Wilson sent General John J. Pershing and a force of 11,000 soldiers deep inside Mexico. For nearly a year, Pershing's troops chased Villa through northern Mexico, but missing their quarry, they returned home in 1917. Carranza then pressed his own war against the bandits and in 1917 put through a new liberal constitution. Mexico was establishing a more orderly government, almost in spite of Wilson's actions rather than because of them.

PROBLEMS IN LATIN AMERICA   In the Caribbean, Wilson found it as hard to act on his ideals as it had been in Mexico. During President Taft's term, from 1909 to 1913, the United States had practiced "dollar diplomacy." The policy had its origin in 1909, when Taft had personally cabled the Chinese government on behalf of American investors interested in forming an international consortium to finance railroad lines in China. In Latin America "dollar diplomacy" worked differently and with somewhat more success. The idea was to encourage American bankers to help prop up the finances of shaky Caribbean governments.

One of the first applications of Wilsonian idealism to foreign policy came when the president renounced dollar diplomacy. The government, he declared, was not supporting any "special groups or interests." Despite Wilson's public stand against using military force to back up American investments, however, he kept the marines in Nicaragua, where they had been sent by President Taft in 1912 to prevent renewed civil war. There they would stay almost continuously until 1933. In 1915 Wilson dispatched more marines, this time to Haiti, after the country experienced two successive revolutions and subsequent government disarray. The U.S. forces stayed until 1934. Turmoil in the Dominican Republic brought U.S. marines to that country in 1916, where they remained until 1924. The presence of U.S. military force in the region only worsened the already prevalent irritation at "Yankee imperialism."

AN UNEASY NEUTRALITY

During the summer of 1914, problems in Mexico and Central America loomed larger in Wilson's thinking than the gathering storm in Europe. When the thunderbolt of war struck Europe in August 1914, Americans were stunned. Whatever the troubles in Mexico, whatever disorders and interventions agitated other countries, it seemed unreal that civilized Europe could

WORLD WAR I IN EUROPE, 1914

- Central powers (Triple Alliance)
- Allied powers (Triple Entente)
- Neutral countries

How did the European system of alliances spread conflict across all of Europe? How was World War I different from previous wars? How did the war in Europe lead to ethnic tensions in the United States?

descend into such an orgy of destruction. But the assassination of the Austrian archduke Franz Ferdinand by a Serbian nationalist, Austria-Hungary's determination to punish Serbia, and Russia's military mobilization in sympathy with Slavic Serbia suddenly triggered a conflict between the two major European system of alliances: the Triple Alliance, or Central powers (Germany, Austria-Hungary, and Italy), and the Triple Entente, or Allied powers (France, Great Britain, and Russia). The sequence of decisions leading to World War I had unfolded with little thought to their consequences. When Russia refused to stop its army's mobilization, Germany, which backed Austria-Hungary, declared war on Russia on August 1, 1914, and on Russia's ally France two days later. Germany then invaded Belgium to get at France, which brought Great Britain into the war on August 4. Japan, eager to seize German holdings in the Pacific, declared war on August 23, and Turkey entered on the side of the Central powers on October 29. Although allied with the Central powers, Italy initially stayed out of the war and in 1915 struck a bargain by which it joined the Allied powers.

As the fighting unfolded, it quickly became apparent that the First World War was unlike any previous conflict in its scope and carnage. Machine guns, high-velocity rifles, aerial bombing, poison gas, flame throwers, land mines, long-range artillery, and armored tanks changed the nature of warfare and produced massive casualties and widespread destruction. Over 61 million men served in the armed forces on both sides, and over 9 million combatants were killed in action. Another 19 million were wounded.

The battlefields of World War I were surreal in their horrors. During the Battle of Verdun, in France, which lasted from February to December 1916, some 32 million artillery shells were fired—1,500 shells for every square meter of the battlefield. Such devastating firepower ravaged the landscape, turning farmland and forests into wasteland.

Trench warfare gave the First World War its lasting character. Most of the great battles of the war involved hundreds of thousands of men crawling out of their muddy, rat-infested trenches and then crossing a no-man's-land to attack enemy positions, only to be pushed back a day or a week later. The 475 miles of trenches provided protection and living space as well as a jumping-off point for large- and small-scale attacks by day or night. Life in the trenches was miserable. In addition to the dangers of enemy fire, soldiers were forced to deal with flooding and such diseases as trench fever and trench foot, which could lead to amputation. Lice and rats were constant companions. The stench was unbearable. Soldiers on both sides ate, slept, and fought among the dead and amid the reek of death.

Fighting on the Western Front

A gun crew firing on entrenched German positions, 1918.

INITIAL REACTIONS   As the trench war along the western front in Belgium and France stalemated, the casualties soared and pressure for U.S. intervention increased. On the first day of the Battle of the Somme, on July 1, 1916, 20,000 British soldiers were killed and 40,000 others were wounded—all in less than twenty-four hours. Shock in the United States over the sudden outbreak of war in Europe gave way to gratitude that an ocean stood between America and the killing fields. President Wilson repeatedly urged Americans to remain "neutral in thought as well as in action."

That was more easily said than done. More than one third of Americans were first- or second-generation immigrants who retained close ties to their old country. Among the 13 million immigrants from the countries at war, the 8 million German Americans were by far the largest group, and the 4 million Irish Americans harbored a deep-rooted enmity toward Britain. These groups instinctively leaned toward the Central powers.

Old-line Americans, largely of British origin, supported the Allied powers. Americans identified also with France, which had contributed to American culture and ideas and to independence itself. Britain and France, if not their ally Russia, seemed the custodians of democracy, while Germany seemed the embodiment of autocracy and militarism. If not a direct threat to the United States, Germany would pose at least a potential threat if it destroyed the balance of power in Europe. High officers of the U.S. government were pro-British in thought from the outset of the war.

A STRAINED NEUTRALITY At first the war in Europe brought a slump in American exports and the threat of a depression, but by the spring of 1915 the Allies' demand for food and military supplies generated an economic boom. France and Britain bought so much from the United States that they soon needed loans to continue making purchases. Early in the war, Secretary of State William Jennings Bryan declared that loans to any warring nation were "inconsistent with the true spirit of neutrality." Technically he was correct, but Wilson, for all his public professions of neutrality, was in fact determined to aid Great Britain. He quietly began approving credit to sustain trade with the Allies. American investors would advance over $2 billion to the Allies before the United States entered the war, and only $27 million to Germany.

The administration nevertheless clung to its official stance of neutrality through two and a half years of warfare in Europe and tried to uphold the traditions of "freedom of the seas," which had guided American policy since the Napoleonic Wars of the early nineteenth century. Trade on the high seas assumed a new importance as the German army's advance through Belgium toward Paris ground down into the stalemate of trench warfare. In a war of attrition, survival depended upon access to supplies, and in such a war British naval power counted for a great deal. In November 1914 the British declared the whole North Sea a war zone and sowed it with mines. Four months later they announced that they would seize ships carrying goods produced by or intended for their enemies.

NEUTRAL RIGHTS AND SUBMARINES British actions, including the blacklisting of companies that traded with the enemy and censoring the mail, raised some old issues of neutral rights, but the German reaction introduced an entirely new question. In the face of the British blockade, whereby only submarines could venture out to harass the enemy, the German government proclaimed a war zone around the British Isles. Enemy ships in those waters were liable to sinking by submarines, the Germans declared. As the chief advantage of U-boat (*Unterseeboot*) warfare was in surprise, it violated the established international procedure of stopping an enemy vessel on the high seas and providing for the safety of passengers and crew before sinking it. Since the British sometimes flew neutral flags as a ruse, neutral ships in this war zone would also be in danger.

The United States pronounced the German policy "an indefensible violation of neutral rights" and warned that Germany would be held to "strict accountability" for any destruction of American lives and property. Then, on May 7, 1915, a German U-boat torpedoed the passenger liner *Lusitania*, which exploded and sank within eighteen minutes. Before the ship's departure from New York, bound for Liverpool, the German embassy had published warnings in American newspapers against travel to the war zone, but 128 Americans were nevertheless among the 1,198 persons lost.

Americans were outraged. To quiet the uproar, Wilson urged patience: "There is such a thing as a man being too proud to fight. There is such a thing as a nation being so right that it does not need to convince others by force that it is right." But his previous demand for "strict accountability" forced him to make a stronger response. On May 13 Secretary of State Bryan reluctantly signed a note demanding that the Germans abandon unrestricted submarine warfare, disavow the sinking of the *Lusitania*, and pay reparations. The Germans responded that the passenger ship was armed (which it was not) and carried a secret cargo of small arms and ammunition (which it did). A second note on June 9 repeated American demands in stronger terms. Bryan, unwilling to risk war over the issue, resigned in protest. His successor, Robert Lansing, signed the note.

In response to the uproar over the *Lusitania*, the German government had secretly ordered U-boat captains to avoid sinking large passenger vessels. When, despite the order, two American lives were lost in the sinking of the New York-bound British liner *Arabic*, the German government declared on September 1, 1915, "Liners will not be sunk by our submarines without

The *Lusitania*

Americans were outraged when a German torpedo sank the *Lusitania* on May 7, 1915.

warning and without safety of the lives of non-combatants, provided that the liners do not try to escape or offer resistance." With this *Arabic* pledge, Wilson's resolute stand seemed to have won a victory for his policy.

THE DEBATE OVER PREPAREDNESS   The *Lusitania* incident and, more generally, the quarrels over protecting neutral commerce during wartime contributed to a growing demand for a stronger U.S. army and navy. After the *Lusitania* sinking the outcry from preparedness advocates grew into a clamor. In his annual message in 1915, Wilson alerted Congress to his plans for war preparedness. The response was far from unanimous. Progressives and pacifists, especially in the rural South and the West, opposed military expansion.

Wilson eventually accepted a compromise between advocates of an expanded force under federal control and advocates of a traditional citizen army. The National Defense Act of 1916 expanded the regular army from 90,000 to 175,000 and permitted a gradual enlargement to 223,000. It also increased the national guard to 440,000. The Naval Construction Act of 1916 authorized between $500 and $600 million for a three-year shipbuilding program.

Forced to relent on military preparedness, progressive opponents of a buildup insisted that the financial burden should rest upon the wealthy people they held responsible for pushing the nation toward war. The income tax became their weapon. Supported by a groundswell of popular support, they wrote into the Revenue Act of 1916 changes that doubled the basic income tax from 1 to 2 percent, lifted the surtax on income over $2 million to 13 percent, added an estate tax graduated up to a maximum of 10 percent, levied a 12.5 percent tax on gross receipts of munitions makers, and added a new tax on corporations. The new taxes amounted to the most clear-cut victory of radical Progressives in the entire Wilson period, a victory that Wilson supported in preparation for the upcoming presidential election.

THE ELECTION OF 1916   As the 1916 election approached, Republicans hoped to regain their normal electoral majority, and Theodore Roosevelt hoped to be their leader again. But in 1912 he had committed the deadly sin of bolting his party, and what was more his eagerness for the United States to enter the war scared many voters. Needing somebody who would draw Bull Moose Progressives back into the fold, the Republican regulars turned to Justice Charles Evans Hughes, a Progressive governor of New York from 1907 to 1910. On the Supreme Court since then, he had neither endorsed a candidate in 1912 nor spoken out on foreign policy.

The Democrats, as expected, chose Wilson once again and in their platform endorsed a program of social legislation, neutrality regarding the war

Peace with Honor

Woodrow Wilson's policies of neutrality proved popular in the 1916 campaign.

in Europe, and reasonable military preparedness. The party further commended women's suffrage to the states and pledged support for a postwar league of nations to enforce peace with collective-security measures against aggressors. The Democrats' most popular issue was a pledge to keep the nation out of the war in Europe. The peace theme, refined in the slogan "He kept us out of war," became the rallying cry of the Wilson campaign.

The candidates in the 1916 presidential election were remarkably similar. Both Wilson and Hughes were the sons of preachers; both were attorneys and former professors; both had been Progressive governors; both were known for their pristine integrity. Theodore Roosevelt highlighted the similarities between them when he called the bearded Hughes a "whiskered Wilson." Wilson, however, proved to be the better campaigner. In the end, Wilson's twin pledges of peace and Progressivism, a unique combination of issues forged in the legislative and diplomatic crucibles of 1916, brought victory. The final vote showed a Democratic sweep of the Far West and the South, enough for victory in the Electoral College, by 277 to 254, and in the popular vote, by 9 million to 8.5 million. Wilson also carried many social-justice Progressives who in 1912 had supported the Bull Moose campaign.

LAST EFFORTS FOR PEACE   Immediately after the election, Wilson offered to mediate an end to the European war, but neither side was willing to abandon its major war aims. Wilson then decided to make one more appeal, in the hope that public opinion would force the hands of the warring governments. Speaking before the Senate, he asserted that this would have to be a "peace without victory," for only a "peace among equals" could endure.

Although Wilson did not know it, he was already too late. Exactly two weeks before he spoke, German military leaders had decided to wage unrestricted submarine warfare on all shipping in the Atlantic. Faced with weakening resources in a war of attrition, the Germans took the calculated risk of provoking American anger in the hope of scoring a quick knockout. On January 31, 1917, Germany announced the new policy, effective the next day: all vessels would be sunk without warning.

On February 3, 1917, Wilson informed a joint session of Congress that the United States had broken diplomatic relations with the German government. He added that he still did not believe the Germans would do what they said they felt at liberty to do—only overt acts would persuade him that they intended to sink neutral ships. In case of such acts, he would take measures to protect American seamen and citizens.

Then, on March 1, news of the so-called Zimmermann telegram broke in the American press. The British had intercepted and decoded an important message from German foreign secretary Arthur Zimmermann to his ambassador in Mexico. The note instructed the envoy to offer an alliance and financial aid to Mexico in case of war between the United States and Germany. In return for diversionary action against the United States, Mexico would recover "the lost territory in Texas, New Mexico, and Arizona." All this was contingent on war with the United States, but an electrified public read in it an aggressive intent. Later in March another bombshell burst when a revolution overthrew Russia's czarist government and established the provisional government of a Russian republic. The fall of the czarist autocracy allowed Americans the illusion that all the major Allied powers were now fighting for constitutional democracy. Not until November 1917 was that illusion shattered, when the Bolsheviks, led by Vladimir Lenin, seized power in Russia and began establishing a Communist dictatorship.

AMERICA'S ENTRY INTO THE WAR

In March 1917 German submarines did the unthinkable: they sank five American merchant vessels. On March 20 Wilson's cabinet unanimously endorsed a declaration of war, and the following day the president called a special session of Congress. When it met on April 2, Wilson asked Congress to recognize the war that imperial Germany was already waging against the United States. The German government had revealed itself as a natural foe of liberty, and Wilson argued in the rhetoric of Progressivism, "the world must be made safe for democracy." The war resolution passed the Senate by a vote of 82 to 6 on April 4. The House concurred, 373 to 50, and Wilson signed the measure on April 6.

How had matters come to this, less than three years after Wilson's proclamation of neutrality? Prominent among the various explanations of America's entrance into the war were the effects of British propaganda and America's deep involvement in trade with the Allies, which some observers then and later credited to the intrigues of war profiteers and munitions makers. Some Americans thought German domination of Europe would be a threat to U.S. security, especially if it meant the destruction or capture of the British navy. Whatever the influence of such factors, they likely would not have been decisive without the issue of submarine warfare. This issue need not have become decisive, either, since such neutrals as Norway, Sweden, and Denmark took relatively heavier losses yet stayed out of the war. But once Wilson had taken a stand for the traditional rights of neutrals and noncombatants, he was to some extent at the mercy of decisions by the German high command.

AMERICA'S EARLY ROLE   The scope of America's role in the European war remained unclear for a time. Few on either side of the Atlantic expected more from the United States than a token military effort. Despite Congress's preparedness measures, the army remained small and untested. The navy also was largely undeveloped. But the U.S. Navy made a major contribution when it persuaded the Allies to adopt a convoy system of escorting merchant ships in groups, resulting in an impressive decrease in Allied shipping losses to German submarines.

Within a month of America's declaration of war, the British and French requested money for supplies, a request Congress had anticipated in the Liberty Loan Act, which added $5 billion to the national debt in "liberty bonds." Of this amount, $3 billion could be lent to the Allied powers. The United States was also willing to furnish naval support, financial credits, supplies, and munitions. But to raise and train a large army, equip it, and send it across a submarine-infested ocean seemed out of the question.

The United States agreed to send a token military force to bolster Anglo-French morale, and on June 26, 1917, the first American contingent, about 14,500 men commanded by General John J. Pershing, began to disembark

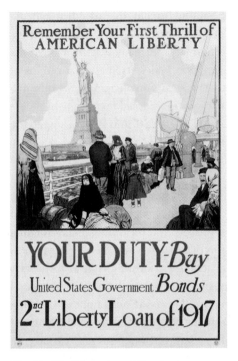

Remember Your First Thrill of
AMERICAN LIBERTY

YOUR DUTY-*Buy*
United States Government *Bonds*
2nd Liberty Loan of 1917

The Thrill of American Liberty

This Liberty Loan poster urges immigrants to do their duty for their new country by buying government bonds.

on the French coast. After reaching Paris, Pershing decided that the war-weary Allies would be unable to mount an offensive by themselves. He therefore requested that Wilson send 1 million American troops by the following spring, and the president obliged.

When the United States entered the war, the combined strength of the regular army and national guard was only 379,000; at the end it would be 3.7 million. The need for such large numbers of troops converted Wilson to the idea of conscription. Under the Selective Service Act of May 18, 1917, all men aged twenty-one to thirty (later, eighteen to forty-five) had to register to be drafted for military service. By July 1917, when the first lottery was held to determine who would actually be drafted to fight in the war, almost 24 million men were registered. In the course of the war, about 2 million Americans crossed the Atlantic, and about 1.4 million of them saw some combat.

MOBILIZING A NATION   Complete economic mobilization on the home front was also necessary to conduct the war efficiently. In 1916 Congress had created a Council of National Defense, which in turn set up other wartime agencies. The U.S. Shipping Board, organized in 1917, within two years was constructing more than forty steel and ninety wooden ships monthly. In 1917 Congress created a Food Administration, headed by Herbert Hoover, a future president who sought to raise crop production while reducing civilian use of foodstuffs. "Food will win the war" was the slogan. Hoover directed a propaganda campaign that "Hooverized" the country with "meatless Tuesdays," "wheatless Wednesdays," "porkless Saturdays," the planting of victory gardens, and the creative use of leftovers. The Fuel Administration introduced the country to daylight saving time and "heatless Mondays" to save fuel.

The War Industries Board (WIB), established in 1917, soon became the most important of all the mobilization agencies. Wilson summoned Bernard Baruch, a brilliant Wall Street investor, to head the board, giving him a virtual dictatorship over the economy. The WIB could allocate raw materials, tell manufacturers what to produce, order construction of new plants, and with presidential approval, fix prices.

A NEW LABOR FORCE   The closing off of foreign immigration from Europe during the war and the movement of almost 4 million men into the armed services created a labor shortage. To meet it, women, African Americans, and other ethnic minorities were encouraged to enter industries and agricultural activities heretofore dominated by white men. Northern businesses sent recruiting agents into the Deep South to find workers for their factories and mills, and over 400,000 southern blacks began the Great Migration northward during the war years, a mass movement that continued unabated through the 1920s. Mexican Americans followed the same migratory pattern. Recruiting agents and newspaper editors portrayed the North as the "land of promise" for southern blacks suffering from their region's depressed agricultural economy and rising racial intimidation and violence. By 1930 the number of African Americans living in the North was triple that of 1910.

But the newcomers were not always welcomed above the Mason-Dixon line. Many native white workers resented the new arrivals, and racial tensions sparked riots in cities across the country. In 1917 over forty African Americans and nine whites were killed during a riot over employment in a defense plant in East St. Louis. Two years later the toll of a Chicago race riot was nearly as high, with twenty-three African Americans and fifteen whites left dead. In these and other incidents of racial violence, the pattern was the same: whites angered by the influx of blacks into their communities would seize upon an incident as an excuse to rampage through black neighborhoods, killing, burning, and looting while white policemen looked the other way or encouraged the mobs.

For women, American intervention in World War I had more positive effects. Initially women supported the war effort in traditional ways. They helped organize war-bond and war-relief drives, conserved foodstuffs and war-related materials, supported the Red Cross, and joined the army nurse corps. But as the scope of the war widened, both government and industry sought to mobilize women workers for service on farms, loading docks, and railway crews, as well as in armaments industries, machine shops, steel and lumber mills, and chemical plants. Many women leaders saw such opportunities as a breakthrough. "At last, after centuries of disabilities and discrimination," said a speaker at a Women's Trade Union League meeting in 1917, "women are coming into the labor [force] and festival of life on equal terms with men."

In fact, however, war-generated changes in female employment were limited and brief. About 1 million women participated in "war work," but they usually were young, single, and already working outside the home. Most returned to their previous jobs once the war ended. In fact, male-dominated unions encouraged women to revert to their stereotypical domestic roles after the war. The Central Federated Union of New York baldly insisted that "the same patriotism which induced women to enter industry during the war should induce them to vacate their positions after the war." The anticipated gains of women in the workforce failed to materialize. In fact, in 1920 the 8.5 million working women made up a smaller percentage of the labor force than women had in 1910. Still, one tangible result of women's contributions to the war effort was Woodrow Wilson's decision to endorse women's suffrage. In the fall of 1918, he told the Senate that giving women the vote was "vital to the winning of the war."

WAR PROPAGANDA   The exigencies of winning the war also led the government to mobilize public opinion. On April 14, 1917, eight days after the declaration of war, Wilson established the Committee on Public Information. Its executive director, George Creel, a Denver journalist, sold Wilson on the idea that the best approach to influencing public opinion was "expression, not repression"—propaganda instead of censorship. Creel organized a propaganda machine to convey the Allies' war aims to the people and, above all, to the enemy, where it might encourage public pressure to end the fighting.

CIVIL LIBERTIES   By arousing public opinion to such a frenzy, the war effort channeled the zeal of Progressivism into grotesque campaigns of "Americanism" and witch hunting. Wilson had foreseen these consequences. "Once lead this people into war," he told a newspaper editor, "and they'll forget there ever was such a thing as tolerance." Popular prejudice equated anything German with disloyalty. Schools even dropped German-language courses.

While mobs hunted spies and chased rumors, the federal government stalked bigger game, with results often as absurd. The Espionage and Sedition Acts of 1917 and 1918 effectively outlawed criticism of government leaders and war policies. These laws led to more than 1,500 prosecutions and 1,000 convictions. Such repression disillusioned many Progressives. Senator Robert La Follette declared that those engaged in such a "witch-hunt" were trying "to throw the country into a state of terror, to coerce public opinion, stifle criticism, suppress discussion of the issues of the war, and put a quietus on all opposition. It is time for the American people to assert and maintain their rights."

The impact of these acts fell with most severity upon radicals. Eugene V. Debs, who had polled over 900,000 votes as the Socialist candidate for president in 1912, was arrested and eventually sentenced to ten years in prison for encouraging draft resistance. In 1920, still in jail, he polled nearly 1 million votes for president.

In an important decision just after the war, the Supreme Court upheld the Espionage and Sedition Acts. *Schenck v. United States* (1919) sustained the conviction of a man for circulating anti-draft leaflets among members of the armed forces. In this case, Justice Oliver Wendell Holmes observed, "Free speech would not protect a man in falsely shouting fire in a theater, and causing a panic." The Sedition Act applied where there was "a clear and present danger" that free speech in wartime might create evils Congress had a right to prevent.

"THE DECISIVE POWER"

American troops played little more than a token role in the European fighting until the end of 1917, when the Allied position turned desperate. In October the Italian lines collapsed in the face of the Austrian offensive. In November, having suffered some 5.5 million casualties and widespread food and ammunition shortages, the Russian provisional republican government succumbed to a revolution led by Vladimir Lenin and his Bolshevik party, which promised the Russian people "peace, land, and bread." With German troops then deep in Russian territory and with armies of "White" Russians organizing to resist the Bolsheviks, Lenin concluded a separate peace with the Germans in the Treaty of Brest-Litovsk (March 3, 1918). The Central powers were then free to concentrate their forces on the western front, and the American war effort became a "race for France," to restore the balance of strength in that arena. French premier Georges Clemenceau appealed to the Americans to accelerate their mobilization. "A terrible blow is imminent," he predicted to an American journalist. "Tell your Americans to come quickly."

THE WESTERN FRONT   On March 21, 1918, Clemenceau's prediction came true when the Germans began the first of several offensives in France and Belgium to try to end the war before the Americans arrived in force. On May 27 the Germans began their next drive along the Aisne River, took Soissons, and pushed on to the Marne River along a forty-mile front. By May

America at War

U.S. soldiers fire an artillery gun in Argonne, France.

1918 there were 1 million fresh U.S. troops in Europe, and for the first time they made a difference. In a counterattack, American forces retook Cantigny on May 28 and held it. During early June a marine brigade blocked the Germans at Belleau Wood, and army troops took Vaux and opposed the Germans at Château-Thierry. Though these actions had limited military significance, their effect on Allied morale was immense. Each was a solid American success, and together they reinforced General Pershing's demand for a separate U.S. army.

Before that could come to pass, the Second Battle of the Marne erupted on July 15, 1918, and proved to be the turning point in the western campaign. On both sides of Reims, the Germans assaulted the French lines. Within three days, however, they had stalled, and the Allies began to roll the German front back into Belgium. On September 12 an army of more than 500,000 staged the first strictly American offensive of the war, aimed at German forces at St.-Mihiel. Within three days the Germans had pulled back. Two weeks later the massive Meuse-Argonne offensive employed U.S. divisions in a drive toward the rail center at Sedan, which supplied the entire German front. The largest American action of the war resulted in 117,000 American casualties, including 26,000 dead. All along the front from Sedan to Flan-

**WORLD WAR I,
THE WESTERN FRONT, 1918**

- - - Western front, March 1918
—— German offensive, spring 1918
→ Allied counteroffensive
—— Western front, November 1918

Why was the war on the western front a stalemate for most of World War I? What was the effect of the arrival of the American troops? Why was the Second Battle of the Marne the turning point of the war?

ders, the Germans were in retreat. "America," wrote a German commander, "thus became the decisive power in the war."

Meanwhile, in an effort to prevent Allied supplies stockpiled in Russia from falling into German hands and to encourage the counter-revolutionary Russian "Whites" in their civil war against the "Reds," fourteen Allied nations sent troops into eastern Russia. On August 2, 1918, some 8,000 Americans joined the expedition and remained on Russian soil until April 1920. But the Allied intervention in Russia was a colossal failure. The Bolsheviks were able to consolidate their power and defeat the Whites. Lenin and the Soviets never forgave the West for attempting to thwart their revolution.

THE FOURTEEN POINTS   As the conflict in Europe was ending, neither the Allies nor the Central powers, despite Wilson's prodding, had stated openly what they hoped to gain through the bloodletting. Wilson insisted that the Americans had no selfish ends. "We desire no conquest, no dominion," he stressed in his war message. Unfortunately for his idealistic purpose, the Bolsheviks later published copies of secret treaties in which the Allies had promised territorial gains in order to win Italy, Romania, and Greece to their side. When an Interallied Conference in Paris late in 1917 failed to agree on a statement of aims, Wilson formulated his own.

With advice from a panel of experts, Wilson drew up a peace plan that would be labeled the Fourteen Points. These he delivered to a joint session of Congress on January 8, 1918, "as the only possible program" for peace. The first five points called for open diplomacy, freedom of the seas, removal of trade barriers, armaments reduction, and an impartial adjustment of colonial claims based upon the interests of the populations involved. Most of the remaining points called upon the Central powers to evacuate occupied lands and allow self-determination for various nationalities, a crucial principle for Wilson. Point 14, the capstone in Wilson's thinking, called for the formation of a "league" of nations to guarantee the independence and territorial integrity of all countries, great and small.

Wilson sincerely believed in the Fourteen Points, but they also served important political purposes. One of their aims was to keep Russia in the war by a more liberal statement of purposes—a vain hope, as it turned out. Another was to reassure the Allied peoples that they were involved in a noble cause. A third was to drive a wedge between the governments of the Central powers and their people by offering a reasonable peace. But the chaos into which Central Europe descended in 1918, as Germany and Austria-Hungary verged on starvation and experienced socialist uprisings, took matters out of Wilson's hands.

THE END OF THE WAR   On September 29, 1918, German general Erich Ludendorff advised his government to seek the best peace terms possible. On October 3 a new chancellor made the first German overtures for peace on the basis of the Fourteen Points. The Allies, after a month of diplomatic fencing, accepted the Fourteen Points as a basis of peace but with two significant reservations: the right to discuss freedom of the seas further and the demand for reparations (financial compensation to the victors) for war damages.

Meanwhile, German morale plummeted, culminating in a naval mutiny. Germany's allies, Bulgaria, Turkey, and Austria-Hungary, dropped out of the war during the early fall of 1918. On November 9 the kaiser, head of the German Empire, abdicated, and a German republic was proclaimed. Two days later, on November 11, 1918, an armistice was signed, ceasing the hostilities. Under the armistice the Germans agreed to evacuate occupied territories, pull back behind the Rhine River, and surrender their navy, railroad equipment, and other matériel. The Germans were assured that the Fourteen Points would be the basis of the peace conference.

During its nineteen months of participation in the war, the United States saw 126,000 of its servicemen killed. Germany's war dead totaled over 2 million, including civilians; France lost 1,375,000 combatants, the United Kingdom had 703,000 military deaths, and Russia lost 1.7 million. The new Europe emerging from the conflagration would be much different: more violent, more polarized, more cynical, less sure of itself, and less capable of decisive action. The United States, for good or ill, would be sucked into the vacuum of power created by the destructiveness of the Great War.

THE FIGHT FOR PEACE

DOMESTIC UNREST Woodrow Wilson made a fateful decision to attend the Paris Peace Conference, which convened on January 18, 1919, and would last almost six months. A president had never left the country for so long, and doing so dramatized all the more Wilson's messianic vision and his desire to ensure his goal of a lasting peace. From one viewpoint it was a shrewd move, for his prestige and determination made a difference in Paris. But during his prolonged trip abroad, he lost touch with political developments at home, where his political coalition was already unraveling under the pressures of wartime discontent. Western farmers complained about the government's control of wheat prices while eastern business leaders chafed at revenue policies designed, according to the *New York Sun*, "to pay for the war out of taxes raised north of the Mason and Dixon Line." Organized labor, despite real gains, groused about inflation and the problems of reconversion to a peacetime economy.

In the midterm elections of 1918, Wilson made matters worse when he defied his advisers and urged voters to elect a Democratic Congress to support his foreign policies. Republicans, who for the most part had supported his war measures, took affront. So, too, did many voters. In elections held a week before the armistice, the Democrats lost control of both houses of

Congress. With an opposition majority in the new Congress, Wilson further weakened his standing by failing to include a single prominent Republican in the American delegation headed for Paris and the treaty negotiations. Former President Taft suggested that Wilson's real intention in going to Paris was "to hog the whole show."

When Wilson reached Europe in December 1918, enthusiastic demonstrations greeted him in Paris. At the conference table, however, he had to deal with some tough-minded statesmen who did not share his utopian zeal. The Paris conference included delegates from all countries that had declared war or broken diplomatic relations with Germany. But it was dominated by the Big Four: the prime ministers of Britain, France, and Italy and the president of the United States. British prime minister David Lloyd George was a gifted politician fresh from electoral victory following a campaign whose slogan declared, "Hang the kaiser." Italy's prime minister, Vittorio Orlando, was there to pick up the spoils promised his country in the secret Treaty of London (1915). French premier Georges Clemenceau, a stern realist, insisted on severe measures to weaken Germany and guarantee French security.

The Big Four

Woodrow Wilson (second from left) with Georges Clemenceau of France and Arthur Balfour of Great Britain at the Paris Peace Conference.

THE LEAGUE OF NATIONS   Woodrow Wilson insisted that his cherished League of Nations come first in the conference and in the treaty. Whatever compromises he might have to make regarding territorial boundaries and financial claims, whatever mistakes might result, Wilson believed that a league of nations committed to collective security would maintain international stability.

Wilson presided over the commission to draft a league charter. Article Ten of the charter, which he called "the heart of the League," pledged members to consult on military and economic sanctions against aggressors. The use of armed force would be a last resort. The League structure would allow each member an equal voice in the Assembly; the Big Five (Britain, France, Italy, Japan, and the United States) and four rotating members would make up the Council; the administrative staff, in Geneva, would make up the Secretariat; and a Permanent Court of International Justice (set up in 1921 and usually called the World Court) could "hear and determine any dispute of an international character."

On February 14, 1919, Wilson delivered the finished draft of the League charter and departed the next day for a month-long visit home. Already he faced rumblings of opposition. Republican Henry Cabot Lodge, chairman of the Senate Foreign Relations Committee, claimed that the League's covenant was unacceptable. His statement of March 4 bore the signatures of thirty-nine Republican senators or senators-elect, more than enough to block ratification.

TERRITORY AND REPARATIONS   Back in Paris, Wilson grudgingly acceded to French demands for territorial concessions and reparations from Germany. The Allied statesmen also agreed that the Allies would occupy a demilitarized German Rhineland for fifteen years and that the League of Nations would administer Germany's coal-rich Saar Basin. France could use Saar mines for fifteen years, after which the region's voters would determine whether to join Germany or France.

In other territorial matters, Wilson had to compromise his principle of national self-determination. There was in fact no way to make Europe's boundaries correspond to ethnic divisions because mixed populations were scattered through Central Europe. In some areas, moreover, national self-determination yielded to other interests, such as trade and defense. The result was a reorganized map of Central Europe in which portions of the former Austro-Hungarian Empire became independent, most notably Czechoslovakia and Yugoslavia, and portions were attached to Poland, Romania, and Italy.

EUROPE AFTER THE TREATY
OF VERSAILLES, 1918

········ 1914 boundaries

[ ] New nations

[ ] Plebiscite areas

[ ] Occupied area

Why was self-determination difficult for states in Central Europe? How did territorial concessions weaken Germany? Why might territorial changes like the creation of the Polish Corridor or the concession of the Sudetenland to Czechoslovakia have created problems in the future?

Ethnic and nationalist tensions continued and would contribute to the crisis that culminated in World War II.

The discussion of reparations was among the longest and most bitter at the conference. Despite a pre-armistice agreement that Germany would be liable only for civilian damages, Clemenceau and Lloyd George proposed reparations for the entire cost of the war. On this point, Wilson made perhaps his most fateful concessions. He agreed to a clause in the treaty by which Germany accepted responsibility for starting the war and for its entire cost. The "war guilt" clause offended Germans and provided a source of persistent bitterness upon which Adolf Hitler would later capitalize.

On May 7, 1919, the victorious powers presented the treaty to the German delegates, who returned three weeks later with 443 pages of criticism protesting that the terms violated the Fourteen Points. A few small changes were made, but when the Germans still refused to sign, the French prepared to move their army across the Rhine River. Finally, on June 28, 1919, the Germans gave up and signed the treaty at Versailles.

WILSON'S LOSS AT HOME   The force of Woodrow Wilson's idealism struck deep, and on July 8, 1919, he returned home with the Versailles Treaty amid a great clamor of popular support. One third of the state legislatures had endorsed the League, as had thirty-three of the nation's forty-eight governors. Wilson called upon the Senate to accept the "great duty" of ratifying the treaty.

Senator Henry Cabot Lodge, however, doubted that the Paris negotiators could make "mankind suddenly virtuous by a statute or written constitution." A powerful Republican who nourished an intense dislike for Wilson, Lodge relished a fight. He knew the undercurrents already stirring up opposition to the treaty: the resentment felt by German, Italian, and Irish groups, the disappointment of liberals with Wilson's compromises on reparations and boundaries, the distractions of demobilization and resulting domestic problems, and the revival of isolationism. Lodge's close friend Theodore Roosevelt, still a popular figure, lambasted Wilson and the League, noting that he keenly distrusted a "man who cares for other nations as much as his own."

The League of Nations Argument in a Nutshell

J. N. "Ding" Darling's summation of the League controversy.

Others agreed. In the Senate a group of "irreconcilables," fourteen Republicans and two Democrats, opposed U.S. participation in the League on any terms. They were mainly western and midwestern Progressives who feared that new foreign commitments would threaten domestic programs and reforms. The irreconcilables would be useful to Lodge's purpose, but he belonged to a larger group of "reservationists," who insisted upon limiting U.S. involvement in the League. Wilson said that he had already amended the covenant to these ends, pointing out that with a veto in the League Council, the United States could not be obligated to do anything against its will.

Lodge, who set more store by the old balance of power than by the new idea of collective security, offered a set of amendments, or reservations. Wilson responded by agreeing to interpretive reservations but to nothing that would reopen the negotiations with Germany and the Allies. He especially opposed the amendments weakening Article Ten of the League of Nations covenant, which provided for collective action by the signatory governments against aggression.

By September, with momentum for the treaty slackening, Wilson decided to go directly to the people. Against the advice of doctors and friends, he set forth on a railroad tour through the Midwest to the West Coast, pounding out speeches on his typewriter between stops. In all he traveled 8,000 miles in twenty-two days, giving thirty-two major addresses and voicing dire warnings of the consequences if the treaty were not approved.

For a while, Wilson seemed to be regaining the initiative, but on October 2, 1919, he suffered a severe stroke, leaving him paralyzed on his left side and an invalid for the rest of his life. For seventeen months his protective wife, Edith, kept him isolated from all but the most essential business. The illness intensified his stubbornness. He might have done better to have secured the best compromise possible, but he refused to yield. As he scoffed to an aide, "Let Lodge compromise."

Lodge was determined to amend the treaty before it was ratified. Between November 7 and 19, the Senate adopted fourteen of Lodge's reservations to the Versailles Treaty, most having to do with the League. Wilson refused to make any compromises or concessions. As a result, the Wilsonians found themselves thrown into an unlikely combination with the irreconcilables, who opposed the treaty under any circumstances. The Senate vote on the treaty with Lodge's reservations was thirty-nine for and fifty-five against. On the question of taking the treaty without reservations, irreconcilables and reservationists combined to defeat ratification again, with thirty-eight for and fifty-three against.

In the face of strong public criticism, however, the Senate voted to reconsider. On March 19, 1920, twenty-one intransigent Democrats deserted Wilson and joined the reservationists, but the treaty once again fell short of a two-thirds majority, by a vote of forty-nine yeas and thirty-five nays. The real winners were the smallest of the three groups in the Senate, neither the Wilsonians nor the reservationists but the irreconcilables.

When Congress declared the war at an end by joint resolution on May 20, 1920, Wilson vetoed the action; it was not until after he left office that a joint resolution officially ended the state of war with Germany and Austria-Hungary, on July 2, 1921. Peace treaties with Germany, Austria, and Hungary were ratified on October 18, 1921, but by then Warren Gamaliel Harding was president of the United States.

Lurching from War to Peace

The Versailles Treaty, for all the time it spent in the Senate before being defeated, was but one issue clamoring for public attention in the turbulent period after the war. Demobilization of the armed forces and the government's war effort proceeded in haphazard fashion. The War Industries Board closed shop on January 1, 1919, and the sudden cancellation of war contracts left workers and business leaders to cope with reconversion to a peacetime economy on their own. Wilson's leadership was missing. He had been preoccupied by the war and the League, and once bedridden by his illness, he became strangely grim and peevish. His rudderless administration floundered through rough waters during its last two years.

THE SPANISH FLU   Amid the initial confusion of postwar life, many Americans confronted a virulent menace that produced far more casualties than the war itself. It became known as the Spanish flu, and its contagion spread around the globe. Erupting in the spring of 1918 and lasting a year, the pandemic killed more than 22 million people throughout the world, twice as many as died in World War I. In the United States alone the flu accounted for over 675,000 deaths, seven times the number of combat deaths in France.

American servicemen returning from France brought the flu with them, and it raced through the congested army camps and naval bases. By September 1918 the epidemic had spread to the civilian population. In that month 10,000 Americans died from the disease. Municipal health officers began fining people for spitting on the sidewalks or sneezing without a handkerchief. Millions of people began wearing surgical masks to work. Phone booths were locked up, as were other public facilities, such as dance halls, poolrooms, and theaters. Even churches and saloons in many communities were declared off-limits. Still the death toll rose. From September 1918 to June 1919, one quarter of the population contracted the illness.

By the spring of 1919, the pandemic had run its course. It ended as suddenly—and as inexplicably—as it had begun. Although another outbreak occurred in the winter of 1920, the population had grown more resistant to its assaults. No disease, plague, war, famine, or natural catastrophe in world history had killed so many people in such a short time.

THE ECONOMIC TRANSITION The problems of postwar readjustment were worsened by widespread labor unrest. Prices continued to rise steeply after the war, and discontented workers, released from wartime constraints, were more willing to strike for their demands. In 1919 more than 4 million workers walked out in thousands of disputes. After a general strike in Seattle, public opinion of militant workers began to turn hostile.

The most celebrated postwar labor confrontation was the Boston police strike, which inadvertently launched a presidential career. On September 9, 1919, most of Boston's police force went out on strike, demanding recognition of their union. Massachusetts governor Calvin Coolidge mobilized the national guard to arrest looters and restore order. After four days the strikers were ready to return, but the police commissioner fired them all. When labor leader Samuel Gompers appealed for their reinstatement, Coolidge responded in words that suddenly turned him into a national figure: "There is no right to strike against the public safety by anybody, anywhere, anytime."

RACIAL FRICTION The summer of 1919 also brought a season of violent race riots, in the North and the South. Whites invaded the black section of Longview, Texas, in search of a teacher who had allegedly accused a white woman of a liaison with a black man. They burned shops and houses and ran several African Americans out of town. A week later in Washington, D.C., reports of black assaults on white women aroused white mobs, and for four days gangs of white and black rioters waged race war in the streets until soldiers and driving rains ended the fighting.

These were but preliminaries to the Chicago riot of late July, in which 38 people were killed, 537 injured, and 1,000 left homeless. It all started on the shores of Lake Michigan, when a black youth's raft drifted into the whites' beach area, and whites started stoning him. The climactic disorders of the summer occurred in the rural area around Elaine, Arkansas, where African-American tenant farmers tried to organize a union. According to official reports, 5 whites and 25 blacks were killed in the violence, but whites told one reporter in the area that in fact more than 100 blacks had died. Altogether twenty-five race riots erupted in 1919.

THE RED SCARE   Public reaction to the wave of labor strikes and race riots reflected the impact of Russia's Bolshevik revolution. A minority of radicals thought America's domestic turbulence, like that in Russia, was the first scene in a drama of world revolution. A much larger public was persuaded that they might be right. After all, Lenin's tiny faction in Russia had exploited confusion to impose its will on the entire nation. Wartime hysteria against all things German was thus readily transformed into a postwar Red Scare.

Fears of revolution in America might have remained latent except for the actions of a lunatic fringe. In April 1919 the postal service intercepted nearly forty homemade mail bombs addressed to prominent citizens. One slipped through and blew off the hands of a Georgia senator's maid. In June another bomb destroyed the front of Attorney General A. Mitchell Palmer's house in Washington.

In June 1919 the Justice Department decided to deport radicals, and Attorney General Palmer set up as the head of the department's new General Intelligence Division the young J. Edgar Hoover, who began to collect files on radicals. Raids began on November 7, 1919, when agents swooped down on the Union of Russian Workers in twelve cities. Many of those arrested were deported without a court hearing. On January 2, 1920, police raids in dozens of cities swept up some 5,000 suspects, many taken from their homes without search warrants. About half of those seized were kept in custody. That same month the New York State legislature expelled five duly elected Socialist members.

Basking in popular approval, Palmer continued to warn of the Red menace, but like other fads and alarms, the ugly mood of intolerance passed. By the summer of 1920, the Red Scare had begun to evaporate. Communist revolutions in Europe died out, leaving Bolshevism isolated in Russia. Bombings tapered off; the wave of strikes and race riots receded. The reactionary attorney general began to seem more threatening to civil liberties than a handful of radicals were to the social order. By September 1920, when a bomb explosion at the corner of Broad and Wall Streets in New York City killed thirty-eight people, Americans were ready to take it for what it was: the work of a crazed mind and not the start of a revolution.

The Red Scare nevertheless left a lasting mark on American life. Part of its legacy was the continuing crusade for "100 percent Americanism" and restrictions on immigration. It also left a stigma on labor unions (already weakened by their internal ethnic and racial tensions) and contributed to the anti-union open-shop campaign—the American plan, its sponsors called it. But for many thoughtful Americans the chief residue of the Great War, President Wilson's physical collapse, and its chaotic aftermath was a profound disillusionment.

MAKING CONNECTIONS

- The Red Scare at the end of World War I led to a wave of nativism and to immigration restriction, outlined in the next chapter.

- This chapter ended by noting the "profound disillusionment" Americans felt with efforts to reform the world. The political aspect of that disillusionment—the return to "normalcy" in the 1920s—is discussed in Chapter 27.

- The treaty ending World War I was designed to cripple Germany's military strength. But as Chapter 29 shows, within two decades Adolf Hitler was leading a rebuilt German military force into World War II.

FURTHER READING

A lucid overview of international events covered in this chapter is Robert H. Ferrell's *Woodrow Wilson and World War I, 1917–1921* (1985). On Wilson's stance toward war, see Ross Gregory's *The Origins of American Intervention in the First World War* (1971). An excellent brief biography is H. W. Brands's *Woodrow Wilson* (2003).

Edward M. Coffman's *The War to End All Wars: The American Military Experience in World War I* (1968) is a detailed presentation of America's military involvement. David M. Kennedy's *Over Here: The First World War and American Society* (1980) surveys the impact of the war on the home front. Maurine Weiner Greenwald's *Women, War, and Work: The Impact of World War I on Women Workers in the United States* (1980) discusses the role of women. Ronald Schaffer's *America in the Great War: The Rise of the War Welfare State* (1991) shows the effect of war mobilization on business organization. Richard Polenberg's *Fighting Faiths: The Abrams Case, the Supreme*

Court, and Free Speech (1987) examines the prosecution of a case under the 1918 Sedition Act.

How American diplomacy fared in the making of peace has received considerable attention. Thomas J. Knock interrelates domestic affairs and foreign relations in his explanation of Wilson's peacemaking in *To End All Wars: Woodrow Wilson and the Quest for a New World Order* (1992).

The problems of the immediate postwar years and chronicled by a number of historians. On the Spanish flu, see John M. Barry's *The Great Influenza: The Epic Story of the Deadliest Plague in History* (2004). Labor tensions are examined in David E. Brody's *Labor in Crisis: The Steel Strike of 1919* (1965) and Francis Russell's *A City in Terror: The 1919 Boston Police Strike* (1975). On racial strife, see William M. Tuttle Jr.'s *Race Riot: Chicago in the Red Summer of 1919* (1970). The fear of Communists is analyzed in Robert K. Murray's *Red Scare: A Study in National Hysteria, 1919–1920* (1955).

26

THE MODERN TEMPER

FOCUS QUESTIONS

· What issues mobilized the reactionary groups of the 1920s?

· How did the new social trends in the 1920s challenge traditional attitudes?

· How did modernism influence American culture?

To answer these questions and access additional review material, please visit www.wwnorton.com/studyspace.

The horrors of World War I dealt a shattering blow to the widespread belief that Western civilization was steadily progressing, a myth that had dominated the public consciousness for a century and had been a powerful stimulus of Progressivism. The editors of *Presbyterian* magazine announced in 1919 that the "world has been convulsed . . . and every field of thought and action has been disturbed. . . . The most settled principles and laws of society . . . have been attacked."

The war's unimaginable carnage produced a postwar disillusionment among young intellectuals that challenged traditional values. A new "modernist" sensibility emerged among artists, writers, and journalists. At once a mood and a movement, as well as a label for a historical era and a cultural style, modernism appeared first in Europe at the end of the nineteenth century and had become a pervasive international force by 1920. It arose out of a widespread recognition that Western civilization had entered an era of bewildering change. New technologies, new modes of transportation and communication, and new scientific discoveries such as quantum mechanics and relativity theory combined to rupture perceptions of reality and generate new forms of artistic expression. Modernism manifested itself in a cluster of diverse intellectual and artistic movements: impressionism, futurism, Dadaism, surrealism, Freudianism. As the French painter Paul Gauguin acknowledged, the upheavals of modernism produced "an epoch of confusion."

At the same time that the war provided an accelerant for modernism, it stimulated volatile social tensions and political radicalism. The postwar wave of strikes, bombings, anti-Communist hysteria, and race riots convinced many Americans that the country had entered a frightening new era of turmoil and turbulence. Conflict abounded. Defenders of tradition located the germs of radicalism in the polyglot cities teeming with immigrants and foreign ideas. The defensive mood of the 1920s fed on a growing tendency to connect American nationalism with nativism, Anglo-Saxon racism, and militant Protestantism.

REACTION IN THE TWENTIES

NATIVISM   That so many political radicals in the United States were immigrants strengthened the suspicion that the seeds of sedition were foreign-born. In the early 1920s over half the white men and one third of the white women working in manufacturing and industry were foreign-born, most of them from central or eastern Europe. That socialism and anarchism were prevalent in those regions made such immigrant workers especially suspicious in the eyes of "old stock" Americans.

The most celebrated case of nativist prejudice involved two Italian-born anarchists, Nicola Sacco and Bartolomeo Vanzetti. Arrested in 1920 for a robbery and murder in South Braintree, Massachusetts, they were tried by a judge who privately referred to them as "anarchist bastards." People then and since have insisted that Sacco and Vanzetti were sentenced more for their political beliefs and their ethnic origin than for any crime they had committed. The case became a great radical and liberal cause of the 1920s, but despite pleas for mercy and worldwide demonstrations on behalf of the two men, Sacco and Vanzetti were sent to the electric chair in 1927. Recent investigations have pointed to their likely guilt.

The surging postwar nativism generated new efforts to restrict immigration. Congress, alarmed at the influx of foreigners after 1919, passed the Emergency Immigration Act of 1921, which restricted European arrivals each year to 3 percent of the foreign-born of any nationality as shown in the 1910 census. A quota law in 1924 reduced the number to 2 percent based on the 1890 census, which included fewer of the "new" immigrants from southern and eastern Europe. This law set a permanent limitation, which became effective in 1929, of slightly over 150,000 immigrants per year based on the "national origins" of the U.S. population as of 1920. In signing the law, President Calvin Coolidge pledged, "America must be kept American."

However inexact the quotas, their purpose was clear: to tilt the balance in favor of the old immigration from northern and western Europe, which was assigned about 85 percent of the total. The law completely excluded people from east Asia. Yet it left the gate open to immigrants from Western Hemisphere countries, so that an ironic consequence was a substantial increase in the Hispanic Catholic population. People of Latin American descent (chiefly Mexicans, Puerto Ricans, and Cubans) became the fastest growing ethnic minority in the country.

THE KLAN   During the postwar years the nativist tradition took on a new form, a revived Ku Klux Klan modeled on the group founded in the South after the Civil War. The new Klan was devoted to "100 percent Americanism" rather than to the old Confederacy, and it restricted its membership to native-born white Protestants. It was determined to protect its warped notion of the American way of life not only from blacks but also from Roman Catholics, Jews, and immigrants. In going nativist, the new Klan spread far outside the South. Its appeal reached areas as widely scattered as Oregon and Maine. It thrived in small towns and cities in the North and especially in the Midwest. And it was preoccupied with the defense of white ("native") women and Christian morals.

Klan Rally

In 1925 40,000 Klan members paraded down Pennsylvania Avenue in Washington, D.C.

The Klan represented a vicious reflex against the modern and the alien, against shifting moral standards, the declining influence of churches, and the social permissiveness of cities and colleges. In the Southwest the Klan became more than anything else a moral crusade. "It is going to drive the bootleggers forever out of this land," declared a Texan. "It is going to bring clean moving pictures . . . clean literature . . . break up roadside parking . . . enforce the laws . . . protect homes." Instead, the Klan terrorized and assaulted blacks and immigrants. Estimates of its peak membership, probably inflated, range from 3 million to 8 million, but the Klan's influence diminished as quickly as its numbers grew. Nativist excitement declined after passage of the 1924 immigration law. The Klan also suffered from recurrent factional quarrels and schisms. And its willing use of violence tarnished its moral pretensions.

FUNDAMENTALISM   While the Klan saw a threat mainly in the "alien menace," many adherents of the old-time religion saw threats from modernism in the churches: new ideas that the Bible should be studied in the light of modern scholarship (the "higher criticism") or that it could be reconciled with scientific theories of evolution. Fearing that such modernist notions had infected schools and even pulpits, fundamentalism, grounded in a literal interpretation of the Bible, took on a new militancy.

Among the rural fundamentalist leaders only William Jennings Bryan, the former presidential candidate and secretary of state, had the following, prestige, and eloquence to make the movement a popular crusade. By 1920 Bryan was showing signs of age, but he remained as silver-tongued as ever. In 1921 he sparked a drive for laws prohibiting the teaching of Darwinian evolution in the public schools. Anti-evolution bills began to appear in legislatures, but the only victories came in the South—and there were few of those.

The climax came in Tennessee, where in 1925 the legislature outlawed the teaching of evolution in public schools and colleges. A young teacher at a high school in Dayton, Tennessee, John T. Scopes, accepted an offer from the American Civil Liberties Union to defend a test case. It soon was a case heard round the world. Before the opening day of the "monkey trial," the streets of Dayton swarmed with publicity hounds, curiosity seekers, evangelists and atheists, hucksters, and a mob of reporters.

The two stars of the show were Bryan, who led the prosecution of Scopes for teaching evolution in violation of Tennessee law, and Clarence Darrow, a renowned Chicago trial lawyer and confessed agnostic, who defended Scopes by challenging the anti-evolution law. The trial quickly became a debate between fundamentalism and modernism. When the judge (a

Courtroom Scene during the Scopes Trial

The media, food vendors, and others flocked to Dayton, Tennessee, for the case against John Scopes, the teacher who taught evolution.

practicing evangelist) damaged Darrow's case by ruling out scientific testimony on evolution, most observers assumed the trial was over.

But the defense rebounded by calling Bryan as an expert witness on biblical interpretation. Darrow, who had once supported Bryan as a presidential candidate, now relentlessly entrapped the statesman in literal-minded interpretations and exposed Bryan's ignorance of biblical history and scholarship. Bryan insisted that a "great fish" had swallowed Jonah, that Joshua had made the sun stand still, that the world was created in 4004 B.C.—all, according to Darrow, "fool ideas that no intelligent Christian on earth believes." It was a bitter scene. At one point the two men, their patience exhausted in the broiling summer heat, lunged at each other, shaking their fists, leading the judge to adjourn the court.

The next day the testimony ended. The only issue before the court, the judge ruled, was whether Scopes had in fact taught evolution. He was found guilty, but the Tennessee Supreme Court, while upholding the law, overruled the $100 fine on a legal technicality. The chief prosecutor accepted the higher court's advice against "prolonging the life of this bizarre case" and dropped the issue. With more prescience than he knew, Bryan had described the trial as a "duel to the death." A few days after it closed, he died of a heart condition aggravated by heat and fatigue.

PROHIBITION   Prohibition of alcoholic beverages offered another example of reforming zeal channeled into a drive for moral righteousness and conformity. Moralists had been campaigning against excessive drink since the eighteenth century. Around 1900, however, the leading temperance organizations, the Women's Christian Temperance Union and the Anti-Saloon League, shifted their efforts from reforming individuals to campaigning for a national prohibition law. The Anti-Saloon League became one of the most effective pressure groups in history, mobilizing Protestant churches behind its single-minded battle to elect "dry" candidates.

The 1916 elections produced in both houses of Congress two-thirds majorities suffering an amendment to the Constitution prohibiting alcoholic beverages. Soon the wartime spirit of sacrifice, the need to use grain for food, and wartime hostility to German-American brewers transformed the cause into a virtual test of patriotism. On December 18, 1917, Congress sent to the states the Eighteenth Amendment, which one year after ratification, on January 16, 1919, banned the manufacture, sale, and transportation of intoxicating liquors nationwide.

Prohibition

A 1926 police raid on a speakeasy.

The new amendment did not keep people from drinking, however. Congress never supplied adequate enforcement, if such were even possible given the public thirst, the spotty support of local officials, and the profits to be made in bootlegging. In Detroit, across the river from Ontario, Canada, where booze was legal, the liquor industry during Prohibition was second in size only to the auto industry. Speakeasies, hip flasks, and cocktail parties were among the social innovations of the era, along with increased drinking by women.

It would be too much to say that Prohibition gave rise to organized crime, for systematic vice, gambling, and extortion had long been practiced and were often tied in with saloons. But Prohibition supplied ruthless, flamboyant criminals, such as "Scarface" Al Capone, with a new, enormous source of income, while the automobile and the submachine gun provided greater mobility and greater firepower. Gangland leaders showed remarkable gifts for exploiting loopholes in the law when they did not simply bribe policemen and politicians.

Capone was by far the most celebrated criminal of the 1920s. In 1927 he pocketed $60 million from his bootlegging, prostitution, and gambling empire, and he flaunted his wealth as well as his open disregard for legal authorities. He bludgeoned to death several conspiring police lieutenants and ordered the execution of dozens of his criminal competitors. Law-enforcement officials began to smash his bootlegging operations in 1929, but they were unable to pin anything on him until a Treasury agent infiltrated his gang and uncovered evidence that was used to convict him later that year of tax evasion. He was sentenced to eleven years in prison.

In the light of the illegal activities of Capone and other members of organized-crime syndicates, it came as no great surprise when a commission in 1931 reported evidence that enforcement of Prohibition had broken down. Still, the commission voted to extend Prohibition, and President Herbert Hoover chose to stand by what he called the "experiment, noble in motive and far-reaching in purpose."

THE ROARING TWENTIES

In many ways the reactionary temper of the 1920s and the repressive movements to which it gave rise seemed the dominant trends of the decade. But they arose in part as reactions to disruptive social and intellectual currents. During those years a new cosmopolitan, urban America confronted provincial small-town and rural America, and cultural conflict reached new levels of tension.

Young urban intellectuals developed an active disdain for the old-fashioned values of the hinterlands. Sinclair Lewis's novel *Main Street* (1920) caricatured the stifling life of the prairie town, depicting a "savorless people, gulping tasteless food, and sitting afterward, coatless and thoughtless, in rocking chairs prickly with inane decorations, listening to mechanical music, saying mechanical things about the excellence of Ford automobiles, and viewing themselves as the greatest race in the world." The banality of small-town life became a pervasive theme in much of the literature of the time, and the heartland responded with counterimages of cities infested with vice, crime, corruption, and foreigners.

THE JAZZ AGE Writer F. Scott Fitzgerald dubbed the postwar era the Jazz Age because young people were willing to experiment with new forms of recreation and sexuality. The new jazz music bubbling up in New Orleans, Kansas City, Memphis, New York City, and Chicago blended African and European traditions to form a distinctive sound characterized by improvisation, "blue notes," and polyrhythm. The syncopated rhythms of jazz were immensely popular among rebellious young adults and helped spawn carefree new dance steps such as the Charleston and the black bottom, gyrations that shocked guardians of morality.

Frankie "Half Pint" Jackson and His Band at the Sunset Cafe, Chicago, 1920s

Jazz emerged in the 1920s as an especially American expression of the modernist spirit. African-American artists bent musical conventions to give fuller rein to improvisation and sensuality.

If people were not listening to ragtime or jazz or to the family radio shows that became the rage in the 1920s, they were frequenting movie theaters. By 1930 there were more than 23,000 theaters around the country, and they drew more than 95 million customers each week. In Muncie, Indiana, a small city of 35,000, nine movie theaters were operating seven days a week. Films became even more popular after the introduction of sound in 1927.

THE NEW MORALITY Much of the shock to traditionalists during the Jazz Age came from the changes in manners and morals evidenced first among young people and especially on college campuses. In *This Side of Paradise* (1920), a novel of student life at Princeton, F. Scott Fitzgerald wrote of "the great current American phenomenon, the 'petting party.'" None of the Victorian mothers, he said, "had any idea how casually their daughters were accustomed to be kissed." From such novels and from magazines and movies, many Americans learned about the cities' wild parties, illegal drinking, promiscuity, and speakeasies.

Sex came to be discussed with surprising frankness during the 1920s. Much of the talk derived from a spreading awareness of Dr. Sigmund Freud, the Viennese father of psychoanalysis. By the 1920s his ideas had begun to infiltrate popular awareness, and in society and literature there was talk of libido, Oedipus complexes, sublimation, and repression.

Fashion also reflected the rebellion against prudishness and a loosening of inhibitions. In 1919 women's skirts were typically six inches above the ground; by 1927 they were at the knees, and the "flapper," with her bobbed hair, rolled stockings, cigarettes, lipstick, and sensuous dancing, was providing a shocking model of the new feminism. The name *flapper* derived from the way female rebels allowed their galoshes to flap around their ankles. Conservative moralists saw the

The "New Woman" of the 1920s

Two flappers dance atop the Sherman Hotel in Chicago, 1926.

flappers as just another sign of a degenerating society. Others saw in the "new woman" an expression of rugged American individualism.

By 1930, however, the thrill of rebellion was waning; the revolution against Victorian morality had run its course. Its extreme expressions in time aroused doubts that the indulgence of lust equaled liberation. And the much-discussed revolution in morals was also greatly exaggerated. The twenties roared for only a small proportion of the population. F. Scott Fitzgerald reminded Americans in 1931 that the Jazz Age was jazzy for only the "upper tenth" of the population. Still, some new folkways had come to stay. In the late 1930s a survey disclosed that among college women almost half had had sexual relations before marriage.

THE WOMEN'S MOVEMENT   At the same time that many women were embracing new sexual mores, all women were being liberated politically. The suffrage movement, which had been in the doldrums since 1896, sprang back to life in the second decade of the new century. In 1912 Alice

Votes for Women

Suffragettes march in New York City in 1912, their children by their side.

Paul, a Quaker social worker, returned from an apprenticeship with the militant suffragists of England to chair the National American Woman Suffrage Association's Congressional Committee. Paul instructed female activists to picket state legislatures, target and "punish" politicians who failed to endorse suffrage, chain themselves to public buildings, provoke police to arrest them, and undertake hunger strikes. By 1917 Paul and her followers were picketing the White House and deliberately inviting arrest, after which they went on hunger strikes in prison.

In 1915 Carrie Chapman Catt had once again become head of the National Woman Suffrage Association (NWSA). For several years, President Woodrow Wilson had evaded the issue of a suffrage amendment, but he supported a plank in the 1916 Democratic platform endorsing state action for women's suffrage. He addressed the NWSA that year, and thereafter he worked closely with its leaders. On June 4, 1919, the Senate finally adopted the Nineteenth Amendment, by a bare two-thirds majority, and after fourteen months the states ratified the women's suffrage amendment on August 21, 1920, the climactic achievement of the Progressive Era.

Women thereafter entered politics in growing numbers, but this development did not suddenly release women from deeply embedded social customs and legal discrimination. Women tended to vote like men on most issues. One group, however, wanted something more. Alice Paul set a new goal, first introduced in Congress in 1923: an equal rights amendment that would eliminate any remaining legal distinctions between the sexes, including the special legislation for the protection of working women put on the books in the previous fifty or so years. It would be another fifty years before Alice Paul would see Congress adopt her amendment in 1972; she did not live to see it fall short of ratification, however.

The sharp increase in the number of women in the workforce during World War I proved short-lived, but in the longer view a steady increase in the number of employed women occurred in the 1920s and 1930s. Working women remained concentrated in traditional occupations: they were mostly domestics, office workers, teachers, clerks, salespeople, dressmakers, milliners, and seamstresses. On the eve of World War II, women's work was little more diversified than it had been at the turn of the century, but by 1940 it would be on the eve of a major transformation.

THE "NEW NEGRO"   The discriminations experienced by African Americans and women display many parallels, and their struggles for equality have frequently coincided. The most significant development in African-American life during the early twentieth century was the Great Migration northward. A massive movement of blacks from the South to the North began in 1915–1916, when rapidly expanding war industries were experiencing a labor shortage, leaving openings for African Americans in the North. Altogether between 1910 and 1920 the Southeast lost some 323,000 blacks, or 5 percent of the 1920 native black population, and by 1930 it had lost another 615,000, or 8 percent of the 1920 African-American population. The migration north led to a slow but steady growth in black political influence. African Americans were freer to speak and act in a northern settling, and they gained political leverage by settling in large cities in states with many electoral votes.

Along with political activity came a bristling spirit of protest, a spirit that received cultural expression in a literary and artistic movement labeled the Harlem Renaissance. Claude McKay, a Jamaican immigrant, was the first significant writer of the movement, which sought to rediscover black folk culture. Poems collected in McKay's *Harlem Shadows* (1922) expressed defiance in such titles as "If We Must Die" and "To the White Fiends." Other emergent black writers included Langston Hughes, Zora Neale Hurston, Countee Cullen, Jean Toomer, and James Weldon Johnson.

The spirit of the "New Negro" also found an outlet in what came to be called Negro nationalism, which exalted blackness, black cultural expression, and at its most extreme, black exclusiveness. The leading spokesman for such views was the flamboyant Marcus Garvey. Racial bias, Garvey said, was so ingrained in whites that it was futile to appeal to their sense of justice. He advised blacks to liberate themselves from the surrounding white culture. "We have outgrown slavery," he declared, "but our minds are still enslaved to the thinking of the Master Race."

Garvey endorsed the "social and political separation of all peoples to the extent that they promote their own ideals and civilization." Such a separatist message appalled other African-American leaders. W.E.B. Du Bois, for example, labeled Garvey "the most dangerous enemy of the Negro race." Garvey and his aides created their own black version of Christianity, organized their own fraternal lodges and community cultural centers, started their own businesses, and published their own newspaper. Garvey's message of racial pride and self-reliance appealed to many blacks who had arrived in the northern cities during the Great Migration and had grown embittered with the hypocrisy of American democracy during the postwar economic slump. Garvey declared that the only lasting hope for blacks was to flee America and build their own republic in Africa.

In 1916 Garvey brought to New York the Universal Negro Improvement Association, which he had started in his native Jamaica two years before. He quickly

Marcus Garvey

Garvey was the founder of the
Universal Negro Improvement
Association and a leading spokesman
for "Negro nationalism" in the 1920s.

enlisted 500,000 members in his association, and claimed as many as 6 million by 1923. At the peak of his popularity, however, Garvey was convicted
of mail fraud. He was imprisoned from
1925 until pardoned and deported to
Jamaica in 1927 by President Calvin
Coolidge. Garvey died in obscurity in
London in 1940, but the memory of his
movement kept alive an undercurrent
of racial pride that would reemerge
later under the slogan of black power.

Even more influential in promoting black rights was the National Association for the Advancement of
Colored People. Founded in 1910, it
was led by northern white liberals
and black leaders such as Du Bois. Its
main strategy focused on getting the
federal government to enforce the
Fourteenth and Fifteenth Amendments. In 1919, the NAACP launched
a campaign against lynching, still a common atrocity in many parts of the
country, most of whose victims were black. An anti-lynching bill making
mob murder a federal offense passed the House in 1922 but lost to a filibuster by southern senators. Nonetheless, the bill stayed before the House
until 1925, and continuing agitation of the issue helped to reduce lynchings,
which declined to one third of what they had been the previous decade.

THE CULTURE OF MODERNISM

After 1920 changes in the realms of science and social thought were
perhaps even more dramatic than those affecting women and African Americans. As the twentieth century advanced, the easy faith in progress and reform
expressed by Progressives fell victim to a series of frustrations and disasters,
including the Great War, the failure of the League of Nations to win approval
in the United States, Woodrow Wilson's physical and political collapse, and
the failure of Prohibition. Startling new findings in physics further shook
prevailing assumptions.

SCIENCE AND SOCIAL THOUGHT   Physicists of the early twentieth century altered the image of the cosmos in bewildering ways. Since Isaac Newton's research in the late seventeenth century, conventional wisdom had held that the universe was governed by laws that the scientific method could ultimately uncover. A world of such certain order and rationality had bolstered hopes of infinite progress in human knowledge.

This rational world of order and certainty disintegrated at the turn of the century when Albert Einstein, a young German physicist, announced his theory of relativity, which maintained that space, time, and mass were not absolutes but were relative to the location and motion of the observer. Newton's eighteenth-century mechanics, according to Einstein's relativity theories, worked well enough at relatively slow speeds, but the more nearly one approached the velocity of light (about 186,000 miles per second), the more all measuring devices would change accordingly, so that yardsticks would become shorter, clocks and heartbeats would slow down, even the aging process would ebb.

Relativity was not the only disconcerting concept that Einstein discovered. The farther one reached out into the universe and the farther one reached down into the minute world of the atom, the more certainty dissolved. The discovery of radioactivity in the 1890s showed that atoms were not irreducible units of matter and that some of them emitted particles of energy. This meant, Einstein noted, that mass and energy were not separate phenomena but interchangeable.

Meanwhile, the German physicist Max Planck had discovered that electromagnetic emissions of energy, whether as electricity or light, came in little bundles that he called quanta. The development of quantum theory suggested that atoms were far more complex than once believed. In 1927 the pioneering German physicist Werner Heisenberg announced that the activities within an atom were ultimately indescribable. One could never know both the position and the velocity of an electron, Heisenberg concluded, because the very process of observation would affect the behavior of the particle, altering its position or velocity.

Heisenberg's "uncertainty principle" meant that human knowledge had limits. Just as Enlightenment thinkers drew on Isaac Newton's principles of gravitation two centuries before to formulate their views on the laws governing society, the ideas of relativity and uncertainty in the twentieth century convinced some people to deny the relevance of absolute values in any sphere of society, thus undermining the concepts of personal responsibility and absolute standards. Anthropologists aided the process by transforming the word *culture*, which had before meant "refinement," into a term for the whole system of ideas, folkways, and institutions within which any group lived. Even the most primitive societies had cultures, and all things being relative, one culture should not impose its value judgments upon another. Two anthropologists, Ruth Benedict and Margaret Mead, were especially effective in spreading this viewpoint.

MODERNIST ART AND LITERATURE   The cluster of scientific ideas associated with Charles Darwin, Sigmund Freud, and Albert Einstein helped inspire a modernist revolution in the minds of many intellectuals and creative artists during the early twentieth century. The modernist world was one in which, as Karl Marx said, "all that is solid melts into air." Modernism arose out of a widespread recognition that Western civilization was entering an era of bewildering change. New technologies, new modes of transportation and communication, and new scientific discoveries combined to transform the nature of everyday life and to generate dramatic new forms of artistic expression and architectural design.

Whereas nineteenth-century writers and artists took for granted an accessible world that could be readily observed and accurately represented, self-willed modernists viewed reality as something to be created rather than copied, expressed rather than reproduced. As a consequence, they concluded that the subconscious regions of the psyche were more interesting and more potent than reason, common sense, and logic.

In the various arts such concerns spawned abstract painting, atonal music, free verse in poetry, stream-of-consciousness narrative, and interior monologues in stories and novels. Writers showed an intense concern with new forms of expression in an effort to violate expectations and shock their audiences.

The chief American prophets of modernism were living in Europe: Ezra Pound and T. S. Eliot in London and Gertrude Stein in Paris. All were deeply concerned with creating new and often difficult styles of modernist expression. Pound, as foreign editor of *Poetry,* served as the conduit through which many American poets achieved publication in the leading journals and magazines promoting experimentalism. At the same time he became the leader of the imagist movement, a revolt against the ornamental verbosity of Victorian poetry in favor of the concrete image.

Ezra Pound's brilliant protégé was the St. Louis–born Harvard graduate T. S. Eliot, who in 1915 contributed to *Poetry* his first major poem, "The Love Song of J. Alfred Prufrock," the musings of an ineffectual man who "after tea and cakes and ices" could never find "the strength to force the moment to its crisis." Eliot went to Oxford in 1913 and soon decided to make England his home and poetry his career. He rejected the nineteenth century's "cheerfulness, optimism, and hopefulness," as well as the traditional notion of poetry as the literal representation of a beautiful world. The modern poet, he insisted, must "be able to see beneath both beauty and ugliness; to see the boredom, and the horror and the glory." Eliot's *The Waste Land* (1922) made few concessions to readers in its obscure allusions, its juxtaposition of unexpected metaphors, its deep sense of postwar disillusionment and melancholy, and its suggestion of a burned-out civilization. The poem became for an alienated younger generation almost the touchstone of the modern temper.

Gertrude Stein, another voluntary exile, settled in Paris in 1903 and became an early champion of experimentalism and a collector of modern art. Long regarded as no more than the literary eccentric who wrote "a rose is a rose is a rose is a rose," she would later be recognized as one of the chief promoters of the modernist prose style. At the time she was known chiefly through her influence on such literary expatriates of the 1920s as Sherwood Anderson and Ernest Hemingway, whom she told, "All of you young people who served in the war, you are the lost generation."

The earliest chronicler of that "lost" generation, F. Scott Fitzgerald, blazed up brilliantly and then quickly flickered out like the tinseled, carefree, sad young characters in his novels. Successful and famous at age twenty-four, having published *This Side of Paradise* in 1920, he, along with his wife, Zelda, experienced and depicted the "greatest, gaudiest spree in history." What gave depth to the best of Fitzgerald's work was what a character in *The Great Gatsby* (1925), his finest novel, called "a sense of the fundamental decencies" amid all the surface gaiety—and almost always a sense of impending doom.

Ernest Hemingway suffered even more from a psychic wound inflicted by an uncaring world. For him literature was a means of defense, a way to strike back, and in the process find a meaning for himself rather than accept one imposed by society. Hemingway's novels *The Sun Also Rises* (1926) and *A Farewell to Arms* (1929) depict a desperate search for "real" life and the doomed, war-tainted love affairs of Americans of the "lost generation." Hundreds of writers tried to imitate Hemingway's terse style, but few had his gift, which lay less in what he had to say than in the way he said it.

THE SOUTHERN RENAISSANCE As modernist literature arose in response to the changes taking place in the United States and Europe, so southern literature of the 1920s reflected a regional world in the midst of rebirth. A southern renaissance in writing emerged from the conflict between the dying world of tradition and the modern commercial world struggling to come to life in the aftermath of the Great War. While in the South the conflict of values aroused the Ku Klux Klan and fundamentalist furies that tried desperately to bring back the world of tradition, it also inspired the creativity of the South's young writers.

Two of the most notable of the new southern writers were Thomas Wolfe and William Faulkner. Fame rushed in first on Wolfe and his native Asheville, North Carolina, which he wrote about in his first novel, *Look Homeward,*

Angel. "Against the Victorian morality and the Bourbon aristocracy of the South," Wolfe had "turned in all his fury," wrote newspaper editor Jonathan Daniels, a former classmate. Despite his lust for experience and knowledge, his demonic drive to escape the encircling hills for the "fabled" world out-side, and his agonized search for some "lost lane-end into heaven," Wolfe never completely severed his roots in the South.

William Faulkner's achievement, more than Wolfe's, was rooted in the coarsely textured social world that produced him. Born near Oxford, Missis-sippi, he grew up there and transmuted his hometown into the fictional Jef-ferson, in Yoknapatawpha County. In writing *Sartoris* (1929), he began to discover that his "own little postage stamp of native soil was worth writing about" and that he "would never live long enough to exhaust it." With *Sar-toris* and the creation of his mythical land of Yoknapatawpha, Faulkner kin-dled a blaze of creative energy. Next, as he put it, he wrote his gut into *The Sound and the Fury* (1929). It was one of the triumphs of the modernist style, but most early readers, taking their cue from the title instead of the critics, believed that its complex prose and themes signified nothing.

Modernism and the southern literary renaissance, both of which emerged from the crucible of the Great War and its aftermath, were products of the 1920s. But the widespread alienation felt by the writers and artists of the 1920s did not survive the decade. The onset of the Great Depression in 1929 sparked a renewed sense of commitment and affirmation in the arts, as if people could no longer afford the art-for-art's-sake emphasis of the 1920s. Alienation would give way to social purpose in the decade to come.

MAKING CONNECTIONS

- The next chapter discusses the growing consumer culture of the 1920s, an economic offshoot of the Roaring Twenties described in this chapter.

- Chapter 28 touches on the changes in literary culture wrought by the Great Depression, from the modernism discussed in this chapter to a recognition of the social role of literature and the cultural "rediscovery of America" in the 1930s.

- The status of women in the workforce did not improve in the 1920s despite the successes of the women's movement. That status changed, at least temporarily, during World War II. In Chapter 30 the rise of Rosie the Riveter is discussed.

FURTHER READING

For a lively survey of the interwar period, start with William E. Leuchtenburg's *The Perils of Prosperity, 1914–32,* 2nd ed. (1993). The best introduction to the culture of the 1920s remains Loren Baritz's *The Culture of the Twenties* (1970). See also Lynn Dumenil's *The Modern Temper: American Culture and Society in the 1920s* (1995).

John Higham's *Strangers in the Land: Patterns of American Nativism, 1860–1925,* 2nd ed. (1988) details the story of immigration restriction. The controversial Sacco and Vanzetti case is thoroughly explored in *Kill Now, Talk Forever: Debating Sacco and Vanzetti,* edited by Richard Newby (2002). For analysis of the revival of Klan activity, see Nancy MacLean's *Behind the Mask of Chivalry: The Making of the Second Ku Klux Klan* (1994).

Women's suffrage is treated extensively in Eleanor Flexner's *Century of Struggle: The Woman's Rights Movement in the United States,* enlarged ed. (1996). See Charles F. Kellogg's *NAACP: A History of the National Association for the Advancement of Colored People* (1967) for his analysis of the pioneering court cases against racial discrimination. Nathan Irvin Huggin's *Harlem Renaissance* (1971) assesses the cultural impact of the Great Migration on New York. On the migration to Chicago see James R. Grossman's *Land of Hope: Chicago, Black Southerners, and the Great Migration* (1989). Nicholas Lemann's *The Promised Land: The Great Black Migration and How It Changed America* (1991) is a fine exposition of the changes brought about by the migration in the both the South and the North.

On southern modernism, see Daniel Joseph Singal's *The War Within: From Victorian to Modernist Thought in the South, 1919–1945* (1982). Stanley Coben's *Rebellion against Victorianism: The Impetus for Cultural Change in 1920s America* (1991) surveys the appeal of modernism among writers, artists, and intellectuals.

27

REPUBLICAN RESURGENCE AND DECLINE

FOCUS QUESTIONS

- How did the conservatism of Harding, Coolidge, and Hoover shape their policies?
- What drove the growth of the American economy in the 1920s?
- What were the causes of the Great Depression?

To answer these questions and access additional review material, please visit www.wwnorton.com/studyspace.

The Progressive political coalition that reelected Woodrow Wilson in 1916 proved to be quite fragile, and by 1920 it had fragmented. It began to show signs of fissure during the war, when radicals and other reformers were disaffected by America's involvement. After the war, Wilson's support continued to erode as his health problems incapacitated him. Organized labor resented the administration's unsympathetic attitude toward the strikes of 1919–1920, and western farmers complained that wartime price controls had discriminated against them. While prominent intellectuals grew disillusioned with the popular support for Prohibition and religious fundamentalism, many among the middle class lost interest in political activism. They instead channeled their energies into building a new business civilization based upon mass production and mass consumption, greater leisure, and the introduction of labor-saving electrical appliances in the home. Moreover, Progressivism's final triumphs at the national level crystallized before the war's end: the Eighteenth Amendment, which outlawed alcoholic beverages, was ratified in 1919, and the Nineteenth Amendment, which extended women's suffrage to the entire country, became law a year later.

Progressivism did not completely disappear in the 1920s, however. Although smaller in number, reformers remained active in Congress during much of the decade even while the White House was in conservative Republican hands. The Progressive impulse for "good government" and extended public services remained strong, especially at the state and local levels, where movements for good roads, education, public health, and social welfare gained momentum during the decade. At the same time, however, the reactionary temper of the times gave rise to the grassroots drive for moral righteousness and conformity, animating the Ku Klux Klan and the fundamentalist and prohibitionist movements.

"NORMALCY"

THE ELECTION OF 1920   After World War I most Americans grew weary of idealistic crusades and suspicious of leaders promoting reform. Woodrow Wilson himself recognized the reactionary temper. "It is only once in a generation," he remarked, "that a people can be lifted above material things. That is why conservative government is in the saddle two-thirds of the time."

When the Republicans met in Chicago in 1920, the Old Guard party regulars found their man in the affable Ohio senator Warren Gamaliel Harding, who had set the tone of his campaign when he told a Boston audience, "America's present need is not heroics, but healing; not nostrums, but normalcy; not revolution, but restoration; not agitation, but adjustment; not surgery, but serenity; not the dramatic, but the dispassionate; not experiment, but equipoise; not submergence in internationality, but sustainment in triumphant nationality." Harding caught the mood of the times—a longing for "normalcy" and contentment with the status quo.

Harding's promise of a "return to normalcy" reflected his own conservative values and folksy personality. The son of an Ohio farmer, he described himself not as an intellectual or a crusader but "just a plain fellow" who was "old-fashioned and even reactionary in matters of faith and morals." Such a description, however, suggests a certain puritan regimen that Harding never practiced. Far from being an old-fashioned moralist in his personal life, he drank bootleg liquor in the midst of Prohibition, smoked and chewed tobacco, relished weekly poker games, and had numerous liaisons with women other than his austere wife, whom he called Duchess. The general public, however, remained unaware of Harding's escapades. Instead, voters saw him as a handsome, charming, gregarious, and lovable politician. A man of self-confessed limitations in vision, leadership, and intellectual power, he once admitted that "I cannot hope to be one of the great presidents, but perhaps I may be remembered as one of the best loved." He got his wish.

The Democrats in 1920 hoped that Harding would not be president at all. James Cox, former newsman and former governor of Ohio, won the presidential nomination of a fragmented Democratic party on the forty-fourth ballot. For vice president the convention named Franklin D. Roosevelt, who as assistant secretary of the navy occupied the same position his Republican cousin Theodore Roosevelt had once held.

The Democrats suffered from the breakup of the Wilsonian coalition and the conservative postwar mood. In the words of the Progressive journalist William Allen White, Americans in 1920 were "tired of issues, sick at heart of ideals, and weary of being noble." The country voted overwhelmingly for Harding's promised "return to normalcy." Harding got 16 million votes to 9 million for Cox, who carried no state outside the Democratic Solid South.

EARLY APPOINTMENTS AND POLICY   Harding in office had much in common with Ulysses Grant. His cabinet, like Grant's, mixed some of the best men in the party with some of the worst. Charles Evans Hughes became a distinguished secretary of state. Herbert Hoover in the Commerce Department, Andrew W. Mellon in the Treasury Department, and Henry A. Wallace in the Agriculture Department were also efficient, forceful figures. Of the others, Secretary of the Interior Albert B. Fall landed in prison and Attorney General Harry M. Daugherty only narrowly escaped prosecution. Many lesser offices went to members of the soon notorious "Ohio gang," headed by Daugherty, a group of Harding's Ohio friends with whom the president met regularly for poker games lubricated with illegal liquor.

Harding and his friends set about dismantling or neutralizing as many components of Progressivism as they could. Harding's four appointments to the Supreme Court were all conservatives, including Chief Justice William Howard Taft, who announced that he had been "appointed to reverse a few decisions." During the 1920s the Taft court struck down a federal child-labor law and a minimum-wage law for women, issued numerous injunctions against striking unions, and made rulings limiting the powers of federal regulatory agencies.

The Harding administration established a pro-business tone reminiscent of the McKinley White House. To sustain economic growth, Secretary of the Treasury Mellon promoted government spending cuts and federal tax reductions. As Ronald Reagan would argue sixty years later, Mellon insisted that tax cuts should go mainly to the rich, on the assumption that wealth in the hands of the few would promote the general welfare through increased capital investment.

At Mellon's behest, Congress first repealed the wartime excess-profits tax and lowered the maximum rate on personal income from 65 percent to 50 percent. Subsequent revenue acts eventually lowered the maximum tax rate to 20 percent. The Revenue Act of 1926 extended further benefits to high-income individuals by lowering estate taxes and repealing the gift tax. Much of the tax money released to the wealthy by these acts seems to have fueled the speculative excess of the late 1920s as much as it boosted consumer spending and entrepreneurial activity. Mellon, however, did balance the federal budget for a time. Government expenditures fell, as did the national debt.

In addition to tax cuts, Mellon favored the time-honored Republican policy of high tariffs. So, too, did spokesmen for several emerging industries. Wartime innovations in chemical and metal processing revived the argument for protection of infant American industries from foreign competition. The Fordney-McCumber Tariff of 1922 dramatically increased rates on chemical and metal products as a safeguard against the revival of German industries that had previously commanded the field. To please the farmers, the new act further extended the duties on imported farm products.

Higher tariffs had unexpected consequences, however. During the war the United States had been transformed from a debtor nation to a creditor nation. Foreign capital had long flowed into the United States, playing an important role in fueling economic expansion. But the private and public credits given the Allies to purchase American supplies during the war had reversed the pattern. Mellon now insisted that the European powers repay all that they had borrowed during the war, but the American tariff walls erected against imports made it all the harder for other nations to sell their products in the United States and thereby acquire dollars with which to repay their war debts. For nearly a decade further extensions of U.S. loans and investments sent more dollars abroad, postponing the settling of accounts.

Rounding out the Republican economic program was a more lenient attitude toward government regulation of corporations. Neither Harding nor his successor, Calvin Coolidge, could dissolve the regulatory agencies created by Progressivism, but they named commissioners who promoted "friendly" government regulation. Harding appointed advocates of big business to the Interstate Commerce Commission, the Federal Reserve Board, and the Federal Trade Commission. One senator characterized the new appointments as "the nullification of federal law by a process of boring from within." Republican senator Henry Cabot Lodge agreed, noting, "We have torn up Wilsonism by the roots."

A CORRUPT ADMINISTRATION   Republican conservatives such as Lodge, Mellon, Coolidge, and Hoover were operating out of a sincere philosophical conviction intended to benefit the nation. By contrast, the crass members of Harding's "Ohio gang" used their White House connections to line their own pockets. In 1923 Harding learned that the head of the Veterans Bureau was systematically looting the government's medical and hospital supplies. The corrupt administrator resigned and fled to Europe, and Harding's general counsel committed suicide.

Not long afterward a close crony of Attorney General Daugherty's also shot himself. The man held no federal appointment, but he had set up an office in the Justice Department from which he peddled influence for a fee. Daugherty himself was implicated in the fraudulent handling of German assets seized after the war. When investigated, he refused to testify on the grounds that he might incriminate himself. Twice brought to court, he was never indicted; possibly the lack of evidence was a result of his destruction of pertinent records. These were but the most visible of the many scandals that touched the Justice Department, the Prohibition Bureau, and other agencies under Harding.

But one major scandal rose above all others. Teapot Dome, like the Watergate break-in fifty years later, became the catchword for an era of government corruption. An oil deposit on federal land in Wyoming, Teapot Dome had been set aside to be administered by the Interior Department under Albert Fall. Fall let private companies exploit the oil deposits, arguing that such contracts were in the government's interest. Yet he acted in secret, without allowing competitive bids.

Suspicion grew when Fall's personal standard of living suddenly skyrocketed. It turned out that he had taken "loans" of about $400,000 (which came in "a little black bag") from oil executives. For the rest of his life, Fall insisted that the loans were unrelated to the oil leases and that he had contrived a good deal for the government, but at best the questionable circumstances revealed his fatal blindness to propriety.

Harding himself avoided public disgrace. How much he knew of the scandals swirling around him remains unclear, but he knew enough to give the

Juggernaut

This 1924 cartoon alludes to the dimensions of the Teapot Dome scandal.

appearance of being troubled. "My God, this is a hell of a job!" he confided to a journalist. "I have no trouble with my enemies, I can take care of my enemies all right. But my damn friends, my God-damn friends. . . . They're the ones that keep me walking the floor nights!" In 1923 Harding left on what would be his last journey, a western speaking tour and a trip to the Alaska Territory. In Seattle he suffered an attack of food poisoning, recovered briefly, then died in a San Francisco hotel.

Not since the death of Lincoln had there been such an outpouring of grief for a "beloved President," for the kindly, ordinary man who found it in his heart (as Wilson had not) to pardon Eugene Debs, the former Socialist candidate who had been jailed for opposing U.S. intervention in World War I. As Harding's funeral train moved toward Washington, D.C., then back to Ohio, millions stood by the tracks to honor their lost leader.

Eventually, however, grief yielded to scorn and contempt. For nearly a decade after Harding's death, scandalous revelations concerning his administrative officials were paraded before congressional committees and then the courts. Harding's extramarital affairs also came to light. As a result of the amorous detours and corrupt associates, Harding's foreshortened administration came to be viewed as one of the worst in history. More recently, however, scholars have suggested that the scandals obscured several accomplishments. Some historians credit Harding with leading the nation out of the turmoil of the postwar years and creating the foundation for the decade's remarkable economic boom. They also stress that he was a hardworking president who played a far more forceful role in shaping economic and foreign policies than was previously believed. Harding also promoted diversity and civil rights. He appointed Jews to key federal positions and criticized the Klan as well as other "factions of hatred and prejudice and violence." No previous president had promoted women's rights as forcefully as Harding did. Still, even Harding's foremost scholarly defender admits that he lacked good judgment and "probably should never have been president."

"SILENT CAL"   The news of Harding's death came when Vice President Calvin Coolidge was visiting his father in the mountain village of Plymouth, Vermont, his birthplace. There, at 2:47 A.M. on August 3, 1923, by the light of a kerosene lamp, Colonel John Coolidge administered the oath of office to

Conservatives in the White House

Warren Harding (left) and Calvin Coolidge (right).

his son. The rustic simplicity of Plymouth, the very name itself, evoked just the image of traditional values and solid integrity that the country would long for amid the wake of the Harding scandals.

Coolidge brought to the White House a clear conviction that the presidency should revert to its passive stance of the Gilded Age and defer to the leadership of Congress. Americans embraced the unflappability of Silent Cal and his conservatism. Even more than Harding, Coolidge identified the nation's welfare with the success of big business. "The chief business of the American people is business," he intoned. "The man who works there worships there." Where Harding had sought to balance the interests of labor, agriculture, and industry, Coolidge focused on industrial development at the expense of the other two areas. He sought to unleash the free-enterprise system, and even more than Harding, he sought to end government regulation and reduce taxes.

THE ELECTION OF 1924   In filling out Harding's unexpired term, Calvin Coolidge successfully distanced himself from the scandals and put two lawyers of undoubted integrity in charge of the prosecutions. A man of honesty and ability, a good administrator who delegated well and managed Republican factions adroitly, he quietly took control of the Republican party machinery and seized the initiative in the campaign for the 1924 nomination, which he won with only token opposition.

The Coolidge luck held as the Democrats again fell victim to internal dissension, prompting humorist Will Rogers's classic statement that "I am a member of no organized political party. I am a Democrat." The party's divisions reflected the deep rift between the new urban culture of the twenties and the more traditional hinterland, a gap that the party could not bridge. It took 103 ballots to bestow a tarnished nomination on John W. Davis, a Wall Street lawyer from West Virginia who could nearly outdo Coolidge in conservatism.

While the Democrats bickered, a new farm-labor coalition mobilized a third-party effort. Meeting in Cleveland on July 4, 1924, farm and labor groups reorganized the Progressive party and nominated Wisconsin senator Robert M. La Follette for president. La Follette also won the support of the Socialist party and the American Federation of Labor.

In the campaign, Coolidge focused on La Follette, whom he called a dangerous radical who would turn America into a "communistic and socialistic state." The country preferred to "keep cool with Coolidge," who swept both the popular and the electoral votes by decisive majorities. Davis took only the solid Democratic South, and La Follette carried only his native Wisconsin.

The New Era

Business executives interpreted the 1924 Republican victory as a vindication of their leadership, and Coolidge saw in the decade's surging prosperity a confirmation of his pro-business philosophy. In fact, the prosperity and technological achievements of the time had much to do with Coolidge's victory over the Democrats and Progressives. Those in the large middle class who before had formed an important part of the Progressive coalition were now absorbed instead into the new corporate and consumer world created by advances in communications, transportation, and business organization. As more and more commentators stressed, the United States was entering a "new era" of advanced capitalism.

THE CONSUMER CULTURE   The economy was changing markedly during the 1920s. Dramatic increases in efficiency meant that the marketplace was flooded with new consumer delights. Goods once available only to the wealthy were now accessible to the general public. Middle-class consumers could own cameras, wristwatches, cigarette lighters, vacuum cleaners, and washing machines. But those enticing new goods would produce economic havoc if people did not abandon their traditional notions of frugality and go on a buying spree. Hence, business leaders, salespersons, and public relations experts began a concerted effort to eradicate what was left of the original Protestant ethic's emphasis on plain living.

The public had to be taught the joys of carefree consumerism, and the new industry of mass advertising obliged. By portraying impulse buying as a therapeutic measure to bolster self-esteem, advertisers shrewdly helped undermine notions of frugality. In his popular novel *Babbitt,* Sinclair Lewis recognized advertising's impact upon middle-class life: "These standard advertised wares—toothpastes, socks, tires, cameras, instantaneous hot water heaters—were the symbols and proofs of excellence."

Inventions in communications, such as motion pictures, radio, and telephones, were also transforming social life and creating a more homogeneous national culture. In 1905 the first movie house opened, in Philadelphia, and within three years there were nearly 10,000 movie theaters nationwide. During the next decade, Hollywood became the center of movie production, spinning out Westerns and the timeless comedies of Mack Sennett's Keystone Company, in which slapstick comedians, most notably Charlie Chaplin, perfected their art, transforming it into a powerful form of social criticism. By the mid-1930s every large city and most small towns had movie theaters, and films replaced oratory as the chief mass entertainment, growing into a multimillion-dollar industry that catered to the working poor as well as to the affluent. In the mid-1920s motion pictures were attracting 50 million people weekly, equal to half the national population.

Radio broadcasting had an even more spectacular growth. The first radio commercial aired in 1922. By the end of that year, there were over 500 stations and some 3 million receivers in action. In 1927 Congress established a Federal Radio Commission to regulate the industry; in 1934 it became the Federal Communications Commission, with authority over other forms of communication as well. Calvin Coolidge was the first president to address the nation by radio, and he did so each month, paving the way for Franklin Roosevelt's popular and influential "fireside chats."

A nationwide mass culture replaced the local and regional economies of the nineteenth century. The leading advertising agency explained in 1926 that the advent of nationally circulated magazines, chain stores,

The Rise of Radio

The radio brings this farm family together and connects them to the outside world. By the end of the 1930s, millions would tune in to newscasts, soap operas, sports events, and church services.

syndicated news features, motion pictures, national brand names, and radio programs was creating "a nation which lives to [the same] pattern everywhere." Nonetheless, even though working-class folk could buy brand goods, phonographs, and radios, as well as movie tickets, the new consumer culture did not erase social distinctions. "Participating in mass culture," as one historian stressed, "made them feel no more mainstream or middle class, no less ethnic, religious, or working class than they already felt."

AIRPLANES, AUTOMOBILES, AND THE ECONOMY   Advances in transportation were equally startling. Wilbur and Orville Wright, owners of a Dayton, Ohio, bicycle shop, built the first airplane, which they flew on a beach near Kitty Hawk, North Carolina, in 1903. The use of planes advanced slowly until the outbreak of war in Europe in 1914. An American aircraft industry developed during the war but foundered in the postwar demobilization. In 1925 the government began to subsidize the industry through airmail contracts, and the following year it started a program of federal aid to air transport and navigation, making available funds for the construction of airports.

Aviation received a psychological boost in 1927 when Charles A. Lindbergh Jr. flew the first transatlantic solo flight, traveling from New York to Paris in thirty-three and a half hours. The scope of the New York City parade honoring

Ford Motor Company's Highland Park Plant, 1913

Gravity slides and chain conveyors contributed to the mass production of automobiles.

Lindbergh surpassed even the celebration of victory in World War I. The accomplishments of Lindbergh and other aviators helped catapult the aviation industry into prominence. By 1930 there were forty-three airline companies in operation in the United States.

Nevertheless, by far the most significant transportation development of the twentieth century was the automobile. The first motor car had been manufactured for sale in 1895, but the founding of the Ford Motor Company in 1903 revolutionized the industry. Ford's reliable Model T (the celebrated Tin Lizzie) appeared in 1908 at a price of $850 (in 1924 it would sell for $290). Henry Ford aimed "to democratize the automobile. When I'm through everybody will be able to afford one, and about everyone will have one." He was right. In 1916 the number of cars manufactured passed 1 million; by 1920 more than 8 million were registered, and in 1929 there were more than 23 million. The production of automobiles stimulated the whole economy by consuming large amounts of steel, rubber, glass, and textiles. It gave rise to a gigantic market for oil products just as the Spindletop gusher heralded the opening of vast southwestern oilfields. The automotive revolution also quickened the movement for good roads, introduced efficient mass-production assembly-line techniques to other industries, speeded transportation and tourism, encouraged the sprawl of suburbs, and sparked real-estate booms in California and Florida.

STABILIZING THE ECONOMY   During the 1920s the efficiency craze, which had been a prominent feature of the Progressive impulse, powered the wheels of mass production and consumption and became a cardinal belief of Republican leaders. As Harding's and Coolidge's dynamic secretary of commerce, Herbert Hoover transformed the trifling Commerce Department into the most active agency of those two Republican administrations. During a period of government retrenchment, Hoover promoted expansion. He sought out new markets for business and sponsored more than 1,000 conferences on product design, production, and distribution. He also extended the wartime emphasis on standardization to include, for example, automobile tires and paving bricks, bedsprings and toilet paper.

Most of all Hoover endorsed the burgeoning trade-association movement. The organization of business trade associations became his favorite instrument for "stabilization," to avoid the waste inherent in competition. Through such associations, executives in a given field would share information on sales, purchases, shipments, production, and prices. The information allowed them to plan with more confidence, the advantages of which included predictable costs, prices, and markets, as well as more stable employment and wages. Sometimes abuses crept in as the associations skirted the edge of legality by engaging in price-fixing and other monopolistic practices, but the Supreme Court in 1925 held the practice of sharing information as such to be within the law.

THE BUSINESS OF FARMING   During the Harding and Coolidge administrations, agriculture remained the weakest sector in the economy, in many ways as weak as it had been during the 1890s, when cities flourished and much of rural America languished. For a brief time after the war, farmers' hopes soared on wings of prosperity. The wartime boom lasted into 1920, and then commodity prices collapsed as European farmers resumed high levels of production. Low prices persisted into 1923, especially in the wheat and corn belts. A bumper cotton crop in 1926 resulted in a price collapse and an early taste of depression in much of the South, where foreclosures and bankruptcies spread.

In some ways, farmers shared the business outlook of the so-called New Era. Many commercial farms, like corporations, were getting larger, more efficient, and more mechanized. By 1930 about 13 percent of all farmers had tractors, and the proportion was even higher on the western plains. Better plows and other new machines were part of the mechanization process that accompanied improved crop yields, fertilizers, and methods of animal breeding.

Farm organizations of the 1920s moved from the attempted alliance with urban labor that had marked the Populist era toward a new view of farmers as profit-conscious business owners. During the postwar farm depression, farm groups formed regional commodity-marketing associations, which enabled them to negotiate ironclad contracts with producers for the delivery of their crops over a period of years. These associations also brought order to the marketing of farm products, requiring uniform standards and grades, efficient handling and advertising, and a business-like organization with professional technicians and executives.

But if concern with marketing co-ops and other business-like approaches drew farmers further from populist traditions, nagging problems still invited political solutions. The most effective political response to the collapse of farm prices of the early 1920s was the formation of the farm bloc, a congressional coalition of western Republicans and southern Democrats that put through a program of agricultural legislation from 1921 to 1923. During that period the farm bloc passed bills exempting farm cooperatives from anti-trust laws and creating new credit banks that could lend to cooperative producing and marketing associations.

In the spring of 1924, Senator Charles L. McNary of Oregon and Representative Gilbert N. Haugen of Iowa introduced a bill to secure "equality for agriculture in the benefits of the protective tariff." Their plan sought to dump American farm surpluses on the world market in order to raise commodity prices in the home market. The goal was to achieve "parity"—that is, to raise domestic farm prices to a point where farmers would have the same purchasing power relative to other commodity prices that they had enjoyed between 1909 and 1914, a time viewed in retrospect as a golden age of American agriculture. A McNary-Haugen bill finally passed both houses of Congress in 1927 and again a year later, only to be vetoed both times by President Coolidge, who criticized the measure as an unsound effort at price-fixing and un-American and unconstitutional to boot. Nonetheless, the bill catapulted the farm problem into the arena of national debate, defined it as a problem of crop surpluses, and revived the political alliance between the South and the West.

SETBACKS FOR UNIONS   Urban workers more than farmers shared in the affluence of the 1920s. "A workman is far better paid in America than anywhere else in the world," a French visitor wrote in 1927, "and his standard of living is enormously higher." Nonfarmworkers gained about 20 percent in real wages between 1921 and 1928, while farm income rose only 10 percent. The benefits of this rise were distributed unevenly, however. Miners and textile workers suffered a decline in real wages. In these and other trades, technological unemployment followed the introduction of new production methods and more efficient machines, because technology eliminated as well as created jobs.

Organized labor did no better than organized agriculture in the 1920s. Even though President Harding had supported the practice of collective bargaining and tried to reduce the twelve-hour workday and the six-day workweek so that laborers "may have time for leisure and family life," he ran into stiff opposition in Congress. Overall, unions suffered a setback after the growth years of the war as the Red Scare and the strikes of 1919 left the uneasy impression that unions practiced political subversion. The brief postwar depression of 1921 further weakened the unions, as did the popularity of open-shop associations. While the open shop in theory implied only the employer's right to hire anyone, in practice it often meant discrimination against unionists and the refusal to recognize unions even in shops where most of the workers belonged to one. Prosperity, propaganda, welfare capitalism, and active hostility combined to cause union membership to drop from about 5 million in 1920 to 3.5 million in 1929.

The Gastonia Strike

These female textile workers pit their strength against that of a national guardsman during the strike at the Loray Mill in Gastonia, North Carolina, in 1929.

PRESIDENT HOOVER, ENGINEER

HOOVER VERSUS SMITH   On August 2, 1927, while on vacation in the Black Hills of South Dakota, President Coolidge passed to reporters slips of paper with the curious statement "I do not choose to run for President in 1928." Exactly what he meant puzzled observers and has since perplexed historians. Apparently he at least half hoped to be drafted at the convention, but his statement cleared the way for Herbert Hoover to mount an active campaign for the Republican nomination. Well before the 1928 Republican Convention in Kansas City, Hoover was too far in the lead to be stopped. The party platform took credit for postwar prosperity, debt and tax reduction, and the high protective tariff that had been in operation since 1922 ("as vital to American agriculture as it is to manufacturing"). It rejected the McNary-Haugen program but promised a farm board to manage crop surpluses more efficiently.

The Democratic nomination went to Governor Alfred E. Smith of New York. The Democratic party had had its fill of factionalism in 1924, and all remained fairly harmonious until Smith revealed in his acceptance speech a desire to liberalize Prohibition. Hoover, by contrast, had pronounced the outlawing of alcoholic beverages "a great social and economic experiment, noble in motive and far-reaching in purpose," and he called for improved enforcement.

The two candidates projected sharply different images. Hoover was the Quaker son of middle America, the successful engineer and businessman from rural Iowa, the brilliant architect of Republican prosperity, a simple man who dressed plainly, spoke tersely, and followed his strong conscience. Smith was the prototype of those things that rural and small-town America distrusted: the son of Irish immigrants, Catholic, and a critic of Prohibition. Outside the large cities such qualities were handicaps he could scarcely surmount, for all his affability and wit. The religious right launched a furious attack on him. The Klan mailed out thousands of postcards proclaiming that the Catholic New Yorker was the Antichrist.

In the third consecutive Republican landslide, Hoover won 21 million popular votes to Smith's 15 million and an even more top-heavy electoral majority of 444 to 87. Hoover even cracked the Solid South, leaving Smith only six Deep South states plus Massachusetts and Rhode Island. The election was above all a vindication of Republican prosperity, but the shattering defeat of the Democrats concealed a major political realignment in the making. Smith had nearly doubled the vote for the Democratic candidate of four years before. Smith's image, though a handicap in the hinterlands, swung big northern cities back into the Democratic column. In the agricultural states of the West, there were signs that some disgruntled farmers had switched over to the Democrats. A coalition of urban workers and unhappy farmers was in the making, and the Great Depression of the 1930s would solidify it.

HOOVER IN CONTROL   The milestone year of 1929 dawned with high hopes. The economy seemed solid, income was rising, and the chief architect of Republican prosperity was about to enter the White House. "I have no fears for the future of our country," Hoover told his inauguration audience. "It is bright with hope."

Forgotten in the rush of later events would be Hoover's credentials as a progressive, humanitarian president. Over the objection of Treasury Secretary Mellon, he announced a plan for tax reductions in the low-income brackets. He shunned corrupt patronage practices, and he refused to countenance "Red hunts" or interference with peaceful picketing of the White

Herbert Hoover

"I have no fears for the future of our country," Hoover told the nation at his inauguration in 1929.

House. He also defended his wife's right to invite prominent blacks to the White House, and he sought more money for all-black Howard University.

Hoover showed greater sympathy than Coolidge for the struggling agricultural sector. In 1929 he pushed through Congress the Agricultural Marketing Act, which established both a Federal Farm Board with a revolving loan fund of $500 million to help farm cooperatives market commodities and a program in which the Farm Board could set up "stabilization corporations" empowered to buy surpluses. To open up glutted markets, he also proposed higher tariffs on imported farm products. After a fourteen-month struggle with competing interests, however, Hoover settled for a generally upward revision of Tariffs on manufactures as well as farm goods. The Hawley-Smoot Tariff of 1930 carried duties to a new high. Average rates went from about 32 to 40 percent. More than 1,000 economists petitioned Hoover to veto the bill because, they predicted, it would raise prices paid by consumers, damage the export trade and thus hurt farmers, promote inefficiency, and provoke foreign reprisals. Events proved them right, but Hoover felt that he had to go along with his party in an election year. That proved to be a disastrous mistake, for it only exacerbated the growing economic depression.

THE ECONOMY OUT OF CONTROL   Depression? Most Americans during the 1920s had come to assume that there would never be another depression. Their misguided optimism proved to be an important factor in generating the economic free fall after 1929. Throughout the 1920s the idea grew that American business had entered a new era of *permanent* growth. Such naive talk helped promote an array of get-rich-quick schemes.

Until 1927 stock values had risen with profits, but then they began to soar on wings of fanciful speculation. Mellon's tax reductions had released money that, with the help of aggressive brokerage houses, found its way to Wall Street. One could now buy stock on margin—that is, make a small down payment (usually 10 percent) and borrow the rest from a broker, who held the stock as security against a down market. If the stock price fell and the buyer failed to provide more cash, the broker could sell the stock to cover his loan.

Gamblers in the market ignored warning signs. By 1927 residential construction and automobile sales were catching up to demand, business inventories had risen, and the rate of consumer spending had slowed. By mid-1929 production, employment, and other gauges of economic activity were declining. Still the stock market rose, driven by excessive confidence and perennial greed. By 1929 the stock market had become a fantasy world. Conservative financiers and brokers who counseled caution went unheeded. Hoover worried, too, and he sought to discourage speculation, but to no avail. On September 4 stock prices wavered, and the next day they dropped. The great bull market staggered on into October, trending downward but with enough good days to keep hope alive. On October 22 a leading bank president told reporters, "I know of nothing fundamentally wrong with the stock market or with the underlying business and credit structure."

THE CRASH AND ITS CAUSES   The next day, stock values tumbled, and the day after that a wild scramble to unload stocks lasted until word arrived that leading bankers had formed a pool to buy stocks and halt the slide. For the rest of the week, stock prices steadied, but after a weekend to think the situation over, stockholders began to unload their portfolios. On Tuesday, October 29, the most devastating single day in the market's history to that point, the index dropped almost 13 percent. The plunge in prices fed on itself as brokers sold the shares they held for buyers who failed to come up with more cash. During October the value of stocks on the New York Stock Exchange fell by an average of 37 percent.

Business and government leaders initially expressed hope. According to President Hoover, "the fundamental business of the country" was sound. Some speculators who got out of the market went back in for bargains but found themselves caught in a slow erosion of values. By 1933 the value of stocks on the New York Stock Exchange was less than 20 percent of the value at the market's 1929 peak.

Caution was now the watchword for consumers and business leaders. Buyers held out for lower prices, orders fell off, wages fell or ceased altogether, and the decline in purchasing power brought further cutbacks in business activity. From 1929 to 1932, personal income declined by more than half, from $82 million to $40 million. Unemployment continued to rise dramatically, from 1.6 million in 1929 to 12.8 million in 1933, from 3 percent to 25 percent of the labor force. Farmers, already in trouble, faced catastrophe as commodity prices were cut in half. More than 9,000 banks closed during this period, hundreds of factories and mines shut down, entire towns were abandoned, and thousands of farms were sold to pay debts. A cloud of gloom spread across the nation.

The stock market crash alone did not cause the Great Depression, but it did reveal major structural flaws in the economy and in government policies. Too many businesses during the 1920s had maintained prices and taken profits while holding down wages. As a result, about one third of the nation's personal income went to only 5 percent of the population. By plowing profits back into expansion rather than raising wages, business brought on a growing imbalance between rising productivity and declining purchasing power. As the demand for goods declined, the rate of investment in new plants and equipment also began to decline. For a time the softness of purchasing power was concealed by an increase in installment buying, and the deflationary effects of high tariffs were concealed by the volume of foreign loans and investments, which supported foreign demand for American goods. But the flow of American capital abroad began to dry up when the stock market became a more attractive investment. Swollen profits and dividends enticed the rich into market speculation. When trouble came, the bloated corporate structure collapsed.

Government policies also contributed to the debacle. Treasury Secretary Mellon's tax reductions led to oversaving by the consuming public, which helped diminish the demand for consumer goods. The growing money supply fed the fever of speculation by lowering interest rates. Hostility toward unions discouraged collective bargaining and may have worsened the prevalent imbalances in income. High tariffs discouraged foreign trade. Lax enforcement of anti-trust laws encouraged concentration, monopolies, and high prices.

Another culprit was the gold standard. The world monetary system remained fragile throughout the 1920s. When economic output, prices, and savings began dropping in 1929, policy makers—certain that they had to keep their currencies tied to gold at all costs—either did nothing or tightened money supplies, thus exacerbating the downward spiral. The only way to restore economic stability within the constraints of the gold standard was to let prices and wages continue to fall. The best policy, Andrew Mellon advised, would be to "liquidate labor, liquidate stocks, liquidate the farmers, liquidate real estate," allowing the downturn to "purge the rottenness out of the system." Such passivity helped turn a recession into the world's worst depression.

THE HUMAN TOLL OF THE DEPRESSION   The devastating collapse of the economy caused immense social hardships across the nation. By 1933 over 13 million people were out of work, and many more found themselves working fewer hours. African Americans and Mexicans were usually the first laid off. Factories shut down, banks closed, and farms went bankrupt; millions of people found themselves not only jobless but also homeless and penniless. Hungry people lined up at churches and soup kitchens; others rummaged through trash cans behind restaurants. Local welfare agencies were swamped with appeals for charity and quickly ran out of funds. Many of the destitute slept on park benches or in back alleys. Others congregated in makeshift shelters in vacant lots. Thousands of desperate men in search of jobs rode the rails. These hobos or tramps, as they were derisively called, sneaked onto empty railway cars and rode from town to town looking for work. During the winter homeless people wrapped themselves in newspapers to keep warm, sarcastically referring to their coverings as Hoover blankets. Some grew weary of their grim fate and ended their lives. Suicide rates soared during the 1930s. America had never before experienced social distress on such a scale.

HOOVER'S EFFORTS AT RECOVERY   Although the policies of public officials helped bring on economic collapse, few political or economic leaders acknowledged the severity of the crisis: all that was needed, they thought, was a slight correction of the market. Those who held to the theory of limited government, such as Andrew Mellon, thought the economy would cure itself. Hoover, however, was unwilling to sit by and let events take their course. In fact, he did more than any previous president had ever done in such dire economic circumstances. Still, his own philosophy, now hardened into dogma, set strict limits on action by the federal government, and he refused to set his philosophy aside even to meet the unprecedented emergency.

Hoover believed that the country's main need was confidence. In speech after speech, he exhorted the public to keep up hope. He asked business and labor leaders to keep the mills and shops open, maintain wage levels, and spread out the work to avoid layoffs—in short, to let the shock fall on corporate profits rather than on purchasing power. In return, union leaders, who had little choice, agreed to refrain from making wage demands and staging strikes.

While reassuring the public, however, Hoover also accelerated the commencement of government construction projects in order to provide jobs, but state and local cutbacks more than offset the new federal spending. At

Hoover's demand the Federal Reserve returned to an easier credit policy, and Congress passed a modest tax reduction to put more purchasing power into people's pockets. The high Hawley-Smoot Tariff, proposed at first to help farmers, brought reprisals abroad, devastating foreign trade.

As always, depression hurt the political party and president in power. Near the city dumps and along railroad tracks, the dispossessed huddled in shacks of tar paper and galvanized iron, in old packing boxes and abandoned cars. These squalid settlements were labeled Hoovervilles; a Hoover flag was an empty pocket turned inside out. Such scornful labels reflected the quick erosion of Hoover's political support. In 1930 the Democrats gained their first national victory since 1916, winning a majority in the House and enough gains in the Senate to control it in coalition with farm state Republicans in the West.

CONGRESSIONAL INITIATIVES   With a new Congress in session, demands for federal action impelled Hoover to stretch his philosophy of

Impact of the Depression

Two children set up shop in a Hooverville in Washington, D.C.

government to its limits. He was ready now to use government resources to at least shore up the financial institutions. In early 1932 the new Congress responded to pleas from the desperate banking sector by setting up the Reconstruction Finance Corporation (RFC) to provide emergency loans to banks, life-insurance companies, building-and-loan societies, farm mortgage associations, and railroads. The RFC staved off some bankruptcies, but Hoover's critics charged that it favored business at the expense of workers. The RFC nevertheless remained a key federal agency through the decade and during World War II.

Further help to the financial structure came with the Glass-Steagall Act of 1932, which increased the availability of commercial loans. It also released about $750 million in gold formerly used to back Federal Reserve notes, countering the effect of foreign withdrawals and domestic hoarding of gold at the same time that it enlarged the supply of credit. For homeowners the Federal Home Loan Bank Act of 1932 created with Hoover's blessing a series of discount banks for home mortgages. They provided savings-and-loan associations with a service much like the one that the Federal Reserve System provided to commercial banks.

Hoover's critics argued that all these measures reflected a dubious "trickle-down" theory. If government could help banks and railroads, asked New York senator Robert F. Wagner, "is there any reason why we should not likewise extend a helping hand to that forlorn American, in every village and every city of the United States, who has been without wages since 1929?" The contraction of credit devastated such debtors as farmers and those who made purchases on the installment plan or held balloon mortgages, whose monthly payments increased over time.

By 1932 members of Congress were filling the hoppers with bills to provide federal relief directly to distressed people. At that point, Hoover might have pleaded "dire necessity," taken the leadership of the relief movement, and salvaged his political fortunes. Instead, he held back and only grudgingly edged toward federal humanitarian relief. On July 21, 1932, he signed the Emergency Relief Act, which avoided a federal dole (direct cash payments to individuals) but gave the RFC $300 million for relief loans to the states, authorized loans of up to $1.5 billion for state and local construction projects, and appropriated $322 million for federal construction.

FARMERS AND VETERANS IN PROTEST Government relief for farmers had long since been abandoned. Faced with total loss, some farmers began to defy the law. Angry mobs stopped foreclosures and threatened to lynch bankers and judges. In Nebraska, farmers burned corn to keep warm;

Anger and Frustration

Unemployed veterans, members of the Bonus Expeditionary Force, clash with Washington, D.C., police at Anacostia Flats in July 1932.

dairy farmers dumped milk into roadside ditches in an effort to raise prices. Like voluntary efforts to reduce the number of acres cultivated, these strikes generally failed, but they vividly dramatized the farmers' frustration and anger.

Fears of organized revolt arose when unemployed World War I veterans converged on Washington, D.C., in the spring of 1932. The "Bonus Expeditionary Force" grew quickly to more than 15,000. Their purpose was to get immediate payment of the cash bonus to war veterans that Congress had voted in 1924 in the form of life insurance payable in 1945 (earlier to heirs of deceased veterans). The House approved a bonus bill, but when the Senate voted it down, most of the veterans went home. The rest, having no place to go, camped in vacant government buildings and in a shantytown within sight of the Capitol. The chief of the Washington police gave the squatters a friendly welcome and won their trust, but a fearful White House fretted. Eager to disperse the destitute veterans, Hoover persuaded Congress to vote funds to buy their tickets home. More left, but others stayed even after Congress adjourned, hoping at least to meet with the embattled president.

Late in July the administration ordered the shantytown razed. In the ensuing melee a policeman panicked, fired into the crowd, and killed two veterans. The secretary of war then dispatched about 700 soldiers under General Douglas MacArthur, who was aided by junior officers Dwight D. Eisenhower and George S. Patton. The soldiers easily drove out the unarmed veterans and their families and burned the shacks. MacArthur self-righteously explained in his report that when dealing with "riotous elements," a show of "obvious strength gains a moral ascendancy." General MacArthur claimed that the "mob," spurred by "the essence of revolution," was about to seize control of the government. To most Americans the Bonus Army was more pathetic than threatening. The spectacle of army troops using tanks to dislodge unarmed veterans did not help Hoover's eroding image.

The stress took its toll on Hoover's health and morale. "I am so tired," he sometimes sighed, "that every bone in my body aches." As the months passed, presidential news conferences grew more strained and less frequent. When friends urged Hoover to seize the reins of leadership, he replied, "I can't be a Theodore Roosevelt" or "I have no Wilsonian qualities." His gloom and growing sense of futility were apparent to the country. In a mood more despairing than rebellious, Americans waited impatiently to see what the next presidential campaign would bring.

MAKING CONNECTIONS

- This chapter discussed setbacks suffered by labor unions during the Republican administrations of the 1920s. In the next chapter, unions win new protections under Franklin Roosevelt's New Deal.

- An element of the "normalcy" discussed in this chapter was American isolation from global affairs. Chapter 29 discusses that isolationism in the context of the coming of World War II.

- The characteristics of American society in the 1920s may be compared with the postwar society and culture of the 1950s, discussed in Chapter 32.

FURTHER READING

A fine synthesis of events immediately following the First World War is Ellis W. Hawley's *The Great War and the Search for a Modern Order: A History of the American People and Their Institutions, 1917–1933* (1979).

On Harding, see Robert K. Murray's *The Harding Era: Warren G. Harding and His Administration* (2000). On Coolidge, see Robert H. Ferrell's *The Presidency of Calvin Coolidge* (1998). On Hoover, see Martin L. Fausold's *The Presidency of Herbert C. Hoover* (1985).

Overviews of the depressed economy are found in Charles P. Kindleberger's *The World in Depression, 1929–1939*, rev. and enlarged ed. (1986) and Peter Fearon's *War, Prosperity, and Depression: The U.S. Economy, 1917–1945* (1987). John A. Garraty's *The Great Depression: An Inquiry into the Causes, Course, and Consequences of the Worldwide Depression of the Nineteen Thirties* (1986) describes how people survived the Depression.

28

NEW DEAL AMERICA

FOCUS QUESTIONS

- What were the social effects of the Great Depression and Franklin Roosevelt's efforts at relief, recovery, and reform?
- Why did the New Deal arouse criticism from both the right and the left?
- How did the New Deal expand the federal government's authority and responsibilities?
- What were the major cultural changes of the 1930s?

To answer these questions and access additional review material, please visit www.wwnorton.com/studyspace.

Upon arriving in the White House in March 1933, Franklin Delano Roosevelt (FDR) inherited a nation mired in the third year of an unprecedented economic depression. No other business slump had been so deep, so long, so baffling, or so painful. One out of every four Americans was unemployed, and in many large cities nearly half the adults were out of work. Some 500,000 Americans had lost homes or farms because they could not make their mortgage payments. Thousands of banks had failed; millions of depositors had lost their life savings. The global depression had also helped accelerate the rise of fascism and communism. Totalitarianism was on the march in Europe and Asia—and democratic capitalism was on the defensive. President Roosevelt and a supportive Congress immediately adopted bold measures to relieve the human suffering, restore confidence, and promote economic recovery. Such initiatives provided the foundation for what came to be called welfare capitalism.

From Hooverism to the New Deal

On June 14, 1932, while the ragtag Bonus Army was still encamped in Washington, D.C., Republicans gathered in Chicago to renominate Herbert Hoover. The delegates went through the motions in a mood of defeat. The Democrats, in contrast, converged on Chicago later in the month confident that they would nominate the next president. New York governor Franklin D. Roosevelt had already lined up most of the delegates, and he won the nomination on the fourth ballot.

In a dramatic gesture, Roosevelt appeared in person to accept the nomination instead of awaiting formal notification. He told the expectant delegates, "I pledge you, I pledge myself to a new deal for the American people." What the New Deal would be in practice Roosevelt had little idea as yet, but he was much more flexible and willing to experiment than Hoover. What was more, his upbeat personality communicated joy and hope, as did his campaign song, "Happy Days Are Here Again."

FRANKLIN ROOSEVELT   Born in 1882 into a wealthy family, educated by governesses and tutors at his father's rambling Hudson River estate, Franklin Roosevelt led the cosmopolitan life of a young patrician. After attending an elite Connecticut boarding school, he earned degrees from Harvard and Columbia Law School. While a law student, he married Anna Eleanor Roosevelt, a niece of President Theodore Roosevelt, his own distant cousin.

In 1910 Franklin Roosevelt won a Democratic seat in the New York State Senate. As a freshman legislator he displayed the contradictory qualities that would characterize his political career: he was an aristocrat with a sincere empathy for common folk, a traditionalist with a penchant for experimenting, an affable charmer with an infectious smile and upturned chin who harbored profound convictions, and a skilled political tactician with a shrewd sense of timing and a distinctive willingness to listen to and learn from others.

In 1912 Roosevelt had backed Woodrow Wilson, and for both of Wilson's terms he served as his assistant secretary of the navy. Then, in 1920, largely on the strength of his name, he gained the Democratic vice-presidential nomination. Political defeat was followed by personal crisis when in 1921, at the age of thirty-nine, Roosevelt contracted polio, which left him permanently crippled, unable to stand or walk without braces. But his prolonged struggle with this disability transformed the snobbish young aristocrat. A friend recalled that Roosevelt emerged from his struggle with polio "completely warm-hearted, with a new humility of spirit" that led him to identify with the poor and the suffering. For seven years, aided by his talented wife, Eleanor, Roosevelt strengthened his body, and in 1928 he ran for governor of New York and won. Reelected by a whopping majority of 700,000 in 1930, he became the Democratic front-runner for the presidency in 1932.

Behind the public facade of a cheery and self-confident politician, Roosevelt was at times a crass manipulator of people and power. Obsessed with gaining the highest office in the land, he was willing to sacrifice all else in his life—marriage, health, staff, friends—to that end. Roosevelt occasionally inflated his own accomplishments and took credit for those of others, but his own strengths and achievements were considerable. A born leader, he had a talent for surrounding himself with capable people and getting the most out of them. Most important, however, was his bulldog determination to succeed, to overcome all obstacles, to triumph over despair and adversity, and in the process to achieve greatness.

THE 1932 CAMPAIGN   Partly to dispel doubts about his health, Roosevelt set forth on a grueling campaign tour in 1932. He blamed the Depression on Hoover and the Republicans, and he began to define what he meant by his New Deal. Like Hoover, Roosevelt made the requisite pledge to balance the budget, but he left open the loophole that he would incur short-term deficits to prevent starvation. He was evasive on the tariff, and on farm policy he offered several options pleasing to farmers but ambiguous enough not to alarm city dwellers. He came out unequivocally for strict regulation of electric companies, and he consistently stood by his party's pledge to repeal the Prohibition amendment. Perhaps most important, he recognized that a mature economy would require imaginative national planning. "The country needs, and, unless I mistake its temper, the country demands bold, persistent experimentation." What came across to voters, however, was less the content of his speeches than his irrepressible confidence.

The dour Hoover, by contrast, had no confidence. Democrats, he argued, ignored the international causes of the Depression. Roosevelt's reckless proposals, Hoover warned, "would destroy the very foundations of our

The "New Deal" Candidate

Governor Franklin D. Roosevelt, the Democratic nominee for president in 1932, campaigning in Topeka, Kansas. Roosevelt's confidence inspired voters.

American system." But few were listening. Frustrated by the persistent Depression, the country wanted a new course, a new leadership, a new deal.

Some voters took a dim view of both major candidates. Those who believed that only a radical departure would suffice supported the Socialist party candidate, Norman Thomas, who polled 882,000 votes, and a few went on to support the Communist party candidate, who won 103,000 votes. The wonder is that a desperate people did not turn in greater numbers to such radical alternatives. Instead, they swept Roosevelt into office by a whopping margin.

THE INAUGURATION   For the last time the country waited four months, until March 4, for a new president and Congress to take office. The Twentieth Amendment, ratified on January 23, 1933, provided that the president would thereafter take office on January 20 and the newly elected Congress on January 3.

Amid spreading destitution and misery, unemployment continued to rise during the bleak winter of 1932–1933, and panic struck the banking system. As bank after bank collapsed, frantic people rushed to their own banks to remove their savings. The run on the banks exacerbated the crisis and paralyzed

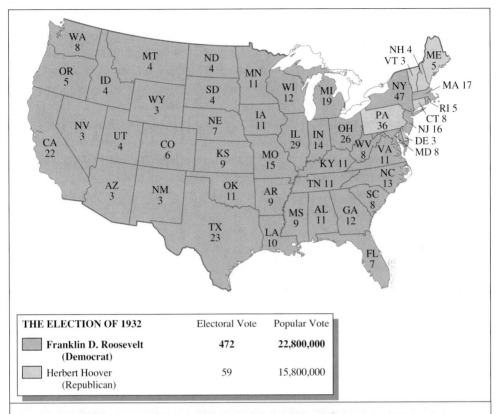

THE ELECTION OF 1932	Electoral Vote	Popular Vote
Franklin D. Roosevelt (Democrat)	472	22,800,000
Herbert Hoover (Republican)	59	15,800,000

Why did Roosevelt appeal to voters struggling during the Depression? What were Hoover's criticisms of Roosevelt's "New Deal"? What policies defined Roosevelt's New Deal during the presidential campaign?

the economy. When the Hoover administration left office, four fifths of the nation's banks were closed, and the country was on the brink of economic paralysis.

The profound crisis of confidence that greeted Roosevelt when he took office on March 4, 1933, gave way to a mood of expectancy. The new president promised vigorous action. He asserted "that the only thing we have to fear is fear itself." He would not merely exhort, he promised: "This nation asks for action, and action now!" He called for "broad executive power to wage a war" against the economic crisis. It was exactly what a distraught nation wanted to hear. One citizen wrote Roosevelt that the speech was "the finest thing this side of heaven. It seemed to give the people, as well as myself, a new hold on life."

COMPETING SOLUTIONS   When Roosevelt and the New Dealers arrived in Washington, they were confronted by three major challenges: reviving the devastated economy, relieving the human misery brought on by the Great Depression, and alleviating the desperate plight of farmers and their families. Roosevelt's "brain trust" of advisers developed conflicting opinions about how best to turn the economy around. Some promoted vigorous enforcement of the anti-trust laws as a means of restoring business competition; others argued for the opposite, saying that anti-trust laws should be suspended so as to enable large corporations to collaborate with the federal government in "managing" the economy. Still others called for a massive expansion of welfare programs and a prolonged infusion of government spending to address the profound human crisis and revive the economy.

For his part, Roosevelt vacillated among these three schools of thought. In part his approach reflected the political reality that conservative southern Democrats controlled the Congress and the president could not risk alienating these powerful proponents of balanced budgets and limited government. Roosevelt's inconsistencies also reflected his own outlook. He was a pragmatist rather than an ideologue. As he once explained, "Take a method and try it. If it fails admit it frankly and try another." Roosevelt's New Deal would therefore take the form of a series of trial-and-error actions.

Roosevelt and his advisers initially settled on a three-pronged strategy to address the problems facing the nation. First, they sought to remedy the financial crisis and provide short-term emergency relief for the jobless. Second, they tried to promote industrial recovery through increased federal spending and cooperative agreements between management and organized labor. Third, they attempted to raise commodity prices (and thereby farm income) by paying farmers to reduce the size of crops and herds. By reducing the overall supply of farm products, prices for grain and meat would eventually rise. None of these initiatives worked perfectly, but their combined effect was to restore hope and energy to a nation paralyzed by fear and uncertainty.

STRENGTHENING THE MONETARY SYSTEM   On his second day in office, Roosevelt followed through on his pledge to act decisively: he called a special session of Congress and declared a four-day bank holiday to halt hysteria and restore confidence in the financial system. It took the Democratic-controlled Congress only seven hours to pass the Emergency Banking Relief Act, which permitted sound banks to reopen and provided managers for those still in trouble. On March 12, 1933, in the first of his radio-broadcast "fireside chats," the president insisted that it was safer to "keep your money in a reopened bank than under the mattress." The following day, deposits in reopened banks exceeded withdrawals. Having ended the bank panic, Roosevelt slashed military pensions and government payrolls and then urged Congress to pass the Twenty-first Amendment, which ended Prohibition.

Those measures were but the beginning of an avalanche of executive and legislative action. Between March 9 and June 16, 1933, the so-called Hundred Days, Congress passed more than a dozen of Roosevelt's major proposals, legislation whose scope was unprecedented in American history.

With the banking crisis over, an acute debt problem continued to paralyze farmers and homeowners as did, along with a lingering distrust of the banks. By early 1933 banks were foreclosing on farm mortgages at the rate of 20,000 per month. By executive decree, Roosevelt reorganized all farm credit agencies into the Farm Credit Administration. Congress then authorized the extensive refinancing of farm mortgages at lower interest rates to stem the tide of foreclosures. The Home Owners' Loan Act provided a similar service to city dwellers through the Home Owners' Loan Corporation, which refinanced mortgage loans at lower monthly payments for strapped homeowners. The Banking Act further shored up confidence in the banking system, by creating the Federal Deposit Insurance Corporation to insure personal bank deposits up to $5,000. It also required commercial banks to separate themselves from investment-brokerage operations.

Roosevelt and Congress also tightened the regulation of Wall Street. The Federal Securities Act required that new stock and bond issues register with the Federal Trade Commission and, later, with the Securities and Exchange Commission, a new agency that regulated the chaotic stock and bond markets.

Throughout 1933 Roosevelt tinkered with devaluation of the currency as a way to raise stock and commodity prices and ease the debt burden on strapped investors and farmers. With the government's official abandonment of the gold standard on April 19, the decline in the value of the dollar increased the prices of commodities and stocks at home.

The Galloping Snail

A vigorous Roosevelt drives Congress to action in this *Detroit News* cartoon from March 1933.

RELIEF MEASURES   Another urgent priority in 1933 was relieving the widespread personal distress caused by the Depression. Hoover had steadfastly resisted using federal funds to provide direct relief for the unemployed. Roosevelt had fewer qualms.

Congress took a first step toward relief with the creation of the Civilian Conservation Corps (CCC), which provided useful jobs to working-class men age eighteen to twenty-five. Nearly 3 million CCC workers thereafter performed a variety of jobs in forests, parks, and recreational areas and on soil-conservation projects. They built roads, bridges, campgrounds, and fish hatcheries; planted trees; taught farmers how to control soil erosion; and fought fires. Directed by army officers and foresters, they worked under military discipline and were perhaps the most direct analogue of an army at war in the whole New Deal. Like the military at the time, CCC camps were racially segregated.

The Federal Emergency Relief Administration (FERA) addressed the broader problems of human distress. Designed as a shared undertaking of the federal government and the state and city governments, it was in fact shaped and directed by the Roosevelt administration. Harry L. Hopkins, a tireless social worker from Iowa who had directed Roosevelt's relief program in New York State, headed the new effort and became the second most powerful figure in the administration. He pushed the FERA with a boundless energy, spending $5 million within two hours of taking office. FERA funds created jobs by financing state construction of over 5,000 public buildings and 7,000 bridges, organized adult literacy programs, financed college education for poor students, and set up day-care centers for low-income families. The FERA also helped local agencies dispense food and clothing to the needy.

The first large-scale experiment with *federal* work relief, which put people directly on the government payroll at competitive wages, came with the formation of the Civil Works Administration (CWA). Created in November 1933, when it had become apparent that the state-sponsored programs funded by the FERA were inadequate, the CWA provided federal jobs and wages to those unable to find work that winter. It was hastily conceived and implemented but during its four-month existence put to work over 4 million people. The agency organized a variety of useful projects: from making highway repairs and laying sewer lines, constructing or improving more than 1,000 airports and 40,000 schools, and providing 50,000 teaching jobs that helped keep rural schools open. As the number of people employed by the CWA soared, the program's costs skyrocketed to over $1 billion. Roosevelt balked at the expenditures and worried that people would become dependent upon federal jobs. So in the spring of 1934, he ordered the CWA dissolved. By April some 4 million workers were again unemployed.

Roosevelt nevertheless continued to favor work relief over the dole (direct cash payment to individuals); he thought the dole was an addictive "narcotic, a subtle destroyer of the human spirit." Real jobs, however, nurtured "self-respect and self-reliance." In 1935, he asked, therefore, for an array of new federal job programs, and Congress responded by passing a $4.8-billion bill providing work relief for the jobless. To manage these programs, Roosevelt created the Works Progress Administration (WPA), headed by Harry Hopkins. Hopkins was told to provide millions of jobs quickly, and as a result some of the new jobs appeared to be make-work or mere "leaning on shovels." But before the WPA died during World War II, it left permanent monuments on the landscape in the form of buildings, bridges, hard-surfaced roads, airports, and schools.

The WPA also employed a wide range of talented Americans in the Federal Theatre Project, the Federal Art Project, the Federal Music Project, and the Federal Writers' Project. Talented writers such as Ralph Ellison, John Cheever, and Saul Bellow found work writing travel guides to the United States, and Orson Welles directed Federal Theatre Project productions. Critics charged that these programs were frivolous, but Hopkins replied that writers and artists needed "to eat just like other people." The National Youth Administration (NYA), also under the WPA, provided part-time employment to students, set up technical training programs, and aided jobless youths. Twenty-seven-year-old Lyndon Johnson was director of an NYA program in Texas, and Richard Nixon, a penniless Duke University law student, found work through the NYA at 35¢ an hour. Although the WPA took care of only about 3 million out of some 10 million jobless at any one time, in all it helped some 9 million Americans weather desperate times before it expired in 1943.

Recovery through Regulation

In addition to rescuing the banks and providing immediate relief for the unemployed, Roosevelt and his advisers promoted the recovery of the agricultural and industrial sectors. Roosevelt's brain trust of university-trained experts, lawyers, and professors initially believed that the trend toward economic concentration was inevitable: big businesses were not going to disappear. The brain trust also believed that the mistakes of the 1920s showed that the only way to operate an integrated economy at full capacity and in the public interest was through stringent regulation and organized central planning in cooperation with big business, not by breaking up huge corporations. The success of gevernment-led economic planning during World War I reinforced such ideas. New recovery programs sprang from those beliefs.

AGRICULTURAL RECOVERY   The sharp decline in crop prices after 1929 meant that many farmers could not afford to plant or harvest their crops. The Agricultural Adjustment Act of 1933 created the Agricultural Adjustment Administration (AAA), which sought to help raise commodity prices by paying farmers to cut back production. The money for the benefits payments made to farmers would be raised from a "processing tax" levied on the businesses that processed farm products for sale (such as cotton gins, flour mills, and meatpacking plants).

As a complement to the AAA, Roosevelt created the Commodity Credit Corporation. This CCC extended loans to farmers above the market price of their crops, which were kept off the market in federal warehouses. If crop prices rose over time, a farmer could repay the loan, retrieve the crops, and sell them. If prices did not rise, the government kept the crops in storage, and the farmer kept the loaned money.

By the time Congress acted on the farm bills in 1933, the growing season was already under way, and the prospect of another bumper cotton crop created an urgent problem. The AAA reluctantly sponsored a plow-under program. To destroy a growing crop was a "shocking commentary on our civilization," Agriculture Secretary Henry Wallace lamented. "I could tolerate it only as a cleaning up of the wreckage from the old days of unbalanced production." In addition to plowing under ripening crops, the AAA encouraged farmers to destroy young livestock as a means of raising prices by reducing supply.

For a while these farm measures worked. By the end of 1934, Wallace could report significant declines in wheat, cotton, and corn production and a simultaneous increase in commodity prices. Farm income increased by 58 percent between 1932 and 1935. The AAA was only partially responsible for the gains, however. The devastating drought that settled over the Great Plains between 1932 and 1935 played a major role in reducing production and creating the epic "dust-bowl" migrations so poignantly evoked in John Steinbeck's novel *The Grapes of Wrath*. Many migrant families had actually been driven off the land by AAA benefit programs that encouraged large farmers to take land worked by tenants and sharecroppers out of cultivation.

Although it created unexpected problems, the AAA achieved successes in boosting the overall farm economy. Many conservatives, however, opposed its sweeping powers, and on January 6, 1936, the Supreme Court, in *United States v. Butler,* ruled the AAA's tax on food processors unconstitutional. The administration hastily devised a new plan to achieve crop reduction indirectly, with the Soil Conservation and Domestic Allotment Act (1936), which it pushed through Congress in six weeks. The new act omitted processing taxes and acreage quotas but provided benefit payments to farmers who engaged in soil-conservation practices and cut back on soil-depleting staple crops. Since the money to pay benefits came out of general funds and not from taxes, the approach was not vulnerable to lawsuits.

The act was an almost unqualified success as an engineering and educational project because it helped heal the scars of erosion and the plague of dust storms. But soil conservation nevertheless failed as a device for limiting production. With their worst lands taken out of production, farmers cultivated their fertile acres more intensively. In response, Congress passed the Agricultural Adjustment Act of 1938, which reestablished the earlier programs but left out the processing taxes. Benefit payments to farmers would come from general federal funds. Increasingly federal farm programs came to dominate the nation's agricultural economy.

INDUSTRIAL RECOVERY   The industrial counterpart to the AAA was the National Industrial Recovery Act (NIRA), passed in 1933. The NIRA had two major components. One created the Public Works Administration (PWA), granting $3.3 billion for public buildings, highway programs, flood control, bridges, tunnels, and aircraft carriers. Under the direction of Interior Secretary Harold L. Ickes, the PWA indirectly served the purpose of work relief. Ickes focused on well-planned permanent improvements, and he used private contractors rather than workers on the government payroll. PWA workers built Virginia's Skyline Drive, New York's Triborough Bridge, the Overseas Highway from Miami to Key West, and Chicago's subway system.

The more controversial and ambitious part of the NIRA created the National Recovery Administration (NRA), headed by the colorful former army general Hugh S. Johnson. Modeled on the War Industries Board of 1917–1918, its purpose was twofold: to stabilize the business sector by reducing chaotic competition through the implementation of codes that set wages and prices and to generate more purchasing power for consumers by providing jobs, defining labor standards, and raising wages. The NRA raised trade-union hopes for the protection of basic hour and wage standards and liberal hopes for comprehensive government planning for the economy.

In each industry, committees representing management, labor, and government drew up fair-practice codes. The labor standards were quite progressive. Every code set a forty-hour workweek and minimum weekly wages of $13 ($12 in the South, where living costs were considered lower), which more than doubled earnings in some cases. Child labor under the age of sixteen was prohibited.

Labor unions, already hard pressed by the economic downturn and a loss of members, were understandably concerned about the NRA's efforts to reduce competition by allowing businesses to cooperate in fixing wages and prices as well as production levels. To gain their support, the NRA included a provision that guaranteed the right of workers to organize unions. While prohibiting employers from interfering with labor-organizing efforts, however, the NRA did not create adequate enforcement measures, nor did it require employers to bargain in good faith with labor representatives.

For a time the NRA worked, and an air of confidence began to replace the depression blues as the downward spiral of wages and prices subsided. But as soon as economic recovery began, critics charged that the larger companies were dominating the code negotiations, that they were using the codes to stifle competition by dividing up markets and entrenching their own positions, and that price-fixing among industry giants was robbing small producers of the chance to compete. The NRA wage codes also excluded agricultural and domestic workers—three out of every four employed African Americans. The effort to develop detailed codes for every industry in the nation proved an administrative nightmare, and the daily annoyances of code enforcement inspired growing hostility among business executives.

By 1935 the NRA had developed more critics than friends, and a full economic recovery was nowhere in sight. In 1935, when the Supreme Court declared the NRA unconstitutional, few mourned. Yet the NRA experiment left an enduring mark. With dramatic suddenness the industry codes had set important new workplace standards, such as the forty-hour workweek and the abolition of child labor. The NRA's endorsement of collective bargaining also spurred union growth.

REGIONAL PLANNING   The wide-ranging scope of the New Deal embraced more than the centralized planning approaches of the NRA. The creation of the Tennessee Valley Authority (TVA) was a truly bold venture to revitalize one of the most underdeveloped and poverty-stricken regions of the country, where disease and illiteracy were rampant.

In May 1933 Congress created the TVA as a multipurpose public corporation. The TVA sought to bring cheap electricity to the Tennessee River valley, build fertilizer plants, provide jobs and recreation, and educate rural folk in the ways of modern life. By 1936 the TVA had six dams completed or under way, and the agency had developed a plan to build nine high dams on the Tennessee River, which would create the "Great Lakes of the South." The TVA, moreover, opened the rivers to navigation, fostered soil conservation and forestry, experimented with fertilizers, and drew new industry to the region.

The TVA's success at generating greater power consumption and lower electricity rates awakened private utilities to the mass consumer markets. It also transported farmers of the valley from the age of kerosene to the age of electricity. Although 90 percent of urban dwellers had electricity by 1930, only ten percent of rural Americans did. Through loans of more than $321 million to rural cooperatives, the Rural Electrification Administration paved the way to the electrification of 288,000 rural households in the Tennessee valley and across the nation.

THE SOCIAL COST OF THE DEPRESSION

Although New Deal programs helped ease the devastation wrought by the Depression, they did not restore prosperity or end the widespread human suffering. Throughout the 1930s the Depression continued to take a toll on ordinary Americans who remained in the throes of a shattered economy that was only slowly working its way back to health.

CONTINUING HARDSHIPS   As late as 1939, some 9.5 million workers (17 percent of the labor force) remained unemployed. Prolonged economic hardship continued to create personal tragedies and tremendous social strains. Poverty led desperate people to do desperate things. Petty theft soared during the 1930s, as did street-corner begging and prostitution. Although the divorce rate dropped, in part because couples could not afford to live separately or pay the legal fees to obtain a divorce, all too often husbands down on their luck simply deserted their wives. A 1940 survey revealed that 1.5 million husbands had left home.

With their future uncertain, married couples often decided not to have children; the birthrate plummeted during the 1930s. Couples with children sometimes could not support them. In 1933 the Children's Bureau reported that one out of every five children was not getting enough to eat. Struggling parents often sent children to live with relatives or friends. Some 900,000 children left home and joined the army of homeless "tramps."

Dust Storm Approaching, 1930s

When a dust storm blew in, it brought utter darkness, as well as the sand and grit that soon covered every surface, both indoors and out.

DUST BOWL MIGRANTS   In the southern plains of the Midwest and the Mississippi River valley, a decade-long drought during the 1930s helped produce an environmental and human catastrophe known as the dust bowl. Colorado, New Mexico, Kansas, Nebraska, Texas, and Oklahoma were the hardest hit. As crops withered, income plummeted. Unrelenting winds swept across the treeless plains, scooping up millions of tons of parched topsoil into billowing dark clouds that floated east across entire states, engulfing farms and towns in what were called black blizzards. A massive dust storm in May 1934 darkened skies from Colorado to the Atlantic seaboard, depositing silt on porches and rooftops as well as on ships in the Atlantic Ocean. In 1937 there were seventy-two major dust storms. The worst of them killed livestock and people and caused railroads to derail and automobiles to career off roads. By 1938 over 25 million acres of prairie land had lost most of its topsoil.

What made these dust storms worse than normal was the transition during the early twentieth century from scattered subsistence farming to widespread industrial agriculture, in which "factory farms" used dry-farming techniques to plant vast acres of wheat, corn, and cotton. The advent of powerful tractors, deep-furrow plows, and mechanical harvesters greatly increased the scale and intensity of farming—and the indebtedness of farmers.

The mercurial cycle of falling crop prices and rising indebtedness led farmers to plant as much and as often as they could. Overfarming and overgrazing disrupted the fragile ecology of the plains by decimating the native prairie grasses that stabilized the nutrient-rich topsoil. Constant plowing loosened vast amounts of dirt that were easily swept up by powerful winds during the devastating drought of the 1930s. Hordes of grasshoppers followed the gigantic dust storms and devoured what meager crops were left standing.

Human misery paralleled the environmental devastation. The dust storms penetrated windows and doors. A Kansas woman reported that the grit "got into cupboards and clothes closets; our faces were as dirty as if we had rolled in the dirt; our hair was gray and stiff and we ground dirt between our teeth." Parched farmers could not pay mortgages, and banks foreclosed on their property. Suicides and divorces soared in the "Dust Bowl" states. With each year, millions of people abandoned their farms.

Uprooted farmers and their families formed a migratory stream rushing from the blighted South and Midwest toward California, buoyed by currents of hope and desperation. The West Coast was rumored to have plenty of jobs. So off they went on a cross-country trek in search of new opportunities. Although frequently lumped together as "Okies," most of the dust-bowl refugees were from cotton belt communities in Arkansas, Texas, and Missouri, as well as Oklahoma. During the 1930s and 1940s, some 800,000 people left those four states and headed to the Far West. Not all were farmers; many were white-collar workers and retailers whose jobs had been tied to the health of the agriculture sector. Most of the dust-bowl migrants were white, and most were young adults in their twenties and thirties who relocated with spouses and children. Some traveled on trains or buses; others hopped a freight train or hitched a ride; most rode in their own cars, the trip taking four to five days on average.

The dust-bowl migrants who had come from cities gravitated to California's urban areas—Los Angeles, San Diego, or San Francisco. Many of the newcomers, however, moved into the San Joaquin Valley, the agricultural heartland of the state. There they discovered that California was no paradise. Only a few of the migrants could afford to buy land. Most found themselves competing with local Latinos and Asians for seasonal work as pickers in the cotton fields or orchards of large corporate farms. Living in tents or crude cabins and frequently on the move, they suffered from exposure and poor sanitation.

They also felt the sting of social prejudice. The writer John Steinbeck explained that "Okie us'ta mean you was from Oklahoma. Now it means you're a dirty son-of-a-bitch. Okie means you're scum. Don't mean nothing in it-self, it's the way they say it." Such hostility toward the migrants drove one third of them to return to their home states. Most of the farmworkers who stayed tended to fall back upon their old folkways rather than assimilate into their new surroundings. These gritty "plain folk" had brought with them their own prejudices, against blacks and ethnic minorities, as well as a potent tradition of evangelical Protestantism and a distinctive style of music vari-ously labeled country, hillbilly, or cowboy. This "Okie" subculture remains a vivid part of California society.

MINORITIES AND THE NEW DEAL   The Depression was especially traumatic for the most disadvantaged groups. However progressive Franklin Roosevelt was on social issues, he failed to assault long-standing patterns of racism and segregation for fear of alienating conservative southern Democrats in Congress. As a result, many of the New Deal programs were for whites only. The Federal Housing Administration, for example, refused to guarantee mortgages on houses purchased by blacks in white neighborhoods. Both the CCC and the TVA practiced racial segregation.

The efforts of the Roosevelt administration to raise crop prices by reduc-ing production proved especially devastating for African Americans and Mexican Americans. To earn the federal payments for reducing crops as pro-vided by the AAA and other New Deal agriculture programs, many farm owners would first take out of cultivation the marginal lands worked by ten-ants and sharecroppers, many of whom were blacks or Latinos. The effect was to drive the landless off farms and eliminate the jobs of many migrant workers. Over 200,000 African-American tenant farmers nationwide were displaced by the AAA.

Mexican Americans suffered even more. Thousands of Mexicans had mi-grated to the United States during the 1920s, most of them settling in Cali-fornia, New Mexico, Arizona, Colorado, Texas, and the midwestern states. But because many Mexican Americans were unable to prove their citizen-ship, either out of ignorance of the regulations or because their migratory work hampered their ability to meet residency requirements, they were de-nied access to the many new federal relief programs under the New Deal. As economic conditions worsened, government officials called for the deporta-tion of Mexican-born Americans to avoid the cost of providing them with public services and relief. By 1935 over 500,000 Mexican Americans and their American-born children had returned to Mexico. The state of Texas alone returned over 250,000 people.

Native Americans were also devastated by the Great Depression. They initially were encouraged by Roosevelt's appointment of John Collier as the commissioner of the Bureau of Indian Affairs (BIA). Collier steadily increased the number of Native Americans employed by the BIA and strove to ensure that Indians gained access to the various New Deal relief programs. Collier's primary objective, however, was passage of the Indian Reorganization Act. He wanted the new legislation to replace the provisions of the 1887 Dawes Act, which had sought to "Americanize" the Indians by breaking up their tribal land and allocating it to individuals. Collier insisted that the Dawes Act had produced only widespread poverty and demoralization. He hoped to reinvigorate Indian cultural traditions by restoring land to tribes, granting Indians the right to charter business enterprises and establish self-governing constitutions, and providing federal funds for vocational training and economic development. The act that Congress finally passed was a much-diluted version of Collier's original proposal, however.

CULTURE IN THE THIRTIES

In view of the celebrated—if exaggerated—alienation of writers, artists, and intellectuals rebelling against the materialism of the 1920s, one might have expected the onset of the Great Depression to have deepened their despair. Instead, it brought a renewed sense of militancy and affirmation, as if society could no longer afford the art-for-art's-sake outlook of the 1920s.

In the summer of 1932, even the "golden boy" of the lost generation, the writer F. Scott Fitzgerald, had declared that "to bring on the revolution, it may be necessary to work within the Communist party." But few remained Communists for long. Being a notoriously independent lot, most left-wing writers rebelled at demands to hew to a shifting party line. And many abandoned communism upon learning that the Soviet leader Joseph Stalin practiced a tyranny more horrible than anything under the czars.

LITERATURE AND THE DEPRESSION   Among the Depression-era writers who addressed themes of immediate social significance two novelists deserve special notice: John Steinbeck and Richard Wright. The single piece of fiction that best captured the ordeal of the Depression, Steinbeck's *The Grapes of Wrath* (1939), treated workers as people rather than ideological tools. Steinbeck had traveled with displaced "Okies" fleeing the Oklahoma dust bowl to pursue jobs in the fields of California's Central Valley. This firsthand experience allowed him to create a vivid tale of the Joad family's painful journey west from Oklahoma.

Among the most talented of the young novelists emerging in the 1930s was Richard Wright, an African American born near Natchez, Mississippi. The grandson of former slaves and the son of a sharecropper who deserted his family, Wright ended his formal schooling in the ninth grade (as valedictorian of his class). He then worked in Memphis and greedily devoured books he borrowed on a white friend's library card, all the while saving up to go north to escape the racism of the segregated South. In Chicago, where he arrived on the eve of the Depression, the Federal Writers' Project gave him a chance to develop his talent. His period as a Communist, from 1934 to 1944, gave him an intellectual framework that did not overpower his fierce independence.

Native Son (1940), Wright's masterpiece, is set in the Chicago he had come to know before moving to New York. It tells the story of Bigger Thomas, a product of the ghetto, a man hemmed in, and finally impelled to murder, by forces beyond his control. Somehow Wright managed to transform into literary power his own bitterness and rage at what he called "the Ethics of Living Jim Crow."

POPULAR CULTURE   While many writers and artists dealt directly with the human suffering and social tensions spawned by the Great Depression, the more popular cultural outlets, such as radio programs and movies, provided patrons with a welcome escape from the decade's grim realities.

By the 1930s radio had become a major source of family entertainment. More than 10 million families owned a radio, and by the end of the decade the number had tripled. Millions of housewives listened to radio "soap operas," ongoing dramas that were broadcast daily in fifteen-minute episodes and derived their name from their sponsors, soap manufacturers.

Late-afternoon radio programs were directed at children home from school. In the evening after supper, families would gather around the radio to listen to newscasts; comedies such as *Amos 'n' Andy* and the husband-and-wife team of George Burns and Gracie Allen; adventure dramas such as *Jack Armstrong, The Lone Ranger, Dick Tracy,* and *The Green Hornet;* and big-band musical programs, all interspersed with commercials. On Sundays most radio stations broadcast church services. Fans could also listen to baseball and football games or boxing matches. Franklin Roosevelt was the first president to take full advantage of the popularity of radio broadcasting. He hosted sixteen "fireside chats" to generate public support for his New Deal initiatives.

Movies were even more popular than radio shows. In the late 1920s what had been silent films were transformed by the introduction of sound. The "talkies" made movies the most popular form of entertainment during the 1930s—much more popular than they are today. The introduction of double features in 1931 and the construction of outdoor drive-in theaters in 1933 also boosted interest and attendance. More than 60 percent of the population—70 million people—saw at least one movie each week.

The movies of the 1930s rarely dealt directly with hard times. Exceptions were film versions of *Gone with the Wind* (1939) and *The Grapes of Wrath* (1940). Much more common were movies intended for pure entertainment; they transported viewers into the realm of adventure, spectacle, humor, and fantasy. People relished shoot-'em-up gangster films, animated cartoons, spectacular musicals, "screwball" comedies, and horror films such as *Dracula* (1931), *Frankenstein* (1931), *The Mummy* (1932), and *Werewolf of London* (1935).

The best way to escape the daily troubles of the Depression was to watch one of the zany comedies of the Marx Brothers, former vaudeville performers.

The Marx Brothers

In addition to their vaudeville antics, the Marx Brothers satirized social issues such as Prohibition.

As one Hollywood insider explained, the movies of the 1930s were intended to "laugh the big bad wolf of the depression out of the public mind." *The Cocoanuts* (1929), *Animal Crackers* (1930), and *Monkey Business* (1931) introduced Americans to the anarchic antics of Chico, Groucho, Harpo, and Zeppo Marx, who combined slapstick humor with verbal wit to create plotless masterpieces of irreverent satire.

The Second New Deal

During Roosevelt's first year in office, his programs and his personal charms generated massive support. The president's travels and speeches, his twice-weekly press conferences, and his radio-broadcast fireside chats brought vitality and warmth from a once-remote White House. In the congressional elections of 1934, the Democrats increased their strength in both the House and the Senate, an almost unprecedented midterm victory for a party in power. Only seven Republican governors remained in office throughout the country.

ELEANOR ROOSEVELT   One of the reasons for Roosevelt's popularity was his wife, Eleanor, who became an enormous political asset and would prove to be one of the most influential and revered leaders of the time. From an early age, Eleanor Roosevelt had embraced social service. Her compassion resulted in part from the loneliness she experienced as she was growing up and in part from the sense of betrayal she felt upon learning in 1918 that her husband was engaged in an extramarital affair with Lucy Mercer, her secretary. In the face of personal troubles, Eleanor Roosevelt "lived to be kind." Compassionate without being maudlin, more stoical than sentimental, she exuded warmth and sincerity, and she challenged the complacency of the comfortable and the affluent.

The First Lady

An intelligent, principled, and candid woman, Eleanor Roosevelt became a political figure in her own right. Here she is serving as guest host for a radio program, ca. 1935.

Eleanor Roosevelt was an activist who redefined the role of the presidential spouse. She was the first woman to address a national political convention, to write a nationally syndicated column, and to hold regular press conferences. A tireless advocate and agitator, Eleanor crisscrossed the nation, representing the president and the New Deal, defying local segregation ordinances to meet with African-American leaders, supporting women's causes and organized labor, highlighting the plight of unemployed youth, and imploring Americans to live up to their egalitarian and humanitarian ideals.

CRITICISM   Public criticism of the New Deal during Franklin Roosevelt's first year in office was muted. But not for long. The Depression's downward slide had been halted, but unemployment remained high (10 million were out of work in 1935, more than 20 percent of the workforce), and prosperity remained elusive. "We have been patient and long suffering," said a farm leader in October 1933. "We were promised a New Deal. Instead we have the same old stacked deck." Even more unsettling to some was the dramatic growth of executive power and the emergence of welfare capitalism, whereby workers developed a sense of entitlement to federal support programs. In 1934 a group of conservative businessmen and politicians, including Alfred E. Smith and John W. Davis, two former Democratic presidential candidates, formed the American Liberty League to oppose New Deal measures as violations of personal and property rights.

More potent threats to Roosevelt came from the hucksters of social panaceas. The most flamboyant of the group was Louisiana's "Kingfish," Senator Huey P. Long. A short, strutting man, Long sported pink suits and pastel shirts, red ties, and two-toned shoes. He was a brilliant but unscrupulous reformer driven by a relentless urge for power and attention. First as Louisiana's governor, then as political boss of the state, Long had delivered tax favors, roads, schools, free textbooks, charity hospitals, and better public services. That he had become a sort of state dictator in the process, using bribery, physical intimidation, and blackmail to achieve his ends, seemed irrelevant to many of his ardent supporters.

In 1933 Long joined Roosevelt in Washington as a Democratic senator. He initially supported the New Deal but quickly grew suspicious of the NRA's collusion with big business. He had also grown jealous of Roosevelt's mushrooming popularity, having developed his own aspirations for the Oval Office. Promoting himself as a true if self-indulgent friend of the people, Long had his own plan for dealing with the Great Depression.

Long's Share-the-Wealth program proposed to confiscate large personal fortunes, guarantee every family a cash grant of $5,000 and every worker an annual income of $2,500, provide pensions to the aged, reduce working hours, pay veterans' bonuses, and ensure a college education for every qualified student. It did not matter to him that his figures failed to add up or that his program offered little to promote an economic recovery. Whether he had a workable plan or not, by early 1935 the charismatic Long was claiming 7.5 million supporters across the country.

Another popular social scheme was hatched by a gray-haired California doctor, Francis E. Townsend. Outraged by the sight of three elderly women raking through garbage cans in Long Beach, Townsend proposed government pensions for the aged. In 1934 he began promoting the Townsend Recovery Plan, which would pay $200 a month to every citizen over sixty who retired from employment and promised to spend the money within the month. The plan had the lure of providing financial security for the aged and stimulating economic growth. Critics noted that the cost of his program for 9 percent of the population would be more than half the national income. Yet Townsend was indifferent to details. "I'm not in the least interested in the cost of the plan," he blandly told a House committee.

A third huckster of panaceas, Father Charles E. Coughlin, the Roman Catholic "radio priest," founded the National Union for Social Justice in 1935. In broadcasts over the CBS network, he promoted schemes for the coinage of silver and made attacks on bankers that increasingly hinted at anti-Semitism.

"The Kingfish"

Huey Long, governor of Louisiana. Although he often led people to believe he was a country bumpkin, Long was a shrewd lawyer and consummate politician.

Coughlin, Townsend, and Long drew support largely from desperate lower-middle-class Americans. Of the three, Long had the widest following. A 1935 survey showed that he could draw 5 million to 6 million votes as a third-party candidate for president in 1936, perhaps enough to undermine Roosevelt's chances of reelection. Beset by pressures from both ends of the political spectrum, Roosevelt hesitated for months before deciding to "steal the thunder" from the left by instituting new programs of reform and social security. "I'm fighting Communism, Huey Longism, Coughlinism, Townsendism," Roosevelt told a reporter in early 1935. He needed "to save our system, the capitalist system," from such "crackpot ideas." Political pressures impelled Roosevelt to move to the left, but so did the growing influence within the administration from Supreme Court justices Louis Brandeis and Felix Frankfurter. These powerful advisers urged Roosevelt to be less cozy with big business and to push for restored competition and heavy taxes on large corporations.

OPPOSITION FROM THE COURT   A series of Supreme Court decisions finally spurred the president to act. On May 27, 1935, the Court killed the National Industrial Recovery Act by a unanimous vote. The defendants in *Schechter Poultry Corporation v. United States,* quickly tagged the "sick-chicken" case, had been convicted of selling an "unfit chicken" and violating other NRA code provisions. The high court ruled that Congress had delegated too much power to the executive branch when it granted the code-making authority to the NRA. Congress had also exceeded its power under the commerce clause by regulating intrastate commerce. The poultry in question, the Court decided, had "come to permanent rest within the state," although earlier it had been moved across state lines. In a press conference soon afterward, Roosevelt fumed: "We have been relegated to the horse-and-buggy definition of interstate commerce." The same line of reasoning, he warned, might endanger other New Deal programs.

LEGISLATIVE ACHIEVEMENTS OF THE SECOND NEW DEAL
To rescue his legislative program from such judicial and political challenges, Roosevelt in 1935 ended the stalemate in Congress and launched the second phase of the New Deal. He demanded several pieces of "must" legislation, most of which Congress passed within a few months.

The National Labor Relations Act, often called the Wagner Act for its sponsor, New York senator Robert Wagner, gave workers the right to bargain with employers through unions of their own choice and prohibited employers from interfering with union activities. A National Labor Relations Board of five members could supervise plant elections and certify unions as bargaining agents where a majority of the workers approved. The board could also investigate the actions of employers and issue "cease-and-desist" orders against specified unfair practices.

The Social Security Act of 1935, Roosevelt announced, was the New Deal's "cornerstone" and "supreme achievement." Indeed, it has proved to be the most significant and far-reaching of all the New Deal initiatives. The concept was by no means new. Progressives during the early 1900s had proposed a federal system of social security for the aged, indigent, disabled, and unemployed. Other nations had already enacted such programs, but the United States remained steadfast in its tradition of individual self-reliance. The Great Depression revived the idea, however, and Roosevelt masterfully guided the legislation through Congress.

The Social Security Act included three major provisions. Its centerpiece was a federally-administered pension fund for retired people over the age of sixty-five and their survivors. Beginning in 1937, workers and employers contributed payroll taxes to establish the fund. Benefit payments started in 1940 and averaged $22 per month, a modest sum even for those depressed times. Roosevelt stressed that the pension program was not intended to guarantee a comfortable retirement; it was designed to supplement other sources of income and protect the elderly from some of the "hazards and vicissitudes of life." Only later did American come to perceive of Social Security as the *primary* source of retirement income for most of the aged.

Social Security

A poster distributed by the government to educate the public about the new Social Security Act.

The Social Security Act also set up a shared federal-state unemployment-insurance program, financed by a payroll tax on employers. In addition, the new legislation committed the national government to a broad range of social-welfare activities based upon the assumption that "unemployables"—people who were unable to work—would remain a state responsibility while the national government would provide work relief for the able-bodied. To that end the law inaugurated federal grants-in-aid for three state-administered public-assistance programs—old-age assistance, aid for dependent children, aid to the blind—and further aid for maternal, child-welfare, and public health services.

Relatively speaking, the new federal program was quite conservative. It was the only government pension program in the world financed by taxes on the earnings of workers: most other countries funded such programs out of general revenues. The Social Security payroll tax was also a regressive tax in that it entailed a single fixed rate for all, regardless of income level. It thus hurt the poor more than the rich, and it also impeded Roosevelt's efforts to revive the economy because it removed from circulation a significant amount of money: the new Social Security tax took money out of workers' pockets and placed it in a pension trust fund, exacerbating the shrinking money supply that was one of the main causes of the Depression. By taking discretionary income away from workers, the government blunted the sharp increase in public consumption needed to restore the health of the economy. In addition, the Social Security system initially excluded 9.5 million workers who most needed the new program: farm laborers, domestic workers, and the self-employed, a disproportionate percentage of whom were African Americans.

Roosevelt regretted the limitations, but he knew that they were necessary compromises in order to see the Social Security Act through Congress and enable it to withstand court challenges. As he replied to an aide who criticized funding the pension program through employee contributions:

> I guess you're right on the economics, but those taxes were never a problem of economics. They are politics all the way through. We put those payroll contributions there so as to give the contributors a moral, legal, and political right to collect their pensions and their unemployment benefits. With those taxes in there, no damn politician can ever scrap my Social Security program.

The last of the major bills making up the second phase of the New Deal was the Revenue Act of 1935, sometimes called the Wealth-Tax Act but popularly known as the soak-the-rich tax. The Revenue Act raised tax rates on income above $50,000. Estate and gift taxes also rose, as did the corporate tax on all but small corporations (those with an annual income below $50,000).

Business leaders fumed over Roosevelt's tax and spending policies. The wealthy resented their loss of status and the growing power of government and labor. They railed against the New Deal and Roosevelt, whom they called a traitor to his own class. Visitors at the home of J. P. Morgan Jr. were cautioned not to mention Roosevelt's name lest it raise Morgan's blood pressure. By "soaking" the rich, Roosevelt stole much of the thunder from the political left, although the results of his tax policy fell short of the promise. The new soak-the-rich tax failed to increase federal revenue significantly, nor did it result in a significant redistribution of income. Still, the prevailing view was that the president had moved in a radical direction. Roosevelt countered by stressing his basic conservatism and asserting that he had no love for socialism: "I am fighting communism. . . . I want to save our system, the capitalistic system." Yet he added that to save it from revolutionary turmoil required a more equal distribution of wealth.

Roosevelt's Second Term

On June 27, 1936, Roosevelt accepted the Democratic party's presidential nomination for a second term. He promised to continue to promote a government motivated by a "spirit of charity" rather than a government "frozen in the ice of its own indifference."

THE ELECTION OF 1936   The popularity of Roosevelt and the New Deal impelled the Republican Convention in 1936 to avoid candidates too closely identified with the "hate-Roosevelt" contingent. The party chose Governor Alfred M. Landon of Kansas, a former Bull Moose Progressive who had endorsed many New Deal programs. He was probably more liberal than most of his backers and clearly more so than the party's platform, which accused the New Deal of usurping power.

The Republicans hoped that the followers of Huey Long, Charles Coughlin, Francis Townsend, and other dissidents would combine to draw enough votes away from Roosevelt to throw the election to them. But that possibility faded when an assassin, the son-in-law of a Louisiana judge whom Long had sought to remove, gunned down the Kingfish in 1935. Coughlin, Townsend, and a remnant of the Long movement supported Representative William Lemke of North Dakota on a Union party ticket, but it was a forlorn effort, polling only 882,000 votes.

In 1936 Roosevelt forged a new electoral coalition that would affect national politics for years to come. While holding the support of most traditional Democrats in the North and the South, the president made strong gains among beneficiaries of New Deal farm programs in the West. In the northern cities he held on to the ethnic groups helped by New Deal welfare measures. Middle-class voters, whose property had been saved by New Deal initiatives, flocked to support him, as did intellectuals stirred by the ferment of new ideas coming from the government. The revived labor movement threw its support to Roosevelt, and in the most profound departure of all African-American voters for the first time cast the majority of their ballots for a Democratic president. "My friends, go home and turn Lincoln's picture to the wall," a Pittsburgh journalist told black Republicans. "That debt has been paid in full." The final tally revealed that 81 percent of those with an income under $1,000 a year opted for Roosevelt, as did 79 percent of those earning between $1,000 and $2,000. By contrast, only 46 percent of those earning over $5,000 voted for FDR.

In his acceptance speech to the Democratic Convention, Roosevelt abandoned efforts to reassure corporate leaders. As the Americans of 1776 had sought freedom from political autocracy, he noted, the Americans of 1936 sought freedom from the "economic royalists." He later claimed that never before had business leaders been "so united against one candidate." They were "unanimous in their hate for me—and I welcome their hatred." Roosevelt campaigned with tremendous buoyancy, and he wound up carrying every state except Maine and Vermont, with a popular vote of 27.7 million to Landon's 16.7 million. Democrats would also dominate Republicans in the new Congress, by 77 to 19 in the Senate and 328 to 107 in the House. After the lopsided victory, Roosevelt rode a wave of popularity into his second term.

THE COURT-PACKING PLAN   Soon after his landslide reelection, however, Roosevelt found himself deluged in a sea of troubles. His second inaugural address, delivered on January 20, 1937, promised even greater reforms. The challenge to American democracy, he maintained, was that millions of citizens "at this very moment are denied the greater part of what the very lowest standards of today call the necessities of life. . . . I see one-third of a nation ill-housed, ill-clad, ill-nourished." He viewed the election of 1936 as a mandate for even more extensive government action, and the overwhelming Democratic majorities in Congress ensured the passage of new legislation to buttress the Second New Deal. But one major roadblock stood in the way: the Supreme Court.

By the end of its 1936 term, the Court had ruled against New Deal programs in seven of the nine major cases it reviewed. Suits against the Social Security and Wagner Acts were pending. Given the conservative bent of the Court, the Second New Deal seemed in danger of being nullified, just as much of the original New Deal had been.

For that reason, Roosevelt resolved to change the Court's philosophy by enlarging the Court, a move for which there was ample precedent and power. Congress, not the Constitution, determines the size of the Court, which at different times has numbered six, seven, eight, nine, and ten justices and in 1937 numbered nine. On February 5 Roosevelt sent his plan to enlarge the Court to Congress, without having consulted congressional leaders. He wanted to create up to fifty new federal judges, including six new Supreme Court justices, and diminish the power of the judges who had served ten or more years or reached the age of seventy.

But the Court-packing maneuver, as opponents quickly tagged the president's scheme, backfired. It was a shade too contrived, much too brazen, and far too political. By implying that some judges were impaired by senility, Roosevelt affronted the elder statesmen of Congress and the Court, especially Justice Louis D. Brandeis, who was both the oldest and the most liberal of the Supreme Court judges. Roosevelt's scheme also ran headlong into a deep-rooted public veneration of the courts and aroused fears that another president might use the precedent for quite different purposes.

As it turned out, unforeseen events derailed Roosevelt's drive to change the Court. A sequence of Court decisions during the spring of 1937 reversed previous judgments in order to uphold the Wagner and Social Security Acts. In addition, a conservative justice resigned, and Roosevelt named to the vacancy one of the most consistent New Dealers, Senator Hugo Black of Alabama.

Roosevelt later claimed he had lost the battle but won the war. The Court had reversed itself on important New Deal legislation, and the president was able to appoint justices in harmony with the New Deal. But the episode created dissension within the Democratic party and blighted Roosevelt's prestige. For the first time, Democrats in large numbers deserted the president, and the Republican opposition found a powerful issue to use against the administration. During the first eight months of 1937, the momentum of Roosevelt's 1936 landslide victory was lost. As Secretary of Agriculture Henry Wallace later remarked, "The whole New Deal really went up in smoke as a result of the Supreme Court fight."

A NEW DIRECTION FOR LABOR   Rebellions meanwhile erupted on other fronts while the Court-packing bill pended. Under the impetus of the New Deal, the labor-union movement stirred anew. John L. Lewis, head of the United Mine Workers, increased membership from 150,000 to 500,000 within a year. Spurred by the mine workers' example, Sidney Hillman of the Amalgamated Clothing Workers and David Dubinsky of the International Ladies Garment Workers joined Lewis in promoting a campaign to organize workers in the mass-production industries. As leaders of some of the few industrial unions (made up of all types of workers) in the American Federation of Labor, they found the smaller, more restrictive craft unions (made up of male workers, with each union limited to a single skilled trade) to be obstacles to organizing the basic industries.

In 1935, with passage of the Wagner Act, the industrial unionists formed a Committee for Industrial Organization (CIO), and craft unionists (in the AFL) began to fear submergence by the mass unions of unskilled workers. Jurisdictional disputes spread among the unions, and in 1936 the AFL expelled the CIO unions, which then formed a permanent structure, called after 1938 the Congress of Industrial Organizations (also known by the initials CIO). The rivalry spurred both groups to greater unionizing efforts.

The CIO's major organizing drives in the automobile and steel industries began in 1936, but they were thwarted by management's use of blacklisting, private detectives, labor spies, vigilante groups, and other forms of intimidation to suppress the unions. Early in 1937 automobile workers spontaneously adopted a new technique, the "sit-down strike," in which workers refused to leave a plant until employers granted collective bargaining rights to their union.

Led by the fiery young autoworker and union organizer Walter Reuther, thousands of employees at the General Motors assembly plants in Flint, Michigan, occupied the factories and stopped all production. Management refused to recognize the union efforts, and the standoff lasted over a month before the company finally relented and signed a contract recognizing the United Automobile Workers. Other automobile manufacturers soon followed suit. And the following month, U.S. Steel capitulated to the Steel Workers Organizing Committee (later the United Steelworkers of America), granting it recognition, a 10 percent wage hike, and a forty-hour workweek.

Having captured two giants of heavy industry, the CIO went on in the next few years to organize much of industrial America: the rubber, oil, and electronics industries and a good part of the textile industry, in which unionists had to fight protracted struggles to organize scattered plants. The slow pace of labor organizing in textiles denied the CIO a major victory in the South comparable to its swift conquest of automobiles and steel in the North, but even down South a labor movement gained a foothold. Union membership in the United States grew from under 3 million in 1933 to 8.5 million in 1940. Wages rose and working conditions improved because of their efforts. Whether by design or accident, union members became solid Democrats.

A SLUMPING ECONOMY   During the years 1935 and 1936 the economy finally showed signs of recovery. By the spring of 1937, economic output had moved above the 1929 level. But worried about deficits and rising inflation, Roosevelt ordered sharp cuts in federal spending. At the same time the Treasury began to reduce disposable income by collecting $2 billion in Social Security from employee paychecks. Private spending could not fill the gap left by reductions in government spending, and big business still lacked the faith to risk large capital investments. The result was the slump of 1937, which was sharper than that of 1929 but was called by the press a recession to distinguish it from the depression. By the end of 1937, an additional 4 million people had been thrown out of work; grim scenes of the earlier depression reappeared. The 1937 recession ignited a fierce debate within the administration. One group, led by Treasury Secretary Henry Morgenthau, favored less federal spending and a balanced budget. The other group, which included Harry Hopkins and Harold Ickes, argued for renewed government spending and stricter enforcement of anti-trust laws.

ECONOMIC POLICY AND LATER REFORMS Roosevelt seemed bewildered by the recession, but he eventually endorsed the ideas of the spenders. In the spring of 1938, he asked Congress to adopt a large-scale spending program intended to increase mass purchasing power, and Congress voted almost $3.3 billion, mainly for public works projects. In a short time the increase in spending reversed the economy's decline, but the recession and Roosevelt's reluctance to adopt massive, sustained government spending forestalled the achievement of full recovery. Only the massive crisis of World War II would return the U. S. economy to full production and full employment.

The 1937 recession further eroded Roosevelt's prestige and dissipated the mandate of the 1936 elections. The only major reforms enacted in Roosevelt's second term were the Wagner-Steagall National Housing Act, the Bankhead-Jones Farm Tenant Act, and the Fair Labor Standards Act. The Housing Act of 1937 set up the U.S. Housing Authority (USHA) in the Department of the Interior, which extended long-term loans to local agencies willing to assume part of the cost of slum clearance and public housing. The agency also subsidized rents for low-income residents.

The Farm Tenant Act, passed in 1937, was to be administered by a new agency, the Farm Security Administration (FSA). The program offered loans to prevent marginally profitable farm owners from sinking into tenancy. It also offered loans to tenants to help them purchase their own farms. But by the late 1930s the idea of small homesteads was doomed to failure. American mythology still exalted the family farm, but in reality the ever-larger agricultural unit predominated. In the end the FSA proved to be little more than another relief operation that tided a few farmers over difficult times. Sadly, a more effective answer to the problem awaited national mobilization for war, which moved many tenants into the military services or defense industries, broadened their horizons, and taught them skills that enabled them to leave the farm altogether.

The Fair Labor Standards Act of 1938 applied only to employees in enterprises that operated in or affected interstate commerce. It set a minimum wage of 40¢ an hour and a maximum workweek of forty hours, to be put into effect over several years. The act also prohibited child labor under the age of sixteen. Southern congressmen howled in opposition to the bill because it raised wages in their region and thus increased employers' expenses.

THE LEGACY OF THE NEW DEAL

SETBACKS FOR THE PRESIDENT   Although critics were unable to defeat the Fair Labor Standards Act, their stiff resistance revealed that an effective opposition to the New Deal was emerging within the president's own party, especially in the conservative southern wing. Southern Democrats were at best uneasy bedfellows of organized labor and African Americans, and more and more of them drifted toward closer cooperation with conservative Republicans. By the end of 1937, a formidable anti-New Deal bloc had developed in Congress.

In 1938 the conservative opposition stymied Roosevelt's proposal to reorganize the executive branch amid cries that it would lead to dictatorship. As the political season of 1938 advanced, Roosevelt unfolded a new idea as momentous as his Court-packing plan: a proposal to reshape the Democratic party in the image of the New Deal. He announced his plan to campaign in Democratic primaries as the party leader with the goal of seeing his own supporters nominated. Instead of succeeding, however, the effort to shape the state elections backfired and broke the spell of presidential invincibility, or what was left of it. As in the Court-packing fight, Roosevelt had risked his prestige while handing his adversaries a combustible issue to use against him. His opponents tagged his intervention in the primaries an attempt to "purge" the Democratic party of its southern conservatives; the word evoked visions of Adolf Hitler and Joseph Stalin, tyrants who had purged their Nazi and Communist parties with blood.

The elections of November 1938 resulted in another setback for the administration, caused in part by the friction among the Democrats. FDR had failed in his efforts to liberalize the party by ousting southern conservatives. The Democratic dominance in the House fell from 229 to 93, in the Senate from 56 to 42. The margins remained large, but the president now headed an increasingly divided party. In his State of the Union message in 1939, Roosevelt for the first time proposed no new reforms. He did manage, however, to put through his plan to reorganize the executive branch. Under the Administrative Reorganization Act of 1939, the president could "reduce, coordinate, consolidate, and reorganize" the agencies of government. With that, Roosevelt's domestic innovations feebly ended.

A HALFWAY REVOLUTION   The New Deal had lost momentum, but it had wrought several enduring changes. By the end of the 1930s, the power of the national government was vastly enlarged over what it had been in 1932, and hope had been restored to people who had grown disconsolate. But the New Deal entailed more than just bigger government and revived public confidence. It also constituted a significant change from the older liberalism embodied in the Progressivism of Theodore Roosevelt and Woodrow Wilson. Those reformers, despite their sharp differences, had assumed that the function of progressive government was to use aggressive regulation to ensure that the people had an equal opportunity to pursue their notions of happiness.

Franklin Roosevelt and the New Dealers went beyond this concept of a regulatory state by insisting that the government not simply *respond* to social crises but also take positive steps to *avoid* them. To this end, the New Deal's various welfare and benefit programs conferred on the government the responsibility to ensure a minimum level of well-being for all Americans. The New Deal had established minimum qualitative standards for labor conditions and public welfare and helped middle-class Americans hold on to their savings, their homes, and their farms. The protection afforded by bank-deposit insurance, unemployment pay, and Social Security pensions would come to be universally accepted as a safeguard against future depressions.

The old Progressive formulation of regulation versus trust-busting was now superseded by the rise of the "broker state," a powerful federal government that mediated among major interest groups. Government's role was to act as an honest broker protecting a variety of interests, not just big business but workers, farmers, consumers, small business, and the unemployed.

In implementing his domestic program, Roosevelt steered a zigzag course between the extremes of laissez-faire capitalism and socialism. The first New Deal had experimented for a time with a managed economy under the NRA but had abandoned that experiment for a turn toward enforcing competition through regulation and priming the economy with increased government spending. This tactic finally produced full employment during World War II.

Roosevelt himself, impatient with political theory, was flexible in developing policy: he kept what worked and discarded what did not. The result was, paradoxically, both profoundly revolutionary and profoundly conservative.

Roosevelt sharply increased the regulatory functions of the federal government and laid the foundation for what would become an expanding welfare system. Despite what his critics charged, however, his initiatives fell far short of socialism; they left the basic capitalist structure in place. In the process of such bold experimentation and dynamic preservation, the New Deal represented a "halfway revolution" that permanently altered the nation's social and political landscape.

MAKING CONNECTIONS

- In the mid-1930s, just as Roosevelt was getting the New Deal into place, the growing conflict in Europe began to consume more and more of his (and America's) attention; Chapter 29 shows how Roosevelt went from combating the Depression to leading the United States into World War II.

- Harry Truman, Roosevelt's successor in the White House, tried unsuccessfully to expand the idea of the New Deal into new areas (national health insurance and federal aid to education, for example), topics covered in Chapter 31.

FURTHER READING

The best recent interpretive survey of the 1930s is David M. Kennedy's *Freedom from Fear: The American People in Depression and War, 1929–1945* (1999). Michael E. Parrish's *Securities Regulation and the New Deal* (1970) and Ellis W. Hawley's *The New Deal and the Problem of Monopoly: A Study in Economic Ambivalence* (1966) analyze government attempts to forestall another market crash.

Alan Brinkley's *The End of Reform: New Deal Liberalism in Recession and War* (1995) suggests that the New Deal reformers did not go far enough in their efforts to curb big business. On the critics of the New Deal, see Alan Brinkley's *Voices of Protest: Huey Long, Father Coughlin, and the Great Depression* (1982). James N. Gregory's *American Exodus: The Dust Bowl Migration and Okie Culture in California* (1989) describes the migratory movement's effect on American culture. On the environmental and human causes of the dust bowl, see Donald Worster, *Dust Bowl: The Southern Plains in the 1930s* (1979).

29

FROM ISOLATION TO GLOBAL WAR

FOCUS QUESTIONS

- What was the impact of isolationism and peace movements on national politics between the two world wars?

- How did the United States respond to German aggression in Europe?

- How did events in Asia lead to Japan's attack on Pearl Harbor and America's entry into the global war?

To answer these questions and access additional review material, please visit www.wwnorton.com/studyspace.

In the late 1930s the winds of war swept across Asia and Europe, abruptly shifting the focus of American politics from domestic to foreign affairs. Another Democratic president had to turn his attention from social and economic reform to military preparedness and war. And the public again had to wrestle with a painful choice: involve the country in volatile world affairs or remain aloof and officially neutral.

POSTWAR ISOLATIONISM

THE LEAGUE AND THE UNITED STATES   Between Woodrow Wilson and Franklin Roosevelt lay two decades of relative isolation from foreign entanglements. The post–World War I mood of indifference to global affairs set the pattern. The voters in 1920 expressed their resistance to international commitments, and President-elect Harding lost little time in disposing of American membership in the League of Nations. The spirit of isolation found other expressions as well: higher tariffs, the Red Scare, and restrictive immigration laws, with which the nation all but shut the door to newcomers.

The United States may have felt the urge to insulate itself from a wicked world, but it could hardly ignore its substantial global interests. American business had expanding worldwide connections. Investments and loans abroad put in circulation the dollars that purchased American exports. America's overseas possessions, moreover, directly involved the country in world affairs, especially in the Pacific. Even the League of Nations was too great an organization to ignore. After 1924 the United States gradually entered into joint efforts with the League on such tasks as policing the international trade in drugs and arms, and American diplomats took part in a variety of economic, cultural, and technical conferences.

WAR DEBTS AND REPARATIONS   Probably nothing did more to heighten American isolationism during the 1920s and 1930s—or anti-American feeling in Europe—than the war-debt tangle. When in 1917 the Allies had begun to exhaust their sources of private credit in the United States, the U.S. government advanced them millions of dollars, first for the war effort and then for postwar reconstruction.

To Americans the repayment of the war debts seemed a simple matter of obligation, but Europeans commonly had a different perception. The French and the British had insisted that they could pay America only as they collected reparations from defeated Germany. Twice during the 1920s the resulting strain on Germany brought the structure of international payments to the verge of collapse, and both times the Reparations Commission called in American bankers to work out rescue plans.

The whole structure finally did collapse during the Great Depression. In 1931 President Hoover negotiated a moratorium on both German reparations and Allied payment of war debts. At the end of 1932, after Hoover's debt moratorium ended, most of the European countries defaulted on their war debts to the United States. In retaliation, Congress passed the Johnson Debt Default Act of 1934, which prohibited private loans to any defaulting government.

ATTEMPTS AT DISARMAMENT   After World War I many Americans decided that the armaments race had caused the war and that arms limitations treaties would bring lasting peace. The United States had no intention of maintaining a large army, but under the naval building program begun in 1916, it had constructed a fleet second only to that of Britain.

Neither the British nor the Americans relished a naval armaments race, but both shared a concern about the alarming growth of Japanese military power. Since 1914 Japanese-American relations had grown increasingly strained as the United States objected to continued Japanese encroachments in Asia. During World War I, Japan had taken China's Shan-tung Peninsula and the islands of Micronesia from its enemy, Germany. In 1917, after the United States entered the war, Viscount Kikujiro Ishii visited Washington to secure American recognition of Japan's expanded position in Asia, dropping hints that Germany had several times tried to get Japan to quit the war. To forestall the loss of an ally in the war, Secretary of State Robert Lansing had signed an ambiguous agreement saying that "Japan has special interests in China." Americans were unhappy with the Lansing-Ishii Agreement, but it was viewed as the only way to keep Japan in the war.

After the war ended, Japanese-American relations deteriorated. To address the problem, President Warren Harding invited eight key countries to the Washington Conference of 1921. It opened with a surprise announcement by the U.S. secretary of state, Charles Evans Hughes, who laid out a disarmament plan to destroy most of the world's navies. Delegates from the United States, Britain, Japan, France, and Italy signed a Five-Power Treaty

The Washington Conference, 1921

The Big Five at the conference were (from left) Kijuro Shidehara (Japan), Arthur Balfour (Great Britain), Charles Evans Hughes (United States), Aristide Briand (France), and Carlo Schanzer (Italy).

(1922), incorporating Hughes's plan for tonnage limits on their navies and a moratorium of ten years, during which no battleships would be built. The five powers also agreed to refrain from further fortification of their Pacific possessions. The agreement in effect partitioned the world: U.S. naval power became supreme in the Western Hemisphere, Japanese power in the western Pacific, and British power from the North Sea to Singapore.

Two other major agreements emerged from the Washington Conference. With the Four-Power Treaty, the United States, Britain, Japan, and France agreed to respect one another's possessions in the Pacific. The Nine-Power Treaties for the first time pledged the signers to support the principle of the Open Door enunciated by Secretary of State John Hay at the turn of the century. The Open Door enabled all nations to compete for trade and investment opportunities in China on an equal footing rather than allow individual nations to create economic monopolies in particular regions of that country. The signers of the Nine-Power Treaties also promised to respect the territorial integrity of China. The powers, in addition to those signing the Five-Power Treaty, were China, Belgium, Portugal, and the Netherlands.

With these agreements in hand, President Harding's supporters could boast of a brilliant diplomatic stroke that relieved citizens of the need to pay for an enlarged navy and defused potential conflicts in the Pacific. Yet the agreements were without obligation and without teeth. The signers of the Four-Power Treaty agreed only to consult, not to help one another. The formal endorsement of the Open Door in the Nine-Power Treaties was just as ineffective, for the United States remained unwilling to use force to uphold the principle. Moreover, the naval-disarmament treaty set tonnage limits only on battleships and aircraft carriers; the race to build cruisers, destroyers, submarines, and other smaller craft continued.

THE KELLOGG-BRIAND PACT   During and after World War I the fanciful ideal of simply abolishing war seized the American imagination. Peace societies thrived, and the glorious vision of ending war by the stroke of a pen culminated in the Kellogg-Briand Pact of 1928. This unique treaty originated when the French foreign minister Aristide Briand proposed to President Calvin Coolidge's secretary of state, Frank B. Kellogg, an agreement whereby the two countries would never go to war with each other. Kellogg countered with a scheme to have all nations sign the pact, an idea all the more acceptable to the many peace organizations of the day.

The Pact of Paris (its official name), signed on August 27, 1928, declared that the signatories "condemn recourse to war . . . and renounce it as an instrument of national policy." Eventually sixty-two nations joined the pact, but all reserved "self-defense" as an escape hatch. The U.S. Senate included a reservation declaring the Monroe Doctrine necessary to America's self-defense and then ratified the agreement by a vote of eighty-five to one. A Virginia senator who voted for "this worthless, but perfectly harmless peace treaty" wrote a friend that he feared it would "confuse the minds of many good people who think that peace may be secured by polite professions of neighborly and brotherly love."

THE "GOOD NEIGHBOR" POLICY In Latin America the spirit of peace and noninvolvement helped allay long-festering resentments against the United States, which had freely intervened in the Caribbean during the first two decades of the century. In 1924 American marines left the Dominican Republic after an eight-year occupation. U.S. troops left Nicaragua a year later but returned in 1926 with the outbreak of disorder and civil war. In 1927 the Coolidge administration negotiated an agreement for U.S.-supervised elections, but one rebel leader, César Augusto Sandino, held out, and the marines stayed until 1933.

In 1930 President Hoover improved America's image in Latin America by permitting publication of a memorandum that denied that the Monroe Doctrine justified U.S. intervention in Latin America. It stopped short of re-pudiating intervention on any grounds, but that fine point hardly blunted the celebration in Latin America. Although Hoover never endorsed this so-called Clark memorandum, named for American diplomat Reuben Clark, he never ordered military intervention in the region. Before he left office, steps had been taken to withdraw American forces from Nicaragua and Haiti.

Franklin D. Roosevelt likewise embraced the policy of the "good neighbor" and soon advanced it in practice. In 1933, at the Seventh Pan-American Conference, the United States supported a resolution declaring that no na-tion "has the right to intervene in the internal or external affairs of another." Under President Roosevelt the marines completed their withdrawal from Nicaragua and Haiti, and in 1934 the president negotiated with Cuba a treaty that abrogated the Platt Amendment (1901), which had given the United States a formal right to intervene in Cuba.

WAR CLOUDS

JAPANESE INCURSIONS INTO CHINA Improving U.S. relations in the Western Hemisphere during the 1930s proved an exception in an other-wise dismal world scene as war clouds darkened over Europe and Asia. Actual conflict erupted first in Asia, where unsettled social and political conditions in China had attracted foreign encroachments since before the turn of the century. In 1929 Chinese nationalist aspirations and China's subsequent clashes with Russia convinced the Japanese that their own extensive investments in Manchuria, including the South Manchurian Railway, were in danger.

Japanese military occupation of Manchuria began with the Mukden incident of 1931, when an explosion destroyed a section of railroad track near that city. The Japanese army based in Manchuria to guard the railway blamed the incident on the Chinese and used it as a pretext to occupy all of Manchuria. In 1932 the Japanese converted Manchuria into the puppet empire of Manchukuo.

The Manchuria incident, as the Japanese called their undeclared war, flagrantly violated the Nine-Power Treaties, the Kellogg-Briand Pact, and Japan's pledges as a member of the League of Nations. But when China asked the League and the United States for help, neither obliged. President Herbert Hoover refused to invoke military or economic sanctions.

In early 1932 Japan's indiscriminate bombing of civilians in Shanghai, China's great port city, aroused Western indignation but no action. When the League of Nations condemned Japanese aggression in 1933, Japan withdrew from the League. Thereafter, hostilities in Manchuria gradually subsided and ended with a truce. An uneasy peace settled upon east Asia for four years, during which time Japan's military leaders extended their political sway in Tokyo.

ITALY AND GERMANY   The rise of the Japanese militarists paralleled the rise of totalitarian dictators in Italy and Germany. In 1922 Benito Mussolini had seized power in Italy after organizing the Fascist movement, a composite of superheated nationalism and socialism. The party's program, and above all Mussolini's promise to restore order and pride in a country fragmented by dissension and self-doubts, enjoyed a wide appeal. Once in power, Mussolini largely abandoned the socialist part of his platform and gradually suppressed all opposition. By 1925 he was wielding dictatorial power as Il Duce (the Leader).

There was always something ludicrous about the strutting Mussolini. Italy, after all, was a minor European power. But Germany was another matter, and most Americans were not amused, even at the beginning, by Il Duce's German counterpart, Adolf Hitler. Hitler's National Socialist German Workers' (Nazi) party duplicated the major features of Italian fascism, including the ancient Roman salute. Hitler capitalized on the weakness of Germany's postwar government, the poverty and despair caused by a severe economic depression, and festering German resentment toward the Versailles Treaty.

Named chancellor on January 30, 1933, Hitler swiftly won dictatorial powers and in 1934 assumed the title of Reichsführer (national leader). The Nazi police state cranked up the engines of tyranny, persecuting Jews, whom Hitler blamed for Germany's troubles, and rearming in defiance of the Versailles Treaty. Hitler flouted international agreements, pulled Germany out of the League of Nations in 1933, and threatened to extend control over all German-speaking peoples. Despite one provocation after another, the European democracies lacked the will to resist.

RUSSIAN RECOGNITION   Isolationist sentiment in the United States grew even more potent during the early 1930s, but one significant exception to American insularity was Roosevelt's decision to favor official recognition of Soviet Russia. By 1933 the reasons for America's refusal to recognize the Bolshevik regime had grown stale. Seen as an expansive market for U.S. goods, the Soviet Union stirred fantasies of an American trade boom, much

Axis Leaders

Mussolini and Hitler in Munich, June 1940.

as China had at the turn of the century. Japanese expansionism in Asia, moreover, gave the Soviet Union and the United States a common foreign-policy concern. Given an opening by the shift of opinion, Roosevelt invited the Soviet commissar for foreign affairs to visit Washington, D.C. After nine days of talks, a formal exchange of notes on November 16, 1933, signaled the renewal of diplomatic relations. The Soviet commissar promised that his country would abstain from promoting communist propaganda in the United States, extend religious freedom to Americans in the Soviet Union, and reopen the question of unpaid Russian debts to the United States.

THE MARCH OF AGGRESSION   After 1932 a catastrophic chain of events in Asia and Europe sent the world hurtling toward disaster. In 1934 Japan renounced the Five-Power Treaty. The next year, Mussolini commenced Italy's conquest of Ethiopia. That same year a referendum in Germany's Saar Basin, held in accordance with the Versailles Treaty, delivered the coal-rich region into the hands of Hitler. In 1936 Hitler's armed forces reoccupied the Rhineland, a direct violation of the Versailles Treaty. The French did nothing to oust the German force, however.

The year 1936 also brought the Spanish Civil War, which began with an uprising of the Spanish armed forces in Morocco, led by General Francisco Franco, against the democratically elected Spanish republic. Over the next three years, Franco established a fascist dictatorship with help from Hitler and Mussolini while the European democracies left the Spanish republic to its fate.

On July 7, 1937, Japanese and Chinese troops clashed at the Marco Polo Bridge, west of Peking, and the incident quickly developed into a full-scale war. World War II had begun in Asia two years before it would erupt in Europe. That same year, Japan joined Germany and Italy in establishing an alliance known as the Rome-Berlin-Tokyo "Axis."

By 1938 the peace of Europe trembled in the balance. Having rebuilt the German military force, Hitler forced the *Anschluss* (union) of Austria with Germany in March 1938. Six months later British and French leaders, recognizing the situation's severity but failing to comprehend Hitler's ruthlessness, sought to appease the German leader by agreeing to abandon the Sudetenland in Czechoslovakia, a country that had probably the second strongest army in central Europe. Germany promptly took the mountainous Sudetenland, largely German in population, which had been given to Czechoslovakia at the Paris Peace Conference in 1919 because of its strategic importance to that new nation's defense.

After promising that the Sudetenland would be his last territorial demand, Hitler in 1939 brazenly broke his pledge. He occupied the remainder

AGGRESSION IN EUROPE, 1935–1939

← Aggressive moves

Axis powers

Keeping in mind the terms of the Treaty of Versailles (see page 725), explain why Hitler began his campaign of expansion by invading the Rhineland and the Sudetenland. Why would Hitler have wanted to retake the Polish Corridor? Why did the attack on Poland begin World War II whereas Hitler's previous invasions of his European neighbors did not?

of Czechoslovakia and seized former German territory from Lithuania. In quick succession the Spanish republic collapsed on March 28, and Mussolini seized the kingdom of Albania on April 7. On September 1, 1939, Hitler launched his conquest of Poland. A few days before, he had signed a nonaggression pact with Soviet Russia. Having deserted Czechoslovakia, Britain and France now honored their commitment to go to war if Poland were invaded.

DEGREES OF NEUTRALITY   During these years of deepening crisis, the Western democracies seemed paralyzed, hoping in vain that each concession would appease the appetites of fascist dictators. Americans retreated more deeply into isolation. The neutrality laws of the 1930s sought to keep the United States insulated from the quarrels of Europe. But while Americans wanted to steer clear of war altogether, their sympathies were more strongly than ever with the Western democracies, and the triumph of fascist aggression in Europe aroused fears for national security. The Neutrality Act of 1935 forbade the sale of arms and munitions to all belligerents (warring nations) whenever the president proclaimed that a state of war existed, and it declared that Americans who traveled on belligerents' ships did so at their own risk. Roosevelt would have preferred discretionary authority to levy an embargo only against aggressors, but he reluctantly accepted the act because it was to be effective for only six months.

Yet on October 3, 1935, just weeks after Roosevelt signed the legislation, Italy invaded Ethiopia, and Roosevelt invoked the act. When Congress reconvened in 1936, it extended the arms embargo and added a provision forbidding loans to belligerents. Then, in July 1936, while Italian troops mopped up the last resistance in Ethiopia, the Spanish Civil War broke out. Roosevelt now became more isolationist than some of the most extreme isolationists. Although the Spanish Civil War involved a fascist uprising against a recognized democratic government, Roosevelt accepted the French and British position that only their nonintervention would keep the fight from spreading to the rest of Europe.

The conflict in Spain led Roosevelt to seek a "moral embargo" on the arms trade, and he encouraged Congress to extend the neutrality laws to cover civil wars. Congress did so in 1937 with only one dissenting vote. The Western democracies then stood by as German and Italian soldiers, planes, and armaments supported Franco's overthrow of Spanish democracy.

In the spring of 1937, Congress passed another neutrality law, which continued restraints on arms sales and loans, forbade Americans to travel on the ships of nations at war, and prohibited the arming of American merchant ships trading with warring nations. The new law also empowered the president to require that goods other than arms or munitions exported to belligerents be sold on a cash-and-carry basis (that is, the nation purchasing the goods would have to pay cash and transport the cargo in its own ships). This was an ingenious scheme to preserve a profitable trade without running the risk of war.

The new law had its first test in July 1937, when Japanese and Chinese forces clashed at the Marco Polo Bridge. Since neither side declared war,

Roosevelt was able to avoid invoking the neutrality law, which would have favored the Japanese, since China had greater need of American arms but few means to get supplies past the Japanese navy. A flourishing trade in munitions to China flowed around the world as ships carried American military equipment across the Atlantic to England, where it was reloaded onto British ships bound for Hong Kong. Roosevelt, by his refusal to invoke the neutrality laws, had challenged strict isolationism.

Roosevelt soon ventured a step further. In Chicago on October 5, 1937, he denounced the "reign of terror and international lawlessness" whereby 10 percent of the world's population threatened the peace of the other 90 percent. He called for a "quarantine" against those nations "creating a state of international anarchy and instability from which there is no escape through mere isolation or neutrality." Public reaction to the speech was mixed, but the president nevertheless quickly backed off from its implications and refused to spell out any program for dealing with aggression.

After the German occupation of Czechoslovakia in 1939, Roosevelt no longer pretended impartiality in the deepening European struggle. He began to educate the public about the menace of unchecked fascism. He urged

Neutrality

A 1938 cartoon shows U.S. foreign policy entangled by the serpent of isolationism.

Congress to repeal the munitions embargo and permit the United States to sell arms on a cash-and-carry basis to Britain and France, but to no avail. "You haven't got the votes," Vice President John Nance Garner told him, "and that's all there is to it." When the Germans attacked Poland on September 1, Roosevelt proclaimed official neutrality but in a radio talk stressed that he would not, like Woodrow Wilson in 1914, ask Americans to remain neutral in thought because "even a neutral has a right to take account of the facts."

Roosevelt summoned Congress into special session and asked again for amendments to the Neutrality Act. "I regret the Congress passed the Act," he confessed. "I regret equally that I signed the Act." Under the Neutrality Act of 1939, Britain and France could buy supplies with cash and take away in their own ships weapons or anything else they wanted. American ships, on the other hand, were excluded from the ports of warring nations and from specified war zones. Roosevelt then designated as a war zone the Baltic Sea and the waters around Great Britain and Ireland, from Norway south to the coast of Spain. One unexpected effect of this move was to relieve Hitler of any inhibitions about using unrestricted submarine warfare to blockade Britain.

Once the great democracies of western Europe faced war, American public opinion, appalled at Hitler's tyranny, rallied to aid its allies without being drawn into the war itself. For a time it seemed that the Western Hemisphere could remain insulated. After the Nazis overran Poland in less than a month, the war settled into a stalemate in early 1940 that began to be called the phony war. What lay ahead, it seemed, was a long war of attrition—much like World War I—in which Britain and France would have the resources to outlast Hitler. That illusion lasted from October 1939 until the spring of 1940.

THE STORM IN EUROPE

BLITZKRIEG   In the spring of 1940 the long winter lull in the European fighting suddenly erupted into Blitzkrieg—lightning war. At dawn on April 9, without warning, Nazi troops occupied Denmark and landed along the Norwegian coast. Denmark fell in a day, Norway within a few weeks. On May 10 Hitler unleashed dive bombers and tank divisions on neutral Belgium and the Netherlands. On May 21 German troops moving down the valley of the Somme River reached the English Channel, cutting off a British force sent to help the Belgians and the French. A desperate evacuation from the French beaches at Dunkirk enlisted every available boat, from warship to tug. Amid the chaos some 338,000 soldiers, about one third of them French, escaped to England.

The Blitz

In London, St. Paul's Cathedral looms above the destruction wrought by German bombs during the Blitz. Churchill's response: "We shall never surrender."

Having outflanked France's heavily fortified defense perimeter, the Maginot Line, the German forces rushed ahead, cutting the French armies to pieces and spreading panic by strafing refugees. On June 14 the Nazi swastika flew over Paris.

AMERICA'S GROWING INVOLVEMENT Britain now stood alone, but its new prime minister, Winston Churchill, breathed defiance. "We shall go on to the end," he pledged; "we shall never surrender." Nevertheless, America seemed suddenly vulnerable as Hitler unleashed his air force against Britain. President Roosevelt called for a military buildup and the production of 50,000 combat planes a year. In 1940 Congress voted more than $17 billion for defense. In response to Churchill's appeal for military supplies, the War and Navy Departments began releasing stocks of arms, planes, and munitions to the British.

The world crisis transformed Roosevelt. Having been stalemated for much of his second term by congressional opposition to his domestic program, he was revitalized by the war in Europe. Nervous cabinet officers, military leaders, and diplomats now encountered a decisive, forceful president willing to exert executive authority on behalf of Britain. Roosevelt acted with remarkable boldness in the face of an American public that still held staunchly to the doctrine of isolationism.

The summer of 1940 brought the desperate Battle of Britain, in which the Royal Air Force finally forced the Germans to give up plans to invade the British Isles. Submarine warfare meanwhile strained the resources of the battered Royal Navy. To relieve the pressure, Churchill urgently requested the transfer of American destroyers to help protect convoys from submarines. Secret negotiations led to an executive agreement under which fifty "overaged" destroyers went to the British in return for ninety-nine-year leases on naval and air bases in Newfoundland, Bermuda, and islands in the

Caribbean. Roosevelt disguised the action as necessary for defense of the hemisphere. Two weeks later, on September 14, 1940, Congress adopted the first peacetime conscription in American history. All 16 million men aged twenty-one to thirty-five were required to register for a year's military service within the United States.

The new state of affairs prompted vigorous debate between "internationalists," who believed national security demanded aid to Britain, and isolationists, who charged that Roosevelt was drawing the United States into an unnecessary war. In 1940 internationalists organized the nonpartisan Committee to Defend America by Aiding the Allies, drawing its strongest support from the East and West Coasts and the South. Two months later isolationists formed the America First Committee. The isolationists argued that a Nazi victory, while distasteful, would pose no threat to American national security.

FDR'S THIRD TERM   In the midst of these profound global crises, the quadrennial presidential campaign came due. Isolationist sentiment was strongest in the Republican party, yet their nominee took a different stance. Wendell L. Willkie was a former Democrat who had voted for Roosevelt in 1932. An Indiana farm boy whose disheveled charm inspired strong loyalty, he openly supported aid to the Allies.

The Nazi victory in France ensured that Roosevelt would decide to run for an unprecedented third term. The president cultivated party unity with his foreign policy and kept a sphinxlike silence about his intentions. The world crisis reconciled southern conservatives to the man whose foreign policy, at least, they supported. At the convention in Chicago, Roosevelt won nomination for a third term with only token opposition. For his new running mate, he tapped his secretary of agriculture, Henry Wallace, a devoted supporter who would appeal to farm voters.

Throughout the summer, Roosevelt assumed the role of a man above the political fray, busy rather with urgent matters of defense and diplomacy. Because Willkie's foreign-policy ideas mirrored Roosevelt's, the Republican nominee was reduced to attacking New Deal red tape and promising to run the programs better. Roosevelt won the election by a comfortable margin of 27 million votes to Willkie's 22 million and by a wider margin, 449 to 82, in the Electoral College. Though the popular vote was closer than in any presidential election since 1916, the dangerous world situation had persuaded a majority of voters to back the Democrats' slogan: "Don't switch horses in the middle of the stream."

THE "ARSENAL OF DEMOCRACY"   Bolstered by the mandate for a third term, Roosevelt moved quickly to provide greater aid to besieged Britain, whose cash was running out. Since direct government loans would arouse memories of earlier war-debt defaults—the Johnson Debt Default Act of 1934 forbade such loans anyway—the president created an ingenious device to bypass that issue and yet supply British needs: the "lend-lease" program. In a fireside chat, Roosevelt told the nation that it must become "the great arsenal of democracy" to help prevent Britain's fall, and to do so it must make new efforts to help the British purchase American supplies. The lend-lease bill, introduced in Congress on January 10, 1941, authorized the president to sell, lend, or lease arms and other equipment and supplies to "any country whose defense the President deems vital to the defense of the United States."

For two months a bitter debate over the lend-lease bill raged in Congress and around the country. Isolationists saw it as the point of no return. Administration supporters denied that lend-lease would lead to American involvement in the war, but they knew that it did increase the risk. Lend-lease became law in early 1941, and Britain and China were the first beneficiaries.

While the nation debated, the war intensified. Italy had officially entered the European war as Hitler's ally in June 1940. In late 1940, as the American presidential campaign approached its climax, Mussolini launched attacks on Greece and, from Italian-controlled Libya, assaulted the British in Egypt. But his troops had to fall back in both cases, and in the spring of 1941 German forces under General Erwin Rommel joined the Italians in Libya, forcing the British to withdraw into Egypt, their resources having been drained to help Greece. In April 1941 Nazi armored divisions overwhelmed Yugoslavia and Greece, and by the end of May airborne forces had subdued the Greek island of Crete, putting Hitler in a position to menace the entire Middle East.

With Hungary, Romania, and Bulgaria forced into the Axis fold, Hitler controlled nearly all of Europe, but his ambition was unbounded. On June 22, 1941, Nazi troops suddenly fell upon the Soviet Union, their ally, hoping to use another lightning stroke to eliminate the potential threat on Germany's eastern front. The Nazis massed 3.6 million soldiers on a 2,000-mile front from the Arctic to the Black Sea. After retreating for four months, however, Russian soldiers and civilians rallied to defend Leningrad, Moscow, and Sevastopol. During the winter of 1941–1942, a ferocious Soviet counterattack proved to be the most important development of the war in Europe. Still, in the summer of 1941 the Nazi juggernaut appeared unstoppable.

Winston Churchill had already decided to provide British support to the Soviet Union in case of such an attack. Roosevelt adopted the same policy, offering American aid to Russia two days after the German invasion in late June 1941. Stalinist Russia, so long as it held out against the Germans, ensured Britain's survival. American aid was now indispensable to Europe's defense, and the logic of lend-lease led to deeper American involvement. To deliver aid to Britain, supply ships had to maneuver through the German submarine "wolf packs" in the North Atlantic. So in April 1941 Roosevelt informed Churchill that the U.S. Navy would extend its patrol areas in the North Atlantic nearly to Iceland.

In August 1941 Roosevelt and Churchill held a secret meeting off the coast of Newfoundland. There they drew up a statement of international principles known as the Atlantic Charter. Their joint statement called for the self-determination of all peoples, economic cooperation, freedom of the seas, and a new international system of collective security. The Soviet Union later endorsed the charter.

Having entered into a joint statement of war aims with the anti-Axis powers, the United States soon became involved in shooting incidents in the North Atlantic. After a German submarine attacked an American battleship, the president ordered American ships to "shoot on sight" any German or Italian raiders ("rattlesnakes of the Atlantic") that ventured into American waters. Five days later the U.S. Navy announced that it would convoy British-bound merchant ships all the way to Iceland.

Further attacks prompted Congress to make the changes in the 1939 Neutrality Act that had been requested by the president. On November 17 Congress removed the bans on arming merchant vessels and allowed them to enter combat zones and belligerent ports. Step-by-step the United States was giving up neutrality and embarking on naval warfare against Germany. Still, Americans hoped to avoid the final step of all-out war. The decision to go to war would be made in response to aggression in an unexpected quarter—the Pacific.

THE STORM IN THE PACIFIC

JAPANESE AGGRESSION After the Nazi victories in Europe during the spring of 1940, America's relations with Japan took a turn for the worse. Japanese militarists, bogged down in the vastness of China, now eyed new temptations in Southeast Asia. They wanted to incorporate into their "Greater East Asia Co-Prosperity Sphere" the oil, rubber, and other strategic materials that their crowded homeland lacked. As it was, Japan depended upon the United States for important supplies, including 80 percent of its fuel.

On September 27, 1940, the Tokyo government signed a Tripartite Pact with Germany and Italy, by which each pledged to declare war on any nation

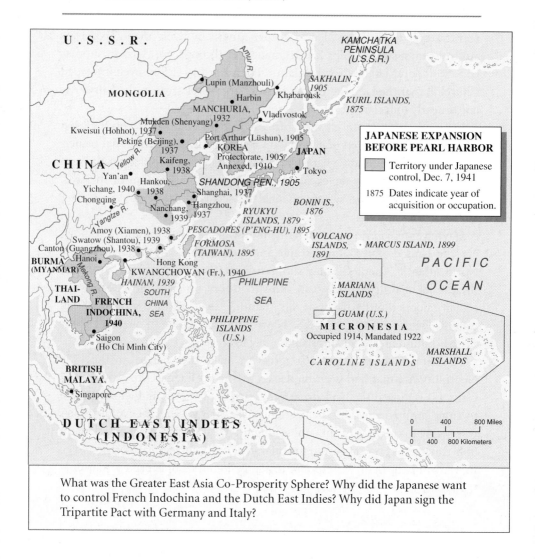

What was the Greater East Asia Co-Prosperity Sphere? Why did the Japanese want to control French Indochina and the Dutch East Indies? Why did Japan sign the Tripartite Pact with Germany and Italy?

that attacked any of them. On April 13, 1941, while the Nazis were sweeping through the Balkans, Japan signed a nonaggression pact with the Soviet Union, and once the Nazis invaded Russia in June, the Japanese were freed of any threat from the north.

In July 1941 Japan announced that it was creating a protectorate over all of French Indochina. Responding to this latest act of aggression, Roosevelt froze all Japanese assets in the United States, he restricted exports of oil to Japan, and he took the armed forces of the Philippines into the U.S. Army and put their commander, General Douglas MacArthur, in charge of all U.S. forces in the Far East. By September 1941 the oil restrictions had tightened into a complete embargo. Forced to secure oil supplies elsewhere, the Japanese army and navy began planning attacks on the Dutch and British colonies in Southeast Asia.

Actions by both sides put the United States and Japan on a collision course leading to war. In his regular talks with the Japanese ambassador, Secretary of State Cordell Hull insisted that Japanese withdrawal from French Indochina and China was the price of renewed trade with the United States. A more flexible position might have strengthened the moderates in Japan. Prime Minister Fumimaro Konoe, however, while known as a man of liberal principles who preferred peace, caved in to pressures from the militants. Perhaps he had no choice.

The Japanese warlords, for their part, seriously misjudged the United States. The desperate wish of the Americans to stay out of the war might still have enabled the Japanese to conquer the British and Dutch colonies in the Pacific. But the warlords decided that they dared not leave the U.S. Navy intact and the Philippines untouched on the flank of their new lifeline to the south.

TRAGEDY AT PEARL HARBOR   Thus a tragedy began to unfold with a fatal certainty, mostly out of sight of the American people, whose attention was focused on the Nazi submarine threat in the Atlantic. Late in August 1941 Prime Minister Konoe proposed a meeting with President Roosevelt. Secretary of State Hull urged the president not to meet unless agreement on fundamental issues could be reached in advance. On September 6 the Japanese government approved a surprise attack on Hawaii and gave Konoe six more weeks in which to reach a settlement.

The Japanese emperor's concern about the risk of an attack afforded the prime minister one last chance to pursue a compromise, but the presence of Japanese troops in China remained a stumbling block to any American agreement. In October, Konoe urged War Minister Hideki Tōjō to consider withdrawal of Japanese forces while saving face by keeping some troops in north China. Instead, the inflexible Tōjō forced Konoe to resign in October. Tōjō became prime minister the next day. The war party was now in complete control of the Japanese government.

By late November, Washington officials knew that war was imminent. Reports of Japanese troop transports moving south from Formosa prompted U.S. officials to send warnings to Pearl Harbor and Manila and to the British government. The massive Japanese movements southward clearly signaled attacks on the British and the Dutch. American leaders had every reason to expect war in the southwest Pacific, but none expected that Japan would

The Attack on Pearl Harbor

This view from an army airfield shows the destruction and confusion brought on by the surprise attack.

commit most of its aircraft carriers to another attack 5,000 miles away, at Pearl Harbor, the major American base in the Pacific.

On the morning of December 7, 1941, American Servicemen decoded the last part of a secret Japanese message breaking off the diplomatic negotiations in Washington. Tōjō instructed Japan's ambassador to deliver the message at 1 P.M. (7:30 A.M. in Honolulu), about a half hour before the attack was to begin, but delays held up delivery by more than an hour. The War Department sent out an alert at noon that something was about to happen, but the message, which went by commercial wire because radio contacts were broken, arrived in Hawaii eight and a half hours later. Even so, the decoded Japanese message did not mention Pearl Harbor specifically, and U.S. military leaders there would probably have assumed the attack was to come in Southeast Asia.

It was still a sleepy Sunday morning in Hawaii when the first Japanese planes roared down the west coast and the central valley of Oahu to begin their assault. For nearly two hours the Japanese planes kept up their fierce attack. Of the eight U.S. battleships in Pearl Harbor, three were sunk, and the others were badly battered. Altogether nineteen ships were sunk or disabled. At the airfields on the island, the Japanese destroyed about 180 planes. Before it was over, the raid had killed more than 2,400 American military personnel and civilians.

The surprise attack fulfilled the dreams of its planners, but it fell short of total success in two ways. The Japanese ignored oil-storage tanks in Hawaii, without which the surviving U.S. ships might have been forced back to the West Coast, and they missed the American aircraft carriers that had fortuitously left port a few days earlier. In the naval war to come, those aircraft carriers would be decisive.

Later that day (December 8 in the western Pacific), Japanese forces invaded the Philippines, Guam, Midway, Hong Kong, and the Malay Peninsula. With one stroke the Japanese had silenced America's debate on neutrality—a suddenly unified and vengeful nation resolutely prepared for the struggle.

The day after the attack on Pearl Harbor, President Roosevelt told Congress that December 7 was "a date which will live in infamy," and he asked for a declaration of war. It was approved with only one dissenting vote, by Representative Jeanette Rankin of Montana, a pacifist who was unable in good conscience to vote for war in 1917 or 1941. On December 11 Germany and Italy impetuously declared war on the United States. The separate wars in Asia and Europe had become one global conflict—and American isolationism was cast aside.

MAKING CONNECTIONS

- During the 1930s the United States tried to stake out a neutral position in the growing world conflict. Compare that effort with earlier American attempts at neutrality, from the Napoleonic Wars of Jefferson's administration onward.

- The American alliance with the Soviet Union described in this chapter proved to be temporary; after the war the Americans and the Soviets would be adversaries in a prolonged cold war, the beginnings of which are outlined in Chapter 31.

- The Japanese conquest of French Indochina would play an important role in the events leading to American involvement in that region, a topic discussed in Chapter 34.

FURTHER READING

The best overview of interwar diplomacy remains Selig Adler's *The Uncertain Giant, 1921–1941: American Foreign Policy between the Wars* (1965). Joan Hoff's *American Business and Foreign Policy, 1920–1933* (1971) highlights the efforts of Republican administrations during the 1920s to promote international commerce. Robert Dallek's *Franklin D. Roosevelt and American Foreign Policy, 1932–1945* (1979) provides a judicious assessment of Roosevelt's foreign policy during the 1930s.

A noteworthy study of America's entry into World War II is Waldo Heinrichs's *Threshold of War: Franklin D. Roosevelt and American Entry into World War II* (1988). See also David Reynolds's *From Munich to Pearl Harbor: Roosevelt's America and the Origins of the Second World War* (2001). Bruce M. Russett's *No Clear and Present Danger: A Skeptical View of the United States Entry into World War II* (1972) provides a critical account of American actions.

On Pearl Harbor, see Gordon W. Prange's *Pearl Harbor: The Verdict of History* (1986). Japan's perspective is described in Akira Iriye's *The Origins of the Second World War in Asia and the Pacific* (1987).

30

THE SECOND WORLD WAR

FOCUS QUESTIONS

· What were the social and economic effects of World War II, especially in the West?

· How did the Allied forces win the war?

· What efforts did the Allies make to shape the postwar world?

To answer these questions and access additional review material, please visit www.wwnorton.com/studyspace.

The Japanese attack on Pearl Harbor ended a period of uneasy neutrality for the United States, and it plunged the nation into a global conflict that would cost the lives of over 400,000 Americans. The war would also transform social and economic life, as well as international affairs. The Second World War would become the most destructive and far-reaching conflict in history. It was so terrible in its intensity and obscene in its cruelties that it altered the image of war itself. Devilish new instruments of destruction were invented—plastic explosives, flame throwers, proximity fuses, rockets, jet airplanes, and atomic weapons—and systematic genocide emerged as an explicit war aim of the Nazis. Racist propaganda flourished on both sides, and intense hatred of the enemy caused many military and civilian prisoners to be executed. The scorching passions of such a total war blanched many moral scruples. Over 50 million deaths resulted from the war, and the physical destruction was incalculable. Whole cities were leveled, nations dismembered, and societies transformed. The world is still coping with the consequences.

America's Early Battles

SETBACKS IN THE PACIFIC   For months after Pearl Harbor, the news from the Pacific was "all bad," as President Roosevelt confessed. The Japanese captured a string of Allied outposts in the three months before the end of December, 1941: Guam, Wake Island, the Gilbert Islands, Hong Kong, Singapore, and Java. The Japanese capture of Rangoon, in Burma (Yangon in present-day Myanmar), in March 1942 cut off the Burma Road, the main supply route to China. By May the Japanese had ousted U.S. forces from the Philippines, and they controlled a new empire that stretched from Burma eastward through the Dutch East Indies and extended to Wake Island and the Gilbert Islands.

The Japanese might have consolidated an almost impregnable empire with the resources they had seized. But the Japanese navy succumbed to what one of its admirals later called victory disease: they decided to push farther into the South Pacific, isolate Australia, and strike again at Hawaii. Japanese planners hoped to destroy the American navy before the productive power of the United States could be brought to bear on the war effort.

Early Defeats

U.S. prisoners of war, captured by the Japanese in the Philippines, 1942.

CORAL SEA AND MIDWAY American forces finally halted the Japanese advance toward Australia in two decisive naval clashes. The Battle of the Coral Sea (May 7–8, 1942) stopped a fleet convoying Japanese troop transports toward New Guinea. Planes from the *Lexington* and the *Yorktown* sank one Japanese aircraft carrier, damaged another, and destroyed smaller ships. American losses were greater, but the Japanese designs on Australia were thwarted.

Less than a month after the Coral Sea conflict, Admiral Isoroku Yamamoto, the Japanese naval commander, led his fleet toward Midway Island, from which he hoped to render Pearl Harbor helpless. This time it was the Japanese who were the victims of surprise. American cryptanalysts had by then broken the Japanese naval code, and Admiral Chester Nimitz, commander of the central Pacific, knew their plan of attack. He reinforced Midway with planes and the carriers *Enterprise, Hornet,* and *Yorktown.*

The first Japanese foray against Midway, on June 4, 1942, severely damaged the American installations on the island, but at the cost of about one third of the Japanese planes. Meanwhile, American torpedo planes and dive bombers caught three of the four Japanese carriers in the process of servicing their planes. The decks of the Japanese ships were cluttered with bombs, gasoline, and planes. Dive bombers sank three of them during the first assault. Later the Japanese lost another carrier, but not before its planes had disabled the *Yorktown.* The only other major American loss was a destroyer. The Japanese defeat at Midway was the turning point of the Pacific war. It demonstrated that aircraft carriers, not battleships, would decide the naval conflict.

SETBACKS IN THE ATLANTIC   Early Allied setbacks in the Pacific were matched by losses in the Atlantic. Since the blitzkrieg of 1940, German submarine "wolf packs" had wreaked havoc in the North Atlantic. In 1942, German U-boats appeared off American shores and began to attack coastal ships, most of them tankers. Nearly 400 ships were lost in American waters before effective countermeasures brought the problem under control. The naval command hastened the building of small escort vessels, meanwhile pressing into patrol service all kinds of surface craft and planes, some of them civilian. During the second half of 1942, these efforts sharply reduced American losses.

MOBILIZATION AT HOME

The attack on Pearl Harbor ended not only the long public debate on isolation and intervention but also the long economic depression that had ravaged the country during the 1930s. The war effort required all of America's immense productive capacity and full employment of the workforce. For 1942 alone the government ordered 60,000 planes, 45,000 tanks, and 8 million tons of merchant shipping. The next year's goals were even higher. Mobilization was in fact already further along than preparedness had been in 1916–1917. The draft had been in effect for more than a year, and the army had grown to more than 1.4 million men by July 1941. Congress quickly extended the term of military service to last until six months after the war's end. Men between the ages of eighteen and forty-five were now subject to conscription. Altogether more than 15 million American men and women would serve in the armed forces during the war. The average soldier or sailor was twenty-six years old, stood five feet eight inches, and weighed 144 pounds, an inch taller and eight pounds heavier than the average recruit in World War I. Less than half the servicemen had finished high school.

ECONOMIC CONVERSION   The economy, too, was already partially mobilized for war, by lend-lease and the defense buildup. Congress had authorized the president to reshuffle government agencies and to allot materials and facilities as needed for defense, with penalties for any agency that failed to comply. The War Production Board, created in 1942, directed the conversion of manufacturing to war production. The Office of Scientific Research and Development mobilized thousands of scientists to design the many technologies and devices that contributed to the war effort, which would include radar, sonar, the proximity fuse, and the bazooka.

   The pressure of wartime needs and the stimulus of government spending more than doubled the gross national product between 1940 and 1945. Government expenditures during the war years soared. The total was about 10 times what America spent in World War I and 100 times the expenditures during the Civil War. The massive infusion of government capital into the economy also encouraged greater centralization and consolidation in private industry. Larger companies tended to win the most government contracts, and the more they won, the larger they became. Conversely, those without government contracts withered and died. In 1942 alone 300,000 businesses shut down.

   America's basic economic problem during the war years was no longer creating jobs but finding workers for the booming shipyards, aircraft factories, and munitions plants. Millions of people who had lived on the margins of the economic system, especially women, were now brought fully into the workforce. Pockets of stubborn poverty did not disappear, but for most civilians the war spelled neither severe hardship nor suffering but a better life than ever before, despite shortages and rationing of consumer goods. Labor unions benefited directly from the dramatic growth of the civilian workforce. Union membership increased significantly during the war years, from about 11 million to 15 million.

ECONOMIC CONTROLS   Increased family income and government spending during the war raised fears of inflation. Some of the available money went into taxes and war bonds, but even so, more purchasing power was sent chasing scarce consumer goods just as industrial production was converting to war needs. Consumer durables such as cars, washing machines, and nondefense housing in fact ceased to be produced at all. In the face of such wartime shortages, only strict restraints would keep prices from soaring out of sight. In 1941 Roosevelt created the Office of Price Administration, and the following year Congress authorized it to set price ceilings. With prices frozen, basic consumer goods had to be allocated through rationing, which began with tires and was gradually extended to other scarce items such as sugar, coffee, meat, and gasoline.

At first, however, wages and farm prices were not tightened, and this complicated matters. War prosperity offered farmers a chance to recover from two decades of distress, and farm-state legislators raised both floors and ceilings on farm prices. Higher food prices reinforced workers' demands for higher wages. To relieve this inflationary pressure, the president won new authority to control wages and farm prices. Businesses and workers chafed at the new controls, and on occasion the government was forced to seize industries threatened by strikes. The coal mines and railroads were nationalized for a short time in 1943. Despite these problems the government's program to stabilize the war economy succeeded. By the end of the war, consumer prices had risen by only about 31 percent, a far better record than the World War I rise of 62 percent.

To make the economic controls work, the government launched a program to encourage conservation of resources. As one popular slogan had it, "Use it up, wear it out, make it do or do without." People collected scrap metal and grew their own food in backyard "victory gardens." In 1942, when the war plants faced a rubber shortage, President Roosevelt asked citizens to turn in "old tires, old rubber raincoats, old garden hoses, rubber shoes, bathing caps, gloves—whatever you have that is made of rubber."

DOMESTIC CONSERVATISM   Despite the government's efforts to encourage sacrifices for the war effort, Americans expressed their discontent with price controls, labor shortages, rationing, and a hundred other petty vexations. They manifested those concerns in a reaction against Roosevelt liberalism at the polls that indicated a growing political conservatism. In 1942 the congressional elections registered a national swing against the New Deal. Republicans gained forty-six seats in the House and nine in the Senate, chiefly in the farm areas of the midwestern states. Democratic losses outside the South strengthened the southern delegation's position within the party, and the delegation itself reflected conservative victories in southern primaries. A coalition of conservatives dismantled "nonessential" New Deal agencies, including the National Youth Adminstration, the Civilian Conservation Corps, and the Farm Security Administration.

Organized labor, despite substantial gains during the war, felt the impact of the conservative trend. In the spring of 1943, when John L. Lewis led the coal miners out on strike, Congress passed the Smith-Connally War Labor Disputes Act, which authorized the government to seize plants useful to the war effort. In 1943 a dozen states adopted laws restricting picketing and other union activities, and in 1944 Arkansas and Florida set in motion a wave of "right-to-work" legislation that outlawed the closed shop (requiring that all employees be union members).

SOCIAL EFFECTS OF THE WAR

MOBILIZATION AND THE DEVELOPMENT OF THE WEST   The dramatic expansion of defense production after 1940 and the mobilization of millions of people in the armed forces accelerated economic development and a population boom in the western states. Nearly 8 million people moved into the states west of the Mississippi River between 1940 and 1950. The Far West experienced the fastest rate of urban growth in the country. Small cities such as Phoenix and Albuquerque mushroomed while Seattle, San Francisco, Los Angeles, and San Diego witnessed dizzying growth. San Diego's population, for example, increased by 147 percent between 1941 and 1945. The migration of workers to new defense jobs in the West had significant demographic effects. Communities with few African Americans witnessed an influx of blacks. Lured by news of job openings and higher wages, African Americans from Texas, Oklahoma, Arkansas, and Louisiana headed west. During the war years, Seattle's African-American population jumped from 4,000 to 40,000, Portland's from 2,000 to 15,000.

CHANGING ROLES FOR WOMEN   The war marked an important watershed in the changing status of women. With millions of men going into military service, the demand for labor shook up old prejudices about sex roles in the workplace—and in the military. Nearly 200,000 women served in the Women's Army Corps (WAC) and the navy's equivalent, Women Accepted for Volunteer Emergency Services (WAVES). Lesser numbers joined the Marine Corps, the Coast Guard, and the Army Air Force.

Over 6 million women entered the workforce during the war, an increase of more than 50 percent and in manufacturing alone an increase of some 110 percent. By 1944 over one third of all American women were in the labor force. Old barriers fell overnight as women became toolmakers, machinists, riveters, crane operators, lumberjacks, stevedores, blacksmiths, and railroad workers. Desperate for laborers, the government launched an intense publicity campaign to draw women into traditional male jobs. "Rosie the Riveter," a beautiful model dressed in overalls, served as the cover girl for the recruiting campaign.

One striking feature of the wartime economy was the larger proportion of older, married women in the workforce. In 1940 about 15 percent of married women were employed outside the home; by 1945, 24 percent were. In the workforce as a whole, married women for the first time outnumbered single women. Many women were eager to get away from the grinding routine of domestic life. One female welder remembered that her wartime job "was the first time I had a chance to get out of the kitchen and work in industry and make a few bucks. This was something I had never dreamed would happen." And it was something that many women did not want to relinquish after the war.

Women in the Military

This navy recruiting poster urged women to join the WAVES (Women Accepted for Volunteer Emergency Service).

AFRICAN AMERICANS IN WORLD WAR II   The most volatile issue ignited by the war was African-American participation in the defense effort. From the start black leaders demanded equality in the armed forces and defense industries. Eventually about 1 million African Americans served in the armed forces, but most were assigned to segregated units. The most important departure from this pattern came with a 1940 decision to integrate officer-candidate schools, except those for air force cadets. A separate military flight school at Tuskegee, Alabama, trained about 600 African-American pilots, many of whom distinguished themselves in combat.

War industries were even less hospitable to integration. "We will not employ Negroes," said the president of North American Aviation. In 1941 A. Philip Randolph, the brilliant head of the Brotherhood of Sleeping Car Porters, organized a March on Washington movement to demand an end to racial discrimination in defense industries. The Roosevelt administration, alarmed at the prospect of a mass descent on the capital, struck a bargain. Randolph called off the march in return for an executive order prohibiting racial discrimination in companies that received federal defense contracts.

African-American leaders quickly broadened their drive for wartime participation into a more inclusive and open challenge to all kinds of discrimination, including racial segregation itself. Membership in the NAACP soared during the war, from 50,000 to 450,000. African Americans could look forward to greater political participation after the Supreme Court, in *Smith v. Allwright* (1944), struck down Texas's whites-only primary on the grounds that Democratic primaries were part of the election process and thus subject to the Fifteenth Amendment.

LATINOS IN THE LABOR FORCE   As rural folk moved to the western cities, many farm counties across the nation experienced a labor shortage. In an ironic about-face, local and federal government authorities who before

Tuskegee Airmen, 1942

One of the last segregated military training schools, the flight school at Tuskegee trained African-American men for combat during World War II.

the war had forced undocumented Mexican laborers back across the border now recruited them to harvest crops. Before it would assist in providing the needed workers, the Mexican government insisted that the United States ensure minimum working and living conditions. The result was the creation of the bracero program in 1942. Mexico agreed to provide seasonal farmworkers in exchange for a promise by the U.S. government not to draft them into military service. The workers were hired on year-long contracts, and American officials provided transportation from the border to their job sites. Under the bracero program some 200,000 Mexican farmworkers entered the western United States. At least that many more crossed the border as undocumented workers.

The rising tide of Mexican Americans in Los Angeles provoked a growing stream of anti-Latino editorials and incidents. Even though Mexican Americans fought in the war with great valor, earning seventeen Congressional Medals of Honor, there was constant conflict between servicemen and Mexican-American gang members and teenage "zoot-suiters" in southern California. In 1943 several thousand off-duty sailors and soldiers, joined by hundreds of local white civilians, rampaged through downtown Los Angeles streets, assaulting Latinos, African Americans, and Filipinos. The violence lasted a week and came to be labeled the zoot-suit riots. (Zoot suits were the flamboyant suits popular in the 1940s and worn by some young Mexican-American men.)

NATIVE AMERICANS AND THE WAR EFFORT   Indians supported the war effort more fully than any other group in American society. Almost one third of eligible Native American men, over 25,000 people, served in the armed forces. Another one fourth worked in defense-related industries. Thousands of Indian women volunteered as nurses or joined the WAVES. As was the case with African Americans, Indians benefited from the experiences afforded by the war. Those who left reservations to work in defense plants or to join the military gained new vocational skills as well as a greater awareness of opportunities available in the larger American society.

Why did so many Native Americans fight in such high numbers for a nation that had stripped them of their land and decimated their heritage? Some felt that they had no choice. Mobilization for the war effort ended many New Deal programs that had provided Indians with jobs. Reservation Indians thus faced the necessity of finding new jobs elsewhere. Others viewed the Nazis and the Japanese warlords as threats to their own homeland. The most common sentiment animating Indian involvement in the war effort, however, seems to have been a genuine sense of patriotism.

Whatever the reasons, Indians distinguished themselves in the military. Unlike their African-American counterparts, Indian servicemen were integrated into regular units. Perhaps the most distinctive activity performed by Indians was their service as "code talkers": every military branch used Indians to encode and decipher messages using their native languages.

INTERNMENT OF JAPANESE AMERICANS   The record on civil liberties during World War II was on the whole better than that during World War I, if only because there was virtually no domestic opposition to the war effort after the attack on Pearl Harbor. Neither German Americans nor Italian Americans faced the harassments meted out to their counterparts in the previous war; few had much sympathy for Hitler or Mussolini. The shameful exception to an otherwise improved record was the treatment accorded to Americans of Japanese descent in the months following the attack on Pearl Harbor. One California barbershop offered "free shaves for Japs" but noted that it was "not responsible for accidents." Others were even blunter. Idaho's governor declared: "A good solution to the Jap problem would be to send them all back to Japan, then sink the island. They live like rats, breed like rats, and act like rats." Such attitudes were widespread, and the government finally succumbed to demands that it force all Japanese, citizens or not, into "war relocation camps" in the interior.

Caught up in the war hysteria and racial prejudice unleashed by the attack on Pearl Harbor, President Roosevelt initiated the removal and confinement of Japanese Americans when he issued Executive Order 9066 on February 19, 1942. More than 60 percent of the internees were U.S. citizens; one third were under the age of nineteen. More than 100,000 people were eventually removed from their homes and businesses. Forced to sell their farms and businesses at great losses, the internees lost both their liberty and their property. Not until 1983 did the government acknowledge the injustice of the internment policy. Five years later Congress voted to give $20,000 and an apology to each of the 60,000 former internees who were still living. .

THE ALLIED DRIVE TOWARD BERLIN

In mid-1942 the "home front" had begun to get news from the war fronts that some of the lines were holding at last. By midyear a fleet of American air and sea subchasers was suppressing German U-boats off the Atlantic coast. This event was all the more important because Allied war plans called for the defeat of Germany first.

WAR AIMS AND STRATEGY   There were good reasons for giving top priority to defeating Hitler: Nazi forces in western Europe and the Atlantic posed a more direct threat to the Western Hemisphere than did Japan, and Germany's war potential exceeded Japan's. Yet Japanese attacks involved Americans directly in the Pacific war from the start, and as a consequence more Americans went to the Pacific than crossed the Atlantic during the first year of fighting.

The Pearl Harbor attack brought British prime minister Winston Churchill to Washington, D.C. for talks about a common war plan. Thus began a successful but not always harmonious wartime alliance between the United States and Great Britain. The meetings in Washington in 1942 affirmed the priority of winning the war against Germany. Agreement on war aims did not bring agreement on strategy, however. When Roosevelt and Churchill met at the White House a second time in 1942, they could not agree on the location of the first attack against the Nazis. American strategists wanted to strike German-held France directly across the English Channel before the end of 1942. With vivid memories of the last war, the British feared a mass bloodletting in trench warfare if they struck prematurely. The Soviets, bearing the brunt of the German attack in the east, insisted that the Western Allies must do something to relieve the pressure along the Russian front. Finally, the Americans accepted Churchill's proposal to invade French North Africa, now allied with Germany .

THE NORTH AFRICAN CAMPAIGN   On November 8, 1942, British and American units commanded by General Dwight D. Eisenhower landed in Morocco and Algeria. Completely surprised, French forces under the Vichy government (which collaborated with the Germans) had little will to resist. Farther east, British forces were pushing German armies back across Libya. Before spring the Germans were caught in a gigantic pair of pincers. By April the British had linked up with American forces. Hammered from all sides and unable to retreat across the Mediterranean, an army of more than 200,000 Germans surrendered on May 12, 1943, leaving all of North Africa in Allied hands.

While the Battle of Tunisia was still unfolding, Roosevelt and Churchill met at Casablanca, Morocco. Stalin declined to leave beleaguered Russia for the meeting but continued to press for the opening of a second front in western Europe. Since the German invasion of Russia in 1941, over 90 percent of German military casualties had occurred on the Russian front. The British and American engagements with German forces in North Africa were minuscule in comparison with the scope and fury of the fighting in Russia.

Churchill and Roosevelt spent eight days at Casablanca, hammering out key strategic decisions. The Americans wanted to launch a massive Allied invasion of German-occupied France as soon as possible, but the British still insisted that such a major assault was premature. They convinced the Americans that they should follow up a victory in North Africa with an assault on Sicily and Italy. Roosevelt and Churchill also decided to step up the bombing of Germany and to increase shipments of military supplies to the Soviet Union and the Nationalist Chinese forces fighting the Japanese.

Before leaving Casablanca, Roosevelt announced, with Churchill's endorsement, that the war would end only with the "unconditional surrender" of all enemies. This demand was designed to reassure Stalin that the Western Allies would not negotiate separately with the Germans. The West desperately needed Soviet cooperation in defeating Germany, and Roosevelt and Churchill were eager to reassure Stalin of their good intentions.

THE BATTLE OF THE ATLANTIC While fighting raged in North Africa, the more crucial Battle of the Atlantic reached its climax on the high seas. Several factors contributed to the success of the Allied effort. Scientists had perfected a variety of detection devices: radar, which the British had already used to advantage in the Battle of Britain, bounced radio waves off objects and registered their position on a screen; sonar detected sound waves from submerged U-boats; sonobuoys, dropped from planes, radioed back their findings; and advanced magnetic equipment enabled aircraft to detect objects underwater.

By early 1943 in the western portion of the North Atlantic, there were at any given time an average of 31 convoys with 145 escorts and 673 merchant ships, as well as a number of heavily escorted troopships. None of the troopships going to Britain or the Mediterranean was lost. The U-boats kept up the Battle of the Atlantic until the war's end, but their commander later admitted that the battle had been lost by the end of May 1943. He credited the difference largely to radar. What he did not know then was that the Allies had a secret weapon: by early 1943 their cryptanalysts were routinely decoding secret messages and telling their subhunters where to look for German U-boats.

SICILY AND ITALY On July 10, 1943, after the Allied victory in the North African campaign, about 250,000 British and American troops landed on Sicily, scoring a complete surprise. The German-Italian collapse in Sicily ended Mussolini's twenty years of Fascist rule. On July 25, 1943, Italy's king notified the dictator of his dismissal as prime minister. A new regime startled the Allies when it offered not only to surrender but also to switch sides in the war. Unfortunately, mutual suspicions prolonged talks until September 3, while the Germans poured reinforcements into Italy. In the confusion the Italian army disintegrated, although most of the navy escaped to Allied ports. A few army units later joined the Allied effort. Mussolini, plucked from imprisonment by a daring German airborne raid, became head of a puppet government in northern Italy.

Therefore the Allied assault on the Italian mainland did not turn into an easy victory. The main landing at Salerno on September 9 encountered heavy German resistance. The Americans, joined by British troops, nevertheless secured beachheads within a week and captured Naples. After a five-month siege of Rome, the Americans finally took the fabled city on June 4, 1944. Yet they enjoyed only a brief moment of glory, for the long-awaited cross-Channel landing in France, begun two days later, quickly became the focus of attention.

THE STRATEGIC BOMBING OF EUROPE   Behind the long-postponed landings on the Normandy beaches lay months of preparation. While waiting, the U.S. Army Air Force and the Royal Air Force (RAF) had attacked Hitler's "Fortress Europe." By 1943 American strategic bombers were full-fledged partners of the RAF in the effort to pound Germany into submission. Yet despite the widespread damage it caused, the strategic air offensive ultimately failed to dismantle German production or, as later studies found, break civilian morale. By the end of 1943, however, new jettisonable gas tanks permitted Allied escort fighters to fly as far as Berlin and back, protecting the bomber groups. Thereafter, heavy losses of both planes and pilots forced the German Luftwaffe to conserve its strength and cease challenging every Allied mission.

With air supremacy assured, the Allies were free to concentrate on their primary urban and industrial targets and, when the time came, to provide cover for the Normandy landings. On April 14, 1944, General Eisenhower assumed control of the Strategic Air Forces for the invasion of German-controlled France. On D-day, June 6, 1944, he told the troops, "If you see fighting aircraft over you, they will be ours."

THE TEHRAN MEETING   Late in November 1943 Churchill and Roosevelt had met with Stalin in Tehran, Iran, to coordinate plans for the invasion of France and a Soviet offensive from the east. After Churchill and Roosevelt assured Stalin that a cross-Channel invasion was finally coming, the Soviet premier in return promised to enter the war against Japan after Germany's defeat. The Allied leaders also agreed to begin plans for a new international

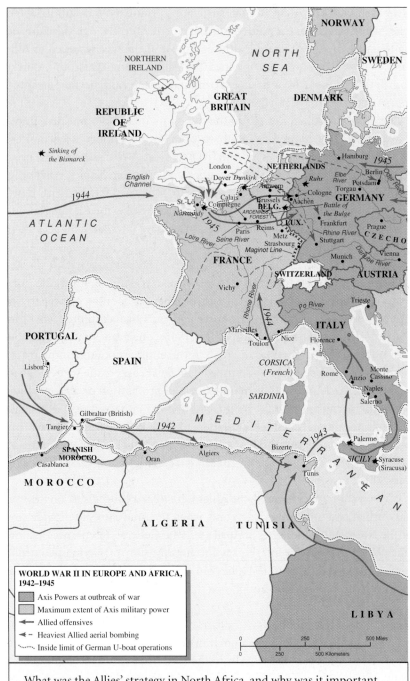

WORLD WAR II IN EUROPE AND AFRICA, 1942–1945

- Axis Powers at outbreak of war
- Maximum extent of Axis military power
- Allied offensives
- Heaviest Allied aerial bombing
- Inside limit of German U-boat operations

What was the Allies' strategy in North Africa, and why was it important for the invasion of Italy? Why did Eisenhower's plan on D-day succeed? What was the Battle of the Bulge? What was the role of strategic bombing in the war? Was it effective?

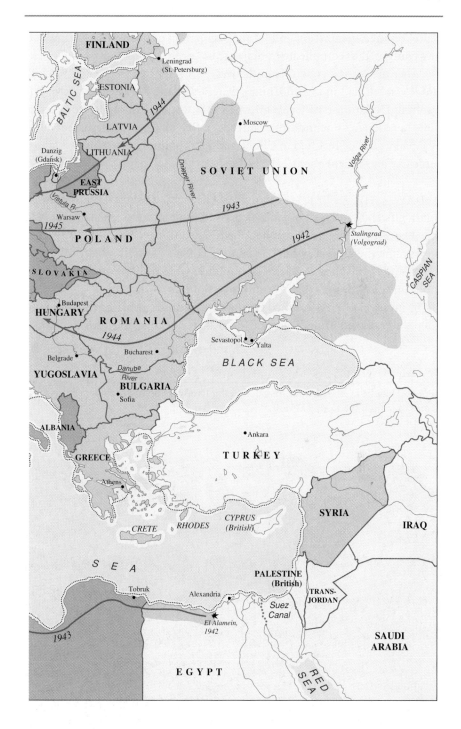

FINLAND

Leningrad
(St. Petersburg)

BALTIC SEA

ESTONIA

LATVIA

1944

Moscow

LITHUANIA

Danzig
(Gdańsk)

EAST
PRUSSIA

SOVIET UNION

Vistula R.

Dnieper River

Volga River

Warsaw

1945

1943

POLAND

1942

Stalingrad
(Volgograd)

CASPIAN SEA

SLOVAKIA

Budapest

HUNGARY

ROMANIA

1944

Sevastopol

Yalta

BLACK SEA

Belgrade

Bucharest

Danube
River

YUGOSLAVIA

BULGARIA

Sofia

ALBANIA

Ankara

GREECE

TURKEY

Athens

CYPRUS
(British)

SYRIA

IRAQ

CRETE

RHODES

SEA

Tobruk

Alexandria

PALESTINE
(British)

TRANS-
JORDAN

Suez
Canal

El Alamein,
1942

1943

RED SEA

SAUDI
ARABIA

EGYPT

peacekeeping organization and for the occupation of postwar Germany. Politics continued to complicate military strategy.

Earlier in November, while on the way to the Tehran meeting, Churchill, and Roosevelt had met with China's general Chiang Kai-shek in Cairo. The resulting Declaration of Cairo affirmed that war against Japan would continue until Japan's unconditional surrender, that all Chinese territories taken by Japan would be restored to China, and that "in due course Korea shall become free and independent."

D-DAY AND AFTER   In early 1944 General Dwight D. Eisenhower, smart, efficient, and well organized, arrived in London to take command at the Supreme Headquarters of the Allied Expeditionary Force (SHAEF) and prepare for the cross-Channel assault on Hitler's "Atlantic Wall." Within a few months over 1 million American soldiers were training along England's southern coast for the cross-Channel invasion.

The invasion of France, called Operation Overlord, surprised the Germans. Eisenhower fooled Hitler's generals into believing that the invasion would

Operation Overlord

General Dwight D. Eisenhower instructing paratroopers before they board their airplanes to launch the D-day assault.

come at Pas de Calais, on the French-Belgian border. Instead, the landings occurred in Normandy, about 200 miles south. Airborne forces dropped behind the beaches during the night while planes and battleships pounded the coastal defenses.

At dawn on June 6, 1944, D-day, the invasion fleet of some 4,000 ships carrying and 150,000 men (57,000 Americans) filled the horizon off the Normandy coast. Overhead, thousands of Allied planes supported the invasion force. Sleepy German soldiers awoke to see the vast armada arrayed before them. Despite Eisenhower's meticulous planning and the imposing array of Allied troops and firepower, the D-day invasion almost failed. Cloud cover and German anti-aircraft fire caused many of the paratroopers and glider pilots to miss their landing zones. Oceangoing landing craft delivered their troops to the wrong locations. Low clouds led the Allied planes to drop their bombs too far inland. The naval bombardment was equally ineffective. In addition, rough seas made many soldiers seasick and capsized dozens of landing craft.

The Landing at Normandy

D-day, June 6, 1944. Before they could huddle under a seawall and begin to root out the region's Nazi defenders, soldiers on Omaha Beach had to cross a fifty-yard stretch that exposed them to bullets fired from machine guns housed in concrete pillboxes.

Over 1,000 men drowned. Waterlogged radios failed to work, and the deafening noise of the artillery and gunfire made oral communication impossible.

On Utah Beach the American troops made it in against relatively light opposition, but farther east, on a four-mile segment designated Omaha Beach, bombardment failed to take out the German defenders, and the Americans were caught in heavily mined water. In just ten minutes 197 of the 205 men in one rifle company were killed or wounded. By nightfall the bodies of some 5,000 killed or wounded Allied soldiers were strewn across Normandy's beaches. German losses were even heavier. Entire units were decimated or captured. Operation Overlord was the greatest military invasion in the annals of warfare and the climactic battle of World War II. With the beachhead secured, the Allied leaders knew that victory was now in their grasp.

Within two weeks after D-day, the Allies had landed 1 million troops, 556,000 tons of supplies, and 170,000 vehicles. They had seized a beachhead sixty miles wide and five to fifteen miles deep. They continued to pour men and supplies onto the beaches and to edge inland through the marshes and hedgerows. A stubborn Hitler issued disastrous orders to contest every inch of land. Field Marshal Erwin Rommel, convinced that all was lost, began to intrigue for a separate peace. Other like-minded German officers, sure that the war was hopeless, tried to kill Hitler at his headquarters on July 20, 1944, but the Führer survived the bomb blast, and hundreds of conspirators and suspects were tortured to death. General Rommel was granted the option of suicide, which he took.

Meanwhile, Hitler's tactics brought calamity to the German forces in western France. On July 25 American units broke out westward into Brittany and eastward toward Paris. On August 15 a joint American-French invasion force landed on the French Mediterranean coast and raced up the Rhône Valley. German resistance in France collapsed. A division of the Free French resistance, aided by American forces, had the honor of liberating Paris on August 25. Hitler's forces retreated toward the German border, and by mid-September most of France and Belgium were cleared of enemy troops.

LEAPFROGGING TO TOKYO

Even in the Pacific, relegated to a lower priority, Allied forces had brought the war within reach of the enemy's homeland by the end of 1944. The war's first American offensive, in fact, had been in the southwest Pacific. There the Japanese, stopped at Coral Sea and Midway, had thrust into the southern Solomon Islands and were building an airstrip on Guadalcanal, from which they would be able to attack Allied transportation routes to Australia. On August 7, 1942, two months before the North Africa landings, the First Marine Division landed on Guadalcanal and seized the airstrip.

MACARTHUR IN NEW GUINEA   Meanwhile, American and Australian forces under General Douglas MacArthur had begun to push the Japanese out of their positions on New Guinea's northern coast. These costly battles, fought through some of the hottest, most humid, and most mosquito-infested swamps in the world, secured the eastern tip of New Guinea by the end of January 1943.

At this stage, American war planners were confronted with two propositions by the leaders of rival branches of the armed service, the army and the navy. The vainglorious MacArthur, sometimes accused of being a legend in his own mind, proposed to move his forces westward along the northern coast of New Guinea toward the Philippines and ultimately to Tokyo. Naval admiral Chester Nimitz argued for a sweep through the islands of the central Pacific to Formosa and China. The combined chiefs of staff agreed to pursue both plans.

During the Battle of the Bismarck Sea (March 2–3, 1943), American bombers sank eight Japanese troopships and ten warships carrying reinforcements. Thereafter the Japanese dared not risk sending transports to reinforce points under siege, making it possible for the Allies to use the tactic of neutralizing Japanese strongholds with air and sea power and moving on, leaving them to die on the vine. Some called it leapfrogging or island-hopping, and it was a major factor contributing to the Allied victory. By the end of 1943, MacArthur's forces controlled the northern coast of New Guinea.

NIMITZ IN THE CENTRAL PACIFIC   Admiral Nimitz's advance through the central Pacific had as its first target Tarawa in the Gilbert Islands. Tarawa was one of the most heavily protected islands in the Pacific. In a pitched battle nearly 1,000 U.S. soldiers, sailors, and marines lost their lives rooting out 4,000 Japanese soldiers who refused to surrender. The Gilbert Islands provided airfields from which the Seventh Air Force began softening up strong points in the Marshall Islands to the northwest. Japanese planes completely abandoned the region.

In the Battle of the Philippine Sea, fought mostly in the air on June 19–20, 1944, the Japanese lost 3 more carriers, 2 submarines, and over 300 planes, at a cost of only 17 U.S. planes. The battle secured the Mariana Islands, and soon large B-29 bombers were winging their way to the first systematic bombing of the Japanese homeland. Defeat in the Marianas convinced General Tōjō that the war was lost. On July 18, 1944, he and his entire cabinet resigned.

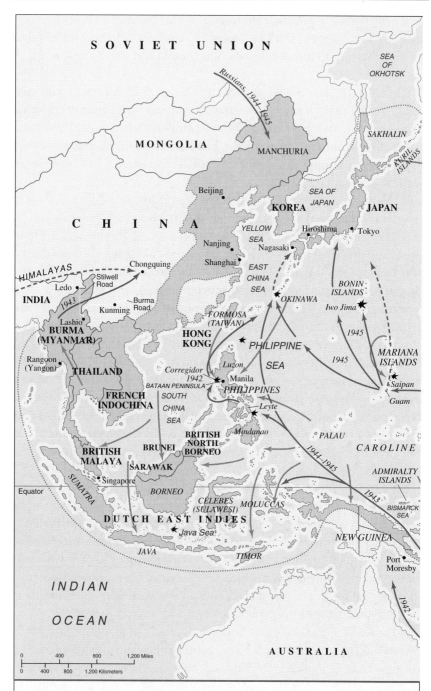

What was "leapfrogging"? Why were the battles in the Marianas a major turning point in the war? What was the significance of the Battle of Leyte Gulf? How did the battle at Okinawa affect how both sides proceeded in the war? Why did Truman decide to drop atomic bombs on Hiroshima and Nagasaki?

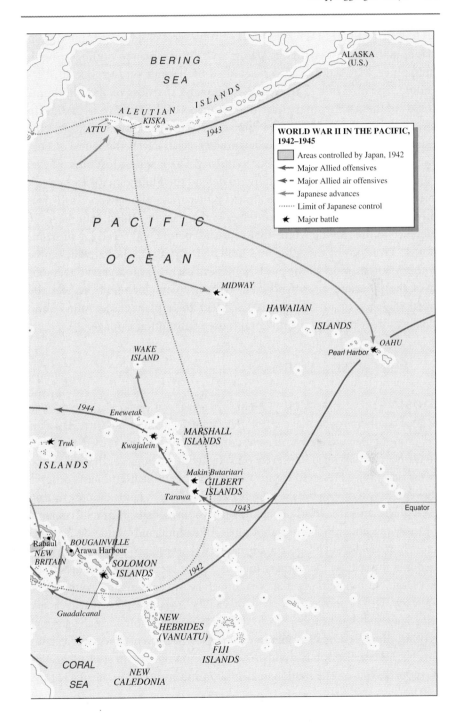

BERING SEA

ALASKA (U.S.)

ALEUTIAN ISLANDS
KISKA
ATTU
1943

PACIFIC

OCEAN

MIDWAY

HAWAIIAN

ISLANDS

OAHU
Pearl Harbor

WAKE ISLAND

1944   Enewetak
Truk   Kwajalein   MARSHALL ISLANDS
ISLANDS
Makin Butaritari
GILBERT ISLANDS
Tarawa
1943   Equator

Rabaul   BOUGAINVILLE
NEW   Arawa Harbour
BRITAIN   SOLOMON ISLANDS
1942

Guadalcanal

NEW HEBRIDES (VANUATU)
FIJI ISLANDS
CORAL   NEW CALEDONIA
SEA

WORLD WAR II IN THE PACIFIC, 1942–1945

- Areas controlled by Japan, 1942
- Major Allied offensives
- Major Allied air offensives
- Japanese advances
- Limit of Japanese control
- ★ Major battle

THE BATTLE OF LEYTE GULF   With New Guinea and the Mariana Islands all but conquered, MacArthur and Nimitz focused on liberating the Philippines. MacArthur's forces assaulted the islands on October 20, 1944, landing first on Leyte. The Japanese, knowing that loss of the Philippines would cut them off from the essential resources of the Dutch East Indies (Indonesia), brought in fleets from three directions. The three encounters that resulted on October 25 came to be known collectively as the Battle of Leyte Gulf, the largest naval engagement in history. The Japanese lost most of their remaining sea power and the ability to defend the Philippines. Also remarkable was the first use of suicide attacks by Japanese pilots, who crash-dived into American ships, killing themselves in the process. Called "kamikazes" (a reference to the "divine wind" that centuries before had saved Japan from a Mongol invasion) by the Allies and "tokkotai" (meaning special attack force) by the Japanese, most of the pilots were not fanatical volunteers. The majority of the thousand or so who died were very young student draftees (between the ages of 17–24) ordered to steer their planes into Allied ships. Whatever their motives, the tokkotai caused substantial damage.

A NEW AGE IS BORN

ROOSEVELT'S FOURTH TERM   In 1944, war or no war, the calendar dictated another presidential election. This time the Republicans turned to a former crime fighter and New York governor, Thomas E. Dewey, as their candidate. No Democrat challenged Roosevelt, but a fight did develop over the second spot on the ticket. Vice President Henry Wallace had aggravated southern conservatives and northern city bosses, who feared his ties with labor unions, so Roosevelt finally chose the relatively unknown Missouri senator Harry S. Truman.

Dewey ran under the same handicap as Alf Landon and Wendell Willkie had before him. He did not propose to dismantle Roosevelt's programs; rather, he argued that it was time for younger men to replace the "tired" old leaders of the New Deal. The problem was that even though he was considerably younger than Roosevelt, Dewey showed few signs of vitality. Although blessed with a silky voice and a stylish wardrobe, he was ill at ease in public, stiff, formal, seemingly arrogant, and worst of all—dull. Roosevelt showed signs of illness and exhaustion, but nevertheless, on November 7, 1945, he was once again elected, this time by a popular vote of 25.6 million to 22 million and an electoral vote of 432 to 99.

CONVERGING MILITARY FRONTS   Meanwhile, Allied forces were mired in war in Europe; complete victory remained elusive. After the quick sweep across France, the Allies lost momentum in the fall of 1944 and settled down to slugging it out along the border of Germany. The armies would fight along this line all winter, but first, on December 16, 1944, the Germans sprang a surprise in the rugged Ardennes Forest, where the Allied line was thinnest. The Nazis advanced along a fifty-mile bulge in the Allied lines in Belgium and Luxembourg (hence the name the Battle of the Bulge) before they stalled at Bastogne. Reinforced by the Allies just before it was surrounded, Bastogne held out for six days against relentless attacks. The American situation remained desperate until December 23, when the weather improved, allowing Allied air power to drop supplies and attack the Germans. On December 26, the besieged American army at Bastogne was relieved.

Germany's sudden counterattack upset Eisenhower's timetable and made continued coordination with the Soviet army even more crucial. The Nazis poured resources into the battle at Bastogne but were unable to hold the eastern front when in January 1945 the Soviets began their final offensive. The destruction of Hitler's last reserve units at the Battle of the Bulge also left open the door to Germany's heartland. The western offensives began in February, and by early March Allied forces were crossing the Rhine River into Germany. By that time the Soviet offensive on the eastern front had also reached the German border.

YALTA AND THE POSTWAR WORLD   As the final offensives against Germany got under way, the Big Three leaders met again, in early February 1945 at Yalta, a resort in southern Russia. While the focus at Tehran in 1943 had been on wartime strategy, the leaders now discussed the shape of the postwar world. Stalin was self-confident, demanding, and sarcastic. He knew that the Soviet forces' control of key areas would ensure that his demands would be met. Two aims loomed large in Roosevelt's thinking. One was the need to ensure that the Soviet Union would join the war against Japan. The other was based upon the lessons he had drawn from the previous world war. Chief among the mistakes to be remedied were the failures of the United States to join the League of Nations and of the Allies to maintain a united front in negotiations with the German aggressors after the war.

The Yalta meeting thus began by calling for a conference to create a new world organization, called the United Nations. The conferees also decided that substantive decisions in the new organization's Security Council would require the agreement of its five permanent members: the United States, Britain, the Soviet Union, France, and China.

GERMANY AND EASTERN EUROPE   With Hitler's Reich stumbling to its doom, the leaders at Yalta had to make arrangements for the postwar governance of Germany. The war map dictated the basic pattern of occupation

The Yalta Conference

Churchill, Roosevelt, and Stalin confer on the shape of the postwar world in February 1945.

zones: the Soviet Union would control eastern Germany, and the Western Allies would control the rich industrial areas of the west. Berlin, isolated within the Soviet zone, would be jointly occupied. Churchill and Roosevelt insisted that liberated France receive a zone along its border with Germany and one in Berlin. Austria was similarly divided, with Vienna, like Berlin, under joint occupation within the Soviet zone. Russian demands for reparations of $20 billion to the Allies, half of which would go to the Soviet Union, were referred to a reparations commission. That commission never reached agreement, although the Soviets took untold amounts of German machinery and equipment from their occupation zone.

With respect to Eastern Europe, where Soviet forces were advancing on a broad front, there was little the Western Allies could do to influence events. Poland became the main focus of Western concern. Britain and France had gone to war in 1939 to defend it, and now, six years later, the course of the war had ironically left Poland's fate in the hands of the Soviets. Events had long foreshadowed the outcome. When they entered Poland in 1944, the Soviets allowed a puppet regime in Lublin to take control of civil administration. The Soviets refused to recognize the legitimacy of Poland's government-in-exile in London, formed by officials who had fled the country following Hitler's invasion in 1939. With Soviet troops at the gates of Warsaw, the underground resistance in the city rose up against the Nazi occupiers. But because the Polish underground supported the Polish government-in-exile, the Soviet armies idled for two months while the Nazis killed thousands of Poles in Warsaw, potential rivals of the Soviets' Lublin puppet government.

At Yalta the Big Three promised to sponsor free elections, democratic governments, and constitutional safeguards of freedom throughout the rest of Europe. The Yalta Declaration of Liberated Europe reaffirmed faith in the principles of the Atlantic Charter and the Declaration of the United Nations, but in the end it made little difference. It may have postponed Communist takeovers in Eastern Europe for a few years, but before long Communist members of coalition governments had purged the opposition. Russia, twice invaded by Germany in the twentieth century, was determined to create compliant buffer states between it and the German state.

YALTA'S LEGACY Critics later attacked the Yalta agreements for "giving" Eastern Europe over to Soviet domination. Some argued that Roosevelt's declining health allowed him to buckle under Stalin's insistent demands. Yet the course of the war shaped the actions at Yalta, not personal diplomacy. The Soviets had the upper hand in Eastern Europe. Perhaps the most bitterly criticized of the Yalta accords was a secret agreement on the Far East, made public after the war. The combined chiefs of staff estimated that Japan could hold out for eighteen months after the defeat of Germany. Costly campaigns thus lay ahead, and the atomic bomb was still an expensive and untested gamble.

Roosevelt thus believed he had no choice but to accept Stalin's demands on postwar arrangements in the Far East, subject technically to agreement later by China's general Chiang Kai-shek. Stalin wanted continued Soviet control of Outer Mongolia through its puppet People's Republic, acquisition of the Kuril Islands from Japan, and recovery of rights and territory lost after the Russo-Japanese War of 1905. Stalin in return promised to enter the war against Japan two or three months after the German defeat, recognize Chinese sovereignty over Manchuria, and conclude a treaty of friendship and alliance with the Chinese Nationalists. Roosevelt's concessions would later appear in a different light, but given their geographic advantages in Asia, as in Eastern Europe, the Soviets were in a position to get what they wanted in any case.

THE COLLAPSE OF THE THIRD REICH By 1945 the collapse of Nazi resistance was imminent, but President Roosevelt did not live to join the celebrations. Throughout 1944 his health had been declining, and on April 12, 1945, while drafting a speech, he died from a cerebral hemorrhage.

Hitler's Germany collapsed less than a month later. The Allied armies rolled up almost unopposed to the Elbe River, where they met advance detachments of Soviets on April 25. Three days later Italian partisans captured and brutally killed Mussolini as he tried to flee. In Berlin, which was under siege by the Soviets, Hitler married his mistress, Eva Braun, in an underground bunker on April 30, just before killing her and himself. On May 2 Berlin fell to the Soviets. That day, German forces in Italy surrendered. On May 7 the Germans signed an unconditional surrender in the Allied headquarters at Reims.

Massive victory celebrations on V-E Day, May 8, 1945, were tempered by the tragedies that had engulfed the world: mourning for the lost president and the death and mutilation of untold millions. Most shocking was the Allied armies' confirmation of the existence of the death camps in which Nazis had sought to apply their "final solution" to the "Jewish problem": the wholesale extermination of some 6 million Jews, along with more than 1 million others from occupied countries.

May 8, 1945

The celebration in New York's City's Times Square on V-E Day.

During the war, reports from Red Cross and underground sources had amassed growing evidence of Germany's systematic genocide against European Jews. Stories appeared in major American newspapers as early as 1942, but they were nearly always buried on inside pages. Reports of such horror seemed beyond belief. In addition, American government officials, even some Jewish leaders, dragged their feet on the question for fear that relief efforts for Jewish refugees might stir latent anti-Semitism at home. Finally Roosevelt had set up a War Refugees Board in 1944. It managed to rescue about 200,000 European Jews and some 20,000 others. But more might have been done. The Allies rejected a plan to bomb the rail lines leading to the largest death camp, Auschwitz, in Poland, although American planes hit industries five miles away. Moreover, few refugees were accepted into the United States. The Allied handling of the Holocaust was inept at best and disgraceful at worst.

A GRINDING WAR AGAINST JAPAN The sobering thought that Japan must still be defeated cast a further pall over the victory celebrations. American forces continued to assault the Japanese Empire in the early months of 1945, but at a heavy cost. On February 19, 1945, U.S. marines invaded Iwo Jima, a volcanic island 760 miles from Tokyo that was needed to provide a fighter escort for bombers over Japan and a landing strip for disabled B-29 bombers. It took nearly six weeks to secure the site from Japanese defenders hiding in caves, and the cost was high: more than 20,000 American casualties, including nearly 7,000 dead.

The fight for Okinawa, beginning on Easter Sunday, April 1, was even bloodier. The island was large enough to afford a staging area for the planned invasion of the Japanese islands, and its capture required the largest amphibious operation of the Pacific war, involving some 300,000 troops. The fight raged until late June, incurring nearly 50,000 American casualties. The Japanese lost an estimated 140,000, including about 42,000 Okinawans. When resistance on Okinawa collapsed, the Japanese emperor instructed his new prime minister to seek peace.

THE ATOMIC BOMB In 1939 physicist Albert Einstein had alerted President Roosevelt to German research on nuclear fission. In response the president in 1940 had launched the $2-billion top-secret Manhattan Project, involving over 120,000 scientists and technicians in several locations. In a laboratory in Los Alamos, New Mexico, under the direction of J. Robert Oppenheimer, a group of physicists worked out the scientific and technical problems of the bomb's construction. On July 16, 1945, the first atomic fireball rose from the desert. Oppenheimer said later that in the bunker where observers watched the test blast, "a few people laughed, a few people cried, most people were silent." President Harry S. Truman, thrust into the presidency upon Roosevelt's death in April, wrote in his diary, "We have discovered the most terrible bomb in the history of the world."

Word of the new weapon changed all strategic calculations. How to use this awful weapon posed profound problems. Some scientists favored a demonstration explosion for the Japanese in a remote area, but that idea was vetoed because only two bombs were available, and even those might misfire. The choice of targets received more consideration. After deciding against Kyōto, Japan's ancient capital and repository of national and religious treasures, priority went to Hiroshima, a port city of 400,000 people in southern Japan, which was a center of war industries, headquarters of the Japanese Second General Army, and command center for the homeland's defenses.

On July 25, 1945, President Truman ordered the atomic bomb dropped if Japan did not surrender before August 3. Although an intense scholarly debate has emerged over the decision to drop the bomb, it is clear that Truman believed that the atomic bomb would save lives by avoiding an American invasion against defenders who would fight like "savages, ruthless, merciless, and fanatic."

The ferocious Japanese defense of Okinawa had convinced military planners that an amphibious invasion of Japan itself, scheduled to begin on November 1, 1945, could cost as many as 250,000 Allied casualties and even more Japanese losses. Moreover, some 100,000 Allied prisoners of war being held in Japan were to be executed when an invasion began. It is important to remember as well that the bombing of cities and the consequent killing of civilians had become accepted military practice during 1945. Once the Japanese navy was destroyed, American ships had roamed the Japanese coastline, shelling targets onshore. American planes had bombed at will and mined the waters of the Inland Sea. Tokyo, Nagoya, and other major cities had been devastated by firestorms created by incendiary bombs. The firebomb raids on Tokyo on a single night in March 1945 killed 100,000 civilians and left over 1 million people homeless. By July more than sixty of Japan's largest cities had been firebombed, resulting in 500,000 deaths and 13 million civilians left homeless. The use of atomic bombs on Japanese cities was thus seen as a logical next step to end the war without an invasion of Japan. As it turned out, American scientists greatly underestimated the physical effects of the atomic bomb. They predicted that 20,000 people would be killed. The number would be much higher.

On July 26 the heads of the American, British, and Chinese governments issued the Potsdam Declaration, demanding that Japan surrender or face "prompt and utter destruction." The deadline passed, and at 8:15 A.M. on

August 6, flying at 31,600 feet, a B-29 bomber named *Enola Gay* released the five-ton uranium bomb nicknamed Little Boy. Forty-three seconds later, as the *Enola Gay* turned sharply to avoid the blast, the bomb tumbled to an altitude of 1,900 feet, where it exploded as planned with the force of 20,000 tons of TNT. A blinding flash of light was followed by a fireball towering to 40,000 feet. The tail gunner on the *Enola Gay* described the scene: "It's like bubbling molasses down there . . . the mushroom is spreading out . . . fires are springing up everywhere . . . it's like a peep into hell."

The shock wave, firestorm, cyclonic winds, and radioactive rain killed some 80,000 people. Dazed survivors wandered the streets, so badly burned that their skin peeled off in large strips. By the end of the year, the death toll had reached 140,000 as the effects of radiation burns and infection took their toll. In addition, 70,000 buildings were destroyed, and four square miles of the city turned to rubble.

Two days after the Hiroshima bombing an opportunistic Soviet Union, eager to share the spoils of victory, hastened to enter the war in Asia. Truman and his aides, frustrated by the stubborn refusal of Japanese military and political

The Bomb

This image shows the wasteland that remained after the atomic bomb "Little Boy" decimated Hiroshima in 1945.

leaders to surrender and fearful that the Soviet Union's entry into the war would complicate negotiations, ordered the second atomic bomb dropped. On August 9 a B-29 aircraft named *Bockscar,* carrying a bomb dubbed Fat Man, flew over its primary target, Kokura. The city was so shrouded in haze and smoke from an earlier air raid, however, that *Bockscar* turned to its secondary target, Nagasaki, where at 11:02 A.M. it dropped its terrifying bomb, killing 36,000 people. That night the Japanese emperor urged his cabinet to surrender on the sole condition that he remain as sovereign. The next day the U.S. government announced its willingness to let the emperor keep his throne, but under the authority of an Allied supreme commander. Frantic exchanges ended with Japanese acceptance of the terms on August 14, 1945, when the emperor himself delivered a radio message announcing the surrender to his people. On September 2, 1945, General MacArthur and other Allied representatives accepted Japan's formal surrender on board the battleship *Missouri.*

THE FINAL LEDGER

Thus ended the most deadly conflict in human history. One estimate has it that 70 million fought in the war, at a cost of some 50 million military and civilian dead, including those murdered in concentration camps. The Soviet Union suffered the greatest losses of all: over 13 million military deaths, more than 7 million civilian deaths, and at least 25 million left homeless. World War II was more costly for the United States than any other foreign war: 292,000 battle deaths and 114,000 other deaths. But in proportion to its population, the United States suffered a loss far smaller than any of the other major Allies or their enemies, and American territory escaped the devastation inflicted on so many other parts of the world.

World War II had profound effects on American life and society. Mobilization for the war stimulated a phenomenal increase in productivity and brought full employment, thus ending the Great Depression and laying the foundation for an era of unprecedented prosperity. New technologies and products developed for military purposes—radar, computers, electronics, plastics and synthetics, jet engines, rockets, atomic energy—began to transform the private sector as well. And new opportunities for women as well as for African Americans and other minorities set in motion changes that would culminate in the civil rights movement of the 1960s and the feminist movement of the 1970s.

The Democratic party benefited from the war effort by solidifying its control of both the White House and Congress. The dramatic expansion of the federal government occasioned by the war continued after 1945. Presidential authority and prestige increased enormously at the expense of congressional and state power. The isolationist sentiment in foreign relations that had been so powerful in the 1920s and 1930s disintegrated as the United States emerged from the war with far-flung global responsibilities and interests. Thus the war's end opened a new era for the United States in the world arena. It accelerated the growth of American power while devastating all other world powers, leaving the United States economically and militarily the strongest nation on earth.

MAKING CONNECTIONS

- The impact of World War II on the home front was much more extensive than that of World War I, especially in the effects of war on race and gender relations.
- The growing domestic conservatism of the war years continued into the 1950s, a topic discussed in the next chapter.
- Dwight D. Eisenhower's success as a military commander and the Allied leader led to his nomination and election as president in 1952. Compare Eisenhower's political experience to the experience of Ulysses S. Grant and other American military leaders.

FURTHER READING

John Keegan's *The Second World War* (1989) surveys the European conflict, while Charles B. MacDonald's *The Mighty Endeavor: The American War in Europe* (1986) concentrates on U.S. involvement. Roosevelt's wartime leadership is analyzed in Eric Larrabee's *Commander in Chief: Franklin Delano Roosevelt, His Lieutenants, and Their War* (1987).

Books on specific European campaigns include Stephen E. Ambrose's *D-Day, June 6, 1944: The Climactic Battle of World War II* (1994) and Charles B. MacDonald's *A Time for Trumpets: The Untold Story of the Battle of the Bulge* (1995). On the Allied commander, see Carlo D'Este's *Eisenhower: A Soldier's Life* (2002).

For the war in the Far East, see John Costello's *The Pacific War, 1941–1945* (1981), Ronald H. Spector's *Eagle against the Sun: The American War with Japan* (1985), John W. Dower's award-winning *War without Mercy: Race and Power in the Pacific War* (1986), and Dan van der Vat's *The Pacific Campaign: The U.S.-Japanese Naval War, 1941–1945* (1991).

An excellent overview of the war's effects on the home front is Michael C. C. Adams's *The Best War Ever: America and World War II* (1994). On economic effects, see Harold G. Vatter's *The U.S. Economy in World War II* (1985).

Susan M. Hartmann's *The Home Front and Beyond: American Women in the 1940s* (1982) treats the new working environment for women. Neil A. Wynn looks at the participation of blacks in *The Afro-American and the Second World War* (1976). The story of the oppression of Japanese Americans is told in Peter Irons's *Justice at War: The Story of the Japanese American Internment Cases* (1983).

A sound introduction to U.S. diplomacy during the conflict can be found in Gaddis Smith's *American Diplomacy during the Second World War, 1941–1945* (1965). To understand the role that Roosevelt played in policy making, consult Warren F. Kimball's *The Juggler: Franklin Roosevelt as Wartime Statesman* (1991).

The issues and events that led to the deployment of atomic weapons are addressed in Martin J. Sherwin's *A World Destroyed: The Atomic Bomb and the Grand Alliance* (1975).

Part Seven

THE
AMERICAN
AGE

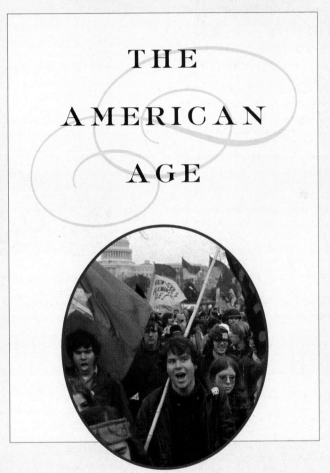

1945

Harry Truman serves as president (1945–1953)

George Kennan outlines the rationale of containment in *Foreign Affairs* (1947)

National Security Act makes permanent the Joint Chiefs of Staff, creates the Central Intelligence Agency and the National Security Council (1947)

Truman Doctrine establishes plan to help postwar Europe (1947)

Dixiecrats nominate Strom Thurmond for president; Truman unexpectedly wins reelection (1948)

House Un-American Activities Committee keeps lists on possible subversives, eventually fueling the outbreak of a second Red Scare (1940s–1950s)

11 top Communist party leaders are convicted under the Smith Act (1949)

1950

Alger Hiss is convicted for lying about espionage; Congress passes McCarran Internal Security Act; Senator Joseph McCarthy begins witch hunt for Communists (1950)

Twenty-second Amendment limits presidents after Truman to two terms (1951)

Dwight D. Eisenhower serves as president (1953–1961)

U.S. executes Julius and Ethel Rosenberg for espionage (1953)

McCarthy hearings are held; Congress votes to censure Senator McCarthy (1954)

1960

Civil Rights Acts do little to achieve equality for black citizens (1957, 1960)

John F. Kennedy serves as president (1961–1963)

Black employment in the upper ranks of the federal civil service increases 88 percent (1961–1963)

Lyndon B. Johnson serves as president following JFK's assassination (1963–1969)

Lyndon Johnson defeats Barry Goldwater in landslide (1964)

Voting Rights Act ends literacy tests in the South (1965)

Johnson decides not to run for reelection; Democratic Convention in Chicago is accompanied by violence (1968)

Martin Luther King Jr. and Robert Kennedy are killed by assassins (1968)

United Nations is created (1945)

Communists take over governments in Eastern Europe (1946–1948)

Civil war erupts in Greece (1946–1947)

India achieves independence (1947)

Marshall Plan funnels $13 billion to Europe (1948–1951)

Soviets blockade West Berlin; U.S. and Allies respond with Berlin airlift (1948)

State of Israel is declared; Arabs begin war to destroy it (1948)

Soviets lift blockade of Berlin and create German Democratic Republic (1949)

NATO is created (1949)

Soviets explode an atomic bomb (1949)

Communists led by Mao Tse-tung win civil war in China; Nationalists under Chiang Kai-shek flee to Formosa (1949)

Korean War (1950–1953)

U.S. helps overthrow governments of Iran (1953) and Guatemala (1954)

Communist Viet Minh defeats French at Dien Bien Phu; Geneva Accords create North Vietnam and South Vietnam (1954)

U.S. sends funds and military advisers to South Vietnam (1954)

Warsaw Pact confirms military alliance of communist Eastern European countries with the Soviet Union (1955)

Egypt nationalizes the Suez Canal Company, causing the Suez War (1956)

Soviet forces crush a liberation movement in Hungary (1956)

Soviets launch *Sputnik* (1957); U.S. launches *Explorer-I* (1958)

Fidel Castro leads a successful revolution in Cuba (1959)

Soviet Yuri Gagarin orbits the earth; American Alan Shepard reaches outer space (1961)

U.S. launches Alliance for Progress and the Peace Corps (1961)

Plot to overthrow Castro fails at Bay of Pigs in Cuba (1961)

Cuban missile crisis (1962)

U.S. presence in Vietnam escalates after Tonkin Gulf resolution (1964)

Cultural Revolution takes place in China (1966–1976)

1945

Women leave the workforce to make room for returning soldiers (1945)

College enrollment quadruples (1945–1970)

Proportion of homeowners increases by 50 percent in the United States (1945–1960)

Benjamin Spock publishes *Common Sense Book of Baby and Child Care* (1946)

Baby boom increases U.S. population by 30 percent (40 million) (1946–1960)

Number of television sets in the U.S. increases from 7,000 to 50 million (1946–1960)

Jackie Robinson becomes first black player in major-league baseball (1947)

Truman bans racial discrimination in federal hiring and orders desegregation of the armed forces (1948)

Returning servicemen use GI Bill to pay for college or job training or to buy homes (1944–1949)

Strikes by auto and steel workers lead to wage and price increases, fueling inflation and leading to a 6 percent rise in the cost of living (1945–1946)

Auto production soars from 2 million to 8 million (1946–1950s)

Greater availability of discretionary income and credit fuels purchases of homes, cars, televisions, and washing machines (1946–1950s)

Technological advances lead to agricultural surpluses (1940s–1970s)

Taft-Hartley Act curbs power of labor unions (1947)

Congress funds construction of 79,000 miles of highways (1947–1956)

1950

Rise of the suburbs (1950s)

Religious revival casts prosperity and conformity in a moral light (1950s)

Beat poets rebel against middle-class life and conformity (1950s)

Arthur Miller, Edward Albee, and Tennessee Williams write plays portraying alienation (1950s–1960s)

Brown v. Board of Education prohibits segregation in public schools, overruling "separate-but-equal" doctrine (1954)

Rosa Parks inspires Montgomery bus boycott (1955)

Martin Luther King establishes SCLC to combat racism (1957)

Arkansas prevents blacks from entering Little Rock's Central High School; Eisenhower sends federal troops to enforce desegregation (1957)

Cesar Chavez organizes the United Farm Workers (1962)

Betty Friedan's *The Feminine Mystique* is published (1963)

200,000 demonstrators take part in the March on Washington (1963)

Bracero program ends (1964)

Gap between blacks' and whites' income continues to increase (1950s)

Eisenhower approves joint U.S.-Canadian development of St. Lawrence Seaway (1954)

Amendments to Social Security Act extend benefits to professionals (1954, 1956)

Government raises minimum wage from 75¢ to $1 per hour (1955)

Eisenhower submits to Congress largest peacetime budget in history (1957)

Government makes agriculture surpluses available to poor Americans through use of food stamps (1959)

Social Security benefits increase 7 percent (1959)

1960

Area Redevelopment Act earmarks $400 million for "distressed areas" (1961)

Kennedy makes $4.9 billion available to cities for mass transit and housing (1962)

Trade Expansion Act leads to tariff cuts between U.S. and Common Market (1962)

Federal allocation of billions of dollars for education, medical care, and housing fuels economic growth (1964)

1970

Richard Nixon serves as president (1969–1974)

Twenty-sixth Amendment gives 18-year-olds the right to vote in all elections (1971)

Watergate break-in occurs (1972)

War Powers Act passes (1973)

Spiro Agnew resigns vice presidency after accepting bribes (1973)

House impeaches Nixon for his role in the Watergate affair (1974)

Nixon resigns (1974); Gerald Ford serves as president (1974–1977)

1980

Gerald Ford pardons Nixon (1974)

Jimmy Carter serves as president (1977–1981)

Moral Majority becomes a political force (1980s)

Ronald Reagan serves as president (1981–1989)

Iran-Contra scandal cripples Reagan's presidency (1986)

George H. W. Bush serves as president (1989–1993)

1990

1999

William J. Clinton serves as president (1993–2001)

Republican-dominated Congress attempts to enact Contract with America, passing 26 bills, only 4 of which become law (1995)

House impeaches Clinton as a result of Monica Lewinsky scandal; Senate votes not to convict him (1999)

George W. Bush serves as president (2001–)

Tet offensive turns U.S. public opinion against the war in Vietnam (1968)

Soviets occupy Czechoslovakia, ending Prague Spring (1968)

Neil Armstrong becomes the first man to walk on the moon (1969)

Nixon travels to China (1972)

U.S. and Soviets sign SALT and begin dé-tente (1972)

Last U.S. combat troops leave Vietnam (April 1973)

South Vietnam falls to Communists (1975)

Mao Tse-tung dies (1976)

Panama Canal treaties are ratified (1977)

Israel and Egypt sign Camp David accords (1978)

U.S. and Soviets sign SALT II (1979)

Soviets invade Afghanistan (1979)

Iranian hostage crisis unfolds (1979–1980)

Iran-Iraq War (1980–1988)

U.S. supports Contras and anti-Communist regimes in Central America (1980s)

U.S. begins development of Strategic Defense Initiative ("Star Wars") (1983)

Mikhail Gorbachev promotes glasnost and perestroika in Soviet Union (1985–1989)

U.S. and Soviets sign treaty eliminating intermediate-range missiles (1987)

Soviets pull out of Afghanistan; Berlin Wall falls; Soviet Empire collapses (1989)

Chinese government kills student protesters in Tiananmen Square (1989)

Germany is reunited (1990)

U.S. and Soviets sign agreement to reduce the number of long-range missiles (1991)

Soviet Union dissolves into 15 autonomous republics (1991)

Operation Desert Storm is put into effect in Iraq (1991)

Former Yugoslavia erupts in violent ethnic conflict among Serbs, Croats, and Bosnian Muslims (1991–1995)

Apartheid ends in South Africa (1991)

NATO intervention in Yugoslavia restores Muslim refugees to Kosovo (1999)

September 11 terrorist attacks (2001)

Civil Rights Act outlaws segregation in public facilities and discriminatory employment practices (1964)

LBJ's "war on poverty" leads to Great Society legislation (1964–1965)

Student activists protest Vietnam War (1964–1970s)

Immigration and Nationality Services Act liberalizes immigration policies (1965)

Separatist black power movement leads to founding of Black Panthers (1966)

Affirmative-action programs encourage hiring of women and members of racial minorities (1960s–1980s)

Evangelical religion experiences national revival (1970s–1980s)

In *Roe v. Wade*, Supreme Court legalizes abortions during first trimester (1973)

Percentage of Americans living below poverty level increases (1979–1983)

90 percent of nation's population growth occurs in sunbelt states (1980s)

Culture of consumerism is characterized by rampant spending and less personal savings (1980s)

Most immigrants to U.S. come from Asia and Latin America (1980s–1990s)

Computer technology revolutionizes the way people live and work (1980s–1990s)

Right-to-life movement emerges (1980s–1990s)

Militia movements spread, culminating in tragedies at Ruby Ridge, Waco, and Oklahoma City (1992–1995)

Federal courts limit affirmative-action programs (1995–1996)

Internet and e-mail spark commercial and communications revolutions (1990s)

Department of Housing and Urban Development is established (1966)

Inflation rises from 3 percent to 12 percent (1967–1974)

1970

Clean Air Act allocates funds for cleaning up air pollution (1970)

Stock-market contraction leads to "Nixon recession"; Nixon freezes wages and prices (1971)

Energy crisis in U.S. occurs because of Arab oil boycott and OPEC price increases (1973)

1980

Inflation reaches 18 percent; mortgage rates reach 15 percent; interest rates peak at 20 percent (1980)

Economic Recovery Tax Act lowers taxes and leads to mounting deficit (1981)

Unemployment reaches 10.4 percent in worst recession since the 1930s (1981–1982)

Federal deficit for 1983 is higher than all previous deficits combined (1983)

Labor union participation decreases (1980s)

Federal debt soars to $1.4 trillion (1987)

Stock market drops 22.6 percent (1987)

Savings-and-Loan crisis is resolved by a $500-billion federal bailout (1989)

1990

NAFTA links economies of Mexico, the U.S., and Canada (1992)

Major federal welfare programs are turned over to the states (1996)

Productivity and profits set records; gap between rich and poor widens (1990s)

Federal government has first surplus in 30 years (1998)

1999

Dow Jones industrial average increases from 3,500 to over 11,000 (1993–1999)

The United States emerged from World War II the preeminent military and economic power in the world. While much of Europe and Asia struggled to recover from the physical devastation of the war, the United States was virtually unscathed, its economic infrastructure intact and operating at peak efficiency. By 1955 the United States, with only 6 percent of the world's population, was producing half the world's goods. In Europe, Japan, and elsewhere, American products and popular culture attracted excited attention.

Yet the specter of a "cold war" cast a pall over the buoyant revival of the economy. The ideological contest with the Soviet Union and Communist China produced numerous foreign crises and sparked a domestic witch hunt for American Communists that far surpassed earlier episodes of political and social repression in the nation's history. Both major political parties accepted the geopolitical assumptions embedded in the ideological cold war with international communism. Both Republican and Democratic presidents affirmed the need to "contain" the spread of Communist influence around the world.

This bedrock assumption eventually embroiled the United States in a costly war in Southeast Asia, which destroyed Lyndon Johnson's presidency and revived isolationist sentiments. The Vietnam War was also the catalyst for a countercultural movement in which young idealists of the "baby-boom" generation promoted many overdue social reforms, including the civil rights and environmental movements. But the youth revolt also contributed to an array of social ills, from street riots to drug abuse to sexual promiscuity. The social upheavals of the 1960s and early 1970s provoked a conservative backlash. Richard Nixon's paranoid reaction to his critics led to the Watergate affair and the destruction of his presidency.

Through all of this turmoil, however, the basic premises of welfare-state capitalism that Franklin Roosevelt had instituted with his New Deal programs remained essentially intact. With only a few exceptions, both Republicans and Democrats after 1945 came to accept the notion that the federal government must assume greater responsibility for the welfare of individuals than had heretofore been the case. Even Ronald Reagan, a sharp critic of liberal social-welfare programs, recognized the need for the federal government to provide a "safety net" for those who could not help themselves.

This fragile consensus on public policy began to disintegrate in the late 1980s amid stunning international events and less visible domestic changes. The internal collapse of the Soviet Union and the disintegration of European communism surprised observers and sent policy makers scurrying to respond to a post–cold war world, in which the United States remained the only legitimate superpower. After forty-five years, American foreign policy was no longer centered on a single adversary, and world politics lost its bipolar quality. During the early 1990s the two Germanys reunited, apartheid in South Africa ended, and Israel and the Palestinians signed a previously unimaginable peace treaty.

At the same time, American foreign policy began to focus less on military power and more on economic competition and technological development. In those arenas, Japan and a reunited Germany challenged the United States for preeminence. By reducing the public's fear of nuclear annihilation, the end of the cold war also reduced American interest in foreign affairs. The presidential election of 1992 was the first since 1936 in which foreign-policy issues played virtually no role. This was an unfortunate development, for post–cold war world affairs remained volatile and dangerous. The implosion of Soviet communism after 1989 unleashed a series of ethnic, nationalist, and separatist conflicts throughout Eurasia. Responding to pleas for assistance, the United States found itself drawn into crises in faraway locations, such as Bosnia, Somalia, Kosovo, Afghanistan, and Iraq.

31

THE FAIR DEAL AND CONTAINMENT

FOCUS QUESTIONS

- What was the economic, social, and political aftermath of World War II?
- What were the origins and early manifestations of the cold war?
- What was Truman's Fair Deal?
- What was the extent of U.S. involvement in the Korean War?
- What were the roots of McCarthyism and the second Red Scare?

To answer these questions and access additional review material, please visit www.wwnorton.com/studyspace.

o sooner did the Second World War end than a "cold war" began. The uneasy wartime alliance between the United States and the Soviet Union had collapsed by the fall of 1945. The two strongest nations to emerge from the carnage of World War II could not bridge their ideological differences over such basic issues as human rights, individual liberties, and religious beliefs. Mutual suspicion and a race to gain influence and control over the so-called third world countries further polarized the two nations. The defeat of Japan and Germany had created power vacuums that sucked the United States and the Soviet Union into an unrelenting war of words fed by clashing geopolitical interests. At the same time the devastation wrought by the war in western Europe and the exhaustion of its peoples led to anti-colonial uprisings in Asia and Africa that threatened to strip Britain and France of their empires. The postwar world was thus an unstable one in which international tensions shaped the contours of domestic politics and culture as well as foreign relations.

Demobilization under Truman

truman's uneasy start "Who the hell is Harry Truman?" Roosevelt's chief of staff asked the president in the summer of 1944. The question was on more lips when, after less than twelve weeks as vice president, Harry Truman took the presidential oath on April 12, 1945. Clearly he was not as charismatic or as magisterial as Franklin Roosevelt, and that was one of the burdens he would bear. Roosevelt and Truman came from quite different backgrounds. For Truman there had been no inherited wealth, no early contact with the great and near great, no European travel, no Harvard— indeed, no college at all. Born in 1884 in western Missouri, Truman grew up in Independence, outside Kansas City. Too nearsighted to join in the activities of other boys, Truman became bookish and introverted. After high school, however, he spent a few years working in Kansas City banks and grew into an outgoing young man.

During World War I, Truman served in France as captain of an artillery battery. Afterward he opened a clothing business, but it failed during the recession of 1922, and Truman then entered politics. In 1934 Missouri sent him to the U.S. Senate, where he remained fairly obscure until he chaired a committee investigating corruption in defense industries during World War II.

Something about Harry Truman evoked the spirit of Andrew Jackson: his decisiveness, his feistiness, his family loyalty. But that was a side of the man the people came to know only as he settled into the presidency. On his first full day as president, as the war in Asia ground on, he remained awestruck. "Boys, if you ever pray, pray for me now," he told a group of reporters. "I don't know whether you fellows ever had a load of hay fall on you, but when they told me yesterday what had happened, I felt like the moon, the stars and all the planets had fallen on me."

Truman favored much of the New Deal and was even prepared to extend its scope, but he was uneasy with many of the most ardent New Deal reformers. Within ninety days of taking office, he had replaced much of the Roosevelt cabinet with his own choices. On the whole his cabinet was more conservative in outlook and included several mediocrities. Truman suffered the further handicap of seeming to be a caretaker for the remainder of Roosevelt's term. Few expected him to run on his own in 1948.

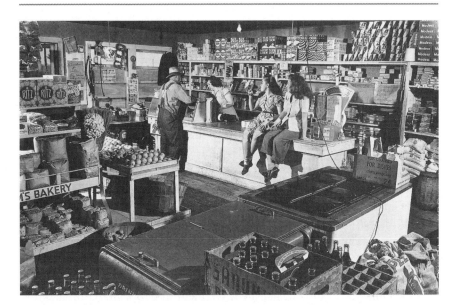

The Eldridge General Store, Fayette County, Illinois

Postwar America quickly demobilized, turning its attention to the pursuit of abundance.

The new president gave a significant clue to his domestic policies on September 6, 1945, when he sent Congress a comprehensive peacetime program that in effect proposed to enlarge the New Deal. Its twenty-one points included expansion of unemployment insurance, a higher minimum wage, a permanent Fair Employment Practices Committee, slum clearance and low-rent housing, regional development of the nation's river valleys, and a public-works program. "Not even President Roosevelt asked for so much at one sitting," charged the House Republican leader. "It's just a plain case of out-dealing the New Deal." But Truman did not have the same success as Roosevelt in getting his legislation through Congress. Beset by other problems, Truman soon saw his new domestic proposals mired in disputes over the transition to a peacetime economy.

CONVERTING TO PEACE The raucous celebrations that greeted Japan's surrender signaled the habitual American response to military victory: a rapid demobilization of the armed forces and a return to more carefree pursuits. The public demanded that the president and Congress bring the troops home as soon as possible. By 1947 the total armed forces had shrunk to 1.5 million from a wartime high of 12 million. By early 1950 the army had been reduced to 600,000 troops.

The military veterans returned to colleges, jobs, wives, and babies. Population growth, which had dropped off sharply in the Depression decade, now soared. Americans born during this postwar period composed what came to be known as the baby-boom generation, an oversize population cohort that would become a dominant force shaping the nation's social and economic life.

The end of the war, with its sudden demobilization and conversion to a peacetime economy, generated labor unrest and strikes but not the postwar depression that many had feared. Several shock absorbers cushioned the economic impact of demobilization: unemployment insurance and other Social Security benefits; the Servicemen's Readjustment Act of 1944, known as the GI Bill of Rights, under which $13 billion was spent for military veterans on education, vocational training, medical treatment, unemployment insurance, and loans for building houses and going into business; and most important, the pent-up demand for consumer goods that was fueled by wartime shortages. Instead of sinking into depression after the war, the economy enjoyed a spurt of private investment in new production facilities and equipment.

CONTROLLING INFLATION The most acute economic problem facing postwar America was not depression but inflation. Released from wartime restraints, businesses demanded higher prices, and workers demanded higher wages, thereby conspiring to frustrate Truman's efforts to maintain stabilization of the economy. The president endorsed "reasonable" wage increases, which he thought businesses could absorb without raising prices, and he considered necessary to sustain consumer purchasing power. Management, however, did not agree. Within six weeks of the war's end, corporations had refused union demands for higher wages and better benefits, and a series of strikes followed in the automotive, steel, mining, petroleum, and railroad industries.

President Truman, miffed at what he considered to be excessive union demands, including a 30 percent wage boost, used powers granted the chief executive during wartime to seize the coal mines and threaten to draft striking railroad workers into the armed forces. A strike in the steel industry finally provided a formula for settling most of the disputes. Truman suggested a pay raise of 18.5¢ per hour, which the Steel Workers accepted but management refused. To break the logjam, the administration in 1946 agreed to let the steel companies increase their prices. That sequence of events became the pattern for settlements in other industries and set a dangerous precedent of price-wage spirals that would plague consumers in the postwar world.

The wartime Office of Price Administration maintained some restraint on price increases while gradually ending the rationing of most goods, and Truman asked for a one-year renewal of its powers. During the winter and spring of 1946, however, business lobbyists campaigned against price controls. Congress extended controls in July, but by then the cost of living had risen by 6 percent. After the 1946 congressional elections, Truman gave up the battle, ending all price controls except those on rent, sugar, and rice.

PARTISAN CONFLICT   Before the 1946 congressional elections, public discontent ran high, with most of it directed against the administration. Labor union supporters tagged Truman "the No. 1 strikebreaker," while much of the public, angry at striking unions, blamed the White House for the strikes. Critics of the administration had a field day coining campaign slogans. The most effective was the simple "Had enough?" attributed to a Boston ad agency: the message was that the Democrats had simply been in power too long. In the end, Republicans won majorities in both houses of Congress for the first time since 1928.

The rising public criticism of organized labor spurred the new Republican Congress to pass the Taft-Hartley Labor Act of 1947 to curb the power of the unions. It banned the closed shop (in which nonunion workers could not be hired) but permitted a union shop (in which workers newly hired were required to join the union) except where banned by state law. The antiunion legislation included provisions forbidding "unfair" union practices such as "featherbedding" (paying for work not done), refusing to bargain in good faith, and contributing to political campaigns. Unions' political action committees were allowed to function only on a voluntary basis, and union leaders had to take oaths declaring that they were not members of the Communist party. Employers were permitted to sue unions for breaking contracts and to speak freely during union campaigns. The act forbade strikes by federal employees and imposed a "cooling-off" period of eighty days on any strike that the president found to be dangerous to the national health or safety.

Truman's veto of the Taft-Hartley bill, which unions called the slave-labor act, restored his credit with labor and brought many unionists who had voted Republican in 1946 back to the Democratic fold. But the bill passed over the president's veto. Its most severe impact was probably on the CIO's Operation Dixie, a drive to win unions a more secure foothold in the South. By 1954 fifteen states, mainly in the South, had used the Taft-Hartley Act's authority to pass "right-to-work" laws forbidding the union shop. Those laws also eroded union strength in the North as many firms began to migrate to right-to-work southern states.

Yet the conflicts between Truman and Congress obscured the high degree of bipartisan cooperation marking matters of government reorganization and foreign policy. In 1947 a bipartisan majority in Congress passed the National Security Act, which created a National Military Establishment, headed by the secretary of defense with subcabinet departments of army, navy, and air force, and the National Security Council (NSC), which included the president, heads of the defense departments, and the secretary of state, among others. The act made permanent the Joint Chiefs of Staff, a wartime innovation, and established the Central Intelligence Agency (CIA) to coordinate global intelligence gathering.

THE COLD WAR

BUILDING THE UN   The hope that the wartime military alliance between the Soviet Union and the United States would carry over into the postwar world proved but another great illusion. The pragmatic Roosevelt had shared no such illusion. He expected that the great powers in the postwar world would have separate geographic spheres of influence but felt he had to temper such realpolitik with an organization "which would satisfy widespread demand in the United States for new idealistic or universalist arrangements for assuring the peace."

On April 25, 1945, two weeks after Roosevelt's death and two weeks before the German surrender, delegates from fifty nations at war with the Axis met in San Francisco to draw up the Charter of the United Nations. Additional members would be admitted by a two-thirds vote of the General Assembly. This body, one of the two major agencies set up by the charter, included delegates from all member nations and was to meet annually in regular session to approve the budget, receive annual reports from UN agencies, and choose members of the Security Council and other bodies.

The Security Council, the other major charter agency, would remain in permanent session and would have "primary responsibility for the maintenance of international peace and security." Its eleven members (fifteen after 1965) included six (later ten) members elected for two-year terms and five permanent members: the United States, the Soviet Union, Britain, France, and China. Each permanent member could veto any question of substance. The Security Council might investigate any dispute, recommend settlement or reference to another UN body—the International Court of Justice at The

Hague, in the Netherlands—and take measures, including the use of military force. The U.S. Senate, in sharp contrast to the reception it gave the League of Nations, ratified the UN charter by a vote of eighty-nine to two.

DIFFERENCES WITH THE SOVIETS   There were signs of trouble in the wartime alliance linking Britain, the Soviet Union, and the United States as early as the spring of 1945, as the Soviet Union set up compliant governments in the nations of Eastern Europe, violating the Yalta promises of democratic elections. Protests against such actions led to Soviet counter-protests that the British and the Americans were negotiating a German surrender in Italy "behind the back of the Soviet Union."

Such was the atmosphere when Truman entered the White House. A few days before the San Francisco conference to organize the United Nations, the president gave Soviet foreign minister Vyacheslav Molotov a tongue lashing in Washington on the Polish situation. "I have never been talked to like that in my life," Molotov protested. "Carry out your agreements," Truman snapped, "and you won't get talked to like that."

On May 12, 1945, four days after victory in Europe, Winston Churchill sent Truman a telegram: "What is to happen about Europe? An iron curtain is drawn down upon [the Russian] front. We do not know what is going on behind [it]. . . . Surely it is vital now to come to an understanding with Russia, or see where we are with her, before we weaken our armies mortally." Nevertheless, as a gesture of goodwill, and over Churchill's protest, the U.S. forces withdrew from the occupation zone in Germany that had been assigned to the Soviet Union at Yalta. Americans still hoped that the Yalta agreements would be carried out, and they were even more eager to have Soviet help in defeating Japan.

Although the Soviets admitted British and American observers to their sectors of Eastern Europe, there was little the Western powers could have done to prevent Soviet control of the region even if they had kept up their military strength. The presence of Soviet armed forces frustrated the efforts of non-Communists to gain political influence in Eastern European countries. Opposition leaders were exiled, silenced, executed, or imprisoned.

Secretary of State James F. Byrnes, who took office in 1945, struggled through 1946 with the problems of postwar treaties. In early 1947 the Council of Foreign Ministers finally produced treaties for Italy, Hungary, Romania, Bulgaria, and Finland that confirmed Soviet control over Eastern Europe, which in Russian eyes seemed but a parallel to American control over Japan and Western control over most of Germany and all of Italy. The Yalta Conference's guarantees of democracy in Eastern Europe had turned out much like the Open Door policy in China, little more than pious rhetoric sugarcoating the realities of power and national interest.

CONTAINMENT   By the beginning of 1947, relations with the Soviet Union had become even more troubled. The year before, Stalin had pronounced international peace impossible "under the present capitalistic development of the world economy." His statement impelled George F. Kennan, counselor of the U.S. embassy in Moscow, to send an 8,000-word dispatch to the State Department, in which he sketched the roots of Soviet policy.

More than a year later Kennan, back at the State Department in Washington, spelled out his ideas for a proper response to the Soviets. In a 1947 article published anonymously in *Foreign Affairs,* he provided a brilliant historical and psychological analysis of Soviet insecurity and postwar intentions. He predicted that the Soviets would try to fill "every nook and cranny available . . . in the basin of world power." Therefore, he insisted, the United States must pursue "a long-term, patient but firm and vigilant *containment* of Russian expansive tendencies."

Kennan's "containment" concept dovetailed with the outlook of Truman and his advisers. They all harbored a growing fear that Soviet aims reached beyond Eastern Europe, posing dangers in the eastern Mediterranean, the Middle East, and western Europe itself. The Soviet Union especially sought access to the Mediterranean region, long important to Russia for purposes of trade and defense. After the war the Soviet Union pressed Turkey for territorial concessions and the right to build naval bases on the Bosporus, an important gateway between the Black Sea and the Mediterranean. In 1946 civil war broke out in neighboring Greece between a British-backed government and a Communist-led faction that held the northern part of the country. In 1947 the British ambassador informed the U.S. government that the British could no longer bear the economic and military burden of aiding Greece and suggested that the United States assume the responsibility.

THE TRUMAN DOCTRINE AND THE MARSHALL PLAN   On March 12, 1947, Truman asked Congress for $400 million in economic and military aid to Greece and Turkey. In his speech to Congress, the president announced what quickly became known as the Truman Doctrine. Although intended as a response to a specific crisis, its rhetoric was universal. "I believe," Truman declared, "that it must be the policy of the United States to support free peoples who are resisting attempted subjugation by armed minorities or by outside pressures." In 1947 Congress passed the Greek-Turkish aid bill and by 1950 had spent $659 million on the program. Turkey achieved economic stability, and Greece defeated the Communist insurrection in 1949.

Such immediate gains created long-term problems, however. The Truman Doctrine marked the beginning of a contest that people began to call a "cold war." Greece and Turkey were but the front lines in an ideological struggle between East and West for world power and influence. That struggle quickly focused on western Europe, where wartime damage had devastated factory production and a severe drought in 1947, followed by a harsh winter, had destroyed crops. Coal shortages in London left only enough fuel to heat and light homes for a few hours each day. In Berlin, people were freezing or starving to death. The transportation system in Europe was in shambles: bridges were out, canals clogged, and rail networks destroyed. Amid the chaos the Communist parties of France and Italy were flourishing.

In the spring of 1947, former general George C. Marshall, who had replaced James Byrnes as secretary of state, called for a program of massive aid to rescue western Europe from disaster and possible Communist subversion. "Our policy," he pledged, "is directed not against country or doctrine, but against hunger, poverty, desperation, and chaos." Marshall offered aid to all European countries, including the Soviet Union, but Moscow refused to participate in the "imperialist" scheme.

In late 1947 Truman submitted his proposal for the European Recovery Program to Congress. Soon thereafter a Communist coup d'état in Czechoslovakia ended the last remaining coalition government in Eastern Europe. The Communist seizure of power in Prague assured congressional passage of the Marshall Plan, which from 1948 until 1951 provided $13 billion to promote European economic recovery.

DIVIDING GERMANY   The Marshall Plan drew the nations of western Europe closer together, but the breakdown of the wartime alliance with the Soviet Union left the problem of postwar Germany unsettled. The German economy had stagnated, requiring the U.S. Army to carry a staggering burden of relief to prevent civilians from starving. Slowly occupation zones evolved into functioning governments. In 1948 the British, French, and Americans merged their zones, and the "West Germans" elected delegates to a federal constitutional convention.

Soviet resentment of the Marshall Plan and the political unification of West Germany led the Soviets, in April 1948, to restrict road and rail traffic into West Berlin; on June 23 they stopped all traffic. The next day, the Soviets cut off electricity to the western sector of the divided city. The Soviets hoped the blockade would force the Allies to give up either Berlin or the plan to unify Germany. It was war by starvation and intimidation, but Truman stood firm. After considering the use of armed convoys to supply West Berlin, he opted for a massive airlift. At the time it seemed like an impossible task. But

THE OCCUPATION OF GERMANY AND AUSTRIA
- French zone
- British zone
- U.S. zone
- Soviet zone

How did the Allies divide Germany and Austria at the Yalta Conference (see page 854)? What was the "iron curtain"? Why did Truman airlift supplies to Berlin?

the Allied air forces quickly brought in planes from around the world, and soon they were flying in up to 13,000 tons of food, coal, and other supplies a day.

The massive airlift went on for months. Finally, on May 12, 1949, after extended talks, the Soviets lifted the blockade. Before the end of the year, the Federal Republic of Germany had a functioning government. At the end of May 1949, an independent German "Democratic" Republic arose in the Soviet-dominated eastern zone, dividing Germany into two independent states.

BUILDING NATO   As relations between the Soviets and western Europe chilled, transatlantic unity ripened into a formal military alliance. On April 4, 1949, diplomats signed the North Atlantic Treaty. Twelve nations were represented: the United States, Britain, France, Belgium, the Netherlands, Luxembourg, Canada, Denmark, Iceland, Italy, Norway, and Portugal. Greece and Turkey joined the alliance in 1952, West Germany in 1955,

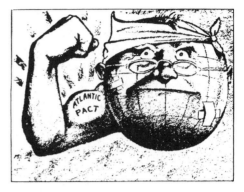

NATO

NATO is depicted as a symbol of renewed strength for a battered Europe.

and Spain in 1982. The treaty pledged that an attack against any one of the members would be considered an attack against all. A council of the North Atlantic Treaty Organization (NATO) would govern the alliance. In 1950 the council voted to create an integrated defense force for western Europe. Five years later the Warsaw Treaty Organization appeared as the Eastern European counterpoint to NATO.

The eventful year of 1948 produced another foreign-policy decision with long-term consequences. Late in 1947 the UN General Assembly voted to partition Palestine into Jewish and Arab states. Despite fierce Arab opposition, Jewish leaders proclaimed the independence of the new State of Israel on May 14, 1948. President Truman, who had been in close touch with Jewish leaders at home and abroad, ordered immediate recognition of the new state; the United States was the first nation to do so.

The neighboring Arab states thereupon attacked Israel, which held its own. UN mediators gradually worked out truce agreements with Israel's Arab neighbors, restoring an uneasy peace by May 11, 1949, when Israel joined the United Nations. But the mutual hatred and intermittent warfare between Israel and the Arab states have festered ever since, complicating U.S. foreign policy, which has aimed to maintain friendship with both sides while insisting on the legitimacy of the Israeli nation.

CIVIL RIGHTS DURING THE 1940S

The social tremors triggered by World War II and the onset of the cold war transformed America's racial landscape. The government-sponsored racism of the German Nazis, the Italian Fascists, and the Japanese imperialists focused attention on the need for the United States to improve its own race relations and to provide for equal rights under the law.

For most of his political career, Harry Truman had shown little concern with the plight of African Americans. He had grown up in western Missouri assuming that blacks and whites preferred to be segregated from one another. As president, however, he began to reassess his convictions. In the fall of 1946, Truman hosted a delegation of civil rights activists who urged the president to condemn the resurgence of the Ku Klux Klan and the lynching of African Americans. Truman soon appointed a Committee on Civil Rights to investigate racist violence and recommend preventive measures. In its report the committee urged the renewal of the Fair Employment Practices Committee and the creation of a permanent civil rights commission to investigate abuses. It also argued that federal aid be denied to any state that mandated segregated schools and public facilities.

On July 26, 1948, Truman banned racial discrimination in the hiring of federal employees. Four days later he issued an executive order ending racial segregation in the armed forces. The air force and navy quickly complied, but the army dragged its feet until the early 1950s. By 1960 the armed forces were the most racially integrated of all organizations.

Jackie Robinson, 1949

Racial discrimination remained widespread throughout the postwar period. In 1947 Jackie Robinson of the Brooklyn Dodgers became the first black to play major-league baseball.

JACKIE ROBINSON Meanwhile, racial segregation was being confronted in a much more public field of endeavor: professional baseball. In April 1947, as the baseball season opened, the National League's Brooklyn Dodgers included the first black player to cross the color line in major-league baseball: Jackie Robinson. Born in Georgia and raised in California, Robinson was an army veteran and baseball player in the Negro leagues. Branch Rickey, president of the Dodgers, selected Robinson to integrate professional baseball not only for his athletic potential but because of his willingness to control his temper in the face of virulent racism. Teammates and opposing players viciously baited Robinson, pitchers threw at him, base runners spiked him, and spectators booed and taunted him in every city. Hotels refused him rooms, and restaurants denied him service. Hate mail arrived by the bucket load. On the other hand, black spectators were electrified by Robinson's courageous example; they turned out in droves to see him play.

As time passed, Robinson won over many racist fans and opposing players through his quiet courage, self-deprecating wit, and determined performance. Soon other teams signed black players. Baseball's pathbreaking efforts also stimulated the integration of football and basketball teams. Jackie Robinson vividly demonstrated that racism, not inferiority, impeded African-American advancement in the postwar era and that segregation need not be a permanent condition of American life.

SHAPING THE FAIR DEAL   As the 1948 election approached, the issue of civil rights presented daunting political challenges. While some Americans applauded Truman's efforts to desegregate the federal workforce, others were appalled. Liberals thought that his efforts were not bold enough. Southern conservative Democrats found him too radical. Truman's chances for winning the election of 1948 seemed bleak.

The president had a game plan for 1948, however. His advisers knew that to win another presidential term he needed the midwestern and western farm belts. In metropolitan areas he needed to carry the union and African-American vote, which Truman wooed by working closely with unions and pressing the cause of civil rights. Truman's advisers counted on the Solid South to stay in the Democratic column. With the South and the West, Truman could afford to lose some New Deal strongholds in the East and still win. This strategy erred chiefly in underrating the rebellion that would take four Deep South states out of Truman's camp because of his support for civil rights.

Truman used his State of the Union message to set the agenda for an election year. The 1948 speech offered something to nearly every group the Democrats hoped to win over. The first goal, Truman remarked, was "to secure fully the essential human rights of our citizens," and he promised a special message later on civil rights. "To protect human resources," he proposed federal aid to education, increased and extended unemployment and retirement benefits, a comprehensive system of health insurance, more federal support for public housing, and extension of rent controls. As one senator put it, the speech "raised all the ghosts of the old New Deal."

THE ELECTION OF 1948   The Republican majority in Congress for the most part spurned the Truman program, an action it would later regret. Scenting victory in November, Republican delegates again nominated Thomas Dewey, the former New York governor. The platform endorsed most of the New Deal reforms as an accomplished fact and approved the administration's bipartisan foreign policy; Dewey promised to run things more efficiently, however.

In July a glum Democratic Convention gathered in Philadelphia expecting to do little more than go through the motions but found itself surprised by a fierce debate over civil rights. To keep from stirring southern hostility, the administration sought a platform plank that opposed racial discrimination only in general terms. Activists, however, sponsored a plank that called on Congress to take action. Minneapolis mayor Hubert H. Humphrey electrified the delegates and set off a ten-minute demonstration when he declared, "The time has arrived for the Democratic party to get out of the shadow of states' rights and walk forthrightly into the bright sunshine of human rights." Segregationist delegates from Alabama and Mississippi instead walked out of the convention.

A group of rebellious southern Democrats, miffed by Truman's progressive civil rights plank, met later in Birmingham, Alabama, and nominated South Carolina governor Strom Thurmond on a States' Rights ticket, which was quickly dubbed the Dixiecrat party. The Dixiecrats sought to draw enough electoral votes to preclude a majority for either major party, throwing the election into the House of Representatives, where they might strike a sectional bargain. A few days later the left wing of the Democratic party gathered in Philadelphia to name Henry A. Wallace on a Progressive party ticket. These splits in the Democratic ranks seemed to spell the final blow to Truman.

"I Stand Pat!"

Truman's support of civil rights for African Americans had its political costs, as this 1948 cartoon suggests.

"Dewey Defeats Truman"

Truman's victory in 1948 was a huge upset, so much so that even the early edition of the *Chicago Daily Tribune* was caught off guard, running this premature headline.

But Truman, undaunted, set out on a 31,000-mile "whistle-stop" train tour, during which he castigated the "do-nothing" Eightieth Congress, provoking cries from his audiences to "Pour it on, Harry!" and "Give 'em hell, Harry." Truman responded, "I don't give 'em hell. I just tell the truth and they think it's hell." Dewey, in contrast, ran a restrained campaign designed to avoid controversy. By so doing, he may have snatched defeat from the jaws of victory.

The polls and the pundits predicted a sure win for Dewey, but on election day Truman chalked up the biggest upset in history, taking 24.2 million votes (49.5 percent) to Dewey's 22 million (45.1 percent) and winning by a thumping margin of 303 to 189 in the Electoral College. Thurmond and Wallace each got more than 1 million votes, but the revolt of right and left had worked to Truman's advantage. The Dixiecrat rebellion backfired by angering black voters, while the Progressive party's radicalism made it hard to tag Truman soft on communism. Thurmond carried four Deep South states, and his success hastened a momentous disruption of the Democratic Solid South. But Truman's victory carried Democratic majorities into Congress.

Truman viewed his upset victory as a vindication for the New Deal and a mandate for moderate liberalism. His 1949 State of the Union message repeated the agenda he had set forth the year before. "Every segment of our

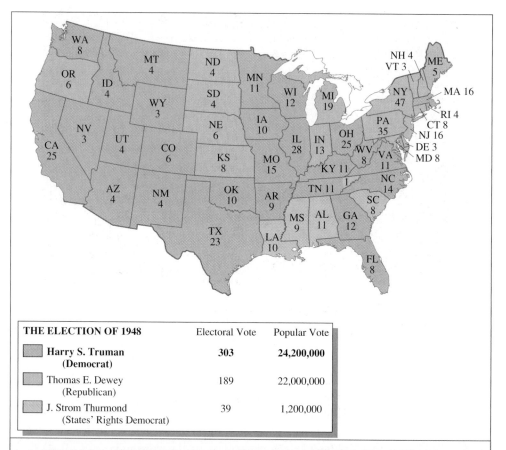

THE ELECTION OF 1948	Electoral Vote	Popular Vote
Harry S. Truman (Democrat)	303	24,200,000
Thomas E. Dewey (Republican)	189	22,000,000
J. Strom Thurmond (States' Rights Democrat)	39	1,200,000

Why did the political pundits predict a Dewey victory? Why was civil rights a divisive issue at the Democratic Convention? How did the candidacies of Thurmond and Wallace help Truman?

population and every individual," he stressed, "has a right to expect from his government a fair deal." Whether deliberately or not, he had invented a tag, the Fair Deal, to distinguish his program from the New Deal.

Some of Truman's Fair Deal proposals became law, but most of them were extensions or enlargements of New Deal programs already in place: a higher minimum wage, expanded Social Security coverage, extension of rent controls, increased farm subsidies, and a sizable slum-clearance and public-housing program. Despite Democratic majorities in Congress, however, the conservative coalition of Southern Democrats and Republicans disdained any drastic departures in domestic policy. Congress balked at civil rights bills, national health insurance, federal aid to education, and a plan to provide subsidies that would support farm income rather than farm prices. Congress also turned down Truman's demand for repeal of the Taft-Hartley Act.

THE COLD WAR HEATS UP

Global concerns, never far from center stage in the postwar world, plagued Truman's second term, as they had his first. Americans began to fear that Communists were infiltrating their society. In his inaugural address, Truman called for an anti-Communist foreign policy resting on four pillars: the United Nations, the Marshall Plan, NATO, and a "bold new plan" for technical assistance to underdeveloped parts of the world, a global Marshall Plan that came to be known as Point Four. This program to aid the postwar world never accomplished its goals, in part because other international problems soon diverted Truman's attention.

"LOSING" CHINA   One of the most intractable problems, the China tangle, was fast unraveling in 1949. The Chinese Nationalists, led by Chiang Kai-shek, had been fighting Mao Tse-tung (Mao Zedong)* and the Communists since the 1920s. The outbreak of war with Japan in 1937 halted the civil war, and both Roosevelt and Stalin believed that the Nationalists would control China after the war.

The commanders of U.S. forces in China during World War II, however, concluded that Chiang's government had become hopelessly corrupt, tyrannical, and inefficient. U.S. policy during and immediately after the war promoted peace between the factions in China. But when the civil war resumed in 1945, American forces ferried Nationalist armies back into the eastern and northern provinces as the Japanese withdrew.

It soon became a losing fight for the Nationalists as the Communists won over the land-hungry peasantry. By late 1949 the Nationalist government had fled to the island of Formosa, which it renamed Taiwan. Truman's critics asked bitterly: "Who lost China?" and a State Department report blamed Chiang for his failure to hold on to the support of the Chinese people. In fact it is hard to imagine how the U.S. government could have prevented a

---

*The traditional (Wade-Giles) transliterations of Chinese with pinyin in parentheses are used in this text up to 1976. After Mao's death the Chinese government adopted the pinyin translations that are widely used today: Mao Tse-tung became Mao Zedong; Peking became Beijing.

"It's the Same Thing."

The Marshall Plan, which distributed aid throughout Europe, is represented in this 1949 cartoon as a modern tractor driven by a prosperous farmer. In the foreground a poor, overworked man is yoked to an old-fashioned "Soviet" plow, forced to go over the ground of the "Marshal Stalin Plan," while Stalin himself tries to persuade others that "it's the same thing without mechanical problems."

Communist victory short of undertaking a massive military intervention, which would have been risky, costly, and unpopular. After 1949, the United States continued to recognize the Nationalist government on Taiwan as the rightful government of China, delaying formal relations with Communist China for thirty years. In an effort to shore up friendly governments in Asia, the United States in 1950 recognized the French-supported government of Emperor Bao Dai in Vietnam and shortly afterward extended aid to the French in their battle against Ho Chi Minh's Vietnamese guerrillas.

As the Communists were securing control in China, U.S. intelligence discovered that the Soviets had set off an atomic explosion. News of the Soviet bomb in 1949 provoked an intense reappraisal of the strategic balance of power in the world, causing Truman in 1950 to order the construction of a hydrogen bomb, a weapon far more powerful than the atomic bomb, lest the Soviets make one first. In addition, the National Security Council recommended rebuilding conventional military forces to provide options other than nuclear war. Such a plan represented a major departure from America's time-honored aversion to keeping large standing armies in peacetime. It was also an expensive proposition. But the American public was growing more receptive to the nation's role as world leader, and an invasion of South Korea by Communist forces from the north clinched the issue for most Americans.

WAR IN KOREA The Japanese had occupied Korea since 1910, and after their defeat and withdrawal in 1945 the victorious Allies faced the difficult task of creating a new Korean nation. Complicating that task was the fact that Soviet troops had advanced into northern Korea and accepted the surrender of Japanese forces above the 38th parallel, while U.S. forces had done the same south of that line. The Soviets quickly organized a Korean government along Stalinist lines, while the Americans set up a Western-style regime in the south.

Like the postwar division of Germany, the victors' decision to divide Korea at the 38th parallel began as a temporary expedient and ended as a permanent fact. With the onset of the cold war, it became clear that Soviet-American agreement on unification was no more likely in Korea than in Germany. By the end of 1948, separate Korean regimes had appeared in the two sectors, and occupation forces had withdrawn. The weakened state of the demobilizing American military contributed to the impression that South Korea was vulnerable to a Communist assault. A growing body of evidence in Soviet archives reveals that Stalin encouraged the North Koreans to use force to unify their country and oust the Americans from the peninsula. The Soviets helped design a war plan that called for North Korean forces to seize Seoul within three days and all of South Korea within a week. Stalin apparently assumed the United States would not intervene.

Over 80,000 North Korean soldiers crossed the boundary on June 25, 1950, and swept down the peninsula. President Truman responded decisively. He and his advisers assumed that the North Korean attack was directed by Moscow and was a brazen indication of the aggressive designs of Soviet communism. Truman made two critical decisions. First, he decided to wage war under the auspices of the United Nations rather than unilaterally. Second, he decided to send troops without asking Congress for a formal declaration of war.

An emergency meeting of the UN Security Council quickly censured the North Korean "breach of peace." The Soviet delegate, who held veto power, was at the time boycotting the council because it would not seat Communist China in place of Nationalist China. On June 27, its first resolution having been ignored, the Security Council called on UN members to "furnish such assistance to the Republic of Korea as may be necessary to repel the armed attack and to restore international peace and security in the area."

Truman ordered American air, naval, and ground forces into action. Eventually U.S. units numbered over 350,000, while the South Koreans contributed 500,000. In all, some fourteen other nations sent another 50,000 men. Later the UN authorized a unified command and put General Douglas MacArthur in charge. The defense of South Korea remained chiefly an American affair and one that set a precedent of profound consequence: war by order of a president rather than by vote of Congress. Yet it had the sanction of the UN Security Council and could technically be considered a "police action," not a war. Other presidents had ordered U.S. troops into action without a declaration of war, but never on such a scale.

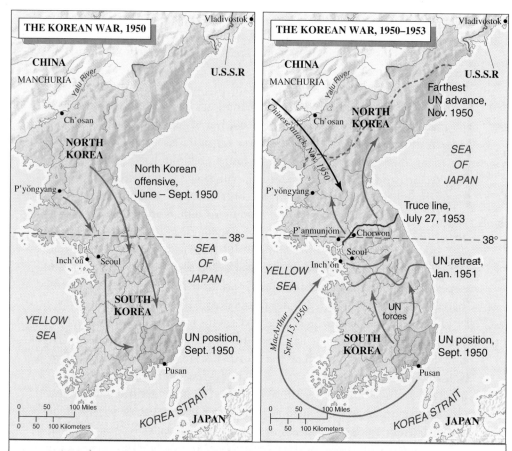

THE KOREAN WAR, 1950

CHINA
MANCHURIA
Yalu River
Vladivostok
U.S.S.R
Ch'osan
NORTH KOREA
P'yŏngyang
North Korean offensive, June – Sept. 1950
38°
Inch'ŏn · Seoul
SEA OF JAPAN
SOUTH KOREA
YELLOW SEA
UN position, Sept. 1950
Pusan
0   50   100 Miles
0   50   100 Kilometers
KOREA STRAIT   JAPAN

THE KOREAN WAR, 1950–1953

CHINA
MANCHURIA
Yalu River
Vladivostok
U.S.S.R
Chinese attacks, Nov. 1950
Ch'osan
NORTH KOREA
Farthest UN advance, Nov. 1950
SEA OF JAPAN
P'yŏngyang
Truce line, July 27, 1953
P'anmunjŏm   Chorwon
38°
Seoul
Inch'ŏn
YELLOW SEA
UN retreat, Jan. 1951
MacArthur Sept. 15, 1950
UN forces
SOUTH KOREA
UN position, Sept. 1950
Pusan
0   50   100 Miles
0   50   100 Kilometers
KOREA STRAIT   JAPAN

How did the surrender of the Japanese in Korea set up the conflict between Soviet-influenced North Korea and U.S.-influenced South Korea? What was MacArthur's strategy for retaking Korea? Why did Truman remove MacArthur from command?

Truman's conviction that the invasion of South Korea was orchestrated by Stalin led to two other decisions that had far-reaching consequences. First, Truman decided that the Korean conflict was actually a diversion for a Soviet invasion of western Europe, so he began a major expansion of American forces in NATO. Second, while dispatching U.S. military units to Korea and Europe, Truman increased assistance to the French troops in Indochina, creating the Military Assistance Advisory Group for Indochina—the start of America's deepening military involvement in Vietnam.

For three months the fighting went badly for the South Korean and UN forces. By September they were barely hanging on to the Pusan perimeter in the southeast corner of Korea. Then, in a brilliant maneuver on September 15, 1950, General MacArthur landed a new force to the North Korean rear at Inch'ŏn. Synchronized with a breakout from Pusan, the sudden blow stampeded the enemy back across the border.

At that point, MacArthur persuaded Truman to allow him to push north and seek to reunify Korea. The Soviet delegate was now back in the Security Council, wielding his veto, so on October 7 the United States got approval for this course from the UN General Assembly, where the veto did not apply. U.S. forces had crossed the North Korean boundary by October 1 and continued northward. President Truman, concerned about broad hints of Communist Chinese intervention, flew 7,000 miles to Wake Island for a conference with General MacArthur on October 15. There the general discounted chances that the Chinese Red Army would act, but if it did, he confidently predicted, "there would be the greatest slaughter."

That same day, Peking announced that Communist China "cannot stand idly by." On October 26 UN units reached the Yalu River, Korea's border with China. MacArthur predicted total victory by Christmas, but on the night of November 25, several hundred thousand Chinese "volunteers" counterattacked. Massive "human-wave" attacks, with the support of tanks and planes, turned the tables on the UN forces, sending them into a desperate retreat just at the onset of winter. It had become "an entirely new war," MacArthur concluded. Soon he was reporting that the war was dragging on because the administration refused to let him blockade the Chinese mainland.

Truman opposed leading the United States into the "gigantic booby trap" of a ground war with China, and the UN forces soon rallied. By January 1951 over 900,000 UN troops under General Matthew Ridgway finally secured their lines below Seoul and then launched a counterattack that in some places carried them back across the 38th parallel in March. When Truman seized the chance and offered negotiations to restore the boundary and end the war, General MacArthur undermined the move by issuing an ultimatum for China to make peace or suffer an attack. Truman decided then that he had no choice but to accept MacArthur's aggressive policy or fire him. Civilian control of the military was at stake, Truman later asserted. On April 11, 1951, the president removed MacArthur, whom he called Mr. Prima Donna, from all his commands and replaced him with Ridgway.

Truman's action set off an uproar across the country, and a tumultuous reception greeted MacArthur upon his first return home since 1937. MacArthur's dramatic speech to a joint session of Congress provided the climactic event. A Senate investigation showcased the administration's arguments, best summarized by General Omar Bradley, chairman of the Joint Chiefs of Staff. The MacArthur strategy, he said, "would involve us in the

September 1950

Soldiers engaged in the recapture of Seoul from the North Koreans.

wrong war at the wrong place at the wrong time and with the wrong enemy." Most Americans found Bradley's logic persuasive.

On June 24, 1951, the Soviet representative at the United Nations proposed a cease-fire in Korea along the 38th parallel, which Secretary of State Dean Acheson accepted in principle a few days later. China and North Korea responded favorably—at the time, General Ridgway's "meat-grinder" offensive was inflicting severe losses. Truce talks started in July, only to drag on for two years while the fighting continued. The chief snags were exchanges of prisoners and the South Korean president's insistence on unification.

By the time a truce was finally reached, on July 27, 1953, Truman had relinquished the White House to Dwight D. Eisenhower. The truce line followed the front at that time, mostly a little north of the 38th parallel, with a demilitarized zone separating the forces; repatriation of prisoners would be voluntary, supervised by a neutral commission. No final peace conference ever took place, and Korea, like Germany, remained divided. The war had cost the United States more than 33,000 deaths and 103,000 wounded or missing. South Korean casualties, all told, were about 1 million, and North Korean and Chinese casualties totaled an estimated 1.5 million.

ANOTHER RED SCARE   The costs of the Korean War included the far-reaching consequences of a second Red Scare, which had grown since 1945 as the domestic counterpart to the cold war abroad and reached a climax during the Korean conflict. Since 1938 the House Un-American Activities Committee (HUAC) had kept up a barrage of accusations about supposed subversives in the federal government.

In 1947 the HUAC subpoenaed nineteen prominent Hollywood writers, producers, and actors, intending to prove that Communist party members dominated the Screen Writers Guild, that they injected subversive propaganda into motion pictures, and that President Roosevelt had brought improper pressure to bear upon the industry to produce pro-Soviet films during the war. Ten of the witnesses, the so-called Hollywood Ten, jointly decided to use the First Amendment as a defense, and each of them refused to answer the question "Are you now or have you ever been a member of the Communist party?" All ten had been members of the party, but they would not answer the question as a matter of principle, claiming that party identification was their business, especially since membership in the Communist party at that time was not illegal in the United States. They were all judged to be in contempt and were sentenced to up to a year in prison. But greater punishment awaited them. The movie industry blacklisted the Hollywood Ten, denying them further work.

In the charged atmosphere of the postwar years, Truman decided that he, too, must become more vigilant in rooting out Communists from the government. On March 21, 1947, therefore, just nine days after he announced the Truman Doctrine, the president signed an executive order setting up procedures for an employee loyalty program in the federal government. Designed partly to protect the president's political flank, it failed to do so mainly because of disclosures of earlier Communist penetrations of the government that were few in number but sensational in character.

The case most embarrassing to the administration involved Alger Hiss, president of the Carnegie Endowment for International Peace, who had served in several government departments, including the State Department. Whittaker Chambers, a former Soviet agent and later an editor of *Time* magazine, told the HUAC in 1948 that Hiss had given him secret documents ten years earlier, when Chambers was spying for the Soviets. Hiss sued for libel, and Chambers produced microfilms of the State Department documents that he claimed Hiss had passed to him. Hiss denied the accusation, whereupon he was indicted and, after one mistrial, convicted in 1950. The charge was perjury, but he was convicted of lying about espionage, for which he could not be tried because the statute of limitations on that crime had expired.

President Truman, taking at face value the many testimonials to Hiss's integrity, had called the charges against him a "red herring." Secretary of State Dean Acheson compounded the damage when, meaning to express compassion, he pledged not "to turn my back on Alger Hiss." The Hiss affair had another political consequence: it raised to national prominence a young California congressman, Richard M. Nixon, who doggedly insisted on pursuing the case and then exploited an anti-Communist stance to win election to the Senate in 1950.

More cases of Communist infiltration surfaced. In 1950 the government disclosed the existence of a British-American spy network that had fed information about the development of the atomic bomb to the Soviet Union. These disclosures led to the arrest of, among others, Julius and Ethel Rosenberg.

JOSEPH MCCARTHY'S WITCH HUNT   Revelations of Soviet spying encouraged politicians in both parties to exploit the public's fears. If a man of such respectability as Hiss was guilty, many wondered, who could be trusted? Early in 1950 a little-known Republican senator from Wisconsin, Joseph R. McCarthy, surfaced as the shrewdest and most ruthless exploiter of the nation's anxieties. He took up the cause of anti-communism with a vengeance, claiming that the State Department was infested with Communists and that he possessed a list of their names. Later there was confusion as to whether he had said there were 205, 81, 57, or "a lot" of names on the list

Joseph McCarthy

Senator McCarthy (left) and his aide Roy Cohn (right) exchange comments during testimony.

and even whether the sheet of paper he brandished contained any such list. Confusion would typically surround McCarthy's charges.

McCarthy never uncovered a single Communist agent in the government. But with the United States at war with Korean Communists in mid-1950, he continued to mobilize true believers behind his crusade. Republicans encouraged him to keep up the game. In 1951 he listed Generals George Marshall and Dwight Eisenhower among the disloyal. He kept up his outrageous campaign without successful challenge until the end of the Korean War.

Fears of Communist espionage led Congress in 1950 to pass the McCarran Internal Security Act over President Truman's veto, requiring Communist and Communist-front organizations to register with the attorney general. Aliens who had belonged to totalitarian parties were barred from admission to the United States. Documents recently uncovered in Russian archives and U.S. security agencies reveal that the Soviets did indeed operate an extensive espionage ring in the United States after World War II. Russian agents recruited several hundred American spies to ferret out secrets regarding atomic weapons, defense systems, and military intelligence.

ASSESSING THE COLD WAR   In retrospect the onset of the cold war takes on an appearance of terrible inevitability. America's preference for international principles such as self-determination and democracy conflicted with the Soviet Union's preference for international spheres of influence and totalitarian control. Russia, after all, had suffered two German invasions in the first half of the twentieth century, and Soviet leaders wanted tame buffer states on their borders for protection.

The people of Eastern Europe were again caught in the middle. But the Communists themselves held to a universal principle: world revolution. And since the time of President James Monroe, Americans had bristled at the thought of foreign intervention in their sphere of influence, the Western Hemisphere. Thus, to create a defensive shield against the spread of communism, the United States signed mutual defense treaties. Under the 1947 Treaty of Rio de Janeiro, the nations of the Western Hemisphere agreed to aid any country in the region that was attacked. In 1951 the United States and Japan signed a treaty that permitted the United States to maintain military forces in Japan. That same year American negotiators signed other mutual defense treaties with the Philippines, Australia, and New Zealand.

The policy initiatives of the Truman years led the country to abandon its long-standing aversion to peacetime alliances. It was a far cry from the world of 1796, when George Washington in his farewell address warned against "those overgrown military establishments which . . . are inauspicious to liberty" and advised his country "to steer clear of permanent alliances with any portion of the foreign world." But then Washington had warned only against participation in the "ordinary" combinations and collusions of Europe, and surely the postwar years had seen extraordinary events and unprecedented new alliances.

MAKING CONNECTIONS

- The cold war had a major impact on American society: among other things, it helped create the "conforming culture" described in the next chapter.

- The New Frontier and Great Society programs of Presidents Kennedy and Johnson, discussed in Chapter 34, accomplished much of what Truman tried to do through his Fair Deal policies.

- The world seemed a dangerous place at the height of the cold war, but when seen from the perspective of the post–cold war world of the 1990s (discussed in Chapters 36 and 37), it had a certain stability that discouraged political violence.

FURTHER READING

The cold war remains a hotly debated topic. The traditional interpretation is best reflected in John Lewis Gaddis's *The United States and the Origins of the Cold War, 1941–1947* (1972) and *We Now Know: Rethinking Cold War History* (1997). Both superpowers, Gaddis argues, were responsible for causing the cold war, but the Soviet Union was more culpable. The revisionist perspective is represented by Gar Alperovitz's *Atomic Diplomacy: Hiroshima and Potsdam: The Use of the Atomic Bomb and the American Confrontation with Soviet Power,* 2nd ed. (1994). Alperovitz places primary responsibility for the conflict on the United States. Also see H. W. Brands's *The Devil We Knew: Americans and the Cold War* (1993) and Melvyn P. Leffler's *A Preponderance of Power: National Security, the Truman Administration, and the Cold War* (1992). On the architect of containment, see David Mayers's *George Kennan and the Dilemmas of U.S. Foreign Policy* (1988).

Arnold A. Offner indicts Truman for clumsy statesmanship in *Another Such Victory: President Truman and the Cold War, 1945–1953* (2002). For a positive assessment of Truman's leadership, see Alonzo L. Hamby's *Beyond the New Deal: Harry S. Truman and American Liberalism* (1973). The domestic policies of the Fair Deal are treated in William C. Berman's *The Politics of Civil Rights in the Truman Administration* (1970), Richard M. Dalfiumes's *Desegregation of the U.S. Armed Forces: Fighting on Two Fronts, 1939–1953* (1969), and Maeva Marcus's *Truman and the Steel Seizure Case: The Limits of Presidential Power* (1977). The most comprehensive biography of Truman is David McCullough's *Truman* (1992).

For an introduction to the tensions in Asia, see Akira Iriye's *The Cold War in Asia: A Historical Introduction* (1974). For the Korean conflict, see Callum A. MacDonald's *Korea: The War before Vietnam* (1986) and Max Hasting's *The Korean War* (1987).

The anti-Communist syndrome is surveyed in David Caute's *The Great Fear: The Anti-Communist Purge under Truman and Eisenhower* (1978). Arthur Herman's *Joseph McCarthy: Reexamining the Life and Legacy of America's Most Hated Senator* (2000) covers McCarthy himself. For a well-documented account of how the cold war was sustained by superpatriotism, intolerance, and suspicion, see Stephen J. Whitfield's *The Culture of the Cold War,* 2nd ed. (1996).

32

THROUGH THE PICTURE WINDOW: SOCIETY AND CULTURE, 1945–1960

FOCUS QUESTIONS

· Why did the U.S. economy expand so rapidly in the postwar period?

· How did strains of conformity and innovation characterize the culture of the 1950s?

· What were the characteristics of America's burgeoning consumer culture?

To answer these questions and access additional review material, please visit www.wwnorton.com/studyspace.

Americans emerged from World War II elated, proud of their military strength and industrial might, and eager to enjoy peacetime prosperity. As the editors of *Fortune* magazine proclaimed in 1946, "This is a dream era, this is what everyone was waiting through the blackouts for. The Great American Boom is on." So it was. An American public that had known deprivation and sacrifice for a decade and a half began to enjoy unprecedented economic growth and seeming social contentment—at least on the surface.

Amid the rising affluence and optimism, however, many social critics, writers, and artists expressed a growing sense of unease. Was postwar society becoming too complacent, too conformist, too materialistic? These questions reflected the perennial tension in American life between idealism and materialism, a tension that arrived with the first settlers and remains with us today. Americans have always struggled to accumulate goods and cultivate goodness. During the postwar era the nation tried to do both. For a while, at least, it appeared to succeed.

PEOPLE OF PLENTY

The dominant feature of post–World War II society was its remarkable prosperity. After a surprisingly brief postwar recession, the economy soared to record heights. The gross national product nearly doubled between 1945 and 1960, and the 1960s witnessed an even more spectacular expansion of the economy. By 1970 the gap between the living standard in the United States and in the rest of the world had become a chasm: with 6 percent of the world's population, Americans produced and consumed nearly two thirds of its goods.

Several factors contributed to this sustained economic surge. The massive federal expenditures to meet military needs during the war had catapulted the economy out of the Depression. High government spending continued to drive the postwar economy, thanks to the tensions generated by the cold war. Military-related research also helped spawn the new glamour industries of the postwar era: chemicals, electronics, and aviation.

Most of the other major industrial nations of the world—England, France, Germany, Japan, the Soviet Union—had been physically devastated during the war, which meant that American manufacturers enjoyed a virtual monopoly on international trade. In addition, the widespread use of new and more efficient machinery and computers led to a 35 percent jump in the productivity of American workers between 1945 and 1955.

The major catalyst in promoting economic expansion after 1945, however, was the unleashing of pent-up consumer demand. During the war, civilians had postponed purchases of major items such as cars and houses and in the process had saved over $150 billion. Now they were eager to buy. The United States after World War II experienced a purchasing frenzy.

THE GI BILL OF RIGHTS   Part of that frenzy was indirectly financed by the federal government. People feared that a sharp postwar drop in military spending and the sudden influx of veterans into the civilian workforce would send the economy into a downward spiral and produce widespread unemployment. Those concerns led Congress to pass the Servicemen's Readjustment Act of 1944. Popularly known as the GI Bill of Rights (*GI* meaning "government issue," a phrase that was stamped on military uniforms and was slang for "serviceman"), it led to the creation of a new government agency, the Veterans Administration. The GI Bill also provided unemployment pay for veterans for one year, preference for veterans seeking government jobs, loans for home construction, access to government hospitals, and generous subsidies for college or professional training.

The infusion of funds into the economy provided by the GI Bill helped fuel the prosperity. Between 1944 and 1956 almost 8 million veterans took advantage of $14.5 billion in GI Bill subsidies to attend college or enroll in job-training programs. Some 5 million veterans bought new homes using GI Bill benefits. These two programs combined to produce a social revolution.

The GI Bill enabled millions of veterans to receive higher education. Before World War II approximately 160,000 Americans graduated from college each year. By 1950 the figure had more than tripled. In 1949 veterans accounted for 40 percent of all college enrollments, and the United States could boast the world's best-educated workforce.

The GI Bill democratized higher education. It provided a generation of working-class Americans with an opportunity to earn a college degree for the first time. In turn a college education served as a lever into the middle class and fostered economic security. But while the GI Bill helped erode class barriers, it was less successful in dismantling racial barriers. Many African-American veterans could not take equal advantage of the education benefits. Most colleges and universities after the war remained racially segregated, by regulation or by practice.

The historically black colleges, most of which were in the South, could not expand quickly enough to meet the demand. In 1940 African-American colleges enrolled 43,000 students; in 1950 the number had soared to 77,000. Yet over 20,000 others were denied admission because of overcrowded facilities. In 1946 only one fifth of the 100,000 African Americans who had applied for education benefits had enrolled.

The return of some 12 million veterans to private life also helped generate the postwar baby boom, which peaked in 1957. Between 1946 and 1960 the population grew by almost 40 million, a whopping 30 percent increase. Such a dramatic growth rate had a host of reverberating effects. Indeed, much of America's social history since the 1940s has been the story of the unusually large baby-boom generation and its progress through the stages of life.

AN EXPANDING CONSUMER CULTURE   The baby boom was accompanied by a postwar construction boom. The proportion of homeowners in the population increased by 50 percent between 1945 and 1960. And

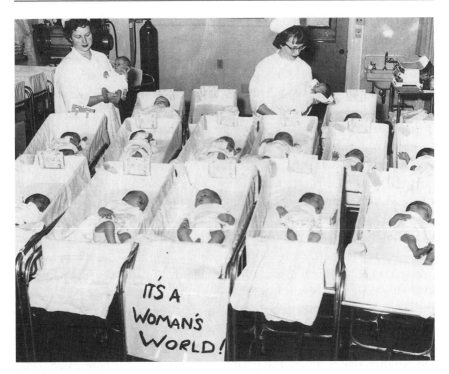

IT'S A
WOMAN'S
WORLD!

The Baby Boom

Much of America's social history since the 1940s has been the story of the baby-boom generation.

those new homes were increasingly filled with the latest electrical appliances: refrigerators, washing machines, sewing machines, vacuum cleaners, freezers, mixers, and television sets. By far the most popular new household product was the TV set. In 1946 there were only 7,000 primitive black-and-white TV sets in the country; by 1960 there were 50 million high-quality sets. Nine out of ten homes had one, and by 1970, 38 percent of homes had the new color sets.

What differentiated the affluence of the post–World War II era from earlier periods of prosperity was its ever-widening dispersion. Although pockets of rural and urban poverty persisted, few noticed such exceptions to the prevailing prosperity during the 1950s. In 1955 union leader George Meany proclaimed that "American labor never had it so good."

On the surface many blacks were also beneficiaries of the wave of prosperity that swept over postwar society. By 1950 African Americans were earning on average more than four times their 1940 wages. While gains had been made, however, African Americans and other minority groups lagged behind whites in their rate of improvement. Indeed, the gap between the average yearly income of whites and blacks widened during the 1950s. Yet the desire to present a united front against communism led commentators to ignore or gloss over issues of racial and economic injustice. Such corrosive neglect would fester and explode during the 1960s, but for now the emphasis was on consensus, conformity, and economic growth.

To perpetuate the postwar prosperity, economists repeated the basic marketing strategy of the 1920s: the public must be taught to consume more and expect more. Economists knew that Americans had more money than ever before. The average adult had twice as much *real* income in 1955 as in the rosy days of the late 1920s before the crash. Still, many people who had undergone the severities of the Depression and the rationing required for the war effort had to be weaned from a decade and a half of imposed frugality in order to nourish the growing consumer culture.

Advertising became a more crucial component of the consumer culture than ever before. Expenditures for TV ads increased 1,000 percent during the 1950s. Such startling growth rates led the president of NBC to claim in 1956 that the primary reason for the postwar economic boom was that "advertising has created an American frame of mind that makes people want more things, better things and newer things." Paying for such "things" was no problem; the age of the credit card had arrived. Between 1945 and 1957 consumer credit soared 800 percent. Whereas families in other industrialized nations were typically saving 10 to 20 percent of their income, American families by the 1960s were saving only 5 percent.

Young Americans especially participated in the consumer culture. By the late 1950s the baby-boom generation was entering its teens, and the disproportionate number of affluent adolescents generated a vast new specialized market for youth-oriented goods ranging from transistor radios, Hula-Hoops, and rock-and-roll records to cameras, surfboards, *Seventeen* magazine, and Pat Boone movies. Most teenagers had far more discretionary income and free time than previous generations had had. Teens in the postwar era knew nothing of depressions or rationing; they were immersed in abundance from an early age and took for granted the notion of carefree consumption.

THE SUBURBAN FRONTIER   The population increase of the 1950s and 1960s was an urban as well as a suburban phenomenon. Dramatic new technological advances in agricultural production reduced the need for manual laborers. Almost 20 million Americans left the land for the city between 1940 and 1970. Much of the urban population growth occurred in the South, the Southwest, and the West, in an arc that stretched from the

Suburban Life

A woman vacuums her living room in Queens, New York, 1953, illustrating the 1950s ideal of domestic contentment facilitated by electrical appliances.

Carolinas to California, regions that by the 1970s were being lumped to-gether and called the sunbelt. The dispersion of air-conditioning through-out these warm regions dramatically enhanced their attractiveness to north-erners. But the Northeast remained the most densely populated area; by the early 1960s, 20 percent of the nation's population lived in the corridor that stretched south from Boston to Norfolk, Virginia.

While more people concentrated in cities, Americans after World War II were simultaneously spreading out within the metropolitan areas. During the 1950s suburbs grew six times faster than cities. By 1970 more people lived in suburbs (76 million) than in central cities (64 million). Suburban development required cars, highways, and government-backed home mort-gages. It also required bold entrepreneurs.

William Levitt, a brassy New York developer, led the suburban revolution. In 1947, on 1,200 acres of Long Island farmland, he built 10,600 houses that were inhabited by more than 40,000 people, mostly adults under thirty-five and their children. Within a few years there were similar Levittowns in Penn-sylvania and New Jersey, and other developers soon followed suit around the country. Expanded automobile production and highway construction facili-tated the rush to the suburbs as more and more people were able to com-mute longer distances to work. Car production soared, and a car-dependent culture soon emerged. Widespread car ownership necessitated an improved road network. Local and state governments built many new roads, but the guiding force was the federal government. In 1947 Congress authorized the construction of 37,000 miles of federal highways, and nine years later it funded 42,000 additional miles of interstate expressways.

The federal government also fostered the suburban revolution through loans to developers and consumers. By insuring loans for up to 95 percent of the value of a house, the Federal Housing Administration made it easy for a builder to borrow money to construct low-cost homes. In addition, military veterans were given substantial assistance with home ownership. A veteran could buy a Levitt house with no down payment and monthly installments of $56. African Americans and other racial minorities, however, were often discriminated against. Contracts for homes in Levittown, Long Island, for example, specifically excluded "members of other than the Caucasian race." Such discrimination, whether explicit or implicit, was widespread; the nation's suburban population in 1970 was 95 percent white.

THE GREAT BLACK MIGRATION   World War II, like World War I, spurred a mass migration of rural southern blacks to the cities of other regions. This second migration was much larger in scope than the first, and its social consequences were much more dramatic. After 1945 more than 5 million southern blacks, mostly farm folk, left their native regions in search of better jobs, higher wages, decent housing, and greater social equality. During the 1950s, for example, the African-American population of Chicago more than doubled. The South Side of Chicago soon became known as the capital of black America. It remains the neighborhood with the largest concentration of African Americans in the nation.

Most black migrants were sharecroppers and farm laborers from the Mississippi Delta, the richest cotton-producing land in the world. For over a century the Delta cotton culture had been dependent upon African-American workers, first as slaves and then as sharecroppers and wage laborers. But a more efficient mechanical cotton picker invented in 1944 changed all that. The new machine could do the work of fifty people, making many farmworkers superfluous. Displaced southern blacks, many of them illiterate and provincial, streamed northward in search of a new promised land only to see many of their dreams dashed. In northern cities such as Chicago, Philadelphia, Newark, Detroit, New York, Boston, and Washington, D.C., African Americans from the rural South confronted harsh new realities. Slumlords often gouged them for rent, employers refused to hire them, and some union bosses denied them membership. Soon the promised land had become for many an ugly nightmare of slum housing, joblessness, illiteracy, dysfunctional families, welfare dependency, street gangs, pervasive crime, and racism.

The unexpected tidal wave of African-American migrants severely taxed the resources of urban governments and the tolerance of white racists. Throughout the North angry whites attacked blacks who dared move into their neighborhoods. Northern cities sought to deal with the migrants and alleviate racial stress by constructing massive all-black public-housing projects to accommodate the newcomers. These overcrowded racial enclaves were essentially segregated prisons. To be sure, many African-American migrants and their children did manage through extraordinary determination and ingenuity to "clear"—to climb out of the teeming ghettos and into the middle class. But most did not. As a consequence the great black migration produced a web of complex social problems in northern cities that in the 1960s would erupt into a crisis.

A CONFORMING CULTURE

In the 1950s social commentators mostly ignored people and cultures outside the mainstream. As evidenced in many of the new look-alike suburbs sprouting up across the land, much of white middle-class social life during the two decades after World War II exhibited an increasingly homogenized character. While fears generated by the cold war initially played a key role in encouraging orthodoxy, corporations and advertisers also came to play an increasingly important role in promoting homogeneity. Suburban life itself encouraged uniformity, since people felt a need for companionship and a sense of belonging as they moved into communities of strangers. "Conformity," predicted a journalist in 1954, "may very well become the central social problem of this age."

CORPORATE LIFE   During World War II big business had grown bigger. The government had relaxed its anti-trust activity, and huge defense contracts promoted corporate concentration and consolidation. In 1940, for example, the 100 largest companies were responsible for 30 percent of all manufacturing output; three years later they were producing 70 percent. After the war fewer and fewer people were self-employed; many now worked for large corporations, with manual labor giving way to mental labor for a large part of the workforce. In the huge companies as well as in similarly large government agencies and universities, the working atmosphere promoted conformity and regimentation rather than individualism.

WOMEN'S "PLACE"   Increasing conformity in middle-class business and corporate life was mirrored in the middle-class home. A special issue of *Life* magazine in 1956 featured the "ideal" middle-class woman, a thirty-two-year-old "pretty and popular" white suburban housewife, mother of four, who had married at age sixteen. Described as an excellent wife, mother, volunteer, and "home manager," she hosted dozens of dinner parties each year, sang in her church choir, worked with the PTA and the Campfire Girls, and was devoted to her husband. "In her daily round," *Life* reported, "she attends club or charity meetings, drives the children to school, does the weekly grocery shopping, makes ceramics, and is planning to study French." *Life's* ideal of the middle-class woman reflected a veritable cult of feminine domesticity that witnessed a dramatic revival in the postwar era. The soaring birthrate reinforced the deeply embedded notion that a woman's place was in the home. "Of all the accomplishments of the American woman," the *Life* cover story proclaimed, "the one she brings off with the most spectacular success is having babies."

Even though millions of women had responded to wartime appeals and joined the traditionally male workforce, afterward they were encouraged—and even forced—to turn their jobs over to the returning veterans and resume

The New Household

A Tupperware party in a middle-class suburban home.

their full-time commitment to home and family. Throughout the postwar era, educators, politicians, ministers, advertisers, and other commentators exalted the cult of domesticity and castigated the few feminists who were encouraging women to broaden their horizons beyond crib and kitchen. Women were to forget any thoughts of continuing their own careers in the workplace and return to their traditional domestic roles. Nonetheless, despite the ideal of women remaining in the home and the stigma associated with violating this norm, the percentage of women working outside the home increased overall during the 1950s.

THE SEARCH FOR COMMUNITY   In several respects, Americans were on the move after World War II. Some 20 percent of the population changed their place of residence each year. One cause of the mobility was the largest corporations' standard policy of relocating their sales and managerial employees. As they moved from central city to suburb, from suburb to suburb, from farm to city, from state to state, people searched for a sense of community and rootedness. Hence Americans, even more than usual, became joiners: they joined civic clubs, garden clubs, car pools, and babysitting groups.

Billy Graham Preaches to Thousands, 1955

The Baptist evangelist used radio and television to promote his huge crusades, as droves of Americans, encouraged by the president, Congress, and billboard advertising, joined churches and attended revival meetings.

Americans also joined churches and synagogues in record numbers. The postwar era witnessed a massive renewal of religious participation. In 1940 less than half the adult population belonged to a church; by 1960 over 65 percent were official communicants. Bible sales soared, and books, movies, and songs with religious themes were stunning commercial successes. The prevailing tone of the popular religious revival of the 1950s was upbeat and soothing. Most ministers assumed that people were not interested in "fire-and-brimstone" harangues from the pulpit; congregants did not want their conscience overburdened with a sense of personal sin or social guilt about issues such as segregation and inner-city poverty. Instead, they wanted to be reassured that their own comfortable way of life was indeed God's will.

CRACKS IN THE PICTURE WINDOW

Yet despite widespread prosperity, all was not well in postwar America. The widely publicized affluence masked festering poverty in rural areas and urban ghettos. People were also profoundly anxious about the meaning of their lives and of life in general in the nuclear age. That tranquilizers were the fastest growing medication suggested that considerable anxiety accompanied the nation's much-trumpeted affluence. Thus one of the most striking aspects of postwar American life was the sharp contrast between the prevailing sentiment that everything was fine and for the best as long as people believed in God, the "American way," and themselves and the increasingly bitter criticism of social life coming from artists, intellectuals, and other commentators.

THE LONELY CROWD   The criticism of postwar life and values began in the early 1950s and quickly gathered momentum. In *The Affluent Society* (1958), for example, the economist John Kenneth Galbraith warned that sustained economic growth would not necessarily solve chronic social problems. He reminded readers that for all of America's vaunted postwar prosperity, the nation had yet to confront, much less eradicate, the chronic poverty plaguing the nation's inner cities and rural hamlets. Postwar cultural critics also questioned the supposed bliss offered by middle-class suburban life. John Keats, in *The Crack in the Picture Window* (1956), launched a savage assault on life in the huge new suburban developments. Suburbanites, he concluded, were locked into a deadly routine, hounded by financial insecurity, engulfed by mass mediocrity, and living, in short, in a "homogeneous, postwar Hell."

Social critics in the 1950s repeatedly cited the huge modern corporation as an important source of regimentation in American life. The most provocative analysis of the docile new corporate character was David Riesman's *The Lonely Crowd* (1950). Riesman, a social psychologist, detected a fundamental shift in the dominant American personality from what he called the "inner-directed" type to the "other-directed" type. Inner-directed people, Riesman argued, possess a deeply internalized set of basic values implanted by strong-minded parents or other elders. Such an assured, self-reliant personality, Riesman claimed, had prevailed in nineteenth-century life. But during the mid–twentieth century a new, other-directed personality had displaced it. In the huge hierarchical corporations that abounded in postwar America, employees who could win friends and influence people thrived; rugged individualists indifferent to personal popularity did not. The other-directed people who adapted to the corporate culture had few internal convictions and standards; they did not follow their conscience so much as adapt to the prevailing standards of the moment. They were concerned more with being well liked than with being independent.

Riesman amassed considerable evidence to show that the other-directed personality was not just an aspect of the business world; its characteristics were widely dispersed throughout middle-class life. One of its sources, Riesman suggested, may have been Dr. Benjamin Spock's influential advice on raising children. Spock's popular manual, *The Common Sense Book of Baby and Child Care,* sold 1 million copies a year between its first appearance in 1946 and 1960. Spock stressed that parents should foster in their children qualities and skills that would enhance their chances in what Riesman called the "popularity market."

YOUTH CULTURE AND DELINQUENCY   Heeding Dr. Spock's advice, most parents of the 1950s tended to be permissive with their children, who occupied a distinctive place in postwar life. One commentator described the American family in 1957 as a "child-centered anarchy." As the baby boomers were reaching adolescence during the 1950s, a distinctive "teen" subculture began to emerge. And as most adults in postwar society were striving to get along and to conform to the values of the club or civic group or corporation, so too were most young people during the 1950s embracing the values of their parents and the capitalist system.

Yet such conformity and striving for popularity masked a great deal of turbulence. During the 1950s a wave of juvenile delinquency swept across middle-class society. By 1956 over 1 million teens a year were being arrested. Car theft was the leading offense, but larceny, rape, and murder were not

Youth Culture

A drugstore soda fountain, a popular outlet for teenagers' consumerism in the 1950s.

uncommon. A Boston judge announced that the entire city was being "terrorized" by juvenile gangs. What was causing the delinquency? J. Edgar Hoover, head of the Federal Bureau of Investigation, insisted that the root of the problem was a lack of religious training in more and more households. Others pointed to the growing number of urban slums, whose "brutish" environment could lead to criminality. Yet those factors failed to explain why so many middle-class kids from God-fearing families were becoming delinquents. One explanation may have been the unprecedented mobility of young people. Access to automobiles enabled teens to escape parental control, and in the words of one journalist, cars provided "a private lounge for drinking and for petting or sex episodes."

ROCK AND ROLL   Many concerned observers blamed the delinquency on a new form of music that emerged during the postwar era: rock and roll. In 1955 *Life* magazine published a long article about a mysterious new "frenzied teenage music craze" that was creating "a big fuss." Alan Freed, a Cleveland disc jockey, had coined the term *rock and roll* in 1951. At a record store he had noticed white teenagers buying rhythm and blues (R&B) records that had heretofore been purchased only by African Americans and Hispanic Americans. Freed began playing R&B records on the air but labeled the music rock and roll (a phrase used in African-American communities to refer to dancing and sex) to surmount the racial barrier.

Freed's radio program was an immediate success, and its popularity helped bridge the gap between "white" and "black" music. African-American singers such as Chuck Berry, Little Richard, and Ray Charles and Hispanic-American performers such as Ritchie Valens (Richard Valenzuela) were suddenly the rage among young white middle-class audiences eager to claim their own cultural style and message.

At the same time, Elvis Presley, a young white truck driver and aspiring singer from Memphis, Tennessee, began experimenting with "rockabilly" music, his unique blend of gospel, country-and-western, and R&B rhythms and lyrics. In 1956 the twenty-one-year-old Presley released "Heartbreak Hotel," and over the next two years the sensual baritone won fourteen gold records and emerged as the most popular entertainer in history. His sexually suggestive stage performances, featuring twisting hips and a gyrating pelvis, drove teenagers wild.

Such hysterics prompted cultural conservatives to urge parents to confiscate and destroy Presley's records because they promoted "a pagan concept of life." A Catholic cardinal denounced Presley as a vile symptom of a new teen "creed of dishonesty, violence, lust and degeneration." Patriotic groups claimed that rock-and-roll music was a tool of Communist insurgents designed to corrupt American youth.

Yet rock and roll survived the assaults and in the process gave

Elvis Presley, 1956

The teenage children of middle-class America made rock and roll a thriving industry in the 1950s and Elvis its first star. The strong beat of rock music combined with the electric guitar, its signature instrument, produced a distinctive new sound.

adolescents a self-conscious sense of belonging to a unique social group with distinctive characteristics and tastes. It also represented an unprecedented intermingling of racial, ethnic, and class identities.

ALIENATION IN THE ARTS Dissatisfaction with the conventions and conformity of American society surfaced not only in rock and roll; it was manifested also in literature as well as in some of the artwork of the times. Many of the best novels and plays of the postwar period reinforced David Riesman's image of modern American society as a "lonely crowd" of individuals, hollow at the core, groping for a sense of belonging and affection. Arthur Miller's much-celebrated play *Death of a Salesman* (1949) explored this theme powerfully. Willy Loman, an aging, confused traveling salesman in decline, centers his life and that of his family on the notion of material success through personal popularity, only to be abruptly told by his boss that he is in fact a failure. Willy, for all his puffery about being well liked, admits that he is "terribly lonely." He has no real friends; even his relations with his family are neither honest nor intimate. When Willy finally realizes that he has been leading a counterfeit existence, he yearns for a life in which "a man is not a piece of fruit," but eventually he is so dumbfounded by his predicament that he decides he can endow his life with meaning only by ending it.

Nor are there many happy endings in the best novels of the postwar period. A brooding sense of resigned alienation dominated literary fiction in the two decades after 1945. The characters in novels such as James Jones's *From Here to Eternity* (1951), Ralph Ellison's *Invisible Man* (1952), Saul Bellow's *Dangling Man* (1944) and *Seize the Day* (1956), William Styron's *Lie Down in Darkness* (1951), and John Updike's *Rabbit, Run* (1961), among many others, tend to be like Willy Loman: restless, tormented, impotent individuals who are unable to fasten on a satisfying self-image and therefore can find neither contentment nor respect in an overpowering or impersonal world.

Many visual artists also explored the theme of desolate loneliness in urban-industrial American life. Virtually all of Edward Hopper's paintings, for example, depict isolated individuals, melancholy, anonymous, and motionless. The silence of his scenes is deafening, the monotony striking, the alienation absorbing.

A group of younger painters in New York City felt that postwar society was so chaotic that it denied any attempt at literal representation. Their anarchic technique came to be called abstract expressionism, and during the late 1940s and 1950s it dominated not only the American art scene but the international field as well. Abstract expressionists included Jackson Pollock,

Robert Motherwell, Willem de Kooning, Arshile Gorky, Clyfford Adolph Gottlieb, and Mark Rothko. "Abstract art," Motherwell declared, "is an effort to close the void that modern men feel."

In practice this meant that the *act* of painting was as important as the result and that art no longer had to represent one's visual surroundings. Instead, it could unapologetically represent the painter's personal thoughts and actions. Wyoming-born Pollock, for example, placed his huge canvases flat on the floor and then walked around each side, pouring and dripping his paint in an effort to "literally be *in* the painting." Such action paintings, with their commanding size, bold form, powerful color contrasts, and rough texture, were vibrant, frenzied, meditative, disorienting, and provocative.

THE BEATS   The desire to liberate self-expression and reject middle-class conventions also animated a small but highly visible and controversial group of young writers, poets, painters, and musicians known as the Beats. These young men—Jack Kerouac, Allen Ginsberg, Gary Snyder, William Burroughs, and Gregory Corso, among others—rebelled against the mundane horrors of middle-class life. The Beats were not lost in despair, however; they strenuously embraced life. But it was life on their own terms, and their terms were shocking to most observers.

The self-described Beats grew out of the bohemian underground in New York's Greenwich Village. Essentially apolitical throughout the 1950s, the Beats sought personal rather than social solutions to their hopes and anxieties. As Jack Kerouac insisted, his friends were not beat in the sense of beaten; they were "mad to live, mad to talk, mad to be saved." Their road to salvation lay in hallucinogenic drugs and alcohol, sex, a penchant for jazz and the street life of urban ghettos, an affinity for Buddhism, and a restless, vagabond spirit that took them speeding back and forth across the country between San Francisco and New York.

This existential mania for intense experience and frantic motion provided the subject matter for the Beats' writing. Ginsberg's long prose poem *Howl*, published in 1956, features an explicit sensuality as well as an impressionistic attempt to catch the color, movement, and dynamism of modern life. Kerouac published his autobiographical novel *On the Road* a year later. In frenzied prose it portrays the Beats' life of "bursting ecstasies" and maniacal traveling. *Howl* and *On the Road* elicited angry sarcasm from many reviewers, but the books enjoyed brisk sales, especially among young people. *On the Road* made the best-seller list, and soon the term *Beat generation* or *beatnik* referred to almost any young rebel who openly dissented from the comfortable ethos of middle-class life.

Allen Ginsberg

Ginsberg, considered the poet laureate of the Beat generation, reads his uncensored poetry to a crowd in Washington Square Park in New York City.

A PARADOXICAL ERA

For all their eccentricities and vitality the Beats had little impact on the prevailing patterns of postwar social and cultural life. The same held true for most of the critics who attacked the smug conformity and excessive materialism they saw pervading their society. The public had become weary of larger social or political concerns in the aftermath of the Depression and the war. Instead, Americans eagerly focused on personal and family goals and material achievements.

Yet those achievements, considerable as they were, eventually created a new set of problems. The benefits of abundance were by no means equally distributed during the 1950s, and millions of people still lived in poverty. For those more fortunate, unprecedented affluence and security fostered greater leisure and independence, which in turn provided opportunities for pursuing more diverse notions of what the good life entailed. Yet the conformist mentality of the cold war era discouraged experimentation. By the mid-1960s tensions between innovation and convention would erupt into open conflict. Many members of the baby-boom generation would become the leaders of the 1960s rebellion against the corporate and consumer cultures and the militarism excited by the cold war. Ironically, the person who would warn Americans of the 1960s of the mounting dangers of the burgeoning "military-industrial complex" was the president who had long symbolized its growth: Dwight D. Eisenhower.

MAKING CONNECTIONS

- The culture of the 1950s laid the groundwork for the counterculture of the 1960s, discussed in Chapters 34 and 35.

- Fruitful comparisons may be made between American culture in the 1950s and the earlier postwar period, the 1920s, which was described in Chapter 26.

- The women's movement of the 1970s, discussed in Chapter 35, was led by women who rejected the cult of domesticity that is described in this chapter.

- The baby boom of the postwar period would have continuing economic, social, political, and cultural significance as its members moved through the life cycle. Follow along in the coming chapters.

FURTHER READING

Two excellent overviews of social and cultural trends in the postwar era are William H. Chafe's *The Unfinished Journey: America since World War II*, 5th ed. (2003) and William E. Leuchtenburg's *A Troubled Feast: America since 1945* (1973). For insights into the cultural life of the 1950s, see Jeffrey Hart's *When the Going Was Good!: American Life in the Fifties* (1982) and David Halberstam's *The Fifties* (1993).

The baby-boom generation and its impact are vividly described in Paul C. Light's *Baby Boomers* (1988). The emergence of the television industry is discussed in Erik Barnouw's *Tube of Plenty: The Evolution of American Television* (1975) and Ella Taylor's *Prime-Time Families: Television Culture in Postwar America* (1989).

A comprehensive account of the process of suburban development is Kenneth T. Jackson's *Crabgrass Frontier: The Suburbanization of the United States*

(1985). Equally good is Tom Martinson's *American Dreamscape: The Pursuit of Happiness in Postwar America* (2000).

The middle-class ideal of family life in the 1950s is examined in Elaine Tyler May's *Homeward Bound: American Families in the Cold War Era* (1988). Thorough accounts of women's issues are found in Wini Breines's *Young, White, and Miserable: Growing up Female in the Fifties* (1992). For an overview of the resurgence of religion in the 1950s, see George M. Marsden's *Religion and American Culture* (1990).

A lively discussion of movies of the 1950s can be found in Peter Biskind's *Seeing Is Believing: How Hollywood Taught Us to Stop Worrying and Love the Fifties* (1983). The origins and growth of rock and roll are surveyed in Carl Belz's *The Story of Rock,* 2nd ed. (1972). Thoughtful interpretive surveys of postwar American literature include Josephine Hendin's *Vulnerable People: A View of American Fiction since 1945* (1978) and Malcolm Bradbury's *The Modern American Novel* (1983). The colorful Beats are brought to life in Steven Watson's *The Birth of the Beat Generation: Visionaries, Rebels, and Hipsters, 1944–1960* (1995).

33

CONFLICT AND DEADLOCK: THE EISENHOWER YEARS

FOCUS QUESTIONS

· What characterized Eisenhower's "dynamic conservatism"?

· What were the central terms of American foreign policy in the 1950s?

· How did the civil rights movement emerge in the 1950s?

· What events led up to the Vietnam War?

To answer these questions and access additional review material, please visit www.wwnorton.com/studyspace.

The New Deal political coalition established by Franklin Roosevelt and sustained by Harry Truman posed a formidable challenge to Republicans after World War II. To counter the potent combination of Solid South white Democrats, African Americans, and members of other minority groups, and organized labor, the Grand Old Party turned to General Dwight David Eisenhower, a military hero capable of attracting independent voters as well as some Democrats. Eisenhower's commitment to a "moderate Republicanism" promised to slow the rate of government expansion while retaining many of the cherished social programs established by Roosevelt and Truman. Eisenhower's two terms as president are often characterized as a lull between two eras of Democratic activism. In Eisenhower's view, however, his administration would restore the authority of state and local governments and restrain the executive branch from political and social "engineering." In the process the former general sought to reinforce traditional virtues and inspire Americans with a vision of a brighter future.

"Time for a Change"

By 1952 the Truman administration had piled up a heavy burden of political liabilities: a bloody stalemate in Korea, renewed wage and price controls at home, reckless charges of subversion and disloyalty among federal employees, and the exposure of corrupt lobbyists and influence peddlers who rigged favors in Washington. The disclosure of government corruption led Truman to fire nearly 250 employees of the Internal Revenue Service. But doubts lingered that he would ever finish the housecleaning.

THE POLITICAL RISE OF EISENHOWER   It was, in a slogan of the day, "time for a change," and Republicans saw public sentiment turning their way as the 1952 election approached. Republican leaders recruited General Dwight D. Eisenhower to be their candidate. Despite his Kansas roots in Republican conservatism, Eisenhower had initially supported Roosevelt and the New Deal, and he admired Roosevelt's wartime leadership. During the Truman years, however, Eisenhower reverted to the political party of his youth. In early 1952 he affirmed that he was a Republican and permitted his name to be entered in party primaries. He won the nomination on the first ballot, then balanced the ticket by selecting as his running mate a youthful Californian, the thirty-nine-year-old senator Richard M. Nixon, who had built a career on strenuous opposition to domestic "subversives."

THE ELECTION OF 1952   The Twenty-second Amendment, ratified in 1951, forbade any president from serving more than two terms. The amendment exempted the current incumbent, Harry Truman, but weary of the war in Korea and harassed by charges of subversion and corruption in his administration, Truman chose to withdraw. In a wide-open Democratic race he supported Illinois governor Adlai E. Stevenson, who roused the Democratic Convention delegates with an eloquent speech welcoming them to Chicago.

The 1952 campaign matched two of the most magnetic personalities ever pitted against each other in a presidential contest, but the race was uneven from the start. Eisenhower, though a political novice, was a world hero who had been in the public eye for a decade. Stevenson was hardly known outside Illinois. The genial Eisenhower, who disliked politics and politicians, pledged to clean up "the mess in Washington." To this he added a promise, late in the campaign, that as president-elect he would secure "an early and honorable" peace in Korea. Stevenson offered a keen intellect spiced with a quick wit, but his resolve to "talk sense" and "tell the truth to the American

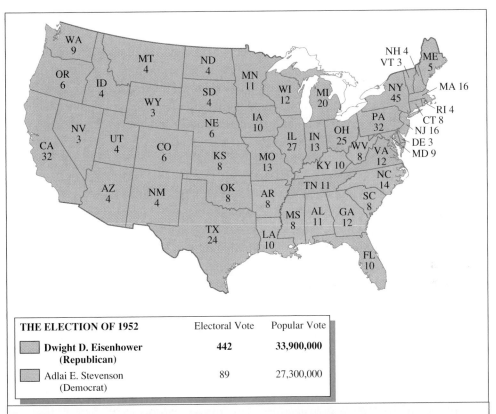

THE ELECTION OF 1952	Electoral Vote	Popular Vote
Dwight D. Eisenhower (Republican)	**442**	**33,900,000**
Adlai E. Stevenson (Democrat)	89	27,300,000

Why was the contest between Stevenson and Eisenhower so lopsided? Why was Eisenhower's victory in the South remarkable? Did Eisenhower's broad appeal help congressional Republicans win more seats?

people" came across as too aloof, a shade too intellectual. The Republicans labeled him an egghead in contrast to Eisenhower, the folksy man of the people, the man of decisive action.

In the end, Stevenson's humor and intellect were no match for Eisenhower's popularity. The war hero triumphed in a landslide of 34 million votes to 27 million. The election marked a turning point in Republican fortunes in the South: for the first time since the 1850s, the South was moving toward a two-party system. Stevenson carried only eight southern states plus West Virginia; Eisenhower picked up five states on the periphery of the Deep South: Florida, Oklahoma, Tennessee, Texas, and Virginia. The "nonpolitical" Eisenhower had made it respectable, even fashionable, to vote Republican in the South. Elsewhere, too, the general made inroads into the New Deal coalition, attracting supporters among the ethnic and religious minorities in the major cities who had long identified with the Democratic party.

The voters, it turned out, liked Ike better than they liked his party. In the 1952 election, Democrats retained most of the governorships, lost control of the House by only eight votes, and broke even in the Senate. The congressional elections two years later would weaken the Republican grip on Congress, and Eisenhower would have to work with a Democratic Congress until he left office.

EISENHOWER'S "HIDDEN-HAND" PRESIDENCY

IKE   Born in Denison, Texas, in 1890, Dwight David Eisenhower grew up in Abilene, Kansas, and attended the U.S. Military Academy at West Point, New York. As a general during World War II, he took command of American forces in the European theater and directed the invasion of North Africa in 1942. In 1944 he assumed the post of supreme commander of Allied forces in preparation for the invasion of German-controlled Europe. After the war, by then the five-star general of the army, Eisenhower became chief of staff and supreme commander of NATO forces, with a brief interlude as president of Columbia University.

Far from being a "do-nothing" president, as some have charged, Eisenhower was an effective leader. The art of leadership, he once explained, did not require "hitting people over the head. Any damn fool can do that. . . . It's persuasion—and conciliation—and education—and patience. That's the only kind of leadership I know—or believe in—or will practice." The public image of Ike was warm, sincere, and unpretentious, a man who rose above partisan politics. Those who were close to him have presented another side, however. When provoked, the genial general could show a fiery temper and release a stream of scalding profanity. One student of Eisenhower's leadership techniques has spoken of a "hidden-hand presidency," in which Ike deliberately cultivated a public image of passivity to hide his active involvement in policy decisions.

"DYNAMIC CONSERVATISM" AT HOME   Eisenhower called his domestic program dynamic conservatism, which meant being "conservative when it comes to money and liberal when it comes to human beings." Budget cutting was a high priority. Eisenhower warned repeatedly against the dangers of "creeping socialism," "huge bureaucracies," and budget deficits. His administration ended wage and price controls and reduced federal farm-price subsidies.

But though Eisenhower chipped away at New Deal programs, his presidency in the end served rather to legitimate the New Deal by keeping its basic structure and premises intact during an era of prosperity. In some ways the administration expanded the New Deal, especially after 1954, when it had the help of Democratic Congresses. Amendments to the Social Security Act in 1954 and 1956 brought coverage to millions in categories formerly excluded: professional people, domestic and clerical workers, farmworkers, and members of the armed forces. The federal minimum wage rose in 1955 from 75¢ to $1 an hour. Federal expenditures for public health rose steadily in the Eisenhower years, and low-income housing continued to be built, although on a much reduced scale. Some farm-related aid programs were actually expanded.

Despite Eisenhower's disapproval of federal electric-power programs, he continued to support government public works projects that served the national interest. Two such programs left major monuments to his presidency: the St. Lawrence Seaway and the interstate highways. The St. Lawrence Seaway, opened in 1959 as a joint venture with Canada, allowed oceangoing ships to reach the Great Lakes. The Federal-Aid Highway Act of 1956 authorized the federal government to contribute 90 percent of the cost of building 42,500 miles of limited-access interstate highways to serve the needs of commerce and defense, as well as the convenience of private citizens. The states provided the remaining 10 percent.

CONCLUDING AN ARMISTICE   America's new global responsibilities in the postwar world continued to absorb Eisenhower's attention. The most pressing problem when he entered office was the painful deadlock in the Korean peace talks. To break the stalemate, Eisenhower took a bold stand. In mid-May 1953 he stepped up aerial bombardment of North Korea, then had Secretary of State John Foster Dulles warn the Chinese of his willingness to use atomic bombs. Whether for that reason or others, negotiations moved quickly toward an armistice along the established border just above the 38th parallel and toward a complicated arrangement for an exchange of prisoners that allowed captives to decide whether to accept or refuse repatriation.

On July 26, 1953, Eisenhower announced the conclusion of the Korean armistice agreement. No one knows if he actually would have forced the issue with atomic weapons. Perhaps the more decisive factors in bringing about a settlement were the mounting Chinese losses and the spirit of uncertainty and caution felt by the Russian Communists after the death of Joseph Stalin on March 5, 1953, six weeks after Ike's inauguration.

COMMUNIST PARTY ORGANIZATION U.S.A-FEB 9, 1950

The Army-McCarthy Hearings, June 1954

The attorney Joseph Welch (hand on head) listening incredulously to Senator Mc-Carthy's claims of Communist infiltration of the U.S. Army.

CONCLUDING A WITCH HUNT   The Korean armistice helped to end the meteoric career of Senator Joseph McCarthy. Convinced that the government was thoroughly infested with Communists and spies, the Wisconsin senator launched a one-man crusade to root them out. Eventually the logic of McCarthy's unscrupulous tactics led to his self-destruction, but not before he had left many careers and reputations in ruins. The Eisenhower Republicans thought their victory in 1952 would curb McCarthy's recklessness, but the senator grew more outlandish in both his charges and his investigative methods.

McCarthy finally overreached himself in the spring of 1954, when as chairman of the Senate's Government Operations Committee he made the absurd charge that the U.S. Army itself was "soft" on communism. The televised Army-McCarthy hearings displayed McCarthy at his worst, scowling at critics, bullying witnesses, repeatedly calling "point of order." He became the perfect foil for the Army's gentle but unflappable counsel, Joseph Welch, whose rapier wit repeatedly drew blood. On December 2, 1954, the Senate voted sixty-seven to twenty-two to "condemn" McCarthy for contempt of the Senate. McCarthy's political career collapsed. For all his attacks and inquiries he had never uncovered one Communist in the government. McCarthyism, Eisenhower joked, had become McCarthywasm. To the end, Eisenhower refused to "get down in the gutter with that guy" and sully the dignity of the presidency. He did work resolutely against McCarthy behind the scenes, but some scholars consider his "hidden-hand" approach to have been ineffective at best and cowardly at worst.

Eisenhower believed that espionage posed a real danger to national security. He denied clemency to Julius and Ethel Rosenberg, who had been convicted of passing atomic secrets to the Russians, on the grounds that they "may have condemned to death tens of millions of innocent people." The Rosenbergs were electrocuted in 1953.

INTERNAL SECURITY   The anti-Communist crusade survived McCarthy's downfall. Even before 1954 Eisenhower stiffened the government security program that Truman had set up in 1947. In 1953 he issued an executive order broadening the basis for firing subversive government workers, replacing Truman's criterion of "disloyalty" with the new category of "security risk." Under the new edict federal workers could lose their jobs because of dubious political associations or personal behavior that might make them careless or vulnerable to blackmail. However, the Supreme Court modified some of the more extreme expressions of this continuation of the Red Scare. In 1953 Eisenhower appointed as chief justice of the Supreme Court former governor Earl Warren of California, a decision he later pronounced the "biggest damnfool mistake I ever made." Warren, who had seemed safely conservative while in electoral politics, led an active Court on issues of civil rights and civil liberties. The Warren Court (1953–1969), under the chief justice's influence, became an important agent of social and political change through the 1960s. In connection with security programs and loyalty requirements, the Court veered back in the direction of traditional individual rights.

FOREIGN INTERVENTION

DULLES AND FOREIGN POLICY   The Eisenhower administration promised new foreign-policy departures under the direction of Secretary of State John Foster Dulles. Grandson of one secretary of state and nephew of another, Dulles pursued a lifetime career as an international lawyer and sometime diplomat. Son of a minister and himself an earnest Presbyterian, Dulles, in the words of the British ambassador, resembled those old zealots of the wars of religion who "saw the world as an arena in which the forces of good and evil were continuously at war." But he was also a man of immense energy, intelligence, and experience.

The foreign-policy planks of the 1952 Republican platform, which Dulles wrote, showed both the moralist and the tactician at work. Truman's policy of containment was needlessly defensive, Dulles thought. Americans instead should promote the "liberation" of sovereign nations from Soviet domination.

"Don't Be Afraid—I Can Always Pull You Back."

Secretary of State John Foster Dulles pushes a reluctant America to the brink of war.

Eisenhower was quick to explain, however, that liberating Eastern Europe from Soviet control would not involve military force. He would promote independence "by every peaceful means, but only by peaceful means."

Yet for all his talk of liberating Eastern Europe, Dulles made no significant departure from the containment strategy created under Truman. Instead, he institutionalized containment in the rigid mold of his cold war rhetoric and extended it to the military strategy of deterrence. Dulles's endorsement of "massive retaliation" was an effort to get, in the slogan soon current, "more bang for the buck." By this time both the United States and the Soviet Union had exploded hydrogen bombs. With the new policy of deterrence, what Winston Churchill called a balance of terror had replaced the old balance of power. The threat of nuclear holocaust was terrifying, but the notion that the United States would risk such a disaster in response to local wars had little credibility.

Dulles's policy of "brinksmanship" depended for its strategic effect upon those very fears of nuclear disaster. He argued in 1956 that in following a tough policy of confronting communism, a nation sometimes had to "go to the brink" of war. Such a firm stand had halted aggression in Korea when America threatened in 1953 to use atomic weapons. Dulles also employed brinksmanship in Indochina in 1954, when U.S. aircraft carriers moved into the South China Sea "both to deter any Red Chinese attack against Indochina and to provide weapons for instant retaliation."

INDOCHINA: THE BACKGROUND TO WAR Like the rest of the old colonial world of Asia and Africa, French Indochina experienced a wave of nationalism after World War II, damaging both the power and the prestige of France. By the early 1950s most of British Asia was independent or on its way to independence: India, Pakistan, Ceylon (now Sri Lanka), Burma (now Myanmar), and the Malay States (now Malaysia). The Dutch and French, however, were less willing to give up their colonies, a situation that created a dilemma for U.S. policy makers. Americans sympathized with the colonial nationalists but wanted Dutch and French help fending off the spread of communism. For the Dutch and the French to maintain control of their colonial empires, they had to reconquer areas that had passed from Japanese occupation into the hands of local patriots. The Truman administration had felt obliged to comply with the Dutch and French pleas for aid.

French Indochina, created in the nineteenth century out of the old kingdoms of Cambodia, Laos, and Vietnam, offered a variation on colonial nationalism. During World War II, opposition to the Japanese occupation of Indochina was led by the Viet Minh (League for the Independence of Vietnam), nationalists who fell under the influence of Communists led by the magnetic rebel Ho Chi Minh. At the end of the war, the Viet Minh controlled part of northern Vietnam, and on September 2, 1945, Ho Chi Minh proclaimed a Democratic Republic of Vietnam, with its capital in Hanoi. Ho had secretly received American help against the Japanese during the war, but his bids for further aid after the war went unanswered. Vietnam was a low priority in U.S. diplomatic concerns, which at the time were focused on restoring western Europe and containing the spread of communism there.

In 1946 the French government recognized Ho's new government as a "free state" within the French colonial union. Before the year was out, however, Ho had opposed French efforts to establish another regime in the southern provinces, and their clash soon expanded into the First Indochina War. This was a troubling development for the U.S. government. On the one hand, the United States resented France's determination to restore colonial rule. Yet Truman was even more determined to see France become a bulwark against communism

Ho Chi Minh

A seasoned revolutionary, Ho Chi Minh cultivated a humble, proletarian image of himself as Uncle Ho, a man of the people.

in Europe. As a result, the American government acquiesced in France's efforts to crush Vietnamese nationalism.

The Viet Minh movement thereafter became more dependent upon the Soviet Union and Communist China for help. In 1950, with the outbreak of fighting in Korea, the struggle in Vietnam took on the appearance of a battleground in the cold war. When the Korean War ended, American aid to the French in Vietnam, begun by the Truman administration, escalated dramatically. By the end of 1953, the Eisenhower administration was paying about two thirds of the cost of the French war effort in Indochina.

But even with lavish U.S. aid the French were unable to suppress the well-organized and tenacious Viet Minh. In 1954 a major French force had been sent to Dien Bien Phu, in the northwest corner of Vietnam, near the Laos border, in the hope of luring Viet Minh guerrillas into the open and overwhelming them with superior firepower. The French instead found themselves surrounded by a superior force that laid siege to their stronghold.

In March 1954 the French government requested an American air strike to relieve the pressure on Dien Bien Phu. Eisenhower seemed to endorse forceful action when he advanced his "domino theory" at a news conference on April 7. He implied that if Indochina fell to the Communists, the rest of Asia would be next. Eisenhower, however, opposed direct U.S. military action unless the British lent support. When they refused, Eisenhower backed away from unilateral action, explaining that it would be a "tragic error to go in alone as a partner of France."

America's decision not to intervene sealed the fate of the besieged French garrison at Dien Bien Phu. On May 7, 1954, the Viet Minh overwhelmed the courageous but vastly outnumbered French resistance. It was the very eve of the day on which an international conference at Geneva took up the question of Indochina. Six weeks later, as French forces continued to suffer defeats in Vietnam, a new French government promised an early settlement. On July 20 representatives of France, Britain, the Soviet Union, the People's Republic of China, and the Viet Minh signed the Geneva Accords and the next day produced their Final Declaration, which proposed to make Laos and Cambodia independent and divide Vietnam at the 17th parallel. The Viet Minh would take power in the north, and the French would remain south of the line until elections in 1956 would reunify Vietnam. American and South Vietnamese representatives refused to join in the accord or to sign the Final Declaration.

Eisenhower announced that although the United States "had not itself been party to or bound by the decision taken at the Conference," any renewal of Communist aggression in Vietnam "would be viewed by us as a matter of grave concern." (He failed to note that the United States had agreed at

Geneva to "refrain from the threat or use of force to disturb" the agreements.) Ho Chi Minh and his government in Hanoi quickly sought to consolidate control throughout the north. In the hinterlands local Communists held kangaroo courts that tried and executed landowners and confiscated their land. Residents of the north who wished to leave for the south did so with American aid. Over 900,000 refugees, most of them Catholics, relocated in the south, causing staggering logistical problems for the struggling new government there.

Power in the south gravitated to a new premier, Ngo Dinh Diem, a Catholic nationalist who had opposed both the French and the Viet Minh. Diem took office during the Geneva talks, after returning from exile at a seminary in New Jersey. In 1954 Eisenhower offered to assist Diem if he would enact democratic reforms and distribute land to the peasants. U.S. aid took the form of CIA and military advisers charged with training Diem's armed forces and police. Eisenhower remained opposed to the use of U.S. combat troops. He was convinced that such military intervention would bog down into a costly stalemate—as it eventually did.

Instead of instituting comprehensive reforms, however, Diem suppressed his political opponents on both the right and the left, offering little or no land distribution and permitting widespread corruption. In 1956 he refused to join in the elections to reunify Vietnam, and the United States endorsed his decision. But Diem's efforts to eliminate all opposition only played into the hands of the Communists, who found more and more recruits among the discontented peasantry. By 1957 guerrilla forces in the south, known as the Viet Cong, had begun attacks on the Diem government, and in 1960 the resistance formed its own political arm, the National Liberation Front. As guerrilla warfare gradually disrupted South Vietnam, Eisenhower was helpless to do anything but "sink or swim with Ngo Dinh Diem."

REELECTION AND FOREIGN CRISES

As the United States continued to forge postwar alliances and bring pressure to bear on foreign governments by practicing brinksmanship, a new presidential campaign unfolded. Despite having suffered a coronary seizure in the fall of 1955 and undergoing an operation for ileitis (an intestinal inflammation) in early 1956, Eisenhower decided to run for reelection. He retained widespread public support, although the Democrats controlled Congress. Meanwhile, new crises in foreign and domestic affairs required him to take decisive action.

A LANDSLIDE FOR IKE   In 1956 the Republican Convention renominated Eisenhower by acclamation and again named Nixon the vice-presidential candidate. The party platform endorsed Eisenhower's "modern Republicanism." The Democrats turned again to Adlai Stevenson, with a platform that revived party issues: less "favoritism" to big business, repeal of the Taft-Hartley Act, increased aid to farmers, and tax relief for those in low-income brackets.

Neither candidate generated much excitement. The Democrats focused their fire on the heir apparent, Richard Nixon, a "man of many masks." Stevenson roused little enthusiasm for two controversial proposals: to replace military conscription with an all-volunteer army and to ban hydrogen-bomb tests by international agreement. Both involved military questions that put Stevenson at a disadvantage by pitting his judgment against that of a successful former general. Voters handed Eisenhower a landslide victory. He lost one border state, Missouri, but in carrying Louisiana became the first Republican to win a Deep South state since Reconstruction; nationally, he carried all but seven states.

CRISIS IN THE MIDDLE EAST   To forestall Soviet penetration in the Middle East, the Eisenhower-Dulles foreign policy cultivated Arab friendship, and in 1955 Dulles had completed his line of alliances across the "northern tier" of the Middle East. Under American sponsorship, Britain had joined Turkey, Iraq, Iran, and Pakistan in the Middle East Treaty Organization (METO), or the Baghdad Pact Organization, as the treaty was commonly called. But after Iraq, the only Arab member, withdrew in 1959, the alliance lost its cohesion and credibility. The Arab states remained aloof from the organization. These were the states of the Arab League (Egypt, Iraq, Jordan, Lebanon, Saudi Arabia, Syria, and Yemen), which had warred on Israel in 1948–1949 and remained committed to its destruction.

The most fateful developments in the Middle East turned on the rise of the Egyptian general Gamal Abdel Nasser, who overthrew King Farouk in 1952. Nasser's nationalist regime soon pressed for the withdrawal of British forces guarding the Suez Canal, the crucial link between the Mediterranean Sea and the Indian Ocean. Eisenhower and Dulles supported Nasser's demand, and in 1954 an Anglo-Egyptian treaty provided for British withdrawal within twenty months. Ownership of the canal remained with the Anglo-French Suez Canal Company, however.

Nasser, like other leaders of the third world, remained unaligned in the cold war and sought to play both sides off against each other. The United States in turn courted Egyptian support by offering a loan to build a huge hydroelectric plant at Aswān on the Nile River. From the outset the administration's proposal

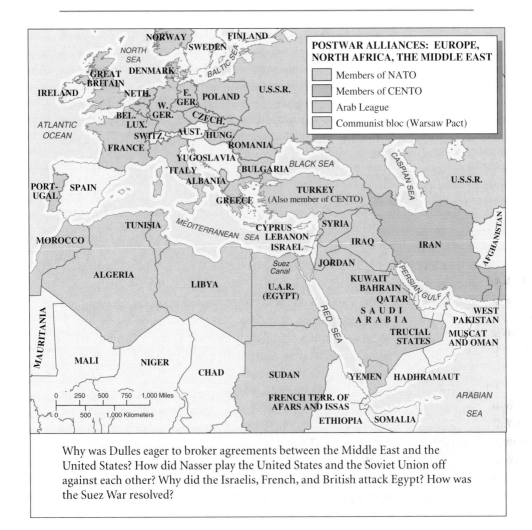

POSTWAR ALLIANCES: EUROPE, NORTH AFRICA, THE MIDDLE EAST

- Members of NATO
- Members of CENTO
- Arab League
- Communist bloc (Warsaw Pact)

Why was Dulles eager to broker agreements between the Middle East and the United States? How did Nasser play the United States and the Soviet Union off against each other? Why did the Israelis, French, and British attack Egypt? How was the Suez War resolved?

was opposed by Jewish constituencies concerned with Egyptian threats to Israel and by southern congressmen who feared the competition from Egyptian cotton. In 1956, when Nasser increased trade with the Soviet bloc and recognized Communist China, Dulles abruptly canceled the loan offer.

The outcome was far from a triumph of American diplomacy. The chief victims, it turned out, were Anglo-French interests in the Suez. Unable to retaliate against the United States, Nasser took control of the Suez Canal Company. The British and the French were furious. While negotiations dragged on, Israeli forces invaded the Gaza Strip and Sinai peninsula. Ostensibly their aim was to root out Arab guerrillas, but actually it was to synchronize with the British and the French, who began bombing Egyptian air bases and occupied Port Said.

The Suez War put the United States in a quandary. Either the administration could support its Western allies and see the troublesome Nasser crushed, or it could defend the UN charter and champion Arab nationalism against imperialist aggression. Eisenhower opted for the latter course, with the unusual result that the Soviet Union sided with the United States. Once the threat of American embargoes had forced the Anglo-French-Israeli to halt their advance against Egypt, the Soviets capitalized on the situation by threatening to use missiles against the Western aggressors. This belated bravado won for the Soviet Union in the Arab world some of the credit actually owed the United States.

REPRESSION IN HUNGARY   In the Soviet Union, Nikita Khrushchev had come out on top in the post-Stalin power struggles. In 1956 Khrushchev had delivered a "secret" speech on the crimes of the Stalin era and had hinted at relaxed policies in neighboring countries. This new policy of "de-Stalinization" put Stalinist leaders in the satellite countries of Eastern Europe on the defensive and emboldened the more independent leaders to take action. Riots in the Polish city of Poznan led to the rise of Wladyslaw Gomulka, a Polish nationalist, as leader of the Polish Communist party. Gomulka managed to win a degree of independence by avoiding an open break with the Soviets.

In Hungary, however, a similar movement got out of hand. On October 23, 1956, fighting broke out in Budapest, followed by the installation of Imre Nagy, a moderate Communist, as head of the government. Again the Soviets seemed content to let de-Stalinization follow its course, and on October 28 they withdrew their forces from Budapest. But Nagy's announcement three days later that Hungary would withdraw from the Warsaw Pact (a military alliance linking the Eastern European countries under Soviet control) brought Soviet tanks back into Budapest. Although Khrushchev was willing to relax relations with the Eastern European satellites, he refused to allow them to break with the Soviet Union or abandon their mutual defense obligations. The Soviets installed a more compliant leader in Hungary, János Kádár, and hauled Nagy off to Moscow, where a firing squad executed him in 1958. It was a tragic ending to an independence movement that at the outset promised the sort of moderation that might have vindicated George Kennan's policy of containment, if not Dulles's notion of liberation.

SPUTNIK   On October 4, 1957, the Soviets launched the first satellite, called *Sputnik*. Americans, until then complacent about their technical superiority, suddenly discovered an apparent "missile gap." If the Soviets were so advanced in rocketry, then perhaps they could hit American cities with missiles. All along Eisenhower had known that the "missile gap" was more illusory than real, but he could not reveal that high-altitude American U-2 spy planes were gathering that information.

Soviet success with *Sputnik* thus frightened the United States, prompting it to increase defense spending, offer NATO allies intermediate-range ballistic missiles pending development of long-range intercontinental ballistic missiles (ICBMs), set up a new agency to coordinate space efforts, and establish a crash program in science education and military research. In 1958 Congress created the National Aeronautics and Space Administration (NASA) to coordinate research and development in the space program. Before the end of the year, NASA had unveiled a program to put a manned craft in orbit, but the first manned U.S. flight, by Commander Alan B. Shepard Jr., did not take place until May 5, 1961. Finally, in 1958 Congress enacted the National Defense Education Act, which authorized federal grants, especially for training in mathematics, science, and modern languages, as well as for student loans and fellowships.

FESTERING PROBLEMS ABROAD

Once the Suez and Hungary crises had faded from the front pages, Eisenhower enjoyed eighteen months of smooth sailing in foreign affairs. Nonetheless, a brief flurry occurred in 1958 over hostile demonstrations in Peru and Venezuela against Vice President Richard Nixon, who was on a goodwill tour of eight Latin American countries. Meanwhile, problems in the Middle East and Europe continued to fester, only to reemerge with new force in 1958. The cold war would again be played out in the Middle East and in Eastern Europe, as well as at America's back door, in Cuba.

THE MIDDLE EAST By 1958 Congress had approved what came to be called the Eisenhower Doctrine, a resolution that promised to extend economic and military aid to Middle East nations and to use armed forces if necessary to assist any such nation against military aggression by Communist country.

Egypt's president Nasser, meanwhile, had emerged from the Suez crisis with heightened prestige, and in 1958 he created the United Arab Republic by (a short-lived) merger with Syria. Then a leftist coup in Iraq, supposedly inspired by Nasser and the Soviets, threw out the pro-Western government there. Lebanon, already unsettled by internal conflict, appealed to the United States for support to fend off a similar fate. Eisenhower immediately ordered 5,000 marines into Lebanon, limiting them to the capital, Beirut, and its airfield. He proposed to go no farther because, he said later, if the government was not strong enough to hold out with such protection, then "we probably should not be there." In October 1958, once the situation had stabilized and the Lebanese factions had reached a compromise, the U.S. forces withdrew.

BERLIN   The problem of Berlin, an island of Western capitalism deep in Soviet-controlled East Germany, continued to fester with little chance of a resolution. Soviet premier Nikita Khrushchev called it a "bone in his throat." West Berlin served as a "showplace" of Western democracy and prosperity in the middle of Communist East Germany, a listening post for Western intelligence gathering, and a funnel through which news and propaganda from the West penetrated what the British leader Winston Churchill had called the iron curtain. Although East Germany had sealed its western frontiers, refugees could still pass from East to West Berlin. On November 10, 1958, however, Khrushchev threatened to give East Germany control of East Berlin and the air lanes into West Berlin. After the deadline he set, May 27, 1959, Western occupation authorities would have to deal with the East German government, in effect recognizing it, or face the possibility of another blockade.

Eisenhower refused to budge from his position on Berlin. At the same time he refused to engage in saber-rattling or even to cancel existing plans to reduce the overall size of the army. Khrushchev, it turned out, was no more eager for confrontation than Eisenhower. Khrushchev's deadline passed almost unnoticed. In September 1959 Khrushchev visited the United States, stopping in New York, Washington D.C., Los Angeles, San Francisco, and Iowa. In talks with Eisenhower, he endorsed "peaceful coexistence," and Eisenhower admitted that the Berlin situation was "abnormal." They agreed to discuss the problem at a summit meeting in the spring.

THE U-2 SUMMIT   The planned summit meeting blew up in Eisenhower's face, however. On May 1, 1960, a Soviet rocket brought down an American U-2 spy plane over the Soviet Union. After a period of international jousting with Khrushchev, Eisenhower took personal responsibility for the incident—an unprecedented action for a head of state—and justified it on grounds of national security. At a summit meeting in Paris five days later, Khrushchev called upon the president to repudiate the U-2 flights, which had been going on for more than three years, and "pass severe judgment on those responsible." When Eisenhower refused, Khrushchev left the meeting.

Fidel Castro

Castro (center) became Cuba's Communist premier in 1959, following years of guerrilla warfare against the Batista regime. He planned a social and agrarian revolution and opposed foreign control of the Cuban economy.

CASTRO'S CUBA Among all of Eisenhower's foreign crises, the greatest thorn in his side was the regime of Fidel Castro, which took power in Cuba on January 1, 1959, after two years of guerrilla warfare against a right-wing dictator. Castro's forces had the support of many Americans who hoped for a new day of democratic government in Cuba. But those hopes were dashed when American television reported unfair trials and summary executions conducted by the victorious leader. When Castro instituted programs of land reform and nationalization of foreign-owned property, relations with the United States worsened. Some observers believed, however, that by rejecting Castro's requests for loans and other help, the U.S. government lost a chance to influence the direction of the Cuban revolution. Some thought, too, that by acting upon the assumption that Communists had the upper hand in his movement, the administration may have ensured that fact.

Castro, on the other hand, eagerly accepted Soviet support. In 1960 he entered a trade agreement to swap Cuban sugar for Soviet oil and machinery. One of Eisenhower's last acts as president, on January 3, 1961, was to suspend diplomatic relations with Cuba. The president also secretly authorized the CIA to begin training a force of Cuban refugees for a new revolution. But the final decision on the use of that force would rest with the next president, John F. Kennedy.

THE EARLY YEARS OF THE CIVIL RIGHTS MOVEMENT

While the cold war had produced a tense stalemate by the mid-1950s, race relations in the United States threatened to destroy the domestic tranquility masking years of injustice. Eisenhower entered office committed to civil rights in principle. During his first three years, public services in Washington, D.C., were desegregated, as were navy yards and veterans' hospitals. Beyond that, however, two aspects of the president's philosophy inhibited vigorous action in enforcing the principle of civil rights: his preference for state or local action over federal involvement and his doubt that laws could change deeply embedded racial attitudes. "I don't believe you can change the hearts of men with laws or decisions," he said. Eisenhower's passive stance meant that leadership in the civil rights field came from the judiciary more than the executive or legislative branch of the government.

In the mid-1930s the NAACP had resolved to test the separate-but-equal doctrine that had upheld racial segregation since the *Plessy* decision in 1896. Charles H. Houston, dean of the Howard University Law School, laid the plans, and his former student Thurgood Marshall served as chief NAACP lawyer. They decided to begin their efforts to integrate society by focusing on higher education. But it took almost fifteen years to persuade the courts that segregated schooling must end. In *Sweatt v. Painter* (1950), the Supreme Court ruled that a separate black law school in Texas was not equal in quality to the state's whites-only schools. The Court ordered the state to remedy the situation.

THE *BROWN* DECISION   By the early 1950s challenges to state laws mandating segregation in the public schools were rising through the appellate courts. Five such cases, from Kansas, Delaware, South Carolina, Virgina, and the District of Columbia—usually cited by reference to the first, *Brown v. Board of Education of Topeka, Kansas*—came to the Supreme Court for joint argument by NAACP attorneys in 1952. Chief Justice Earl Warren wrote the opinion, handed down on May 17, 1954, in which a unanimous Court declared that "in the field of public education the doctrine of 'separate but equal' has no place." In support of its opinion, the Court cited sociological and psychological findings, demonstrating that even if separate facilities were

Civil Rights Stirrings

In the late 1930s the NAACP began to test the constitutionality of racial segregation.

equal in quality, the mere fact of separating people by race engendered feelings of inferiority. A year later, after further argument, the Court directed that the process of racial integration should move "with all deliberate speed."

But Eisenhower refused to force states to comply with the Court's decisions. Privately he maintained "that the Supreme Court decision *set back progress in the South at least fifteen years.* The fellow who tries to tell me you can do these things by *force* is just plain *nuts."* While token integration began as early as 1954 in the border states, hostility mounted in the Deep South and Virginia, led by the newly formed Citizens' Councils. The Citizens' Councils were middle- and upper-class versions of the Ku Klux Klan that spread quickly across the region and eventually included 250,000 members. Instead of physical violence and intimidation, the Councils used economic coercion to discipline blacks who crossed racial boundaries. African Americans who defied white supremacy would lose their jobs, have their insurance policies canceled, or be denied personal loans or home mortgages. The Citizens' Councils grew so powerful in many communities that membership became almost a prerequisite for an aspiring white politician.

Before the end of 1955, opponents of court-ordered interaction grew dangerously belligerent. Virginia senator Harry F. Byrd supplied a rallying cry: "Massive Resistance." In 1956, 101 members of Congress signed a "Southern Manifesto" denouncing the Court's decision in the *Brown* case as "a clear abuse of judicial power." In six southern states at the end of 1956, not a single black child attended school with whites.

THE MONTGOMERY BUS BOYCOTT   The essential role played by the NAACP and the courts in providing a legal lever for the civil rights movement often overshadows the courageous contributions of individual African Americans who took great personal risks to challenge segregation. In Montgomery, Alabama, for example, on December 1, 1955, Rosa Parks, a black seamstress committed to gaining equal rights, was arrested for refusing to give up her seat on a city bus to a white man. As was the case in many southern communities, Montgomery had a local ordinance that required blacks to give up their bus or train seat to a white when asked. The next night black community leaders met in the Dexter Avenue Baptist Church to organize a massive bus boycott.

In Dexter Avenue's twenty-six-year-old pastor, Martin Luther King Jr., the movement found a charismatic leader. Born in Atlanta, the grandson of a slave and the son of a minister, King possessed intelligence, courage, and eloquence. After graduating from Morehouse College in Atlanta, he attended divinity school and earned a doctorate in philosophy from Boston University before accepting a call to preach in Montgomery. He inspired the civil-rights movement with a compelling call for nonviolent disobedience based upon the Gospels, the writings of Henry David Thoreau, and the example of Mahatma Gandhi in India. To his antagonists he said, "We will soon wear you down by our capacity to suffer, and in winning our freedom we will so appeal to your heart and conscience that we will win you in the process."

The Montgomery bus boycott achieved a remarkable solidarity. For months, blacks formed carpools, hitchhiked, or simply walked. But the white civic leaders held out against the boycott and against the pleas of a bus company tired of losing money. The boycotters finally won a federal case they had initiated against bus segregation, and in 1956 the Supreme Court affirmed that "the separate but equal doctrine can no longer be safely followed as a correct statement of the law." The next day, King and other African Americans boarded the buses.

To keep alive the spirit of the boycott, King and a group of associates in 1957 organized the Southern Christian Leadership Conference. Several days later King found an unexploded dynamite bomb on his front porch. Two hours later he addressed his congregation:

I'm not afraid of anybody this morning. Tell Montgomery they can keep shooting and I'm going to stand up to them; tell Montgomery they can keep bombing and I'm going to stand up to them. If I had to die tomorrow morning I would die happy because I've been to the mountain top and I've seen the promised land and it's going to be here in Montgomery.

Montgomery, Alabama

Martin Luther King Jr., here facing arrest for leading a civil rights march, advocated nonviolent resistance to racial segregation.

THE CIVIL RIGHTS ACT Despite President Eisenhower's reluctance to take the lead in desegregating schools, he supported the right of African Americans to vote. In 1956, hoping to exploit divisions between northern and southern Democrats and to reclaim some of the black vote for the Republicans, Eisenhower proposed legislation that became the Civil Rights Act of 1957, the first civil rights law passed since Reconstruction. It finally got through the Senate, after a year's delay, with the help of majority leader Lyndon B. Johnson, a Texas Democrat who won southern acceptance by watering it down. The Civil Rights Act established the Civil Rights Commission and a new Civil Rights Division in the Justice Department, which could seek injunctions to prevent interference with the right to vote. Yet by 1959 the Civil Rights Act had not added a single southern black to the voting rolls. Neither did the Civil Rights Act of 1960, which provided for federal court referees to register African Americans where a court found a "pattern and practice" of discrimination. This act, too, lacked teeth and depended upon vigorous presidential enforcement to achieve any real results.

DESEGREGATION IN LITTLE ROCK A few weeks after passage of the Civil Rights Act of 1957, Arkansas governor Orval Faubus called out the

National Guard to prevent nine African-American students from entering Little Rock's Central High School under a federal court order. A conference between the president and the governor proved fruitless, but on court order Governor Faubus withdrew the National Guard. When the students tried to enter the school, a hysterical white mob forced local authorities to remove them. At that point, Eisenhower, who had said two months before that he could not "imagine any set of circumstances that would ever induce me to send federal troops," ordered 1,000 paratroopers to Little Rock to protect the black students, and he placed the National Guard on federal service. The soldiers stayed through the school year.

In the summer of 1958, Faubus decided to close the high schools of Little Rock rather than allow integration, and court proceedings dragged on into 1959 before the schools could be reopened. In that year massive resistance to integration in Virginia collapsed when both state and federal courts struck down state laws that had cut off funds to integrated schools. Thereafter, "massive resistance" for the most part was confined to the Deep South, where five states—from South Carolina west through Louisiana—still opposed even token integration.

ASSESSING THE EISENHOWER YEARS

Dwight Eisenhower entered office in 1953 after being elected in a landslide and held high approval ratings for ending the Korean War and his strong handling of foreign crises. He won a second landslide election in 1956. Yet support for the president did not translate into support for his party. Eisenhower's decisive win failed to swing a congressional majority for Republicans in either house, leaving the country in the hands of a Republican president and a Democratic Congress. Eisenhower was thus the first president to face three successive Congresses controlled by the opposition party. This meant that he could manage few initiatives in domestic policy, although he did oversee the admission of the first states that are not contiguous to the continental forty-eight: Alaska became the forty-ninth state on January 3, 1959, and Hawaii became the fiftieth on August 21, 1959.

During Eisenhower's second term the country experienced an economic slump, a drop in tax revenues, and a large federal deficit. The country also suffered the embarrassments of the U-2 spy-plane incident and Cuba's falling into the Communist orbit. Emotional issues such as civil rights, defense policy, and corrupt aides compounded Eisenhower's troubles. The president's reluctance to enforce civil rights rulings and his unwillingness to speak out on behalf of racial equality undermined his efforts to promote the general welfare. One observer called the Eisenhower years "the time of the great postponement," during which the president left domestic and foreign policies "about where he found them in 1953."

Yet opinion of Eisenhower's presidency has improved with time. Even critics now grant that Eisenhower succeeded in ending the war in Korea and settling the dust raised by Senator Joseph McCarthy. Although Eisenhower failed to end the cold war and in fact institutionalized global confrontation, he did sense the limits of American power and kept its application to low-risk situations. He also tried to restrain the arms race. Although he took few initiatives in addressing social and racial issues, he did sustain the major innovations of the New Deal. Although he tolerated unemployment of as much as 7 percent, he saw to it that inflation remained minimal during his two terms.

Eisenhower's January 17, 1961, farewell address to the American people showed his remarkable foresight in his own area of expertise, the military. He highlighted, perhaps better than anyone else could have, the dangers of a huge military establishment in a time of peace: "In the councils of government we must guard against the acquisition of unwarranted influence, whether sought or unsought, by the military-industrial complex. The potential for the disastrous rise of misplaced power exists and will persist." Eisenhower confessed that his great disappointment was that he could affirm only that "war has been avoided," not that "a lasting peace is in sight."

MAKING CONNECTIONS

- The civil rights movement of the 1950s aimed to achieve the racial integration of public services and equal access to political rights. This struggle would continue into the 1960s and then move in several new directions, as discussed in Chapter 34.

- American involvement in Vietnam grew in the 1950s but remained limited to an advisory role. Escalation to an active fighting role came under Lyndon Johnson in 1965, a topic also covered in Chapter 34.

- Eisenhower's hands-off approach to the presidency was reminiscent of the Gilded Age presidencies and those of the 1920s. See Chapters 18, 22, and 27.

FURTHER READING

Scholarship on the Eisenhower years is extensive. A carefully balanced overview of the period is Chester J. Pach Jr. and Elmo Richardson's *The Presidency of Dwight D. Eisenhower,* rev. ed. (1991). For the manner in which Eisenhower conducted foreign policy, see Robert A. Divine's *Eisenhower and the Cold War* (1981). Tom Wicker deems Eisenhower a better person than a president in *Dwight D. Eisenhower* (2002).

For the buildup of American involvement in Indochina, consult Lloyd C. Gardner's *Approaching Vietnam: From World War II through Dien Bien Phu, 1941–1954* (1988) and David L. Anderson's *Trapped by Success: The Eisenhower Administration and Vietnam, 1953–1961* (1991). How the Eisenhower Doctrine came to be implemented is traced in Stephen E. Ambrose and Douglas G. Brinkley's *Rise to Globalism: American Foreign Policy since 1938,* 8th ed. (1997).

The impact of the Supreme Court during the 1950s is the focus of Archibald Cox's *The Warren Court: Constitutional Decision as an Instrument of Reform* (1968). A masterful study of the important Warren Court decision on school desegregation is James T. Patterson's *Brown v. Board of Education: A Civil Rights Milestone and Its Troubled Legacy* (2001).

For the story of the early years of the civil rights movement, see Taylor Branch's *Parting the Waters: America in the King Years, 1954–1963* (1988) and Robert Weisbrot's *Freedom Bound: A History of America's Civil Rights Movement* (1990).

34

NEW FRONTIERS: POLITICS AND SOCIAL CHANGE IN THE 1960s

FOCUS QUESTIONS

- What were the goals of Kennedy's New Frontier and Johnson's Great Society?
- What were the achievements of the civil rights movement and the ensuing splinter movements?
- What factors led to America's growing involvement in Vietnam and the rising opposition to it?
- How did Kennedy try to combat communism in Cuba?

To answer these questions and access additional review material, please visit www.wwnorton.com/studyspace.

For those pundits who considered the social and political climate of the 1950s dull, the following decade would provide a striking contrast. The 1960s were years of extraordinary turbulence and innovation in public affairs—as well as tragedy and trauma. Many social ills that had been simmering for decades suddenly forced their way onto the national agenda. At the same time the deeply entrenched assumptions of cold war ideology led the country into the longest, most controversial, and least successful war in its history.

The New Frontier

KENNEDY VERSUS NIXON   In 1960 there was little sense of dramatic change on the horizon. The presidential election that year featured two candidates—Richard M. Nixon and John F. Kennedy—who initially symbolized the bland politics of the 1950s. Though better known than Kennedy because of his eight years as Eisenhower's vice president, Nixon had developed the reputation of a cunning chameleon, the Tricky Dick who concealed his duplicity behind a series of masks.

Nixon possessed great ability, however, as well as tenacious energy and a compulsive love for politics, the more combative the better. Born in suburban Los Angeles in 1913, he grew up in a Quaker family that struggled to make ends meet. After law school and military service in the Pacific during World War II, Nixon jumped into the political arena in 1946 as a Republican and surprised observers by unseating a popular congressman in southern California. He arrived in Washington eager to reverse the tide of New Deal liberalism. Four years later he won election to the Senate. In his campaigns, Nixon unleashed scurrilous personal attacks on his opponents, shrewdly manipulating the growing anti-Communist hysteria. Yet Nixon became a respected, effective legislator, and by 1950 he was the most requested Republican speaker in the country. His rapid rise to political stardom led to his being offered the vice-presidential nomination in 1952 and 1956. He was an active, highly visible vice president.

Kennedy lacked such experience and exposure. He boasted an abundance of assets, including a widely publicized record of heroism in World War II, a glamorous young wife, a Harvard education, and a large, wealthy family. Yet the handsome forty-three-year-old candidate lacked national prominence and political distinction. Kennedy's record in the Senate was mediocre.

During his campaign for the Democratic nomination, however, Kennedy had shown that he had energy, grace, and ambition. As the first Catholic to run for the presidency since Al Smith in 1928, he strove to dispel the impression that his religion was a major political liability. In his acceptance speech at the Democratic Convention, Kennedy found the stirring rhetoric that would stamp the rest of his campaign and his presidency: "We stand today on the edge of a New Frontier—the frontier of unknown opportunities and perils—a frontier of unfulfilled hopes and threats."

The turning point in the presidential campaign came when Richard Nixon agreed to debate his less prominent opponent on television. During the first of four debates, some 70 million viewers saw Nixon, still weak from a recent illness, perspiring heavily and looking haggard, uneasy, and even

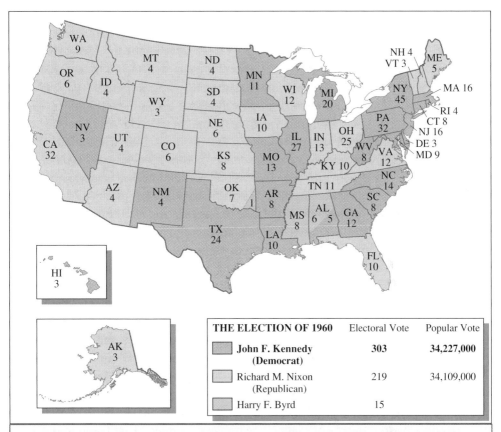

THE ELECTION OF 1960

	Electoral Vote	Popular Vote
John F. Kennedy (Democrat)	303	34,227,000
Richard M. Nixon (Republican)	219	34,109,000
Harry F. Byrd	15	

How did the election of 1960 represent a sea change in American presidential politics? What three events shaped the campaign? How did Kennedy win the election in spite of winning fewer states than Nixon?

sinister before the camera. Kennedy, on the other hand, projected a cool poise that made him seem equal, if not superior, in his fitness for the office. Kennedy's popularity immediately shot up in the polls.

When the votes were counted, Kennedy and his running-mate, Lyndon Johnson of Texas, had won the closest presidential election since 1888. The winning margin was only 118,574 votes out of the 68 million cast. Kennedy's wide lead in the electoral vote, 303 to 219, belied the paper-thin margin in several key states.

THE NEW ADMINISTRATION   John F. Kennedy was the youngest person ever elected president, and his cabinet appointments highlighted youth. He sought to attract the "best and the brightest" minds, men who would inject a tough, dispassionate, pragmatic, and vigorous outlook into government affairs. To that end he asked Robert McNamara, one of the whiz kids who had reorganized the Ford Motor Company, to bring his managerial magic to bear on the Department of Defense. Kennedy appointed Harvard professor McGeorge Bundy, whom he called "the second smartest man I know," as special assistant for national security affairs and chose as his secretary of state Dean Rusk, a career diplomat and former Rhodes scholar. When critics attacked the appointment of Kennedy's thirty-five-year-old brother Robert as attorney general, the president quipped, "I don't see what's wrong with giving Bobby a little experience before he goes into law practice."

The inaugural ceremonies set the tone of elegance and youthful vigor that would come to be called the Kennedy style. After the poet Robert Frost paid tribute to the administration in verse, Kennedy dazzled listeners with his uplifting rhetoric. "Let every nation know," he proclaimed, ". . . that we shall pay any price, bear any burden, meet any hardship, support any friend, oppose any foe, to assure the survival and success of liberty. And so, my fellow Americans: ask not what your country can do for you—ask what you can do for your country." Spines tingled; the glittering atmosphere and inspiring language of the inauguration seemed to herald an era of fresh promise and youthful energy.

THE KENNEDY RECORD   Despite his idealistic rhetoric, however, Kennedy had a difficult time launching his New Frontier domestic program. Elected by a razor-thin margin, he did not have a popular mandate. Nor did he show much skill in dealing with a Democratic majority in a Congress controlled by conservative southerners. Congress blocked his efforts to increase federal aid to education, provide health insurance for the aged, and create a Department of Urban Affairs.

Administration proposals did nevertheless win some notable victories in Congress. They included a new Housing Act that appropriated nearly $5 billion for urban renewal over four years, an increase in the minimum wage, and enhanced Social Security benefits. Just two months into his administration, Kennedy launched the celebrated Peace Corps to supply volunteers for educational and technical service in underdeveloped countries. Kennedy also won support for an accelerated program to land astronauts on the moon before the end of the decade. Congress readily approved a series of broad foreign-aid programs to help Latin American nations, dubbed the Alliance for Progress. Another important initiative was a bold tax-reduction bill intended to accelerate economic growth. Passed in 1964, after Kennedy's death, it

Kennedy versus Nixon

John Kennedy's poise and precision in the debates with Richard Nixon impressed viewers and voters.

provided a surprisingly potent boost to the economy. Perhaps Kennedy's most significant legislative accomplishment was the Trade Expansion Act of 1962, which eventually led to tariff cuts averaging 35 percent on goods traded between the United States and the European Economic Community (the Common Market).

THE WARREN COURT   Under Chief Justice Earl Warren the Supreme Court continued to be a decisive influence on domestic life during the 1960s. In *Gideon v. Wainwright* (1963), the Court required that every felony defendant be provided a lawyer regardless of the defendant's ability to pay. In 1964 the Court ruled in *Escobedo v. Illinois* that a person accused of a crime must also be allowed to consult a lawyer before being interrogated by police. Two years later, in *Miranda v. Arizona,* the Court issued perhaps its most bitterly criticized ruling when it ordered that an accused person in police custody be informed of certain basic rights: the right to remain silent; the right to know that anything said can be used against the individual in court; and the right to have a defense attorney present during interrogation. In addition, the Court established rules for police to follow in informing suspects of their legal rights before questioning could begin.

Expansion of the Civil Rights Movement

The most important developments in domestic life during the 1960s occurred in civil rights. John F. Kennedy was initially reluctant to challenge conservative southern Democrats on the race issue. He also was never as personally committed to civil rights as his brother Robert, the attorney general. Despite a few dramatic gestures of support for African-American leaders, President Kennedy only belatedly grasped the moral and emotional significance of what would become the most widespread reform movement of the decade. Eventually, however, his conscience was pricked by the grassroots civil rights movement led by Martin Luther King Jr., a movement that would profoundly change the contours of American life.

SIT-INS AND FREEDOM RIDES   After the Montgomery bus boycott of 1955–1956, King's philosophy of "militant nonviolence" inspired thousands to challenge segregation and discrimination with direct action. At the same time, lawsuits to desegregate the schools activated thousands of parents and young people. The momentum generated a genuine mass movement when four black college students courageously sat down and demanded service at a "whites-only" Woolworth's lunch counter in Greensboro, North Carolina, on February 1, 1960. Within a week the "sit-in" movement had spread to six more towns in the state, and within two months demonstrations had occurred in fifty-four cities in nine states.

In 1960 student activists, black and white, formed the Student Nonviolent Coordinating Committee (SNCC), which worked with King's Southern Christian Leadership Conference to spread the civil rights movement. The sit-ins became "kneel-ins" at churches and "wade-ins" at segregated public swimming pools. During the year after the Greensboro sit-ins, over 3,600 black and white activists spent time in jail. In many communities they were struck with clubs, poked with cattle prods, pelted with rocks, burned with cigarettes, and subjected to unending verbal abuse. Nonetheless, the protesters refused to retaliate.

In May 1961 the Congress of Racial Equality sent a group of black and white "freedom riders" on buses to test a federal ruling that had banned segregation on buses and trains and in their depots. In Alabama, mobs attacked the young travelers with fists and pipes, burned one of the buses, and assaulted Justice Department observers, but the demonstrators persisted, drawing national attention and generating new support for their cause. Yet President Kennedy was not inspired by the courageous freedom riders. Preoccupied with the Berlin crisis, he ordered an aide to tell them to "call it off."

Former president Harry Truman called the bus activists northern "busybodies." It fell to Attorney General Robert Kennedy to use federal marshals to protect the freedom riders during the summer of 1961.

FEDERAL INTERVENTION   In 1962 Governor Ross Barnett of Mississippi, a rabid racist who believed that God made "the Negro different to punish him," defied a court order and refused to allow James Meredith, an African-American student, to enroll at the University of Mississippi. Attorney General Robert Kennedy intervened again, but a violent white mob prevented the federal marshals he dispatched from enforcing the law. Federal troops had to intervene, and Meredith was registered at Ole Miss, but only after two deaths and many injuries.

Everywhere, it seemed, African-American activists and white supporters were challenging deeply entrenched patterns of segregation and prejudice. In 1963 Martin Luther King launched a series of demonstrations in Birmingham, Alabama, where Police Commissioner Eugene "Bull" Connor proved the perfect foil for King's tactic of nonviolent civil disobedience. Connor's policemen used dogs, tear gas, electric cattle prods, and fire hoses

Birmingham, Alabama, May 1963

Eugene "Bull" Connor's police unleash dogs on civil rights demonstrators.

on the protesters while millions of outraged Americans watched the confrontations on television.

King, who was arrested and jailed during the demonstrations, wrote his now-famous Letter from a Birmingham City Jail, a stirring defense of his nonviolent strategy that became a classic of the civil rights movement. "One who breaks an unjust law," he stressed, "must do so openly, lovingly, and with a willingness to accept the penalty." In his letter, King signaled a shift in his strategy for social change. Heretofore he had emphasized the need to educate southern whites about the injustice of segregation and other patterns of discrimination. Now he focused more on gaining federal enforcement of the law and new legislation by provoking racists to display their violent hatred in public.

Southern traditionalists defied efforts to promote racial integration. In 1963 Governor George Wallace dramatically stood in the doorway of a building at the University of Alabama to block the enrollment of African-American students, but he stepped aside in the face of insistent federal marshals. Later that night NAACP official Medgar Evers was shot to death as he returned to his home in Jackson, Mississippi.

The high point of the integrationist phase of the civil rights movement occurred on August 28, 1963, when over 200,000 blacks and whites marched down the Mall in Washington, D.C., toward the Lincoln Memorial, singing "We Shall Overcome." The March on Washington for Jobs and Freedom was the largest civil rights demonstration in American history. Standing in front of Lincoln's statue, Martin Luther King delivered one of the century's memorable speeches: "Even though we face the difficulties of today and tomorrow, I still have a dream. It is a dream chiefly rooted in the American dream . . . one day . . . the sons of former slaves and the sons of former slave-owners will be able to sit together at the table of brotherhood." Such racial harmony had not yet arrived, however. Two weeks later a bomb exploded in a Birmingham church, killing four African-American girls who had arrived early for Sunday school.

Yet King's dream—shared and promoted by thousands of other activists—survived. The intransigence and violence that civil rights workers encountered won converts to their cause across the country and forced whites nationwide to confront the myths of their own virtue and innocence with the brutal facts of racial hatred. Persuaded by his brother Robert, a man of greater conviction, compassion, and vision, and by the pressure of events, President Kennedy finally decided that enforcement of existing statutes was not enough; new legislation was needed to deal with the race question. In 1963 he told the nation that racial discrimination "has no place in American life or law," and he endorsed an ambitious civil rights bill intended to end

"I Have a Dream," August 28, 1963

Protesters in the March on Washington make their way to the Lincoln Memorial, where Martin Luther King Jr. delivered his now-famous speech.

discrimination in public facilities, desegregate public schools, and protect black voters. Southern conservatives, however, quickly blocked the bill in Congress. The backlash that had surfaced in the South in the 1930s in response to the expansion of Franklin Roosevelt's New Deal continued to shape Democratic politics in the region.

Although Kennedy saw his support among southern voters plummet, he remained committed to the bill. As he told Martin Luther King: "This is a very serious fight. We're in this up to the neck. The worst trouble would be to lose the fight in Congress. . . . A good many programs I care about may go down the drain as a result of this [bill]—We may all go down the drain . . . so we are putting a lot on the line."

FOREIGN FRONTIERS

EARLY SETBACKS   John F. Kennedy's record in foreign affairs was mixed, more spectacularly so than his domestic record. Upon taking office, he discovered that there was in the works a secret CIA operation designed to prepare 1,500 anti-Castro Cubans for an invasion of their homeland. The Joint Chiefs of Staff endorsed the plan; analysts reported that the invasion would inspire Cubans on the island to rebel against Castro. But the scheme, poorly conceived and poorly executed, had little chance of succeeding. When the invasion force landed at Cuba's Bay of Pigs on April 17, 1961, it was brutally subdued in two days, and over 1,000 men were captured.

Two months after the Bay of Pigs disaster, Kennedy met Soviet premier Nikita Khrushchev in Vienna. The volatile Khrushchev tried to bully the inexperienced Kennedy. He threatened to limit Western access to Berlin, the divided city located 100 miles within Communist East Germany. Kennedy was shaken by the aggressive Soviet stand. Upon his return home he demonstrated his resolve by mobilizing army reserve and national guard units. The Soviets responded by erecting the Berlin Wall, cutting off movement between East and West Berlin.

THE CUBAN MISSILE CRISIS   A year later, in the fall of 1962, Khrushchev and the Soviets posed another serious challenge, this time just ninety miles south of Florida. Khrushchev granted Fidel Castro's request for nuclear missiles in Cuba to protect the island from future American-sponsored invasions and to redress the strategic imbalance caused by the presence of U.S. missiles in Turkey aimed at the Soviet Union. While such missiles would hardly alter the worldwide military balance, they would be placed in areas not covered by American radar systems and, if launched, would go undetected, arriving without warning. More important to Kennedy was the psychological effect of American acquiescence to a Soviet presence on its doorstep. Khrushchev's apparent purpose was to demonstrate his toughness to both Chinese and Soviet critics of his earlier advocacy of peaceful coexistence. But he misjudged the American response.

On October 14, 1962, U.S. intelligence flights discovered Soviet missile sites under construction in Cuba. Although the Soviet actions violated no law or treaty, the administration immediately decided that the missiles had to be removed; the only question was how. In a series of secret meetings, the Executive Committee of the National Security Council debated whether to launch a "surgical" air strike or a naval blockade of Cuba. President Kennedy wisely opted for a blockade, but since that would technically represent an act of war, it was called a *quarantine*. It offered the advantage of forcing the Soviets to shoot first, if matters came to that, and it left open options of stronger action. Monday, October 22, began the most perilous week in world history. On that day the president announced the discovery of the missile sites in Cuba and the U.S. naval quarantine of the island nation.

Tensions grew as Khrushchev blustered that Kennedy had pushed humankind "to the abyss of a world nuclear-missile war." Soviet ships, he declared, would ignore the quarantine. But on Wednesday, October 24, five Soviet supply ships stopped short of the American ships. Two days later the Soviets offered to withdraw the missiles in return for a public pledge by the United States not to invade Cuba.

In the aftermath of the crisis, the United States took several symbolic steps to relax tensions: an agreement to sell surplus wheat to the Soviets, the installation of a "hot-line" telephone between Washington and Moscow to provide instant contact between the heads of government, and the removal of obsolete American missiles from Turkey, Italy, and Britain. The United States also negotiated a treaty with Soviet and British representatives to end nuclear testing in the atmosphere. The treaty, ratified in September 1963, was an important move toward greater international cooperation on nuclear proliferation.

KENNEDY AND VIETNAM   As tensions with the Soviet Union were easing, a crisis was developing in Southeast Asia. Events there would lead to the greatest American foreign-policy debacle of the century. During John Kennedy's "thousand days" in office, the turmoil of Indochina never preoccupied public attention for any extended period, but it dominated international diplomatic debates from the time the administration entered office.

In South Vietnam Premier Ngo Dinh Diem had failed to deliver promised social and economic reforms. His repressive tactics, directed not only against Communists but also against the Buddhist majority and other critics, played into the hands of his enemies. In 1961 White House assistant Walt Rostow and General Maxwell Taylor, the first in a long line of presidential emissaries to South Vietnam's capital, Saigon, proposed a major increase in the U.S. military presence, but Kennedy instead dispatched more military "advisers." When he took office, there had been 2,000 U.S. troops in South Vietnam; by the end of 1963, there were 16,000, none of whom had been officially committed to battle.

But the American-supported Diem regime continued to be its own worst enemy. By mid-1963 growing Buddhist demonstrations against Diem ignited the public discontent in South Vietnam and created consternation abroad. The spectacle of Buddhist monks setting themselves on fire on Saigon streets in protest of Diem's iron-fisted rule shocked Americans but brought from the Diem regime only a sarcastic comment by the premier's sister-in-law about "barbecued monks."

By the fall of 1963, the Kennedy administration had decided that Diem was a lost cause. When dissident Vietnamese generals proposed a coup d'état, the

U.S. ambassador assured them that the Kennedy administration would not stand in the way. On November 1 the insurgent military leaders seized the government and murdered Diem. Yet the generals provided no more stability than had earlier regimes, and successive coups set South Vietnam's government spinning from one military leader to another.

KENNEDY'S ASSASSINATION   By the fall of 1963, President Kennedy seemed to recognize the intractability of the situation in Vietnam. Some of his aides later argued that Kennedy would never have allowed a dramatic escalation of U.S. military involvement in Vietnam. Others strongly disagreed. The question is endless because it is unanswerable, and it is unanswerable because on November 22, 1963, while visiting Dallas, Texas, Kennedy was shot twice in the throat and head and died almost immediately. A few hours later Dallas police arrested Lee Harvey Oswald, a twenty-four-year-old ex-marine drifter who had worked in the Texas School Book Depository, from which the shots had been fired at Kennedy. Yet before Oswald could be thoroughly interrogated, he, too, was killed. Two days after his arrest, as television cameras covered his transfer to another jail, Jack Ruby, a Dallas nightclub owner, stepped from the crowd of onlookers and fatally shot Oswald in the abdomen.

Oswald's death ignited a controversy over the assassination that still simmers. In December 1963 President Johnson appointed a commission to investigate Kennedy's murder. Headed by Chief Justice Earl Warren, it concluded that Oswald had acted alone. Yet many people were (and are) not convinced, and since 1963 dozens of conspiracy theories have been proposed. Some blame the CIA or the Mafia; others point at Fidel Castro, whom the CIA had once tried to assassinate. Still others insist that Cuban exiles in Miami, angered by Kennedy's failure to rescue their comrades during the Bay of Pigs fiasco, were behind the assassination. Whatever the actual story of the assassination, Kennedy's tragic death enshrined him in the public imagination as a martyred leader cut down in the prime of his career.

Lyndon Johnson and the Great Society

Lyndon Johnson took the presidential oath of office on board the plane that brought John F. Kennedy's body back to Washington from Dallas. Fifty-five years old, Johnson had spent twenty-six years on the Washington scene and had served nearly a decade as Senate Democratic leader, where he had displayed the greatest gift for compromise since Henry Clay. Johnson brought to the White House a marked change of style from his predecessor.

A self-made and self-centered man, he had used gritty determination and shrewd manipulation to work his way out of a hardscrabble rural Texas homeland to become one of Washington's most powerful figures. He had none of Kennedy's elegance. He was a bundle of conflicting elements: earthy, idealistic, domineering, insecure, gregarious, ruthless, and compassionate. His ego was as huge as his ambition.

Those who viewed Johnson as a stereotypical southern conservative ignored his long-standing admiration for Franklin Roosevelt, the depth of his concern for the poor, and his heartfelt commitment to the cause of civil rights. Though a novice in foreign affairs in the domestic arena during the 1950s, Johnson had been unsurpassed in his ability to shepherd legislation through the gauntlet of special-interest lobbyists and Congress. He had once bragged that "Ike couldn't pass the Lord's Prayer in Congress without me." Johnson wanted to be the greatest president, the one who did the most good for the most people. And he would let nothing stand in the way of his grand ambition. He ended up promising far more than he could accomplish, raising false hopes and stoking fiery resentments.

POLITICS AND POVERTY

Domestic policy was Johnson's first priority. He exploited the nation's grief after the assassination by declaring that Kennedy's legislative program, stymied in congressional committees, would be passed. Johnson loved the political infighting and legislative detail that Kennedy had loathed. The logjam in Congress that had blocked Kennedy's program broke under Johnson's forceful leadership, and a torrent of legislation poured through. At the top of Johnson's agenda were the stalled measures for tax reduction and civil rights. In 1962 Kennedy had announced an unusual plan to jump-start the sluggish economy: a tax cut designed to stimulate consumer spending.

The Johnson Treatment

Lyndon Johnson used powerful body language to intimidate and manipulate anyone who dared disagree with him.

Congressional Republicans opposed the idea because it would increase the federal budget deficit. And polls showed that public opinion was also skeptical. So Kennedy postponed the proposed tax cut for a year; it was still bogged down in Congress when the president was assassinated. Johnson broke the logjam, and the Revenue Act of 1964 provided a needed boost to the economy.

Likewise, the Civil Rights Act that Kennedy had presented to Congress in 1963 was brought to fruition in 1964 by Johnson's forceful leadership. The bill prohibited racial segregation in public facilities such as bus terminals, restaurants, theaters, and hotels. And it outlawed long-standing racial discrimination in the registration of voters and the hiring of employees. President Johnson revived bipartisan efforts on its behalf, and the bill passed the House in February 1964. In the Senate, however, southern legislators launched a filibuster that lasted two months. Johnson finally prevailed, and the civil rights bill became law on July 2. But the new president knew it had come at a political price. On the night after signing it, Johnson told an aide that "we have just delivered the South to the Republican Party for a long time to come."

In addition to fulfilling Kennedy's major promises, Johnson launched an ambitious legislative program of his own. In his 1964 State of the Union address, he added to his must-do list a bold new idea that bore the Johnson brand: "This Administration today, here and now, declares unconditional war on poverty in America." The particulars of this "war on poverty" were to come later, the product of a task force at work before Johnson took office.

Americans had rediscovered poverty in 1962, when the social critic Michael Harrington published a powerful exposé titled *The Other America.* Harrington argued that more than 40 million people were mired in a "culture of poverty." Unlike the upwardly mobile immigrant poor at the turn of the century, the modern poor were impervious to hope. President Kennedy had learned of *The Other America* in 1963 and asked his advisers to investigate the problem and suggest solutions. Upon taking office, Lyndon Johnson announced that he wanted an anti-poverty package that was "big and bold, that would hit the nation with real impact." Money for the program would come from the economic growth expected from the tax reduction of more than $10 billion that had passed in 1964.

The administration's war on poverty was embodied in an economic-opportunity bill that incorporated a wide range of programs: a Job Corps for inner-city youths, a Head Start program for disadvantaged preschoolers, work-study programs for college students, grants to farmers and rural businesses, loans to employers willing to hire the chronically unemployed, the Volunteers in Service to America (a domestic Peace Corps), and the Community Action Program, which would provide "maximum feasible participation" of the poor in directing neighborhood programs designed for their benefit. Speaking at Ann Arbor, Michigan, Johnson called for a "Great Society" resting on "abundance and liberty for all. The Great Society demands an end to poverty and racial injustice, to which we are fully committed in our time." In theory it was liberalism triumphant; in practice its considerable achievements were accompanied by administrative bungling, corruption, and misguided idealism.

THE ELECTION OF 1964 As the 1964 election approached, Johnson was conceded the Democratic nomination from the start. He chose as his running mate Hubert H. Humphrey of Minnesota, the prominent liberal senator with the seemingly permanent smile and inexhaustible supply of optimism and energy.

The Republicans, meeting in San Francisco, were determined to offer an alternative to Johnson's liberalism. By 1960 Arizona senator Barry Goldwater, a millionaire department-store owner, had emerged as the leader of the party's conservative wing. A movement to nominate Goldwater had begun as early as 1961, mobilizing conservative activists to capture party caucuses and contest primaries. In 1964 they took an early lead, and Goldwater swept the all-important California primary. Thus his forces controlled the Republican Convention.

Goldwater displayed an unusual gift for frightening voters. Accusing the administration of waging a "no-win" war in Vietnam, he urged wholesale bombing of North Vietnam and left the impression of being trigger-happy. He also savaged Johnson's war on poverty and the New Deal tradition. At times he was foolishly candid. In Tennessee he proposed the sale of the Tennessee Valley Authority; in St. Petersburg, Florida, a major retirement community, he questioned the value of Social Security. He had voted against both the nuclear test ban and the 1964 Civil Rights Act. Republican campaign buttons claimed, "In your heart, you know he's right." Democrats responded, "In your guts, you know he's nuts."

Johnson, on the other hand, appealed to the middle of the political spectrum. In contrast to Goldwater's bellicose rhetoric on Vietnam, he made a pledge that won great applause at the time and much comment later: "We are not about to send American boys nine or ten thousand miles from home to do what Asian boys ought to be doing for themselves."

The election was a landslide. Johnson polled 61 percent of the total vote; Goldwater carried only Arizona and five states in the Deep South. Johnson won the electoral vote by a whopping 486 to 52. In the Senate the Democrats increased their majority by two (68 to 32) and in the House by thirty-seven (295 to 140).

LANDMARK LEGISLATION   In 1965 Johnson took advantage of his electoral mandate to launch his Great Society program. It would, he promised, end poverty, renovate the decaying central cities, provide every young American with the chance to attend college, protect the health of the elderly, enhance cultural life, clean up the air and water, and make the highways safer and prettier.

To accomplish those goals, the Johnson administration pushed legislation through the Congress at a pace unseen since Franklin Roosevelt's Hundred Days. Priority went to health insurance and aid to education, proposals that had languished since President Truman had proposed them in 1945. The proposal for a comprehensive medical-insurance plan had long been stalled by the American Medical Association's ardent opposition. But now that Johnson had the votes, the AMA joined Republicans in supporting a bill serving those over age sixty-five. The act not only created the Medicare insurance program for the aged but also included another program, Medicaid, which provided states with federal grants to help cover medical payments for the indigent.

Five days after Johnson submitted his Medicare program, he sent to Congress his proposal for a massive increase in federal aid to elementary and secondary education. Such proposals had been ignored since the 1940s, blocked alternately by issues of segregation and separation of church and state. Now Johnson and congressional leaders devised a means of extending aid to "poverty-impacted" school districts regardless of their public or parochial character.

The momentum generated by these measures had already begun to carry others along, and it continued through the following year. Altogether the tide of Great Society legislation carried 435 bills through the Congress. Among them was the Appalachian Regional Development Act of 1966, which allocated federal funds for programs to enhance the standard of living in remote mountain areas that had long been pockets of desperate poverty. The Housing and Urban Development Act of 1965 provided for construction of 240,000 housing units. Rent supplements for low-income families followed in 1966, and in that year there began a new Department of Housing and Urban Development, headed by Robert C. Weaver, the first African-American cabinet member.

THE IMMIGRATION ACT   Little noticed among the legislation flowing from Congress was a major new immigration bill that had originated in the Kennedy White House. President Johnson signed the Immigration and Nationality Services Act of 1965 in a ceremony held on Liberty Island in New York Harbor. In his speech, Johnson stressed that the new law would redress the wrong done to those "from southern and eastern Europe" and the "developing continents" of Asia, Africa, and Latin America. It would do so by abolishing the discriminatory quotas based on national origins that had governed immigration policy since the 1920s.

The new law treated all nationalities and races equally. In place of national quotas, it created hemispheric ceilings on visas issued: 170,000 for persons from outside the Western Hemisphere, 120,000 for persons from within. It also stipulated that no more than 20,000 people could come from any one country each year. The new act allowed the entry of immediate family members of American residents without limit. Most of the annual visas were to be given on a first-come, first-served basis to "other relatives" of American residents, and only a small proportion (about 10 percent) were allocated to those with special talents or job skills. During the 1960s became the largest contingent of new Americans.

ASSESSING THE GREAT SOCIETY   The Great Society programs included several successes. The Highway Safety Act and the Traffic Safety Act established safety standards for automobile manufacturers and highway design, and the scholarships provided for college students under the Higher Education Act were quite popular. Many Great Society initiatives aimed at improving the health, nutrition, and education of poor Americans, young and old, made headway. So, too, did efforts to clean up air and water pollution. Some of Johnson's ambitious programs were hastily designed or mismanaged, however, and others were vastly underfunded. Medicare, for example, removed incentives for hospitals to control costs, and medical bills skyrocketed. The Great Society helped reduce the number of people living in poverty, but it did so largely by providing federal welfare payments, not by finding them productive jobs. The war on poverty ended up being as disappointing as the war in Vietnam. Often funds appropriated for various programs never made it through the tangled bureaucracy to the needy. Widely publicized cases of welfare fraud placed a powerful weapon in the hands of those opposed to liberal social programs. By 1966 middle-class resentment over the cost and waste of the Great Society programs helped generate a strong conservative backlash that fueled a Republican resurgence at the polls.

FROM CIVIL RIGHTS TO BLACK POWER

CIVIL RIGHTS LEGISLATION   Among the successes of the Great Society was a landmark piece of civil rights legislation: the Civil Rights Act of

1964, the most far-reaching civil rights measure ever enacted. It outlawed racial discrimination in hotels, restaurants, and other public accommodations. In addition, its provisions enabled the attorney general to bring suits to end school desegregation, relieving parents of that painful burden. Federally assisted programs and private employers alike were required to eliminate discrimination. An Equal Employment Opportunity Commission administered a ban on job discrimination by race, religion, national origin, or sex.

The Civil Rights Act increased the momentum of the movement. Early in 1965 Martin Luther King announced a voter-registration drive aimed at the 3 million unregistered African Americans in the South. On March 7 civil rights protesters began a march for voting rights from Selma, Alabama, to Montgomery, only to be violently dispersed by state troopers and a mounted posse. A federal judge then agreed to allow the march, and President Johnson provided federal troops for protection. By March 25, when the demonstrators reached Montgomery, they numbered 35,000, and King delivered a rousing address from the steps of the state capitol.

Several days before the march, President Johnson went before Congress with a moving plea for voting rights legislation. The resulting Voting Rights Act of 1965 ensured all citizens the right to vote. It authorized the attorney general to dispatch federal examiners to register voters. In states or counties where fewer than half the adults had voted in 1964, the act suspended literacy tests and other devices commonly used to defraud citizens of the vote. By the end of the year, some 250,000 African Americans were newly registered.

BLACK POWER   Amid this success, however, the civil rights movement began to fragment. On August 11, 1965, less than a week after the passage of the Voting Rights Act, Watts, a predominantly black and poor neighborhood in Los Angeles, exploded in a frenzy of riots and looting. When the uprising ended, thirty-four were dead, almost 4,000 rioters were in jail, and property damage exceeded $35 million. The Watts upheaval marked the beginning of four long hot summers of racial conflagration. Riots in 1966 erupted in Chicago and Cleveland and in forty other American cities. The following summer, Newark and Detroit burst into flames. Detroit provided the most graphic instance of urban violence as tanks rolled through the streets to restore order.

In retrospect, it was understandable that the civil rights movement would shift its focus to the plight of urban blacks. By the mid-1960s about 70 percent of African Americans lived in metropolitan areas, most of them in central-city ghettos that had been bypassed by the postwar prosperity. It seems clear, also in retrospect, that the nonviolent tactics that had worked in the rural South would not work in the northern cities. In the North racial problems resulted from segregated residential patterns not amenable to changes in the law. Moreover, northern white ethnic groups did not have the cultural heritage that southern whites shared with blacks by virtue of their living together in the South for so many generations. A special Commission on Civil Disorders noted that, unlike earlier race riots, which had been started by whites, the urban upheavals of the middle 1960s were initiated by African Americans themselves in an effort to destroy what they could not stomach and what civil rights legislation seemed unable to change.

In the midst of the violence, a new philosophy of racial separatism began to emerge. By 1966 "black power" had become the rallying cry of young activists. Radical members of SNCC had become estranged from Martin Luther King's theories of nonviolence. When Stokely Carmichael, a twenty-five-year-old graduate of Howard University, became head of SNCC in 1966, he adopted a separatist philosophy of black power and ousted whites from the organization. "We reject an American dream defined by white people and must work to construct an American reality defined by Afro-Americans," said a SNCC position paper. H. Rap Brown, who succeeded Carmichael as head of SNCC in 1967, even urged blacks to "get you some guns" and "kill the honkies." Meanwhile, Carmichael had moved on to the Black Panther party, founded in Oakland, California, in 1966. Headed by Huey P. Newton, Bobby Seale, and Eldridge Cleaver, the self-professed urban revolutionaries terrified the public. Eventually the Panthers fragmented in spasms of violence, much of which the FBI and local police officials helped to provoke.

The most articulate spokesman for black power was one of the earliest, Malcolm X (formerly Malcolm Little, with the X denoting his lost African surname). Malcolm had risen from a ghetto childhood involving narcotics and crime to become the chief disciple of Elijah Muhammad, a Black Muslim prophet who rejected Christianity as "the religion of white devils" and encouraged black culture and black pride. By 1964 Malcolm had broken with Elijah Muhammad and founded an organization committed to fostering alliances between African

Malcolm X

Malcolm X was the black power movement's most influential spokesman.

Americans blacks and the nonwhite peoples of the world. He had also begun to abandon his earlier separatist agenda and violent tactics. But Malcolm was gunned down in Harlem by Black Muslim assassins in early 1965. With him went the most effective voice for urban black militancy. What made the assassination especially tragic was that just months before Malcolm had begun to abandon his strident anti-white rhetoric and preach a biracial message of social change.

Although widely publicized and highly visible, the black power movement never attracted more than a small minority of African Americans. Only about 15 percent of blacks labeled themselves separatists. The preponderant majority continued to identify with the philosophy of nonviolent integration promoted by Martin Luther King and organizations such as the NAACP.

Yet the black power movement, despite its strident language and violence, had two positive effects upon the civil rights movement. First, it prompted African Americans to take greater pride in their racial heritage. As Malcolm X often pointed out, prolonged slavery and institutionalized racism had eroded the self-esteem of many blacks in the United States. "The worst crime the white man has committed," he declared, "has been to teach us to hate ourselves." He and others helped blacks appreciate their African roots and their American accomplishments. It was Malcolm X who insisted that blacks call themselves African Americans as a symbol of pride in their roots and as a spur to learning more about their history as a people.

Second, the black power phenomenon forced King and other mainstream African-American leaders and organizations to launch a new stage in the civil rights movement, focusing attention on the economic plight of poor inner-city blacks. Legal access to restaurants, schools, and other public accommodations, King pointed out, meant little to people mired in a culture of urban poverty. They needed jobs and decent housing as much as they needed legal rights. The time had come for radical measures "to provide jobs and income for the poor." Yet as King and others sought to escalate the war on poverty at home, the war in Vietnam was consuming more and more of America's resources and energies.

The Tragedy of Vietnam

As domestic violence was escalating in America's inner cities, the war in Vietnam reached new levels of intensity and destruction. At the time of President Kennedy's death, there were 16,000 American military advisers in Vietnam. Lyndon Johnson inherited a commitment to prevent a Communist takeover in South Vietnam along with a reluctance to assume the military burden for fighting the war. One president after another had done just enough to avoid being charged with having lost Vietnam. Johnson did the same, fearing that any other course would undermine his influence and endanger his Great Society programs in Congress. But this path took him and the United States deeper into intervention in Southeast Asia. Early on Johnson doubted that Vietnam was worth American military involvement. In May 1964 he told his national security adviser, McGeorge Bundy, that he had spent a sleepless night worrying about Vietnam: "It looks to me like we are getting into another Korea. . . . I don't think we can fight them 10,000 miles away from home. . . . I don't think it's worth fighting for. And I don't think we can get out. It's just the biggest damned mess that I ever saw."

ESCALATION   The official sanction for America's "escalation"—a Defense Department term favored in the Vietnam era—was the Tonkin Gulf resolution, approved by Congress on August 7, 1964. On that day, Johnson reported in a national television address that two American destroyers had been attacked by North Vietnamese vessels on August 2 and 4 in the Gulf of Tonkin, off the coast of North Vietnam. Although he described the attacks as unprovoked, in truth the destroyers had been monitoring South Vietnamese raids against two North Vietnamese islands—raids planned by American advisers. Even though there was no tangible evidence of an attack on the American ships, the Tonkin Gulf resolution authorized the president to "take all necessary measures to repel any armed attack against the forces of the United States and to prevent further aggression."

Three months after his landslide victory over Goldwater, Johnson made the crucial decisions that would shape American policy in Vietnam for the next four years. Viet Cong guerrilla attacks on American forces in February 1965 led Johnson to launch Operation Rolling Thunder, the first sustained bombing of North Vietnam, which was intended to stop the flow of soldiers and supplies into the south. Six months later analysts concluded that the bombing had had little effect on the supplies pouring down the Ho Chi Minh Trail from North Vietnam through Laos into South Vietnam. Still, the bombing continued.

In March 1965 the new U.S. army commander in Vietnam, General William C. Westmoreland, requested and got the first installment of combat troops, ostensibly to defend American airfields. By the end of 1965, there were 184,000 U.S. troops in Vietnam; in 1966 there were 385,000. As combat operations increased throughout South Vietnam, so did American casualties, announced each week on the nightly news, along with the "body count" of alleged enemy dead.

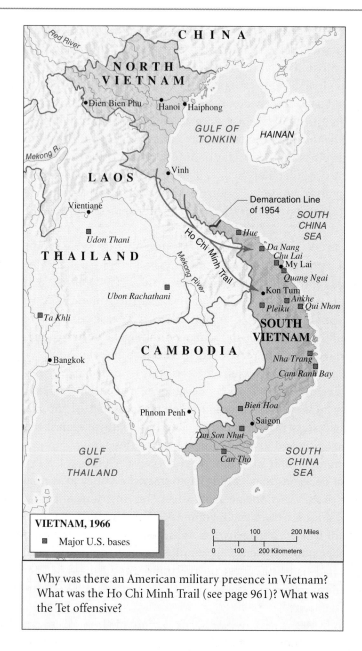

VIETNAM, 1966

◼ Major U.S. bases

0   100   200 Miles

0   100   200 Kilometers

Why was there an American military presence in Vietnam? What was the Ho Chi Minh Trail (see page 961)? What was the Tet offensive?

THE CONTEXT FOR POLICY   Lyndon Johnson's decision to "Americanize" the Vietnam War, so ill-starred in retrospect, was entirely consistent with the foreign-policy principles pursued by all presidents after World War II. The version of the containment theory articulated in the Truman Doctrine, endorsed by Dwight Eisenhower, and reaffirmed by John Kennedy, pledged

The Tet Offensive

Many Vietnamese were driven from their homes during the bloody street battles of the 1968 Tet offensive. Here, following a lull in the fighting, civilians carrying a white flag approach U.S. Marines.

opposition to the advance of communism anywhere in the world. Secretary of State Dean Rusk frequently warned that Thailand, Burma, and the rest of Southeast Asia would fall "like dominoes" to communism if American forces withdrew from Vietnam. Military intervention was thus a logical culmination of the assumptions widely shared by the foreign-policy establishment and leaders of both political parties since the early days of the cold war.

Nor did the United States "stumble into a quagmire" blindly in Vietnam, as some commentators maintained. Johnson insisted from the start that military involvement must not reach levels that would provoke the Chinese or Soviets to intervene with their own forces. He therefore exercised a tight rein over the bombing campaign, once boasting that "they can't even bomb an outhouse without my approval." Such a restrictive policy meant, in effect, that military victory was never possible. America's goal was not to win the war in a conventional sense by capturing enemy territory but to prevent the North Vietnamese and the Viet Cong from winning and, eventually, to force

"How Deep Do You Figure We'll Get Involved, Sir?"

Although U.S. soldiers were first sent to Vietnam as noncombatant advisers, they soon found themselves involved in a quagmire of fighting.

a negotiated settlement with the North Vietnamese. This meant that America would have to maintain a military presence as long as the enemy retained the will to fight.

As it turned out, American public support for the war eroded faster than the will of the North Vietnamese leaders to tolerate devastating casualties and destruction. Systematic opposition to the war broke out on college campuses with the escalation of 1965. By 1967 anti-war demonstrations in New York City and at the Pentagon were attracting massive support. Nightly television accounts of the fighting— Vietnam was the first war to receive extended television coverage and hence was dubbed the living-room war—contradicted the official optimism.

In a war of political will, North Vietnam had the advantage. Johnson and his advisers grievously underestimated the tenacity of North Vietnam's commitment to unify Vietnam and expel the United States. While the United States fought a limited war for limited objectives, the Vietnamese Communists fought a total war for their survival. Just as General Westmoreland was assuring Johnson and the American public that his forces in early 1968 were on the verge of gaining the upper hand, the Communists again displayed their cunning and tenacity.

THE TURNING POINT   On January 31, 1968, the first day of the Vietnamese New Year (Tet), the Viet Cong and the North Vietnamese defied a holiday truce to launch a wave of surprise assaults on American and South Vietnamese forces throughout South Vietnam. The old capital city of Hue fell to the Communists, and Viet Cong units temporarily occupied the grounds of the U.S. embassy in Saigon. Within a few days, however, American and South Vietnamese forces organized a devastating counterattack. General Westmoreland justifiably proclaimed the Tet offensive a major defeat for the

Viet Cong. But while Viet Cong casualties were enormous, the psychological impact of the surprise attacks on the American public was more telling. The scope and intensity of the offensive contradicted upbeat claims by commanders that the war was going well. *Time* and *Newsweek* soon ran anti-war editorials urging American withdrawal. Polls showed that Johnson's popularity had declined to 35 percent, lower than that of any president in polling history. In 1968 the United States was spending $322,000 on every enemy soldier killed in Vietnam; the poverty programs at home received only $53 per person.

During 1968 Lyndon Johnson grew increasingly isolated. He suffered from depression and bouts of paranoia. The secretary of defense reported that a task force of prominent soldiers and civilians saw no prospect for a military victory; the stalemated war was undermining the Great Society programs. The Democratic party was also fragmenting. Robert Kennedy, now a senator from New York, was considering a run for the presidency in order to challenge Johnson's Vietnam policy. Senator Eugene McCarthy of Minnesota had already decided to oppose Johnson in the Democratic primaries. With anti-war students rallying to his candidacy, McCarthy polled 42 percent of the vote to Johnson's 48 percent in New Hampshire's March primary. It was a remarkable showing for a little-known senator. Each presidential primary now promised to become a referendum on Johnson's Vietnam policy.

On March 31 Johnson made a dramatic decision. He announced a limited halt to the bombing of North Vietnam and fresh initiatives for a negotiated cease-fire. Then he added a stunning postscript: "I shall not seek, and I will not accept, the nomination of my party for another term as your President." Although American combat troops would remain in Vietnam for seven more years and the casualties would mount, the quest for military victory had ended. Now the question was how the most powerful nation in the world could extricate itself from Vietnam with a minimum of damage to its prestige. It would not be easy. When direct negotiations with the North Vietnamese finally began in Paris in May 1968, they immediately bogged down over North Vietnam's demand for a halt to the bombing by the United States as a precondition for further discussion.

SIXTIES CRESCENDO

A TRAUMATIC YEAR   Change moved at a fearful pace throughout the 1960s, but 1968 was the most turbulent and the most traumatic year of all. On April 4, only four days after Johnson's withdrawal from the presidential race, Martin Luther King was gunned down in Memphis, Tennessee. The assassin, James Earl Ray, had expressed hostility toward African Americans, but Americans continue to debate whether he was a pawn in an organized conspiracy. King's death set off an outpouring of grief among whites and blacks. It also set off riots in over sixty American cities.

Two months later, on June 5, Robert Kennedy was shot in the head by a young Palestinian who resented Kennedy's strong support of Israel. Kennedy died on the day after he had convincingly defeated Eugene McCarthy in the California Democratic primary, thereby momentarily assuming leadership of the anti-war forces in the race for the nomination for president.

CHICAGO AND MIAMI   In August 1968 Democratic delegates gathered inside a Chicago convention hall to nominate Vice President Hubert Humphrey, while almost 20,000 police and national guardsmen and a small army of television reporters stood watch over several thousand diverse protesters herded together miles away in a public park. Chicago mayor Richard J. Daley, who had given "shoot-to-kill" orders to police during the April riots following the King assassination, warned that he would not tolerate disruptions. Nonetheless, riots broke out and were televised nationwide. As demonstrators chanted "The whole world is watching," police attacked the crowds with tear gas and billy clubs.

The Democratic party's liberal tradition was clearly in disarray, a fact that gave heart to the Republicans, who gathered in Miami Beach to nominate Richard Nixon and celebrate a remarkable political comeback. Nixon's narrow loss to Kennedy in 1960 had been followed by a disastrous defeat in the California gubernatorial race two years later. In what he labeled his "last press conference," he vowed never again to run for office. Yet Nixon displayed his remarkable resilience by returning to national politics in 1964, when he crisscrossed the nation in support of Goldwater's candidacy. For the next several years he remained active in politics, and in 1968 he was ready to take advantage of Johnson's crumbling popularity. He offered a vision of stability and order that appealed to a majority of Americans, soon to be called the silent majority.

But others were ready as well to challenge the Democratic party regulars. George Wallace, the Democratic governor of Alabama, ran as a third candidate in the campaign, on the American Independent party ticket. Wallace had made his political reputation as a brazen defender of segregation, but in his campaign for national office in 1968 he moderated his position on the race issue. And he appealed even more candidly than Nixon to the fears generated by rioting anti-war protesters, the welfare system, and the growth of

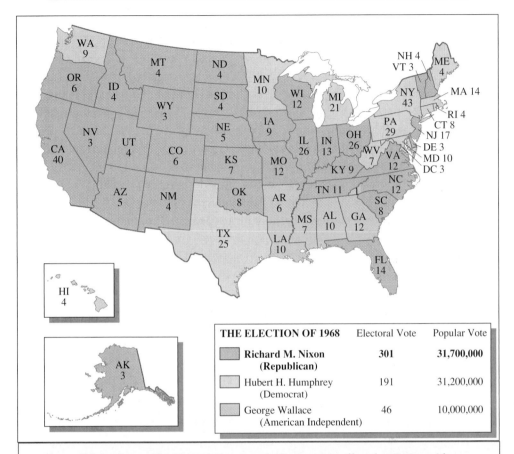

THE ELECTION OF 1968	Electoral Vote	Popular Vote
Richard M. Nixon (Republican)	301	31,700,000
Hubert H. Humphrey (Democrat)	191	31,200,000
George Wallace (American Independent)	46	10,000,000

How did the riots at the Chicago Democratic Convention affect the 1968 presidential campaign? How did Nixon engineer his political comeback? What was Wallace's appeal to over 10 million voters?

the federal government. Wallace's platform was compelling in its simplicity: rioters would be shot, the war in Vietnam won, states' rights and law and order restored, open-housing laws repealed, and welfare cheats jailed.

Wallace's reactionary candidacy generated considerable appeal outside his native South, especially in white working-class communities, where resentment of Johnson's Great Society liberalism was rife. Although never a possible winner, Wallace had to be taken seriously: he could deny Humphrey or Nixon an electoral majority and thereby throw the choice into the House of Representatives, which could provide an appropriate climax to a chaotic year.

NIXON AGAIN   It did not happen that way. Richard Nixon enjoyed an enormous early lead in the polls, which narrowed as the 1968 election approached. George Wallace's campaign was hurt by his outspoken running mate, retired air force general Curtis LeMay, who suggested using nuclear weapons in Vietnam. In October 1968 Hubert Humphrey infuriated Johnson and the party bosses when he announced that, if elected, he would stop bombing North Vietnam "as an acceptable risk for peace."

In the end, Nixon and his running mate, Governor Spiro Agnew of Maryland, eked out a narrow victory of about 500,000 votes, a margin of about 1 percentage point. The electoral vote was more decisive, 301 to 191. Wallace won 10 million votes, 13.5 percent of the total, the best showing by a third-party candidate since Robert La Follette headed the Progressive ticket in 1924. All but one of Wallace's 46 electoral votes were from the Deep South. Nixon swept all but four of the states west of the Mississippi, while Humphrey's support came almost exclusively from the Northeast.

So at the end of a turbulent year, near the end of a traumatic decade, a nation on the verge of violent chaos looked to Richard Nixon to provide what he had promised in the campaign: "peace with honor" in Vietnam and a middle ground on which a majority of Americans, silent or otherwise, could come together.

MAKING CONNECTIONS

- The reform movements of the 1960s galvanized the baby-boom generation into a new youth movement, described in the next chapter, that continued through the early 1970s.

- The conflict in Vietnam, America's longest war, would come to a bitter end for U.S. forces, but the divisions it spawned still echo today.

- The Immigration and Nationality Act of 1965 would have profound and unexpected consequences on American society, described in Chapter 37.

- The success of the civil rights movement in the 1960s led to similar movements by women, gays, Native Americans, and Latinos, as we will see in the next chapter.

FURTHER READING

A dispassionate analysis of Kennedy's life is Thomas C. Reeves's *A Question of Character: A Life of John F. Kennedy* (1991). The best study of the Kennedy administration's domestic policies is Irving Bernstein's *Promises Kept: John F. Kennedy's New Frontier* (1991). For details on the assassination, see David W. Belin's *Final Disclosure: The Full Truth about the Assassination of President Kennedy* (1988).

The most comprehensive biography of LBJ is Robert Dallek's two-volume work, *Lone Star Rising: Lyndon Johnson and His Times, 1908–1960* (1991) and *Flawed Giant: Lyndon B. Johnson and His Times, 1960–1973* (1998). On the Johnson administration, see Vaughn Davis Bornet's *The Presidency of Lyndon B. Johnson* (1984).

Among the works that interpret liberal social policy during the 1960s, John Schwarz's *America's Hidden Success: A Reassessment of Twenty Years of Public Policy* (1983) offers a glowing endorsement of Democratic programs. For a contrasting perspective, see Charles Murray's *Losing Ground: American Social Policy, 1950–1980,* rev. ed. (1994).

On foreign policy, see *Kennedy's Quest for Victory: American Foreign Policy, 1961–1963* (1989), edited by Thomas G. Paterson. To learn more about Kennedy's problems in Cuba, see Mark White's *Missiles in Cuba: Kennedy, Khrushchev, Castro and the 1962 Crisis* (1997). See also Aleksandr Fursenko and Timothy Naftali's *"One Hell of a Gamble": Khrushchev, Castro and Kennedy, 1958–1964* (1997).

American involvement in Vietnam has received voluminous treatment from all political perspectives. For an excellent overview, see Larry Berman's *Planning a Tragedy: The Americanization of the War in Vietnam* (1982) and *Lyndon Johnson's War: The Road to Stalemate in Vietnam* (1989), as well as Stanley Karnow's *Vietnam: A History,* rev. ed. (1991). An excellent analysis of policy making concerning the Vietnam War is David M. Barrett's *Uncertain Warriors: Lyndon Johnson and His Vietnam Advisors* (1993). An excellent account of the military involvement is Robert D. Schulzinger's A *Time for War: The United States and Vietnam, 1941–1975* (1997). On the legacy of the Vietnam War, see Arnold R. Isaacs's *Vietnam Shadows: The War, Its Ghosts, and Its Legacy* (1997).

Many scholars have dealt with various aspects of the civil rights movement and race relations in the 1960s. See especially Carl M. Brauer's *John F. Kennedy and the Second Reconstruction* (1977), David Garrow's *Bearing the Cross: Martin Luther King, Jr., and the Southern Christian Leadership Conference*

(1986), Adam Fairclough's *To Redeem the Soul of America: The Southern Christian Leadership Conference and Martin Luther King, Jr.* (1987). William H. Chafe's *Civilities and Civil Rights: Greensboro, North Carolina, and the Black Struggle for Freedom* (1980) details the original sit-ins. An award-winning study of racial and economic inequality in a representative American city is Thomas J. Sugrue's *The Origins of the Urban Crisis: Race and Inequality in Postwar Detroit* (1996).

35

REBELLION AND REACTION IN THE 1960s AND 1970s

FOCUS QUESTIONS

- What characterized the rebellion and struggles for rights in the 1970s?
- How did the war in Vietnam end?
- What was the Watergate incident, and how did it lead to Nixon's resignation?
- How did the Carter administration deal with the Middle East?

To answer these questions and access additional review material, please visit www.wwnorton.com/studyspace.

As Richard Nixon entered the White House in early 1969, he faced a nation whose social fabric was in tatters. Everywhere, it seemed, traditional institutions and notions of authority were under attack. The traumatic events of 1968 revealed how deeply divided American society had become and how difficult a task Nixon faced in carrying out his pledge to restore social harmony. The stability he promised proved elusive. His policies and his combative temperament served to heighten rather than reduce societal tensions. Those tensions reflected profound fissures in the postwar consensus promoted by Eisenhower and inherited by Kennedy and Johnson. Ironically, many of the same forces that had promoted the flush times of the Eisenhower years—the baby boom, the containment doctrine of anti-communism, and the superficial focus on the consumer culture—helped generate the social upheaval of the 1960s and 1970s.

THE ROOTS OF REBELLION

YOUTH REVOLT   By the early 1960s the postwar baby boomers were maturing. Now young adults, they differed from their elders in that they had experienced neither economic depression nor a major war. In record numbers they were attending colleges and universities: college enrollment quadrupled between 1945 and 1970. Many universities had become sprawling institutions increasingly dependent upon research contracts from giant corporations and the federal government. As these "multiversities" grew more bureaucratic and hierarchical, they unwittingly invited resistance from students wary of involvement in what President Eisenhower had called the military-industrial complex.

The Greensboro student sit-ins in 1960 not only precipitated a decade of civil rights activism but also signaled an end to the supposed apathy that had enveloped college campuses and social life during the 1950s. Although primarily concerned with the rights and status of black people, the sit-ins, marches, protests, principles, and sacrifices associated with the civil rights movement provided inspiring models and rhetoric for other groups demanding justice, freedom, and equality.

During 1960–1961 a small but significant number of white students joined the sit-in movement. They and many others were also inspired by President Kennedy's direct appeals to their youthful idealism. Soon, however, it became clear that politics was mixed with principle in the president's position on civil rights. Later, as criticism of escalating American involvement in Vietnam mounted, more and more young people grew disillusioned with the government, corporations, and parental authority. By the mid-1960s a full-fledged youth revolt had erupted across the country, and rebels began to flow into two distinct yet frequently overlapping movements: the New Left and the counterculture.

THE NEW LEFT   The explicitly political strain of the youth revolt coalesced when Tom Hayden and Al Haber, two student radicals at the University of Michigan, formed Students for a Democratic Society (SDS) in 1960. Two years later Hayden drafted what became known as the Port Huron Statement: "We are the people of this generation, bred in at least moderate comfort, housed in universities, looking uncomfortably to the world we inherit."

Hayden's manifesto focused on the absence of individual freedom in modern life. The country, he insisted, was dominated by huge organizational structures—governments, corporations, universities—all of which conspired to oppress and alienate the individual. Inspired by the example of African-American activism in the South, Hayden declared that students had the power to restore "participatory democracy" to American life by wresting "control of the educational process from the administrative bureaucracy" and then forging links with other dissident movements. He and others adopted the term New Left to distinguish their efforts at grassroots democracy from those of the Old Left of the 1930s, which had espoused an orthodox version of Marxism.

In the fall of 1964, students at the University of California at Berkeley took Hayden's program to heart. When the university's chancellor announced that sidewalk solicitations for political causes would no longer be allowed, several hundred students staged a sit-in. Over 2,000 more joined in and after a tense standoff the administration relented.

The program and tactics of the SDS soon spread to universities across the country, but the focus changed as escalating involvement in Vietnam brought a dramatic expansion of the military draft and millions of young men faced the grim prospect of participating in an increasingly unpopular war. In fact, however, Vietnam, like virtually every other war, was a poor man's fight. In 1965–1966, thanks to deferments and exemptions, college students made up only 2 percent of all military inductees. Yet several thousand male collegians would flee to Canada or Sweden to escape the draft, while hundreds of thousands engaged in various protests against a war they considered immoral.

During the eventful spring of 1968—when Lyndon Johnson announced he would not run for reelection and Martin Luther King was assassinated—campus unrest reached a climax with the disruption of Columbia University in New York City. Mark Rudd, an SDS leader, and a small group of radicals protested the university's insensitive decision to disrupt a neighboring African-American community in order to build a new gymnasium. The students occupied some campus buildings, and the protest quickly spread. During the following week more buildings were occupied, faculty and administrative offices were ransacked, and classes were canceled. University officials finally called in the New York City police. While arresting the protesters, officers injured a number of innocent bystanders. Their excessive force angered many unaligned students, who then joined militants in staging a strike that shut down the university for the remainder of the semester. That spring similar clashes among students, administrators, and police occurred

Upheaval in Chicago

The violence that accompanied the 1968 Democratic National Convention in Chicago seared the nation.

at Harvard, Cornell, and San Francisco State.

At the 1968 Democratic Convention in Chicago, the polarization of American society reached a bizarre climax. Inside the tightly guarded convention hall, Democrats were nominating Lyndon Johnson's faithful vice-president, Hubert Humphrey, while Chicago's streets roiled with anti-war dissenters. The outlandish behavior of the anarchic protesters provoked an equally outlandish response from Chicago's Mayor Richard Daley and his army of police. As a national television audience watched, many police officers went berserk, clubbing and gassing demonstrators as well as bystanders caught up in the chaotic scene. The televised spectacle lasted three days and generated a wave of anger among many middle-class Americans, anger that Richard Nixon and the Republicans shrewdly exploited at their nominating convention in Miami Beach. At the same time, the Chicago riots helped fragment the anti-war movement.

During 1968 the SDS fractured into rival factions, the most extreme of which called itself the Weathermen, a name derived from a lyric by Bob Dylan: "You don't need a weatherman to know which way the wind blows." These hardened young activists launched a campaign of violence and disruption, firebombing university and government buildings and killing innocent people, as well as several of their own. Government forces arrested most of them, and the rest went into hiding. By 1971 the New Left was dead as a political movement. In large measure it had committed suicide by abandoning the democratic and pacifist principles that had inspired participants and given the movement its moral legitimacy. The larger anti-war movement also began to fade. There would be a wave of student protests against the Nixon administration in 1970–1971, but thereafter campus unrest virtually disappeared as American troops returned home from Vietnam and the draft ended.

If the social mood was changing during Richard Nixon's presidency, a large segment of the public persisted in the quest for social justice. A *New York Times* survey of college campuses in 1969 revealed that many students were refocusing their attention on the environment. This new ecological awareness would blossom in the 1970s into one of the most compelling items on the nation's social agenda.

THE COUNTER CULTURE   The numbing events of 1968 led other disaffected activists away from radical politics altogether, toward another manifestation of the sixties youth revolt: the counterculture. Long hair, blue jeans, tie-dyed shirts, sandals, mind-altering drugs, rock music, and group living arrangements were more important than revolutionary ideology or mass protest to the hippies, the direct descendants of the Beats of the 1950s. These advocates of the counterculture were, like their New Left peers, primarily young whites alienated by the Vietnam War, racism, political corruption and parental demands, runaway technology, and a crass corporate mentality that equated the good life with material goods. Disillusioned with organized political action, they embraced the credo announced by the zany Harvard professor Timothy Leary, "Turn on to the scene, tune in to what's happening, and drop out."

For some the counterculture entailed the study and practice of Asian religions, such as Buddhism. For others it centered on the frequent use of hallucinogenic drugs such as LSD. Collective living in urban enclaves such as San Francisco's Haight-Ashbury district and New York's East Village was the rage for a while, until conditions grew so crowded and violent that residents migrated elsewhere. Rural communes also attracted bourgeois rebels. During the 1960s and early 1970s thousands of inexperienced romantics flocked to the countryside, eager to liberate themselves from parental and institutional restraints, live in harmony with nature, and coexist in an atmosphere of love and openness. Only a handful of their utopian homesteads survived more than a few months, however.

Huge outdoor rock-music concerts were also a popular source of community for hippies. The largest of these was the Woodstock Music and Art Fair, held in 1969 on a 600-acre farm near the tiny rural town of Bethel, New York. For three days some 500,000 "flower children" reveled in good music and cheap marijuana. But the carefree spirit of the Woodstock festival was short-lived. When promoters tried to replicate the scene four months later, this time at a Rolling Stones concert at the Altamont speedway, near San Francisco, members of the Hell's Angels motorcycle gang beat a man to death in front of the stage.

Just as the 1968 Democratic Convention in Chicago marked the end of the New Left as a vital political force, the violence at Altamont sharply diminished the appeal of the counterculture. Moreover, many of the flower children grew tired of their riches-to-rags existence and returned to college to become lawyers, doctors, politicians, or accountants. The search on the part of alienated youth for a better society and a good life was strewn with both comic and tragic aspects, and it reflected the deep social ills that had been allowed to fester throughout the post–World War II period.

FEMINISM   The ideal of liberation spawned during the 1960s helped accelerate a powerful women's rights crusade. Like the New Left the new feminism drew much of its inspiration and many of its initial tactics from the civil rights movement. Its aim was to challenge the cult of domesticity that had been touted as the ideal during the 1950s.

Woodstock

The Woodstock music festival drew nearly half a million people to a farm in Bethel, New York. The concert was billed as three days of "peace, music, . . . and love."

The mainstream women's movement was led by Betty Friedan. Her influential book *The Feminine Mystique* (1963) launched a new phase of female protest on a national level. Women, Friedan wrote, had actually lost ground during the years after World War II, when many left wartime jobs and settled down in suburbia to care for their children. Advertisers and women's magazines promoted the "feminine mystique" of blissful domesticity. In Friedan's view the middle-class home had become "a comfortable concentration camp" where women saw their individual potential suffocated in an atmosphere of mindless materialism, daytime TV, and neighborhood gossip.

The Feminine Mystique inspired many women who felt trapped in a domestic rut. In 1966 Friedan and other activists founded the National Organization for Women (NOW), whose membership grew rapidly. NOW spearheaded efforts to end job discrimination on the basis of sex, legalize abortion, and obtain federal and state support for child-care centers.

Pressured by NOW, Congress and the Supreme Court in the early 1970s advanced the cause of sexual equality. Under Title IX of the Educational Amendments Act of 1972, colleges were required to institute "affirmative-action" programs to ensure equal opportunities for women in such areas as admissions, faculty and staff hiring, and athletics. In the same year, Congress overwhelmingly approved the equal-rights amendment to the Constitution. And in 1973 the Supreme Court, in *Roe v. Wade,* struck down state laws forbidding abortions during the first three months of pregnancy, a ruling based on the constitutional right to privacy. Meanwhile, many bastions of male education, including Yale and Princeton, led a new movement for coeducation that swept the nation.

By the end of the 1970s, however, sharp disputes between moderate and radical feminists

Feminist Awakenings

In 1967 Syracuse University student Kathy Switzer challenged the Boston Marathon's tradition of excluding women. Officials tried to pull Switzer from the course, but with the aid of fellow runners she completed the race. Women did not become official entrants until 1971.

had fragmented the women's movement. The movement's failure to broaden its appeal much beyond the confines of the white middle class caused reform efforts to stagnate. In 1982 the equal-rights amendment died, several states short of ratification. The very success of NOW's efforts to liberalize state abortion laws helped generate a powerful backlash, especially among Catholics and fundamentalist Protestants, who mounted a "right-to-life" crusade that remains a potent political force.

Yet the success of the women's movement endured despite setbacks. The growing political power of women and their expanding presence in the workforce combined to become one of the most significant developments of the era. By 1976 over half the married women in America and nine out of ten female college graduates were employed outside the home, a development that one economist called "the single most outstanding phenomenon of this century." Many career women, however, did not regard themselves as feminists; they took jobs because they and their families needed the money to achieve higher levels of material comfort. Whatever the motives, women were changing traditional sex roles and child-rearing practices to accommodate the two-career family, which had replaced the established pattern of male breadwinner and female housekeeper as the new American norm.

HISPANIC RIGHTS   The activism that animated the crusade for women's rights also spread to various ethnic minority groups. The labor shortages during World War II had led defense industries to offer Hispanic Americans their first significant access to skilled-labor jobs. As was the case with African Americans, service in the military during the war years helped to heighten an American identity among Hispanic Americans and increase their desire for equal rights and opportunities.

But equality was elusive. After World War II, Hispanic Americans still faced widespread discrimination in hiring, housing, and education. Poverty was widespread. In 1960, for example, the median income of a Mexican-American family was only 62 percent of that of a family in the general population. Hispanic-American activists during the 1950s and 1960s mirrored the efforts of black civil rights leaders. They, too, denounced segregation, promoted efforts to improve the quality of public education, and struggled to increase Hispanic-American political influence and economic opportunities.

One of the most popular initiatives was the use of the term *Chicano* as an inclusive label for all Mexican immigrants, Spanish Americans in New Mexico, old Californios (descendants of the inhabitants of California before it was seized by the United States, most of whom were Indians or of mixed ancestry), and Tejanos (descendants of the inhabitants of Texas before it became independent).* In southern California, students formed Young Chicanos for Community Action, a social-service group designed to promote self-reliance and local involvement within Hispanic-American neighborhoods. Wearing brown berets, the members protested the disproportionate number of Hispanics being killed in the Vietnam War and demanded improvements in their neighborhood schools.

Unlike their African-American counterparts, however, Hispanic-American leaders faced an awkward dilemma: what should they do about the continuing stream of undocumented Mexicans flowing across the border? Many Mexican Americans argued that their hopes for economic advancement and social equality were put at risk by the daily influx of Mexican laborers willing to accept low-paying jobs in the United States. Mexican-American leaders thus helped end the bracero program in 1964 (which trucked in day laborers, from Mexico) and in 1962 formed the United Farm Workers (UFW, originally the National Farm Workers Association) to represent Mexican-American migrant workers.

The founder of the UFW was Cesar Chavez. Born in 1927 in Yuma, Arizona, to Mexican immigrant parents, Chavez moved with his family to California in 1939. There they joined thousands of other migrant farmworkers traversing the state, moving from job to job, living in tents, cars, or ramshackle cabins. In 1944, at age seventeen, Chavez joined the navy. After the war he married and found work, first as a sharecropper raising strawberries and then as a migrant laborer in apricot orchards. In 1952 Chavez joined the Community Service Organization (CSO), a social-service group that sought to educate and organize the migrant poor so that they could become self-reliant. He founded new CSO chapters and was named general director in 1958.

Chavez left the organization in 1962 when it refused to back his proposal to establish a union for farmworkers. Other CSO leaders believed that it was impossible to organize migrant workers into an effective union. They thought the migrant workers were too mobile, too poor, too illiterate, too ethnically diverse, and too easily replaced by braceros. Moreover, farmworkers did not enjoy protected status under the National Labor Relations Act of 1935 (the Wagner Act). Unlike industrial laborers they were not guaranteed

---

*Hispanic, a term used in the United States to refer to people who are from, or trace their ancestry to, Spanish-speaking Latin America or Spain, came to be used increasingly after 1945 in conjunction with growing efforts to promote economic and social justice for those people.(Although frequently used as a synonym for Hispanic, the term Latino technically refers only to people of Latin American descent.)

the right to organize or the right to receive a minimum wage. Nor did federal regulations govern the safety of their workplace.

Despite such obstacles, Chavez resolved to organize the migrant farmworkers. His fledgling Farm Workers Association gained national attention in 1965 when it joined a strike by Filipino farmworkers against the corporate grape farmers in California's San Joaquin Valley. Chavez's charisma and Catholic piety, his insistence upon nonviolent tactics, his reliance upon college-student volunteers, his skillful alliance with organized labor and religious groups—all combined to attract media interest and popular support.

Still, the grape strike itself brought no tangible gains. So Chavez organized a nationwide consumer boycott of grapes. Two years later, in 1970, the grape strike and consumer boycott finally succeeded in bringing twenty-six grape growers to the bargaining table. They signed formal contracts recognizing the UFW, and soon migrant workers throughout the West were benefiting from Chavez's strenuous efforts on their behalf. Wages increased, and working conditions improved. In 1975 the California state legislature passed a bill that required growers to bargain collectively with the elected representatives of the farmworkers.

The chief strength of the Hispanic movement lay less in the duplication of the civil rights strategies than in the rapid growth of the Hispanic population. In 1960 Hispanics in the United States numbered slightly more than 3 million; by 1970 they had increased to 9 million, and by 2006 they numbered over 40 million, making them the largest minority in the country.

United Farm Workers

Cesar Chavez (center) with organizers of the grape boycott. In 1968 Chavez ended a three-week fast by taking communion and breaking bread with Senator Robert Kennedy.

NATIVE AMERICAN RIGHTS

American Indians—many of whom had begun calling themselves Native Americans—also emerged as a political force in the late 1960s. Two conditions combined to make Indian rights a priority: first, white Americans felt a persistent sense of guilt for the destructive policies of their ancestors toward a people who had, after all, first settled the continent; second, the plight of the Native American minority was more desperate than that of any other group in the country. Indian unemployment was 10 times the national rate, life expectancy was 20 years lower than the national average, and the suicide rate was 100 times higher than that for whites.

Although President Lyndon Johnson recognized the poverty of the Native Americans and attempted to funnel federal anti-poverty-program funds into reservations, militants within the Indian community became impatient with the pace of change. They organized protests and demonstrations against local, state, and federal agencies. In 1963 two Chippewas (Ojibwas) living in Minneapolis, George Mitchell and Dennis Banks, founded the American Indian Movement (AIM) to promote "red power." The leaders of AIM occupied Alcatraz Island in San Francisco Bay in 1969, claiming the site "by right of discovery." And in 1972 a sit-in at the Department of the Interior's Bureau of Indian Affairs (BIA) in Washington attracted national attention to their cause. The BIA was then—and still is—widely viewed as the worst-managed federal agency. Instead of finding creative ways to promote tribal autonomy and economic self-sufficiency, the BIA has served as a classic example of government paternalism gone awry.

Indian protesters subsequently discovered a more effective tactic than direct action and sit-ins: they went into federal courts armed with copies of old treaties and demanded that these become the basis for restitution. In Alaska, Maine, and Massachusetts they won significant settlements that provided legal recognition of their tribal rights and financial compensation at levels that upgraded the standard of living on several reservations.

GAY RIGHTS   The liberationist impulses of the 1960s also encouraged homosexuals to organize and assert their right to equal treatment. On June 27, 1969, New York City police raided the Stonewall Inn, a Greenwich Village bar popular with gay men. The patrons fought back, and the struggle spilled into the streets. Hundreds of other gays and their supporters joined the fracas against the police. Rioting lasted throughout the weekend. When it ended, homosexuals had forged a new sense of solidarity and a new organization, the Gay Liberation Front.

As news of the Stonewall riots spread across the country, the gay rights movement assumed national proportions. One of its main tactics was to encourage people to "come out," to make public their homosexuality. This was by no means an easy decision. By professing their homosexuality, gays faced social ostracism, physical assault, exclusion from the military and civil service, and discrimination in the workplace. Yet despite the risks, thousands of homosexuals did come out. By 1973 almost 800 gay and lesbian organizations had been formed across the country, and every major city had a visible gay community and cultural life.

Like the civil rights crusade and the women's movement, however, the campaign for gay rights soon suffered from internal divisions and aroused a conservative backlash. Gay activists engaged in fractious disputes over tactics and objectives, and conservative moralists and Christian fundamentalists launched a nationwide counterattack and succeeded in repealing new local laws banning discrimination against homosexuals. By the end of the 1970s, the gay movement had lost its initial momentum and was struggling to salvage many of its hard-won gains.

Nixon and Vietnam

The numerous liberation movements of the 1960s fundamentally changed the tone and texture of American social life. By the early 1970s, however, the national mood was swinging back toward conservatism. The election of Richard Nixon in 1968 and the rise of George Wallace as a serious political force on the right reflected the emergence of the "silent majority," those white working-class and middle-class citizens who were determined to regain control of a society they feared was awash in permissiveness. Large as the gap was between the "silent majority" and the varied forces of dissent, the two sides agreed on one thing: that the Vietnam War remained the dominant event of the time. Until the war was ended and all American troops were returned home, the nation would find it difficult to achieve the equilibrium that the new president had promised.

GRADUAL WITHDRAWAL   Nixon and his special assistant for national security, Dr. Henry Kissinger, claimed to have a plan to achieve "peace with honor" in Vietnam. Peace, however, was long in coming and not very honorable when it arrived. The Nixon administration, even while withdrawing U.S. forces, held to a policy that refused to let the North Vietnamese dominate Indochina. By the time a settlement was reached, in 1973, another 20,000 Americans had died, the morale of the American army had been shattered, millions of Asians had been killed or wounded, and fighting was continuing in Southeast Asia. In the end, Nixon's policy gained little that the president could not have accomplished in 1969.

The administration's new strategy in Vietnam moved along three fronts. The first front was the deadlocked Paris peace talks, where American negotiators demanded the withdrawal of North Vietnamese forces from South Vietnam and the preservation of the U.S.-supported regime of President Nguyen Van Thieu. The North Vietnamese and Viet Cong negotiators insisted on retaining a Communist military presence in the south, however, and on reunifying the Vietnamese people under a Communist-dominated government. There was no common ground on which to come together. Hidden from public awareness and from America's South Vietnamese allies were secret meetings between Henry Kissinger and the North Vietnamese.

On the second front, Nixon tried to defuse domestic unrest generated by the war. To this end he sought to "Vietnamize" the conflict by turning over most of the combat missions to Vietnamese units and sharply reducing the number of U.S. ground forces. To assuage the South Vietnamese, he provided more equipment and training for their troops. From a peak of 560,000 in 1969, U.S. combat units were withdrawn at a steady pace. By 1973 only 50,000 troops remained in Vietnam. In late 1969 Nixon also established a lottery system that clarified the likelihood of being drafted: only those with low lottery numbers would have to go. Nixon was more successful in reducing anti-war activity than in forcing concessions from the North Vietnamese in Paris.

On the third front, while reducing the number of troops in Vietnam, Nixon and Kissinger secretly expanded the air war in an effort to persuade the enemy to come to terms. On March 18, 1969, U.S. planes began Operation Menu, a fourteen-month-long bombing of Communist forces in Cambodia. Over 100,000 tons of bombs were dropped, four times the tonnage dropped on Japan during World War II. Congress did not learn of those raids until 1970, when Nixon announced what he called an "incursion" by U.S. troops into supposedly "neutral" Cambodia to "clean out" North Vietnamese staging areas.

DIVISIONS AT HOME   News of the Cambodia "incursion" came on the heels of another incident that rekindled public indignation against the war. Late in 1969 the story of the My Lai Massacre broke. During the next two years the public learned the gruesome tale of Lieutenant William Calley, who in 1968 had ordered the murder of over 300 Vietnamese civilians in the village of My Lai. Twenty-five officers were charged with complicity in the massacre and subsequent cover-up, but only Calley was convicted of murder. Nixon then granted him parole.

The loudest public outcry against Nixon's Indochina policy occurred in the wake of the Cambodian "incursion," in the spring of 1970. Campuses across the country witnessed a new wave of protests that closed hundreds of colleges and universities. At Kent State University, the Ohio National Guard was called in to quell rioting, during which the campus Reserve Officers' Training Corps (ROTC) building was burned down by anti-war protesters. Pelted by rocks and verbal taunts, the poorly trained guardsmen panicked and opened fire on the demonstrators, killing four bystanders. Eleven days later, on May 15, Mississippi highway patrolmen riddled a dormitory at Jackson State College with bullets, killing two African-American students. Although an official investigation of the Kent State episode condemned the "casual and indiscriminate shooting," polls indicated that the public supported the national guard; students had "got what they were asking for."

The following year, 1971, the *New York Times* began publishing excerpts from a secret Defense Department study on the Vietnam War. The so-called Pentagon Papers, leaked to the press by a former Pentagon official, Daniel

Kent State University

National guardsmen shot and killed four bystanders during antiwar demonstrations on the campus of Kent State University in Ohio.

Ellsberg, confirmed what many critics of the war had long suspected: Congress and the public had not received the full story on the Gulf of Tonkin incident of 1964. Contingency plans for American entry into the war were being drawn up even while President Johnson was promising that combat troops would never be sent to Vietnam. The Nixon administration attempted to block publication of the Pentagon Papers, arguing that it would endanger national security and prolong the war. By a vote of six to three, the Supreme Court ruled against the government. Newspapers throughout the country began publication the next day.

WAR WITHOUT END   Although Nixon's decision in the spring of 1970 to use American forces to root out Communist bases in Cambodia did bring a tactical victory, it also served to widen a war he had promised to end. Moreover, his hopes that the South Vietnamese units replacing U.S. forces could hold their own against the North Vietnamese were dashed when they suffered repeated defeats in 1971 and 1972. Disorganized, poorly led, and lacking tenacity, the South Vietnamese soldiers had to call upon U.S. airpower to fend off North Vietnamese offensives.

The deteriorating ground war along with mounting divisions at home and the approach of the 1972 presidential elections combined to produce a shift in the American negotiating position in Paris. In the summer of 1972, Henry Kissinger dropped his insistence upon the removal of all North Vietnamese troops from the south before the withdrawal of the remaining U.S. troops. On October 26, only a week before the presidential election, he announced, "Peace is at hand." But the Thieu regime in South Vietnam objected to the plan for a cease-fire, fearful that the continued presence of North Vietnamese troops in the south virtually guaranteed an eventual Communist victory. Hanoi then stiffened its position by demanding that Thieu resign.

The Paris peace talks broke off on December 16, 1972, and Nixon told his military advisers that only a massive show of American airpower would make the North Vietnamese more cooperative at the negotiating table. Two days later the reelected Nixon unleashed furious B-52 raids on Hanoi and Haiphong. The so-called Christmas bombings aroused worldwide protest, but Henry Kissinger claimed Nixon's "jugular diplomacy" worked, for the talks in Paris soon resumed.

On January 27, 1973, the United States, North and South Vietnam, and the Viet Cong signed an "agreement on ending the war and restoring peace in Vietnam." The agreement showed that despite the Christmas bombings, the North Vietnamese never altered their basic stance: they kept 150,000 troops in the south and remained committed to the reunification of Vietnam under one government. What had changed since the previous fall was the willingness of the South Vietnamese, who were never allowed to participate in the negotiations, to accept these terms, albeit reluctantly, on the basis of Nixon's promise that the United States would respond "with full force" to any Communist violation of the agreement.

On March 29, 1973, the last U.S. combat troops left Vietnam. On that same day 587 American prisoners of war, most of them downed pilots, were released from Hanoi. Within a period of months, however, the war between north and south resumed, and the Communist forces gained the advantage. In Cambodia and Laos, where fighting had been more sporadic, Communist victory also seemed inevitable.

In 1975 the North Vietnamese launched a full-scale armored invasion against the south. President Thieu appealed to Washington for assistance, but the Democratic majority in Congress refused, and on April 30, 1975, Americans watched on television as North Vietnamese tanks rolled into Saigon, soon to be renamed Ho Chi Minh City. The scene at the U.S. embassy in Saigon, where thousands of terrified Vietnamese fought to board the last departing helicopters, was a poignant and tragic ending to America's greatest foreign-policy disaster.

The longest war in U.S. history was finally over, leaving in its wake a bitter legacy. The Vietnam war, described as a noble crusade on behalf of democratic ideals, instead suggested that democracy was not easily transferable to third world regions lacking experience with civil liberties and representative government. The war eroded respect for the military so thoroughly that many young Americans came to regard military service as inherently corrupting and ignoble. The war, fought to show the world that the United States was united in its anti-communist convictions, divided Americans more drastically than any event since the Civil War. The Vietnam War cost the nation some 58,000 deaths and $150 billion. Little wonder the dominant public reaction to the war's end was the urge to "put Vietnam behind us" and revert to a noninterventionist foreign policy.

Nixon and Middle America

Richard Nixon had been elected in 1968 as the representative of Middle America, those middle-class citizens fed up with the liberal politics and cultural radicalism of the 1960s. Nixon selected men for his cabinet and White House staff who would restore conservative values and carry out his orders with blind obedience. John Mitchell, the gruff attorney general who had been a senior partner in Nixon's New York law firm, was the new president's closest confidant. H. R. "Bob" Haldeman, an imperious former advertising executive, served as Nixon's chief of staff. As Haldeman explained, "Every President needs a son of a bitch, and I'm Nixon's. I'm his buffer, I'm his bastard." He was succeeded in 1973 by General Alexander Haig, whom Nixon described as "the meanest, toughest, most ambitious son of a bitch I ever knew." John Ehrlichman, a Seattle attorney and college schoolmate of Haldeman's, served as chief domestic policy adviser. As secretary of state, Nixon tapped his old friend William Rogers, who had served as attorney general under Eisenhower. Rogers's control over foreign policy was quickly preempted by Henry Kissinger, a distinguished Harvard political scientist who served as national security adviser before becoming secretary of state in 1973. Kissinger came to dominate the Nixon administration's diplomatic planning and emerged as one of the most respected and internationally famous members of the staff. Nixon often had to mediate the tensions between Rogers and Kissinger, noting that the secretary of state considered the German-born Kissinger "Machiavellian, deceitful, egotistical, arrogant, and insulting," while Kissinger viewed Rogers as "vain, emotional, unable to keep a secret, and hopelessly dominated by the State Department bureaucracy."

DOMESTIC AFFAIRS   A major reason for Richard Nixon's election in 1968 was the effective "southern strategy" fashioned by his campaign staffers. To garner support among Republican delegates from the South and then win over southern voters in the election, Nixon had assured southern conservatives that he would slow federal enforcement of civil rights laws and appoint pro-southern justices to the Supreme Court. Once in office, Nixon strove to follow through on his pledges. He appointed no African Americans to his cabinet and refused to meet with the Congressional Black Caucus. In 1970 he launched a concerted effort to block congressional renewal of the Voting Rights Act of 1965 and to delay implementation of court orders requiring the desegregation of school districts in Mississippi. The Democratic-controlled Congress then extended the Voting Rights Act over Nixon's veto. The Supreme Court, in the first decision made under the new chief justice, Warren Burger—a Nixon appointee—ordered the integration of the Mississippi public schools. During Nixon's first term, and despite his wishes, affirmative action made major inroads, and more schools were desegregated than in all the Kennedy-Johnson years combined.

Nixon's attempts to block desegregation efforts in urban areas also failed. The Burger Court ruled unanimously in *Swann v. Charlotte-Mecklenburg*

Board of Education (1971) that school systems must bus students out of their neighborhood if necessary to achieve racial integration. Protests over deseg-regation now occurred more in the North and the West than in the South as white families in Boston, Denver, and other cities denounced the destruction of "the neighborhood school." Busing opponents won a limited victory when the Supreme Court ruled in 1974 that requiring the transfer of stu-dents from the inner city to the suburbs was unconstitutional. That ruling, along with the *Board of Regents of the University of California v. Bakke* (1978) decision, which restricted the use of quotas to achieve racial balance in uni-versity classrooms, marked the transition of desegregation from an issue of simple justice to a more tangled thicket of conflicting group and individual rights.

It also reflected the growing conservatism of the Supreme Court, a trend encouraged by Nixon. The litany of liberal decisions during the 1960s had made the Warren Court a prime target for conservatives who resented what they regarded as the federal government's excessive protection of the "unde-serving." Fate and the aging of the justices on the Warren Court gave Nixon the chance to make four new appointments. Only one, William Rehnquist, would consistently support Nixon's conservative interpretation of the Con-stitution, but overall the tenor of the Court did shift toward a more moder-ate stance.

Nixon also fervently desired to reverse the welfare-state policies of his De-mocratic predecessors. But the administration never succeeded in develop-ing a comprehensive domestic agenda acceptable to Congress. Meanwhile, the Democratic Congress moved forward with new legislation: the right of eighteen-year-olds to vote in national elections (1970) and, under the Twenty-sixth Amendment (1971), in state and local elections as well; in-creases in Social Security benefits tied to the inflation rate; a rise in food-stamp funding; the Occupational Safety and Health Act (1970); and the Federal Election Campaign Act (1972). Moreover, in response to Nixon's proposal to decentralize responsibility for various programs, Congress passed a five-year revenue-sharing plan in 1972 that would distribute $30 billion of federal revenues to the states for use as they saw fit.

During Nixon's first term, Americans in large numbers began to lobby for government action to protect and improve the natural environment. In 1970 hundreds of thousands of activists rallied across the country in support of the first annual Earth Day. In response, Congress established new programs to control water pollution and passed the Clean Air Act (1970) over Nixon's veto. Congress also created the Environmental Protection Agency (EPA) to oversee federal guidelines for controlling air pollution, toxic wastes, and water quality. The EPA began requiring developers to perform environmental-impact studies before new construction could begin. The agency also set fuel-efficiency standards for automobiles and required manufacturers to reduce the level of carbon monoxide emissions from car engines.

ECONOMIC MALAISE The major domestic development during the Nixon years was a floundering economy. Exacerbated by the expense of the Vietnam War, the annual inflation rate began to rise in 1967, when it was at 3 percent. By 1973 it had reached 9 percent; a year later it was at 12 percent, and it remained in double digits for most of the 1970s. Unemployment, at a low of 3.3 percent when Nixon took office, climbed to 6 percent by the end of 1970 and threatened to keep rising. Somehow the American economy was undergoing a recession and an inflation at the same time. Economists coined the term *stagflation* to describe the syndrome that defied the orthodox laws of economics.

The economic malaise had at least three deep-rooted causes. First, the Johnson administration had attempted to pay for both the Great Society's social-welfare programs and the war in Vietnam without a major tax increase, thereby generating larger federal deficits, a major expansion of the money supply, and rapid price inflation. Second and more important, by the late 1960s American goods faced stiff competition in international markets from West Germany, Japan, and other emerging industrial powers. This development sharply reduced the export of American goods and generated a growing trade deficit. Third, the economy had grown heavily dependent upon cheap sources of energy.

Just as domestic petroleum reserves began to dwindle and dependence upon foreign sources increased, the nations in the Organization of Petroleum Exporting Countries (OPEC), centered in the Middle East, resolved to use their oil as a political and economic weapon. In 1973, after the United States sent massive aid to Israel during the Yom Kippur War, OPEC announced that it would not sell oil to nations supporting Israel and that it was raising its prices by 400 percent. American motorists thereafter faced long lines at gas stations, schools and offices closed temporarily, factories cut production, and the inflation rate soared.

Another condition leading to stagflation was the flood of new workers—mainly baby boomers and women—entering the labor market. From 1965 to 1980, the workforce grew by 40 percent, almost 30 million workers, a figure greater than the total labor force of France or West Germany. The number of new jobs created could not keep up, leaving many unemployed. At the same time, worker productivity declined, further increasing prices in the face of rising demand.

Stagflation posed a new set of economic problems, but the Nixon administration responded with old remedies. First it tried to reduce the federal deficit by raising taxes and cutting the budget. When the Democratic Congress refused to cooperate with that approach, the White House encouraged the Federal Reserve Board to reduce the money supply by raising interest rates. But that move backfired when the stock market quickly collapsed, plunging the economy into the "Nixon recession." A sense of desperation seized the White House. In 1969, when asked about government restrictions on wages and prices, Nixon had been adamant: "Controls. Oh, my God, no! ... We'll never go to controls." On August 15, 1971, however, he reversed himself. He froze all wages and prices for ninety days, yet the economy still floundered. By 1973 the wage and price guidelines were made voluntary and were therefore almost entirely ineffective. Stagflation continued to plague the economy for the rest of the decade.

Nixon Triumphant

Confronting a Congress controlled by Democrats, Richard Nixon focused his energies on foreign policy, where presidential initiatives were less restricted and where he, in tandem with Henry Kissinger, achieved several

Race to the Moon

In July 1969 a program begun by President Kennedy reached its goal: putting a man on the moon.

major breakthroughs. He also continued to support the American space program and the efforts to beat the Soviets to the moon. In July 1969 astronaut Neil Armstrong became the first person to walk on the moon. This extraordinary achievement buoyed American spirits at a time when troops were still mired in Vietnam, cities were boiling over with racial unrest, and the economy was languishing. Similarly, Nixon's foreign-policy successes gave Americans new confidence in their government. His administration managed to improve U.S. relations with the major powers of the Communist world—China and the Soviet Union—and fundamentally shift the pattern of the cold war.

By 1969 Nixon had perceived that a new multipolar world order was emerging to replace the conventional cold war confrontation between the United States and the Soviet Union. Since 1945 the United States had lost its monopoly on nuclear weapons and its overwhelming economic dominance and geopolitical influence. The rapid rise of competing power centers in Europe, China, and Japan complicated international relations—China had replaced the United States as the Soviet Union's most threatening competitor—but also provided strategic opportunities, which Nixon and Kissinger seized.

In early 1970 Nixon announced a significant alteration in American foreign policy. The United States could no longer be the world's policeman against communism; the long-standing containment policy developed by President Truman must be revised: "America cannot—and will not—conceive *all* the plans, design *all* the programs, execute *all* the decisions, and undertake *all* the defense of the free nations of the world." In explaining what became known as the Nixon Doctrine, the president declared that "our interests must shape our commitments, rather than the other way around." The United States, he

The United States and China

With President Richard Nixon's visit to China in 1972, the United States formally recognized China's Communist government. Here Nixon and Chinese premier Chou En-lai drink a toast.

and Kissinger stressed, must become more strategic and more realistic in its commitments, and it would begin to establish selected partnerships with Communist countries in areas of mutual interest.

CHINA   In 1971 Henry Kissinger made a secret trip to Peking to explore the possibility of U.S. recognition of China. In 1972 Nixon himself arrived in Peking and made recognition an official and public fact. The irony of the event was overwhelming. Richard Nixon, the former anti-Communist crusader who had condemned the State Department for "losing" China in 1949, had accomplished a diplomatic feat that his Democratic predecessors could not. Yet it was because Nixon had been such an ardent anti-Communist that he could pull off the recognition of China: he could not be accused of going soft on communism.

DÉTENTE   China sought the breakthrough in relations with the United States because its festering rivalry with the Soviet Union, with which it shares a long border, had become increasingly bitter. Soviet leaders, troubled by the Sino-American agreements, were also eager to ease tensions with the United States now that they had, as the result of a huge arms buildup following the Cuban missile crisis, achieved virtual parity with the United States in nuclear weapons. Once again Nixon surprised the world, announcing that he would visit Moscow in 1972 for discussions with Leonid Brezhnev, the Soviet premier.

What became known as détente with the Soviets offered the promise of a more orderly and restrained competition between the two superpowers. Nixon and Brezhnev signed the Strategic Arms Limitation Talks (SALT) agreement, which set ceilings on the number of long-range nuclear missiles each nation could possess and limited the construction of antiballistic missile systems. In effect the Soviets were allowed to retain a greater number of missiles with greater destructive power while the United States retained a lead in the total number of warheads. No limitations were placed on new weapons systems, though each side agreed to work toward a permanent freeze on all nuclear weapons.

SHUTTLE DIPLOMACY   The Nixon-Kissinger initiatives in the Middle East were less dramatic and less conclusive than the agreements with China and the Soviet Union, but they did show that America recognized Arab power in the region and its own dependence upon oil from Islamic states, which were fundamentally opposed to the existence of Israel. After Israel recovered from the initial shock of the Arab attacks that triggered the Yom Kippur War of 1973, it recaptured the Golan Heights and seized additional Syrian territory. Henry Kissinger initiated the negotiations leading to a cease-fire and exerted pressure to prevent Israel from taking more Arab territory. American reliance upon Arab oil led to closer ties with Egypt and its president, Anwar el-Sadat, and more restrained support for Israel. Although Kissinger's "shuttle diplomacy," involving numerous visits to the capitals of the Middle East, won acclaim from all sides, it failed to find a comprehensive peace formula for the troubled region. It also ignored the problem of establishing a homeland for Palestinian refugees. But Kissinger's efforts did lay groundwork for the accord between Israel and Egypt in 1977.

THE ELECTION OF 1972   Nixon's foreign-policy achievements allowed him to stage the presidential campaign of 1972 as a triumphal procession. The first threat to his reelection came from the Democratic governor of Alabama, George Wallace, who had the potential to deprive the Republicans of conservative votes. But on May 15, 1972, Wallace was shot by a deranged man. Paralyzed below the waist, Wallace was forced to withdraw from the campaign. Meanwhile, the Democrats were further ensuring Nixon's victory by nominating Senator George S. McGovern of South Dakota, a steadfast liberal who embodied anti-war principles and embraced progressive social-welfare policies. At the Democratic Convention, party reforms contributed to McGovern's nomination by increasing the representation of women, African Americans, and other minorities, but those reforms alienated the party regulars.

In 1972 Nixon won the greatest victory of any Republican presidential candidate in history, capturing 520 electoral votes to only 17 for McGovern. During the course of the campaign, McGovern complained about the "dirty tricks" of the Nixon administration, most especially the curious incident during the summer of 1972 in which burglars were caught breaking into the headquaters of the Democratic National Committee in the Watergate apartment complex in Washington, D.C. McGovern's accusations seemed shrill and biased at the time. Nixon and his staff made plans for "four more years" as the investigation of the fateful Watergate break-in unfolded.

WATERGATE

During the trial of the accused Watergate burglars in January 1973, the relentless prodding of Judge John J. Sirica led one of the accused to tell the full story of the Nixon administration's complicity in the episode. James McCord, a former CIA agent and security chief of the Committee to Re-elect the President (CREEP), was the first of many informers in a melodrama that unfolded over two years. It ended in the first resignation of a president in American history, the conviction and imprisonment of twenty-five officials of the Nixon administration, including four cabinet members, and the most serious constitutional crisis since the impeachment trial of President Andrew Johnson.

UNCOVERING THE COVER-UP   The trail of evidence pursued by Judge Sirica, a grand jury, several special prosecutors, and a televised Senate investigatory committee headed by Democrat Samuel J. Ervin Jr. of North Carolina led directly to the White House. No evidence surfaced that Nixon had ordered the break-in or that he had been aware of plans to burglarize the Democratic National Committee headquarters. From the start, however, Nixon participated in the cover-up, using his presidential powers to discredit and block the investigation. Perhaps most alarming was that the Watergate burglary proved to be just one small part of a larger pattern of corruption and criminality sanctioned by the Nixon White House. Having developed a compulsive view of his presidency as being above the law, Nixon had ordered intelligence agencies to spy on his most outspoken opponents, open their mail, and even burglarize their homes in an effort to uncover compromising information.

The Watergate cover-up began to unravel as various people, including John Dean, legal counsel to the president, began to cooperate with prosecutors. It unraveled further in 1973 when L. Patrick Gray, acting director of the FBI, resigned after confessing that he had destroyed several incriminating documents. On April 30 top Nixon aides John Ehrlichman and Bob Haldeman resigned, together with Attorney General Richard Kleindienst. A few days later Nixon nervously assured the public in a television address, "I'm not a crook." New evidence suggested otherwise. John Dean, whom Nixon had dismissed, testified before the Ervin committee and a rapt television audience that Nixon had approved the cover-up. In another bombshell disclosure, a White House aide told the committee that Nixon had installed a taping system in the White House and that many of the conversations about Watergate had been recorded.

A year-long legal battle for the "Nixon tapes" began. Pleading "executive privilege," Nixon refused to release them. On July 24, 1974, in *United States v. Richard M. Nixon,* the Supreme Court ruled unanimously that the president must surrender all of the tapes. A few days later the House Judiciary Committee voted to recommend three articles of impeachment: obstruction of justice through the payment of "hush money" to witnesses and the withholding of evidence, abuse of power through the use of federal agencies to deprive citizens of their constitutional rights, and defiance of Congress by withholding the tapes. Before the House of Representatives could meet to vote on impeachment, however, Nixon handed over the complete set of White House tapes. On August 9, 1974, fully aware that the evidence on the tapes implicated him in the cover-up, Richard Nixon resigned from office, the only president ever to do so.

Nixon's Resignation

Having resigned his office, Richard Nixon waves farewell outside the White House on August 9, 1974.

THE EFFECTS OF WATERGATE   Vice President Spiro Agnew did not succeed Nixon because Agnew had been forced to resign in October 1973 for accepting bribes from contractors before and during his term as vice president. The vice president at the time of Nixon's resignation was Gerald Ford, the former Michigan congressman and House minority leader, whom Nixon had appointed, with congressional approval, under the provisions of the Twenty-fifth Amendment (ratified in 1967). President Ford insisted that he had no intention of pardoning Nixon, who was still liable for criminal prosecution. But a month after Nixon's resignation, on September 8, the new president issued the pardon, explaining that it was necessary to end the national obsession with the Watergate scandals. Many Americans suspected that Nixon and Ford had made a deal, though there was no evidence to confirm the speculation.

If there was a silver lining in Watergate's dark cloud, it was the vigor and resilience of the institutions that had brought a president down: the press, Congress, the courts, and an aroused public opinion. The Watergate revelations led Congress to pass several pieces of legislation designed to curb executive power in the future. The War Powers Act (1973) requires a president to inform Congress within forty-eight hours if U.S. troops are deployed in combat abroad and to withdraw troops after sixty days unless Congress specifically approves their stay. In an effort to correct abuses of campaign funds, Congress enacted legislation in 1974 that set new ceilings on political contributions and expenditures. In reaction to the Nixon claim of "executive privilege" as a means of withholding evidence, Congress strengthened the 1966 Freedom of Information Act to require prompt responses to requests for information from government files and to place on government agencies the burden of proof for classifying information as secret.

An Unelected President

While the Watergate crisis dominated the Washington scene, major domestic and foreign problems received little executive attention. Stagflation, the perplexing combination of inflation and recession, worsened, as did the oil crisis. At the same time, Henry Kissinger, who assumed control over the management of foreign policy, watched helplessly as the South Vietnamese forces began to crumble before North Vietnamese attacks, attempted with limited success to establish a framework for peace in the Middle East, and supported a CIA role in the overthrow of the popularly elected Marxist president of Chile.

THE FORD YEARS   Gerald Ford inherited those simmering problems, as well as the burden of being an unelected president. An amiable, honest man, Ford enjoyed widespread popular support for only a short time. "I am a Ford, not a Lincoln," he candidly recognized upon becoming vice president. His pardon of Nixon generated a storm of criticism. The *New York Times* called it "an unconscionable act."

As president, Ford adopted the posture he had developed as a conservative minority leader in the House: a nay-saying leader of the opposition who believed that the federal government exercised too much power over domestic affairs. In his fifteen months as president, Ford vetoed thirty-nine bills, outstripping Herbert Hoover's record in less than half the time. By resisting congressional pressure to reduce taxes and increase federal spending, he succeeded in plummeting the economy into the deepest recession since the Great Depression. Unemployment jumped to 9 percent in 1975, and the federal deficit hit a record the next year. Ford rejected wage and price controls to curb inflation, preferring voluntary restraints.

In foreign policy, Ford retained Henry Kissinger as secretary of state and attempted to pursue Nixon's goals of stability in the Middle East, rapprochement with China, and détente with the Soviet Union. Late in 1974 Ford met with Soviet leader Leonid Brezhnev and accepted the framework for another arms-control agreement that was to serve as the basis for SALT II. Meanwhile, Kissinger's tireless shuttling between Cairo and Tel Aviv produced an agreement: Israel promised to return to Egypt most of the Sinai territory captured in the 1967 war, and the two nations agreed to rely upon negotiations rather than force to settle future disagreements.

These limited but significant achievements should have enhanced Ford's image, but they were drowned in the sea of criticism and carping that followed the loss of South Vietnam to North Vietnam in the spring of 1975. Not only had a decade of American effort in Vietnam proved futile, but the Khmer Rouge, the Cambodian Communist movement, had also won a resounding victory, plunging Cambodia into a fanatic bloodbath. And the OPEC oil cartel was threatening another worldwide boycott while other third world nations denounced the United States as a depraved imperialistic power.

THE ELECTION OF 1976   In the midst of the turmoil, the Democrats could hardly wait for the 1976 election. At the Republican Convention, Ford managed to thwart a powerful challenge for the nomination from the former California governor and Hollywood actor Ronald Reagan. The Democrats chose Jimmy Carter, a former naval officer and engineer turned peanut farmer who had served one term as governor of Georgia. Carter capitalized on the post-Watergate cynicism by promising never to "tell a lie to the American people" and by citing his independence from traditional Washington power politics.

To the surprise of many pundits, the little-known Carter revived the New Deal coalition of southern whites, blacks, urban labor, and ethnic groups to win the election, with 41 million votes to Ford's 39 million. Polls showed that the Carter victory benefited from a heavy turnout of African Americans in the South, where Carter swept every state but Virginia. Minnesota senator Walter F. Mondale, Carter's liberal running mate and a favorite among blue-collar workers and the urban poor, also gave the ticket a big boost. The real story of the election, however, was the low voter turnout. Almost half of America's eligible voters, apparently alienated by Watergate and the lackluster candidates, chose to sit out the election.

THE CARTER INTERREGNUM

EARLY SUCCESSES   During the first two years of his term, Jimmy Carter enjoyed several successes. His administration included more African Americans, Hispanics, and women than any before. He offered amnesty to the thousands of young men who had fled the country rather than serve in Vietnam, closing one of the remaining open wounds of that traumatic event.

He reformed the civil service to provide rewards for meritorious performance, and he created new cabinet-level Departments of Energy and Education. Carter also pushed through Congress significant environmental initiatives, including a bill to regulate strip mining and a "superfund" to clean up chemical-waste sites.

His success was short-lived, however. In the summer of 1979, when renewed violence in the Middle East produced a second fuel shortage, motorists were again forced to wait in long lines for limited supplies of gasoline that they regarded as excessively expensive. Soon they directed their frustration at the White House. Opinion polls showed Carter with an approval rating of only 26 percent, lower than Nixon's during the worst moments of the Watergate crisis.

Several of Carter's early foreign-policy initiatives also got caught in political crossfires. Soon after his inauguration, Carter vowed that "the soul of our foreign policy" should be the defense of human rights abroad. But the human rights campaign aroused opposition from two sides: those who feared that it sacrificed a detached appraisal of national interest for high-level moralizing and those who believed that human rights were important but that the administration was applying the standard inconsistently.

THE CAMP DAVID ACCORDS   Carter's crowning diplomatic achievement was the arrangement of a peace agreement between Israel and Egypt. In 1978 Carter invited Egypt's president Anwar el-Sadat and Israel's prime minister Menachem Begin to Camp David, the presidential retreat in Maryland, for two weeks of difficult negotiations. The first part of the eventual agreement required Israel to return all land in the Sinai peninsula in exchange for Egyptian recognition of Israel's sovereignty. This agreement was successfully implemented in 1982, when the last Israeli settler vacated the peninsula. But the second part of the agreement, calling for Israel to negotiate with Sadat a resolution to the Palestinian refugee dilemma, began to unravel soon after the Camp David summit. Still, Carter and Secretary of State Cyrus Vance had orchestrated a dramatic display of high-level diplomacy that, whatever its limitations, made an all-out war between Israel and the Arab world less likely. It also represented a significant first step toward a comprehensive settlement of the region's volatile tensions.

MOUNTING TROUBLES   Carter's crowning failure was his mismanagement of the economy. In effect he inherited a bad situation and let it worsen. Carter employed the same economic policies as Nixon and Ford to fight stagflation, but he reversed the order of the federal "cure," preferring to fight unemployment first with a tax cut and increased public spending.

The Camp David Accords

Egyptian president Anwar el-Sadat (left), Jimmy Carter (center), and Israeli prime minister Menachem Begin (right) at the announcement of the Camp David Accords, September 1978.

Unemployment declined slightly, from 8 to 7 percent in 1977, but inflation soared; at 5 percent when he took office, it reached 10 percent in 1978 and kept rising. During one month in 1980, it measured an annual rate of 18 percent. Like previous presidents, Carter then reversed himself to fight the other side of the economic malaise. By midterm he was delaying tax reductions and vetoing government spending programs that he had proposed in his first year. The result was the worst of all possible worlds—a deepened recession and inflation averaging between 12 and 13 percent per year.

IRAN   Then the Iranian crisis exploded, producing a year-long barrage of unwelcome events that epitomized the inability of the United States to control world affairs. The crisis began in 1979 with the overthrow of the shah of Iran, long a staunch American ally and right-wing dictator. The revolutionaries who toppled the shah's government rallied around Ayatollah Ruhollah Khomeini, a fundamentalist Muslim leader who symbolized the militant Islamic values the shah had tried to replace with Western ways. Khomeini's hatred of the United States dated back to 1953, when the CIA had sponsored the overthrow of Iran's prime minister, Mohammed Mossadegh, an ardent nationalist who sought to rid his country of Western influence and interests. The 1953 coup had restored the shah's regime to power.

Late in 1979 Carter allowed the exiled shah to enter the United States to undergo cancer treatment. A few days later, on November 4, a frenzied mob stormed the U.S. embassy in Tehran and seized the staff. Khomeini applauded the mob action and demanded the shah's return, along with all his wealth, in exchange for the release of the fifty-two American hostages still held captive.

Carter was furious, but his options were limited. He appealed to the United Nations, but Khomeini scoffed at UN requests for the release of the hostages. Carter then froze all Iranian assets in the United States and appealed to American allies to organize a trade embargo of Iran. The trade restrictions were only partially effective—even America's most loyal European allies did not want to lose access to Iranian oil.

So a frustrated Carter, hounded by a public and press demanding "action," authorized a rescue attempt by U.S. commandos in April 1980. The raid was aborted in the Iranian desert because of helicopter malfunctions, however, and it ended with eight fatalities when a U.S. helicopter collided with a transport plane. Carter's presidency died with the failed raid. Secretary of State Cyrus Vance resigned in protest against the risky venture. Meanwhile, nightly television coverage of the taunting Iranian rebels generated a near obsession with the seeming impotence of the United States and the fate of the hostages. On January 20, 1981, the crisis ended after 444 days of captivity when Carter released several billion dollars of Iranian assets to ransom the kidnapped hostages. By then, however, Ronald Reagan had been elected president, and Carter was headed into retirement.

The turbulent and often tragic events of the 1970s—the Communist conquest of South Vietnam, the Watergate scandal and Nixon's resignation, the energy shortage and stagflation, and the Iranian hostage episode—provoked among Americans what Carter labeled a "crisis of confidence." By 1980 American power and prestige seemed to be on the decline, the economy remained in a shambles, and the sexual revolution launched in the 1960s, with the questions it raised for the family and other basic social and political institutions, had sparked a backlash of resentment in Middle America. With theatrical timing, Ronald Reagan emerged to tap the growing reservoir of public frustration and transform his political career into a crusade to make America "stand tall again." He told his supporters that there was "a hunger in this land for a spiritual revival, a return to a belief in moral absolutes." The United States, he declared, remained the "greatest country in the world. We have the talent, we have the drive, we have the imagination. Now all we need is the leadership."

MAKING CONNECTIONS

· Foreign affairs in the 1970s showed the changing patterns of the cold war. The next chapter details the end of both the cold war and the Soviet Union.

· Presidents Nixon and Ford tried, with limited success, to decrease the power of the federal government over domestic affairs. President Reagan was much more successful at advancing the conservative agenda, another topic covered in the next chapter.

· The rebellion and turbulence of the 1960s and 1970s became less apparent in the following decade; as Chapter 37 shows, however, that turbulence reappeared, in a somewhat different form, in the 1990s.

FURTHER READING

An engaging overview of the cultural trends of the 1960s is Maurice Isserman and Michael Kazin's *America Divided: The Civil War of the 1960s* (1999). The New Left is assessed in Irwin Unger's *The Movement: A History of the American New Left, 1959–1972* (1974). On the Students for a Democratic Society, see Kirkpatrick Sale's *SDS* (1973) and Allen J. Matusow's *The Unraveling of America: A History of Liberalism in the 1960s* (1984). Also useful is Todd Gitlin's *The Sixties: Years of Hope, Days of Rage,* rev. ed. (1993).

Two influential assessments of the counterculture by sympathetic commentators are Theodore Roszak's *The Making of a Counterculture: Reflections on the Technocratic Society and Its Youthful Opposition* (1969) and Charles A. Reich's *The Greening of America* (1970). A good scholarly analysis of the hippies that takes them seriously is Timothy Miller's *The Hippies and American Values* (1991).

The best study of the women's liberation movement is Ruth Rosen's *The World Split Open: How the Modern Women's Movement Changed America* (2000). The organizing efforts of Cesar Chavez are detailed in Ronald B. Taylor's *Chavez and the Farm Workers* (1975). The struggles of Native Americans for recognition and power are sympathetically described in Stan Steiner's *The New Indians* (1968).

On Nixon, see Melvin Small's *The Presidency of Richard Nixon* (1999). For a solid overview of the Watergate scandal, see Stanley I. Kutler's *The Wars of Watergate: The Last Crisis of Richard Nixon* (1990). For the way the Republicans handled foreign affairs, consult Tad Szulc's *The Illusion of Peace: Foreign Policy in the Nixon Years* (1978).

The loss of Vietnam and the end of American involvement there are traced in Larry Berman's *No Peace, No Honor: Nixon, Kissinger, and Betrayal in Vietnam* (2001). William Shawcross's *Sideshow: Kissinger, Nixon and the Destruction of Cambodia*, rev. ed. (2002), deals with the broadening of the war, while Larry Berman's *Planning a Tragedy: The Americanization of the War in Vietnam* (1982) assesses the final impact of American involvement. The most comprehensive treatment of the anti-war movement in the United States is Tom Wells's *The War Within: America's Battle over Vietnam* (1994).

A comprehensive treatment of the Ford administration is contained in John Robert Greene's *The Presidency of Gerald R. Ford* (1995). The best overview of the Carter administration is Burton I. Kaufman's *The Presidency of James Earl Carter, Jr.* (1993). A work more sympathetic to the Carter administration is John Dumbrell's *The Carter Presidency: A Re-evaluation* (1993). Gaddis Smith's *Morality, Reason, and Power: American Diplomacy in the Carter Years* (1986) provides an overview. Background on how the Middle East came to dominate much of American policy is found in William B. Quandt's *Decade of Decisions: American Policy toward the Arab-Israeli Conflict, 1967–1976* (1977).

36

A CONSERVATIVE INSURGENCY

FOCUS QUESTIONS

- What were the demographic, social, and economic reasons for the rise of Ronald Reagan and Republican conservatism?

- How did changing relations between the United States and the Soviet Union lead to the end of the cold war?

- What characterized the economy and the society of the 1980s?

- What were the causes and the aftermath of the Gulf War?

To answer these questions and access additional review material, please visit www.wwnorton.com/studyspace.

President Jimmy Carter and his embattled Democratic administration hobbled through 1979. The economy remained sluggish, double-digit inflation continued unabated, and failed efforts to free the hostages in Iran made the administration appear indecisive. Carter's inability to persuade the nation to embrace his energy conservation program revealed mortal flaws in his reading of the public mood and his understanding of legislative politics.

While the lackluster Carter administration was foundering, Republican conservatives were forging an aggressive plan to win the White House in 1980 and to assault the New Deal welfare-state mentality in Washington. Those plans centered on the popularity and charisma of Ronald Reagan, the Hollywood actor turned California governor and prominent political commentator. Reagan was not a deep thinker, but he was a superb analyst of the public mood, an unabashed patriot, and a committed champion of conservative

The Great Communicator

Ronald Reagan in 1980, shortly before his election.

principles. He was also charming and cheerful, a likable politician renowned for his folksy anecdotes and optimistic outlook. Where the dour Carter denounced the evils of free-enterprise capitalism and scolded Americans in an attempt to get them to revive long-forgotten virtues of frugality, a sunny Reagan promised a "revolution of ideas" designed to unleash the capitalist spirit, restore national pride, and regain international respect.

During the late 1970s Reagan's simple message promoting a restoration of American pride and prosperity offered an uplifting alternative to Carter's vision of a constrained future. Reagan wanted to increase military spending, dismantle the "bloated" federal bureaucracy, reduce taxes and regulations, and in general, shrink the role of the government. He also wanted to affirm old-time morality by banning abortions and reinstituting prayer in public schools. Reagan's appeal derived from his remarkable skills as a public speaker and his dogmatic commitment to a few overarching ideas and simple themes. As a true believer and an able compromiser, he combined the fervor of a revolutionary with the pragmatism of a diplomat.

Such attributes won Reagan two presidential terms, in 1980 and 1984, and ensured the election of his successor, George H. W. Bush, in 1988. Just how revolutionary the Reagan era was remains a subject of intense partisan debate. What cannot be denied, however, is that Reagan's actions and beliefs set the tone for the decade's political and economic life.

THE REAGAN REVOLUTION

THE MAKING OF A PRESIDENT As the 1980 election approached, the Republicans eagerly anticipated the contest with a struggling Jimmy Carter. Their candidate, Ronald Reagan, had initially appeared as an even more improbable presidential possibility than Carter had four years earlier.

Born in Illinois in 1911, Reagan graduated from tiny Eureka College and then worked as a radio announcer and sportscaster before heading to Hollywood in 1937. In 1964 Reagan entered the political limelight when he delivered a rousing speech on behalf of Barry Goldwater at the Republican Convention. During two terms as governor of California (1967–1975), he displayed a commitment to conservative principles as well as a political realism and an openness to compromise. Nevertheless, by the middle 1970s Reagan's brand of free-enterprise conservatism still appeared too extreme for a national audience.

THE MOVE TO REAGAN   By the eve of the 1980 election, however, Reagan had become the beneficiary of three developments that made his conservative vision of America much more viable. First, the 1980 census revealed that the population was aging, and large numbers of retirees were moving from the liberal Northeast to the conservative sunbelt states of the South and the West. This development meant that demographic forces were carrying the electorate toward Reagan's conservative position.

Second, in the 1970s the country experienced a major revival of evangelical religion. No longer simply a local or provincial phenomenon, Christian evangelicals and fundamentalists had bought television and radio stations and were operating schools and universities. The Reverend Jerry Falwell's Moral Majority expressed the major goals of the religious right wing: free enterprise should remain free, big government should be shrunk, abortion should be outlawed, prayer in public schools should be reinstated, Darwinian evolution should be replaced in schoolbooks by the biblical story of creation, and Soviet communism should be opposed as a form of pagan totalitarianism. The moralistic zeal and financial resources of the religious right made its adherents effective opponents of liberal political candidates and programs. They rallied to Reagan's call for the strengthening of traditional values and local government.

A third factor contributing to the conservative resurgence was a well-organized and well-financed backlash against the feminist movement. During the 1970s women who opposed the social goals of feminism formed counterorganizations with names like Women Who Want to Be Women and Females Opposed to Equality. Spearheading those efforts was Phyllis Schlafly, a right-wing Republican activist from Illinois. Schlafly orchestrated the campaign to defeat the equal-rights amendment and thereafter served as the galvanizing force behind a growing anti-feminist movement. She characterized feminists as a "bunch of bitter women seeking a constitutional cure for their personal problems," and she urged women to embrace their "God-given" roles as wives and mothers. Feminists, she charged, were "anti-family, anti-children, and pro-abortion."

Many of Schlafly's supporters also participated in a mushrooming anti-abortion, or "pro-life," movement. By 1980 the National Right to Life Committee, supported by the National Conference of Catholic Bishops, boasted 11 million members representing all religious denominations. The intensity of its members' commitment made it a powerful political force in its own right, and the Reagan campaign was quick to highlight its own support for traditional "family values," gender roles, and the "rights" of the unborn. Such hot-button cultural issues helped persuade many northern Democrats to support Reagan. Whites alienated by the increasingly liberal social agenda of the Democratic party became a crucial element in Reagan's electoral strategy.

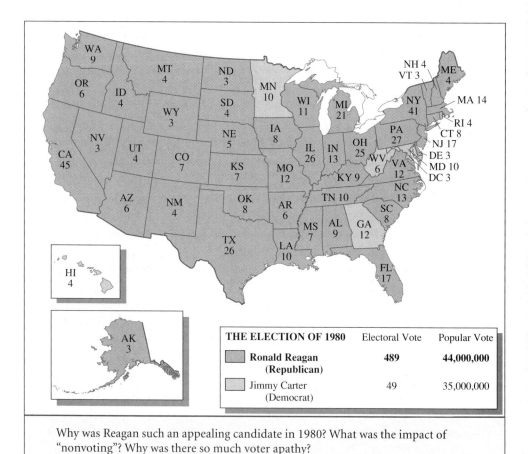

THE ELECTION OF 1980	Electoral Vote	Popular Vote
Ronald Reagan (Republican)	489	44,000,000
Jimmy Carter (Democrat)	49	35,000,000

Why was Reagan such an appealing candidate in 1980? What was the impact of "nonvoting"? Why was there so much voter apathy?

THE ELECTION OF 1980   By 1980 voters were flocking to Reagan's cheery promises of a new era of less government, lower taxes, renewed prosperity, waning inflation, and revived military strength and national pride. His "supply-side" economic proposals, soon dubbed Reaganomics by supporters and voodoo economics by critics, suggested that the stagflation of the 1970s had resulted from excessive taxes that weakened the incentive to work, save, and reinvest. The solution was to slash tax rates. For a long-suffering nation it was, in theory, an alluring economic panacea.

On election day, Reagan swept to a decisive victory, with 489 electoral votes to 49 for Carter, who carried only six states. The popular vote proved equally lopsided: 44 million (51 percent) to 35 million (41 percent), with 7 percent going to John Anderson, a moderate Republican who had bolted the party after Reagan's nomination and ran on an independent ticket.

In addition to affirming Reagan's conservative agenda, the 1980 election reflected the triumph of what one political scientist called the "largest mass movement of our time"—nonvoting. Almost as striking as Reagan's one-sided victory was the fact that his total votes represented only 28 percent of registered voters. Only 53 percent of eligible voters cast ballots in the 1980 election.

There were various explanations for the high level of voter apathy among working-class Americans. Some observers stressed the disillusionment with government that grew out of the Watergate affair. Others believed that the Democratic party had alienated its traditional blocs of support among common folk. Democratic leaders no longer spoke eloquently on behalf of those at the bottom of America's social scale. By embracing a fiscal conservatism indistinguishable from that of the Republicans, as Carter had done, Democrats had lost their appeal among blue-collar workers and the urban poor. When viewed in this light, Reagan's lopsided triumph represented both a resounding victory for conservative Republicans and a self-inflicted defeat by a fractured Democratic party. Flush with a sense of power and destiny, President-elect Ronald Reagan headed toward Washington with a blueprint for dismantling the welfare state.

REAGAN'S FIRST TERM

REAGANOMICS   Ronald Reagan brought to Washington a simple conservative philosophy. "Government is not the solution to our problem," he insisted; "government is the problem." Reagan credited Calvin Coolidge and Coolidge's Treasury secretary, Andrew Mellon, with demonstrating that by reducing taxes and easing government regulation of business, free-market capitalism would revive the economy. By cutting taxes and domestic federal spending and by following a supply-side economic program, he claimed, a surging economy would produce *more* government revenues, which in turn would help reduce the budget deficit.

Unlike Carter, Reagan increased defense spending, reduced social spending, and persuaded Congress to pass a sweeping tax-reform proposal. Enough Democrats—mostly sympathetic southern conservatives dubbed boll weevils—supported the measures to pass them by overwhelming majorities. On August 1, 1981, Reagan signed the Economic Recovery Tax Act, which cut personal income taxes by 25 percent, lowered the maximum rate from 70 to 50 percent for 1982, cut the capital gains tax by one third, and offered a broad array of other tax concessions.

The new legislation embodied an idea that went back to Alexander Hamilton, George Washington's Treasury secretary: more money in the hands of the affluent would benefit society at large, since the wealthy would engage in productive consumption and investment. A closer parallel was Treasury Secretary Andrew Mellon's tax-reduction program of the 1920s. The difference was that the Reagan tax cuts were accompanied by massive increases in defense spending, which generated ever-mounting federal deficits. Reagan's advisers insisted that the unbalanced budgets were only temporary; the new tax plan would fuel economic growth and thereby boost tax revenues as personal income and corporate profits skyrocketed. But it did not work out that way. By the summer of 1983, a major economic recovery was under way, but the federal deficits had grown ever larger, so much so that the president, who in 1980 had pledged to balance the federal budget by 1983, had in fact run up debts larger than those of all his predecessors combined.

Bankers and investors feared that the rising federal debt would send interest rates soaring, a fear expressed in sagging bond and stock markets. A business slump and rising unemployment continued through most of 1982. That year the federal deficit doubled. Aides finally convinced Reagan that to reassure the public about deficits and the threat of inflation, the government needed "revenue enhancements," a euphemism for tax increases. With Reagan's support, Congress passed a new tax bill in 1982 that would raise almost $100 billion. During the midterm elections of 1982, Reagan urged voters to "stay the course" and appealed for more time to let his economic program take effect. Meanwhile, the economic slump persisted through 1982, with unemployment standing at 10.4 percent, and the congressional Republicans experienced moderate losses in the elections.

THE DEFENSE BUILDUP   Reagan's conduct of foreign policy reflected his belief that trouble in the world stemmed mainly from Moscow. He charged that the Soviets were "prepared to commit any crime, to lie, to cheat" and do anything necessary to promote world communism. Reagan and Secretary of Defense Caspar Weinberger embarked on a major buildup of nuclear and conventional weapons to close the gap that they claimed had developed between Soviet and U.S. military forces.

In 1983 Reagan escalated the nuclear arms race by authorizing the Defense Department to develop a Strategic Defense Initiative, a complex defense system meant to destroy enemy missiles in outer space well before they reached their targets. Despite skepticism among the media and many scientists that such a "Star Wars"defense system could be built, it forced the Soviets to launch an expensive research and development program of their own to keep pace.

Reagan borrowed the rhetoric of Harry Truman, John Foster Dulles, and John F. Kennedy's inaugural address to express American resolve in the face of "Communist aggression anywhere in the world." Détente deteriorated even further when the Soviets imposed martial law in Poland during the winter of 1981. The crackdown came after Polish workers, united under the banner of an independent union called Solidarity, challenged the Communist monopoly of power. As with the Soviet interventions in Hungary in 1956 and Czechoslovakia in 1968, there was little the United States could do except register protest and impose economic sanctions against Poland's Communist government.

THE AMERICAS   Reagan's foremost international concern, however, was in Central America, where he detected the most serious Communist threat. The tiny nation of El Salvador, caught up since 1980 in a brutal struggle between Communist-supported revolutionaries and right-wing extremists, received U.S. economic and military assistance. Reagan stopped short of sending troops, but he did increase the number of military advisers and the amount of financial aid to the Salvadoran government.

Even more troubling was the situation in Nicaragua. The State Department claimed that the Cuban-sponsored Sandinista government, which had only recently taken control of the country after ousting a corrupt dictator, was funneling Soviet and Cuban arms to leftist Salvadoran rebels. In response the Reagan administration ordered the CIA to train and supply guerrilla bands of disgruntled Nicaraguans, tagged Contras, who staged attacks on Sandinista bases and officials from sanctuaries in Honduras. In supporting these "freedom fighters," Reagan sought not only to impede the

"Shhhhhh. It's Top Secret."

A comment on the Reagan administration's covert operations in Nicaragua.

traffic in arms to Salvadoran rebels but also to overthrow the Communist Sandinistas.

Critics of Reagan's anti-Sandinista policy accused the Contras of being mostly right-wing fanatics who indiscriminately killed civilians as well as Sandinista soldiers. They also feared that the United States might eventually commit its own combat forces, thus threatening another Vietnam-like intervention.

THE MIDDLE EAST The Middle East remained a tinderbox of geopolitical conflict throughout the 1980s. No peaceable end seemed possible in the bloody Iran-Iraq War, which had erupted in 1980, entangled as it was with the passions of Islamic fundamentalism. In 1984 both sides began to attack tankers in the Persian Gulf, a major source of the world's oil. Although the Reagan administration harbored no affection for either nation, it viewed Iranian fundamentalism as the greater threat and funneled aid to Iraq, a policy with unforeseen and grave consequences.

American diplomats continued to see Israel as the strongest ally in the region, all the while seeking to encourage moderate Arab groups and anti-Communist governments. Continuing chaos in Lebanon, where ethnic and religious tensions erupted into near anarchy, threatened both Israel's borders and America's goals for the region. The capital, Beirut, became a battleground for rival Muslim and Christian factions, the army of the Palestine Liberation Organization (PLO), Syrian invaders cast as peacekeepers, and Israelis responding to PLO attacks.

French, Italian, and U.S. forces moved into Beirut as "peacekeepers," but in such small numbers as to become targets themselves. On October 23, 1983, an Islamic suicide bomber drove a truck laden with explosives into the U.S. Marine headquarters at the Beirut airport. The explosion left 241 Americans dead. On February 7, 1984, Reagan announced that the marines would be redeployed on warships offshore. The Israeli forces pulled back to southern Lebanon, while the Syrians remained in eastern Lebanon and imposed a tenuous peace upon the faction-ridden country.

GRENADA   In a fortunate turn for the Reagan administration, an easy military triumph closer to home eclipsed news of the debacle in Lebanon. On the tiny Caribbean island of Grenada, a leftist government had admitted Cuban workers to build a new airfield and had signed military agreements with several Communist-bloc countries. Appeals from the governments of neighboring islands led Reagan in 1983 to order 1,900 soldiers to invade the island, depose the radical regime, and evacuate a group of American students at Grenada's medical school. The UN General Assembly condemned the action, but most Grenadans and their neighbors applauded it, and the intervention was immensely popular in the United States.

REAGAN'S SECOND TERM

By 1983 prosperity had returned, and inflation had subsided; the Reagan economic program seemed to be working as touted. A dramatic fall in oil prices following the fragmentation of the OPEC cartel helped fuel the economic expansion.

THE ELECTION OF 1984   By 1984 Reagan had restored strength and vitality to the White House and the nation. His prospects for reelection were bright. The Democratic nominee, former Minnesota senator and vice president Walter Mondale, faced an uphill struggle. Mondale won a lot of media attention by choosing as his running mate a woman, New York representative Geraldine Ferraro. Attention soon turned to Ferraro's husband's dubious business finances, however. In any case, Reagan's skill and confidence at campaigning outshone Mondale, and the economic recovery made it difficult for the Democratic nominee to attract interest, much less generate enthusiasm. In the end, Reagan won almost 59 percent of the popular vote and lost only Minnesota and the District of Columbia. His coattails were not as long as they had been in 1980, however. Republicans gained only fifteen seats in the House, leaving them still greatly outnumbered by Democrats, 253 to 182. They also lost two Senate seats, creating a margin of only 53 to 47.

THE REAGAN DOCTRINE   In his 1985 State of the Union message, the reelected president clarified what had come to be called the Reagan Doctrine in foreign affairs. The United States, he proclaimed, would support anti-Communist forces around the world seeking to "defy Soviet-supported aggression." In effect, he was challenging the isolationism that followed the nation's humbling experience in Vietnam. America, he promised, would not hesitate to intervene in the world's hot spots.

Yet for all his stern talk about the Soviet Union being "an evil empire," Reagan was determined to reach an arms-control agreement with the Soviets. In Geneva in 1985, he met with Mikhail Gorbachev, the innovative

Foreign Relations

A light moment at a meeting between U.S. president Ronald Reagan (left) and Soviet premier Mikhail Gorbachev (right).

new leader of the Soviet Union. The two signed several cultural and scientific agreements and issued a statement on arms-limitations talks, but no treaty was in the offing. Nearly a year after the Geneva summit, on sudden notice and with limited preparation, Gorbachev and Reagan met in Iceland for two days to discuss arms reductions. Early reports predicted a major breakthrough, including a total ban on nuclear weapons, but the talks collapsed over disagreement on Reagan's commitment to the Strategic Defense Initiative. After the Iceland meeting the two nations reduced the scope of their discussions in order to break the impasse.

The logjam impeding the arms negotiations suddenly broke when Gorbachev announced that he was willing to deal separately on a medium-range missile treaty. After nine months of strenuous negotiations, Reagan and Gorbachev met amid much fanfare in Washington on December 9, 1987, and signed a treaty to eliminate intermediate-range (300- to 3,000-mile) nuclear forces. It was an epochal event, not only because it marked the first time that the two nations had agreed to destroy a whole class of weapons systems but also because it represented a key first step toward the eventual end of the arms race altogether. Under the terms of the treaty, the United States would destroy 859 missiles, and the Soviets would eliminate 1,752. Provision was also made for on-site inspections by each side to verify compliance. Still, this winnowing of weapons would represent only 4 percent of the total number of nuclear missiles on both sides. Arms-control advocates thus looked toward a second and more comprehensive treaty that would eliminate long-range strategic missiles.

THE IRAN-CONTRA AFFAIR   During the fall of 1986, the Reagan administration suffered a double blow. In the midterm elections, Democrats regained control of the Senate by fifty-five to forty-five. For his final two years in office, Reagan would face an opposition Congress. What was worse, on election day reports surfaced that the United States, with Israeli assistance, had secretly selling arms to Iran in the hope of securing the release of American hostages held in Lebanon by extremist Islamic groups with close ties to Iran. Such action contradicted Reagan's repeated public insistence that his administration would never negotiate with terrorists.

There was more to the story. Over the next several months, revelations reminiscent of the Watergate affair disclosed a more complicated series of covert activities carried out by administration officials. At the center of what came to be dubbed Irangate was the much-decorated marine lieutenant colonel Oliver North. An aide to the National Security Council who specialized in counterterrorism, North had been scheming to use the profits from the secret sale of military weapons to Iran to subsidize the

Contra rebels fighting in Nicaragua even though Congress had voted to ban such aid.

Under increasing criticism and amid growing doubts about his credibility and his ability, Reagan appointed both an independent counsel and a three-man commission, led by former Republican senator John Tower, to investigate the scandal. The Tower Commission issued a report early in 1987 that placed much of the responsibility for the bungled Iran-Contra affair on Reagan's loose management style. He seemed unaware of what his staffers were doing.

The investigations of the independent counsel led to six indictments in 1988. A Washington jury found Oliver North guilty of three relatively minor charges but innocent of nine more serious counts, apparently reflecting the jury's reasoning that he had acted as an agent of higher-ups. His conviction was later overturned on appeal. The Iran-Contra affair left support for the Nicaraguan Contras badly eroded in Congress, and it undermined much of Reagan's popularity.

THE POOR, THE HOMELESS, AND THE VICTIMS OF AIDS

The 1980s were years of vivid contrast. Despite unprecedented affluence there were countless beggars in the streets and homeless people sleeping in door-ways, in cardboard boxes, and on ventilation grates. A variety of factors caused the shortage of low-cost housing: the government had given up on building public housing, urban-renewal programs had demolished blighted areas but provided no housing for those they displaced, and owners had abandoned un-profitable buildings in poor neighborhoods or converted them into expensive condominiums, a process called gentrification.

After new medications enabled the deinstitutionalization of the mentally ill, many individuals ended up on the streets because the promised commu-nity mental-health services failed to materialize. By the summer of 1988, the *New York Times* estimated, more than 45 percent of New York's adults were living in poverty, totally outside the labor force, for lack of skills, drug use, and other problems.

Still another group cast aside were those suffering from the frightening new malady that had come to be known as AIDS (acquired immuno defi-ciency syndrome). At the beginning of the decade, public health officials had begun to report that gay men and intravenous drug users were especially at risk for contracting AIDS. Those infected with the virus that causes AIDS showed signs of fatigue, developed a strange combination of infections, and eventually died; people contracted the virus (HIV) by coming into contact with the blood or body fluids of an infected person. The Reagan administra-tion showed little interest in AIDS in part because it initially was viewed as a "gay" disease. Patrick Buchanan, the conservative spokesman who served as White House director of communications, said that homosexuals had "declared war on nature, and now nature is extracting an awful retribution."

THE REAGAN LEGACY   Although Ronald Reagan had declared in 1981 his intention to "curb the size and influence of the federal establishment," the welfare state remained intact when Reagan left office. Neither the Social Security system nor Medicare was dismantled or overhauled, nor were any other major welfare programs. And the federal agencies that Reagan had threatened to abolish, such as the Department of Education, not only remained in place in 1989 but saw their budgets grow. The federal budget as a percentage of the gross domestic product was actually higher when Reagan left office than when he had entered. Moreover, he did not try to push through Congress the incendiary social issues championed by the religious right, such as allowing prayer in public schools and a ban on abortions.

Yet Ronald Reagan succeeded in redefining the national political agenda and accelerated the conservative insurgency that had been developing for over twenty years. Reagan's critics highlighted his lack of intellectual sophistication and his indifference to day-to-day administrative details. His greatest successes were in renewing America's soaring sense of possibilities, bringing inflation under control, stimulating the longest sustained period of peacetime prosperity in history, and helping to light the fuse of democratic freedom in Eastern Europe. The fact that Reagan's tax policies widened the gap between the rich and the poor and created huge budget deficits for future presidents to confront did not diminish the popularity of the Great Communicator.

THE ELECTION OF 1988   As a new presidential election unfolded, eight Democratic presidential candidates engaged in a wild scramble for their party's nomination. As the primary season progressed, however, it soon became a two-man race, between Massachusetts governor Michael Dukakis and Jesse Jackson, the African-American civil rights activist who had been one of Martin Luther King's chief lieutenants. Dukakis eventually won out and managed a difficult reconciliation with the Jackson forces that left the Democrats unified and confident as the fall campaign began.

The Republicans nominated Reagan's two-term vice president, George H. W. Bush, who after a bumpy start had easily cast aside his rivals in the primaries. As Reagan's handpicked heir, Bush claimed credit for the administration's successes, but like all vice presidents he also faced the challenge of defining his own political identity. Yet at the Republican Convention, Bush delivered a forceful address that sharply enhanced his stature. The most

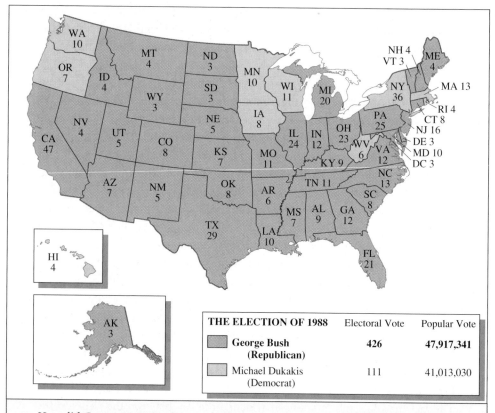

THE ELECTION OF 1988	Electoral Vote	Popular Vote
George Bush (Republican)	**426**	**47,917,341**
Michael Dukakis (Democrat)	111	41,013,030

How did George H. W. Bush overtake Dukakis's lead in the polls? What was the role of race and class in the election results? Who didn't vote in the election of 1988?

memorable line was a defiant statement on taxes: "Congress will push me to raise taxes, and I'll say no, and they'll push, and I'll say no, and they'll push again. And I'll say to them: Read my lips: *no new taxes.*"

In a campaign given over to mudslinging, the Bush partisans attacked Dukakis as a camouflaged liberal who would increase federal spending, raise taxes, gut the defense budget, and refuse to intervene to prevent Communist aggression abroad. The Republican onslaught took its toll against the less organized, less focused Dukakis campaign. Moreover, the Republicans continued to benefit from the population growth in the sunbelt states, the shift of population from the Democratic cities to the Republican suburbs, and from the votes of many moderate and conservative Democrats and independents. Dukakis captured only ten states plus the District of Columbia, with clusters in the Northeast, Midwest, and Northwest. Bush carried the rest, with a margin of about 54 percent to 46 percent in the popular vote and 426 to 111 in the Electoral College.

THE BUSH ADMINISTRATION

George H. W. Bush viewed himself as a guardian president rather than an activist. He lacked Reagan's visionary outlook and skill as a speaker. Bush was a pragmatic caretaker eager to avoid "stupid mistakes" and to find a way to get along with the Democratic majority in Congress. "We don't need to remake society," he announced. Bush sought to consolidate the programs that Reagan had put in place rather than launch his own array of programs and policies.

THE DEMOCRACY MOVEMENT ABROAD   Bush entered the White House with more foreign-policy experience than most presidents, and he found the spotlight of the world stage more congenial than wrestling with the intractable problems of the inner cities and the deficit. Within two years of his inauguration, George Bush would lead the United States into two wars. Throughout most of 1989, however, he merely had to sit back and observe the dissolution of one totalitarian or authoritarian regime after another. For the first time in years, global democracy was suddenly on the march in a sequence of mostly bloodless revolutions that took the world by surprise.

Although in China a democracy movement came to a tragic end in 1989 when government forces mounted a deadly assault on demonstrators in Beijing's (Peking's) Tiananmen Square, Eastern Europe had an entirely different experience. Mikhail Gorbachev set events in motion by responding to Soviet economic problems with policies of perestroika (restructuring) and glasnost (openness), a loosening of central economic planning and censorship. His foreign policy sought rapprochement and trade with the West, and he aimed to relieve the Soviet economy of burdensome military costs.

Gorbachev backed off from Soviet imperial ambitions. Early in 1989 Soviet troops left Afghanistan after spending nine years bogged down in civil war there. Then in July in Paris, Gorbachev repudiated the Brezhnev Doctrine, which asserted the right of the Soviet Union to intervene in the internal affairs of other Communist countries. The days when Soviet tanks would roll through Warsaw and Prague were over, and leaders in the Eastern-bloc countries found themselves beset by demands for democratic reform. With opposition strength building, the old regimes fell with surprisingly little bloodshed. Communist party rule ended first in Poland and Hungary, then in Czechoslovakia and Bulgaria. In Romania the year of peaceful revolution ended in a bloodbath when the Romanian people were joined by the army in a bloody uprising against the brutal dictator Nicolae Ceauşescu. He and his wife were captured, tried, and then executed on Christmas Day.

The most spectacular event in the collapse of the Soviet Empire in Eastern Europe came on November 9, 1989, when the chief symbol of the cold war—the Berlin Wall—was torn down by Germans, and the East German government succumbed to popular pressures for change. With the borders to the West fully open, the Communist government of East Germany collapsed, a freely elected government came to power, and on October 3, 1990, the five states of East Germany were united with West Germany. The reunified German nation remained in NATO, and the Warsaw Pact alliance was dissolved.

The reform impulse that Gorbachev helped unleash in the Eastern-bloc countries careened out of control within the Soviet Union, however.

Dissolution of the Soviet Empire

West Germans hacking away at the Berlin Wall on November 11, 1989, two days after all crossings between East Germany and West Germany were opened.

Gorbachev proved unusually adept at political restructuring. While yielding to the Communist monopoly of government, he built a new presidential system that gave him, if anything, increased powers. His skills did not extend to an antiquated economy that resisted change, however. The revival of ethnic allegiances added to the instability. Although Russia proper included slightly over half the Soviet Union's population, it was only one of fifteen constituent republics, most of which began to seek autonomy, if not independence.

Gorbachev's popularity in the Soviet Union shrank as it grew abroad. It especially eroded among the Communist hard-liners, who saw in his reforms the unraveling of their bureaucratic and political empire. On August 18, 1991, a cabal of political and military leaders tried to seize the reins of power in Russia. They accosted Gorbachev at his vacation retreat in the Crimea and demanded that he sign a decree proclaiming a state of emergency and transferring his powers to them. He replied, "Go to hell," whereupon he was placed under house arrest. Twelve hours later the Soviet news agency reported to the world that Gorbachev was "ill" and had temporarily transferred his powers to his vice president and an eight-member emergency

Action against Gorbachev

In August 1991, one day after Mikhail Gorbachev was placed under house arrest by Communists planning a coup, Russian Federation president Boris Yeltsin (holding papers) makes a speech criticizing the plotters.

committee. Political parties were suspended, newspapers were silenced, a curfew was announced, and street demonstrations were banned. Tanks and armored vehicles surrounded government buildings in Moscow. The new leaders promised to end the "chaos and anarchy" they claimed were bedeviling the country.

But the coup was doomed from the start. Poorly planned and clumsily implemented, it lacked effective coordination. The plotters failed to arrest popular leaders such as Boris Yeltsin, the president of the Russian republic, and they neglected to close the airports or cut off telephone and television communications. Most important, the plotters failed to recognize the strength of the democratic idealism unleashed by Gorbachev's reforms.

As the political drama unfolded in the Soviet Union, foreign leaders spoke out against the coup. On August 20 President Bush, after a day of indecision, responded favorably to Yeltsin's request for support and convinced other leaders to join him in refusing to recognize the legitimacy of the new Soviet government. The next day, word began to seep out that the plotters had given up and were fleeing. Several committed suicide, and a newly released Gorbachev ordered the others arrested. But Gorbachev's freedom did not bring a restoration of his power. Boris Yeltsin emerged as the most popular political figure in the country. Gorbachev reclaimed the title of president, but he was forced to resign as head of the Communist party and admit that he had made a grave mistake in appointing the men who had turned against him.

What began as a reactionary coup turned into a powerful accelerant for stunning changes in the Soviet Union. Most of the fifteen republics proclaimed their independence, with the Baltic republics of Latvia, Lithuania, and Estonia regaining the status of independent nations. The Communist party apparatus was dismantled, prompting celebrating crowds to topple statues of Lenin and other Communist heroes.

The aborted coup accelerated Soviet and American efforts to reduce the stockpiles of nuclear weapons. In 1991 President Bush announced that the United States would destroy all its tactical nuclear weapons on land and at sea in Europe and Asia, take its long-range bombers off twenty-four-hour-alert status, and initiate discussions with the Soviet Union for the purpose of instituting sharp cuts in nuclear missiles with multiple warheads. Bush explained that the prospect of a Soviet invasion of western Europe was "no longer a realistic threat," and this transformation presented an unprecedented opportunity for reducing the threat of nuclear holocaust. The Soviets responded by announcing reciprocal cutbacks. As Colin Powell, Chairman of the Joint Chiefs of Staff, remarked, the cold war "has vaporized before our eyes."

By the end of 1991, the Soviet Union had dissolved into a new—and fragile—Commonwealth of Independent States made up of eleven autonomous republics (Georgia joined in 1993). Held together by little other than historic ties and contiguous borders, the federated republics soon suffered outbreaks of ethnic tensions and separatist movements. With the Communist party dissolved, the Soviet Union dismantled, and continuing economic woes creating obstacles to his leadership, Mikhail Gorbachev resigned as president at the end of 1991. Boris Yeltsin, now a national hero, replaced him.

The dilution of the Soviet military threat led the U.S. Defense Department in 1992 to withdraw large numbers of personnel from military bases in Asia and Europe. The Pentagon also announced a plan to shrink the armed forces by 500,000 troops over the next five years. In 1992 Bush and Yeltsin declared their intention to reduce their combined arsenals of nuclear weapons from about 22,500 to no more than 7,000 by 2003. All land-based multiple-warhead missiles were to be destroyed.

PANAMA The end of the cold war did not spell the end of international tensions and conflicts, however. Indeed, in some respects the world became more unstable. Before the end of 1989, American troops were engaged in battle in Panama, where General Manuel Noriega, as chief of the Panamanian Defense Forces since 1983, was head of the government in fact if not in title. Years earlier Noriega had worked secretly with the CIA, providing information about developments in Central America. At the same time he got involved in the lucrative—and illegal—drug trade. In 1988 federal grand juries in Miami and Tampa indicted Noriega and fifteen others on charges of international drug smuggling, gunrunning, and laundering the profits through Panamanian banks.

In 1989 Panama's National Assembly named Noriega head of the government and proclaimed that Panama "is declared to be in a state of war" with the United States. The next day, December 16, 1989, an American marine in Panama was killed. President Bush ordered an invasion of Panama in order to capture Noriega, bring him to the United States so that he could face the charges against him, and install a government headed by opposition leaders.

The 12,000 U.S. military personnel already in Panama were quickly joined by 12,000 more, and in the early morning of December 20 five military task forces struck at strategic targets in the country. Twenty-three U.S. servicemen were killed in the action, and estimates of Panamanians killed and wounded were as high as 4,000, including many civilians. Noriega was captured, and he was detained in a U.S. federal prison for well over a year before his trial began in late 1991. He was convicted in 1992 on eight counts of racketeering and drug distribution.

THE GULF WAR   Months after Panama had moved to the background of public attention, Saddam Hussein, dictator of Iraq, focused attention on the Middle East when his army suddenly invaded neighboring Kuwait on August 2, 1990. Kuwait had raised its production of oil, contrary to agreements with OPEC. The resulting drop in oil prices offended the Iraqi regime, deep in debt and heavily dependent upon oil revenues.

Saddam Hussein did not expect the firestorm of world indignation his assault on Kuwait ignited. The UN Security Council quickly voted unanimously to condemn the invasion and demand withdrawal. American secretary of state James Baker and Soviet foreign minister Eduard Shevardnadze issued a joint statement of condemnation. The Security Council then endorsed Resolution 661, an embargo on trade with Iraq.

President Bush condemned Iraq's "naked aggression" and dispatched planes and troops to Saudi Arabia on a "wholly defensive" mission: to protect Saudi Arabia. British forces soon joined in, as did troops from a half

The Gulf War

U.S. soldiers adapt to desert conditions during Operation Desert Shield, December 1990.

dozen Arab nations. On August 22 Bush ordered the mobilization of American reserve forces for the operation, now dubbed Desert Shield.

A flurry of peace efforts sent diplomats scurrying, but without result. Iraq refused to yield. On January 10 Congress began to debate whether to authorize the use of U.S. armed forces. The outcome was uncertain to the end, but on January 12 a resolution for the use of force passed in the House, by a vote of 250 to 183, and in the Senate, by 52 to 47.

By January 1991 an allied force of over thirty nations was committed to Operation Desert Storm when the first missiles began to hit Iraq at about 2:30 A.M. on January 17, Baghdad time. Saddam Hussein concentrated his forces in Kuwait, expecting an allied attack northward into that country. But the Iraqis were outflanked when 200,000 allied troops, largely American, British, and French, turned up on the undefended Iraqi border with Saudi Arabia, far to the west. The allied ground assault began on February 24 and lasted only four days. Thousands of Iraqi soldiers surrendered, and there was a quick breakthrough into Kuwait.

On February 28, six weeks after the fighting began, President Bush called for a cease-fire, the Iraqis accepted, and the shooting ended. There were 137 American fatalities. The lowest estimate of Iraqi fatalities, civilian and military, was around 100,000. The coalition forces occupied about one fifth of Iraq. The consequences of the brief but intense Persian Gulf War, the "mother of all battles" in Saddam Hussein's words, would be played out in the future in ways no one predicted.

MAKING CONNECTIONS

- Much of what characterized the 1980s, from economic and social policy to presidential leadership style, was reminiscent of the late nineteenth century as well as the 1920s and 1950s.

- Another parallel between the late nineteenth century and the 1980s was a rise in immigration and a change in immigration patterns. These changes are discussed in Chapter 37.

- Chapter 37 also shows how the economic and political conservatism of the 1980s became much more ideological in the early 1990s.

FURTHER READING

Two brief accounts of Reagan's presidency are David Mervin's *Ronald Reagan and the American Presidency* (1990) and Michael Schaller's *Reckoning with Reagan: America and Its President in the 1980s* (1992).

On Reaganomics, see David A. Stockman's *The Triumph of Politics: How the Reagan Revolution Failed* (1986) and Robert Lekachman's *Greed Is Not Enough: Reaganomics* (1982). On the issue of arms control, see Strobe Talbott's *Deadly Gambits: The Reagan Administration and the Stalemate in Nuclear Arms Control* (1984).

For Reagan's foreign policy in Central America, see James Chace's *Endless War: How We Got Involved in Central America and What Can Be Done* (1984) and Walter LaFeber's *Inevitable Revolutions: The United States in Central America*, 2nd ed. (1993). Insider views of Reagan's foreign policy are offered in Alexander M. Haig Jr.'s *Caveat: Realism, Reagan, and Foreign Policy* (1984) and Caspar W. Weinberger's *Fighting for Peace: Seven Critical Years in the Pentagon* (1990).

On Reagan's second term, see Jane Mayer and Doyle McManus's *Landslide: The Unmaking of the President, 1984–1988* (1988). For a masterful work on the Iran-Contra affair, see Theodore Draper's *A Very Thin Line: The Iran Contra Affairs* (1991). Several collections of essays include varying assessments of the Reagan years. Among these are *The Reagan Revolution?* (1988), edited by B. B. Kymlicka and Jean V. Matthews; *The Reagan Presidency: An Incomplete Revolution?* (1990), edited by Dilys M. Hill, Raymond A. Moore, and Phil Williams, and *Looking Back on the Reagan Presidency* (1990), edited by Larry Berman.

On the 1988 campaign, see Jack W. Germond and Jules Witcover's *Whose Broad Stripes and Bright Stars? The Trivial Pursuit of the Presidency, 1988* (1989) and Sidney Blumenthal's *Pledging Allegiance: The Last Campaign of the Cold War* (1990). For a social history of the decade, see John Ehrman's *The Eighties: America in the Age of Reagan* (2005).

37

TRIUMPH AND TRAGEDY: AMERICA AT THE TURN OF THE CENTURY

FOCUS QUESTIONS

- How did demographic patterns change in the 1980s and 1990s?
- What led to the Democratic resurgence of the early 1990s and the Republican landslide of 1994?
- Why did the economy and stock market surge during the 1990s?
- What were the consequences of the rise of global terrorism and the terrorist assaults on the United States?

To answer these questions and access additional review material, please visit www.wwnorton.com/studyspace.

The United States entered the final decade of the twentieth century triumphant. American vigilance in the cold war had led to the stunning collapse of the Soviet Union and the birth of democratic capitalism in eastern Europe. The United States was now the world's only superpower. By the mid-1990s the American economy would become the marvel of the world as remarkable gains in productivity afforded by new technologies created the greatest period of prosperity in modern history. Yet no sooner did the century come to an end than America's comfortable sense of physical and material security was shattered by a shocking terrorist assault that would kill thousands, plummet the economy into recession, and call into question conventional notions of national security and personal safety.

AMERICA'S CHANGING MOSAIC

DEMOGRAPHIC SHIFTS   During the 1980s and 1990s the nation's population grew by 20 percent, or some 50 million people, boosting the total to over 296 million in 2006. The much-discussed baby-boom generation—the 43 million people born between 1946 and 1964—entered middle age. This generation's maturation and its preoccupation with practical concerns such as raising families, paying for college, and buying houses helped explain the surge of political conservatism during the 1980s.

During the last quarter of the twentieth century, the sunbelt states of the South and the West continued to lure residents from the Midwest and the Northeast. Fully 90 percent of the nation's total population growth during the 1980s occurred in southern or western states. These population shifts forced a massive redistricting of the House of Representatives, with Florida, California, and Texas gaining seats and states such as New York losing seats.

Americans at the end of the twentieth century tended to settle in large communities. This continuing move to urban areas largely reflected trends in the job market, as the "postindustrial" economy continued to shift from manufacturing to professional-service industries, particularly those specializing in telecommunications and information processing. By 2000 fewer than 2 million people out of a total population of 290 million worked on farms.

Women continued to enter the workforce in large numbers. In 1970, 38 percent of the workforce was female; in 2000 the figure was almost 50 percent. Women made up over one third of the new doctors (up from 4 percent in 1970), 40 percent of the new lawyers (up from 8 percent in 1970), and 23 percent of the new dentists (up from less than 1 percent in 1970).

The decline of the traditional family unit continued. In 2006 less than 65 percent of children lived with two parents, down from 85 percent in 1970. And more people were living alone than ever before, largely as a result of high divorce rates or a growing practice of delaying marriage until well into the twenties. The number of single mothers increased 35 percent during the decade. The rate was much higher for African Americans: in 2000 fewer than 32 percent of African-American children lived with both parents, down from 67 percent in 1960.

Young African Americans in particular faced shrinking economic opportunities at the start of the twenty-first century. The urban poor more than others were victimized by high rates of crime and violence, with young black men suffering the most. In 2000 the leading cause of death among African-American men between the ages of fifteen and twenty-four was homicide.

Over 25 percent of African-American men aged twenty to twenty-nine were in prison, on parole, or on probation, while only 4 percent were enrolled in college. Nearly 40 percent of African-American men were functionally illiterate.

THE NEW IMMIGRANTS The racial and ethnic composition of the country was also changing rapidly at the turn of the century. By 2006 the United States had more foreign-born and first-generation residents than ever before. Over 30 percent of Americans claimed African, Asian, Latino, or American Indian ancestry. Latinos represented 13 percent of the total population, African Americans 11 percent, Asians about 4 percent, and American Indians almost 1 percent. The rate of increase among those four groups was twice as fast as it had been during the 1970s.

The primary cause of this dramatic change in the nation's ethnic mix was a surge of immigration. During the 1990s legal immigration to the United States totaled over 10 million people, 40 percent higher than in the previous

Illegal Immigration

Increasing numbers of Chinese risked their savings and their lives trying to gain entry to the United States. These illegal immigrants are trying to keep warm after being forced to swim ashore when the freighter carrying them to the United States ran aground near Rockaway Beach in New York City in June 1993.

decade and more than in any other decade. These figures do not include the hundreds of thousands of undocumented aliens, mostly Mexicans and Haitians. In 2000 the United States welcomed more than twice as many immigrants as all other countries in the world combined. For the first time in the nation's history, the majority of immigrants came not from Europe but from other parts of the world: Asia, Latin America, and Africa. Among the legal immigrants, Mexicans made up the largest share, averaging over 100,000 a year.

THE COMPUTER REVOLUTION   While demographic shifts and immigration were changing the nation's appearance, technological changes were transforming its behavior. A dramatic revolution in information technology produced a surge in productivity and prosperity during the 1980s and 1990s. Cellular phones, laser printers, VCRs and then DVDs, fax machines, personal computers, and iPods became commonplace. The computer age had arrived.

The idea of a programmable machine that would rapidly perform mental tasks had been around since the eighteenth century, but it took the crisis of World War II to gather the intellectual and financial resources needed to develop such a "computer." A team of engineers at the University of Pennsylvania created ENIAC (electronic numerical integrator and computer), the first all-purpose, all-electronic digital computer. Unveiled in 1946, it could perform 5,000 operations per second. ENIAC took up 3,000 cubic feet of space and housed 18,000 vacuum tubes (glass canisters designed to amplify electric current), 70,000 resistors, 10,000 capacitors, and 6,000 switches.

With the invention in 1971 of the microprocessor—a computer on a silicon chip, the functions that had once been performed by computers taking up an entire room could be performed by a microchip circuit the size of a postage stamp. Engineers soon incorporated microchips into television sets, wristwatches, automobiles, kitchen appliances, and spacecraft.

The invention of the microchip made possible the personal computer. In 1975 an engineer named Ed Roberts developed the prototype of the so-called personal computer. The Altair 8800 was imperfect and cumbersome, with no display, no keyboard, and not enough memory to do anything useful. But its potential excited a Harvard sophomore named Bill Gates. Gates improved the software of the Altair 8800, dropped out of college, and formed a company called Microsoft to market the new system. By 1977 Gates and others had helped transform the personal computer from a machine for hobbyists to a mass consumer product.

By the end of the 1980s, there were 60 million personal computers in the United States, and people began to talk about an "information superhighway,"

The Computer Age

Beginning with the cumbersome electronic numerical integrator and computer (ENIAC), pictured here in 1946, computer technology flourished, leading to the development of personal computers in the 1980s and the popularization of the Internet in the 1990s.

a worldwide network of linked computers and databases connected by fiber-optic lines that facilitated high-speed transmission. During the 1990s the development of the Internet and electronic mail meant that anyone with a personal computer and a modem could travel on the information super-highway. Such advances enabled instantaneous communication across the continents.

CULTURAL CONSERVATISM

Cultural conservatives helped elect Ronald Reagan and George Bush in the 1980s, but they were disappointed with the results. Once in office, neither president had, in the eyes of those conservatives, adequately addressed their moral agenda, including a complete ban on abortions and the restoration of prayer in public schools. By the 1990s a new generation of young conservative activists, mostly political independents or Republicans, had emerged as a force to be reckoned with in national affairs. They were more ideological, more libertarian, more partisan, and more impatient than their predecessors.

THE RELIGIOUS RIGHT Although quite diverse, cultural conservatives tended to be evangelical Christians or orthodox Catholics who joined together to exert increasing religious pressure on the political process. In 1989 the television evangelist Pat Robertson organized the Christian Coalition to replace Jerry Falwell's Moral Majority as the flagship organization of the resurgent religious right. The Christian Coalition encouraged religious conservatives to vote, run for public office, and support only those candidates who shared the organization's views.

The Christian Coalition chose the Republican party, with its well-organized grassroots movement in every state, as the best vehicle for transforming the religious right's pro-family campaign into public policies. The Christian Coalition encouraged its supporters to withhold political support from any candidate who did not provide an ironclad promise to support the coalition's school-prayer, anti-abortion, anti–gay rights positions. In addition to promoting "traditional family values," it urged politicians to "radically downsize and delimit government."

As a centrist professional politician, George Bush initially tried to keep the cultural conservatives at arm's length, only to find himself the target of their attacks. His successor, the Democrat Bill Clinton, also underestimated the growing strength of organized groups such as the Christian Coalition. In the 1994 congressional elections, religious conservatives went to the polls in record numbers, and 70 percent of them voted Republican. One third of the voters identified themselves as "white, evangelical, born-again Christians." In many respects they took control of the political and social agendas in the 1990s.

BUSH TO CLINTON

For months after the Persian Gulf War in 1991, George H. W. Bush seemed unbeatable. But the aftermath of Desert Storm was mixed, with Saddam Hussein's grip on Iraq still intact. Despite his image of strength abroad, Bush began to look weak even on foreign policy. The Soviet Union, meanwhile, stumbled on to its surprising end. On December 25, 1991, the Soviet flag over the Kremlin was replaced by the flag of the Russian Federation. The cold war had ended not just with the collapse of the Soviet Union but with the dismemberment of its fifteen constituent republics. As a result, the United States had become the world's only superpower.

"Containment" of the Soviet Union, the bedrock of American foreign policy for more than four decades, had lost its reason for being. Bush struggled to interpret the fluid new international scene. He spoke of a "new world order" but never defined it. By his own admission he had trouble with "the vision thing." The dynamic international situation, in fact, did not lend itself to a simple vision—unless the answer was to drift into isolation, a great temptation with foreign dangers seemingly on the decline. By the end of 1991, a listless Bush faced a challenge in the Republican primary from the feisty television commentator and former White House aide Patrick Buchanan.

RECESSION AND DOWNSIZING For the Bush administration and for the nation, the most devastating development in the early 1990s was a prolonged economic recession that began in 1990. The first major economic setback in more than eight years, it grew into the longest, if not the deepest, since the Great Depression. During 1991, 25 million workers—about 20 percent of the labor force—were unemployed at some point.

What made this recession unusual was that its victims included a large number of white-collar workers. In the corporate world, terms such as *restructuring* and *downsizing* ruled the day as companies began to reduce personnel, switch employees to part-time status to reduce the cost of benefits, and find other ways to cut labor costs. At the same time the country was experiencing a continuing imbalance in foreign trade and soaring expenditures on defense and public-entitlement programs. During 1991 a $150-billion annual deficit had become a $450-billion shortfall.

A Senate-committee analysis of the stagnant economy confirmed a chilling fact: under the Bush administration "the average standard of living has actually declined." The euphoria over the allied victory in the Gulf War quickly gave way to anxiety and resentment generated by the depressed economy. At the end of 1991, *Time* magazine declared that "no one, not even George Bush" could deny "that the economy was sputtering."

Whatever the reasons for the recession, the cure remained elusive. Although the Federal Reserve Board began cutting interest rates, the economy remained in the doldrums through 1992. The Democratic Congress and the Republican president squabbled over legislation to promote economic recovery but little was done to prod new growth or reduce the hemorrhaging deficits. With his domestic policies in disarray and his foreign policy abandoned, George Bush tried a clumsy balancing act in addressing the recession, on the one hand acknowledging that "people are hurting" while on the other urging Americans that "this is a good time to buy a car."

THE THOMAS HEARINGS AND THE WOMEN'S MOVEMENT Other developments contributed to the erosion of President Bush's popularity, among them the retirement in 1991 of the first African-American Supreme Court justice, Thurgood Marshall, after twenty-four years on the bench. To succeed him Bush named Clarence Thomas, an African-American federal judge whose views delighted conservative senators. Thomas questioned the wisdom of the minimum wage, the use of school busing to achieve desegregation, and affirmative-action hiring programs, and he preached "black self-help," once declaring that all civil rights leaders ever did was "bitch, bitch, bitch, moan, and whine."

Such opinions promised trouble for Thomas's confirmation hearings in the Democratic Senate, but an unexpected explosion occurred when Anita Hill, a soft-spoken law professor at the University of Oklahoma, charged that Thomas had sexually harassed her when she worked for him at a federal agency. Pro-Thomas senators orchestrated an often-savage and sometimes absurd cross-examination of Hill. The televised hearings revealed that either Hill or Thomas had lied, and the committee's tie vote reflected the doubt. The full Senate then confirmed Thomas by the margin of fifty-two to forty-eight.

The Thomas hearings sparked a resurgence in the women's movement. Many women grew incensed at the treatment of Anita Hill, and an unprecedented number of women ran for national and local offices in 1992. The Thomas confirmation struggle thus widened the gender gap for a Republican party already less popular with women than with men.

TAX TURMOIL President Bush had already set a political trap for himself when he declared at the 1988 Republican Convention: "Read my lips. No new taxes." Fourteen months into his presidency, he had decided that the growing federal budget deficit was a greater risk than violating his no-tax pledge. After intense negotiations with congressional Democrats, Bush had announced that reducing the federal deficit required "tax revenue increases." Bush's backsliding set off a revolt among House Republicans, but a bipartisan majority (with most Republicans still opposed) finally approved a tax increase, raising the top personal rate from 28 to 31 percent, disallowing certain deductions in the upper brackets, and raising various excise taxes. Conservative Republicans would not let George Bush forget his abandoned pledge.

DEMOCRATIC RESURGENCE As the Republicans divided over tax policy and social issues, the Democrats sought to present an image of centrist forces in control. For several years the Democratic Leadership Council, in which Arkansas governor William Jefferson Clinton figured prominently, had pushed the party from the liberal left to the center of the political spectrum. Clinton strove to move the Democrats closer to the mainstream of political opinion. A graduate of Georgetown University, he had won a Rhodes scholarship to Oxford and then earned a law degree from Yale, where he met and married Hillary Rodham. By 1979, at age thirty-two, he was back in his native Arkansas, serving as the youngest governor in the country. He served three more terms as governor and in the process emerged as a dynamic young leader committed to winning back the middle-class whites who had voted Republican during the 1980s. Democrats had grown so liberal, he argued, that they had alienated their key constituency, the "vital center."

A self-described moderate, Clinton promised to cut the defense budget, provide tax relief for the middle class, and create a massive economic-aid package for the former republics of the Soviet Union seeking to embrace democratic capitalism. Handsome, witty, intelligent, and a compelling speaker, Clinton projected an image of youthful energy and optimism, reminding many political observers of John F. Kennedy. But underneath the veneer of Clinton's charisma were several flaws. He often seemed so determined to become president that he was willing to sacrifice consistency and principle. He made extensive use of polls to shape his stance on issues, pandered to special-interest groups, and flip-flopped on controversial subjects, leading critics to

The 1992 Presidential Campaign

Presidential candidate Bill Clinton and his running mate, Al Gore, brought youthful enthusiasm to the campaign trail.

label him Slick Willie. Said one former opponent in Arkansas: "He'll be what people want him to be. He'll do or say what it will take to get elected." Even more enticing to the media and more embarrassing to Clinton were charges that he was a chronic adulterer and that he had manipulated the ROTC program during the Vietnam War to avoid the draft. Clinton's evasive denials of both allegations could not dispel a lingering distrust of his character.

Yet after a series of bruising party primaries, Clinton emerged as the front-runner by the time of the nominating convention in the summer of 1992. Once nominated, Clinton chose Senator Albert Gore Jr. of Tennessee as his running mate. So the candidates were two southern Baptists from adjoining states.

Flushed with their convention victory and sporting a ten-point lead in the polls, the Clinton-Gore team stressed economic issues to win over working-class white and African-American voters. Clinton won the election with 370 electoral votes and about 43 percent of the vote, Bush received 168 electoral votes and 39 percent of the vote, and off-and-on independent candidate H. Ross Perot of Texas garnered 18 percent of the popular vote but no electoral votes. A puckish billionaire, Perot found a big audience for his simplified explanations of public problems and his offers to just "get under the hood and fix them."

DOMESTIC POLICY IN CLINTON'S FIRST TERM

Clinton had run a brilliant campaign, portraying himself as an outsider untainted by Washington politics and inertia. Yet his inexperience in international affairs and congressional maneuvering led to several missteps in his first year as president. Like George Bush before him, Clinton reneged on several campaign promises. He abandoned his proposed middle-class tax cut in order to keep down the federal deficit. Nine days into office he backed down when the Pentagon and Congress strongly opposed his attempt to allow professed homosexuals to serve in the military; subsequently he announced an ambiguous policy concerning gays in the military that came to be known as don't ask, don't tell. In Clinton's first two weeks in office, his approval rating dropped 20 percent.

THE ECONOMY Clinton entered office determined to reduce the federal deficit without damaging the economy. To this end, on February 17, 1993, he proposed higher taxes for corporations and for individuals in higher tax brackets and called for an economic-stimulus package for "investment" in public works (transportation, utilities, and the like) and "human capital" (education, skills, health, and welfare). Clinton's hotly contested deficit-reduction package passed by 218 to 216 in the House and 51 to 50 in the Senate, with Vice President Gore breaking the tie.

Equally contested was the North American Free Trade Agreement (NAFTA), which the Bush administration had negotiated with Canada and Mexico. The debate over its congressional approval revived old arguments on the tariff, pro and con. Clinton stuck with his party's tradition of low tariffs and urged approval of NAFTA, which would make North America the largest free-trade area in the world. He and his supporters argued that tariff reductions would open up foreign markets to American industries. Opponents of the bill, including wealthy gadfly Ross Perot and organized labor, favored barriers that would discourage cheaper foreign products and believed that with NAFTA the country would hear a "giant sucking sound" of American jobs being drawn to Mexico. Yet Clinton prevailed, winning solid Republican support while losing a sizable minority of Democrats, mostly from the South, where executives predicted that textile mills would lose business to "cheap-labor" countries.

HEALTH-CARE REFORM Clinton's major public-policy initiative was a new federal health-care plan. Sentiment for health-care reform spread as annual medical costs skyrocketed and some 39 million Americans went without insurance either by choice or out of necessity. Universal medical coverage as proposed by Clinton would entitle every citizen and documented immigrant to health insurance. First Lady Hillary Clinton chaired the health-care-plan task force and became the administration's lead witness on the plan before congressional committees. The bill aroused intense opposition from the pharmaceutical and insurance industries, however. By the summer of 1994, Clinton's health-insurance plan was doomed. Republican senators began a filibuster to prevent a vote on the bill. Lacking the votes to stop the filibuster, the Democrats acknowledged defeat and gave up the fight for universal medical coverage.

MISTRUST OF GOVERNMENT AND THE MILITIA MOVEMENT While Clinton sparred with Republicans in Washington, a grassroots militia movement spread across the country in the 1990s, a manifestation of the paranoid and populist strain in cultural politics. In Waco, Texas, a confrontation between federal authorities and a cultlike militia group called the Branch Davidians sparked a tragedy. The Davidians, an apocalyptic religious sect headed by a charismatic loony named David Koresh, was found to be

Oklahoma City

The Alfred P. Murrah Federal Building in Oklahoma City after it was bombed on April 19, 1995, in what was then the deadliest terrorist act on U.S. soil.

stockpiling weapons, engaging in child abuse, and violating immigration laws. On February 28, 1993, agents from the Treasury Department's Bureau of Alcohol, Tobacco, and Firearms (BATF) entered the sect's compound, where they were met with gunfire. Four agents and two Branch Davidians were killed, and twenty people were injured. The next day the FBI took over the siege of the compound, waging fruitless psychological warfare against the Branch Davidians. On April 19, the fifty-first day of the televised siege, FBI agents recklessly attacked the compound with armored vehicles and tear gas. Amid the commotion the compound caught fire and quickly burned to the ground. At least seventy-seven people died in the inferno.

On the second anniversary of the Waco incident, April 19, 1995, a massive truck bomb exploded in front of the federal office building in Oklahoma City, Oklahoma. The entire front portion of the nine-story building collapsed, killing 168 people, 19 of them children in the building's day-care center. Six hundred others were injured. Within days the FBI had arrested Timothy McVeigh and Terry Nichols and charged them with the bombing. A third man pleaded guilty to separate charges of conspiring to produce explosives. All three men were militia members who hated the federal government and had been incensed by the way the BATF and the FBI had dealt with the Branch Davidians at Waco. The Oklahoma City bombing shocked and saddened the nation. It brought to public attention the rise of right-wing militia groups and revealed the depth of anti-government sentiment among those fringe groups.

REPUBLICAN INSURGENCY

During 1994 Bill Clinton began to see his presidency unravel. Unable to get either health-care reform or welfare-reform bills through the

Democratic Congress and having failed to carry out his campaign pledge for middle-class tax relief, he and his party found themselves on the defensive.

In the midterm elections of 1994, the Democrats suffered a humbling defeat. It was the first election since 1952 in which Republicans captured both houses of Congress. In both the majority was solid: 52 to 48 in the Senate, a majority that soon increased when two Democrats declared themselves Republicans, and 230 to 204 in the House. Not a single Republican incumbent was defeated. Republicans also won a net gain of eleven governorships and fifteen state legislatures.

THE CONTRACT WITH AMERICA   A Georgian named Newton Leroy Gingrich led the Republican insurgency in Congress. Gingrich, a brilliant former history professor with an oversize ego, had helped mobilize religious and social conservatives associated with the Christian Coalition. In early 1995 he became the first Republican Speaker of the House in forty-two years. Gingrich announced that "we are at the end of an era." Liberalism was dead, and the Democratic party was dying. He dismissed Bill and Hillary Clinton as "counterculture McGoverniks." Gingrich pledged to start a new reign of congressional Republican dominance that would dismantle the "corrupt liberal welfare state." He was aided by freshman Republicans promoting what he called the Contract with America. The ten-point contract outlined an anti-big-government program with less regulation, less environmental conservation, term limits for members of Congress, a line-item veto for the president, welfare reform, and a balanced-budget amendment.

By April 13, exactly 100 days after taking office, the congressional Republicans had passed twenty-six bills stemming from the Contract with America and had failed to pass only two. Nonetheless, only four of those twenty-six bills succeeded in becoming law. The much-ballyhooed GOP revolution and the Contract with America fizzled out. The revolution that the imperious Gingrich touted was far too ambitious to be carried out in so limited a time with so slim a majority and so little sense of crisis. What is more, many of the congressional Republican freshmen were scornful of compromise and were amateurs at legislative procedure, and they limited Gingrich's ability to maneuver. The Senate rejected many of the bills that had been passed in the House as senators were less under Gingrich's spell and not party to the Contract with America anyway. The "Republican revolution" of 1994 fizzled out, too, because Newt Gingrich became such an unpopular figure, both in Congress and among the electorate. He was too ambitious, too slick, too aggressive, too rambunctious. Clinton's lieutenants effectively portrayed him as an extremist. And beyond all those factors, a presidential veto stood in the path of the Contract with America. President Clinton shrewdly moved to the political center and co-opted much of the Republican agenda. His distinctive strength—at least in the eyes of his supporters—resided in his agile responsiveness to changing public moods. To Clinton the Republican victory in the 1994 congressional elections and in the passage of the Contract with America initiatives bore a simple message: he must recapture the political center by radically changing his own agenda.

LEGISLATIVE BREAKTHROUGH In the late summer of 1996, as lawmakers were preparing to adjourn and participate in the presidential nominating conventions, the 104th Congress broke through its partisan gridlock and passed a flurry of important legislation that President Clinton quickly signed, including bills increasing the minimum wage and broadening access to health insurance.

Even more significant was a comprehensive welfare-reform measure that ended the federal government's open-ended guarantee of aid to the poor, a guarantee that had been in place since 1935. The Personal Responsibility and Work Opportunity Act of 1996 turned over the major federal welfare programs to the states, which would receive federal grants to fund them. The bill also limited the amount of time during which a person could receive welfare benefits funded by federal money and required that at least half of a state's welfare recipients have jobs or be enrolled in job-training programs by 2002. States failing to meet the deadline would have their federal funds cut.

The Republican-sponsored welfare-reform legislation passed the Senate by a vote of seventy-four to twenty-four. It had the effect of cutting $56 billion over six years from various welfare programs, several of which dated back to Franklin Roosevelt's New Deal. Liberals charged that Clinton was abdicating Democratic social principles in order to gain reelection amid the conservative climate of the times. Clinton and his centrist advisers, dismissed the criticism, however. With his reelection bid at stake, the president was determined to live up to his 1992 campaign pledge to "end welfare as we know it." Clinton also knew that most voters in both parties were eager to see major cuts in federal entitlement programs.

THE 1996 CAMPAIGN After clinching the Republican presidential nomination in 1996, Senate majority leader Bob Dole resigned his seat in order to devote his attention to defeating Bill Clinton. As the 1996 presidential campaign unfolded, however, Clinton maintained a large lead in the polls. With an improving economy and no major foreign-policy crises to confront, personal and partisan issues surged into prominence. Concern about Dole's age (seventy-three) and his acerbic manner, as well as rifts in the Republican party between economic and social conservatives over issues such as abortion and gun control, hampered Dole's efforts to generate widespread support.

On November 5, 1996, Clinton won again, with an electoral vote of 379 to 159 and 49 percent of the popular vote. Dole received 41 percent of the popular vote, and independent candidate Ross Perot got 8 percent. The Republicans lost eight seats in the House but retained a 227 to 207 advantage over the Democrats in the House; in the Senate, Republicans gained two seats for a 55 to 45 majority. The resulting deadlock reflected the conservative mood of the times.

ECONOMIC AND SOCIAL TRENDS OF THE 1990S

THE "NEW ECONOMY" As the twentieth century came to a close, the United States benefited from a prolonged period of unprecedented prosperity. Buoyed by low inflation, high employment, declining federal budget deficits, dramatic improvements in productivity, the rapid globalization of economic life, and the astute leadership of Federal Reserve Board chairman Alan Greenspan, business and industry witnessed record profits.

During the late 1990s the stock market soared. In 1993 the Dow Jones industrial average hit 3,500. By 1996 it had topped 6,000. During 1998 it reached 9,000, defying the predictions of experts that the economy could not sustain such performance. In 1998 unemployment was only 4.3 percent, the lowest since 1970. Inflation was a measly 1.7 percent. People talked of the onset of a new economy, one that was centered on high-tech companies and would defy the boom-and-bust cycles of the previous hundred years. "It is possible," Greenspan suggested, "that we have moved 'beyond history.' "

In the 1990s much of the growth in the economy resulted from efforts to promote favored free markets on a world scale: global markets without tariffs and other barriers to free trade. More and more gigantic corporations such as IBM and General Electric had become international in scope. This phenomenon encouraged free-trade agreements such as NAFTA as well as most-favored-nation treatment for Communist China and other countries. With such agreements in place, American companies could easily "outsource" much of their production to plants in countries with lower labor costs. Increasingly, therefore, blue-collar labor lost ground to cheap foreign labor in assembly plants or "sweatshops" elsewhere in the world.

RACE INITIATIVES   After the triumphs of the civil rights movement in the 1960s, the momentum for minority advancement had run out—except for gains in college admissions and employment under the rubric of affirmative action. The conservative mood during the mid-1990s manifested itself in the Supreme Court. In 1995 the Court ruled against election districts redrawn to create African-American or Latino majorities and narrowed federal affirmative-action programs.

   In 1996 two major steps were taken against affirmative action in college admissions. In *Hopwood v. Texas*, a federal court ruled that considering race to achieve a diverse student body at the University of Texas was "not a compelling interest under the Fourteenth Amendment." Later that year the state of California passed Proposition 209, an initiative that ruled out race, sex, ethnicity, and national origin as criteria for preferring any group. These rulings eviscerated affirmative-action programs and drastically reduced African-American enrollments, thereby prompting second thoughts. In addition, the nation still had not addressed intractable problems that lay beyond civil rights—that is, problems of dependency: illiteracy, poverty, unemployment, urban decay, and slums.

THE SCANDAL MACHINE   During his first term, President Clinton was dogged by allegations of improper involvement in the Whitewater Development Corporation. In 1978, as governor of Arkansas, he had invested in a resort project on the White River in northern Arkansas. The project turned out to be a fraud and a failure, and the Clintons took a loss on their investment. In 1994 Kenneth Starr, a Republican, was appointed to serve as independent counsel in an investigation of the Whitewater case. Although Starr had a reputation for fairness, many observers believed that his unwillingness to end the investigation and his former position in the Bush administration suggested a taint of partisanship. While revealing that Hillary Clinton had handled some legal work for the Whitewater enterprise, Starr's investigation did not uncover evidence that the Clintons were directly involved in the fraud, although a number of their close associates had been caught in the web and convicted of various charges, some related to Whitewater and some not.

   Besides Whitewater, Starr's team of investigators looked into the allegations of Paula Jones that Clinton had sexually harassed her while he was governor of Arkansas and she was a state employee. In the course of the investigation, it surfaced that the president may have had a sexual affair with a former White House intern, Monica Lewinsky, and may have pressed her to lie about it under oath. Clinton publicly denied the affair, but the tawdry scandal would not disappear. In August 1998 President Clinton agreed to testify before a grand jury convened to investigate the sexual allegations. He was the first president in history to testify before a grand jury. On August 17, with the nation anxiously awaiting the results, Clinton recanted his earlier denials and acknowledged having had "inappropriate intimate physical contact" with Monica Lewinsky. Public reaction to Clinton's stunning about-face was mixed. A majority of Americans expressed sympathy for the president because of his public humiliation and wanted the matter dropped. Clinton's credibility had suffered a serious blow on account of his reckless lack of self-discipline and his efforts to deny and then cover up the sordid scandal.

Meanwhile, Kenneth Starr continued his tenacious investigation. On September 9, 1998, he submitted to Congress a 445-page report and eighteen boxes of supporting material. The Starr Report found "substantial and creditable" evidence of presidential wrongdoing. Drawing upon the evidence, the Republican-controlled House Judiciary Committee voted 21 to 16 to recommend a full impeachment inquiry into the allegations of perjury and obstruction of justice by the president. On October 8 the House of Representatives voted 258 to 176 to begin a wide-ranging impeachment

Impeachment

Representative Edward Pease, a member of the House Judiciary Committee, covers his face during the vote on the third of four articles of impeachment charging President Clinton with "high crimes and misdemeanors," December 1998.

inquiry of President Clinton. Thirty-one Democrats joined the Republicans in supporting the investigation. On December 19, 1998, William Jefferson Clinton became the second president to be impeached by the House of Representatives. The House officially approved two articles of impeachment, charging Clinton with lying under oath to a federal grand jury and obstructing justice.

The Senate trial of President Clinton began on January 7, 1999, with the swearing in of Chief Justice William Rehnquist to preside and the senators as jurors. Five weeks later, on February 12, the Senate acquitted the president. Rejecting the first charge of perjury, ten Republicans and all forty-five Democrats voted "not guilty." On the charge of obstruction of justice, the Senate split fifty-fifty (which meant acquittal, since sixty-seven votes were needed for conviction). In both instances, senators had a hard time interpreting Clinton's philandering as constituting "high crimes and misdemeanors," the constitutional requirement for removal of a president from office. Clinton's supporters portrayed him as the victim of a puritanical special prosecutor and partisan conspiracy run amok. His critics lambasted him as a lecherous man without honor or integrity. Both characterizations were incomplete. Politically astute, charismatic, and well-informed, Clinton had as much ability and potential as any president. Yet he was also shamelessly self-indulgent. The result was a scandalous presidency punctuated by dramatic achievements in welfare reform, economic growth, and foreign policy.

Foreign-Policy Challenges

Like Woodrow Wilson, Lyndon Johnson, and Jimmy Carter before him, Bill Clinton was a Democratic president who came into office determined to focus on the nation's domestic problems only to find himself mired in foreign entanglements that had no easy resolution. Clinton continued the Bush administration's intervention in Somalia, on the northeastern horn of Africa, where collapse of the government early in 1991 had left the country in anarchy, prey to tribal marauders. President Bush in 1992 had gained UN sanction for a military force led by American troops to relieve hunger and restore peace. In early 1993 U.S. troop levels peaked and began to shrink with the arrival of international forces. The Somalian operation proved successful at its primary mission, but it never solved the political problems that lay at the root of the population's starvation and civil strife.

Clinton and the Middle East

President Clinton presides as Israeli prime minister Yitzhak Rabin (left) and PLO leader Yasir Arafat (right), agree to a peace accord between Israel and the Palestinians, September 1993.

THE MIDDLE EAST   Clinton also continued George Bush's policy of sponsoring patient negotiations between the Arabs and the Israelis. A new development was the inclusion of the PLO in the negotiations. In 1993 a draft agreement between Israel and the PLO provided for the restoration of Palestinian self-rule in the occupied Gaza Strip and in Jericho, on the West Bank of the Jordan River, in an exchange of land for peace as provided in UN Security Council resolutions. A formal signing occurred at the White House on September 13, 1993. With President Clinton presiding, Israeli prime minister Yitzhak Rabin and PLO leader Yasir Arafat exchanged handshakes, and their foreign ministers signed the agreement.

The Middle East peace process suffered a terrible blow in early November 1995, however, when Yitzhak Rabin was assassinated at a peace rally in Tel Aviv by an Israeli Jewish zealot who resented Rabin's efforts to negotiate with the Palestinians. Some observers feared that the assassin had killed the peace process as well when seven months later conservative hard-liner Benjamin Netanyahu narrowly defeated the U.S.-backed Shimon Peres in the Israeli elections. Yet in October 1998 Clinton brought Arafat, King Hussein of Jordan, and Netanyahu together at a conference center in Wye Mills, Maryland, where they reached an agreement. Under the Wye River Accord, Israel surrendered land in return for security guarantees by the Palestinians. As hard-liners attempted to derail the tenuous peace process, Netanyahu called elections early, and the Israeli public swept into power former general Ehud Barak, who promised to jump-start the peace process.

THE BALKANS   Bill Clinton's foreign policy also addressed the chaotic transition in eastern Europe from Soviet domination to independence. With the collapse of Communist power, ethnic and religious hatreds resurfaced, often leading to violent clashes. When Yugoslavia imploded in 1991, fanatics and tyrants incited ethnic conflict as four of its six republics seceded. Serb minorities, backed by Serbia itself, stirred up civil wars in Croatia and Bosnia. In Bosnia especially the war involved "ethnic cleansing"—driving Muslims from their homes and towns. In 1995 American negotiators finally persuaded the foreign ministers of Croatia, Bosnia, and the new Federal Republic of Yugoslavia to agree to a comprehensive peace plan. To enforce the agreement, 60,000 NATO troops would be dispatched to Bosnia as part of a peacekeeping operation. A cease-fire went into effect in October 1995.

In 1998 the Balkan tinderbox flared up again, this time in the Yugoslav province of Kosovo, a region long considered sacred by Christian Serbs. By 1989, however, over 90 percent of the 2 million Kosovars were ethnic Albanian Muslims. In that year, Yugoslav president Slobodan Milošević decided to reassert Serbian control over the province. He stripped Kosovo of its autonomy and established de facto martial law. When the Albanian Kosovars resisted and large numbers of Muslim men began to join the Kosovo Liberation Army, Serbian soldiers and state police ruthlessly suppressed them and launched another program of "ethnic cleansing," burning Albanian villages, murdering men, raping women, and displacing hundreds of thousands of Muslim Albanian Kosovars.

On March 24, 1999, NATO, relying heavily upon American military resources and leadership, launched air strikes against Yugoslavia. After seventy-two days of unrelenting bombardment, Milošević sued for peace on NATO's terms. An agreement was reached on June 3, 1999. As the Albanian Kosovars began to return to Kosovo, however, large numbers of Serbs, fearful of Muslim retribution, began to leave, and some of them were killed. Members of the Kosovo Liberation Army stepped into the vacuum left by the departing Serbs and began to take control of the province.

GLOBALIZATION   The deepening involvement of the United States in the complex affairs of eastern Europe symbolized the broadening scope of globalization. As the proliferation of global-spanning information and communications technologies shrank time and distance, a cornucopia of consumer goods was produced, distributed, marketed, and purchased by multinational companies all over the world, not just in the United States. Unlike the 1950s and 1960s, when the United States enjoyed a near monopoly on international commerce because of the devastation of European and Asian economies during World War II, the rest of the world was now aggressively competing with American businesses. Yet as more nations entered the world economy and experienced prosperity, they benefited corporations in the United Stated by buying more American goods and sending more and better goods to the United States. U.S. exports rose dramatically in the last twenty years of the twentieth century. In 1970 American exports totaled $43 billion; in 2000 they totaled $1.2 trillion. Globalization benefited American consumers as well, by making available many more products–and at lower prices.

By the end of the twentieth century, the American economy had become global dependent; foreign trade had become central to American prosperity–and to American politics. "The global economy," said a leading bank executive, "is defined by capital, ideas, and energy, not by artificial, geographic or political boundaries." Foreign government and foreign investors had become the primary purchasers of U.S. government bonds. Driven by a ferocious desire to cut production costs, large corporations moved more and more of their production overseas. Outsourcing work "offshore" to developing countries, where wages were low, became the rage. By 2000 over one third of the production of American multinational companies was occurring abroad, compared with only 9 percent in 1980. Likewise, executives in multinational countries became more multinational themselves. A growing number of chief executive officers were of a different nationality than that of the company they headed. By the end of the twentieth century, the American economy had become internationalized to such a profound extent that global concerns exercised an overwhelming influence on American domestic and foreign policies.

THE ELECTION OF 2000

The election of 2000 revealed that American voters were split evenly along partisan lines. The two major-party candidates for president, Democratic vice president Al Gore and Texas Republican governor George W. Bush, son of the former president, presented sharply contrasting views on the role of the federal government, tax cuts, environmental policies, and the best way to preserve Social Security and Medicare. Gore, a Tennessee native and Harvard graduate whose father had been a senator, favored an active federal government that would preserve Social Security and subsidize prescription-medicine expenses for the elderly. He criticized proposed Republican tax cuts as catering to the wealthy. An environmental activist, Gore reaffirmed his support for the Environmental Protection Agency and the Interior Department.

Bush, on the other hand, sought to transfer power from the federal government to the states, particularly in regard to the environment and education. He promoted more drilling for oil on federal land, and he endorsed the use of vouchers (cash grants) to enable parents to send their children to private schools. In international affairs, Bush questioned the need to maintain U.S. peacekeeping forces in Bosnia and the continuing expense of other global military commitments.

In the end the election was the one of the closest—and most controversial—in history. The television networks initially reported that Gore had narrowly won the state of Florida and its decisive twenty-five electoral votes. Later in the evening, however, the networks reversed themselves, saying that Florida was too close to call. The final tally in Florida showed Bush with a razor-thin lead, but state law required a recount. For the first time in 125 years, the results of a presidential election remained in doubt for weeks after the voting.

As a painstaking hand count of presidential ballots proceeded in Florida, supporters of Bush and Gore pursued victory through legal maneuvers in the Florida courts and the U.S. Supreme Court; each side accused the other of trying to steal the election. The stalemated political drama continued for five weeks. At last, on December 12, 2000, the Supreme Court halted the statewide manual recounts in Florida. In the case known as *Bush v. Gore*, a bare five-to-four majority ruled that any new recount would clash with existing Florida law. Bush was deemed the winner in Florida by the slimmest of margins: 537 votes. Although Gore amassed a 540,000-vote lead nationwide, he lost in the Electoral College by two votes when he lost Florida.

The 2000 election revealed the remarkable balance that had emerged in national politics. Not since the 1880s had the two major parties been so evenly divided. Republicans retained a slim lead in the House, 49.2 percent to 47.9 percent. The number of senators was split down the middle, fifty-fifty. Some 71 percent of city residents voted for Gore while only 26 percent chose Bush. Conversely, 59 percent of rural voters cast ballots for Bush while only 37 percent opted for Gore. Gore won fewer than one third of the votes in the South and lost his home state of Tennessee. Bush won the mountain West and the South while Gore dominated the Northeast, the West Coast, and the industrial Midwest. Women favored Gore over Bush by 11 percentage points, exactly the reverse of the male voters.

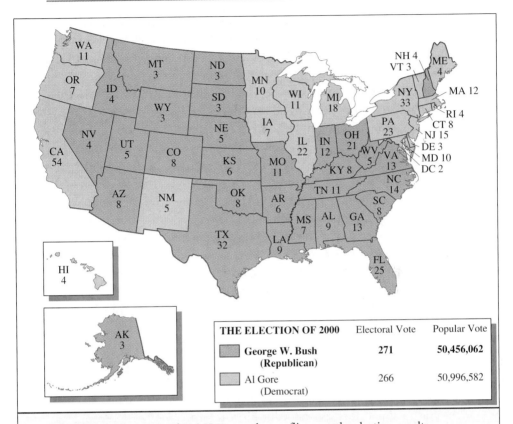

THE ELECTION OF 2000	Electoral Vote	Popular Vote
George W. Bush (Republican)	271	50,456,062
Al Gore (Democrat)	266	50,996,582

Why was the election so close? How was the conflict over the election results resolved? How were differences between urban and rural voters key to the outcome of the election?

COMPASSIONATE CONSERVATISM

THE SECOND BUSH PRESIDENCY During the 2000 election campaign, commentators criticized George W. Bush's political inexperience and lack of knowledge about world affairs. As president-elect he addressed those concerns by naming to his cabinet seasoned public figures. His vice-president, Richard "Dick" Cheney, is a former congressman from Wyoming who served as secretary of defense under the senior George Bush. Colin Powell, a former army general and chairman of the Joint Chiefs of Staff, became the first African-American secretary of state. Donald Rumsfeld, secretary of defense under Gerald Ford, returned to that position in the Bush administration. Bush named former Missouri senator John Ashcroft attorney general.

Bush not only arrived in the White House amid the controversy of a disputed election, but he also inherited a sputtering economy and a falling stock market. By the spring of 2000, the high-tech companies that had led the soaring stock market during the 1990s had begun to stall. Many of the dazzling new dot-com businesses declared bankruptcy. Greed fed by record profits and speculative excesses had led businesses, investors, and consumers to take dangerous risks; many leading corporate executives, it turned out, had engaged in unethical practices that undermined the economy. The Internet bubble burst in 2001. Stock values collapsed, stealing over $2 trillion from household wealth. Consumer confidence and capital investment plummeted with the stock market. By March 2001 the economy was in recession for the first time in over a decade.

Bush's disputed election and the political balance in Congress did not prevent the new president from launching an ambitious legislative agenda. Confident that he could win over Democrats, he promised within months of his inauguration to provide "an explosion of legislation" promoting his goal of "compassionate conservatism." The top item on Bush's wish list was a $1.6-trillion tax cut intended to stimulate the sagging economy. The Senate eventually trimmed the cut to $1.35 trillion over eleven years, and Bush signed it into law on June 7, 2001.

NO CHILD LEFT BEHIND In addition to tax reduction, one of President Bush's top priorities was education reform. In late 2001 Congress passed a comprehensive education-improvement plan called No Child Left Behind, and the president signed the bill in early 2002. It required states to set new learning standards and ensure that all students were "proficient" at reading and math by 2014. It also mandated that all teachers be "highly qualified" in their subject area by 2005, allowed children in low-performing schools to transfer to other schools, and required states to submit annual reports of students' scores on standardized tests. Schools and school districts that fell short of the new standards were eligible for financial and technical assistance, but if progress did not occur the federal government would issue a series of sanctions culminating in the state's taking over deficient school districts. States soon criticized the program, noting that it provided insufficient funds for remedial programs and that poor school districts, many of them in blighted inner cities or rural areas, would be especially hard pressed to meet the guidelines.

EXPLOITING THE ENVIRONMENT The Bush administration's environmental policies ignited a firestorm of controversy. The president refused to sign the Kyōto Protocol, an international agreement among dozens of nations setting limits on the emissions of carbon dioxide and other gases contributing to global climate change. Bush argued that the treaty would harm the economy. Administration officials also sought to roll back restrictions on economic development posed by long-standing environmental regulations. In addition, they wanted to allow more logging in national forests and open up more federal land, including wildlife sanctuaries, to exploration for energy sources in the face of dramatic increases in oil and gasoline prices. Like Ronald Reagan before him, Bush appointed former industry executives to federal agencies responsible for enforcing environmental regulations, and he exempted the Defense Department from many environmental restrictions. James Jeffords, a Republican turned independent and the ranking minority member of the Senate Environment and Public Works Committee, predicted that the Bush administration would "go down in history as the greatest disaster for public health and the environment in the history of the United States."

Yet the Bush administration did take several steps to protect the environment. The EPA ordered General Electric to spend hundreds of millions of dollars to remove toxic chemicals it had deposited into New York's Hudson River. It also established the first limits on diesel-fuel emissions for trucks and off-road vehicles. And Bush appropriated funds to begin chipping away at a huge deferred-maintenance backlog at the national parks.

GLOBAL TERRORISM

With the collapse of the Soviet Union and the end of the cold war, world politics had grown more unstable during the 1990s. The basic premise of American foreign policy was "unipolar": to maintain the nation's leadership role in global affairs. Yet a simmering mistrust of America's geopolitical and dominance economic glolaization festered internationally. Where ideologies such as capitalism and communism had earlier been the cause of conflict and tension in foreign relations, issues of religion, ethnicity, and clashing cultural values now divided peoples.

Nations were no longer the sole actors on the stage of world politics. Instead, nebulous multinational groups inspired by religious fanaticism and anti-American rage were using high-tech terrorism to gain notoriety and exact vengeance. The very rootlessness of the zealots—their alienation from their native societies and their ability to infiltrate other countries and cultures—proved to be an ironic strength. Well-financed and well-armed terrorists flourished in the cracks of foundering nations such as Sudan, Somalia, Pakistan, Yemen, and Afghanistan. Throughout the 1990s the United States had fought a losing secret war against organized terrorism. The ineffectiveness of Western intelligence agencies in tracking the movements and intentions of militant extremists became tragically evident in the late summer of 2001.

SEPTEMBER 11, 2001: A DAY OF INFAMY   At 8:45 on the morning of September 11, 2001, the world watched in horror as a commercial airliner hijacked by Islamic terrorists slammed into the north tower of the World Trade Center in New York City. A second hijacked jumbo jet, traveling at 500 miles per hour, hit the south tower eighteen minutes later. The fuel-laden planes turned the majestic buildings into infernos. The twin towers, both 110 stories tall and filled with thousands of people, collapsed from the intense heat. Surrounding buildings also crumpled. The entire southern end of Manhattan—ground zero—became a hellish scene of twisted steel, suffocating smoke, and wailing sirens.

While the catastrophic drama in New York was unfolding, a third hijacked plane crashed into the Pentagon in Washington, D.C. A fourth commandeered airliner, thought to be headed for the White House, missed its mark when passengers, who had heard reports of the earlier incidents via cell phones, assaulted the hijackers to prevent the plane from being used as a weapon. During the struggle in the cockpit, the plane went out of control and plummeted into the Pennsylvania countryside, killing all on board.

The hijackings represented the costliest terrorist assault on the United States in the nation's history. There were 266 passengers and crew members aboard the crashed jets. More than 100 civilians and military personnel were killed at the Pentagon. The death toll at the World Trade Center was over 2,600, with many firefighters, police officers, and rescue workers among the dead. Hundreds of those killed were foreign nationals working in the financial district; some eighty nations lost citizens in the attacks. The terrorists also destroyed a powerful symbol of America: the World Trade Center towers were the central offices of global capitalism.

The terrorist attacks of September 11 created shock and chaos, grief and anger. They also prompted an unprecedented display of national unity and patriotism. People rushed to donate blood, food, and money. Volunteers clogged military-recruiting centers. American flags were in evidence everywhere. Citizens around the world held vigils at U.S. embassies. World leaders offered condolences and support. For the first time in its history, NATO invoked Article V of its charter, which states that an attack on any member will be considered an attack on all.

September 11, 2001

Smoke pours out of the north tower of the World Trade Center as the south tower bursts into flames after being struck by a second hijacked airplane. Both towers collapsed about an hour later.

Within hours of the hijackings, officials had identified the nineteen terrorists as members of al Qaeda (the Base), a well-financed worldwide network of Islamic extremists led by a wealthy Saudi renegade, Osama bin Laden. Years before, bin Laden had declared holy war on the United States, Israel, and the Saudi monarchy. For several years he had been using remote bases in war-torn Afghanistan as terrorist training centers. Collaboring with bin Laden's terrorist agenda was Afghanistan's ruling Taliban, a coalition of radical Islamists that had emerged in the mid-1990s following the forced withdrawal of Soviet troops from Afghanistan. Taliban leaders provided bin Laden with a safe haven in exchange for his financial and military support against the Northern Alliance, a cluster of rebel groups opposed to Taliban rule. Bin Laden sought to mobilize Muslim militants into a global army energized by local causes. As many as 20,000 recruits from twenty countries circulated through his training camps. Most of the terrorists received religious indoctrination and basic infantry training to prepare them to fight for the Taliban. A smaller group was selected by al Qaeda for elite training to organize secret cells around the world and engage in urban warfare, assassination, demolition, and sabotage.

WAR ON TERRORISM The September 11 terrorist assault on the United States changed the course of the new presidency, the nation, and the world. The economy, already in decline, went into a free fall. With people world wide reluctant to fly, airlines laid off tens of thousands of employees. Insurance companies struggled to pay off an estimated $30 billion in claims resulting from the attacks. On Wall Street, markets plummeted in anticipation of a deeper recession combined with a war against terrorism.

President Bush, who had never professed to know much about international relations or world affairs and had shown only disdain for Bill Clinton's "multilateralism," was thrust onto center stage as commander in chief of a wounded nation eager for vengeance. The Bush administration immediately forged an international coalition to strike at terrorism worldwide. The coalition demanded that Afghanistan's Taliban government surrender the terrorists or risk military attack. In a televised address on September 20, Bush warned Americans that the war against terrorism would be a lengthy campaign involving covert action as well as conventional military forces, which would target not only terrorists but also the groups and governments that abet them. "Every nation in every region," he said, "now has a decision to make: either you are with us or you are with the terrorists."

On October 7, after the Taliban defiantly refused to turn over bin Laden, the United States and its allies launched a ferocious military campaign— Operation Enduring Freedom—to locate and punish terrorists or "those harboring terrorists." U.S. and British cruise missiles and bombers destroyed Afghan military installations and al Qaeda training camps. The coalition found key allies in neighboring Pakistan and in Afghanistan's Northern Alliance. U.S. military commanders used new high-tech weapons—precision-guided bombs, spy satellites, and laser-targeting devices—that enabled American forces to engage the enemy and occupy territory without risking soldiers' lives.

On December 9, only two months after the American-led military campaign in Afghanistan had begun, the Taliban regime collapsed. With its collapse, the war in Afghanistan devolved into a high-stakes manhunt for the elusive Osama bin Laden and an international network of terrorists operating in sixty countries.

In December 2001 Afghanistan's long-feuding factions, minus the Taliban, signed a UN-brokered peace agreement that created an interim government, led by Hamid Karzai, an exiled tribal leader who had reentered the country in October to rally opposition to the Taliban. While the American-led coalition forces continued to track down al Qaeda stragglers and search for bin Laden, the interim Afghan government faced the stern challenge of providing basic services and creating stability in a faction-ridden, war-torn country.

TERRORISM AT HOME While the military campaign continued in Afghanistan, officials in Washington worried that terrorists might launch additional attacks in the United States with biological, chemical, or even nuclear weapons. To address the threat and to help restore public confidence, President Bush created a new federal agency, the Office of Homeland Security, and a new federal agency, the Transportation Security Administration, assumed responsibility for screening airline passengers. At the same time, President Bush and a supportive Congress created new legislation, known as the USA Patriot Act, which gave government agencies the right to eavesdrop on confidential conversations between prison inmates and their lawyers and permitted terrorist suspects to be tried in military courts. Such tribunals would have less stringent standards regarding the burden of proof than civilian courts: they could be held in secret, they allowed for the admission of hearsay and illegally obtained information as evidence, and they required only a two-thirds majority for conviction. Civil liberties groups voiced grave concerns that the measures jeopardized constitutional rights and protections. But the crisis atmosphere after September 11 caused most people to support these extraordinary steps.

MIDDLE EAST TURMOIL The Middle East again exploded in violence in the new century. Seven years of relative calm ended when Israeli-Palestinian peace talks in Oslo collapsed in 2000. Disputes over the fate of Jerusalem, a holy city to Jews, Christians, and Muslims, undermined any new accords between the Israelis and the Palestinians. Frustrated by the collapse of negotiations, Palestinians again declared an intifada, or uprising. In October 2000 street demonstrations in the Israeli-controlled West Bank and Gaza Strip gave way to a series of suicide bombings against Israeli soldiers and civilians. Israeli troops retaliated. Hundreds of casualties resulted, many of them children.

In February 2001 Israeli voters, angry with the increasing violence, elected the party of Ariel Sharon, a militant conservative. As their prime minister, Sharon vowed that there would be no negotiating with the Palestinians as long as their intifada continued. Sharon's government responded to attacks with air strikes and armored assaults on Palestinian-controlled areas. Israeli

Bush and the Middle East

President George W. Bush addresses soldiers in July 2002 as part of an appeal to Congress to speed approval of increased defense spending after the September 11 terrorist attacks.

agents also assassinated leaders of Hamas and Islamic Jihad, two Palestinian terrorist organizations.

THE BUSH DOCTRINE In the fall of 2002, President Bush unveiled a new national security doctrine that marked a distinct shift from that of previous administrations. Containment and deterrence had been the guiding strategic concepts of the cold war. Now, President Bush declared, the growing menace posed by "shadowy networks" of terrorist groups and unstable rogue nations with "weapons of mass destruction," required a new doctrine of preemptive military action. "If we wait for threats to fully materialize," he explained, "we will have waited too long. In the world we have entered, the only path to safety is the path of action. And this nation will act."

A SECOND GULF WAR During 2002 and 2003 Iraq emerged as the focus of the Bush administration's new policy of "preemptive" military action to prevent terrorism and destroy weapons of mass destruction. Following the Persian Gulf War of 1991, UN inspectors had gone to Iraq to search for such biological and chemical weapons. Iraqi leader Saddam Hussein never accepted the legitimacy of those efforts, and in the fall of 1998 he had ordered the UN inspectors to leave. Thereafter, American officials grew increasingly concerned about Iraq's illegal possession of biological and chemical weapons as well as its support of global terrorism. In September 2002 President Bush urged the UN to confront the "grave and gathering danger" posed by Hussein's dictatorial regime in Iraq. He warned that the United States would act alone if the UN did not respond. In October, Congress approved a resolution proposed by Bush authorizing him to use "all means that he determines to be appropriate, including force" to defend the United States against the threat posed by Iraq. On November 8 the UN Security Council passed Resolution 1441 ordering Iraq to disarm immediately or face "serious consequences." Faced with growing international pressure, Hussein grudgingly allowed UN weapons inspectors to return to Iraq "without conditions."

As the UN inspectors resumed their efforts, however, the Iraqi government continued its partial cooperation and stalling tactics. President Bush gained the support of Great Britain and Spain in proposing a new UN resolution that would authorize military action to ensure that Iraq eliminated its weapons of mass destruction. "The United States," Bush insisted, "will not permit the world's most dangerous regimes to threaten us with the world's most destructive weapons."

During early 2003 American and British military units began to assemble in the Persian Gulf. France, China, Germany, and Russia opposed the American-led effort to use force against Iraq, arguing that the UN inspectors should be given more time to complete their task. Secretary of State Colin Powell's efforts to marshal international support for the forceful American stance proved fruitless. On March 17 the United States, Great Britain, and Spain withdrew their proposed Security Council resolution, announcing that diplomatic efforts had failed. President Bush issued an ultimatum to Saddam Hussein: he and his sons must leave Iraq within forty-eight hours or face a U.S.-led invasion. Hussein refused. Two days later, on March 19, American and British forces, supported by what George Bush called the "coalition of the willing," attacked Iraq.

Operation Iraqi Freedom involved a massive bombing campaign followed closely by a fast-moving invasion across the Iraqi desert from bases in Kuwait. Some 250,000 American soldiers, sailors, and marines were joined by 50,000 British troops as well as small contingents from other countries, including Australia and Poland. President Bush explained that the purpose of the invasion was to "disarm Iraq, to free its people, and defend the world from grave danger." Critics at home and abroad, however, saw the allied assault as an imperialist effort to control Iraqi oil and impose a capitalist democracy on an Arab country. On April 9, after only three weeks of intense

A Continued Presence in Iraq

U.S. military police patrol the market in Abu Ghraib, on the outskirts of Baghdad.

fighting amid sweltering heat and blinding sandstorms, allied forces occupied Baghdad, the capital of Iraq. Iraqis cheered as U.S. soldiers toppled an enormous statue of Saddam Hussein in the city center. Saddam's Baathist regime and his inept army collapsed and fled a week later. On May 1, 2003, an exuberant President Bush declared that the war was essentially over. "The battle of Iraq," he said, "is one victory in a war on terror that began on September 11, 2001, and still goes on."

The complicated Iraqi military campaign was a brilliantly orchestrated demonstration of intense firepower, daring maneuver, and complex logistical support. No one had predicted such a quick and decisive victory—or so few casualties among the allied forces. The six-week war came at a cost of fewer than 200 combat deaths among the 300,000 coalition troops. Over 2,000 Iraqi soldiers were killed; civilian casualties numbered in the tens of thousands.

Secretary of Defense Donald Rumsfeld saw the Iraq War as an opportunity to showcase America's new military strategy, with its focus on airpower, precision weaponry, sophisticated communications, and mobile ground forces adept at stealth and speed. Yet winning the peace proved far more difficult than winning the war. No sooner had Saddam Hussein's tyranny been destroyed than the allies faced the daunting task of restoring order and installing a democratic government in a chaotic Iraq torn by age-old religious feuds and ethnic tensions. Looting was rampant and basic services nonexistent. Saddam Hussein and many of his lieutenants evaded capture and organized insurgent attacks against the allied forces and the interim Iraqi government. Violence engulfed the war-torn country. Vengeful Islamic jihadists (holy warriors) from around the world streamed into Iraq to wage a merciless campaign of terror and sabotage against the coalition forces and their Iraqi allies.

Defense Department analysts had greatly underestimated the difficulty of pacifying and reconstructing postwar Iraq. As Secretary Rumsfeld told his staff in October 2003, the invasion of Iraq was the easy part. The allies now faced "a long, hard slog" in their effort to install a new Iraqi government and restore basic services in the midst of a growing guerrilla insurgency. By the fall of 2003, President Bush was forced to admit that substantial numbers of American troops (around 150,000) would remain in Iraq much longer than originally anticipated and that rebuilding the fractured nation would take much longer than expected. Victory on the battlefields of Iraq did not bring peace to the Middle East. Militant Islamic groups seething with hatred for the United States remained a constant global threat. In addition, the dispute over the Iraq War strained relations between the Anglo-American alliance and France, Germany, and Russia, all of which opposed the war.

Throughout 2003 and 2004 the Iraqi insurgency and its campaign of terror grew in scope and savagery. Near-daily suicide car bombings and roadside ambushes of U.S. military convoys wreaked havoc among Iraqi civilians and allied troops. Terrorists kidnapped foreign civilians and beheaded several of them in grisly rituals videotaped for the world to see. In the United States the euphoria of battlefield victory turned to dismay as the casualties and the expense of the Iraqi occupation soared. In the face of mounting criticism, President Bush urged Americans to "stay the course," insisting that a democratic Iraq would bring stability to the volatile Middle East and thereby blunt the momentum of Islamic terrorism.

But the president's credibility suffered a sharp blow in January 2004 when administration officials admitted that no weapons of mass destruction—the primary reason for launching the invasion—had been found in Iraq. The chief weapons inspector told Congress that the intelligence reports about Saddam's supposed secret weapons were "almost all wrong." Shocking revelations in April 2004 of American soldiers' torturing Iraqi prisoners further eroded public confidence in Bush's handling of the war and its aftermath.

By September 2004 American military deaths in Iraq had reached 1,000, and during 2006 they were well over 2,500. Although Saddam Hussein was captured in December 2003 and Iraqi citizens elected their first democratic government in January 2005 and approved a new constitution nine months later, Iraq seemed less secure than ever. The continuing guerrilla war in Afghanistan and the new one in Iraq strained American military resources and the federal budget. The Defense Department was forced to call up thousands of members of U.S. Army Reserve and National Guard units, and military recruiters found it increasingly difficult to meet their quotas.

THE ELECTION OF 2004 Growing public concern about the mayhem in Iraq complicated George Bush's campaign for a second term. Throughout 2004 his approval rating plummeted. And in the new century the electorate had become deeply polarized. A Gallup poll showed that Bush had the support of 91 percent of Republicans and only 17 percent of Democrats, the widest partisan gap in the poll's history. Visceral cultural issues such as abortion, school prayer, stem-cell research, and gay marriage continued to divide voters and inflame political discourse.

The 2004 Election

President George W. Bush (center) and Democratic candidate Senator John Kerry (left) participate in the second presidential debate, a town-hall style exchange held at Washington University in St. Louis, Missouri.

A ferocious partisanship dominated civic commentary in the early years of the century. Democrats still fumed over the contested election results of 2000. When asked about the intensity of his critics, a combative George Bush declared the furor "a compliment. It means I'm willing to take a stand." One of his advisers explained it more bluntly: "He likes being hated. It lets him know he's doing the right thing."

The 2004 presidential campaign was punctuated by negative attacks on each candidate as the two parties sought to galvanize their loyalists. Campaign rhetoric was especially caustic because both sides saw so much at stake. Democrats worried that the tide of Republican conservatism might sweep them into irrelevance. Republicans worried that the "jobless" economic recovery and deepening commitment in Iraq might derail their political momentum.

The Democratic nominee, Senator John Kerry of Massachusetts, was a decorated Vietnam War veteran who had helped organize the Vietnam Veterans against the War in the early 1970s. During the 2004 campaign, Kerry lambasted the Bush administration for misleading the nation on the issue of weapons of mass destruction in Iraq and for its inept handling of the Iraq occupation, implying that the United States was foundering in another Vietnam-like quagmire. Kerry charged that the Iraq War was hurting the war on global terror. He also highlighted the record budget deficits occurring under the Republican leadership. Bush countered that the tortuous efforts to create a democratic government in Iraq would enhance America's long-term security. The president also promised to continue his efforts to reform the Social Security pension program and the tax code and to reduce unemployment by restoring sustained economic growth.

On election day the exit polls suggested a Kerry victory, but in the end the election hinged on the crucial swing state of Ohio. No Republican had ever lost Ohio and still won the presidency. After an anxious night viewing returns from Ohio and even considering the contested ballots, Kerry conceded the election. "The outcome," he stressed, "should be decided by voters, not a protracted legal battle." By narrowly winning Ohio, Bush garnered 286 electoral votes to Kerry's 251. The 2004 election was remarkable for its high voter turnout. Almost 120 million people voted, some 15 million more than in the disputed 2000 election.

Bush won the popular vote by 50.73 to 48.27 percent, the narrowest margin won by any incumbent president. Yet in some respects the close election was not so close. Bush received 3.5 million more votes nationwide than Kerry, and Republicans increased their control of both the House and the Senate. As was true in the 2000 election, Bush and the Republicans dominated in the South, the Midwest, and the Rocky Mountain states while the

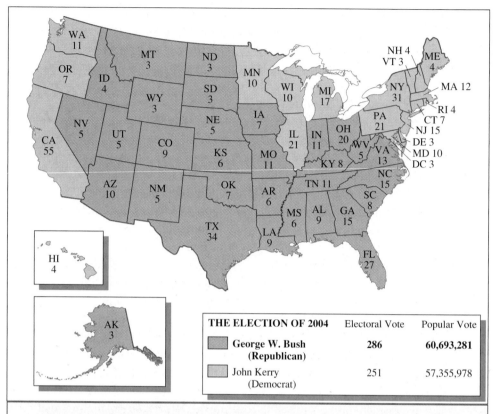

THE ELECTION OF 2004	Electoral Vote	Popular Vote
George W. Bush (Republican)	286	60,693,281
John Kerry (Democrat)	251	57,355,978

How did the war in Iraq polarize the electorate? In what ways did the election of 2004 give Republicans a mandate?

Democrats controlled the West Coast, the Northeast, and the states bordering the Great Lakes. Trumpeting "the will of the people at my back," Bush pledged to bring democracy and security to Iraq, overhaul the tax code and eliminate the estate tax, revamp Social Security, trim the federal budget deficit, limit awards for medical malpractice lawsuits, pass an energy bill, and create more jobs. "I earned capital in the campaign, political capital, and now I intend to spend it," he told reporters.

SECOND-TERM BLUES

Yet like many modern presidents, George Bush sputtered in his second term. In 2005 he pushed through Congress an energy bill and a Central

American Free Trade Act. But his effort to privatize Social Security retirement accounts went nowhere, and soaring budget deficits made repeal of the estate tax politically impossible.

The retirement of Sandra Day O'Connor from the Supreme Court in July 2005 ignited a fierce political debate over combustible issues such as abortion, gay marriage, and affirmative action. Militants on the left and on the right exerted unrelenting pressure on the White House, but Bush's shrewd decision to nominate John G. Roberts Jr., a socially conservative circuit court judge, stalemated critics because Roberts's legal credentials were impeccable. Yet the fractious cultural debates did not subside. No sooner had the Senate overwhelmingly confirmed Roberts (seventy-eight to twenty-two) than Chief Justice William Rehnquist died. Bush then named Roberts the new chief justice and nominated Harriet E. Miers, a longtime friend and former personal lawyer turned White House legal counsel, to replace O'Connor. Critics, many of them Republican conservatives, denounced Miers as a legal mediocrity and a presidential crony. The furor led Miers to withdraw her nomination in late October 2005, a humiliating development for President Bush that further hobbled his stalled legislative efforts. Her withdrawal coincided with the indictment of Vice President Richard Cheney's chief of staff, Lewis Libby, for perjury and obstruction of justice relating to an investigation of administration officials who purportedly had revealed the identity of a covert CIA agent in a supposed act of political revenge. To address concerns that the Bush administration was sputtering in its second term and heal the ruptures within the Republican coalition, Bush nominated to the Supreme Court Samuel Alito Jr., a federal judge and a favorite of conservatives.

HURRICANE KATRINA   In the summer of 2005, President Bush's eroding public support suffered another blow, this time when a natural disaster turned into a political crisis. In late August a killer hurricane named Katrina slammed into the Gulf coast, devastating large areas of Alabama, Mississippi, and Louisiana. Coastal towns such as Gulfport and Biloxi, Mississippi, were blown away. The sultry metropolis of New Orleans was virtually destroyed as levees and flood walls holding back the Mississippi River and Lake Pontchartrain burst, inundating three quarters of the city, most of which is below sea level and below the Mississippi River.

New Orleans had always been at war with its environment. Since its founding in the early eighteenth century, the sodden city surrounded by mosquito-infested swamps and regularly visited by floods had placed its faith in engineering to keep back the surrounding water. This time nature

Hurricane Katrina

Cars and buildings are partially submerged on Canal Street, a central thoroughfare in New Orleans, September 3, 2005.

won. After Katrina roared through the city, whole neighborhoods lay underwater, often up to the roofline. Nearly 500,000 New Orleans residents were displaced, most of them poor and many of them African American. Looting was so widespread that officials declared martial law; the streets were awash with soldiers and police. Katrina's awful wake left over 1,000 people dead in three states and millions homeless and hopeless. "The magnitude of the situation is untenable," Louisiana's governor lamented. "It's just heartbreaking."

Local political officials and the Federal Emergency Management Agency (FEMA) were caught unprepared as the catastrophe unfolded. Disaster plans were incomplete; communication and coordination were sorely lacking; confusion and incompetence abounded. Evacuation plans proved faulty, and government red tape compounded the misery. A wave of public outrage crashed against the Bush administration. Republican senator David Vitter of Louisiana gave the federal relief effort "a failing grade, across the board." Already-high gasoline prices skyrocketed as the hurricane shut down refineries, oil platforms, and pipelines. In the face of blistering criticism,

President Bush accepted responsibility for the balky federal response to the disaster and accepted the resignation of the FEMA director. Rebuilding the Gulf coast would take a long time and a lot of money.

Hurricane Katrina was one of the worst natural disasters in American history. Although many thousands more people were killed in the hurricanes that destroyed Galveston, Texas, in 1900 and devastated the Lake Okeechobee area of Florida in 1928, the dollar cost of Katrina's fury was much greater. Experts predicted that it would take $200 billion to restore the Gulf coast. More worrisome were claims made by a growing number of scientists that the increasing frequency and potency of hurricanes were a dreadful manifestation of global warming, a controversial phenomenon supposedly caused by carbon dioxide emissions from industrial smokestacks and automobile exhaust rising into the atmosphere and depleting the earth's protective ozone layer. Depleted ozone causes the temperature of the earth and the oceans to rise, thereby affecting climate and, according to some scientists, making weather more extreme. Americans already insecure in the face of global terrorism wrestled with the anxiety of a planet suddenly turned unstable and unpredictable.

The havoc wreaked by Katrina was only partly the result of natural forces run amok, however. Environmental calamities usually expose human failings. And in washing away property and lives, Katrina revealed all the elements of a disaster waiting to happen: poor planning, social inequalities, embedded corruption, and racial injustice. The destruction of New Orleans could have been mitigated or avoided altogether if, for example, warnings about the weakness of the aging levees had been heeded. The failure of the levees revealed scandalous breaches in public policy and public leadership. New Orleans had come to depend upon the Army Corps of Engineers for its lifeline of levees and pumps designed to keep the Mississippi River and Lake Pontchartrain at bay. Yet the city's flood-control funding had been reduced by 44 percent since 2001. The weakening of wetlands protections to favor developers had also made the city far more vulnerable to the flood surge generated by hurricanes. Marshes absorb storm water, but much of the wetland surrounding New Orleans had disappeared as a result of strenuous efforts to reroute the Mississippi River in order to facilitate the passage of ships and, ironically, provide better flood control. Realigning the river had prevented silt from building up in the Delta and nourishing the wetlands. The natural calamity was made much worse by human action—and inaction.

A STALLED PRESIDENCY George Bush bore the brunt of public indignation over the federal response to the Katrina disaster. By the fall of 2006, the White House was beset by political problems, a sputtering economy, and growing public dissatisfaction with the president's performance. Bush's job-approval rating fell below 40 percent, an all-time low. Even his support among Republicans crumbled, and many social conservatives felt betrayed by his sporadic attention to their concerns. The editors of the *Economist,* an influential conservative newsmagazine, declared in June 2005 that Bush had become "the least popular re-elected president since Richard Nixon became embroiled in the Watergate fiasco." The skyrocketing gasoline prices and the federal budget deficit fueled public frustration. President Bush and Congress had overseen the largest increase in federal spending since Franklin Roosevelt. The president's efforts to reform the tax code, Social Security, and immigration laws languished during his second term, and the turmoil and violence in Iraq showed no signs of abating. Senator Chuck Hagel, a Nebraska Republican, declared in 2005 that "we're losing in Iraq." The drumbeat of disillusionment prompted President Bush to acknowledge "setbacks" in Iraq and flaws in the intelligence reports that provided the rationale for going to war. At the end of 2005, the embattled president visited the recovering Gulf coast. His purpose, explained an aide, was "to give people a sense of hope." George Bush might have done the same for his presidency. It, too, needed an infusion of hope and energy as he reached the midpoint of his second term.

FURTHER READING

On George H. W. Bush's presidency, see *Leadership and the Bush Presidency: Prudence or Drift in an Era of Change?* edited by Ryan J. Barilleaux and Mary E. Stuckey (1992) and Charles Tiefer's *The Semi-Sovereign Presidency: The Bush Administration's Strategy for Governing without Congress* (1994). Among the journalistic accounts of the presidential election of 1992, the best narrative is Jack W. Germond and Jules Witcover's *Mad as Hell: Revolt at the Ballot Box, 1992* (1993). The best scholarly study is Theodore J. Lowi and Benjamin Ginsberg's *Democrats Return to Power: Politics and Policy in the Clinton Era* (1994).

Analysis of the Clinton years can be found in Joe Klein's *The Natural: The Misunderstood Presidency of Bill Clinton* (2002). Clinton's impeachment is assessed in Richard A. Posner's *An Affair of State: The Investigation, Impeachment, and Trial of President Clinton* (1999).

On changing demographic trends, see Sam Roberts's *Who We Are Now: The Changing Face of America in the Twenty-First Century* (2004). On social and cultural life in the 1990s, see Haynes Johnson's *The Best of Times: Amer-*

ica in the Clinton Years (2001). The onset and growth of the AIDS epidemic are traced in *And the Band Played On: Politics, People, and the AIDS Epidemic* (1987) by Randy Shilts.

Aspects of fundamentalist and apocalyptic movements are the subject of Paul Boyer's *When Time Shall Be No More: Prophecy Belief in Modern American Culture* (1992), George M. Marsden's *Understanding Fundamentalism and Evangelicalism* (1991), and Ralph E. Reed's *Politically Incorrect: The Emerging Faith Factor in American Politics* (1994).

On the invention of the computer and the Internet, see Paul E. Ceruzzi's *A History of Modern Computing,* 2nd ed. (2003) and Janet Abbate's *Inventing the Internet* (1999). The booming economy of the 1990s is well analyzed in Joseph E. Stiglitz's *The Roaring Nineties: A New History of the World's Most Prosperous Decade* (2003). On the rising stress within the workplace, see Jill Andresky Fraser's *White-Collar Sweatshop: The Deterioration of Work and Its Rewards in Corporate America* (2001). Aspects of corporate restructuring and downsizing are the subject of Bennett Harrison's *Lean and Mean: The Changing Landscape of Corporate Power in the Age of Flexibility* (1994).

For further treatment of the end of the cold war, see Michael R. Beschloss's *At the Highest Levels: The Inside Story of the End of the Cold War* (1993) and Richard Crockatt's *The Fifty Years War: The United States and the Soviet Union in World Politics, 1941–1991* (1995). On the Persian Gulf conflict, see Lester H. Brune's *America and the Iraqi Crisis, 1990–1992: Origins and Aftermath* (1993). On the transformation of American foreign policy, see James Mann's *Rise of the Vulcans: The History of Bush's War Cabinet* (2004), Claes G. Ryn's *America the Virtuous: Crisis of Democracy and the Quest for Empire* (2003), and Stephen M. Walt's *Taming American Power: The Global Response to U.S. Primacy* (2005).

The disputed 2000 presidential election is the focus of Jeffrey Toobin's *Too Close to Call: The Thirty-Six-Day Battle to Decide the 2000 Election* (2001). On the attacks of September 11, 2001, and their aftermath, see *The Age of Terror: America and the World after September 11,* edited by Strobe Talbott and Nayan Chanda (2001).

GLOSSARY

Agricultural Adjustment Act (1933) New Deal legislation that established the Agricultural Adjustment Administration (AAA) to improve agricultural prices by limiting market supplies; declared unconstitutional in *United States v. Butler* (1936).

Alamo, Battle of the Siege in the Texas War for Independence, 1836, in which the San Antonio mission fell to the Mexicans, and Davy Crockett and Jim Bowie died.

***Alexander v. Holmes County Board of Education* (1969)** Case fifteen years after the *Brown* decision in which the U.S. Supreme Court ordered an immediate end to segregation in public schools.

Alien and Sedition Acts (1798) Four measures passed during the undeclared war with France that limited the freedoms of speech and press and restricted the liberty of noncitizens.

America First Committee Largely midwestern isolationist organization supported by many prominent citizens, 1940–41.

American Anti-Slavery Society National abolitionist organization founded in 1833 by New York philanthropists Arthur and Lewis Tappan, propagandist Theodore Dwight Weld, and others.

American Colonization Society Organized in 1816 to encourage colonization of free blacks to Africa; West African nation of Liberia founded in 1822 to serve as a homeland for them.

American Federation of Labor Founded in 1881 as a federation of trade unions, the AFL under president Samuel Gompers successfully pushed for the eight-hour workday.

American Protective Association Nativist, anti-Catholic secret society founded in Iowa in 1887 and active until the end of the century.

American System Program of internal improvements and protective tariffs promoted by Speaker of the House Henry Clay in his presidential campaign of 1824; his proposals formed the core of Whig ideology in the 1830s and 1840s.

Antietam, Battle of (Battle of Sharpsburg) One of the bloodiest battles of the Civil War, fought to a standoff on September 17, 1862, in western Maryland.

Anti-Federalists Forerunners of Thomas Jefferson's Democratic-Republican party; opposed the Constitution as a limitation on individual and states' rights, which led to the addition of a Bill of Rights to the document.

Appomattox Court House, Virginia Site of the surrender of Confederate general Robert E. Lee to Union general Ulysses S. Grant on April 9, 1865, marking the end of the Civil War.

Army-McCarthy hearings Televised U.S. Senate hearings in 1954 on Senator Joseph McCarthy's charges of disloyalty in the Army; his tactics contributed to his censure by the Senate.

Atlanta Compromise Speech to the Cotton States and International Exposition in 1895 by educator Booker T. Washington, the leading black spokesman of the day; black scholar W. E. B. Du Bois gave the speech its derisive name and criticized Washington for encouraging blacks to accommodate segregation and disenfranchisement.

Atlantic Charter Issued August 12, 1941, following meetings in Newfoundland between President Franklin D. Roosevelt and British prime minister Winston Churchill, the charter signaled the allies' cooperation and stated their war aims.

Atomic Energy Commission Created in 1946 to supervise peacetime uses of atomic energy.

Axis powers In World War II, the nations of Germany, Italy, and Japan.

Aztec Mesoamerican people who were conquered by the Spanish under Hernando Cortés, 1519–28.

baby boom Markedly higher birth rate in the years following World War II; led to the biggest demographic "bubble" in American history.

Bacon's Rebellion Unsuccessful 1676 revolt led by planter Nathaniel Bacon against Virginia governor William Berkeley's administration because it had failed to protect settlers from Indian raids.

***Bakke v. Board of Regents of California* (1978)** Case in which the U.S. Supreme Court ruled against the California university system's use of racial quotas in admissions.

balance of trade Ratio of imports to exports.

Bank of the United States Proposed by the first secretary of the treasury, Alexander Hamilton, the bank opened in 1791 and operated until 1811 to issue a uniform currency, make business loans, and collect tax monies. The Second Bank of the United States was chartered in 1816 but was not renewed by President Andrew Jackson twenty years later.

barbary pirates Plundering pirates off the Mediterranean coast of Africa; President Thomas Jefferson's refusal to pay them tribute to protect American ships sparked an undeclared naval war with North African nations, 1801–1805.

barbed wire First practical fencing material for the Great Plains was invented in 1873 and rapidly spelled the end of the open range.

Battle of the Currents Conflict in the late 1880s between inventors Thomas Edison and George Westinghouse over direct versus alternating electric current; Westinghouse's alternating current (AC), the winner, allowed electricity to travel over long distances.

Bay of Pigs Invasion Hoping to inspire a revolt against Fidel Castro, the CIA sent 1,500 Cuban exiles to invade their homeland on April 17, 1961, but the mission was a spectacular failure.

Bill of Rights First ten amendments to the U.S. Constitution, adopted in 1791 to guarantee individual rights and to help secure ratification of the Constitution by the states.

Black Codes (1865–66) Laws passed in southern states to restrict the rights of former slaves; to combat the codes, Congress passed the Civil Rights Act of 1866 and the Fourteenth Amendment and set up military governments in southern states that refused to ratify the amendment.

Black Power Post-1966 rallying cry of a more militant civil rights movement.

Bland-Allison Act (1878) Passed over President Rutherford B. Hayes's veto, the inflationary measure authorized the purchase each month of 2 to 4 million dollars' worth of silver for coinage.

"Bleeding" Kansas Violence between pro- and antislavery settlers in the Kansas Territory, 1856.

Bloody Shirt, Waving the Republican references to Reconstruction-era violence in the South, used effectively in northern political campaigns against Democrats.

Bonus Expeditionary Force Thousands of World War I veterans, who insisted on immediate payment of their bonus certificates, marched on Washington in 1932; violence ensued when President Herbert Hoover ordered their tent villages cleared.

Boston Massacre Clash between British soldiers and a Boston mob, March 5, 1770, in which five colonists were killed.

Boston Tea Party On December 16, 1773, the Sons of Liberty, dressed as Indians, dumped hundreds of chests of tea into Boston harbor to protest the Tea Act of 1773, under which the British exported to the colonies millions of pounds of cheap—but still taxed—tea, thereby undercutting the price of smuggled tea and forcing payment of the tea duty.

Boxer Rebellion Chinese nationalist protest against Western commercial domination and cultural influence, 1900; a coalition of American, European, and Japanese forces put down the rebellion and reclaimed captured embassies in Peking (Beijing) within the year.

brain trust Group of advisers—many of them academics—that Franklin D. Roosevelt assembled to recommend New Deal policies during the early months of his presidency.

Branch Davidians Religious cult that lived communally near Waco, Texas, and was involved in a fiery 1993 confrontation with federal authorities in which dozens of cult members died.

Brook Farm Transcendentalist commune in West Roxbury, Massachusetts, populated from 1841 to 1847 principally by writers (Nathaniel Hawthorne, for one) and other intellectuals.

Brown v. Board of Education of Topeka (1954) U.S. Supreme Court decision that struck down racial segregation in public education and declared "separate but equal" unconstitutional.

Budget and Accounting Act of 1921 Created the Bureau of the Budget and the General Accounting Office.

Bull Run, Battles of (First and Second Manassas) First land engagement of the Civil War took place on July 21, 1861, at Manassas Junction, Virginia, at which surprised Union troops quickly retreated; one year later, on August 29–30, Confederates captured the federal supply depot and forced Union troops back to Washington.

Bunker Hill, Battle of First major battle of the Revolutionary War; it actually took place at nearby Breed's Hill, Massachusetts, on June 17, 1775.

"Burned-Over District" Area of western New York strongly influenced by the revivalist fervor of the Second Great Awakening; Disciples of Christ and Mormons are among the many sects that trace their roots to the phenomenon.

Burr conspiracy Scheme by Vice-President Aaron Burr to lead the secession of the Louisiana Territory from the United States; captured in 1807 and charged with treason, Burr was acquitted by the U.S. Supreme Court.

***Bush v. Gore* (2000)** U.S. Supreme Court case that determined the winner of the disputed 2000 presidential election.

Calhoun Resolutions In making the proslavery response to the Wilmot Proviso, Senator John C. Calhoun argued that barring slavery in Mexican acquisitions would violate the Fifth Amendment to the Constitution by depriving slaveholding settlers of their property.

Calvinism Doctrine of predestination expounded by Swiss theologian John Calvin in 1536; influenced the Puritan, Presbyterian, German and Dutch Reformed, and Huguenot churches in the colonies.

Camp David Accords Peace agreement between Israeli prime minister Menachem Begin and Egyptian president Anwar Sadat, brokered by President Jimmy Carter in 1978.

carpetbaggers Northern emigrants who participated in the Republican governments of the Reconstruction South.

Chancellorsville, Battle of Confederate general Robert E. Lee won his last major victory and General "Stonewall" Jackson died in this Civil War battle in northern Virginia on May 1–4, 1863.

Chattanooga, Battle of Union victory in eastern Tennessee on November 23–25, 1863; gave the North control of important rail lines and cleared the way for General William T. Sherman's march into Georgia.

Chinese Exclusion Act (1882) Halted Chinese immigration to the United States.

Civil Rights Act of 1866 Along with the Fourteenth Amendment, guaranteed the rights of citizenship to freedmen.

Civil Rights Act of 1957 First federal civil rights law since Reconstruction; established the Civil Rights Commission and the Civil Rights Division of the Department of Justice.

Civil Rights Act of 1964 Outlawed discrimination in public accommodations and employment.

clipper ships Superior oceangoing sailing ships of the 1840s to 1860s that cut travel time in half; the clipper ship route around Cape Horn was the fastest way to travel between the coasts of the United States.

closed shop Hiring requirement that all workers in a business must be union members.

Coercive Acts/Intolerable Acts (1774) Four parliamentary measures in reaction to the Boston Tea Party that forced payment for the tea, disallowed colonial trials of British soldiers, forced their quartering in private homes, and set up a military government.

cold war Term for tensions, 1945–89, between the Soviet Union and the United States, the two major world powers after World War II.

***Commonwealth v. Hunt* (1842)** Landmark ruling of the Massachusetts supreme court establishing the legality of labor unions.

Compromise of 1850 Complex compromise mediated by Senator Henry Clay that headed off southern secession over California statehood; to appease the South it included a stronger fugitive slave law and delayed determination of the slave status of the New Mexico and Utah territories.

Compromise of 1877 Deal made by a special congressional commission on March 2, 1877, to resolve the disputed presidential election of 1876; Republican Rutherford B. Hayes, who had lost the popular vote, was declared the winner in exchange for the withdrawal of federal troops from the South, marking the end of Reconstruction.

Congress of Industrial Organizations (CIO) Umbrella organization of semi-skilled industrial unions, formed in 1935 as the Committee for Industrial Organization and renamed in 1938.

Congress of Racial Equality (CORE) Civil rights organization started in 1944 and best known for its "freedom rides," bus journeys challenging racial segregation in the South in 1961.

conspicuous consumption Phrase referring to extravagant spending to raise social standing, coined by Thorstein Veblen in *The Theory of the Leisure Class* (1899).

Constitutional Convention Meeting in Philadelphia, May 25–September 17, 1787, of representatives from twelve colonies—excepting Rhode Island—to revise the existing Articles of Confederation; convention soon resolved to produce an entirely new constitution.

containment General U.S. strategy in the cold war that called for containing Soviet expansion; originally devised in 1947 by U.S. diplomat George F. Kennan.

Continental Army Army authorized by the Continental Congress, 1775–84, to fight the British; commanded by General George Washington.

Continental Congress Representatives of a loose confederation of colonies met first in Philadelphia in 1774 to formulate actions against British policies; the Second Continental Congress (1775–89) conducted the war and adopted the Declaration of Independence and the Articles of Confederation.

convict leasing System developed in the post–Civil War South that generated income for the states and satisfied planters' need for cheap labor by renting prisoners out; the convicts, however, were often treated poorly.

Copperheads Northerners opposed to the Civil War.

Coral Sea, Battle of the Fought on May 7–8, 1942, near the eastern coast of Australia, it was the first U.S. naval victory over Japan in World War II.

cotton gin Invented by Eli Whitney in 1793, the machine separated cotton seed from cotton fiber, speeding cotton processing and making profitable the cultivation of the more hardy, but difficult to clean, short-staple cotton; led directly to the dramatic nineteenth-century expansion of slavery in the South.

counterculture "Hippie" youth culture of the 1960s, which rejected the values of the dominant culture in favor of illicit drugs, communes, free sex, and rock music.

court-packing plan President Franklin D. Roosevelt's failed 1937 attempt to increase the number of U.S. Supreme Court justices from nine to fifteen in order to save his Second New Deal programs from constitutional challenges.

Credit Mobilier scandal Millions of dollars in overcharges for building the Union Pacific Railroad were exposed; high officials of the Ulysses S. Grant administration were implicated but never charged.

Cuban missile crisis Caused when the United States discovered Soviet offensive missile sites in Cuba in October 1962; the U.S.-Soviet confrontation was the cold war's closest brush with nuclear war.

crop-lien system Merchants extended credit to tenants based on their future crops, but high interest rates and the uncertainties of farming often led to inescapable debts (debt peonage).

D-Day June 6, 1944, when an Allied amphibious assault landed on the Normandy coast and established a foothold in Europe from which Hitler's defenses could not recover.

Dartmouth College v. Woodward (1819) U.S. Supreme Court upheld the original charter of the college against New Hampshire's attempt to alter the board of trustees; set precedent of support of contracts against state interference.

Declaration of Independence Document adopted on July 4, 1776, that made the break with Britain official; drafted by a committee of the Second Continental Congress including principal writer Thomas Jefferson.

Deism Enlightenment thought applied to religion; emphasized reason, morality, and natural law.

Department of Homeland Security Created to coordinate federal antiterrorist activity following the 2001 terrorist attacks on the World Trade Center and Pentagon.

Depression of 1893 Worst depression of the century, set off by a railroad failure, too much speculation on Wall Street, and low agricultural prices.

Dixiecrats Deep South delegates who walked out of the 1948 Democratic National Convention in protest of the party's support for civil rights legislation and later formed the States' Rights (Dixiecrat) party, which nominated Strom Thurmond of South Carolina for president.

Dominion of New England Consolidation into a single colony of the New England colonies—and later New York and New Jersey—by royal governor Edmund Andros in 1686; dominion reverted to individual colonial governments three years later.

Donner Party Forty-seven surviving members of a group of migrants to California were forced to resort to cannibalism to survive a brutal winter trapped in the Sierra Nevadas, 1846–47; highest death toll of any group traveling the Overland Trail.

Dred Scott v. Sandford **(1857)** U.S. Supreme Court decision in which Chief Justice Roger B. Taney ruled that slaves could not sue for freedom and that Congress could not prohibit slavery in the territories, on the grounds that such a prohibition would violate the Fifth Amendment rights of slaveholders.

due-process clause Clause in the Fifth and the Fourteenth amendments to the U.S. Constitution guaranteeing that states could not "deprive any person of life, liberty, or property, without due process of law."

Dust Bowl Great Plains counties where millions of tons of topsoil were blown away from parched farmland in the 1930s; massive migration of farm families followed.

Eighteenth Amendment (1919) Prohibition amendment that made illegal the manufacture, sale, or transportation of alcoholic beverages.

Ellis Island Reception center in New York Harbor through which most European immigrants to America were processed from 1892 to 1954.

Emancipation Proclamation (1863) President Abraham Lincoln issued a preliminary proclamation on September 22, 1862, freeing the slaves in the Confederate states as of January 1, 1863, the date of the final proclamation.

Embargo Act of 1807 Attempt to exert economic pressure instead of waging war in reaction to continued British impressment of American sailors; smugglers easily circumvented the embargo, and it was repealed two years later.

Emergency Banking Relief Act (1933) First New Deal measure that provided for reopening the banks under strict conditions and took the United States off the gold standard.

Emergency Immigration Act of 1921 Limited U.S. immigration to 3 percent of each foreign-born nationality in the 1910 census; three years later Congress restricted immigration even further.

encomienda System under which officers of the Spanish conquistadores gained ownership of Indian land.

ENIAC Electronic Numerical Integrator and Computer, built in 1944, the early, cumbersome ancestor of the modern computer.

Enlightenment Revolution in thought begun in the seventeenth century that emphasized reason and science over the authority of traditional religion.

Enola Gay American B-29 bomber that dropped the atomic bomb on Hiroshima, Japan, on August 6, 1945.

Environmental Protection Agency (EPA) Created in 1970 during the first administration of President Richard M. Nixon to oversee federal pollution control efforts.

Equal Rights Amendment Amendment to guarantee equal rights for women, introduced in 1923 but not passed by Congress until 1972; it failed to be ratified by the states.

Era of Good Feelings Contemporary characterization of the administration of popular Democratic-Republican president James Monroe, 1817–25.

Erie Canal Most important and profitable of the barge canals of the 1820s and 1830s; stretched from Buffalo to Albany, New York, connecting the Great Lakes to the East Coast and making New York City the nation's largest port.

Espionage and Sedition Acts (1917–18) Limited criticism of government leaders and policies by imposing fines and prison terms on those who acted out in opposition to in the First World War; the most repressive measures passed up to that time.

Fair Deal Domestic reform proposals of the second Truman administration (1949–53); included civil rights legislation and repeal of the Taft-Hartley Act, but only extensions of some New Deal programs were enacted.

Fair Employment Practices Commission Created in 1941 by executive order, the FEPC sought to eliminate racial discrimination in jobs; it possessed little power but represented a step toward civil rights for African Americans.

Family and Medical Leave Act (1993) Allowed certain workers to take twelve weeks of unpaid leave each year for family health problems, including birth or adoption of a child.

Farmers' Alliance Two separate organizations (Northwestern and Southern) of the 1880s and 1890s that took the place of the Grange, worked for similar causes, and attracted landless, as well as landed, farmers to their membership.

Federal Trade Commission Act (1914) Established the Federal Trade Commission to enforce existing antitrust laws that prohibited business combinations in restraint of trade.

The Federalist Collection of eighty-five essays that appeared in the New York press in 1787–88 in support of the Constitution; written by Alexander Hamilton, James Madison, and John Jay but published under the pseudonym "Publius."

Federalist party One of the two first national political parties, it favored a strong central government.

Fence-Cutters' War Violent conflict in Texas, 1883–84, between large and small cattle ranchers over access to grazing land.

"Fifty-four forty or fight" Democratic campaign slogan in the presidential election of 1844, urging that the northern border of Oregon be fixed at 54°40′ north latitude.

***Fletcher v. Peck* (1810)** U.S. Supreme Court decision in which Chief Justice John Marshall upheld the initial fraudulent sale contracts in the Yazoo Fraud cases; Congress paid $4.2 million to the original speculators in 1814.

Fort Laramie Treaty (1851) Restricted the Plains Indians from using the Overland Trail and permitted the building of government forts.

Fort McHenry Fort in Baltimore Harbor unsuccessfully bombarded by the British in September 1814; Francis Scott Key, a witness to the battle, was moved to write the words to "The Star-Spangled Banner."

Fort Sumter First battle of the Civil War, in which the federal fort in Charleston (South Carolina) Harbor was captured by the Confederates on April 14, 1861, after two days of shelling.

"forty-niners" Speculators who went to northern California following the discovery of gold in 1848; the first of several years of large-scale migration was 1849.

Fourteen Points President Woodrow Wilson's 1918 plan for peace after World War I; at the Versailles peace conference, however, he failed to incorporate all of the points into the treaty.

Fourteenth Amendment (1868) Guaranteed rights of citizenship to former slaves, in words similar to those of the Civil Rights Act of 1866.

franchise The right to vote.

"free person of color" Negro or mulatto person not held in slavery; immediately before the Civil War, there were nearly a half million in the United States, split almost evenly between North and South.

Free Soil party Formed in 1848 to oppose slavery in the territory acquired in the Mexican War; nominated Martin Van Buren for president in 1848, but by 1854 most of the party's members had joined the Republican party.

Free Speech Movement Founded in 1964 at the University of California at Berkeley by student radicals protesting restrictions on their right to demonstrate.

Freedmen's Bureau Reconstruction agency established in 1865 to protect the legal rights of former slaves and to assist with their education, jobs, health care, and landowning.

French and Indian War Known in Europe as the Seven Years' War, the last (1755–63) of four colonial wars fought between England and France for control of North America east of the Mississippi River.

Fugitive Slave Act of 1850 Gave federal government authority in cases involving runaway slaves; so much more punitive and prejudiced in favor of slaveholders than the 1793 Fugitive Slave Act had been that Harriet Beecher Stowe was inspired to write *Uncle Tom's Cabin* in protest; the new law was part of the Compromise of 1850, included to appease the South over the admission of California as a free state.

Fundamentalism Anti-modernist Protestant movement started in the early twentieth century that proclaimed the literal truth of the Bible; the name came from *The Fundamentals*, published by conservative leaders.

Gadsden Purchase (1853) Thirty thousand square miles in present-day Arizona and New Mexico bought by Congress from Mexico primarily for the Southern Pacific Railroad's transcontinental route.

Gentlemen's Agreement (1907) United States would not exclude Japanese immigrants if Japan would voluntarily limit the number of immigrants coming to the United States.

Gettysburg, Battle of Fought in southern Pennsylvania, July 1–3, 1863; the Confederate defeat and the simultaneous loss at Vicksburg spelled the end of the South's chances in the Civil War.

***Gibbons v. Ogden* (1824)** U.S. Supreme Court decision reinforcing the "commerce clause" (the federal government's right to regulate interstate commerce) of the Constitution; Chief Justice John Marshall ruled against the State of New York's granting of steamboat monopolies.

***Gideon v. Wainwright* (1963)** U.S. Supreme Court decision guaranteeing legal counsel for indigent felony defendants.

The Gilded Age Mark Twain and Charles Dudley Warner's 1873 novel, the title of which became the popular name for the period from the end of the Civil War to the turn of the century.

Glass-Owen Federal Reserve Act (1913) Created a Federal Reserve System of regional banks and a Federal Reserve Board to stabilize the economy by regulating the supply of currency and controlling credit.

Glass-Steagall Act (Banking Act of 1933) Established the Federal Deposit Insurance Corporation and included banking reforms, some designed to control speculation. A banking act of the Hoover administration, passed in 1932 and also known as the Glass-Steagall Act, was designed to expand credit.

Good Neighbor Policy Proclaimed by President Franklin D. Roosevelt in his first inaugural address in 1933, it sought improved diplomatic relations between the United States and its Latin American neighbors.

grandfather clause Loophole created by southern disfranchising legislatures of the 1890s for illiterate white males whose grandfathers had been eligible to vote in 1867.

Granger movement Political movement that grew out of the Patrons of Husbandry, an educational and social organization for farmers founded in 1867; the Grange had its greatest success in the Midwest of the 1870s, lobbying for government control of railroad and grain elevator rates and establishing farmers' cooperatives.

Great Awakening Fervent religious revival movement in the 1720s through the 1740s that was spread throughout the colonies by ministers like New England Congregationalist Jonathan Edwards and English revivalist George Whitefield.

Great Compromise (Connecticut Compromise) Mediated the differences between the New Jersey and Virginia delegations to the Constitutional Convention by providing for a bicameral legislature, the upper house of which would have equal representation and the lower house of which would be apportioned by population.

Great Depression Worst economic depression in American history; it was spurred by the stock market crash of 1929 and lasted until World War II.

Great Migration Large-scale migration of southern blacks during and after World War I to the North, where jobs had become available during the labor shortage of the war years.

Great Society Term coined by President Lyndon B. Johnson in his 1965 State of the Union address, in which he proposed legislation to address problems of voting rights, poverty, diseases, education, immigration, and the environment.

Greenback party Formed in 1876 in reaction to economic depression, the party favored issuance of unsecured paper money to help farmers repay debts; the movement for free coinage of silver took the place of the greenback movement by the 1880s.

habeas corpus, writ of An essential component of English common law and of the U.S. Constitution that guarantees that citizens may not be imprisoned without due process of law; literally means, "you must have the body."

Half-Breeds During the presidency of Rutherford B. Hayes, 1877–81, a moderate Republican party faction led by Senator James G. Blaine that favored some reforms of the civil service system and a restrained policy toward the defeated South.

Harlem Renaissance African-American literary and artistic movement of the 1920s and 1930s centered in New York City's Harlem district; writers Langston Hughes, Jean Toomer, Zora Neale Hurston, and Countee Cullen were among those active in the movement.

Harpers Ferry, Virginia Site of abolitionist John Brown's failed raid on the federal arsenal, October 16–17, 1859; he intended to arm the slaves, but ten of his compatriots were killed, and Brown became a martyr to his cause after his capture and execution.

Hartford Convention Meeting of New England Federalists on December 15, 1814, to protest the War of 1812; proposed seven constitutional amendments (limiting embargoes and changing requirements for officeholding, declaration of war, and admission of new states), but the war ended before Congress could respond.

Hawley-Smoot Tariff Act (1930) Raised tariffs to an unprecedented level and worsened the depression by raising prices and discouraging foreign trade.

Haymarket Affair Riot during an anarchist protest at Haymarket Square in Chicago on May 4, 1886, over violence during the McCormick Harvester Company strike; the deaths of eleven, including seven policemen, helped hasten the demise of the Knights of Labor, even though they were not responsible for the riot.

Hessians German soldiers, most from Hesse-Cassel principality (hence the name), paid to fight for the British in the Revolutionary War.

holding company Investment company that holds controlling interest in the securities of other companies.

Homestead Act (1862) Authorized Congress to grant 160 acres of public land to a western settler, who had only to live on the land for five years to establish title.

Homestead Strike Violent strike at the Carnegie Steel Company near Pittsburgh in 1892 that culminated in the disintegration of the Amalgamated Association of Iron and Steel Workers, the first steelworkers' union.

House Un-American Activities Committee (HUAC) Formed in 1938 to investigate subversives in the government; best-known investigations were of Hollywood no tables and of former State Department official Alger Hiss, who was accused in 1948 of espionage and Communist party membership.

Hundred Days Extraordinarily productive first three months of President Franklin D. Roosevelt's administration in which a special session of Congress enacted fifteen of his New Deal proposals.

impeachment Bringing charges against a public official; for example, the House of Representatives can impeach a president for "treason, bribery, or other high crimes and misdemeanors" by majority vote, and after the trial the Senate can remove the president by a vote of two-thirds.

implied powers Federal powers beyond those specifically enumerated in the U.S. Constitution; the Federalists argued that the "elastic clause" of Article I, Section 8, of the Constitution implicitly gave the federal government broad powers, while the Antifederalists held that the federal government's powers were explicitly limited by the Constitution.

"In God We Trust" Phrase placed on all new U.S. currency as of 1954.

indentured servant Settler who signed on for a temporary period of servitude to a master in exchange for passage to the New World; Virginia and Pennsylvania were largely peopled in the seventeenth and eighteenth centuries by English indentured servants.

Independent Treasury Act (1840) Promoted by President Martin Van Buren, the measure sought to stabilize the economy by preventing state banks from printing unsecured paper currency and establishing an independent treasury based on specie.

Indian Peace Commission Established in 1867 to end the Indian wars in the West, the commission's solution was to contain the Indians in a system of reservations.

Indian Removal Act (1830) Signed by President Andrew Jackson, the law permitted the negotiation of treaties to obtain the Indians' lands in exchange for their relocation to what would become Oklahoma.

Industrial Workers of the World Radical union organized in Chicago in 1905 and nicknamed the Wobblies; its opposition to World War I led to its destruction by the federal government under the Espionage Act.

internal improvements In the early national period the phrase referred to road building and the development of water transportation.

Interstate Commerce Commission Reacting to the U.S. Supreme Court's ruling in *Wabash Railroad* v. *Illinois* (1886), Congress established the ICC to curb abuses in the railroad industry by regulating rates.

Iran-Contra affair Scandal of the second Reagan administration involving sale of arms to Iran in partial exchange for release of hostages in Lebanon and use of the arms money to aid the Contras in Nicaragua, which had been expressly forbidden by Congress.

Iron Curtain Term coined by Winston Churchill to describe the cold war divide between western Europe and the Soviet Union's eastern European satellites.

Irreconcilables Group of isolationist U.S. senators who fought ratification of the Treaty of Versailles, 1919–20, because of their opposition to American membership in the League of Nations.

Jamestown, Virginia Site in 1607 of the first permanent English settlement in the New World.

Jay's Treaty Treaty with Britain negotiated in 1794 by Chief Justice John Jay; Britain agreed to vacate forts in the Northwest Territories, and festering disagreements (border with Canada, prewar debts, shipping claims) would be settled by commission.

Jim Crow Minstrel show character whose name became synonymous with post-Reconstruction laws revoking civil rights for freedmen and with racial segregation generally.

Judiciary Act of 1801 Enacted by the lame duck Congress to allow the Federalists, the losing party in the presidential election, to reorganize the judiciary and fill the open judgeships with Federalists.

Kansas-Nebraska Act (1854) Law sponsored by Illinois senator Stephen A. Douglas to allow settlers in newly organized territories north of the Missouri border to decide the slavery issue for themselves; fury over the resulting nullification of the Missouri Compromise of 1820 led to violence in Kansas and to the formation of the Republican party.

Kellogg-Briand Pact Representatives of sixty-two nations in 1928 signed the pact (also called the Pact of Paris) to outlaw war.

Kentucky and Virginia Resolutions (1798–99) Passed in response to the Alien and Sedition Acts, the resolutions advanced the state-compact theory that held states could nullify an act of Congress if they deemed it unconstitutional.

King William's War (War of the League of Augsburg) First (1689–97) of four colonial wars between England and France.

King's Mountain, Battle of Upcountry South Carolina irregulars defeated British troops under Patrick Ferguson on October 7, 1780, in what proved to be the turning point of the Revolutionary War in the South.

Knights of Labor Founded in 1869, the first national union picked up many members after the disastrous 1877 railroad strike but lasted, under the leadership of Terence V. Powderly, only into the 1890s; supplanted by the American Federation of Labor.

Know-Nothing (American) party Nativist, anti-Catholic third party organized in 1854 in reaction to large-scale German and Irish immigration; the party's only presidential candidate was Millard Fillmore in 1856.

Korean War Conflict touched off in 1950 when Communist North Korea invaded South Korea, which had been under U.S. control since the end of World War II; fighting largely by U.S. forces continued until 1953.

Ku Klux Klan Organized in Pulaski, Tennessee, in 1866 to terrorize former slaves who voted and held political offices during Reconstruction; a revived organization in the 1910s and 1920s stressed white, Anglo-Saxon, fundamentalist Protestant supremacy; the Klan revived a third time to fight the civil rights movement of the 1950s and 1960s in the South.

Land Ordinance of 1785 Directed surveying of the Northwest Territory into townships of thirty-six sections (square miles) each, the sale of the sixteenth section of which was to be used to finance public education.

League of Nations Organization of nations to mediate disputes and avoid war established after World War I as part of the Treaty of Versailles; President Woodrow Wilson's "Fourteen Points" speech to Congress in 1918 proposed the formation of the league.

Lecompton Constitution Controversial constitution drawn up in 1857 by proslavery Kansas delegates seeking statehood; rejected in 1858 by an overwhelmingly antislavery electorate.

Legal Tender Act (1862) Helped the U.S. government pay for the Civil War by authorizing the printing of paper currency.

Lend-Lease Act (1941) Permitted the United States to lend or lease arms and other supplies to the Allies, signifying increasing likelihood of American involvement in World War II.

Levittown Low-cost, mass-produced development of suburban tract housing built by William Levitt on Long Island in 1947.

Lexington and Concord, Battle of The first shots fired in the Revolutionary War, on April 19, 1775, near Boston; approximately 100 minutemen and 250 British soldiers were killed.

Leyte Gulf, Battle of Largest sea battle in history, fought on October 25, 1944, and won by the United States off the Philippine island of Leyte; Japanese losses were so great that they could not rebound.

Liberty party Abolitionist political party that nominated James G. Birney for president in 1840 and 1844; merged with the Free Soil party in 1848.

Lincoln-Douglas debates Series of senatorial campaign debates in 1858 focusing on the issue of slavery in the territories; held in Illinois between Republican Abraham Lincoln, who made a national reputation for himself, and incumbent Democratic senator Stephen A. Douglas, who managed to hold onto his seat.

Little Bighorn, Battle of Most famous battle of the Great Sioux War took place in 1876 in the Montana Territory; combined Sioux and Cheyenne warriors massacred a vastly outnumbered U.S. Cavalry commanded by Lieutenant Colonel George Armstrong Custer.

Lost Colony English expedition of 117 settlers, including Virginia Dare, the first English child born in the New World; colony disappeared from Roanoke Island in the Outer Banks sometime between 1587 and 1590.

Louisiana Purchase President Thomas Jefferson's 1803 purchase from France of the important port of New Orleans and 828,000 square miles west of the Mississippi River to the Rocky Mountains; it more than doubled the territory of the United States at a cost of only $15 million.

Lusitania British passenger liner sunk by a German U-boat, May 7, 1915, creating a diplomatic crisis and public outrage at the loss of 128 Americans (roughly 10 percent of the total aboard); Germany agreed to pay reparations, and the United States waited two more years to enter World War I.

Lyceum movement Founded in 1826, the movement promoted adult public education through lectures and performances.

maize Indian corn, native to the New World.

Manhattan Project Secret American plan during World War II to develop an atomic bomb; J. Robert Oppenheimer led the team of physicists at Los Alamos, New Mexico.

Manifest Destiny Imperialist phrase first used in 1845 to urge annexation of Texas; used thereafter to encourage American settlement of European colonial and Indian lands in the Great Plains and Far West.

Marbury v. Madison **(1803)** First U.S. Supreme Court decision to declare a federal law—the Judiciary Act of 1801—unconstitutional; President John Adams's "midnight appointment" of Federalist judges prompted the suit.

March on Washington Civil rights demonstration on August 28, 1963, where the Reverend Martin Luther King, Jr., gave his "I Have a Dream" speech on the steps of the Lincoln Memorial.

Marshall Plan U.S. program for the reconstruction of post–World War II Europe through massive aid to former enemy nations as well as allies; proposed by General George C. Marshall in 1947.

massive resistance In reaction to the *Brown* decision of 1954, U.S. senator Harry Byrd encouraged southern states to defy federally mandated school integration.

Maya Pre-Columbian society in Mesoamerica before about A.D. 900.

Mayflower Compact Signed in 1620 aboard the *Mayflower* before the Pilgrims landed at Plymouth, the document committed the group to majority-rule government; remained in effect until 1691.

Maysville Road Bill Federal funding for a Kentucky road, vetoed by President Andrew Jackson in 1830.

McCarran Internal Security Act (1950) Passed over President Harry S. Truman's veto, the law required registration of American Communist party members, denied them passports, and allowed them to be detained as suspected subversives.

***McCulloch v. Maryland* (1819)** U.S. Supreme Court decision in which Chief Justice John Marshall, holding that Maryland could not tax the Second Bank of the United States, supported the authority of the federal government versus the states.

McNary-Haugen Bill Vetoed by President Calvin Coolidge in 1927 and 1928, the bill to aid farmers would have artificially raised agricultural prices by selling surpluses overseas for low prices and selling the reduced supply in the United States for higher prices.

Meat Inspection Act (1906) Passed largely in reaction to Upton Sinclair's *The Jungle*, the law set strict standards of cleanliness in the meatpacking industry.

mercantilism Limitation and exploitation of colonial trade by an imperial power.

Mestizo Person of mixed Native American and European ancestry.

Mexican War Controversial war with Mexico for control of California and New Mexico, 1846–48; the Treaty of Guadalupe Hidalgo fixed the border at the Rio Grande and extended the United States to the Pacific coast, annexing more than a half-million square miles of potential slave territory.

Midway, Battle of Decisive American victory near Midway Island in the South Pacific on June 4, 1942; the Japanese navy never recovered its superiority over the U.S. navy.

Military Reconstruction Act (1867) Established military governments in ten Confederate states—excepting Tennessee—and required that the states ratify the Fourteenth Amendment and permit freedmen to vote.

minstrel show Blackface vaudeville entertainment popular in the decades surrounding the Civil War.

Miranda v. Arizona **(1966)** U.S. Supreme Court decision required police to advise persons in custody of their rights to legal counsel and against self-incrimination.

Missouri Compromise Deal proposed by Kentucky senator Henry Clay to resolve the slave/free imbalance in Congress that would result from Missouri's admission as a slave state; in the compromise of March 20, 1820, Maine's admission as a free state offset Missouri, and slavery was prohibited in the remainder of the Louisiana Territory north of the southern border of Missouri.

Molly Maguires Secret organization of Irish coal miners that used violence to intimidate mine officials in the 1870s.

Monitor **and** *Merrimack,* **Battle of the** First engagement between ironclad ships; fought at Hampton Roads, Virginia, on March 9, 1862.

Monroe Doctrine President James Monroe's declaration to Congress on December 2, 1823, that the American continents would be thenceforth closed to colonization but that the United States would honor existing colonies of European nations.

Moral Majority Televangelist Jerry Falwell's political lobbying organization, the name of which became synonymous with the religious right—conservative evangelical Protestants who helped ensure President Ronald Reagan's 1980 victory.

Mormons Founded in 1830 by Joseph Smith, the sect (officially, the Church of Jesus Christ of Latter-Day Saints) was a product of the intense revivalism of the "Burned-Over District" of New York; Smith's successor Brigham Young led 15,000 followers to Utah in 1847 to escape persecution.

Montgomery bus boycott Sparked by Rosa Parks's arrest on December 1, 1955, a successful year-long boycott protesting segregation on city buses; led by the Reverend Martin Luther King.

Muckrakers Writers who exposed corruption and abuses in politics, business, meat-packing, child labor, and more, primarily in the first decade of the twentieth century; their popular books and magazine articles spurred public interest in progressive reform.

Mugwumps Reform wing of the Republican party which supported Democrat Grover Cleveland for president in 1884 over Republican James G. Blaine, whose influence peddling had been revealed in the Mulligan letters of 1876.

***Munn v. Illinois* (1877)** U.S. Supreme Court ruling that upheld a Granger law allowing the state to regulate grain elevators.

NAFTA Approved in 1993, the North American Free Trade Agreement with Canada and Mexico allowed goods to travel across their borders free of tariffs; critics argued that American workers would lose their jobs to cheaper Mexican labor.

National Aeronautics and Space Administration (NASA) In response to the Soviet Union's launching of *Sputnik*, Congress created this federal agency in 1957 to coordinate research and administer the space program.

National Association for the Advancement of Colored People (NAACP) Founded in 1910, this civil rights organization brought lawsuits against discriminatory practices and published *The Crisis*, a journal edited by African-American scholar W. E. B. Du Bois.

National Defense Education Act (1958) Passed in reaction to America's perceived inferiority in the space race, the appropriation encouraged education in science and modern languages through student loans, university research grants, and aid to public schools.

National Industrial Recovery Act (1933) Passed on the last of the Hundred Days, it created public-works jobs through the Federal Emergency Relief Administration and established a system of self-regulation for industry through the National Recovery Administration, which was ruled unconstitutional in 1935.

National Organization for Women Founded in 1966 by writer Betty Friedan and other feminists, NOW pushed for abortion rights and nondiscrimination in the workplace, but within a decade it became radicalized and lost much of its constituency.

National Road First federal interstate road, built between 1811 and 1838 and stretching from Cumberland, Maryland, to Vandalia, Illinois.

National Security Act (1947) Authorized the reorganization of government to coordinate military branches and security agencies; created the

National Security Council, the Central Intelligence Agency, and the National Military Establishment (later renamed the Department of Defense).

National Youth Administration Created in 1935 as part of the Works Progress Administration, it employed millions of youths who had left school.

nativism Anti-immigrant and anti-Catholic feeling in the 1830s through the 1850s; the largest group was New York's Order of the Star-Spangled Banner, which expanded into the American, or Know-Nothing, party in 1854.

naval stores Tar, pitch, and turpentine made from pine resin and used in shipbuilding; an important industry in the southern colonies, especially North Carolina.

Navigation Acts Passed by the English Parliament to control colonial trade and bolster the mercantile system, 1650–1775; enforcement of the acts led to growing resentment by colonists.

Neutrality Acts Series of laws passed between 1935 and 1939 to keep the United States from becoming involved in war by prohibiting American trade and travel to warring nations.

New Deal Franklin D. Roosevelt's campaign promise, in his speech to the Democratic National Convention of 1932, to combat the Great Depression with a "new deal for the American people"; the phrase became a catchword for his ambitious plan of economic programs.

New England Anti-Slavery Society Abolitionist organization founded in 1832 by William Lloyd Garrison of Massachusetts, publisher of the *Liberator*.

New Freedom Democrat Woodrow Wilson's political slogan in the presidential campaign of 1912; Wilson wanted to improve the banking system, lower tariffs, and, by breaking up monopolies, give small businesses freedom to compete.

New Frontier John F. Kennedy's program, stymied by a Republican Congress and his abbreviated term; his successor Lyndon B. Johnson had greater success with many of the same concepts.

New Harmony Founded in Indiana by British industrialist Robert Owen in 1825, the short-lived New Harmony Community of Equality was one of the few nineteenth-century communal experiments not based on religious ideology.

New Left Radical youth protest movement of the 1960s, named by leader Tom Hayden to distinguish it from the Old (Marxist-Leninist) Left of the 1930s.

New Nationalism Platform of the Progressive party and slogan of former president Theodore Roosevelt in the presidential campaign of 1912; stressed government activism, including regulation of trusts, conservation, and recall of state court decisions that had nullified progressive programs.

New Orleans, Battle of Last battle of the War of 1812, fought on January 8, 1815, weeks after the peace treaty was signed but prior to its ratification; General Andrew Jackson led the victorious American troops.

New South *Atlanta Constitution* editor Henry W. Grady's 1886 term for the prosperous post–Civil War South he envisioned: democratic, industrial, urban, and free of nostalgia for the defeated plantation South.

Nineteenth Amendment (1920) Granted women the right to vote.

Nisei Japanese Americans; literally, "second generation."

normalcy Word coined by future president Warren G. Harding as part of a 1920 campaign speech—"not nostrums, but normalcy"—signifying his awareness that the public was tired of progressivism, war, and sacrifice.

North Atlantic Treaty Organization (NATO) Defensive alliance founded in 1949 by ten western European nations, the United States, and Canada to deter Soviet expansion in Europe.

Northwest Ordinance of 1787 Created the Northwest Territory (area north of the Ohio River and west of Pennsylvania), established conditions for self-government and statehood, included a Bill of Rights, and permanently prohibited slavery.

nullification Concept of invalidation of a federal law within the borders of a state; first expounded in the Kentucky and Virginia Resolutions (1798), cited by South Carolina in its Ordinance of Nullification (1832) of the Tariff of Abominations, used by southern states to explain their secession from the Union (1861), and cited again by southern states to oppose the *Brown* v. *Board of Education* decision (1954).

Nullification Proclamation President Andrew Jackson's strong criticism of South Carolina's Ordinance of Nullification (1832) as disunionist and potentially treasonous.

Office of Price Administration Created in 1941 to control wartime inflation and price fixing resulting from shortages of many consumer goods, the OPA imposed wage and price freezes and administered a rationing system.

Okies Displaced farm families from the Oklahoma dust bowl who migrated to California during the 1930s in search of jobs.

Old Southwest In the antebellum period, the states of Alabama, Mississippi, Louisiana, Texas, Arkansas, and parts of Tennessee, Kentucky, and Florida.

Oneida Community Utopian community founded in 1848; the Perfectionist religious group practiced universal marriage until leader John Humphrey Noyes, fearing prosecution, escaped to Canada in 1879.

OPEC Organization of Petroleum Exporting Countries.

Open Door Policy In hopes of protecting the Chinese market for U.S. exports, Secretary of State John Hay unilaterally announced in 1899 that Chinese trade would be open to all nations.

Operation Desert Storm Multinational allied force that defeated Iraq in the Gulf War of January 1991.

Operation Dixie CIO's largely ineffective post–World War II campaign to unionize southern workers.

Oregon fever Enthusiasm for emigration to the Oregon Country in the late 1830s and early 1840s.

Ostend Manifesto Memorandum written in 1854 from Ostend, Belgium, by the U.S. ministers to England, France, and Spain recommending purchase or seizure of Cuba in order to increase the United States' slaveholding territory.

Overland (Oregon) Trail Route of wagon trains bearing settlers from Independence, Missouri, to the Oregon Country in the 1840s through the 1860s.

overseer Manager of slave labor on a plantation.

Panic of 1819 Financial collapse brought on by sharply falling cotton prices, declining demand for American exports, and reckless western land speculation.

Panic of 1837 Major economic depression lasting about six years; touched off by a British financial crisis and made worse by falling cotton prices, credit and currency problems, and speculation in land, canals, and railroads.

Panic of 1857 Economic depression lasting about two years and brought on by falling grain prices and a weak financial system; the South was largely protected by international demand for its cotton.

Panic of 1873 Severe six-year depression marked by bank failures and railroad and insurance bankruptcies.

Peace of Paris Signed on September 3, 1783, the treaty ending the Revolutionary War and recognizing American independence from Britain also established the border between Canada and the United States, fixed the western border at the Mississippi River, and ceded Florida to Spain.

Pendleton Civil Service Act (1883) Established the Civil Service Commission and marked the end of the spoils system.

Pentagon Papers Informal name for the Defense Department's secret history of the Vietnam conflict; leaked to the press by former official Daniel Ellsberg and published in the *New York Times* in 1971.

Pequot War Massacre in 1637 and subsequent dissolution of the Pequot Nation by Puritan settlers, who seized the Indians' lands.

Personal Responsibility and Work Opportunity Act (1996) Welfare reform measure that mandated state administration of federal aid to the poor.

Philippine Sea, Battle of the Costly Japanese defeat of June 19–20, 1944; led to the resignation of Premier Tojo and his cabinet.

Pilgrims Puritan Separatists who broke completely with the Church of England and sailed to the New World aboard the *Mayflower,* founding Plymouth Colony on Cape Cod in 1620.

Pinckney's Treaty Treaty with Spain negotiated by Thomas Pinckney in 1795; established United States boundaries at the Mississippi River and the thirty-first parallel and allowed open transportation on the Mississippi.

planter In the antebellum South, the owner of a large farm worked by twenty or more slaves.

Platt Amendment (1901) Reserved the United States' right to intervene in Cuban affairs and forced newly independent Cuba to host American naval bases on the island.

Plessy v. Ferguson **(1896)** U.S. Supreme Court decision supporting the legality of Jim Crow laws that permitted or required "separate but equal" facilities for blacks and whites.

poll tax Tax that must be paid in order to be eligible to vote; used as an effective means of disenfranchising black citizens after Reconstruction, since they often could not afford even a modest fee.

popular sovereignty Allowed settlers in a disputed territory to decide the slavery issue for themselves.

Populist party Political success of Farmers' Alliance candidates encouraged the formation in 1892 of the National People's party (later renamed the Populist party); active until 1912, it advocated a variety of reform issues, including free coinage of silver, income tax, postal savings, regulation of railroads, and direct election of U.S. senators.

Pottawatomie Massacre Murder of five proslavery settlers in eastern Kansas led by abolitionist John Brown on May 24–25, 1856.

Potsdam Conference Last meeting of the major Allied powers, the conference took place outside Berlin from July 17 to August 2, 1945; United States president Harry Truman, Soviet dictator Joseph Stalin, and British prime minister Clement Atlee finalized plans begun at Yalta.

Proclamation of Amnesty and Reconstruction President Lincoln's plan for reconstruction, issued in 1863, allowed southern states to rejoin the Union if 10 percent of the 1860 electorate signed loyalty pledges, accepted emancipation, and had received presidential pardons.

Proclamation of 1763 Royal directive issued after the French and Indian War prohibiting settlement, surveys, and land grants west of the Appalachian Mountains; although it was soon overridden by treaties, colonists continued to harbor resentment.

Progressive party Created when former president Theodore Roosevelt broke away from the Republican party to run for president again in

1912; the party supported progressive reforms similar to the Democrats but stopped short of seeking to eliminate trusts.

Progressivism Broad-based reform movement, 1900–17, that sought governmental help in solving problems in many areas of American life, including education, public health, the economy, the environment, labor, transportation, and politics.

Protestant Reformation Reform movement that resulted in the establishment of Protestant denominations; begun by German monk Martin Luther when he posted his "Ninety-five Theses" (complaints of abuses in the Catholic church) in 1517.

Pullman Strike Strike against the Pullman Palace Car Company in the company town of Pullman, Illinois, on May 11, 1894, by the American Railway Union under Eugene V. Debs; the strike was crushed by court injunctions and federal troops two months later.

Pure Food and Drug Act (1906) First law to regulate manufacturing of food and medicines; prohibited dangerous additives and inaccurate labeling.

Puritans English religious group that sought to purify the Church of England; founded the Massachusetts Bay Colony under John Winthrop in 1630.

Quartering Act (1765) Parliamentary act requiring colonies to house and provision British troops.

Radical Republicans Senators and congressmen who, strictly identifying the Civil War with the abolitionist cause, sought swift emancipation of the slaves, punishment of the rebels, and tight controls over the former Confederate states after the war.

Railroad Strike of 1877 Violent but ultimately unsuccessful interstate strike, which resulted in extensive property damage and many deaths.

Reaganomics Popular name for President Ronald Reagan's philosophy of "supply side" economics, which combined tax cuts, less government spending, and a balanced budget with an unregulated marketplace.

Reconstruction Finance Corporation Federal program established in 1932 under President Herbert Hoover to loan money to banks and other institutions to help them avert bankruptcy.

Red Scare Fear among many Americans after World War I of Communists in particular and noncitizens in general, a reaction to the Russian Revolution, mail bombs, strikes, and riots.

Redcoats Nickname for British soldiers, after their red uniform jackets.

Redeemers/Bourbons Conservative white Democrats, many of whom had been planters or businessmen before the Civil War, who reclaimed control of the South following the end of Reconstruction.

Regulators Groups of backcountry Carolina settlers who protested colonial policies; North Carolina royal governor William Tryon retaliated at the Battle of Alamance on May 17, 1771.

Report on Manufactures First secretary of the treasury Alexander Hamilton's 1791 analysis that accurately foretold the future of American industry and proposed tariffs and subsidies to promote it.

Republican party Organized in 1854 by antislavery Whigs, Democrats, and Free Soilers in response to the passage of the Kansas-Nebraska Act; nominated John C. Frémont for president in 1856 and Abraham Lincoln in 1860.

Republicans Political faction that succeeded the Anti-Federalists after ratification of the Constitution; led by Thomas Jefferson and James Madison, it soon developed into the Democratic-Republican party.

Reservationists Group of U.S. senators led by Majority Leader Henry Cabot Lodge who would only agree to ratification of the Treaty of Versailles subject to certain reservations, most notably the removal of Article X of the League of Nations Covenant.

Revolution of 1800 First time that an American political party surrendered power to the opposition party; Jefferson, a Democratic-Republican, had defeated incumbent Adams, a Federalist, for president.

right-to-work State laws enacted to prevent imposition of the closed shop; any worker, whether or not a union member, could be hired.

***Roe v. Wade* (1973)** U.S. Supreme Court decision requiring states to permit first-trimester abortions.

Roosevelt Corollary (1904) President Theodore Roosevelt announced in what was essentially a corollary to the Monroe Doctrine that the United States could intervene militarily to prevent interference from European powers in the Western Hemisphere.

Romanticism Philosophical, literary, and artistic movement of the nineteenth century that was largely a reaction to the rationalism of the previous century; romantics valued emotion, mysticism, and individualism.

Rough Riders The 1st U.S. Volunteer Cavalry, led in battle in the Spanish-American War by Theodore Roosevelt; they were victorious in their only battle near Santiago, Cuba, and Roosevelt used the notoriety to aid his political career.

Santa Fe Trail Beginning in the 1820s, a major trade route from St. Louis, Missouri, to Santa Fe, New Mexico Territory.

Saratoga, Battle of Major defeat of British general John Burgoyne and more than 5,000 British troops at Saratoga, New York, on October 17, 1777.

Scalawags Southern white Republicans—some former Unionists—who served in Reconstruction governments.

***Schenck v. U.S.* (1919)** U.S. Supreme Court decision upholding the wartime Espionage and Sedition Acts; in the opinion he wrote for the case, Justice Oliver Wendell Holmes set the now-familiar "clear and present danger" standard.

scientific management Analysis of worker efficiency using measurements like "time and motion" studies to achieve greater productivity; introduced by Frederick Winslow Taylor in 1911.

Scottsboro case (1931) In overturning verdicts against nine black youths accused of raping two white women, the U.S. Supreme Court established precedents in *Powell* v. *Alabama* (1932), that adequate counsel must be appointed in capital cases, and in *Norris* v. *Alabama* (1935), that African Americans cannot be excluded from juries.

Second Great Awakening Religious revival movement of the early decades of the nineteenth century, in reaction to the growth of secularism and rationalist religion; began the predominance of the Baptist and Methodist churches.

Second Red Scare Post–World War II Red Scare focused on the fear of Communists in U.S. government positions; peaked during the Korean War and declined soon thereafter, when the U.S. Senate censured Joseph McCarthy, who had been a major instigator of the hysteria.

Seneca Falls Convention First women's rights meeting and the genesis of the women's suffrage movement; held in July 1848 in a church in Seneca Falls, New York, by Elizabeth Cady Stanton and Lucretia Coffin Mott.

"separate but equal" Principle underlying legal racial segregation, which was upheld in *Plessy* v. *Ferguson* (1896) and struck down in *Brown* v. *Board of Education* (1954).

Servicemen's Readjustment Act (1944) The "GI Bill of Rights" provided money for education and other benefits to military personnel returning from World War II.

settlement houses Product of the late nineteenth-century movement to offer a broad array of social services in urban immigrant neighborhoods; Chicago's Hull House was one of hundreds of settlement houses that operated by the early twentieth century.

Seventeenth Amendment (1913) Progressive reform that required U.S. senators to be elected directly by voters; previously, senators were chosen by state legislatures.

Seward's Folly Secretary of State William H. Seward's negotiation of the purchase of Alaska from Russia in 1867.

Shakers Founded by Mother Ann Lee Stanley in England, the United Society of Believers in Christ's Second Appearing settled in Watervliet, New York, in 1774 and subsequently established eighteen additional communes in the Northeast, Indiana, and Kentucky.

sharecropping Type of farm tenancy that developed after the Civil War in which landless workers—often former slaves—farmed land in exchange for farm supplies and a share of the crop; differed from tenancy in that the terms were generally less favorable.

Shays's Rebellion Massachusetts farmer Daniel Shays and 1,200 compatriots, seeking debt relief through issuance of paper currency and lower taxes, stormed the federal arsenal at Springfield in the winter of 1787 but were quickly repulsed.

Sherman Anti-Trust Act (1890) First law to restrict monopolistic trusts and business combinations; extended by the Clayton Anti-Trust Act of 1914.

Sherman Silver Purchase Act (1890) In replacing and extending the provisions of the Bland-Allison Act of 1878, it increased the amount of silver periodically bought for coinage.

Shiloh, Battle of At the time it was fought (April 6–7, 1862), Shiloh, in western Tennessee, was the bloodiest battle in American history; afterward, General Ulysses S. Grant was temporarily removed from command.

single tax Concept of taxing only landowners as a remedy for poverty, promulgated by Henry George in *Progress and Poverty* (1879).

Sixteenth Amendment (1913) Legalized the federal income tax.

Smith-Connally War Labor Disputes Act (1943) Outlawed labor strikes in wartime and allowed the president to take over industries threatened by labor disputes.

***Smith v. Allwright* (1944)** U.S. Supreme Court decision that outlawed all-white Democratic party primaries in Texas.

Social Darwinism Application of Charles Darwin's theory of natural selection to society; used the concept of the "survival of the fittest" to justify class distinctions and to explain poverty.

social gospel Preached by liberal Protestant clergymen in the late nineteenth and early twentieth centuries; advocated the application of Christian principles to social problems generated by industrialization.

Social Security Act (1935) Created the Social Security system with provisions for a retirement pension, unemployment insurance, disability insurance, and public assistance (welfare).

Sons of Liberty Secret organizations formed by Samuel Adams, John Hancock, and other radicals in response to the Stamp Act; they impeded British officials and planned such harassments as the Boston Tea Party.

South Carolina Exposition and Protest Written in 1828 by Vice-President John C. Calhoun of South Carolina to protest the so-called Tariff of Abominations, which seemed to favor northern industry; introduced the concept of state interposition and became the basis for South Carolina's Nullification Doctrine of 1833.

Southeast Asia Treaty Organization (SEATO) Pact among mostly western nations signed in 1954; designed to deter Communist expansion and cited as a justification for U.S. involvement in Vietnam.

Southern Christian Leadership Conference (SCLC) Civil rights organization founded in 1957 by the Reverend Martin Luther King, Jr., and other civil rights leaders.

Southern renaissance Literary movement of the 1920s and 1930s that included such writers as William Faulkner, Thomas Wolfe, and Robert Penn Warren.

Spanish flu Unprecedentedly lethal influenza epidemic of 1918 that killed more than 22 million people worldwide.

spoils system The term—meaning the filling of federal government jobs with persons loyal to the party of the president—originated in Andrew Jackson's first term; the system was replaced in the Progressive Era by civil service.

Sputnik First artificial satellite to orbit the earth; launched October 4, 1957, by the Soviet Union.

Stalwarts Conservative Republican party faction during the presidency of Rutherford B. Hayes, 1877–81; led by Senator Roscoe B. Conkling of New York, Stalwarts opposed civil service reform and favored a third term for President Ulysses S. Grant.

Stamp Act (1765) Parliament required that revenue stamps be affixed to all colonial printed matter, documents, dice, and playing cards; the Stamp Act Congress met to formulate a response, and the act was repealed the following year.

Standard Oil Company Founded in 1870 by John D. Rockefeller in Cleveland, Ohio, it soon grew into the nation's first industry-dominating trust; the Sherman Anti-Trust Act (1890) was enacted in part to combat abuses by Standard Oil.

staple crop Important cash crop, for example, cotton or tobacco.

steamboats Paddlewheelers that could travel both up- and down-river in deep or shallow waters; they became commercially viable early in the nineteenth century and soon developed into America's first inland freight and passenger service network.

Stimson Doctrine In reaction to Japan's 1932 occupation of Manchuria, Secretary of State Henry Stimson declared that the United States would not recognize territories acquired by force.

Strategic Defense Initiative ("Star Wars") Defense Department's plan during the Reagan administration to build a system to destroy incoming missiles in space.

Student Non-violent Coordinating Committee Founded in 1960 to coordinate civil rights sit-ins and other forms of grassroots protest.

Students for a Democratic Society (SDS) Major organization of the New Left, founded at the University of Michigan in 1960 by Tom Hayden and Al Haber.

Sugar Act (Revenue Act of 1764) Parliament's tax on refined sugar and many other colonial products; the first tax designed solely to raise revenue for Britain.

Taft-Hartley Act (1947) Passed over President Harry Truman's veto, the law contained a number of provisions to control labor unions, including the banning of closed shops.

tariff Federal tax on imported goods.

Tariff of Abominations (Tariff of 1828) Taxed imported goods at a very high rate; the South hated the tariff because it feared it would provoke Britain to reject American cotton.

Tariff of 1816 First true protective tariff, intended strictly to protect American goods against foreign competition.

Tax Reform Act (1986) Lowered federal income tax rates to 1920s levels and eliminated many loopholes.

Teapot Dome Harding administration scandal in which Secretary of the Interior Albert B. Fall profited from secret leasing to private oil companies of government oil reserves at Teapot Dome, Wyoming, and Elk Hills, California.

tenancy Renting of farmland by workers who owned their own equipment; tenant farmers kept a larger percentage of the crop than did sharecroppers.

Tennessee Valley Authority Created in 1933 to control flooding in the Tennessee River Valley, provide work for the region's unemployed, and produce inexpensive electric power for the region.

Tenure of Office Act (1867) Required the president to obtain Senate approval to remove any official whose appointment had also required Senate approval; President Andrew Johnson's violation of the law by firing Secretary of War Edwin Stanton led to the Radical Republicans retaliating with Johnson's impeachment.

Tertium Quid Literally, the "third something": states' rights and strict constructionist Republicans under John Randolph who broke with President Thomas Jefferson but never managed to form a third political party.

Tet Offensive Surprise attack by the Viet Cong and North Vietnamese during the Vietnamese New Year of 1968; turned American public opinion strongly against the war in Vietnam.

Tippecanoe, Battle of On November 7, 1811, Indiana governor William Henry Harrison (later president) defeated the Shawnee Indians at the Tippecanoe River in northern Indiana; victory fomented war fever against the British, who were believed to be aiding the Indians.

Title IX Part of the Educational Amendments Act of 1972 that required colleges to engage in "affirmative action" for women.

Tonkin Gulf Resolution (1964) Passed by Congress in reaction to supposedly unprovoked attacks on American warships off the coast of North Vietnam; it gave the president unlimited authority to defend U.S. forces and members of SEATO.

Tories Term used by Patriots to refer to Loyalists, or colonists who supported the Crown after the Declaration of Independence.

Townshend Acts (1767) Parliamentary measures (named for the chancellor of the exchequer) that punished the New York Assembly for failing to house British soldiers, taxed tea and other commodities, and established a Board of Customs Commissioners and colonial vice-admiralty courts.

Trail of Tears Cherokees' own term for their forced march, 1838–39, from the southern Appalachians to Indian lands (later Oklahoma); of 15,000 forced to march, 4,000 died on the way.

Transcendentalism Philosophy of a small group of mid-nineteenth-century New England writers and thinkers, including Ralph Waldo Emerson, Henry David Thoreau, and Margaret Fuller; they stressed "plain living and high thinking."

Transcontinental railroad First line across the continent from Omaha, Nebraska, to Sacramento, California, established in 1869 with the linkage of the Union Pacific and Central Pacific railroads at Promontory, Utah.

Truman Doctrine President Harry S. Truman's program of post–World War II aid to European countries—particularly Greece and Turkey—in danger of being undermined by communism.

trust Companies combined to control competition.

Twenty-first Amendment (1933) Repealed prohibition on the manufacture, sale, and transportation of alcoholic beverages, effectively nullifying the Eighteenth Amendment.

Twenty-second Amendment (1951) Limited presidents to two full terms of office or two terms plus two years of an assumed term; passed in reaction to President Franklin D. Roosevelt's unprecedented four elected terms.

Twenty-sixth Amendment (1971) Lowered the voting age from twenty-one to eighteen.

U.S.S. *Maine* Battleship that exploded in Havana Harbor on February 15, 1898, resulting in 266 deaths; the American public, assuming that the Spanish had mined the ship, clamored for war, and the Spanish-American War was declared two months later.

Uncle Tom's Cabin Harriet Beecher Stowe's 1852 antislavery novel popularized the abolitionist position.

Underground Railroad Operating in the decades before the Civil War, the "railroad" was a clandestine system of routes and safehouses through which slaves were led to freedom in the North.

Understanding clause Added to state constitutions in the late nineteenth century, it allowed illiterate whites to circumvent literacy tests for voting by demonstrating that they understood a passage in the Constitution; black citizens would be judged by white registrars to have failed.

Underwood-Simmons Tariff (1913) In addition to lowering and even eliminating some tariffs, it included provisions for the first federal income tax, made legal the same year by the ratification of the Sixteenth Amendment.

Unitarianism Late eighteenth-century liberal offshoot of the New England Congregationalist church; rejecting the Trinity, Unitarianism professed the oneness of God and the goodness of rational man.

United Farm Workers Union for the predominantly Mexican-American migrant laborers of the Southwest, organized by César Chavez in 1962.

United Nations Organization of nations to maintain world peace, established in 1945 and headquartered in New York.

Universal Negro Improvement Association Black nationalist movement active in the United States from 1916 to 1923, when its leader Marcus Garvey went to prison for mail fraud.

Universalism Similar to Unitarianism, but putting more stress on the importance of social action, Universalism also originated in Massachusetts in the late eighteenth century.

V-E Day May 8, 1945, the day World War II officially ended in Europe.

vertical integration Company's avoidance of middlemen by producing its own supplies and providing for distribution of its product.

veto President's constitutional power to reject legislation passed by Congress; a two-thirds vote in both houses of Congress can override a veto.

Vicksburg, Battle of The fall of Vicksburg, Mississippi, to General Ulysses S. Grant's army on July 4, 1863, after two months of siege was a turning point in the war because it gave the Union control of the Mississippi River.

Virginia and New Jersey Plans Differing opinions of delegations to the Constitutional Convention: New Jersey wanted one legislative body with equal representation for each state; Virginia's plan called for a strong central government and a two-house legislature apportioned by population.

Volstead Act (1919) Enforced the prohibition amendment, beginning January 1920.

Voting Rights Act of 1965 Passed in the wake of Martin Luther King's Selma to Montgomery March, it authorized federal protection of the right to vote and permitted federal enforcement of minority voting rights in individual counties, mostly in the South.

Wabash Railroad v. Illinois (1886) Reversing the U.S. Supreme Court's ruling in *Munn* v. *Illinois*, the decision disallowed state regulation of interstate commerce.

Wade-Davis Bill (1864) Radical Republicans' plan for reconstruction that required loyalty oaths, abolition of slavery, repudiation of war debts, and denial of political rights to high-ranking Confederate officials; President Lincoln refused to sign the bill.

Wagner Act (National Labor Relations Act of 1935) Established the National Labor Relations Board and facilitated unionization by regulating employment and bargaining practices.

War Industries Board Run by financier Bernard Baruch, the board planned production and allocation of war materiel, supervised purchasing, and fixed prices, 1917–19.

War of 1812 Fought with Britain, 1812–14, over lingering conflicts that included impressment of American sailors, interference with shipping, and collusion with Northwest Territory Indians; settled by the Treaty of Ghent in 1814.

War on Poverty Announced by President Lyndon B. Johnson in his 1964 State of the Union address; under the Economic Opportunity Bill signed later that year, Head Start, VISTA, and the Jobs Corps were created, and grants and loans were extended to students, farmers, and businesses in efforts to eliminate poverty.

War Production Board Created in 1942 to coordinate industrial efforts in World War II; similar to the War Industries Board in World War I.

War Relocation Camps Internment camps where Japanese Americans were held against their will from 1942 to 1945.

Warren Court The U.S. Supreme Court under Chief Justice Earl Warren, 1953–69, decided such landmark cases as *Brown v. Board of Education* (school desegregation), *Baker v. Carr* (legislative redistricting), and *Gideon v. Wainwright* and *Miranda v. Arizona* (rights of criminal defendants).

Washington Armaments Conference Leaders of nine world powers met in 1921–22 to discuss the naval race; resulting treaties limited to a specific ratio the carrier and battleship tonnage of each nation (Five-Power Naval Treaty), formally ratified the Open Door to China (Nine–Power Treaty), and agreed to respect each other's Pacific territories (Four-Power Treaty).

Watergate Washington office and apartment complex that lent its name to the 1972–74 scandal of the Nixon administration; when his knowledge of the break-in at the Watergate and subsequent coverup was revealed, Nixon resigned the presidency under threat of impeachment.

Webster-Ashburton Treaty Settlement in 1842 of U.S.-Canadian border disputes in Maine, New York, Vermont, and in the Wisconsin Territory (now northern Minnesota).

Webster-Hayne debate U.S. Senate debate of January 1830 between Daniel Webster of Massachusetts and Robert Hayne of South Carolina over nullification and states' rights.

Whig Party Founded in 1834 to unite factions opposed to President Andrew Jackson, the party favored federal responsibility for internal improvements; the party ceased to exist by the late 1850s, when party members divided over the slavery issue.

Whigs Another name for revolutionary Patriots.

Whiskey Rebellion Violent protest by western Pennsylvania farmers against the federal excise tax on corn whiskey, 1794.

Whitewater Development Corporation Failed Arkansas real estate investment that kept President Bill Clinton and his wife Hillary under investigation by Independent Counsel Kenneth Starr throughout the Clinton presidency; no charges were ever brought against either of the Clintons.

Wilderness, Battle of the Second battle fought in the thickly wooded Wilderness area near Chancellorsville, Virginia; in the battle of May 5–6, 1864, no clear victor emerged, but the battle served to deplete the Army of Northern Virginia.

Wilderness Road Originally an Indian path through the Cumberland Gap, it was used by over 300,000 settlers who migrated westward to Kentucky in the last quarter of the eighteenth century.

Wilmot Proviso Proposal to prohibit slavery in any land acquired in the Mexican War, but southern senators, led by John C. Calhoun of South Carolina, defeated the measure in 1846 and 1847.

Works Progress Administration (WPA) Part of the Second New Deal, it provided jobs for millions of the unemployed on construction and arts projects.

Wounded Knee, Battle of Last incident of the Indians Wars took place in 1890 in the Dakota Territory, where the U.S. Cavalry killed over 200 Sioux men, women, and children who were in the process of surrender.

writs of assistance One of the colonies' main complaints against Britain, the writs allowed unlimited search warrants without cause to look for evidence of smuggling.

XYZ Affair French foreign minister Tallyrand's three anonymous agents demanded payments to stop French plundering of American ships in 1797; refusal to pay the bribe led to two years of sea war with France (1798–1800).

Yalta Conference Meeting of Franklin D. Roosevelt, Winston Churchill, and Joseph Stalin at a Crimean resort to discuss the postwar world on February 4–11, 1945; Soviet leader Joseph Stalin claimed large areas in eastern Europe for Soviet domination.

Yazoo Fraud Illegal sale of the Yazoo lands (much of present-day Alabama and Mississippi) by Georgia legislators; by 1802 it had become a tangle of conflicting claims that the U.S. Supreme Court settled in *Fletcher* v. *Peck* (1810).

yellow journalism Sensationalism in newspaper publishing that reached a peak in the circulation war between Joseph Pulitzer's *New York World* and William Randolph Hearst's *New York Journal* in the 1890s; the papers' accounts of events in Havana Harbor in 1898 led directly to the Spanish-American War.

yeoman farmers Small landowners (the majority of white families in the South) who farmed their own land and usually did not own slaves.

Yorktown, Battle of Last battle of the Revolutionary War; General Lord Charles Cornwallis along with over 7,000 British troops surrendered at Yorktown, Virginia, on October 17, 1781.

Zimmermann telegram From the German foreign secretary to the German minister in Mexico, February 1917, instructing him to offer to recover Texas, New Mexico, and Arizona for Mexico if it would fight the United States to divert attention from Germany in case of war.

APPENDIX

THE DECLARATION OF INDEPENDENCE

WHEN IN THE COURSE OF HUMAN EVENTS, it becomes necessary for one people to dissolve the political bands which have connected them with another, and to assume the Powers of the earth, the separate and equal station to which the Laws of Nature and of Nature's God entitle them, a decent respect to the opinions of mankind requires that they should declare the causes which impel them to the separation.

We hold these truths to be self-evident, that all men are created equal, that they are endowed by their Creator with certain unalienable rights, that among these are Life, Liberty, and the pursuit of Happiness. That to secure these rights, Governments are instituted among Men, deriving their just powers from the consent of the governed. That whenever any Form of Government becomes destructive of these ends, it is the Right of the People to alter or to abolish it, and to institute new Government, laying its foundation on such principles and organizing its powers in such form, as to them shall seem most likely to effect their Safety and Happiness. Prudence, indeed, will dictate that Governments long established should not be changed for light and transient causes; and accordingly all experience hath shown, that mankind are more disposed to suffer, while evils are sufferable, than to right themselves by abolishing the forms to which they are accustomed. But when a long train of abuses and usurpations, pursuing invariably the same Object evinces a design to reduce them under absolute Despotism, it is their right, it is their duty, to throw off such Government, and to provide new Guards for their future security.—Such has been the patient sufferance of these Colonies; and such is now the necessity which constrains them to alter their former Systems of Government. The history of the present King of Great Britain is a history of repeated injuries and usurpations, all having in direct object the establishment of an absolute Tyranny over these States. To prove this, let Facts be submitted to a candid world.

He has refused his Assent to Laws, the most wholesome and necessary for the public good.

He has forbidden his Governors to pass Laws of immediate and pressing importance, unless suspended in their operation till his Assent should be obtained; and when so suspended, he has utterly neglected to attend to them.

He has refused to pass other Laws for the accommodation of large districts of people, unless those people would relinquish the right of Representation in the Legislature, a right inestimable to them and formidable to tyrants only.

He has called together legislative bodies at places unusual, uncomfortable, and distant from the depository of their public Records, for the sole purpose of fatiguing them into compliance with his measures.

He has dissolved Representative Houses repeatedly, for opposing with manly firmness his invasions on the rights of the people.

He has refused for a long time, after such dissolutions, to cause others to be elected; whereby the Legislative powers, incapable of Annihilation, have returned to the People at large for their exercise; the State remaining in the mean time exposed to all dangers of invasion from without, and convulsions within.

He has endeavoured to prevent the population of these States; for that purpose obstructing the Laws of Naturalization of Foreigners; refusing to pass others to encourage their migrations hither, and raising the conditions of new Appropriations of Lands.

He has obstructed the Administration of Justice, by refusing his Assent to Laws for establishing Judiciary powers.

He has made Judges dependent on his Will alone, for the tenure of their offices, and the amount and payment of their salaries.

He has erected a multitude of New Offices, and sent hither swarms of Officers to harass our People, and eat out their substance.

He has kept among us, in times of peace, Standing Armies without the Consent of our legislatures.

He has affected to render the Military independent of and superior to the Civil Power.

He has combined with others to subject us to a jurisdiction foreign to our constitution, and unacknowledged by our laws; giving his Assent to their Acts of pretended Legislation:

For quartering large bodies of armed troops among us:

For protecting them, by a mock Trial, from Punishment for any Murders which they should commit on the Inhabitants of these States:

For cutting off our Trade with all parts of the world:

For imposing taxes on us without our Consent:

For depriving us of many cases, of the benefits of Trial by jury:

For transporting us beyond Seas to be tried for pretended offences:

For abolishing the free System of English Laws in a neighbouring Province, establishing therein an Arbitrary government, and enlarging its

Boundaries so as to render it at once an example and fit instrument for introducing the same absolute rule into these Colonies:

For taking away our Charters, abolishing our most valuable Laws, and altering fundamentally the Forms of our Governments:

For suspending our own Legislatures, and declaring themselves in vested with Power to legislate for us in all cases whatsoever.

He has abdicated Government here, by declaring us out of his Protection and waging War against us.

He has plundered our seas, ravaged our Coasts, burnt our towns, and destroyed the lives of our people.

He is at this time transporting large armies of foreign mercenaries to compleat the works of death, desolation, and tyranny, already begun with circumstances of Cruelty & perfidy scarcely paralleled in the most barbarous ages, and totally unworthy the Head of a civilized nation.

He has constrained our fellow Citizens taken Captive on the high Seas to bear Arms against their Country, to become the executioners of their friends and Brethren, or to fall themselves by their Hands.

He has excited domestic insurrections amongst us, and has endeavoured to bring on the inhabitants of our frontiers, the merciless Indian Savages, whose known rule of warfare, is an undistinguished destruction of all ages, sexes, and conditions.

In every stage of these Oppressions We have Petitioned for Redress in the most humble terms: Our repeated Petitions have been answered only by repeated injury. A Prince, whose character is thus marked by every act which may define a Tyrant, is unfit to be the ruler of a free people.

Nor have We been wanting in attention to our British brethren. We have warned them from time to time of attempts by their legislature to extend an unwarrantable jurisdiction over us. We have reminded them of the circumstances of our emigration and settlement here. We have appealed to their native justice and magnanimity, and we have conjured them by the ties of our common kindred to disavow these usurpations, which, would inevitably interrupt our connections and correspondence. They too must have been deaf to the voice of justice and of consanguinity. We must, therefore, acquiesce in the necessity, which denounces our Separation, and hold them, as we hold the rest of mankind, Enemies in War, in Peace Friends.

WE, THEREFORE, the Representatives of the UNITED STATES OF AMERICA, in General Congress, Assembled, appealing to the Supreme Judge of the world for the rectitude of our intentions, do, in the Name, and by Authority of the good People of these Colonies, solemnly publish and declare, That these United Colonies are, and of Right ought to be FREE AND INDEPENDENT STATES; that they are Absolved from all Allegiance to the

British Crown, and that all political connection between them and the State of Great Britain, is and ought to be totally dissolved; and that as Free and Independent States, they have full Power to levy War, conclude Peace, contract Alliances, establish Commerce, and to do all other Acts and Things which Independent States may of right do. And for the support of this Declaration, with a firm reliance on the Protection of Divine Providence, we mutually pledge to each other our Lives, our Fortunes, and our sacred Honor.

The foregoing Declaration was, by order of Congress, engrossed, and signed by the following members:

John Hancock

NEW HAMPSHIRE
Josiah Bartlett
William Whipple
Matthew Thornton

MASSACHUSETTS BAY
Samuel Adams
John Adams
Robert Treat Paine
Elbridge Gerry

RHODE ISLAND
Stephen Hopkins
William Ellery

CONNECTICUT
Roger Sherman
Samuel Huntington
William Williams
Oliver Wolcott

NEW YORK
William Floyd
Philip Livingston
Francis Lewis
Lewis Morris

NEW JERSEY
Richard Stockton
John Witherspoon
Francis Hopkinson
John Hart
Abraham Clark

PENNSYLVANIA
Robert Morris
Benjamin Rush
Benjamin Franklin
John Morton
George Clymer
James Smith
George Taylor
James Wilson
George Ross

DELAWARE
Caesar Rodney
George Read
Thomas M'Kean

MARYLAND
Samuel Chase
William Paca
Thomas Stone
Charles Carroll, of Carrollton

VIRGINIA
George Wythe
Richard Henry Lee
Thomas Jefferson
Benjamin Harrison
Thomas Nelson, Jr.
Francis Lightfoot Lee
Carter Braxton

NORTH CAROLINA
William Hooper
Joseph Hewes
John Penn

SOUTH CAROLINA
Edward Rutledge
Thomas Heyward, Jr.
Thomas Lynch, Jr.
Arthur Middleton

GEORGIA
Button Gwinnett
Lyman Hall
George Walton

Resolved, that copies of the declaration be sent to the several assemblies, conventions, and committees, or councils of safety, and to the several commanding officers of the continental troops; that it be proclaimed in each of the united states, at the head of the army.

ARTICLES OF CONFEDERATION

To all to whom these Presents shall come, we the undersigned Delegates of the States affixed to our Names send greeting.

Whereas the Delegates of the United States of America in Congress assembled did on the fifteenth day of November in the Year of our Lord One Thousand Seven Hundred and Seventy-seven, and in the Second Year of the Independence of America agree to certain articles of Confederation and perpetual Union between the States of Newhampshire, Massachusetts-bay, Rhodeisland and Providence Plantations, Connecticut, New York, New Jersey, Pennsylvania, Delaware, Maryland, Virginia, North-Carolina, South-Carolina and Georgia in the Words following, viz.

Articles of Confederation and perpetual Union between the States of Newhampshire, Massachusetts-bay, Rhodeisland and Providence Plantations, Connecticut, New-York, New-Jersey, Pennsylvania, Delaware, Maryland, Virginia, North-Carolina, South-Carolina and Georgia.

Article I. The stile of this confederacy shall be "The United States of America."

Article II. Each State retains its sovereignty, freedom and independence, and every power, jurisdiction and right, which is not by this confederation expressly delegated to the United States, in Congress assembled.

Article III. The said States hereby severally enter into a firm league of friendship with each other, for their common defence, the security of their liberties, and their mutual and general welfare, binding themselves to assist each other, against all force offered to, or attacks made upon them, or any of them, on account of religion, sovereignty, trade or any other pretence whatever.

ARTICLE IV. The better to secure and perpetuate mutual friendship and intercourse among the people of the different States in this Union, the free inhabitants of each of these States, paupers, vagabonds and fugitives from justice excepted, shall be entitled to all privileges and immunities of free citizens in the several States; and the people of each State shall have free ingress and regress to and from any other State, and shall enjoy therein all the privileges of trade and commerce, subject to the same duties, impositions and restrictions as the inhabitants thereof respectively, provided that such restrictions shall not extend so far as to prevent the removal of property imported into any State, to any other State of which the owner is an inhabitant; provided also that no imposition, duties or restriction shall be laid by any State, on the property of the United States, or either of them.

If any person guilty of, or charged with treason, felony, or other high misdemeanor in any State, shall flee from justice, and be found in any of the United States, he shall upon demand of the Governor or Executive power, of the State from which he fled, be delivered up and removed to the State having jurisdiction of his offence.

Full faith and credit shall be given in each of these States to the records, acts and judicial proceedings of the courts and magistrates of every other State.

ARTICLE V. For the more convenient management of the general interests of the United States, delegates shall be annually appointed in such manner as the legislature of each State shall direct, to meet in Congress on the first Monday in November, in every year, with a power reserved to each State, to recall its delegates, or any of them, at any time within the year, and to send others in their stead, for the remainder of the year.

No State shall be represented in Congress by less than two, nor by more than seven members; and no person shall be capable of being a delegate for more than three years in any term of six years; nor shall any person, being a delegate, be capable of holding any office under the United States, for which he, or another for his benefit receives any salary, fees or emolument of any kind.

Each State shall maintain its own delegates in a meeting of the States, and while they act as members of the committee of the States.

In determining questions in the United States, in Congress assembled, each State shall have one vote.

Freedom of speech and debate in Congress shall not be impeached or questioned in any court, or place out of Congress, and the members of Congress shall be protected in their persons from arrests and imprisonments, during the time of their going to and from, and attendance on Congress, except for treason, felony, or breach of the peace.

Article VI. No State without the consent of the United States in Congress assembled, shall send any embassy to, or receive any embassy from, or enter into any conference, agreement, alliance or treaty with any king, prince or state; nor shall any person holding any office of profit or trust under the United States, or any of them, accept of any present, emolument, office or title of any kind whatever from any king, prince or foreign state; nor shall the United States in Congress assembled, or any of them, grant any title of nobility.

No two or more States shall enter into any treaty, confederation or alliance whatever between them, without the consent of the United States in Congress assembled, specifying accurately the purposes for which the same is to be entered into, and how long it shall continue.

No State shall lay any imposts or duties, which may interfere with any stipulations in treaties, entered into by the United States in Congress assembled, with any king, prince or state, in pursuance of any treaties already proposed by Congress, to the courts of France and Spain.

No vessels of war shall be kept up in time of peace by any State, except such number only, as shall be deemed necessary by the United States in Congress assembled, for the defence of such State, or its trade; nor shall any body of forces be kept up by any State, in time of peace, except such number only, as in the judgment of the United States, in Congress assembled, shall be deemed requisite to garrison the forts necessary for the defence of such State; but every State shall always keep up a well regulated and disciplined militia, sufficiently armed and accoutred, and shall provide and constantly have ready for use, in public stores, a due number of field pieces and tents, and a proper quantity of arms, ammunition and camp equipage.

No State shall engage in any war without the consent of the United States in Congress assembled, unless such State be actually invaded by enemies, or shall have received certain advice of a resolution being formed by some nation of Indians to invade such State, and the danger is so imminent as not to admit of a delay, till the United States in Congress assembled can be consulted: nor shall any State grant commissions to any ships or vessels of war, nor letters of marque or reprisal, except it be after a declaration of war by the United States in Congress assembled, and then only against the kingdom or state and the subjects thereof, against which war has been so declared, and under such regulations as shall be established by the United States in Congress assembled, unless such State be infested by pirates, in which case vessels of war may be fitted out for that occasion, and kept so long as the danger shall continue, or until the United States in Congress assembled shall determine otherwise.

ARTICLE VII. When land-forces are raised by any State of the common defence, all officers of or under the rank of colonel, shall be appointed by the Legislature of each State respectively by whom such forces shall be raised, or in such manner as such State shall direct, and all vacancies shall be filled up by the State which first made the appointment.

ARTICLE VIII. All charges of war, and all other expenses that shall be incurred for the common defence or general welfare, and allowed by the United States in Congress assembled, shall be defrayed out of a common treasury, which shall be supplied by the several States, in proportion to the value of all land within each State, granted to or surveyed for any person, as such land and the buildings and improvements thereon shall be estimated according to such mode as the United States in Congress assembled, shall from time to time direct and appoint.

The taxes for paying that proportion shall be laid and levied by the authority and direction of the Legislatures of the several States within the time agreed upon by the United States in Congress assembled.

ARTICLE IX. The United States in Congress assembled, shall have the sole and exclusive right and power of determining on peace and war, except in the cases mentioned in the sixth article—of sending and receiving ambassadors—entering into treaties and alliances, provided that no treaty of commerce shall be made whereby the legislative power of the respective States shall be restrained from imposing such imposts and duties on foreigners, as their own people are subjected to, or from prohibiting the exportation or importation of and species of goods or commodities whatsoever—of establishing rules for deciding in all cases, what captures on land or water shall be legal, and in what manner prizes taken by land or naval forces in the service of the United States shall be divided or appropriated—of granting letters of marque and reprisal in times of peace—appointing courts for the trial of piracies and felonies committed on the high seas and establishing courts for receiving and determining finally appeals in all cases of captures, provided that no member of Congress shall be appointed a judge of any of the said courts.

The United States in Congress assembled shall also be the last resort on appeal in all disputes and differences now subsisting or that hereafter may arise between two or more States concerning boundary, jurisdiction or any other cause whatever; which authority shall always be exercised in the manner following. Whenever the legislative or executive authority or lawful agent of any State in controversy with another shall present a petition to Congress, stating the matter in question and praying for a hearing, notice thereof shall be given by order of Congress to the legislative or executive authority of the other State in controversy, and a day assigned for the appearance of the parties by their lawful agents, who shall then be directed to appoint by joint consent, commissioners or judges to constitute a court for hearing and determining the matter in question: but if they cannot agree, Congress shall name three persons out of each of the United States, and from the list of such persons each party shall alternately strike out one, the petitioners beginning, until the number shall be reduced to thirteen; and from that number not less than seven, nor more than nine names as Congress shall direct, shall in the presence of Congress be drawn out by lot, and the persons whose names shall be so drawn or any five of them, shall be commissioners or judges, to hear and finally determine the controversy, so always as a major part of the judges who shall hear the cause shall agree in the determination: and if either party shall neglect to attend at the day appointed, without reasons, which Congress shall judge sufficient, or being present shall refuse to strike, the Congress shall proceed to nominate three persons out of each State, and the Secretary of Congress shall strike in behalf of such party absent or refusing; and the judgment and sentence of the court to be appointed, in the manner before prescribed, shall be final and conclusive; and if any of the parties shall refuse to submit to the authority of such court, or to appear or defend their claim or cause, the court shall nevertheless proceed to pronounce sentence, or judgment, which shall in like manner be final and decisive, the judgment or sentence and other proceedings being in either case transmitted to Congress, and lodged among the acts of Congress for the security of the parties concerned: provided that every commissioner, before he sits in judgment, shall take an oath to be administered by one of the judges of the supreme or superior court of the State where the case shall be tried, "well and truly to hear and determine the matter in question, according to the best of his judgment, without favour, affection or hope of reward:" provided also that no State shall be deprived of territory for the benefit of the United States.

All controversies concerning the private right of soil claimed under different grants of two or more States, whose jurisdiction as they may respect such lands, and the states which passed such grants are adjusted, the said grants or either of them being at the same time claimed to have originated antecedent to such settlement of jurisdiction, shall on the petition of either party to the Congress of the United States, be finally determined as near as may be in the same manner as is before prescribed for deciding disputes respecting territorial jurisdiction between different States.

The United States in Congress assembled shall also have the sole and exclusive right and power of regulating the alloy and value of coin struck by their own authority, or by that of the respective States—fixing the standard of weights and measures throughout the United States—regulating the trade and managing all affairs with the Indians, not members of any of the States, provided that the legislative right of any State within its own limits be not infringed or violated—establishing and regulating post-offices from one State to another, throughout all of the United States, and exacting such postage on the papers passing thro' the same as may be requisite to defray the expenses of the said office—appointing all officers of the land forces, in the service of the United States, excepting regimental officers—appointing all the officers of the naval forces, and commissioning all officers whatever in the service of the United States—making rules for the government and regulation of the said land and naval forces, and directing their operations.

The United States in Congress assembled shall have authority to appoint a committee, to sit in the recess of Congress, to be denominated "a Committee of the States," and to consist of one delegate from each State; and to appoint such other committees and civil officers as may be necessary for managing the general affairs of the United States under their direction—to appoint one of their number to preside, provided that no person be allowed to serve in the office of president more than one year in any term of three years; to ascertain the necessary sums of money to be raised for the service of the United States, and to appropriate and apply the same for defraying the public expenses—to borrow money, or emit bills on the credit of the United States, transmitting every half year to the respective States an account of the sums of money so borrowed or emitted,—to build and equip a navy—to agree upon the number of land forces, and to make requisitions from each State for its quota, in proportion to the number of white inhabitants in such State; which requisition shall be binding, and thereupon the Legislature of each State shall appoint the regimental officers, raise the men and cloath, arm and equip them in a soldier like manner, at the expense of the United States; and the officers and men so cloathed, armed and equipped shall march to the place appointed, and within the time agreed on by the United States in Congress assembled: but if the United States in Congress assembled shall, on consideration of circumstances judge proper that any State should not raise men, or should raise a smaller number of men than the quota thereof, such extra number shall be raised, officered, cloathed, armed and equipped in the same manner as the quota of such State, unless the legislature of such State shall judge that such extra number cannot be safely spared out of the same, in which case they shall raise officer, cloath, arm and equip as many of such extra number as they judge can be safely spared. And the officers and men so cloathed, armed and equipped, shall march to the place appointed, and within the time agreed on by the United States in Congress assembled.

The United States in Congress assembled shall never engage in a war, nor grant letters of marque and reprisal in time of peace, nor enter into any treaties or alliances, nor coin money, nor regulate the value thereof, nor ascertain the sums and expenses necessary for the defence and welfare of the United States, or any of them, nor emit bills, nor borrow money on the credit of the United States, nor appropriate money, nor agree upon the number of vessels to be built or purchased, or the number of land or sea forces to be raised, nor appoint a commander in chief of the army or navy, unless nine States assent to the same: nor shall a question on any other point, except for adjourning from day to day be determined, unless by the votes of a majority of the United States in Congress assembled.

The Congress of the United States shall have power to adjourn to any time within the year, and to any place within the United States, so that no period of adjournment be for a longer duration than the space of six months, and shall publish the journal of their proceedings monthly, except such parts thereof relating to treaties, alliances or military operations, as in their judgment require secresy; and the yeas and nays of the delegates of each State on any question shall be entered on the Journal, when it is desired by any delegate; and the delegates of a State, or any of them, at his or their request shall be furnished with a transcript of the said journal, except such parts as are above excepted, to lay before the Legislatures of the several States.

ARTICLE X. The committee of the States, or any nine of them, shall be authorized to execute, in the recess of Congress, such of the powers of Congress as the United States in Congress assembled, by the consent of nine States, shall from time to time think expedient to vest them with; provided that no power be delegated to the said committee, for the exercise of which, by the articles of confederation, the voice of nine States in the Congress of the United States assembled is requisite.

ARTICLE XI. Canada acceding to this confederation, and joining in the measures of the United States, shall be admitted into, and entitled to all the advantages of this Union: but no other colony shall be admitted into the same, unless such admission be agreed to by nine States.

ARTICLE XII. All bills of credit emitted, monies borrowed and debts contracted by, or under the authority of Congress, before the assembling of the United States, in pursuance of the present confederation, shall be deemed and considered as a charge against the United States, for payment and satisfaction whereof the said United States, and the public faith are hereby solemnly pledged.

ARTICLE XIII. Every State shall abide by the determinations of the United States in Congress assembled, on all questions which by this confederation are submitted to them. And the articles of this confederation shall be inviolably observed by every State, and the Union shall be perpetual; nor shall any alteration at any time hereafter be made in any of them; unless such alteration be agreed to in a Congress of the United States, and be afterwards confirmed by the Legislatures of every State.

And whereas it has pleased the Great Governor of the world to incline the hearts of the Legislatures we respectively represent in Congress, to approve of, and to authorize us to ratify the said articles of confederation and perpetual union. Know ye that we the undersigned delegates, by virtue of the power and authority to us given for that purpose, do by these presents, in the name and in behalf of our respective constituents, fully and entirely ratify and confirm each and every of the said articles of confederation and perpetual union, and all and singular the matters and things therein contained: and we do further solemnly plight and engage the faith of our respective constituents, that they shall abide by the determinations of the United States in Congress assembled, on all questions, which by the said confederation are submitted to them. And that the articles thereof shall be inviolably observed by the States we respectively represent, and that the Union shall be perpetual.

In witness thereof we have hereunto set our hands in Congress. Done at Philadelphia in the State of Pennsylvania the ninth day of July in the year of our Lord one thousand seven hundred and seventy-eight, and in the third year of the independence of America.

THE CONSTITUTION OF THE UNITED STATES

WE THE PEOPLE OF THE UNITED STATES, in order to form a more perfect Union, establish Justice, insure domestic Tranquility, provide for the common defence, promote the general Welfare, and secure the Blessings of Liberty to ourselves and our Posterity, do ordain and establish this Constitution for the United States of America.

ARTICLE. I.

Section. 1. All legislative Powers herein granted shall be vested in a Congress of the United States, which shall consist of a Senate and House of Representatives.

Section. 2. The House of Representatives shall be composed of Members chosen every second Year by the People of the several States, and the Electors in each State shall have the Qualifications requisite for Electors of the most numerous Branch of the State Legislature.

No Person shall be a Representative who shall not have attained to the Age of twenty five Years, and been seven Years a Citizen of the United States, and who shall not, when elected, be an Inhabitant of that State in which he shall be chosen.

Representatives and direct Taxes shall be apportioned among the several States which may be included within this Union, according to their respective Numbers, which shall be determined by adding to the whole Number of free Persons, including those bound to Service for a Term of Years, and excluding Indians not taxed, three fifths of all other Persons. The actual Enumeration shall be made within three Years after the first Meeting of the Congress of the United States, and within every subsequent Term of ten Years, in such Manner as they shall by Law direct. The Number of Representatives shall not exceed one for every thirty Thousand, but each State shall have at Least one Representative; and until such enumeration shall be made, the State of New Hampshire shall be entitled to chuse three, Massachusetts eight, Rhode-Island and Providence Plantations one, Connecticut five, New-York six, New Jersey four, Pennsylvania eight, Delaware one, Maryland six, Virginia ten, North Carolina five, South Carolina five, and Georgia three.

When vacancies happen in the Representation from any state, the Executive Authority thereof shall issue Writs of Election to fill such Vacancies.

The House of Representatives shall chuse their Speaker and other Officers; and shall have the sole Power of Impeachment.

Section. 3. The Senate of the United States shall be composed of two Senators from each State, chosen by the legislature thereof, for six Years; and each Senator shall have one Vote.

Immediately after they shall be assembled in Consequence of the first Election, they shall be divided as equally as may be into three Classes. The Seats of the Senators of the first Class shall be vacated at the Expiration of the second Year, of the second Class at the Expiration of the fourth Year, and of the third Class at the Expiration of the sixth Year, so that one third maybe chosen every second Year; and if Vacancies happen by Resignation, or otherwise, during the Recess of the Legislature of any State, the Executive thereof may make temporary Appointments until the next Meeting of the Legislature, which shall then fill such Vacancies.

No Person shall be a Senator who shall not have attained to the Age of thirty Years, and been nine Years a Citizen of the United States, and who shall not, when elected, be an Inhabitant of that State for which he shall be chosen.

The Vice President of the United States shall be President of the Senate, but shall have no Vote, unless they be equally divided.

The Senate shall chuse their other Officers, and also a President pro tempore, in the Absence of the Vice President, or when he shall exercise the Office of President of the United States.

The Senate shall have the sole Power to try all Impeachments. When sitting for that Purpose, they shall be on Oath or Affirmation. When the President of the United States is tried, the Chief Justice shall preside: And no Person shall be convicted without the Concurrence of two thirds of the Members present.

Judgment in Cases of Impeachment shall not extend further than to removal from Office, and disqualification to hold and enjoy any Office of honor, Trust or Profit under the United States: but the Party convicted shall nevertheless be liable and subject to Indictment, Trial, Judgment and Punishment, according to Law.

Section. 4. The Times, Places and Manner of holding Elections for Senators and Representatives, shall be prescribed in each State by the Legislature thereof; but the Congress may at any time by Law make or alter such Regulations, except as to the Places of chusing Senators.

The Congress shall assemble at least once in every Year, and such Meeting shall be on the first Monday in December, unless they shall by Law appoint a different Day.

Section. 5. Each House shall be the Judge of the Elections, Returns and Qualifications of its own Members, and a Majority of each shall constitute a Quorum to do Business; but a smaller Number may adjourn from day to day, and may be authorized to compel the Attendance of absent Members, in such Manner, and under such Penalties as each House may provide.

Each House may determine the Rules of its Proceedings, punish its Members for disorderly Behaviour, and, with the Concurrence of two thirds, expel a Member.

Each House shall keep a Journal of its Proceedings, and from time to time publish the same, excepting such Parts as may in their Judgment require Secrecy; and the Yeas and Nays of the Members of either House on any question shall, at the Desire of one fifth of those Present, be entered on the Journal.

Neither House, during the Session of Congress, shall, without the Consent of the other, adjourn for more than three days, not to any other Place than that in which the two Houses shall be sitting.

Section. 6. The Senators and Representatives shall receive a Compensation for their Services, to be ascertained by Law, and paid out of the Treasury of the United States. They shall in all Cases, except Treason, Felony and Breach of the Peace, be privileged from Arrest during their Attendance at the Session of their respective Houses, and in going to and returning from the same; and for any Speech or Debate in either House, they shall not be questioned in any other Place.

No Senator or Representative shall, during the Time for which he was elected, be appointed to any civil Office under the Authority of the United States, which shall have been created, or the Emoluments whereof shall have been encreased during such time; and no Person holding any Office under the United States, shall be a Member of either House during his Continuance in Office.

Section. 7. All Bills for raising Revenue shall originate in the House of Representatives; but the Senate may propose or concur with Amendments as on other Bills.

Every Bill which shall have passed the House of Representatives and the Senate shall, before it become a Law, be presented to the President of the United States; If he approve he shall sign it, but if not he shall return it, with his Objections to that House in which it shall have originated, who shall enter the Objections at large on their Journal, and proceed to reconsider it. If after such Reconsideration two thirds of that House shall agree to pass the Bill, it shall be sent, together with the Objections, to the other House, by which it shall likewise be reconsidered, and if approved by two thirds of that House, it shall become a Law. But in all such Cases the Votes of both Houses shall be determined by yeas and Nays, and the Names of the Persons voting for and against the Bill shall be entered on the Journal of each House respectively. If any Bill shall not be returned by the President within ten Days (Sundays excepted) after it shall have been presented to him, the Same shall be a Law, in like Manner as if he had signed it, unless the Congress by their Adjournment prevent its Return, in which Case it shall not be a Law.

Every Order, Resolution, or Vote to which the Concurrence of the Senate and House of Representatives may be necessary (except on a question of Adjournment) shall be presented to the President of the United States; and before the Same shall take Effect, shall be approved by him, or being disapproved by him, shall be repassed by two thirds of the Senate and House of Representatives, according to the Rules and Limitations prescribed in the Case of a Bill.

Section. 8. The Congress shall have Power To lay and collect Taxes, Duties, Imposts and Excises, to pay the Debts and provide for the common Defence and general Welfare of the United States; but all Duties, Imposts and Excises shall be uniform throughout the United States;

To borrow Money on the credit of the United States;

To regulate Commerce with foreign Nations, and among the several States, and with the Indian Tribes;

To establish an uniform Rule of Naturalization, and uniform Laws on the subject of Bankruptcies throughout the United States;

To coin Money, regulate the Value thereof, and of foreign Coin, and fix the Standard of Weights and Measures;

To provide for the Punishment of counterfeiting the Securities and current Coin of the United States;

To establish Post Offices and Post Roads;

To promote the Progress of Science and useful Arts, by securing for limited Times to Authors and Inventors the exclusive Right to their respective Writings and Discoveries;

To constitute Tribunals inferior to the supreme Court;

To define and punish Piracies and Felonies committed on the high Seas, and Offences against the Law of Nations;

To declare War, grant Letters of Marque and Reprisal, and make Rules concerning Captures on land and Water;

To raise and support Armies, but no Appropriation of Money to that Use shall be for a longer Term than two Years;

To provide and maintain a Navy;

To make Rules for the Government and Regulation of the land and naval Forces;

To provide for calling forth the Militia to execute the Laws of the Union, suppress Insurrections and repel Invasions;

To provide for organizing, arming, and disciplining, the Militia, and for governing such Part of them as may be employed in the Service of the United States, reserving to the States respectively, the Appointment of the Officers, and the Authority of training the Militia according to the discipline prescribed by Congress.

To exercise exclusive Legislation in all Cases whatsoever, over such District (not exceeding ten Miles square) as may, by Cession of Particular States, and the Acceptance of Congress, become the Seat of the Government of the United States, and to exercise like Authority over all Places purchased by the Consent of the Legislature of the State in which the Same shall be, for the Erection of Forts, Magazines, Arsenals, dock-Yards, and other needful Buildings;—And

To make all Laws which shall be necessary and proper for carrying into Execution the foregoing Powers, and all other Powers vested by this Constitution in the Government of the United States, or in any Department or Officer thereof.

Section. 9. The Migration or Importation of such Persons as any of the States now existing shall think proper to admit, shall not be prohibited by the Congress prior to the Year one thousand eight hundred and eight, but a Tax or duty may be imposed on such Importation, not exceeding ten dollars for each Person.

The Privilege of the Writ of Habeas Corpus shall not be suspended, unless when in Cases of Rebellion or Invasion the public Safety may require it.

No Bill of Attainder or ex post facto Law shall be passed.

No Capitation, or other direct, Tax shall be laid, unless in Proportion to the Census or Enumeration herein before directed to be taken.

No Tax or Duty shall be laid on Articles exported from any State.

No Preference shall be given by any Regulation of Commerce or Revenue to the Ports of one State over those of another: nor shall Vessels bound to, or from, one State, be obliged to enter, clear, or pay Duties in another.

No Money shall be drawn from the Treasury, but in Consequence of Appropriations made by Law; and a regular Statement and Account of the Receipts and Expenditures of all public Money shall be published from time to time.

No Title of Nobility shall be granted by the United States: And no Person holding any Office of Profit or trust under them, shall, without the Consent of the Congress, accept of any present, Emolument, Office, or Title, of any kind whatever, from any King, Prince, or foreign State.

Section 10. No State shall enter into any Treaty, Alliance, or Confederation; grant Letters of Marque and Reprisal; coin Money; emit Bills of Credit; make any Thing but gold and silver Coin a Tender in Payment of Debts; pass any Bill of Attainder, ex post facto Law, or Law impairing the Obligation of Contracts, or grant any Title of Nobility.

No State shall, without the Consent of the Congress, lay any Imposts or Duties on Imports or Exports, except what may be absolutely necessary for executing its inspection Laws: and the net Produce of all Duties and Imposts, laid by any State on Imports or Exports, shall be for the Use of the Treasury of the United States; and all such Laws shall be subject to the Revision and Controul of the Congress.

No State shall, without the Consent of Congress, lay any Duty of Tonnage, keep Troops, or Ships of War in time of Peace, enter into any Agreement or Compact with another State, or with a foreign Power, or engage in War, unless actually invaded, or in such imminent Danger as will not admit of delay.

ARTICLE. II.

Section. 1. The executive Power shall be vested in a President of the United States of America. He shall hold his Office during the term of four Years, and, together with the Vice President, chosen for the same Term, be elected, as follows:

Each State shall appoint, in such Manner as the Legislature thereof may direct, a Number of Electors, equal to the whole Number of Senators and Representatives to which the State may be entitled in the Congress: but no Senator or Representative, or Person holding an Office of Trust or Profit under the United States, shall be appointed an Elector.

The Electors shall meet in their respective States, and vote by Ballot for two Persons, of whom one at least shall not be an Inhabitant of the same State with themselves. And they shall make a List of all the Persons voted for, and of the Number of Votes for each; which List they shall sign and certify, and transmit sealed to the Seat of the Government of the United States, directed to the President of the Senate. The President of the Senate shall, in the Presence of the Senate and House of Representatives, open all the Certificates, and the Votes shall then be counted. The Person having the greatest Number of Votes shall be the President, if such Number be a Majority of the whole Number of Electors appointed; and if there be more than one who have such Majority, and have an equal Number of Votes, then the House of Representatives shall immediately chuse by Ballot one of them for President; and if no Person have a Majority, then from the five highest on the List the said House shall in like Manner chuse the President. But in chusing the President, the Votes shall be taken by States, the Representation from each State having one Vote; A quorum for this Purpose shall consist of a Member or Members from two thirds of the States, and a Majority of all the States shall be necessary to a Choice. In every Case, after the Choice of the President, the Person having the greatest Number of Votes of the Electors shall be the Vice President. But if there should remain two or more who have equal Votes, the Senate shall chuse from them by Ballot the Vice President.

The Congress may determine the Time of chusing the Electors, and the Day on which they shall give their Votes; which Day shall be the same throughout the United States.

No Person except a natural born Citizen, or a Citizen of the United States, at the time of the Adoption of this Constitution, shall be eligible to the Office of President; neither shall any Person be eligible to that Office who shall not have attained to the Age of thirty five Years, and been fourteen Years a Resident within the United States.

In Case of the Removal of the President from Office, or of his Death, Resignation, or Inability to discharge the Powers and Duties of the said Office, the Same shall devolve on the Vice President, and the Congress may by Law provide for the Case of Removal, Death, Resignation or Inability, both of the President and Vice President, declaring what Officer shall then act as

President, and such Officer shall act accordingly, until the Disability be removed, or a President shall be elected.

The President shall, at stated Times, receive for his Services, a Compensation, which shall neither be encreased or diminished during the Period for which he shall have been elected, and he shall not receive within that Period any other Emolument from the United States, or any of them.

Before he enters on the Execution of his Office, he shall take the following Oath or Affirmation:—"I do solemnly swear (or affirm) that I will faithfully execute the Office of President of the United States, and will to the best of my Ability, preserve, protect and defend the Constitution of the United States."

Section. 2. The President shall be Commander in Chief of the Army and Navy of the United States, and of the Militia of the several States, when called into the actual Service of the United States; he may require the Opinion, in writing, of the principal Officer in each of the executive Departments, upon any Subject relating to the Duties of their respective Offices, and he shall have Power to grant Reprieves and Pardons for Offences against the United States, except in Cases of Impeachment.

He shall have Power, by and with the Advice and Consent of the Senate, to make Treaties, provided two thirds of the Senators present concur; and he shall nominate, and by and with the Advice and Consent of the Senate, shall appoint Ambassadors, other public Ministers and Consuls, Judges of the supreme Court, and all other Officers of the United States, whose Appointments are not herein otherwise provided for, and which shall be established by Law; but the Congress may by Law vest the Appointment of such inferior Officers, as they think proper, in the President alone, in the Courts of Law, or in the Heads of Departments.

The President shall have Power to fill up all Vacancies that may happen during the Recess of the Senate, by granting Commissions which shall expire at the End of their next Session.

Section. 3. He shall from time to time give to the Congress Information of the State of the Union, and recommend to their Consideration such Measures as he shall judge necessary and expedient; he may, on extraordinary Occasions, convene both Houses, or either of them, and in Case of Disagreement between them, with Respect to the Time of Adjournment, he may adjourn them to such Time as he shall think proper; he shall receive Ambassadors and other public Ministers; he shall take Care that the Laws be faithfully executed, and shall Commission all the Officers of the United States.

Section. 4. The President, Vice President and all civil Officers of the United States, shall be removed from Office on Impeachment for, and Conviction of, Treason, Bribery, or other high Crimes and Misdemeanors.

Article. III.

Section. 1. The judicial Power of the United States, shall be vested in one supreme Court, and in such inferior Courts as the Congress may from time to time ordain and establish. The Judges, both of the supreme and inferior Courts, shall hold their Offices during good Behavior, and shall, at stated Times, receive for their Services, a Compensation, which shall not be diminished during their Continuance in Office.

Section. 2. The judicial Power shall extend to all Cases, in Law and Equity, arising under this Constitution, the Laws of the United States, and Treaties made, or which shall be made, under their Authority;—to all Cases affecting Ambassadors, other public Ministers and Consuls;—to all Cases of admiralty and maritime Jurisdiction;—the Controversies to which the United States shall be a Party;—to Controversies between two or more States;—between a State and Citizens of another State;—between Citizens of different States;—between Citizens of the same State claiming Lands under Grants of different States, and between a State, or the Citizens thereof, and foreign States, Citizens or Subjects.

In all cases affecting Ambassadors, other public Ministers and Consuls, and those in which a State shall be Party, the supreme Court shall have original Jurisdiction. In all the other Cases before mentioned, the supreme Court shall have appellate Jurisdiction, both as to Law and Fact, with such Exceptions, and under such Regulations as the Congress shall make.

The Trial of all Crimes, except in Cases of Impeachment, shall be by Jury; and such Trial shall be held in the State where the said Crimes shall have been committed; but when not committed within any State, the Trial shall be at such Place or Places as the Congress may by Law have directed.

Section. 3. Treason against the United States, shall consist only in levying War against them, or in adhering to their Enemies, giving them Aid and Comfort. No Person shall be convicted of Treason unless on the Testimony of two Witnesses to the same overt Act, or on Confession in open Court.

The Congress shall have Power to declare the Punishment of Treason, but no Attainder of Treason shall work Corruption of Blood, or Forfeiture except during the Life of the Person attainted.

ARTICLE. IV.

Section. 1. Full Faith and Credit shall be given in each State to the public Acts, Records, and judicial Proceedings of every other State. And the Congress may by general Laws prescribe the Manner in which such Acts, Records and Proceedings shall be proved, and the Effect thereof.

Section. 2. The Citizens of each State shall be entitled to all Privileges and Immunities of Citizens in the several States.

A Person charged in any State with Treason, Felony, or other Crime, who shall flee from Justice, and be found in another State, shall on Demand of the executive Authority of the State from which he fled, be delivered up, to be removed to the State having Jurisdiction of the Crime.

No Person held to Service or Labour in one State, under the Laws thereof, escaping into another, shall, in Consequence of any Law or Regulation therein, be discharged from such Service or Labour, but shall be delivered up on Claim of the Party to whom such Service or Labour may be due.

Section. 3. New States may be admitted by the Congress into this Union; but no new State shall be formed or erected within the Jurisdiction of any other State; nor any State be formed by the Junction of two or more States, or Parts of States, without the consent of the Legislatures of the States concerned as well as of the Congress.

The Congress shall have Power to dispose of and make all needful Rules and Regulations respecting the Territory or other Property belonging to the United States; and nothing in this Constitution shall be so construed as to Prejudice any Claims of the United States, or of any particular States.

Section. 4. The United States shall guarantee to every State in this Union a Republican Form of Government, and shall protect each of them against Invasion; and on Application of the Legislature, or of the Executive (when the Legislature cannot be convened) against domestic Violence.

ARTICLE. V.

The Congress, whenever two thirds of both Houses shall deem it necessary, shall propose Amendments to this Constitution, or, on the Application of the

Legislatures of two thirds of the several States, shall call a Convention for proposing Amendments, which, in either Case, shall be valid to all Intents and Purposes, as Part of this Constitution, when ratified by the Legislatures of three fourths of the several States, or by Conventions in three fourths thereof, as the one or the other Mode of Ratification may be proposed by the Congress; Provided that no Amendment which may be made prior to the Year One thousand eight hundred and eight shall in any Manner affect the first and fourth Clauses in the Ninth Section of the first Article; and that no State, without its Consent, shall be deprived of its equal Suffrage in the Senate.

ARTICLE. VI.

All Debts contracted and Engagements entered into, before the Adoption of this Constitution, shall be as valid against the United States under this Constitution, as under the Confederation.

This Constitution, and the Laws of the United States which shall be made in Pursuance thereof; and all Treaties made, or which shall be made, under the Authority of the United States, shall be the supreme Law of the Land; and the Judges in every State shall be bound thereby, any Thing in the Constitution or Laws of any State to the Contrary notwithstanding.

The Senators and Representatives before mentioned, and the Members of the several State Legislatures, and all executive and judicial Officers, both of the United States and of the several States, shall be bound by Oath or Affirmation, to support this Constitution; but no religious Test shall ever be required as a Qualification to any Office or public Trust under the United States.

ARTICLE. VII.

The Ratification of the Conventions of nine States, shall be sufficient for the Establishment of this Constitution between the States so ratifying the Same.

Done in Convention by the Unanimous Consent of the States present the Seventeenth Day of September in the Year of our Lord one thousand seven hundred and Eighty seven and of the Independence of the United States of America the Twelfth. In witness thereof We have hereunto subscribed our Names,

G⁰. WASHINGTON—Presdᵗ.
and deputy from Virginia.

New Hampshire	{ John Langdon { Nicholas Gilman		{ Geo: Read Gunning Bedford jun
		Delaware	{ John Dickinson
Massachusetts	{ Nathaniel Gorham { Rufus King		Richard Bassett { Jaco: Broom
Connecticut	{ Wᵐ Samˡ Johnson { Roger Sherman		{ James McHenry
		Maryland	{ Dan of St Thoˢ Jenifer
New York: . . .	Alexander Hamilton		{ Danˡ Carroll
		Virginia	{ John Blair— { James Madison Jr.
New Jersey	{ Wil: Livingston David A. Brearley. Wᵐ Paterson. Jona: Dayton		
		North Carolina	{ Wᵐ Blount { Richᵈ Dobbs Spaight. { Hu Williamson
Pennsylvania	{ B Franklin Thomas Mifflin Robᵗ Morris Geo. Clymer Thoˢ FitzSimons Jared Ingersoll James Wilson Gouv Morris	South Carolina	{ J. Rutledge Charles Cotesworth Pinckney Charles Pinckney Pierce Butler.
		Georgia	{ William Few { Abr Baldwin

AMENDMENTS TO THE CONSTITUTION

ARTICLES IN ADDITION TO, and Amendment of the Constitution of the United States of America, proposed by Congress, and ratified by the Legislatures of the several States, pursuant to the fifth Article of the original Constitution.

AMENDMENT I.

Congress shall make no law respecting an establishment of religion, or prohibiting the free exercise thereof; or abridging the freedom of speech, or of the press; or the right of the people peaceably to assemble, and to petition the Government for a redress of grievances.

AMENDMENT II.

A well regulated Militia, being necessary to the security of a free State, the right of the people to keep and bear Arms, shall not be infringed.

AMENDMENT III.

No Soldier shall, in time of peace be quartered in any house, without the consent of the Owner, nor in time of war, but in a manner to be prescribed by law.

AMENDMENT IV.

The right of the people to be secure in their persons, houses, papers, and effects, against unreasonable searches and seizures, shall not be violated, and no Warrants shall issue, but upon probable cause, supported by Oath or affirmation, and particularly describing the place to be searched, and the persons or things to be seized.

AMENDMENT V.

No person shall be held to answer for a capital, or otherwise infamous crime, unless on a presentment or indictment of a Grand Jury, except in cases arising in the land or naval forces, or in the Militia, when in actual service in time of War or public danger; nor shall any person be subject for the same offence to be twice put in jeopardy of life or limb; nor shall be compelled in any criminal case to be a witness against himself, nor be deprived of life, liberty, or property, without due process of law; nor shall private property be taken for public use, without just compensation.

AMENDMENT VI.

In all criminal prosecutions, the accused shall enjoy the right to a speedy and public trial, by an impartial jury of the State and district wherein the crime shall have been committed, which district shall have been previously ascertained by law, and to be informed of the nature and cause of the accusation;

to be confronted with the witnesses against him; to have compulsory process for obtaining witnesses in his favor, and to have the Assistance of Counsel for his defence.

AMENDMENT VII.

In Suits at common law, where the value in controversy shall exceed twenty dollars, the right of trial by jury shall be preserved, and no fact tried by a jury, shall be otherwise re-examined in any Court of the United States, than according to the rules of the common law.

AMENDMENT VIII.

Excessive bail shall not be required, nor excessive fines imposed, nor cruel and unusual punishments inflicted.

AMENDMENT IX.

The enumeration in the Constitution, of certain rights, shall not be construed to deny or disparage others retained by the people.

AMENDMENT X.

The powers not delegated to the United States by the Constitution, nor prohibited by it to the States, are reserved to the States respectively, or to the people. [The first ten amendments went into effect December 15, 1791.]

AMENDMENT XI.

The Judicial power of the United States shall not be construed to extend to any suit in law or equity, commenced or prosecuted against one of the United States by Citizens of another State, or by Citizens or Subjects of any Foreign State. [January 8, 1798.]

AMENDMENT XII.

The Electors shall meet in their respective states, and vote by ballot for President and Vice-President, one of whom, at least, shall not be an inhabitant of the same state with themselves; they shall name in their ballots the person voted for as President, and in distinct ballots the person voted for as Vice-President, and they shall make distinct lists of all persons voted for as President, and of all persons voted for as Vice President, and of the number of votes for each, which lists they shall sign and certify, and transmit sealed to the seat of the government of the United States, directed to the President of the Senate;—The President of the Senate shall, in the presence of the Senate and House of Representatives, open all the certificates and the votes shall then be counted;—The person having the greatest number of votes for President, shall be the President, if such number be a majority of the whole number of Electors appointed; and if no person have such majority, then from the persons having the highest numbers not exceeding three on the list of those voted for as President, the House of Representatives shall choose immediately, by ballot, the President. But in choosing the President, the votes shall be taken by states, the representation from each state having one vote; a quorum for this purpose shall consist of a member or members from two-thirds of the states, and a majority of all the states shall be necessary to a choice. And if the House of Representatives shall not choose a President whenever the right of choice shall devolve upon them, before the fourth day of March next following, then the Vice-President shall act as President, as in the case of the death or other constitutional disability of the President.— The person having the greatest number of votes as Vice-President, shall be the Vice-President, if such number be a majority of the whole number of Electors appointed, and if no person have a majority, then from the two highest numbers on the list, the Senate shall choose the Vice-President; a quorum for the purpose shall consist of two-thirds of the whole number of Senators, and a majority of the whole number shall be necessary to a choice. But no person constitutionally ineligible to the office of President shall be eligible to that of Vice-President of the United States. [September 25, 1804.]

AMENDMENT XIII.

Section 1. Neither slavery nor involuntary servitude, except as a punishment for crime whereof the party shall have been duly convicted, shall exist within the United States, or any place subject to their jurisdiction.

Section 2. Congress shall have power to enforce this article by appropriate legislation. [December 18, 1865.]

AMENDMENT XIV.

Section 1. All persons born or naturalized in the United States, and subject to the jurisdiction thereof, are citizens of the United States and of the State wherein they reside. No State shall make or enforce any law which shall abridge the privileges or immunities of citizens of the United States; nor shall any State deprive any person of life, liberty, or property, without due process of law; nor deny to any person within its jurisdiction the equal protection of the laws.

Section 2. Representatives shall be apportioned among the several States according to their respective numbers, counting the whole number of persons in each State, excluding Indians not taxed. But when the right to vote at any election for the choice of electors for President and Vice President of the United States, Representatives in Congress, the Executive and Judicial officers of a State, or the members of the Legislature thereof, is denied to any of the male inhabitants of such State, being twenty-one years of age, and citizens of the United States, or in any way abridged, except for participation in rebellion, or other crime, the basis of representation therein shall be reduced in the proportion which the number of such male citizens shall bear to the whole number of male citizens twenty-one years of age in such State.

Section 3. No person shall be a Senator or Representative in Congress, or elector of President and Vice President, or hold any office, civil or military, under the United States, or under any State, who, having previously taken an oath, as a member of Congress, or as an officer of the United States, or as a member of any State legislature, or as an executive or judicial officer of any State, to support the Constitution of the United States, shall have engaged in insurrection or rebellion against the same, or given aid or comfort to the enemies thereof. But Congress may by a vote of two-thirds of each House, remove such disability.

Section 4. The validity of the public debt of the United States, authorized by law, including debts incurred for payment of pensions and bounties for services in suppressing insurrection or rebellion, shall not be questioned. But neither the United States nor any State shall assume or pay any debt or obligation incurred in aid of insurrection or rebellion against the United States, or any claim for the loss or emancipation of any slave; but all such debts, obligations and claims shall be held illegal and void.

Section 5. The Congress shall have power to enforce, by appropriate legislation, the provisions of this article. [July 28, 1868.]

Amendment XV.

Section 1. The right of citizens of the United States to vote shall not be denied or abridged by the United States or by any State on account of race, color, or previous condition of servitude—

Section 2. The Congress shall have power to enforce this article by appropriate legislation.—[March 30, 1870.]

Amendment XVI.

The Congress shall have power to lay and collect taxes on incomes, from whatever source derived, without apportionment among the several States, and without regard to any census or enumeration. [February 25, 1913.]

Amendment XVII.

The Senate of the United States shall be composed of two senators from each State, elected by the people thereof, for six years; and each Senator shall have one vote. The electors in each State shall have the qualifications requisite for electors of the most numerous branch of the State legislature.

When vacancies happen in the representation of any State in the Senate, the executive authority of such State shall issue writs of election to fill such vacancies: *Provided,* That the legislature of any State may empower the executive thereof to make temporary appointments until the people fill the vacancies by election as the legislature may direct.

This amendment shall not be so construed as to affect the election or term of any senator chosen before it becomes valid as part of the Constitution. [May 31, 1913.]

AMENDMENT XVIII.

After one year from the ratification of this article, the manufacture, sale, or transportation of intoxicating liquors within, the importation thereof into, or the exportation thereof from the United States and all territory subject to the jurisdiction thereof for beverage purposes is hereby prohibited.

The Congress and the several States shall have concurrent power to enforce this article by appropriate legislation.

This article shall be inoperative unless it shall have been ratified as an amendment to the Constitution by the legislatures of the several States, as provided in the Constitution, within seven years from the date of the submission thereof to the States by Congress. [January 29, 1919.]

AMENDMENT XIX.

The right of citizens of the United States to vote shall not be denied or abridged by the United States or by any State on account of sex.

The Congress shall have power by appropriate legislation to enforce the provisions of this article. [August 26, 1920.]

AMENDMENT XX.

Section 1. The terms of the President and Vice-President shall end at noon on the twentieth day of January, and the terms of Senators and Representatives at noon on the third day of January, of the years in which such terms would have ended if this article had not been ratified; and the terms of their successors shall then begin.

Section 2. The Congress shall assemble at least once in every year, and such meeting shall begin at noon on the third day of January, unless they shall by law appoint a different day.

Section 3. If, at the time fixed for the beginning of the term of the President, the President-elect shall have died, the Vice-President-elect shall become President. If a President shall not have been chosen before the time fixed for the beginning of his term, or if the President-elect shall have failed to qualify, then the Vice-President-elect shall act as President until a President shall have qualified; and the Congress may by law provide for the case wherein neither a President-elect nor a Vice-President-elect shall have qualified, declaring who shall then act as President, or the manner in which one who is to act shall be selected, and such person shall act accordingly until a President or Vice-President shall have qualified.

Section 4. The Congress may by law provide for the case of the death of any of the persons from whom the House of Representatives may choose a President whenever the right of choice shall have devolved upon them, and for the case of the death of any of the persons from whom the Senate may choose a Vice-President whenever the right of choice shall have devolved upon them.

Section 5. Sections 1 and 2 shall take effect on the 15th day of October following the ratification of this article.

Section 6. This article shall be inoperative unless it shall have been ratified as an amendment to the Constitution by the legislatures of three-fourths of the several States within seven years from the date of its submission. [February 6, 1933.]

AMENDMENT XXI.

Section 1. The eighteenth article of amendment to the Constitution of the United States is hereby repealed.

Section 2. The transportation or importation into any State, Territory or possession of the United States for delivery or use therein of intoxicating liquors, in violation of the laws thereof, is hereby prohibited.

Section 3. This article shall be inoperative unless it shall have been ratified as an amendment to the Constitution by convention in the several States, as provided in the Constitution, within seven years from the date of the submission thereof to the States by the Congress. [December 5, 1933.]

AMENDMENT XXII.

Section 1. No person shall be elected to the office of the President more than twice, and no person who has held the office of President, or acted as President, for more than two years of a term to which some other person was elected President shall be elected to the office of the President more than once. But this Article shall not apply to any person holding the office of President when this Article was proposed by the Congress, and shall not prevent any person who may be holding the office of President, or acting as President, during the term within which this Article becomes operative from holding the office of President or acting as President during the remainder of such term.

Section 2. This article shall be inoperative unless it shall have been ratified as an amendment to the Constitution by the legislatures of three-fourths of the several states within seven years from the date of its submission to the States by the Congress. [February 27, 1951.]

Amendment XXIII.

Section 1. The District constituting the seat of government of the United States shall appoint in such manner as the Congress may direct:

A number of electors of President and Vice-President equal to the whole number of Senators and Representatives in Congress to which the District would be entitled if it were a State, but in no event more than the least populous State; they shall be in addition to those appointed by the States, but they shall be considered, for the purposes of the election of President and Vice-President, to be electors appointed by a State; and they shall meet in the District and perform such duties as provided by the twelfth article of amendment.

Section 2. The Congress shall have the power to enforce this article by appropriate legislation. [March 29, 1961.]

Amendment XXIV.

Section 1. The right of citizens of the United States to vote in any primary or other election for President or Vice President, for electors for President or Vice President, or for Senator or Representative in Congress, shall not be denied or abridged by the United States or any State by reason of failure to pay any poll tax or other tax.

Section 2. The Congress shall have power to enforce this article by appropriate legislation. [January 23, 1964.]

AMENDMENT XXV.

Section 1. In case of the removal of the President from office or of his death or resignation, the Vice President shall become President.

Section 2. Whenever there is a vacancy in the office of Vice President, the President shall nominate a Vice President who shall take office upon confirmation by a majority vote of both Houses of Congress.

Section 3. Whenever the President transmits to the President pro tempore of the Senate and the Speaker of the House of Representatives his written declaration that he is unable to discharge the powers and duties of his office, and until he transmits to them a written declaration to the contrary, such powers and duties shall be discharged by the Vice President as Acting President.

Section 4. Whenever the Vice President and a majority of either the principal officers of the executive departments or of such other body as Congress may by law provide, transmit to the President pro tempore of the Senate and the Speaker of the House of Representatives their written declaration that the President is unable to discharge the powers and duties of his office, the Vice President shall immediately assume the powers and duties of the office as Acting President.

Thereafter, when the President transmits to the President pro tempore of the Senate and the Speaker of the House of Representatives his written declaration that no inability exists, he shall resume the powers and duties of his office unless the Vice President and a majority of either the principal officers of the executive departments or of such other body as Congress may by law provide, transmit within four days to the President pro tempore of the Senate and the Speaker of the House of Representatives their written declaration that the President is unable to discharge the powers and duties of his office. Thereupon Congress shall decide the issue, assembling within forty-eight hours for that purpose if not in session. If the Congress, within twenty-one days after receipt of the latter written declaration, or, if Congress is not in session, within twenty-one days after Congress is required to assemble, determines by two-thirds vote of both Houses that the President is unable to discharge the powers and duties of his office, the Vice President shall continue to discharge the same as Acting President; otherwise, the President shall resume the powers and duties of his office. [February 10, 1967.]

Amendment XXVI.

Section 1. The right of citizens of the United States, who are eighteen years of age or older, to vote shall not be denied or abridged by the United States or by any State on account of age.

Section 2. The Congress shall have power to enforce this article by appropriate legislation [June 30, 1971.]

Amendment XXVII.

No law, varying the compensation for the services of the Senators and Representatives shall take effect, until an election of Representatives shall have intervened. [May 8, 1992.]

PRESIDENTIAL ELECTIONS

Year	Number of States	Candidates	Parties	Popular Vote	% of Popular Vote	Electoral Vote	% Voter Participation
1789	11	**GEORGE WASHINGTON**	No party			69	
		John Adams	designations			34	
		Other candidates				35	
1792	15	**GEORGE WASHINGTON**	No party			132	
		John Adams	designations			77	
		George Clinton				50	
		Other candidates				5	
1796	16	**JOHN ADAMS**	Federalist			71	
		Thomas Jefferson	Democratic-Republican			68	
		Thomas Pinckney	Federalist			59	
		Aaron Burr	Democratic-Republican			30	
		Other candidates				48	
1800	16	**THOMAS JEFFERSON**	Democratic-Republican			73	
		Aaron Burr	Democratic-Republican			73	
		John Adams	Federalist			65	
		Charles C. Pinckney	Federalist			64	
		John Jay	Federalist			1	
1804	17	**THOMAS JEFFERSON**	Democratic-Republican			162	
		Charles C. Pinckney	Federalist			14	

Year	Number of States	Candidates	Parties	Popular Vote	% of Popular Vote	Electoral Vote	% Voter Participation
1808	17	**JAMES MADISON**	Democratic-Republican			122	
		Charles C. Pinckney	Federalist			47	
		George Clinton	Democratic-Republican			6	
1812	18	**JAMES MADISON**	Democratic-Republican			128	
		DeWitt Clinton	Federalist			89	
1816	19	**JAMES MONROE**	Democratic-Republican			183	
		Rufus King	Federalist			34	
1820	24	**JAMES MONROE**	Democratic-Republican			231	
		John Quincy Adams	Independent			1	
1824	24	**JOHN QUINCY ADAMS**	Democratic-Republican	108,740	30.5	84	26.9
		Andrew Jackson	Democratic-Republican	153,544	43.1	99	
		Henry Clay	Democratic-Republican	47,136	13.2	37	
		William H. Crawford	Democratic-Republican	46,618	13.1	41	
1828	24	**ANDREW JACKSON**	Democratic	647,286	56.0	178	57.6
		John Quincy Adams	National-Republican	508,064	44.0	83	

Year	Number of States	Candidates	Parties	Popular Vote	% of Popular Vote	Electoral Vote	% Voter Participation
1832	24	ANDREW JACKSON	Democratic	688,242	54.5	219	55.4
		Henry Clay	National-Republican	473,462	37.5	49	
		William Wirt	Anti-Masonic	101,051	8.0	7	
		John Floyd	Democratic			11	
1836	26	MARTIN VAN BUREN	Democratic	765,483	50.9	170	57.8
		William H. Harrison	Whig			73	
		Hugh L. White	Whig	739,795	49.1	26	
		Daniel Webster	Whig			14	
		W. P. Mangum	Whig			11	
1840	26	WILLIAM H. HARRISON	Whig	1,274,624	53.1	234	80.2
		Martin Van Buren	Democratic	1,127,781	46.9	60	
1844	26	JAMES K. POLK	Democratic	1,338,464	49.6	170	78.9
		Henry Clay	Whig	1,300,097	48.1	105	
		James G. Birney	Liberty	62,300	2.3		
1848	30	ZACHARY TAYLOR	Whig	1,360,967	47.4	163	72.7
		Lewis Cass	Democratic	1,222,342	42.5	127	
		Martin Van Buren	Free Soil	291,263	10.1		
1852	31	FRANKLIN PIERCE	Democratic	1,601,117	50.9	254	69.6
		Winfield Scott	Whig	1,385,453	44.1	42	
		John P. Hale	Free Soil	155,825	5.0		
1856	31	JAMES BUCHANAN	Democratic	1,832,955	45.3	174	78.9
		John C. Frémont	Republican	1,339,932	33.1	114	
		Millard Fillmore	American	871,731	21.6	8	

Year	Number of States	Candidates	Parties	Popular Vote	% of Popular Vote	Electoral Vote	% Voter Participation
1860	33	**ABRAHAM LINCOLN**	Republican	1,865,593	39.8	180	81.2
		Stephen A. Douglas	Democratic	1,382,713	29.5	12	
		John C. Breckinridge	Democratic	848,356	18.1	72	
		John Bell	Constitutional Union	592,906	12.6	39	
1864	36	**ABRAHAM LINCOLN**	Republican	2,206,938	55.0	212	73.8
		George B. McClellan	Democratic	1,803,787	45.0	21	
1868	37	**ULYSSES S. GRANT**	Republican	3,013,421	52.7	214	78.1
		Horatio Seymour	Democratic	2,706,829	47.3	80	
1872	37	**ULYSSES S. GRANT**	Republican	3,596,745	55.6	286	71.3
		Horace Greeley	Democratic	2,843,446	43.9	66	
1876	38	Rutherford B. Hayes	Republican	4,036,572	48.0	185	81.8
		Samuel J. Tilden	Democratic	4,284,020	51.0	184	
1880	38	**JAMES A. GARFIELD**	Republican	4,453,295	48.5	214	79.4
		Winfield S. Hancock	Democratic	4,414,082	48.1	155	
		James B. Weaver	Greenback-Labor	308,578	3.4		
1884	38	**GROVER CLEVELAND**	Democratic	4,879,507	48.5	219	77.5
		James G. Blaine	Republican	4,850,293	48.2	182	
		Benjamin F. Butler	Greenback-Labor	175,370	1.8		
		John P. St. John	Prohibition	150,369	1.5		
1888	38	**BENJAMIN HARRISON**	Republican	5,477,129	47.9	233	79.3
		Grover Cleveland	Democratic	5,537,857	48.6	168	
		Clinton B. Fisk	Prohibition	249,506	2.2		
		Anson J. Streeter	Union Labor	146,935	1.3		

Year	Number of States	Candidates	Parties	Popular Vote	% of Popular Vote	Electoral Vote	% Voter Participation
1892	44	GROVER CLEVELAND	Democratic	5,555,426	46.1	277	74.7
		Benjamin Harrison	Republican	5,182,690	43.0	145	
		James B. Weaver	People's	1,029,846	8.5	22	
		John Bidwell	Prohibition	264,133	2.2		
1896	45	WILLIAM MCKINLEY	Republican	7,102,246	51.1	271	79.3
		William J. Bryan	Democratic	6,492,559	47.7	176	
1900	45	WILLIAM MCKINLEY	Republican	7,218,491	51.7	292	73.2
		William J. Bryan	Democratic; Populist	6,356,734	45.5	155	
		John C. Wooley	Prohibition	208,914	1.5		
1904	45	THEODORE ROOSEVELT	Republican	7,628,461	57.4	336	65.2
		Alton B. Parker	Democratic	5,084,223	37.6	140	
		Eugene V. Debs	Socialist	402,283	3.0		
		Silas C. Swallow	Prohibition	258,536	1.9		
1908	46	WILLIAM H. TAFT	Republican	7,675,320	51.6	321	65.4
		William J. Bryan	Democratic	6,412,294	43.1	162	
		Eugene V. Debs	Socialist	420,793	2.8		
		Eugene W. Chafin	Prohibition	253,840	1.7		
1912	48	WOODROW WILSON	Democratic	6,296,547	41.9	435	58.8
		Theodore Roosevelt	Progressive	4,118,571	27.4	88	
		William H. Taft	Republican	3,486,720	23.2	8	
		Eugene V. Debs	Socialist	900,672	6.0		
		Eugene W. Chafin	Prohibition	206,275	1.4		

Year	Number of States	Candidates	Parties	Popular Vote	% of Popular Vote	Electoral Vote	% Voter Participation
1916	48	**WOODROW WILSON**	Democratic	9,127,695	49.4	277	61.6
		Charles E. Hughes	Republican	8,533,507	46.2	254	
		A. L. Benson	Socialist	585,113	3.2		
		J. Frank Hanly	Prohibition	220,506	1.2		
1920	48	**WARREN G. HARDING**	Republican	16,143,407	60.4	404	49.2
		James M. Cox	Democratic	9,130,328	34.2	127	
		Eugene V. Debs	Socialist	919,799	3.4		
		P. P. Christensen	Farmer-Labor	265,411	1.0		
1924	48	**CALVIN COOLIDGE**	Republican	15,718,211	54.0	382	48.9
		John W. Davis	Democratic	8,385,283	28.8	136	
		Robert M. La Follette	Progressive	4,831,289	16.6	13	
1928	48	**HERBERT C. HOOVER**	Republican	21,391,993	58.2	444	56.9
		Alfred E. Smith	Democratic	15,016,169	40.9	87	
1932	48	**FRANKLIN D. ROOSEVELT**	Democratic	22,809,638	57.4	472	56.9
		Herbert C. Hoover	Republican	15,758,901	39.7	59	
		Norman Thomas	Socialist	881,951	2.2		
1936	48	**FRANKLIN D. ROOSEVELT**	Democratic	27,752,869	60.8	523	61.0
		Alfred M. Landon	Republican	16,674,665	36.5	8	
		William Lemke	Union	882,479	1.9		
1940	48	**FRANKLIN D. ROOSEVELT**	Democratic	27,307,819	54.8	449	62.5
		Wendell L. Willkie	Republican	22,321,018	44.8	82	
1944	48	**FRANKLIN D. ROOSEVELT**	Democratic	25,606,585	53.5	432	55.9
		Thomas E. Dewey	Republican	22,014,745	46.0	99	

Year	Number of States	Candidates	Parties	Popular Vote	% of Popular Vote	Electoral Vote	% Voter Participation
1948	48	**HARRY S. TRUMAN**	Democratic	24,179,345	49.6	303	53.0
		Thomas E. Dewey	Republican	21,991,291	45.1	189	
		J. Strom Thurmond	States' Rights	1,176,125	2.4	39	
		Henry A. Wallace	Progressive	1,157,326	2.4		
1952	48	**DWIGHT D. EISENHOWER**	Republican	33,936,234	55.1	442	63.3
		Adlai E. Stevenson	Democratic	27,314,992	44.4	89	
1956	48	**DWIGHT D. EISENHOWER**	Republican	35,590,472	57.6	457	60.6
		Adlai E. Stevenson	Democratic	26,022,752	42.1	73	
1960	50	**JOHN F. KENNEDY**	Democratic	34,226,731	49.7	303	62.8
		Richard M. Nixon	Republican	34,108,157	49.5	219	
1964	50	**LYNDON B. JOHNSON**	Democratic	43,129,566	61.1	486	61.9
		Barry M. Goldwater	Republican	27,178,188	38.5	52	
1968	50	**RICHARD M. NIXON**	Republican	31,785,480	43.4	301	60.9
		Hubert H. Humphrey	Democratic	31,275,166	42.7	191	
		George C. Wallace	American Independent	9,906,473	13.5	46	
1972	50	**RICHARD M. NIXON**	Republican	47,169,911	60.7	520	55.2
		George S. McGovern	Democratic	29,170,383	37.5	17	
		John G. Schmitz	American	1,099,482	1.4		

Year	States	Candidates	Party	Popular Vote	% of Popular Vote	Electoral Vote	% Voter Participation
1976	50	**JIMMY CARTER**	Democratic	40,830,763	50.1	297	53.5
		Gerald R. Ford	Republican	39,147,793	48.0	240	
1980	50	**RONALD REAGAN**	Republican	43,901,812	50.7	489	52.6
		Jimmy Carter	Democratic	35,483,820	41.0	49	
		John B. Anderson	Independent	5,719,437	6.6		
		Ed Clark	Libertarian	921,188	1.1		
1984	50	**RONALD REAGAN**	Republican	54,451,521	58.8	525	53.1
		Walter F. Mondale	Democratic	37,565,334	40.6	13	
1988	50	**GEORGE H. W. BUSH**	Republican	47,917,341	53.4	426	50.1
		Michael Dukakis	Democratic	41,013,030	45.6	111	
1992	50	**BILL CLINTON**	Democratic	44,908,254	43.0	370	55.0
		George H. W. Bush	Republican	39,102,343	37.4	168	
		H. Ross Perot	Independent	19,741,065	18.9		
1996	50	**BILL CLINTON**	Democratic	47,401,185	49.0	379	49.0
		Bob Dole	Republican	39,197,469	41.0	159	
		H. Ross Perot	Independent	8,085,295	8.0		
2000	50	**GEORGE W. BUSH**	Republican	50,455,156	47.9	271	50.4
		Al Gore	Democrat	50,997,335	48.4	266	
		Ralph Nader	Green	2,882,897	2.7		
2004	50	**GEORGE W. BUSH**	Republican	62,040,610	50.7	286	60.7
		John F. Kerry	Democrat	59,028,444	48.3	251	

Candidates receiving less than 1 percent of the popular vote have been omitted. Thus the percentage of popular vote given for any election year may not total 100 percent.

Before the passage of the Twelfth Amendment in 1804, the electoral college voted for two presidential candidates; the runner-up became vice-president.

ADMISSION OF STATES

Order of Admission	State	Date of Admission	Order of Admission	State	Date of Admission
1	Delaware	December 7, 1787	26	Michigan	January 26, 1837
2	Pennsylvania	December 12, 1787	27	Florida	March 3, 1845
3	New Jersey	December 18, 1787	28	Texas	December 29, 1845
4	Georgia	January 2, 1788	29	Iowa	December 28, 1846
5	Connecticut	January 9, 1788	30	Wisconsin	May 29, 1848
6	Massachusetts	February 7, 1788	31	California	September 9, 1850
7	Maryland	April 28, 1788	32	Minnesota	May 11, 1858
8	South Carolina	May 23, 1788	33	Oregon	February 14, 1859
9	New Hampshire	June 21, 1788	34	Kansas	January 29, 1861
10	Virginia	June 25, 1788	35	West Virginia	June 30, 1863
11	New York	July 26, 1788	36	Nevada	October 31, 1864
12	North Carolina	November 21, 1789	37	Nebraska	March 1, 1867
13	Rhode Island	May 29, 1790	38	Colorado	August 1, 1876
14	Vermont	March 4, 1791	39	North Dakota	November 2, 1889
15	Kentucky	June 1, 1792	40	South Dakota	November 2, 1889
16	Tennessee	June 1, 1796	41	Montana	November 8, 1889
17	Ohio	March 1, 1803	42	Washington	November 11, 1889
18	Louisiana	April 30, 1812	43	Idaho	July 3, 1890
19	Indiana	December 11, 1816	44	Wyoming	July 10, 1890
20	Mississippi	December 10, 1817	45	Utah	January 4, 1896
21	Illinois	December 3, 1818	46	Oklahoma	November 16, 1907
22	Alabama	December 14, 1819	47	New Mexico	January 6, 1912
23	Maine	March 15, 1820	48	Arizona	February 14, 1912
24	Missouri	August 10, 1821	49	Alaska	January 3, 1959
25	Arkansas	June 15, 1836	50	Hawaii	August 21, 1959

POPULATION OF THE UNITED STATES

Year	Number of States	Population	% Increase	Population per Square Mile
1790	13	3,929,214		4.5
1800	16	5,308,483	35.1	6.1
1810	17	7,239,881	36.4	4.3
1820	23	9,638,453	33.1	5.5
1830	24	12,866,020	33.5	7.4
1840	26	17,069,453	32.7	9.8
1850	31	23,191,876	35.9	7.9
1860	33	31,443,321	35.6	10.6
1870	37	39,818,449	26.6	13.4
1880	38	50,155,783	26.0	16.9
1890	44	62,947,714	25.5	21.1
1900	45	75,994,575	20.7	25.6
1910	46	91,972,266	21.0	31.0
1920	48	105,710,620	14.9	35.6
1930	48	122,775,046	16.1	41.2
1940	48	131,669,275	7.2	44.2
1950	48	150,697,361	14.5	50.7
1960	50	179,323,175	19.0	50.6
1970	50	203,235,298	13.3	57.5
1980	50	226,504,825	11.4	64.0
1985	50	237,839,000	5.0	67.2
1990	50	250,122,000	5.2	70.6
1995	50	263,411,707	5.3	74.4
2000	50	281,421,906	6.8	77.0

IMMIGRATION TO THE UNITED STATES, FISCAL YEARS 1820–2005

Year	Number	Year	Number	Year	Number	Year	Number
1820–1989	55,457,531	1871–80	2,812,191	1921–30	4,107,209	1971–80	4,493,314
1820	8,385	1871	321,350	1921	805,228	1971	370,478
		1872	404,806	1922	309,556	1972	384,685
1821–30	143,439	1873	459,803	1923	522,919	1973	400,063
1821	9,127	1874	313,339	1924	706,896	1974	394,861
1822	6,911	1875	227,498	1925	294,314	1975	386,914
1823	6,354	1876	169,986	1926	304,488	1976	398,613
1824	7,912	1877	141,857	1927	335,175		103,676
1825	10,199	1878	138,469	1928	307,255	1977	462,315
1826	10,837	1879	177,826	1929	279,678	1978	601,442
1827	18,875	1880	457,257	1930	241,700	1979	460,348
1828	27,382	1881–90	5,246,613	1931–40	528,431	1980	530,639
1829	22,520	1881	669,431	1931	97,139	1981–90	7,338,062
1830	23,322	1882	788,992	1932	35,576	1981	596,600
1831–40	599,125	1883	603,322	1933	23,068	1982	594,131
1831	22,633	1884	518,592	1934	29,470	1983	559,763
1832	60,482	1885	395,346	1935	34,956	1984	543,903
1833	58,640	1886	334,203	1936	36,329	1985	570,009
1834	65,365	1887	490,109	1937	50,244	1986	601,708
1835	45,374	1888	546,889	1938	67,895	1987	601,516
1836	76,242	1889	444,427	1939	82,998	1988	643,025
1837	79,340	1890	455,302	1940	70,756	1989	1,090,924
1838	38,914	1891–1900	3,687,564	1941–50	1,035,039	1990	1,536,483
1839	68,069	1891	560,319	1941	51,776	1991–2000	9,090,857
1840	84,066	1892	579,663	1942	28,781	1991	1,827,167
1841–50	1,713,251	1893	439,730	1943	23,725	1992	973,977
1841	80,289	1894	285,631	1944	28,551	1993	904,292
1842	104,565	1895	258,536	1945	38,119	1994	804,416
		1896	343,267	1946	108,721		

Year	Number	Year	Number	Year	Number	Year	Number
1843	52,496	1897	230,832	1947	147,292	1995	720,461
1844	78,615	1898	229,299	1948	170,570	1996	915,900
1845	114,371	1899	311,715	1949	188,317	1997	798,378
1846	154,416	1900	448,572	1950	249,187	1998	660,477
1847	234,968					1999	644,787
1848	226,527	**1901–10**	**8,795,386**	**1951–60**	**2,515,479**	2000	841,002
1849	297,024	1901	487,918	1951	205,717	**2001–5**	**4,904,341**
1850	369,980	1902	648,743	1952	265,520	2001	1,058,902
		1903	857,046	1953	170,434	2002	1,059,356
1851–60	**2,598,214**	1904	812,870	1954	208,177	2003	705,827
1851	379,466	1905	1,026,499	1955	237,790	2004	957,883
1852	371,603	1906	1,100,735	1956	321,625	2005	1,122,373
1853	368,645	1907	1,285,349	1957	326,867		
1854	427,833	1908	782,870	1958	253,265		
1855	200,877	1909	751,786	1959	260,686		
1856	200,436	1910	1,041,570	1960	265,398		
1857	251,306						
1858	123,126	**1911–20**	**5,735,811**	**1961–70**	**3,321,677**		
1859	121,282	1911	878,587	1961	271,344		
1860	153,640	1912	838,172	1962	283,763		
		1913	1,197,892	1963	306,260		
1861–70	**2,314,824**	1914	1,218,480	1964	292,248		
1861	91,918	1915	326,700	1965	296,697		
1862	91,985	1916	298,826	1966	323,040		
1863	176,282	1917	295,403	1967	361,972		
1864	193,418	1918	110,618	1968	454,448		
1865	248,120	1919	141,132	1969	358,579		
1866	318,568	1920	430,001	1970	373,326		
1867	315,722						
1868	138,840						
1869	352,768						
1870	387,203						

Source: U.S. Immigration and Naturalization Service, 2006.

IMMIGRATION BY REGION AND SELECTED COUNTRY OF LAST RESIDENCE, FISCAL YEARS 1820–2004

Region and Country of Last Residence[1]	1820	1821–30	1831–40	1841–50	1851–60	1861–70	1871–80	1881–90
All countries	8,385	143,439	599,125	1,713,251	2,598,214	2,314,824	2,812,191	5,246,613
Europe	7,690	98,797	495,681	1,597,442	2,452,577	2,065,141	2,271,925	4,735,484
Austria-Hungary	—[2]	—[2]	—[2]	—[2]	—[2]	7,800	72,969	353,719
Austria	—[2]	—[2]	—[2]	—[2]	—[2]	484[3]	63,009	226,038
Hungary	—[2]	—[2]	—[2]	—[2]	—[2]	7,124[3]	9,960	127,681
Belgium	1	27	22	5,074	4,738	6,734	7,221	20,177
Czechoslovakia	—[4]	—[4]	—[4]	—[4]	—[4]	—[4]	—[4]	—[4]
Denmark	20	169	1,063	539	3,749	17,094	31,771	88,132
France	371	8,497	45,575	77,262	76,358	35,986	72,206	50,464
Germany	968	6,761	152,454	434,626	951,667	787,468	718,182	1,452,970
Greece	—	20	49	16	31	72	210	2,308
Ireland[5]	3,614	50,724	207,381	780,719	914,119	435,778	436,871	655,482
Italy	30	409	2,253	1,870	9,231	11,725	55,759	307,309
Netherlands	49	1,078	1,412	8,251	10,789	9,102	16,541	53,701
Norway-Sweden	3	91	1,201	13,903	20,931	109,298	211,245	568,362
Norway	—[6]	—[6]	—[6]	—[6]	—[6]	—[6]	95,323	176,586
Sweden	—[6]	—[6]	—[6]	—[6]	—[6]	—[6]	115,922	391,776
Poland	5	16	369	105	1,164	2,027	12,970	51,806
Portugal	35	145	829	550	1,055	2,658	14,082	16,978
Romania	—[7]	—[7]	—[7]	—[7]	—[7]	—	11	6,348
Soviet Union	14	75	277	551	457	2,512	39,284	213,282
Spain	139	2,477	2,125	2,209	9,298	6,697	5,266	4,419
Switzerland	31	3,226	4,821	4,644	25,011	23,286	28,293	81,988
United Kingdom[5,8]	2,410	25,079	75,810	267,044	423,974	606,896	548,043	807,357
Yugoslavia	—[9]	—[9]	—[9]	—[9]	—[9]	—[9]	—[9]	—[9]
Other Europe	—	3	40	79	5	8	1,001	682

Asia	6	30	55	141	41,538	64,759	124,160	69,942
China[10]	1	2	8	35	41,397	64,301	123,201	61,711
Hong Kong	—[11]	—[11]	—[11]	—[11]	—[11]	—[11]	—[11]	—[11]
India	1	8	39	36	43	69	163	269
Iran	—[12]	—[12]	—[12]	—[12]	—[12]	—[12]	—[12]	—[12]
Israel	—[13]	—[13]	—[13]	—[13]	—[13]	—[13]	—[13]	—[13]
Japan	—[14]	—[14]	—[14]	—[14]	—[14]	186	149	2,270
Korea	—[15]	—[15]	—[15]	—[15]	—[15]	—[15]	—[15]	—[15]
Philippines	—[16]	—[16]	—[16]	—[16]	—[16]	—[16]	—[16]	—[16]
Turkey	1	20	7	59	83	131	404	3,782
Vietnam	—[11]	—[11]	—[11]	—[11]	—[11]	—[11]	—[11]	—[11]
Other Asia	3	—[11]	1	11	15	72	243	1,910
America	387	11,564	33,424	62,469	74,720	166,607	404,044	426,967
Canada & Newfoundland [17,18]	209	2,277	13,624	41,723	59,309	153,878	383,640	393,304
Mexico[18]	1	4,817	6,599	3,271	3,078	2,191	5,162	191,319
Caribbean	164	3,834	12,301	13,528	10,660	9,046	13,957	29,042
Cuba	—[12]	—[12]	—[12]	—[12]	—[12]	—[12]	—[12]	—[12]
Dominican Republic	—[20]	—[20]	—[20]	—[20]	—[20]	—[20]	—[20]	—[20]
Haiti	—[20]	—[20]	—[20]	—[20]	—[20]	—[20]	—[20]	—[20]
Jamaica	—[21]	—[21]	—[21]	—[21]	—[21]	—[21]	—[21]	—[21]
Other Caribbean	164	3,834	12,301	13,528	10,660	9,046	13,957	29,042
Central America	2	105	44	368	449	95	157	404
El Salvador	—[20]	—[20]	—[20]	—[20]	—[20]	—[20]	—[20]	—[20]
Other Central America	2	105	44	368	449	95	157	404
South America	11	531	856	3,579	1,224	1,397	1,128	2,304
Argentina	—[20]	—[20]	—[20]	—[20]	—[20]	—[20]	—[20]	—[20]
Colombia	—[20]	—[20]	—[20]	—[20]	—[20]	—[20]	—[20]	—[20]
Ecuador	—[20]	—[20]	—[20]	—[20]	—[20]	—[20]	—[20]	—[20]
Other South America	11	531	856	3,579	1,224	1,397	1,128	2,304
Other America	—[22]	—[22]	—[22]	—[22]	—[22]	—[22]	—[22]	—[22]
Africa	1	16	54	55	210	312	358	857
Oceania	1	2	9	29	158	214	10,914	12,574
Not specified [22]	300	33,030	69,902	53,115	29,011	17,791	790	789

Region and Country of Last Residence[1]	1891–1900	1901–10	1911–20	1921–30	1931–40	1941–50	1951–60	1961–70
All countries	3,687,564	8,795,386	5,735,811	4,107,209	528,431	1,035,039	2,515,479	3,321,677
Europe	3,555,352	8,056,040	4,321,887	2,463,194	347,566	621,147	1,325,727	1,123,492
Austria-Hungary	592,707[23]	2,145,266[23]	896,342[23]	63,548	11,424	28,329	103,743	26,022
Austria	234,081[3]	668,209[3]	453,649	32,868	3,563[24]	24,860[24]	67,106	20,621
Hungary	181,288[3]	808,511[3]	442,693	30,680	7,861	3,469	36,637	5,401
Belgium	18,167	41,635	33,746	15,846	4,817	12,189	18,575	9,192
Czechoslovakia	—[4]	—[4]	3,426[4]	102,194	14,393	8,347	918	3,273
Denmark	50,231	65,285	41,983	32,430	2,559	5,393	10,984	9,201
France	30,770	73,379	61,897	49,610	12,623	38,809	51,121	45,237
Germany	505,152[23]	341,498[23]	143,945[23]	412,202	114,058[24]	226,578[24]	477,765	190,796
Greece	15,979	167,519	184,201	51,084	9,119	8,973	47,608	85,969
Ireland[5]	388,416	339,065	146,181	211,234	10,973	19,789	48,362	32,966
Italy	651,893	2,045,877	1,109,524	455,315	68,028	57,661	185,491	214,111
Netherlands	26,758	48,262	43,718	26,948	7,150	14,860	52,277	30,606
Norway-Sweden	321,281	440,039	161,469	165,780	8,700	20,765	44,632	32,600
Norway	95,015	190,505	66,395	68,531	4,740	10,100	22,935	15,484
Sweden	226,266	249,534	95,074	97,249	3,960	10,665	21,697	17,116
Poland	96,720[23]	—[23]	4,813[23]	227,734	17,026	7,571	9,985	53,539
Portugal	27,508	69,149	89,732	29,994	3,329	7,423	19,588	76,065
Romania	12,750	53,008	13,311	67,646	3,871	1,076	1,039	2,531
Soviet Union	505,290[23]	1,597,306[23]	921,201[23]	61,742	1,370	571	671	2,465
Spain	8,731	27,935	68,611	28,958	3,258	2,898	7,894	44,659
Switzerland	31,179	34,922	23,091	29,676	5,512	10,547	17,675	18,453
United Kingdom[5,8]	271,538	525,950	341,408	339,570	31,572	139,306	202,824	213,822
Yugoslavia	—[9]	—[9]	1,888[9]	49,064	5,835	1,576	8,225	20,381
Other Europe	282	39,945	31,400	42,619	11,949	8,486	16,350	11,604

Asia	427,642	153,249	37,028	16,595	112,059	247,236	323,543	74,862
China[10]	34,764	9,657	16,709	4,928	29,907	21,278	20,605	14,799
Hong Kong	75,007	15,541[11]	—[11]	—[11]	—[11]	—[11]	—[11]	—[11]
India	27,189	1,973	1,761	496	1,886	2,082	4,713	68
Iran	10,339	3,388	1,380	195	241[12]	—[12]	—[12]	—[12]
Israel	29,602	25,476	476[13]	—[13]	—[13]	—[13]	—[13]	—[13]
Japan	39,988	46,250	1,555	1,948	33,462	83,837	129,797	25,942
Korea	34,526	6,231	107[15]	—[15]	—[15]	—[15]	—[15]	—[15]
Philippines	98,376	19,307	4,691	528[16]	—[16]	—[16]	—[16]	—[16]
Turkey	10,142	3,519	798	1,065	33,824	134,066	157,369	30,425
Vietnam	4,340	335[11]	—[11]	—[11]	—[11]	—[11]	—[11]	—[11]
Other Asia	63,369	21,572	9,551	7,435	12,739	5,973	11,059	3,628
America	1,716,374	996,944	354,804	160,037	1,516,716	1,143,671	361,888	38,972
Canada & Newfoundland[17,18]	413,310	377,952	171,718	108,527	924,515	742,185	179,226	3,311
Mexico[18]	453,937	299,811	60,589	22,319	459,287	219,004	49,642	971[19]
Caribbean	470,213	123,091	49,725	15,502	74,899	123,424	107,548	33,066
Cuba	208,536	78,948	26,313	9,571	15,901[12]	—[12]	—[12]	—[12]
Dominican Republic	93,292	9,897	5,627	1,150[20]	—[20]	—[20]	—[20]	—[20]
Haiti	34,499	4,442	911	191[20]	—[20]	—[20]	—[20]	—[20]
Jamaica	74,906	8,869[21]	—[21]	—[21]	—[21]	—[21]	—[21]	—[21]
Other Caribbean	58,980	20,935[21]	16,874	4,590	58,998	123,424	107,548	33,066
Central America	101,330	44,751	21,665	5,861	15,769	17,159	8,192	549
El Salvador	14,992	5,895	5,132	673[20]	—[20]	—[20]	—[20]	—[20]
Other Central America	86,338	38,856	16,533	5,188	15,769	17,159	8,192	549
South America	257,954	91,628	21,831	7,803	42,215	41,899	17,280	1,075
Argentina	49,721	19,486	3,338	1,349[20]	—[20]	—[20]	—[20]	—[20]
Colombia	72,028	18,048	3,858	1,223[20]	—[20]	—[20]	—[20]	—[20]
Ecuador	36,780	9,841	2,417	337[20]	—[20]	—[20]	—[20]	—[20]
Other South America	99,425	44,253	12,218	4,894	42,215	41,899	17,280	1,075
Other America	19,630	59,711	29,276	25	31[22]	—[22]	—[22]	—[22]
Africa	28,954	14,092	7,367	1,750	6,286	8,443	7,368	350
Oceania	25,122	12,976	14,551	2,483	8,726	13,427	13,024	3,965
Not specified[22]	93	12,491	142	—	228	1,147	33,523[25]	14,063

Region and Country of Last Residence[1]	1971–80	1981–89	1990–99	1991–2000	2001	2002	2003	2004	Total 184 Years 1820–2004
All countries	4,493,314	5,801,579	9,781,496	9,095,417	1,064,318	1,063,732	705,827	946,142	69,869,450
Europe	800,368	637,524	1,291,299	1,359,737	177,833	177,652	102,843	130,151	39,049,276
Austria-Hungary	16,028	20,152	N/A	24,882	2,318	4,016	2,181	3,683	4,379,862
Austria	9,478	14,566	5,094	15,500	1,004	2,657	1,163	2,442	1,851,712
Hungary	6,550	5,586	11,003	9,382	1,314	1,359	1,018	1,241	1,682,074
Belgium	5,329	6,239	5,783	7,090	1,002	842	518	746	220,754
Czechoslovakia[27]	6,023	6,649	7,597	9,816	1,921	1,862	1,474	1,870	162,744
Czech Republic	N/A	N/A	723	N/A	N/A	N/A	N/A	N/A	N/A
Slovak Republic	N/A	N/A	3,010	N/A	N/A	N/A	N/A	N/A	N/A
Denmark	4,439	4,696	5,785	6,079	741	655	436	568	378,891
France	25,069	28,088	26,879	35,820	5,431	4,596	2,933	4,209	840,576
Germany	74,414	79,809	60,082	92,606	22,093	21,058	8,102	10,270	7,237,594
Germany, East	N/A	N/A	105	N/A	N/A	N/A	N/A	N/A	N/A
Germany, West	N/A	N/A	7,338	N/A	N/A	N/A	N/A	N/A	N/A
Greece	92,369	34,490	15,403	26,759	1,966	1,516	914	1,213	736,272
Ireland	11,490	22,229	67,975	56,950	1,550	1,419	1,010	1,518	4,787,580
Italy	129,368	51,008	23,365	62,722	3,377	2,837	1,904	2,495	5,446,443
Netherlands	10,492	10,723	12,334	13,308	1,895	2,305	1,329	1,713	394,782
Norway-Sweden	10,472	13,252	15,720	17,893	2,561	2,097	1,520	2,011	2,172,036
Norway	3,941	3,612	4,618	5,178	588	464	386	457	760,792
Sweden	6,531	9,640	11,102	12,715	1,973	1,633	1,134	1,554	1,265,817
Poland	37,234	64,888	180,035	163,747	12,355	13,304	11,016	13,972	820,730
Portugal	101,710	36,365	25,428	22,916	1,654	1,320	821	1,062	529,034
Romania	12,393	27,361	55,303	51,203	6,224	4,525	3,311	4,064	274,168
Russia	N/A	N/A	110,921	N/A	N/A	N/A	N/A	N/A	N/A
Soviet Union[28]	38,961	42,898	126,115	462,874	55,099	55,464	33,563	36,646	4,087,352
Former Soviet Republics[29]	N/A	N/A	255,552						
Spain	39,141	17,689	14,310	17,157	1,889	1,603	1,107	1,453	308,357
Switzerland	8,235	7,561	8,840	11,841	1,796	1,503	867	1,193	376,639
United Kingdom	137,374	140,119	138,380	151,866	20,258	18,057	11,220	16,680	5,337,231
Yugoslavia[28]	30,540	15,984	25,923	66,557	21,937	28,100	8,296	13,211	274,372

Former Yugoslavian States	N/A	N/A	61,389						
Other Europe	9,287	7,324	822,161	57,651	11,766	10,573	10,321	11,574	283,859
Asia	1,588,178	2,416,278	2,965,360	2,795,672	337,566	326,871	236,039	314,489	10,029,817
China, People's Republic	124,326	306,108	410,736	419,114	50,821	55,974	37,395	45,942	1,523,622
Hong Kong	113,467	83,848	78,016	109,779	10,307	7,952	5,020	5,421	440,709
India	164,134	221,977	371,925	363,060	65,916	66,864	47,157	65,472	1,064,185
Iran	45,136	101,267	129,055	68,556	8,063	7,730	4,709	5,898	271,807
Israel	37,713	38,367	33,814	39,397	4,925	4,938	3,719	5,206	195,725
Japan	49,775	40,654	60,112	67,942	10,464	9,150	6,724	8,652	565,176
Korea	267,638	302,782	187,794	164,166	19,933	20,114	12,177	19,441	878,079
Philippines	354,987	477,485	526,835	503,945	50,870	48,674	43,258	54,632	1,728,032
Taiwan	N/A	N/A	112,464	N/A	N/A	N/A	N/A	N/A	N/A
Turkey	13,399	20,028	26,178	38,212	3,477	3,934	3,332	4,489	465,771
Vietnam	172,820	266,027	443,173	286,145	34,648	32,425	21,270	30,064	862,829
Other Asia	244,783	557,735	769,425	735,356	78,142	69,116	51,278	69,272	2,033,882
Africa	80,779	144,096	374,149	354,939	50,209	56,135	45,640	62,510	903,578
Oceania	41,242	38,401	49,040	55,845	7,253	6,536	5,102	6,929	286,287
America	1,982,735	2,564,698	4,529,512	4,486,806	473,351	478,777	306,793	407,471	19,220,746
Canada	169,939	132,296	138,165	191,987	30,203	27,299	16,555	22,437	4,584,066
Mexico	640,294	975,657	2,756,513	2,249,421	204,844	217,318	114,984	173,664	6,848,960
Caribbean	741,126	759,416	1,023,237	978,787	96,958	94,240	67,660	81,893	4,022,715
Cuba	264,863	135,142	170,675	169,322	26,073	27,520	8,722	15,385	995,732
Dominican Republic	148,135	209,899	365,598	335,251	21,256	22,474	26,157	30,049	945,323
Haiti	56,335	118,510	179,725	179,644	22,535	19,189	11,942	13,502	481,569
Jamaica	137,577	184,481	182,552	169,227	15,099	14,567	13,082	13,565	655,040
Other Caribbean	134,216	111,384	124,687	125,343	11,995	10,490	7,757	9,392	945,051
Central America	134,640	321,845	611,597	526,915	73,063	66,520	53,435	60,299	1,599,860
El Salvador	34,436	133,938	274,989	215,798	31,054	30,539	27,915	29,285	609,258
Other Central America	100,204	187,907	336,608	311,117	42,009	35,981	25,520	31,014	990,602
South America	295,741	375,026	569,650	539,656	68,279	73,400	54,155	69,177	2,054,956
Argentina	29,897	21,374	27,431	26,644	3,459	3,811	3,217	4,672	172,921
Colombia	77,347	99,066	140,685	128,499	16,333	18,488	14,455	17,887	491,015
Ecuador	50,077	43,841	81,204	76,592	9,694	10,564	7,040	8,351	268,008
Other South America	138,420	210,745	320,330	307,921	38,793	40,537	29,443	38,267	1,123,012
Other America	995	458	595	40	4	3	4	1	110,189
Unknown or not reported	N/A	N/A	2,486	42,418	18,106	17,761	9,410	24,592	379,746

Source: U.S. Immigration and Naturalization Service, 2006.

[1]Data for years prior to 1906 relate to country whence alien came; data from 1906–79 and 1984–89 are for country of last permanent residence; and data for 1980–99 refer to country of birth. Because of changes in boundaries, changes in lists of countries, and lack of data for specified countries for various periods, data for certain countries, especially for the total period 1820–2004, are not comparable throughout. Data for specified countries are included with countries to which they belonged prior to World War I.

[2]Data for Austria and Hungary not reported until 1861.

[3]Data for Austria and Hungary not reported separately for all years during the period.

[4]No data available for Czechoslovakia until 1920.

[5]Prior to 1926, data for Northern Ireland included in Ireland.

[6]Data for Norway and Sweden not reported separately until 1871.

[7]No data available for Romania until 1880.

[8]Since 1925, data for United Kingdom refer to England, Scotland, Wales, and Northern Ireland.

[9]In 1920, a separate enumeration was made for the Kingdom of Serbs, Croats, and Slovenes. Since 1922, the Serb, Croat, and Slovene Kingdom recorded as Yugoslavia.

[10]Beginning in 1957, China includes Taiwan.

[11]Data not reported separately until 1952.

[12]Data not reported separately until 1925.

[13]Data not reported separately until 1949.

[14]No data available for Japan until 1861.

[15]Data not reported separately until 1948.

[16]Prior to 1934, Philippines recorded as insular travel.

[17]Prior to 1920, Canada and Newfoundland recorded as British North America. From 1820 to 1898, figures include all British North America possessions.

[18]Land arrivals not completely enumerated until 1908.

[19]No data available for Mexico from 1886 to 1893.

[20]Data not reported separately until 1932.

[21]Data for Jamaica not collected until 1953. In prior years, consolidated under British West Indies, which is included in "Other Caribbean."

[22]Included in countries "Not specified" until 1925.

[23]From 1899 to 1919, data for Poland included in Austria-Hungary, Germany, and the Soviet Union.

[24]From 1938 to 1945, data for Austria included in Germany.

[25]Includes 32,897 persons returning in 1906 to their homes in the United States.

[26]Data for fiscal year 1998 have been revised due to changes in the count for asylees and cancellation of removal. The previously reported total was 660,477.

[27]Prior to 1993, data include independent republics; beginning in 1993, data are for unknown republic only.

[28]Prior to 1992, data include independent republic; beginning in 1992, data are for Yugoslavia only.

[29]Prior to 1992, data include previously independent republics only; beginning in 1992, data are for all former republics except Russia.

— represents zero.

NOTE: From 1820 to 1867, figures represent alien passengers arrived at seaports; from 1868 to 1891 and 1895 to 1897, immigrant aliens arrived; from 1892 to 1894 and 1898 to 1989, immigrant aliens admitted for permanent residence. From 1892 to 1903, aliens entering by cabin class were not counted as immigrants. Land arrivals were not completely enumerated until 1908. For this table, fiscal year 1843 covers 9 months ending September 1843; fiscal years 1832 and 1850 cover 15 months ending December 31 of the respective years; and fiscal year 1868 covers 6 months ending June 30, 1868.

PRESIDENTS, VICE-PRESIDENTS, AND SECRETARIES OF STATE

	President	*Vice-President*	*Secretary of State*
1.	George Washington, Federalist 1789	John Adams, Federalist 1789	Thomas Jefferson 1789 Edmund Randolph 1794 Timothy Pickering 1795
2.	John Adams, Federalist 1797	Thomas Jefferson, Dem.-Rep. 1797	Timothy Pickering 1797 John Marshall 1800
3.	Thomas Jefferson, Dem.-Rep. 1801	Aaron Burr, Dem.-Rep. 1801 George Clinton, Dem.-Rep. 1805	James Madison 1801
4.	James Madison, Dem.-Rep. 1809	George Clinton, Dem.-Rep. 1809 Elbridge Gerry, Dem.-Rep. 1813	Robert Smith 1809 James Monroe 1811
5.	James Monroe, Dem.-Rep. 1817	Daniel D. Tompkins, Dem.-Rep. 1817	John Q. Adams 1817
6.	John Quincy Adams, Dem.-Rep. 1825	John C. Calhoun, Dem.-Rep. 1825	Henry Clay 1825
7.	Andrew Jackson, Democratic 1829	John C. Calhoun, Democratic 1829 Martin Van Buren, Democratic 1833	Martin Van Buren 1829 Edward Livingston 1831 Louis McLane 1833 John Forsyth 1834
8.	Martin Van Buren, Democratic 1837	Richard M. Johnson, Democratic 1837	John Forsyth 1837
9.	William H. Harrison, Whig 1841	John Tyler, Whig 1841	Daniel Webster 1841

President	Vice-President	Secretary of State
10. John Tyler, Whig and Democratic 1841	None	Daniel Webster 1841 Hugh S. Legaré 1843 Abel P. Upshur 1843 John C. Calhoun 1844
11. James K. Polk, Democratic 1845	George M. Dallas, Democratic 1845	James Buchanan 1845
12. Zachary Taylor, Whig 1849	Millard Fillmore, Whig 1848	John M. Clayton 1849
13. Millard Fillmore, Whig 1850	None	Daniel Webster 1850 Edward Everett 1852
14. Franklin Pierce, Democratic 1853	William R. King, Democratic 1853	William L. Marcy 1853
15. James Buchanan, Democratic 1857	John C. Breckinridge, Democratic 1857	Lewis Cass 1857 Jeremiah S. Black 1860
16. Abraham Lincoln, Republican 1861	Hannibal Hamlin, Republican 1861 Andrew Johnson, Unionist 1865	William H. Seward 1861
17. Andrew Johnson, Unionist 1865	None	William H. Seward 1865
18. Ulysses S. Grant, Republican 1869	Schuyler Colfax, Republican 1869 Henry Wilson, Republican 1873	Elihu B. Washburne 1869 Hamilton Fish 1869
19. Rutherford B. Hayes, Republican 1877	William A. Wheeler, Republican 1877	William M. Evarts 1877

	President	Vice-President	Secretary of State
20.	James A. Garfield, Republican 1881	Chester A. Arthur, Republican 1881	James G. Blaine 1881
21.	Chester A. Arthur, Republican 1881	None	Frederick T. Frelinghuysen 1881
22.	Grover Cleveland, Democratic 1885	Thomas A. Hendricks, Democratic 1885	Thomas F. Bayard 1885
23.	Benjamin Harrison, Republican 1889	Levi P. Morton, Republican 1889	James G. Blaine 1889 John W. Foster 1892
24.	Grover Cleveland, Democratic 1893	Adlai E. Stevenson, Democratic 1893	Walter Q. Gresham 1893 Richard Olney 1895
25.	William McKinley, Republican 1897	Garret A. Hobart, Republican 1897 Theodore Roosevelt, Republican 1901	John Sherman 1897 William R. Day 1898 John Hay 1898
26.	Theodore Roosevelt, Republican 1901	Charles Fairbanks, Republican 1905	John Hay 1901 Elihu Root 1905 Robert Bacon 1909
27.	William H. Taft, Republican 1909	James S. Sherman, Republican 1909	Philander C. Knox 1909
28.	Woodrow Wilson, Democratic 1913	Thomas R. Marshall, Democratic 1913	William J. Bryan 1913 Robert Lansing 1915 Bainbridge Colby 1920
29.	Warren G. Harding, Republican 1921	Calvin Coolidge, Republican 1921	Charles E. Hughes 1921
30.	Calvin Coolidge, Republican 1923	Charles G. Dawes, Republican 1925	Charles E. Hughes 1923 Frank B. Kellogg 1925

	President	Vice-President	Secretary of State
31.	Herbert Hoover, Republican 1929	Charles Curtis, Republican 1929	Henry L. Stimson 1929
32.	Franklin D. Roosevelt, Democratic 1933	John Nance Garner, Democratic 1933 Henry A. Wallace, Democratic 1941 Harry S. Truman, Democratic 1945	Cordell Hull 1933 Edward R. Stettinius, Jr. 1944
33.	Harry S. Truman, Democratic 1945	Alben W. Barkley, Democratic 1949	Edward R. Stettinius, Jr. 1945 James F. Byrnes 1945 George C. Marshall 1947 Dean G. Acheson 1949
34.	Dwight D. Eisenhower, Republican 1953	Richard M. Nixon, Republican 1953	John F. Dulles 1953 Christian A. Herter 1959
35.	John F. Kennedy, Democratic 1961	Lyndon B. Johnson, Democratic 1961	Dean Rusk 1961
36.	Lyndon B. Johnson, Democratic 1963	Hubert H. Humphrey, Democratic 1965	Dean Rusk 1963
37.	Richard M. Nixon, Republican 1969	Spiro T. Agnew, Republican 1969 Gerald R. Ford, Republican 1973	William P. Rogers 1969 Henry Kissinger 1973
38.	Gerald R. Ford, Republican 1974	Nelson Rockefeller, Republican 1974	Henry Kissinger 1974
39.	Jimmy Carter, Democratic 1977	Walter Mondale, Democratic 1977	Cyrus Vance 1977 Edmund Muskie 1980

	President	Vice-President	Secretary of State
40.	Ronald Reagan, Republican 1981	George H. W. Bush, Republican 1981	Alexander Haig 1981 George Schultz 1982
41.	George H. W. Bush, Republican 1989	J. Danforth Quayle, Republican 1989	James A. Baker 1989 Lawrence Eagleburger 1992
42.	William J. Clinton, Democrat 1993	Albert Gore, Jr., Democrat 1993	Warren Christopher 1993 Madeleine Albright 1997
43.	George W. Bush, Republican 2001	Richard B. Cheney, Republican 2001	Colin L. Powell 2001 Condoleezza Rice 2005

CREDITS

PART 4: **p. 385,** The Granger Collection; **p. 386,** The Granger Collection and the Library of Congress; **p. 387,** The Granger Collection and The Granger Collection; **p. 388,** Library of Congress and the Library of Congress; **p. 389,** Library of Congress, **p. 390,** Library of Congress.

CHAPTER 15: **p. 393,** Bettmann/Corbis; **p. 395,** Prints and Photographs Division, Schomburg Center for Research, The New York Public Library; **p. 397,** Bettmann/Corbis; **p. 400,** The Charleston Museum; **p. 405,** Library of Congress; **p. 409,** The Granger Collection; **p. 411,** (*left*) The Granger Collection and (*right*) Collection of the New-York Historical Society.

CHAPTER 16: **p. 416,** The Granger Collection; **p. 420,** The Granger Collection; **p. 423,** The Granger Collection; **p. 425,** The Granger Collection; **p. 427,** The Granger Collection; **p. 437,** The Granger Collection; **p. 439,** Library of Congress; **p. 441,** Library of Congress.

CHAPTER 17: **p. 447,** Library of Congress; **p. 452,** Bettmann/Corbis; **p. 454,** Bettmann/Corbis; **p. 465,** (*top*) Library of Congress and (*bottom*) Library of Congress; **p. 470,** Library of Congress; **p. 472,** National Archives; **p. 475,** Library of Congress; **p. 478,** Bettmann/Corbis; **p. 480,** Bettmann/Corbis; **p. 484,** Library of Congress.

CHAPTER 18: **p. 488,** Library of Congress; **p. 490,** Library of Congress; **p. 492,** Library of Congress; **p. 495,** Library of Congress; **p. 499,** Library of Congress; **p. 507,** Bettmann/Corbis; **p. 512,** Library of Congress; **p. 515,** Library of Congress.

PART 5: **p. 521,** The Granger Collection; **p. 522,** The Granger Collection, Bettmann/Corbis; **p. 523,** The Granger Collection; **p. 524,** Library of Congress and Library of Congress; **p. 525,** Warder Collection and The Granger Collection; **p. 526,** The Granger Collection.

CHAPTER 19: **p. 527,** Library of Congress; **p. 533,** The Granger Collection; **p. 539,** Library of Congress; **p. 540,** Warder Collection; **p. 542,** Kansas State Historical Society; **p. 547,** Warder Collection; **p. 550,** Bettmann/Corbis; **p. 554,** Western Historical Collections, University of Oklahoma Library.

CHAPTER 20: **p. 558,** Library of Congress; **p. 560,** Alfred Stieglitz, *The Hand of Man,* 1902, photogravure, P.1978.112, Amon Carter Museum; **p. 562,** Union Pacific Museum; **p. 567,** Warder Collection; **p. 569,** Carnegie Library of Pittsburgh; **p. 570,** Pierpont Morgan Library; **p. 571,** The Granger Collection; **p. 576,** T.V. Powderly Photographic Collection, The American Catholic History Research Center and University Archives, The Catholic University of America, Washington, D.C.; **p. 580,** Walter P. Reuther Library, Wayne State University.

CHAPTER 21: **p. 585,** Library of Congress; **p. 589,** Culver Pictures; **p. 590,** Bettmann/Corbis; **p. 594,** The Byron Collection, Museum of the City of New York; **p. 595,** William Williams Papers, Manuscripts and Archives Division, The New York Public

Library, Astor, Lenox and Tilden Foundations; **p. 598,** Brown Brothers; **p. 601,** Old York Library; **p. 602,** Library of Congress; **p. 610,** The Salvation Army National Archives; **p. 611,** University of Illinois at Chicago.

CHAPTER 22: **p. 616,** Library of Congress; **p. 620,** Library of Congress; **p. 623,** Warder Collection; **p. 626,** Bettmann/Corbis; **p. 631,** Library of Congress; **p. 634,** Kansas State Historical Society; **p. 638,** Library of Congress.

PART 6: **p. 643,** Library of Congress; **p. 644,** Bettmann/Corbis and Bettmann/Corbis; Bettmann/Corbis and Library of Congress; **p. 645,** Bettmann/Corbis and Library of Congress; **p. 646,** AP/Wide World Photos and Bettmann/Corbis; Bettmann/Corbis and Bettmann/Corbis; **p. 647,** Bettmann/Corbis and AP/Wide World Photos; **p. 649,** Library of Congress.

CHAPTER 23: **p. 651,** Bettmann/Corbis; **p. 655,** Hawaii State Archives; **p. 658,** Library of Congress; **p. 661,** Library of Congress; **p. 663,** National Archives; **p. 669,** Bettmann/Corbis; **p. 670,** Bettmann/Corbis.

CHAPTER 24: **p. 674,** Library of Congress; **p. 678,** Library of Congress; **p. 679,** Bettmann/Corbis; **p. 682** (*top*) Collection of the New-York Historical Society and (*bottom*) Library of Congress; **p. 685,** Library of Congress; **p. 689,** Library of Congress; **p. 691,** Library of Congress; **p. 694,** Warder Collection; **p. 697,** Warder Collection.

CHAPTER 25: **p. 703,** Library of Congress; **p. 705,** Bettmann/Corbis; **p. 709,** National Archives; **p. 711,** The New York Times; **p. 713,** Bettmann/Corbis; **p. 716,** Bettmann/Corbis; **p. 720,** Bettmann/Corbis; **p. 724,** Mary Evans Picture Library; **p. 727,** Courtesy of the "Ding" Darling Wildlife Foundation.

CHAPTER 26: **p. 734,** Bettmann/Corbis; **p. 736,** Bettmann/Corbis; **p. 738,** Bettmann/Corbis; **p. 739,** Bettmann/Corbis; **p. 741,** Ramsey Archive; **p. 742,** Bettmann/Corbis; **p. 743,** Bettmann/Corbis; **p. 746,** AP/Wide World Photos.

CHAPTER 27: **p. 752,** Bettmann/Corbis; **p. 757,** © The Washington Post. Reprinted with permission; **p. 758,** Hulton Archive; **p. 761,** Bettmann/Corbis; **p. 762,** From the Collections of The Henry Ford; **p. 766,** Bettmann/Corbis; **p. 768,** Herbert Hoover Presidential Library; **p. 772,** Bettmann/Corbis; **p. 774,** New York Daily News, DailyNewsPix.

CHAPTER 28: **p. 777,** Bettmann/Corbis; **p. 780,** AP/Wide World Photos; **p. 783,** National Archives; **p. 790,** National Archives; **p. 795,** Bettmann/Corbis; **p. 796,** Hulton Archive; **p. 798,** Bettmann/Corbis; **p. 800,** Library of Congress.

CHAPTER 29: **p. 810,** Bettmann/Corbis; **p. 812,** AP/Wide World Photos; **p. 816,** National Archives; **p. 820,** © 1938, The Washington Post. Reprinted with permission; **p. 822,** British Information Services; **p. 828,** Library of Congress.

CHAPTER 30: **p. 831,** Bettmann/Corbis; **p. 832,** Warder Collection; **p. 837,** Library of Congress; **p. 838,** AP/Wide World Photos; **p. 846,** Eisenhower Presidential Library; **p. 847,** National Archives; **p. 854,** National Archives; **p. 856,** National Archives; **p. 859,** Hulton Archive.

Part 7: p. 863, Bill Eppridge/Getty Images; **p. 864,** Bettman/Corbis, Bettmann/Corbis and AP/Wide World Photos; **p. 865,** Hy Peskin/Getty Images, New York Public Library and AP/Wide World Photos; **p. 866,** AP/Wide World Photos, Bettmann/Corbis and Bettmann/Corbis; Bettmann/Corbis and Bettmann/Corbis; **p. 869,** Bettman/Corbis.

Chapter 31: p. 871, Bettmann/Corbis; **p. 873,** University of Louisville; **p. 881,** Hartford Courant; **p. 882,** Hy Peskin/Getty Images; **p. 884,** © 1948, The Washington Post. Reprinted with permission; **p. 885,** Bettmann/Corbis; **p. 888,** Library of Congress; **p. 892,** Bettmann/Corbis; **p. 894,** Yale Joel/Getty Images.

Chapter 32: p. 898, Hulton Archive; **p. 901,** AP/Wide World Photos; **p. 903,** Bettmann/Corbis; **p. 906,** Fogg Art Museum, Harvard University; **p. 907,** PNI/Archive Photos; **p. 910,** Hulton Archive; **p. 911,** AP/Wide World Photos; **p. 914,** AP/Wide World Photos.

Chapter 33: p. 917, Bettmann/Corbis; **p. 922,** Bettmann/Corbis; **p. 924,** "Don't Be Afraid—I Can Always Pull You Back," from Herblock's Special for Today (Simon & Schuster, 1958); **p. 925,** Photoworld; **p. 933,** AP/Wide World Photos; **p. 935,** University of Louisville; **p. 937,** Black Star/Stock Photo.

Chapter 34: p. 941, Bettmann/Corbis; **p. 945,** National Archives; **p. 947,** National Archives; **p. 949,** Hulton Archive; **p. 953,** Time & Life Pictures; **p. 959,** National Archives; **p. 963,** Bettmann/Corbis; **p. 964,** The Newark Star-Ledger.

Chapter 35: p. 971, Bettmann/Corbis; **p. 974,** Magnum Photos; **p. 976,** John Dominis/Getty Images; **p. 977,** Bettmann/Corbis; **p. 980,** AP/Wide World Photos; **p. 984,** Valley News Dispatch; **p. 990,** NASA Kennedy Space Center; **p. 991,** John Dominis/Getty Images; **p. 995,** AP/Wide World Photos; **p. 999,** AP/Wide World Photos.

Chapter 36: p. 1003, Bettmann/Corbis; **p. 1004,** Bettmann/Corbis; **p. 1010,** Los Angeles Times Syndicate; **p. 1012,** AP/Wide World Photos; **p. 1018,** Woodfin Camp; **p. 1019,** AP/Wide World Photos; **p. 1022,** Bettmann/Corbis.

Chapter 37: p. 1025, Bettmann/Corbis; **p. 1027,** AP/Wide World Photos; **p. 1029,** Library of Congress; **p. 1033,** Chris Wilkins/Getty Images; **p. 1036,** AP/Wide World Photos; **p. 1041,** AP/Wide World Photos; **p. 1043,** AP/Wide World Photos; **p. 1051,** Bettmann/Corbis; **p. 1054,** Bettmann/Corbis; **p. 1056,** Bettmann/Corbis; **p. 1058,** Bettmann/Corbis; **p. 1062,** Bettmann/Corbis.

INDEX

Page numbers in *italics* refer to illustrations.

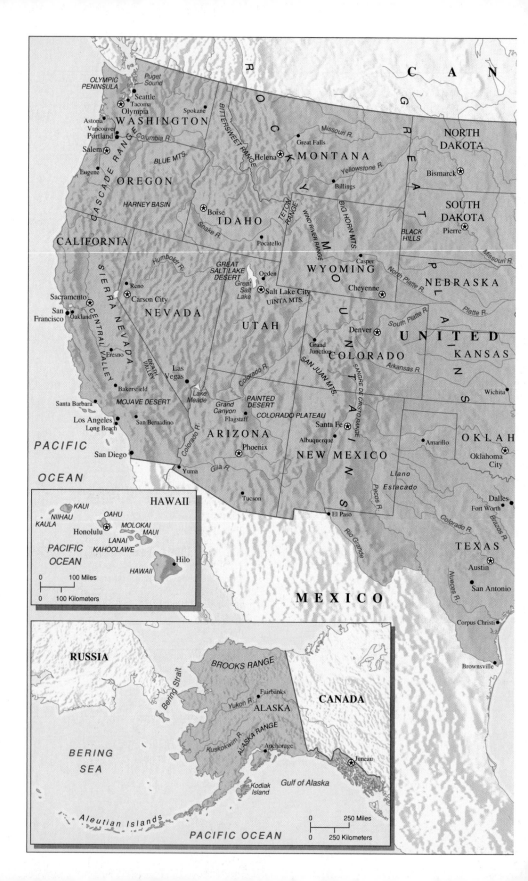

OLYMPIC
PENINSULA
Puget Sound
Seattle
Tacoma
Olympia
Astoria
Vancouver
Portland
Salem
Eugene
WASHINGTON
Spokane
BLUE MTS.
OREGON
HARNEY BASIN
CASCADE RANGE
Columbia R.
BITTERSWEET RANGE
Great Falls
Helena
MONTANA
Missouri R.
Yellowstone R.
Billings
NORTH
DAKOTA
Bismarck
SOUTH
DAKOTA
Pierre
BLACK
HILLS
TETON RANGE
BIG HORN MTS.
WIND RIVER RANGE
Boise
IDAHO
Snake R.
Pocatello
CALIFORNIA
Reno
Carson City
NEVADA
Humboldt R.
GREAT
SALT LAKE
DESERT
Ogden
Great
Salt
Lake
Salt Lake City
UINTA MTS.
WYOMING
Casper
Cheyenne
NEBRASKA
North Platte R.
Platte R.
Missouri R.
Sacramento
San
Francisco
Oakland
SIERRA NEVADA
CENTRAL VALLEY
Fresno
DEATH VALLEY
UTAH
Denver
Grand
Junction
COLORADO
South Platte R.
Arkansas R.
UNITED
KANSAS
Wichita
G
R
E
A
T
P
L
A
I
N
S
R   O   C   K   Y
M   O   U   N   T   A   I   N   S
Las
Vegas
Lake
Mead
Bakersfield
Santa Barbara
Los Angeles
Long Beach
San Bernadino
San Diego
MOJAVE DESERT
Grand
Canyon
Flagstaff
Colorado R.
PAINTED
DESERT
COLORADO PLATEAU
SAN JUAN MTS.
Santa Fe
Albuquerque
SANGRE DE CRISTO RANGE
Amarillo
OKLAH
Oklahoma
City
PACIFIC
OCEAN
Colorado R.
Yuma
Gila R.
ARIZONA
Phoenix
Tucson
NEW MEXICO
Llano
Estacado
Pecos R.
El Paso
Dalles
Fort Worth
Colorado R.
Brazos R.
TEXAS
Austin
San Antonio
Rio Grande
Nueces R.
Corpus Christi
Brownsville
MEXICO

HAWAII
KAUI
NIIHAU
KAULA
OAHU
Honolulu
MOLOKAI
MAUI
LANAI
KAHOOLAWE
PACIFIC
OCEAN
HAWAII
Hilo
0   100 Miles
0   100 Kilometers

RUSSIA
BROOKS RANGE
Bering Strait
Fairbanks
Yukon R.
ALASKA
CANADA
BERING
SEA
Kuskokwim R.
ALASKA RANGE
Anchorage
Juneau
Kodiak
Island
Gulf of Alaska
Aleutian Islands
PACIFIC OCEAN
0   250 Miles
0   250 Kilometers

C   A   N

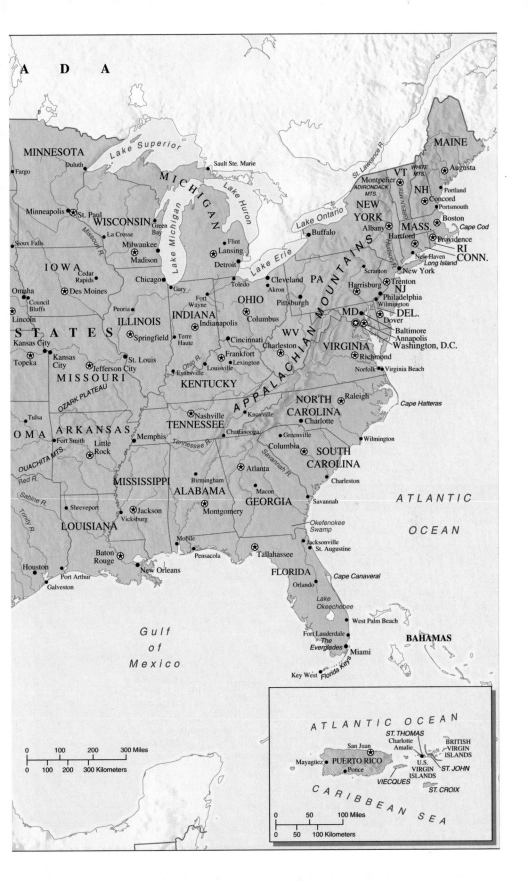

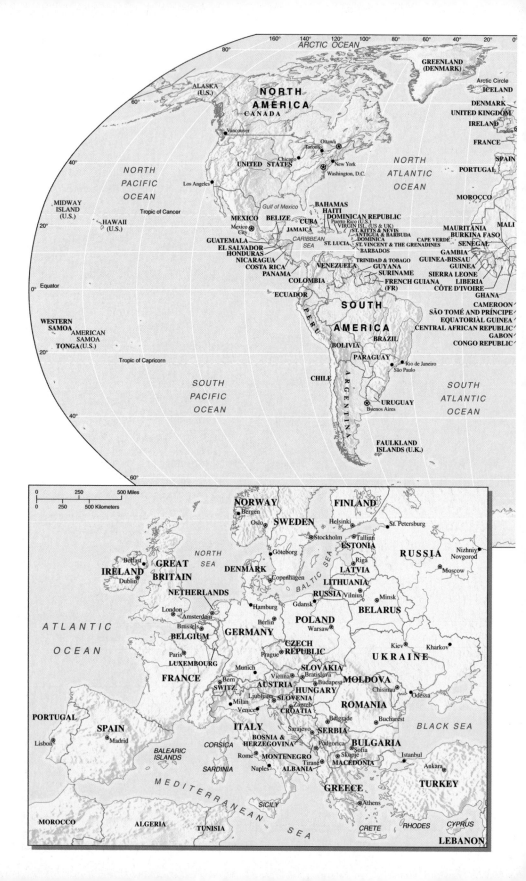

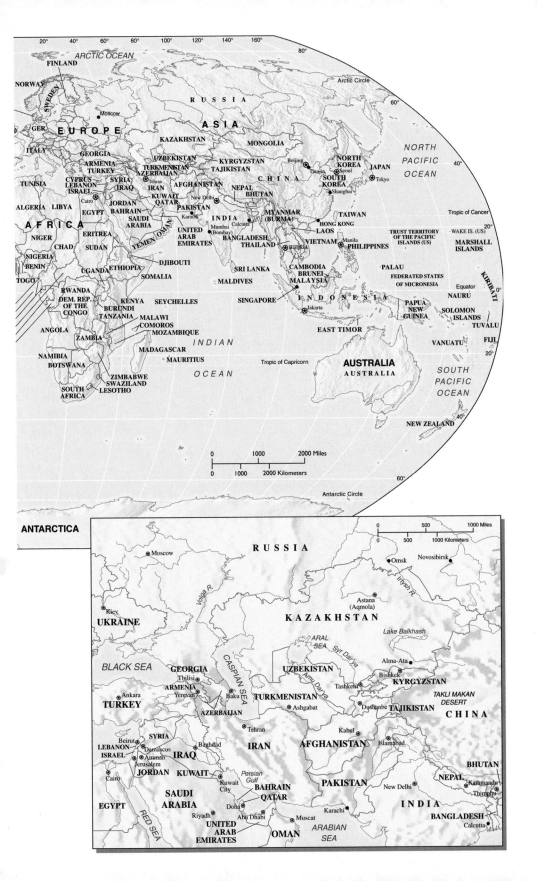

Top map:

20° 40° 60° 80° 100° 120° 140° 160° 80°

ARCTIC OCEAN

FINLAND

Arctic Circle

NORWAY

SWEDEN

R U S S I A

60°

Moscow

GER.

EUROPE

A S I A

ITALY

KAZAKHSTAN

MONGOLIA

NORTH
PACIFIC
OCEAN

GEORGIA

UZBEKISTAN

KYRGYZSTAN

ARMENIA
TURKEY

TURKMENISTAN

Beijing

NORTH
KOREA

JAPAN

40°

TAJIKISTAN

Seoul

AZERBAIJAN

Tianjin

SOUTH

Tokyo

CYPRUS

SYRIA

Tehran

AFGHANISTAN

C H I N A

KOREA

TUNISIA

LEBANON

IRAN

NEPAL

Shanghai

ISRAEL

IRAQ

New Delhi

BHUTAN

ALGERIA

LIBYA

JORDAN

KUWAIT

PAKISTAN

TAIWAN

Tropic of Cancer

EGYPT

BAHRAIN

Cairo

QATAR

Karachi

INDIA

MYANMAR
(BURMA)

HONG KONG

A F R I C A

SAUDI
ARABIA

Mumbai
(Bombay)

Calcutta

LAOS

TRUST TERRITORY
OF THE PACIFIC
ISLANDS (US)

WAKE IS. (US)

20°

NIGER

CHAD

YEMEN OMAN

UNITED
ARAB
EMIRATES

VIETNAM

Manila

MARSHALL
ISLANDS

ERITREA

SUDAN

BANGLADESH

NIGERIA

THAILAND

Bangkok

PHILIPPINES

BENIN

DJIBOUTI

SRI LANKA

CAMBODIA

PALAU

TOGO

UGANDA

ETHIOPIA

SOMALIA

MALDIVES

BRUNEI

FEDERATED STATES
OF MICRONESIA

Equator

KIRIBATI

RWANDA

DEM. REP.
OF THE
CONGO

KENYA

SEYCHELLES

SINGAPORE

MALAYSIA

I N D O N E S I A

NAURU

BURUNDI

TANZANIA

MALAWI

Jakarta

PAPUA
NEW
GUINEA

SOLOMON
ISLANDS

TUVALU

ANGOLA

COMOROS

MOZAMBIQUE

I N D I A N

EAST TIMOR

ZAMBIA

MADAGASCAR

VANUATU

FIJI

20°

NAMIBIA

MAURITIUS

Tropic of Capricorn

AUSTRALIA

SOUTH
PACIFIC
OCEAN

BOTSWANA

O C E A N

A U S T R A L I A

ZIMBABWE

SWAZILAND

SOUTH
AFRICA

LESOTHO

0   1000   2000 Miles

0 1000 2000 Kilometers

NEW ZEALAND

40°

60°

Antarctic Circle

ANTARCTICA

Bottom map:

0   500   1000 Miles

0   500   1000 Kilometers

Moscow

R U S S I A

Omsk

Novosibirsk

Irtysh R.

Astana
(Aqmola)

Kiev

K A Z A K H S T A N

Lake Balkhash

UKRAINE

Volga R.

ARAL
SEA

Syr Darya

Alma-Ata

BLACK SEA

GEORGIA

CASPIAN SEA

UZBEKISTAN

Bishkek

KYRGYZSTAN

Tbilisi

Amu Darya

Tashkent

ARMENIA

Yerevan

Baku

TAKLI MAKAN
DESERT

Ankara

TURKMENISTAN

Dushanbe

TAJIKISTAN

C H I N A

TURKEY

AZERBAIJAN

Ashgabat

Tehran

Kabul

SYRIA

Beirut

LEBANON

Damascus

Baghdad

IRAN

AFGHANISTAN

Islamabad

BHUTAN

ISRAEL

Amman

IRAQ

NEPAL

Jerusalem

Kathmandu

Cairo

JORDAN

KUWAIT

Persian
Gulf

PAKISTAN

New Delhi

Thimphu

Kuwait
City

BAHRAIN

Karachi

I N D I A

SAUDI

QATAR

EGYPT

ARABIA

Doha

BANGLADESH

Riyadh

Abu Dhabi

Muscat

Calcutta

UNITED
ARAB
EMIRATES

OMAN

ARABIAN
SEA

RED SEA